INDEX TO PERIODICAL LITERATURE FOR THE STUDY
OF THE NEW TESTAMENT

NEW TESTAMENT TOOLS
AND STUDIES

EDITED BY

BRUCE M. METZGER, Ph.D., D.D., L.H.D., D. Theol., D. Litt.

Professor of New Testament Language and Literature, Emeritus
Princeton Theological Seminary
and
Corresponding Fellow of the British Academy

AND

BART D. EHRMAN, Ph.D.

James A. Gray Professor of Religious Studies
University of North Carolina at Chapel Hill

VOLUME XXXI

INDEX TO PERIODICAL LITERATURE FOR THE STUDY OF THE NEW TESTAMENT

COMPILED BY

WATSON E. MILLS, Th.D., Ph.D.

BRILL

LEIDEN · BOSTON

2004

This book is printed on acid-free paper.

Library of Congress Cataloging-in-Publication Data

Mills, Watson E.
    Index to periodical literature for the study of the New Testament / by Watson E. Mills.
        p. cm. — (New Testament tools and studies, ISSN 0077-8842 ; v. 31)
    Includes bibliographical references and index.
    ISBN 90-04-12616-3 (alk. paper)
        1. Bible. N.T.—Periodicals—Bibliography. I. Title. II. Series.

Z7772.L1 M5497
[BS410]
016.225'05-dc22

                                                                            2003066450

ISSN 0077-8842
ISBN 90 04 12616 3

© Copyright 2004 by Koninklijke Brill NV, Leiden, The Netherlands

PRINTED IN THE NETHERLANDS

for Alex
the light of my life
with all of my love and affection
and with great appreciation

Table of Contents

Preface

This bibliography provides citations to journal articles that bear upon the critical study of books of the New Testament. Approximately 185 scholarly journals are indexed in the more than 15,000 entries that follow.

Each of the twenty-seven books of the Christian Bible is treated in canonical order. Within each book, the method of citation is by a specific textual unit. The arrangement of these units is the longer unit, e.g., 3:1-4:2, before the shorter, e.g., 3:1-18. Within each set of textual units, journal references are arranged chronologically beginning with the earliest. If two or more works occur with the same publication year the arrangement is alphabetical by the author's last name. Works are cited that have publication dates falling between 1900 and 2000. If a particular journal article discusses more than one textual unit within a given canonical book or several canonical books, the reference is repeated for each of the different textual units. In each of these conventions, I have followed the example of Günter Wagner, *An Exegetical Bibliography of the New Testament* (1982ff) and Paul-Émile Langevin, *Biblical Bibliography* (3 volumes 1970-1983).

No work of scholarship stands on its own; bibliographic works perhaps even less so. This project rests upon the shoulders of many works that have come before, and in several cases, continue. Most notable among these are: Wagner, Langevin, *Elenchus Bibliographicus, New Testament Abstracts,* and *Ephemerides theologicae Lovanienses*. Also, I have especially depended upon three earlier volumes in this series edited by Bruce M. Metzger: *Index to Periodical Literature on Christ and the Gospels* (1961, 1966, updated 1988); *An Index to Periodical Literature on the Apostle Paul* (1966,

1970, updated 1993); and A.J. Mattill and Mary B. Mattill, *A Classified Bibliography of Periodical Literature on the Acts of the Apostles: 1960-1985* (1966, updated 1986).

Thanks are due to several people who have contributed to this project. Irene Palmer oversaw the initial data entry. She was assisted by Carol Lucas and Alesa Jones. My colleague Rollin S. Armour assisted greatly in proofreading especially non-English titles. I gratefully acknowledge my editor at Brill, Louise Schouten, for help and support throughout this project.

Watson E. Mills
Mercer University
July 2003

Abbreviations

ABR	Australian Biblical Review (Melbourne)
AfTJ	African Theological Journal (Tanzania)
AJBI	Annual of the Japanese Biblical Institute (Tokyo)
AmER	American Ecclesiastical Review (Washington)
Ant	Antonianum (Rome)
AsSeign	Assemblées du Seigneur (Paris)
ATR	Anglican Theological Review (New York)
AUSS	Andrews University Seminary Studies (Berrien Springs MI)
BA	Biblical Archaeologist (New Haven CN)
BB	Bible Bhashyam: An Indian Biblical Quarterly (Vadavathoor)
BI	Biblical Illustrator (Nashville)
Bib	Biblica (Rome)
BibFe	Biblia y fe: Revista de teologia bíblica (Madrid)
BibInt	Biblical Interpretation (Leiden)
BibL	Bibel und Leben (Düsseldorf)
BibN	Biblische Notizen: Beiträge zur exegetischen Diskussion (Bamberg)
BibO	Bibbia e Oriente (Milan)
BibTo	Bible Today (Colegeville MN)
Bij	Bijdragen (Nijmegen)
BJRL	Bulletin of the John Rylands University Library (Manchester)
BK	Bibel und Kirche (Stuttgart)

BL	Bibel und Liturgie (Vienna)
BLE	Bulletin de Littérature Eccleésiastique (Toulouse)
BLOS	Bulletin de liaison sur l'origine des Synoptiques (Orléans)
BLT	Brethren Life and Thought (Chicago)
BR	Biblical Research (Chicago)
BSac	Bibliotheca Sacra (Dallas)
BT	Bible Translator (London)
BTB	Biblical Theology Bulletin (Jamaica NY)
Bur	Burgense: Collectanea Scientifica (Burgos)
BVC	Bible et Vie Chretienne (Paris)
BZ	Biblische Zeitschrift (Paderborn)
Cath	Catholica: Vierteljahresschrift füur ökumenische Theologie (Münster)
CBQ	Catholic Biblical Quarterly (Washington)
CC	Christian Century (Chicago)
CEJ	Christian Education Journal (Glen Ellyn IL)
Chr	Christus (Paris)
ChrM	Christian Ministry (Chicago)
CICR	Communio: International Catholic Review (Spokane WA)
CJ	Concordia Journal (St. Louis MO)
Conci	Concilium (London)
CT	Christianity Today (Washington)
CThM	Currents in Theology and Mission (St. Louis MO)
CTJ	Calvin Theological Journal (Grand Rapids)
CTM	Concordia Theological Monthly (St. Louis MO)
CTQ	Concordia Theological Quarterly (Fort Wayne IN)
CuBí	Cultura Bíblica (Madrid)

Dir	Direction (Fresno CA)
Div	Divinitas pontificiae academiae theologicae Romanae commentarii (Rome)
DR	Downside Review (Bath)
DTT	Dansk Teologisk Tidsskrift (Cophenhagen)
EAJT	East Asia Journal of Theology (Singapore)
EB	Estudios Bíblicos (Madrid)
EE	Estudios Eclesiásticos (Madrid)
EGLMBS	Eastern Great Lakes and Midwest Biblical Society (Chicago)
ÉgT	Église et théologie (Ottawa)
Emmanuel	Emmanuel (New York)
EMQ	Evangelical Missions Quarterly (Washington)
EQ	Evangelical Quarterly (London)
ErAu	Erbe und Auftrag (Beuron)
ERT	Evangelical Review of Theology (New Delhi)
EstT	Estudios Teológicos (Guatemala City)
ET	Expository Times (Edinburgh)
ETL	Ephemerides Theologicae Lovanienses (Louvain)
ETR	Etudes Théologiques et Religieuses (Montpellier)
EV	Esprit et Vie (Langres)
EvT	Evangelische Theologie (Munich)
ExA	Ex Auditu (Princeton)
FilN	Filologia Neotestamentaria (Cordoba)
FM	Faith and Mission (Wake Forest NC)
Forum	Forum (Sonoma CA)
FV	Foi et Vie (Paris)
GeistL	Geist und Leben (Würzburg)
Greg	Gregorianum (Rome)

GTJ   Grace Theological Journal (Winona Lake IN)
GTT   Gereformeered Theologisch Tijdschrift (Aalten)
HBT   Horizons in Biblical Theology (Pittsburg PA)
HeyJ   Heythrop Journal (Oxford)
HTR   Harvard Theological Review (Cambridge MA)
HTS   Hervormde Teologiese Studies (Pretoria)
IBS   Irish Biblical Studies (London)
IJT   Indian Journal of Theology (Serampore)
IKaZ   Internationale Katholische Zeitschrift: Communio
             (Frankfurt)
Int   Interpretation (Richmond VA)
IRM   International Review of Mission (London)
ITQ   Irish Theological Quarterly (Maynooth)
JAAR   Journal of the American Academy of Religion
             (Atlanta)
JBL   Journal of Biblical Literature (Atlanta)
JETS   Journal of the Evangelical Theological Society
             (Wheaton IL)
JSNT   Journal for the Study of the New Testament (Sheffield)
JTS   Journal of Theological Studies (Oxford)
JTSA   Journal of Theology for Southern Africa (Rondebosch)
K   Kairos: Zeitschrift für Religionswissenschaft und
             Theologie (Salzburg)
KD   Kerygma and Dogma (Göttingen)
LB   Linguistica Biblica (Bonn)
LouvS   Louvain Studies (Louvain)
LTJ   Lutheran Theological Journal (Adelaide)
LV   Lumen Vitae (Washington)
MeliT   Melita Theologia (La Valetta)

MSR	Mélanges de Science Religieuse (Lille)
MTZ	Münchener theologische Zeitschrift (München)
NedTT	Nederlands theologisch tijdschrift ('s-Gravenhage)
Neo	Neotestamentica (Pretoria)
NovT	Novum Testamentum (Leiden)
NRT	La Nouvelle revue théologique (Louvain)
NTS	New Testament Studies (Cambridge)
NTT	Norsk teologisk tidsskrift (Oslo)
Para	Paraclete (Wheaton IL)
ParSpirV	Parola, spirito e vita: Quaderni di lettura biblica (Bologna)
Pneuma	Pneuma: The Journal of the Society for Pentecostal Studies (Chicago)
Point	Point (Papua, New Guinea)
Pres	Presbyterion (St. Louis)
PRS	Perspectives in Religious Studies (Macon GA)
PSB	Princeton Seminary Bulletin (Princeton NJ)
PV	Parole di vita (Torino)
QR	Quarterly Review (Nashville TN)
RafT	Revue Africaine de Théologie (Alger)
RB	Revue biblique (Paris)
RBib	Rivista Biblica (Bologna)
RechSR	Recherches de science religieuse (Paris)
RevB	Revista Biblica (Buenos Aires)
RevExp	Review and Expositor (Louisville KY)
RevQ	Revue de Qumran (Paris)
RevSR	Revue des Sciences religieuses (Strasbourg)
RHPR	Revue d'histoire et de philosophie religieuses (Strasbourg)

RivBib	Rivista Biblica (Brescia)
RoczTK	Roczniki Teologiczno-Kanoniczne (Lublin)
RQ	Restoration Quarterly (Austin TX)
RR	Reformed Review (Holland MI)
RSB	Religious Studies Bulletin (Calgary)
RSPT	Revue des Sciences Philosophiques et Théologiques (Paris)
RT	Revue Thomiste (Paris)
RTL	Revue théologique de Louvain (Louvain)
RTR	Reformed Theological Review (Melbourne)
Sale	Salesianum (Rome)
Salm	Salmanticensis (Salamanca)
SBFLA	Studii Biblici Franciscani Liber Annuus (Jerusalem)
SBLSP	Society of Biblical Literature Seminar Papers (Atlanta)
SBT	Studia Biblica et Theologica (Pasadena CA)
ScE	Science et Esprit (Montreal)
Scr	Scripture: Quarterly of the Catholic Biblical Association (Edinburgh)
ScrSA	Scriptura: Journal of Bible and Theology in South Africa (Stellenbosch, South Africa)
SE	Sciences Ecclésiastiques (Montreal)
SEÅ	Svensk Exegetisk Årsbok (Lund)
SEAJT	South East Asia Journal of Theology (Singapore)
SEcu	Studi Ecumenici (Verona)
SémBib	Sémiotique et Bible (Lyon)
Semeia	Semeia (Atlanta)
SJT	Scottish Journal of Theology (Edinburgh)
SkrifK	Skrif en Kerk (Pretoria)

SM	Studia Missionalia (Wuppertal-Barmen)
SNTU-A	Studien zum NT und seiner Umwelt (Linz)
Soj	Sojourners (Washington)
SouJT	Southwestern Journal of Theology (Fort Worth TX)
SR	Studies in Religion/Sciences religieuses (Toronto)
ST	Studies in Theology (London)
StTheol	Studia Theologica (Copenhagen)
SVTQ	St. Vladimir's Theological Quarterly (New York)
TBe	Theologische Beiträge (Tübingen)
TD	Theology Digest (St. Louis)
TEd	Theological Educator (New Orleans LA)
TextK	Texte und Kontexte: Exegetische Zeitschrift (Berlin)
TGl	Theologie und Glaube (Paderborn, Germany)
Theology	Theology (London)
ThEv	Theologia evangelica (Pretoria)
TLZ	Theologische Literaturzeitung (Leipzig)
TQ	Theologische Quartalschift (Tübingen)
TriJ	Trinity Journal (Deerfield IL)
TS	Theological Studies (Woodstock)
TT	Theology Today (Notre Dame IN)
TTZ	Trierer Theologische Zeitschrift (Trier)
TynB	Tyndale Bulletin (Cambridge)
TZ	Theologische Zeitschrift (Basel)
USQR	Union Seminary Quarterly Review (New York)
VC	Vigiliae Christianae (Amsterdam)
VD	Verbum Domini (Rome)
VS	La vie spirituelle (Paris)
WLQ	Wisconsin Lutheran Quarterly (Mequon WI)
Worship	Worship (Collegeville MN)

WTJ	Westminster Theological Journal (Philadelphia)
WW	Word and World (Saint Paul MN)
ZAW	Zeitschrift für die alttestamentliche Wissenschaft (Berlin)
ZKT	Zeitschrift für Katholische Theologie (Innsbruck)
ZMiss	Zeitschrift für Mission (Basel)
ZNW	Zeitschrift für die neutestamentliche Wissenschaft (Berlin)
ZRGG	Zeitschrift für Religions- und Geistesgeschichte (Erlangen)
ZTK	Zeitschrift für Theologie und Kirche (Tübingen)

Matthew

__1-4__

1   L. Nortjé, "Die Abraham motief in Matteus 1-4," *SkrifK* 19 (1998): 46-56.

__1-2__

2   Myles M. Bourke, "The Literary Genius of Matthew 1-2," *CBQ* 22 (1960): 160-75.

3   E. Galbiati, "Evangeli," *BibO* 4 (1962): 20-29.

4   C. H. Cave, "St. Matthew's Infancy Narrative," *NTS* 9 (1962-1963): 382-90.

5   Edgar M. Krentz, "The Extent of Matthew's Prologue," *JBL* 83 (1964): 409-14.

6   Rudolf Pesch, "Der Gottessohn im matthäischen Evangelienprolog (Mt. 1-2): Beobachtungen zu den Zitationsformeln der Reflexionszitate," *Bib* 48 (1967): 416-19.

7   D. Ashbeck, "The Literary Genre of Matthew 1-2," *BibTo* 57 (1971): 572-78.

8   B. De Solages, "Réflexions sur les évangiles de l'enfance," *BLE* 72 (1971): 37-42.

9   S. Muñoz Iglesias, "Midrás y Evangelios de la Infancia," *EB* 31 (1972): 331-59.

10   Kurt Schubert, "Die Kindheitsgeschichten Jesu im Lichte der Religionsgeschichte des Judentums," *BL* 45 (1972): 224-40.

11   J. O. Tuni, "La Tipología Israel-Jesús en Mt. 1-2," *EE* 47 (1972): 361-76.

12   E. Galbiati, "Genere letterario e storia in Matteo 1-2," *BibO* 15 (1973): 3-16.

13   A. Vicent Cernuda, "La dialéctica *gennô-tiktô* en Mt. 1-2," *Bib* 55 (1974): 408-17.

14   Dan O. Via, "Narrative World and Ethical Response: The Marvelous and Righteousness in Matthew 1-2," *Semeia* 12 (1978): 123-49.

15   Raymond E. Brown, "Gospel Infancy Narrative Research from 1976 to 1986: Part I (Matthew)," *CBQ* 48 (1986): 468-83.

16   J. Cosslett Quin, "The Infancy Narratives with Special Reference to Matthew 1 and 2," *IBS* 9 (1987): 63-69.

17   B. T. Benedict, "The Genres of Matthew 1-2: Light from 1 Timothy 1:4," *RB* 97 (1990): 31-53.

18   C. Thomas, "The Nativity Scene," *BibTo* 28 (1990): 26-33.

1:1-25

19   E. Pascual, "La Genealogia de Jesus segun S. Mateo," *EB* 23 (1964): 109-49.

20   O. Da Spinetoli, "Les généalogies de Jésus et leur signification," *AsSeign* NS 9 (1974): 6-19.

21   J. Schaberg, "The Foremothers and the Mother of Jesus," *Conci* 206 (1989): 112-19.

22   Lynlea Rodger, "The Infancy Stories of Matthew and Luke: An Examination of the Child as a Theological Metaphor," *HBT* 19 (1997): 58-81.

23   Wim J. C. Weren, "The Five Women in Matthew's Geneology," *CBQ* 59 (1997): 288-305.

1:1-18

24   Barclay M. Newman, "Matthew 1:1-18: Some Comments and a Suggested Restructuring," *BT* 2 (1976): 209-12.

1:1-17

25   Jacques Dupont, "La genealogia di Gesu secondo Matteo 1,1-17," *BibO* 4 (1962): 3-6.

26   H. Milton, "The Structure of the Prologue to St. Matthew's Gospel," *JBL* 81 (1962): 175-81.

27   K. H. Schelkle, "Die Frauen im Stammbaum Jesu," *BK* 18 (1963): 113-15.

28   J. E. Bruns, "Matthew's Genealogy of Jesus," *BibTo* 1 (1964): 980-85.

29   L. Ramlot, "Les genealogies bibliques. Un genre littéraire oriental," *BVC* 60 (1964): 53-70.

30   H. Schöllig, "Die Zählung der Generationen im matthäischen Stammbaum," *ZNW* 59 (1968): 261-68.

31   E. L. Abel, "The Genealogies of Jesus ὁ Χριστός," *NTS* 20 (1974): 203-10.

32   D. E. Nineham, "The Genealogy in St. Matthew's Gospel and Its Significance for the Study of the Gospels" *BJRL* 58 (1976): 421-44.

33   Herman C. Waetjen, "The Genealogy as the Key to the Gospel According to Matthew," *JBL* 95 (1976): 205-30.

34   Franz Schnider and Werner Stenger, "Die Frauen im Stammbaum Jesu nach Matthäus. Strukturale Beobachtungen zu Mt. 1, 1-17" *BZ* 23 (1979): 187-96.

35   W. Hammer, "L'intention de la génélogie de Matthieu," *ÉTR* 55 (1980): 305-306.

36   André Feuillet, "Observations sur les deux généalogies de Jésus-Christ de saint Matthieu (1,1-17) et de saint Luc (3,23-38)," *EV* 98 (1988): 605-608.

37   R. P. Nettelhorst, "The Genealogy of Jesus," *JETS* 31 (1988): 169-72.

38   Thomas H. Graves, "Matthew 1:1-17," *RevExp* 86 (1989): 595-600.

39   H. Hempelmann, " 'Das dürre Blatt im Heiligen Buch.' Mt. 1,1-17 und der Kampf wider die Erniedrigung Gottes," *TBe* 21 (1990): 6-23.

40   Nancy de Chazal, "The Women in Jesus' Family Tree," *Theology* 97 (1994): 413-19.

41   John Nolland, "The Four (Five) Women and Other Annotations in Matthew's Genealogy," *NTS* 43 (1997): 527-39.

42   John Nolland, "Genealogical Annotation in Genesis as Background for the Matthean Genealogy of Jesus," *TynB* 47 (1996): 115-22.

43   K-H. Ostmeyer, "Der Stammbaum des Verheissencn: theologische Implikationen der Namen und Zahlen in Mt 1.1-17," *NTS* 46 (2000): 175-92.

1:1

44   Sebastián Bartina, "Jesus, el Cristo, ben David ben Abraham (Mt. 1,1): Los appelidos de la Biblia y su traduccion al castellano," *EB* 18 (1959): 375-93.

45   W. Barnes Tatum, " 'The Origin of Jesus Messiah' (Matt. 1:1, 18a): Matthew's Use of the Infancy Traditions" *JBL* 96 (1977): 523-35.

46   John Nolland, "What Kind of Genesis Do We Have in Matt 1.1?" *NTS* 42 (1996): 463-71.

1:2-16

47   Anton Vögtle, "Die Genealogie Mt. 1,2-16 und die mätthaische Kindheitsgeschichte (I. Teil)," *BZ* 8 (1964): 45-58.

48   C. T. Davis, "The Fulfillment of Creation: A Study of Matthew's Genealogy," *JAAR* 41 (1973): 520-35.

1:3-4

49   Richard J. Bauckham, "Tamar's Ancestry and Rahab's Marriage: Two Problems in the Matthean Genealogy," *NovT* 37 (1995): 313-29.

1:3

50   John P. Heil, "The Narrative Roles of the Women in Matthew's Genealogy," *Bib* 72 (1991): 538-45.

1:5

51   Yair Zakovitch, "Rahab als Mutter des Boaz in der Jesus-Genealogie (Matth. 1,5)," *NovT* 17 (1975): 1-5.

52   A. T. Hanson, "Rahab the Harlot in Early Christian Tradition" *JSNT* (1978): 53-60.

53   Jerome D. Quinn, "Is Ῥαχάβ in Mt. 1,5 Rahab of Jericho?" *Bib* 62 (1981): 225-28.

54   Raymond E. Brown, "Rachab in Mt. 1,5 Probably Is Rahab of Jericho," *Bib* 63 (1982): 79-80.

55   John P. Heil, "The Narrative Roles of the Women in Matthew's Genealogy," *Bib* 72 (1991): 538-45.

1:6

56   John P. Heil, "The Narrative Roles of the Women in Matthew's Genealogy," *Bib* 72 (1991): 538-45.

1:16

57   Bruce M. Metzger, "On the Citation of Variant Readings of Matt. 1,16," *JBL* 77 (1958): 361-63.

58   John P. Heil, "The Narrative Roles of the Women in Matthew's Genealogy," *Bib* 72 (1991): 538-45.

59   John Nolland, "A Text-Critical Discussion of Matthew 1:16," *CBQ* 58 (1996): 665-73.

1:17

60   John M. Jones, "Subverting the Textuality of Davidic Messianism: Matthew's Presentation of the Genealogy and the Davidic Title," *CBQ* 56 (1994): 256-72.

1:18-2:25

61   Ingo Broer, "Die Bedeutung der 'Jungfrauengeburt' im Matthäusevangelium," *BibL* 12 (1971): 248-60.

62   A. Knockaert and C. van der Plancke, "Catéchèses de l'annonciation," *LV* 34 (1979): 79-121.

63   M. Herranz Marco, "Substrato arameo en el relato de la Anunciación a José," *EB* 38 (1979-1980): 35-55, 237-68.

1:18-2:23

64   C. T. Davis, "Tradition and Redaction in Matthew 1:18-2:23," *JBL* 90 (1971): 404-21.

65   M. J. Down, "The Matthaean Birth Narratives: Matthew 1:18-2:23," *ET* 90 (1978): 51-52.

66   E. A. Ahirika, "The Theology of Matthew in the Light of the Nativity Story," *BB* 16 (1990): 5-19.

67   David R. Bauer, "The Kingship of Jesus in the Matthean Infancy Narrative: A Literary Analysis," *CBQ* 57 (1995): 306-23.

1:18-2:19

68   J. M. Germano, "Nova et vetera in pericopam de sancto Joseph," *VD* 46 (1968): 351-60.

1:18-25

69   Reginald H. Fuller, "The Virgin Birth: Historical Fact or Kerygmatic Truth?" *BR* 1 (1957): 1-8.

70   F. Dumermuth, "Bemerkung zu Jesu Menschwerdung," *TZ* 20 (1964): 52-53.

71   M. Krämer, "Die globale Analyse des Stiles in Mt. 1,18-25," *Bib* 45 (1964): 4-22.

72   M. Krämer, "Zwei Probleme aus Mt. 1:18-25: Vers 20 und 25" *Sale* 26 (1964): 303-33.

73   Otto A. Piper, "The Virgin Birth: The Meaning of the Gospel Accounts," *Int* 18 (1964): 131-48.

74   André Pelletier, "L'Annonce à Joseph," *RechSR* 54 (1966): 67-68.

75   Joseph A. Fitzmyer, "The Virginal Conception of Jesus in the New Testament," *TS* 34 (1973): 541-75.

76   Kenneth Grayston, "Matthieu 1:18-25: Essai d'interprétation," *RTP* 23 (1973): 221-32.

77   Alois Stöger, "Giuseppe 'uomo giusto' in Mt. 1,18-25," *RBib* 21 (1973): 287-300.

78   Franz Schnider and Werner Stenger, " 'Mit der Abstammung Jesu Christi verhielt es sich so: . . .' Strukturale Beobachtungen zu Mt. 1,18-25," *BZ* 25 (1981): 255-64.

79   Raymond E. Brown, "The Annunciation to Joseph (Matthew 1:18-25)," *Worship* 61 (1987): 482-92.

80   Fred L. Horton, "Parenthetical Pregnancy: The Conception and Birth of Jesus in Matthew 1:18-25," *SBLSP* 26 (1987): 175-89.

81   T. Kronholm, "Den Kommande Hiskia," *SEÅ* 54 (1989): 109-17.

82   P. T. Stramare, "L'Annunciazione a Giuseppe in Mt. 1:18-25: Analisi letteraria e significato teologico," *BibO* 31 (1989): 3-14.

83   P. T. Stramare, "L'Annunciazione a Giuseppe in Mt. 1:18-25: Analisi letteraria e significato teologico," *BibO* 31 (1989): 199-217.

84   Richard N. Longenecker, "Whose Child Is This?" *CT* 34 (1990): 25-28.

85   Sheila Klassen-Wiebe, "Matthew 1:18-25," *Int* 46 (1992): 392-95.

86   Dale C. Allison, "Divorce, Celibacy and Joseph," *JSNT* 49 (1993): 3-10.

87   John Nolland, "No Son-of-God Christology in Matthew 1.18-25," *JSNT* 62 (1996): 3-12.

1:18-24

88   A. Bouton, "C'est toi qui lui donneras le nom de Jésus," *AsSeign* NS 8 (1972): 17-25.

1:18-21

89   F. J. Steinmetz, "Der Zweifel des Josef, der Heilige Geist und das neue Leben. Meditationsanregungen zu Mt. 1,18-21.24," *GeistL* 47 (1974): 465-68.

90   Laurence Cantwell, "The Parentage of Jesus: Mt. 1:18-21," *NovT* 24 (1982): 304-15.

1:18

91   W. Barnes Tatum, " 'The Origin of Jesus Messiah' (Matt. 1:1, 18a): Matthew's Use of the Infancy Traditions" *JBL* 96 (1977): 523-35.

92   James Lagrand, "How was the Virgin Mary 'Like a Man': A Note on Mt. 1:18b and Related Syriac Christian Texts," *NovT* 22 (1980): 97-107

1:19

93   Ceslaus Spicq, " 'Joseph, son mari, étant juste. . .' (Mt. 1, 19)," *RB* 70 (1964): 206-14.

94   David Hill, "A Note on Matthew 1:19," *ET* 76 (1965): 133-34.

95   A. Tosato, "Joseph, Being a Just Man (Matt. 1:19)," *CBQ* 41 (1979): 547-51.

96   A. Vicent Cernuda, "El domicilio de José y la fama de María," *EB* 46 (1988): 5-25.

1:20

97   Pierre Grelot, "La naissance d'Isaac et celle de Jésus," *NRT* 104 (1972): 462-87, 561-85.

1:21-59

98   Frans Neirynck, "Apò tóte ērxato and the Structure of Matthew," *ETL* 64 (1988): 21-59.

1:21

99   J. M. Germano, "Privilegium nominis messianici a S. Joseph imponendi (Is. 7,14; Mt. 1,21, 23, 25)," *VD* 47 (1969): 151-62.

100   A. R. C. McLellan, "Choosing a Name for the Baby," *ET* 93 (1981): 80-82.

1:22-23

101   Willem S. Prinsloo, "Jesaja 7 (1996): 14 en die maagdelike geboorte," *SkrifK* 18 (1997): 323-27.

1:22

102   James W. Scott, "Matthew's Intention to Write History," *WTJ* 47 (1985): 68-82.

1:23-25

103   Andreas Schmidt, "Der mögliche Text von P. Oxy. III 405, Z 39-45," *NTS* 37 (1991): 160.

1:23

104   H. E. W. Turner, "Expository Problems: The Virgin Birth," *ET* 68 (1956): 12-17.

105   Robert G. Bratcher, "A Study of Isaiah 7:14: Its Meaning and Use in the Masoretic Text, the Septuagint and the Gospel of Matthew," *BT* 9 (1958): 98-125.

106   M. McNamara, "The Emmanuel Prophecy and Its Context-III," *Scr* 15 (1963): 80-88.

107   J. Brennan, "Virgin and Child in Isaiah 7:14," *BibTo* 1 (1964): 968-74.

108   J. M. Germano, "Privilegium nominis messianici a S. Joseph imponendi (Is. 7,14; Mt. 1,21, 23, 25)," *VD* 47 (1969): 151-62.

109   C. H. Dodd, "New Testament Translation Problems I," *BT* 27 (1976): 301-11.

110   John T. Willis, "The Meaning of Isaiah 7:14 and Its Application in Matthew 1:23," *RQ* 21 (1978): 1-18.

111   J. M. James, "The God Who Is with Us," *ET* 91 (1979): 78-79.

112   Frederick Anderson, "The Virgin Birth," *RevExp* 1 (1904): 28-43.

113   Georges Arnera, "Du rocher d'Esaie aux douze montagnes d'Hermas," *ÉTR* 59 (1984): 215-20.

114   F. J. Steinmetz, "Der Zweifel des Josef, der Heilige Geist und das neue Leben: Meditationsanregungen zu Mt. 1,18-21.24," *GeistL* 47 (1974): 465-68.

1:25

115   J. M. Germano, "Privilegium nominis messianici a S. Joseph imponendi (Is. 7,14; Mt.1, 21, 23, 25)," *VD* 47 (1969): 151-62.

2-3

116   M. S. Enslin, "The Christian Stories of the Nativity," *JBL* 59 (1940): 314-38.

117   A. R. C. Leaney, "The Birth Narratives in St. Luke and St. Matthew," *NTS* 8 (1962): 158-66.

118   Armand Beauduini, "The Infancy Narratives: A Confession of Faith," *LV* 39 (1984): 167-77.

2:1-23

119   R. Couffignal, "Le conte merveilleux des mages et du cruel Hérode," *RT* 89 (1989): 97-117.

2:1-12

120   H. J. Richards, "The Three Kings (Mt. II 1-12)," *Scr* 8 (1956): 23-28.2:1-12

121   E. Galbiati, "Esegesi degli Evangeli festivi. L'Adorazione dei Magi (Matt. 2,1-12). (Festa dell'Epifania)," *BibO* 4 (1962): 20-29.

122   F. Kerstiens, "Unterwegs im Glauben: Homilie zum Feste Epiphanie," *BibL* 6 (1965): 303-306.

123   J. N. M. Wifngaards, "The Episode of the Magi and Christian Kerygma," *IJT* 61 (1967): 30-41.

124   Paul Gächter, "Die Magierperikope (Mt. 2,1-12)," *ZKT* 90 (1968): 257-95.

125   W. A. Schulze, "Nachtrag zu meinem Aufsatz: Zur Geschichte der Auslegung von Matth. 2:1-12," *TZ* 31 (1975): 150-60.

126   Raymond E. Brown, "The Meaning of the Magi: The Significance of the Star," *Worship* 49 (1975): 574-82.

127   W. A. Schulze, "Zur Geschichte der Auslegung von Matth. 2,1-12," *TZ* 31 (1975): 150-60.

128   David C. Steinmetz, "Gedanken zum Dreikönigstag: Reflexionen über die Huldigung der Magier in Mt. 2," *GeistL* 50 (1977): 401-408.

129   G. Schmahl, "Magier aus dem Osten und die Heiligen Drei Könige," *TTZ* 87 (1978): 295-303.

130   Robert W. Bertram, "An Epiphany Crossing: Programming Matthew 2:1-12 for Readers Today," *CThM* 7 (1980): 328-36.

131   Antonio Charbel, "Mateo 2:1-12: los Magos en el ambiente del Reino Nabateo," *RevB* 46 (1984): 147-58.

132   Elmer Matthias, "The Epiphany of Our Lord," *CJ* 10 (1984): 231.

133   William E. Phipps, "The Magi and Halley's Comet," *TT* 43 (1986): 88-92.

134   Donald P. Senior, "Matthew 2:1-12," *Int* 46 (1992): 395-98.

135   Elian Cuvillier, "La Visite des Mages dans l'Evangile de Matthieu (Matthieu 2,1-12)," *FV* 98 (1999): 75-85.

136   John Holland, "The Sources for Matthew 2:1-12," *CBQ* 60
       (1998): 283-300.

137   Christophe Raimbault, "Une analyse structurelle de
       l'adoration des mages en Mt 2,1-12," *EB* 56 (1998):
       221-35.

138   Kathleen Weber, "The Image of Sheep and Goats in
       Matthew 25:31-46," *CBQ* 59 (1997): 657-78.

139   M. A. Powell, "The Magi as Wise Men: Re-examining a
       Basic Supposition," *NTS* 46 (2000): 1-20.

140   David C. Sim, "The Magi: Gentiles or Jews?" *HTS* 55
       (1999): 980-1000.

2:1-7

141   Antonio Charbel, "Mt. 2,1.7: I Magi erano Nabatei?" *RBib*
       20 (1972): 571-83.

2:2

142   Nigel Turner, "The New-Born King: Mt. 2:2," *ET* 68
       (1957): 122.

143   R. A. Rosenberg, "The a Star of the Messiah
       'Reconsidered'," *Bib* 53 (1972): 105-109.

144   M. Küchler, "Wir haben seinen Stern gesehen . . . ," *BK* 44
       (1989): 179-86.

2:6

145   Homer Heater, "Matthew 2:6 and Its Old Testament
       Sources," *JETS* 26 (1983): 395-97.

146   A. J. Petrotta, "A Closer Look at Matt. 2:6 and Its Old
       Testament Sources," *JETS* 28 (1985): 47-52.

147   A. J. Petrotta, "An Even Closer Look at Matt 2:6 and Its
       Old Testament Sources," *JETS* 33 (1990): 311-15.

2:7

148   Alasdair B. Gordon, "The Fate of Judas according to Acts
       1:18," *EQ* 43 (1971): 97-100.

2:9

149   Kim Paffenroth, "Science or Story? The Star of
       Bethlehem," *ET* 106 (1994): 78-79.

2:11

150   Gonzague Ryckmans, "De l'or, de l'encens et de la myrrhe," *RB* 58 (1951): 372-76.

151   G. W. van Beek, "Frankincense and Myrrh," *BA* 23 (1960): 70-95.

152   S. Barting, "Casa o caserio? Los magos en Belen," *EB* 25 (1966): 355-57.

153   D. H. C. Read, "Three Gaudy Kings," *ET* 91 (1979): 84-86.

154   Joachim Kügler, "Gold, Weihrauch und Myrrhe: Eine Notiz zu Mt 2,11," *BibN* 87 (1997): 24-33.

2:13-23

155   André Paul, "La fuite en Égypte et le retour en Galilée," *AsSeign* NS 11 (1971): 19-28.

156   A. R. C. McLellan, "Into Egypt," *ET* 95 (1983): 84-86.

157   Thomas H. Graves, "A Story Ignored: An Exegesis of Matthew 2:13-23," *FM* 5 (1987): 66-76.

158   Richard J. Erickson, "Divine Injustice? Matthew's Narrative Strategy and the Slaughter of the Innocents," *JSNT* 64 (1996): 5-27.

2:13-18

159   David Daube, "The Earliest Structure of the Gospels," *NTS* 5 (1958-1959): 184-87.

2:13-15

160   N. Walker, "The Alleged Matthaean Errata," *NTS* 9 (1962-1963): 391-94.

2:13

161   K. Rahner, "Nimm das Kind und seine Mutter," *GeistL* 30 (1957): 14-22.

2:15

162   Sebastián Bartina, "Y desde Egipto lo he proclamado hijo mio (Mt. 2,15)," *EB* 29 (1970): 157-60.

163   Tracy L. Howard, "The Use of Hosea 11:1 in Matthew 2:15. An Alternative Solution," *BSac* 143 (1986): 314-28.

2:16-23

164　David L. Bartlett, "Jeremiah 31:15-20," *Int* 32 (1978): 73-78.

2:16-18

165　Richard T. France, "Herod and the Children of Bethelem," *NovT* 21 (1979): 98-120.

2:17-18

166　M. Quesnel, "Les citations de Jérémie dans l'évangile selon saint Matthieu," *EB* 47 (1989): 513-27.

2:17

167　M. J. J. Menken, "The References of Jeremiah in the Gospel According to Matthew (Mt. 2,17; 16,14; 27,9)," *ETL* 60 (1984): 5-24.

168　James W. Scott, "Matthew's Intention to Write History," *WTJ* 47 (1985): 68-82.

2:18-25

169　F. L. Filas, "Karl Rahner, Saint Joseph's Doubt," *TD* 6 (1958): 169-73.

2:18

170　David L. Bartlett, "Jeremiah 31:15-20," *Int* 32 (1978): 73-78.

171　Bob Becking, " 'A Voice Was Heared in Ramah': Some Remarks on Structure and Meaning of Jeremiah 31,15-17," *BZ* NS 38 (1994): 229-42.

2:20

172　Michal Wojciechowski, "Herod and Antipater? A Supplementary Clue to Dating the Birth of Jesus," *BibN* 44 (1988): 61-62.

2:21

173　R. R. Lewis, "*Epiblēma rakous agnaphou* (Mt. 2,21)," *ET* 45 (1933-1934): 185.

2:23

174　W. Caspari, "Nazwraioc Mt. 2,23 nach alttestamentlichen Voraussetzungen," *ZNW* 21 (1922): 122-27.

175   J. A. Bain, "Did Joseph Belong to Bethlehem or to Nazareth?" *ET* 47 (1935-1937): 93.

176   E. Zolli, "Nazarenus Vocabitur," *ZNW* 49 (1958): 135-36.

177   J. G. Rembry, "Quoniam Nazaraeus vocabitur (Mt. 2,23)," *SBFLA* 12 (1961-1962): 46-65.

178   J. A. Sanders, "*Nazōraios* in Matt. 2,23," *JBL* 84 (1965): 169-72.

179   Ernst Zuckschwerdt, "Ναζωραῖος in Matth. 2,23," *TZ* 31 (1975): 65-77.

180   W. Barnes Tatum, "Matthew 2:23: Wordplay and Misleading Translations," *BT* 27 (1976): 135-38.

181   H. P. Rüger, "Nazareth/Nazara Nazarenos/Nazaraios," *ZNW* 72 (1981): 257-63.

3-4

182   E. M. Wainwright, "Reading Matthew 3—4: Jesus—Sage, Seer, Sophia, Son of God," *JSNT* 77 (2000): 25-43.

3:1-12

183   B. Marconcini, "Tradizione e redazione in Mt. 3,1-12," *RBib* 19 (1971): 165-86.

184   B. Marconcini, "La predicazione del Battista in Marco e Luca confrontata con la redazione di Matteo," *RBib* 20 (1972): 451-66.

185   B. Marconcini, "La predicazione del Battista," *BibO* 15 (1973): 49-60.

3:1-5

186   Jean Doignon, "L'Argumentation d'Hilaire de Poitiers dans l'Exemplum de la Tentation de Jesus (In Matthaeum, 3,1-5)," *BT* 29 (1978): 126-28.

3:1

187   Gerd Häfner, " 'Jene Tage' (Mt 3:1) und der Umfang des matthäischen 'Prologs': Ein Beitrag zur Frage nach der Struktur des Mt-Ev," *BZ* NS 37 (1993): 43-59.

3:4

188 Hans Windisch, "Die Notiz über Tracht und Speise des Täufers Johannes und ihre Entsprechungen in der Jesusüberlieferung," *ZNW* 32 (1933): 65-87.

3:7-12

189 Alan Kirk, "Upbraiding Wisdom: John's Speech and the Beginning of Q," *NovT* 40 (1998): 1-16.

3:7-10

190 Carl Kazmierski, "The Stones of Abraham: John the Baptist and the End of Torah (Matt. 3,7-10 Par. Luke 3,7 - 9)," *Bib* 68 (1987): 22-40.

3:10

191 John P. Brown, "The Ark of the Covenant and the Temple of Janus," *BZ* 30 (1986): 20-35.

3:11-12

192 Günther Schwarz, "To de Achuron Katakausei," *ZNW* 72 (1981): 264-71.

193 Harry T. Fleddermann, "John and the Coming One (Matt. 3:11-12–Luke 3:16-17)," *SBLSP* 23 (1984): 377-84.

194 J. Daryl Charles, " 'The Coming One'/'Stronger One' and His Baptism: Matt. 3:11-12, Mark 1:8, Luke 3:16-17," *Pneuma* 11 (1989): 37-50.

3:11

195 N. Krieger, "Barfuss Busse Tun," *NovT* 1 (1956): 227-28.

196 L. W. Barnard, "A Note on Matt. 3.11 and Luke 3.16," *JTS* 8 (1957): 107.

197 P. G. Bretscher, "Whose Sandals? (Matt. 3,11)," *JBL* 86 (1967): 81-87.

3:12

198 James S. Alexander, "A Note on the Interpretation of the Parable of the Threshing Floor at the Conference at Carthage of A.D. 411," *JTS* 24 (1973): 512-19.

3:13-4:25

199 Mark McVann, "One of the Prophets: Matthew's Testing Narrative as a Rite of Passage," *BTB* 23 (1993): 14-20.

3:13-4:11

200   Benno Przybylski, "The Role of Mt. 3:13-4:11 in the Structure and Theology of the Gospel of Matthew," *BTB* 4 (1974): 222-35.

3:13-17

201   M. Dutheil, "Le Baptême de Jésus. Éléments d'interprétation," *SBFLA* 6 (1955-1956): 85-124.

202   Placide Roulin and Giles Carton, "Le Baptême du Christ," *BVC* 25 (1959): 39-48.

203   A. Viard, "Baptême du Seigneur," *EV* 85 (1975): 2-3.

204   Curtis W. Freeman, "Matthew 3:13-17," *Int* 47 (1993): 285-89.

3:15

205   F. D. Coggan, "Note on St. Matthew 3:15," *ET* 60 (1949): 258.

206   J. M. Ross, "St. Matthew 3:15," *ET* 61 (1949): 30-31.

207   Richard T. France, "The Servant of the Lord in the Teaching of Jesus," *TynB* 19 (1968): 26-52.

208   Otto Eissfeldt, "πληρῶσαι πᾶσαν δικαιοσύνην in Matthäus 3:15," *ZNW* 61 (1970): 209-15.

209   Robert G. Bratcher, " 'Righteousness' in Matthew," *BT* 40 (1989): 228-35.

3:16

210   Günther Schwarz, " 'Wie eine Taube'?" *BibN* 89 (1997): 27-29.

4:1-11

211   Jaroslav J. Pelikan, "The Temptation of the Church: A Study of Matthew 4:1-11," *CTM* 22 (1951): 251-59.

212   C. U. Wolf, "The Continuing Temptation of Christ in the Church. Searching and Preaching on Matthew 4:1-11," *Int* 20 (1966): 288-301.

213   William R. Stegner, "Wilderness and Testing in the Scrolls and in Matthew 4:1-11," *BR* 18 (1967): 18-27.

214   P. Pokorný, "The Temptation Stories and their Intention," *NTS* 20 (1974): 115-27.

215   Balmer H. Kelly, "An Exposition of Matthew 4:1-11," *Int*
       29 (1975): 57-62.

216   Kenneth Grayston, "The Temptations," *ET* 88 (1977):
       143-44.

217   Dieter Zeller, "Die Versuchungen Jesu in der
       Logienquelle," *TTZ* 89 (1980): 61-73.

218   Wilhelm Wilkens, "Die Versuchung Jesu nach Matthäus,"
       NTS 28 (1982): 479-89.

219   Walter Wink, "Matthew 4:1-11," *Int* 37 (1983): 392-97.

220   Lamar Williamson, "Matthew 4:1-11," *Int* 38 (1984):
       51-55.

221   William R. Stegner, "The Temptation Narrative: A Study
       in the Use of Scripture by Early Jewish Christians," *BR* 35
       (1990): 5-17.

222   Hugh M. Humphrey, "Temptation and Authority:
       Sapiential Narratives in Q," *BTB* 21 (1991): 43-50.

223   Marlis Gielen, " 'Und führe uns nicht in Versuchung' Die
       6. Vater-Unser Bitte—eine Anfechtung für das biblische
       Gottesbild?" *ZNW* 89 (1998): 201-16.

224   Christoph Kähler, "Satanischer Schriftgebrauch: Zur
       Hermeneutik von Mt 4,1-11//Lk 4,1-13," *TLZ* 119 (1994):
       857-67.

4:3

225   R. L. Mowery, "Subtle Differences: The Matthean 'Son of
       God' References," *NovT* 32 (1990): 193-200.

4:4

226   George D. Kilpatrick, "Matthew iv.4," *JTS* 45 (1944):
       176-77.

4:5-7

227   Niels Hyldahl, "Die Versuchung auf der Zinne des
       Tempels," *StTheol* 15 (1961): 113-27.

4:6

228   R. L. Mowery, "Subtle Differences: The Matthean 'Son of
       God' References," *NovT* 32 (1990): 193-200.

4:8

229   George D. Kilpatrick, "Three Problems of New Testament Text," *NovT* 21 (1979): 289-92.

230   D. Durken, "Mountains and Matthew," *BibTo* 28 (1990): 304-307.

4:12-7:29

231   F. Genuyt, "Evangile de Matthieu, chapitres 4,12-7,29," *SémBib* 62 (1991): 2-20.

4:12-23

232   A. Duprez, "Le programme de Jesus, selon Matthieu," *AsSeign* NS 34 (1973): 9-18.

233   T. Harley Hall, "An Exposition of Matthew 4:12-23," *Int* 29 (1975): 63-67.

4:12-17

234   Frans Neirynck, "*Apò tóte ērxato* and the Structure of Matthew," *ETL* 64 (1988): 21-59.

4:12-16

235   G. G. Gamba, "Gesù si stabilisce a Cafarnao (Mt. 4,12-16)," *BibO* 16 (1974): 109-32.

4:14-16

236   George M. Soares-Prabhu, "Matthew 4:14-16: A Key to the Origin of the Formula Quotations of Matthew," *IJT* 20 (1971): 70-91.

4:15

237   H. Dixon Slingerland, "The Transjordanian Origin of St. Matthew's Gospel," *JSNT* 1 (1979): 18-28.

4:17-5:12

238   Warren Carter, "Narrative/Literary Approaches to Matthean Theology: The 'Reign of the Heavens' as an Example," *JSNT* 67 (1997): 3-27.

4:17

239   Kazimierz Romaniuk, "Repentez-vous, car le Royaume des Cieux est tout proche (Matt. iv.17 par.)," *NTS* 12 (1965-1966): 259-69.

4:18-22

240   M. H. Franzmann, "Studies in Discipleship: I. The Calling of the Disciples (Mt. 4:18-22; 1:1-4:16)," *CTM* 31 (1960): 607-25.

241   Warren Carter, "Matthew 4:18-22 and Matthean Discipleship: An Audience-Oriented Perspective," *CBQ* 59 (1997): 58-75.

4:18-19

242   J. D. M. Derrett, "Esan gar Halieis (Mark 1:16). Jesus' Fisherman and the Parable of the Net," *NovT* 22 (1980): 108-37.

4:23-25

243   K.-S. Krieger, "Das Publikum der Bergpredigt (Mt. 4.23-25)," *K* 28 (1986): 98-119.

5-7

244   J. H. Farmer, "An Analysis of the Sermon on the Mount," *RevExp* 1 (1904): 71-80.

245   O. Hammelsbeck, "Die Bergpredigt in Andacht und Unterricht," *EvT* 5 (1938): 212-21.

246   F. C. Grant, "The Sermon on the Mount," *ATR* 24 (1942): 131-44.

247   P.-É. Bonnard, "Le Sermon sur la montagne," *RTP* 3 (1953): 233-46.

248   C. Kopp, "Die Stätte der Bergpredigt und Brotvermehrung," *BK* 8 (1953): 10-16.

249   Henlee Barnette, "The Ethic of the Sermon on the Mount," *RevExp* 53 (1956): 23-33.

250   Huber Drumwright, "A Homiletic Study of the Sermon on the Mount: The Ethical Motif," *SouJT* 5 (1962): 65-76.

251   J. Héring, "Le Sermon sur la Montagne dans la nouvelle traduction anglaise de la Bible," *RHPR* 42 (1962): 122-32.

252   J. Schmid, "Ich aber sage euch: Der Anruf der Bergpredigt," *BK* 19 (1964): 75-79.

253   Ernst Lerle, "Realisierbare Forderungen der Bergpredigt?" *KD* 16 (1970): 32-40.

254   Morris A. Inch, "Matthew and the House-Churches," *EQ* 43 (1971): 196-202.

255   G. Schmahl, "Gültigkeit und Verbindlichkeit der Bergpredigt," *BibL* 14 (1973): 180-87.

256   G. Menestrina, "Matteo 5-7 e Luca 6,20-49 nell'Evangelo di Tommaso," *BibO* 18 (1976) 65-67.

257   Frans Neirynck, "The Sermon on the Mount in the Gospel Synopsis," *ETL* 52 (1976): 350-57.

258   Karlmann Beyschlag, "Zur Geschichte der Bergpredigt in der Alten Kirche," *ZTK* 74 (1977): 291-322.

259   G. Bornkamm, "Der Aufbau der Bergpredigt," *NTS* 24 (1978): 419-32.

260   R. M. Grant, "The Sermon on the Mount in Early Christianity," *Semeia* 12 (1978): 215-31.

261   Michel Bouttier, "Hésiode et le sermon sur la montagne," *NTS* 25 (1978-1979): 129-30.

262   A.-L. Descamps, "Le Discours sur la montagne: Esquisse de théologie biblique," *RTL* 12 (1981): 5-39.

263   W. Egger, "I titoli delle pericope bibliche come chiave di lettura," *RBib* 29 (1981): 33-43.

264   E. Bader, "Bergpredigt, sozialphilosophische Aspekte," *BL* 56 (1983): 144-49.

265   Francisco Montagnini, "Echi del discorso del monte nella Didaché," *BibO* 25 (1983): 137-43.

266   Daniel T. W. Chow, "A Study of the Sermon on the Mount: With Special Reference to Matthew 5:21-48," *EAJT* 2 (1984): 312-14.

267   J. Nagórny, "Kazanie na górze (Mt. 5-7) jako moralne oredize nowego przymierza," *RoczTK* 32 (1985): 5-21.

268   Christoph Burchard, "Le thème du Sermon sur la Montogne," *ÉTR* 62 (1987): 1-17.

269   Karin Bornkamm, "Umstrittener 'Spiegel eines Christlichen lebens': Luthers Auslegung der Bergpredigt in seinen Wochenpredigten von 1530 bis 1532," *ZTK* 85 (1988): 409-54.

270   Charles E. Carlston, "Betz on the Sermon on the Mount: A Critique," *CBQ* 50 (1988): 47-57.

271   Stanley Hauerwas, "The Sermon on the Mount, Just War and the Quest for Peace," *Conci* 195 (1988): 36-43.

272   Robert J. Miller, "The Lord's Prayer and Other Items from the Sermon on the Mount," *Forum* 5 (1989): 177-86.

273   Richard E. Strelan, "The Gospel in the Sermon on the Mount," *LTJ* 23 (1989): 19-26.

274   J. G. Williams, "Paraenesis, Excess, and Ethics: Matthew's Rhetoric in the Sermon on the Mount," *Semeia* 50 (1990): 163-87.

275   H. D. Betz, "The Sermon on the Mount: In Defense of a Hypothesis," *BR* 36 (1991): 74-80.

276   Ernest W. Saunders, "A Response to H. D. Betz on the Sermon on the Mount," *BR* 36 (1991): 81-87.

277   Klyne R. Snodgrass, "A Response to H. D. Betz on the Sermon on the Mount," *BR* 36 (1991): 88-94.

278   Loyd Allen, "The Sermon on the Mount in the History of the Church," *RevExp* 89 (1992): 245-62.

279   William B. Tolar, "The Sermon on the Mount from an Exegetical Perspective," *SouJT* 35 (1992): 4-12.

280   James L. Bailey, "Sermon on the Mount: Model for Community," *CThM* 20 (1993): 85-94.

281   Jonathan A. Draper, "The Genesis and Narrative Trust of the Paraenesis in the Sermon on the Mount," *JSNT* 75 (1999): 25-48.

282   Paul Hoffmann, "Betz and Q," *ZNW* 88 (1997): 197-210.

5:1-7:29

283   William R. Farmer, "The Sermon on the Mount: A Form-Critical and Redactional Analysis of Matt. 5:1-7:29," *SBLSP* 25 (1986): 56-87.

5:1-20

284   E. Nellessen, "Aufbruch und Vollendung der Königsherrschaft: Eine Meditation zu den Perikopen des Allerheiligenfestes," *BibL* 9 (1968): 222-29.

285   J. Salguero, "Las Bienaventuranzas evangélicas," *CuBí* 29 (1972): 73-90.

286   W. J. Dumbrell, "The Logic of the Role of the Law in Matthew 5:1-20," *NovT* 23 (1981): 1-21.

5:1-12

287   F. Buchholz, "Predigt über Matthäus 5,1-12," *EvT* 14 (1954): 97-104.

288   H. Frankemölle, "Die Makarismen (Mt. 5,1-12; Lk. 6,20-23)," *BZ* 15 (1971): 52-75.

289   P.-E. Jacquemin, "Les béatitudes selon saint Matthieu," *AsSeign* NS 66 (1973): 50-63.

290   A. Viard, "Les béatitudes," *EV* 85 (1975): 5-6.

291   Robert A. Guelich, "The Matthean Beatitudes: 'Entrance-Requirements' of Eschatological Blessings," *JBL* 95 (1976): 415-34.

292   William R. Domeris, " 'Blessed Are You . . .' " *JTSA* 73 (1990): 67-76.

5:1-10

293   André Paul, "Béatitudes," *Chr* 22 (1975): 326-29.

294   Dalmazio Mongillo, "Les Béatitudes et la béatitude: Le dynamisme de la Somme de théologie de Thomas d'Aquin: une lecture de la Ia-IIae q 69," *RSPT* 78 (1994): 373-88.

5:1-8

295   Barclay M. Newman, "Some Translational Notes on the Beatitudes," *BT* 26 (1975): 106-20.

5:1-2

296   Dale C. Allison, "Jesus and Moses (Mt. 5:1-2)," *ET* 98 (1987): 203-204.

5:1

297   Jindrich Mánek, "On the Mount—On the Plain (Mt. 5:1 - Lk. 6:17)," *NovT* 9 (1967): 124-31.

5:2-12

298   Patrick J. Hartin, "Call to Be Perfect through Suffering (James 1,2-4): The Concept of Perfection in the Epistle of

James and the Sermon on the Mount," *Bib* 77 (1996): 477-92.

5:2

299   Joseph Sickenberger, "Zwei neue Äusserungen zur Ehebruchklausel bei Matthäus," *ZNW* 42 (1949): 202-209.

5:3-7:29

300   A. M. Perry, "The Framework of the Sermon on the Mount," *JBL* 54 (1935): 103-15.

5:3-12

301   Georg Braumann, "Zum traditionsgeschichtlichen Problem der Seligpreisungen Mt. 5:3-12," *NovT* 4 (1960-1961): 253-60.

302   Georg Strecker, "Die Makarismen der Bergpredigt," *NTS* 17 (1970-1971): 255-75.

303   Joseph Coppens, "Les Béatitudes," *ETL* 50 (1974): 256-60.

304   Jacques Dupont, "Introduction aux Béatitudes," *NRT* 98 (1976): 97-108.

305   H. D. Betz, "Die Makarismen der Bergpredigt (Matthäus 5:3-12)," *ZTK* 75 (1978): 3-19.

306   G. Bleickert, "Die Seligpreisungen: Eine meditative Erschliessung," *GeistL* 51 (1978): 326-38.

307   N. J. McEleney, "The Beatitudes of the Sermon on the Mount/Plain," *CBQ* 43 (1981): 1-13.

308   J. Pantelis, "Los Pobres en espíritu. Bienaventurados en el Reino de Dios. Mateo 5,3-12," *RevB* 51 (1989): 1-9.

309   Klemens Stock, "Der Weg der Freude: Die acht Seligpreisungen (I)," *GeistL* 62 (1989): 360-73.

310   Klemens Stock, "Der Gott der Freude: Die acht Seligpreisungen (II)," *GeistL* 62 (1989): 433-46.

311   Michel Gourgues, "Sur l'articulation des béatitudes matthénnes (Mt 5:3-12) (1997): une proposition," *NTS* 44 (1998): 340-56.

312   K. C. Hanson, "How Honorable! How Shameful! A Cultural Analysis of Matthew's Makarisms and Reproaches," *Semeia* 68 (1994): 81-111.

5:3-10

313   H. Spämann, "Die acht Seligkeiten: Eine Meditation zu Mt. 5,3-10," *BibL* 5 (1964): 131-36.

314   A. G. Van Aarde, "A Study of the New Testament Beatitude and the Beatitude Series in Matthew 5:3-10: A New Approach to 'Gattungsforschung'," *HTS* suppl 5 (1994): 151-79.

5:3-6

315   C. Michaelis, "Die π Alliteration der Subjektsworte der ersten 4 Seligpreisungen in Mt. V 3-6 und ihre Bedeutung für den Aufbau der Seligpreisungen bei Mt., Lk. und in Q," *NovT* 10 (1968): 148-61.

5:3-5

316   Felix Böhl, "Die Demut ('*nwh*) als höchste der Tugenden: Bemerkungen zu Mt. 5,3,5," *BZ* 20 (1976): 217-23.

5:3

317   M. Knepper, "Die 'Armen' der Bergpredigt Jesu," *BK* 8 (1953): 19-27.

318   Ernest Best, "Matthew 5:3," *NTS* 7 (1961): 255-58.

319   Simon Légasse, "Les Pauvres en Esprit et les 'Volontaires' de Qumran," *NTS* 8 (1961-1962): 336-45.

320   C. H. Dodd, "New Testament Translation Problems I," *BT* 27 (1976): 301-11.

321   Günther Schwarz, " 'Ihnen gehört das Himmelreich' (Matthäus V.3)," *NTS* 23 (1977): 341-43.

322   A. M. Ambrozic, "Reflections on the First Beatitude," *CICR* 17 (1990): 95-104.

323   Robert H. Smith, " 'Blessed Are the Poor in (Holy) Spirit'? (Matthew 5:3)," *WW* 18 (1998): 389-96.

5:4

324   P. Schempp, "Die zweite Seligpreisung," *EvT* I (1934-1935): 10-23.

325   W. Tebbe, "Die zweite Seligpreisung (Matth. 5,4)," *EvT* 12 (1952-1953): 121-28.

326   M. Kehl, " 'Selig die Trauernden. denn sie werden getröstet werden'," *GeistL* 73 (2000): 96-97.

5:6

327   J. M. Bover, "Beati qui esurivunt et sitiunt iustitiam (Mt. 5,6)," *EE* 16 (1942): 9-26.

328   Robert G. Bratcher, " 'Righteousness' in Matthew," *BT* 40 (1989): 228-35.

329   Wiard Popkes, "Die Gerechtigkeitstradition im Matthäusevangelium," *ZNW* 80 (1989): 1-23.

330   A. Sicari, "The Hunger and Thirst of Christ," *CICR* 18 (1991): 590-602.

5:9

331   B. W. Bacon, "The Blessing of the Peacemakers," *ET* 41 (1929- 1930): 58-60.

332   Rudolf Schnackenburg, "Die Sellgpreisung der Friedensstifter (Mt. 5,9) im Mattäischen Kontext," *BZ* 26 (1982): 161-78.

333   Joachim Gnilka, "Selig, die Frieden stiften," *IKaZ* 18 (1989): 97-103.

5:10

334   Robert G. Bratcher, " 'Righteousness' in Matthew," *BT* 40 (1989): 228-35.

335   Wiard Popkes, "Die Gerechtigkeitstradition im Matthäusevangelium," *ZNW* 80 (1989): 1-23.

336   Nicholas T. Wright, "Thy Kingdom come: Living the Lord's Prayer," *CC* 114 (1997): 268-70.

5:11-12

337   Werner Stenger, "Die Seligpreisungen der Geschmähten (Mt. 5,11-12; Lk. 6,22-23)," *K* 28 (1986): 33-60.

338   Pieter J. Maartens, "Critical Dialogue in Theory and Practice of Literary Interpretation: A Study of Semiotic Relations in Matthew 5:11 and 12," *LB* 65 (1991): 5-24.

5:11

339   Michael W. Holmes, "The Text of Matthew 5:11," *NTS* 32 (1986): 283-86.

5:12

340   Jacques Dupont, "Réjouissez-vous et exultez," in *Les Béatitudes*. Tome II: La bonne nouvelle. Paris: Gabalda, 1969. 2:320-38.

341   M. Corbin, "Votre récompense est grande dans les cieux," *Chr* 28 (1981): 65-77.

342   Arland J. Hultgren, "Forgive Us, as We Forgive (Matthew 6:12)," *WW* 16 (1996): 284-90.

343   Bastiaan Van Elderen, "When Do We Forgive?" *CTJ* 33 (1998): 169-75.

5:13-16

344   J. B. Soucek, "Salz der Erde und Licht der Welt. Zur Exegese von Matth. 5:13-16," *TZ* 19 (1962): 169-79.

345   H. Rusche, "Ihr, Salz der Erde, Licht der Welt!" *BibL* 14 (1973): 215-17.

346   Simon Légasse, "Les chrétiens 'sel de la terre', 'lumiere du monde'," *AsSeign* NS 36 (1974): 17-25.

347   A. Viard, "Les disciples du Christ au service du monde," *EV* 85 (1975): 6-8.

348   M. Krämer, "Ihr seid das Salz der Erde . . . Ihr seid das Licht der Welt," *MTZ* 28 (1977): 133-57.

5:13-14

349   Günther Schwarz, "Matthäus v. 13a und 14a: Emendation und Rückübersetzung," *NTS* 17 (1970-1971): 80-86.

5:13

350   A. J. Mee, "Ye Are the Salt of the Earth (Mt. 5,13)," *ET* 46 (1934-1935): 476-77.

351   J. H. Morrison, "Ye Are the Salt of the Earth! (Mt. 5,13)," *ET* 46 (1934-1935): 525.

352   Sigvard Hellestam, "Mysteriet med saltet," *SEÅ* 55 (1990): 59-63.

353   Kenneth Grayston, "The Decline of Temptation--and the Lord's Prayer," *SJT* 46 (1993): 279-95.

354   Marc Philonenko, "La sixième demande du 'Notre Père' et le livre des Jubilés," *RHPR* 78 (1998): 27-37.

5:14

355   K. M. Campbell, "The New Jerusalem in Matthew 5:14," *SJT* 31 (1978): 335-63.

356   J. D. M. Derrett, "The Light and the City: Mt. 5:14," *ET* 103 (1992): 174-75.

5:15

357   Joachim Jeremias, "Die Lampe unter dem Scheffel," *ZNW* 39 (1940): 237-40.

358   J. D. M. Derrett, "Light Under a Bushel: The Hanukkah Lamp?" *ET* 78 (1966-1967): 18.

359   Robert F. Shedinger, "The Textual Relationship Between P45 and Shem-Tob's Hebrew Matthew," *NTS* 43 (1997): 58-71.

5:17-37

360   L. Deiss, "La loi nouvelle," *AsSeign* NS 37 (1971): 19-33.

5:17-21

361   T. David Gordon, "Critique of Theonomy: A Taxonomy," *WTJ* 56 (1994): 23-43.

5:17-20

362   Eduard Schweizer, "Matth. 5,17-20. Anmerkungen zum Gesetzesverständnis des Matthäus," *TLZ* 77 (1952): 479-84.

363   André Feuillet, "Morale Ancienne et Morale Chrétienne d'après Mt. 5.17-20; Comparaison avec la Doctrine de l'Épître aux Romains," *NTS* 17 (1970-1971): 123-37.

364   Robert Banks, "Matthew's Understanding of the Law: Authenticity and Interpretation in Matthew 5:17-20," *JBL* 93 (1974): 226-42.

365   Léopold Sabourin, "Matthieu 5,17-20 et le rôle prophétique de la Loi," *SE* 30 (1978): 303-11.

366   Ulrich Luz, "Die Erfüllung des Gesetzes bei Matthäus," *ZTK* (1978-1979): 398-435.

367   C. Heubüly, "Mt. 5:17-20: Ein Beitrag zur Theologie des Evangelisten Matthäus," *ZNW* 71 (1980): 143-49.

368   Christine Heutuot, "Mt. 5,17-20," *ZNW* 71 (1980): 143-49.

5:17

369   C. F. D. Moule, "Fulfillment-Words in the New Testament: Use and Abuse," *NTS* 14 (1968): 293-320.

370   J. W. Deenick, "The Fourth Commandment and Its Fulfillment," *RTR* 28 (1969): 54-61.

371   William R. Eichhorst, "The Issue of Biblical Inerrancy in Definition and Defense," *GTJ* 10 (1969): 3-17.

372   H. van de Sandt, "An Explanation of Rom. 8:4a," *Bij* 37 (1976): 361-78.

373   D. H. C. Read, " 'Thou Shalt Not!'—Says Who?" *ET* 88 (1977): 209-11.

374   S. Clive Thexton, "The Word of God in the Old Testament," *ET* 93 (1981): 50-51.

375   Warren Carter, "Jesus' 'I have come' Statements in Matthew's Gospel," *CBQ* 60 (1998): 44-62.

5:18

376   A. M. Honeyman, "Matthew 5:18 and the Validity of the Law," *NTS* 1 (1954-1955): 141-42.

377   W. Auer, "Jota unum aut unus apex non praeteribit a lege," *BK* 14 (1959): 97-103.

378   Robert G. Hamerton-Kelly, "Attitudes to the Law in Matthew's Gospel: A Discussion of Matthew 5:18," *BR* 17 (1972): 19-32.

379   Günther Schwarz, "ἰῶτα ἓν ἢ μία κεραία (Matthäus 5:18)," *ZNW* 66 (1975): 268-69.

5:19-20

380   Benedict T. Viviano, "Matthew, Master of Ecumenical Infighting," *CThM* 10 (1983): 325-32.

5:20

381 H. Günther, "Die Gerechtigkeit des Himmelreiches in der Bergpredigt," *KD* 17 (1971): 113-26.

382 Harvey Lange, "The Greater Righteousness," *CThM* 5 (1978): 116-21.

383 Robert G. Bratcher, " 'Righteousness' in Matthew," *BT* 40 (1989): 228-35.

384 Wiard Popkes, "Die Gerechtigkeitstradition im Matthäusevangelium," *ZNW* 80 (1989): 1-23.

5:21-48

385 Victor Hasler, "Das Herzstück der Bergpredigt," *TZ* 15 (1959): 90-106.

386 Robert A. Guelich, "The Antitheses of Matthew V. 21-48: Traditional and/or Redactional?" *NTS* 22 (1976): 444-57.

387 Daniel T. W. Chow, "A Study of the Sermon on the Mount: With Special Reference to Matthew 5:21-48," *EAJT* 2 (1984): 312-14.

388 John R. Levison, "Responsible Initiative in Matthew 5:21-48," *ET* 98 (1987): 231-34.

389 D. J. Harrington, "Not to Abloish, but to Fulfill," *BibTo* 27 (1989): 333-37.

5:21-22

390 C. F. D. Moule, "Matthew 5,21-22," *ET* 50 (1938-1939): 189-90.

391 H.-J. Iwand, "Du sollst nicht töten," *EvT* 10 (1950-1951): 145-53.

5:21

392 C. Jaeger, "À propos de deux passages du sermon sur la montagne (Matthieu 6,13; 5,21 et 33)," *RHPR* 18 (1938): 415-18.

393 M. Weise, "Mt. 5:21f.—ein Zeugnis sakraler Rechtsprechung in der Urgemeinde," *ZNW* 49 (1958): 116-23.

394 C. F. D. Moule, "Uncomfortable Words. Part I. The Angry Word: Matthew 5:21f.," *ET* 81 (1969): 10-13.

395   C. F. D. Moule, "The Angry Word: Mt. 5:21f.," *ET* 81 (1969-1970): 10-13.

5:22

396   Ernest C. Colwell, "Has *Raka* a Parallel in the Papyri?" *JBL* 53 (1934): 351-54.

397   P. Wernberg-Moller, "A Semitic Idiom in Matt. v.22," *NTS* 3 (1956-57): 71-73.

398   F. Bussby, "Note on Matthew 5:22 and Matthew 6:7 in the Light of Qumran," *ET* 76 (1964-1965): 26.

399   Robert A. Guelich, "Mt. 5,22: Its Meaning and Integrity," *ZNW* 64 (1973): 39-52.

5:22

400   David A. Black, "The Text of Matthew 5:22a Revisited," *NovT* 30 (1988): 1-8.

5:23

401   Joachim Jeremias, "Lass allda deine Gabe (Mt. 5,23f.)," *ZNW* 36 (1937): 150-54.

5:25-26

402   Ernest Lussier, "The Biblical Theology on Purgatory," *AmER* 142 (1960): 225-33.

403   George B. Caird, "Expounding the Parables: The Defendant," *ET* 77 (1965-1966): 36-39.

5:27-32

404   Will Deming, "Mark 9:42-10:12, Matthew 5:27-32, and b. Nid, 13b: A First Century Discussion of Male Sexuality," *NTS* 36 (1990): 130-41.

5:27-28

405   Hubert Ordon, "Jezusowa interpretatacja zakazu cudzolóstwa," *RoczTK* 31 (1984): 81-90.

5:28

406   Klaus Haacker, "Der Rechtssatz Jesu zum Thema Ehebruch," *BZ* 21 (1977): 113-16.

5:29-30

407   Herbert W. Basser, "The Meaning of 'Shtuth', Gen. 4.11
        in Reference to Matthew 5.29-30 and 18.8-9," *NTS* 31
        (1985): 148-51.

5:29

408   Henri Clavier, "Matthieu 5,29 et la non-résistance," *RHPR*
        37 (1957): 44-57.

5:30a

409   S. D. Currie, "Matthew 5:30a: Resistance or Protest?"
        HTR 57 (1964): 140-45.

5:31

410   G. J. Wenham, "Matthew and Divorce: An Old Crux
        Revisited," *JSNT* 22 (1984): 95-107.

411   Phillip H. Wiebe, "Jesus' Divorce Exception," *JETS* 32
        (1989): 327-33.

5:31-32

412   Augustine Stock, "Matthean Divorce Texts," *BTB* 8
        (1978): 24-33.

413   Charles C. Ryrie, "Biblical Teaching on Divorce and
        Remarriage," *GTJ* 3 (1982): 177-92.

414   B. N. Wambacq, "Matthieu 5,31-32: Possibilité de Divorce
        ou Obligation de Rompre une Union Illiégitime," *NRT* 104
        (1982): 34-49.

5:32

415   Heinrich Baltensweiler, "Die Ehebruchsklauseln bei
        Matthaeus: zu Matth. 5:32; 19:9," *TZ* 15 (1959): 340-56.

416   John J. O'Rourke, "A Note on an Exception: Mt. 5:32
        (19:9) and 1 Cor 7:12 Compared," *HeyJ* 5 (1964):
        299-302.

417   H. G. Coiner, "Those 'Divorce and Remarriage'
        Passages," *CTM* 39 (1968): 367-84.

418   Richard N. Soulen, "Marriage and Divorce: A Problem in
        New Testament Interpretation," *Int* 23 (1969): 439-50.

419   Gerhard Schneider, "Jesu Wort über die Ehescheidung in der Überlieferung des Neuen Testaments," *TTZ* 80 (1971): 65-87.

420   P. T. Stramare, "Matteo Divorzista?" *Div* 15 (1971): 213-35.

421   Henri Crouzel, "Le Texte Patristique de Matthieu V.32 et XIX.9," *NTS* 19 (1972): 98-119.

422   Antonio Vargas-Machuca, "Los casos de 'divorcio' admitidos por San Mateo (5,32 y 19,9). Consecuencias para la teologia actual," *EE* 50 (1975): 5-54.

423   John J. Kilgallen, "To What Are the Matthean Exception-Texts (5,32 and 19,9) an Exception?" *Bib* 61 (1980): 102-105.

424   William A. Heth, "Another Look at the Erasmian View of Divorce and Remarriage," *JETS* 25 (1982): 263-72.

425   Ben Witherington, "Matthew 5.32 and 19.9—Exception or Exceptional Situation?" *NTS* 31 (1985): 571-76.

426   Markus Bockmuehl, "Matthew 5.32; 19.9 in the Light of Pre-Rabbinic Halakhah," *NTS* 35 (1989): 291-95.

427   Don T. Smith, "The Matthean Exception Clauses in the Light of Matthew's Theology and Community," *SBT* 17 (1989): 55-82.

428   Michael W. Holmes, "The Text of the Matthean Divorce Passages: A Comment on the Appeal to Harmonization in Textual Decisions," *JBL* 109 (1991): 651-54.

429   William A. Heth, "Divorce and Remarriage: The Search for an Evangelical Hermeneutic," *TriJ* 16 (1995): 63-100.

430   Duane Warden, "The Words of Jesus on Divorce," *RQ* 39 (1997): 141-53.

5:33-37

431   Paul S. Minear, "Yes or No: The Demand for Honesty in the Early Church," *NovT* 13 (1971): 1-13.

432   Gerhard Dautzenberg, "Ist das Schwurverbot Mt. 5,33-37; Jak 5,12 ein Beispiel für die Torakritik Jesu?" *BZ* 25 (1981): 47-66.

433   Julián Carrón Pérez, "The Second Commandment in the New Testament: Your Yes Is Yes, Your No Is No," *CICR* 20 (1993): 5-25.

434   Don B. Garlington, "Oath-Taking in the Community of the New Age (Matthew 5:33-37)," *TriJ* 16 (1995): 139-70.

435   Bernd Kollmann, "Das Schwurverbot Mt 5,33-37/Jak 5,12 im Spiegel antiker Eidkritik," *BZ* NS 40 (1996): 179-93.

5:33

436   C. Jaeger, "À propos de deux passages du sermon sur la montagne (Matthieu 6,13; 5,21 et 33)," *RHPR* 18 (1938): 415-18.

5:34-37

437   Gustav Stählin, "Zum Gebrauch von Beteuerungsformeln im Neuen Testament," *NovT* 5 (1962): 115-43.

5:35

438   Dennis C. Duling, " 'Do Not Swear . . . by Jerusalem' Because It Is the City of the Great King," *JBL* 110 (1991): 291-309.

5:37

439   Lucile L. Brandt, "The Christian Yea and Nay," *BLT* 22 (1977): 245-50.

5:38-48

440   Jerome Rausch, "The Principle of Nonresistance and Love of Enemy in Mt. 5,38-48," *CBQ* 28 (1966): 31-41.

441   Fritz Neugebauer, "Die dargebotene Wange und Jesu Gebot der Feindesliebe: Erwägungen zu Lk. 6,27-36//Mt. 5,38-48," *TLZ* 110 (1985): 865-76.

5:38-42

442   Harald Sahlin, "Traditionskritische Bemerkungen zu zwei Evangelienperikopen," *StTheol* 33 (1979): 6

443   Markus Rathey, "Talion im NT? Zu Mt. 5,38-42," *ZNW* 82 (1991): 264-66.

444   Dale C. Allison, "Anticipating the Passion: The Literary Reach of Matthew 26:47-27:56," *CBQ* 56 (1994): 701-14.

5:38-39

445   H. E. Bryant, "Matthew 5,38.39," *ET* 48 (1936-37): 236-37.

5:38

446   David Daube, "Matthew v.38f," *JTS* 45 (1944): 177-87.

5:39-47

447   Edgar V. McKnight and Charles H. Talbert, "Can the Griesbach Hypothesis Be Falsified?" *JBL* 91 (1972): 338-68.

5:39-42

448   Harald Sahlin, "Ett svårt ställe i Bergspredikan (Mt. 5:39-42)," *SEÅ* 51/52 (1986-1987): 214-218.

5:39-41

449   Lewis R. Donelson, " 'Do Not Resist Evil' and the Question of Biblical Authority," *HBT* 10 (1988): 33-46.

5:39

450   E. W. Archer, "Matthew v. 39," *ET* 42 (1930-1931): 190-91.

451   H. E. Bryant, "Matthew 6,13 and 5,39," *ET* 47 (1935-1936): 93-95.

452   Marcus J. Borg, "A New Context for Romans XIII," *NTS* 19 (1973): 205-18.

453   K.-S. Krieger, "Fordert Mt. 5:39b das passive Erdulden von Gewalt? Ein kleiner Beitrag zur Redaktionskritik der 5 Antithese," *BibN* 54 (1990): 28-32.

5:43-48

454   O. Bayer, "Sprachbewegung und Weltveränderung. Ein systematischer Versuch als Auslegung von Mt. 5,43-48," *EvT* 35 (1975): 309-21.

455   Bonnie B. Thurston, "Matthew 5:43-48," *Int* 41 (1987): 170-73.

5:43-44

456   O. J. F. Seitz, "Love your Enemies," *NTS* 16 (1969-1970): 39-54.

5:43

457   M. Smith, "Mt. 5.43: 'Hate Thine Enemy'," *HTR* 45 (1952): 71-73.

458   Olof Linton, "St. Matthew 5,43," *StTheol* 18 (1964): 66-80.

5:44-48

459   Patrick J. Hartin, "Call to Be Perfect through Suffering (James 1,2-4): The Concept of Perfection in the Epistle of James and the Sermon on the Mount," *Bib* 77 (1996): 477-92.

5:44

460   Marcus J. Borg, "A New Context for Romans XIII," *NTS* 19 (1973): 205-18.

5:46

461   E. M. Sidebottom, " 'Reward' in Matthew v.46, etc.," *ET* 67 (1955-1956): 219-20.

462   Marcus J. Borg, "A New Context for Romans XIII," *NTS* 19 (1973): 205-18.

5:48

463   H. Bruppacher, "Was sagte Jesus in Matthäus 5,48?" *ZNW* 58 (1967): 145.

464   Léopold Sabourin, "Why Is God Called 'Perfect' in Mt. 5:48?" *BZ* 24 (1980): 266-68.

465   Robert H. Smith, "The End in Matthew (5:48 and 28:20): How to Preach It and How Not To," *WW* 19 (1999): 303-13.

6:1-18

466   Christian Dietzfelbinger, "Die Frömmigkeitsregeln von Mt. 6,1-18 als Zeugnisse frühchristlicher Geschichte," *ZNW* 75 (1985): 184-201.

6:1

467   Robert G. Bratcher, " 'Righteousness' in Matthew," *BT* 40 (1989): 228-35.

468   Wiard Popkes, "Die Gerechtigkeitstradition im Matthäusevangelium," *ZNW* 80 (1989): 1-23.

6:2

469   E. Klostermann, "Zum Verständnis von Mt. 6,2," *ZNW* 47 (1956): 280-81.

470   N. J. McEleney, "Does the Trumpet Sound or Resound? An Interpretation of Matthew 6,2," *ZNW* 76 (1985): 43-46.

6:4

471   Paul Ellingworth, " 'In Secret' (Matthew 6.4, 6, 18)," *BT* 40 (1989): 446-47.

472   Günther Schwarz, "ὁ βλέπτων ἐν τῷ κρυπτῶι," *BibN* 54 (1990): 38-41.

6:5-15

473   Scott L. Tatum, "Great Prayers of the Bible," *SouJT* 14 (1972): 29-42.

474   Philip B. Harner, "Matthew 6:5-15," *Int* 4 (1987): 173-78.

6:5-13

475   Richard J. Dillon, "On the Christian Obedience of Prayer (Matthew 6:5-13)," *Worship* 59 (1985): 413-26.

476   Lewis J. Prockter, "The Blind Spot: New Testament Scholarship's Ignorance of Rabbinic Judaism," *ScrSA* 48 (1994): 1-12.

6:6

477   Paul Ellingworth, " 'In Secret' (Matthew 6.4, 6, 18)," *BT* 40 (1989): 446-47.

478   Günther Schwarz, "ὁ βλέτων ἐν τῷ κρυπτῶι," *BibN* 54 (1990): 38-41.

6:7

479   F. Bussby, "Note on Matthew v.22 and Matthew vi.7 in the Light of Qumran," *ET* 76 (1964-1965): 26.

6:9-15

480   W. Stiller, *"Vaterunser,* Biblische Erwägungen," *TGl* 42 (1952): 49-52.

481   T. W. Manson, "The Lord's Prayer," *BJRL* 38 (1955-1956): 99-113, 436-48.

482   W. Fresenius, "Beobachtungen und Gedanken zum Gebet des Herrn," *EvT* 20 (1960): 235-39.

483   Georges Casalis, "Das Vater Unser und die Weltlage," *EvT* 29 (1969): 357-71.

6:9-13

484   O. Schäfer, "Das Vaterunser, das Gebet des Christen," *TGl* 35 (1943): 1-6.

485   Joachim Jeremias, "The Lord's Prayer in Modern Research," *ET* 71 (1959-1960): 141-46.

486   D. W. Shriver, "The Prayer that Spans the World. An Exposition: Social Ethics and the Lord's Prayer," *Int* 21 (1967): 274-88.

487   Günther Schwarz, "Matthäus vi.9-13, Lukas xi.2-4," *NTS* 15 (1968-1969): 233-47.

488   Daniel C. Arichea, "Translating the Lord's Prayer (Matthew 6.9-13)," *BT* 31 (1980): 219-23.

489   L. Gil, "Versiones del *Pater noster* al castellaño en el Siglo de Oro," *FilN* 1 (1988): 175-91.

490   W. M. Buchan, "Research on the Lord's Prayer," *ET* 100 (1989): 336-39.

491   Robert J. Miller, "The Lord's Prayer and Other Items from the Sermon on the Mount," *Forum* 5 (1989): 177-86.

492   D. A. Templeton, "The Lord's Prayer as Eucharist in Daily Life," *IBS* 11 (1989): 133-40.

493   R. G. Kratz, "Die Gnade des täglichen Brots: Späte Psalmen auf dem Weg zum Vaterunser," *ZTK* 89 (1992): 1-40.

494   F. Urbanek, " 'Vater im Himmel': das alte Vaterunser in sprachlicher Neuauflage," *LB* 66 (1992): 39-54.

495   Rick W. Byargeon, "Echoes of Wisdom in the Lord's Prayer (Matt 6:9-13)," *JETS* 41 (1998): 353-65.

496   Warren Carter, "Recalling the Lord's Prayer: The Authorial Audience and Matthew's Prayer as Familiar Liturgical Experience," *CBQ* 57 (1995): 514-30.

497   Günther Schwarz, "Das Gebet der Gebete (Mt 6,9-13//Lk 11,2-4)," *BibN* 70 (1993): 21-24.

498   Alistair I. Wilson, "The Disciples' Prayer: A Fresh Look at a Familiar Text," *RTR* 57 (1998): 136-50.

499   L. Cardellino, "Il 'Padrenostro'," *BibO* 46 (1999): 129-207.

500   F. Pierno, "Appunti sull'evoluzione testuale del *Padre nostro* nelle versioni bibliche italiane del Quattro-Cinquecentesche," *RivBib* 48 (2000): 55-68.

<u>6:9-11</u>

501   F. Hauck, "ἄρτος ἐπιούσιος," *ZNW* 33 (1934): 199-202.

<u>6:9</u>

502   James Swetnam, "Hallowed Be Thy Name," *Bib* 52 (1971): 556-63.

503   David J. Clark, "Our Father in Heaven," *BT* 30 (1979): 210-13.

504   Monsengwo Pasinya, "Lokola biso tokolimbisaka baninga (Mt. 6,9 par.): Incidence théologique d'une traduction," *RAfT* 12 (1988): 15-21.

505   Willem A. VanGemeren, "'Abba' in the Old Testament?" *JETS* 31 (1988): 386-98.

<u>6:10</u>

506   Kair A. Syreeni, "Between Heaven and Earth: On the Structure of Matthew's Symbolic Universe," *JSNT* 40 (1990): 9-13.

507   Marc Philonenko, "La troisème demande du 'Notre Père' et l'hymne de Nabuchodonosor," *RHPR* 72 (1992): 23-31.

<u>6:11</u>

508   Matthew Black, "The Aramaic of τὸν ἄρτον ἡμῶν τὸν ἐπιούσιον, Matt. vi.11 Luke xi.3," *JTS* 42 (1941): 186-89.

509   G. H. P. Thompson, "Thy Will Be Done in Earth as It Is in Heaven (Matthew vi. II)," *ET* 70 (1959-1960): 379- 81.

510   J. Starcky, "La Quatrième Demande du Pater," *HTR* 64 (1971): 401-409.

511   B. Hemmerdinger, "Un élément pythagoricien dans le Pater," *ZNW* 63 (1972): 121.

512   Bernard Orchard, "The Meaning of τὸν ἐπιούσιον (Mt. 6:11 = Lk. 11:3)," *BTB* 3 (1973): 274-82.

513   R. ten Kate, "Geef ons Heden ons 'Dagelijks Brood'," *NedTT* 32 (1978): 125-39.

514   Henri Bourgoin, "Epiousios Expliqué par la Notion de Prefixe Vide," *Bib* 60 (1979): 91-96.

515   Delores Aleixandre, "En torno a la cuarta peticion del Padrenuestro," *EB* 45 (1987): 325-36.

516   H. Heinen, "Göttliche Sitometrie: Beobachtungen zur Brotbitte des Vaterunsers," *TTZ* 99 (1990): 72-79.

517   Arland J. Hultgren, "The Bread Petition of the Lord's Prayer," *ATR* 11 (1990): 41-54.

518   L. Ramaroson, " 'Notre part de nourriture'," *ScE* 43 (1991): 87-115.

519   R. G. Kratz, "Die Gnade des täglichen Brots: Späte Psalmen auf dem Weg zum Vaterunser," *ZTK* 89 (1992): 1-40.

6:12

520   E. Sjöberg, "Das Licht in dir. Zur Deutung von Matth. 6,12f. Par.," *StTheol* 5 (1952): 89-105.

6:12

521   F. C. Burkitt, " 'As We Have Forgiven' (Matt. 6:12)," *JTS* 33 (1932): 253-55.

522   F. C. Fensham, "The Legal Background of Mt. 6:12," *NovT* 4 (1960-1961): 1-2.

523   J. M. Ford, "The Forgiveness Clause in the Matthean Form of the Our Father," *ZNW* 59 (1968): 127-31.

524   Samuel T. Lachs, "On Matthew 6:12," *NovT* 17 (1975): 6-8.

6:13

525 H. E. Bryant, "Matthew 6,13 and 5,39," *ET* 47 (1935-1936): 93-95.

526 C. Jaeger, "À propos de deux passages du sermon sur la montagne (Matthieu 6,13; 5,21 et 33)," *RHPR* 18 (1938): 415-18.

527 J. N. Hoare, "Lead us not into Temptation," *ET* 50 (1938-1939): 333.

528 A. J. B. Higgins, " 'Lead Us Not into Temptation': Some Latin Variants," *JTS* 46 (1945): 179-83.

529 W. Powell, "Lead Us Not into Temptation," *ET* 67 (1955-1956): 177-78.

530 J. B. Bauer, "Liberia nos a malo," *VD* 34 (1956): 12-15

531 M. H. Sykes, "And Do Not Bring Us to the Test," *ET* 73 (1961-1962): 189-90.

532 Michael B. Walker, "Lead Us Not into Temptation," *ET* 73 (1961-1962): 287.

533 J. Carmignac, "La portée d'une négation devant un verbe au causatif," *RB* 72 (1965): 218-26.

534 G. Smith, "Matthaean 'Additions' to Lord's Prayer," *ET* 82 (1970-1971): 54-55.

535 Buetubela Balembo, "Et ne nous sournets pas à la tentation. La difficile actualisation de Mt. 6,13," *RAfT* 10 (1986): 5-13.

536 Pierre Grelot, "L'épreuve de la Tentation," *EV* 99 (1989): 280-84.

537 Wiard Popkes, "Die letzte Bitte des Vater-Unser: Formgeschichtliche Beobachtungen zum Gebet Jesu," *ZNW* 81 (1990): 1-20.

538 Stanley E. Porter, "Mt. 6:13 and Lk. 11:4: 'Lead Us not into Temptation'," *ET* 101 (1990): 359-62.

539 E. Moore, "Lead Us Not into Temptation," *ET* 102 (1991): 171-72.

6:13

540   Davis McCaughey, "Matthew 6.13a: The Sixth Petition in the Lord's Prayer," *ABR* 33 (1985): 31-40.

6:18

541   Paul Ellingworth, " 'In Secret' (Matthew 6.4, 6, 18)," *BT* 40 (1989): 446-47.

542   Günther Schwarz, "ὁ βλέπων ἐν τῷ κρυπτῶι" *BibN* 54 (1990): 38-41.

6:22-23

543   Dale C. Allison, "The Eye is the Lamp of the Body (Matthew 6.22-23 = Luke 11.34-36)," *NTS* 33 (1987): 61-83.

544   Marc Philonenko, "La parabole sur la lampe (Luc 11:33-36) et les horoscopes qoumâniens," *ZNW* 79 (1988): 145-51.

545   John H. Elliott, "The Evil Eye and the Sermon on the Mount: Contours of a Pervasive Belief in Social Scientific Perspective," *BibInt* 2 (1994): 51-84.

6:24-34

546   Karl Barth, "Predigt über Matth. 6,24-34," *EvT* 2 (1935): 331-38.

547   P.-E. Jacquemin, "Les options du chretien," *AsSeign* NS 39 (1972): 18-27.

548   Charles E. Carlston, "Matthew 6:24-34," *Int* 41 (1987): 179-83.

6:24

549   H. P. Rüger, "Μαμωνᾶς," *ZNW* 64 (1973): 127-31.

550   Hans C. Brennecke, " 'Niemand kann zwei Herren dienen': Bemerkungen zur Auslegung von Mt 6:24//Lk 16:13 in der Alten Kirche," *ZNW* 88 (1997): 157-69.

6:25-34

551   H. D. Betz, "Kosmogonie und Ethik in der Bergpredigt," *ZTK* 81 (1984): 139-71.

552 C. Lejeune, "Les oiseaux et les lis. Lecture 'écologique' de Matthieu 6,25-34," *Hokhma* 44 (1990): 3-20.

553 J. J. Bartolomé, "Los pájaros y los lirios: Una aproximación a la cuestión ecológica desde Mt. 6,25-34," *EB* 49 (1991): 165-90.

554 John N. Jones, " 'Think of the Lilies' and Prov 6:6-11," *HTR* 88 (1995): 175-77.

555 Oda Wischmeyer, "Matthäus 6,25-34 par: Die Spruchreihe vom Sorgen," *ZNW* 85 (1994): 1-22.

6:25

556 Detlev Dormeyer, "Das Verständnis von Arbeit im Neuen Testament im Horizont der Naherwartung," *HTS* 45 (1989): 801-14.

6:26

557 J. F. Healey, "Models of Behavior: Matt. 6:26," *JBL* 108 (1989): 497-98.

6:27

558 Patrick P. Saydon, "Some Biblico-Liturgical Passages Reconsidered," *MeliT* 18 (1966): 10-17.

559 Günther Schwarz, "Prostheinae epi teen Helikian autou Pechun hena," *ZNW* 71 (1980): 244-47.

6:28

560 Peter Katz, "πῶς αὐξάνουσιν, Matt. VI. 28," *JTS* 5 (1954): 207-209.

561 J. Enoch Powell, "Those 'Lilies of the Field' Again," *JTS* 33 (1982): 490-92.

562 James M. Robinson and Christoph Heil, "Zeugnisse eines schriftlichen, griechischen vorkanonischen Textes: Mt 6,18b Aleph, P Oxy 655 I,1-17 und Q 12,27," *ZNW* 89 (1998): 30-44.

6:29

563 Warren Carter, " 'Solomon in All His Glory': Inter-textuality and Matthew 6:29," *JSNT* 65 (1997): 3-25.

6:33

564   W. H. P. Hatch, "A Note on Matthew 6:33," *HTR* 38 (1945): 270-72.

565   Thomas E. Schmidt, "Burden, Barrier, Blasphemy: Wealth in Matt. 6:33, Luke 14:33, and Luke 16:15," *TriJ* 9 (1988): 171-89.

566   Robert G. Bratcher, " 'Righteousness' in Matthew," *BT* 40 (1989): 228-35.

567   Wiard Popkes, "Die Gerechtigkeitstradition im Matthäusevangelium," *ZNW* 80 (1989): 1-23.

7:1-12

568   N. J. McEleney, "The Unity and Theme of Matthew 7:1-12," *CBQ* 56 (1994): 490-500.

7:1

569   F. J. Steinmetz and Friedrich Wulf, "Richtet Nicht," *GeistL* 42 (1969): 71-75.

570   George S. Hendry, "Judge Not: A Critical Test of Faith," *TT* 40 (1983): 113-29.

571   J. D. M. Derrett, "Christ and Reproof (Matthew 7.1-5//Luke 6.37-42)," *NTS* 34 (1988): 271-81.

572   Bernd Kollmann, "Jesu Verbot des Richtens und die Gemeindedisziplin," *ZNW* 88 (1997): 170-86.

7:2

573   H. P. Rüger, "Mit welchem Mass ihr messt, wird euch gemessen werden," *ZNW* 60 (1969): 174-82.

7:3-5

574   G. B. King, "A Further Note on the Mote and the Beam (Matt. 7:3-5; Luke 6:41-42)," *HTR* 26 (1933): 73-76.

7:5

575   C. Daniel, " 'Faux Prophète': Surnom des Esséniens dans le Sermon sur la Montagne," *RevQ* 7 (1969): 45-79.

7:6

576   A. M. Perry, "Pearls before Swine," *ET* 46 (1934-1935): 381-82.

577   T. F. Glasson, "Chiasmus in St. Matthew vii.6," *ET* 68 (1956-1957): 302.

578   Günther Schwarz, "Matthäus vii 6a. Emendation und Rückübersetzung," *NovT* 14 (1972): 18-25.

579   Thomas J. Bennett, "Matthew 7:6—A New Interpretation," *WTJ* 49 (1987): 371-86.

580   Hermann von Lips, "Schweine füttert man, Hunde nicht. Ein Versuch, das Rätsel von Matthäus 7:6 zu lösen," *ZNW* 79 (1988): 165-86.

581   Stephen Llewelyn, "Mt. 7:6a: Mistranslation or Interpretation," *NovT* 31 (1989): 97-103.

7:7-8

582   John D. Crossan, "Aphorism in Discourse and Narrative," *Semeia* 43 (1988): 121-40.

7:7

583   Otto A. Piper, "In Search of Christ's Presence," *Int* 12 (1958): 16-27.

7:8

584   David Hellholm, "En textgrammatisk konstruktion I Matteus-evangeliet," *SEÅ* 51 (1986-1987): 80-89.

585   Willem A. VanGemeren, " 'Abba' in the Old Testament? *JETS* 31 (1988): 386-98.

7:11

586   Robert F. Shedinger, "The Textual Relationship Between P45 and Shem-Tob's Hebrew Matthew," *NTS* 43 (1997): 58-71.

7:12

587   H.-W. Bartsch, "Traditionsgeschichtliches zur 'Goldenen Regel' und zum Aposteldekret," *ZNW* 75 (1984): 128-32.

588   W. Wolbert, "Die Goldene Regel und das ius talionis," *TTZ* 95 (1986): 169-81.

589   P. Ricoeur, "The Golden Rule: Exegetical and Theological Perplexities," *NTS* 36 (1990): 392-97.

7:13-14

590   J. D. M. Derrett, "The Merits of the Narrow Gate," *JSNT* 15 (1982): 20-29.

591   E. P. Nacpil, "The Way To Life: Matt. 7:13-14," *EAJT* 11 (1983): 130-32.

592   Martino Conti, "La via della beatitudine e della rovina secondo il Salmo I," *Ant* 61 (1986): 3-39.

7:13

593   Rod Parrott, "Entering the Narrow Door: Matt. 7:13//Luke 13:22-24," *Forum* 5 (1989): 111-20.

7:13a

594   Günther Schwarz, "Matthäus vii.13a," *NovT* 12 (1970): 229-32.

7:14

595   David A. Black, "Remarks on the Translation of Matthew 7:14" *FilN* 2 (1989): 193-95.

596   G. H. R. Horsley, "τί at Matthew 7:14: 'Because' not 'How'," *FilN* 3 (1990): 141-43.

7:14b

597   A. J. Mattill, " 'The Way of Tribulation'," *JBL* 98 (1979): 531-46.

7:15-23

598   David Hill, "The False Prophets and Charismatics: Structure and Interpretation in Matthew 7:15-23," *Bib* 57 (1976): 327-48.

7:15

599   Otto Böcher, "Wölfe in Schafspelzen. Zum religionsgeschichtlichen Hintergrund von Matth. 7,15," *TZ* 24 (1968): 405-26.

7:21-27

600   A. Ornella, "Les chrétiens seront jugés," *AsSeign* NS 40 (1973): 16-27.

7:21-23

601   H. D. Betz, "Eine Episode im Jungsten Gericht," *ZTK* 78 (1981): 1-30.

602   Alberto Maggi, "Nota sull'uso τῷ σῷ ονοματι e ανομια in Mt. 7:21-23" *FilN* 3 (1990): 145-49.

7:22

603   Eduard Schweizer, "Observance of the Law and Charismatic Activity in Matthew," *NTS* 16 (1970): 213-30.

7:24-27

604   Walter Magass, " 'Er aber schlief' (Mt. 8,24)," *LB* 29/30 (1973): 55-59.

7:27

605   George Howard, "A Note on Codex Sinaiticus and Shem-Tob's Hebrew Matthew," *NTS* 38 (1992): 187-204.

7:24-26

8:1-11:1

606   I. Fransen, "La Charte de l'Apôtre," *BVC* 37 (1961): 34-45.

8-9

607   William G. Thompson, "Reflections on the Composition of Mt. 8:1-9:34," *CBQ* 33 (1971): 365-88.

608   B. F. Drewes, "The Composition of Matthew 8-9," *SEAJT* 12 (1972): 92-101.

609   C. Burger, "Jesu Taten nach Matthäus 8 und 9," *ZTK* 70 (1973): 272-87.

610   Jack D. Kingsbury, "Observations on the 'Miracle Chapters' of Matthew 8-9," *CBQ* 40/4 (1978): 559-73.

611   Jeremy Moiser, "The Structure of Matthew 8-9: A Suggestion." *ZNW* 76/1 (1985): 117-18.

8:1-13

> 612   Marcel Bastin, "Jesus Worked Miracles: Texts from Mt. 8," *LV* 39/2 (1984): 131-39.

8:1-4

> 613   John J. Pilch, "Understanding Biblical Healing: Electing the Appropriate Model," *BTB* 18 (1988): 60-66.

> 614   Jack D. Kingsbury, "Retelling the 'Old, Old Story': The Miracle of the Cleansing of the Leper as an Approach to the Theology of Matthew," *CThM* 4/6 (1977): 342-49.

> 615   Marcel Bastin, "Jesus Worked Miracles: Texts from Mt. 8," *LV* 39/2 (1984): 131-39.

8:5-13

> 616   H. F. D. Sparks, "The Centurion's παῖς," *JTS* 42 (1941): 179-80.

> 617   Rudolf Schnackenburg, "Zur Traditionsgeschichte von Joh, 4, 46-54," *BZ* 8 (1964): 58-88.

> 618   E. F. Siegman, "St. John's Use of the Synoptic Material," *CBQ* 30/2 (1968): 182-98.

> 619   J. D. M. Derrett, "Law in the New Testament: The Syro-Phoenician Woman and the Centurion of Capernaum," *NovT* 15 (1973): 161-86.

> 620   Christoph Burchard, "Zu Matthäus 8,5-13," *ZNW* 84 (1993): 278-88.

> 621   Robert A. J. Gagnon, "The Shape of Matthew's Q Text of the Centurion at Capernaum: Did It Mention Delegations?" *NTS* 40 (1994): 133-42.

8:9

> 622   M. Frost, "I Also Am a Man under Authority," *ET* 45 (1933-1934): 477-78.

> 623   C. F. Hogg, "The Lord's Pleasure in the Centurion's Faith," *ET* 47 (1935-1936): 44-45.

8:11-12

> 624   Dale C. Allison, "Who Will Come from East and West," *IBS* 11 (1989): 158-70.

625   Dieter Zeller, "Das Logion Mt. 8,11f., Lk. 13,28f., und das Motiv der 'Völkerwallfahrt'," *BZ* 15 (1971): 222-37; 16 (1972): 84-93.

626   W. Grimm, "Zum Hintergrund von Mt. 8,11f., Lk. 13,28f.," *BZ* 16 (1972): 255-56.

8:12

627   B. Schwank, "Dort wird Heulen und Zähneknirschen sein," *BZ* 16 (1972): 121-22.

8:14-15

628   Marcel Bastin, "Jesus Worked Miracles: Texts from Mt. 8," *LV* 39 (1984): 131-39.

8:15

629   Günther Schwarz, " 'Er berührte ihre Hand'?" *BibN* 73 (1994): 33-35.

8:16-22

630   Marcel Bastin, "Jesus Worked Miracles: Texts from Mt. 8," *LV* 39 (1984): 131-39.

8:16-17

631   Alva J. McClain, "Was Christ Punished for Our Diseases?" *GTJ* 6 (1965): 3-6.

8:17

632   M. J. J. Menken, "The Source of the Quotation from Isaiah 53:4 in Matthew 8:17," *NovT* 39 (1997): 313-27.

633   Daniel Patte, "Textual Constraints, Ordinary Readings, and Critical Exegeses: An Androcritical Perspective," *Semeia* 62 (1993): 59-79.

8:18-22

634   Jack D. Kingsbury, "On Following Jesus: The 'Eager' Scribe and the 'Reluctant' Disciple (Matthew 8:18-22)," *NTS* 34 (1988): 45-59.

635   Jarmo Killunen, "Der nachfolgewillige Schriftgelehrte: Matthäus 8:19-20 im verständnis des Evangelisten," *NTS* 37 (1991): 268-79.

8:20

636   P. Maurice Casey, "The Son of Man Problem," *ZNW* 67 (1976): 147-54.

637   P. Maurice Casey, "The Jackals and the Son of Man (Matt. 8.20//Luke 9.58)," *JSNT* 23 (1985): 3-22.

638   M. H. Smith, "No Place for a Son of Man," *Forum* 4 (1988): 83-107.

639   François Martin, "The Image of Shepherd in the Gospel of St. Matthew," *ScE* 27 (1975): 261-301.

8:21-22

640   A. Ehrhardt, "Lass die Toten ihre Toten begraben," *StTheol* 6 (1953): 128-64.

641   Byron McCane, "Let the Dead Bury Their Own Dead: Secondary Burial and Matthew 8:21-22," *HTR* 83 (1990): 31-43.

8:21

642   Roy A. Harrisville, "Jesus and the Family," *Int* 23 (1969): 425-38.

8:22

643   F. Perles, "Zwei Übersetzungsfehler im Text der Evangelien," *ZNW* 19 (1919-1920): 96.

644   F. Perles, "Noch einmal Mt. 8:22," *ZNW* 25 (1926): 286.

645   H. G. Klemm, "Das Wort von der Selbstbestattung der Toten," *NTS* 16 (1969-1970): 60-75.

646   Günther Schwarz, "*Aphes tous Nekrous Thapsai tous heauton nekrous*," *ZNW* 72 (1981): 272-76.

647   Markus Bockmuehl, " 'Let the Dead Bury Their Dead' (Matt 8:22//Luke 9:60) (1997): Jesus and the Halakhah," *JTS* NS 49 (1998): 553-81.

8:23-27

648   J. Duplacy, "Et il y eut un grand calme . . . La tempête apaisée (Matthieu 8:23-27)," *BVC* 74 (1967): 15-28.

649   Paul F. Feiler, "The Stilling of the Storm in Matthew: A Response to Günther Bornkamm," *JETS* 26 (1983): 399-406.

8:24

650   Walter Magass, " 'Er aber schlief' (Mt. 8,24)," *LB* 29/30 (1973): 55-59.

651   Günther Schwarz, " 'Ein grosses Beben entstand auf dem Meer'? (Matthäus 8,24)," *BibN* 74 (1994): 31-32.

8:28-34

652   Anton Vögtle, "Die historische und theologische Tragweite der heutigen Evangelienforschung," *ZKT* 86 (1964): 385-417.

653   Musa W. Dube, "Consuming a Colonial Cultural Bomb: Translating Badimo into 'Demons' in the Setswana Bible," *JSNT* 73 (1999): 33-59.

8:29

654   R. L. Mowery, "Subtle Differences: The Matthean 'Son of God' References," *NovT* 32 (1990): 193-200.

9-27

655   George D. Kilpatrick, "The Historic Present in the Gospels and Acts," *ZNW* 68 (1977): 258-62.

9:1-8

656   Frans Neirynck, "Les accords mineurs et la rédaction des évangiles L'épisode du paralytique (Mt. IX,1-8; Lc. V,17-26 pa.r; Mc. II,1-12)," *ETL* 50 (1974): 215-30.

9:2

657   Robert H. Thouless, "Miracles and Physical Research," *Theology* 72 (1969): 253-58.

9:8

658   Wolfgang Schenk, "Den Menschen, Mt. 9:8," *ZNW* 54 (1963): 272-75.

659   Juan Leal, " 'Qui Dedit Potestatem Talem Hominibus' (Mt. 9,8)," *VD* 44 (1966): 53-59.

9:9-26

660   F. Genuyt, "Evangile de Matthieu 9,9-26," *SémBib* 64 (1991): 3-14.

9:9-13

661   Rudolf Pesch, "Manifestation de la miséricorde de Dieu (Mt. 9)," *AsSeign* NS 41 (1971): 15-24.

662   Michael Theobald, "Der Primat der Synchronie vor der Diachronie als Grundaxiom der Literaturkritik: Methodische Erwägungen an Hand von Mk. 2,13-17, Mt. 9,9-13," *BZ* 22 (1978): 161-86.

663   Mark Kiley, "Why 'Matthew' in Matt. 9, 9-13?" *Bib* 65 (1984): 347-51.

9:9

664   Barnabas Lindars, "Matthew, Levi, Lebbaeus and the Value of the Western Text," *NTS* 4 (1957-1958): 220-22.

665   Rudolf Pesch, "Levi-Matthäus (Mc. 2,14//Mt. 9,9; 10,3): Ein Beitrag zur Lösung eines alten Problems," *ZNW* 59 (1968): 40-56.

9:13-14

666   José O'Callaghan, "Tres casos de armonización en Mt. 9," *EB* 47 (1989): 131-34.

9:13

667   David Hill, "On the Use and Meaning of Hosea vi.6 in Matthew's Gospel," *NTS* 24 (1977): 107-19.

668   Warren Carter, "Jesus' 'I have come' Statements in Matthew's Gospel," *CBQ* 60 (1998): 44-62.

669   Mary Hinkle-Edin, "Learning What Righteousness Means: Hosea 6:6 and the Ethic of Mercy in Matthew's Gospel," *WW* 18 (1998): 355-63.

9:14-17

670   Juan Fernández, "La cuestion de ayuno (Mt. 9,14-17; Mc. 2,18-22; Lu. 5,33-39)," *CuBí* 19 (1962): 162-69.

671   Philippe Rolland, "Les Prédécesseurs de Marc: Les Sources Pré-synoptiques de Mc II,18-22 et Parallèles," *RB* 89 (1982): 370-405.

672   George J. Brooke, "The Feast of New Wine and the Question of Fasting," *ET* 95 (1984): 175-76.

9:14-15

673   J. C. O'Neill, "The Source of the Parables of the Bridegroom and the Wicked Husbandman," *JTS* 39 (1988): 485-89.

9:17

674   A. E. Harvey, "New Wine in Old Skins: II. Priest," *ET* 84 (1973): 200-203.

9:18-26

675   E. Galbiati, "Gesù guarisce l'emorroissa e risuscita la figlia di Giairo (Matt. 9,18-26)," *BibO* 6 (1964): 225-30.

676   Everett R. Kalin, "Matthew 9:18-26: An Exercise in Redaction Criticism," *CThM* 15 (1988): 39-47.

9:18-25

677   Roger L. Omanson, "A Question of Harmonization— Matthew 9:18-25," *BT* 42 (1991): 241.

9:18

678   José O'Callaghan, "La Variante *eis/elthon* en Mt. 9,18," *Bib* 62 (1981): 104-106.

9:20-22

679   Manfred Hutter, "Ein Altorientalischer Bittegestus in Mt. 9,20-22," *ZNW* 75 (1984): 133-35.

9:24

680   R. C. Fuller, "The Healing of Jairus' Daughter," *Scr* 3 (1948): 53.

9:28

681   Angelo Lancellotti, "La Casa Pietro a Cafarnao nel Vangeli Sinottici: Redazione e Tradizione," *Ant* 58 (1983): 48-69.

9:32-34

682 Pierre Guillemette, "La Forme des Récits d'Exorcisme de Bultmann: Un Dogme a Reconsidérer," *ÉgT* 11 (1980): 177-93.

683 R. F. Collins, "Jesus' Ministry to the Deaf and Dumb," *MeliT* 35 (1984): 12-36.

9:35-11:1

684 Joseph A. Grassi, "The Last Testament-Succession Literary Background of Matthew 9:35-11:1 and Its Significance," *BTB* 7 (1977): 172-76.

685 Schuyler Brown, "The Mission to Israel in Matthew's Central Section (Mt. 9:35-11:1)," *ZNW* 69 (1978): 73-90.

686 Robert E. Morosco, "Matthew's Formation of a Commissioning-Type Scene out of the Story of Jesus' Commissioning of the Twelve," *JBL* 104 (1984): 539-56.

9:35-10:8

687 Beverly R. Gaventa, "The Unqualified Twelve," *CC* 110 (1993): 549.

9:35-38

688 O. Weber, "Predigt über Matth. 9,35-38," *EvT* 8 (1948-1949): 117-23.

9:36

689 François Martin, "The Image of Shepherd in the Gospel of St. Matthew," *ScE* 27 (1975): 261-301.

9:37

690 B. Charette, "A Harvest for the People? An Interpretation of Matthew 9:37f.," *JSNT* 38 (1990): 29-35.

10:1-11:1

691 Elian Cuvillier, "Coopération interprétative et questionnement du lecteur dans le récit d'envoi en mission," *RHPR* 76 (1996): 139-55.

10:1-42

692 F. Genuyt, "Evangile de Matthieu 10,1-42," *SémBib* 65 (1992): 3-17.

10:1-16

693   F. W. Beare, "The Mission of the Disciples and the Mission Charge: Matthew 10 and Parallels," *JBL* 89 (1970): 1-13.

10:1-8

694   Hans W. Huppenbauer, "Die Zumutung: 'Siehe, ich sende euch. . . !' " *ZMiss* 23 (1997): 2-6.

10:3

695   Rudolf Pesch, "Levi-Matthäus (Mc 2,14 // Mt. 9,9; 10,3): Ein Beitrag zur Lösung eines alten Problems," *ZNW* 59 (1968): 40- 56.

10:5-6

696   Morna D. Hooker, "Uncomfortable Words: X. The Prohibition of Foreign Missions," *ET* 82 (1971): 361-65.

697   Roman Bartnicki, "Der Bereich der Tätigkeit der Jünger nach Mt. 10,5b-6," *BZ* 31 (1987): 250-56.

698   Axel von Dobbeler, "Die Restitution Israels und die Bekehrung der Heiden. Das Verhältnis von Mt 10.5b.6 und Mt 28.18-20 unter dem Aspekt der Komplementarität. Erwägungen zum Standort des Matthäusevangeliums," *ZNW* 91 (2000): 18-44.

10:7-8

699   Martino Conti, "Il mandato di Cristo (Mt. 10.7-8.11-15)," *Ant* 47 (1972): 17-68.

10:8

700   Musa W. Dube, "Consuming a Colonial Cultural Bomb: Translating Badimo into 'Demons' in the Setswana Bible," *JSNT* 73 (1999): 33-59.

10:9-10

701   Martino Conti, "Fondamenti biblici della poverti nel ministero apostolico (Mt. 10,9-10)," *Ant* 46 (1971): 393-426.

10:10

702   J. Andrew Kirk, "Did 'Officials' in the New Testament Church Receive a Salary?" *ET* 84 (1973): 105-108.

703   José O'Callaghan, "Dos retoques antioquenos: Mt. 10,10; Mc. 2,20," *Bib* 68 (1987) 564-67.

704   Günther Schwarz, "προφῆς αὐτοῦ oder τῆς μισθοῦ αὐτοῦ?" *BibN* 56 (1991): 25.

10:11-15

705   Martino Conti, "Il mandato di Cristo (Mt. 10.7-8.11-15)," *Ant* 47 (1972): 17-68.

10:13

706   J. A. Montgomery, "New Testament Notes," *JBL* 56 (1937): 51-52.

10:14

707   Édouard Delebecque, " 'Secouez la Poussière de vos Pieds . . . sur l'Hellénisme de Luc IX,5," *RB* 89 (1982): 177-84.

708   Bruce A. Stevens, "Jesus as the Divine Warrior," *ET* 941 (1983): 326-29.

10:15

709   R. M. Grant, "Like Children," *HTR* 39 (1946): 71-73.

10:16

710   Paul de Vries, "The Taming of the Shrewd," *CT* 34 (1990): 14-17.

10:17-23

711   Dale C. Allison, "Anticipating the Passion: The Literary Reach of Matthew 26:47-27:56," *CBQ* 56 (1994): 701-14.

10:17-19

712   Matthew Mahoney, "Luke 21:14-15: Editorial Rewriting or Authenticity?" *ITQ* 47 (1980): 220-38.

10:19

713   Ragnar Leivestad, "An Interpretation of Matt. 10:19," *JBL* 71 (1952): 179-81.

10:21

714   Pierre Grelot, "Miche 7,6 dans les évangiles et dans la littérature rabbinique," *Bib* 67 (1986): 363-77.

10:23

715   Jacques Dupont, "Vous n'aurez pas achevé les villes d'Israël avant que le fils de l'homme ne vienne (Mat. X 23)," *NovT* 2 (1957-1958): 228-44.

716   E. Bammel, "Matthäus 10,23," *StTheol* 15 (1961): 79-92.

717   Royce Clark, "Eschatology and Matthew 10:23," *RQ* 6 (1963): 73-81.

718   Royce Clark, "Matthew 10:23 and Eschatology (II)," *RQ* 8 (1965): 53-69.

719   Charles H. Giblin, "Theological Perspective and Matthew 10:23b," *TS* 29 (1968): 637-61.

720   Scot McKnight, "Jesus and the End-Time: Matthew 10:23," *SBLSP* 25 (1986): 501-20.

721   Roman Bartnicki, "Das Trostwort an die Jünger in Matth. 10,23," *TZ* 43 (1987): 311-19.

722   Volker Hampel, " 'Ihr werdet mit den Städten Israels nicht zu Ende kommen'," *TZ* 45 (1989): 1-31.

10:24-33

723   Susan R. Garrett, "Matthew 10:24-33," *Int* 47 (1993): 166-69.

10:24-31

724   Edward May, "Outlines on the Swedish Gospels (Alternate Series)," *CTM* 29 (1958): 277-91.

10:25

725   W. C. B. MacLaurin, "Beelzeboul," *NovT* 20 (1978): 156-60.

10:26-31

726   Dale C. Allison, "Matthew 10:26-31 and the Problem of Evil," *SVTQ* 32 (1988): 293-308.

10:28

727   I. Howard Marshall, "Uncomfortable Words. VI. 'Fear Him Who Can Destroy both Soul and Body in Hell'," *ET* 81 (1970): 276-82.

728   Chaim Milikowsky, "Which Gehenna: Retribution and Eschatology in the Synoptic Gospels and in Early Jewish Texts," *NTS* 34 (1988): 238-49.

729   Robert F. Shedinger, "The Textual Relationship Between P45 and Shem-Tob's Hebrew Matthew," *NTS* 43 (1997): 58-71.

10:29

730   T. Hirunuma, "ἄνευ τοῦ πατρός: 'Without (of) the Father'," *FilN* 3 (1990): 53-62.

10:30

731   Dale C. Allison, "The Hairs on Your Head Are Numbered," *ET* 101 (1990): 334-36.

10:32-33

732   G. W. H. Lampe, "St. Peter's Denial," *BJRL* 55 (1973): 346-68.

733   Paul Hoffmann, "Der Menschensohn in Lukas 12:8," *NTS* 44 (1998): 357-79.

10:32

734   Barnabas Lindars, "Jesus as Advocate: A Contribution to the Christology Debate," *BJRL* 62 (1980): 476-97.

10:34-39

735   M. Vidal, "Seguimiento de Cristo y evangelización. Variación sobre un tema de moral neotestamentaria (Mt. 10,34-39)," *Sale* 18 (1971): 289-312.

10:34-36

736   T. A. Roberts, "Some Comments on Matthew x.34-36 and Luke xii.51-53," *ET* 69 (1957-1958): 304-306.

10:34-35

737   Warren Carter, "Jesus' 'I have come' Statements in Matthew's Gospel," *CBQ* 60 (1998): 44-62.

10:34

738   Matthew Black, "The Violent Word," *ET* 81 (1969-1970): 115-18.

739   David C. Sim, "The Sword Motif in Matthew 10:34," *HTS* 56 (2000): 84-104.

10:39

740   Tomas Arvedson, "Phil. 2,6 und Mt. 10,39," *StTheol* 5 (1952): 49-51.

10:40-42

741   Savas Agourides, " 'Little Ones' in Matthew," *BT* 35 (1984): 329-34.

10:40

742   H. K. Stothard, "Apostolic Authority," *CT* 14 (1969): 116-19.

11:1

743   David Hellholm, "En textgrammatisk konstruktion I Matteusevangeliet," *SEÅ* 51 (1986-1987): 80-89.

11:2-26

744   Selma Hirsch, "Studien zu Matthäus 11,2-26," *TZ* 5 (1949): 241-60.

11:2-19

745   John P. Meier, "John the Baptist in Matthew's Gospel," *JBL* 99 (1980): 383-405.

746   Wilhelm Wilkens, "Die Täuferüberlieferung des Matthäus und ihre Verarbeitung durch Lukas," *NTS* 40 (1994): 542-57.

11:2-15

747   Walter Vogels, "Performers and Receivers of the Kingdom: A Semiotic Analysis of Matthew 11:2-15," *ScE* 42 (1991): 335-36.

11:2-11

748   Sarah Henrich, "Matthew in Minneapolis and in Israel," *WW* 19 (1999): 201-209.

11:2-6

749   Jan Lambrecht, " 'Are You the One Who Is to Come, or Shall We Look for Another?' The Gospel Message of Jesus Today," *LouvS* 8 (1980): 115-18.

750   R. F. Collins, "Jesus' Ministry to the Deaf and Dumb," *MeliT* 35 (1984): 12-36.

751   Walter Wink, "Jesus' Reply to John: Matt. 11:2-6//Luke 7:18-23," *Forum* 5 (1989): 121-28.

11:3

752   Carroll Simcox, "Is Anybody Good Enough to Be Antichrist?" *CT* 102 (1985): 582-85.

11:6

753   C. L. Mitton, "Stumbling Block Characteristics of Jesus," *ET* 82 (1970-1971): 168-72.

11:7-19

754   Jack T. Sanders, "The Criterion of Coherence and the Randomness of Charisma: Poring Through Some Aporias in the Jesus Tradition," *NTS* 44 (1998): 1-25.

11:7-15

755   J. A. T. Robinson, "Elijah, John and Jesus," *NTS* 4 (1958): 263-81.

11:7-8

756   C. Daniel, "Les Esséniens et 'Ceux qui sont dans les maisons des rois'," *RevQ* 6 1967): 261-77.

11:7

757   Günther Schwarz, " 'Ein Rohr, vom Wind bewegt'?" *BibN* 83 (1996): 19-21.

11:10

758   W. C. Kaiser, "The Promise of the Arrival of Elijah in Malachi and the Gospels," *GTJ* 3 (1982): 221-33.

11:11

759   Benedict T. Viviano, "The Least in the Kingdom: Matthew 11:11. Its Parallel in Luke 7:28 (Q), and Daniel 4:14," *CBQ* 62 (2000): 41-54.

11:12-13

760   P. W. Barnett, "Who Were the *'Biastai'*?" *RTR* 363 (1977): 65-70.

761   Stephen Llewelyn, "The Traditionsgeschichte of Matt 11:12-13, par Luke 16:16," *NovT* 36 (1994): 330-49.

11:12

762   Georg Braumann, "Dem Himmelreich wird Gewalt angetan (Mt. 11,12 par.)," *ZNW* 52 (1961): 104-109.

763   W. E. Moore, "*Biazō, arpazō* and Cognates in Josephus," *NTS* 21 (1975): 519-43.

764   B. E. Thiering, "Are the 'Violent Men' False Teachers?" *NovT* 21 (1979): 293-97.

765   Sharon Karam, "Flannery O'Connor: A Modern Apocalyptic," *BibTo* 18 (1980): 182-86.

766   W. E. Moore, "Violence to the Kingdom: Josephus and the Syrian Churches," *ET* 100 (1989): 174-77.

767   Paolo Papone, "Il regno dei cieli soffre violenza? (Mt. 11:12)," *RBib* 38 (1990): 375-76.

11:14

768   W. C. Kaiser, "The Promise of the Arrival of Elijah in Malachi and the Gospels," *GTJ* 3 (1982): 221-33.

11:16-19

769   Olof Linton, "The Parable of the Children's Game," *NTS* 22 (1976): 159-79.

770   Harald Sahlin, "Traditionskritische Bemerkungen zu zwei Evangelien-perikopen," *StTheol* 33 (1979): 6.

11:16-17

771   José O'Callaghan, "La variante 'se gritan . . . diciendo', de Mt. 11,16-17," *EE* 61 (1986): 67-70.

11:19

772   P. Maurice Casey, "The Son of Man Problem," *ZNW* 67 (1976): 147-54.

773   C. Deutsch, "Wisdom in Matthew: Transformation of a Symbol," *NovT* 32 (1990): 13-47.

11:20-24

774   Joseph A. Comber, "The Composition and Literary Characteristics of Matt. 11:20-24." *CBQ* 39 (1977): 497-504.

11:22-23

775   Robert F. Shedinger, "The Textual Relationship Between P45 and Shem-Tob's Hebrew Matthew," *NTS* 43 (1997): 58-71.

11:24-30

776   W. D. Davies, " 'Knowledge' in the Dead Sea Scrolls and Matthew 11:24-30," *HTR* 46 (1953): 113-39.

11:25-30

777   K. G. Steck, "Über Matthäus 11,25-30," *EvT* 15 (1955): 343-49.

778   A. M. Hunter, "Crux Criticorum. Matt. xi.25-30: A Re-appraisal," *NTS* 8 (1961-1962): 241-49.

779   R. Beauvery, "La sagesse se rend justice," *AsSeign* (1974): 17-24.

780   L. Randellini, "L'inno di giubulo: Mt. 11,25-30; Lc. 10,20-24)," *RBib* 22 (1974): 183-235.

781   Kenneth O. Gangel, "Leadership: Coping with Cultural Corruption," *BSac* 144 (1987): 450-60.

782   Dale C. Allison, "Two Notes on a Key Text: Matthew 11:25-30," *JTS* 39 (1988): 477-85.

783   C. Deutsch, "Wisdom in Matthew: Transformation of a Symbol," *NovT* 32 (1990): 13-47.

11:25-27

784   Harold A. Guy, "Matthew 11,25-27; Luke 10,21-22," *ET* 49 (1937-1938): 236-37.

785   W. Grundmann, "Die *ēpiois* in der urchristlichen Paränese," *NTS* 5 (1958-1959): 188-205.

786   W. Grimm, "Der Dank für die empfangene Offenbarung bei Jesus und Josephus," *BZ* 17 (1973): 249-56.

11:27

787   Paul Winter, "Matthew 11:27 and Luke 10:22 from the First to the Fifth Century. Reflections on the Development of the Text," *NovT* 1 (1956): 112-48.

788   W. Grundmann, "Matth. xi.27 und die Johanneischen 'Der Vater-Der Sohn'-Stellen," *NTS* 12 (1965-66): 42-49.

789   Jesse Sell, "Johannine Traditions in Logion 61 of the Gospel of Thomas," *PRS* 7 (1980): 24-37.

11:28-30

790   J. B. Bauer, "Das milde Joch und die Ruhe, Matth. 11, 28-30," *TZ* 17 (1961): 99-106.

791   H. D. Betz, "The Logion of the Easy Yoke and of Rest," *JBL* 86 (1967): 10-24.

792   Graham N. Stanton, "Salvation Proclaimed: Matthew 11:28-30: Comfortable Words?" *ET* 94 (1982): 3-9.

793   S. Bacchiocchi, "Matthew 11:28-30: Jesus' Rest and the Sabbath," *AUSS* 22 (1984): 289-316.

794   Martin Hengel, "Die Einladung Jesu (Mt. 11,28-30)," *TBe* 18 (1987): 113-19.

795   B. Charette, " 'To Proclaim Liberty to the Captives': Matthew 11:28-30 in the Light of OT Prophetic Expectation," *NTS* 38 (1992): 290-97.

11:28

796   G. N. Curnock, "A Neglected Parallel (Mt. 11,28 and Ex. 33,14)," *ET* 44 (1932-1933): 141.

797   James J. C. Cox, "Bearers of Heavy Burdens: A Significant Textual Variant," *AUSS* 9 (1971): 1-15.

11:29

798   M. Maher, " 'Take My Yoke upon You' (Matt. xi.29)," *NTS* 22 (1975-1976): 97-103.

11:29b

799   K. Luke, "The Syriac Text of Matthew 11:29b and John 1:32-33," *BB* 16 (1990): 177-91.

12:1-14

800   John M. Hicks, "The Sabbath Controversy in Matthew: An Exegesis of Matthew 12:1-14," *RQ* 27 (1984): 79-91.

12:1-8

801   Pierre Benoit, "Les épis arrachés (Mt. 12,1-8 et par.)," *SBFLA* 13 (1962-1963): 76-92.

802   Joseph A. Grassi, "The Five Loaves of the High Priest," *NovT* 7 (1964-1965): 119-22.

803   Edgar V. McKnight and Charles H. Talbert, "Can the Griesbach Hypothesis Be Falsified?" *JBL* 91 (1972): 338-68.

804   Matty Cohen, "La Controverse de Jésus et des Pharisiens à Propos de la Cueillette des Epis, selon l'Évangile de Saint Matthieu," *MSR* 34 (1977): 3-12.

12:7

805   Mary Hinkle-Edin, "Learning What Righteousness Means: Hosea 6:6 and the Ethic of Mercy in Matthew's Gospel," *WW* 18 (1998): 355-63.

12:18-21

806   Richard Beaton, "Messiah and Justice: A Key to Matthew's Use of Isaiah 42.1-4?" *JSNT* 75 (1999): 5-23.

12:18

807   C. Tassin, "Matthieu 'targumiste?' L'exemple de Mt. 12,18 (= Is 42,1)," *EB* 48 (1990): 199-214.

12:22-37

808   Roland Meynet, "Qui Donc Est 'Le Plus Fort'? Analyse Rhétorique de Mc. 3,22-30; Mt. 12,22-37; Luc. 11,14-26," *RB* 90 (1983): 334-50.

12:22-32

809   David Peel, "Missing the Signs of the Kingdom," *ET* 99 (1988): 114-15.

12:22-30

810   R. F. Collins, "Jesus' Ministry to the Deaf and Dumb," *MeliT* 35 (1984): 12-36.

12:22-24

811   Pierre Guillemette, "La forme des récits d'exorcisme de Bultmann: Un dogme à reconsidérer," *ÉgT* 11 (1980): 177-93.

12:24

812   W. C. B. MacLaurin, "Beelzeboul," *NovT* 20 (1978): 156-60.

12:25-32

813   Chrys C. Caragounis, "Kingdom of God, Son of Man and Jesus' Self-Understanding," *TynB* 40 (1989): 3-23.

12:28

814   Cyril S. Rodd, "Spirit or Finger," *ET* 72 (1960-1961): 157-58.

815   Robert G. Hamerton-Kelly, "A Note on Matthew 12:28 Par. Luke 11:20," *NTS* 11 (1965): 167-69.

816   Chrys C. Caragounis, "Kingdom of God, Son of Man and Jesus' Self-Understanding," *TynB* 40 (1989): 223-38.

12:30-31

817   J. G. Williams, "A Note on the 'Unforgivable Sin' Logion," *NTS* 12 (1965): 75-77.

12:31-32

818   M. Eugene Boring, "The Unforgivable Sin Logion Mark 3:28-29//Matt. 12:31-32//Luke 12:10: Formal Analysis and History of the Tradition," *NovT* 18 (1976): 258-79.

12:31

819   Gerhard L. Miller, "Purgatory," *TD* 33 (1986): 31-36.

12:32

820   Jan Lambrecht, "Ware Verwantschap en Eeuwige Zonde: Ontstaan en Structuur van Mc. 3:20-35," *Bij* 29 (1968): 114-50.

821   P. Maurice Casey, "The Son of Man Problem," *ZNW* 67 (1976): 147-54.

822   Chrys C. Caragounis, "Kingdom of God, Son of Man and Jesus' Self-Understanding," *TynB* 40 (1989): 223-38.

12:38-42

823 P. Seidelin, "Das Jonaszeichen," *StTheol* 5 (1952): 119-31.

824 Otto Glombitza, "Das Zeichen des Jona (Zum Verständnis von Matth. xii. 38-42)," *NTS* 8 (1961-1962): 359-66.

825 John Howton, "The Sign of Jonah," *SJT* 15 (1962): 288-304.

826 Edgar V. McKnight and Charles H. Talbert, "Can the Griesbach Hypothesis Be Falsified?" *JBL* 91 (1972): 338-68.

827 Théo Pfrimmer, "De l'interprétation en théologie pratique," *ÉTR* 73 no 4 (1998): 543-55.

828 W. G. Thirion, "'n Eksegeties-hermeneutiese ondersoek van die Jona-gegewens in Matteus 12:38ev," *SkrifK* 18 (1997): 154-75.

12:38

829 A. K. M. Adam, "The Sign of Jonah: A Fish-Eye View," *Semeia* 51 (1990): 177-91.

12:40

830 Harvey K. McArthur, " 'On the Third Day'," *NTS* 18 (1971): 81-86.

831 Santiago G. Oporto, "The Sign of Jonah," *TD* 32 (1985): 49-53.

13-19

832 André Feuillet, "Dans le sillage de Vatican II. Réflexions sur quelques versets de Jn. 6 (vv. 14-15 et 67-69) et sur le realisme historique du Quatrime évangile," *Div* 30 (1986): 3-52.

13:1-37

833 Hugo Lattanzi, "Eschatologici Sermonis Domini Logica Interpretatio," *Div* 11 (1967): 71-92.

13:1-23

834 Joachim Jeremias, "Palästinakundliches zum Gleichnis vom Säemann (Mark 4:3-8 Par.)," *NTS* 13 (1966): 48-53.

835 Jacques Dupont, "Le semeur est sorti pour semer (Mt. 13)," *AsSeign* 46 (1974): 18-27.

836   David Wenham, "The Interpretation of the Parable of the Sower," *NTS* 20 (1974): 299-319.

837   Harvey H. Potthoff, "Homiletical Resources: The Sermon as Theological Event Interpretations of Parables," *QR* 4 (1984): 76-102.

838   J. G. du Plessis, "Pragmatic Meaning in Matthew 13:1-23," *Neo* 21 (1987): 33-56.

839   P. Mark Achtemeier, "Matthew 13:1-23," *Int* 44 (1990): 61-65.

13:1-9

840   Mark L. Bailey, "The Kingdom in the Parables of Matthew 13," *BSac* 155 (1998): 29-38, 172-88, 266-79, 449-59.

13:1-3

841   Barclay M. Newman, "To Teach or Not to Teach (A Comment on Matthew 13.1-3)," *BT* 34 (1983): 139-43.

13:2-52

842   A. del Agua Pérez, "Eclesiología como discurso narrado: Mt 13,2-52: Teoría y práctica del análisis de discursos narrados en los evangelios," *EE* 72 (1997): 217-69.

13:3-9

843   L. Ramaroson, " 'Parole-semence' ou 'peuple-semence' dans la Parabole du Semeur?" *ScE* 40 (1988): 91-101.

13:4-7

844   José O'Callaghan, "Dos variantes en la parábola del sembrador," *EB* 48 (1990): 267-70.

13:5-6

845   John Horman, "The Source of the Version of the Parable of the Sower in the Gospel of Thomas," *NovT* 21 (1979): 326-43.

13:7

846   José O'Callaghan, "La Variante 'Ahogaron' en Mt. 13,7," *Bib* 68 (1987): 402-403.

13:8

847   Jean Bernardi, "Cent, soixante et trente," *RB* 36 (1991): 398-402.

848   Robert K. McIver, "One Hundred-Fold Yield--Miraculous
       or Mundane? Matthew 13:8,23; Mark 4:8,20; Luke 8:8,"
       NTS 40 (1994): 606-608.

13:11

849   Lucien Cerfaux, "La connaissance des secrets du Royaume
       d'après Matt. xiii. 11 et par.," *NTS* 2 (1955-1956): 238-49.

13:12

850   G. Linkeskog, "Logia-Studien," *StTheol* 4 (1951-1952):
       129-89.

13:13-17

851   Mark L. Bailey, "The Kingdom in the Parables of Matthew
       13," *BSac* 155 (1998): 29-38, 172-88, 266-79, 449-59.

13:13-15

852   Dan O. Via, "Matthew on the Understandability of the
       Parables," *JBL* 84 (1965): 430-32.

13:15

853   David S. New, "The Occurrence of Auton in Matthew
       13:15 and the Process of Text Assimilation," *NTS* 37
       (1991): 478-80.

13:20-23

854   W. Link, "Die Geheimnisse des Himmelreichs," *EvT* 2
       (1935): 115-27.

13:21

855   Jan Joosten, "The Text of Matthew 13:21a and Parallels in
       the Syriac Tradition," *NTS* 37 (1991): 153-59.

13:23

856   Robert K. McIver, "One Hundred-Fold Yield--Miraculous
       or Mundane? Matthew 13:8,23; Mark 4:8,20; Luke 8:8,"
       NTS 40 (1994): 606-608.

13:24-30

857   Charles E. Carlston, "A Positive Criterion of
       Authenticity?" *BR* 7 (1962): 33-44.

858   William G. Doty, "An Interpretation: Parable of the Weeds
       and Wheat," *Int* 25 (1971): 185-93.

859   Domenico Ellena, "Thematische Analyse der Wachstumsgleichnisse," *LB* 23 (1973): 48-62.

860   David R. Catchpole, "John the Baptist, Jesus and the Parable of the Tares," *SJT* 31 (1978): 557-71.

861   Mark L. Bailey, "The Kingdom in the Parables of Matthew 13," *BSac* 155 (1998): 29-38, 172-88, 266-79, 449-59.

862   Richard E. Strelan, "A Ripping Yarn: Matthew 13:24-30," *LTJ* 30 (1996): 22-29.

13:24

863   Harvey H. Potthoff, "Homiletical Resources: The Sermon as Theological Event Interpretations of Parables," *QR* 4 (1984): 76-102.

13:31-32

864   Otto Kuss, "Zur Senfkornparabel," *TGl* 41 (1951): 40-49.

865   Harvey K. McArthur, "The Parable of the Mustard Seed," *CBQ* 33 (1971): 198-210.

866   John A. Sproule, "The Problem of the Mustard Seed," *GTJ* 1 (1980): 37-42.

13:32

867   W. Harold Mare, "The Smallest Mustard Seed: Matthew 13:32," *GTJ* 9 (1968): 3-9.

868   Robert F. Shedinger, "The Textual Relationship Between P45 and Shem-Tob's Hebrew Matthew," *NTS* 43 (1997): 58-71.

13:33

869   Robert W. Funk, "Beyond Criticism in Quest of Literacy: The Parable of the Leaven," *Int* 25 (1971): 149-70.

870   Domenico Ellena, "Thematische Analyse der Wachstumsgleichnisse," *LB* 23 (1973): 48-62.

871   Elizabeth Waller, "The Parable of the Leaven: A Sectarian Teaching and the Inclusion of Women," *USQR* 35 (1980): 99-109.

872   Günther Schwarz, " 'Verbarg es in drei Sea Mehl'? (Matthäus 13,33//Lukas 13,20.21)," *BibN* 86 (1997): 60-62.

13:39

873 Raymond E. Gingrich, "Adumbrations of Our Lord's Return: Political Alignments," *GTJ* 9 (1968): 3-14.

13:44-52

874 Delmar Jacobson, "An Exposition of Matthew 13:44-52," *Int* 29 (1975): 277-82.

875 Harvey H. Potthoff, "Homiletical Resources: The Sermon as Theological Event Interpretations of Parables," *QR* 4 (1984): 76-102.

13:44-46

876 Charles W. Hedrick, "The Treasure Parable in Matthew and Thomas," *Forum* 2 (1986): 41-56.

877 Jeffrey A. Gibbs, "Parables of Atonement and Assurance: Matthew 13:44-46," *CTQ* 51 (1987): 19-40.

878 Paul W. Meyer, "Context as a Bearer of Meaning in Matthew," *USQR* 42 (1988): 69-72.

13:44

879 J. D. M. Derrett, "Law in the New Testament: The Treasure in the Field," *ZNW* 54 (1963): 31-42.

880 Walter Magass, " 'Der Schatz im Acker' (Mt. 13, 44): Von der Kirche als einem Tauschphänomen- Paradigmatik und Transformation," *LB* 21 (1973): 2-18.

881 George Howard, "A Note on Codex Sinaiticus and Shem-Tob's Hebrew Matthew," *NTS* 38 (1992): 187-204.

13:47-50

882 Domenico Ellena, "Thematische Analyse der Wachstumsgleichnisse," *LB* 23 (1973): 48-62.

883 William G. Morrice, "The Parable of the Dragnet and the Gospel of Thomas," *ET* 95 (1984): 269-73.

13:47-49

884 J. D. M. Derrett, "Esan gar Halieis (Mark 1:16). Jesus' Fishermen and the Parable of the Net," *NovT* 22 (1980): 108-37.

13:52

885   J. Becker, "Erwägungen zu Fragen der Neutestamentlichen Exegese," *BZ* 13 (1969): 99-102.

886   Dieter Zeller, "Zu Einer Jüdischen Vorlage von Mt. 13, 52," *BZ* 20 (1976): 223-26.

887   Donald A. Hagner, "New Things from the Scribe's Treasure Box (Mt 13:52)," *ET* 109 (1998): 329-34.

13:53-18:35

888   David W. Gooding, "Structure littéraire de Matthieu 13:53 à 18:35," *RB* 85 (1978): 227-52.

13:53

889   David Hellholm, "En textgrammatisk konstruktion I Matteus-evangeliet," *SEÅ* 51 (1986-1987): 80-89.

13:55

890   George W. Buchanan, "Jesus and the Upper Class," *NovT* 7 (1965): 195-206.

14:1-2

891   Philippe Rolland, "La question synoptique demande-t-elle une response compliquée?" *Bib* 70 (1989): 217-23.

14:3-12

892   John P. Meier, "John the Baptist in Matthew's Gospel," *JBL* 99 (1980): 383-405.

14:3

893   Lamar Cope, "The Death of John the Baptist in the Gospel of Matthew; or, the Case of the Confusing Conjunction," *CBQ* 38 (1976): 515-19.

894   Terence L. Donaldson, " 'For Herod Had Arrested John' (Matt 14:3): Making Sense of an Unresolved Flashback," *SR* 28 (1999): 35-48.

14:13-21

895   A. G. Van Aarde, "The Miraculous Multiplication of Loaves: Historical Criticism in Perspective," *HTS* suppl 5 (1994): 180-203.

896   F. de Stefano and L. Sperco, "Una rilettura del miracolo della moltiplicazione del pani," *BibO* 41 (1999): 65-75.

14:13-14

897   Frans Neirynck, "The Matthew-Luke Agreements in Matt. 14:13-14 and Lk. 9:10-11 (par. Mk. 6:30-34): The Two-Source Theory behind the Impasse," *ETL* 60 (1984): 25-44.

14:16

898   Jerome Murphy-O'Connor, "The Structure of Matthew XIV-XVII." *RB* 82 (1975): 360-84.

899   Joseph A. Grassi, " 'You Yourselves Give Them to Eat': An Easily Forgotten Command of Jesus," *BibTo* 97 (1978): 1704-09.

14:22-33

900   Charles R. Carlisle, "Jesus' Walking on the Water: A Note on Matthew 14.22-33," *NTS* 31 (1985): 151-55.

901   David Hill, "The Walking on the Water: A Geographic or Linguistic Answer?" *ET* 99 (1988): 267-69.

14:22-23

902   Andreas Dettwiler, "La conception matthéenne de la foi (à l'exemple de Matthieu 14:22-33)," *ÉTR* 73 (1998): 333-47.

14:22-24

903   Edward J. Kilmartin, "A First Century Chalice Dispute," *SE* 12 (1960): 403-408.

14:23

904   D. Durken, "Mountains and Matthew," *BibTo* 28 (1990): 304-307.

14:28-33

905   J. D. M. Derrett, "Der Wasserwandel in christilicher und buddhistischer Perspektive," *ZRGG* 41 (1989): 193-214.

14:28-31

906   Evald Lövestam, "Wunder und Symbolhandlung: Eine Studie über Matthäus 14:28-31," *KD* 8 (1962): 124-35.

14:28

907   Ralph Stehley, "Boudhisme et Nouveau Testament: Apropos de la Marche de Pierre sur l'Eau," *RHPR* 57 (1977): 433-37.

15:1-20

908   Gregory Murray, "What Defiles a Man?" *DR* 106 (1988): 297-98.

15:4-6

909   J. D. M. Derrett, "KORBAN, HO ESTIN ŌRON," *NTS* 16 (1970): 364-68.

15:5

910   Joseph A. Fitzmyer, "The Aramaic Qorbān Inscription from Jebel Hallet el-Ṭûri and Mark 7:11//Matt. 15:5," *JBL* 78 (1959): 60-65.

911   Z. W. Falk, "On Talmudic Vows," *HTR* 59 (1966): 309-12.

15:6

912   José O'Callaghan, "La variante 'palabra' o 'precepto' en Mt. 15,6," *EE* 61 (1986) 421-23.

15:13-26

913   Howard Horton, "The Gates of Hades Shall Not Prevail Against It," *RQ* 5 (1961): 1-5.

15:17

914   C. Jaeger, "Remarques philologiques sur quelques passages des Synoptiques," *RHPR* 16 (1936): 246-49.

15:21-29

915   Gerard Mussies, "Jesus and 'Sidon' in Matthew 15//Mark 7," *Bij* 58 (1997): 264-78.

15:21-28

916   J. I. Hasler, "The Incident of the Syro-Phoenician Woman (Mt. 15,21-28, Mk. 7,14-30)," *ET* 45 (1933-1934): 459-61.

917   P. D. Hamilton, "The Syro-Phoenician Woman: Another Suggestion," *ET* 46 (1934-1935): 477-78.

918   C. E. Garritt, "The Syro-Phoenician Woman," *ET* 47 (1935-1936): 43.

919   James D. Smart, "Jesus, the Syro-Phoenician Woman and the Disciples," *ET* 50 (1938-1939): 469-72.

920   Roy A. Harrisville, "The Woman of Canaan. A Chapter in the History of Exegesis," *Int* 20 (1966): 274-87.

921   P. E. Scherer, "A Gauntlet with a Gift in It. From Text to Sermon on Matthew 15:21-28 and Mark 7:24-30," *Int* 20 (1966): 387-99.

922   W. Storch, "Zur Perikope von der Syrophonizierin," *BZ* 14 (1970): 256-57.

923   T. Lovison, "La pericopa della Cananea Mt. 15,21-28," *RBib* 19 (1971): 273-305.

924   K. Gatzweiler, "Un pas vers l'universalisme: la Cananéenne (Mt. 15)," *AsSeign* 51 (1972): 15-24.

925   Simon Légasse, "L'épisode de la Cananéenne d'après Mt. 15,21-28," *BLE* 73 (1972): 21-40.

926   Scott L. Tatum, "Great Prayers of the Bible," *SouJT* 14 (1972): 29-42.

927   J. D. M. Derrett, "Law in the New Testament: The Syro-Phoenician Woman and the Centurion of Capernaum," *NovT* 15 (1973): 161-86.

928   Mark C. Thompson, "Matthew 15:21-28," *Int* 35 (1981): 279-84.

929   Alice Dermience, "La pericope de la Cananeenne (Matt. 15:21-28): redaction et théologie," *ETL* 58 (1982): 25-49.

930   John P. Meier, "Matthew 15:21-28," *Int* 40 (1986): 397-402.

931   Elian Cuvillier, "Particularisme et universalisme chez Matthieu: Quelques hypothèses à l'épreuve du texte," *Bib* 78 (1997): 481-502.

932   Robert W. Dahlen, "The Savior and the Dog: An Exercise in Hearing," *WW* 17 (1997): 269-77.

933   Musa W. Dube, "Readings Of Semoya: Batswana Women's Interpretations Of Matthew 15:21-28," *Semeia* 73 (1996): 111-29.

934   Jim Perkinson, "A Canaanitic Word in the Logos of Christ; or The Difference the Syro-Phoenician Woman Makes to Jesus," *Semeia* 75 (1996): 61-85.

935   P. Pokorný, "From a Puppy to the Child: Some Problems of Contemporary Biblical Exegesis Demonstrated from Mark 7:24-30 and Matthew 15:21-28," *NovT* 41 (1995): 321-37.

936   J. Martin C. Scott, "Matthew 15:21-28: A Test-Case for Jesus' Manners," *JSNT* 63 (1996): 21-44.

15:22

937   Günther Schwarz, "Syrophoinikissa - Cananaia," *NTS* 30 (1984): 626-28.

938   Musa W. Dube, "Consuming a Colonial Cultural Bomb: Translating Badimo into 'Demons' in the Setswana Bible," *JSNT* 73 (1999): 33-59.

15:27

939   Daniel P. Leyrer, "Matthew 15:27--The Canaanite Woman's Great Faith," *WLQ* 96 (1999): 218-19.

15:29-31

940   R. F. Collins, "Jesus' Ministry to the Deaf and Dumb," *MeliT* 35 (1984): 12-36.

15:29

941   D. Durken, "Mountains and Matthew," *BibTo* 28 (1990): 304-307.

15:32-39

942   Joseph Knackstedt, "Die beiden Brotvermehrungen im Evangelium," *NTS* 10 (1963-1964): 309-35.

15:35-36

943   José O'Callaghan, "Consideraciones críticas sobre Mt. 15,35-36a," *Bib* 67 (1986): 360-62.

16:1-20

944   L. Perrin, "Interpréter, c'est recevoir un 'plus': la révélation et la filiation. Une lecture de Mt. 16,1-20," *SémBib* 55 (1989): 19-28.

16:1-19

945   B. Willaert, "La connexion littéraire entre la première prédiction de la passion et la confession de Pierre chez les synoptiques," *ETL* 32 (1956): 24-45.

16:1-8

946   Nikolaus Walter, "Eine Vormatthäische Schilderung der Auferstehung Jesus," *NTS* 19 (1973): 415-29.

16:1-4

947   A. K. M. Adam, "The Sign of Jonah: A Fish-Eye View," *Semeia* 51 (1990): 177-91.

948   X. Quinzá Lleó, "La reflexión bíblica sobre los signos de los tiempos," *EB* 48 (1990): 317-34.

16:5-12

949   Robert C. Newman, "Breadmaking with Jesus," *JETS* 40 (1997): 1-11.

16:13-26

950   James L. Boyce, "Transformed for Disciple Community: Matthew in Pentecost," *WW* 13 (1993): 308-17.

16:13-23

951   Anton Vögtle, "Messiasbekenntnis und Petrusverheissung. Zur Komposition Mt. 16,13-23 par.," *BZ* 1 (1957): 252-72; 2 (1958): 85-103.

952   William J. Tobin, "The Petrine Primacy Evidence of the Gospels," *LV* 23 (1968): 27-70.

953   André Feuillet, "Chercher à presuader Dieu," *NovT* 12 (1970): 350-60.

954   Edgar V. McKnight and Charles H. Talbert, "Can the Griesbach Hypothesis Be Falsified?" *JBL* 91 (1972): 338-68.

955   Bruce T. Dahlberg, "The Topological Use of Jeremiah 1:4-19 in Matthew 16:13-23," *JBL* 94 (1975): 73-80.

956   Jean Galot, "La première profession de foi chrétienne," *EV* 97 (1987): 593-99.

16:13-20

957   Gilles Gaide, " 'Tu es le Christ' . . . 'Tu es Pierre' (Mt. 16)," *AsSeign* 52 (1974): 16-26.

958   Paul S. Berge, "An Exposition of Matthew 16:13-20," *Int* 29 (1975): 283-88.

959   M. J. Suggs, "Matthew 16:13-20," *Int* 39 (1985): 291-95.

960   Wallace W. Bubar, "Killing Two Birds with One Stone: The Utter De(con)struction of Matthew and His Church," *BibInt* 3 (1995): 144-57.

16:13-19

961   Tord Forberg, "Peter: The High Priest of the New Covenant?" *EAJT* 4 (1986): 113-21.

16:13-16

962   E. Thurneysen, "Predigt über Matthäus 16,13-16, 21-28," *EvT* 3 (1936): 127-35.

16:13

963   Simone Frutiger, "Les lectures d'Evangile ou les textes disjoints: Matthieu 16:13 à 25:46," *FV* 82 (1983): 59-75.

16:14

964   M. J. J. Menken, "The References of Jeremiah in the Gospel According to Matthew (Mt. 2,17; 16,14; 27,9)," *ETL* 60 (1984): 5-24.

965   Benjamin G. Wright, "A Previously Unnoticed Greek Variant of Matt. 16:14: 'Some Say John the Baptist . . . '," *JBL* 105 (1986): 694-97.

16:15

966   Pierre Ganne, "La Personne du Christ: 'Qui Dites-Vous que je Suis?'," *NRT* 104 (1982): 3-21.

16:16-19

967   J. Hadzega, "Mt. 16,16-19 in der neueren Literatur der Orthodoxen," *TGl* 26 (1934): 458-64.

968   Julius R. Mantey, "What of Priestly Absolution," *CT* 13 (1969): 233-391.

969   Jan Lambrecht, " 'Du bist Petrus': Mt. 16,16-19 und das Papsttum," *SNTU-A* 11 (1986): 5-32.

16:16-18

970   J. K. Elliott, "Kēphas: Simōn Petros, o Petros: An Examination of New Testament Usage," *NovT* 14 (1972): 241-56.

16:16-17

971   Jean Doignon, "Pierre 'Fondement de l'Église' et Foi de la Confession de Pierre 'Base de l'Église' chez Hilaire de Poitiers," *RSPT* 66 (1982): 417-25.

972   François Refoulé, "Le parallèle Matthieu 16/16-17—Galates 1/15-16 réexaminé," *ÉTR* 67/2 (1992): 161-75.

16:16

973   Colin Brown, "The Hermeneutics of Confession and Accusation," *CTJ* 30 (1995): 460-71.

16:17-19

974   H. Hirschberg, "Simon Bariona and the Ebionites," *JBL* 61 (1942): 171-91.

975   A. Oepke, "Der Herrnspruch über die Kirche Mt. 16,17-19 in der neuesten Forschung," *StTheol* 2 (1948): 110-65.

976   O. J. F. Seitz, "Upon This Rock: A Critical Re-examination of Matt. 16,17-19," *JBL* 69 (1950): 329-40.

977   E. L. Allen, "On This Rock," *JTS* 5 (1954): 59-62.

978   Otto Betz, "Felsenmann und Felsengemeinde," *ZNW* 48 (1957): 49-77.

979   Dan O. Via, "Jesus and His Church in Matthew 16:17-19," *RevExp* 55 (1958): 22-39.

980   Veselin Kesich, "The Problem of Peter's Primacy," *SVTQ* 4/2 (1961): 2-25.

981   Peter Milward, "Prophetic Perspective and the Primacy of Peter," *AmER* 144 (1961): 122-29.

982   Robert H. Gundry, "The Narrative Framework of Matthew 16:17-19," *NovT* 7/1 (1964): 1-9.

983   M. García Cordero, "Concepción jerárquica de la Iglesia en el Nuevo Testamento," *Sale* 18 (1971): 233-87.

984   Max Wilcox, "Peter and the Rock: A Fresh Look at Matthew 16:17-19," *NTS* 22/1 (1975): 73-88.

985   Christoph Kahler, "Zur Form- und Traditionsgeschichte von Matth. 16:17-19," *NTS* 23/1 (1976): 36-58.

986   Ian S. Kemp, "The Blessing, Power and Authority of the Church: A Study in Matthew 16:17-19," *ERT* 6/1 (1982): 9-22.

987   Bernard P. Robinson, "Peter and His Successors: Tradition and Redaction in Matthew 16:17-19," *JSNT* 21 (1984): 85-104.

988   Joachim Gnilka, " 'Tu es, Petrus'. Die Petrus-Verheissung in Mt. 16,17-19," *MTZ* 38 (1987): 3-17.

989   Ulrich Luz, "Das Primatwort Matthäus 16:17-19 aus wirkungsgeschichtlicher Sicht," *NTS* 37 (1991): 415-33.

990   Christian Grappe, "Mt. 16,17-19 et le récit de la Passion," *RHPR* 72 (1992): 33-40.

16:17

991   H. Lehman, "Du bist Petrus," *EvT* 13 (1953): 44-66.

16:18-20

992   V. Burch, "The 'Stone' and the 'Keys' (Mt. 16,18ff.)," *JBL* 52 (1933): 147-52.

16:18-19

993   K. L. Carroll, "Thou Art Peter," *NovT* 6 (1963-1964): 268-76.

994   O. Da Spinetoli, "La Portata Ecclesiologica Di Mt. 16,18-19," *Ant* 42/3 (1967): 357-75.

995   Julius R. Mantey, "Distorted Translations in John 20:23; Matthew 16:18-19 and 18:18," *RevExp* 78/3 (1981): 409-16.

996   Benedict T. Viviano, "Matthew, Master of Ecumenical Infighting," *CThM* 10/6 (1983): 325-32.

997   Joel Marcus, "The Gates of Hades and the Keys of the Kingdom," *CBQ* 50/3 (1988): 443-55.

16:18

998   J. E. L. Oulton, "An Interpretation of Matthew 16,18," *ET* 48 (1936-1937): 525-26.

999   Bruce M. Metzger, "The New Testament View of the Church," *TT* 19 (1962): 369-80.

1000   George Howard, "The Meaning of Petros-Petra," *RQ* 10/4 (1967): 217-21.

1001   Luther L. Grubb, "The Church Reaching Tomorrow's World," *GTJ* 12/3 (1971): 13-22.

1002   Palémon Glorieux, "Deux Eloges de la Sainte par Pierre d'Ailly," *MSR* 29/3 (1972): 113-29.

1003   J. W. Roberts, "The Meaning of Ekklesia in the New Testament," *RQ* 15/1 (1972): 27-36.

1004   D. Broughton Knox, "De-Mythologising the Church," *RTR* 32/2 (1973): 48-55.

1005   Peter Lampe, "Das Spiel mit dem Petrusnamen-Matt. xvi.18," *NTS* 25/2 (1979): 221-27.

1006   C. Buzzetti, " 'You Are a Rock, Peter. . .' in Italy," *BT* 34/3 (1983): 308-11.

1007   Colin Brown, "The Gates of Hell: An Alternative Approach," *SBLSP* 26 (1987): 357-67.

1008   Pierre Grelot, " 'Sur cette pierre je bâtirai mon Église' (Mt. 16,18b)," *NRT* 109/5 (1987): 641-59.

1009   Augustine Stock, "Is Matthew's Presentation of Peter Ironic?" *BTB* 17/2 (1987): 64-69.

1010   J. D. M. Derrett, " 'Thou Art the Stone, and upon This Stone'," *DR* 106 (1988): 276-85.

1011   Raimund Lülsdorff, "Vom Stein zum Felsen: Anmerkungen zur biblischen Begründung des Petrusamtes nach Mt. 16:18," *Cath* 44/4 (1990): 274-83.

1012   Ulrich Luz, "The Primacy Text (Mt. 16:18)," *PSB* 12/1 (1991): 41-55.

1013   Jack P. Lewis, " 'The Gates of Hell Shall Not Prevail Against It' (Matt 16:18): A Study of the History of Interpretation," *JETS* 38 (1995): 349-67.

16:19

1014   Henry J. Cadbury, "The Meaning of John 20,23, Matthew 16,19, and Matthew 18,18," *JBL* 58 (1939): 251-54.

1015   Julius R. Mantey, "The Mistranslation of the Perfect Tense in John 20,23,.Mt. 16,19, and Mt. 18,18," *JBL* 58 (1939): 243-49.

1016   Julius Gross, "Die Schlüsselgewalt nach Haimo von Auxerre," *ZRGG* 9 (1957): 30-41.

1017   S. V. McCasland, "Matthew Twists the Scriptures," *JBL* 80 (1961): 143-48.

1018   J. A. Emerton, "Binding and Loosing: Forgiving and Retaining," *JTS* 15 (1962): 325-31.

1019   Julius R. Mantey, "Evidence that the Perfect Tense in John 20:23 and Matthew 16:19 Is Mistranslated," *JETS* 16/3 (1973): 129-38.

1020   Paul Elbert, "The Perfect Tense in Matthew 16:19 and Three Charismata," *JETS* 17/3 (1974): 149-55.

1021   J. D. M. Derrett, "Binding and Loosing (Matt. 16:19; Matt. 18:18; John 20:23)," *JBL* 102 (1983): 112-17.

1022   Herbert W. Basser, "Derrett's 'Binding' Reopened," *JBL* 104 (1985): 297-300.

1023   Richard H. Hiers, " 'Binding' and 'Loosing': The Matthean Authorizations," *JBL* 104/2 (1985): 233-50.

1024   Dennis C. Duling, "Binding and Loosing: Matthew 16:19; Matthew 18:18; John 20:23," *Forum* 3 (1987): 3-31.

1025   Georg Korting, "Binden oder lösen: Zur Verstockungs- und Befreiungstheologie in Mt. 16,19; 18:18-21:35 und Joh 15,1-17; 2,23," *SNTU-A* 14 (1989): 39-91.

1026   Kair A. Syreeni, "Between Heaven and Earth: On the Structure of Matthew's Symbolic Universe," *JSNT* 40 (1990): 9-13.

16:20

1027   Herbert W. Basser, "Marcus's 'Gates': A Response," *CBQ* 52 (1990): 307-308.

16:21-28

1028   E. Thurneysen, "Predigt über Matthäus 16,13-16, 21-28,"
        EvT 3 (1936): 127-35.

16:21-27

1029   James M. Efird, "Matthew 16:21-27," *Int* 35/3 (1981):
        284-89.

16:21-26

1030   Bruce J. Malina, " 'Let Him Deny Himself' (Mark 8:34 &
        par): A Social Psychological Model of Self-Denial," *BTB*
        24 (1994): 106-19.

16:21-23

1031   B. Willaert, "La connexion littéraire entre la première
        prédiction de la passion et la confession de Pierre chez les
        synoptiques," *ETL* 32 (1956): 24-45.

16:21

1032   Donald J. Verseput, "Jesus' Pilgrimage to Jerusalem and
        Encounter in the Temple: A Geographical Motif in
        Matthew's Gospel," *NovT* 36 (1994): 105-21.

16:22

1033   Henri Clavier, "Notes sur un Motclef du Johannisme et de
        la Sotériologie Biblique: Hilasmos," *NovT* 10/4 (1968):
        287-304.

16:26

1034   José O'Callaghan, "Nota Critica a Mc 8,36," *Bib* 64/1
        (1983): 116-17.

17:1-13

1035   Sigfred Pedersen, "Die Proklamation Jesu als des
        Eschatologischen Offenbarungsträgers," *NovT* 17/4
        (1975): 241-64.

17:1-9

1036   A. C. Winn, "Worship as a Healing Experience: An
        Exposition of Matthew 17:1-9," *Int* 29/1 (1975): 68-72.

17:1-8

1037   Dale C. Allison, "Anticipating the Passion: The Literary
        Reach of Matthew 26:47-27:56," *CBQ* 56 (1994): 701-14.

17:1

1038   D. Durken, "Mountains and Matthew," *BibTo* 28 (1990): 304-307.

1039   Robert F. Shedinger, "The Textual Relationship Between P45 and Shem-Tob's Hebrew Matthew," *NTS* 43 (1997): 58-71.

17:4

1040   José O'Callaghan, "Discusion Critica en Mt. 17,4," *Bib* 65/1 (1984): 91-93.

17:7

1041   José O'Callaghan, "Mt. 17,7: Revision Critica," *Bib* 66/3 (1985): 422-23.

17:10-13

1042   John P. Meier, "John the Baptist in Matthew's Gospel," *JBL* 99 (1980): 383-405.

17:11

1043   W. C. Kaiser, "The Promise of the Arrival of Elijah in Malachi and the Gospels," *GTJ* 3/2 (1982): 221-33.

17:14-20

1044   Gregory E. Sterling, "Jesus as Exorcist: An Analysis of Matthew 17:14-20; Mark 9:14-29; Luke 9:37-43a," *CBQ* 55 (1993): 467-93.

17:17

1045   C. Jaeger, "Remarques philologiques sur quelques passages des Synoptiques," *RHPR* 16 (1936): 246-49.

17:20

1046   R. Merkelbach and D. Hagedorn, "Ein neues Fragment aus Porphyrios 'Gegen die Christen'," *VC* 20/2 (1966): 86-90.

17:22-20:19

1047   David McClister, " 'Where Two or Three Are Gathered Together': Literary Structure as a Key to Meaning in Matthew 17:22-20:19," *JETS* 39 (1996): 549-58.

17:22-27

1048   Donald J. Verseput, "Jesus' Pilgrimage to Jerusalem and Encounter in the Temple: A Geographical Motif in Matthew's Gospel," *NovT* 36 (1994): 105-21.

17:22

1049   J. Vara, "Dos conjeturas textuales sobre Mateo 25,21.23 y Mateo 26,32/17,22 y par.," *Salm* 33 (1986): 81-86.

17:24-27

1050   J. D. M. Derrett, "Peter's Penny: Fresh Light on Matthew 17:24-27," *NovT* 6/1 (1963): 1-15.

1051   Hugh W. Montefiore, "Jesus and the Temple Tax," *NTS* 11/1 (1964): 60-71.

1052   Simon Légasse, "Jésus et l'impôt du Temple (Matthieu 17, 24-27)," *SE* 24 (1972): 361-77.

1053   N. J. McEleney, "Mt. 17:24-27: Who Paid the Temple Tax?" *CBQ* 38/2 (1976): 178-92.

1054   Richard J. Cassidy, "Matthew 17:24-27: A Word on Civil Taxes," *CBQ* 41/4 (1979): 571-80.

1055   David E. Garland, "Matthew's Understanding of the Temple Tax (Matt. 17:24-27)," *SBLSP* 26 (1987): 190-209.

1056   A. G. van Aarde, "Resonance and Reception: Interpreting Mt. 17:24-27 in Context," *ScrSA* 29 (1989): 1-12.

1057   A. G. van Aarde, "A Silver Coin in the Mouth of a Fish: A Miracle of Nature, Ecology, Economy and the Politics of Holiness," *HTS* suppl 5 (1994): 204-28.

1058   Warren Carter, "Paying the Tax to Rome as Subversive Praxis: Matthew 17.24-27," *JSNT* 76 (1999): 3-31.

17:25

1059   José O'Callaghan, "Discusion Critica en Mt. 17:25," *FilN* 3 (1990): 151-53.

17:26

1060   Tjitze Baarda, "Geven als vreemdeling. Over de herkomst van een merkwaardige variant van ms 713 in Mattheus 17:26," *NedTT* 42 (1988): 99-113.

17:27

1061   H. A. Homeau, "On Fishing for Staters: Matthew 17:27,"
       ET 85/11 (1974): 340-42.

1062   Günther Schwarz, "ΑΝΟΙΞΑΣ ΤΟ ΣΤΟΜΑ ΑΥΤΟΥ
       (Matthäus 17.27)," *NTS* 38 (1992): 138-41.

18-25

1063   Daniel Patte, "Bringing Out of the Gospel-Treasure: What
       Is New and What Is Old: Two Parables in Matthew
       18-23," *QR* 10 (1990): 79-108.

18:1-6

1064   David Wenham, "A Note on Mark 9:33-42/Matt.
       18:1-6/Luke 9:46-50," *JSNT* 14 (1982): 113-18.

18:1-5

1065   Daniel Patte, "Jesus' Pronouncement about Entering the
       Kingdom Like a Child: A Structural Exegesis," *Semeia* 29
       (1983): 3-42.

18:3

1066   Daniel Patte, "Entering the Kingdom Like Children: A
       Structural Exegesis," *SBLSP* 21 (1982): 371-96.

1067   Vernon K. Robbins, "Pronouncement Stories and Jesus'
       Blessing of Children," *SBLSP* 21 (1982): 407-30.

18:6

1068   J. D. M. Derrett, "Two Harsh Sayings Of Christ
       Explained," *DR* 103 (1985): 218-29.

18:8-14

1069   H. B. Kossen, "Quelques remarques sur l'ordre des
       paraboles dans Luc xv et sur la construction de Matthieu
       xviii.8-14," *NovT* 1 (1956): 75-80.

18:8-9

1070   Herbert W. Basser, "The Meaning of 'Shtuth', Gen. 4.11
       in Reference to Matthew 5.29-30 and 18.8-9," *NTS* 31/1
       (1985): 148-51.

18:14

1071   Savas Agourides, " 'Little Ones' in Matthew," *BT* 35/3
       (1984): 329-34.

18:15-20

1072   James L. Boyce, "Transformed for Disciple Community: Matthew in Pentecost," *WW* 13 (1993): 308-17.

1073   Estella B. Horning, "The Rule of Christ: An Exposition of Matthew 18:15-20," *BLT* 38 (1993): 69-78.

18:15-18

1074   V. C. Pfitzner, "Purified Community-Purified Sinner: Expulsion from the Communion According to Matthew 18:15-18 and 1 Corinthians 5:1-5," *ABR* 30 (1982): 34-55.

1075   Elaine Ramshaw, "Power and Forgiveness in Matthew 18," *WW* 18 (1998): 397-404.

18:15-17

1076   F. García Martínez, "La reprehensión fraterna en Qumran y Mt. 18,15-17," *FilN* 2/1 (1989): 23-40.

18:15

1077   Gerhard Barth, "Auseinandersetzungen um die Kirchenzucht im Umkreis des Matthäusevangeliums," *ZNW* 69/3 (1978): 158-77.

18:17

1078   S. Hobhouse, "Let Him Be unto Thee as the Gentile and the Publican (Mt. 18,17)," *ET* 49 (1937-1938): 43-44.

18:18-21:35

1079   Georg Korting, "Binden oder lösen: Zur Verstockungs- und Befreiungstheologie in Mt. 16,19; 18:18-21:35 und Joh 15,1-17; 2,23," *SNTU-A* 14 (1989): 39-91.

18:18

1080   Henry J. Cadbury, "The Meaning of John 20,23, Matthew 16,19, and Matthew 18,18," *JBL* 58 (1939): 251-54.

1081   Julius R. Mantey, "The Mistranslation of the Perfect Tense in John 20,23, Mt. 16,19, and Mt. 18,18," *JBL* 58 (1939): 243-49.

1082   Julius R. Mantey, "What of Priestly Absolution," *CT* 13/9 (1969): 233-391.

1083   Julius R. Mantey, "Distorted Translations in John 20:23; Matthew 16:18-19 and 18:18," *RevExp* 78/3 (1981): 409-16.

1084   J. D. M. Derrett, "Binding and Loosing (Matt. 16:19; Matt. 18:18; John 20:23)," *JBL* 102 (1983): 112-17.

1085   Herbert W. Basser, "Derrett's 'Binding' Reopened," *JBL* 104 (1985): 297-300.

1086   Richard H. Hiers, " 'Binding' and 'Loosing': The Matthean Authorizations," *JBL* 104/2 (1985): 233-50.

1087   Dennis C. Duling, "Binding and Loosing: Matthew 16:19; Matthew 18:18; John 20:23," *Forum* 3 (1987): 3-31.

1088   Kair A. Syreeni, "Between Heaven and Earth: On the Structure of Matthew's Symbolic Universe," *JSNT* 40 (1990): 9-13.

18:19-20

1089   E. C. Ratcliff, "The Prayer of St. Chrysostom: A Note on Cranmer's Rendering and Its Background," *ATR* 42 (1960): 1-9.

1090   J. Caba, "El poderde la petición comunitaria (Mt. 18,19-20)," *Greg* 54 (1973): 609-54.

1091   J. D. M. Derrett, "Where Two or Three Are Convened in My Name . . . .': A Sad Misunderstanding," *ET* 91/3 (1979): 83-86.

18:20

1092   Pietro Bolognesi, "Matteo 18:20 e la dottrina della Chiesa," *BibO* 29 (1987): 1671-77.

18:21-35

1093   Erhardt Guttgemanns, "Narrative Analyse Synoptischer Texte," *LB* 25 (1973): 50-73.

1094   Harvey H. Potthoff, "Homiletical Resources: The Sermon as Theological Event Interpretations of Parables," *QR* 4/2 (1984): 76-102.

1095   Donald P. Senior, "Matthew 18:21-35," *Int* 41/4 (1987): 403-407.

1096   Beat Weber, "Vergeltung oder Vergebung!? Matthäus
        18,21-35 auf dem Hintergrund des 'Erlassjahres'," *TZ* 50
        (1994): 124-51.

1097   S. E. Hylen, "Forgiveness and Life in Community," *Int* 54
        (2000): 146-57.

18:21-22

1098   Elaine Ramshaw, "Power and Forgiveness in Matthew
        18," *WW* 18 (1998): 397-404.

18:23-35

1099   L. G. Kelly, "Cultural Consistency in Translation," *BT*
        21/4 (1970): 170-75.

1100   Christian Dietzfelbinger, "Das Gleichnis von der
        erlassenen Schuld. Eine theologische Untersuchung von
        Matthäus 18,23-35," *EvT* 32 (1972): 437-51.

1101   Martinus C. de Boer, "Ten Thousand Talents: Matthew's
        Interpretation and Redaction of the Parable of the
        Unforgiving Servant (Matt. 18:23-35)," *CBQ* 50 (1988):
        214-32.

18:23-34

1102   Bernard B. Scott, "The King's Accounting: Matthew
        18:23-34. *JBL* 104/3 (1985): 429-42.

18:23-24

1103   Beat Weber, "Alltagswelt und Gottesreich: Überlegungen
        zum Verstehenshintergrund des Gleichnisses vom
        'Schalksknecht'," *BZ* NS 37 (1993): 161-82.

19:1-12

1104   Dale C. Allison, "Divorce, Celibacy and Joseph," *JSNT* 49
        (1993): 3-10.

19:1-9

1105   Duane Warden, "The Words of Jesus on Divorce," *RQ* 39
        (1997): 141-53.

19:1

1106   David Hellholm, "En textgrammatisk konstruktion I
        Matteusevangeliet," *SEÅ* 51 (1986-1987): 80-89.

1107   Donald J. Verseput, "Jesus' Pilgrimage to Jerusalem and Encounter in the Temple: A Geographical Motif in Matthew's Gospel," *NovT* 36 (1994): 105-21.

19:3-13

1108   John J. Pilch, "Marriage in the Lord," *BibTo* 102 (1979): 2010-13.

19:3-12

1109   David R. Catchpole, "The Synoptic Divorce Material as a Traditio-Historical Problem," *BJRL* 57/1 (1974): 92-127.

1110   Francis J. Moloney, "Matthew 19,3-12 and Celibacy. A Redactional and Form Critical Study," *JSNT* 1/2 (1979): 42-60.

1111   Charles C. Ryrie, "Biblical Teaching on Divorce and Remarriage," *GTJ* 3/2 (1982): 177-92.

1112   Craig L. Blomberg, "Marriage, Divorce, Remarriage, and Celibacy: An Exegesis of Matthew 19:3-12," *TriJ* 11 (1990): 161-96.

19:3-9

1113   Augustine Stock, "Matthean Divorce Texts," *BTB* 8/1 (1978): 24-33.

1114   M. J. Molldrem, "A Hermeneutic of Pastoral Care and the Law/Gospel Paradigm Applied to the Divorce Texts of Scripture," *Int* 45 (1991): 43-54.

19:4-6

1115   Gladys Lewis, "A Christian Lifestyle for Families," *SouJT* 22/1 (1979): 74-83.

19:4

1116   David A. Black, "Conjectural Emendations in the Gospel of Matthew," *NovT* 31/1 (1989): 1-15.

19:9

1117   Heinrich Baltensweiler, "Die Ehebruchsklausen bei Matthaeus: zu Matth 5:32; 19:9," *TZ* 15 (1959): 340-56.

1118   John J. O'Rourke, "A Note on an Exception: Mt. 5:32 (19:9) and 1 Cor 7:12 Compared," *HeyJ* 5 (1964): 299-302.

1119   H. G. Coiner, "Those 'Divorce and Remarriage' Passages," *CTM* 39/6 (1968): 367-84.

1120   Richard N. Soulen, "Marriage and Divorce: A Problem in New Testament Interpretation," *Int* 23/4 (1969): 439-50.

1121   L. Ramaroson, "Une nouvelle interprétation de la 'clausule' de Mt. 19, 9," *SE* 23 (1971): 247-51.

1122   P. T. Stramare, "Matteo Divorzista?" *Div* 15/2 (1971): 213-35.

1123   Antonio Vargas-Machuca, "Los casos de 'divorcio' admitidos por San Mateo (5,32 y 19,9). Consecuencias para la teologia actual," *EE* 50 (1975): 5-54.

1124   John J. Kilgallen, "To What Are the Matthean Exception-Texts (5,32 and 19,9) An Exception?" *Bib* 61/1 (1980): 102-05.

1125   Henri Crouzel, "Quelques remarques concernant le texte patristique de Mt. 19,9," *BLE* 82 (1981): 82-92.

1126   Carroll D. Osburn, "The Present Indicative in Matthew 19:9," *RQ* 24/4 (1981): 193-203.

1127   William A. Heth, "Another Look at the Erasmian View of Divorce and Remarriage," *JETS* 25/3 (1982): 263-72.

1128   G. J. Wenham, "Matthew and Divorce: An Old Crux Revisited," *JSNT* 22 (1984): 95-107.

1129   Ben Witherington, "Matthew 5.32 and 19.9—Exception or Exceptional Situation?" *NTS* 31/4 (1985): 571-76.

1130   G. J. Wenham, "The Syntax of Matthew 19.9," *JSNT* 28 (1986): 17-23.

1131   Markus Bockmuehl, "Matthew 5.32, 19.9 in the Light of Pre-Rabbinic Halakhah," *NTS* 35/2 (1989): 291-95.

1132   Don T. Smith, "The Matthean Exception Clauses in the Light of Matthew's Theology and Community," *SBT* 17/1 (1989): 55-82.

1133   Phillip H. Wiebe, "Jesus' Divorce Exception," *JETS* 32 (1989): 327-33.

1134   Corrado Marucci, "Clausole matteane e critica testuale. In merito alla teoria di H. Crouzel sul testo originale di Mt. 19,9," *RBib* 38 (1990): 301-25.

19:10-12

1135   C. Daniel, "Esséniens et Eunuques (Matthieu 19,10-12)," *RevQ* 6 (1968): 353-90.

1136   Jean-Marie van Cangh, "Fondement Angelique de la Vie Religieuse," *NRT* 95/6 (1973): 635-47.

1137   Roger Balducelli, "The Decision for Celibacy," *TS* 36/2 (1975): 219-42.

1138   Thaddee Matura, "Le Celibat dans le Nouveau Testament," *NRT* 97/6 (1975): 481-500.

1139   G. G. Gamba, "La 'Eunuchia' per il Regno Deicieli. Annotazioni in Margineamatteo 19,10-12," *Sale* 42/2 (1980): 243-87.

1140   Christian Wolff, "Niedrigkeit und Verzicht in Wort und Weg Jesu und in der apostolischen Existenz des Paulus," *NTS* 34/2 (1988): 183-96.

19:12

1141   Q. Quesnell, " 'Made Themselves Eunuchs for the Kingdom of Heaven'," *CBQ* 30/3 (1968): 335-58.

1142   Heinrich Greeven, "Ehe nach dem Neuen Testament," *NTS* 15/4 (1969): 365-88.

1143   J. Kodell, "The Celibacy Logion in Matthew 19:12," *BTB* 8/1 (1978): 19-23.

1144   William A. Heth, "Another Look at the Erasmian View of Divorce and Remarriage," *JETS* 25/3 (1982): 263-72.

1145   Pierre-Rene Cote, "Les eunuques pour le Royaume (Mt. 19,12)," *ÉgT* 17/3 (1986): 321-34.

1146   William A. Heth, "Unmarried 'For the Sake of the Kingdom' (Matthew 19:12) in the Early Church," *GTJ* 8/1 (1987): 55-88.

19:13-15

1147   Daniel Patte, "Jesus' Pronouncement about Entering the Kingdom Like a Child: A Structural Exegesis," *Semeia* 29 (1983): 3-42.

19:16-30

1148   A. F. J. Klijn, "The Question of the Rich Young Man in a Jewish-Christian Gospel," *NovT* 8 (1966): 149-15.

1149   J. M. R. Tillard, "Le Propos de Pauvreté et l'Exigence Evangélique," *NRT* 100/2 (1978): 207-32.

1150   Robert L. Thomas, "The Rich Young Man in Matthew," *GTJ* 3/2 (1982): 235-60.

19:16-22

1151   Gregory Murray, "The Rich Young Man," *DR* 103 (1985): 144-46.

1152   Reginald H. Fuller, "The Decalogue in the NT," *Int* 43/3 (1989): 243-55.

19:16

1153   John W. Wenham, "Why Do You Ask Me About the Good? A Study of the Relation between Text and Source Criticism," *NTS* 28/1 (1982): 116-25.

19:17

1154   Eric F. Osborn, "Origen and Justification: The Good Is One," *ABR* 24/1 (1976): 18-29.

19:24

1155   José O'Callaghan, "Examen critico de Mt. 19,24," *Bib* 69/3 (1988): 401-05.

19:28

1156   Fred W. Burnett, "Παλιγγενεσίᾳ in Matt. 19:28: A Window on the Matthean Community?" *JSNT* 17 (1983): 60-72.

1157   J. D. M. Derrett, "Παλιγγενεσίᾳ (Matthew 19.28)," *JSNT* 20 (1984): 51-58.

1158   David C. Sim, "The Meaning of *palingenesia* in Matthew 19.28," *JSNT* 50 (1993): 12.

19:30

1159   José O'Callaghan, "Nota crítica sobre Mt. 19,30," *EB* 48 (1990): 271-73.

20:1-16

1160   W. T. Williams, "The Parable of the Labourers in the Vineyard (Mt. 20,1-16)," *ET* 50 (1938-1939): 526.

1161   C. L. Mitton, "Expounding the Parables: The Workers in the Vineyard," *ET* 77 (1965-1966): 307-11.

1162   L. J. Crampton, "St. Gregory's Homily XIX and the Institution of Septuagesima Sunday," *DR* 86 (1968): 162-66.

1163   Antonio Orbe, "San Ireneo y la parábola de los obreros de la viñ: Mt. 20,1-16," *EE* 46 (1971): 35-62, 183-206.

1164   Erhardt Guttgemanns, "Narrative Analyse Synoptischer Texte," *LB* 25 (1973): 50-73.

1165   D. A. Nelson, "An Exposition of Matthew 20:1-16," *Int* 29/3 (1975): 288-92.

1166   Frédéric Manns, "L'Arrière-Plan Socio-Economique de la Parabole des Ouvriers de la Onzième Heure et ses Limites," *Ant* 55/1 (1980): 258-68.

1167   Franz Schnider, "Von der Gerechtigkeit Gottes: Beobachtungen zum Gleichnis von den Arbeitern im Weinberg (Matt. 20:1-16)," *K* 23/1 (1981): 88-95.

1168   Robert T. Fortna, "You Have Made Them Equal to Us!" *JTSA* 72 (1990): 66-72.

1169   Ulrich Busse, "In Souveränität--anders," *BZ* NS 40 (1996): 61-72.

1170   B. Rod Doyle, "The Place of the Parable of the Labourers in the Vineyard in Matthew 20:1-16," *ABR* 42 (1994): 39-58.

20:1-15

1171   Rudolf Hoppe, "Gleichnis und Situation," *BZ* 28/1 (1984): 1-21.

20:1-6

1172   John G. Strelan, "Sermon Study: Matthew 20:1-6," *LTJ* 20/1 (1986): 19-21.

<u>20:1</u>

1173   Gerhard Sellen, "Gleichnisstrukturen," *LB* 31 (1974): 89-115.

<u>20:4</u>

1174   F. C. Glover, "Workers for the Vineyard, Mt. 20,4," *ET* 86 (1975): 310-11.

<u>20:16</u>

1175   E. F. Sutcliffe, "Many Are Called But Few Are Chosen," *ITQ* 28 (1961): 126-31.

<u>20:20-28</u>

1176   Ndubuisi B. Akuchie, "The Servants and the Superstars: An Examination of Servant Leadership in Light of Matthew 20:20-28," *CEJ* 14 (1993): 39-47.

<u>20:20-21</u>

1177   Emily R. Cheney, "The Mother of the Sons of Zebedee," *JSNT* 68 (1997): 13-21.

<u>20:21</u>

1178   José O'Callaghan, "Fluctuación textual en Mt. 20, 21.26.27," *Bib* 71/4 (1990): 553-58.

1179   Dale C. Allison, "Anticipating the Passion: The Literary Reach of Matthew 26:47-27:56," *CBQ* 56 (1994): 701-14.

<u>20:26</u>

1180   José O'Callaghan, "Fluctuación textual en Mt. 20, 21.26.27," *Bib* 71/4 (1990): 553-58.

<u>20:28</u>

1181   Mogens Müller, "Mattaeusevangeliets Messiasbillede: et forsg pa at bestemme Mattaeusevangeliets forstaelse af Jesu messianitet," *SEÅ* (1986-1987): 51/52 168-79.

1182   Warren Carter, "Jesus' 'I have come' Statements in Matthew's Gospel," *CBQ* 60 (1998): 44-62.

<u>21</u>

1183   Sarah Henrich, "Matthew in Minneapolis and in Israel," *WW* 19 (1999): 201-209.

21:1-23:39

    1184   Donald J. Verseput, "Jesus' Pilgrimage to Jerusalem and Encounter in the Temple: A Geographical Motif in Matthew's Gospel," *NovT* 36 (1994): 105-21.

21:1-17

    1185   Renate Brandscheidt, "Messias und Tempel: Die alttestamentlichen Zitate in Mt. 21,1-17," *TTZ* 99 (1990): 36-48.

21:1-11

    1186   Roman Bartnicki, "Das Zitat von Zach IX, 9-10 und die Tiere im Berichte von Matthäus über den Einzug Jesu in Jerusalem (Mt. XXI,1-11)," *NovT* 18/3 (1976): 161-66.

21:1

    1187   D. Durken, "Mountains and Matthew," *BibTo* 28 (1990): 304-307.

21:4

    1188   James W. Scott, "Matthew's Intention to Write History," *WTJ* 47/1 (1985): 68-82.

21:5-7

    1189   A. Frenz, "Mt. XXI.5.7," *NovT* 13 (1971): 259-60.

21:11

    1190   Paul W. Meyer, "Matthew 21:11," *Int* 40/2 (1986): 180-85.

21:15

    1191   Savas Agourides, " 'Little Ones' in Matthew," *BT* 35/3 (1984): 329-34.

21:17

    1192   George Howard, "A Note on Codex Sinaiticus and Shem-Tob's Hebrew Matthew," *NTS* 38 (1992): 187-204.

21:18-19

    1193   H.-W. Bartsch, "Die 'Verfluchung' des Feigenbaums," *ZNW* 53 (1962): 256-60.

21:27-31

    1194   Piet DeVries and Friedrich Wulf, "Gleichnisse vom Vater und Seinen Söhnen," *GeistL* 44/1 (1971): 74-75.

21:28-22:14

1195 A. Ogawa, "Paraboles de l'Israel Véritable? Reconsidération Critique de Mt. XXI.28-XXII.14," *NovT* 21/2 (1979): 121-49.

21:28-32

1196 J. Ramsey Michaels, "The Parable of the Regretful Son," *HTR* 61 (1968): 15-26.

1197 J. D. M. Derrett, "The Parable of the Two Sons," *StTheol* 25 (1971): 109-16.

1198 Helmut Merkel, "Das Gleichnis von den 'ungleichen Söhnen' (Matth. xxi.28-32)," *NTS* 20 (1974): 254-61.

1199 W. L. Richards, "Another Look at the Parable of the Two Sons," *BR* 23 (1978): 5-14.

21:28-31

1200 Gerhard Sellen, "Gleichnisstrukturen," *LB* 31 (1974): 89-115.

1201 Jean Doignon, "L'exégèse latine de la parabole des deux fils (Matth. 21:28-31): Hilaire de Poitiers devant le problème de l'obéisance a Dieu," *RHPR* 65/1 (1985): 53-59.

21:31

1202 Henry Osborn, "A Quadruple Quote in the Triumphal Entry Account in Warao," *BT* 18/1 (1967): 301-21.

21:33-48

1203 J. C. O'Neill, "The Source of the Parables of the Bridegroom and the Wicked Husbandmen," *JTS* 39 (1988): 485-89.

21:33-46

1204 John D. Crossan, "The Parable of the Wicked Husbandmen," *JBL* 90/4 (1971): 451-65.

1205 Jack D. Kingsbury, "The Parable of the Wicked Husbandmen and the Secret of Jesus' Divine Sonship in Matthew: Some Literary-Critical Observations," *JBL* 105 (1986): 643-55.

1206   C. Wrembek, "Das Gleichnis vom königlichen Hochzeitsmahl und vom Mann ohne hochzeitliches Gewand. Eine geistliche-theologische Erwägung zu Mt. 22,1-14," *GeistL* 64/1 (1991): 17-40.

1207   Wim J. C. Weren, "The Use of Isaiah 5,1-7 in the Parable of the Tenants (Mark 12,1-12; Matthew 21,33-46)," *Bib* 79 (1998): 1-26.

21:33-43

1208   Fred B. Craddock, "Homiletical Studies: Exegesis and Exposition of Gospel Lections for the Season after Pentecost," *QR* 1/4 (1981): 5-42.

21:33-41

1209   Jane E. Newell and Raymond R. Newell, "The Parable of the Wicked Tenants," *NovT* 14/3 (1972): 226-37.

21:38-42

1210   Edwin K. Broadhead, "An Example of Gender Bias in UBS3," *BT* 40/3 (1989): 336-38.

21:41

1211   K. H. Kuhn, "Kakie Kakos in the Sahidic Version of Matthew 21:41," *JTS* 36/2 (1985): 390-93.

21:43

1212   R. Swaeles, "L'Arrière-fond scripturaire de Matt. xxi. 43 et son lien avec Matt. xxi. 44," *NTS* 6 (1959-1960): 310-13.

1213   W. H. Gispen, "Het Oude Testament over de Toekomst van Israel," *GTT* 60 (1960): 50-63.

22:1-14

1214   H. Schlier, "Der Ruf Gottes (Mt. 22,1-14)," *GeistL* 28 (1955): 241-47.

1215   Eta Linnemann, "Überlegungen zur Parabel vom grossen Abendmahl, Lc 14,15-24 Mt,22 1-14," *ZNW* 51 (1960): 246-55.

1216   Otto Glombitza, "Das grosse Abendmahl: Luk. 14:12-24," *NovT* 5 (1962): 10-16.

1217 Victor Hasler, "Die königliche Hochzeit, Matth. 22,1-14," *TZ* 18 (1962): 25-35.

1218 Dan O. Via, "The Relationship of Form to Content in the Parable: The Wedding Feast," *Int* 25 (1971): 171-84.

1219 Chan-Hie Kim, "The Papyrus Invitation," *JBL* 94/3 (1975): 391-402.

1220 Fred B. Craddock, "Homiletical Studies: Exegesis and Exposition of Gospel Lections for the Season after Pentecost," *QR* 1/4 (1981): 5-42.

1221 C. Wrembek, "Das Gleichnis vom königlichen Hochzeitsmahl und vom Mann ohne hochzeitliches Gewand. Eine geistlich theologische Erwägung zu Mt. 22,1-14," *GeistL* 64/1 (1991): 17-40.

1222 Richard J. Bauckham, "The Parable of the Royal Wedding Feast (Matthew 22:1-14) and the Parable of the Lame Man and the Blind Man (Apocryphon of Ezekial)," *JBL* 115 (1996): 471-88.

1223 A. G. Van Aarde, "A Historical-Critical Classifcation of Jesus' Parables and the Metaphoric Narration of the Wedding Feast in Matthew 22:1-14," *HTS* suppl 5 (1994): 229-47.

22:1-10

1224 Erhardt Guttgemanns, "Narrative Analyse Synoptischer Texte," *LB* 25 (1973): 50-73.

1225 Gerhard Sellen, "Gleichnisstrukturen," *LB* 31 (1974): 89-115.

1226 Eugene E. Lemcio, "The Parables of the Great Supper and the Wedding Feast. History, Redaction and Canon," *HBT* 8/1 (1986): 1-26.

1227 Elaine Wainwright, "God Wills to Invite All to the Banquet," *IRM* 77 (1988): 185-93.

1228 Peter Dschulnigg, "Positionen des Gleichnisverständnisses im 20. Jahrhundert," *TZ* 45/4 (1989): 335-51.

22:1-4

1229   W. Trilling, "Zur Überlieferungsgeschichte des Glechnisses vom Hochzeitsmahl," *BZ* 4 (1960): 251-65.

22:1

1230   Paul H. Ballard, "Reasons for Refusing the Great Supper," *JTS* 23/2 (1972): 341-50.

22:2-10

1231   R. W. Resenhöfft, "Jesu Gleichnis von den Talenten, Ergänzt durch die Lukas-Fassung," *NTS* 26/3 (1979-1980): 318-31.

22:11-14

1232   Erhardt Guttgemanns, "Narrative Analyse Synoptischer Texte," *LB* 25 (1973): 50-73.

22:11-13

1233   J. B. Bauer, "De Veste Nuptiali (Mt. 22,11-13)," *VD* 43 (1965): 15-18.

1234   David C. Sim, "The Man without the Wedding Garment (Matthew 22:11-13)," *HeyJ* 31 (1990): 165-78.

22:12

1235   K. R. Cripps, "A Note on Matthew xxii.12," *ET* 69 (1957-1958): 30.

22:13

1236   C. Jaeger, "Remarques philologiques sur quelques passages des Synoptiques," *RHPR* 16 (1936): 246-49.

22:14

1237   E. F. Sutcliffe, "Many Are Called But Few Are Chosen," *ITQ* 28 (1961): 126-31.

1238   Ben F. Meyer, "Many (=All) Are Called, But Few (=Not All) Are Chosen," *NTS* 36/1 (1990): 89-97.

22:15-22

1239   Fred B. Craddock, "Homiletical Studies: Exegesis and Exposition of Gospel Lections for the Season after Pentecost," *QR* 1/4 (1981): 5-42.

1240   David T. Owen-Ball, "Rabbinic Rhetoric and the Tribute Passage," *NovT* 35 (1993): 1-14.

22:21

1241 Charles H. Giblin, " 'The Things of God' in the Questions Concerning Tribute to Caesar," *CBQ* 33/4 (1971): 510-27.

22:30

1242 Thaddee Matura, "Le Celibat dans le Nouveau Testament," *NRT* 97/6 (1975): 481-500.

1243 Robert C. Newman, "The Ancient Exegesis of Genesis 6:2,4," *GTJ* 5/1 (1984): 13-36.

22:31-32

1244 D. M. Cohn-Sherbok, "Jesus' Defence of the Resurrection of the Dead," *JSNT* 11 (1981): 64-73.

22:32

1245 Frédéric Manns, "La technique du 'Al Tiqra' dans les évangiles," *RevSR* 64 (1990): 1-7.

22:34-40

1246 Carl A. Clark, "The Neglected Commandment I (Matthew 22:34-40)," *SouJT* 3 (1960): 61-73.

1247 Robert Douglas, "The Neglected Commandment II (Matthew 22:34-40)," *SouJT* 3 (1960): 74-77.

1248 Arland J. Hultgren, "The Double Commandment of Love in Mt. 22:34-40," *CBQ* 36 (1974): 373-78.

1249 Oscar S. Brooks, "The Function of the Double Love Command in Matthew 22:34-40," *AUSS* 36 (1998): 7-22.

1250 Wayne E. Oates, "A Biblical Perspective on Addiction," *RevExp* 91 (1994): 71-75.

22:35

1251 Tjitze Baarda, "Nomikos in Syriac Texts," *NovT* 41 (1999): 383-89.

22:39

1252 John Wilson and Nicholas Wilson, "Loving Your Neighbor As Yourself," *Theology* 101 (1998): 411-20.

22:40

1253 Terence L. Donaldson, "The Law that 'Hangs' (Mt. 22:40): Rabbinic Formulation and Matthean Social World," *SBLSP* (1990): 14-33.

23:1-12

1254   Benedict T. Viviano, "Social World and Community Leadership: The Case of Matthew 23:1-12, 34," *JSNT* 39 (1990): 3-21.

23:2-7

1255   M. A. Powell, "Do and Keep What Moses Says," *JBL* 114 (1995): 419-35.

23:2

1256   José O'Callaghan, "La variante neotestamentaria levadura de los panes," *Bib* 67 (1986): 98-100.

1257   Kenneth G. C. Newport, "A Note on the 'Seat of Moses'," *AUSS* 28 (1990): 53-58.

23:4

1258   George Howard, "A Note on Codex Sinaiticus and Shem-Tob's Hebrew Matthew," *NTS* 38 (1992): 187-204.

23:5-6

1259   Hyam Z. Maccoby, "The Washing of Cups," *JSNT* 14 (1982): 3-15.

23:8-10

1260   J. D. M. Derrett, "Mt. 23,8-10: A Midrash on Is. 54,13 and Jer. 31,33-34," *Bib* 62/3 (1981): 372-86.

23:8-9

1261   R. S. Barbour, "Uncomfortable Words. VIII: Status and Titles," *ET* 82/5 (1971): 137-42.

23:9

1262   John T. Townsend, "Matthew 23:9," *JTS* 12 (1961): 56-59.

1263   W. C. Robinson, "The Virgin Birth: A Broader Base," *CT* 17/5 (1972): 238-40.

23:10

1264   Ceslaus Spicq, "Une allusion au docteur de justice dans Matthieu 23:10?" *RB* 66 (1959): 387-96.

1265   Bruce W. Winter, "The Messiah as the Tutor: The Meaning of Kathegetes in Matthew 23:10," *TynB* 42 (1991): 152-57.

<u>23:15</u>

1266 H. J. Flowers, "Matthew 23:15," *ET* 73 (1961): 67-69.

1267 John Hoad, "On Matthew 23:15: A Rejoinder," *ET* 73 (1962): 211-12.

1268 Paul S. Minear, "Yes or No: The Demand for Honesty in the Early Church," *NovT* 13 (1971): 1-13.

1269 John Nolland, "Proselytism or Politics in Horace Satires 1, 4, 138-143?" *VC* 33/4 (1979): 347-55.

<u>23:23</u>

1270 Dietrich Correns, "Die Verzehntung der Raute. Luk XI 42 und M Schebi IX I," *MeliT* 6/2 (1963): 110-12.

1271 Peter Harvey, "Vision and Obligation," *DR* 85 (1967): 62-70.

1272 Robert A. Wild, "The Encounter between Pharisaic and Christian Judaism: Some Early Gospel Evidence," *NovT* 27/2 (1985): 105-24.

<u>23:24-30</u>

1273 J. D. M. Derrett, "Receptacles and Tombs (Mt. 23,24-30)," *ZNW* 77 (1986): 255-66.

<u>23:24-26</u>

1274 Fred B. Craddock, "Homiletical Studies: Exegesis and Exposition of Gospel Lections for the Season after Pentecost," *QR* 1/4 (1981): 5-42.

<u>23:25-35</u>

1275 Robert J. Miller, "The Rejection of the Prophet in Q," *JBL* 107 (1988): 225-40.

<u>23:25-27</u>

1276 John C. Poirier, "A Reply to Hyam Maccoby," JSNT 76 (1999): 115-18.

<u>23:25-26</u>

1277 Robert A. Wild, "The Encounter between Pharisaic and Christian Judaism: Some Early Gospel Evidence," *NovT* 27/2 (1985): 105-24.

<u>23:25</u>

1278 J. M. Ross, "Which Zachariah?" *IBS* 9 (1987): 70-73.

23:26

1279   Günther Schwarz, " 'Reinige . . . das Innere des Bechers'? (Matthäus 23,26)," *BibN* 75 (1994): 31-34.

23:27-28

1280   Samuel T. Lachs, "On Matthew 23:27-28," *HTR* 68/3 (1975): 385-88.

23:27

1281   Günther Schwarz, " 'Unkenntliche Gräber'? (Lukas XI. 44)," *NTS* 23/2 (1977): 345-46.

23:29-24:2

1282   Ross E. Winkle, "The Jeremiah Model for Jesus in the Temple," *AUSS* 24/2 (1986): 155-72.

23:29-36

1283   H. Pernot, "Matthieu XXIII,29-36. Luc XI,47-51," *RHPR* 13 (1933): 262-67.

23:29-32

1284   L. Cardellino, "Mt 23,29-32 e ii preteso antigiudaismo di Matteo," *RivBib* 48 (2000): 27-53.

23:34-40

1285   Robert Douglas, "The Neglected Commandment II (Matthew 22:34-40)," *SouJT* 3 (1960): 74-77.

23:34-39

1286   C. Deutsch, "Wisdom in Matthew: Transformation of a Symbol," *NovT* 32 (1990): 13-47.

23:34

1287   Benedict T. Viviano, "Social World and Community Leadership: The Case of Matthew 23:1-12, 34," *JSNT* 39 (1990): 3-21.

23:35

1288   J. Barton Payne, " 'Zachariah Who Perished'," *GTJ* 8/3 (1967): 33-35.

23:37-39

1289   H. van der Kwaak, "Die Klage über Jerusalem (Matth. xxiii. 37-39)," *NovT* 8 (1966): 156-70.

23:39

1290   Eduard Lohse, "Hosianna," *NovT* 6/2 (1963): 113-19.

1291   Dale C. Allison, "Matt. 23:39 = Luke 13:35b as a Conditional Prophecy," *JSNT* 18 (1983): 75-84.

24-25

1292   André Feuillet, "La synthèse eschatologique de saint Matthieu XXIV-XXV," *RB* 56 (1949): 340-64; 57 (1950): 62-91; 180-211.

1293   M. Miguéns, "Anotaciones sobre Mateo cc. 24-25," *SBFLA* 6 (1955-1956): 125-95.

1294   P. Géoltrain, "Notes sur Matthieu 24-25," *FV* 5 (1967): 26-35.

1295   Morris A. Inch, "Matthew and the House-Churches," *EQ* 43/4 (1971): 196-202.

1296   John F. Walvoord, "Christ's Olivet Discourse on the End of the Age," *BSac* 128 (1971): 109-16.

1297   John F. Walvoord, "Christ's Olivet Discourse on the Time of the End," *BSac* 129 (1972): 20-32.

1298   Henry G. Waterman, "The Sources of Paul's Teaching on the Second Coming of Christ in 1 and 2 Thessalonians," *JETS* 18/2 (1975): 105-13.

1299   Bruce A. Ware, "Is the Church in View in Matthew 24-25?" *BSac* 138 (1981): 158-72.

24:1-2:15

1300   John F. Walvoord, "Will Israel Build a Temple in Jerusalem?" *BSac* 125 (1968): 99-106.

24:1-41

1301   David L. Turner, "The Structure and Sequence of Matthew 24:1-41: Interaction with Evangelical Treatments," *GTJ* 10 (1989): 3-27.

24:1-36

1302   Hugo Lattanzi, "Eschatologici Sermonis Domini Logica Interpretatio," *Div* 11/1 (1967): 71-92.

24:1-28

1303   Ingo Broer, "Redaktionsgeschichtliche Aspekte von Mt 24:1-28," *NovT* 35 (1993): 209-33.

24:3-28

1304   Willem S. Vorster, "A Reader-Response Approach to Matthew 24:3-28," *HTS* 47 (1991): 1099-1108.

24:3

1305   Raymond E. Gingrich, "Adumbrations of Our Lord's Return: Political Alignments," *GTJ* 9/1 (1968): 3-14.

1306   D. Durken, "Mountains and Matthew," *BibTo* 28 (1990): 304-307.

24:4-14

1307   John F. Walvoord, "Christ's Olivet Discourse on the Time of the End: Prophecies Fulfilled in the Present Age," *BSac* 128 (1971): 206-14.

24:9-13

1308   Justin Taylor, " 'The Love of Many Will Grow Cold': Matt. 24:9-13 and the Neronian Persecution," *RB* 96/3 (1989): 352-57.

24:10-12

1309   David Wenham, "A Note on Matthew 24:10-12," *TynB* 31 (1980): 150-62.

24:12

1310   Raymond E. Gingrich, "Adumbrations of Our Lord's Return: Global Iniquity," *GTJ* 8/3 (1967): 17-32.

1311   Domingo Muñoz León, "Jesus y la apocaliptica pesimista (a proposito de Lc 18:8b y Mt. 24:12)," *EB* 46/4 (1988): 457-95.

24:14

1312   Raymond E. Gingrich, "Adumbrations of Our Lord's Return: Political Alignments," *GTJ* 9/1 (1968): 3-14.

24:15-22

1313   John F. Walvoord, "Posttribulationism Today. Part IV: Post-tribulational Denial of Imminency and Wrath," *BSac* 133 (1976): 108-18.

24:15-20

1314   Gordon D. Fee, "A Text-Critical Look at the Synoptic
        Problem," *NovT* 22/1 (1980): 12-28.

24:15-16

1315   Thomas S. McCall, "How Soon the Tribulation Temple?"
        BSac 128 (1971): 341-51.

24:15

1316   G. C. Aalders, "De 'Gruwel der Verwoesting'," *GTT* 60
        (1960): 1-5.

24:20

1317   Graham N. Stanton, " 'Pray That Your Flight May Not Be
        in Winter or on a Sabbath'," *JSNT* 37 (1989): 17-30.

1318   E. K.-C. Wong, "The Matthean Understanding of the
        Sabbath: A Response to G. N. Stanton," *JSNT* 44 (1991):
        3-18.

24:26-29

1319   Bonnie B. Thurston, " 'Do This': A Study on the
        Institution of the Lord's Supper," *RQ* 30/4 (1988): 207-17.

24:26-28

1320   Hjerl-Hansen Borge, "Did Christ Know the Qumran Sect?
        Jesus and the Messiah of the Desert: An Observation
        Based on Matthew 24:26-28," *RevQ* 1 (1959): 495-508.

24:27-30

1321   John F. Walvoord, "Christ's Coming to Reign," *BSac* 123
        (1966): 195-203.

24:29-34

1322   John F. Walvoord, "The Parable of the Talents," *BSac* 129
        (1972): 206-10.

24:29-31

1323   John S. Kloppenborg, "Didache 16:6-8 and Special
        Matthaean Tradition," *ZNW* 70/1 (1979): 54-67.

24:29

1324   G. C. Fuller, "The Olivet Discourse: An Apocalyptic
        Time-Table," *WTJ* 28/2 (1966): 157-63.

24:30

1325 A. J. B. Higgins, "The Sign of the Son of Man (Matt. 24:30)," *NTS* 9 (1962-1963): 380-82.

1326 T. F. Glasson, "The Ensign of the Son of Man (Matt. 24:30)," *JTS* 15 (1964): 299-300.

1327 Donald V. Etz, "Comets in the Bible," *CT* 18/6 (1973): 338-40.

24:34

1328 S. Joseph Kidder, " 'This Generation' in Matthew 24:34," *AUSS* 21/3 (1983): 203-209.

1329 Neil D. Nelson, " 'This Generation' in Matt 24:34: A Literary Critical Perspective," *JETS* 38 (1995): 369-85.

24:35

1330 George Howard, "A Note on Codex Sinaiticus and Shem-Tob's Hebrew Matthew," *NTS* 38 (1992): 187-204.

24:36-44

1331 Marcelo A. Cisneros, "La inseguridad como mensaje Mt 24,36-44," *RevB* 60 (1998): 309-12.

1332 Sarah Henrich, "Matthew in Minneapolis and in Israel," *WW* 19 (1999): 201-209.

24:37-39

1333 Edgar V. McKnight and Charles H. Talbert, "Can the Griesbach Hypothesis Be Falsified?" *JBL* 91/3 (1972): 338-68.

24:42

1334 Nunzio Conte, " 'Il Signore Vostre Viene' (Mt. 24,42) l'Aspetto Escatologico della Liturgia. Domenica Idiavento A," *Sale* 47/3 (1985): 511-27.

24:51

1335 Otto Betz, "The Dichotomized Servant and the End of Judas Iscariot," *RevQ* 5/17 (1964): 43-58.

25:1-13

1336 J. M. Ford, "The Parable of the Foolish Scholars (Matt. 25:1-13)," *NovT* 9 (1967): 107-23.

1337 L. Deiss, "La parabole des dix vierges (Mt. 25,1-13)," *AsSeign* NS 63 (1971): 20-32.

1338 Karl P. Donfried, "The Allegory of the Ten Virgins (Matt. 25:1-13) as a Summary of Matthean Theology," *JBL* 93 (1974): 415-28.

1339 Gerhard Sellen, "Gleichnisstrukturen," *LB* 31 (1974): 89-115.

1340 Karl P. Donfried, "The Ten Virgins (Mt. 25:1-13)," *TD* 23 (1975): 106-10.

1341 W. Schrenk, "Auferweckung der Toten oder Gericht nach den Werken. Tradition und Redaktion in Mattäus XXV: 1-13," *NovT* 20/4 (1978): 278-99.

1342 Nancy J. Duff, "Wise and Foolish Maidens, Matthew 25:1-13," *USQR* 40/3 (1985): 55-58.

25:1-12

1343 Patrick P. Saydon, "Some Biblico-Liturgical Passages Reconsidered," *MeliT* 18/1 (1966): 10-17.

1344 Martino Conti, "La Sacra Scrittura nella Predicazione di San Bernardino," *Ant* 55/4 (1980): 549-72.

25:1-3

1345 Walter Magass, " 'Er aber schlief' (Mt. 8,24)," *LB* 29/30 (1973): 55-59.

25:1

1346 Joachim Jeremias, "*Lampdes*. Mt. 25,1.3f," *ZAW* 56 (1965): 196-201.

25:14-30

1347 E. Kamlah, "Kritik und Interpretation der Parabel von den anvertrauten Geldern," *KD* 14 (1968): 28-38.

1348 Erhardt Guttgemanns, "Narrative Analyse Synoptischer Texte," *LB* 25 (1973): 50-73.

1349 Gerhard Sellen, "Gleichnisstrukturen," *LB* 31 (1974): 89-115.

1350 L. C. McGauchy, "The Fear of Yahweh and the Mission of Judaism: A Postexilic Maxim and Its Early Christian

Expansion in the Parable of the Talents," *JBL* 94 (1975): 235-45.

1351   David C. Steinmetz, "Matthew 25:14-30," *Int* 34/2 (1980): 172-76.

1352   Daniel Lys, "Contre le salut par les oeuvres dans la prédiction des talents," *ÉTR* 64 (1989): 331-40.

1353   Carolyn Dipboye, "Matthew 25:14-30--To Survive or To Serve?" *RevExp* 92 (1995): 507-12.

25:21-23

1354   J. Vara, "Dos conjeturas textuales sobre Mateo 25,21.23 y Mateo 26,32/17,22 y par.," *Salm* 33 (1986): 81-86.

25:26

1355   J. Mutch, "The Man with the One Talent," *ET* 41 (1930-1931): 332-34.

1356   Helge K. Nielsen, "Er den 'dovne' tjener doven? Om oversaettelsen af ὀκνηρός i Matth 25,26," *DTT* 53 (1990): 106-15.

25:30

1357   A. Marcus Ward, "Uncomfortable Words: IV. Unprofitable Servants," *ET* 81/7 (1970): 200-203.

25:31-46

1358   C. F. Burney, "St. Matthew 25:31-46 as a Hebrew Poem," *JTS* (1912-1913): 414-24.

1359   A. T. Cadoux, "The Parable of the Sheep and the Goats," *ET* 41 (1929-1930): 559-62.

1360   J. A. T. Robinson, "The 'Parable' of the Sheep and the Goats," *NTS* 2 (1955-1956): 225-37.

1361   J. Ramsey Michaels, "Apostolic Hardships and Righteous Gentiles," *JBL* 84 (1965): 27-37.

1362   H. E. W. Turner, "Expounding the Parables: The Parable of the Sheep and the Goats," *ET* 77 (1965-1966): 243-46.

1363   John F. Walvoord, "Christ's Coming to Reign," *BSac* 123 (1966): 195-203.

1364 Norman K. Bakken, "The New Humanity: Christ and the Modern Age: A Study in the Christ-Hymn: Philippians 2:6-11," *Int* 22/1 (1968): 71-82.

1365 Lamar Cope, "Matthew 25:31-46: 'The Sheep and the Goats' Reinterpreted," *NovT* 11 (1969): 32-44.

1366 J.-C. Ingelaere, "La 'parabole' du Jugement Dernier (Matthieu 25,31-46)," *RHPR* 50 (1970): 23-60.

1367 Dietfried Gewalt, "Matthäus 25,31-46 im Erwartungshorizont heutiger Exgese," *LB* 25/26 (1973): 9-21.

1368 Erhardt Guttgemanns, "Narrative Analyse synoptischer Texte," *LB* 25 (1973): 50-73.

1369 Richard C. Oudersluys, "The Parable of the Sheep and Goats (Matthew 25:31-46): Eschatology and Mission, Then and Now," *RR* 26/3 (1973): 151-61.

1370 Max A. Chevallier, "Note à propos de l'exégèse de Mt. 25:31-46," *RevSR* 48 (1974): 398-400.

1371 Tibor Horvath, "3 Jn 11: An Early Ecumenical Creed?" *ET* 85/11 (1974): 339-40.

1372 A. J. Mattill, "Matthew 25:31-46 Relocated," *RQ* 17/2 (1974): 107-14.

1373 P.-É. Bonnard, "Matt. 25:31-46: Questions de lecture et d'interprétation," *FV* 76 (1977): 81-87.

1374 Rudolf Brändle, "Jean Chrysostome—l'importance de Matth 25,31-46 pour son Éthique," *VC* 31/1 (1977): 47-52.

1375 David R. Catchpole, "The Poor on Earth and the Son of Man in Heaven: A Reappraisal of Matthew 25:31-46," *BJRL* 61/2 (1979): 355-97.

1376 Rudolf Brändle, "Zur Interpretation von Mt. 25:31-46 im Matthäuskommentar des Origenes," *TZ* 36 (1980): 17-25.

1377 André Feuillet, "Le Caractère universel: Du Jugement et la Charite sans Frontières en Mt. 25,31-46," *NRT* 102/2 (1980): 179-96.

1378 Lauree H. Meyer, "Understanding Ministry," *BLT* 25/1 (1980): 28-31.

1379   Martin Tripole, "A Church for the Poor and the World: At Issue with Moltmann's Ecclesiology," *TS* 42/4 (1981): 645-59.

1380   X. Pikaza, "La estructura de Mateo y su influencia en 25:31-46," *Salm* 30 (1983): 11-40.

1381   John M. Court, "Right and Left: The Implications for Matthew 25.31-46," *NTS* 31/2 (1985): 223-33.

1382   Werner Fuchs, "Meditacao sobre Mateus 25:31-46," *EstT* 27/2 (1987): 81-186.

1383   Dan O. Via, "Ethical Responsibility and Human Wholeness in Matthew 25:31-46," *HTR* 80/1 (1987): 79-100.

1384   J. J. Lapoorta, "Exegesis and Proclamation: 'Whatever You Did for One of the Least of These . . . You Did for Me' (Matt. 25:31-46)," *JTSA* 68 (1989): 103-109.

1385   E. Farahian, "Relire Matthieu 25,31-46," *Greg* 72 (1991): 437-57.

1386   Manfred Hutter, "Mt. 25:31-46 in der Deutung Manis," *NovT* 33 (1991) 276-82.

1387   J. Sayer, " 'Ich hatte Durst, und ihr gabt mir zu trinken'. Zum Ansatz einer Theologie der menschlichen Grundbedürfnisse nach Mt. 25,31ff. im Rahmen der Pastoral der Befreiung," *MTZ* 42 (1991): 151-67.

1388   Klaus Wengst, "Wie aus Böcken Ziegen wurden (Mt 25,32f): Zur Entstehung und Verbreitung einer Forschungslegende oder: Wissenschaft als 'stille Post'," *EvT* 54 (1994): 491-500.

25:31-33

1389   Wilfred Tooley, "The Shepherd and Sheep Image in the Teaching of Jesus," *NovT* 7/1 (1964): 15-25.

25:31

1390   James H. Smylie, "Uncle Tom's Cabin Revisited: The Bible, the Romantic Imagination and the Sympathies of Christ," *Int* 27/1 (1973): 67-85.

25:32-33

1391   J. D. M. Derrett, "Unfair to Goats (Mt 25:32-33)," *ET* 108
        (1997): 177-78.

25:32

1392   François Martin, "The Image of Shepherd in the Gospel of
        St. Matthew," *ScE* 27 (1975): 261-301.

25:35

1393   Joseph A. Grassi, " 'I Was Hungry and You Gave Me
        Something to Eat'," *BTB* 11/3 (1981): 81-84.

25:37-26:3

1394   W. D. McHardy, "Matthew 25:37-26:3 in 074," *JTS* 46
        (1945): 190-91.

25:40

1395   G. Gross, "Die 'geringsten Brüder' Jesu in Mt. 25:40 in
        Auseinandersetzung mit der neueren Exegese," *BibL* 5
        (1964): 172-80.

1396   Michael Wilson, "Violence and Nonviolence in the Cure
        of Disease and the Healing of Patients," *CC* 87 (1970):
        756-58.

25:41-46

1397   P. H. Bligh, "Eternal Fire, Eternal Punishment, Eternal
        Life (Mt. 25,41.46)," *ET* 83 (1971-72): 9-11.

25:46

1398   Simone Frutiger, "Les lectures d'Evangile ou les textes
        disjoints: Matthieu 16:13 à 25:46," *FV* 82 (1983): 59-75.

26-28

1399   K. G. Kuhn, "Jesus in Gethsemane," *EvT* 12 (1952-1953):
        260-85.

1400   S. J. Rieckert, "The Narrative Coherence in Matthew
        26-28," *Neo* 16 (1982): 53-74.

26-27

1401   Nils A. Dahl, "Die Passionsgeschichte bei Matthäus," *NTS*
        2 (1955): 17-32.

26:1-27:61

1402   Donald P. Senior, "The Gospel of Matthew and the
        Passion of Jesus: Theological and Pastoral Perspectives,"
        WW 18 (1998): 372-79.

26:1

1403   David Hellholm, "En textgrammatisk konstruktion I
        Matteus-evangeliet," *SEÅ* 51 (1986-1987): 80-89.

26:3

1404   Robert F. Shedinger, "The Textual Relationship Between
        P45 and Shem-Tob's Hebrew Matthew," *NTS* 43 (1997):
        58-71.

26:6-13

1405   Ronald F. Thiemann, "The Unnamed Woman at Bethany,"
        TT 44/2 (1987): 179-88.

1406   James F. Coakley, "The Anointing at Bethany and the
        Priority of John," *JBL* 107/2 (1988): 241-56.

1407   Guy Wagner, "L'oncion de Béthanie: Essai sur la genèse
        du récit de Marc 14/3-9 et sa reprise par Matthieu, Luc et
        Jean," *ÉTR* 72 (1997): 437-46.

26:13

1408   A. Strobel, "Zum Verständnis von Mat. 26:13," *NTS* 2
        (1957-1958): 199-227.

1409   J. H. Greenlee, "For Her Memorial: Mt. 26:13, Mk. 14:9,"
        ET 71 (1959-1960): 245.

26:15

1410   P. Colella, "Trenta denari," *RBib* 21 (1973): 325-27.

26:23

1411   Robert F. Shedinger, "The Textual Relationship Between
        P45 and Shem-Tob's Hebrew Matthew," *NTS* 43 (1997):
        58-71.

26:26-28

1412   D. B. Carmichael, "David Daube on the Eucharist and the
        Passover Seder," *JSNT* 42 (1991): 45-67.

26:27

1413 Phillip Sigal, "Another Note to 1 Corinthians 10.16," *NTS* 29/1 (1983): 134-39.

26:28

1414 J. M. R. Tillard, "L'Eucharistie, Purification de l'Église Pérégrinante," *NRT* 84 (1962): 449-74, 579-97.

1415 Lynne C. Boughton, " 'Being Shed for You/Many': Time-Sense and Consequences in the Synoptic Cup Citations," *TynB* 48 (1997): 249-70.

26:29-31

1416 E. Bammel, "P^{64} (^{67}) and the Last Supper." *JTS* 24/1 (1973): 189.

26:31

1417 François Martin, "The Image of Shepherd in the Gospel of St. Matthew," *ScE* 27 (1975): 261-301.

26:32

1418 J. Vara, "Dos conjeturas textuales sobre Mateo 25,21.23 y Mateo 26,32/17,22 y par.," *Salm* 33 (1986): 81-86.

1419 Domingo Muñoz León, " 'Iré delante de vosotros a Galilea' (Mt. 26,32 y par.). Sentido mesiánico y posible sustrato arameo del logion," *EB* 48 (1990): 215-41.

26:34

1420 G. Zuntz, "A Note on Matthew 26:34 and 26:75," *JTS* 50 (1949): 182-83.

1421 Herbert Dennett, "The Need for a Neutral Idiom," *BT* 17 (1966): 39-41.

26:36-28:20

1422 T. Kayalaparampil, "Passion and Resurrection in the Gospel of Matthew," *BB* 16 (1990): 41-51.

26:36-46

1423 Anna M. Aagaard, "Doing God's Will: Matthew 26:36-46," *IRM* 77 (1988): 221-28.

1424 Marlis Gielen, " 'Und führe uns nicht in Versuchung' Die 6. Vater-Unser Bitte—eine Anfechtung für das biblische Gottesbild?" *ZNW* 89 (1998): 201-16.

1425   Kevin Madigan, "Ancient and High-Medieval Interpretations of Jesus in Gethsemane: Some Reflections on Tradition and Continuity in Christian Thought," *HTR* 88 (1995): 157-73.

26:47-27:56

1426   Dale C. Allison, "Anticipating the Passion: The Literary Reach of Matthew 26:47-27:56," *CBQ* 56 (1994): 701-14.

26:50

1427   J. P. Wilson, "Matthew 26,50," *ET* 41 (1929-1930): 334.

1428   F. Rehkopf, "Mt. 26:50: Ἑταῖρε, ἐφ᾽ ὃ πάρει," *ZNW* 52 (1961): 109-15.

1429   G. M. Lee, "Matthew 26:50," *ET* 81 (1969-1970): 55.

1430   James L. Boyer, "Relative Clauses in the Greek New Testament: A Statistical Study," *GTJ* 9/2 (1988): 233-56.

26:52

1431   H. Kosmala, "Matthew 26:52. A Quotation from the Targum ," *NovT* 4 (1960-61): 3-5.

26:56-28:2

1432   Philip Burton, "Fragmentum Vindobonense 563: Another Latin- Gothic Bilingual?" *JTS* NS 47 (1996): 141-56.

26:56

1433   James W. Scott, "Matthew's Intention to Write History," *WTJ* 47/1 (1985): 68-82.

26:57-27:2

1434   Birger Gerhardsson, "Confession and Denial before Men: Observation on Matt. 26:57-27:2," *JSNT* 13 (1981): 46-66.

26:63

1435   R. L. Mowery, "Subtle Differences: The Matthean 'Son of God' References," *NovT* 32 (1990): 193-200.

1436   Colin Brown, "The Hermeneutics of Confession and Accusation," *CTJ* 30 (1995): 460-71.

1437   J. D. M. Derrett, " 'I Adjure Thee' (Matthew 26,63)," *DR* 115 (1997): 225-34.

26:64

1438   F. Segarra, "Algunas observaciones sobre los principales textos escatológicos de Nuestro Señor: S. Mateo, XXVI,64," *EE* 15 (1936): 47-66.

1439   David R. Catchpole, "The Answer of Jesus to Caiaphas (Matthew 26:64)," *NTS* 17/2 (1971): 213-26.

1440   Renatus Kempthorne, "The Marcan Text of Jesus' Answer to the High Priest (Mark 14:62)," *NovT* 19/3 (1977): 197-208.

26:68

1441   Frans Neirynck, "Tis estin o paisas se." *ETL* 63/1 (1987): 5-47.

26:69-75

1442   N. J. McEleney, "Peter's Denials—How Many? To Whom?" *CBQ* 52 (1990): 467-72.

26:69-72

1443   Dietfried Gewalt, "Die Verleugnung des Petrus," *LB* 43 (1978): 113-44.

26:75

1444   G. Zuntz, "A Note on Matthew 26:34 and 26:75," *JTS* 50 (1949): 182-83.

27:1-26

1445   J. Escande, "Judas et Pilate prisonniers d'une même Structure (Mt. 27,1-26)," *FV* 18 (1979): 92-100.

27:2-66

1446   G. M. Lee, "The Guard at the Tomb," *Theology* 72 (1969): 169-75.

27:3-10

1447   Donald P. Senior, "A Case Study in Matthean Creativity: Matthew 27:3-10," *BR* 19 (1974): 23-36.

1448   L. Desautels, "La mort de Judas (Mt. 27,3-10; Ac 1,15-26)," *ScE* 38 (1986): 221-39.

27:8

1449   J. D. M. Derrett, "Akeldama (Acts 1:19)," *Bij* 56 (1995): 122-32.

27:9-10

1450   M. Quesnel, "Les citations de Jérémie dans l'évangile selon saint Matthieu," *EB* 47 (1989): 513-27.

27:9

1451   E. F. Sutcliffe, "Matthew 27,9," *JTS* 3 (1952): 227-28.

1452   M. J. J. Menken, "The References of Jeremiah in the Gospel According to Matthew (Mt. 2,17; 16,14; 27,9)," *ETL* 60/1 (1984): 5-24.

1453   James W. Scott, "Matthew's Intention to Write History," *WTJ* 47/1 (1985): 68-82.

27:19

1454   A. Oepke, "Noch einmal das Weib des Pilatus," *TLZ* 73 (1948): 743-46.

1455   J. D. M. Derrett, "Haggadah and the Account of the Passion," *DR* 97 (1979): 308-15.

1456   F. M. Gillman, "The Wife of Pilate (Matthew 27:19)," *LouvS* 17 (1992): 152-65.

1457   Roland Kany, "Die Frau des Pilatus und ihr Name: Ein Kapitel aus der Geschichte neutestamentlicher Wissenschaft," *ZNW* 86 (1995): 104-10.

27:24-25

1458   Frank J. Matera, "His Blood Be on Us and Our Children," *BibTo* 27 (1989): 345-50.

1459   T. B. Cargal, " 'His Blood Be Upon Us and Upon Our Children': A Matthean Double Entendre?" *NTS* 37/1 (1991): 102-12.

27:24

1460   Marc Philonenko, "Le sang du Juste (I Hénoch 47:1-4; Matthieu 27:24)" *RHPR* 73 (1993): 395-99.

27:25

1461   Robert H. Smith, "Matthew 27:25: The Hardest Verse in Matthew's Gospel," *CThM* 17 (1990): 421-28.

27:27

1462   Wallace M. Alston, "Christ and the Military Mind," *Int* 30/1 (1976): 26-35.

27:35

1463 Joseph A. Fitzmyer, "Crucifixion in Ancient Palestine, Qumran Literature, and the New Testament," *CBQ* 40/4 (1978): 493-513.

27:37-44

1464 Terence L. Donaldson, "The Mockers and the Son of God (Matthew 27:37-44): Two Characters in Matthew's Story of Jesus," *JSNT* 41 (1991): 3-18.

27:37

1465 Brian K. Blount, "A Socio-Rhetorical Analysis of Simon of Cyrene: Mark 15:21 and Its Parallels," *Semeia* 64 (1994): 171-98.

27:44-54

1466 Hartmut Gese, "Psalm 22 und das Neue Testament," *ZTK* 65/1 (1968): 1-22.

27:45-53

1467 A. G. Van Aarde, "Matthew 27:45-53 and the Turning of the Tide in Israel's History," *BTB* 28 (1998): 16-26.

1468 F. Smith, "The Strangest 'Word' of Jesus," *ET* 44 (1932-1933): 259-61.

1469 D. H. C. Read, "The Cry of Dereliction," *ET* 68 (1956-1957): 260-62.

1470 S. Lewis Johnson, "The Death of Christ," *BSac* 125 (1968): 10-19.

1471 Scott C. Layton, "Leaves from an Onomastician's Notebook," *ZAW* 108 (1996): 608-20.

1472 Paul S. Minear, "The Messiah Forsaken . . . Why?" *HBT* 17 (1995): 62-83.

1473 Louis Painchaud, "Le Christ vainqueur de la mort dans l'Evangile selon Philippe, une exégèse valentinienne de Matt 27:46," *NovT* 38 (1996): 382-92.

27:49

1474 Stephen Pennells, "The Spear Thrust," *JSNT* 19 (1983): 99-115.

27:50

1475   A. LaCocque, "Le grand cri de Jesus dans Matthieu 27:50," *ÉTR* 75 (2000): 161-87.

27:51-54

1476   W. G. Essame, "Matthew 27:51-54 and John 5:25-29," *ET* 76 (1964-1965): 103.

1477   Frank J. Matera, "Matthew 27:51-54," *Int* 38 (1984): 55-59.

1478   Ronald D. Witherup, "The Death of Jesus and the Raising of the Saints: Matthew 27:51-54," *SBLSP* (1987): 574-85.

1479   G. J. Swart, "Twee aardbewings of een? Die assosiasie van literêre motiewe in die eksegese van Matteus 27:51-54 & 28:2-4," *HTS* 49 (1993): 255-65.

27:51-53

1480   Josef Blinzler, "Zur Erklärung von Mt. 27,51b-53," *TGl* 34 (1943): 91-93.

1481   Paul K. Jewett, "Can We Learn from Mariology?" *CC* 84/32 (1967): 1019-21.

1482   Donald P. Senior, "The Death of Jesus and the Resurrection of the Holy Ones (Mt. 27:51-53)," *CBQ* 38 (1976): 312-29.

1483   Rafael Aguirre, "El Reino de Dios y la muerte de Jesús en el evangelio de Mateo," *EE* 54 (1979): 363-82.

1484   Rafael Aguirre, "Cross and Kingdom in Matthew's Theology," *TD* 29/2 (1981): 149-52.

1485   John W. Wenham, "When Were the Saints Raised?" *JTS* 32/1 (1981): 150-52.

1486   David Hill, "Matthew 27:51-53 in the Theology of the Evangelist," *IBS* 7 (1985): 76-87.

1487   S. P. Botha, "'n Opstanding met verheerlikte liggame in Matteus 27:51b-53? 'n Noukeurige lees van die teks," *HTS* 52 (1996): 270-84.

1488   Donald P. Senior, "Revisiting Matthew's Special Material in the Passion Narrative," *ETL* 70 (1994): 417-24.

27:51

1489   Marinus de Jonge, "Matthew 27:51 in Early Christian Exegesis," *HTR* 79/1 (1986): 67-79.

27:55

1490   Günther Schwarz, "ἀπὸ μακρόθεν/ἐπὶ τῆς ὁδοῦ," *BibN* 20 (1983): 56-57.

27:56

1491   Emily R. Cheney, "The Mother of the Sons of Zebedee," *JSNT* 68 (1997): 13-21.

27:57-28:20

1492   P. H. Lai, "Production du sens par la foi. Autorités religieuses contestées/fondées. Analyse structurale de Matthieu 27,57-28,20," *RechSR* 61 (1973): 65-96.

1493   L. Pham, "Sinn-Erzeugung durch den Glauben-Widerlegte: Begründete Religiöse Authoritäten: Strukturale Analyse von Matth 27,57-28,20," *LB* 32 (1974): 1-37.

1494   Charles H. Giblin, "Structural and Thematic Correlation in the Matthaean Burial-Resurrection Narrative (Matt. 27:57-28:20)," *NTS* 21 (1974-1975): 406-20.

27:57-28:15

1495   C. Turiot, "Sémiotique et lisibilité du texte évangélique," *RechSR* 73 (1985): 161-75.

27:57-60

1496   W. Boyd Barrick, "The Rich Man from Arimathea (Matt. 27:57-60) and 1QIsa," *JBL* 96/2 (1977): 235-39.

27:59

1497   D. Moody Smith, "Mark 15:46: The Shroud of Turin as a Problem of History and Faith," *BA* 46/4 (1983): 251-54.

1498   Jacques Winandy, "Les vestiges laissés dans le tombeau et la foi du disciple (Jn 20,1-9)," *NRT* 110/2 (1988) 212-19.

27:61

1499   Emily R. Cheney, "The Mother of the Sons of Zebedee," *JSNT* 68 (1997): 13-21.

27:62-66

1500   Nikolaus Walter, "Eine vormatthäische Schilderung der Auferstehung Jesu," *NTS* 19/4 (1973): 415-29.

28:1-18

1501   Edgar V. McKnight and Charles H. Talbert, "Can the Griesbach Hypothesis Be Falsified?" *JBL* 91/3 (1972): 338-68.

28:1-10

1502   Paul S. Minear, "Matthew 28:1-10," *Int* 38/1 (1984): 59-63.

1503   Cynthia A. Jarvis, "Matthew 28:1-10," *Int* 42 (1988): 63-68.

1504   Dorothy J. Weaver, "Matthew 28:1-10," *Int* 46 (1992): 399-402.

28:1-8

1505   Nikolaus Walter, "Eine vormatthäische Schilderung der Auferstehung Jesu," *NTS* 19/4 (1973): 415-29.

28:1-3

1506   C. A. Webster, "St. Matthew 28,1.3," *ET* 42 (1930-1931): 381-82.

28:1

1507   G. R. Driver, "Two Problems in the New Testament," *JTS* 16 (1965): 327-37.

1508   Warren Carter, " 'To see the tomb': Matthew's Women at the Tomb," *ET* 107 (1996): 201-205.

1509   Emily R. Cheney, "The Mother of the Sons of Zebedee," *JSNT* 68 (1997): 13-21.

1510   Michael Winger, "When Did the Women Visit the Tomb?" *NTS* 40 (1994): 284-88.

28:2-4

1511   Nikolaus Walter, "Eine Vormatthaische Schilderung derr Aufer-stehung Jesus," *NTS* 19/4 (1973): 415-29.

1512   G. J. Swart, "Twee aardbewings of een? Die assosiasie van literêre motiewe in die eksegese van Matteus 27:51-54 & 28:2-4," *HTS* 49 (1993): 255-65.

28:2

1513 A. Krücke, "Der Engel am Grabe Christi," *ZNW* 33 (1934): 313-17.

28:4

1514 G. M. Lee, "The Guard at the Tomb," *Theology* 72 (1969): 169-75.

28:7

1515 A. G. Van Aarde, "'Ηγέρθη ἀπὸ τῶν νεκρῶν (Mt. 28:7): A Textual Evidence on the Separation of Judaism and Christianity," *Neo* 23 (1989): 219-33.

28:9-10

1516 Frans Neirynck, "John and the Synoptics: The Empty Tomb Stories," *NTS* 30/2 (1984): 161-87.

1517 Frans Neirynck, "Note on Mt 28,9-10," *ETL* 71 (1995): 161-65.

28:11-15

1518 G. M. Lee, "The Guard at the Tomb," *Theology* 72 (1969): 169-75.

1519 Nikolaus Walter, "Eine vormatthäische Schilderung der Auferstehung Jesu," *NTS* 19/4 (1973): 415-29.

28:16-20

1520 H. M. Parker, "The Great Commission," *Int* 2 (1948): 74-75.

1521 Robert D. Culver, "What Is the Church's Commission? Some Exegetical Issues in Matthew 28:16-20," *JETS* 10/2 (1967): 115-26.

1522 Ulrich Luck, "Herrenwort und Geschichte in Matth. 28,16-20," *EvT* 27 (1967): 494-508.

1523 Bruce J. Malina, "The Literary Structure and Form of Matt. 28:16-20," *NTS* 17 (1970-1971): 87-103.

1524 J. Zumstein, "Matthieu 28:16-20," *RTP* 22 (1972): 14-33.

1525 Jack D. Kingsbury, "The Composition and Christology of Matthew 28:16-20," *JBL* 93/4 (1974): 573-84.

1526   James Tanis, "Reformed Pietism and Protestant Missions,"
        HTR 67/1 (1974): 65-73.

1527   Charles H. Giblin, "A Note on Doubt and Reassurance in
        Mt. 28:16-20," *CBQ* 37 (1975): 68-75.

1528   Grant R. Osborne, "Redaction Criticism and the Great
        Commission: A Case Study Toward a Biblical
        Understanding of Inerrancy," *JETS* 19/2 (1976): 73-85.

1529   Luis M. Bermejo, "The Alleged Infallibility of Councils,"
        Bij 38/2 (1977): 128-62.

1530   John P. Meier, "Two Disputed Questions in Matt.
        28:16-20," *JBL* 96/3 (1977): 407-24.

1531   L. G. Parkhurst, "Matthew 28:16-20 Reconsidered," *ET* 90
        (1979): 179-80.

1532   Jacques Matthey, "The Great Commission According to
        Matthew," *IRM* 69 (1980): 161-73.

1533   Oscar S. Brooks, "Matthew 28:16-20 and the Design of the
        First Gospel," *JSNT* 10 (1981): 2-18.

1534   Benedict T. Viviano, "Matthew, Master of Ecumenical
        Infighting," *CThM* 10/6 (1983): 325-32.

1535   C. Manus, " 'King-Christology': The Result of a Critical
        Study of Matt. 28:16-20 as an Example of Contextual
        Exegesis in Africa," *ScrSA* 39 (1991): 25-42.

1536   David P. Scaer, "The Relation of Matthew 28:16-20 to the
        Rest of the Gospel," *CTQ* 55 (1991): 245-66.

1537   Cynthia M. Campbell, "Matthew 28:16-20," *Int* 46 (1992):
        402-405.

1538   W. D. Davies and Dale C. Allison, "Matt. 28:16-20: Texts
        Behind the Text," *RHPR* 72 (1992): 89-98.

1539   Cilliers Breytenbach, "Meditation zu Matthäus 28,16-20,"
        ZMiss 19 (1993): 2-5.

1540   Olaf H. Schumann, "Ein Missionsbefehl?" *ZMiss* 20
        (1994): 130-32.

1541   George M. Soares-Prabhu, "Two Mission Commands: An
        Interpretation of Matthew 28:16-20 in the Light of a
        Buddhist Text," *BibInt* 2 (1994): 264-82.

1542 Peter Stuhlmacher, "Zur missionsgeschichtlichen Bedeutung von Mt 28,16-20," *EvT* 59 (1999): 108-30.

28:17

1543 J. Kwik, "Some Doubted," *ET* 77 (1965-1966): 181.

1544 I. P. Ellis, "But Some Doubted," *NTS* 14 (1967-1968): 574-80.

1545 E. Margaret Howe, " 'But Some Doubted' (Matt. 28:17). A Re-Appraisal of Factors Influencing the Easter Faith of the Early Christian Community," *JETS* 18/3 (1975): 173-80.

1546 Kenneth Grayston, "The Translation of Matthew 28:17," *JSNT* 21 (1984): 105-109.

1547 K. L. McKay, "The Use of *Hoi De* in Matthew 28.17," *JSNT* 24 (1985): 71-72.

1548 P. W. van der Horst, "Once More: The Translation of *Hoi De* in Matthew 28.17," *JSNT* 27 (1986): 27-30.

28:18-20

1549 J. Czerski, "Christozentrische Ekklesiologie im Matthäusevangelium," *BibL* 12 (1971): 55-66.

1550 Everett F. Harrison, "Did Christ Command World Evangelism?" *CT* 18/4 (1973): 210-14.

1551 Peter T. O'Brien, "The Great Commission of Matthew 28:18-20," *RTR* 35/3 (1976): 66-78.

1552 Schuyler Brown, "The Matthean Community and the Gentile Mission," *NovT* 22/3 (1980): 193-221.

1553 Gerhard Friedrich, "Die Formale Struktur von Mt. 28,18-20," *ZTK* 80/2 (1983): 137-83.

1554 Axel von Dobbeler, "Die Restitution Israels und die Bekehning der Heiden. Das Verhältnis von Mt 10.5b.6 und Mt 28.18-20 unter dem Aspekt der Komplementarität. Erwägungen zum Standort des Matthäusevangeliums," *ZNW* 91 (2000): 18-44.

28:18-19

1555 Dale Cowling, "Being the Church Today," *SouJT* 17/2 (1975): 65-72.

28:18

1556   Kair A. Syreeni, "Between Heaven and Earth: On the Structure of Matthew's Symbolic Universe," *JSNT* 40 (1990): 9-13.

28:19-20

1557   E. Luther Copeland, "The Great Commission and Missions," *SouJT* 9/2 (1967): 79-89.

1558   Robert D. Culver, "What Is the Church's Commission?" *BSac* 125 (1968): 239-53.

1559   Luther L. Grubb, "The Church Reaching Tomorrow's World," *GTJ* 12/3 (1971): 13-22.

1560   J. M. Ras, "Matteus 28:19-20: Enkele tekskritiese en eksegetiese opmerkings aan die hand van Nestle- Aland se 27e uitgawe van die Griekse Nuwe Testament," *HTS* 54 (1998): 810-31.

28:19

1561   D. R. A. Hare and D. J. Harrington, "Make Disciples of All the Gentiles (Matthew 28:19)," *CBQ* 37 (1975): 359-69.

1562   John P. Meier, "Nations or Gentiles in Matthew 28:19," *CBQ* 39/1 (1977): 94-102.

1563   Luise Abramowski, "Die Entstehung der Dreigliedrigen Taufformel- ein Versuch-mit einem Exkurs: Jesus der Naziräer," *ZTK* 81/4 (1984): 417-46.

1564   David R. Plaster, "Baptism by Triune Immersion," *GTJ* 6/2 (1985): 383-90.

1565   S. H. Kio, "Understanding and Translating 'Nations' in Mt. 28:19," *BT* 41 (1990): 230-38.

1566   T. C. de Kruijf, "Go therefore and Make Disciples of All Nations," *Bij* 54 (1993): 19-29.

1567   David P. Kuske, "Exegetical Brief: The Meaning of matheteusate in Matthew 28:19," *WLQ* 94 (1997): 115-21.

28:20

1568   Robert H. Smith, "The End in Matthew (5:48 and 28:20): How to Preach It and How Not To," *WW* 19 (1999): 303-13.

Mark

1:1-8:26

1569   Frans Neirynck, "Mark and His Commentators: Mark 1,1-8,26," *ETL* 65 (1989): 381-89.

1:1-3:36

1570   Eduard Schweizer, "Die theologische Leistung des Markus," *EvT* 24 (1964): 337-55.

1:1-15

1571   O. J. F. Seitz, "Praeparatio Evangelica in the Markan Prologue," *JBL* 82 (1963): 201-206.

1572   Leander E. Keck, "The Introduction to Mark's Gospel," *NTS* 12 (1965-1966): 352-70.

1573   Hugolinus Langkammer, "Tradycja i redakcja w prologu Ewangelii Marka (1,1-15)," *RoczTK* 20 (1973): 37-57.

1574   Gerhard Dautzenberg, "Die Zeit des Evangeliums. Mk 1,1-15 und die Konzeption des Markusevangeliums," *BZ* 21 (1977): 219-34.

1575   Gerhard Dautzenberg, "Die Zeit des Evangeliums. Mk 1,1-15 und die Konzeption des Markusevangeliums [Pt. 2]," *BZ* 22/1 (1978): 76-91.

1576   Robert A. Guelich, "The Beginning of the Gospel," *BR* 27 (1982): 5-15.

1577   M. Eugene Boring, "Mark 1:1-15 and the Beginning of the Gospel," *Semeia* 52 (1990): 43-81.

1578   Klauspeter Blaser, "Der Stärkere: biblische Besinnung zu Mk 1:1-15 par," *ZMiss* 17/1 (1991): 3-7.

1579   Jan Lambrecht, "John the Baptist and Jesus in Mark 1:1-15: Markan Redaction of Q?" *NTS* 38 (1992): 357-84.

1580   Paul J. Sankey, "Promise and Fulfilment: Reader-Response to Mark 1:1-15," *JSNT* 58 (1995): 3-18.

<u>1:1-13</u>

1581   Richard T. France, "The Beginning of Mark," *RTR* 49 (1990): 11-19.

<u>1:1-8</u>

1582   Harald Sahlin, "Zwei Fälle von harmonisicrendem Einfluss des Matthäusevangeliums auf das Markus-Evangelium," *StTheol* 13 (1959): 166-79.

1583   Paul Ternant, "Le ministère de Jean, commencement de l'Evangile, Mc 1,1-8," *AsSeign* 6 (1969): 41-53.

<u>1:1-6</u>

1584   Ernest C. Colwell, "The Significance of Grouping New Testament Manuscripts," *NTS* 4 (1957-1958): 73-92.

1585   Ismo Dunderberg, "Q and the Beginning of Mark," *NTS* 41 (1995): 501-11.

<u>1:1-4</u>

1586   Jean Delorme, "Evangile et Récit (1996): La narration evangélique en Marc," *NTS* 43 (1997): 367-84.

<u>1:1</u>

1587   J. A. Emerton, "Some New Testament Notes," *JTS* 11 (1960): 329-36.

1588   Paul Lamarche, " 'Commencement de l'Evangile de Jesus, Christ, Fils de Dieu' (Mc I,1)," *NRT* 92/10 (1970): 1024-36.

1589   Mario Galizzi, "Vangelo di Gesu Cristo, figlio di Dio (Mc 1,1)," *PV* 18 (1973): 51-70.

1590   Gerhard Arnold, "Mk 1:1 und Eröffnungswendungen in griechischen und lateinischen Schriften," *ZNW* 68 (1977): 123-27.

1591   J. Slomp, "Are the Words 'Son of God' in Mark 1.1 Original?" *BT* 28 (1977): 143-50.

1592   André Feuillet, "Le 'Commencement' de l'économie chrétienne d'après He ii.3-4; Mc i.1 et Ac i.1-2," *NTS* 24 (1977-1978): 163-74.

1593   Mario Galizzi, "Inizio del Vangelo di Gesù il Cristo, il Figlio di Dio," *PV* 26 (1981): 404-18.

1594   Alexander Globe, "The Caesarean Omission of the Phrase 'Son of God' in Mark 1:1," *HTR* 75 (1982): 209-18.

1595   Detlev Dormeyer, "Die Kompositionsmetapher 'Evangelium Jesu Christi, des Sohnes Gottes' Mk 1:1: ihre theologische und literarische Aufgabe in Markus," *NTS* 33/3 (1987): 452-68.

1596   Eugene A. LaVerdiere, "Looking Ahead to the Year of Mark," *Emmanuel* 93 (1987): 494-501.

1597   Donald H. Juel and Patrick R. Keifert, "A Markan Epiphany: Lessons from Mark 1," *WW* 8 (1988): 80-85.

1598   Peter M. Head, "A Text-Critical Study of Mark 1:1: 'The Beginning of the Gospel of Jesus Christ'," *NTS* 37 (1991): 621-29.

1599   William F. McInerny, "An Unresolved Question in the Gospel Called Mark: 'Who Is This Whom Even Wind and Sea Obey'?" *PRS* 23 (1996): 255-68.

1600   Tae H. Kim, "The Anarthrous *yios theou* in Mark 15,39 and the Roman Imperial Cult," *Bib* 79 (1998): 221-41.

1:2-13

1601   Eugene A. LaVerdiere, "Mark's Gospel in Miniature," *Emmanuel* 93 (1987): 546-53.

1602   Frank J. Matera, "The Prologue as the Interpretative Key to Mark's Gospel," *JSNT* 34 (1988): 3-20.

1603   R. P. Merendino, "Testi anticotestamentari in Mc 1,2-8," *RBib* 35 (1987): 3-25.

1604   Eugene A. LaVerdiere, "In the Following of Christ. The Eucharist in the Gospel According to Mark—II. Locusts, Wild Honey, and the Bread of Angels," *Emmanuel* 106 (2000): 68-76.

1:2-6

1605   M.-É. Boismard, "Évangile des Ébionites et problème synoptique (Mc. I,2-6 et par.)," *RB* 73 (1966): 321-52.

1606   Frans Neirynck, "Une nouvelle théorie synoptique (À propos de Mc. I,2-6 et par.). Notes critiques," *ETL* 44 (1968): 141-53.

1:2-3

1607   Klyne R. Snodgrass, "Streams of Tradition Emerging from Isaiah 40:1-5 and Their Adaptation in the New Testament," *JSNT* 8 (1980): 24-45.

1608   L. Schenke, "Gibt es im Markusevangelium eine Präexistenzchristologie?" *ZNW* 91 (2000): 45-71.

1:2

1609   C. T. Ruddick, "Behold, I Send My Messenger," *JBL* 88 (1969): 381-417.

1610   Michael D. Goulder, "On Putting Q to the Test," *NTS* 24 (1977-1978): 218-34.

1611   J. M. Ross, "The 'Harder Reading' in Textual Criticism," *BT* 33 (1982): 138-39.

1612   Christopher M. Tuckett, "On the Relationship between Matthew and Luke," *NTS* 30 (1984): 130-42.

1:3-4

1613   Alfonso Ortega, "Nueva vision de Marcos I,3-4," *Salm* 9 (1962): 599-607.

1:3

1614   C. Buzzetti, "Parallels in the Synoptic Gospels: A Case Study," *BT* 34 (1984): 425-431.

1:40-3:6

1615   Mario Galizzi, "Gesù ha scelto l'uomo (Mc 1,40-3,6)," *PV* 21 (1976): 31-37.

1:4-11

1616   Donald H. Juel and Patrick R. Keifert, "A Markan Epiphany: Lessons from Mark 1," *WW* 8 (1988): 80-85.

1617   Paul S. Berge, "The Beginning of the Good News: The Epiphany Gospels in Mark and John," *WW* 17 (1997): 94-101.

1:4-8

1618   Christian Wolff, "Zur Bedeutung Johannes des Täufers im Markusevangelium," *TLZ* 102 (1977): 857-65.

1:4-5

1619   R. Trevijano Etcheverría, "La tradiciáon sobre el Bautista en Mc. 1,4-5 y par.," *Bur* 12 (1971): 9-39.

1:4

1620   Herman Ljungvik, "Randanmärkningar till 1963 års bibelkommités översättningsförslag," *SEÅ* 34 (1969): 147-69.

1621   J. K. Elliott, "Ho baptizōn and Mark i.4," *TZ* 31 (1975): 14-15.

1622   Theodore Mueller, "An Application of Case Grammar to Two New Testament Passages," *CTQ* 43 (1979): 320-25.

1623   Paul Ellingworth, "Translating Parallel Passages in the Gospels," *BT* 34 (1983): 401-407.

1624   Johan C. Thom, "Markus 1:4 in die Nuwe Afrikaanse Vertaling," *HTS* 49 (1993): 934-41.

1:5

1625   John S. Kloppenborg, "City and Wasteland: Narrative World and the Beginning of the Sayings Gospel (Q)," *Semeia* 52 (1990): 145-60.

1:6-11

1626   Edmond Jacquemin, "Le baptême du Christ. Mt 3,13-17; Mc 1,6b-11; Lc 3,15s.21s," *AsSeign* 12 (1969): 48-66.

1:7-8

1627   François Martin, "Le baptême dans l'Esprit: Tradition du Nouveau Testament et vie de l'Église," *NRT* 106 (1984): 23-58.

1628   Balembo Buetubela, "Le message de Jean Baptiste en Mc 1,7-8," *RAfT* 9 (1985): 165-73.

1629   L. Schenke, "Gibt es im Markusevangelium eine Präexistenzchristologie?" *ZNW* 91 (2000): 45-71.

1:7

1630   W. R. Weeks, "Mark 1:7," *ET* 73 (1961-1962): 54.

1631   René Kieffer, "A Christology of Superiority in the Synoptic Gospels," *RSB* 3/2 (1983): 61-75.

1:8

1632   F. J. Botha, "'Εβάπτισα in Mark i.8," *ET* 64 (1952-1953): 286.

1633   J. E. Yates, "The Form of Mark 1:8b: 'I Baptized You with Water; He Will Baptize You with the Holy Spirit'," *NTS* 4 (1957-1958): 334-38.

1634   Norman K. Bakken, "Uma nova criaçao: o Cristo para o nosso tempo," *EstT* 24/2 (1984): 118-28.

1635   J. Daryl Charles, " 'The Coming One'/'Stronger One' and His Baptism: Matthew 3:11-12, Mark 1:8, Luke 3:16-17," *Pneuma* 11 (1989): 37-50.

1:9-15

1636   Ulrich Mell, "Jesu Taufe durch Johannes (Markus 1,9-15)--zur narrativen Christologie vom neuen Adam," *BZ* NS 40 (1996): 161-78.

1:9-13

1637   Eugene A. LaVerdiere, "The Baptism of the Lord," *Emmanuel* 94 (1988): 6-13, 21.

1638   Jeffrey B. Gibson, "Jesus' Wilderness Temptation according to Mark," *JSNT* 53 (1994): 3-34.

1:9-11

1639   Herbert Braun, "Entscheidende Motive in den Berichten über die Taufe Jesu von Markus bis Justin," *ZTK* 50 (1953): 39-43.

1640   C. E. B. Cranfield, "The Baptism of Our Lord: A Study of St. Mark 1:9-11," *SJT* 8 (1955): 53-63.

1641   André Feuillet, "Le Baptême de Jésus d'après l'Évangile selon Saint Marc (1,9-11)," *CBQ* 21 (1959): 468-90.

1642   Placide Roulin and Giles Carton, "Le Baptême du Christ," *BVC* 25 (1959): 39-48.

1643   S. Lewis Johnson, "The Baptism of Christ," *BSac* 123 (1966): 220-29.

1644   Dieter Zeller, "Jesu Taufe—ein literarischer Zugang zu Markus 1,9-11," *BK* 23 (1968): 90-94.

1645   Lars Hartman, "Dop, ande och barnaskap. Några traditionshistoriska överväganden till Mk 1:9-11 par," *SEÅ* 37/38 (1972): 88-106.

1646   Giuseppe Segalla, "La predicazione dell'amore nella tradizione presinottica," *RBib* 20 (1972): 481-528.

1647   Antonio Vargas-Machuca, "La narración del bautismo de Jesus (Mc 1,9-11) y la exégesis reciente. ¿Visión real o 'género didáctico'?" *CuBi* 30 (1973): 131-41.

1648   Georg Richter, "Zu den Tauferzählungen Mk 1:9-11 und Joh 1:32-34," *ZNW* 65 (1974): 43-56.

1649   A. Tosato, "Il battesimo di Gesu e alcuni passi trascurati dello Pseudo-Filone," *Bib* 56 (1975): 405-409.

1650   Stephen Gero, "The Spirit as a Dove at the Baptism of Jesus," *NovT* 18 (1976): 17-35.

1651   Paul Garnet, "The Baptism of Jesus and the Son of Man Idea," *JSNT* 9 (1980): 49-65.

1652   Gerhard Sellin, "Das Leben des Gottessohnes: Taufe und Verklärung Jesu als Bestandteile eines vormarkinischen 'Evangeliums'," *K* 25/3-4 (1983): 237-53.

1653   Sigfred Pedersen, "Die Gotteserfahrung bei Jesus," *StTheol* 41 (1987): 127-56.

1654   Ernst L. Schnellbächer, "Sachgemässe Schriftauslegung," *NovT* 30 (1988): 114-31.

1655   James R. Edwards, "The Baptism of Jesus According to the Gospel of Mark," *JETS* 34 (1991): 43-57.

1656   Donald H. Juel, "The Baptism of Jesus," *WW* Supplement 1 (1992): 119-26.

1657   L. Schenke, "Gibt es im Markusevangelium eine Präexistenzchristologie?" *ZNW* 91 (2000): 45-71.

1:9-10

1658   Helmut Gollwitzer, "Zur Frage der 'Sündlosigkeit Jesu," *EvT* 31 (1971): 496-506.

1:9

1659   Theodor Lorenzmeier, "Wider das Dogma von der Sündlosigkeit Jesu," *EvT* 31 (1971): 452-71.

1660   Jean-Marie van Cangh, "La Galilée dans l'évangile de Marc: un lieu théologique?" *RB* 79 (1972): 59-75.

1:10-11

1661   Jean Delorme, "Le discours de l'intertextualité dans le discours exégétique," *SémBib* 15 (1979): 56-62.

1:10

1662   Herman Ljungvik, "Randanmärkningar till 1963 års bibelkommités översättningsförslag," *SEÅ* 34 (1969): 147-69.

1663   Paul Ellingworth, "Translating Parallel Passages in the Gospels," *BT* 34 (1983): 401-407.

1664   C. Buzzetti, "Parallels in the Synoptic Gospels: A Case Study," *BT* 35 (1984): 425-31.

1665   Ernst M. Dörrfuss, "Wie eine Taube: Überlegungen zum Verständnis von Mk 1:10," *BibN* 57 (1991): 7-13.

1666   David Ulansey, "The Heavenly Veil Torn: Mark's Cosmic Inclusio" *JBL* 110 (1991):123-25.

1667   Günther Schwarz, " 'Wie eine Taube'?" *BibN* 89 (1997): 27-29.

1:11

1668   W. Dekker, "De 'geliefde Zoon' in de synoptische evangeliën," *NTT* 16 (1961-1962): 94-106.

1669   George D. Kilpatrick, "The Order of Some Noun and Adjective Phrases in the New Testament," *NovT* 5 (1962): 111-14.

1670   P. G. Bretscher, "Exodus 4:22-23 and the Voice from Heaven," *JBL* 87 (1968): 301-11.

1671   I. Howard Marshall, "Son of God or Servant of Yahweh? A Reconsideration of Mark 1:11," *NTS* 15 (1968-1969): 326-36.

1672   C. H. Dodd, "New Testament Translation Problems II," *BT* 28 (1977): 101-16.

1673   Alfredo Scattolon, "L'ἀγαπητός sinottico nella luce della tradizione giudaica," *RBib* 26 (1978): 3-32.

1674   Gerhard Schneider, "Christologische Aussagen des 'Credo' im Lichte des Neuen Testaments," *TTZ* 89 (1980): 282-92.

1675   Norman K. Bakken, "Uma nova criaçao: o Cristo para o nosso tempo," *EstT* 24/2 (1984): 118-28.

1:12-15

1676   F. Smyth-Florentin, "Jésus, le Fils du Père, vainqueur de Satan. Mt 4,1-11; Mc 1,12-15; Lc 4,1-13," *AsSeign* 14 (1973): 56-75.

1:12-13

1677   Peter Doble, "The Temptations," *ET* 72 (1960-1961): 91-93.

1678   Raymond E. Brown, "Incidents That Are Units in the Synoptic Gospels but Dispersed in St. John," *CBQ* 23 (1961): 143-60.

1679   André Feuillet, "L'épisode de la Tentation d'après l'Évangile selon Saint Marc (I,12-13)," *EB* 19 (1960): 49-73. See also *TD* 12 (1964): 79-82.

1680   Jacques Dupont, "L'origine du récit des tentations de Jésus au désert," *RB* 73 (1966): 30-76.

1681   J. González Faus, "Las tentaciones de Jesus y la tentacion cristiana," *EE* 47 (1972): 155-88.

1682   Antonio Vargas-Machuca, "La tentacion de Jesus segun Mc. 1,12-13, ¿Hecho real o relato de tipo haggadico?" *EE* 48 (1973): 163-90.

1683   Frans Neirynck, "Réponse à P. Rolland," *ETL* 60/4 (1984): 363-66.

1684   Philippe Rolland, "L'arrière-lond sémitique des évangiles synoptiques," *ETL* 60 (1984): 358-62.

1685   Curtis C. Mitchell, "The Practice of Fasting in the New Testament," *BSac* 147 (1990): 455-69.

1686   Marlis Gielen, " 'Und führe uns nicht in Versuchung' Die 6. Vater-Unser Bitte—eine Anfechtung für das biblische Gottesbild?" *ZNW* 89 (1998): 201-16.

1687   Jan W. van Henten, "The First Testing of Jesus: A Rereading of Mark 1.12-13," *NTS* 45 no 3 (1999): 349-66.

1688 L. Schenke, "Gibt es im Markusevangelium eine Präexistenzchristologie?" *ZNW* 91 (2000): 45-71.

1:12

1689 Otto Betz, "Early Christian Cult in the Light of Qumran," *RSB* 2 (1982): 73-85.

1690 Wilhelm Wilkens, "Die Versuchung Jesu nach Matthäus," *NTS* 28/4 (1982): 479-89.

1691 René Kieffer, "A Christology of Superiority in the Synoptic Gospels," *RSB* 3/2 (1983): 61-75.

1:13

1692 W. A. Schulze, "Der Heilige und die wilden Tiere. Zur Exegese von Mk 1,13b," *ZNW* 46 (1955): 280-83.

1:14-8:30

1693 Eugene A. LaVerdiere, "Jesus the Christ," *Emmanuel* 94 (1988): 74-81.

1:14-3:35

1694 B. M. F. van Iersel, "Concentric Structures in Mark 1:14-3:35 (4:1): With Some Observations on Method," *BibInt* 3 (1995): 75-98.

1:14-3:6

1695 Eugene A. LaVerdiere, "Jesus and the Call of the First Disciples," *Emmanuel* 94 (1988): 154-59, 173.

1:14-45

1696 Eugene A. LaVerdiere, "Jesus and the Call of the First Disciples: A New Teaching with Authority," *Emmanuel* 94 (1988): 190-97.

1:14-20

1697 Herman Ljungvik, "Randanmärkningar till 1963 års bibelkommités översättningsförslag," *SEÅ* 34 (1969): 147-69.

1698 Jean Brière, "Jésus agit par ses disciples. Mc 1,14-20," *AsSeign* 34 (1973): 32-46.

1699 John H. Reumann, "Mark 1:14-20," *Int* 32 (1978): 405-10.

1700 Vernon K. Robbins, "Mark 1:14-20: An Interpretation at the Intersection of Jewish and Graeco-Roman Traditions," *NTS* 28 (1982): 220-36.

1701 Paul S. Berge, "The Beginning of the Good News: The Epiphany Gospels in Mark and John," *WW* 17 (1997): 94-101.

1:14-15

1702 James L. Mays, "Jesus Came Preaching: A Study and Sermon on Mark 1:14-15," *Int* 26 (1972): 30-41.

1703 Karl-Georg Reploh, " 'Evangelium' bei Markus. Das Evangelium des Markus als Anruf an die Gemeinde zu Umkehr und Glaube (1,14-15)," *BK* 27 (1972): 110-14.

1704 J. J. A. Kahmann, "Marc 1,14-15 en hun plaats in het geheel van het Marcusevangelie," *Bij* 38 (1977): 84-98.

1705 John E. Alsup, "Mark 1:14-15," *Int* 33 (1979): 394-98.

1706 Klemens Stock, "La venuta del Regno," *ParSpirV* 8 (1983): 103-18.

1707 Augustine Stock, "Hinge Transitions in Mark's Gospel," *BTB* 15 (1985): 27-31.

1708 Rinaldo Fabris, "San Pietro apostolo nella prima chiesa," *SM* 35 (1986): 41-70.

1709 Andreas Lindemann, "Erwägungen zum Problem einer 'Theologie der synoptischen Evangelien'," *ZNW* 77/1-2 (1986): 1-33.

1710 Donald H. Juel and Patrick R. Keifert, "A Markan Epiphany: Lessons from Mark 1," *WW* 8 (1988): 80-85.

1711 Gustavo Gutiérrez, "Mark 1:14-15," *RevExp* 88 (1991): 427-31.

1:14

1712 Franz Mußner, "Die Bedeutung von Mk 1,14f. für die Reichgottesverkündigung," *TTZ* 66 (1957): 257-75.

1713 Jean-Marie van Cangh, "La Galilée dans l'évangile de Marc: un lieu théologique?" *RB* 79 (1972): 59-75.

1714 Matthew Vellanickal, "Faith and Conversion," *BB* 8 (1982): 29-41.

1:15

1715   Matthew Black, "The Kingdom of God Has Come," *ET* 63 (1951-1952): 289-90.

1716   Herbert Braun, "'Umkehr' in spatjüdisch-häretischer und in frühchristlicher Sicht," *ZTK* 50 (1953): 243-58.

1717   Robert F. Berkey, "ΕΓΓΙΖΕΙΝ, PHTHANEIN, and Realized Eschatology," *JBL* 82 (1963): 177-87.

1718   Lars Hartman, "Baptism 'Into the Name of Jesus' and Early Christology: Some Tentative Considerations," *StTheol* 28 (1974): 21-48.

1719   Norman K. Bakken, "Uma nova criaçao: o Cristo para o nosso tempo," *EstT* 24/2 (1984): 118-28.

1720   John M. McDermott, "Gegenwärtiges und kommendes Reich Gottes," *IKaZ* 15/2 (1986): 142-44.

1721   Paul S. Pudussery, " 'Repent and Believe in the Gospel'," *BB* 16 (1990): 95-113.

1722   Jean Delorme, "Evangile et Récit (1996): La narration évangélique en Marc," *NTS* 43 (1997): 367-84.

1:16-2:17

1723   Juan I. Alfaro, "Exegesis Pastoral, Mc 1:16-2:17: Un desafio para hoy," *RevB* 50/2-3 (1988): 171-82.

1:16-39

1724   Michael D. Goulder, "On Putting Q to the Test," *NTS* 24 (1977-1978): 218-34.

1725   Christopher M. Tuckett, "On the Relationship between Matthew and Luke," *NTS* 30 (1984): 130-42.

1:16-20

1726   Rudolf Schnackenburg, "Zur formgeschichtlichen Methode in der Evangelienforschung," *ZKT* 85 (1963): 16-32.

1727   Rudolf Pesch, "Berufung und Sendung, Nachfolge und Mission. Eine Studie zu Mk 1,16-20," *ZKT* 91 (1969): 1-31.

1728   A.-L. Descamps, "Aux origines du ministère: La pensée de Jesus," *RTL* 2 (1971): 3-45; 3 (1972): 121-59.

1729   James Donaldson, " 'Called to Follow': A Twofold Experience of Discipleship in Mark," *BTB* 5 (1975): 67-77.

1730   Luigi Di Pinto, "Seguitemi, vi farò diventare pescatori di uomini (Mc 1,16-20)," *ParSpirV* 2 (1980): 83-104.

1731   Francis J. Moloney, "The Vocation of the Disciples in the Gospel of Mark," *Sale* 43 (1981): 487-516.

1732   Samuel O. Abogunrin, "The Three Variant Accounts of Peter's Call: A Critical and Theological Examination of the Texts," *NTS* 31 (1985): 587-602.

1733   Claude Coulot, "Les figures du maître et de ses disciples dans les premières communautés chrétiennes," *RevSR* 59/1 (1985): 1-11.

1:16

1734   Sebastián Bartina, "La red esparavel del Evangelio (Mt 4.18; Mc 1,16)," *EB* 19 (1960): 215-27.

1735   J. D. M. Derrett, "ἦσαν γὰρ ἁλιεῖς (Mk. 1,16). Jesus' Fishermen and the Parable of the Net," *NovT* 22 (1980): 108-37.

1736   Paul Ellingworth, "Translating Parallel Passages in the Gospels," *BT* 34 (1983): 401-407.

1737   C. Buzzetti, "Parallels in the Synoptic Gospels: A Case Study," *BT* 35 (1984): 425-31.

1738   Lars Lode, "The Presentation of New Information," *BT* 35 (1984): 101-108.

1:17-18

1739   Helmut Gollwitzer, "Zur Frage der 'Sündlosigkeit Jesu'," *EvT* 31 (1971): 496-506.

1:17

1740   Jindrich Mánek, "Fishers of Men," *NovT* 2 (1957-1958): 138-41.

1:18

1741   Otto Betz, "Donnersöhne, Menschenfischer und der Davidische Messias," *RevQ* 3 (1961): 41-70.

1:20

1742   Günther Schwarz, "Καὶ εὐθὺς ἐκάλεσεν αὐτούς (Markus 1:20a)," *BibN* 48 (1989): 19-20.

1:21-3:19

1743   David L. Dungan, "Synopses of the Future," *Bib* 66/4 (1985): 457-92.

1:21-2:12

1744   David E. Garland, " 'I Am the Lord Your Healer': Mark 1:21-2:12," *RevExp* 85/2 (1988): 327-43.

1:21-45

1745   Dany Dideberg and Pierre M. Beernaert, " 'Jésus vint en Galilée.' Essai sur la structure de Marc 1,21-45," *NRT* 98 (1976): 306-23.

1:21-39

1746   Perry V. Kea, "Perceiving the Mystery: Encountering the Reticence of Mark's Gospel," *EGLMBS* 4 (1984): 181-94.

1:21-34

1747   Rudolf Pesch, "Ein Tag vollmächtigen Wirkens Jesu in Kapharnaum (Mk 1,21-34, 35-39)," *BibL* 9 (1968): 114-28, 177-95, 261-77.

1:21-28

1748   Jean Brière, "Le cri et le secret. Signification d'un exorcisme. Mc 1,21-28," *AsSeign* 35 (1973): 34-46.

1749   A. Viard, "Quatrième Dimanche (Mc 1,21-28)," *EV* 86 (1976): 8-10.

1750   Helge K. Nielsen, "Ein Beitrag zur Beurteilung der Tradition über die Heilungstätigkeit," *SNTU-A* 4 (1979): 5-26.

1751   Georges Casalis, "Jesús, el exorcista," *BibFe* 6 (1980): 28-40.

1752   Pierre Guillemette, "La Forme des Récits d'Exorcisme de Bultmann: Un Dogme a Reconsidérer," *ÉgT* 11/2 (1980): 177-93.

1753   Paul J. Achtemeier, "The Ministry of Jesus in the Synoptic Gospels," *Int* 35 (1981): 157-69.

1754   Alfred Suhl, "Überlegungen zur Hermeneutik an Hand von Mk 1:21-28," *K* 26/1-2 (1984): 28-38.

1755   Enzo Bianchi, "Esei da costui!" *ParSpirV* 19 (1989): 109-38.

1:21

1756   Robert H. Stein, "The 'Redaktionsgeschichtlich' Investigation of a Markan Seam (Mc 1:21f.)," *ZNW* 61 (1970): 70-94.

1:22

1757   H. J. Flowers, "Ὡς ἐξουσίαν ἔχων," *ET* 66 (1954-1955): 254.

1758   D. F. Hudson, "Ὡς ἐξουσίαν ἔχων," *ET* 67 (1955-1956): 17.

1759   A. W. Argyle, "The Meaning of ἐξουσία in Mark 1:22, 27," *ET* 80 (1969-1970): 343.

1760   William R. Domeris, "The Office of the Holy One," *JTSA* 54 (1986): 35-38.

1:23-28

1761   Léopold Sabourin, "The Miracles of Jesus (II). Jesus and the Evil Powers," *BTB* 4 (1974): 115-75.

1762   J. González Faus, "Jesus y los demonios: Intróducción cristológica a la lucha por la justicia," *EE* 52 (1977): 487-519.

1763   Peter Pimentel, "The 'Unclean Spirits' of St. Mark's Gospel," *ET* 99 (1987-1988): 173-75.

1:24-25

1764   R. Trevijano Etcheverría, "El trasfondo apocalípticode Mc. 1,24.25; 5,7.8 y par.," *Bur* 11 (1970): 117-33.

1:24

1765   Franz Mußner, "Ein Wortspiel in Mk 1:24?" *BZ* 4/2 (1960): 285-86.

1766   Otto Bächli, " 'Was habe ich mit dir zu schaffen?' Eine formelhafte Frage im Alten Testament und Neuen Testament," *TZ* 33 (1977): 69-80.

1767   Pierre Guillemette, "Mc 1,24 est-il une formule de défense magique?" *ScE* 30 (1978): 81-96.

1768   A. Marcello Buscemi, "La prolessi nel Nuovo Testamento," *SBFLA* 35 (1985): 37-68.

1769   William R. Domeris, "The 'Holy One of God' as a Title for Jesus," *Neo* 19 (1985): 9-17.

1770   Francis Watson, "The Social Function of Mark's Secrecy Theme," *JSNT* 24 (1985): 49-69.

1:25

1771   Bernd Kollmann, "Jesu Schweigegebote an die Dämonen," *ZNW* 82 (1991): 267-73.

1:27

1772   A. W. Argyle, "The Meaning of ἐξουσία in Mark 1:22, 27," *ET* 80 (1968-1969): 343.

1773   William R. Domeris, "The Office of the Holy One," *JTSA* 54 (1986): 35-38.

1:29-39

1774   Gilles Gaide, "De l'admiration à la foi. Mc 1,29-39," *AsSeign* 36 (1974): 39-48.

1:29-34

1775   Angelo Lancellotti, "La Casa Pietro a Cafarnao nel Vangeli Sinottici. Redazione e Tradizione," *Ant* 58/1 (1983): 48-69.

1:29-31

1776   Maria L. Rigato, "Tradizione e redazione in Mc. 1,29-31 (e paralleli). La guarigione della suocera di Simon Pietro," *RBib* 17 (1969): 139-74.

1777   Rainer Riesner, "Wie sicher ist die Zwei-Quellen-Theorie?" *TBe* 8 (1977): 49-73.

1778   Albert Fuchs, "Entwicklungsgeschichtliche Studie zu Mk 1,29-31 par Mt 8,14-15 par Lk 4.38-39: Macht über Fieber und Dämonen," *SNTU-A* 6-7 (1981-1982): 21-76.

1779   C. Buzzetti, "Parallels in the Synoptic Gospels: A Case Study," *BT* 35 (1984): 425-31.

1780 Eugene A. LaVerdiere, "In the Following of Christ. The Eucharist in the Gospel According to Mark—III. The Eucharist and the Gospel of God," *Emmanuel* 106 (2000): 221-23, 227-33.

1:30-4:35

1781 Ched Myers, "Binding the Strong Man: Jesus's First Campaign of Nonviolent Direct Action, Mark 1:30-4:35," *Soj* 16 (1987): 28-32.

1:30

1782 George Howard, "Stylistic Inversion and the Synoptic Tradition," *JBL* 97 (1978): 375-89.

1:31

1783 Günther Schwarz, " 'Er berührte ihre Hand'?" *BibN* 73 (1994): 33-35.

1:32-34

1784 T. W. Kowalski, "Les sources pré-synoptiques de Marc 1,32-34 et parallèles. Phénoménes d'amalgame et indépendance mutuelle immédiate des évangélistes synoptiques," *RechSR* 60 (1972): 541-73.

1785 Jozef Verheyden, "Mark 1:32-34 and 6:53-56: Tradition or Redaction?" *ETL* 64/4 (1988): 415-28.

1:34

1786 Klemens Stock, "La conoscenza religiosa nel Nuovo Testamento (i demoni, Mc 1,34)," *ParSpirV* 18 (1988): 93-112.

1:35-39

1787 Rudolf Pesch, "Ein Tag vollmächtigen Wirkens Jesu in Kapharnaum (Mk 1,21-34, 35-39)," *BibL* 9 (1968): 114-28, 177-95, 261-77.

1788 Manfred Wichelhaus, "Am ersten Tage der Woche. Mk. i,35-39 und die didaktischen Absichten des Markus-Evangelisten," *NovT* 11 (1969): 45-66.

1789 Robert Schlarb, "Die Suche nach dem Messias: ζητέω als Terminus technicus der markinischen Messianologie," *ZNW* 81 (1990): 155-70.

1:35

1790 Walter Kirchschlager, "Jesu Gebetsverhalten als Paradigma zu Mk 1,35," *K* 20 (1978): 303-10.

1791 Gregory Murray, "Did Luke Use Mark?" *DR* 104 (1986): 268-71.

1792 Benny R. Crockett, "The Function of Mathetological Prayer in Mark," *IBS* 10 (1988): 123-39.

1:38

1793 Günther Schwarz, " 'Auch den anderen Städten'? (Lukas iv.43a)," *NTS* 23 (1976-1977): 344.

1794 D. O. Wretlind, "Jesus' Philosophy of Ministry: A Study of a Figure of Speech in Mark 1:38," *JETS* 20 (1977): 321-23.

1:39-45

1795 Rainer Dillmann, "Die Bedeutung neuerer exegetischer Methoden für eine biblisch orientierte Pastoral: Aufgezeigt an Mk 1,39-45 - der Heilung eines Aussätzigen," *TGl* 80 (1990): 116-30.

1796 Edwin K. Broadhead, "Christology as Polemic and Apologetic: The Priestly Portrait of Jesus in the Gospel of Mark," *JSNT* 47 (1992): 21-34.

1:39

1797 Jean-Marie van Cangh, "La Galilée dans l'évangile de Marc: un lieu théologique?" *RB* 79 (1972): 59-75.

1:40-45

1798 Charles C. Ryrie, "The Cleansing of the Leper," *BSac* 113 (1956): 262-67.

1799 André Paul, "La guérison d'un lépreux: Approche d'un récit de Marc," *NRT* 92 (1970): 592-604.

1800 Gilles Gaide, "Guérison d'un lépreux: Mc 1,40-45," *AsSeign* 4/37 (1971): 53-61.

1801 M. Herranz Marco, "La curación de un leproso según San Marcos (Mc 1,40-45)," *EB* 31 (1972): 399-433.

1802 C. H. Cave, "The Leper: Mark 1:40-45," *NTS* 25 (1978-1979): 245-50.

1803 André Fossion, "From the Bible Text to the Homily: Cure of a Leper," *LV* 35 (1980): 279-90.

1804 M.-É. Boismard, "La guérison du lépreux (Mc 1,40-45 et par.)," *Salm* 28 (1981): 283-91.

1805 Vittorio Fusco, "Il segreto messianico nell'episodio del lebbroso (Mc. 1,40-45)," *RBib* 29 (1981): 273-313.

1806 Lars Lode, "The Presentation of New Information," *BT* 35 (1984): 101-108.

1807 Frans Neirynck, "Papyrus Egerton 2 and the Healing of the Leper," *ETL* 61/1 (1985): 153-60.

1808 John J. Pilch, "Understanding Biblical Healing: Selecting the Appropriate Model," *BTB* 18 (1988): 60-66.

1809 Michal Wojciechowski, "The Touching of the Leper (Mark 1:40-45) as a Historical and Symbolic Act of Jesus," *BZ* 33/1 (1989): 114-19.

1810 C.-B. Amphoux, "Étude synoptique: La purification du lépreux (Mt 8,2-4 / Mc 1,40-45 / Lc 5,12-16 / Egerton 2)," *BLOS* 4 (1990): 3-12.

1811 Dominique Hermant, "La purification du lépreux (Mt 8,1-4; Mc 1,40-45; Lc 5,12-16)," *BLOS* 4 (1990): 13-22.

1812 Philippe Rolland, "Préliminaires à la première multiplication des pains," *BLOS* 3 (1990): 12-18.

1813 Philippe Rolland, "Propos intempestifs sur la guérison du lépreux," *BLOS* 4 (1990): 23-27.

1814 Carl Kazmierski, "Evangelist and Leper: A Socio-Cultural Study of Mark 1:40-45," *NTS* 38 (1992): 37-50.

1815 W. R. G. Loader, "Challenged at the Boundaries: A Conservative Jesus in Mark's Tradition," *JSNT* 63 (1996): 45-61.

1:40-44

1816 Gregory Murray, "Five Gospel Miracles," *DR* 108 (1990): 79-90.

1:41

1817 Kenneth W. Clark, "The Theological Relevance of Textual Variation in Current Criticism of the Greek New Testament," *JBL* 85 (1966): 1-16.

1:45

1818   Frederick W. Danker, "Mark 1:45 and the Secrecy Motif,"
        CTM 37 (1966): 492-99.

1819   J. K. Elliott, "The Conclusion of the Pericope of the
        Healing the Leper and Mark i.45," *JTS* 22 (1971): 153-57.

1820   J. K. Elliott, "Is ὁ ἐξελθὼν a Title for Jesus in Mark
        1:45?" *JTS* 27 (1976): 402-405.

1821   James Swetnam, "Some Remarks on the Meaning of ὁ δὲ
        ἐξελθὼν in Mark 1:45," *Bib* 68/2 (1987): 245-49.

2:1-3:6

1822   Cesare Bissoli, "Le cinque controversie galilaiche," *PV*
        15/3 (1970): 217-32.

1823   Joanna Dewey, "The Literary Structure of the Controversy
        Stories in Mark 2:1-3:6," *JBL* 92/3 (1973): 394-401.

1824   Pierre M. Beernaert, "Jésus controversé: Structure et
        théologie de Marc 2,1-3,6," *NRT* 95 (1973): 129-49.

1825   David J. Clark, "Criteria for Identifying Chiasm," *LB* 35
        (1975): 63-72.

1826   Ronald J. Kernaghan, "History and Redaction in the
        Controversy Stories in Mark 2:1-3:6," *SBT* 9 (1979):
        23-47.

1827   Ulrich B. Müller, "Zur Rezeption gesetzeskritischer
        Jesusüberlieferung im Frühen Christentum," *NTS* 27/2
        (1980-1981): 158-85.

1828   Darrell J. Doughty, "The Authority of the Son of Man,"
        ZNW 74/3-4 (1983): 161-81.

1829   James D. G. Dunn, "Mark 2:1-3:6: A Bridge Between
        Jesus and Paul on the Question of the Law," *NTS* 30/3
        (1984): 395-415.

1830   Eugene A. LaVerdiere, "Jesus and the Call of the First
        Disciples: Conflict with the Scribes and Pharisees,"
        Emmanuel 94 (1988): 264-69, 272-73, 292.

2:1-28

1831   Verner Hoefelmann, "O caminho da paixao de Jesus na
        perspectiva do evangelista Marcos," *EstT* 26/2 (1986):
        99-119.

<u>2:1-17</u>

1832 Jean Calloud, "Toward a Structural Analysis of the Gospel of Mark," *Semeia* 16 (1979): 133-65.

<u>2:1-13</u>

1833 Jean Delorme, "Marc 2,1-13—ou l'ouverture des frontières," *SémBib* 30 (1983): 1-14.

1834 Edwin K. Broadhead, "Christology as Polemic and Apologetic: The Priestly Portrait of Jesus in the Gospel of Mark," *JSNT* 47 (1992): 21-34.

<u>2:1-12</u>

1835 Allen Cabaniss, "A Fresh Exegesis of Mark 2:1-12," *Int* 11 (1957): 324-27.

1836 R. T. Mead, "The Healing of the Paralytic—A Unit?" *JBL* 80 (1961): 348-54.

1837 G. G. Gamba, "Considerazioni in margine alla poetica di Mc 2,1-12," *Sale* 28 (1966): 324-49.

1838 Robert J. Maddox, "The Function of the Son of Man according to the Synoptic Gospels," *NTS* 15 (1968-1969): 45-74.

1839 Gilles Gaide, "Le paralytique pardonné et guéri: Mc 2,1-12," *AsSeign* 4/38 (1970): 79-88.

1840 Alfred Blenker, "Tilgivelse i Jesu forkyndelse," *DTT* 34 (1971): 105-109.

1841 Detlev Dormeyer, " 'Narrative Analyse' von Mk 2,1-12," *LB* 31 (1974): 68-88.

1842 Léopold Sabourin, "The Miracles of Jesus (II). Jesus and the Evil Powers," *BTB* 4 (1974): 115-75.

1843 H. J. Klauck, "Die Frage der Sündenvergebung in der Perikope von der Heilung des Gelähmten Mk 2,1-12 Parr," *BZ* 25/2 (1981): 223-48.

1844 C. Buzzetti, "Parallels in the Synoptic Gospels: A Case Study," *BT* 35 (1984): 425-31.

1845 Lars Lode, "The Presentation of New Information," *BT* 35 (1984): 101-108.

1846 J. Bishop, "Parabole and Parrhesia in Mark," *Int* 40/1 (1986): 39-52.

1847 Albert Fuchs, "Offene Probleme der Synoptikerforschung: Zur Geschichte der Perikope Mk 2,1-12 par Mt 9,1-8 par Lk 5,17-26," *SNTU-A* 15 (1990): 73-99.

1848 Isabelle Parlier, "L'autorité qui révèle la foi et l'incrédulité: Marc 2/1-12," *ÉTR* 67/2 (1992): 243-47.

1849 Robert C. Dykstra, "The Unreality of God," *PSB* NS 20 (1999): 183-88.

2:1-10

1850 Paul J. Achtemeier, "The Ministry of Jesus in the Synoptic Gospels," *Int* 35 (1981): 157-69.

2:1-3

1851 Pierre M. Beernaert, "Jésus Controversé: Structure et Théologie de Marc 2,1-3, 6," *NRT* 95/2 (1973): 129-49.

2:1-2

1852 John Vannorsdall, "Mark 2:1-2," *Int* 36/1 (1982): 58-63.

1853 Ivor Bailey, "The Cripple's Story," *ET* 99 (1987-1988): 110-12.

2:2-12

1854 Gregory Murray, "Five Gospel Miracles," *DR* 108 (1990): 79-90.

2:3-11

1855 F. C. Synge, "A Matter of Tenses—Fingerprints of an Annotator in Mark," *ET* 88 (1976-1977): 168-71.

2:3-5

1856 E. Rasco, " 'Cuatro' y 'la fe': ¿quiénes y de quién? (Mc 2,3b.5a)," *Bib* 50 (1969): 59-67.

2:3

1857 Michael D. Goulder, "On Putting Q to the Test," *NTS* 24 (1977-1978): 218-34.

1858 Christopher M. Tuckett, "On the Relationship between Matthew and Luke," *NTS* 30 (1984): 130-42.

2:4

1859   Herman Ljungvik, "Randanmärkningar till 1963 års bibelkommités översättningsförslag," *SEÅ* 34 (1969): 147-69.

1860   Günther Schwarz, "ἀπεστέγασαν τὴν στέγην (Markus 2:4c)," *BibN* 54 (1990): 41.

2:5-10

1861   J. Michl, "Sündenvergebung in Christus nach dem Glauben der frühen Kirche," *MTZ* 24 (1973): 25-35.

2:5-7

1862   Paul Ellingworth, "Translating Parallel Passages in the Gospels," *BT* 34 (1983): 401-407.

2:5

1863   Harvie Branscomb, " 'Son, Thy Sins are Forgiven' (Mark 2:5)," *JBL* 53 (1934): 53-60.

1864   E. M. Sidebottom, "The So-Called Divine Passive in the Gospel Tradition," *ET* 87 (1975-1976): 200-204.

2:6-12

1865   Joseph Keller, "Jesus and the Critics: A Logico-Critical Analysis of the Marcan Confrontation," *Int* 40/1 (1986): 29-38.

2:6

1866   Pierre M. Beernaert, "Jésus Controversé: Structure et Théologie de Marc 2,1-3, 6," *NRT* 95/2 (1973): 129-49.

2:7

1867   John Thorley, "Aktionsart in New Testament Greek: Infinitive and Imperative," *NovT* 31 (1989): 290-315.

2:8-9

1868   Ronald Ross, "Was Jesus Saying Something or Doing Something? (Mark 2:8-9)," *BT* 41 (1990): 441-42.

2:8

1869   Philippe Rolland, "L'arrière-lond sémitique des évangiles synoptiques," *ETL* 60 (1984): 358-62.

1870   Philippe Rolland, "Jésus connaissait leurs pensées," *ETL* 62 (1986): 118-21.

2:9

1871   Faith Hunter and Geoffrey Hunter, " 'Which Is Easier'?"
        ET 105 (1993): 12-13.

2:10-28

1872   André Feuillet, "L'ἐξουσία du Fils de l'homme (d'après
        Mc, 2:10-28 et par.)," *RechSR* 42 (1954): 161-92.

1873   Christopher M. Tuckett, "The Present Son of Man," *JSNT*
        14 (1982): 58-81.

2:10

1874   George H. Boobyer, "Mark 2:10a and the Interpretations
        of the Healing of the Paralytic," *HTR* 47 (1954): 115-20.

1875   Christian P. Ceroke, "Is Mark 2:10 a Saying of Jesus?"
        CBQ 22 (1960): 369-90.

1876   I. Howard Marshall, "The Synoptic Son of Man Sayings in
        Recent Discussion," *NTS* 12 (1965-1966): 327-51.

1877   L. S. Hay, "The Son of Man in Mark 2:10 and 2:28," *JBL*
        89 (1970): 69-75.

1878   Lars Hartman, "Baptism 'Into the Name of Jesus' and
        Early Christology: Some Tentative Considerations,"
        StTheol 28 (1974): 21-48.

1879   P. Maurice Casey, "The Son of Man Problem," *ZNW* 67/3
        (1976): 147-54.

1880   George Howard, "Stylistic Inversion and the Synoptic
        Tradition," *JBL* 97 (1978): 375-89.

2:11-16

1881   Herman Ljungvik, "Randanmärkningar till 1963 års
        bibelkommités översättningsförslag," *SEÅ* 34 (1969):
        147-69.

2:11-12

1882   Frans Neirynck, "Les accords mineurs et la rédaction des
        évangiles: L'épisode du paralytique," *ETL* 50 (1974):
        215-30.

2:11

1883   José O'Callaghan, "Tres casos de armonización en Mt 9,"
        EB 47 (1989): 131-34.

2:12

1884 Martin J. Higgins, "New Testament Result Clauses with Infinitive," *CBQ* 23 (1961): 233-41.

1885 Angelo Lancellotti, "La Casa Pietro a Cafarnao nel Vangeli Sinottici: Redazione e Tradizione," *Ant* 58/1 (1983): 48-69.

1886 Lars Lode, "Narrative Paragraphs in the Gospels and Acts," *BT* 34/3 (1983): 322-35.

2:13-17

1887 Paul Lamarche, "The Call to Conversion and Faith. The Vocation of Levi (Mark 2:13-17)," *LV* 25 (1970): 301-12.

1888 A.-L. Descamps, "Aux origines du ministère: La pensée de Jesus," *RTL* 2 (1971): 3-45; 3 (1972): 121-59.

1889 Paul Lamarche, "L'appel de Levi. Marc 2,13-17," *Chr* 23 (1976): 107-18.

1890 Michael Theobald, "Der Primat der Synchronie vor der Diachronie als Grundaxion der Literaturkritik. Methodische Erwägungen an Hand von Mk 2,13-17, Mt 9,9-13," *BZ* 22/2 (1978): 161-86.

1891 Martin Völkel, " 'Freund der Zöllner und Sünder'," *ZNW* 69 (1978): 1-10.

1892 Balembo Buetubela, "La vocation de Lévi et le repas avec les pécheurs (Mc 2,13-17)," *RAfT* 3 (1979): 47-60.

1893 Eugene A. LaVerdiere, "In the Following of Christ. The Eucharist in the Gospel According to Mark—IV. Jesus and the First Disciples," *Emmanuel* 106 (2000): 292-300.

2:13-14

1894 Francis J. Moloney, "The Vocation of the Disciples in the Gospel of Mark," *Sale* 43 (1981): 487-516.

1895 Jean Magne, "La vocation de Matthieu," *BLOS* 3 (1990): 3-6.

2:14-17

1896 John R. Donahue, "Tax Collectors and Sinners: An Attempt at Identification," *CBQ* 33 (1971): 39-61.

2:14-16

1897   Fritz Herrenbrück, "Wer waren die 'Zöllner'?" *ZNW* 72 (1981): 178-94.

1898   Fritz Herrenbrück, "Zum Vorwurf der Kollaboration des Zöllners mit Rom," *ZNW* 78 (1987): 186-99.

2:14

1899   Rudolf Pesch, "Levi-Matthäus (Mc 2,14 / Mt 9,9; 10,3): Ein Beitrag zur Lösung eines alten Problems," *ZNW* 59 (1968): 40-56.

1900   Beltran Villegas, "Peter, Philip and James of Alphaeus," *NTS* 33 (1987): 292-94.

2:15-3:6

1901   Mary A. Tolbert, "Is It Lawful on the Sabbath To Do Good or To Do Harm: Mark's Ethics of Religious Practice," *PRS* 23 (1996): 199-214.

2:15-17

1902   Paul De Maat, "Hoe Krijgt Marcus 2:15-17 betekenis?" *Bij* 44/2 (1983): 194-207.

1903   Robert G. Bratcher, "Unusual Sinners," *BT* 39 (1988): 335-37.

1904   Jean Magne, "Le repas avec les pécheurs," *BLOS* 5 (1990): 17-20.

2:15-16

1905   H.-W. Bartsch, "Zur Problematik eines Monopoltextes des Neuen Testaments. Das Beispiel Markus 2, Vers 15 und 16," *TLZ* 105 (1980): 91-96.

1906   H.-W. Bartsch, "Ein neuer Textus Receptus für das griechische Neue Testament?" *NTS* 27 (1980-1981): 585-92.

2:15

1907   Elizabeth S. Malbon, "Τῇ οἰκίᾳ αὐτοῦ: Mark 2:15 in Context," *NTS* 31/2 (1985): 282-92.

1908   David M. May, "Mark 2:15: the home of Jesus or Levi?" *NTS* 39 (1993): 147-49.

2:16-17

1909   J. Alonso Díaz, "La parábola del médico en Mc. 2,16-17," *CuBí* 16 (1959): 10-12.

2:16

1910   Donald E. Cook, "A Gospel Portrait of the Pharisees," *RevExp* 84 (1987): 221-33.

1911   George D. Kilpatrick, "Two Studies of Style and Text in the Greek New Testament," *JTS* 41 (1990): 94-98.

1912   D. Neufeld, "Jesus' Eating Transgressions and Social Impropriety in the Gospel of Mark: A Social Scientific Approach," *BTB* 30 (2000): 15-26.

2:17

1913   G. M. Lee, " 'They that are Whole Need Not a Physician'," *ET* 76 (1964-1965): 254.

1914   C. Buzzetti, "Parallels in the Synoptic Gospels: A Case Study," *BT* 35 (1984): 425-31.

2:18-28

1915   David Daube, "Responsibilities of Master and Disciples in the Gospels," *NTS* 19 (1972-1973): 1-15.

1916   Jean Calloud, "Toward a Structural Analysis of the Gospel of Mark," *Semeia* 16 (1979): 133-65.

2:18-22

1917   Harvey K. McArthur, "The Dependence of the Gospel of Thomas on the Synoptics," *ET* 71 (1959-1960): 286-87.

1918   Juan Fernández, "La cuestión de ayuno (Mt 9,14-17; Mc 2,18-22; Lu 5,33-39)," *CuBí* 19 (1962): 162-69.

1919   John O'Hara, "Christian Fasting. Mark 2,18-22," *Scr* 19 (1967): 82-95.

1920   G. Schille, "Was ist ein Logion?" *ZNW* 61 (1970): 172-82.

1921   Gilles Gaide, "Question sur le jeûne. Mc 2,18-22," *AsSeign* 39 (1972): 44-54.

1922   Robert Banks, "Jesus and Custom," *ET* 84 (1972-1973): 265-69.

1923   J. A. Ziesler, "The Removal of the Bridegroom: A Note on Mark 2:18-22 and Parallels," *NTS* 19 (1972-1973): 190-94.

1924 Rainer Riesner, "Wie sicher ist die Zwei-Quellen-Theorie?" *TBe* 8 (1977): 49-73.

1925 Pieter J. Maartens, "Mark 2:18-22: An Exercise in Theoretically- Founded Exegesis," *ScrSA* 2 (1980): 1-54.

1926 Philippe Rolland, "Les Prédécesseurs de Marc: Les Sources Présynoptiques de Mc II,18-22 et Paralleles," *RB* 89/3 (1982): 370-405.

1927 R. S. Good, "Jesus, Protagonist of the Old, in Luke 5:33-39," *NovT* 25/1 (1983): 19-36.

1928 Curtis C. Mitchell, "The Practice of Fasting in the New Testament," *BSac* 147 (1990): 455-69.

2:18-20

1929 André Feuillet, "La controverse sur le jeûne (Mc 2,18-20; Mt 9,14-15; Lc 5,33-35)," *NRT* 90 (1968): 113-36; 252-77.

1930 Frans Neirynck, "Les expressions doubles chez Marc et le problème synoptique," *ETL* 59/4 (1983): 303-30.

2:18

1931 José O'Callaghan, "Tres casos de armonización en Mt 9," *EB* 47 (1989): 131-34.

2:19-20

1932 Roderic Dunkerley, "The Bridegroom Passage," *ET* 64 (1952-1953): 303-304.

1933 Augustin George, "Comment Jésus a-t-il perçu sa propre mort?" *LV* 101 (1971): 34-59.

1934 J. C. O'Neill, "The Source of the Parables of the Bridegroom and the Wicked Husbandmen," *JTS* 39 (1988): 485-89.

2:19

1935 Franz G. Cremer, " 'Die Söhne des Brautgemachs' (Mk 2,19 parr) in der griechischen und lateinischen Schrifterklärung," *BZ* 11 (1967): 246-53.

2:20-22

1936 Paul Ellingworth, "Translating Parallel Passages in the Gospels," *BT* 34 (1983): 401-407.

2:20

1937 José O'Callaghan, "Dos retoques antioquenos: Mt' 10,10; Mc 2,20," *Bib* 68/4 (1987): 564-67.

2:21-22

1938 L. Paul Trudinger, "The Word on the Generation Gap. Reflections on a Gospel Metaphor," *BTB* 5 (1975): 311-15.

1939 Vernon K. Robbins, "Picking Up the Fragments: From Crossan's Analysis to Rhetorical Analysis," *Forum* 1 (1985): 31-64.

1940 J. D. M. Derrett, "Modes of Renewal (Mk. 2:21-22)," *EQ* 72 (2000): 3-12.

2:21

1941 Ferdinand Hahn, "Die Bildworte vom neuen Flicken und vom jungen Wein (Mk. 2,21f. parr)," *EvT* 31 (1971): 357-75.

2:23-6:6

1942 Eugene A. LaVerdiere, "Jesus and the New Israel," *Emmanuel* 94 (1988): 322-29.

2:23-3:6

1943 Henri Troadec, "Le Fils de l'Homme est Maitre même du sabbat (Marc 2,23-3,6)," *BVC* 21 (1958): 73-83.

1944 A. Duprez, "Deuz affrontements un jour de sabbat. Mc 2:23-3:6," *AsSeign* 40 (1972): 43-53.

2:23-28

1945 Joseph A. Grassi, "The Five Loaves or the High Priest," *NovT* 7 (1964-1965): 119-22.

1946 Arland J. Hultgren, "The Formation of the Sabbath Pericope in Mark 2:23-28," *JBL* 91/1 (1971): 38-43.

1947 Bernard Jay, "Jesus et le sabbat. Simples notes a propos de Marc 2/23-28," *ÉTR* 50 (1975): 65-68.

1948 Hermann Aichinger, "Quellenkritische Untersuchung der Perikope vom Ährenraufen am Sabbat: Mk 2,23-28 par, Mt 12,1-8 par, Lk 6,1-5," *SNTU-A* 1 (1976): 110-53.

1949   G. G. Gamba, "Struttura letteraria e significato dottrinale di Marco 2,23-28 e 3,1-6," *Sale* 40 (1978): 529-82.

1950   Lars Lode, "The Presentation of New Information," *BT* 35 (1984): 101-108.

1951   Stanley N. Olson, "Christ for All of Life: Mark's Miracle Stories for 1985," *CThM* 12 (1985): 90-99.

1952   P. Maurice Casey, "Culture and Historicity: The Plucking of the Grain in Mark 2:23-28," *NTS* 34/1 (1988): 1-23.

1953   Edwin K. Broadhead, "Christology as Polemic and Apologetic: The Priestly Portrait of Jesus in the Gospel of Mark," *JSNT* 47 (1992): 21-34.

1954   Rod Parrott, "Conflict and Rhetoric in Mark 2:23-28," *Semeia* 64 (1994): 117-37.

1955   Rainer Dillmann, "Die Bedeutung der semantischen Analyse für die Textpragmatik," *BibN* 79 (1995): 5-9.

2:23

1956   H.-J. Schoeps, "Jesus et la Loi juive," *RHPR* 33 (1953): 1-20.

2:24

1957   Donald E. Cook, "A Gospel Portrait of the Pharisees," *RevExp* 84 (1987): 221-33.

2:26

1958   Alan D. Rogers, "Mark 2:26," *JTS* 2 (1951): 44.

1959   C. S. Morgan, " 'When Abiathar Was High Priest,' (Mark 2:26)," *JBL* 98 (1979): 409-10.

1960   J. H. van Halsema, "Het raadsel als literaire vorm in Marcus en Johannes," *GTT* 83/1 (1983): 1-17.

1961   Craig A. Evans, "Patristic Interpretation of Mark 2:26: 'When Abiathar was High Priest'," *VC* 40/2 (1986): 183-86.

2:27-28

1962   Félix Gils, " 'Le sabbat a été fait pour l'homme et non l'homme pour le sabbat' (Mc II,27). Réflexions à propos de Mc II,27-28," *RB* 69 (1962): 506-23.

1963   J. M. Casciaro Ramírez, "General, Generic and Indefinite: The Use of the Term 'Son of Man' in Aramaic Sources and in the Teaching of Jesus," *JSNT* 29 (1987): 21-56.

2:27

1964   Félix Gils, " 'Le sabbat a été fait pour l'homme et non l'homme pour le sabbat' (Mc II,27). Réflexions à propos de Mc II,27-28," *RB* 69 (1962): 506-23.

1965   Rüdiger Bartelmus, "Mk 2:27 und die ältesten Fassungen des Arbeitsruhegebotes im AT: biblisch-theologische Beobachtungen zur Sabbatfrage," *BibN* 41 (1988): 41-64.

2:28

1966   L. S. Hay, "The Son of Man in Mark 2:10 and 2:28," *JBL* 89 (1970): 69-75.

1967   P. Maurice Casey, "The Son of Man Problem," *ZNW* 67/3 (1976): 147-54.

1968   Douglas J. Moo, "Jesus and the Authority of the Mosaic Law," *JSNT* 20 (1984): 3-49.

3:1-4:20

1969   James R. Edwards, "Markan Sandwiches: The Significance of Interpolations in Markan Narratives," *NovT* 31 (1989): 193-216.

3:1-12

1970   B. Marconcini, "La predicazione del Battista in Marco e Luca confrontata con la redazione di Matteo," *RBib* Supp. 20 (1972): 451-66.

3:1-7

1971   Edwin K. Broadhead, "Christology as Polemic and Apologetic: The Priestly Portrait of Jesus in the Gospel of Mark," *JSNT* 47 (1992): 21-34.

3:1-6

1972   Jean Levie, "L'évangile araméen de S. Matthieu est-il la source de l'évangile de S. Marc?" *NRT* 76 (1954): 689-715, 812-43.

1973   Cyril S. Rodd, "Are the Ethics of Jesus Situation Ethics?" *ET* 79 (1967-1968): 167-70.

1974   P. Géoltrain, "La violation du sabbat: Une lecture de Marc 3,1-6," *FV* 69/3 (1970): 70-90.

1975   Léopold Sabourin, "The Miracles of Jesus (III): Healings, Resuscitations, Nature Miracles," *BTB* 5 (1975): 146-200.

1976   Christian Dietzfelbinger, "Vom Sinn der Sabbatheilungen Jesu," *EvT* 38 (1978): 281-98.

1977   G. G. Gamba, "Struttura letteraria e significato dottrinale di Marco 2,23-28 e 3,1-6," *Sale* 40 (1978): 529-82.

1978   Jürgen Sauer, "Traditionsgeschichtliche Überlegungen Zu Mk 3,1-6," *ZNW* 73/3-4 (1982): 183-203.

1979   J. D. M. Derrett, "Christ and the Power of Choice: Mark 3:1-6," *Bib* 65/2 (1984): 168-88.

1980   Lars Lode, "The Presentation of New Information," *BT* 35 (1984): 101-108.

1981   Wolfgang Feneberg, "Das Neue Testament: Sprache der Liebe—Zum Problem des Antijudaismus," *ZKT* 107 (1985): 333-40.

1982   Stephen H. Smith, "Mark 3:1-6: Form, Redaction and Community Function," *Bib* 75 (1994): 153-74.

3:2

1983   A. Marcello Buscemi, "La prolessi nel Nuovo Testamento," *SBFLA* 35 (1985): 37-68.

1984   Lino Cignelli, "La grecità biblica," *SBFLA* 35 (1985): 203-48.

3:4

1985   John Thorley, "Aktionsart in New Testament Greek: Infinitive and Imperative," *NovT* 31 (1989): 290-315.

3:6

1986   H.-J. Schoeps, "Jesus et la Loi juive," *RHPR* 33 (1953): 1-20.

1987   C. Daniel, "Les 'Hérodiens' du Nouveau Testament sont-ils des Esséniens?" *RevQ* 6 (1967): 31-53.

1988   W. J. Bennett, "The Herodians of Mark's Gospel," *NovT* 17/1 (1975): 9-14.

1989   Augustine Stock, "Jesus, Hypocrites, and Herodians," *BTB* 16/1 (1986): 3-7.

3:7-19

1990   Lucien Cerfaux, "La mission de Galilée dans la tradition synoptique," *ETL* 27 (1951): 369-89; 28 (1952): 629-47.

3:7-12

1991   Leander E. Keck, "Mark 3:7-12 and Mark's Christology," *JBL* 84/4 (1965): 341-58.

1992   T. A. Burkill, "Mark 3:7-12 and the Alleged Dualism in the Evangelist's Miracle Material," *JBL* 87/4 (1968): 409-17.

1993   W. Egger, "Die Verborgenheit in Mk 3,7-12," *Bib* 50 (1969): 466-90.

1994   Alois Stöger, "Sohn Gottes im Markusevangelium (II). Meditation (Mk 3,7-12; 5,1-12)," *BL* 49 (1976): 112-15.

3:7-8

1995   George Howard, "Stylistic Inversion and the Synoptic Tradition," *JBL* 97 (1978): 375-89.

3:8

1996   George D. Kilpatrick, "Two Studies of Style and Text in the Greek New Testament," *JTS* 41 (1990): 94-98.

3:9

1997   Günther Schwarz, "Ἵνα πλοιάριον προσκαπτερῇ αὐτῷ: Markus 3.9," *NTS* 33/1 (1987): 151-52.

3:10

1998   Martin J. Higgins, "New Testament Result Clauses with Infinitive," *CBQ* 23 (1961): 233-41.

3:13-35

1999   John Painter, "When Is a House Not a Home? Disciples and Family in Mark 3.13-35," *NTS* 45 (1999): 498-513.

3:13-19

2000   A.-L. Descamps, "Aux origines du ministère: La pensée de Jesus," *RTL* 2 (1971): 3-45; 3 (1972): 121-59.

2001   Francis J. Moloney, "The Vocation of the Disciples in the Gospel of Mark," *Sale* 43 (1981): 487-516.

3:13-16

2002   Josef Sudbrack, "Berufung, Gebet, Sendung: Die Einsetzung der zwölf Apostel nach Markus 3,13-16," *GeistL* 50 (1977): 387-90.

3:13

2003   Lino Cignelli, "La grecità biblica," *SBFLA* 35 (1985): 203-48.

3:14

2004   Ernest Best, "Mark's Use of the Twelve," *ZNW* 69/1-2 (1978): 11-35.

3:16-19

2005   Michael D. Goulder, "On Putting Q to the Test," *NTS* 24 (1977-1978): 218-34.

2006   Christopher M. Tuckett, "On the Relationship between Matthew and Luke," *NTS* 30 (1984): 130-42.

3:16-17

2007   Harald Sahlin, "Emendationsvorschläge zum griechischen Text des Neuen Testaments I," *NovT* 24 (1982): 160-79.

3:17

2008   Severin M. Grill, "Die Donnersöhne Mk 3.17 nach dem syrischen Text," *BL* 23 (1955-1956): 137-38.

2009   Otto Betz, "Donnersöhne, Menschenfischer und der davidische Messias," *RevQ* 3 (1961): 41-70.

2010   Randall Buth, "Mark 3:17· BONEPEΓEM and Popular Etymology," *JSNT* 10 (1981): 29-33.

3:18-19

2011   J.-A. Morin, "Les deux derniers des Douze: Simon le Zelote et Judas Iskariôth," *RB* 80 (1973): 332-58.

3:18

2012   Beltran Villegas, "Peter, Philip and James of Alphaeus," *NTS* 33 (1987): 292-94.

2013   Roger L. Omanson, "Lazarus and Simon," *BT* 40 (1989): 416-19.

3:19-30

    2014   Lamar Cope, "The Beelzebul Controversy, Mark 3:19-30 and Parallels: A Model Problem in Source Analysis," *SBLSP* 1/1 (1971): 251-56.

3:19-21

    2015   Anthony O. Nkwoka, "Mark 3:19b-21: A Study on the Charge of Fanaticism against Jesus," *BB* 15 (1989): 205-21.

3:19-20

    2016   Frans Neirynck, "The Order of the Gospels and the Making of a Synopsis," *ETL* 61/1 (1985): 161-66.

3:19

    2017   Yoël Arbeitman, "The Suffix of Iscariot," *JBL* 99 (1980): 122-23.

3:20-35

    2018   Jan Lambrecht, "Ware Verwantschap en Eeuwige Zonde: Ontstaan en Structuur van Mc. 3:20-35," *Bij* 29/2 (1968): 114-50.

    2019   Gilles Gaide, "Les deux 'maisons': Mc 3,20-35," *AsSeign* 21/41 (1971): 39-53.

    2020   David M. May, "Mark 3:20-35 from the Perspective of Shame/Honor," *BTB* 17/3 (1987): 83-87.

    2021   Eugene A. LaVerdiere, "Teaching for the New Israel," *Emmanuel* 94 (1988): 383-89.

    2022   George Aichele, "Jesus' Uncanny 'Family Scene'," *JSNT* 74 (1999): 29-49.

3:20-25

    2023   John D. Crossan, "Mark and the Relatives of Jesus," *NovT* 15 (1973): 81-113.

3:20-21

    2024   P. J. Gannon, "Could Mark Employ αὐτός in 3,21 Referring to ὄχλος in 3,20?" *CBQ* 15 (1953): 400-61.

    2025   Francesco Spadafora, "Lo studio della koinè nella esegesi. Mc. 3:20-21," *RBib* 4 (1956): 93-113, 193-217.

2026   Martin Avanzo, "María en las primeras tradiciones evangelicas," *RevB* 38 (1976): 49-57.

2027   Angelo Lancellotti, "La Casa Pietro a Cafarnao nel Vangeli Sinottici. Redazione e Tradizione," *Ant* 58/1 (1983): 48-69.

2028   Robert Schlarb, "Die Suche nach dem Messias: ζητέω als Terminus technicus der markinischen Messianologie," *ZNW* 81 (1990): 155-70.

2029   Detlev Dormeyer, "Dialogue with the Text: Interactional Bible Interpretation," *ScrSA* 33 (1990): 55-64.

2030   Meinrad Limbeck, "Hindernisse fürs Christsein: Zur Verkündigung des Markusevangeliums," *BL* 64 (1991): 164-68.

3:20

2031   Martin J. Higgins, "New Testament Result Clauses with Infinitive," *CBQ* 23 (1961): 233-41.

2032   Ernest Best, "Mark 3:20, 21, 31-35," *NTS* 22/3 (1975-1976): 309-19.

2033   Klemens Stock, "La familia di Gesù se vergogna di lui: Mc 3,20s," *ParSpirV* 20 (1989): 105-26.

3:21

2034   Henry Wansbrough, "Mark iii.21—Was Jesus Out of His Mind?" *NTS* 18 (1971-1972): 233-35.

2035   David Wenham, "The Meaning of Mark III.21," *NTS* 21/2 (1974-1975): 295-300.

2036   Ernest Best, "Mark 3:20, 21, 31-35," *NTS* 22/3 (1975-1976): 309-19.

2037   George E. Rice, "Is Bezae a Homogeneous Codex," *PRS* 11 (1984): 39-54.

2038   D. Neufeld, "Eating, Ecstacy, and Exorcism," *BTB* 26 (1996): 152-62.

2039   Jack T. Sanders, "The Criterion of Coherence and the Randomness of Charisma: Poring Through Some Aporias in the Jesus Tradition," *NTS* 44 (1998): 1-25.

3:22-30

2040 Roland Meynet, "Qui Donc Est 'Le Plus Fort'? Analyse Rhétorique de Mc 3,22-30; Mt 12,22-37; Luc 11,14-26," *RB* 90/3 (1983): 334-50.

2041 Douglas E. Oakman, "Rulers' Houses, Thieves, and Usurpers: The Beelzebul Pericope," *Forum* 4 (1988): 109-23.

3:22-26

2042 J. D. M. Derrett, "Trees Walking, Prophecy, and Christology," *StTheol* 35/1 (1981): 33-54.

3:22-23

2043 Lars Lode, "The Presentation of New Information," *BT* 35 (1984): 101-108.

3:22

2044 W. C. B. MacLaurin, "Beelzeboul," *NovT* 20/2 (1978): 156-60.

2045 Philippe Rolland, "Jésus connaissait leurs pensées," *ETL* 62 (1986): 118-21.

3:23-30

2046 Chrys C. Caragounis, "Kingdom of God, Son of Man and Jesus' Self-Understanding," *TynB* 40 (1989): 3-23; 223-38.

3:27

2047 H.-W. Bartsch, "Das Thomas-Evangelium und die synoptischen Evangelien. Zu G. Quispel's Bemerkungen zum Thomas-Evangelium," *NTS* 6 (1959-1960): 249-61.

2048 Simon Légasse, " 'Homme Fort' de Luc XI,21-22," *NovT* 5 (1962): 5-9.

3:28-30

2049 Robert J. Maddox, "The Function of the Son of Man according to the Synoptic Gospels," *NTS* 15 (1968-1969): 45-74.

3:28-29

2050 Owen E. Evans, "The Unforgiveable Sin," *ET* 68 (1956-1957): 240-44.

2051   Robin Scroggs, "The Exaltation of the Spirit by Some Early Christians," *JBL* 84/4 (1965): 359-73.

2052   M. Eugene Boring, "The Unforgivable Sin Logion Mark 3:28-29/Matt 12:31-32/Luke 12:10: Formal Analysis and History of the Tradition," *NovT* 18/4 (1976): 258-79.

2053   James D. G. Dunn, "Prophetic 'I'-Sayings and the Jesus Tradition: The Importance of Testing Prophetic Utterances within Early Christianity," NTS 24 (1977-1978): 175-98.

2054   P. Maurice Casey, "Aramaic Idiom and Son of Man Sayings," *ET* 96 (1984-1985): 233-36.

3:28

2055   Evald Lövestam, "Logiet om hädelse mot den helige Ande (Mark. 3:28f. par. Matt. 12:31f.; Luk. 12:10)," *SEÅ* 33/34 (1968): 101-17.

2056   M. Eugene Boring, "How May We Identify Oracles of Christian Prophets in the Synoptic Tradition? Mark 3:28, 29 as a Test Case," *JBL* 91/4 (1972): 501-20.

2057   Robert Holst, "Re-examining Mark 3:28f. and Its Parallels," *ZNW* 63 (1972): 122-24.

3:29

2058   M. Eugene Boring, "How May We Identify Oracles of Christian Prophets in the Synoptic Tradition? Mark 3:28, 29 as a Test Case," *JBL* 91/4 (1972): 501-20.

2059   Ernest Best, "An Early Sayings Collection," *NovT* 18/1 (1976): 1-16.

2060   J. C. O'Neill, "The Unforgivable Sin," *JSNT* 19 (1983): 37-42.

2061   Baird Tipson, "A Dark Side of 17th Century English Protestantism: The Sin Against the Holy Spirit," *HTR* 77/3-4 (1984): 301-30.

2062   Byron L. Rohrig, "You Cannot Be Too Bad to Be Forgiven," *CC* 105 (1988): 863.

3:30

2063   Francesco Spadafora, "Entusiasmo della folla frenato dagli apostolie proposito energico dei parenti di Gesù (Mc 3,30s)?" *RBib* 4 (1956): 98-113.

3:31-35

2064   Paul Gächter, "Die 'Brüder' Jesu," *ZKT* 75 (1953): 458-59.

2065   Ekkart Sauser, "Ungewohnte Väteraussagen über Maria," *TTZ* 79 (1970): 306-13.

2066   Guy Lafon, "Qui est dedans? Qui est dehors? Une lecture de Marc 3,31-35," *Chr* 21 (1974): 41-47.

2067   Ernest Best, "Mark 3:20, 21, 31-35," *NTS* 22/3 (1975-1976): 309-19.

2068   Martin Avanzo, "María en las primeras tradiciones evangelicas," *RevB* 38 (1976): 49-57.

2069   Bertrand Buby, "A Christology of Relationship in Mark," *BTB* 10/4 (1980): 149-54.

2070   Angelo Lancellotti, "La Casa Pietro a Cafarnao nel Vangeli Sinottici: Redazione e Tradizione," *Ant* 58/1 (1983): 48-69.

2071   Robert W. Funk, "From Parable to Gospel: Domesticating the Tradition," *Forum* 1/3 (1985): 3-24.

2072   Enzo Bianchi, "La nuova famiglia di Gesù," *ParSpirV* 14 (1986): 179-92.

2073   Detlev Dormeyer, "Dialogue with the Text: Interactional Bible Interpretation," *ScrSA* 33 (1990): 55-64.

2074   Robert Schlarb, "Die Suche nach dem Messias: ζητέω als Terminus technicus der markinischen Messianologie," *ZNW* 81 (1990): 155-70.

2075   M. H. Smith, "Kinship Is Relative: Mark 3:31-35 and Parallels," *Forum* 6 (1990): 80-94.

2076   Meinrad Limbeck, "Hindernisse fürs Christein: Zur Verkündigung des Markusevangeliums," *BL* 64 (1991): 164-68.

3:33

2077   M. Philip Scott, "Chiastic Structure: A Key to the Interpretation of Mark's Gospel," *BTB* 15 (1985): 17-26.

3:34-35

2078   George Howard, "Harmonistic Readings in the Old Syriac Gospels," *HTR* 73 (1980): 473-91.

4:1-8:26

2079   Norman R. Petersen, "The Composition of Mark 4:1-8:26," *HTR* 73 (1980): 185-217.

4:1-34

2080   D. W. Riddle, "Mark 4:1-34: The Evolution of a Gospel Source," *JBL* 56 (1937): 77-90.

2081   C. H. Cave, "The Parables and the Scriptures," *NTS* 11 (1964-1965): 374-87.

2082   Eduard Lohse, "Die Gottesherrschatt in den Gleichnissen Jesu," *EvT* 18 (1958): 145-57.

2083   George H. Boobyer, "The Redaction of Mark 4:1-34," *NTS* 8 (1961-1962): 59-70.

2084   Birger Gerhardsson, "The Parable of the Sower and Its Interpretation," *NTS* 14 (1967-1968): 165-93.

2085   David Wenham, "The Synoptic Problem Revisited: Some New Suggestions about the Composition of Mark 4:1-34," *TynB* 23 (1972): 3-38.

2086   Diego A. Losada, "Las parábolas de crecimiento en el evangelio de Marcos," *RevB* 38 (1976): 113-25.

2087   Gerhard Sellen, "Allegorie und 'Gleichnis': Zur Formenlehre der synoptischen Gleichnisse," *ZTK* 75 (1978): 281-335.

2088   C. C. Marcheselli, "Le parabole del vangelo di Marco," *RBib* 29 (1981): 405-15.

2089   Gerhard Sellin, "Textlinguistische und Semiotische Erwägungen zu Mk. 4:1-34," *NTS* 29/4 (1983): 508-30.

2090   Eugene A. LaVerdiere, "Teaching in Parables," *Emmanuel* 94 (1988): 439-45, 453.

2091   Christopher M. Tuckett, "Mark's Concerns in the Parables Chapter (Mark 4,1-34)," *Bib* 69/1 (1988): 1-26.

2092   Greg Fay, "Introduction to Incomprehension: The Literary Structure of Mark 4:1-34," *CBQ* 51/1 (1989): 65-81.

2093 Gerhard Dautzenberg, "Mk 4:1-34 als Belehrung über das Reich Gottes: Beobachtungen zum Gleichniskapitel," *BZ* 34/1 (1990): 38-62.

2094 Philip H. Sellew, "Oral and Written Sources in Mark 4:1-34," *NTS* 36 (1990): 234-67.

4:1-20

2095 Charles C. McDonald, "The Relevance of the Parable of the Sower," *BibTo* 26 (1966): 1822-27.

2096 Eduard Schweizer, "Du texte à la prédication. Marc 4:1-20," *ÉTR* 43 (1968): 256-64.

2097 T. K. Seim, "Apostolat og forkynnelse. En studie til Mk. 4.1-20," *DTT* 35 (1969): 206-22.

2098 John Drury, "The Sower, the Vineyard, and the Place of Allegory in the Interpretation of Mark's Parables," *JTS* 24/2 (1973): 367-79.

2099 John W. Bowker, "Mystery and Parable: Mark 4:1-20," *JTS* 25/2 (1974): 301-17.

2100 Eduard Schweizer, "From the New Testament Text to the Sermon. Mark 4:1-20," *RevExp* 72 (1975): 181-88.

2101 Eugene E. Lemcio, "External Evidence for the Structure and Function of Mark IV.1-20, VII.14-23, and VIII.14-21," *JTS* 29/2 (1978): 323-38.

2102 Craig A. Evans, "On the Isaianic Background of the Parable of the Sower," *CBQ* 47/3 (1985): 464-68.

2103 James R. Edwards, "Markan Sandwiches: The Significance of Interpolations in Markan Narratives," *NovT* 31 (1989): 193-216.

2104 Michael Stahl, "Vom Verstehen des Neuen Testaments in der einen Welt," *ZMiss* 16/4 (1990): 224-35.

2105 Joel Marcus, "Blanks and Gaps in the Markan Parable of the Sower," *BibInt* 5 (1997): 247-62.

4:1-9

2106 John Horman, "The Source of the Version of the Parable of the Sower in the Gospel of Thomas," *NovT* 21/4 (1979): 326-43.

4:3-20

2107   I. Howard Marshall, "Tradition and Theology in Luke 8:5-15," *TynB* 20 (1969): 56-75.

2108   Francis J. McCool, "The Preacher and the Historical Witness of the Gospels," *TS* 21 (1960): 517-43.

2109   Domenico Ellena, "Thematische Analyse der Wachstumsgleichnisse," *LB* 23/24 (1973): 48-62.

2110   H.-J. Geischer, "Verschwenderische Güte. Versuch über Markus 4,3-9," *EvT* 38 (1978): 418-27.

2111   Gerhard Lohfink, "Das Gleichnis vom Sämann: Mk 4,3-9," *BZ* 30/1 (1986): 36-69.

2112   Gerhard Lohfink, "Die Not der Exegese mit der Reich-Gottes- Verkündigung Jesu," *TQ* 168 (1988): 1-15.

2113   Mary A. Tolbert, "How the Gospel of Mark Builds Character," *Int* 47 (1993): 347-57.

2114   Terence J. Keegan, "The Parable of the Sower and Mark's Jewish Leaders," *CBQ* 56 (1994): 501-18.

4:3-8

2115   William Neil, "Expounding the Parables: II. The Sower (Mark 4:3-8)," *ET* 77 (1965-1966): 74-77.

2116   Joachim Jeremias, "Palästinakundliches zum Gleichnis vom Säemann (Mark. IV.3-8 Par.)," *NTS* 13 (1966-1967): 48-53.

2117   Ulrich Busse, "Der verrückte Bauer: Mk 4,3-8—Gotteserfahrung in der Jesustradition," *K* 29 (1987): 166-75.

2118   Sigfred Pedersen, "Die Gotteserfahrung bei Jesus," *StTheol* 41 (1987): 127-56.

4:3

2119   John Thorley, "Aktionsart in New Testament Greek: Infinitive and Imperative," *NovT* 31 (1989): 290-315.

4:4-7

2120   José O'Callaghan, "Dos vartantes en la parábola del sembrador," *EB* 48 (1990): 267-70.

4:4

2121 H.-W. Bartsch, "Das Thomas-Evangelium und die synoptischen Evangelien. Zu G. Quispel's Bemerkungen zum Thomas-Evangelium," *NTS* 6 (1959-1960): 249-61.

2122 J. A. L. Lee, "Some Features of the Speech of Jesus in Mark's Gospel," *NovT* 27 (1985): 1-26.

4:5-6

2123 Michal Wojciechowski, "Une autre division de Mc 4:5-6," *BibN* 28 (1985): 38.

4:6

2124 Harald Sahlin, "Emendationsvorschläge zum griechischen Text des Neuen Testaments I," *NovT* 24 (1982): 160-79.

4:7

2125 José O'Callaghan, "La Variante 'Ahogaron' en Mt 13,7," *Bib* 68/3 (1987): 402-403.

4:8

2126 Robert K. McIver, "One Hundred-Fold Yield--Miraculous or Mundane? Matthew 13:8,23; Mark 4:8,20; Luke 8:8," *NTS* 40 (1994): 606-608.

4:9

2127 Eric F. F. Bishop, "῎Ακούειν ἀκουέτω: Mark 4:9, 23," *BT* 7 (1956): 38-40.

2128 Clemens Roggenbuck, "Mk 4:9: eine Weck-Formel?" *BibN* 3 (1977): 27-32.

4:10-12

2129 William Manson, "The Purpose of the Parables: A Re-Examination of St. Mark 4:10-12," *ET* 68 (1956-1957): 132-35.

2130 E. F. Siegman, "Teaching in Parables," *CBQ* 23 (1961): 161-81.

2131 Peter Lampe, "Die markinische Deutung des Gleichnisses vom Sämann Markus 4:10-12," *ZNW* 65 (1974): 140-50.

2132 Léopold Sabourin, "The Parables of the Kingdom," *BTB* 6 (1976): 115-60.

2133   J. R. Kirkland, "The Earliest Understanding of Jesus' Use
        of Parables: Mark 4:10-12 in Context," *NovT* 19/1 (1977):
        1-21.

2134   F. C. Synge, "A Plea for the Outsiders: Commentary on
        Mark 4,10-12," *JTSA* 30 (1980): 53-58.

2135   G. K. Falusi, "Jesus' Use of Parables in Mark with Special
        Reference to Mark 4:10-12," *IJT* 31 (1982): 35-46.

2136   Perry V. Kea, "Perceiving the Mystery: Encountering the
        Reticence of Mark's Gospel," *EGLMBS* 4 (1984): 181-94.

2137   Joel Marcus, "Mark 4:10-12 and Markan Epistemology,"
        JBL 103/4 (1984): 557-74.

2138   Vincent Parkin, "Mark Chapter 4:10-12: An Exegesis,"
        IBS 8 (1986): 179-82.

2139   Michael D. Goulder, "Those Outside (Mark 4:10-12),"
        NovT 33 (1991): 289-302.

2140   Chris L. Mearns, "Parables, Secrecy and Eschatology in
        Mark's Gospel," *SJT* 44 (1991): 423-42.

4:10-11

2141   Angelo Lancellotti, "La Casa Pietro a Cafarnao nel
        Vangeli Sinottici: Redazione e Tradizione," *Ant* 58/1
        (1983): 48-69.

2142   Jack T. Sanders, "The Criterion of Coherence and the
        Randomness of Charisma: Poring Through Some Aporias
        in the Jesus Tradition," *NTS* 44 (1998): 1-25.

4:10

2143   Ernest Best, "Mark's Use of the Twelve," *ZNW* 69/1-2
        (1978): 11-35.

2144   Philippe Rolland, "L'arrière-lond sémitique des évangiles
        synoptiques," *ETL* 60 (1984): 358-62.

4:11-12

2145   Günter Haufe, "Erwägungen zum Ursprung der
        sogenannten Parabeltheorie Markus 4,11-12," *EvT* 32
        (1972): 413-21.

2146   Michel Hubaut, "Le 'mystère' révélé dans les paraboles
        (Mc 4,11-12)," *RTL* 5 (1974): 454-61.

4:11

2147 W. von Loewenich, "Luther und die Gleichnistheorie von Mc 4,11s," *TLZ* 77 (1952): 483-88.

2148 J. Arthur Baird, "A Pragmatic Approach to Parable Exegesis: Some New Evidence on Mark 4:11, 33-34," *JBL* 76 (1957): 201-207.

2149 Béda Rigaux, "Révélation des mystères et perfection à Qumran et dans le Nouveau Testament," *NTS* 4 (1957-1958): 237-62.

2150 Klaus Haacker, "Erwägungen zu Mc IV,11," *NovT* 14/3 (1972): 219-25.

2151 Schuyler Brown, "The Secret of the Kingdom of God," *JBL* 92/1 (1973): 60-74.

2152 Rudolph Obermüller, "Hablar de la revelación según el Nuevo Testamento: Un estudio terminológico," *RevB* 39 (1977): 117-27.

2153 Robert Hill, "Synoptic 'basileia' and Pauline 'mysterion'," *EB* 45/3-4 (1987): 309-24.

4:12

2154 C. H. Peisker, "Konsekutives ἵνα in Markus 4:12," *ZNW* 59 (1968): 126-27.

2155 Craig A. Evans, "A Note on the Function of Isaiah, vi,9-10 in Mark, iv," *RB* 88 (1981): 234-35.

2156 Kazimierz Romaniuk, "Exégèse du Noveau Testament et Ponctuation," *NovT* 23/3 (1981): 195-209.

2157 Michal Wojciechowski, "Sur hina dans Mc 4:12," *BibN* 28 (1985): 36-37.

4:13-20

2158 Félix Casá, "Parabolas y catequesis," *RevB* 38 (1976): 97-111.

2159 Meinrad Limbeck, "Hindernisse fürs Christsein: Zur Verkündigung des Markusevangeliums," *BL* 64 (1991): 164-68.

4:13

2160   Juan Mateos, "Algunas notas sobre el Evangelio de Marcos (part 1," *FilN* 3 (1989): 197-204; 159-66.

4:14-20

2161   Francis J. McCool, "The Preacher and the Historical Witness of the Gospels," *TS* 21 (1960): 517-43.

4:15

2162   Herman Ljungvik, "Översättningsförslag och språkliga förklingar till skilde ställen i Nya Testamentet," *SEÅ* 30 (1965): 102-20.

2163   Harald Sahlin, "Emendationsvorschläge zum griechischen Text des Neuen Testaments I," *NovT* 24 (1982): 160-79.

4:20

2164   Robert K. McIver, "One Hundred-Fold Yield--Miraculous or Mundane? Matthew 13:8,23; Mark 4:8,20; Luke 8:8," *NTS* 40 (1994): 606-608.

4:21

2165   J. M. Bover, " 'Nada hay encubierto que no se descubra' (Mc 4,21 par)," *EB* 13 (1954): 319-23.

2166   W. G. Essame, "Καὶ ἔλεγεν in Mark 4:21, 24, 26, 30," *ET* 77 (1965-1966): 121.

2167   Gerhard Schneider, "Das Bildwort von der Lampe. Zur Traditionsgeschichte eines Jesus-Wortes," *ZNW* 61 (1970): 183-209.

4:22-24

2168   José O'Callaghan, "Posible identificación de P^{44} C *recto* b como Mc 4,22-24," *Bib* 52 (1971): 398-400.

4:23

2169   Eric F. F. Bishop, " 'Ακούειν ἀκουέτω: Mark 4:9, 23," *BT* 7 (1956): 38-40.

4:24-34

2170   A. Marcello Buscemi, "La prolessi nel Nuovo Testamento," *SBFLA* 35 (1985): 37-68.

4:24-29

2171   Franz Mußner, "Gleichnisauslegung und Heilsgeschichte. Dargetan am Gleichnis von der wachsenden Saat (Mc 4,24-29)," *TTZ* 64 (1955): 257-66.

2172   Michael McCormick, "Two Leaves from the Lost Uncial Codex 0167: Mark 4:24-29 and 4:37-41," *ZNW* 70/3-4 (1979): 238-42.

4:24-25

2173   Howard A. Hatton, "Unraveling the Agents and Events," *BT* 37/4 (1986): 417-20.

4:24

2174   Léon Vaganay, "Existe-t-il chez Marc quelques traces du Sermon sur la Montagne?" *NTS* 1 (1954-1955): 193-200.

2175   W. G. Essame, "Καὶ ἔλεγεν in Mark 4:21, 24, 26, 30," *ET* 77 (1965-1966): 121.

2176   H. P. Rüger, " 'Mit welchem Mass ihr meßt, wird euch gemessen werden'," *ZNW* 6 (1969): 174-82.

2177   J. B. Bauer, "Et Adicietur Vobis Credentibus Mark 4,24f.," *ZNW* 71/3-4 (1980): 248-51.

2178   C. Buzzetti, "Parallels in the Synoptic Gospels: A Case Study," *BT* 34 (1984): 425-31.

4:25

2179   Paul Glaue, "Einige Stellen: die Bedeutung des Codex D charakterisieren," *NovT* 2 (1957-1958): 310-15.

2180   Juan Mateos, "Algunas notas sobre el Evangelio de Marcos," *FilN* 3 (1990): 159-66.

4:26-34

2181   Jacques Dupont, "Deux paraboles du Royaume. Mc 4,26-34," *AsSeign* 2/42 (1970): 50-59.

4:26-32

2182   Nils A. Dahl, "Parables of Growth," *StTheol* 5 (1951): 132-66.

4:26-30

2183   Jacques Dupont, " 'Le royaume des cieux est semblable à . . .'," *BibO* 6 (1964): 247-53.

4:26-29

2184 Jacques Dupont, "La parabole de la semence qui pousse toute seule (Marc 4,26-29)," *RechSR* 55 (1967): 367-92.

2185 Rainer Stuhlmann, "Beobachtungen und Überlegungen zu Markus IV.26-29," *NTS* 19/2 (1972-1973): 153-62.

2186 Domenico Ellena, "Thematische Analyse der Wachstumsgleichnisse," *LB* 23/24 (1973): 48-62.

2187 Harald Sahlin, "Zum Verständnis der christologischen Anschauung des Markusevangeliums," *StTheol* 31 (1977): 1-19.

2188 Claude N. Pavur, "The Grain is Ripe: Parabolic Meaning in Mark 4:26-29," *BTB* 17/1 (1987): 21-23.

2189 J. D. M. Derrett, "Ambivalence: Sowing and Reaping at Mark 4,26-29," *EB* 48 (1990): 489-510.

2190 George Aichele, "Two Theories of Translation with Examples from the Gospel of Mark," *JSNT* 47 (1992): 95-116.

2191 Gerd Theissen, "Der Bauer und die von selbst Frucht bringende Erde: Naiver Synergismus in Mk 4,26-29?" *ZNW* 85 (1994): 167-82.

2192 A. Strobel, "Zum Motiv der selbstwachsenden Saat (Markus 4.26-29)," *BibN* 100 (1999): 34-35.

4:26

2193 W. G. Essame, "Καὶ ἔλεγεν in Mark 4:21, 24, 26, 30," *ET* 77 (1965-1966): 121.

4:28

2194 E. J. Vardaman, "The Earliest Fragments of the New Testament," *ET* 83 (1971-1972): 374-76.

2195 Maurice Baillet, "Les manuscrits de la Grotte 7 de Qumrân et le Nouveau Testament," *Bib* 53 (1972): 508-16.

2196 Pierre Benoit, "Note sur les fragments grecs de la grotte 7 de Qumrân," *RB* 79 (1972): 321-24.

2197 Eugene Fisher, "New Testament Documents among the Dead Sea Scrolls?" *BibTo* 61 (1972): 835-41.

2198   José O'Callaghan, "Notas sobre 7Q tomadas en el 'Rockefeller Museum' de Jerusalém," *Bib* 53 (1972): 517-33.

2199   C. H. Roberts, "On Some Presumed Papyrus Fragments of the New Testament from Qumran," *JTS* 23 (1972): 446-47.

2200   Léopold Sabourin, "A Fragment of Mark at Qumran?" *BTB* 2 (1972): 308-12.

4:30-32

2201   Otto Kuss, "Zur Senfkorn-Parabel," *TGl* 41 (1951): 40-46.

2202   Ernst Fuchs, "Was wird in der Exegese des Neuen Testaments interpretiert?" *ZTK* 56 (1959): 31-48.

2203   Otto Kuss, "Zum Sinngehalt des Doppelgleichnisses vom Senfkorn und Sauerteig," *Bib* 40 (1959): 641-53.

2204   Franz Mußner, "1QHodajoth und das Gleichnis vom Senfkorn (Mk 4:30-32 Par)," *BZ* 4/1 (1960): 128-30.

2205   Jacques Dupont, "Les paraboles du sénevé et du levain," *NRT* 89 (1967): 897-913.

2206   H.-P. Hertzsch, "Jésus herméneute. Une étude de Mc 4,30-32," *FV* 70 (1971): 109-16.

2207   Domenico Ellena, "Thematische Analyse der Wachstumsgleichnisse," *LB* 23/24 (1973): 48-62.

2208   Robert W. Funk, "The Looking-Glass Tree Is for the Birds. Ezekiel 17:22-24; Mark 4:30-32," *Int* 27 (1973): 3-9.

2209   Alberto Casalegno, "La parabola del granello di senape (Mc. 4,30-32)," *RBib* 26 (1978): 139-61.

2210   Olof Linton, "Coordinated Sayings and Parables in the Synoptic Gospels: Analysis versus Theories," *NTS* 26 (1979-1980): 139-63.

2211   Giuseppe Pace, "La senapa del vangelo," *BibO* 22 (1980): 119-23.

2212   John A. Sproule, "The Problem of the Mustard Seed," *GTJ* 1/1 (1980): 37-42.

2213   Richard J. Bauckham, "The Parable of the Vine: Rediscovering a Lost Parable of Jesus," *NTS* 33/1 (1987): 84-101.

4:30

2214   H.-W. Bartsch, "Eine bisher übersehene Zitierung der LXX in Mark 4,30," *TZ* 15 (1959): 126-28.

2215   W. G. Essame, "Καὶ ἔλεγεν in Mark 4:21, 24, 26, 30," *ET* 77 (1965-1966): 121.

4:32

2216   Martin J. Higgins, "New Testament Result Clauses with Infinitive," *CBQ* 23 (1961): 233-41.

4:33-34

2217   J. Arthur Baird, "A Pragmatic Approach to Parable Exegesis: Some New Evidence on Mark 4:11, 33-34," *JBL* 76 (1957): 201-207.

4:35-8:30

2218   L. F. Rivera, "La liberación en el éxodo. El éxodo de Marcos y la revelación del líder (4,35-8,30)," *RevB* 33 (1971): 13-26.

4:35-8:26

2219   Paul J. Achtemeier, "Toward the Isolation of Pre-Markan Miracle Catenae," *JBL* 89/3 (1970): 265-91.

2220   Paul J. Achtemeier, "The Origin and Function of the Pre-Marcan Miracle Catenae," *JBL* 91 (1972): 198-221.

4:35-8:21

2221   Ched Myers, "The Miracle of One Loaf," *Soj* 16 (1987): 31-34.

4:35-5:43

2222   K. M. Fisher and Urban C. Von Wahlde, "The Miracles of Mark 4:35-5:43: Their Meaning and Function in the Gospel Framework," *BTB* 11/1 (1981): 13-16.

2223   F. Mosetto, "I miracoli di Gesù prima del vangelo di Marco: 'Chi è costui'?" *PV* 27 (1982): 187-207.

2224   Mark McVann, "Baptism, Miracles, and Boundary Jumping in Mark," *BTB* 21 (1991): 151-57.

4:35-5:20

2225   Eugene A. LaVerdiere, "Journey to the Gentiles," *Emmanuel* 94 (1988): 554-61.

4:35-41

2226 Eric F. F. Bishop, "Jesus and the Lake," *CBQ* 13 (1951): 398-414.

2227 Paul J. Achtemeier, "Person and Deed: Jesus and the Storm-Tossed Sea," *Int* 16 (1962): 169-76.

2228 G. Schille, "Die Seesturmerzählung Markus 4:35-41 als Beispiel neutestamentlicher Aktualisierung," *ZNW* 56 (1965): 30-40.

2229 Ferdinand Staudinger, "Die neutestamentlichen Wunder in der Verkündigung," *ErAu* 44 (1968): 355-66.

2230 Paul Lamarche, "La tempête apaisée," *AsSeign* 43 (1969): 43-53.

2231 T. M. Suriano, " 'Who Then Is This?' . . . Jesus Masters the Sea," *BibTo* 79 (1975): 449-56.

2232 F. C. Synge, "A Matter of Tenses—Fingerprints of an Annotator in Mark," *ET* 88 (1976-1977): 168-71.

2233 George M. Soares-Prabhu, "And There Was a Great Calm: A 'Dhvani' Reading of the Stilling of the Storm (Mark 4,35-41)," *BB* 5 (1979): 295-308.

2234 Albert Fuchs, "Die 'Seesturmperikope' Mk. 4:35-41 par im Wandel der urkirchlichen Verkündigung," *SNTU-A* 15 (1990): 101-33.

2235 Meinrad Limbeck, "Hindernisse fürs Christein: Zur Verkündigung des Markusevangeliums," *BL* 64 (1991): 164-68.

2236 William F. McInerny, "An Unresolved Question in the Gospel Called Mark: 'Who Is This Whom Even Wind and Sea Obey'?" *PRS* 23 (1996): 255-68.

4:35-39

2237 Pamela Thimmes, "The Biblical Sea-Storm Type-Scene: A Proposal," *EGLMBS* 10 (1990): 107-22.

4:36

2238 Philippe Rolland, "L'arrière-lond sémitique des évangiles synoptiques," *ETL* 60 (1984): 358-62.

2239 Karl F. Ulrichs, " '. . . und viele miteinander waren bei ihm': Ein textkritischer und formgeschichtlicher Vorschlag zu Mk 4:36b," *ZNW* 88 (1997): 187-96.

4:37-41

2240 Michael McCormick, "Two Leaves from the Lost Uncial Codex 0167: Mark 4:24-29 and 4:37-41," *ZNW* 70/3-4 (1979): 238-42.

4:37

2241 George D. Kilpatrick, "The Order of Some Noun and Adjective Phrases in the New Testament," *NovT* 5 (1962): 111-14.

4:38

2242 Rainer Riesner, "Das Boot vom See Gennesaret," *BK* 41 (1986): 135-38.

4:39

2243 Lino Cignelli, "La grecità biblica," *SBFLA* 35 (1985): 203-48.

4:40

2244 J. B. Bauer, "Procellam cur sedarit Salvator," *VD* 35 (1957): 89-96.

5:1-43

2245 Helge K. Nielsen, "Ein Beitrag zur Beurteilung der Tradition über die Heilungstätigkeit," *SNTU-A* 4 (1979): 5-26.

2246 Gail R. O'Day, "Hope beyond Brokenness. A Markan Reflection on the Gift of Life," *CThM* 15 (1988): 244-51.

5:1-21

2247 Tullio Aurelio, "Mistero del regno e unione con Gesù: Mc 5:1-21," *BibO* 19 (1977): 59-68.

5:1-20

2248 T. Hawthorn, "The Gerasene Demoniac: A Diagnosis (Marc 5:1-20 and Luke 8:26-39)," *ET* 66 (1954-1955): 79-80.

2249 J. P. Louw, "De bezetene en de kudde, Marc. 5:1-20. Een hypothese," *NedTT* 13 (1958): 59-61.

2250 Harald Sahlin, "Die Perikope vom gerasenischen Besessenen und der Plan des Markusevangeliums," *StTheol* 18 (1964): 159-72.

2251 Paul Lamarche, "Le possédé de Gérasa," *NRT* 90 (1968): 581-97.

2252 John Bligh, "The Gerasene Demoniac and the Resurrection of Christ," *CBQ* 31 (1969): 383-90.

2253 Cyrille Argebti, "A Meditation on Mark 5:1-20," EcumRev 23 (1971): 398-408.

2254 Léopold Sabourin, "The Miracles of Jesus (II). Jesus and the Evil Powers," *BTB* 4 (1974): 115-75.

2255 J. González Faus, "Jesus y los demonios: Intróducción cristológica a la lucha por la justicia," *EE* 52 (1977): 487-519.

2256 J. D. M. Derrett, "Contributions to the Study of the Gerasene Demoniac," *JSNT* 3 (1979): 2-17.

2257 Sjef van Tilborg, "Het strukturalisme binnen de exegese: een variant van het burgerlijke denken," *Bij* 40 (1979): 364-79.

2258 Georges Casalis, "Jesús, el exorcista," *BibFe* 6 (1980): 28-40.

2259 Pierre Guillemette, "La Forme des Récits d'Exorcisme de Bultmann: Un Dogme a Reconsiderer," *ÉgT* 11/2 (1980): 177-93.

2260 Ulrich B. Müller, "Zur Rezeption gesetzeskritischer Jesusüberlieferung im Frühen Christentum," *NTS* 27/2 (1980-1981): 158-85.

2261 Andrea Strus, "Cristo, Liberatore Dell'Uomo, Nella Catechesi di Pietro, Secondo Mc 5:1-20," *Sale* 44/1 (1982): 35-60.

2262 Peter Pimentel, "The 'Unclean Spirits' of St. Mark's Gospel," *ET* 99 (1987-1988): 173-75.

2263 Carol S. LaHurd, "Reader Response to Ritual Elements in Mark 5:1-20," *BTB* 20 (1990): 154-60.

2264 Gregory Murray, "Five Gospel Miracles," *DR* 108 (1990): 79-90.

2265   Eric K. Wefald, "The Separate Gentile Mission in Mark: A Narrative Explanation of Markan Geography, the Two Feeding Accounts and Exorcisms," *JSNT* 60 (1995): 3-26.

2266   Donald H. Juel, "Plundering Satan's House: Mark 5:1-20," *WW* 17 (1997): 278-81.

5:1-12

2267   Alois Stöger, "Sohn Gottes im Markusevangelium (II). Meditation," *BL* 49 (1976): 112-15.

5:2-20

2268   Juan Mateos, "Términos relacionados con 'Légion' en Mc 5:2-20," *FilN* 1 (1988): 211-16.

5:7-8

2269   R. Trevijano Etcheverría, "El trasfondo apocalípticode Mc. 1,24.25; 5,7.8 y par.," *Bur* 11 (1970): 117-33.

5:7

2270   T. A. Burkill, "Concerning Mark 5:7 and 5:18-20," *StTheol* 11 (1957): 159-66.

2271   Otto Bächli, " 'Was habe ich mit dir zu schaffen?' Eine formelhafte Frage im Alten Testament und Neuen Testament," *TZ* 33 (1977): 69-80.

5:10

2272   Günther Schwarz, " 'Aus der Gegend' (Markus v.10)," *NTS* 22 (1975-1976): 214-15.

5:13

2273   Kamila Blessing, "Call not Unclean: The Pigs in the Story of the Legion of Demons," *EGLMBS* 10 (1990): 92-106.

5:18-20

2274   T. A. Burkill, "Concerning Mark 5:7 and 5:18-20," *StTheol* 11 (1957): 159-66.

5:18

2275   M. Ebner, "Im Schatten der Grossen. Kleine Erzählfiguren im Markusevangelium," *BZ* 44 (2000): 56-76.

5:20

2276   S. Thomas Parker, "The Decapolis Reviewed," *JBL* 94 (1975): 437-41.

5:21-6:1

2277   Gerald West, "Constructing Critical and Contextual Readings with Ordinary Readers: Mark 5:21-6:1," *JTSA* 92 (1995): 60-69.

5:21-43

2278   Jean Potin, "Guérison d'une hémorroisse et résurrection de la fille de Jaïre. Mc 5,21-43," *AsSeign* 44 (1969): 38-47.

2279   Liliane Dambrine, "Guérison de la femme hémorroïsse et résurrection de la fille de Jaïre. Un aspect de la lecture d'un texte: Mc 5:21-43; Mt 9:18-26; Lc 8:40-56," *FV* 70 (1971): 75-81.

2280   Léopold Sabourin, "The Miracles of Jesus (III): Healings, Resuscitations, Nature Miracles," *BTB* 5 (1975): 146-200.

2281   J. D. M. Derrett, "Mark's Technique: The Haemorrhaging Woman and Jairus' Daughter," *Bib* 63/4 (1982): 474-505.

2282   Vincenzo Scippa, "Ricerche preliminari per uno studio su Mc 5,21-43 secondo la Redaktionsgeschichte," *RBib* 31 (1983): 385-404.

2283   James R. Edwards, "Markan Sandwiches: The Significance of Interpolations in Markan Narratives," *NovT* 31 (1989): 193-216.

2284   Eugene A. LaVerdiere, "Women in the New Israel," *Emmanuel* 95 (1989): 34-41, 56.

2285   Liz L. McCloskey, "Hearing and Healing Hedda Nussbaum: A Reflection on Mark 5:21-43," *CC* 106 (1989): 178-79.

2286   Lone Fatum, "En kvindehistorie om tro og køn," *DTT* 53 (1990): 278-99.

2287   Gregory Murray, "Five Gospel Miracles," *DR* 108 (1990): 79-90.

2288   Tom Shepherd, "Intercalation in Mark and the Synoptic Problem," *SBLSP* 30 (1991): 687-97.

5:22-43

2289   F. C. Synge, "A Matter of Tenses—Fingerprints of an Annotator in Mark," *ET* 88 (1976-1977): 168-71.

2290   Dominique Hermant, "La femme au flux de sang et la fille de Jaïre (Mt 9,18-26; Mc 5,22-43; Lc 8,41-56)," *BLOS* 5 (1990): 8-16.

5:22-24

2291   Jean Martucci, "Les récits de miracle: influence des récits de l'Ancien Testament sur ceux du Nouveau," *SE* 27 (1975): 133-46.

5:22

2292   Rudolf Pesch, "Jarïus (Mk 5:22/Lk 8:41)," *BZ* 14/2 (1970): 252-56.

5:24-34

2293   Vernon K. Robbins, "The Woman Who Touched Jesus' Garment: Socio-rhetorical Analysis of the Synoptic Accounts," *NTS* 33 (1987): 502-15.

2294   Mary A. Beavis, "Women as Models of Faith in Mark," *BTB* 18 (1988): 3-9.

2295   Willard M. Swartley, "The Role of Women in Mark's Gospel: A Narrative Analysis," *BTB* 27 (1997): 16-22.

5:25-34

2296   Marla J. Selvidge, "Mark 5:25-34 and Leviticus 15:19-20: A Reaction to Restrictive Purity Regulations," *JBL* 103 (1984): 619-23.

2297   Jean Delorme, "Jésus et l'hémorroïsse ou le choc de la rencontre (Marc 5,25-34)," *SémBib* 44 (1986): 1-17.

2298   Hisako Kinukawa, "The Story of the Hemorrhaging Woman (Mark 5:25-34) Read from a Japanese Feminist Context," *BibInt* 2 (1994): 283-93.

2299   W. R. G. Loader, "Challenged at the Boundaries: A Conservative Jesus in Mark's Tradition," *JSNT* 63 (1996): 45-61.

5:30

2300   Robert H. Thouless, "Miracles and Physical Research," *Theology* 72 (1969): 253-58.

2301   A. Marcello Buscemi, "La prolessi nel Nuovo Testamento," *SBFLA* 35 (1985): 37-68.

5:33

2302   Harald Sahlin, "Emendationsvorschläge zum griechischen
        Text des Neuen Testaments I," *NovT* 24 (1982): 160-79.

5:33-43

2303   Jean Martucci, "Les récits de miracle: influence des récits
        de l'Ancien Testament sur ceux du Nouveau," *SE* 27
        (1975): 133-46.

5:34

2304   Georg Braumann, "Die Schuldner und die Sünderin Luk.
        VII.36-50," *NTS* 10/4 (1963-1964): 487-93.

5:35-42

2305   S. M. Reynolds, "The Zero Tense in Greek: A Critical
        Note," *WTJ* 32 (1969): 68-72.

5:39

2306   R. E. Ker, "St. Mark v.39," *ET* 65 (1953-1954): 315-16; 66
        (1954-1955): 125.

2307   W. Powell, "St. Mark v,39," *ET* 66 (1954-1955): 61, 215.

5:41

2308   Enrique López-Dóriga, "Y cogiendo la mano de la niña le
        dice: Talitha koumi (Mc 5,41). Nota exegético-filológica,"
        EE 39 (1964): 377-81.

5:42

2309   Jeremy Moiser, " 'She Was Twelve Years Old' (Mark
        5.42): A Note on Jewish-Gentile Controversy in Mark's
        Gospel," *IBS* 3 (1981): 179-86.

2310   Frank England, "Afterthought: An Excuse or an
        Opportunity?" *JTSA* 92 (1995): 56-59.

6

2311   Erdmann Schott, "Die Aussendungsrede Mt 10. Mc 6. Lc
        9. 10," *ZNW* 7 (1906): 140-150.

6:1-8

2312   Michael D. Goulder, "Mark 6:1-8 and Parallels," *NTS* 24/2
        (1977-1978): 235-40.

6:1-6

2313   Erich Grässer, "Jesus in Nazareth (Mark 6:1-6a): Notes on the Redaction and Theology of St. Mark," *NTS* 16 (1969-1970): 1-23.

2314   David Hill, "The Rejection of Jesus at Nazareth: Luke 4:16-30," *NovT* 13/3 (1971): 161-80.

2315   John D. Crossan, "Mark and the Relatives of Jesus," *NovT* 15 (1973): 81-113.

2316   Charles Perrot, "Jésus à Nazareth. Mc 6,1-6," *AsSeign* 45 (1974): 40-49.

2317   Martin Avanzo, "María en las primeras tradiciones evangelicas," *RevB* 38 (1976): 49-57.

2318   R. L. Sturch, "The 'Πατρίς' of Jesus," *JTS* 28 (1977): 94-96.

2319   Bernhard Mayer, "Überlieferungs-und Redaktions-geschichtliche Überlegungen zu Mk 6,1-6a," *BZ* 22/2 (1978): 187-98.

2320   Bertrand Buby, "A Christology of Relationship in Mark," *BTB* 10/4 (1980): 149-54.

2321   Eugene A. LaVerdiere, "Jesus' Native Place and the Apostolic Mission," *Emmanuel* 95 (1989): 74-79.

6:2-7

2322   Michael D. Goulder, "On Putting Q to the Test," *NTS* 24 (1977-1978): 218-34.

2323   Christopher M. Tuckett, "On the Relationship between Matthew and Luke," *NTS* 30 (1984): 130-42.

6:3-44

2324   Joseph Knackstedt, "De duplici miraculo multiplicationis panum," *VD* 41 (1963): 39-51, 140-53.

6:3

2325   Alexander Jones, "Reflections on a Recent Dispute," *Scr* 8 (1956): 13-22.

2326   Richard A. Batey, "Is Not This the Carpenter?" *NTS* 30 (1984): 249-58.

6:4

2327   Brian A. Mastin, " 'Jesus Said Grace'," *SJT* 24 (1971): 449-56.

2328   J. B. Bauer, "Das 'Regelwort' Mk 6,4par und EvThom 31," *BZ* NS 41 (1997): 95-98.

6:6-13

2329   John Bradshaw, "Oral Transmission and Human Memory," *ET* 92 (1980-1981): 303-307.

2330   Dale C. Allison, "The Pauline Epistles and the Synoptic Gospels: The Pattern of the Parallels," *NTS* 28/1 (1982): 1-32.

2331   J. D. M. Derrett, "Peace, Sandals and Shirts," *HeyJ* 24 (1983): 253-65.

2332   Eugene A. LaVerdiere, "The Apostolic Mission: A New Exodus," *Emmanuel* 95 (1989): 138-44.

2333   Elian Cuvillier, "Coopération interprétative et questionnement du lecteur dans le récit d'envoi en mission," *RHPR* 76 (1996): 139-55.

6:6

2334   Philippe Rolland, "Le sommaire de Marc 6,6b et l'envoi des Douze en mission," *BLOS* 5 (1990): 21-23.

6:7-13:30

2335   Lucien Cerfaux, "La mission de Galilée dans la tradition synoptique," *ETL* 27 (1951): 369-89; 28 (1952): 629-47.

6:7-30

2336   James R. Edwards, "Markan Sandwiches: The Significance of Interpolations in Markan Narratives," *NovT* 31 (1989): 193-216.

6:7-13

2337   Rudolf Schnackenburg, "Zur formgeschichtlichen Methode in der Evangelienforschung," *ZKT* 85 (1963): 16-32.

2338   Jean Delorme, "La mission des Douze en Galilée. Mc 6,7-13," *AsSeign* 46 (1974): 43-50.

2339   James Donaldson, " 'Called to Follow': A Twofold Experience of Discipleship in Mark," *BTB* 5 (1975): 67-77.

2340   Gregory Murray, "Did Luke Use Mark?" *DR* 104 (1986): 268-71.

6:7-12

2341   Eugene A. LaVerdiere, "Take Nothing on the Journey," *Emmanuel* 91 (1985): 382-85.

6:7

2342   Ernest Best, "Mark's Use of the Twelve," *ZNW* 69/1-2 (1978): 11-35.

6:10-11

2343   John Thorley, "Aktionsart in New Testament Greek: Infinitive and Imperative," *NovT* 31 (1989): 290-315.

6:10

2344   G. M. Lee, "Two Notes on St. Mark," *NovT* 18/1 (1976): 36.

6:11

2345   George B. Caird, "Uncomfortable Words: II. Shake Off the Dust from Your Feet," *ET* 81/2 (1969-1970): 40-43.

2346   Édouard Delebecque, "Secouez la Poussière de vos Pieds . . . sur l'Hellénisme de Luc IX,5," *RB* 89/2 (1982): 177-84.

6:12-13

2347   A. R. C. Leaney, "Dominical Authority for the Ministry of Healing," *ET* 65 (1953-1954): 121-23.

6:14-8:30

2348   Frank J. Matera, "The Incomprehension of the Disciples and Peter's Confession (Mark 6,14-8,30)," *Bib* 70/2 (1989): 153-72.

6:14-29

2349   Alice Bach, "Calling the Shots: Directing Salomé's Dance of Death," *Semeia* 74 (1996): 103-26.

2350   Jean Delorme, "John The Baptist's Head--The Word
        Perverted: A Reading of a Narrative (Mark 6:14-29),"
        Semeia 81 (1998): 115-29.

6:14-22

2351   Jacob Jervell, "Herodes Antipas og hans plass i evangelie-
        overleveringen," *NTT* 61 (1960): 28-40.

2352   Joseph B. Tyson, "Jesus and Herod Antipas," *JBL* 79
        (1960): 239-46.

2353   K.-S. Krieger, "Die Herodianer im Markusevangelium:
        Ein Versuch ihrer Identifizierung," *BibN* 59 (1991): 49-56.

6:14-16

2354   Johannes M. Nützel, "Zum Schicksal der eschatologischen
        Propheten," *BZ* 20 (1976): 59-94.

2355   Eugene A. LaVerdiere, "Herod and John the Baptizer,"
        Emmanuel 95 (1989): 202-208.

2356   Frans Neirynck, "Marc 6:14-16 et par.," *ETL* 65/1 (1989):
        105-109.

2357   S. J. Nortjé, "John the Baptist and the Resurrection
        Traditions in the Gospels," *Neo* 23 (1989): 349-58.

2358   Philippe Rolland, "La question synoptique demande-t-elle
        une réponse compliquée?" *Bib* 70/2 (1989): 217-23.

6:14-15

2359   Richard A. Horsley, "Like One of the Prophets of Old:
        Two Types of Popular Prophets at the Time of Jesus,"
        CBQ 47 (1985): 435-63.

6:14

2360   G. Schille, "Prolegomena zur Jesusfrage," *TLZ* 93 (1968):
        481-88.

2361   Sasagu Arai, "Zum 'Tempelwort' Jesu in
        Apostelgeschichte 6:14," *NTS* 34/3 (1988): 397-410.

2362   Frans Neirynck, "ΚΑΙ ΕΛΕΓΟΝ en Mc 6,14," *ETL* 65/1
        (1989): 110-18.

6:16

2363   Heinrich Greeven, "Erwägungen zur synoptischen
        Textkritik," *NTS* 6 (1959-1960): 282-96.

6:17-29

2364   I. de la Potterie, "Mors Johannis Baptistae (Mc 6,17-29)," *VD* 44 (1966): 142-51.

2365   Diego A. Losada, "La muerte de Juan el Bautista. Mc 6,17-29," *RevB* 39 (1977): 143-54.

2366   Eugene A. LaVerdiere, "The Death of John the Baptizer," *Emmanuel* 95 (1989): 374-81, 402.

2367   Jennifer A. Glancy, "Unveiling Masculinity: The Construction of Gender in Mark 6:17-29," *BibInt* 2 (1994): 34-50.

6:17-25

2368   E. W. Deibler, "Translating from Basic Structure," *BT* 19 (1968): 14-16.

6:17-20

2369   George Aichele, "Two Theories of Translation with Examples from the Gospel of Mark," *JSNT* 47 (1992): 95-116.

6:17

2370   Willem S. Vorster, "Concerning Semantics, Grammatical Analysis, and Bible Translation," *Neo* 8 (1974): 21-41.

6:18

2371   Paul Ellingworth, "Translating Parallel Passages in the Gospels," *BT* 34 (1983): 401-407.

2372   Lino Cignelli, "La grecità biblica," *SBFLA* 35 (1985): 203-48.

6:20

2373   David A. Black, "The Text of Mark 6:20," *NTS* 34/1 (1988): 141-45.

2374   Kazimierz Romaniuk, "Eporei ou epoiei en Mc 6,20?" *ETL* 69 (1993): 140-41.

6:21-29

2375   Frédéric Manns, "Marc 6,21-29 à la lumière des dernières fouilles du Machéronte," *SBFLA* 31 (1981): 287-90.

6:22

2376   William Lillie, "Salome or Herodias," *ET* 65 (1953-1954):
         251.

2377   J. M. Ross, "The 'Harder Reading' in Textual Criticism,"
         BT 33 (1982): 138-39.

6:30-8:27

2378   A.-M. Denis, "Une théologie de la vie chrétienne chez
         saint Marc (VI,30-VIII,27)," *VS* 41 (1959): 416-27.

6:30-8:26

2379   Corina Combet-Galland, "Analyse structurale de Marc
         6,30 à 8,26," *FV* 77 (1978): 34-46.

6:30-8:21

2380   F. C. Synge, "Common Bread. The Craftsmanship of a
         Theologian," *Theology* 75 (1972): 131-35.

6:30-7:30

2381   P.-É. Bonnard, "La méthode historico-critique appliquée
         à Marc 6,30 à 7,30," *FV* 77 (1978): 6-18.

6:30-46

2382   R. Trevijano Etcheverría, "Crisis mesiánica en la
         multiplicacion de los panes (Mc 6,30-46 y Jn 6,1-15)," *Bur*
         16 (1974): 413-39.

2383   R. Trevijano Etcheverría, "La multiplicación de los panes
         (Mc 6,30-46; 8,1-10 y par.)," *Bur* 15 (1974): 435-65.

2384   Jean Martucci, "Les récits de miracle: influence des récits
         de l'Ancien Testament sur ceux du Nouveau," *SE* 27
         (1975): 133-46.

6:30-45

2385   Andreas Pangritz, "Die Speisung der Fünftausend:
         Anmerkungen zu Markus 6:30-45," *TextK* 6 (1979): 5-40.

6:30-44

2386   Austin M. Farrer, "Loaves and Thousands," *JTS* 4 (1953):
         1-14.

2387   Jean Levie, "L'évangile araméen de S. Matthieu est-il la source de l'évangile de S. Marc?" *NRT* 76 (1954): 689-715, 812-43.

2388   Georg Ziener, "Die Brotwunder im Markusevangelium," *BZ* 4 (1960): 282-85.

2389   E. Schuyler English, "A Neglected Miracle," *BSac* 126 (1969): 300-305.

2390   Jean-Marie van Cangh, "Le thème des poissons dans les récits évangéliques de la multiplication des pains," *RB* 78 (1971): 71-83.

2391   T. M. Suriano, "Eucharist Reveals Jesus: The Multiplication of the Loaves," *BibTo* 58 (1972): 642-51.

2392   R. Trevijano Etcheverría, "Historia de milagro y cristolo gía en la multiplicacion de los panes," *Bur* 17 (1976): 9-38.

2393   Lamar Williamson, "An Exposition of Mark 6:30-44," *Int* 30 (1976): 169-73.

2394   Giuseppe Pace, "La prima moltiplicazione dei pani. Topografia," *BibO* 21 (1979): 85-91.

2395   Sarrae Masuda, "The Good News of the Miracle of the Bread: The Tradition and Its Markan Redaction," *NTS* 28 (1982): 191-219.

2396   Donald P. Senior, "The Eucharist in Mark: Mission, Reconciliation, Hope," *BTB* 12 (1982): 67-72.

2397   Ulrich H. J. Körtner, "Das Fischmotiv im Speisungswunder," *ZNW* 75/1 (1984): 24-35.

2398   Fritz Neugebauer, "Die wunderbare Speisung (Mk 6:30-44 parr) und Jesu Identität," *KD* 32/4 (1986): 254-77.

2399   A. G. Van Aarde, "Die wonderbaarlike vermeerdering van brood (Matt 14:13-21 en par): Historiese kritiek in perspektief," *HTS* 42 (1986): 229-56.

2400   Eric K. Wefald, "The Separate Gentile Mission in Mark: A Narrative Explanation of Markan Geography, the Two Feeding Accounts and Exorcisms," *JSNT* 60 (1995): 3-26.

6:30-34

2401 Jean Delorme, "Jésus, les apôtres et la foule: Mc 6,30-34," *AsSeign* 2/47 (1970): 44-58.

2402 Frans Neirynck, "The Matthew-Luke Agreements in Matthew 14:13-14 and Luke 9:10-11: The Two-Source Theory behind the Impasse," *ETL* 60/1 (1984): 25-44.

2403 Michael Pettem, "Le premier récit de la multiplication des pains et le problème synoptique," *SR* 14/1 (1985): 73-83.

6:30-32

2404 Elian Cuvillier, "Coopération interprétative et questionnement du lecteur dans le récit d'envoi en mission," *RHPR* 76 (1996): 139-55.

6:30

2405 Hugh W. Montefiore, "Revolt in the Desert? (Mark 6:30ff.)," *NTS* 8 (1961-1962): 135-41.

2406 Giuseppe Frizzi, "L'ἀπόστολος delle tradizioni sinottiche (Mc, Q, Mt, Lc. e Atti)," *RBib* 22 (1974): 3-37.

2407 P.-É. Bonnard, "La méthode historico-critique appliquée à Marc 6,30 à 7,30," *FV* 77 (1978): 6-18.

6:31-46

2408 Edwin K. Broadhead, "Linguistics and Christology: A Critical Note on Mark 6:31,32-46," *ABR* 42 (1994): 69-70.

6:31-44

2409 Gerhard Friedrich, "Die beiden Erzählungen von der Speisung in Mark 6,31-44; 8,1-9," *TZ* 20 (1964): 10-22.

6:31

2410 Lino Cignelli, "La grecità biblica," *SBFLA* 35 (1985): 203-48.

6:32-15:47

2411 Morton Smith, "Mark 6:32-15:47 and John 6:1-19:42," *SBLSP* 8/2 (1978): 281-88.

6:32-56

2412 Siegfried Mendner, "Zum Problem 'Johannes und die Synoptiker'," *NTS* 4 (1957-1958): 282-307.

6:33-38

2413   Philippe Rolland, "L'arrière-lond sémitique des évangiles synoptiques," *ETL* 60 (1984): 358-62.

6:34-44

2414   Alan Richardson, "The Feeding of the Five Thousand: Mark 6:34-44," *Int* 9 (1955): 144-49.

2415   Alkuin Heising, "Exegese und Theologie der alt- und neutestamentlichen Speisewunder," *ZKT* 86 (1964): 80-96.

2416   Alkuin Heising, "Das Kerygma der wunderbaren Fischvermehrung (Mk 6,34-44 parr)," *BibL* 10 (1969): 52-57.

6:34

2417   Ethelbert Stauffer, "Zum apokalyptischen Festmahl in Mk 6,34ff.," *ZNW* 46 (1955): 264-66.

2418   Wilfred Tooley, "The Shepherd and Sheep Image in the Teaching of Jesus," *NovT* 7 (1964-1965): 15-25.

6:35-44

2419   B. M. F. van Iersel, "Die wunderbare Speisung und das Abendmal in der synoptischen Tradition (Mk 6:35-44, 8:1-20)," *NovT* 7/3 (1964-1965): 167-94.

2420   Eugene A. LaVerdiere, "In Hundreds and Fifties," *Emmanuel* 91 (1985): 425-29.

6:37

2421   Joseph A. Grassi, " 'You Yourselves Give Them to Eat': An Easily Forgotten Command of Jesus," *BibTo* 97 (1978): 1704-1709.

6:38

2422   George H. Boobyer, "The Eucharistic Interpretation of the Miracles of the Loaves in St. Mark's Gospel," *JTS* 3 (1952): 161-71.

2423   George H. Boobyer, "The Miracles of the Loaves and the Gentiles in St. Mark's Gospel," *SJT* 6 (1953): 77-87.

2424   Eero Repo, "Fünf Brote und zwei Fische," *SNTU-A* 3 (1978): 99-113.

6:43

2425   J. D. M. Derrett, "Crumbs in Mark," *DR* 102 (1984): 12-21.

6:45-8:26

2426   Vincent K. Pollard, "The 'Lukan Omission' of Mark 6:45-8:26," *BibTo* 29 (1967): 2032-34.

6:45-56

2427   Eugene A. LaVerdiere, "Resisting the Mission to the Nations," *Emmanuel* 96 (1990): 22-28.

6:45-53

2428   Stephen H. Smith, "Bethsaida via Gennesaret: The Enigma of the Sea-Crossing in Mark 6,45-53," *Bib* 77 (1996): 349-74.

6:45-52

2429   Eric F. F. Bishop, "Jesus and the Lake," *CBQ* 13 (1951): 398-414.

2430   Thierry Snoy, "La rédaction marcienne de la marche sur les eaux," *ETL* 44 (1968): 205-41, 433-81.

2431   Jacob Kremer, "Jesu Wandel auf dem See nach Mk 6,45-52. Auslegung und Meditation," *BibL* 10 (1969): 221-32.

2432   Léopold Sabourin, "The Miracles of Jesus (III): Healings, Resuscitations, Nature Miracles," *BTB* 5 (1975): 146-200.

2433   Hubert Ritt, "Der 'Seewandel Jesu' (Mk 6,45-52 Par)," *BZ* 23/1 (1979): 71-84.

2434   Christian Hartlich, "Ist die historisch-kritische Methode überholt?" *Conci* 16 (1980): 534-38.

2435   René Kieffer, "Deux types d'exégèse à base linguistique," *Conci* 15 (1980): 19-28.

2436   Grant R. Osborne, "Round Four: The Redaction Debate Continues," *JETS* 28 (1985): 399-410.

6:45-42

2437   William F. McInerny, "An Unresolved Question in the Gospel Called Mark: 'Who Is This Whom Even Wind and Sea Obey'?" *PRS* 23 (1996): 255-68.

6:45

2438   John O'Hara, "Two Bethsaidas or One?" *Scr* 15 (1963): 24-27.

2439   Wilhelm Wildens, "Die Auslassung von Mark. 6,45 bei Lukas im Lichte der Komposition Luk. 9,1-50," *TZ* 32/4 (1976): 193-200.

6:46

2440   Benny R. Crockett, "The Function of Mathetological Prayer in Mark," *IBS* 10 (1988): 123-39.

6:48

2441   Maurice Baillet, "Les manuscrits de la Grotte 7 de Qumrân et le Nouveau Testament," *Bib* 54 (1973): 340-50.

2442   Pierre Benoit, "Nouvelle Note sur les Fragments Grecs de la Grotte 7 de Qumrân," *RB* 80/1 (1973): 5-12.

2443   Harry T. Fleddermann, " 'And He Wanted to Pass by Them' (Mark 6:48c)," *CBQ* 45/3 (1983): 389-95.

6:49

2444   David Hill, "The Walking on the Water: A Geographical or Linguistic Answer?" *ET* 99 (1987-1988): 267-69.

6:50

2445   Johannes Brinktrine, "Die Selbstaussage Jesu ἐγώ εἰμι," *TGl* 47 (1957): 34-36.

6:51-52

2446   J. Renié, "Une antilogie évangelique (Mc 6,51-52; Mt 14,32-33)," *Bib* 36 (1955): 223-26.

6:52-53

2447   E. J. Vardaman, "The Earliest Fragments of the New Testament," *ET* 83 (1971-1972): 374-76.

2448   Maurice Baillet, "Les manuscrits de la Grotte 7 de Qumrân et le Nouveau Testament," *Bib* 53 (1972): 508-16.

2449   Eugene Fisher, "New Testament Documents among the Dead Sea Scrolls?" *BibTo* 61 (1972): 835-41.

2450   José O'Callaghan, "Notas sobre 7Q tomadas en el 'Rockefeller Museum' de Jerusalén," *Bib* 53 (1972): 517-33.

2451   C. H. Roberts, "On Some Presumed Papyrus Fragments of
        the New Testament from Qumran," *JTS* 23 (1972): 446-47.

2452   Léopold Sabourin, "A Fragment of Mark at Qumran?"
        BTB 2 (1972): 308-12.

2453   Gordon D. Fee, "Some Dissenting Notes on 7Q5 = Mark
        6:52-53," *JBL* 92 (1973): 109-12.

2454   Colin J. Hemer, "A Note on 7Q5," *ZNW* 65 (1974):
        155-57.

2455   Camille Focant, "Un fragment du second évangile à
        Qumrân: 7Q5 = Mc 6,52-53?" *RTL* 16 (1985): 447-54.

2456   Hans-Udo Rosenbaum, "Cave 7Q5! Gegen die erneute
        Inanspruchnahme des Qumran-Fragments 7Q5 als
        Bruchstueck der aeltesten Evangelien-Handschrift," *BZ*
        31/2 (1987): 189-205.

2457   Ferdinand Rohrhirsch, "Das Qumranfragment 7Q5," *NovT*
        30 (1988): 97-99.

2458   José O'Callaghan, "Sobre el papiro de Marcos en
        Qumrán," *FilN* 5 (1992): 191-97.

2459   Carsten P. Thiede, "Greek Qumran Fragment 7Q5:
        Possibilities and Impossibilities," *Bib* 75 (1994): 394-98.

6:53-56

2460   Jozef Verheyden, "Mark 1:32-34 and 6:53-56: Tradition or
        Redaction?" *ETL* 64/4 (1988): 415-28.

6:53

2461   Pierre Benoit, "Note sur les fragments grecs de la grotte 7
        de Qumrân," *RB* 79 (1972): 321-24.

2462   Giovanni Rinaldi, "Traversata del lago e sbarco a
        Genezaret in 'Marco' 6,53," *BibO* 17 (1975): 43-46.

6:55

2463   Harald Sahlin, "Emendationsvorschläge zum griechischen
        Text des Neuen Testaments I," *NovT* 24 (1982): 160-79.

7:1-23

2464   H.-J. Schoeps, "Jesus et la Loi juive," *RHPR* 33 (1953):
        1-20.

2465   A. W. Argyle, " 'Outward' and 'Inward' in Biblical Thought," *ET* 68 (1956-1957): 196-99.

2466   John P. Brown, "Synoptic Parallels in the Epistles and Form-History," *NTS* 10 (1963-1964): 27-48.

2467   Cyril S. Rodd, "Are the Ethics of Jesus Situation Ethics?" *ET* 79 (1967-1968): 167-70.

2468   N. J. McEleney, "Authenticating Criteria and Mark 7:1-23," *CBQ* 34/4 (1972): 431-60.

2469   Hans Hübner, "Mark VII.1-23 und das 'Jüdisch-Hellenistische' Gesetzesverständnis," *NTS* 22/3 (1975-1976): 319-45.

2470   Jan Lambrecht, "Jesus and the Law. An Investigation of Mark 7:1-23," *ETL* 53 (1977): 24-82.

2471   Phillip Sigal, "Matthean Priority in the Light of Mark 7," *EGLMBS* 3 (1983): 76-95.

2472   Andreas Pangritz, "Jesus und das 'System der Unreinheit': oder Fernando Belo die Leviten gelesen," *TextK* 24 (1984): 28-46.

2473   Daniel R. Schwartz, "Viewing the Holy Utensils (P. Ox. V,840)," *NTS* 32 (1986): 153-59.

2474   Michael FitzPatrick, "From Ritual Observance to Ethics: The Argument of Mark 7:1-23," *ABR* 35 (1987): 22-27.

2475   Gregory Murray, "What Defiles a Man?" *DR* 106 (1988): 297-98.

2476   Eugene A. LaVerdiere, "Jesus and the Tradition of the Elders," *Emmanuel* 96 (1990): 278-85.

2477   Eugene A. LaVerdiere, "Tradition, Traditions, and the Word of God," *Emmanuel* 96 (1990): 206-209, 212-16.

2478   Meinrad Limbeck, "Hindernisse fürs Christsein: Zur Verkündigung des Markusevangeliums," *BL* 64 (1991): 164-68.

2479   Elian Cuvillier, "Tradition et rédaction en Marc 7:1-23," *NovT* 34/2 (1992): 169-92.

2480   Gregory Salyer, "Rhetoric, Purity, and Play: Aspects of Mark 7:1-23," *Semeia* 64 (1994): 139-69.

2481   Enrique Nardoni, "Lo puro y lo impuro en Marcos 7:1-23: La respuesta del lector," *RevB* 59 (1997): 135-54.

<u>7:1-8</u>

2482   Rudolf Pesch, "Pur et impur: Précepte humain et commandement divin, Mc 7,1-8, 14-15, 21-23," *AsSeign* 53 (1970): 50-59.

2483   Richard C. Brand, "Clean and Unclean," *ET* 98/1 (1986-1987): 16-17.

<u>7:2</u>

2484   W. Storch, "Zur Perikope von der Syrophonizierin. Mk 7,2 und Ri 1,7," *BZ* 14/2 (1970): 256-57.

2485   J. H. van Halsema, "Het raadsel als literaire vorm in Marcus en Johannes," *GTT* 83/1 (1983): 1-17.

2486   D. Neufeld, "Jesus' Eating Transgressions and Social Impropriety in the Gospel of Mark: A Social Scientific Approach," *BTB* 30 (2000): 15-26.

<u>7:3</u>

2487   P. R. Weis, "A Note on πυγμῇ," *NTS* 3 (1956-1957): 233-36.

2488   S. M. Reynolds, "Πυγμῇ (Mark 7:3) as 'Cupped Hand'," *JBL* 85 (1966): 87-88.

2489   Martin Hengel, "Mc 7:3 πυγμῇ: Die Geschichte einer exegetischen Aporie und der Versuch ihrer Lösung," *ZNW* 60 (1969): 182-98.

2490   S. M. Reynolds, "A Note on Dr. Hengel's Interpretation of *pygmē* in Mark 7:3," *ZNW* 62 (1971): 295-96.

2491   W. D. McHardy, "Mark 7:3: A Reference to the Old Testament?" *ET* 87 (1975-1976): 119.

2492   J. M. Ross, " 'With the Fist'," *ET* 87 (1975-1976): 374-75.

2493   Malcolm Lowe, "Who Were the Ἰουδαῖοι?" *NovT* 18 (1976): 101-30.

2494   T. C. Skeat, "A Note on πυγμῇ in Mark 7:3," *JTS* 41 (1990): 525-27.

7:4

2495   Eric F. F. Bishop, "'Aπ' ἀγορᾶς: Mark vii.4," *ET* 61 (1949-1950): 219.

7:6

2496   Pierre Grelot, "Miche 7,6 dans les evangiles et dans la littrature rabbinique," *Bib* 67/3 (1986): 363-77.

7:8-9

2497   J. A. Smit, "Mark 7:8-9 in Counter-Determining Context," *Neo* 25 (1991): 17-28.

7:9-13

2498   J. D. M. Derrett, "Κορβᾶν, ὅ ἐστιν, Δῶρον," *NTS* 16/4 (1969-1970): 364-68.

7:10

2499   R. Barraclough, "Being Pharisaic Christians. A Study of Mark 7:10b and Matthew 15:41," *IBS* 22 (2000): 2-25.

7:11

2500   Joseph A. Fitzmyer, "The Aramaic Qorbān Inscription from Jebel Hallet el-Ṭûri and Mark 7:11/Matt 15:5," *JBL* 78 (1959): 60-65.

2501   George W. Buchanan, "Some Vow and Oath Formulas in the New Testament," *HTR* 58 (1965): 319-26.

7:14-30

2502   J. I. Hasler, "The Incident of the Syrophoenician Woman (Matt 15:21-28, Mark 7:14-30)," *ET* 45 (1933-1934): 459-61.

7:14-23

2503   Diego A. Losada, "Las parábolas de crecimiento en el evangelio de Marcos," *RevB* 38 (1976): 113-25.

2504   Eugene E. Lemcio, "External Evidence for the Structure and Function of Mark IV.1-20, VII.14-23, and VIII.14-21," *JTS* 29/2 (1978): 323-38.

2505   Richard C. Brand, "Clean and Unclean," *ET* 98/1 (1986-1987): 16-17.

7:14-15

2506   Rudolf Pesch, "Pur et impur: Précepte humain et commandement divin, Mc 7,1-8, 14-15, 21-23," *AsSeign* 53 (1970): 50-59.

7:14

2507   John Thorley, "Aktionsart in New Testament Greek: Infinitive and Imperative," *NovT* 31 (1989): 290-315.

7:15

2508   Harvey K. McArthur, "The Dependence of the Gospel of Thomas on the Synoptics," *ET* 71 (1959-1960): 286-87.

2509   Helmut Merkel, "Markus 7,15—das Jesuswort über die innere Verunreinigung," *ZRGG* 20 (1968): 340-63.

2510   Charles E. Carlston, "The Things that Defile (Mark 7:15) and the Law in Matthew and Mark," *NTS* 15/1 (1968-1969): 75-96.

2511   Jean Domon, "Du texte au sermon: Mc 7,15," *ÉTR* 45 (1970): 349-54.

2512   George D. Kilpatrick, "Jesus, His Family and His Disciples," *JSNT* 15 (1982): 3-19.

2513   Heikki Räisänen, "Jesus and the Food Laws: Reflectings on Mark 7.15," *JSNT* 16 (1982): 79-100.

7:18-19

2514   Harald Sahlin, "Zum Verständnis der christologischen Anschauung des Markusevangeliums," *StTheol* 31 (1977): 1-19.

7:21-23

2515   Rudolf Pesch, "Pur et impur: Précepte humain et commandement divin, Mc 7,1-8, 14-15, 21-23," *AsSeign* 53 (1970): 50-59.

2516   Harald Sahlin, "Emendationsvorschläge zum griechischen Text des Neuen Testaments I," *NovT* 24 (1982): 160-79.

7:22-26

2517   Donato Baldi, "Il problema del sito di Bethsaida e delle moltiplicazioni dei pani," *SBFLA* 10 (1959-1960): 120-46.

7:23-30

2518   Jim Perkinson, "A Canaanitic Word in the Logos of
       Christ; or The Difference the Syro-Phoenician Woman
       Makes to Jesus," *Semeia* 75 (1996): 61-85.

7:24-37

2519   Eugene A. LaVerdiere, "Jesus among the Gentiles,"
       Emmanuel 96 (1990): 338-45.

7:24-31

2520   T. A. Burkill, "The Syrophoenician Woman: The
       Congruence of Mark 7:24-31," *ZNW* 57 (1966): 23-37.

2521   T. A. Burkill, "The Historical Development of the Story of
       the Syrophoenician Woman," *NovT* 9 (1967): 161-77.

2522   Gerard Mussies, "Jesus and 'Sidon' in Matthew 15/Mark
       7," *Bij* 58 (1997): 264-78.

7:24-30

2523   Elmer A. McNamara, "The Syro-Phoenician Woman,"
       AmER 127 (1952): 360-69.

2524   J. Alonso Díaz, "Cuestión sinóptica y universalidad del
       mensaje cristiano en el pasaje evangélico de la mujer
       cananea," *CuBí* 20 (1963): 274-79.

2525   Roy A. Harrisville, "The Woman of Canaan: A Chapter in
       the History of Exegesis," *Int* 20 (1966): 274-87.

2526   P. E. Scherer, "A Gauntlet with a Gift in It: From Text to
       Sermon on Matthew 15:21-28 and Mark 7:24-30," *Int* 20
       (1966): 387-99.

2527   Barnabas Flammer, "Die Syrophoenizerin. Mk 7,24-30,"
       TQ 148 (1968): 463-78. See the English translation, "The
       Syro-Phoenician Woman (Mk 7:24-30)," *TD* 18 (1970):
       19-24.

2528   Léopold Sabourin, "The Miracles of Jesus (II). Jesus and
       the Evil Powers," *BTB* 4 (1974): 115-75.

2529   Alice Dermience, "Tradition et rédaction dans la péricope
       de la Syrophénicienne: Marc 7,24-30," *RTL* 8 (1977):
       15-29.

2530   Balembo Buetubela, "La Syrophénicienne: Mc 7,24-30.
       Étude littéraire et exégétique," *RAfT* 2 (1978): 245-56.

2531   Georges Casalis, "Jesús, el exorcista," *BibFe* 6 (1980): 28-40.

2532   Pierre Guillemette, "La Forme des Récits d'Exorcisme de Bultmann: Un Dogme a Reconsiderer," *ÉgT* 11/2 (1980): 177-93.

2533   Gerd Theissen, "Lokal- und Sozialkolorit in der Geschichte von der Syrophönischen Frau (Mk 7:24-30)," *ZNW* 75/3-4 (1984): 202-25.

2534   Giuseppe Barbaglio, "Gesù e i non ebrei: la sirofenicia," *ParSpirV* 16 (1987): 101-14.

2535   Peter Pimentel, "The 'Unclean Spirits' of St. Mark's Gospel," *ET* 99 (1987-1988): 173-75.

2536   Mary A. Beavis, "Women as Models of Faith in Mark," *BTB* 18 (1988): 3-9.

2537   Francis Dufton, "The Syrophoenician Woman and Her Dogs," *ET* 100 (1988-1989): 417.

2538   David Rhoads, "Jesus and the Syrophoenician Woman in Mark: A Narrative-Critical Study," *JAAR* 62 (1994): 343-75.

2539   Judith M. Gundry-Volf, "Spirit, Mercy, and the Other," *TT* 51 (1995): 508-23.

2540   P. Pokorný, "From a Puppy to the Child: Some Problems of Contemporary Biblical Exegesis Demonstrated from Mark 7:24-30 and Matthew 15:21-28," *NovT* 41 (1995): 321-37.

2541   W. R. G. Loader, "Challenged at the Boundaries: A Conservative Jesus in Mark's Tradition," *JSNT* 63 (1996): 45-61.

2542   Willard M. Swartley, "The Role of Women in Mark's Gospel: A Narrative Analysis," *BTB* 27 (1997): 16-22.

2543   Pierre-Yves Brandt, "De l'usage de la frontière dans la rencontre entre Jésus et la Syrophénicienne," *ÉTR* 74 no 2 (1999): 173-88.

7:26

2544   A. W. Argyle, "Did Jesus Speak Greek?" *ET* 67 (1955-1956): 92-93.

2545 Günther Schwarz, "Συροφοινίκισσα-Χαναναία (Markus 7:26; Matthäus 15:22)," *NTS* 30/4 (1984): 626-28.

2546 R. S. Sugirtharajah, "The Syrophoenician Woman," *ET* 98/1 (1986-1987): 13-15.

2547 J. K. Elliott, "'Ερωτᾶν and ἐπερωτᾶν in the New Testament," *FilN* 2 (1989): 205-206.

7:27-9:1

2548 Ernst Haenchen, "Die Komposition von Mk VII,27-IX,1 und Par.," *NovT* 6 (1963): 81-109.

7:28

2549 M. Ebner, "Im Schatten der Grossen. Kleine Erzählfiguren im Markusevangelium," *BZ* 44 (2000): 56-76.

7:30

2550 P.-É. Bonnard, "La méthode historico-critique appliquée à Marc 6,30 à 7,30," *FV* 77 (1978): 6-18.

7:31-37

2551 Jean Delorme, "Guérison d'un sourd-bègue: Mc 7,31-37," *AsSeign* 2/54 (1972): 33-44.

2552 R. F. Collins, "Jesus' Ministry to the Deaf and Dumb," *MeliT* 35/1 (1984): 12-36.

2553 Mary A. Beavis, "The Trial before the Sanhedrin (Mark 14:53-65): Reader Response and Greco-Roman Readers," *CBQ* 49 (1987): 581-96.

7:31

2554 S. Thomas Parker, "The Decapolis Reviewed," *JBL* 94 (1975): 437-41.

7:34-37

2555 Ulrich B. Müller, "Zur Rezeption gesetzeskritischer Jesusüberlieferung im frühen Christentum," *NTS* 27/2 (1980-1981): 158-85.

7:34

2556 Isaac Rabinowitz, " 'Be Opened' = ephphatha (Mark 7:34): Did Jesus Speak Hebrew?" *ZNW* 53 (1962): 229-38.

2557 Louis Leloir, "Ephphatha," *AsSeign* 65 (1963): 31-41.

2558   Fred L. Horton, "Nochmals Εφφαθα in MK 7:34," *ZNW* 77/1 (1986): 101-108.

7:35

2559   Tom Baird, "Translating Orthō's at Mark 7:35," *ET* 92 (1980-1981): 337-38.

7:36

2560   James W. Leitch, "The Injunctions of Silence in Mark's Gospel," *ET* 66 (1954-1955): 178-82.

8:1-20

2561   B. M. F. van Iersel, "Die wunderbare Speisung und das Abendmal in der synoptischen Tradition (Mk 6:35-44, 8:1-20)," *NovT* 7/3 (1964-1965): 167-94.

8:1-10

2562   Joseph Knackstedt, "De duplici miraculo multiplicationis panum," *VD* 41 (1963): 39-51, 140-53.

2563   Jean-Marie van Cangh, "Le thème des poissons dans les récits évangéliques de la multiplication des pains," *RB* 78 (1971): 71-83.

2564   T. M. Suriano, "Eucharist Reveals Jesus: The Multiplication of the Loaves," *BibTo* 58 (1972): 642-51.

2565   R. Trevijano Etcheverría, "La multiplicación de los panes (Mc 6,30-46; 8,1-10 y par.)," *Bur* 15 (1974): 435-65.

2566   R. Trevijano Etcheverría, "Historia de milagro y cristolo gía en la multiplicacion de los panes," *Bur* 17 (1976): 9-38.

2567   Sarrae Masuda, "The Good News of the Miracle of the Bread: The Tradition and Its Markan Redaction," *NTS* 28 (1982): 191-219.

2568   Donald P. Senior, "The Eucharist in Mark: Mission, Reconciliation, Hope," *BTB* 12 (1982): 67-72.

2569   Eugene A. LaVerdiere, "The Evening of the Third Day," *Emmanuel* 91 (1985): 502-507.

2570   Eric K. Wefald, "The Separate Gentile Mission in Mark: A Narrative Explanation of Markan Geography, the Two Feeding Accounts and Exorcisms," *JSNT* 60 (1995): 3-26.

<u>8:1-9</u>

2571   Austin M. Farrer, "Loaves and Thousands," *JTS* 4 (1953): 1-14.

2572   Gerhard Friedrich, "Die beiden Erzählungen von der Speisung in Mark 6,31-44; 8,1-9," *TZ* 20 (1964): 10-22.

2573   Alkuin Heising, "Exegese und Theologie der alt- und neutestamentlichen Speisewunder," *ZKT* 86 (1964): 80-96.

2574   E. Schuyler English, "A Neglected Miracle," *BSac* 126 (1969): 300-305.

<u>8:3</u>

2575   Frederick W. Danker, "Mark 8:3," *JBL* 82 (1963): 215-16.

<u>8:4-6</u>

2576   Lars Lode, "Narrative Paragraphs in the Gospels and Acts," *BT* 34/3 (1983): 322-35.

<u>8:6</u>

2577   Brian A. Mastin, " 'Jesus Said Grace'," *SJT* 24 (1971): 449-56.

<u>8:7</u>

2578   Lino Cignelli, "La grecità biblica," *SBFLA* 35 (1985): 203-48.

<u>8:8</u>

2579   J. D. M. Derrett, "Crumbs in Mark," *DR* 102 (1984): 12-21.

<u>8:10-13</u>

2580   Robert Schlarb, "Die Suche nach dem Messias: ζητέω als Terminus technicus der markinischen Messianologie," *ZNW* 81 (1990): 155-70.

<u>8:10</u>

2581   F. Pili, "Dalmanutha (Mc 8,10)," *BibO* 13 (1971): 227-30.

2582   Wilhelm Bruners, "'Und fuhr in das Gebiet von Dalmanutha' (Mk 8,10): Begegnung mit einer biblischen Landschaft - ein Tagebuch," *BL* 57 (1984): 200-207.

<u>8:11-26</u>

2583   Eugene A. LaVerdiere, "Who Do You Say That I Am?" *Emmanuel* 96 (1990): 506-509.

8:11-13

2584 Thierry Snoy, "Les miracles dans l'évangile de Marc. Examen de quelques études récentes," *RTL* 3 (1972): 449-66; 4 (1973): 58-101.

2585 Jeffrey B. Gibson, "Jesus' Refusal to Produce a 'Sign' (Mark 8:11-13)," *JSNT* 38 (1990): 37-66.

8:11-12

2586 Olof Linton, "The Demand for a Sign from Heaven (Mk 8,11-12 and Parallels)," *StTheol* 19 (1965): 112-29.

2587 James Swetnam, "No Sign of Jonah," *Bib* 66/1 (1985): 126-30.

2588 Gregory Murray, "The Sign of Jonah," *DR* 107 (1989): 224-25.

8:12-38

2589 Max Meinertz, " 'Dieses Geschlecht' im Neuen Testament," *BZ* 1 (1957): 283-89.

8:12

2590 Gustav Stählin, "Zum Gebrauch von Beteuerungsformeln im Neuen Testament," *NovT* 5 (1962): 115-43.

2591 George W. Buchanan, "Some Vow and Oath Formulas in the New Testament," *HTR* 58 (1965): 319-26.

2592 Dino Merli, "Il segno di Giona," *BibO* 14 (1972): 61-77.

2593 Jeffrey B. Gibson, "Mark 8:12a: Why Does Jesus 'Sigh Deeply'?" *BT* 38/1 (1987): 122-25.

2594 Jeffrey B. Gibson, "Another Look at Why Jesus 'Sighs Deeply': anastenazo in Mark 8:12a," *JTS* NS 47 (1996): 131-40.

8:14-21

2595 Otto Kuss, "Zum Sinngehalt des Doppelgleichnisses vom Senfkorn und Sauerteig," *Bib* 40 (1959): 641-53.

2596 Jindrich Mánek, "Mark viii,14-21," *NovT* 7 (1964-1965): 10-14.

2597 Eugene E. Lemcio, "External Evidence for the Structure and Function of Mark IV.1-20, VII.14-23, and VIII.14-21," *JTS* 29/2 (1978): 323-38.

2598   Norman A. Beck, "Reclaiming a Biblical Text: The Mark 8:14-21 Discussion about Bread in the Boat," *CBQ* 43/1 (1981): 49-56.

2599   Robert M. Fowler, "Thoughts on the History of Reading Mark's Gospel," *EGLMBS* 4 (1984): 120-30.

2600   L. W. Countryman, "How Many Baskets Full? Mark 8:14-21," *CBQ* 47/4 (1985): 643-55.

2601   Jeffrey B. Gibson, "The Rebuke of the Disciples in Mark 8:14-21," *JSNT* 27 (1986): 31-47.

2602   W. Braun, "Were the New Testament Herodians Essenes? A Critique of an Hypothesis," *RevQ* 14 (1989): 75-88.

8:15

2603   Georg Ziener, "Das Bildwort vom Sauerteig Mk 8,15," *TTZ* 67 (1958): 247-48.

2604   Jacob Jervell, "Herodes Antipas og hans plass i evangelie-overleveringen," *NTT* 61 (1960): 28-40.

2605   Athanase Negōitā and C. Daniel, "L'énigme du levain. Ad Mc. viii,15; Mt. xvi,6; et Lc. xii,1," *NovT* 9 (1967): 306-14.

2606   C. L. Mitton, "Leaven," *ET* 84 (1972-1973): 339-43.

2607   K.-S. Krieger, "Die Herodianer im Markusevangelium: Ein Versuch ihrer Identifizierung," *BibN* 59 (1991): 49-56.

8:19-20

2608   J. D. M. Derrett, "Crumbs in Mark," *DR* 102 (1984): 12-21.

8:21

2609   Eugene A. LaVerdiere, " 'Do You Still Not Understand?' Mark 8:21," *Emmanuel* 96 (1990): 382-89, 454-63.

8:22-10:52

2610   Ernest Best, "Discipleship in Mark: Mark 8:22-10:52," *SJT* 23/3 (1970): 323-37.

2611   Ched Myers, "Embracing the Way of Jesus: A Catechism of the Cross," *Soj* 16 (1987): 27-30.

8:22-30

2612 Eugene A. LaVerdiere, "Jesus Christ, the Son of God," *Emmanuel* 96 (1990): 524-26.

8:22-26

2613 R. Beauvery, "La guérison d'un aveugle à Bethsaïde (Mc. 8:22-26)," *NRT* 90/10 (1968): 1083-91.

2614 Earl S. Johnson, "Mark 8:22-26: The Blind Man from Bethsaida," *NTS* 25/3 (1978-1979): 370-83.

2615 J. K. Howard, "Men as Trees, Walking: Mark 8.22-26," *SJT* 37 (1984): 163-70.

2616 Augustine Stock, "Hinge Transitions in Mark's Gospel," *BTB* 15 (1985): 27-31.

2617 J.-F. Collange, "La déroute de L'aveugle (Mc 8,22-26): Écriture et pratique chrétienne," *RHPR* 66/1 (1986): 21-28.

2618 Paolo Neri, "Per guarire il cieco di Betsaida (Mc 8,22-26)," *BibO* 30 (1988): 138.

8:22

2619 John O'Hara, "Two Bethsaidas or One?" *Scr* 15 (1963): 24-27.

8:23

2620 John Ellington, "Mark 8:23," *BT* 34 (1983): 443-44.

8:24

2621 Herman Ljungvik, "Översättningsförslag och språkliga förklingar till skilde ställen i Nya Testamentet," *SEÅ* 30 (1965): 102-20.

2622 G. M. Lee, "Mark viii.24," *NovT* 20/1 (1978): 74.

2623 Juan Mateos, "Algunas notas sobre el Evangelio de Marcos (part 3)," *FilN* 4 (1991): 193-203.

8:25

2624 Joel Marcus, "A Note on Markan Optics," *NTS* 45 (1999): 250-56.

8:26

2625 J. I. Miller, "Was Tischendorf Really Wrong? Mark 8:26b Revisited," *NovT* 28/2 (1986): 97-103.

2626 J. M. Ross, "Another Look at Mark 8:26," *NovT* 29/2 (1987): 97-99.

8:27-10:52

2627 Hejne Simonsen, "Mark 8,27-10,52 i Markusevangeliets komposition," *DTT* 27 (1956): 83-99.

8:27-9:13

2628 René Lafontaine and Pierre M. Beernaert, "Essai sur la structure de Marc, 8,27-9,13," *RechSR* 57 (1969): 543-61.

8:27-9:9

2629 T. F. Glasson, "The Uniqueness of Christ: The New Testament Witness," *EQ* 43 (1971): 25-35.

8:27-9:1

2630 James L. Mays, "An Exposition of Mark 8:27-9:1," *Int* 30/2 (1976): 174-78.

8:27-35

2631 Adelbert Denaux, "La confession de Pierre et la première annonce de la Passion. Mc 8,27-35," *AsSeign* 55 (1974): 31-39.

8:27-33

2632 B. Willaert, "La connexion littéraire entre la premiere prediction de la passion et la confession de Pierre chez les synoptiques," *ETL* 32 (1956): 24-45.

2633 Josef Ernst, "Petrusbekenntnis—Leidensankündigung—Satanswort (Mk 8,27-33). Tradition und Redaktion," *Cath* 32 (1978): 46-73.

2634 Hendrikus Boers, "Reflections on the Gospel of Mark: A Structural Investigation," *SBLSP* 26 (1987): 255-67.

2635 Hans Klein, "Das Bekenntnis des Petrus und die Anfänge des Christusglaubens im Urchristentum," *EvT* 47 (1987): 176-92.

2636 William F. McInerny, "An Unresolved Question in the Gospel Called Mark: 'Who Is This Whom Even Wind and Sea Obey'?" *PRS* 23 (1996): 255-68.

8:27-30

2637   Raymond E. Brown, "Incidents That Are Units in the Synoptic Gospels but Dispersed in St. John," *CBQ* 23 (1961): 143-60.

2638   Rudolf Pesch, "Das Messiasbekenntnis des Petrus (Mk 8,27-30). Neuverhandlung einer alten Frage," *BZ* 17 (1973): 178-95; 18 (1974): 20-31.

2639   Harald Sahlin, "Zum Verständnis der christologischen Anschauung des Markusevangeliums," *StTheol* 31 (1977): 1-19.

2640   Hubert Ordon, "Literacko-teologiczne przygotowanie perykopy o wyznaniu Piotra," *RoczTK* 29 (1982): 97-109.

2641   Léopold Sabourin, "About Jesus' Self-Understanding," *RSB* 3/3 (1983): 129-34.

2642   Lyle D. Vander Broek, "Literary Context in the Gospels," *RR* 39/2 (1986): 113-17.

8:27-29

2643   Kurt Schubert, "Die Juden und die Römer," *BL* 36 (1962): 235-42.

8:27

2644   G. Schille, "Prolegomena zur Jesusfrage," *TLZ* 93 (1968): 481-88.

2645   Harald Sahlin, "Emendationsvorschläge zum griechischen Text des Neuen Testaments I," *NovT* 24 (1982): 160-79.

8:28

2646   Carl H. Kraeling, "Was Jesus Accused of Necromancy?" (Mk 8:28) *JBL* 59 (1940): 147-57.

2647   Athol Gill, "Women Ministers in the Gospel of Mark," *ABR* 35 (1987): 14-21.

2648   S. J. Nortjé, "John the Baptist and the Resurrection Traditions in the Gospels," *Neo* 23 (1989): 349-58.

8:29-9:1

2649   H. P. Hamann, "A Plea for Commonsense in Exegesis," *CTQ* 42 (1978): 115-29.

8:29

    2650   H. Frankemölle, "Judische Messiaserwartung und christlicher Messiasglaube: Hermeneutische Anmerkungen im Kontext des Petrusbekenntnisses Mk 8,29," *K* 20 (1978): 97-109.

8:30

    2651   James W. Leitch, "The Injunctions of Silence in Mark's Gospel," *ET* 66 (1954-1955): 178-82.

8:31-11:10

    2652   C. J. Reedy, "Mark 8:31-11:10 and the Gospel Ending," *CBQ* 34/2 (1972): 188-97.

8:31-39

    2653   Andreas H. Snyman, "Style and Meaning in Romans 8:31-39," *Neo* 18 (1984): 94-103.

8:31-38

    2654   Rudolf Schnackenburg, "Zur formgeschichtlichen Methode in der Evangelienforschung," *ZKT* 85 (1963): 16-32.

8:31-37

    2655   Bruce J. Malina, " 'Let Him Deny Himself' (Mark 8:34 & par): A Social Psychological Model of Self-Denial," *BTB* 24 (1994): 106-19.

8:31-34

    2656   Robert J. Maddox, "The Function of the Son of Man according to the Synoptic Gospels," *NTS* 15 (1968-1969): 45-74.

8:31-33

    2657   Eugene A. LaVerdiere, "First Prophetic Announcement of the Passion," *Emmanuel* 96 (1990): 574-79.

8:31

    2658   J. B. Bauer, "Drei Tage," *Bib* 39 (1958): 354-58.

    2659   Jacques Dupont, "Ressuscité 'le troisième jour'," *Bib* 40 (1959): 742-61.

2660   Georg Strecker, "Die Leidens- und Auferstehungs-
        voraussagen im Markusevangelium (Mk 8,31; 9,31;
        10,32-34)," *ZTK* 64 (1964): 16-39.

2661   I. Howard Marshall, "The Synoptic Son of Man Sayings in
        Recent Discussion," *NTS* 12 (1965-1966): 327-51.

2662   Richard T. France, "The Servant of the Lord in the
        Teaching of Jesus," *TynB* 19 (1968): 26-52.

2663   Joachim Jeremias, "Gesù predice la sua passione: Morte e
        resurrezione (Mc 8,31 par etc.)," *PV* 15 (1970): 81-93.

2664   W. J. Bennett, "The Son of Man," *NovT* 17/2 (1975):
        113-29.

2665   Marcel Bastin, "L'annonce de la passion et les critères de
        l'historicíte," *RevSR* 50 (1976): 289-329; 51 (1977):
        187-213.

2666   Bruce A. Stevens, " 'Why Must the Son of Man Suffer?'
        The Divine Warrior in the Gospel of Mark," *BZ* 31 (1987):
        101-10.

2667   Juan Mateos, "Algunas notas sobre el Evangelio de
        Marcos (part 2)," *FilN* 3 (1990): 159-66.

8:32

2668   George Aichele, "Jesus' Frankness," *Semeia* 69-70 (1995):
        261-80.

8:33

2669   F. Bussby, "Mark viii.33: A Mistranslation from the
        Aramaic?" *ET* 61 (1949-1950): 159.

2670   Tomas Arvedson, "Lärjungaskapets 'demoni'. Några
        reflexioner till Mk 8,33 par.," *SEÅ* 28/29 (1963): 54-63.

8:34-9:1

2671   John P. Brown, "Synoptic Parallels in the Epistles and
        Form-History," *NTS* 10 (1963-1964): 27-48.

2672   Willem S. Vorster, "On Early Christian Communities and
        Theological Perspectives," *JTSA* 59 (1987): 26-34.

8:34-35

2673   J. G. Griffiths, "The Disciple's Cross," *NTS* 16
        (1969-1970): 358-64.

2674   Robert C. Tannehill, "Reading It Whole: The Function of Mark 8:34-35 in Mark's Story," *QR* 2 (1982): 67-78.

8:34

2675   Günther Schwarz, " 'ἀπαρνησάσθω ἑαυτὸν . . . ?' (Markus VIII,34 parr)," *NovT* 17/2 (1975): 109-12.

2676   Günther Schwarz, "Der Nachfolgespruch Markus 8:34b,c parr: Emendation und Rückübersetzung," *NTS* 33/2 (1987): 255-65.

2677   John Thorley, "Aktionsart in New Testament Greek: Infinitive and Imperative," *NovT* 31 (1989): 290-315.

8:35-38

2678   Klaus Berger, "Zu den sogenannten Sätzen heiligen Rechts," *NTS* 17 (1970-1971): 10-40.

2679   Ernest Best, "An Early Sayings Collection," *NovT* 18/1 (1976): 1-16.

8:35

2680   C. H. Dodd, "Some Johannine 'Herrenworte' with Parallels in the Synoptic Gospels," *NTS* 2 (1955-1956): 75-86.

2681   Josef Sudbrack, " 'Wer sein Leben um meinetwillen verliert . . .' (Mk 8,35). Biblische Überlegungen zur Grundlegung christlicher Existenz," *GeistL* 40 (1967): 161-70.

2682   William A. Beardslee, "Saving One's Life by Losing It," *JAAR* 47 (1979): 57-72.

2683   Walter Rebell, " 'Sein Leben verlieren' (Mark 8.35 parr.) als Strukturmoment vor- und nachösterlichen Glaubens," *NTS* 35/2 (1989): 202-18.

8:36

2684   George Howard, "Harmonistic Readings in the Old Syriac Gospels," *HTR* 73 (1980): 473-91.

2685   José O'Callaghan, "Nota crítica a Mc 8,36," *Bib* 64/1 (1983): 116-17.

8:37

2686   M. Herranz Marco, " '¿Que dará el hombre a cambio de su alma?' (Mc 8,37)," *CuBi* 31 (1974): 23-26.

2687   B. Janowski, "Auslösung des verwirkten Lebens: Zur Geschichte und Struktur der biblischen Lösegeldvorstellung," *ZTK* 79 (1982): 25-59.

8:38

2688   Ernst Käsemann, "Sätze heiligen Rechtes im Neuen Testament," *NTS* 1 (1954-1955): 248-60.

2689   H. P. Owen, "The Parousia of Christ in the Synoptic Gospels," *SJT* 12 (1959): 171-92.

2690   George R. Beasley-Murray, "The Parousia in Mark," *RevExp* 75/4 (1978): 565-81.

2691   Barnabas Lindars, "Jesus as Advocate: A Contribution to the Christology Debate," *BJRL* 62/2 (1979-1980): 476-97.

2692   J. M. Ross, "Some Unnoticed Points in the Text of the New Testament," *NovT* 25 (1983): 59-72.

2693   E. A. Obeng, "The 'Son of Man' Motif and the Intercession of Jesus," *AfTJ* 19 (1990): 155-67.

2694   Paul Hoffmann, "Der Menschensohn in Lukas 12:8," *NTS* 44 (1998): 357-79.

9:1-8

2695   Markus Öhler, "Die Verklärung (Mk 9:1-8): Die Ankunft der Herrschaft Gottes auf der Erde," *NovT* 38 (1996): 197-217.

9:1

2696   Stephen S. Smalley, "The Delay of the Parousia," *JBL* 83 (1964): 41-54.

2697   Norman Perrin, "The Composition of Mark ix,1," *NovT* 11 (1969): 67-70.

2698   Charles L. Holman, "The Idea of an Imminent Parousia in the Synoptic Gospels," *SBT* 3 (1973): 15-31.

2699   Ian A. Moir, "The Reading of Codex Bezae (D-05) at Mark 9:1," *NTS* 20 (1973-1974): 105.

2700 Heinrich Greeven, "Nochmals Mk IX.1 in Codex Bezae," *NTS* 23/3 (1976-1977): 305-308.

2701 Kent E. Brower, "Mark 9:1: Seeing the Kingdom in Power," *JSNT* 6 (1980): 17-41.

2702 Enrique Nardoni, "A Redactional Interpretation of Mark 9:1," *CBQ* 43/3 (1981): 365-84.

2703 Barry S. Crawford, "Near Expectation in the Sayings of Jesus," *JBL* 101/2 (1982): 225-44.

2704 Dietfried Gewalt, "1 Thess 4,15-17; 1 Kor 15,51 und Mk 9,1: Zur Abgrenzung eines 'Herrenwortes'," *LB* 51 (1982): 105-13.

2705 John J. Kilgallen, "Mark 9:1: The Conclusion of a Pericope," *Bib* 63/1 (1982): 81-83.

2706 Heinz Giesen, "Mk 9,1—ein Wort Jesu über die nahe Parusie?" *TTZ* 92 (1983): 134-48.

2707 Robert H. Smith, "Wounded Lion: Mark 9:1 and Other Missing Pieces," *CThM* 11/6 (1984): 333-49.

2708 David R. Jackson, "The Priority of the Son of Man Sayings," *WTJ* 47 (1985): 83-96.

2709 David Wenham and A. D. A. Moses, " 'There Are Some Standing Here . . .': Did They Become the 'Reputed Pillars' of the Jerusalem Church? Some Reflections on Mark 9:1, Galatians 2:9 and the Transfiguration," *NovT* 36 (1994): 146-63.

9:2-13

2710 Charles Masson, "La transfiguration de Jesus (Marc 9:2-13)," *RTP* 97 (1964): 1-14.

2711 Sigfred Pedersen, "Die Proklamation Jesu als des eschatologischen Offenbarungsträgers," *NovT* 17 (1975): 241-64.

9:2-10

2712 Michel Coune, "Radieuse Transfiguration. Mt 17,1-9; Mc 9,2-10; Lc 9,28-36," *AsSeign* 15 (1973): 44-84.

9:2-9

2713 Ernst L. Schnellbächer, "Sachgemässe Schriftauslegung," *NovT* 30 (1988): 114-31.

2714   Paul S. Berge, "The Beginning of the Good News: The
        Epiphany Gospels in Mark and John," *WW* 17 (1997):
        94-101.

9:2-8

2715   George B. Caird, "The Transfiguration," *ET* 67
        (1955-1956): 291-94.

2716   Anthony Kenny, "The Transfiguration and the Agony in
        the Garden," *CBQ* 19 (1957): 444-52.

2717   André Feuillet, "Les perspectives propres à chaque
        évangéliste dans les récits de la transfiguration," *Bib* 39
        (1958): 281-301.

2718   S. Lewis Johnson, "The Transfiguration of Christ," *BSac*
        124 (1967): 133-43.

2719   Robert H. Stein, "Is the Transfiguration a Misplaced
        Resurrection Account?" *JBL* 95/1 (1976): 79-96.

2720   Bruce D. Chilton, "The Transfiguration: Dominical
        Assurance and Apostolic Vision," *NTS* 27/1 (1980-1981):
        115-24.

2721   James M. Robinson, "Jesus: From Easter to Valentinus (or
        the Apostles' Creed)," *JBL* 101 (1982): 5-37.

2722   Walter Wink, "Mark 9:2-8," *Int* 36/1 (1982): 63-67.

2723   Gerald O'Collins, "Luminous Appearances of the Risen
        Christ," *CBQ* 46 (1984): 247-54.

2724   Jean Galot, "Révélation du Christ et liturgie juive," *EV* 98
        (1988): 145-52.

2725   Jürgen Seim, "Offenbarung: Predigt über Markus 9.2-8,"
        EvT 50 (1990): 275-78.

2726   A. del Agua Pérez, "The Narrative of the Transfiguration
        as a Derashic Scenification of a Faith Confession," *NTS* 39
        (1993): 340-54.

9:2-3

2727   L. F. Rivera, "El misterio del Hijo del Hombre en la
        transfiguración (Mr 9,2-3)," *RevB* 28 (1966): 19-34, 79-89.

9:2

2728 Wolfgang Gerber, "Die Metamorphose Jesu, Mark. 9,2f. par.," *TZ* 23 (1967): 385-95.

2729 Foster R. McCurley, " 'And After Six Days' (Mark 9:2): A Semitic Literary Device," *JBL* 93/1 (1974): 67-81.

2730 Ernst L. Schnellbächer, "Καὶ μετὰ ἡμέρας ἓξ (Markus 9:2)," *ZNW* 71/3 (1980): 252-57.

2731 Jean Galot, "La prima professione di fede cristiana," *CC* 132 (1981): 27-40.

9:4

2732 D. Baly, "The Transfiguration Story," *ET* 82 (1970-1971): 82-83.

2733 Jeremy Moiser, "Moses and Elijah," *ET* 96 (1984-1985): 216-17.

2734 John P. Heil, "A Note on 'Elijah with Moses' in Mark 9,4," *Bib* 80 (1999): 115.

9:5-7

2735 J. D. M. Derrett, "Peter and the Tabernacles," *DR* 108 (1990): 37-48.

9:5

2736 Paul Ellingworth, "How Is Your Handbook Wearing?" *BT* 30 (1979): 236-41.

2737 José O'Callaghan, "Discussio Critica en Mt 17,4," *Bib* 65/1 (1984): 91-93.

2738 Benedict T. Viviano, "Rabbouni and Mark 9:5," *RB* 97 (1990): 207-18.

9:7

2739 W. Dekker, "De 'geliefde Zoon' in de synoptische evangeliën," *NTT* 16 (1961-1962): 94-106.

2740 P. G. Bretscher, "Exodus 4:22-23 and the Voice from Heaven," *JBL* 87 (1968): 301-11.

2741 Michael D. Goulder, "On Putting Q to the Test," *NTS* 24 (1977-1978): 218-34.

2742 Alfredo Scattolon, "L'ἀγαπητός sinottico nella luce della tradizione giudaica," *RBib* 26 (1978): 3-32.

2743 Christopher M. Tuckett, "On the Relationship between Matthew and Luke," *NTS* 30 (1984): 130-42.

9:8

2744 Nigel M. Watson, "Willi Marxsen's Approach to Christology," *ET* 97 (1985-1986): 36-42.

9:9-13

2745 Matthew Black, "The Theological Appropriation of the Old Testament by the New Testament," *SJT* 39/1 (1986): 1-17.

9:9-12

2746 Robert J. Maddox, "The Function of the Son of Man according to the Synoptic Gospels," *NTS* 15 (1968-1969): 45-74.

9:9

2747 James W. Leitch, "The Injunctions of Silence in Mark's Gospel," *ET* 66 (1954-1955): 178-82.

9:11-13

2748 Percy J. Heawood, "Mark ix.11-13," *ET* 64 (1952-1953): 239.

2749 C. C. Oke, "The Rearrangement and Transmission of Mark ix.11-13," *ET* 64 (1952-1953): 187-88.

2750 Johannes M. Nützel, "Zum Schicksal der eschatologischen Propheten," *BZ* 20 (1976): 59-94.

2751 Joseph A. Fitzmyer, "More about Elijah Coming First," *JBL* 104 (1985): 295-96.

2752 Joel Marcus, "Mark 9:11-13: 'As It Has Been Written'," *ZNW* 80/1 (1989): 42-63.

2753 Justin Taylor, "The Coming of Elijah, Mt 17,10-13 and Mk 9,11-13: The Development of the Texts," *RB* 98 (1991): 107-19.

9:11

2754 Dale C. Allison, "Elijah Must Come First," *JBL* 103 (1984): 256-58.

9:12-13

2755   J. D. M. Derrett, "Herod's Oath and the Baptist's Head (With an Appendix on Mk IX.12-13, Mal III.24, Micah VII.6)," *BZ* 9 (1965): 49-59, 233-46.

9:12

2756   J. Neville Birdsall, "The Withering of the Fig Tree," *ET* 73 (1961-1962): 191.

2757   Richard T. France, "The Servant of the Lord in the Teaching of Jesus," *TynB* 19 (1968): 26-52.

2758   W. J. Bennett, "The Son of Man," *NovT* 17/2 (1975): 113-29.

2759   W. C. Kaiser, "The Promise of the Arrival of Elijah in Malachi and the Gospels," *GTJ* 3/2 (1982): 221-33.

9:13

2760   S. J. Nortjé, "John the Baptist and the Resurrection Traditions in the Gospels," *Neo* 23 (1989): 349-58.

9:14-29

2761   Jean Levie, "L'évangile araméen de S. Matthieu est-il la source de l'évangile de S. Marc?" *NRT* 76 (1954): 689-715, 812-43.

2762   Harald Riesenfeld, "De fientlige andarna (Mk 9:14-29)," *SEÅ* 22/23 (1957): 64-74.

2763   Wolfgang Schenk, "Tradition und Redaktion in der Epileptiker-perikope, Mk 9:14-29," *ZNW* 63 (1972): 76-94.

2764   Paul J. Achtemeier, "Miracles and the Historical Jesus: A Study of Mark 9:14-29," *CBQ* 37/4 (1975): 471-91.

2765   Gerhard Barth, "Glaube und Zweifel in den synoptischen Evangelien," *ZTK* 72 (1975): 269-92.

2766   Gerd Petzke, "Die historische Frage nach den Wundertaten Jesu: Dargestellt am Beispiel des Exorzismus Mark. ix. 14-29 par," *NTS* 22 (1975-1976): 180-204.

2767   J. González Faus, "Jesus y los demonios: Intróducción cristológica a la lucha por la justicia," *EE* 52 (1977): 487-519.

2768   Hermann Aichinger, "Zur Traditionsgeschichte der Epileptiker- Perikope Mk 9,14-29 par Mt 17,14-21 par Lk 9,37-43a," *SNTU-A* 3 (1978): 114-43.

2769   H. D. Betz, "The Early Christian Miracle Story: Some Observations on the Form Critical Problem," *Semeia* 11 (1978): 69-81.

2770   Georges Casalis, "Jesús, el exorcista," *BibFe* 6 (1980): 28-40.

2771   R. F. Collins, "Jesus' Ministry to the Deaf and Dumb," *MeliT* 35/1 (1984): 12-36.

2772   Peter Pimentel, "The 'Unclean Spirits' of St. Mark's Gospel," *ET* 99 (1987-1988): 173-75.

2773   Gail R. O'Day, "Hope beyond Brokenness. A Markan Reflection on the Gift of Life," *CThM* 15 (1988): 244-51.

2774   Meinrad Limbeck, "Hindernisse fürs Christsein: Zur Verkündigung des Markusevangeliums," *BL* 64 (1991): 164-68.

2775   Gregory E. Sterling, "Jesus as Exorcist: An Analysis of Matthew 17:14-20; Mark 9:14-29; Luke 9:37-43a," *CBQ* 55 (1993): 467-93.

9:14-27

2776   Philippe Rolland, "La guérison de l'enfant épileptique," *BLOS* 5 (1990): 3-7.

9:14-19

2777   Dominique Stein, "Une lecture psychanalytique de la Bible," *RSPT* 72 (1988): 95-108.

9:14-17

2778   Pierre Guillemette, "La Forme des Récits d'Exorcisme de Bultmann: Un Dogme a Reconsiderer," *ÉgT* 11/2 (1980): 177-93.

9:17-27

2779   Paul Ellingworth, "How Is Your Handbook Wearing?" *BT* 30 (1979): 236-41.

9:24

2780   Rolf J. Erler, "Eine kleine Beobachtung an Karl Barths Lebensweg mit den Menschen 'ganz unten': 'Ich glaube, lieber Herr, hilf meinem Unglauben' (Mk 9:24)," *EvT* 47 (1987): 166-70.

9:26

2781   Martin J. Higgins, "New Testament Result Clauses with Infinitive," *CBQ* 23 (1961): 233-41.

9:28-29

2782   Benny R. Crockett, "The Function of Mathetological Prayer in Mark," *IBS* 10 (1988): 123-39.

9:30-37

2783   Jean Brière, "Le Fils de l'homme livré aux hommes. Mc 9,30-37," *AsSeign* 56 (1974): 42-52.

2784   Paul J. Achtemeier, "An Exposition of Mark 9:30-37," *Int* 30/2 (1976): 178-83.

9:30-32

2785   Dominique Hermant, "La deuxième annonce de la Passion (Histoire du texte)," *BLOS* 1 (1989): 14-18.

9:30

2786   Jean-Marie van Cangh, "La Galilée dans l'évangile de Marc: un lieu théologique?" *RB* 79 (1972): 59-75.

9:31

2787   Jacques Dupont, "Ressuscité 'le troisième jour'," *Bib* 40 (1959): 742-61.

2788   Georg Strecker, "Die Leidens- und Auferstehungs-voraussagen im Markusevangelium (Mk 8,31; 9,31; 10,32-34)," *ZTK* 64 (1964): 16-39.

2789   Richard T. France, "The Servant of the Lord in the Teaching of Jesus," *TynB* 19 (1968): 26-52.

2790   Matthew Black, "The 'Son of Man' Passion Sayings in the Gospel Tradition," *ZNW* 60 (1969): 1-8.

2791   Marcel Bastin, "L'annonce de la passion et les critères de l'historicíte," *RevSR* 50 (1976): 289-329; 51 (1977): 187-213.

9:33-50

2792   Léon Vaganay, "Le schématisme du discours
        communautaire à la lumière de la critique des sources," *RB*
        60 (1953): 203-44.

2793   Jean Levie, "L'évangile araméen de S. Matthieu est-il la
        source de l'évangile de S. Marc?" *NRT* 76 (1954):
        689-715, 812-43.

2794   B. C. Butler, "M. Vagarnay and the 'Community
        Discourse'," *NTS* 1 (1954-1955): 283-90.

2795   Harry T. Fleddermann, "The Discipleship Discourse
        (Mark 9:33-50)," *CBQ* 43/1 (1981): 57-75.

2796   Dale C. Allison, "The Pauline Epistles and the Synoptic
        Gospels: The Pattern of the Parallels," *NTS* 28/1 (1982):
        1-32.

2797   Christopher M. Tuckett, "Paul and the Synoptic Mission
        Discourse?" *ETL* 60 (1984): 376-81.

2798   Urban C. Von Wahlde, "Mark 9:33-50: Discipleship: The
        Authority That Serves," *BZ* 29/1 (1985): 49-67.

9:33-42

2799   David Wenham, "A Note on Mark 9:33-42/Matt.
        18:1-6/Luke 9:46-50," *JSNT* 14 (1982): 113-18.

9:33-41

2800   David R. Catchpole, "The Poor on Earth and the Son of
        Man in Heaven: A Reappraisal of Matthew 25:31-46,"
        BJRL 61/2 (1978-1979): 355-97.

2801   M. S. Hostetler, "The Development of Meaning,"
        Theology 82 (1979): 251-59.

9:33-37

2802   Gustav Kafka, "Bild und Wort in den Evangelien," *MTZ*
        2 (1951): 263-87.

2803   Simon Légasse, "L'exercice de l'autorité dans l'Église
        d'après les évangiles synoptiques," *NRT* 85 (1963):
        1009-22.

2804   Rudolf Schnackenburg, "Zur formgeschichtlichen
        Methode in der Evangelienforschung," *ZKT* 85 (1963):
        16-32.

2805   Andrea Strus, "Mc. 9,33-37. Problema dell'autenticità e dell' interpretazione," *RBib* Supp. 20 (1972): 589-619.

2806   J. G. Inrig, "Called to Serve: Toward a Philosophy of Ministry," *BSac* 140 (1983): 335-49.

2807   Vernon K. Robbins, "Pronouncement Stories and Jesus' Blessing of Children: A Rhetorical Approach," *Semeia* 29 (1983): 43-74.

2808   Dominique Hermant, "La première scène d'enfants (Mt 18,1-5; Mc 9,33-37; Lc 9,46-48)," *BLOS* 3 (1990): 7-11.

9:33-34

2809   George D. Kilpatrick, "Διαλέγεσθαι and διαλογίζεσθαι in the New Testament," *JTS* 11 (1960): 338-40.

2810   Tjitze Baarda, "To the Roots of the Syriac Diatessaron Tradition," *NovT* 28 (1986): 1-25.

9:33

2811   Angelo Lancellotti, "La Casa Pietro a Cafarnao nel Vangeli Sinottici: Redazione e Tradizione," *Ant* 58/1 (1983): 48-69.

9:35

2812   Ernest Best, "Mark's Use of the Twelve," *ZNW* 69/1-2 (1978): 11-35.

2813   Vernon K. Robbins, "Picking Up the Fragments: From Crossan's Analysis to Rhetorical Analysis," *Forum* 1 (1985): 31-64.

9:36

2814   Philippe Rolland, "Préliminaires à la première multiplication des pains," *BLOS* 3 (1990): 12-18.

9:37-42

2815   Ernest Best, "An Early Sayings Collection," *NovT* 18/1 (1976): 1-16.

9:37-41

2816   John P. Brown, "Synoptic Parallels in the Epistles and Form-History," *NTS* 10 (1963-1964): 27-48.

9:37-39

2817 A. Calmet, "Pour nous Contre nous? Marc 9,37-39," *BVC* 79 (1968): 52-53.

9:37

2818 C. H. Dodd, "Some Johannine 'Herrenworte' with Parallels in the Synoptic Gospels," *NTS* 2 (1955-1956): 75-86.

2819 Eugene E. Lemcio, "The Unifying Kerygma of the New Testament," *JSNT* 33 (1988): 3-17.

9:38-48

2820 Jean Delorme, "Jésus enseigne ses disciples: Mc 9,38-48," *AsSeign* 2/57 (1971): 53-62.

9:38-40

2821 E. A. Russell, "A Plea for Tolerance (Mk 9.38-40)," *IBS* 8 (1986): 154-60.

2822 X. Pikaza, "Exorcismo, poder y evangelio: Trasfondo histórico y eclesial de Mc 9,38-40," *EB* 57 no 1-4 (1999): 539-64.

9:38-39

2823 Jacques Schlosser, "L'exorciste étranger," *RevSR* 56 (1982): 229-39.

9:38

2824 William G. Morrice, "Translating the Greek Imperative," *BT* 24 (1973): 129-34.

2825 J. M. Ross, "Some Unnoticed Points in the Text of the New Testament," *NovT* 25 (1983): 59-72.

9:40

2826 E. M. Sidebottom, "The So-Called Divine Passive in the Gospel Tradition," *ET* 87 (1975-1976): 200-204.

2827 Heinrich Baltensweiler, "'Wer nicht gegen uns (euch) ist, ist für uns (euch)!' Bemerkungen zu Mk 9,40 und Lk 9,50," *TZ* 40 (1984): 130-36.

2828 Vernon K. Robbins, "Picking Up the Fragments: From Crossan's Analysis to Rhetorical Analysis," *Forum* 1 (1985): 31-64.

2829   Alfonso de la Fuente, "A favor o en contra de Jesús: El logión de Mc 9,40 y sus paralelos," *EB* 53 (1995): 449-59.

9:41

2830   James H. Smylie, "Uncle Tom's Cabin Revisited: The Bible, the Romantic Imagination and the Sympathies of Christ," *Int* 27/1 (1973): 67-85.

9:42-10:12

2831   Will Deming, "Mark 9:42-10:12, Matthew 5:27-32, and b. Nid, 13b: A First Century Discussion of Male Sexuality," *NTS* 36/1 (1990): 130-41.

9:42-50

2832   Gustav Kafka, "Bild und Wort in den Evangelien," *MTZ* 2 (1951): 263-87.

2833   J. D. M. Derrett, "Salted with Fire," *Theology* 76 (1973): 364-68.

9:42

2834   George Howard, "Harmonistic Readings in the Old Syriac Gospels," *HTR* 73 (1980): 473-91.

2835   Lars Lode, "The Presentation of New Information," *BT* 35 (1984): 101-108.

2836   J. D. M. Derrett, "μύλος ὀνικὸς (Mk 9,42 Par)," *ZNW* 76/3 (1985): 284.

2837   J. D. M. Derrett, "Two Harsh Sayings of Christ Explained," *DR* 103 (1985): 218-29.

9:43-47

2838   C. L. Mitton, "Threefoldness in the Teaching of Jesus," *ET* 75 (1963-1964): 228-30.

2839   Helmut Koester, "Mark 9:43-47 and Quintilian 8.3.75," *HTR* 71 (1978): 151-53.

2840   J. P. Meyer, "The Debate on the Resurrection of the Dead: An Incident from the Ministry of the Historical Jesus?" *JSNT* 77 (2000): 3-24.

9:43

2841   Hildebrecht Hommel, "Herrenworte im Lichte sokratischer Überlieferung," *ZNW* 57 (1966): 1-23.

9:44-46

2842   J. M. Ross, "Some Unnoticed Points in the Text of the New Testament," *NovT* 25 (1983): 59-72.

9:49-50

2843   Wolfgang Nauck, "Salt as a Metaphor in Instructions for Discipleship," *StTheol* 6 (1952): 165-78.

9:49

2844   Oscar Cullmann, "Que signifie le sel dans la parabole de Jésus (Mc 9,49s par.)," *RHPR* 37 (1957): 36-43.

2845   Tjitze Baarda, "Mark 9:49," *NTS* 5 (1958-1959): 318-21.

2846   Heinrich Zimmermann, " 'Mit Feuer gesalzen werden': Eine Studie zu Mk 9:49," *TQ* 139 (1959): 28-39.

2847   Günther Schwarz, "πᾶς πυρὶ ἁλισθήσεται," *BibN* 11 (1980): 45.

2848   Weston W. Fields, " 'Everyone Will Be Salted With Fire' (Mark 9:49)," *GTJ* 6/2 (1985): 299-304.

9:50

2849   J. B. Bauer, "Quod si sal infatuatum fuerit," *VD* 29 (1951): 228-30.

2850   Günther Schwarz, "Καλὸν τὸ ἅλας," *BibN* 7 (1978): 32-35.

2851   Michael Lattke, "Salz der Freundschaft in Mk 9,50c," *ZNW* 75/1 (1984): 44-59.

2852   Sigvard Hellestam, "Mysteriet med saltet," *SEÅ* 55 (1990): 59-63.

10:1-16

2853   Paul T. Eckel, "Mark 10:1-16," *Int* 42/3 (1988): 285-91.

10:1-12

2854   Rainer Riesner, "Wie sicher ist die Zwei-Quellen-Theorie?" *TBe* 8 (1977): 49-73.

2855   A.-L. Descamps, "Les textes évangéliques sur le mariage," *RTL* 9 (1978): 259-86.

2856   James R. Mueller, "The Temple Scroll and the Gospel Divorce Texts," *RevQ* 10 (1980): 247-56.

2857   Robert W. Herron, "Mark's Jesus on Divorce: Mark 10:1-12 Reconsidered," *JETS* 25/3 (1982): 273-81.

2858   Eugene A. LaVerdiere, "The Question of Divorce. Part 1: Is It Lawful?" *Emmanuel* 97 (1991): 454-60.

2859   Eugene A. LaVerdiere, "The Question of Divorce. Part 2: Cardiosclerosis," *Emmanuel* 97 (1991): 514-20.

2860   Duane Warden, "The Words of Jesus on Divorce," *RQ* 39 (1997): 141-53.

<u>10:1-11</u>

2861   Paul Ellingworth, "How Is Your Handbook Wearing?" *BT* 30 (1979): 236-41.

<u>10:2-16</u>

2862   Jean Delorme, "Le mariage, les enfants et les disciples de Jésus. Mc 10,2-16," *AsSeign* 58 (1974): 42-51.

<u>10:2-12</u>

2863   H.-J. Schoeps, "Jesus et la Loi juive," *RHPR* 33 (1953): 1-20.

2864   Wilfrid J. Harrington, "Jesus' Attitude towards Divorce," *ITQ* 37 (1970): 199-209.

2865   David R. Catchpole, "The Synoptic Divorce Material as a Traditio-Historical Problem," *BJRL* 57/1 (1974-1975): 92-127.

2866   R. Trevijano Etcheverría, "Matrimonio y divorcio en Mc 10,2-12 y par.," *Bur* 18 (1977): 113-51.

2867   John J. Pilch, "Marriage in the Lord," *BibTo* 102 (1979): 2010-13.

2868   Robert H. Stein, " 'Is It Lawful for a Man to Divorce His Wife'?" *JETS* 22 (1979): 115-21.

2869   Antonio Vargas-Machuca, "Divorcio e indisolubilidad del matrimonio en la Sagrada Escritura," *EB* 39 (1981): 19-61.

<u>10:2-9</u>

2870   Richard N. Soulen, "Marriage and Divorce: A Problem in New Testament Interpretation," *Int* 23/4 (1969): 439-50.

2871   Gerhard Schneider, "Jesu Wort über die Ehescheidung in
        der Überlieferung des Neuen Testaments," *TTZ* 80 (1971):
        65-87.

10:2

2872   George Howard, "Stylistic Inversion and the Synoptic
        Tradition," *JBL* 97 (1978): 375-89.

2873   Augustine Stock, "Matthean Divorce Texts," *BTB* 8/1
        (1978): 24-33.

2874   Paul Ellingworth, "Text and Context in Mark 10:2, 10,"
        JSNT 5 (1979): 63-66.

10:5

2875   Klaus Berger, "Hartherzigkeit und Gottes Gesetz: Die
        Vorgeschichte des antijüdischen Vorwurfs in Mc 10:5,"
        ZNW 61/1 (1970): 1-47.

10:6

2876   Francesco Vattioni, "A propos de Marc 10,6," *ScE* 20
        (1968): 433-36.

10:7-22

2877   Reginald H. Fuller, "The Decalogue in the NT," *Int* 43/3
        (1989): 243-55.

10:8

2878   T. A. Burkill, "Two into One: The Notion of Carnal Union
        in Mark 10:8; 1 Cor 6:16; Eph 5:31," *ZNW* 62 (1971):
        115-20.

10:10-12

2879   Charles C. Ryrie, "Biblical Teaching on Divorce and
        Remarriage," *GTJ* 3/2 (1982): 177-92.

2880   B. N. Wambacq, "Matthieu 5,31-32: Possibilité de Divorce
        ou Obligation de Rompre une Union Illiégitime," *NRT*
        104/1 (1982): 34-49.

2881   Eugene A. LaVerdiere, "The Question of Divorce. Part 3:
        In the Roman World," *Emmanuel* 97 (1991): 566-69,
        582-84.

10:10

2882 Paul Ellingworth, "Text and Context in Mark 10:2, 10," *JSNT* 5 (1979): 63-66.

2883 Angelo Lancellotti, "La Casa Pietro a Cafarnao nel Vangeli Sinottici. Redazione e Tradizione," *Ant* 58/1 (1983): 48-69.

10:11-12

2884 H. G. Coiner, "Those 'Divorce and Remarriage' Passages (Matt. 5:32; 19:9; 1 Cor. 7:10-16), with Brief Reference to the Mark and Luke Passages," *CTM* 39 (1958): 367-84.

2885 Klaus Berger, "Zu den sogenannten Sätzen heiligen Rechts," *NTS* 17 (1970-1971): 10-40.

2886 Bernadette J. Brooten, "Konnten Frauen im alten Judentum die Scheidung betreiben? Überlegungen zu Mk 10,11-12 und 1 Kor 7,10-11," *EvT* 42 (1982): 65-80.

2887 Bernadette J. Brooten, "Zur Debatte über das Scheidungsrecht der jüdischen Frau," *EvT* 43 (1983): 466-78.

10:11

2888 Gerhard Delling, "Das Logion Mark x.11 [und seine Abwandlungen] im Neuen Testament," *NovT* 1 (1956): 263-74.

2889 Peter Katz, "Mark 10:11 Once Again," *BT* 11 (1960): 152.

2890 E. Bammel, "Markus 10:11f. und das jüdische Eherecht," *ZNW* 61/1 (1970): 95-101.

2891 Berndt Schaller, " 'Commits Adultery with Her', Not 'Against Her', Mark 10:11," *ET* 83 (1971-1972): 107-108.

2892 Ernest Best, "An Early Sayings Collection," *NovT* 18/1 (1976): 1-16.

2893 Werner Stenger, "Zur Rekonstruktion eines Jesusworts anhand der synoptischen Ehescheidungslogien," *K* 26 (1984): 194-205.

10:13-16

2894 Howard C. Kee, " 'Becoming a Child' in the Gospel of Thomas," *JBL* 82 (1963): 307-14.

2895   Jürgen Sauer, "Der ursprüngliche 'Sitz im Leben' von Mk 10,13-16," *ZNW* 72/1 (1981): 27-50.

2896   John D. Crossan, "Kingdom and Children: A Study in the Aphoristic Tradition," *Semeia* 29 (1983): 75-95.

2897   J. D. M. Derrett, "Why Jesus Blessed the Children," *NovT* 25/1 (1983): 1-18.

2898   Daniel Patte, "Jesus' Pronouncement about Entering the Kingdom Like a Child: A Structural Exegesis," *Semeia* 29 (1983): 3-42.

2899   Vernon K. Robbins, "Pronouncement Stories and Jesus' Blessing of Children: A Rhetorical Approach," *Semeia* 29 (1983): 43-74.

2900   Guy Bedouelle, "Reflection on the Place of the Child in the Church: 'Suffer the Little Children to Come unto Me'," *CICR* 12 (1985): 349-67.

2901   Anthony O. Nkwoka, "Mark 10:13-16: Jesus' Attitude to Children and Its Modern Challenges," *AfTJ* 14 (1985): 100-10.

2902   Vernon K. Robbins, "Picking Up the Fragments: From Crossan's Analysis to Rhetorical Analysis," *Forum* 1 (1985): 31-64.

2903   Gerhard Ringshausen, "Die Kinder der Weisheit. Zur Auslegung von Mk 10:13-16 par," *ZNW* 77/1 (1986): 34-63.

2904   Larry L. Eubanks, "Mark 10:13-16," *RevExp* 91 (1994): 401-405.

2905   James L. Bailey, "Experiencing the Kingdom as a Little Child: A Rereading of Mark 10:13-16," *WW* 15 (1995): 58-67.

2906   Friedrich Beisser, "Markus 10, 13-16 (parr)--doch ein Text für die Kindertaufe," *KD* 41 (1995): 244-51.

2907   P. J. J. Botha, "'Laat die kindertjies na My toe kom. . .': kindwees in die wêreld van Jesus (Deel I)," *SkrifK* 20 (1999): 302-25.

2908   Jerome Murphy-O'Connor, "Jesus and the Money Changers (Mark 11:15-17; John 2:13-17)," *RevB* 107 (2000): 42-55.

10:13

2909   James H. Smylie, "Uncle Tom's Cabin Revisited: The Bible, the Romantic Imagination and the Sympathies of Christ," *Int* 27/1 (1973): 67-85.

10:14

2910   Jack P. Lewis, "Mark 10:14, Koluein, and Baptizein," *RQ* 21/3 (1978): 129-34.

10:15

2911   F. A. Schilling, "What Means the Saying about Receiving the Kingdom of God as a Little Child (τὴν βασιλείαν τοῦ θεοῦ ὡς παιδίον)? Mark 10:15; Luke 18:17," *ET* 77 (1965-1966): 56-58.

10:17-31

2912   Herbert Braun, " 'Umkehr' in spätjüdisch- häretischer und in früh- christlicher Sicht," *ZTK* 50 (1953): 243-58.

2913   Walther Zimmerli, "Die Frage des Reichen nach dem ewigen Leben (Mc 10,17-31 par.)," *EvT* 19 (1959): 90-97.

2914   Nikolaus Walter, "Zur Analyse von Mc 10:17-31," *ZNW* 53 (1962): 206-18.

2915   A. F. J. Klijn, "The Question of the Rich Young Man in a Jewish-Christian Gospel," *NovT* 8 (1966): 149-55.

2916   Benito C. Abad, "Problemas acerca de la riqueza y seguimiento de Jesús en Mc 10:17-31," *CuBi* 26 (1969): 218-22.

2917   A.-L. Descamps, "Aux origines du ministère: La pensée de Jesus," *RTL* 2 (1971): 3-45; 3 (1972): 121-59.

2918   E. P. Sanders, "Mark 10:17-31 and Parallels," *SBLSP* 1/1 (1971): 257-70.

2919   Ottmar Fuchs, "Funktion und Prozedur herkömmlicher und neuerer Methoden in der Textauslegung," *BibN* 10 (1979): 48-69.

2920   Georges Casalis, "For Human Beings, Impossible!" *Conci* 187 (1986): 36-47.

10:17-30

2921   Simon Légasse, "Tout quitter pour suivre le Christ. Mc 10,17-30," *AsSeign* 59 (1974): 43-54.

10:17-27

2922   É. Florival, "Vends tes biens et suis-moi," *BVC* 37 (1961): 16-33.

2923   Bernard Jay, "Le jeune homme riche. Notes homilétiqes sur Marc 10:17-27," *ÉTR* 53 (1978): 252-58.

2924   William J. Carl, "Mark 10:17-27 (28-31)," *Int* 33/3 (1979): 283-88.

10:17-22

2925   Henry Chadwick, "The Shorter Text of Luke 12:15-20," *HTR* 50 (1957): 249-58.

2926   Henri Troadec, "La vocation de l'homme riche," *VS* 120 (1969): 138-48.

2927   P. J. Riga, "Poverty as Counsel and as Precept," *BibTo* 65 (1973): 1123-28.

2928   Jean-Marie van Cangh, "Fondement Angélique de la Vie Religieuse," *NRT* 95/6 (1973): 635-47.

2929   M. L. O'Hara, "Jesus' Reflections on a Psalm," *BibTo* 90 (1977): 1237-40.

2930   Morris M. Faierstein, "Why Do the Scribes Say That Elijah Must Come First?" *JBL* 100 (1981): 75-86.

2931   Gregory Murray, "The Rich Young Man," *DR* 103 (1985): 144-46.

10:17-18

2932   Theodor Lorenzmeier, "Wider das Dogma von der Sündlosigkeit Jesu," *EvT* 31 (1971): 452-71.

10:18

2933   G. M. Lee, "Studies in Texts: Mark 10:18," *Theology* 70 (1967): 167-68.

2934   Benito C. Abad, " 'Nadie es bueno sino sólo Dios' (Mc 10:18)," *CuBi* 26 (1969): 106-108.

10:19

2935   Kenneth J. Thomas, "Liturgical Citations in the Synoptics," *NTS* (1975-1976): 205-14.

2936   W. D. MacHardy, "Mark 10:19: A Reference to the Old Testament?" *ET* 107 (1996): 143.

10:20

2937   Lino Cignelli, "La grecità biblica," *SBFLA* 35 (1985): 203-48.

10:21

2938   Giuseppe Segalla, "La predicazione dell'amore nella tradizione presinottica," *RBib* 20 (1972): 481-528.

2939   Jean Galot, "Le fondement évangélique du voeu religieux de pauvreté," *Greg* 56 (1975): 441-67.

10:23-31

2940   David Malone, "Riches and Discipleship: Mark 10:23-31," *BTB* 9/2 (1979): 78-88.

10:23-27

2941   Simon Légasse, "Jesus a-t-il Announce le Conversion Finale d'Israel? (a propos de Marc x.23-7)," *NTS* 10/4 (1963-1964): 480-87.

10:24-25

2942   José O'Callaghan, "Examen critico de Mt 19,24," *Bib* 69/3 (1988): 401-405.

10:25

2943   William A. Beardslee, "Uses of the Proverb in the Synoptic Gospels," *Int* 24 (1970): 61-73.

2944   Ernest Best, "Uncomfortable Words: VII. The Camel and the Needle's Eye (Mark 10:25)," *ET* 82/3 (1970-1971): 83-89.

2945   Raimund Köbert, "Kamel und Schiffstau: Zu Markus 10,25 (Par.) und Koran 7,40/38," *Bib* 53 (1972): 229-33.

2946   Allan Boesak, "The Eye of the Needle," *IRM* 72 (1983): 7-10.

2947   J. D. M. Derrett, "A Camel through the Eye of a Needle," *NTS* 32/3 (1986): 465-70.

10:28-31

2948 William J. Carl, "Mark 10:17-27 (28-31)," *Int* 33/3 (1979): 283-88.

10:28

2949 Gerd Theissen, " 'Wir haben alles verlassen' (Mk X,28)," *NovT* 19/3 (1977): 161-96.

10:29-30

2950 Henri Clavier, "L'ironie dans l'enseignement de Jésus," *NovT* 1 (1956): 3-20.

2951 J. Garcia Burillo, "El ciento por uno (Mc 10,29-30 par). Historia de las interpretaciones y exégesis," *EB* 36 (1977): 173-203; 37 (1978): 29-55.

10:29-31

2952 David M. May, "Leaving and Receiving: A Social-Scientific Exegesis of Mark 10:29-31," *PRS* 17 (1990): 141-54.

10:29

2953 Hildebrecht Hommel, "Herrenworte im Lichte sokratischer Überlieferung," *ZNW* 57 (1966): 1-23.

2954 George E. Rice, "Is Bezae a Homogeneous Codex," *PRS* 11 (1984): 39-54.

2955 Robert H. Gundry, "Mark 10:29: Order in the List," *CBQ* 59 (1997): 465-75.

10:30-32

2956 Harald Sahlin, "Emendationsvorschläge zum griechischen Text des Neuen Testaments I," *NovT* 24 (1982): 160-79.

10:30

2957 George E. Rice, "Is Bezae a Homogeneous Codex," *PRS* 11 (1984): 39-54.

10:31-33

2958 J. H. van Halsema, "Het raadsel als literaire vorm in Marcus en Johannes," *GTT* 83/1 (1983): 1-17.

10:31

2959 José O'Callaghan, "Nota crítica sobre Mt 19,30," *EB* 48 (1990): 271-73.

10:32-52

2960   Dan O. Via, "Mark 10:32-52—A Structural, Literary and Theological Interpretation," *SBLSP* 9/2 (1979): 187-203.

10:32-41

2961   Ernest Best, "Mark's Use of the Twelve," *ZNW* 69/1-2 (1978): 11-35.

10:32-34

2962   Georg Strecker, "Die Leidens- und Auferstehungsvoraussagen im Markusevangelium (Mk 8,31; 9,31; 10,32-34)," *ZTK* 64 (1964): 16-39.

2963   Richard T. France, "The Servant of the Lord in the Teaching of Jesus," *TynB* 19 (1968): 26-52.

2964   Ray McKinnis, "An Analysis of Mark 10:32-34," *NovT* 18/2 (1976): 81-100.

10:32

2965   Marla J. Selvidge, " 'And Those Who Followed Feared' (Mark 10:32)," *CBQ* 45/3 (1983): 396-400.

10:33-34

2966   Marcel Bastin, "L'annonce de la passion et les critères de l'historicíte," *RevSR* 50 (1976): 289-329; 51 (1977): 187-213.

10:34

2967   J. B. Bauer, "Drei Tage," *Bib* 39 (1958): 354-58.

2968   Jacques Dupont, "Ressuscité 'le troisième jour'," *Bib* 40 (1959): 742-61.

10:35-45

2969   Augustin George, "Le Service du Royaume (Marc 10,35-45)," *BVC* 25 (1959): 15-19.

2970   Jean Radermakers, "Revendiquer ou servir? Mk 10,35-45," *AsSeign* 60 (1975): 28-39.

2971   James D. Smart, "Mark 10:35-45," *Int* 33/3 (1979): 288-93.

2972   Jürgen Denker, "Identidad y mundo vivencial (Lebenswelt): en torno a Marcos 10:35-45 y Timoteo 2:5s," *RevB* 46/1-2 (1984): 159-69.

2973   Lyle D. Vander Broek, "Literary Context in the Gospels," *RR* 39/2 (1986): 113-17.

2974   Patrick H. Reardon, "The Cross, Sacraments and Martyrdom: An Investigation of Mark 10:35-45," *SVTQ* 36/1-2 (1992): 103-15.

10:35-40

2975   André Feuillet, "La coupe et le baptême de la Passion (Mc x,35-40; cf. Mt xx,20-23; Lc xii,50)," *RB* 74 (1967): 356-91.

2976   Simon Légasse, "Approche de l'épisode préévangélique des fils de Zébédée," *NTS* 20/2 (1973-1974): 161-77.

10:37

2977   José O'Callaghan, "Fluctuación textual en Mt 20,21.26,27," *Bib* 71/4 (1990): 553-58.

10:38-40

2978   J. D. M. Derrett, "Christ's Second Baptism (Lk 12:50; Mk 10:38-40)," *ET* 100 (1988-1989): 294-95.

10:38-39

2979   Otto Kuss, "Zur Frage einer vorpaulinischen Todestaufe," *MTZ* 4 (1953): 1-17.

2980   Gerhard Delling, "Βάπτισμα βαπτισθῆναι," *NovT* 2 (1957-1958): 92-115.

2981   W. E. Moore, "One Baptism," *NTS* 10 (1963-1964): 504-16.

2982   Eugene A. LaVerdiere, "Can You Drink the Cup?" *Emmanuel* 89 (1983): 490-95.

10:38

2983   Georg Braumann, "Leidenskelch und Todestaufe (Mc 10:38f.)," *ZNW* 56 (1965): 178-83.

2984   François Martin, "Le baptême dans l'Esprit: Tradition du Nouveau Testament et vie de l'Église," *NRT* 106 (1984): 23-58.

10:41-45

2985   Simon Légasse, "L'exercice de l'autorité dans l'Église d'après les évangiles synoptiques," *NRT* 85 (1963): 1009-22.

2986   David Seeley, "Rulership and Service in Mark 10:41-45," *NovT* 35 (1993): 234-50.

2987   Oda Wischmeyer, "Herrschen als Dienen--Mk 10,41-45," *ZNW* 90 (1999): 28-44.

10:42

2988   Ulrich Hedinger, "Jesus und die Volksmenge: Kritik der Qualifizierung der óchloi in der Evangelienauslegung," *TZ* 32 (1976): 201-206.

10:43-44

2989   William A. Beardslee, "Uses of the Proverb in the Synoptic Gospels," *Int* 24 (1970): 61-73.

2990   Ernest Best, "An Early Sayings Collection," *NovT* 18/1 (1976): 1-16.

2991   José O'Callaghan, "Fluctuación textual en Mt 20,21.26,27," *Bib* 71/4 (1990): 553-58.

10:45

2992   Paul E. Davies, "Did Jesus Die as a Martyr-Prophet?" *BR* 2 (1957): 19-30.

2993   J. A. Emerton, "The Aramaic Background of Mark 10:45," *JTS* 11 (1960): 334-35.

2994   J. A. Emerton, "Some New Testament Notes," *JTS* 11 (1960): 329-36.

2995   John P. Brown, "Synoptic Parallels in the Epistles and Form-History," *NTS* 10 (1963-1964): 27-48.

2996   André Feuillet, "Le logion sur la rançon," *RSPT* 51 (1967): 365-402.

2997   Richard T. France, "The Servant of the Lord in the Teaching of Jesus," *TynB* 19 (1968): 26-52.

2998   Louis Simon, "De la situation de l'Église au sermon: Marc 10:45," *ÉTR* 46 (1971): 3-11.

2999   Jürgen Roloff, "Anfänge der soteriologischen Deutung des Todes Jesu (MK. X.45 und XII.27)," *NTS* 19/1 (1972-1973): 38-64.

3000   Paul E. Davies, "Did Jesus Die as a Martyr-Prophet?" *BR* 19 (1974): 37-47.

3001   P. Maurice Casey, "The Son of Man Problem," *ZNW* 67/3 (1976): 147-54.

3002   W. J. Moulder, "The Old Testament Background and the Interpretation of Mark 10:45," *NTS* 24/1 (1977-1978): 120-27.

3003   Marco Adinolfi, "Il servo di JHWH nel logion del servizio e del riscatto (Mc. 10,45)," *BibO* 21 (1979): 43-61.

3004   N. Hoffmann, " 'Stellvertretung': Grundgestalt und Mitte des Mysteriums. Ein Versuch trinitätstheologischer Begründung christlicher Sühne," *MTZ* 30 (1979): 161-91.

3005   Barnabas Lindars, "Salvation Proclaimed. VII. Mark 10,45: A Ransom for Many," *ET* 93 (1981-1982): 292-95.

3006   B. Janowski, "Auslösung des verwirkten Lebens: Zur Geschichte und Struktur der biblischen Lösegeldvorstellung," *ZTK* 79 (1982): 25-59.

3007   David J. Lull, "Interpreting Mark's Story of Jesus' Death: Toward a Theology of Suffering," *SBLSP* 24 (1985): 1-12.

3008   Uwe Wegner, "Deu Jesus um sentido salvífico para sua morte: consideraçoes sobre Mc. 14:24 e 10:45," *EstT* 26/3 (1986): 209-46.

3009   David Seeley, "Was Jesus Like a Philosopher? The Evidence of Martyrological and Wisdom Motifs in Q, Pre-Pauline Traditions, and Mark," *SBLSP* 28 (1989): 540-49.

3010   J. Becker, "Die neutestamentliche Rede vom Sühnetod Jesu," *ZTK* 8 (1990): 29-49.

3011   Dieter Vieweger and Annette Böckler, "Ich gebe Ägypten als Lösegeld für dich': Mk 10,45 und die jüdische Tradition zu Jes 43,3b.4," *ZAW* 108 (1996): 594-607.

3012   Adela Y. Collins, "The Signification of Mark 10:45 among Gentile Christians," *HTR* 90 (1997): 371-82.

10:46-52

3013   André Paul, "Guérison de Bartimée. Mc 10,46-52," *AsSeign* 61 (1972): 44-52.

3014   Vernon K. Robbins, "The Healing of Blind Bartimaeus (10:46-52) in the Marcan Theology," *JBL* 92 (1973): 224-43.

3015   Dennis C. Duling, "Solomon, Exorcism, and the Son of David," *HTR* 68 (1975): 235-52.

3016   Ernest L. Stoffel, "An Exposition of Mark 10:46-52," *Int* 30/3 (1976): 288-92.

3017   Paul J. Achtemeier, " 'And He Followed Him': Miracles and Discipleship in Mark 10:46-52," *Semeia* 11 (1978): 115-45.

3018   H. D. Betz, "The Early Christian Miracle Story: Some Observations on the Form-Critical Problem," *Semeia* 11 (1978): 69-81.

3019   Earl S. Johnson, "Mark 10:46-52: Blind Bartimaeus," *CBQ* 40/2 (1978): 191-204.

3020   Helge K. Nielsen, "Ein Beitrag zur Beurteilung der Tradition über die Heilungstätigkeit," *SNTU-A* 4 (1979): 5-26.

3021   Claude Chapalain, "Marc 10,46-52: Plan de travail," *SémBib* 20 (1980): 12-16.

3022   Joseph A. Mirro, "Bartimaeus: The Miraculous Cure," *BibTo* 20 (1982): 221-25.

3023   Jacques Dupont, "L'aveugle de Jéricho recouvre la vue et suit Jésus," *RAfT* 8 (1984): 165-81.

3024   Augustine Stock, "Hinge Transitions in Mark's Gospel," *BTB* 15 (1985): 27-31.

3025   Walter Brueggemann, "Theological Education: Healing the Blind Beggar," *CC* 103/5 (1986): 114-16.

3026   Jacques Dupont, "Blind Bartimaeus (Mark 10:46-52)," *TD* 33/2 (1986): 223-28.

3027   Michael G. Steinhauser, "The Form of the Bartimaeus Narrative (Mark 10.46-52)," *NTS* 32/4 (1986): 583-95.

3028   Stephen H. Smith, "The Literary Structure of Mark
        11:1-12:40," *NovT* 31/2 (1989): 104-24.

3029   John N. Suggit, "Exegesis and Proclamation: Bartimaeus
        and Christian Discipleship (Mark 10:46-52)," *JTSA* 74
        (1991): 57-63.

3030   Sophie Schlumberger, "Le récit de la foi de Bartimée
        (Marc 10/46-52)," *ÉTR* 68 (1993): 73-81.

10:47-48

3031   Evald Lövestam, "Die Davidssohnsfrage," *SEÅ* 27/28
        (1962): 72-82.

10:50

3032   R. Alan Culpepper, "Mark 10:50: Why Mention the
        Garment?" *JBL* 101 (1982): 131-32.

3033   Michael G. Steinhauser, "Part of a 'Call Story'?" *ET* 94
        (1982-1983): 204-206.

10:51

3034   William G. Morrice, "The Imperatival ἵνα," *BT* 23 (1972):
        326-30.

10:52

3035   Georg Braumann, "Die Schuldner und die Sünderin Luk.
        VII.36-50," *NTS* 10/4 (1963-1964): 487-93.

11:1-13:37

3036   T. A. Burkill, "Strain on the Secret: An Examination of
        Mark 11:1-13:37," *ZNW* 51 (1960): 31-46.

3037   Ched Myers, "The Lesson of the Fig Tree: Mark
        11:1-13:37—Jesus' Second Campaign of Nonviolent
        Direct Action," *Soj* 16 (1987): 30-33.

11:1-13:2

3038   Kaj Bollmann, "Die Rolle des Tempels im Neuen
        Testament (Mk 11,1-13,2): Beitrag zur Diskussion über
        'Die Einheit der Bibel'," *TextK* 7 (1980): 19-31.

11:1-12:44

3039   John P. Heil, "The Narrative Strategy and Pragmatics of
        the Temple Theme in Mark," *CBQ* 59 (1997): 76-100.

11:1-12:40

3040   Stephen H. Smith, "The Literary Structure of Mark 11:1-12:40," *NovT* 31/2 (1989): 104-24.

11:1-12:12

3041   Jan W. Doeve, "Purification du Temple et dessèchement du figuier: Sur la structure du 21ème chapitre de Matthieu et parallèles," *NTS* 1 (1954-1955): 297-308.

11:1-25

3042   Paul B. Duff, "The March of the Divine Warrior and the Advent of the Greco-Roman King: Mark's Account of Jesus' Entry into Jerusalem," *JBL* 111 (1992): 55-71.

11:1-14

3043   A. B. Kolenkow, "Two Changing Patterns: Conflicts and the Necessity of Death—John 2 and 12 and Markan Parallels," *SBLSP* 9/1 (1979): 123-26.

11:1-13

3044   J. H. van Halsema, "Het raadsel als literaire vorm in Marcus en Johannes," *GTT* 83/1 (1983): 1-17.

11:1-11

3045   Brian A. Mastin, "The Date of the Triumphal Entry," *NTS* 16 (1969-1970): 76-82.

3046   Roman Bartnicki, "Mesjański charakter perykopy Marka o wjeździe Jezusa do Jerozolimy (Mk 11,1-11)," *RoczTK* 20 (1973): 5-16.

11:1-10

3047   J. D. M. Derrett, "Law in the New Testament: The Palm Sunday Colt," *NovT* 13 (1971): 241-58.

3048   André Paul, "L'entrée de Jésus à Jérusalem," *AsSeign* 19 (1971): 4-26.

3049   Roman Bartnicki, "Il carattere messianico delle pericopi di Marco e Matteo sull'ingresso di Gesù in Gerusalemme (Mc. 11,1-10; Mt. 21,1-9)," *RBib* 25 (1977): 5-27.

3050   W. A. Visser 't Hooft, "Triumphalism in the Gospels," *SJT* 38 (1985): 491-504.

11:1-7

3051   F. C. Synge, "A Matter of Tenses—Fingerprints of an Annotator in Mark," *ET* 88 (1976-1977): 168-71.

11:1-4

3052   Guy Wagner, "Le figuier stérile et la destruction du temple: Marc 11:1-4 et 20-26," *ÉTR* 62/3 (1987): 335-42.

11:1

3053   Werner Schauch, "Der Ölberg: Exegese zu einer Ortsangabe besonders bei Matthäus und Markus," *TLZ* 77 (1952): 391-96.

11:2-7

3054   Walter Bauer, "The Colt on Palm Sunday," *JBL* 72 (1953): 220-29.

11:3

3055   Robert G. Bratcher, "A Note on Mark xi.3 Ὁ κύριος αὐτοῦ χρείν ἔχει," *ET* 64 (1952-1953): 93.

3056   Henry Osborn, "A Quadruple Quote in the Triumphal Entry Account in Warao," *BT* 18/1 (1967): 30-32.

3057   J. M. Ross, "Names of God: A Comment on Mark 11.3 and Parallels," *BT* 35 (1984): 443.

11:9-10

3058   John D. Crossan, "Redaction and Citation in Mark 11:9-10 and 11:17," *BR* 17 (1972): 33-50.

11:9

3059   José L. Sicre, "El uso del Salmo 118 en la Cristología Neotestamentaria," *EE* 52 (1977): 73-90.

11:11-14

3060   Michal Wojciechowski, "Marc 11.14 et Targum Gen. 3.22: les fruits de la loi enlevés à Israël," *NTS* 33/2 (1987): 287-89.

11:11

3061   Ernest Best, "Mark's Use of the Twelve," *ZNW* 69/1-2 (1978): 11-35.

11:12-25

3062   Douglas E. Oakman, "Cursing Fig Trees and Robbers'
        Dens: Pronouncement Stories Within Social-Systemic
        Perspective: Mark 11:12-25 and Parallels," *Semeia* 64
        (1994): 253-72.

11:12-21

3063   James R. Edwards, "Markan Sandwiches: The
        Significance of Interpolations in Markan Narratives,"
        NovT 31 (1989): 193-216.

3064   Emmette Weir, "Fruitless Fig Tree--Futile Worship," *ET*
        106 (1995): 330.

11:12-14

3065   Gerhard Münderlein, "Die Verfluchung des Fegenbaumes
        (Mk. XI. 12-14)," *NTS* 10 (1963): 88-104.

3066   Hugues Cousin, "Le figuier désséche. Un exemple de
        l'actualisation de la geste évangélique: Mc 11,12-14,
        20-25; Mt 21,18-22," *FV* 70 (1971): 82-93.

3067   J. D. M. Derrett, "Figtrees in the New Testament," *HeyJ*
        14 (1973): 249-65.

3068   Kazimierz Romaniuk, " 'Car ce n'était pas la saison des
        figues . . .' (Mk 11:12-14 parr)," *ZNW* 66 (1975): 275-78.

3069   Heinz Giesen, "Der Verdorrte Feigenbaum—Eine
        Symbolische Aussage? zu Mk 11,12-14.20f.," *BZ* 20
        (1976): 95-111.

3070   L. A. Loslie, "The Cursing of the Fig Tree: Tradition
        Criticism of a Marcan Pericope (Mark 11:12-l4, 20-25),"
        SBT 7 (1977): 3-18.

3071   Lyle D. Vander Broek, "Literary Context in the Gospels,"
        RR 39/2 (1986): 113-17.

3072   Bettina von Kienle, "Mk 11:12-14.20-25: der verdorrte
        Feigenbaum," *BibN* 57 (1991): 17-25.

3073   Günther Schwarz, "Jesus und der Feigenbaum am Wege
        (Mk 11:12-14, 20-25/Mt 21:18-22)," *BibN* 61 (1992):
        36-37.

3074   Brent Kinman, "Lucan Eschatology and the Missing Fig
        Tree," *JBL* 113 (1994): 669-78.

3075   Christfried Böttrich, "Jesus und der Feigenbaum Mk 11:12-14,20-25 in der Diskussion," *NovT* 39 (1997): 328-59.

11:13

3076   C. W. F. Smith, "Fishers of Men: Footnotes on a Gospel Figure," *HTR* 52 (1959): 187-203.

3077   Cornelis J. den Heyer, " 'Want Het was de tijd niet voor vijgen'," *GTT* 76/3 (1976): 129-40.

3078   Günther Schwarz, "'Απὸ μακρόθεν / ἐπὶ τῆς ὁδοῦ," *BibN* 20 (1983): 56-57.

3079   Wendy J. Cotter, "For It Was Not the Season for Figs," *CBQ* 48/1 (1986): 62-66.

11:15-19

3080   T. W. Manson, "The Cleansing of the Temple," *BJRL* 33 (1950-1951): 271-82.

3081   F. A. Cooke, "The Cleansing of the Temple," *ET* 63 (1951-1952): 321-22.

3082   S. Jérôme, "La violence de Jésus," *BVC* 41 (1961): 13-17.

3083   Neill Q. Hamilton, "Temple Cleansing and Temple Bank," *JBL* 83 (1964): 365-72.

3084   J. D. M. Derrett, "The Zeal of the House and the Cleansing of the Temple," *DR* 95 (1977): 79-94.

3085   A. B. Kolenkow, "Two Changing Patterns: Conflicts and the Necessity of Death—John 2 and 12 and Markan Parallels," *SBLSP* 9/1 (1979): 123-26.

3086   R. Alan Culpepper, "Mark 11:15-19," *Int* 34/2 (1980): 176-81.

3087   Victor P. Furnish, "War and Peace in the New Testament," *Int* 38 (1984): 363-79.

3088   Egon Spiegel, "War Jesus gewalttätig? Bemerkungen zur Tempelreinigung," *TGl* 75 (1985): 239-47.

3089   Jacob Neusner, "Penningväxlarna i templet (Mark 11:15-19): Mishnas förklaring [M. Sheqalim 1:3]," *SEÅ* 53 (1988): 63-68.

242 PERIODICAL LITERATURE FOR THE STUDY OF THE NEW TESTAMENT

3090 Jacob Neusner, "Money-Changers in the Temple: The Mishnah's Explanation," *NTS* 35/2 (1989): 287-90.

3091 George W. Buchanan, "Symbolic Money-Changers in the Temple?" *NTS* 37 (1991): 280-90.

3092 David Seeley, "Jesus' Temple Act," *CBQ* 55 (1993): 263-83.

11:15-18

3093 J. D. M. Derrett, "No Stone upon Another: Leprosy and the Temple," *JSNT* 30 (1987): 3-20.

3094 Paula F. Qualls, "Mark 11:15-18: A Prophetic Challenge," *RevExp* 93 (1996): 395-402.

3095 H. D. Betz, "Jesus and the Purity of the Temple (Mark 11:15-18): A Comparative Approach," *JBL* 116 (1997): 455-72.

3096 P. Maurice Casey, "Culture and Historicity: The Cleansing of the Temple," *CBQ* 59 (1997): 306-32.

3097 David Seeley, "Jesus' Temple Act Revisited: A Response to P. Maurice Casey," *CBQ* 62 (2000): 55-63.

11:15-17

3098 Joachim Jeremias, "Zwei Miszellen: 1. Antik-Jüdische Münzdeutungen. 2. Zur Geschichtlichkeit der Tempelreinigung," *NTS* 23/2 (1976-1977): 177-79.

3099 Paul Ellingworth, "Translating Parallel Passages in the Gospels," *BT* 34 (1983): 401-407.

3100 Robert J. Miller, "The (A)Historicity of Jesus' Temple Demonstration: A Test Case in Methodology," *SBLSP* 30 (1991): 235-52.

11:15

3101 Étienne Trocmé, "L'expulsion des marchands du Temple," *NTS* 15 (1968-1969): 1-22.

11:16

3102 J. M. Ford, "Money 'Bags' in the Temple (Mark 11:16)," *Bib* 57 (1976): 249-53.

11:17

3103   John D. Crossan, "Redaction and Citation in Mark 11:9-10 and 11:17," *BR* 17 (1972): 33-50.

3104   Craig A. Evans, "Jesus' Action in the Temple: Cleansing or Portent of Destruction?" *CBQ* 51 (1989): 237-70.

11:18-19

3105   Robert Schlarb, "Die Suche nach dem Messias: ζητέω als Terminus technicus der markinischen Messianologie," *ZNW* 81 (1990): 155-70.

11:20-26

3106   Guy Wagner, "Le figuier stérile et la destruction du temple: Marc 11:1-4 et 20-26," *ÉTR* 62/3 (1987): 335-42.

11:20-25

3107   John Coutts, "The Authority of Jesus and of the Twelve in St. Mark's Gospel," *JTS* 8 (1957): 111-18.

3108   Hugues Cousin, "Le figuier désséche. Un exemple de l'actualisation de la geste évangélique: Mc 11,12-14, 20-25; Mt 21,18-22," *FV* 70 (1971): 82-93.

3109   L. A. Loslie, "The Cursing of the Fig Tree: Tradition Criticism of a Marcan Pericope (Mark 11:12-l4, 20-25)," *SBT* 7 (1977): 3-18.

3110   Bettina von Kienle, "Mk 11:12-14.20-25: der verdorrte Feigenbaum," *BibN* 57 (1991): 17-25.

3111   Günther Schwarz, "Jesus und der Feigenbaum am Wege (Mk 11:12-14, 20-25/Mt 21:18-22)," *BibN* 61 (1992): 36-37.

3112   Christfried Böttrich, "Jesus und der Feigenbaum Mk 11:12-14,20-25 in der Diskussion," *NovT* 39 (1997): 328-59.

11:20-24

3113   J. G. Kahn, "La parabole du figuier stérile et les arbres récalcitrants de la Genèse," *NovT* 13 (1971): 38-45.

11:20

3114   Heinz Giesen, "Der verdorrte Feigenbaum—Eine symbolische Aussage? zu Mk 11,12-14.20f.," *BZ* 20 (1976): 95-111.

11:22-23

3115   Gerhard Barth, "Glaube und Zweifel in den synoptischen Evangelien," *ZTK* 72 (1975): 269-92.

11:22

3116   H.-W. Bartsch, "Ein neuer Textus Receptus für das griechische Neue Testament?" *NTS* 27 (1980-1981): 585-92.

3117   J. D. M. Derrett, "Moving Mountains and Uprooting Trees," *BibO* 30 (1988): 231-44.

11:23-25

3118   Giancarlo Biguzzi, "Mc. 11,23-25 e il Pater," *RBib* 27 (1979): 57-68.

11:23

3119   Ernest Best, "An Early Sayings Collection," *NovT* 18/1 (1976): 1-16.

3120   Günther Schwarz, "Πίστιν ὡς κόκκον σινάπεως," *BibN* 25 (1984): 27-35.

11:24-25

3121   Benny R. Crockett, "The Function of Mathetological Prayer in Mark," *IBS* 10 (1988): 123-39.

11:24

3122   John D. Crossan, "Aphorism in Discourse and Narrative," *Semeia* 43 (1988): 121-40.

11:27-12:12

3123   Young-Heon Lee, "Jesus und die jüdische Autorität: eine exegetische Untersuchung zu Mk 11,27-12,12," *ZKT* 106/4 (1984): 505-506.

11:27-33

3124   Jacob Kremer, "Jesu Antwort auf die Frage nach seiner Vollmacht. Eine Auslegung von Mk 11,27-33," *BibL* 9 (1968): 128-36.

3125   G. S. Shae, "The Question on the Authority of Jesus," *NovT* 16 (1974): 1-29.

3126   Corrado Marucci, "Die implizite Christologie in der sogenannten Vollmachtsfrage," *ZKT* 108 (1986): 292-300.

3127   J. D. M. Derrett, "Questioning Jesus's Authority (Mark 11:27-33)," *DR* 116 (1998): 257-70.

11:27

3128   Eric F. F. Bishop, "Jesus Walking or Teaching in the Temple," *ET* 63 (1951-1952): 226-27.

3129   Heinrich Greeven, "Erwägungen zur synoptischen Textkritik," *NTS* 6 (1959-1960): 282-96.

12:1-37

3130   David Daube, "The Earliest Structure of the Gospels," *NTS* 5 (1958-1959): 174-87.

12:1-12

3131   Harvey K. McArthur, "The Dependence of the Gospel of Thomas on the Synoptics," *ET* 71 (1959-1960): 286-87.

3132   Martin Hengel, "Das Gleichnis von den Weingärtnern Mc 12:1-12 im Lichte der Zenonpapyri und der rabbinischen Gleichnisse," *ZNW* 59 (1968): 1-39.

3133   H. J. Klauck, "Das Gleichnis vom Mord im Weinberg (Mk 12,1-12; Mt 21,33-46; Lk 20,9-19)," *BibL* 11 (1970): 118-45.

3134   John D. Crossan, "The Parable of the Wicked Husbandmen," *JBL* 90/4 (1971): 451-65.

3135   John Drury, "The Sower, the Vineyard, and the Place of Allegory in the Interpretation of Mark's Parables," *JTS* 24/2 (1973): 367-79.

3136   Erhardt Güttgemanns, "Narrative Analyse Synoptischer Texte," *LB* 25/26 (1973): 50-73.

3137   Dino Merli, "La parabola dei vignaioli infedeli (Mc. 12,1-12)," *BibO* 15 (1973): 97-108.

3138   Klyne R. Snodgrass, "The Parable of the Wicked Husbandmen: Is the Gospel of Thomas Version the Original?" *NTS* 21 (1974-1975): 142-44.

3139 Craig A. Evans, "On the Vineyard Parables of Isaiah 5 and Mark 12," *BZ* 28 (1984): 82-86.

3140 A. Cornette, "Notes sur la parabole des vignerons," *FV* 84/1-2 (1985): 42-48.

3141 Corina Combet-Galland, "La vigne et l'écriture, histoire de reconnaissances: Marc 12:1-12," *ÉTR* 62/4 (1987): 489-502.

3142 E. Van Eck and A. G. Van Aarde, "A Narratological Analysis of Mark 12:1-12: The Plot of the Gospel of Mark in a Nutshell," *HTS* 45/4 (1989): 778-800.

3143 Aaron A. Milavec, "The Identity of 'the Son' and 'the Others': Mark's Parable of the Wicked Husbandmen Reconsidered," *BTB* 20 (1990): 30-37.

3144 Wim J. C. Weren, "The Use of Isaiah 5,1-7 in the Parable of the Tenants (Mark 12,1-12; Matthew 21,33-46)," *Bib* 79 (1998): 1-26.

12:1-11

3145 Louis Panier, "Analyse sémiotique: 'Pour commencer'," *SémBib* 38 (1985): 1-31.

3146 Jürgen Wehnert, "Die Teilhabe der Christen an der Herrschaft mit Christus--eine eschatologische Erwartung des frühen Christentums," *ZNW* 88 (1997): 81-96.

12:1-8

3147 M. Herranz Marco, "Las espigas arrancadas en sabado (Mt 12,1-8 par.): Tradición y elaboración literaria," *EB* 28 (1969): 313-48.

3148 John D. Crossan, "The Servant Parables of Jesus," *Semeia* 1 (1974): 17-62.

3149 William G. Morrice, "Murder Amongst the Vines," *ET* 97/5 (1985-1986): 145-47.

12:1

3150 Gerhard Sellin, "Gleichnisstrukturen," *LB* 31 (1974): 89-115.

12:6

3151 W. Dekker, "De 'geliefde Zoon' in de synoptische evangeliën," *NTT* 16 (1961-1962): 94-106.

3152   Alfredo Scattolon, "L'ἀγαπητός sinottico nella luce della tradizione giudaica," *RBib* 26 (1978): 3-32.

12:9-11

3153   William G. Morrice, "Translating the Greek Imperative," *BT* 24 (1973): 129-34.

12:10

3154   F. F. Bruce, "The Corner Stone," *ET* 84 (1972-1973): 231-35.

12:12-17

3155   Arthur Ogle, "What Is Left for Caesar," *TT* 35/3 (1978): 254-64.

12:12

3156   Robert Schlarb, "Die Suche nach dem Messias: ζητέω als Terminus technicus der markinischen Messianologie," *ZNW* 81 (1990): 155-70.

12:13-17

3157   Augustin George, "Jésus devant le problème politique," - *LV* 105 (1971): 5-17.

3158   Kenzo Tagawa, "Jésus critiquant l'idéologie théocratique. Une étude de Mc 12,13-17," *FV* 70 (1971): 117-25.

3159   Reinhard Breymayer, "Zur Pragmatik des Bildes. Semiotische Beobachtungen zum Streitgespräch Mk 12,13-17 ('Der Zinsgroschen') unter Berücksichtigung der Spieltheorie," *LB* 13/14 (1972): 19-51.

3160   E. A. Russell, "Church and State in the New Testament," *ITQ* 44 (1977): 192-207.

3161   Sjef van Tilborg, "Het strukturalisme binnen de exegese: een variant van het burgerlijke denken," *Bij* 40 (1979): 364-79.

3162   John R. Donahue, "A Neglected Factor in the Theology of Mark," *JBL* 101 (1982): 563-94.

3163   H. G. Klemm, "De Censu Caesaris. Beobachtungen zu J. Duncan M. Derrett's Interpretation der Perikope Mk. 12:13-17 Par," *NovT* 24/3 (1982): 234-54.

3164 John D. Crossan, "Mark 12:13-17," *Int* 37/4 (1983): 397-401.

3165 Klaus Haacker, "Kaisertribut und Gottesdienst," *TBe* 17 (1986): 285-92.

3166 Uwe Wegner, "O que fazem os denários de César na Palestina?" *EstT* 29/1 (1989): 87-105.

3167 David T. Owen-Ball, "Rabbinic Rhetoric and the Tribute Passage," *NovT* 35 (1993): 1-14.

3168 William R. Herzog, "Dissembling, a Weapon of the Weak: The Case of Christ and Caesar in Mark 12:13-17 and Romans 13:1-7," *PRS* 21 (1994): 339-60.

3169 Jack T. Sanders, "The Criterion of Coherence and the Randomness of Charisma: Poring Through Some Aporias in the Jesus Tradition," *NTS* 44 (1998): 1-25.

12:13

3170 C. Daniel, "Les 'Hérodiens' du Nouveau Testament sont-ils des Esseniens?" *RevQ* 6 (1967): 31-53.

3171 W. J. Bennett, "The Herodians of Mark's Gospel," *NovT* 17/1 (1975): 9-14.

3172 Augustine Stock, "Jesus, Hypocrites, and Herodians," *BTB* 16/1 (1986): 3-7.

12:15-16

3173 Paul C. Finney, "The Rabbi and the Coin Portrait (Mark 12:15b, 16): Rigorism Manqué," *JBL* 112 (1993): 629-44.

12:15

3174 Philippe Rolland, "Jésus connaissait leurs pensées," *ETL* 62 (1986): 118-21.

3175 John Thorley, "Aktionsart in New Testament Greek: Infinitive and Imperative," *NovT* 31 (1989): 290-315.

12:16

3176 L. Y. Rahmani, " 'Whose Likeness and Inscription is This?' (Mark 12:16)," *BA* 49/1 (1986): 60-61.

12:17

3177 Jan N. Sevenster, " 'Geeft den keizer wat des keizers is, en Gode wat Gods is'," *NedTT* 17 (1961): 21-31.

3178 Charles H. Giblin, " 'The Things of God' in the Question Concerning Tribute to Caesar," *CBQ* 33/4 (1971): 510-27.

3179 Maurice Baillet, "Les manuscrits de la Grotte 7 de Qumrân et le Nouveau Testament," *Bib* 54 (1973): 340-50.

3180 Pierre Benoit, "Nouvelle Note sur les Fragments Grecs de la Grotte 7 de Qumrân," *RB* 80/1 (1973): 5-12.

3181 Heda Jason, "Der Zinsgroschen: Analyse der Erzählstruktur," *LB* 41/42 (1977): 49-87.

3182 Victor P. Furnish, "War and Peace in the New Testament," *Int* 38 (1984): 363-79.

3183 James I. Packer, "How to Recognize a Christian Citizen," *CT* 29/7 (1985): 4-8.

3184 Benedict T. Viviano, "Render unto Caesar," *BibTo* 26 (1988): 272-76.

12:18-27

3185 Giles Carton, "Comme des anges dans le ciel (Marc 12,18-27)," *BVC* 28 (1959): 46-52.

3186 Sebastián Bartina, "Jesús y los saduceos: 'El Dios qe Abraham, de Isaac y de Jacob' es 'El que hace existir'," *EB* 21 (1962): 151-60.

3187 Franz Mußner, "Jesu Lehre über das kommende Leben nach den Synoptikern," *Conci* 6 (1970): 692-95.

3188 Antonio Ammassari, "Gesù ha veramente insegnato la risurrezione!" *BibO* 15 (1973): 65-73.

3189 François Vouga, "Controverse sur la résurrection des morts," *LV* 179 (1986): 49-61.

3190 Marius Reiser, "Das Leben nach dem Tod in der Verkündigung Jesu," *ErAu* 66 (1990): 381-90.

3191 J. P. Meyer, "The Debate on the Resurrection of the Dead: An Incident from the Ministry of the Historical Jesus?" *JSNT* 77 (2000): 3-24.

12:18-23

3192 Peter Bolt, "What Were the Sadducees Reading? An Enquiry into the Literary Background of Mark 12:18-23," *TynB* 45 (1994): 369-94.

12:20-23

3193 J. D. M. Derrett, "Marcan Priority and Marcan Skill," *BibO* 29 (1987): 135-40.

12:24-27

3194 F. Gerald Downing, "The Resurrection of the Dead: Jesus and Philo," *JSNT* 15 (1982): 42-50.

12:26-27

3195 F.-P. Dreyfus, "L'argument scripturaire de Jésus en faveur de la résurrection des morts (Marc XII,26-27)," *RB* 66 (1959): 213-25.

3196 D. M. Cohn-Sherbok, "Jesus' Defence of the Resurrection of the Dead," *JSNT* 11 (1981): 64-73.

3197 Hans C. Cavallin, "Jesus gör de döda levande," *SEÅ* 50/51 (1985): 40-49.

12:26

3198 J. G. Janzen, "Resurrection and Hermeneutics: On Exodus 3:6 in Mark 12:26," *JSNT* 23 (1985): 43-58.

12:28-40

3199 Étienne Trocmé, "Jésus et les lettrés d'après Marc 12:28-40," *FV* 84/1-2 (1985): 33-41.

12:28-34

3200 Jay B. Stern, "Jesus' Citation of Dt 6,5 and Lv 19,18 in the Light of Jewish Tradition," *CBQ* 28 (1966): 312-16.

3201 Josef Ernst, "Die Einheit von Gottes- und Nächstenliebe in der Verkündigung Jesu," *TGl* 60 (1970): 3-14.

3202 Giuseppe Segalla, "La predicazione dell'amore nella tradizione presinottica," *RBib* 20 (1972): 481-528.

3203 Ludwig Berg, "Das neutestamentliche Liebesgebot. Prinzip der Sittlichkeit," *TTZ* 83 (1974): 129-45.

3204 Arland J. Hultgren, "The Double Commandment of Love in Mt 22:34-40: Its Sources and Composition," *CBQ* 36 (1974): 373-78.

3205 Ferdinand Hahn, "Neutestamentliche Grundlagen einer christlichen Ethik," *TTZ* 86 (1977): 31-41.

3206   Simon Légasse, "L'étendue de l'amour interhumain d'après le Nouveau Testament: limites et promesses," *RTL* 8 (1977): 137-59, 293-304.

3207   Walter Diezinger, "Zum Liebesgebot Mk XII,28-34 und Parr," *NovT* 20/2 (1978): 81-83.

3208   George W. Hoyer, "Mark 12:28-34," *Int* 33/3 (1979): 293-98.

3209   Morris M. Faierstein, "Why Do the Scribes Say That Elijah Must Come First?" *JBL* 100 (1981): 75-86.

3210   Gregory Murray, "The Questioning of Jesus," *DR* 101 (1984): 271-75.

3211   G. Ghiberti, "Il primo di tutti i comandamenti (Mc 12,28-34)," *ParSpirV* 11 (1985): 97-110.

3212   O. Bucher, "The Scribe of Mark 12," *BibTo* 38 (2000): 95-97.

12:28-31

3213   M. Miguéns, "Amour, alpha et omega de l'existence, Mc 12,28-31," *AsSeign* 62 (1970): 53-62.

12:28

3214   Norbert Lohfink, "Das Hauptgebot im Alten Testament," *GeistL* 36 (1963): 271-81.

3215   Norbert Lohfink, "Il 'comandamento primo' nell'Antico Testamento," *BibO* 7 (1965): 49-60.

3216   Lino Cignelli, "La grecità biblica," *SBFLA* 35 (1985): 203-48.

12:29-30

3217   Kenneth J. Thomas, "Liturgical Citations in the Synoptics," *NTS* (1975-1976): 205-14.

12:31

3218   Hugh W. Montefiore, "Thou Shalt Love Thy Neighbour as Thyself," *NovT* 5 (1962): 157-70.

12:33

3219   James Van Vurst, "The Scribe's Insight," *BibTo* 25 (1987): 37-41.

12:34

3220 Bonaventura Rinaldi, "Νουνεχῶς," *BibO* 20 (1978): 26.

3221 John Thorley, "Aktionsart in New Testament Greek: Infinitive and Imperative," *NovT* 31 (1989): 290-315.

12:35-37

3222 Robert P. Gagg, "Jesus und die Davidssohnfrage: Zur Exegese von Markus 12,35-37," *TZ* 7 (1951): 18-30.

3223 Otto Betz, "Donnersöhne, Menschenfischer und der davidische Messias," *RevQ* 3 (1961): 41-70.

3224 Evald Lövestam, "Die Davidssohnsfrage," *SEÅ* 27/28 (1962): 72-82.

3225 Joseph A. Fitzmyer, "The Son of David Tradition and Mt 22:41-46 and Parallels," *Conci* 10/2 (1966): 40-46.

3226 Gerhard Schneider, "Die Davidssohnfrage (Mk 12,35-37)," *Bib* 53 (1972): 65-90.

3227 Fritz Neugebauer, "Die Davidssohnfrage (Mark XII,35-37 Parr.) und der Menschensohn," *NTS* 21/1 (1974-1975): 81-108.

3228 Dennis C. Duling, "Solomon, Exorcism, and the Son of David," *HTR* 68 (1975): 235-52.

12:35-36

3229 W. R. G. Loader, "Christ at the Right Hand - Ps. cx. 1 in the New Testament," *NTS* 24 (1977-1978): 199-217.

12:35

3230 Gerhard Schneider, "Zur Vorgeschichte des christologischen Prädikats 'Sohn Davids'," *TTZ* 80 (1971): 247-53.

12:37-40

3231 Harry T. Fleddermann, "A Warning About the Scribes (Mark 12:37b-40)," *CBQ* 44/1 (1982): 52-67.

12:38-44

3232 Paul Ternant, "La dévotion contrefaite et l'authentique générosité," *AsSeign* 63 (1971): 53-63.

12:40

3233   J. D. M. Derrett, " 'Eating Up the Houses of Widows':
Jesus' Comment on Lawyers?" *NovT* 14/1 (1972): 1-9.

12:41-44

3234   Louis Simon, "Le sou de la veuve. Marc 12/41-4," *ÉTR* 44
(1969): 115-26.

3235   Joachim Jeremias, "Zwei Miszellen: 1. Antik-Jüdische
Münzdeutungen. 2. Zur Geschichtlichkeit der
Tempelreinigung," *NTS* 23/2 (1976-1977): 177-79.

3236   Eugene A. LaVerdiere, "The Widow's Mite," *Emmanuel*
92 (1986): 341.

3237   Gregory Murray, "Did Luke Use Mark?" *DR* 104 (1986):
268-71.

3238   Mary A. Beavis, "Women as Models of Faith in Mark,"
BTB 18 (1988): 3-9.

3239   Elizabeth S. Malbon, "The Poor Widow in Mark and Her
Poor Rich Readers," *CBQ* 53 (1991): 589-604.

3240   R. S. Sugirtharajah, "The Widow's Mites Revalued," *ET*
103/2 (1992-1993): 42-43.

3241   Darcy D. Jensen, "The Widow's Mite," *WW* 17 (1997):
282-88.

3242   Geoffrey V. Smith, "A Closer Look at the Widow's
Offering: Mark 12:41-44," *JETS* 40 (1997): 27-36.

3243   Willard M. Swartley, "The Role of Women in Mark's
Gospel: A Narrative Analysis," *BTB* 27 (1997): 16-22.

12:42

3244   Daniel Sperber, "Mark 12:42 and its Metrological
Background. A Study in Ancient Syriac Versions," *NovT*
9 (1967): 178-90.

12:44

3245   Harald Sahlin, "Emendationsvorschläge zum griechischen
Text des Neuen Testaments I," *NovT* 24 (1982): 160-79.

13

3246   Brian K. Blount, "Preaching the Kingdom: Mark's Apocalyptic Call for Prophetic Engagement," *PSB* suppl 3 (1994): 33-56.

3247   Peter Bolt, "Mark 13: An Apocalyptic Precursor to the Passion Narrative," *RTR* 54 (1995): 10-32.

3248   Adela Y. Collins, "The Apocalyptic Rhetoric of Mark 13 in Historical Context," *BR* 41 (1996): 5-36.

3249   J. K. Elliott, "The Position of the Verb in Mark with Special Reference to Chapter 13," *NovT* 38 (1996): 136-44.

3250   Sophie Schlumberger, "Appel au Lecteur! (Lecture de Marc 13)," *FV* 98 (1999): 87-96.

13:1-37

3251   Charles Perrot, "Essai sur le Discours eschatologique (Mc. XIII,1-37; Mt. XXIV,1-36; Lc. XXI,5-36)," *RechSR* 47 (1959): 481-514.

3252   Ingo Hermann, "Die Gefährdung der Welt und ihre Erneuerung: Auslegung von Mk 13.1-37," *BibL* 7 (1966): 305-309.

3253   Hugo Lattanzi, "Eschatologici sermonis Domini logica interpretatio," *Div* 11 (1967): 71-92.

3254   John Kallikuzhuppil, "The Glorification of the Suffering Church," *BB* 9 (1983): 247-57.

13:1-2

3255   Stephen H. Smith, "The Literary Structure of Mark 11:1-12:40," *NovT* 31/2 (1989): 104-24.

13:2

3256   Jacques Dupont, "Il n'en sera pas laissé pierre sur pierre (Marc 13,2; Luc 19,44)," *Bib* 52 (1971): 301-20.

3257   Jacques Schlosser, "La parole de Jésus sur la fin du temple," *NTS* 36 (1990): 398-414.

13:3-37

3258   Ton Veerkamp, "Am Ende nur die Hoffnung," *TextK* 28 (1985): 4-31.

13:3

3259 Werner Schauch, "Der Ölberg: Exegese zu einer Ortsangabe besonders bei Matthäus und Markus," *TLZ* 77 (1952): 391-96.

13:5-37

3260 Willem S. Vorster, "Literary Reflections on Mark 13:5-37: A Narrated Speech of Jesus," *Neo* 21 (1987): 203-24.

13:5-27

3261 Geert Hallbäck, "Der Anonyme Plan: Analyse von Mark 13,5-27 im Hinblick auf die Relevanz der apokalyptischen Rede für die Problematik der Aussage," *LB* 49 (1981): 38-53.

13:9-13

3262 Helen R. Graham, "A Markan Theme: Endurance in Time of Persecution," *BibTo* 23 (1985): 297-304.

3263 Helen R. Graham, "A Passion Prediction for Mark's Community: Mark 13:9-13," *BTB* 16/1 (1986): 18-22.

13:9-10

3264 George D. Kilpatrick, "Mark 13:9-10," *JTS* 9 (1958): 81-86.

13:9

3265 Frederick W. Danker, "Double-Entendre in Mark 13:9," *NovT* 10/2 (1968): 162-63.

13:10

3266 Austin M. Farrer, "An Examination of Mark 13:10," *JTS* 7 (1956): 75-79.

3267 James W. Thompson, "The Gentile Mission as an Eschatological Necessity," *RQ* 14/1 (1971): 18-27.

3268 Charles L. Holman, "The Idea of an Imminent Parousia in the Synoptic Gospels," *SBT* 3 (1973): 15-31.

3269 Philippe Rolland, "Luc, témoin de la forme primitive du Discours eschatologique," *BLOS* 2 (1989): 9-11.

13:11

3270 Matthew Mahoney, "Luke 21:14-15: Editorial Rewriting or Authenticity?" *ITQ* 47/3 (1980): 220-38.

13:12

3271   Roy A. Harrisville, "Jesus and the Family," *Int* 23/4 (1969): 425-38.

3272   Pierre Grelot, "Miche 7,6 dans les évangiles et dans la littrature rabbinique," *Bib* 67/3 (1986): 363-77.

3273   B. M. F. van Iersel, "Failed Followers in Mark: Mark 13:12 as a Key for the Identification of the Intended Readers," *CBQ* 58 (1996): 244-63.

13:14-20

3274   Sidney G. Sowers, "The Circumstances and Recollection of the Pella Flight," *TZ* 26 (1970): 305-20.

3275   John J. Gunther, "The Fate of the Jerusalem Church: The Flight to Pella," *TZ* 29 (1973): 81-94.

13:14-18

3276   Gordon D. Fee, "A Text-Critical Look at the Synoptic Problem," *NovT* 22/1 (1980): 12-28.

13:14

3277   Harold A. Guy, "Mark xiii.14: ὁ ἀναγινώσκων νοείτω," *ET* 65 (1953-1954): 30.

3278   Béda Rigaux, "Βδέλυγμα τῆς ἐρημώσεως (Mc 13,14; Mt 4,15)," *Bib* 40 (1959): 675-83.

3279   G. C. Aalders, "De 'gruwel der verwoesting'," *GTT* 60 (1960): 1-5.

3280   R. H. Shaw, "A Conjecture on the Signs of the End," *ATR* 47 (1965): 96-102.

3281   Ernest Best, "The Gospel of Mark: Who Was the Reader?" *IBS* 11 (1989): 124-32.

13:17-18

3282   Paul Glaue, "Einige Stellen: die Bedeutung des Codex D charakterisieren," *NovT* 2 (1957-1958): 310-15.

13:18-27

3283   John R. Donahue, "A Neglected Factor in the Theology of Mark," *JBL* 101 (1982): 563-94.

13:18

3284   Graham N. Stanton, " 'Pray That Your Flight May Not Be in Winter or on a Sabbath' (Matthew 24:20)," *JSNT* 37 (1989): 17-30.

13:20

3285   H. P. Owen, "The Parousia of Christ in the Synoptic Gospels," *SJT* 12 (1959): 171-92.

3286   Philippe Rolland, "Luc, témoin de la forme primitive du Discours eschatologique," *BLOS* 2 (1989): 9-11.

13:21-23

3287   Thierry Snoy, "Les miracles dans l'évangile de Marc. Examen de quelques études récentes," *RTL* 3 (1972): 449-66; 4 (1973): 58-101.

3288   Marinus de Jonge, "The Earliest Christian Use of Christos: Some Suggestions," *NTS* 32 (1986): 321-43.

13:22-27

3289   Philippe Rolland, "Luc, témoin de la forme primitive du Discours eschatologique," *BLOS* 2 (1989): 9-11.

13:22

3290   John Thorley, "Aktionsart in New Testament Greek: Infinitive and Imperative," *NovT* 31 (1989): 290-315.

13:24-27

3291   Franz Mußner, "Die Wiederkunft des Menschensohnes nach Markus 13,24-27 und 14,61-62," *BK* 16 (1961): 105-107.

3292   John S. Kloppenborg, "Didache 16:6-8 and Special Matthaean Tradition," *ZNW* 70/1 (1979): 54-67.

3293   Paul S. Minear, "Some Archetypal Origins of Apocalyptic Predictions," *HBT* 1 (1979): 105-35.

3294   Peter Maser, "Sonne und Mond: exegetische Erwägungen zum Fortleben der Spätantik-jüdischen in der frühchristlichen Kunst," *K* 25/1-2 (1983): 41-67.

13:24-32

3295   W. Sibley Towner, "An Exposition of Mark 13:24-32," *Int* 30/3 (1976): 292-96.

13:24-25

> 3296   B. M. F. van Iersel, "The Sun, Moon, and Stars of Mark 13,24-25 in a Greco-Roman Reading," *Bib* 77 (1996): 84-92.

13:26-27

> 3297   Martin Stowasser, "Mk 13,26f und die urchristliche Rezeption des Menschensohns: Eine Anfrage an Anton Vögtle," *BZ* NS 39 (1995): 246-52.

13:26

> 3298   George R. Beasley-Murray, "The Parousia in Mark," *RevExp* 75/4 (1978): 565-81.

13:27

> 3299   Paul T. Coke, "Angels of the Son of Man," *SNTU-A* 3 (1978): 91-98.

> 3300   Harald Sahlin, "Emendationsvorschläge zum griechischen Text des Neuen Testaments I," *NovT* 24 (1982): 160-79.

13:28-34

> 3301   John R. Donahue, "A Neglected Factor in the Theology of Mark," *JBL* 101 (1982): 563-94.

13:28-32

> 3302   Allan McNicol, "The Lesson of the Fig Tree in Mark 13:28-32: A Comparison between Two Exegetical Methodologies," *RQ* 27/4 (1984): 193-207.

13:28-31

> 3303   J. D. M. Derrett, "Figtrees in the New Testament," *HeyJ* 14 (1973): 249-65.

13:28-29

> 3304   Jacques Dupont, "La parabole du figuier qui bourgeonne (Mc xiii,28-29 et par.)," *RB* 75 (1968): 526-48.

13:30-32

> 3305   Brian M. Nolan, "Some Observations on the Parousia and New Testament Eschatology," *ITQ* 36 (1969): 283-314.

13:30

> 3306   Evald Lövestam, "En problematisk eskatologisk utsaga: Mark. 13:30 par.," *SEÅ* 28/29 (1963): 64-80.

3307   Barry S. Crawford, "Near Expectation in the Sayings of Jesus," *JBL* 101/2 (1982): 225-44.

3308   Heinz Giesen, "Christliche Existenz in der Welt und der Menschensohn: Versuch einer Neuinterpretation des Terminwortes Mk 13,30," *SNTU-A* 8 (1983): 18-69.

3309   Franz Mußner, "Wer ist 'dieses Geschlecht' in Mk 13,30 parr.?" *K* 29 (1987): 23-28.

13:32-37

3310   John B. Trotti, "Mark 13:32-37," *Int* 32/4 (1978): 410-15.

13:32

3311   Max Meinertz, " 'Dieses Geschlecht' im Neuen Testament," *BZ* 1 (1957): 283-89.

3312   Sosio Pezzella, "Marco 13,32 e la scienza di Cristo," *RBib* 7 (1959): 147-52.

3313   Giuseppe Segalla, "Il figlio non conosce il giorno della parusia," *PV* 10 (1965): 250-54.

3314   Jacques Winandy, "Le logion de l'ignorance (Mc, XIII,32; Mt, XXIV,36)," *RB* 75 (1968): 63-79.

13:33-37

3315   Evald Lövestam, "Le portier qui veille la nuit, Mc 13,33-37," *AsSeign* 2 (1969): 44-53.

3316   Richard J. Bauckham, "Synoptic Parousia Parables and the Apocalypse," *NTS* 23 (1976-1977): 162-76; 29 (1983): 129-34.

13:34-37

3317   John D. Crossan, "The Servant Parables of Jesus," *Semeia* 1 (1974): 17-62.

14:1-16:8

3318   Ched Myers, "The Last Days of Jesus, Mark 14:1-16:8: Collapse and Restoration of Discipleship," *Soj* 16 (1987): 32-36.

3319   John P. Heil, "The Narrative Strategy and Pragmatics of the Temple Theme in Mark," *CBQ* 59 (1997): 76-100.

<u>14:1-15:47</u>

3320 Matthew Vellanickal, "The Passion Narrative in the Gospel of Mark," *BB* 9 (1983): 258-78.

<u>14:1-52</u>

3321 John P. Heil, "Mark 14:1-52: Narrative Structure and Reader Response," *Bib* 71/3 (1990): 305-32.

<u>14:1-25</u>

3322 Frederick W. Danker, "The Literary Unity of Mark 14:1-25," *JBL* 85/4 (1966): 467-72.

<u>14:1-11</u>

3323 James R. Edwards, "Markan Sandwiches: The Significance of Interpolations in Markan Narratives," *NovT* 31 (1989): 193-216.

<u>14:1-2</u>

3324 Robert Schlarb, "Die Suche nach dem Messias: ζητέω als Terminus technicus der markinischen Messianologie," *ZNW* 81 (1990): 155-70.

<u>14:2</u>

3325 Christoph Burchard, "Fussnoten zum neutestamentlichen Griechisch," *ZNW* 61 (1970): 157-71.

3326 Ulrich Hedinger, "Jesus und die Volksmenge: Kritik der Qualifizierung der óchloi in der Evangelienauslegung," *TZ* 32 (1976): 201-206.

<u>14:3-9</u>

3327 André Légault, "An Application of the Form-Critique Method to the Anointings in Galilee (Lk 7,36-50) and Bethany (Mt 26,6-13; Mk 14,3-9; Lk 12,1-8)," *CBQ* 16 (1954): 131-45.

3328 Harald Sahlin, "Zum Verständnis der christologischen Anschauung des Markusevangeliums," *StTheol* 31 (1977): 1-19.

3329 Winsome Munro, "The Anointing in Mark 14:3-9 and John 12:1-8," *SBLSP* 9/1 (1979): 127-30.

3330   Franz Schnider, "Christusverkündigung und Jesuserzählungen: Exegetische Überlegungen zu Mk 14,3-9," *K* 24 (1982): 171-80.

3331   John N. Suggit, "An Incident from Mark's Gospel," *JTSA* 50 (1985): 25-55.

3332   Richard C. Brand, "Grace Is Everywhere," *ET* 97/9 (1985-1986): 277-78.

3333   Mary A. Beavis, "Women as Models of Faith in Mark," *BTB* 18 (1988): 3-9.

3334   James F. Coakley, "The Anointing at Bethany and the Priority of John," *JBL* 107/2 (1988): 241-56.

3335   Stephen C. Barton, "Mark as Narrative: The Story of the Anointing Woman (Mark 14:3-9)," *ET* 102 (1990-1991): 230-34.

3336   Phyllis Anderson, "Mark 14:3-9 and the Ordination of Women," *CThM* 22 (1995): 451-53.

3337   Kristine Carlson, "The Ministry of Women: Texts for the Celebration," *WW* 15 (1995): 367-72.

3338   Willard M. Swartley, "The Role of Women in Mark's Gospel: A Narrative Analysis," *BTB* 27 (1997): 16-22.

3339   Guy Wagner, "L'oncion de Béthanie: Essai sur la genèse du récit de Marc 14/3-9 et sa reprise par Matthieu, Luc et Jean," *ÉTR* 72 (1997): 437-46.

14:3

3340   Friedrich Wulf, " 'Der Geist ist willig, das Fleisch schwach' (Mk 14,3b)," *GeistL* 37 (1964): 241-43.

14:4

3341   J. B. Bauer, "Ut Quid Perditio Ista?—zu Mk 14,4f. und Parr.," *NovT* 3 (1959): 54-56.

3342   R. Deichgräber, "Die Gemeinderegel (1QS) X4," *RevQ* 2 (1960): 277-80.

14:8

3343   Robert Holst, "The One Anointing of Jesus: Another Application of the Form-Critical Method," *JBL* 95 (1976): 435-46.

14:9

3344   J. H. Greenlee, "Εἰς μνημόσυνον αὐτῆς: 'For Her Memorial': Mt xxvi.13, Mk xiv.9," *ET* 71 (1959-1960): 245.

3345   C. J. Maunder, "A *Sitz im Leben* for Mark 14:9," *ET* 99/3 (1987-1988): 78-80.

3346   Jean Delorme, "Evangile et Récit (1996): La narration évangélique en Marc," *NTS* 43 (1997): 367-84.

14:10

3347   J.-A. Morin, "Les deux derniers des Douze: Simon le Zelote et Judas Iskariôth," *RB* 80 (1973): 332-58.

3348   Yoël Arbeitman, "The Suffix of Iscariot," *JBL* 99 (1980): 122-23.

14:11

3349   Tjitze Baarda, "Markus 14:11: ἐπηγγείλαντο: 'Bron' of 'Redaktie'?" *GTT* 73 (1973): 65-75.

14:12-31

3350   Donald P. Senior, "The Eucharist in Mark: Mission, Reconciliation, Hope," *BTB* 12 (1982): 67-72.

14:12-17

3351   F. C. Synge, "A Matter of Tenses—Fingerprints of an Annotator in Mark," *ET* 88 (1976-1977): 168-71.

14:12-16

3352   Jean Delorme, "La Cène et la Pâque dans le Nouveau Testament," *LV* 31 (1957): 9-48.

3353   Philippe Rolland, "La préparation du repas pascal," *BLOS* 2 (1989): 3-8.

14:12

3354   Arthur G. Arnott, " 'The First Day of Unleavened . . .' Mt 26.17, Mk 14.12, Lk 22.7," *BT* 35 (1984): 235-38.

14:14-15:20

3355   J. D. M. Derrett, "The Upper Room and the Dish," *HeyJ* 26 (1985): 373-82.

14:16

3356   Wolfgang Feneberg, "Das Neue Testament: Sprache der Liebe—Zum Problem des Antijudaismus," *ZKT* 107 (1985): 333-40.

14:17-26

3357   S. Dockx, "Le récit du repas pascal. Marc 14,17-26," *Bib* 46 (1965): 445-53.

14:18-25

3358   F. C. Synge, "Mark 14:18-25: Supper and Rite," *JTSA* 4 (1973): 38-43.

14:18

3359   D. Neufeld, "Jesus' Eating Transgressions and Social Impropriety in the Gospel of Mark: A Social Scientific Approach," *BTB* 30 (2000): 15-26.

14:20-22

3360   J. Neville Birdsall, "The Withering of the Fig Tree," *ET* 73 (1961-1962): 191.

14:21-28

3361   James LaGrand, "The First of the Miracle Stories According to Mark (1:21-28)," *CThM* 20 (1993): 479-84.

3362   Paul S. Berge, "The Beginning of the Good News: The Epiphany Gospels in Mark and John," *WW* 17 (1997): 94-101.

14:21

3363   Jens Christensen, "Menneskesønnen gaar bort, som der staar skrevet om ham," *DTT* 19 (1956): 83-92.

3364   I. Howard Marshall, "The Synoptic Son of Man Sayings in Recent Discussion," *NTS* 12 (1965-1966): 327-51.

3365   P. Maurice Casey, "The Son of Man Problem," *ZNW* 67/3 (1976): 147-54.

14:22-25

3366   J.-B. du Roy, "Le dernier repas de Jésus," *BVC* 26 (1959): 44-52.

3367   J. Steinbeck, "Das Abendmahl Jesu unter Berücksichtigung moderner Forschung," *NovT* 3 (1959): 70-79.

3368   Heinz Schürmann, "Die Symbolhandlungen Jesu als eschatologische Erfüllungszeichen: Eine Rückfrage nach dem historischen Jesus," *BibL* 11 (1970): 29-41, 73-78.

3369   Enrique Nardoni, "Por una communidad libre. La última cena segun Mc 14,22-25 y el éxodo," *RevB* 33 (1971): 27-42.

3370   Giuseppe Barbaglio, "L'istituzione dell'eucaristia (Mc 14,22-25; 1 Cor 11,23-24 e par.)," *ParSpirV* 7 (1983): 125-41.

3371   William J. Carl, "Mark 14:22-25," *Int* 39/3 (1985): 296-301.

3372   J. Becker, "Die neutestamentliche Rede vom Sühnetod Jesu," *ZTK* 8 (1990): 29-49.

3373   H. Schlier, "Das neue Passa. Mk 14.22-25," *IKaZ* 29 (2000): 155-59.

14:22-24

3374   Heinz Schürmann, "Die Semitismen im Einsetzungsbericht bei Markus und bei Lukas," *ZKT* 73 (1951): 72-77.

14:22-23

3375   Brian A. Mastin, " 'Jesus Said Grace'," *SJT* 24 (1971): 449-56.

14:22

3376   Paul E. Davies, "Did Jesus Die as a Martyr-Prophet?" *BR* 2 (1957): 19-30.

3377   B. E. Thiering, " 'Breaking of Bread' and 'Harvest' in Mark's Gospel," *NovT* 12 (1970): 1-12.

3378   Joachim Jeremias, " 'This is My Body'," *ET* 83 (1971-1972): 196-203.

3379   Richard J. Dillon, " 'As One Having Authority' (Mark 1:22): The Controversial Distinction of Jesus' Teaching," *CBQ* 57 (1995): 92-113.

14:24-25

3380   Willem A. Saayman, "The Eucharist in Mission Perspective," *ThEv* 18/2 (1985): 18-24.

3381   J. M. Casciaro Ramírez, "The Original Aramaic Form of Jesus' Interpretation of the Cup," *JTS* 41 (1990): 1-12.

14:24

3382   J. A. Emerton, "The Aramaic Underlying τὸ αἷμά μου τῆς διαθήκης," *JTS* 6 (1955): 238-40.

3383   J. A. Emerton, "τὸ αἷμά μου τῆς διαθήκης: The Evidence of the Syriac Versions," *JTS* 13 (1962): 111-17.

3384   J. A. Emerton, "Mark 14:24 and the Targum to the Psalter," *JTS* 15 (1964): 58-59.

3385   Richard T. France, "The Servant of the Lord in the Teaching of Jesus," *TynB* 19 (1968): 26-52.

3386   Wilfried Pigulla, "Das für viele vergossene Blut," *MTZ* 23 (1972): 72-82.

3387   N. Hoffmann, " 'Stellvertretung': Grundgestalt und Mitte des Mysteriums. Ein Versuch trinitätstheologischer Begründung christlicher Sühne," *MTZ* 30 (1979): 161-91.

3388   Uwe Wegner, "Deu Jesus um sentido salvífico para sua morte: consideraçoes sobre Mc. 14:24 e 10:45," *EstT* 26/3 (1986): 209-46.

3389   P. Maurice Casey, "The Original Aramaic Form of Jesus' Interpretation of the Cup," *JTS* 41 (1990): 1-12.

3390   Lynne C. Boughton, " 'Being Shed for You/Many': Time-Sense and Consequences in the Synoptic Cup Citations," *TynB* 48 (1997): 249-70.

14:25

3391   Jean Delorme, "La Cène et la Pâque dans le Nouveau Testament," *LV* 31 (1957): 9-48.

3392   Barry S. Crawford, "Near Expectation in the Sayings of Jesus," *JBL* 101/2 (1982): 225-44.

3393   Balembo Buetubela, "Le produit de la vigne et le vin nouveau: Analyse exégétique de Mc 14.25," *RAfT* 8 (1984): 5-16.

3394 Michal Wojciechowski, "Le Nazireat et la Passion (Mc 14,25a; 15,23)," *Bib* 65/1 (1984): 94-96.

3395 Ray C. Jones, "The Lord's Supper and the Concept of Anamnesis," *WW* 6/4 (1986): 434-45.

3396 Jack T. Sanders, "The Criterion of Coherence and the Randomness of Charisma: Poring Through Some Aporias in the Jesus Tradition," *NTS* 44 (1998): 1-25.

3397 J. P. Meyer, "The Debate on the Resurrection of the Dead: An Incident from the Ministry of the Historical Jesus?" *JSNT* 77 (2000): 3-24.

14:26-31

3398 Max Wilcox, "The Denial Sequence in Mark xiv.26-31, 66-72," *NTS* 17 (1970-1971): 426-36.

3399 Jerome H. Neyrey, "The Absence of Jesus' Emotions—The Lucan Redaction of Lk 22,39-49," *Bib* 61/2 (1980): 153-71.

14:26

3400 Werner Schauch, "Der Ölberg: Exegese zu einer Ortsangabe besonders bei Matthäus und Markus," *TLZ* 77 (1952): 391-96.

3401 John Ellington, "The Translation of ὑμνέω, 'Sing a Hymn' in Mark 14:26 and Matthew 26:30," *BT* 30 (1979): 445-46.

14:27-28

3402 Wilfred Tooley, "The Shepherd and Sheep Image in the Teaching of Jesus," *NovT* 7 (1964-1965): 15-25.

3403 Thorwald Lorenzen, "Ist der Auferstandene in Galiläa erschienen? Bemerkungen zu einem Aufsatz von B. Steinseifer," *ZNW* 64 (1973): 209-21.

14:27

3404 John D. Crossan, "Redaction and Citation in Mark 11:9-10, 17 and 14:27," *SBLSP* 2 (1972): 17-60.

3405 R. P. Schroeder, "The 'Worthless' Shepherd. A Study of Mark 14:27," *CThM* 2 (1975): 342-44.

14:28

3406 P. Cornelius Odenkirchen, " 'Praecedam vos in Galilaeam'," *VD* 46 (1968): 193-223.

3407 Jean-Marie van Cangh, "La Galilée dans l'évangile de Marc: un lieu théologique?" *RB* 79 (1972): 59-75.

3408 Robert H. Stein, "A Short Note on Mark 14:28 and 16:7," *NTS* 20 (1973-1974): 445-52.

3409 B. M. F. van Iersel, " 'To Galilee' or 'in Galilee' in Mark 14:28 and 16:7?" *ETL* 58 (1982): 365-70.

3410 Domingo Muñoz León, " 'Iré delante de vosotros a Galilea' (Mt 26,32 y par). Sentido mesiánico y posible sustrato arameo del logion," *EB* 48 (1990): 215-41.

1:29-31

3411 John G. Cook, "In Defence of Ambiguity: Is There a Hidden Demon in Mark 1:29-31?" *NTS* 43 (1997): 184-208.

14:30

3412 Cuthbert Lattey, "A Note on Cockcrow," *Scr* 6 (1953-1954): 53-55.

3413 Markus Ohler, "Der zweimalige Hahnschrei der Markuspassion: Zur Textüberlieferung von Mk 14,30.68.72," *ZNW* 85 (1994): 145-50.

14:32-15:47

3414 Raymond E. Brown, "The Passion according to Mark," *Worship* 59 (1985): 116-26.

14:32-42

3415 J. A. Colunga, "La agonía de Jésus en Getsemaní," *CuBí* 16 (1959): 13-17.

3416 Raymond E. Brown, "Incidents That Are Units in the Synoptic Gospels but Dispersed in St. John," *CBQ* 23 (1961): 143-60.

3417 R. S. Barbour, "Uncomfortable Words: VIII. Status and Titles," *ET* 82/5 (1970-1971): 137-42.

3418 Werner H. Kelber, "Mark 14:32-42: Gethsemane. Passion Christology and Discipleship Failure," *ZNW* 63 (1972): 166-87.

3419 Sjef van Tilborg, "A Form-Criticism of the Lord's Prayer," *NovT* 14/2 (1972): 94-105.

3420 Werner Mohn, "Gethsemane (Mk 14:32-42)," *ZNW* 64/3 (1973): 195-208.

3421 Rinaldo Fabris, "La preghiera del Getsemani," *PV* 19 (1974): 258-67.

3422 Gene Szarek, "A Critique of Kelber's 'The Hour of the Son of Man and the Temptation of the Disciples: Mark 14:32-42'," *SBLSP* 6 (1976): 111-18.

3423 Joseph Thomas, "La scène du jardin selon Marc 14:32-42," *Chr* 28 (1981): 350-60.

3424 Thomas Söding, "Gebet und Gebetsmahnung Jesu in Getsemane: eine redaktionskritische Auslegung von Mk 14:32-42," *BZ* 31/1 (1987): 76-100.

3425 Benny R. Crockett, "The Function of Mathetological Prayer in Mark," *IBS* 10 (1988): 123-39.

3426 Reinhard Feldmeier, "Die Krisis des Gottessohnes: die markinische Gethsemaneperikope als Markuspassion," *TLZ* 113 (1988): 234-36.

3427 Karen E. Smith, "Mark 14:32-42," *RevExp* 88 (1991): 433-37.

3428 Charles W. Hedrick, "Representing Prayer in Mark and Chariton's Chaereas and Callirhoe," *PRS* 22 (1995): 239-57.

3429 Kevin Madigan, "Ancient and High-Medieval Interpretations of Jesus in Gethsemane: Some Reflections on Tradition and Continuity in Christian Thought," *HTR* 88 (1995): 157-73.

3430 Marlis Gielen, " 'Und führe uns nicht in Versuchung' Die 6. Vater- Unser Bitte—eine Anfechtung für das biblische Gottesbild?" *ZNW* 89 (1998): 201-16.

14:35-51

3431   John Bligh, "Christ's Death Cry (Mark 14:35-51)," *HeyJ* 1 (1960): 142-46.

14:36

3432   S. V. McCasland, " 'Abba, Father'," *JBL* 72 (1953): 79-91.

3433   Thor Boman, "Der Gebetskampf Jesu," *NTS* 10 (1963-1964): 261-73.

3434   Wilhelm Vischer, "Abba," *ÉTR* 54 (1979): 683-86.

3435   Joseph A. Grassi, "Abba, Father (Mark 14:36): Another Approach," *JAAR* 50/3 (1982): 449-58.

3436   Mark Riley, " 'Lord Save My Life' (Ps 116:4) as a Generative Text for Jesus' Gethsemane Prayer (Mark 14:36a)," *CBQ* 48/4 (1986): 655-59.

3437   E. A. Obeng, "Abba, Father: The Prayer of the Sons of God," *ET* 99 (1987-1988): 363-66.

14:39

3438   John J. Pilch, "Death with Honor: The Mediterranean Style Death of Jesus in Mark," *BTB* 25 (1995): 65-70.

14:41

3439   George H. Boobyer, "Ἀπέχει in Mark 14:41," *NTS* 2 (1955-1956): 44-48.

3440   Patrick P. Saydon, "Some Biblico-Liturgical Passages Reconsidered," *MeliT* 18/1 (1966): 10-17.

3441   Klaus W. Müller, "Apechei (Mk 14:41): absurda lectio," *ZNW* 77/1-2 (1986): 83-100.

3442   Robert G. Bratcher, "Unusual Sinners," *BT* 39 (1988): 335-37.

14:42-47

3443   W. Boyd Barrick, "The Rich Man from Arimathea (Matt 27:57-60) and 1QIsaᵃ," *JBL* 96 (1977): 235-39.

14:43-16:8

3444   Mark McVann, "The Passion in Mark: Transformation Ritual," *BTB* 18 (1988): 96-101.

14:43-52

3445   Gerhard Schneider, "Die Verhaftung Jesu: Traditionsgeschichte von Mk 14:43-52," *ZNW* 63/3 (1972): 188-209.

3446   Simon Légasse, "L'arrestation de Jésus d'après Marc 14/43-52," *ÉTR* 68 (1993): 241-47.

3447   Detlev Dormeyer, "Joh 18:1-14 Par Mk 14.43-53: Methodologische Überlegungen zur Rekonstruktion einer vorsynoptischen Passionsgeschichte," *NTS* 41 (1995): 218-39.

14:43-51

3448   Jean Cantinat, "Jesus devant le Sanhedrin," *NRT* 75 (1953): 300-308.

14:43

3449   Donald P. Senior, " 'With Swords and Clubs . . .': The Setting of Mark's Community and His Critique of Abusive Power," *BTB* 17 (1987): 10-20.

14:44

3450   C. Buzzetti, "Parallels in the Synoptic Gospels: A Case Study," *BT* 34 (1984): 425-31.

14:45

3451   F. W. Belcher, "A Comment on Mark xiv.45," *ET* (1952-1953): 240.

14:47

3452   Benedict T. Viviano, "The High Priest's Servant's Ear: Mark 14:47," *RB* 96 (1989): 71-80.

14:49

3453   A. W. Argyle, "The Meaning of καθ' ἡμέραν in Mark xiv.49," *ET* 63 (1951-1952): 354.

3454   William G. Morrice, "The Imperatival ἵνα," *BT* 23 (1972): 326-30.

14:50

3455   Thorwald Lorenzen, "Ist der Auferstandene in Galiläa erschienen? Bemerkungen zu einem Aufsatz von B. Steinseifer," *ZNW* 64 (1973): 209-21.

3456   L. Paul Trudinger, "Davidic Links with the Betrayal of
       Jesus: Some Further Observations," *ET* 86 (1974-1975):
       278-79.

14:51-52

3457   Albert Vanhoye, "La fuite du jeune homme nu (Mc
       14,51-52)," *Bib* 52 (1971): 401-406.

3458   Robin Scroggs and Kent I. Groff, "Baptism in Mark:
       Dying and Rising with Christ," *JBL* 92 (1973): 531-48.

3459   Harry T. Fleddermann, "The Flight of a Naked Young
       Man (Mark 14:51-52)," *CBQ* 41/3 (1979): 412-18.

3460   Michael R. Cosby, "Mark 14:51-52 and the Problem of
       Gospel Narrative," *PRS* 11/3 (1984): 219-31.

3461   Marvin W. Meyer, "The Youth in the Secret Gospel of
       Mark," *Semeia* 49 (1990): 129-53.

3462   Howard M. Jackson, "Why the Youth Shed His Cloak and
       Fled Naked: The Meaning and Purpose of Mark
       14:51-52," *JBL* 116 (1997): 273-89.

3463   Michael J. Haren, "The Naked Young Man: A Historian's
       Hypothesis on Mark 14,51-52," *Bib* 79 (1998): 525-31.

14:53-15:1

3464   Gerhard Schneider, "Gab es Eine vorsynoptische Szene
       'Jesus vor dem Synedrium'?" *NovT* 12/1 (1970): 22-39.

3465   Gerhard Schneider, "Jesus vor dem Synedrium," *BibL* 11
       (1970): 1-15.

14:53-65

3466   Kurt Schubert, "Die Juden und die Römer," *BL* 36 (1962):
       235-42.

3467   Donald H. Juel, "The Function of the Trial of Jesus in
       Mark's Gospel," *SBLSP* 5 (1975): 83-104.

3468   Mary A. Beavis, "The Trial before the Sanhedrin (Mark
       14:53-65): Reader Response and Greco-Roman Readers,"
       CBQ 49 (1987): 581-96.

14:53-62

3469   William F. McInerny, "An Unresolved Question in the Gospel Called Mark: 'Who Is This Whom Even Wind and Sea Obey'?" *PRS* 23 (1996): 255-68.

14:53

3470   Paul Winter, "Markus 14:53b, 55-56: Ein Gebilde des Evangelisten," *ZNW* 53 (1962): 260-63.

14:54

3471   George W. Buchanan, "Mark 14:54," *ET* 54 (1956): 27.

3472   Josef Ernst, "Noch einmal: Die Verleugnung Jesu durch Petrus (Mk 14,54.66-72)," *Cath* 30 (1976): 207-26.

3473   George Howard, "Stylistic Inversion and the Synoptic Tradition," *JBL* 97 (1978): 375-89.

14:55-65

3474   Raymond E. Brown, "Incidents That Are Units in the Synoptic Gospels but Dispersed in St. John," *CBQ* 23 (1961): 143-60.

14:55-64

3475   Jean Cantinat, "Jesus devant le Sanhedrin," *NRT* 75 (1953): 300-308.

3476   Georg Braumann, "Markus 15:2-5 und Markus 14:55-64," *ZNW* 52 (1961): 273-78.

3477   Dieter Lührmann, "Markus 14:55-64: Christologie und Zerstörung des Tempels im Markusevangelium," *NTS* 27 (1980-1981): 457-74.

14:55-56

3478   Paul Winter, "Markus 14:53b, 55-56: Ein Gebilde des Evangelisten," *ZNW* 53 (1962): 260-63.

14:58

3479   Gerd Theissen, "Die Tempelweissagung Jesu. Prophetie im Spannungsfeld von Stadt und Land," *TZ* 32 (1976): 144-58.

3480   Giancarlo Biguzzi, "Mc. 14,58: un tempio ἀχειροποίητον," *RBib* 26 (1978): 225-40.

3481   B. Prete, "Formazione e storicità del detto di Gesù sul tempio secondo Mc. 14,58," *BibO* 27 (1985): 3-16.

14:61-64

3482   Jacob Kremer, " 'Sohn Gottes': Zur Klärung des biblischen Hoheitstitels Jesu," *BL* 46 (1973): 3-21.

3483   Klaus Berger, "Die königlichen Messiastraditionen des Neuen Testaments," *NTS* 20 (1973-1974): 1-44.

3484   Craig A. Evans, "In What Sense Blasphemy? Jesus before Caiaphas in Mark 14:61-64," *SBLSP* 30 (1991): 215-34.

14:61-62

3485   Franz Mußner, "Die Wiederkunft des Menschensohnes nach Markus 13,24-27 und 14,61-62," *BK* 16 (1961): 105-107.

3486   W. R. G. Loader, "Christ at the Right Hand—Ps. cx. 1 in the New Testament," *NTS* 24 (1977-1978): 199-217.

14:61

3487   Evald Lövestam, "Die Frage des Hohenpriesters (Mark 14,61 par. Matth. 26,63)," *SEÅ* 26/27 (1961): 93-107.

3488   J. C. O'Neill, "The Silence of Jesus," *NTS* 15/2 (1968-1969): 153-69.

3489   Joel Marcus, "Mark 14:61: 'Are You the Messiah-Son-of-God'?" *NovT* 31 (1989): 125-41.

14:62

3490   E. J. Tinsley, "The Sign of the Son of Man (Mk 14,62)," *SJT* 8 (1955): 297-306.

3491   J. A. T. Robinson, "The Second Coming: Mark 14:62," *ET* 67 (1955-1956): 336-40.

3492   Harvey K. McArthur, "Mark xiv.62," *NTS* 4 (1957-1958): 156-58.

3493   H. P. Owen, "The Parousia of Christ in the Synoptic Gospels," *SJT* 12 (1959): 171-92.

3494   T. F. Glasson, "The Reply to Caiaphas (Mark 14:62)," *NTS* 7 (1960-1961): 88-93.

3495   A. M. Goldberg, "Sitzend zur Rechten der Kraft. Zur Gottesbezeichnung Gebura in der frühen rabbinischen Literatur," *BZ* 8 (1964): 284-93.

3496   I. Howard Marshall, "The Synoptic Son of Man Sayings in Recent Discussion," *NTS* 12 (1965-1966): 327-51.

3497   Norman Perrin, "Mark XIV.62: The End Product of a Christian Pesher Tradition?" *NTS* 12 (1965-1966): 150-55.

3498   F. H. Borsch, "Mark 14:62 and I Enoch 62:5," *NTS* 14 (1967-1968): 565-67.

3499   Renatus Kempthorne, "The Marcan Text of Jesus' Answer to the High Priest (Mark 14:62)," *NovT* 19/3 (1977): 197-208.

3500   George R. Beasley-Murray, "The Parousia in Mark," *RevExp* 75/4 (1978): 565-81.

3501   Antonio Vargas-Machuca, "¿Por qué condenaron a muerte a Jesús de Nazaret?" *EE* 54 (1979): 441-70.

3502   Dennis C. Duling, "Insights from Sociology for New Testament Christology: A Test Case," *SBLSP* 24 (1985): 351-68.

3503   Matthew Black, "The Theological Appropriation of the Old Testament by the New Testament," *SJT* 39/1 (1986): 1-17.

14:64

3504   Paul Lamarche, "Le 'blasphème' de Jésus devant le Sanhédrin," *RechSR* 50 (1962): 74-85.

3505   David R. Catchpole, "You Have Heard His Blasphemy," *TynB* 16 (1965): 10-18.

14:65-72

3506   Michael D. Goulder, "On Putting Q to the Test," *NTS* 24 (1977-1978): 218-34.

3507   Christopher M. Tuckett, "On the Relationship between Matthew and Luke," *NTS* 30 (1984): 130-42.

14:65

3508   Paul Glaue, "Einige Stellen: die Bedeutung des Codex D charakterisieren," *NovT* 2 (1957-1958): 310-15.

3509   Robert H. Gundry, "1Q Isaiah 50,6 and Mark 14,65," *RevQ* 2 (1960): 559-67.

3510   Frans Neirynck, "ΤΙΣ ΕΣΤΙΝ Ο ΠΑΙΣΑΣ ΣΕ: Mt 26,68/Lk 22,64 (diff. Mk 14,65)," *ETL* 63/1 (1987): 5-47.

14:66-72

3511   Jean Cantinat, "Jesus devant le Sanhedrin," *NRT* 75 (1953): 300-308.

3512   Max Wilcox, "The Denial Sequence in Mark xiv.26-31, 66-72," *NTS* 17 (1970-1971): 426-36.

3513   Josef Ernst, "Noch einmal: Die Verleugnung Jesu durch Petrus (Mk 14,54.66-72)," *Cath* 30 (1976): 207-26.

3514   Dietfried Gewalt, "Die Verleugnung des Petrus," *LB* 43 (1978): 113-44.

3515   Kim E. Dewey, "Peter's Denial Reexamined: John's Knowledge of Mark's Gospel," *SBLSP* 9/1 (1979): 109-12.

3516   N. J. McEleney, "Peter's Denials—How Many? To Whom?" *CBQ* 52 (1990): 467-72.

14:68-72

3517   J. D. M. Derrett, "The Reason for the Cock-Crowings," *NTS* 29 (1983): 142-44.

14:68

3518   W. J. P. Boyd, "Peter's Denials—Mark 14:68, Luke 22:57," *ET* 67 (1955-1956): 341.

3519   Markus Ohler, "Der zweimalige Hahnschrei der Markuspassion: Zur Textüberlieferung von Mk 14,30.68.72," *ZNW* 85 (1994): 145-50.

14:72

3520   G. M. Lee, "Mark, xiv.72: ἐπιβαλὼν ἔκλαιεν," *ET* 61 (1949-1950): 160.

3521   J. Neville Birdsall, "Τὸ ῥῆμα ὡς εἶπεν αὐτῷ ὁ Ιησοῦς: Mark 14:72," *NovT* 2 (1957-1958): 272-75.

3522   G. M. Lee, "Mark 14,72: *epibalōn eklaien*," *Bib* 53 (1972): 411-12.

3523   Eugene A. LaVerdiere, "Peter Broke Down and Began to Cry," *Emmanuel* 92 (1986): 70-73.

3524   Markus Ohler, "Der zweimalige Hahnschrei der Markuspassion: Zur Textüberlieferung von Mk 14,30.68.72," *ZNW* 85 (1994): 145-50.

3525   Günther Schwarz, " 'Und er begann zu weinen' (Markus 14,72)," *BibN* 78 (1995): 18-20.

15:1-46

3526   Christopher M. Tuckett, "On the Relationship between Matthew and Luke," *NTS* 30 (1984): 130-42.

15:1-26

3527   Marinus de Jonge, "The Earliest Christian Use of Christos: Some Suggestions," *NTS* 32 (1986): 321-43.

15:1-15

3528   Donald H. Juel, "The Function of the Trial of Jesus in Mark's Gospel," *SBLSP* 5 (1975): 83-104.

15:1

3529   Michael D. Goulder, "On Putting Q to the Test," *NTS* 24 (1977-1978): 218-34.

15:2-21

3530   Klaus Berger, "Die königlichen Messiastraditionen des Neuen Testaments," *NTS* 20 (1973-1974): 1-44.

15:2-5

3531   Georg Braumann, "Markus 15:2-5 und Markus 14:55-64," *ZNW* 52 (1961): 273-78.

3532   Jack T. Sanders, "The Criterion of Coherence and the Randomness of Charisma: Poring Through Some Aporias in the Jesus Tradition," *NTS* 44 (1998): 1-25.

15:2

3533   Klaus Haacker, "Einige Fälle von 'erlebter Rede' im Neuen Testament," *NovT* 12 (1970): 70-77.

3534   Klaus Berger, "Zum Problem der Messianität Jesu," *ZTK* 71 (1974): 1-30.

15:3

3535   Martin J. Higgins, "New Testament Result Clauses with Infinitive," *CBQ* 23 (1961): 233-41.

3536   Marinus de Jonge, "The Earliest Christian Use of Christos: Some Suggestions," *NTS* 32 (1986): 321-43.

15:7-15

3537   Hyam Z. Maccoby, "Jesus and Barabbas," *NTS* 16 (1969-1970): 55-60.

3538   Robert L. Merritt, "Jesus Barabbas and the Paschal Pardon," *JBL* 104 (1985): 57-68.

15:7

3539   Alois Bajsić, "Pilatus, Jesus und Barabbas," *Bib* 48 (1967): 7-28.

3540   Günter Scholz, " 'Joseph von Arimathäa' und 'Barabbas'," *LB* 57 (1985): 81-94.

15:8

3541   G. M. Lee, "Mark xv.8," *NovT* 20 (1978): 74.

15:9-14

3542   C.-I. Foulon-Piganiol, "Le rôle du peuple dans le procès de Jesus: Une hypothèse juridique et théologique," *NRT* 98 (1976): 627-37.

15:9

3543   Klaus Haacker, "Einige Fälle von 'erlebter Rede' im Neuen Testament," *NovT* 12 (1970): 70-77.

15:10

3544   Anselm C. Hagedorn and Jerome H. Neyrey, " 'It Was Out of Envy that They Handed Jesus Over' (Mark 15:10): The Anatomy of Envy and the Gospel of Mark," *JSNT* 69 (1998): 15-56.

15:13

3545   Ulrich Hedinger, "Jesus und die Volksmenge: Kritik der Qualifizierung der óchloi in der Evangelienauslegung," *TZ* 32 (1976): 201-206.

3546   John Thorley, "Aktionsart in New Testament Greek: Infinitive and Imperative," *NovT* 31 (1989): 290-315.

15:16-27

3547   F. C. Synge, "A Matter of Tenses—Fingerprints of an Annotator in Mark," *ET* 88 (1976-1977): 168-71.

15:16-32

3548   Thomas E. Schmidt, "Mark 15:16-32: The Crucifixion Narrative and the Roman Triumphal Procession," *NTS* 41 (1995): 1-18.

15:18

3549   Klaus Berger, "Zum Problem der Messianität Jesu," *ZTK* 71 (1974): 1-30.

15:20-39

3550   Kenneth E. Bailey, "The Fall of Jerusalem and Mark's Account of the Cross," *ET* 102 (1991-1992): 102-105.

15:21-41

3551   José R. Scheifler, "El Salmo 22 y la Crucifixión del Señor," *EB* 24 (1965): 5-83.

3552   Daniel Guichard, "La reprise du psaume 22 dans le récit de la mort de Jésus," *FV* 87/5 (1988): 59-64.

15:21

3553   G. M. Lee, "Mark 15:21: 'The Father of Alexander and Rufus'," *NovT* 17/4 (1975): 303.

3554   Marion L. Soards, "Tradition, Composition, and Theology in Jesus' Speech to the 'Daughters of Jerusalem' (Luke 23,26-32)," *Bib* 68/2 (1987): 221-44.

3555   Brian K. Blount, "A Socio-Rhetorical Analysis of Simon of Cyrene: Mark 15:21 and Its Parallels," *Semeia* 64 (1994): 171-98.

15:22-39

3556   William F. McInerny, "An Unresolved Question in the Gospel Called Mark: 'Who Is This Whom Even Wind and Sea Obey'?" *PRS* 23 (1996): 255-68.

15:22-32

3557   Philippe Rolland, "Jésus est mis en croix," *BLOS* 6 (1990): 11-17.

15:22-29

3558   Miguel de Burgos Nuñez, "La communión de Dios con el crucificado. Cristología de Marcos 15,22-39," *EB* 37 (1978): 243-66.

15:23

3559   Michal Wojciechowski, "Le Nazireat et la Passion (Mc 14,25a; 15,23)," *Bib* 65/1 (1984): 94-96.

15:24

3560   Joseph A. Fitzmyer, "Crucifixion in Ancient Palestine, Qumran Literature, and the New Testament," *CBQ* 40/4 (1978): 493-513.

15:25

3561   Sebastián Bartina, "Ignolum *episēmon* gabex," *VD* 36 (1958): 16-37.

3562   Matthew Mahoney, "A New Look at 'The Third Hour' of Mark 15:25," *CBQ* 28 (1966): 292-99.

3563   Bonaventura Rinaldi, "Ora terza, sesta, nona, le ore della Passione di Cristo," *BibO* 23 (1981): 86.

15:26

3564   Klaus Berger, "Zum Problem der Messianität Jesu," *ZTK* 71 (1974): 1-30.

15:28

3565   Peter R. Rodgers, "Mark 15:28," *EQ* 69/1 (1989): 81-84.

15:29

3566   Klaus Haacker, "Einige Fälle von 'erlebter Rede' im Neuen Testament," *NovT* 12 (1970): 70-77.

15:32

3567   Harald Sahlin, "Emendationsvorschläge zum griechischen Text des Neuen Testaments I," *NovT* 24 (1982): 160-79.

15:33-16:8

3568   Ton Veerkamp, "Vom ersten Tag nach jenem Sabbat: Der Epilog des Markusevangeliums: 15:33-16:8," *TextK* 13 (1982): 5-34.

15:33-39

3569   M. Josuttis, "Die permanente Passion. Predigt über Markus 15,33-39," *EvT* 38 (1978): 160-63.

3570   Frank J. Matera, "The Death of Jesus according to Luke: A Question of Sources," *CBQ* 47 (1985): 469-85.

3571 F. Pérez Herrero, "Mc 15.33-39: muerte de Jesús y revelación de Dios," *Bur* 40 (1999): 369-99.

15:33-34

3572 Bonaventura Rinaldi, "Ora terza, sesta, nona, le ore della Passione di Cristo," *BibO* 23 (1981): 86.

15:33

3573 R. M. Grández, "Las tinieblas en la muerte de Jésus: Historia de la exégesis de Lc 23,44-45a," *EB* 47 (1989): 177-223.

15:34-39

3574 Paul Glaue, "Einige Stellen: die Bedeutung des Codex D charakterisieren," *NovT* 2 (1957-1958): 310-15.

3575 Hartmut Gese, "Psalm 22 und das Neue Testament," *ZTK* 65/1 (1968): 1-22.

15:34-37

3576 Heribert Schützeichel, "Der Todesschrei Jesu: Bemerkungen zu einer Theologie des Kreuzes," *TTZ* 83 (1974): 1-16.

3577 Lorraine Caza, "Le relief que Marc a donné au cri de la croix," *ScE* 39 (1987): 171-91.

15:34

3578 Julius R. Mantey, "The Causal Use of εἰς in the New Testament," *JBL* 70 (1951): 45-48.

3579 D. H. C. Read, "The Cry of Dereliction," *ET* 68 (1956-1957): 260-62.

3580 Martin Rehm, "Eli, Eli lamma sabachthani," *BZ* 2 (1958): 275-78.

3581 Joachim Gnilka, " 'Mein Gott, mein Gott, warum hast du mich verlassen?' (Mk 15,34 Par.)," *BZ* 3 (1959): 294-97.

3582 John Wilkinson, "Seven Words from the Cross," *SJT* 17 (1964): 69-82.

3583 Frederick W. Danker, "The Demonic Secret in Mark: A Reexamination of the Cry of Dereliction (15:34)," *ZNW* 61 (1970): 48-69.

3584   John H. Reumann, "Psalm 22 at the Cross: Lament and Thanksgiving for Jesus Christ," *Int* 28/1 (1974): 39-58.

3585   L. Paul Trudinger, " 'Eli, Eli, Lama Sabachthani?' A Cry of Derelicition? or Victory?" *JETS* 17 (1974): 235-38.

3586   S. J. Kistemaker, "The Seven Words from the Cross," *WTJ* 38 (1976): 182-91.

3587   Harald Sahlin, "Zum Verständnis der christologischen Anschauung des Markusevangeliums," *StTheol* 31 (1977): 1-19.

3588   R. Rubinkiewicz, "Mk 15,34 i Hbr 1,8-9 w świetle tradycji targumicznej," *RoczTK* 25 (1978): 59-67.

3589   Haim H. Cohn, "Jesus' Cry on the Cross: An Alternative View," *ET* 93 (1981-1982): 215-17.

3590   Christoph Burchard, "Markus 15,34," *ZNW* 74/1 (1983): 1-11.

3591   J.-C. Sagne, "The Cry of Jesus on the Cross," *Conci* 169 (1983): 52-58.

3592   David Atkinson, "A Cry of Faith," *ET* 96 (1984-1985): 146-47.

3593   Michael Jinkins and Stephen Reid, "God's Forsakenness: The Cry of Dereliction as an Utterance Within the Trinity," *HBT* 19 (1997): 33-57.

15:35-39

3594   Kent E. Brower, "Elijah in the Markan Passion Narrative," *JSNT* 18 (1983): 85-101.

15:36

3595   G. M. Lee, "Two Notes on St. Mark," *NovT* 18/1 (1976): 36.

15:37-39

3596   Harry L. Chronis, "The Torn Veil: Cultus and Christology in Mark 15:37-39," *JBL* 101/1 (1982): 97-114.

3597   Howard M. Jackson, "The Death of Jesus in Mark and the Miracle from the Cross," *NTS* 33/1 (1987): 16-37.

15:38

3598 André Pelletier, "La tradition synoptique du 'voile déchire' a la lumière des réalités archéologiques," *RechSR* 46 (1958): 161-80.

3599 Marinus de Jonge, "De berichten over het scheuren van het voorhangsel bij Jezus' dood in de synoptische evangeliën," *NTT* 21 (1966-1967): 90-114.

3600 Paul Lamarche, "La mort du Christ et le voile du temple selon Marc," *NRT* 96 (1974): 583-99.

3601 Simon Légasse, "Les voiles du Temple de Jérusalem," *RB* 87 (1980): 560-89.

3602 Marinus de Jonge, "Two Interesting Interpretations of the Rending of the Temple-Veil in the Testaments of the Twelve Patriarchs," *Bij* 46 (1985): 350-62.

3603 S. Motyer, "The Rending of the Veil: A Markan Pentecost?" *NTS* 33/1 (1987): 155-57.

3604 David Ulansey, "The Heavenly Veil Torn: Mark's Cosmic Inclusio" *JBL* 110 (1991):123-25.

15:39

3605 Robert G. Bratcher, "A Note on υἱὸς θεοῦ," *ET* 68 (1956-1957): 27-28.

3606 J. Ramsey Michaels, "The Centurion's Confession and the Spear Thrust," *CBQ* 29 (1967): 102-109.

3607 P. H. Bligh, "A Note on υἱὸς θεοῦ in Mark 15:39," *ET* 80 (1968-1969): 51-53.

3608 T. F. Glasson, "Mark 15:39: The Son of God," *ET* 80 (1968-1969): 286.

3609 Harold A. Guy, "Son of God in Mark 15:39," *ET* 81 (1969-1970): 151.

3610 Philip B. Harner, "Qualitative Anarthrous Predicate Nouns: Mark 15:39 and John 1:1," *JBL* 92 (1973): 75-87.

3611 Klemens Stock, "Das Bekenntnis des Centurio. Mk 15,39 im Rahmen des Markusevangeliums," *ZKT* 100 (1978): 289-301.

3612   Gerhard Schneider, "Christologische Aussagen des 'Credo' im Lichte des Neuen Testaments," *TTZ* 89 (1980): 282-92.

3613   Earl S. Johnson, "Is Mark 15:39 the Key to Mark's Christology?" *JSNT* 31 (1987): 3-22.

3614   Ernst L. Schnellbächer, "Sachgemässe Schriftauslegung," *NovT* 30 (1988): 114-31.

3615   Tae H. Kim, "The Anarthrous *yios theou* in Mark 15,39 and the Roman Imperial Cult," *Bib* 79 (1998): 221-41.

3616   M. Ebner, "Im Schatten der Grossen. Kleine Erzählfiguren im Markusevangelium," *BZ* 44 (2000): 56-76.

3617   Adela Y. Collins, "Mark and His Readers: The Son of God among Greeks and Romans," *HTR* 93 (2000): 85-100.

15:40-16:8

3618   Édouard Dhanis, "L'ensevelissement de Jésus et la visite au tombeau dans l'évangile de saint Marc (Mc. XV,40-XVI,8)," *Greg* 39 (1958): 367-410.

3619   Patrick J. Hartin, "The Role of the Women Disciples in Mark's Narrative," *ThEv* 26 (1993): 91-102.

15:40-47

3620   John D. Crossan, "Mark and the Relatives of Jesus," *NovT* 15 (1973): 81-113.

3621   Luise Schottroff, "Maria Magdalena und die Frauen am Grabe Jesu," *EvT* 42 (1982): 3-25.

15:40-41

3622   Augustine Stock, "Hinge Transitions in Mark's Gospel," *BTB* 15 (1985): 27-31.

3623   Paul Danove, "The Characterization and Narrative Function of the Women at the Tomb," *Bib* 77 (1996): 4-97.

15:40

3624   M. Barnouin, " 'Marie, Mère de Jacques et de José' (Marc 15.40): Quelques observations," *NTS* 42 (1996): 472-74.

15:42-47

3625   J. Spencer Kennard, "The Burial of Jesus," *JBL* 74 (1955): 227-38.

3626   Raymond E. Brown, "The Burial of Jesus," *CBQ* 50 (1988): 233-45.

15:43

3627   Günter Scholz, " 'Joseph von Arimathäa' und 'Barabbas'," *LB* 57 (1985): 81-94.

15:44-45

3628   Gerald O'Collins and Daniel Kendall, "Did Joseph of Arimathea Exist?" *Bib* 75 (1994): 235-41.

15:46

3629   Michael D. Goulder, "On Putting Q to the Test," *NTS* 24 (1977-1978): 218-34.

3630   D. Moody Smith, "Mark 15:46: The Shroud of Turin as a Problem of History and Faith," *BA* 46/4 (1983): 251-54.

15:47

3631   Paul Danove, "The Characterization and Narrative Function of the Women at the Tomb," *Bib* 77 (1996): 4-97.

16

3632   Richard W. Swanson, " 'They Said Nothing'," *CThM* 20 (1993): 471-78.

16:1-20

3633   Gerald O'Collins, "Mary Magdalene as Major Witness to Jesus' Resurrection," *TS* 48 (1987): 631-46.

16:1-13

3634   A.-L. Descamps, "La structure des récits évangéliques de la résurrection," *Bib* 40 (1959): 726-41.

16:1-9

3635   Ched Myers, "Who Will Roll away the Stone?: A Meditation on Mark's Easter Story," *Soj* 23 (1994): 20-23.

16:1-8

3636   Gabriel Hebert, "The Resurrection Narrative in St. Mark's Gospel," *ABR* 7 (1959): 58-65.

3637   Josef A. Sint, "Die Auferstehung Jesu in der Verkündigung der Urgemeinde," *ZKT* 84 (1962): 129-51.

3638   E. Galbiati, "È risorto, non è qui (Marco 16,1-8)," *BibO* 5 (1963): 67-72.

3639   Jean Delorme, "Les femmes au tombeau, Mc 16,1-8," *AsSeign* 2 (1969): 58-67.

3640   Erhardt Güttgemanns, "Linguistische Analyse von Mk 16,1-8," *LB* 11/12 (1972): 13-53.

3641   Robert H. Smith, "New and Old in Mark 16:1-8," *CTM* 43/8 (1972): 518-27.

3642   Peter Stuhlmacher, " 'Kritischer müssten mir die Historisch-Kritischen sein!'," *TQ* 3 (1973): 244-51.

3643   Antonio Ammassari, "Il racconto degli awenimenti della mattina di Pasqua secondo Marco 16,1-8," *BibO* 16 (1974): 49-64.

3644   F. C. Synge, "Mark 16.1-8," *JTSA* 11 (1975): 71-73.

3645   Harald Sahlin, "Zum Verständnis der christologischen Anschauung des Markusevangeliums," *StTheol* 31 (1977): 1-19.

3646   Robert H. Stein, "Was the Tomb Really Empty?" *JETS* 20 (1977): 23-29.

3647   John D. Crossan, "A Form for Absence: The Markan Creation of Gospel," *Semeia* 12 (1978): 41-55.

3648   Craig A. Evans, "Mark's Use of the Empty Tomb Tradition," *SBT* 8 (1978): 50-55.

3649   Heinz-Wolfgang Kuhn, "Predigt über Markus 16,1-8," *EvT* 38 (1978): 155-60.

3650   F.-J. Niemann, "Die Erzählung vom leeren Grab bei Markus," *ZKT* 101 (1979): 188-99.

3651   Andreas Lindemann, "Die Osterbotschaft des Markus. Zur theologischen Interpretation von Mark 16.1-8," *NTS* 26/3 (1979-1980): 298-17.

3652   Frans Neirynck, "Marc 16,1-8. Tradition et rédaction," *ETL* 56 (1980): 56-88.

3653   Henning Paulsen, "Mark 16:1-8," *NovT* 22/2 (1980): 138-75.

3654   Luise Schottroff, "Maria Magdalena und die Frauen am Grabe Jesu," *EvT* 42 (1982): 3-25.

3655   Heinz Giesen, "Der Auferstandene und seine Gemeinde: Zum Inhalt und zur Funktion des ursprünglichen Markusschlusses (16,1-8)," *SNTU-A* 12 (1987): 99-139.

3656   Zane C. Hodges, "The Women and the Empty Tomb," *BSac* 123 (1966): 301-309.

3657   Philippe Rolland, "La découverte du tombeau vide," *BLOS* 6 (1990): 3-10.

3658   J. M. Strijdom and A. G. Van Aarde, "Markus 16:1-8 in die konteks van 'n konstruksie van die Markaanse gemeente," *HTS* 46 (1990): 153-89.

3659   Peter Bolt, "Mark 16:1-8: The Empty Tomb of a Hero?" *TynB* 47 (1996): 27-37.

3660   Paul Danove, "The Characterization and Narrative Function of the Women at the Tomb," *Bib* 77 (1996): 4-97.

3661   William F. McInerny, "An Unresolved Question in the Gospel Called Mark: 'Who Is This Whom Even Wind and Sea Obey'?" *PRS* 23 (1996): 255-68.

16:1-2

3662   Michael Winger, "When Did the Women Visit the Tomb?" *NTS* 40 (1994): 284-88.

16:1

3663   Michael D. Goulder, "On Putting Q to the Test," *NTS* 24 (1977-1978): 218-34.

3664   Christopher M. Tuckett, "On the Relationship between Matthew and Luke," *NTS* 30 (1984): 130-42.

16:2

3665   Frans Neirynck, "ἀνατείλαντος τοῦ ἡλίου (Mc 16,2)," *ETL* 54 (1978): 70-103.

16:4

3666   D. W. Palmer, "The Origin, Form, and Purpose of Mark XVI.4 in Codex Bobbiensis," *JTS* 27/1 (1976): 113-22.

16:5-7

3667   J. H. McIndoe, "The Young Man at the Tomb," *ET* 80 (1968-1969): 125.

16:5

3668   Robin Scroggs and Kent I. Groff, "Baptism in Mark: Dying and Rising with Christ," *JBL* 92 (1973): 531-48.

3669   Michel Gourgues, "À propos du symbolisme christologique et baptismal de Marc 16:5," *NTS* 27 (1980-1981): 672-78.

3670   Allan K. Jenkins, "Young Man or Angel?" *ET* 94/8 (1982-1983): 237-40.

3671   Eugene A. LaVerdiere, "Robed in Radiant White," *Emmanuel* 90 (1984): 138-42.

16:6

3672   Robert Schlarb, "Die Suche nach dem Messias: ζητέω als Terminus technicus der markinischen Messianologie," *ZNW* 81 (1990): 155-70.

16:7-8

3673   Ralf Oppermann, "Eine Beobachtung in Bezug auf das Problem des Markusschlusses," *BibN* 40 (1987): 24-29.

3674   Andrew T. Lincoln, "The Promise and the Failure: Mark 16:7-8," *JBL* 108/2 (1989): 283-300.

3675   Joel F. Williams, "Literary Approaches to the End of Mark's Gospel," *JETS* 42 (1999): 21-35.

16:7

3676   P. Cornelius Odenkirchen, " 'Praecedam vos in Galilaeam'," *VD* 46 (1968): 193-223.

3677   Bernd Steinseifer, "Der Ort der Erscheinungen des Auferstandenen," *ZNW* 62/3 (1971): 232-65.

3678   Jean-Marie van Cangh, "La Galilée dans l'évangile de Marc: un lieu théologique?" *RB* 79 (1972): 59-75.

3679   Thorwald Lorenzen, "Ist der Auferstandene in Galiläa erschienen? Bemerkungen zu einem Aufsatz von B. Steinseifer," *ZNW* 64 (1973): 209-21.

3680   Robert H. Stein, "A Short Note on Mark 14:28 and 16:7," *NTS* 20 (1973-1974): 445-52.

3681   B. M. F. van Iersel, " 'To Galilee' or 'in Galilee' in Mark 14:28 and 16:7?" *ETL* 58 (1982): 365-70.

3682   Eugene A. LaVerdiere, "The End, a Beginning," *Emmanuel* 90 (1984): 484-91.

3683   George E. Rice, "Is Bezae a Homogeneous Codex," *PRS* 11 (1984): 39-54.

3684   Knut Backhaus, " 'Dort werdet ihr Ihn sehen' (Mk 16,7): Die redaktionelle Schlußnotiz des zweiten Evangeliums als dessen christologische Summe," *TGl* 76 (1986): 277-94.

3685   Domingo Muñoz León, " 'Iré delante de vosotros a Galilea' (Mt 26,32 y par). Sentido mesiánico y posible sustrato arameo del logion," *EB* 48 (1990): 215-41.

16:8

3686   C. F. D. Moule, "St. Mark xvi.8 Once More," *NTS* 2 (1955-1956): 58-59.

3687   Jesús Luzarraga, "Retraducción semítica de φοβέομαι en Mc 16,8," *Bib* 50 (1969): 497-510.

3688   Robert P. Meye, "Mark 16:8: The Ending of Mark's Gospel," *BR* 15 (1969): 33-43.

3689   P. W. van der Horst, "Can a Book End with γάρ? A Note On Mark 16:8," *JTS* 23 (1972): 121-24.

3690   Thomas E. Boomershine, "Mark 16:8 and the Apostolic Commission," *JBL* 100/2 (1981): 225-39.

3691   Thomas E. Boomershine and Gilbert L. Bartholomew, "The Narrative Technique of Mark 16:8," *JBL* 100/2 (1981): 213-23.

3692   Gerald O'Collins, "The Fearful Silence of Three Women (Mark 16:8c)," *Greg* 69/3 (1988): 489-503.

3693   Roberto Vignolo, "Una finale reticente: interpretazione narrativa di Mc 16:8," *RBib* 38 (1990): 129-89.

16:9-20

3694   Ernest C. Colwell, "Mark 16:9-20 in the Armenian Version," *JBL* 56 (1937): 369-86.

3695   Kenneth W. Clark, "The Theological Relevance of Textual Variation in Current Criticism of the Greek New Testament," *JBL* 85 (1966): 1-16.

3696   Frans Wagenaars, "Structura Litteraria et Momentum Theologicum Pericopae Mc 16:9-20," *VD* 45/1 (1967): 19-22.

3697   G. W. Trompf, "The First Resurrection Appearance and the Ending of Mark's Gospel," *NTS* 18 (1971-1972): 308-30.

3698   G. W. Trompf, "The *Markusschluß* in Recent Research," *ABR* 21 (1973): 15-26.

3699   Barclay M. Newman, " 'Verses Marked with Brackets. . .'," *BT* 30 (1979): 233-36.

3700   John C. Thomas, "A Reconsideration of the Ending of Mark," *JETS* 26 (1983): 407-19.

3701   Ton Veerkamp, "Das Hinauswerfen der Dämonen: Ein echter Markusschluss," *TextK* 17 (1983): 26-43.

3702   Stanley N. Helton, "Churches of Christ and Mark 16:9-20," *RQ* 36 (1994): 33-52.

16:11

3703   Tjitze Baarda, "An Unexpected Reading in the West-Saxon Gospel Text of Mark 16.11," *NTS* 41 (1995): 458-65.

16:13-23

3704   Anton Vögtle, "Messiasbekenntnis und Petrusverheissung: Zur Komposition Mt 16:13-23 par.," *BZ* 1 (1957): 252-72.

16:14-20

3705   Félix Asensio, "Trasfondo profético-evangélico πᾶσα ἐξουσία de la 'Gran Mision'," *EB* 27 (1968): 27-48.

16:14-18

3706   Emmanuele Testa, "I 'Discorsi di Missione' di Gesù," *SBFLA* 29 (1979): 7-41. a

3707   Dale C. Allison, "Paul and the Missionary Discourse," *ETL* 61 (1985): 369-75.

16:15-20

3708   Paul Ternant, "La prédication universelle de l'Évangile du Signeur, Mc 16,15-20," *AsSeign* 2 (1969): 38-48.

3709   Gilles Becquet, "La mission universelle de l'Église par la foi et ses signes (Mc 16,15-20)," *EV* 80 (1970): 297-300.

16:19-20

3710   Brian K. Donne, "The Significance of the Ascension of Jesus Christ in the New Testament," *SJT* 30 (1977): 555-68.

16:19

3711   W. R. G. Loader, "Christ at the Right Hand—Ps. cx. 1 in the New Testament," *NTS* 24 (1977-1978): 199-217.

16:21-22

3712   James C. G. Greig, "Eukairos," *ET* 65 (1953-1954): 158-59.

16:30-44

3713   Eugene A. LaVerdiere, "The Breaking of the Bread," *Emmanuel* 95 (1989): 554-60, 577.

16:41

3714   Eugene A. LaVerdiere, "It Was a Huge Stone," *Emmanuel* 92 (1986): 394-400.

16:66-72

3715   Gregory Murray, "Saint Peter's Denials," *DR* 103 (1985): 296-98.

Luke

1:1-13:9

3716   John M. Sergeant, "The Ox Unmuzzled: A New Beginning," *ET* 110 (1998): 46-49.

3717   Rainer Dillmann, "Das Lukasevangelium als Tendenzschrift: Leserlenkung und Leseintention in Lk 1,1-4," *BZ* NS 38 (1994): 87-93.

1-4

3718   Gilberto Marconi, "Il Bambino da Vedere: l'Estetica Lucana Nel Cantico di Simeone e Dintorni," *Greg* 72/4 (1991): 629-54.

1:1-4:22

3719   Thomas L. Brodie, "A New Temple and a New Law," *JSNT* 5 (1979): 21-45.

1-3

3720   Martin Völkel, "Exegetische Erwägungen zum Verständnis des Begriffs κατεκσῆςim Lukanischen Prolog," *NTS* 20 (1973-1974): 289-99.

1-2

3721   J. Casper, "Und Jesus nahm zu," *BL* 11 (1939-1940): 9-12.

3722   H. T. Kuist, "Sources of Power in the Nativity Hymns. An Exposition of Luke 1 and 2," *Int* 2 (1948): 288-98.

3723   J. S. Pedro, "Valor apologético de la infancia de Jesús," *CuBí* 11 (1954): 39-40.

3724   Paul Winter, "Two Notes on Luke 1-2 with Regard to the Theory of 'Imitation Hebraisms'," *ST* 7 (1954): 158-65.

3725   Paul Winter, "Some Observations on the Language in the Birth and Infancy Stories of the Third Gospel," *NTS* 1 (1954-1955): 111-21.

3726   Nigel Turner, "The Relation of Luke i and ii to Hebraic Sources and to the Rest of Luke-Acts," *NTS* 2 (1955-1956): 100-109.

3727   Paul Winter, " 'Nazareth' and 'Jerusalem' in Luke i and ii," *NTS* 3 (1956-1957): 136-42.

3728   Michael D. Goulder and M. L. Sanderson, "St. Luke's Genesis," *JTS* 8 (1957): 12-30.

3729   Paul Winter, "Lukanische Miszellen," *ZNW* 59 (1958): 65-77.

3730   Paul Winter, "The Main Literary Problem of the Lucan Infancy Story," *ATR* 40 (1958): 257-64.

3731   H. H. Oliver, "The Lucan Birth Stories and the Purpose of Luke-Acts," *NTS* 10 (1963-1964): 202-26.

3732   Heinz Schürmann, "Aufbau, Eigenart und Geschichtswert von Lukas 1-2," *BK* 21 (1966): 106-11.

3733   A. Smitmans, "Die Hymnen der Kindheitsgeschichte nach Lukas," *BK* 21 (1966): 115-18.

3734   Gerhard Voss, "Die Christusverkündigung der Kindheits-geschichte im Rahmen des Lukasevangeliums," *BK* 21 (1966): 112-15.

3735   W. Barnes Tatum, "The Epoch of Israel: Luke i-ii and the Theological Plan of Luke-Acts," *NTS* 13 (1966-1967): 184-95.

3736   C. T. Ruddick, "Birth Narratives in Genesis and Luke," *NovT* 12 (1970): 343-48.

3737   Anton Vögtle, "Offene Fragen zur lukanischen Geburts- und Kindheitsgeschichte," *BL* 11 (1970): 51-67.

3738   André Feuillet, "Observations sur les récits de l'enfance chez S. Luc," *EV* 82 (1972): 721-24.

3739   S. Muñoz Iglesias, "Midráš y Evangelios de la Infancia," *EE* 47 (1972): 331-59.

3740   A. Vicent Cernuda, "El paralelismo de γεννωυ τικτωεν Lc 1-2," *Bib* 55 (1974): 260-64.

3741   Réne Laurentin, "Les évangiles de l'enfance," *LV* 119 (1974): 84-105.

3742   M. Sinoir, "Jesus et sa Mère d'après les rècits lucaniens de l'enfance," *EV* 84 (1974): 625-34.

3743   F. Gryglewicz, "Die Herkunft der Hymnen des Kind-heitsevangeliums des Lucas," *NTS* 21 (1974-1975): 265-73.

3744　J. M. Ford, "Zealotism and the Lukan Infancy Narratives," *NovT* 18 (1976): 280-92.

3745　Reginald H. Fuller, "The Conception/Birth of Jesus as a Christological Moment," *JSNT* 1 (1978): 37-1.

3746　Jean Galot, "Riflessioni sul primo atto di fede cristiana. Maria la prima credente," *CC* 1 (1978): 27-39.

3747　G. De Rosa, "Storia e teologia nei racconti dell'infanzia di Gesù," *CC* 4 (1978): 11-37.

3748　Tavares A. Augusto, "Infancy Narratives and Historical Criticism," *TD* 28 (1980): 53-54.

3749　G. Jankowski, "In jenen Tagen: Der politische Kontext zu Lukas 1-2," *TextK* 12 (1981): 5-17.

3750　Léopold Sabourin, "Recent Views on Luke's Infancy Narratives," *RSB* 1/1 (1981): 18-25.

3751　Agnès Gueuret, "Luc 1-2: Analyse sémiotique," *SémBib* 25 (1982): 35-42.

3752　Réne Laurentin, "Vérité des Évangiles de l'enfance," *NRT* 105 (1983): 691-710.

3753　A. J. B. Higgins, "Luke 1-2 in Tatian's *Diatessaron*," *JBL* 103 (1984): 193-222.

3754　Réne Laurentin, "La speranza dei giusti in Lc 1-2," *ParSpirV* 9 (1984): 123-36.

3755　Raymond E. Brown, "Gospel Infancy Narrative Research From 1976 to 1986: Part II (Luke)," *CBQ* 48/4 (1986): 660-80.

3756　C. R. Hutcheon, " 'God is with Us': The Temple in Luke-Acts," *SVTQ* 44 (2000): 3-33.

1:1-53

3757　V. Casas, "Dios colmó a los hambrientos," *BibFe* 9 (1983): 288-99.

1:1-5

3758　Eugene Seraphin, "The Edict of Caesar Augustus," *CBQ* 7 (1945): 91-96.

1:1-4

3759   W. C. van Unnik, "Remarks on the Purpose of Luke's Historical Writing (Luke 1:1-4)," *NedTT* 9 (1955): 323-31.

3760   D. E. Nineham, "Eyewitness Testimony and the Gospel Tradition," *JTS* 9 (1958): 13-25, 243-1.

3761   D. J. Sneed, "An Exegesis of Luke 1:1-4 with Special Regard to Luke's Purpose as a Historian," *ET* 83 (1971-1972): 40-43.

3762   É. Samain, "L'Évangile de Luc: un témoignage ecclésial et missionnaire," *AsSeign* NS 34 (1973): 60-73.

3763   Schuyler Brown, "The Prologues of Luke-Acts in Their Relation to the Purpose of the Author," *SBLSP* 5 (1975): 1-14.

3764   G. Menestrina, "L'incipit dell'espitola 'Ad Diognetum,' Luca 1:1-4 et Atti 1:1-2," *BibO* 19 (1977): 215-18.

3765   Vernon K. Robbins, "Prefaces in Greco-Roman Biography and Luke-Acts," *SBLSP* 8/2 (1978): 193-208.

3766   Roger L. Omanson, "A Note on Luke 1.1-4," *BT* 30 (1979): 446-47.

3767   Richard J. Dillon, "Previewing Luke's Project from his Prologue (Luke 1:1-4)," *CBQ* 43 (1981): 205-27.

3768   Franz Mußner, "Die Gemeinde des Lukasprologs," *SNTU-A* 6/7 (1981-1982): 113-30.

3769   Erhardt Güttgemanns, "In welchem Sinne ist Lukas 'Historiker'? Die Beziehungen von Luk 1,1-4 und Papias zur antiken Rhetorik," *LB* 54 (1983): 9-26.

3770   Robert H. Stein, "Luke 1:1-4 and Traditionsgeschichte," *JETS* 26 (1983): 421-30.

3771   Terrance Callan, "The Preface of Luke-Acts and Historiography," *NTS* 31 (1985): 576-81.

3772   Roland Kany, "Der lukanische Bericht von Tod und Auferstehung Jesu aus der Sicht eines hellenistischen Romanlesers," *NovT* 28/1 (1986): 75-90.

3773   James M. Dawsey, "The Origin of Luke's Positive Perception of the Temple," *PRS* 18 (1991): 5-22.

1:1

3774   J. B. Bauer, *"Polloi* Lk 1,1," *NovT* 4 (1960-1961): 263-66.

3775   E. G. Rupp, "A Great and Mighty Wonder!" *ET* 89 (1977-1978): 81-82.

3776   A. Salas, "Dios derribó a los poderosos," *BibFe* 9 (1983): 274-87.

3777   L. C. A. Alexander, "What If Luke Had Never Met Theophilus?" *BibInt* 8 (2000): 161-70.

1:2

3778   André Feuillet, "Témoins oculaires et serviteurs de la parole," *NovT* 15 (1973): 241-59.

1:3

3779   J. Kurzinger, "Lk 1,3: . . . ἀκριβῶς καθεξῆς σοι γράψαι," *BZ* 18 (1974): 249-55.

3780   Brigitte Kahl, "Armenevangelium und Heidenevangelium: 'Sola Scriptura' und die ökumenische Traditions-Problematik," *TLZ* 110 (1985): 779-81.

3781   Mark Janse, "L'importance de la position d'un mot 'accessoire'," *Bib* 77 no 1 (1996): 93-97.

1:5-2:1

3782   Mario Galizzi, "Vangelo dell'infanzia (Lc 1,5-2,1)," *PV* 21 (1976): 455-64.

1:5-2:20

3783   H. L. MacNeill, "The *Sitz im Leben* of Luke 1,5-2,20," *JBL* 65 (1946): 123-30.

1:5-55

3784   John J. Kilgallen, "A Consideration of Some of the Women in the Gospel of Luke," *SM* 40 (1991): 27-55.

1:5-37

3785   Lynlea Rodger, "The Infancy Stories of Matthew and Luke: An Examination of the Child as a Theological Metaphor," *HBT* 19 (1997): 58-81.

1:5-25

3786   Daniel Gerber, "Luc 1/5-25: La poursuite d'un récit qui s'achève," *ÉTR* 72 (1997): 505-14.

1:5-23

> 3787 Robert Gnuse, "The Temple Theophanies of Jaddus, Hyrcanus, and Zechariah," *Bib* 79 (1998): 457-72.

1:5-15

> 3788 R. F. Collins, "Jesus' Ministry to the Deaf and Dumb," *MeliT* 35/1 (1984): 12-36.

1:5

> 3789 David L. Jones, "Luke's Unique Interest in Historical Chronology," *SBLSP* 19 (1989): 378-87.

> 3790 Günther Schwarz, "'Εξ ἐφημερίας 'Αβιά?" *BibN* 53 (1990): 30-31.

1:12-15

> 3791 F. Smyth-Florentin, "Jésus, le Fils du Père, vainqueur de Satan," *AsSeign* 14 (1973): 56-75.

1:14

> 3792 L. Alexander, "Luke's Preface in the Context of Greek Preface-Writing," *NovT* 28/1 (1986): 48-74.

1:15

> 3793 B. Sussarellu, "De praevia sanctificatione Praecursoris," *SBFLA* 3 (191-1953): 37-110.

1:17

> 3794 Carlos Mesters, "Restabelecer a Justiça de Deus No Meio Do Povo: Vida e Luta Do Profeta Elias: Sobre a Missao Profética," *EstT* 24/2 (1984): 129-47.

1:22

> 3795 Heinrich Baarlink, "Friede im Himmel: die lukanische Redaktion von Lk 19,38 und Ihre Deutung," *ZNW* 76/3 (1985): 170-86.

1:25

> 3796 Paul Winter, "Ὅτι Recitativum in Luke 1:25, 61; 2:23," *HTR* 48 (1955): 213-18.

1:26-56

> 3797 K. Butting, "Eine Freundin Gottes: Luk. 1,26-56," *TextK* 21 (1984): 42-49.

3798   Roland Meynet, "Dieu Donne Son Nom à Jésus: Analyse
       Rhétorique de Lc. 1:26-56 et de 1 Sam. 2:1-10," *Bib* 66/1
       (1985): 39-72.

3799   Raymond E. Brown, "The Annunciation to Mary, the
       Visitation and the Magnificat (Luke 1:26-56)," *Worship* 62
       (1988): 249-59.

1:26-45

3800   H. Vermeyen, "Mariologie als Befreiung. Luke 1:26-45,
       56 im Kontext," *ZKT* 105 (1983): 168-83.

1:26-38

3801   Reginald H. Fuller, "The Virgin Birth: Historical Fact or
       Kerygmatic Truth?" *BR* 1 (1957): 1-8.

3802   Otto A. Piper, "The Virgin Birth. The Meaning of the
       Gospel Accounts," *Int* 18 (1964): 131-48.

3803   Hugolinus Langkammer, "The Soteriological Character of
       Mary's Fiat," *SBFLA* 15 (1964-1965): 293-301.

3804   Pierre Benoit, "L'Annonciation (Lc 1)," *AsSeign* NS 8
       (1972): 39-50.

3805   B. Prete, "Il racconto dell'Annunziazione di Luca
       1,26-38," *BibO* 15 (1973): 75-88.

3806   D. Moody Smith, "Luke 1:26-38," *Int* 29 (1975): 411-17.

3807   Alois Stöger, " 'Wir sind Gottes Volk!' Bibelmeditation
       über Luke 1:26-38," *BL* 50 (1977): 250-1.

3808   A. Knockaert and C. Van Der Plancke, "Catéchèse de
       l'annonciation," *LV* 34 (1979): 79-121.

3809   A. M. Serra, "L'annunciazione a Maria (Lc 1,26-38), un
       formulario di alleanza?" *PV* 25 (1980): 164-71.

3810   Klemens Stock, "Die Berufung Marias (Luke 1:26-38),"
       Bib 61 (1980): 457-91.

3811   Klemens Stock, "Lo Spirito su Maria (Lc 1,26-38),"
       ParSpirV 4 (1981): 88-98.

3812   Eugene A. LaVerdiere, "Be It Done to Me," *Emmanuel* 90
       (1984): 184-90.

3813   Detlev Dormeyer, "Die Rolle der Imagination im Leseprozess bei unterschiedlichen Leseweisen von Lk 1,26-38," *BZ* NS 39 (1995): 161-80.

3814   David T. Landry, "Narrative Logic in the Annunciation to Mary," *JBL* 114 (1995): 65-79.

1:26-31

3815   Charles H. Talbert, "Luke 1:26-31," *Int* 39 (1985): 288-91.

1:26-28

3816   Martin Conway, "Your Will Be Done: Mission in Christ's Way," *IRM* 75 (1986): 423-59.

1:27

3817   C. H. Dodd, "New Testament Translation Problems," *BT* 27/3 (1976): 301-305; 28 (1977): 101-16.

3818   J. Carmignac, "The Meaning of παρθένος in Lk 1,27: A Reply to C. H. Dodd," *BT* 28 (1977): 327-30.

1:28-42

3819   A. Salas, "El Avemaria (Lc 1,28.42)," *BibFe* 10 (1984): 1-103.

1:28

3820   F. Stummer, "Beiträge zur Exegese der Vulgata," *ZAW* 62 (1949-1950): 11-67.

3821   P. Franquesa, "Sugerencias en torno a Luke 1:28," *CuBí* 11 (1954): 320-22.

3822   Juan Leal, "El saludo del Angel a la Virgen," *CuBí* 11 (1954): 293-301.

3823   Raimund Köbert, "Lc. 1:28, 42 in den syrischen Evangelien," *Bib* 42/2 (1961): 229-30.

3824   A. Strobel, "Der Gruss an Maria (Lc 1:28): Eine philologische Betrachtung zu seinem Sinngehalt," *ZNW* 53/1-2 (1962): 86-110.

3825   D. Yubero, "Maria, 'el Señor es contigo'," *CuBí* 31 (1974): 91-96.

3826   G. M. Verd, " 'Gratia plena' (Lc 1,28). Sentido de una traduccion," *EE* 50 (1975): 357-89.

3827   Léopold Sabourin, "Recent Views on Luke's Infancy
        Narratives," *RSB* 1/1 (1981): 18-25.

3828   C. Buzzetti, "Κεχαριτωμένη, 'Favoured' (Lk 1:28), and
        the Italian Common Language New Testament," *BT* 33
        (1982): 243.

3829   Édouard Delebecque, "Sur la salutation de Gabriel à Marie
        (Lc 1,28)," *Bib* 65 (1984): 31-55.

3830   I. de la Potterie, "Κεχαριτωμένηεν Lc 1,28: Étude
        philologique," *Bib* 68 (1987): 357-82.

1:31

3831   B. Schellenberger, "Die Jungfrau wird schwanger
        werden," *GeistL* 53 (1980): 38-40.

1:32-34

3832   Georg Richter, "Zu den Tauferzählungen Mk 1:9-11 und
        Joh 1:32-34," *ZNW* 65 (1974): 43-56.

1:32-33

3833   J. G. Sobosan, "Completion of Prophecy: Jesus in Lk
        1:32-33," *BTB* 4 (1974): 317-23.

1:32

3834   Frederick W. Danker, "Politics of the New Age According
        to St. Luke," *CThM* 12 (1985): 338-45.

1:33

3835   D. H. C. Read, "Recognizing Jesus as King Today," *ET* 92
        (1980-1981): 81-82.

1:34-35

3836   Gerhard Schneider, "Lk 1,34.35 als redaktionelle Einheit,"
        BZ 15 (1971): 255-59.

1:34

3837   H.-J. Vogel, "Zur Textgeschichte von Lc 1,34ff.," *ZNW* 43
        (1950-1951): 256-60.

3838   N. L. Martinez, "Porque no conozco varón," *CuBí* 11
        (1954): 333-35.

3839   Josef Gewiess, "Die Marienfrage, Lk. 1:34," *BZ* 5/2
        (1961): 221-54.

3840 Hans Quecke, "Lk. 1:34 in den alten Übersetzungen und im Protevangelium des Jakobus," *Bib* 44/4 (1963): 499-10.

3841 J. B. Bauer, "Philologische Bemerkungen zu Lk. 1:34," *Bib* 45/4 (1964): 535-40.

3842 Hans Quecke, "Lk. 1:34 im Diatessaron," *Bib* 45/1 (1964): 85-88.

3843 M. Orsatti, "Verso la decodificazione di un insolita espressione (Luke 1:34)," *RBib* 29 (1981): 343-57.

1:35

3844 Tjitze Baarda, "Dionysios Bar Salibi and the Text of Luke 1:35," *VC* 17 (1963): 225-29.

3845 Pierre Grelot, "La naissance d'Issac et celle de Jésus," *NRT* 104 (1972): 462-87, 561-85.

3846 F. W. Schlatter, "The Problem of John 1:3b-4a," *CBQ* 34/1 (1972): 54-58.

3847 A. Vicent Cernuda, "La presunta sustantivacion de *gennōmenon* en Lc 1,35b," *EB* 33 (1974): 265-73.

3848 Léopold Sabourin, "Two Lukan Texts (1:35; 3:22)," *RSB* 1 (1981): 29-32.

3849 S. Brock, "Passover, Annunciation and Epiclesis: Some Remarks on the Term *Aggen* in the Syriac Versions of Luke 1:35," *NovT* 24 (1982): 222-33.

3850 Silverio Zedda, "Lc 1,35b, 'Colui che nascerà santo sarà chiamato Figlio di Dio': I. Breve storia dell'esegesi recente," *RBib* 33 (1985): 29-43.

3851 Silverio Zedda, "Lc 1,35b, 'Colui che nascerà santo sarà chiamato Figlio di Dio': II. Questioni sintattiche ed esegesi," *RBib* 33 (1985): 165-89.

3852 Gerald Bostock, "Virgin Birth or Human Conception?" *ET* 97/9 (1986-1987): 260-63.

1:39-56

3853 J. G. Cepeda, "La Virgen, poetisa Sagrada," *CuBi* 11 (1954): 391-94.

3854 C. L'Eplattenier, "Une série pour l'Avent," *ETL* 57 (1982): 569-82.

3855 P. Raffin, "L'Annonciation et l'espérance (Luke 1:39-56)," *EV* 83 (1983): 241-42.

1:39-47

3856 J. P. Martin, "Luke 1:39-47," *Int* 36 (1982): 394-99.

1:39-45

3857 P.-E. Jacquemin, "La Visitation (Lc 1)," *AsSeign* NS 8 (1972): 64-75.

3858 J. M. Salgado, "La visitation de la Sainte Vierge Marie: exercice de sa Maternité Spirituelle," *Div* 16 (1972): 445-1.

3859 H. B. Beverly, "Luke 1:39-45," *Int* 30 (1976): 396-400.

1:41-50

3860 E. Galbiati, "La Visitazione (Luke 1:41-50)," *BibO* 4 (1962): 139-44.

1:42

3861 Raimund Köbert, "Lc. 1:28, 42 in den Syrischen Evangelien," *Bib* 42/2 (1961): 229-30.

1:45-46

3862 Wilhelm Vischer, "Luke 1:45-46," *ÉTR* 30 (1955): 17-19.

3863 Randall Buth, "Hebrew Poetic Tenses and the Magnificat," *JSNT* 21 (1984): 67-83.

1:46-56

3864 J. R. Harris, "Mary or Elisabeth?" *ET* 41 (1929-1930): 266-67.

3865 J. R. Harris, "Again the Magnificat," *ET* 42 (1930-1931): 188-90.

3866 Paul Winter, "Magnificat and Benedictus: Maccabaean Psalms?" *BJRL* 37 (1954-1955): 328-47.

3867 J. G. Davies, "The Ascription of the Magnificat to Mary," *JTS* 15 (1964): 307-308.

3868 D. R. Jones, "The Background and Character of the Lukan Psalms," *JTS* 19 (1968): 19-50.

3869 P.-E. Jacquemin, "Le Magnificat (Lc 1)," *AsSeign* NS 66 (1973): 28-40.

3870 P. Schmidt, "Maria in der Sicht des Magnifikat," *GeistL* 46 (1973): 417-30.

3871 Robert C. Tannehill, "The Magnificat as Poem," *JBL* 93 (1974): 263-75.

3872 P. Schmidt, "Maria und das Magnificat," *Cath* 29 (1975): 230-46.

3873 Walter Vogels, "Le Magnificat, Marie et Israel," *ÉgT* 6 (1975): 279-96.

3874 Luise Schottroff, "Das Magnificat und die älteste Tradition über Jesus von Nazareth," *ET* 38 (1978): 298-313.

1:46-55

3875 V. Hamp, "Der alttestamentliche Hintergrund des Magnifikat," *BK* 8/3 (1953): 17-23.

3876 Kathryn Sullivan, "His Lowly Maid," *Worship* 36 (1962): 374-79.

3877 Stephen Benko, "The Magnificat: A History of the Controversy," *JBL* 86 (1967): 263-75.

3878 D. Minguez, "Poética generativa del Magnificat," *Bib* 61 (1980): 55-77.

3879 Jacques Dupont, "Il cantico della Vergine Maria (Lc 1,46-55)," *ParSpirV* 3 (1981): 89-105.

3880 Léopold Sabourin, "Recent Views on Luke's Infancy Narratives," *RSB* 1/1 (1981): 18-25.

3881 X. Pikaza, "Engrandece mi alma al Señor," *BibFe* 9 (1983): 238-48.

3882 A. Salas, "Magnificat," *BibFe* 9 (1983): 1-98.

3883 Bruce H. Grigsby, "Compositional Hypotheses for the Lucan 'Magnificat': Tensions for the Evangelical," *EQ* 56 (1984): 159-72.

3884 Gail R. O'Day, "Singing Woman's Song: A Hermeneutic of Liberation," *CThM* 12 (1985): 203-10.

3885 Alberto Valentini, "Magnifcat e lopera lucana," *RBib* 33 (1985): 395-423.

3886 Willem S. Vorster, "Die Lukaanse Liedere," *HTS* 1 (1989): 17-34.

3887 Mark Hillmer, "Luke 1:46-55," *Int* 48 (1994): 390-94.

3888 Curtis A. Jahn, "Exegesis and Sermon Study of Luke 1:46-55: The Magnificat (1997): Megalynei e psyche mou ton kirion," *WLQ* 95 (1998): 248-69.

3889 Dirk Schinkel, "Das Magnifikat Lk 1,46-55--ein Hymnus in Harlekinsjacke?" *ZNW* 90 (1999): 273-79.

3890 Antonio M. Slesinski, "The Event of Mercy: Mary's Divine Maternity and the Magnificat," *CICR* 22 (1995): 652-67.

1:49

3891 Paul Winter, "Lc 1,49 und Targum Yerushalmi Again," *ZNW* 46 (1955): 140-41.

3892 A. Manrique, "El poderoso ha hecho maravillas," *BibFe* 9 (1983): 259-64.

1:50

3893 H. J. Klauck, "Gottesfürchtige im Magnificat?" *NTS* 43 (1997): 134-39.

1:51

3894 P. L. Schoonheim, "Der alttestamentliche Boden der Vokabel *uperêphanos,* Lukas i,51," *NovT* 8 (1966): 235-46.

3895 M. C. Crespo, "Dios dispersó a los soberbios," *BibFe* 9 (1983): 265-78.

1:54-55

3896 E. Gallego, "Dios acogió a Israel. La fidelidad del amor," *BibFe* 9 (1983): 300-11.

1:56

3897 H. Vermeyen, "Mariologie als Befreiung. Luke 1:26-45, 56 im Kontext," *ZKT* 105 (1983): 168-83.

1:57

3898 V. Soria, "El nacimiento de Juan el Bautista," *CuBí* 16 (1959): 120-23.

1:59-63

3899 Gerard Mussies, "Vernoemen in de antieke wereld: De historische achtergrond van Luk. 1,59-63," *NTT* 42 (1988): 114-25.

1:61

3900 Paul Winter, " "Οτι Recitativum in Luke 1:25, 61; 2:23," *HTR* 48 (1955): 213-18.

1:67-79

3901 Joachim Gnilka, "Der Hymnus des Zacharias," *BZ* 6/2 (1962): 215-38.

3902 C. L'Eplattenier, "Une série pour l'Avent," *ETL* 57 (1982): 569-82.

1:68-79

3903 Phillip Vielhauer, "Das Benedictus des Zacharias (Lk 1,68-79)," *ZTK* 49 (191): 255-72.

3904 Paul Winter, "Magnificat and Benedictus: Maccabaean Psalms?" *BJRL* 37 (1954-1955): 328-47.

3905 Albert Vanhoye, "Structure du 'Benedictus'," *NTS* 12 (1965-1966): 382-89.

3906 O. Haggenmüller, "Der Lobgesang des Zacharias (Luke 1:68-79)," *BibL* 9 (1968): 249-60.

3907 D. R. Jones, "The Background and Character of the Lukan Psalms," *JTS* 19 (1968): 19-50.

3908 Pierre Auffret, "Note sur la structure littéraire de Luke 1:68-79," *NTS* 24 (1977-1978): 248-58.

3909 J. Reuss, "Studien zur Lukas-Erklärung des Presbyters Hesychius von Jerusalem," *Bib* 59 (1978): 562-71.

3910 M. del Oro, "Benedictus de Zacarias (Luc 1,68-79) ¿Indicios de una cristologia arcaica?" *RevB* 45 (1983): 145-77.

3911 J. S. Croatto, "El 'Benedictus' Como Memoria de la Alianza: Estructura y Teología de Lucas 1:68-79," *RevB* 47/4 (1985): 207-19.

3912 Helmer Ringgren, "Luke's Use of the Old Testament," *HTR* 79/1-3 (1986): 227-35.

3913   François Rousseau, "Les Structures du Benedictus (Luc 1:68-79)," *NTS* 32/2 (1986): 268-82.

3914   Warren Carter, "Zechariah and the Benedictus (Luke 1,68-79): Practicing What He Preaches," *Bib* 69 (1988): 239-47.

3915   Jesús Luzarraga, "El Benedictus (Lc 1,68-79) a través del arameo," *Bib* 80 (1999): 305-59.

3916   Allan McNicol, "Rebuilding the House of David: The Function of the Benedictus in Luke-Acts," *RQ* 40 (1998): 25-38.

1:80

3917   A. S. Getser, "The Youth of John the Baptist: A Deduction from the Break in the Parallel Account of the Lucan Infancy Story," *NovT* 1 (1956): 70-75.

2-3

3918   A. R. C. Leaney, "The Birth Narratives in St. Luke and St. Matthew," *NTS* 8 (1961-1962): 158-66.

2:1-21

3919   J. Riedl, "Zur lukanischen Weihnachtsbotschaft," *BL* 39 (1966): 341-50.

3920   H. Tsuchiya, "The History and the Fiction in the Birth Stories of Jesus: An Observation on the Thought of Luke the Evangelist," *AJBI* 1 (1975): 73-90.

2:1-20

3921   E. Galbiati, "Il Natale (Luke 2:1-20)," *BibO* 2 (1960): 214-19.

3922   F. Kamphaus, " 'Es geschah in jenen Tagen . . . ' Besinnung zum Weihnachtsevangelium Luke 2:1-20," *BibL* 9 (1968): 299-302.

3923   Jan Lambrecht, "The Child in the Manger: A Meditation on Luke 2:1-20," *LouvS* 5 (1974-1975): 331-35.

3924   Raymond E. Brown, "The Meaning of the Manger: The Significance of the Shepherds," *Worship* 50 (1976): 18-38.

3925   Max A. Chevallier, "L'analyse littéraire des textes du Nouveau Testament," *RHPR* 57 (1977): 367-78.

3926   Charles T. Knippel, "The Nativity of Our Lord," *CJ* 11 (1985): 228-29.

3927   Mark I. Wegener, "Luke 2:1-20," *Int* 48 (1994): 394-97.

2:1-12

3928   E. Galbiati, "L'adorazione dei Magi (Luke 2:1-12)," *BibO* 4 (1962): 20-29.

2:1-10

3929   A. M. Wolff, "Der Kaiser und das Kind: Ein Auslegung von Luk 2,1-10," *TextK* 12 (1981): 18-31.

2:1-7

3930   G. Ogg, "The Quirinius Question Today," *ET* 79 (1967-1968): 231-36.

3931   J. D. M. Derrett, "Further Light on the Narratives of the Nativity," *NovT* 17 (1975): 81-108.

2:1-5

3932   P. W. Barnett, "'Ἀπογραφή and ἀπογράφεσθαι in Luke 2:1-5," *ET* 85 (1973-1974): 377-80.

2:1-2

3933   Robert H. Smith, "Caesar's Decree (Luke 2:1-2): Puzzle or Key," *CThM* 7 (1980): 343-51.

2:1

3934   E. Neuhäusler, "Die Herrlichkeit des Herrn," *BibL* 8 (1967): 233-35.

3935   T. P. Wiseman, " 'There Went Out a Decree from Caesar Augustus . . . ," *NTS* 33 (1987): 497.

3936   Royce L. B. Morris, "Why Αὔγουστος? A Note to Luke 2:1," *NTS* 38 (1992): 142-44.

2:2-24

3937   Patrick P. Saydon, "Some Biblico-Liturgical Passages Reconsidered," *MeliT* 18/1 (1966): 10-17.

2:2

3938   G. Ogg, "The Quirinius Question Today," *ET* 79/8 (1967-1968): 231-36.

3939   W. Brindle, "The Census and Quirinius: Luke 2:2," *JETS* 27 (1984): 43-1.

3940   J. Daoust, "Le recensement de Quirinius," *EV* 94 (1984): 366-67.

3941   Klaus Haacker, "Erst unter Quirinius? Ein Übersetzungs-vorschlag zu Lk 2,2," *BibN* 38/39 (1987): 39-43.

2:4-5

3942   George D. Kilpatrick, "Luke 2:4-5 and Leviticus 25:10," *ZNW* 80/3-4 (1989): 264-65.

2:7

3943   D. Yubero, "Una opinión original del 'Brocense'," *CuBí* 11 (1954): 3-6.

3944   E. Pax, "Denn sie fanden keinen 'Platz in der Herberge'. Jüdisches und frühchristliches Herbergswesen," *BibL* 6 (1965): 285-98.

3945   Eugene A. LaVerdiere, "Jesus the First-Born," *Emmanuel* 89 (1983): 544-48.

3946   Eugene A. LaVerdiere, "Wrapped in Swaddling Clothes," *Emmanuel* 90 (1984): 542-46.

3947   Eugene A. LaVerdiere, "No Room for them in the Inn," *Emmanuel* 91 (1985): 51-57.

3948   Hildegard Must, "A Diatessaric Rendering in Luke 2:7," *NTS* 32/1 (1986): 136-43.

3949   J. L. Ottey, "In a Stable Born Our Brother," *ET* 98/3 (1986-1987): 71-73.

3950   L. Paul Trudinger, "No Room in the Inn: A Note on Luke 2:7," *ET* 102 (1990-1991): 172-73.

3951   Joachim Kügler, "Die Windeln Jesu als Zeichen: Religionsgeschichtliche Anmerkungen zu SPARGANOO in Lk," *BibN* 77 (1995): 20-28; 81 (1996): 8-14.

3952   Jacques Winandy, "Du kataluma ä la crêche," *NTS* 44 (1998): 618-22.

2:8-39

3953   C. L'Eplattenier, "Une série pour l'Avent," *ETL* 57 (1982): 569-82.

2:8-14

3954   F. J. Steinmetz, "Nachtwache. Eine Betrachtung zu Luke 2:8-14," *GeistL* 55 (1982): 465-67.

20:9-19

3955   Frank Stagg, "Luke's Theological Use of Parables," *RevExp* 94 (1997): 215-29.

20:9-16

3956   R. Alan Culpepper, "Parable as Commentary: The Twice-Given Vineyard (Luke 20:9-16)," *PRS* 26 (1999): 147-68.

2:10-12

3957   Jacques Winandy, "Le signe de la mangeoire et des langes," *NTS* 43 (1997): 140-46.

2:11

3958   Friedrich Wulf, "Gott im Menschen Jesus. Auslegung und Meditation von Johannes 1:14; Phil 2:7; Lk 2:11," *GeistL* 42 (1969): 273-73.

3959   B. Prete, " 'Oggi vi è nato . . . il Salvatore che è il Cristo Signore' (Lc 2,11)," *RBib* 34 (1986): 289-325.

2:12

3960   A. Pritchard, "Our True Selves," *ET* 94 (1982-1983): 81-82.

3961   John Killinger, "Christmas and Abortion," *ChrM* 16/6 (1985): 26-27.

3962   Joachim Kügler, "Die Windeln Jesu als Zeichen: Religions-geschichtliche Anmerkungen zu SPARGANOO in Lk," *BibN* 77 (1995): 20-28; 81 (1996): 8-14.

2:14

3963   E. R. Smothers, *"En anthrôpois eudokias,"* *RechSR* 24 (1934): 86-93.

3964   C. C. Tarelli, "An Interpretation of Luke 2,14," *ET* 48 (1936-1937): 322.

3965   A. L. Williams, "Men of Good-Will (Lk 2,14)," *ET* 50 (1938-1939): 283-84.

3966   C.-H. Hunzinger, "Neues Licht auf Lc 2,14," *ZNW* 44 (191-1953): 85-90.

3967   Joseph A. Fitzmyer, "Peace upon Earth among Men of His Good Will (Lk 2:14)," *TS* 19 (1958): 225-27.

3968   C.-H. Hunzinger, "Ein weiterer Beleg zu Lc 2,14 *anthrōpoi eudokias*," *ZNW* 49 (1958): 129-30.

3969   R. Deichgräber, "Lc. 2:14: *anthrōpoi eudokais*," *ZNW* 51/1-2 (1960): 132.

3970   Raimund Köbert, "Sabrâ Tabâ Im Syrischen Tatian Luc 2:14," *Bib* 42/1 (1961): 90-91.

3971   H. Rusche, " 'Et in terra pax hominibus bonae voluntatis', Erklärung, Deutung and Betrachtung zum Engelchor in Luke 2:14," *BibL* 2 (1961): 229-34.

3972   Eric F. F. Bishop, "Men of God's Good Pleasure," *ATR* 48 (1966): 63-69.

3973   J. Riedl, " 'Ehre sei Gott in der Höhe'. Meditation über Lukas 2:14," *BK* 21 (1966): 119-22.

3974   Günther Schwarz, "Der Lobgesang der Engel (Lk 2,14)," *BZ* 15 (1971): 260-64.

3975   C. H. Dodd, "New Testament Translation Problems," *BT* 27/3 (1976): 301-305; 28 (1977): 101-16.

3976   E. Hansack, "Luke 2:14: 'Friede den Menschen auf Erden, die guten Willens sind'?" *BZ* 21 (1977): 117-18.

3977   F. V. Mills, "The Christmas Music of St. Luke," *ET* 93 (1981-1982): 49.

3978   Paul R. Berger, "Luke 2:14: ἀνθρώποις εὐδοκίας. Die auf Gottes Weisung mit Wohlgefallen beschenkten Menschen," *ZNW* 74 (1983): 129-44.

3979   Paul R. Berger, "Menschen ohne 'Gottes Wohlgefallen' Lk. 2:14," *ZNW* 76/1-2 (1985): 119-22.

3980   K. Smyth, " 'Peace on Earth to Men . . . ' (Luke 2,14)," *IBS* 9 (1987): 27-34.

3981   Manuel Guerra Gómez, "Análisis filológico-teológio y traducción del himno de los ángeles en Belén," *Bur* 30 (1989): 31-86.

3982 A. P. B. Breytenbach, "Lukas 2:14 vanuit 'n Joods-Christelike perspektief," *HTS* 50 (1994): 272-80.

3983 J. D. M. Derrett, "ἄ)nqrwpoi eu)doki¿aj (Lk 2:14b)," *FilN* 11 (1998): 101-106.

3984 Albert M. Wolters, "*Anthropoi Eudokias* (Luke 2:14) and *'Nsy Rswn* (4Q416)," *JBL* 113 (1994): 291-92.

2:15-20

3985 G. Zananiri, "Les bergers de Noël (Luke 2:15-20)," *EV* 81 (1981): 340-41.

3986 Kikuo Matsunaga, "Pondering Mary," *EAJT* 4/2 (1986): 14-17.

2:15

3987 Christoph Burchard, "Fußnoten zum neutestamentlichen Griechisch II," *ZNW* 69 (1978): 143-57.

3988 Christoph Burchard, "A Note on ῥῆμα in JosAs 17:1f.; Luke 2:15, 17; Acts 10:37," *NovT* 27 (1985): 281-95.

2:17

3989 Paul Ellingworth, "Luke 2:17: Just Who Spoke to the Shepherds?" *BT* 31 (1980): 447.

3990 Christoph Burchard, "A Note on ῥῆμα in JosAs 17:1f.; Luke 2:15, 17; Acts 10:37," *NovT* 27 (1985): 281-95.

2:19

3991 Ben F. Meyer, "But Mary Kept All These Things," *CBQ* 26 (1964): 31-49.

3992 F. Meyer, "Tradition und Meditation. Meditation über Luke 2:19," *BibL* 12 (1971): 285-87.

3993 D. Ogston, "A Time for Pause," *ET* 89 (1977-1978): 50-1.

3994 G. Bellia, " 'Confrontando nel suo cuore.' Custodia sapienziale di Maria in Luke 2:19b," *BibO* 25 (1983): 215-28.

3995 Werner Bieder, "Das Volk Gottes in Erwartung von Licht und Lobpreis," *TZ* 40/2 (1984): 137-48.

2:21

3996 E. Galbiati, "La Circoncisione di Gesù (Luke 2:21)," *BibO* 8 (1966): 37-45.

3997   Lucien Legrand, "On l'appela du nom de Jésus (Luke 2:21)," *RB* 89 (1982): 481-91.

3998   P. T. Stramare, "La circoncisione di Gesù: Signifcato esegetico e teologico," *BibO* 26 (1984): 193-203.

2:22-1

3999   Klemens Stock, "Maria nel tempio (Lc 2,22-1)," *ParSpirV* 6 (1982): 114-25.

2:22-40

4000   E. Galbiati, "La Presentazione al tempio (Luke 2:22-40)," *BibO* 6 (1964): 28-37.

4001   Augustin George, "La présentation de Jésus au Temple (Lc 2)," *AsSeign* NS 11 (1971): 29-39.

4002   Raymond E. Brown, "The Presentation of Jesus (Luke 2:22-40)," *Worship* 51 (1977): 2-11.

4003   P. T. Stramare, "La presentazione di Gesu al tempio (Luke 2:22-40)," *BibO* 25 (1983): 63-71.

4004   Marion L. Soards, "Luke 2:22-40," *Int* 44 (1990): 400-405.

4005   Frederick Strickert, "The Presentation of Jesus: The Gospel of Inclusion: Luke 2:22-40," *CThM* 22 (1995): 33-37.

2:22-38

4006   P. Figueras, "Syméon et Anne, ou le témoignage de la loi et des prophètes," *NovT* 20 (1978): 84-99.

4007   M. Miyoshi, "Jesu Darstellung oder Reinigung im Tempel unter Berücksichtigung von 'Nunc Dimittis' Luke 2:22-38," *AJBI* 4 (1978): 85-115.

2:22-35

4008   Josef Sudbrack, "Gesetz und Geist: Jesu Darstellung im Tempel (Lk 2,22-35)," *GeistL* 48 (1975): 462-66.

2:22-32

4009   G. Ravini, "Esegesi degli Evangeli festivi," *BibO* 1 (1959): 17-19.

2:22

4010   P. T. Stramare, "Compiuti i giorni della loro purificazione (Luke 2:22): gli avvenimenti del Nuovo Testamento conclusivi di un disegno," *BibO* 24 (1982): 199-205.

4011   A. R. C. McLellan, "What the Law Required," *ET* 94 (1982-1983): 82-83.

2:23

4012   Paul Winter, "῝Οτι Recitativum in Luke 1:25, 61; 2:23," *HTR* 48 (1955): 213-18.

4013   P. T. Stramare, " 'Sanctum Domino vocabitur' (Luke 2:23): Il crocevia dei riti è la Santità," *BibO* 25 (1983): 21-34.

2:25-39

4014   P. Figueras, "Syméon et Anne, ou le témoignage de la loi et des prophètes," *NovT* 20 (1978): 84-99.

2:27-33

4015   Pierre Grelot, "Le Cantique de Siméon," *RB* 93/4 (1986): 481-509.

2:29-32

4016   J. Reuss, "Studien zur Lukas-Erklärung des Presbyters Hesychius von Jerusalem," *Bib* 59 (1978): 562-71.

4017   Klaus Berger, "Das Canticum Simeonis (Lk. 2:29-32)," *NovT* 27 (1985): 27-39.

4018   Robert C. Tannehill, "Israel in Luke-Acts: A Tragic Story," *JBL* 104 (1985): 69-85.

2:31

4019   George D. Kilpatrick, "*Laoi* at Luke ii.31 and Acts iv.25, 27," *JTS* 16 (1965): 127.

2:32

4020   A. Smitmans, " 'Ein Licht zur Erleuchtung der Völker' (Luke 2:32). Meditation über das *Nunc dimittis*," *BK* 24 (1969): 138-39.

4021   A. Simon-Muñoz, "Cristo, luz de los gentiles: Puntualizationes sobre Lc 2,32," *EB* 46 (1988): 27-44.

4022 John J. Kilgallen, "Jesus, Savior, the Glory of Your People Israel," *Bib* 75 (1994): 305-28.

2:34-35

4023 W. Wiskirchen, "Das Zeichen des Widerspruchs. Homilie über Luke 2:34b-35," *BibL* 4 (1963): 138-42.

4024 J. D. M. Derrett, "Antilegomenon, romphaia, dialogismoi (Lk 2:34-35): The Hidden Context," *FilN* 6 (1993): 207-18.

2:34

4025 Harold A. Guy, "The Virgin Birth in St. Luke," *ET* 68 (1956-1957): 157-58.

2:35

4026 Pierre Benoit, "Et Toi-Même, Un Glaive Te Transpercera L'âme! (Luc 2:35)," *CBQ* 25 (1963): 251-61.

4027 I. Bailey, "Parental Heart-Break," *ET* 89 (1977-1978): 85-86.

2:36-37

4028 M. P. John, "Luke 2,36-37: How Old Was Anna?" *BT* 26 (1975): 247.

4029 A. T. Varela, "Luke 2:36-37: Is Anna's Age What is Really in Focus?" *BT* 27 (1976): 446.

4030 J. K. Elliott, "Anna's Age," *NovT* 30 (1988): 100-102.

2:39

4031 J. A. Bain, "Did Joseph Belong to Bethlehem or to Nazareth?" *ET* 47 (1935-1936): 93.

2:40-1

4032 Otto Glombitza, "Der zwölfjährige Jesus, Luk 2:40-1: Ein Beitrag zur Exegese der lukanischen Vorgeschichte," *NovT* 5 (1962): 1-4.

2:41-52

4033 J. K. Elliott, "Does Luke 2:41-52 Anticipate the Resurrection?" *ET* 83 (1971-1972): 87-89.

4034 G. Schmahl, "Luke 2:41-52 und die Kindheitserzählung des *Thomas* 19:1-5. Ein Vergleich," *BibL* 15 (1974): 249-58.

4035   John F. Jansen, "Luke 2:41-52," *Int* 30 (1976): 400-404.

4036   Raymond E. Brown, "The Finding of the Boy Jesus in the Temple: A Third Christmas Story," *Worship* 51 (1977): 474-85.

4037   P. W. van der Horst, "Notes on the Aramaic Background of Luke 2:41-1," *JSNT* 7 (1980): 61-66.

4038   Elisabeth Schüssler Fiorenza, "Luke 2:41-52," *Int* 36 (1982): 399-403.

4039   J. D. M. Derrett, "An Apt Student's Matriculation," *EB* 58 (2000): 101-22.

2:41-51

4040   B. M. F. van Iersel, "Finding of Jesus in the Temple: Some Observations on the Original Form of Luke 2:41-51a," *NovT* 4 (1960): 161-73.

4041   H. J. de Jonge, "Sonship, Wisdom, Infancy: Luke 2:41-51a," *NTS* 24 (1977-1978): 317-54.

2:41-50

4042   John J. Kilgallen, "Luke 2:41-50: Foreshadowing of Jesus, Teacher," *Bib* 66/4 (1985): 553-59.

2:42-1

4043   E. Galbiati, "Gesù giovinetto nel tempio (Luke 2:42-1)," *BibO* 2 (1960): 21-25.

2:43-46

4044   J. R. Gray, "Was Our Lord an Only Child?" *ET* 71 (1959-1960): 53.

2:49

4045   Patrick J. Temple, " 'House' or 'Business' in Luke 2:49?" *CBQ* 1 (1939): 342-1.

4046   E. R. Smothers, "A Note on Luke ii,49," *HTR* 45 (191): 67-69.

4047   Paul Winter, "Lc 2,49 and Targum Yerushalmi," *ZNW* 45 (1954): 145-79.

4048   W. C. Robinson, "The Virgin Birth—A Broader Base," *CT* 17/5 (1972): 238-40.

4049   J. Bishop, "The Compulsion of Love," *ET* 85 (1973-1974): 371-73.

4050   F. D. Weinert, "The Multiple Meanings of Luke 2:49 and their Significance," *BTB* 13 (1983): 19-22.

4051   Juan M. Lozano, "Jesucristo en la Espiritualidad de San Antonio María Claret," *EE* 60 (1985): 157-79.

4052   Dennis D. Sylva, "The Cryptic Clause ἐν τοῖς τοῦ πατρός μου δεῖ εἶναί με in Luke," *ZNW* 78 (1987): 132-40.

2:50

4053   S. M. Harris, "My Father's House," *ET* 94 (1982-1983): 84-85.

2:51

4054   Ben F. Meyer, "But Mary Kept All These Things," *CBQ* 26 (1964): 31-49.

2:1

4055   Patrick J. Temple, "Christ's Holy Youth According to Luke 2:1," *CBQ* 3 (1941): 243-50.

4056   B. Couroyer, "À propos de Luke 2:1," *RB* 86 (1979): 92-101.

3-4

4057   Walt Russell, "The Anointing With the Holy Spirit in Luke-Acts," *TriJ* 7/1 (1986): 47-63.

3:1-22

4058   Ben Witherington, "Jesus and the Baptist: Two of a Kind?" *SBLSP* 18 (1988): 225-44.

3:1-20

4059   Ivor Buse, "St. John and 'The First Synoptic Pericope'," *NovT* 3 (1959-1960): 57-61.

3:1-18

4060   William D. Howden, "Good News: Repent," *ChrM* 16/6 (1985): 28.

3:1-12

4061   B. Marconcini, "La predicazione del Battista in Marco e Luca confrontata con la redazione di Matteo," *RBib* 20 Suppl. (1972): 451-66.

3:1-6

4062   E. Galbiati, "Esegesi degli Evangeli festivi. Preparate la via del Signore," *BibO* 5 (1963): 213-15.

4063   J. Mas, "Domingo 2. de Adviento. Ciclo C.: 1. lectura, Baruc 5:1-9; 2. lectura, Filipenses 1:4-6, 8-11; 3. lectura, Lucas 3:1-6," *CuBi* 27 (1970): 343-46.

3:1-4

4064   Walter Brueggemann, "Luke 3:1-4," *Int* 30 (1976): 404-409.

3:1-2

4065   R. M. Grant, "The Occasion of Luke 3:1-2," *HTR* 33 (1940): 151-54.

3:1

4066   D. R. Fotheringham, "Bible Chronology," *ET* 48 (1936-1937): 234-35.

4067   E. Neuhäusler, "Nach mir kommt, der stärker ist als ich. Homilie zum Evangelium des 4. Adventssonntags (Luke 3:1)," *BibL* 4 (1963): 277-81.

4068   A. Strobel, "Plädoyer für Lukas: Zur Stimmigkeit des chronistischen Rahmens von Lk 3.1," *NTS* 41 (1995): 466-69.

3:2-22

4069   E. J. Christiansen, "Taufe als Initiation in der Apostelgeschichte," *ST* 40/1 (1986): 55-79.

3:2-3

4070   Gerd Theissen, "Lokalkoloritforschung in den Evangelien: Plädoyer für die Erneuerung einer alten Fragestellung," *EvT* 45 (1985): 481-99.

3:2

4071   Gerhard Lohfink, " 'Da erging das Wort des Herrn . . . ' Homilie zum 4. Adventssonntag," *BibL* 5 (1964): 271-74.

3:3-22

4072   Harry T. Fleddermann, "The Beginning of Q," *SBLSP* 15 (1985): 153-59.

3:3-14

4073   Helmut Gollwitzer, "Predigt über Lukas 3,3-14," *EvT* 11 (1951-191): 145-51.

3:3

4074   Homer Heater, "A Textual Note on Luke 3:33," *JSNT* 28 (1986): 25-29.

3:7-9

4075   Carl Kazmierski, "The Stones of Abraham: John the Baptist and the End of Torah (Matt 3,7-10 par. Luke 3,7-9)," *Bib* 68 (1987): 22-40.

4076   Alan Kirk, "Upbraiding Wisdom: John's Speech and the Beginning of Q," *NovT* 40 (1998): 1-16.

3:10-18

4077   B. L. Robertson, "Luke 3:10-18," *Int* 36 (1982): 404-409.

3:10-14

4078   S. V. McCasland, " 'Soldiers on Service': The Draft among the Hebrews," *JBL* 62 (1943): 59-71.

4079   Harald Sahlin, "Die Früchte der Umkehr," *ST* 1 (1948): 54-68.

3:14-30

4080   D. Seccombe, "Luke and Isaiah," *NTS* 27 (1980-1981): 21-59.

3:15-17

4081   Mark E. Wangerin, "The Baptism of Our Lord," *CJ* 11 (1985): 231-32.

4082   Sheila Klassen-Wiebe, "Luke 3:15-17,21-22," *Int* 48 (1994): 397-401.

3:15

4083   Edmond Jacquemin, "Le baptême du Christ. Mt 3,13-17; Mc1,6b-11; Lc 3,15s.21s.," *AsSeign* 12 (1969): 48-66.

3:16-17

4084   Harry T. Fleddermann, "John and the Coming One (Matt 3:11-12//Luke 3:16-17)," *SBLSP* 14 (1984): 377-84.

4085   J. Daryl Charles, " 'The Coming One'/'Stronger One' and His Baptism: Matthew 3:11-12, Mark 1:8, Luke 3:16-17," *Pneuma* 11 (1989): 37-50.

4086   Alan Kirk, "Upbraiding Wisdom: John's Speech and the Beginning of Q," *NovT* 40 (1998): 1-16.

3:16

4087   T. F. Glasson, "Water, Wind and Fire (Luke iii.16): An Orphic Initiation," *NTS* 3 (1956-1957): 69-71.

4088   L. W. Barnard, "A Note on Matt. iii.11 and Luke iii.16," *JTS* 8 (1957): 107.

4089   P. Proulx and Luis Alonso Schökel, "Las Sandalias del Mesías Esposo," *Bib* 59 (1978): 1-37.

3:17

4090   James S. Alexander, "A Note on the Interpretation of the Parable of the Threshing Floor at the Conference at Carthage of A.D. 411," *JTS* 24/2 (1973): 512-19.

4091   Günther Schwarz, "Τὸ δὲ ἄχυρον κατακαύσει," *ZNW* 72 (1981): 272-76.

3:18-23

4092   R. F. Collins, "Jesus' Ministry to the Deaf and Dumb," *MeliT* 35/1 (1984): 12-36.

3:19-21

4093   Richard J. Erickson, "The Jailing of John and the Baptism of Jesus: Luke 3:19-21," *JETS* 36 (1993): 455-66.

3:21-38

4094   J. Rius-Camps, "Constituye Lc 3,21-38 un solo periodo? Propuesta de un cambio de puntuación," *Bib* 65 (1984): 189-209.

3:21-22

4095   M. Dutheil, "Le Baptême de Jésus. Éléments d'interprétation," *SBFLA* 6 (1955-1956): 85-124.

4096   Placide Roulin and Giles Carton, "Le Baptême du Christ," *BVC* 25 (1959): 39-48.

4097   G. H. P. Thompson, "Called-Proved-Obedient: A Study in the Baptism and Temptation Narratives of Matthew and Luke," *JTS* 11 (1960): 1-12.

4098   R. F. Collins, "Luke 3:21-22: Baptism or Anointing?" *BibTo* 84 (1976): 821-31.

4099   Max A. Chevallier, "L'analyse littéraire des textes du Nouveau Testament," *RHPR* 57 (1977): 367-78.

4100   Mark E. Wangerin, "The Baptism of Our Lord," *CJ* 11 (1985): 231-32.

4101   Sheila Klassen-Wiebe, "Luke 3:15-17,21-22," *Int* 48 (1994): 397-401.

4102   Günther Schwarz, " 'Wie eine Taube'?" *BibN* 89 (1997): 27-29.

3:21

4103   Edmond Jacquemin, "Le baptême du Christ. Mt 3,13-17; Mc 1,6b-11; Lc 3,15s.21s.," *AsSeign* 12 (1969): 48-66.

3:22

4104   Léopold Sabourin, "Two Lukan Texts (1:35; 3:22)," *RSB* 1 (1981): 29-32.

3:23-38

4105   G. Bolsinger, "Die Ahnenreihe Christi nach Matthäus und Lukas," *BK* 12 (1957): 112-17.

4106   K. H. Schelkle, "Die Frauen im Stammbaum Jesu," *BK* 18 (1963): 113-15.

4107   M. Byskov, "Verus Deus - verus homo, Luc 3:23-28," *ST* 26 (1972): 25-32.

4108   P. Seethaler, "Eine kleine Bemerkung zu den Stammbäumen Jesu nach Matthäus und Lukas," *BZ* 16 (1972): 256-57.

4109   E. L. Abel, "The Genealogies of Jesus *o Khristos*," *NTS* 20 (1973-1974): 203-10.

4110   O. Da Spinetoli, "Les généalogies de Jésus et leur signification: Mt 1,1-25; Lc 3,23-38," *AsSeign* 9 (1974): 6-19.

4111 George E. Rice, "Luke 3:22-38 in Codex Bezae: The Messianic King," *AUSS* 17 (1979): 203-208.

4112 Ernst Lerle, "Die Ahnenverzeichnisse Jesu. Versuch einer christologischen Interpretation," *ZNW* 72 (1981): 112-17.

4113 André Feuillet, "Observations sur les deux généalogies de Jésus-Christ de saint Matthieu (1,1-17) et de saint Luc (3,23-38)," *EV* 98 (1988): 605-608.

4114 Dieter Böhler, "Jesus als Davidssohn bei Lukas und Micha," *Bib* 79 (1998): 532-38.

4115 Lynlea Rodger, "The Infancy Stories of Matthew and Luke: An Examination of the Child as a Theological Metaphor," *HBT* 19 (1997): 58-81.

3:23

4116 G. Ogg, "The Age of Jesus When He Taught," *NTS* 5 (1958-1959): 291-98.

4117 G. M. Lee, "Luke iii,23," *ET* 79 (1967-1968): 310.

4118 A. Salas, "José, el padre," *BibFe* 6 (1980): 304-32.

4119 John W. Miller, "Jesus' 'Age Thirty Transition': A Psychohistorical Probe," *SBLSP* 15 (1985): 45-56.

3:33

4120 Homer Heater, "A Textual Note on Luke 3:33," *JSNT* 28 (1986): 25-29.

3:36

4121 Gert J. Steyn, "The Occurrence of 'Kainam' in Luke's Genealogy," *ETL* 65 (1989): 409-11.

4:1-13

4122 G. S. Freeman, "The Temptation," *ET* 48 (1936-1937): 45.

4123 G. H. P. Thompson, "Called-Proved-Obedient: A Study in the Baptism and Temptation Narratives of Matthew and Luke," *JTS* 11 (1960): 1-12.

4124 Jacques Dupont, "Les Tentations de Jésus dans le Récit de Luc," *SE* 14/1 (1962): 7-29.

4125 H. Swanston, "The Lukan Temptation Narrative," *JTS* 17 (1966): 71.

4126   F. Smyth-Florentin, "Jésus, le Fils du Père, vainqueur de Satan," *AsSeign* 14 (1973): 56-75.

4127   P. Pokorný, "The Temptation Stories and Their Intention," *NTS* 20 (1973-1974): 115-27.

4128   Wilhelm Wilkens, "Die Versuchungsgeschichte, Luk. 4,1-13, und die Komposition des Evangeliums," *TZ* 30 (1974): 262-72.

4129   D. C. Hester, "Luke 4:1-13," *Int* 31 (1977): 53-59.

4130   Dieter Zeller, "Die Versuchungen Jesu in der Logienquelle," *TTZ* 89 (1980): 61-73.

4131   J. A. Davidson, "The Testing of Jesus," *ET* 94 (1982-1983): 113-15.

4132   Paul J. Achtemeier, "Enigmatic Bible Passages: It's the Little Things that Count," *BA* 46 (1983): 30-31.

4133   F. Gerald Downing, "Cynics and Christians," *NTS* 30/4 (1984): 584-93.

4134   Albert Fuchs, "Versuchung Jesu," *SNTU-A* 9 (1984): 95-159.

4135   Elliott J. Bush, "A Fruitful Wilderness," *ChrM* 16/2 (1985): 24-26.

4136   Bill Kellermann, "A Confusion Before the Cross: Confronting Temptation [Pt. 2 of 6]," *Soj* 14/2 (1985): 32-35.

4137   Christoph Kähler, "Satanischer Schriftgebrauch: Zur Hermeneutik von Mt 4,1-11/Lk 4,1-13," *TLZ* 119 (1994): 857-67.

4138   Kim Paffenroth, "The Testing of the Sage: 1 Kings 10:1-13 and Q 4:1-13 (Lk 4:1-13)," *ET* 107 (1996): 142-43.

4139   Marlis Gielen, " 'Und führe uns nicht in Versuchung' Die 6. Vater- Unser Bitte—eine Anfechtung für das biblische Gottesbild?" *ZNW* 89 (1998): 201-16.

4:1-12

4140   Roy Yates, "Jesus and the Demonic in the Synoptic Gospels," *ITQ* 44 (1977): 39-57.

4:1-11

> 4141   A. Knockaert and C. Van Der Plancke, "Catéchèses de la tentation," *LV* 34 (1979): 123-53.

4:1

> 4142   Philippe Rolland, "L'arrière-fond sémitique des évangiles synoptiques," *ETL* 60 (1984): 358-62.

4:4

> 4143   Robert Hodgson, "On the *Gattung* of Q: A Dialogue with James M. Robinson," *Bib* 66/1 (1985): 73-95.

4:5-8

> 4144   R. Morgenthaler, "Roma - Sedes Satanae. Röm, 13,1ff. im Lichte von Luk. 4,5-8," *TZ* 12 (1956): 289-304.

4:9-12

> 4145   Niels Hyldahl, "Die Versuchung auf der Zinne des Tempels," *ST* 15 (1961): 113-27.

4:13

> 4146   Heinrich Baarlink, "Friede im Himmel: die lukanische Redaktion von Lk 19,38 und Ihre Deutung," *ZNW* 76/3 (1985): 170-86.

4:14-44

> 4147   C. Escudero Freire, "Jesús profeta, libertador del hombre: Visión lucana de su ministerio terrestre," *EE* 51 (1976): 463-96.

> 4148   A. del Agua Pérez, "El cumplimiento del Reino de Dios en la misión de Jesús: Programa del Evangelico de Lucas (Luke 4:14-44)," *EB* 38 (1979-1980): 269-93.

4:14-15

> 4149   É. Samain, "L'Évangile de Luc: un témoignage ecclésial et missionnaire," *AsSeign* 34 (1973): 60-73.

4:16-5:11

> 4150   Michael D. Goulder, "On Putting Q to the Test," *NTS* 24 (1977-1978): 218-34.

4:16-44

> 4151   Sharon H. Ringe, "Luke 4:16-44: A Portrait of Jesus as Herald of God's Jubilee," *EGLMBS* 1 (1981): 73-84.

4:16-30

4152 Bruno Violet, "Zum rechten Verständnis der Nazarethperikope Lc 4,16-30," *ZNW* 37 (1938): 251-71.

4153 Hugh Anderson, "Broadening Horizons: The Rejection at Nazareth. Pericope of Luke 4:16-30 in Light of Recent Critical Trends," *Int* 18 (1964): 259-75.

4154 A. Strobel, "Das apokalyptische Terminproblem in der sogenannten Antrittspredigt Jesu," *TLZ* 92 (1967): 251-54.

4155 David Hill, "The Rejection of Jesus at Nazareth: Luke 4:16-30," *NovT* 13/3 (1971): 161-80.

4156 H. J. B. Combrink, "The Structure and Significance of Luke 4:16-30," *Neo* 7 (1973): 27-47.

4157 Charles Perrot, "Luc, 4,16-30 et la lecture biblique de l'ancienne Synagogue," *RevSR* 47 (1973): 324-40.

4158 Donald R. Miesner, "The Circumferential Speeches of Luke-Acts: Patterns and Purpose," *SBLSP* 8/2 (1978): 223-37.

4159 M. Rodgers, "Luke 4:16-30: A Call for a Jubilee Year?" *RTR* 40 (1981): 72-82.

4160 R. Albertz, "Die 'Antrittspredigt' Jesu im Lukasevangelium auf ihrem alttestamentlichen Hintergrund," *ZAW* 74 (1983): 182-206.

4161 J. Kodell, "Luke's Gospel in a Nutshell (Luke 4:16-30)," *BTB* 13 (1983): 16-18.

4162 Paul Löffer, "Jesus und die Nicht-Juden," *ZMiss* 10/2 (1984): 66-69.

4163 Joseph B. Tyson, "The Jewish Public in Luke-Acts," *NTS* 30/4 (1984): 574-83.

4164 B.-J. Koet, " 'Today this Scripture Has Been Fulfilled in Your Ears': Jesus' Explanation of Scripture in Luke 4,16-30," *Bij* 47 (1986): 368-94.

4165 T. V. Walker, "Luke 4:16-30," *RevExp* 85 (1988): 321-24.

4166 Jeffrey S. Siker, "First to the Gentiles: A Literary Analysis of Luke 4:16-30," *JBL* 111 (1992): 73-90.

4167   Charles A. Kimball, "Jesus' Exposition of Scripture in Luke 4:16-30: An Inquiry in Light of Jewish Hermeneutics," *PRS* 21 (1994): 179-202.

4168   Robert F. O'Toole, "Does Luke Also Portray Jesus As the Christ in Luke 4,16-30?" *Bib* 76 (1995): 498-522.

4169   L. Paul Trudinger, "Two Lukan Gospel Stories: Key to the Significance of the Dominical Sacraments in the Life of the Early Church," *DR* 118 (2000): 17-26.

4:16-21

4170   É. Samain, "Le discours-programme de Nazareth (Lc 4)," *AsSeign* NS 20 (1973): 17-27.

4171   Patrick D. Miller, "Luke 4:16-21," *Int* 29 (1975): 417-21.

4172   John Momis, "Renew the Face of the Earth," *Point* 9 (1980): 7-15.

4173   Georges Casalis, "Un Nouvel An. Luke 4:16-21," *ÉTR* 56 (1981): 148-58.

4174   K. H. Schelkle, "Jesus und Paulus lesen die Bibel," *BK* 36 (1981): 277-79.

4175   Guillermo J. Garlatti, "Evangelización y liberación de los pobres," *RevB* 49 (1987): 1-15.

4176   Dirk Monshouwer, "The Reading of the Prophet in the Synagogue at Nazareth," *Bib* 72 (1991): 90-99.

4:16

4177   J. Bishop, "The Place of Habit in the Spiritual Life," *ET* 91 (1980-1981): 374-75.

4:17

4178   Tjitze Baarda, "Anoixas - Anaptyxas: Over de Vaststelling van de Tekst van Lukas 4,17 in het Diatessaron," *NedTT* 40/3 (1986): 199-208.

4:18-19

4179   J. E. Murray, "The Beatitudes," *Int* 1 (1947): 374-76.

4180   Heinrich Baarlink, "Ein gnädiges Jahr des Herrn und Tage der Vergeltung," *ZNW* 73 (1982): 204-20.

4181   Robert Hodgson, "On the *Gattung* of Q: A Dialogue with James M. Robinson," *Bib* 66/1 (1985): 73-95.

4:18

4182   Bonaventura Rinaldi, "Proclamare ai prigionieri la liberazione (Luke 4:18)," *BibO* 18 (1976): 241-45.

4183   S. Dawson, "The Spirit's Gift of Sight," *ET* 90 (1978-1979): 241-42.

4184   Léopold Sabourin, "Evangelize the Poor (Luke 4:18)," *RSB* 1 (1981): 101-109.

4185   Gerhard Sauter, "Leiden und 'Handeln'," *EvT* 45 (1985): 435-58.

4:21-30

4186   É. Samain, "Aucun prophète n'est bien reçu dans sa patrie (Lc 4)," *AsSeign* 35 (1973): 63-72.

4:21

4187   Karl F. Ulrichs, "Some Notes on Ears in Luke-Acts, especially in Lk 4.21," *BibN* 98 (1999): 28-31.

4:22-30

4188   Donald G. Miller, "Luke 4:22-30," *Int* 40/1 (1986): 53-58.

4:22

4189   John Nolland, "Impressed Unbelievers as Witnesses to Christ (Luke 4:22a)," *JBL* 98 (1979): 219-29.

4190   John Nolland, "Words of Grace (Luke 4,22)," *Bib* 65 (1984): 44-60.

4191   Feargus O'Fearghail, "Rejection in Nazareth: Lk 4,22," *ZNW* 75 (1984): 60-72.

4:23-24

4192   John J. Kilgallen, "Provocation in Luke 4:23-24," *Bib* 70/4 (1989): 511-16.

4:23

4193   John Nolland, "Classical and Rabbinic Parallel to 'Physician, heal yourself' (Luke 4:23)," *NovT* 21 (1979): 193-209.

4:25-27

4194   L. C. Crockett, "Luke 4:25-27 and Jewish-Gentile Relations in Luke-Acts," *JBL* 88 (1969): 177-83.

4195   Günther Schwarz, "Versuch einer Wiederherstellung des geistigen Eigentums Jesu," *BibN* 53 (1990): 32-37.

4:25

4196   B. E. Thiering, "The Three and a Half Years of Elijah," *NovT* 23 (1981): 41-55.

4:27

4197   Gerald Bostock, "Jesus as the New Elisha," *ET* 92 (1980-1981): 39-41.

4:29-30

4198   Tjitze Baarda, "The Flying Jesus: Luke 4:29-30 in the Syriac Diatessaron," *VC* 40/4 (1986): 313-41.

4:38-39

4199   Albert Fuchs, "Entwicklungsgeschichtliche Studie zu Mark 1:29-31 par Matthew 8:14-15 par Luke 4:38-39: Macht über Fieber und Dämonen," *SNTU-A* 6/7 (1981-1982): 21-76.

4:39

4200   J. D. M. Derrett, "Getting on Top of a Demon," *EQ* 65 (1993): 99-109.

4:42

4201   Gregory Murray, "Did Luke Use Mark?" *DR* 104 (1986): 268-71.

4:43

4202   Günther Schwarz, "Auch den anderen Städten?" *NTS* 23 (1976-1977): 344.

4:44

4203   D. R. Fotheringham, "St. Luke 4:44," *ET* 45 (1933-1934): 237.

5:1-6:19

4204   Michael Theobald, "Die Anfänge der Kirche: Zur Struktur von Lk. 5:1-6:19," *NTS* 30 (1984): 91-108.

5:1-11

4205   Heinz Schürmann, "Die Verheissung an Simon Petrus. Auslegung von Lukas 5:1-11," *BibL* 5 (1964): 18-24.

4206 K. Zillessen, "Das Schiff des Petrus und die Gefährten vom andern Schiff (Lc 5,1-11)," *ZNW* 57 (1966): 137-39.

4207 Günter Klein, "Die Berufung des Petrus," *ZNW* 58 (1967): 1-44.

4208 Jean Delorme, "Luc v.1-11: Analyse Structurale et Histoire de la Rédaction," *NTS* 18 (1971-1972): 331-50.

4209 K.-H. Crumbach, "Der 'reiche Fischzug' als Berufungsgeschichte. Eine Meditation zu Lk 5,1-11," *GeistL* 47 (1974): 228-31.

4210 Heinz Schürmann, "La promesse à Simon-Pierre: Lc 5,1-11," *AsSeign* 36 (1974): 63-70.

4211 Jean Delorme, "Linguistique, Sémiotique, Exégèse: à propos du Séminaire de Durham," *SémBib* 6 (1977): 35-59.

4212 A. Viard, "La Parole de Dieu et la mission de Pierre," *EV* 87 (1977): 8.

4213 J. D. M. Derrett, "Ἦσαν γὰρ ἁλεῖς (Mark 1:16). Jesus' Fisherman and the Parable of the Net," *NovT* 22/2 (1980): 108-37.

4214 George E. Rice, "Luke's Thematic Use of the Call to Discipleship," *AUSS* 20 (1981): 51-58.

4215 Samuel O. Abogunrin, "The 3 Variant Accounts of Peter's Call: Critical, Theological Examination of the Texts," *NTS* 31 (1985): 587-602.

4216 Claude Coulot, "Les figures du maître et de ses disciples dans les premières communautés chrétiennes," *RevSR* 59/1 (1985): 1-11.

4217 W. Schlichting, " 'Auf dein Wort hin' (Lukas 5,1-11)," *TBe* 17 (1986): 113-17.

4218 J. Rius-Camps, "Simón (Pedro) se autoexcluye de la llamada de Jesús al seguimiento," *EB* 57 (1999): 565-87.

5:1

4219 George D. Kilpatrick, "Three Problems of New Testament Text," *NovT* 21 (1979): 289-92.

4220 J. Rius-Camps, "El καὶ αὐτὸςen los encabezamientos lucanos, ¿una fórmula anadórica?" *FilN* 2 (1989): 187-92.

5:4-6

4221 Friedrich Wulf and M. Velte, " 'Auf dein Wort hin . . .' Meditationen zu Lukas 5,4-6," *GeistL* 44 (1971): 309-12.

5:4

4222 J. A. Fishbaugh, "New Life in the Depths of His Presence," *ET* 90 (1978-1979): 146-48.

5:6

4223 A. Viard, "La Parole de Dieu dans l'Église du Christ," *EV* 87 (1977): 7-11.

5:8

4224 D. P. Davies, "Luke 5:8 (Simon Peter)," *ET* 79 (1967-1968): 382.

4225 Anthony Pope, "More on Luke 5:8," *BT* 41 (1990): 442-43.

5:10

4226 J. D. M. Derrett, "James and John as Co-rescuers from Peril (Luke 5:10)," *NovT* 22 (1980): 299-303.

4227 F. Deltombe, "Désormais tu rendras la vie à des hommes (Luke 5:10)," *RB* 89 (1982): 492-97.

5:11

4228 Karl Barth, "Predigt über Luk. 5,11," *EvT* 1 (1934-1935): 129-37.

5:12-16

4229 J. K. Elliott, "The Healing of the Leper in the Synoptic Parallels," *TZ* 34 (1978): 175-76.

4230 Frans Neirynck, "Papyrus Egerton 2 and the Healing of the Leper," *ETL* 61 (1985): 153-60.

4231 Dominique Hermant, "La purification du lépreux (Mt 8,1-4; Mc 1,40-45; Lc 5,12-16)," *BLOS* 4 (1990): 12-18.

5:12

4232 Christoph Burchard, "Fußnoten zum neutestamentlichen Griechisch II," *ZNW* 69 (1978): 143-57.

5:15-26

4233 Gary W. Light, "Luke 5:15-26," *Int* 48 (1994): 279-82.

5:17-26

4234   Frans Neirynck, "Les accords mineurs et la rédaction des
        évangiles: L'épisode du paralytique (Mt. IX,1-8; Lc.
        V,17-26 par.; Mc. II,1-12)," *ETL* 50 (1974): 215-30.

4235   Albert Fuchs, "Offene Probleme der Synoptikerforschung:
        Zur Geschichte der Perikope Mk 2,1-12 par Mt 9,1-8 par
        Lk 5,17-26," *SNTU-A* 15 (1990): 73-99.

4236   Lytta Basset, "La culpabilité, paralysie du coeur:
        Réinterprétation du récit de la guérison paralysé (Lc
        5/17-26)," *ÉTR* 71 no 3 (1996): 331-45.

5:17

4237   Christoph Burchard, "Fußnoten zum neutestamentlichen
        Griechisch II," *ZNW* 69 (1978): 143-57.

5:18

4238   Michael D. Goulder, "On Putting Q to the Test," *NTS* 24
        (1977-1978): 218-34.

5:24

4239   José O'Callaghan, "Tres casos de armonización en Mt 9,"
        EB 47 (1989): 131-34.

5:26

4240   A. T. Rich, "Luke 5,26," *ET* 44 (1932-1933): 428.

4241   J. H. M. Dabb, "Luke 5:26," *ET* 45 (1933-1934): 45.

5:27-28

4242   Juan Fernández, "Vocacion de Mateo 'el publicano',"
        CuBí 19 (1962): 45-50.

5:28

4243   Philippe Rolland, "L'arrière-fond sémitique des évangiles
        synoptiques," *ETL* 60 (1984): 358-62.

5:29-35

4244   C. B. Cousar, "Luke 5:29-35," *Int* 40 (1986): 58-63.

5:33-6:11

4245   George E. Rice, "Luke 5:33-6:11: Release for the
        Captives," *AUSS* 20 (1982): 23-28.

4246   George E. Rice, "Luke 5:33-6:11: Release from Cultic
        Tradition," *AUSS* 20 (1982): 127-32.

5:33-39

4247   Juan Fernández, "La cuestion de ayuno (Mt 9,14-17; Mc 2,18-22; Lu 5,33-39)," *CuBi* 19 (1962): 162-69.

4248   Bo Reicke, "Die Fastenfrage nach Luk. 5,33-39," *TZ* 30 (1974): 321-28.

4249   Philippe Rolland, "Les Prédécesseurs de Marc: Les Sources Présynoptiques de Mc II,18-22 et Parallèles," *RB* 89/3 (1982): 370-405.

4250   R. S. Good, "Jesus, Protagonist of the Old, in Luke 5:33-39," *NovT* 25/1 (1983): 19-36.

5:33-35

4251   André Feuillet, "La controverse sur le jeûne (Mc 2,18-20; Mt 9,14-15; Lc 5,33-35)," *NRT* 90 (1968): 113-36, 21-77.

5:33

4252   José O'Callaghan, "Tres casos de armonización en Mt 9," *EB* 47 (1989): 131-34.

5:36-39

4253   A. Kee, "The Old Coat and the New Wine," *NovT* 12 (1970): 13-21.

4254   L. Paul Trudinger, "The Word on the Generation Gap: Reflexions on a Gospel Metaphor," *BTB* 5 (1975): 311-15.

5:39

4255   Jacques Dupont, "Vin Vieux, Vin Nouveau (Luc 5:39)," *CBQ* 25 (1963): 286-304.

4256   George J. Brooke, "The Feast of New Wine (Qumran Temple Scroll 19,11-21) and the Question of Fasting," *ET* 95 (1983-1984): 175-76.

4257   Gregory J. Riley, "Influence of Thomas Christianity on Luke 12:14 and 5:39," *HTR* 88 (1995): 229-35.

6:1-13

4258   Dennis J. Ireland, "A History of Recent Interpretation of the Parable of the Unjust Steward," *WTJ* 51 (1989): 293-318.

6:1-5

4259   Hermann Aichinger, "Quellenkritische Untersuchung der Perikope vom Ährenraufen am Sabbat. Mk 2,23-28 par Mt 12,1-8 par Lk 6,1-5," *SNTU-A* 1 (1976): 110-53.

4260   W. Dietrich, " ' . . . den Armen das Evangelium zu verkünden': Vom befreienden Sinn biblischer Gesetze," *TZ* 41 (1985): 31-43.

6:1

4261   B. Cohen, "The Rabbinic Law Presupposed by Matthew 12:2 and Luke 6:1," *HTR* 23 (1930): 91-92.

4262   E. Mezger, "Le Sabbat 'second-premier' de Luc," *TZ* 32 (1976): 138-43.

4263   J. T. Buchanan, "The 'Second-First Sabbath' (Luke 6:1)," *JBL* 97 (1978): 259-62.

4264   E. Isaac, "Another Note on Luke 6:1," *JBL* 100 (1981): 96-97.

4265   T. C. Skeat, "The 'Second-First' Sabbath (Luke 6:1): The Final Solution," *NovT* 30 (1988): 103-106.

4266   Jean Bernardi, "Des chiffres et des lettres: le texte de Luc 6,1," *RB* 101 (1994): 62-66.

4267   Hans Klein, "Am ersten Sabbat: Eine Konjektur zu Lk 6,1," *ZNW* 87 (1996): 290-93.

6:4

4268   E. Bammel, "The Cambridge Pericope: The Addition to Luke 6:4 in Codex Bezae," *NTS* 32/3 (1986): 404-26.

6:5-15

4269   P. Courthial, "La Parabole du Semeur en Luke 6:5-15," *ÉTR* 47 (1972): 397-420.

6:5

4270   J. D. M. Derrett, "Luke 6:5d Reexamined," *NovT* 37 (1995): 232-28.

6:7

4271   J. A. L. Lee, "A Non-Aramaism in Luke 6:7," *NovT* 33 (1991): 28-34.

6:14

4272   Michael D. Goulder, "On Putting Q to the Test," *NTS* 24 (1977-1978): 218-34.

6:16

4273   Johannes Beutler, "Lk 6:16: Punkt Oder Komma?" *BZ* 35/2 (1991): 231-33.

6:17-49

4274   Raymond E. Brown, "Le 'Beatitudini' secondo Luca," *BibO* 7 (1965): 3-8.

4275   L. J. Topel, "The Lukan Version of the Lord's Sermon," *BTB* 11 (1981): 48-53.

6:17-26

4276   P.-E. Jacquemin, "Les Béatitudes selon saint Luc (Lc 6)," *AsSeign* NS 37 (1971): 80-91.

4277   David L. Tiede, "Luke 6:17-26," *Int* 40 (1986): 63-68.

4278   Wayne Muschamp, "The Beatitudes from the Sermon on the Plain: An Exegesis of Luke 6:17-26," *LTJ* 27 (1993): 58-64.

6:17-25

4279   H. Kahlefeld, "Selig ihr Armen," *BibL* 1 (1960): 55-61.

4280   J. Salguero, "Las Bienaventuranzas evangélicas," *CuBi* 29 (1972): 73-90.

4281   A. Viard, "Les Béatitudes et leur contre-partie," *EV* 87 (1977): 8-10.

6:17

4282   Jindrich Mánek, "On the Mount—On the Plain (Mt. 5:1, Lk. 6:17)," *NovT* 9 (1967): 124-31.

6:20-49

4283   A. M. Perry, "The Framework of the Sermon on the Mount," *JBL* 54 (1935): 103-15.

4284   G. Menestrina, "Matteo 5-7 e Luca 6:20-49 nell'Evangelo di Tommaso," *BibO* 18 (1976): 65-67.

4285   David R. Catchpole, "Jesus and the Community of Israel: The Inaugural Discourse in Q," *BJRL* 68 (1985-1986): 296-316.

4286 Leif E. Vaage, "Composite Texts and Oral Myths: The Case of the 'Sermon' (6:20b-49)," *SBLSP* 19 (1989): 424-39.

4287 David J. Clark, "The Sermon on the Plain: Structure and theme in Luke 6.20-49," *BT* 47 (1996): 428-34.

4288 Paul Hoffmann, "Betz and Q," *ZNW* 88 (1997): 197-210.

6:20-31

4289 H. Deim, "Predigt über Lukas 6,20-31," *EvT* 14 (1954): 241-46.

6:20-26

4290 Georg Strecker, "Die Makarismen der Bergpredigt," *NTS* 17 (1970-1971): 255-75.

4291 Joseph Coppens, "Les Béatitudes," *ETL* 50 (1974): 256-60.

4292 N. J. McEleney, "The Beatitudes of the Sermon on the Mount/Plain," *CBQ* 43 (1981): 1-13.

4293 Christopher M. Tuckett, "The Beatitudes: A Source-Critical Study, with a Reply by M. D. Goulder," *NovT* 25 (1983): 193-216.

4294 William R. Domeris, "Biblical Perspectives on the Poor," *JTSA* 57 (1986): 57-61.

6:20-23

4295 H. Frankemölle, "Die Makarismen (Mt 5,1-12; Lk 6,20-23)," *BZ* 15 (1971): 1-75.

4296 M. Eugene Boring, "Criteria of Authenticity: The Lucan Beatitudes as a Test Case," *Forum* 1 (1985): 3-38.

4297 M. Eugene Boring, "The Historical-Critical Method's Criteria of Authenticity: The Beatitudes in Q and Thomas as a Test Case," *Semeia* 44 (1988): 9-44.

6:20-21

4298 Eduard Schweizer, "Formgeschichtliches zu den Seligpreisungen Jesu," *NTS* 19 (1972-1973): 121-26.

6:20

4299 M. Knepper, "Die 'Armen' der Bergpredigt Jesu," *BK* 8/1 (1953): 19-27.

6:22-23

4300　John S. Kloppenborg, "Blessing and Marginality: The 'Persecution Beatitude' in Q, Thomas, and Early Christianity," *Forum* 2 (1986): 36-56.

4301　Werner Stenger, "Die Seligpreisungen der Geschmähten (Mt 5,11-12; Lk 6,22-23)," *K* 28 (1986): 33-60.

6:22

4302　Patrick P. Saydon, "Some Biblico-Liturgical Passages Reconsidered," *MeliT* 18/1 (1966): 10-17.

4303　Günther Schwarz, "Lukas 6,22a.23c.26. Emendation, Rückübersetzung, Interpretation," *ZNW* 66 (1975): 269-74.

6:23

4304　Günther Schwarz, "Lukas 6,22a.23c.26. Emendation, Rückübersetzung, Interpretation," *ZNW* 66 (1975): 269-74.

6:24-27

4305　Hans Klein, "Gerichtsankündigung und Liebesforderung: Lk 6.24 und 27 innerhalb der Botschaft des frühen Christentums," *NTS* 42 (1996): 421-33.

6:24-26

4306　P. Klein, "Die lukanischen Weherufe Luke 6:24-26," *ZNW* 71 (1980): 150-59.

6:26

4307　Günther Schwarz, "Lukas 6,22a.23c.26. Emendation, Rückübersetzung, Interpretation," *ZNW* 66 (1975): 269-74.

6:27-38

4308　A. Viard, "L'amour des ennemis," *EV* 87 (1977): 10-11.

6:27-36

4309　Dieter Lührmann, "Liebet eure Feinde (Lk 6,27-36; Mt 5,39-48)," *ZTK* 69 (1972): 412-38.

4310　Fritz Neugebauer, "Die dargebotene Wange und Jesu Gebot der Feindesliebe: Erwägungen zu Lk. 6:27-36; Matt. 5:38-48," *TLZ* 110/12 (1985): 865-75.

4311　Jürgen Sauer, "Traditionsgeschichtliche Erwägungen zu den synoptischen und paulinischen Aussagen über

Feindesliebe und Wiedervergeltungsverzicht," *ZNW* 76 (1985): 1-28.

6:27-29

4312   Marcus J. Borg, "A New Context for Romans XIII," *NTS* 19/2 (1972-1973): 205-18.

6:27-28

4313   O. J. F. Seitz, "Love your Enemies," *NTS* 16 (1969-1970): 39-54.

6:27

4314   Günther Schwarz, "ἀγαπᾶτε τοὺς ἐχθροὺς ὑμῶν: Mt 5,44a / Lk 6,27a (35a)," *BibN* 12 (1980): 32-34.

4315   V. J. Jahnke, " 'Love Your Enemies': The Value of New Perspectives," *CThM* 15 (1988): 267-73.

6:29

4316   Gerhard Lohfink, "Der ekklesiale Sitz im Leben der Aufforderung Jesu zum Gewaltverzicht (Matt. 5:39-42/Luke 6:29)," *TQ* 162 (1982): 236-53.

4317   Robert W. Funk, "The Beatitudes and Turn the Other Cheek: Recommendations and Polling," *Forum* 2 (1986): 103-28.

6:31

4318   H.-W. Bartsch, "Traditionsgeschichtliches zur 'goldenen Regel' und zum Aposteldekret," *ZNW* 75 (1984): 128-32.

4319   P. Ricoeur, "The Golden Rule: Exegetical and Theological Perplexities," *NTS* 36 (1990): 392-97.

6:32-35

4320   W. C. van Unnik, "Die Motivierung der Feindesliebe in Lukas vi,32-35," *NovT* 8 (1966): 284-300.

6:32

4321   Marcus J. Borg, "A New Context for Romans XIII," *NTS* 19/2 (1972-1973): 205-18.

6:35

4322   Marcus J. Borg, "A New Context for Romans XIII," *NTS* 19/2 (1972-1973): 205-18.

4323   Günther Schwarz, "ἀγαπᾶτε τοὺς ἐχθροὺς ὑμῶν: Mt 5,44a / Lk 6,27a (35a)," *BibN* 12 (1980): 32-34.

4324   Günther Schwarz, "Μηδὲν ἀπελπίζοντες," *ZNW* 71 (1980): 133-35.

4325   P. Ricoeur, "The Golden Rule: Exegetical and Theological Perplexities," *NTS* 36 (1990): 392-97.

6:37-42

4326   J. D. M. Derrett, "Christ and Reproof (Matthew 7:1-5/Luke 6:37-42)," *NTS* 34/2 (1988): 271-81.

6:38

4327   Gordon D. Fee, "A Text-Critical Look at the Synoptic Problem," *NovT* 22/1 (1980): 12-28.

6:39-45

4328   Augustin George, "Le disciple fraternel et efficace (Lc 6)," *AsSeign* NS 39 (1972): 68-77.

6:41-42

4329   G. B. King, "A Further Note on the Mote and the Beam (Matt. 7:3-5; Luke 6:41-42)," *HTR* 26 (1933): 73-76.

6:43-46

4330   M. Krämer, "Hütet euch vor den falschen Propheten. Eine überlieferungsgeschichtliche Untersuchung zu Mt 7:15-23/Lk 6:43-46/Mt 12:33-37," *Bib* 57 (1976): 349-77.

6:48-7:5

4331   Edouard Massaux, "Deux Fragments d'un Manuscrit Oncial de la Vulgate," *ETL* 37 (1961): 112-17.

7:1-10

4332   H. F. D. Sparks, "The Centurion's *pais*," *JTS* 42 (1941): 179-80.

4333   E. F. Siegman, "St. John's Use of the Synoptic Material," *CBQ* 30/2 (1968): 182-98.

4334   J. D. M. Derrett, "Law in the New Testament: The Syro-Phoenician Woman and the Centurion of Capernaum," *NovT* 15 (1973): 161-86.

4335   Augustin George, "Guérison de l'esclave d'un centurion (Lc 7)," *AsSeign* NS 40 (1973): 66-77.

4336 J. A. G. Haslam, "The Centurion at Capernaum: Luke 7:1-10," *ET* 96 (1984-1985): 109-10.

4337 Keith Pearce, "The Lucan Origins of the Raising of Lazarus," *ET* 96 (1984-1985): 359-61.

4338 Robert A. J. Gagnon, "Luke's Motives for Redaction in the Account of the Double Delegation in Luke 7:1-10," *NovT* 36 (1994): 122-45.

7:2-8:3

4339 D. A. S. Ravens, "The Setting of Luke's Account of the Anointing: Luke 7.2-8.3," *NTS* 34 (1988): 282-92.

7:3-7

4340 Robert A. J. Gagnon, "Statistical Analysis and the Case of the Double Delegation in Luke 7:3-7a," *CBQ* 55 (1993): 709-31.

7:8

4341 M. Frost, " 'I Also Am a Man Under Authority'," *ET* 45 (1933-1934): 477-78.

7:11-17

4342 A. Del Riego, "La resurrección del hijo de la viuda de Naín. Commentario-meditación," *CuBí* 22 (1965): 354-59.

4343 Paul Ternant, "La résurrection du fils de la veuve de Naïm (Lc 7)," *AsSeign* NS 41 (1971): 69-79.

4344 F. A. J. Macdonald, "Pity or Compassion?" *ET* 92 (1980-1981): 344-46.

4345 Walter Vogels, "A Semiotic Study of Luke 7:11-17," *ÉgT* 14 (1983): 273-92.

4346 Keith Pearce, "The Lucan Origins of the Raising of Lazarus," *ET* 96 (1984-1985): 359-61.

4347 Thomas L. Brodie, "Towards Unravelling Luke's Use of the Old Testament: Luke 7:11-17 as an Imitation of 1 Kings 17:17-24," *NTS* 32/2 (1986): 247-67.

4348 Sabine Demel, "Jesu Umgang mit Frauen nach dem Lukasevangelium," *BibN* 57 (1991): 41-95.

7:11-16

4349   E. Galbiati, "La risurrezione del giovane di Naim (Lc 7:11-16)," *BibO* 4 (1962): 175-77.

7:11-13

4350   Edouard Massaux, "Deux Fragments d'un Manuscrit Oncial de la Vulgate," *ETL* 37 (1961): 112-17.

7:12-22

4351   Robert J. Karris, "Luke's Soteriology of *With-ness*," *CThM* 12 (1985): 346-1.

7:14

4352   Philippe Gafner, "Le cercueil et la rosée--Le mot soros en Luc 7.14," *BibN* 87 (1997): 13-16.

7:16

4353   Patrick P. Saydon, "Some Biblico-Liturgical Passages Reconsidered," *MeliT* 18/1 (1966): 10-17.

4354   Dorotej Filipp, "The Influence of the Moravian Mission on the Orthodox Church in Czechoslovakia," *IRM* 74 (1985): 219-29.

7:18-35

4355   Ben Witherington, "Jesus and the Baptist: Two of a Kind?" *SBLSP* 18 (1988): 225-44.

4356   Wilhelm Wilkens, "Die Täuferüberlieferung des Matthäus und ihre Verarbeitung durch Lukas," *NTS* 40 (1994): 542-57.

7:18-23

4357   Jan Lambrecht, " 'Are You the One Who is to Come, or Shall We Look for Another?' The Gospel Message of Jesus Today," *LouvS* 8/2 (1980): 115-18.

4358   I. Kerr, "The Signs of Jesus," *ET* 94 (1982-1983): 49-51.

4359   Walter Wink, "Jesus' Reply to John: Matt 11:2-6/Luke 7:18-23," *Forum* 5 (1989): 121-28.

7:18

4360   P. Habandi, "Eine wieder aktuelle Frage. Zu Lukas 7,18ff.: 'Bist du es, der kommen soll, oder sollen wir auf einen andern warten'?" *ZMiss* 6 (1980): 195-98.

7:22

> 4361   Wolfgang Beinert, "Jesus Christus: das Ursakrament Gottes," *Cath* 38/4 (1984): 340-51.

7:24-35

> 4362   Jack T. Sanders, "The Criterion of Coherence and the Randomness of Charisma: Poring Through Some Aporias in the Jesus Tradition," *NTS* 44 (1998): 1-25.

7:24-25

> 4363   C. Daniel, "Les Esséniens et 'Ceux qui sont dans les maisons des rois'," *RevQ* 6 (1967): 261-77.

7:24

> 4364   Günther Schwarz, " 'Ein Rohr, vom Wind bewegt'?" *BibN* 83 (1996): 19-21.

7:27

> 4365   Michael D. Goulder, "On Putting Q to the Test," *NTS* 24 (1977-1978): 218-34.

> 4366   W. C. Kaiser, "The Promise of the Arrival of Elijah in Malachi and the Gospels," *GTJ* 3/2 (1982): 221-33.

7:28

> 4367   J. H. Greenlee, "Some Examples of Scholarly 'Agreement in Error'," *JBL* 77 (1958): 363-64.

7:29-30

> 4368   G. Gander, "Notule sur Luc 7,29-30," *VC* 19 (1951): 141-44.

7:31-35

> 4369   Olof Linton, "The Parable of the Children's Game," *NTS* 22/2 (1975-1976): 159-79.

> 4370   C. Siburt, "The Game of Rejecting God: Luke 7:31-35," *RQ* 19 (1976): 207-10.

> 4371   Wendy J. Cotter, "The Parable of the Children in the Market-Place, Q (Lk) 7:31-35," *NovT* 29 (1987): 289-304.

> 4372   Wendy J. Cotter, "Children Sitting in the Agora: Q (Luke) 7:31-35," *Forum* 5 (1989): 63-82.

7:31-32

4373 Dieter Zeller, "Die Bildlogik des Gleichnisses Mt 11,16f. / Lk 7,31f," *ZNW* 68 (1977): 21-57.

7:33-34

4374 Leif E. Vaage, "Q and the Historical Jesus: Some Peculiar Sayings," *Forum* 5 (1989): 159-76.

7:33

4375 Otto Böcher, "Johannes der Täufer kein Brot (Luk. vii.33)?" *NTS* 18 (1971-1972): 90-92.

4376 S. L. Davies, "John the Baptist and Essene Kashruth," *NTS* 29 (1983): 569-71.

7:34

4377 P. Maurice Casey, "The Son of Man Problem," *ZNW* 67/3 (1976): 147-54.

4378 Antonio Orbe, "El Hijo del hombre come y bebe (Mt 11,19; Lc 7,34)," *Greg* 58 (1977): 13-55.

4379 Martin Völkel, "Freund der Zöllner und Sünder," *ZNW* 69 (1978): 1-10.

4380 Robert J. Karris, "Luke's Soteriology of *With-ness*," *CThM* 12 (1985): 346-1.

7:36-50

4381 R. K. Orchard, "On the Composition of Luke vii,36-50," *JTS* 38 (1937): 243-45.

4382 André Légault, "An Application of the Form-Critique Method to the Anointing in Galilee (Lc 7,36-50) and Bethany (Mt 26,6-13; Mk 14,3-9; Lk 12,1-8)," *CBQ* 16 (1954): 131-45.

4383 Georg Braumann, "Die Schuldner und die Sünderin Luk. VII.36-50," *NTS* 10/4 (1963-1964): 487-93.

4384 K. Löning, "Ein Platz für die Verlorenen. Zur Formkritik zweier neutestamentlicher Legenden (Lk 7,36-50)," *BibL* 12 (1971): 198-208.

4385 L. Ramaroson, "Simon et la pécheresse anonyme (Lc 7,36-50)," *SE* 24 (1972): 379-83.

4386   J. K. Elliott, "The Anointing of Jesus," *ET* 85 (1973-1974): 105-107.

4387   André Feuillet, "Les deux onctions faites sur Jésus, et Marie-Madeleine," *RT* 75 (1975): 357-94.

4388   Robert Holst, "The One Anointing of Jesus: Another Application of the Form-Critical Method," *JBL* 95 (1976): 435-46.

4389   T. McCaughey, "Paradigms of Faith in the Gospel of St. Luke," *ITQ* 45 (1978): 177-84.

4390   Martin Völkel, " 'Freund der Zöllner und Sünder'," *ZNW* 69 (1978): 1-10.

4391   M. Sabbe, "The Footwashing in John 13 and Its Relation to the Synoptic Gospels," *ETL* 58 (1982): 279-308.

4392   Thomas L. Brodie, "Luke 7:36-50 as an Internalization of 2 Kings 4:1-37: A Study in Luke's Use of Rhetorical Imitation," *Bib* 64 (1983): 457-85.

4393   C. Légaré, "Jésus et la pécheresse. Analyse de Luc 7:36-50," *SémBib* 29 (1983): 19-45.

4394   J. P. Sauzède, "Une série pour le Carême," *ÉTR* 58 (1983): 59-71.

4395   Keith Pearce, "The Lucan Origins of the Raising of Lazarus," *ET* 96 (1984-1985): 359-61.

4396   Christian D. Kettler, "The Vicarious Repentance of Christ in the Theology of John McLeod Campbell and R. C. Moberly," *SJT* 38/4 (1985): 19-43.

4397   John J. Kilgallen, "John the Baptist, the Sinful Woman and the Pharisee," *JBL* 104/4 (1985): 675-79.

4398   James F. Coakley, "The Anointing at Bethany and the Priority of John," *JBL* 107 (1988): 241-56.

4399   Mauro Láconi, "Fede e amore: La peccatrice perdonata (Lc 7,36-50)," *ParSpirV* 17 (1988): 143-55.

4400   Bernard-Marie Ferry, "La pécheresse pardonnée (Lc 7:36-50): pourquoi verse-t-elle des pleurs," *EV* 99 (1989): 174-76.

4401   Antony Hurst, "The Woman with the Ointment," *ET* 101 (1989-1990): 304.

4402   Sabine Demel, "Jesu Umgang mit Frauen nach dem Lukasevangelium," *BibN* 57 (1991): 41-95.

4403   John J. Kilgallen, "A Proposal for Interpreting Luke 7:36-50," *Bib* 72/3 (1991): 305-30.

4404   James L. Resseguie, "Luke 7:36-50," *Int* 46 (1992): 285-90.

4405   John J. Kilgallen, "Forgiveness of Sins (Luke 7:36-50)," *NovT* 40 (1998): 105-16.

4406   Ingrid R. Kitzberger, "Love and Footwashing: John 13:1-20 and Luke 7 (1992): 36-50 Read Intertextually," *BibInt* 2 (1994): 190-206.

4407   Roland Meynet, " 'Celui à qui est remis peu, aime un peu . . .' (Lc 7:36-50)," *Greg* 75 (1994): 267-80.

4408   Barbara E. Reid, " 'Do You See This Woman?' Luke 7:36-50 as a Paradigm for Feminist Hermeneutics," *BR* 40 (1995): 37-49.

4409   Frank Stagg, "Luke's Theological Use of Parables," *RevExp* 94 (1997): 215-29.

4410   Robert C. Tannehill, "Should We Love Simon the Pharisee? Hermeneutical Reflections on the Pharisees in Luke," *CThM* 21 (1994): 424-33.

4411   Evelyn R. Thibeaux, " 'Known to Be a Sinner': The Narrative Rhetoric of Luke 7:36-50," *BTB* 23 (1993): 151-60.

7:36-38

4412   Simon Légasse, "Jésus et les prostituées," *RTL* 7 (1976): 137-54.

7:37-48

4413   John Chryssavgis, "The Notion of 'Divine Eros' in the Ladder of St. John Climacus," *SVTQ* 29/3 (1985): 191-200.

7:39-50

4414   Guy Wagner, "L'oncion de Béthanie: Essai sur la genèse du récit de Marc 14/3-9 et sa reprise par Matthieu, Luc et Jean," *ÉTR* 72 (1997): 437-46.

7:41-43

4415   J. Maiworm, "Umgekehrte Gleichnisse," *BK* 10 (1955): 82-85.

4416   Gerhard Sellin, "Gleichnisstrukturen," *LB* 31 (1974): 89-115.

7:41-42

4417   John J. Kilgallen, "Luke 7:41-42 and Forgiveness of Sins," *ET* 111 (1999): 46-47.

7:45

4418   Joachim Jeremias, "Lukas 7:45: *eiselthon*," *ZNW* 51/1-2 (1960): 131.

7:46

4419   K. Weiss, "Der westliche Text von Lc 7,46 und sein Wert," *ZNW* 46 (1955): 241-45.

7:47

4420   L. Ramaroson, " 'Le premier, c'est l'amour' (Lc 7,47a)," *SE* 39 (1987): 319-29.

8:1-10

4421   Ruth A. Foster and William D. Shiell, "The Parable of the Sower and the Seed in Luke 8:1-10: Jesus' Parable of Parables," *RevExp* 94 (1997): 259-67.

8:1-3

4422   Ben Witherington, "On the Road with Mary Magdalene, Joanna, Susanna, and Other Disciples (Luke 8:1-3)," *ZNW* 70 (1979): 243-48.

4423   Sister Philsy, "Diakonia of Women in the New Testament," *IJT* 32 (1983): 110-18.

4424   David C. Sim, "The Women Followers of Jesus: The Implications of Luke 8:1-3," *HeyJ* 30 (1989): 51-62.

4425   Robert J. Karris, "Women and Discipleship in Luke," *CBQ* 56 (1994): 1-20.

8:4-21

4426   S. A. Panimolle, " 'Fate attenzione a come ascoltate!' (Lc 8,4-21," *ParSpirV* 1 (1980): 95-119.

8:4-18

> 4427   M. Miguéns, "La predicazione di Gesù in parabole," *BibO* 1 (1959): 35-40.

> 4428   Frank Stagg, "Luke's Theological Use of Parables," *RevExp* 94 (1997): 215-29.

8:4-15

> 4429   David Wenham, "The Interpretation of the Parable of the Sower," *NTS* 20 (1973-1974): 299-319.

> 4430   J. Toy, "The Parable of the Sower and its Interpretation," *ET*92 (1980-1981): 116-18.

8:4

> 4431   Michael B. Walker, "Luke 8:4," *ET* 75 (1963-1964): 151.

8:5-15

> 4432   I. Howard Marshall, "Tradition and Theology in Luke 8:5-15," *TynB* 20 (1969): 56-75.

8:7

> 4433   José O'Callaghan, "La Variante 'Ahogaron' en Mt 13,7," *Bib* 68/3 (1987): 402-403.

8:8

> 4434   Robert K. McIver, "One Hundred-Fold Yield--Miraculous or Mundane? Matthew 13:8,23; Mark 4:8,20; Luke 8:8," *NTS* 40 (1994): 606-608.

8:9-10

> 4435   E. F. Siegman, "Teaching in Parables," *CBQ* 23 (1961): 161-81.

8:10

> 4436   Lucien Cerfaux, "La connaissance des secrets du Royaume d'après Matt. xiii. et par.," *NTS* 2 (1955-1956): 238-49.

8:12

> 4437   John Ferguson, "Mary Magdalene," *ET* 97/9 (1985-1986): 275-76.

8:14-15

> 4438   J. Gervais, "Les épines étouffantes (Luc 8,14-15)," *ET* 84 (1972-1973): 5-40.

8:18

4439 G. Lindeskog, "Logia-Studien," *ST* 4 (1951-191): 129-89.

4440 C. Bamberg, " 'Gebt acht, dass ihr gut hört!' (Lk 8:18). Zur christlichen Wortmeditation," *GeistL* 50 (1977): 390-94.

8:22

4441 Christoph Burchard, "Fußnoten zum neutestamentlichen Griechisch II," *ZNW* 69 (1978): 143-57.

4442 Philippe Rolland, "L'arrière-fond sémitique des évangiles synoptiques," *ETL* 60 (1984): 358-62.

8:26-39

4443 T. Hawthorn, "The Gerasene Demoniac: A Diagnosis (Marc 5:1-20 and Luke 8:26-39)," *ET* 66 (1954-1955): 79-80.

4444 Anton Vögtle, "Die historische und theologische Tragweite der heutigen Evangelienforschung," *ZKT* 86 (1964): 385-471.

4445 Lee Meyer, "Towards Wholeness: The Christian Ministry of Health and Healing," *Point* 10/2 (1981): 62-70.

4446 J. M. García Pérez, "El endemoniado de Gerasa (Lc 8,26-39)," *EB* 44 (1986): 117-46.

8:33

4447 C. H. Cave, "The Obedience of Unclean Spirits," *NTS* 11 (1964-1965): 93-97.

8:40-56

4448 Liliane Dambrine, "Guérison de la femme hémorroïsse et résurrection de la fille de Jaïre. Un aspect de la lecture d'un texte: Mc 5:21-43; Mt 9:18-26; Lc 8:40-56," *FV* 70 (1971): 75-81.

8:41-56

4449 Dominique Hermant, "Le femme au flux de sang et la fille de Jaïre (Mt 9:18-26; Mc 5:22-43; Lc 8:41-56)," *BLOS* 5 (1990): 8-16.

8:41

4450 Rudolf Pesch, "Jaïrus (Mk 5:22/Lk 8:41)," *BZ* 14/2 (1970): 21-56.

8:42-48

4451 S. T. Kimbrough, "Preachers: Actors in a Drama," *ChrM* 16/2 (1985): 22-24.

8:43-48

4452 T. McCaughey, "Paradigms of Faith in the Gospel of St. Luke," *ITQ* 45 (1978): 177-84.

8:1

4453 R. C. Fuller, "The Healing of Jairus' Daughter," *Scr* 3 (1948): 53.

9-10

4454 Michael D. Goulder, "From Ministry to Passion in John and Luke," *NTS* 29 (1983): 561-68.

9:1-50

4455 Wilhelm Wilkens, "Die Auslassung von Mark 6:45-8:26 bei Lukas im Lichte der Komposition Lukas 9:1-50," *TZ* 32 (1976): 193-200.

4456 David P. Moessner, "Luke 9:1-50: Luke's Preview of the Journey of the Prophet Like Moses of Deuteronomy," *JBL* 102 (1983): 575-605.

4457 Robert F. O'Toole, "Luke's Message in Luke 9,1-50," *CBQ* 49 (1987): 74-89.

9:1-34

4458 J. G. Davies, "The Prefiguration of the Ascension in the Third Gospel," *JTS* 6 (1955): 229-33.

9:1-6

4459 Gregory Murray, "Did Luke Use Mark?" *DR* 104 (1986): 268-71.

9:1

4460 Michael D. Goulder, "On Putting Q to the Test," *NTS* 24 (1977-1978): 218-34.

9:5

4461 Édouard Delebecque, "Sur un hellénisme de Saint Luc," *RB* 87 (1980): 590-93.

4462 Édouard Delebecque, " 'Secouez la Poussière de vos Pieds . . . sur l'Hellénisme de Luc IX,5," *RB* 89/2 (1982): 177-84.

9:7-62

4463 D. A. S. Ravens, "Luke 9:7-62 and the Prophetic Role of Jesus," *NTS* 36 (1990): 119-29.

9:7-9

4464 Philippe Rolland, "La question synoptique demande-t-elle une response compliquée?" *Bib* 70/2 (1989): 217-23.

9:10-17

4465 William R. Stegner, "Lucan Priority in the Feeding of the Five Thousand," *BR* 21 (1976): 19-28.

4466 J. P. Sauzède, "Une série pour le Carême," *ÉTR* 58 (1983): 59-71.

9:10-11

4467 M.-É. Boismard, "The Two-Source Theory at an Impasse," *NTS* 26 (1979-1980): 1-17.

4468 Frans Neirynck, "The Matthew-Luke Agreements in Matt 14:13-14 and Lk 9:10-11 (Par. Mk 6:30-34): The Two Source Theory Behind the Impasse," *ETL* 60/1 (1984): 25-44.

9:11-17

4469 F. Prod'homme, "Le pain qui rassasie les multitudes (Lc 9)," *AsSeign* NS 32 (1971): 55-67.

9:11-13

4470 Philippe Rolland, "L'arrière-fond sémitique des évangiles synoptiques," *ETL* 60 (1984): 358-62.

9:13

4471 Joseph A. Grassi, " 'You Yourselves Give Them to Eat': An Easily Forgotten Command of Jesus," *BibTo* 97 (1978): 1704-1709.

9:16

4472   S. Brock, "Note on Luke 9:16 [Codex Bezae Cantabrigiensis]," *JTS* 14 (1963): 391-93.

9:18-27

4473   M. Corbin, "Le Christ de Dieu. Méditation théologique sur Luc 9:18-27," *NRT* 99 (1977): 641-80.

4474   M. J. Kingston, "Suffering," *ET* 94 (1982-1983): 144-45.

9:18-24

4475   D. E. Miller, "Luke 9:18-24," *Int* 37 (1983): 64-68.

9:18-22

4476   B. Willaert, "La connexion littéraire entre la première prédiction de la passion et la confession de Pierre chez les synoptiques," *ETL* 32 (1956): 24-45.

4477   Anton Vögtle, "Messiasbekenntnis und Petrusverheissung. Zur Komposition Mt 16,13-23 par," *BZ* NF 1 (1957): 21-72; 2 (1958): 85-103.

9:20

4478   Rudolf Bultmann, "Die Frage nach dem messianischen Bewusstsein Jesu und das Petrus-Bekenntnis," *ZNW* 19 (1919-1920): 165-74.

9:21-24

4479   Bruce J. Malina, " 'Let Him Deny Himself' (Mark 8:34 & par): A Social Psychological Model of Self-Denial," *BTB* 24 (1994): 106-19.

9:22

4480   John M. Perry, "The Three Days in the Synoptic Passion Predictions," *CBQ* 48/4 (1986): 637-54.

4481   Frans Neirynck and Timothy A. Friedrichsen, "Note on Luke 9:22," *ETL* 65/4 (1989): 390-94.

4482   Timothy A. Friedrichsen, "Luke 9,22 - A Matthean Foreign Body?" *ETL* 72 (1996): 398-407.

4483   Robert H. Gundry, "The Refusal of Matthean Foreign Bodies to be Exorcised from Luke 9,22; 10,25-28," *ETL* 75 (1999): 104-22.

9:23-24

4484   D. H. C. Read, "At the Centre of the Self," *ET* 5 (1986): 142-44.

9:23

4485   D. R. Fletcher, "Condemned to Die. The Logion on Cross-Bearing: What Does It Mean?" *Int* 18 (1964): 156-64.

9:25

4486   José O'Callaghan, "Nota Critica a Mc 8,36," *Bib* 64/1 (1983): 116-17.

9:27

4487   Charles L. Holman, "The Idea of an Imminent Parousia in the Synoptic Gospels," *SBT* 3 (1973): 15-31.

9:28-36

4488   Michel Coune, "Radieuse Transfiguration. Mt 17,1-9; Mc 9,2-10; Lc 9,28-36," *AsSeign* 15 (1973): 44-84.

4489   Daniel H. Pokorný, "The Transfiguration of Our Lord," *CJ* 11 (1985): 17-18.

4490   Barbara E. Reid, "Voices and Angels: What were They Talking About at the Transfiguration? A Redaction-Critical Study of Luke 9:28-36," *BR* 34 (1989): 19-31.

4491   Michael Rogness, "The Transfiguration of Our Lord: Luke 9:28-36," *WW* 9 (1989): 71-75.

4492   A. del Agua Pérez, "La transfiguración como preludio del 'Exodo' de Jesús en Lc 9,29-36: Estudio derásico y teológico," *Salm* 40 (1993): 5-19.

4493   Robert J. Miller, "Source Criticism and the Limits of Certainty: The Lukan Transfiguration Story as a Test Case," *ETL* 74 (1998): 127-44.

4494   Joseph B. Tyson, "Jews and Judaism in Luke-Acts (1992): Reading as a Godfearer," *NTS* 41 (1995): 19-38.

9:28-31

4495   F. V. Pratt, "The Exodus of Jesus (Lk 9,28-31)," *ET* 41 (1929-1930): 376-77.

9:31

4496   Jindrich Mánek, "The New Exodus of the Books of Luke," *NovT* 2 (1957-1958): 8-23.

4497   André Feuillet, "L' 'Exode' de Jésus et le déroulement du mystère rédempteur d'après S. Luc et S. Jean," *RT* 77 (1977): 181-206.

4498   Susan R. Garrett, "Exodus from Bondage: Luke 9:31 and Acts 12:1-24," *CBQ* 1 (1990): 656-80.

4499   Peter M. Renju, "The Exodus of Jesus (Luke 9.31)," *BT* 46 (1995): 213-18.

9:33

4500   José O'Callaghan, "Discusion Critica en Mt 17,4," *Bib* 65/1 (1984): 91-93.

9:34

4501   Michael D. Goulder, "On Putting Q to the Test," *NTS* 24 (1977-1978): 218-34.

9:37-43

4502   Hermann Aichinger, "Zur Traditionsgeschichte der Epileptiker-Perikope Mk 9,14-29 par Mt 17,14-21 par Lk 9,37-43a," *SNTU-A* 3 (1978): 114-43.

4503   Gregory E. Sterling, "Jesus as Exorcist: An Analysis of Matthew 17:14-20; Mark 9:14-29; Luke 9:37-43a," *CBQ* 55 (1993): 467-93.

9:44

4504   Marcel Bastin, "L'annonce de la passion et les critères de l'historicité," *RevSR* 50 (1976): 289-329.

9:46-56

4505   J. Kodell, "Luke and the Children: The Beginning and End of the Great Interpolation (Luke 9:46-56; 18:9-23)," *CBQ* 49 (1987): 415-30.

9:46-50

4506   B. C. Butler, "M. Vaganay and the 'Community Discourse'," *NTS* 1 (1954-1955): 283-90.

4507   David Wenham, "A Note on Mark 9:33-42/Matt. 18:1-6/Luke 9:46-50," *JSNT* 14 (1982): 113-18.

9:46-48

4508   Dominique Hermant, "La première scène d'enfants (Mt 18,1-5; Mc 9,33-37; Lc 9,46-48)," *BLOS* 3 (1990): 7-11.

9:50

4509   Heinrich Baltensweiler, " 'Wer nicht gegen uns (euch) ist, ist für uns (euch)': Bemerkungen zu Mk 9,40 und Lk 9,50," *TZ* 40 (1984): 130-36.

9:51-19:48

4510   William A. Beardslee, "Saving One's Life By Losing It," *JAAR* 47 (1979): 57-72.

9:51-19:46

4511   Paul Kariamadam, "The Composition and Meaning of the Lucan Travel Narrative (Luke 9,51-19,46)," *BB* 13 (1987): 179-98.

4512   Frank J. Matera, "Jesus' Journey to Jerusalem (Luke 9.51-19.46): A Conflict with Israel," *JSNT* 51 (1993): 57-77.

9:51-19:44

4513   James L. Resseguie, "Interpretation of Luke's Central Section (Luke 9:51-19:44) Since 1856," *SBT* 5/2 (1975): 3-36.

4514   James L. Resseguie, "Point of View in the Central Section of Luke (9:51-19:44)," *JETS* 25 (1982): 41-47.

4515   H. K. Farrel, "The Structure and Theology of Luke's Central Section," *TriJ* 7 (1986): 33-54.

9:51-19:28

4516   Gerhard Sellin, "Komposition, Quellen und Funktion des lukanischen Reiseberichtes," *NovT* 20 (1978): 100-35.

4517   J. L. Espinel, "La vida-viaje de Jesús hacia Jerusalén (Luke 9:51-19:28)," *CuBí* 37 (1980): 29-38.

9:51-19:27

4518   H. LaPointe, "L'espace-temps de Lc 9,51-19,27," *ÉgT* 1 (1970): 275-90.

4519   G. Ogg, "The Central Section of the Gospel according to St. Luke," *NTS* 18 (1971-1972): 39-53.

4520   G. W. Trompf, "La section médiane de l'évangile de Luc: L'organisation des documents," *RHPR* 53 (1973): 141-54.

9:51-18:15

4521   W. Grundmann, "Fragen der Komposition des lukanischen 'Reiseberichts'," *ZNW* 50 (1959): 21-70.

9:51-18:14

4522   W. Gasse, "Zum Reisebericht des Lukas," *ZNW* 34 (1935): 293-99.

4523   C. C. McCown, "The Geography of Luke's Central Section," *JBL* 57 (1938): 51-66.

4524   D. Gill, "Observations on the Lukan Travel Narrative and Some Related Passages," *HTR* 63 (1970): 199-221.

4525   P. von der Osten-Sacken, "Zur Christologie des lukanischen Reiseberichts," *EvT* 33 (1973): 476-96.

4526   G. W. Trompf, "La section médiane de l'évangile de Luc: L'organisation des documents," *RHPR* 53 (1973): 141-54.

4527   John W. Wenham, "Synoptic Independence and the Origin of Luke's Travel Narrative," *NTS* 27 (1980-1981): 507-15.

9:51-62

4528   W. Hülsbusch, "Mit Jesus auf dem Weg nach Jerusalem," *BL* 12 (1971): 121-26.

4529   J. W. Drane, "Simon the Samaritan and the Lucan Concept of Salvation History," *EQ* 47 (1975): 131-37.

4530   B. G. Powley, "Time and Place," *ET* 94 (1983): 371-72.

4531   Paul J. Nuechterlein, "The Work of René Girard as a New Key to Biblical Hermeneutics," *CThM* 26 (1999): 196-209.

9:51-56

4532   Thomas L. Brodie, "The Departure for Jerusalem (Luke 9:51-56) as a Rhetorical Imitation of Elijah's Departure for the Jordan (2 Kgs 1:1-2:6)," *Bib* 70/1 (1989): 96-109.

9:51

4533   André Feuillet, "L' 'Exode' de Jésus et le déroulement du mystère rédempteur d'après S. Luc et S. Jean," *RT* 77 (1977): 181-206.

4534   J. Rius-Camps, "El καὶ αὐτόςεν los encabezamientos lucanos, ¿una fórmula anadórica?" *FilN* 2 (1989): 187-92.

9:1-56

4535   C. Kenneth Lysons, "The Seven Deadly Sins Today, Pt. 3: Anger," *ET* 97/10 (1985-1986): 302-304.

9:54-56

4536   J. M. Ross, "The Rejected Words of Luke 9,54-56," *ET* 84 (1972-1973): 85-88.

9:57-62

4537   C. Küven, "Weisung für die Nachfolge. Eine Besinnung über Lukas 9:57-62," *BibL* 2 (1961): 49-1.

4538   Otto Glombitza, "Die christologische Aussage des Lukas in seiner Gestaltung der drei Nachfolgeworte Lukas IX,57-62," *NovT* 13 (1971): 14-23.

4539   Thomas L. Brodie, "Luke 9:57-62: A Systematic Adaptation of the Divine Challenge to Elijah (1 Kings 19)," *SBLSP* 19 (1989): 237-45.

4540   Jon M. Isaak, "Textual Indeterminancy and Determinancy: Klaus Berger's History-of-Effect Hermeneutic (Luke 9:57-62)," *BTB* 29 (1999): 138-44.

9:57-58

4541   Leif E. Vaage, "Q and the Historical Jesus: Some Peculiar Sayings," *Forum* 5 (1989): 159-76.

9:58

4542   P. Maurice Casey, "The Son of Man Problem," *ZNW* 67/3 (1976): 147-54.

4543   P. Maurice Casey, "The Jackals and the Son of Man (Matt. 8.20//Luke 9.58)," *JSNT* 23 (1985): 3-22.

4544   M. H. Smith, "No Place for a Son of Man," *Forum* 4/4 (1988): 83-107.

9:60

4545   H. G. Klemm, "Das Wort von der Selbstbestattung der Toten," *NTS* 16 (1969-1970): 60-75.

4546   Markus Bockmuehl, " 'Let the Dead Bury Their Dead'
       (Matt 8:22/Luke 9:60) (1997): Jesus and the Halakhah,"
       JTS NS 49 (1998): 553-81.

9:61-62

4547   Michael G. Steinhauser, "Putting One's Hand to the Plow:
       The Authenticity of Q 9:61-62," *Forum* 5 (1989): 151-58.

9:61

4548   Édouard Delebecque, "Sur un hellénisme de Saint Luc,"
       RB 87 (1980): 590-93.

9:62

4549   H. J. Blair, "Putting One's Hand to the Plough," *ET* 79
       (1967-1968): 342-43.

10:1-24

4550   Richard J. Dillon, "Early Christian Experience in the
       Gospel Sayings," *BibTo* 21 (1983): 83-88.

10:1-20

4551   A. Lignee, "La mission des soixante-douze (Lc 10),"
       AsSeign NS 45 (1974): 64-74.

10:1-7

4552   Rudolf Schnackenburg, "Zur Traditionsgeschichte von Joh
       4,46-54," *BZ* 8 (1964): 58-88.

10:1

4553   Bruce M. Metzger, "Seventy or Seventy-Two Disciples,"
       NTS 5 (1958-1959): 299-306.

4554   S. Jellicoe, "St. Luke and the Seventy(-Two)," *NTS* 6
       (1959-1960): 319-21.

10:2-16

4555   Ulrich Luz, "Q 10:2-16; 11:14-23," *SBLSP* 15 (1985):
       101-102.

4556   James M. Robinson, "The Mission and Beelzebul: Pap Q
       10:2-16; 11:14-23," *SBLSP* 15 (1985): 97-99.

10:4

4557   A. P. O'Hagan, "Greet No One on the Way (Lk 10,4b),"
       SBFLA 16 (1965-1966): 69-84.

4558   Bernhard Lang, "Grussverbot oder Besuchsverbot?" *BZ* 26 (1982): 75-79.

10:6

4559   William Klassen, " 'A Child of Peace' in First Century Context," *NTS* 27 (1980-1981): 488-506.

10:7

4560   Édouard Delebecque, "Sur un hellénisme de Saint Luc," *RB* 87 (1980): 590-93.

4561   A. E. Harvey, " 'The Workman is Worthy of His Hire': Fortunes of a Proverb in the Early Church," *NovT* 2 (1982): 209-21.

4562   Günther Schwarz, "Τῆς τροφῆς αὐτοῦ oder τῆς μισθοῦ αὐτοῦ?" *BibN* 56 (1991): 25.

10:11

4563   A. Viard, "Exigences de la vie chrétienne," *EV* 87 (1977): 345-48.

10:13

4564   M. Miyoshi, "Das jüdische Gebet Sema und die Abfolge der Traditionsstücke in Luke 10:13," *AJBI* 7 (1981): 70-123.

10:17-20

4565   David Crump, "Jesus: The Victorious Scribal-Intercessor in Luke's Gospel," *NTS* 38 (1992): 51-65.

10:18

4566   Ulrich B. Müller, "Vision und Botschaft. Erwägungen zur prophetischen Struktur der Verkündigung Jesu," *ZTK* 74 (1977): 416-48.

4567   Samuel Vollenweider, "Ich Sah den Satan wie einen Blitz vom Himmel fallen (Lk. 10:18)," *ZNW* 79/3-4 (1988): 187-203.

4568   Julian V. Hills, "Luke 10:18—Who Saw Satan Fall?" *JSNT* 46 (1992): 25-40.

4569   Joel Marcus, "Jesus' Baptismal Vision," *NTS* 41 (1995): 512-21.

10:19

4570   Pierre Grelot, "Étude critique de Luc 10:19," *RechSR* 69 (1981): 87-100.

10:20-24

4571   L. Randellini, "L'inno di giubulo: Mt. 11,25-30; Lc. 10,20-24," *RBib* 22 (1974): 183-235.

10:21-24

4572   Frank Stagg, "Luke's Theological Use of Parables," *RevExp* 94 (1997): 215-29.

10:21-22

4573   Harold A. Guy, "Matthew 11,25-27; Luke 10,21-22," *ET* 49 (1937-1938): 236-37.

4574   K. J. Scaria, "Jesus' Prayer and Christian Prayer," *BB* 7 (1981): 160-85, 201-24.

10:21

4575   Alois Stöger, "Jesu Jubelruf: Quelle seiner Freude. Meditation über Lk 10,21f.," *BL* 50 (1977): 187-91.

10:22

4576   Paul Winter, "Matthew 11:27 and Luke 10:22 from the First to the Fifth Century: Reflections on the Development of the Text," *NovT* 1 (1956): 112-48.

4577   W. Grundmann, "Die *nēpioi* in der Urchristlichen Paranese," *NTS* 5 (1958-1959): 188-205.

4578   Jesse Sell, "Johannine Traditions in Logion 61 of the Gospel of Thomas," *PRS* 7/1 (1980): 24-37.

10:23-37

4579   E. Galbiati, "Esegesi degli Evangeli festivi," *BibO* 1 (1959): 17-19.

10:23-24

4580   W. Grimm, "Selige Augenzeugen, Luk. 10,23f. Alttestamentlicher Hintergrund und ursprünglicher Sinn," *TZ* 26 (1970): 172-83.

4581   M. Eugene Boring, "A Proposed Reconstruction of Q: 10:23-24," *SBLSP* 18 (1988): 456-71.

10:25-42

4582   Gary Phillips, " 'What is Written? How are You Reading?'
        Gospel, Intertextuality and Doing Likewise: Reading Luke
        10:25-42 Otherwise," *Semeia* 69-70 (1995): 111-47.

10:25-38

4583   Browning Ware, "Preaching to the Power Brokers," *FM*
        3/1 (1985): 50-56.

10:25-37

4584   C. H. Lindijer, "Oude en Nieuwe Visies op de Gelijkenis
        van de Barmhartige Samaritaan," *NedTT* 15 (1960): 11-23.

4585   Robert W. Funk, " 'How Do You Read?' A Sermon on
        Luke 10:25-37," *Int* 18 (1964): 56-61.

4586   Erhardt Güttgemanns, "Narrative Analyse Synoptischer
        Texte," *LB* 25/26 (1973): 50-73.

4587   G. Crespy, "The Parable of the Good Samaritan: An Essay
        in Structural Research," trans. John Kirby, *Semeia* 2
        (1974): 27-50.

4588   John D. Crossan, "The Good Samaritan: Towards a
        Generic Definition of Parable," *Semeia* 2 (1974): 82-112.

4589   Robert W. Funk, "The Good Samaritan as Metaphor,"
        Semeia 2 (1974): 74-81.

4590   Jan Lambrecht, "The Message of the Good Samaritan,"
        LouvS 5 (1974): 121-35.

4591   Daniel Patte, "An Analysis of Narrative Structure and the
        Good Samaritan," *Semeia* 2 (1974): 1-26.

4592   Daniel Patte, "Comments on the Article of John D.
        Crossan," *Semeia* 2 (1974): 117-21.

4593   Gerhard Sellin, "Lukas als Gleichniserzählen: Die
        Erzählung vom barmherzigen Samariter (Lk 10,25-37),"
        ZNW 65 (1974): 166-89.

4594   Robert C. Tannehill, "Comments on the Articles of Daniel
        Patte and John D. Crossan," *Semeia* 2 (1974): 113-16.

4595   Paul Ternant, "Le bon Samaritain (Lc 10)," *AsSeign* NS 46
        (1974): 66-77.

4596   Jean Delorme, "Linguistique, Sémiotique, Exégèse: à propos du Séminaire de Durham," *SémBib* 6 (1977): 35-59.

4597   Dietfried Gewalt, "Der 'Barmherzige Samariter': Zu Lukas 10:25-37," *EvT* 38 (1978): 403-17.

4598   René Kieffer, "Analyse sémiotique et commentaire. Quelques réflexions à propos d'études de Luc 10:25-37," *NTS* 25 (1979): 454-68.

4599   Peter R. Jones, "The Love Command in Parable: Luke 10:25-37," *PRS* 6 (1979): 224-42.

4600   Walter Wink, "The Parable of the Compassionate Samaritan: A Communal Exegesis Approach," *RevExp* 76 (1979): 199-217.

4601   M. J. Kingston, "Love Cannot Be Contained By Rules," *ET* 91 (1979-1980): 339-40.

4602   André Feuillet, "Le bon Samaritain (Luc 10,25-37): Sa signification christologique et l'universalisme de Jésus," *EV* 90 (1980): 337-51.

4603   Robert W. Funk, "The Prodigal Samaritan," *JAAR* 48 (1981): 83-97.

4604   T. Sorg, "Zwischen Jerusalem und Jericho: Predigt über Lukas 10,25-37," *TBe* 14 (1983): 1-5.

4605   Dennis M. Sweetland, "The Good Samaritan and Martha and Mary," *BibTo* 21 (1983): 325-30.

4606   Norman H. Young, "The Commandment to Love Your Neighbour as Yourself and the Parable of the Good Samaritan," *AUSS* 21 (1983): 265-72.

4607   F. Scott Spencer, "2 Chronicles 28:5-15 and the Parable of the Good Samaritan," *WTJ* 46 (1984): 317-49.

4608   P. Y. Bourdil, "L'église, un Monde et sa Pensée," *RHPR* 65/3 (1985): 297-314.

4609   Pamela Thimmes, "The Language of Community: Metaphors, Systems of Convictions, Ethnic, and Gender Issues in Luke 10:25-37 and 10:38-42," *SBLSP* 21 (1991): 698-713.

4610   Juan C. Cevallos, "The Good Samaritan: A Second
        Reading of the Law (Luke 10:25-37)," *TEd* 56 (1997):
        49-58.

4611   Corina Combet-Galland, "L'amour, au jeu de la loi et du
        hasard: La parabole du 'Bon Samaritain' et le débat
        qu'elle bouscule (Lc 10/25-37)," *ÉTR* 71 (1996): 321-30.

4612   Mike Graves, "Luke 10:25-37: The Moral of the 'Good
        Samaritan' Story?" *RevExp* 94 (1997): 269-75.

4613   John J. Kilgallen, "The Plan of the 'Nomikos' (Luke
        10:25-37)," *NTS* 42 (1996): 615-19.

4614   Frank Stagg, "Luke's Theological Use of Parables,"
        RevExp 94 (1997): 215-29.

4615   Brett Younger, "Luke 10:25-37--Preaching like the Good
        Samaritan," *RevExp* 90 (1993): 393-98.

10:25-28

4616   Robert H. Gundry, "The Refusal of Matthean Foreign
        Bodies to be Exorcised from Luke 9,22; 10,25-28," *ETL*
        75 (1999): 104-22.

10:27

4617   John S. Piper, "Is Self-Love Biblical?" *CT* 21 (1977):
        1150-53.

10:29-38

4618   J. D. M. Derrett, "Law in the New Testament: Fresh Light
        on the Parable of the Good Samaritan," *NTS* 11
        (1964-1965): 22-37.

10:29-37

4619   W. J. Masson, "The Parable of the Good Samaritan," *ET*
        48 (1936-1937): 179-81.

4620   F. H. Wilkinson, "Oded: Proto-Type of the Good
        Samaritan," *ET* 69 (1957-1958): 94.

4621   L. Ramaroson, "Comme 'Le Bon Samaritain' ne chercher
        qu'à aimer (Lc 10,29-37)," *Bib* 56 (1975): 533-36.

4622   G. Burn, "The Parable of the Bad Exegete: A Note on
        Luke 10:29-37," *ET* 111 (2000): 299-300.

10:29

4623 E. Biser, "Wer ist meiner Nächster?" *GeistL* 48 (1975): 406-14.

4624 L. Paul Trudinger, "Once Again, Now, 'Who Is My Neighbour'?" *EQ* 48 (1976): 160-63.

4625 Norman H. Young, "Once Again, Now, 'Who Is My Neighbour?' A Comment," *EQ* 49 (1977): 178-79.

10:30-37

4626 H. Binder, "Das Gleichnis vom barmherzigen Samariter," *TZ* 15 (1959): 176-94.

4627 C. Daniel, "Les Esséniens et l'arrière-fond historique de la parabole du Bon Samaritain," *NovT* 11 (1969): 71-104.

4628 W. C. Linss, "Example Stories," *CThM* 17 (1990): 447-53.

4629 Uwe Wegner, "Repensando Uma Velha Pergunta: Quem é Meu Próximo?" *EstT* 30/1 (1990): 59-73.

10:30-35

4630 E. Biser, "Wer ist meiner Nächster?" *GeistL* 48 (1975): 406-14.

10:30

4631 H. G. Klemm, "Schillers ethisch-ästhetische Variationen zum Thema Lk 10,30ff.," *KD* 17 (1971): 127-40.

4632 Gerhard Sellin, "Gleichnisstrukturen," *LB* 31 (1974): 89-115.

10:31-35

4633 Michel Gourgues, "The Priest, the Levite, and the Samaritan Revisited: A Critical Note on Luke 10:31-35," *JBL* 117 (1998): 709-13.

10:31-32

4634 Christoph Burchard, "Fußnoten zum neutestamentlichen Griechisch II," *ZNW* 69 (1978): 143-57.

10:34

4635 Günter Scholz, "Aesthetische Beobachtungen am Gleichnis vom reichen Mann und armen Lazarus und von drei anderen Gleichnissen," *LB* 43 (1978): 67-74.

4636   J. R. Royce, "A Philonic Use of πανδοχεῖον," *NovT* 23
        (1981): 193-94.

10:35

4637   Douglas E. Oakman, "The Buying Power of Two Denarii,"
        Forum 3 (1987): 33-38.

10:36

4638   R. S. Clucas, "The Neighbour Questions," *ThEv* 17
        (1984): 49-50.

10:37

4639   J. W. Drane, "Simon the Samaritan and the Lucan Concept
        of Salvation History," *EQ* 47 (1975): 131-37.

10:38-42

4640   E. Laland, "Die Martha-Maria-Perikope Lukas 10,38-42,"
        ST 13 (1959): 70-86.

4641   A. Knockaert, "Analyse structurale du texte biblique," *LV*
        33 (1978): 331-40.

4642   F. Castel, "Luc 10.38-42," *ÉTR* 55 (1980): 560-65.

4643   J. A. Davidson, "Things to be Understood and Things to
        be Done," *ET* 94 (1982-1983): 306-307.

4644   Eugene A. LaVerdiere, "The One Thing Required,"
        Emmanuel 89 (1983): 398-403.

4645   James F. Coakley, "The Anointing at Bethany and the
        Priority of John," *JBL* 107 (1988): 241-56.

4646   France Beydon, "A Temps Nouveau, Nouvelles Questions:
        Luc 10:38-42," *FV* 88 (1989): 25-32.

4647   Jutta Brutscheck, "Lukanische Anliegen in der
        Maria-Martha-Erzählung zu Lk 10:38-42," *GeistL* 62
        (1989): 84-96.

4648   Robert W. Wall, "Martha and Mary (Luke 10:38-42) in the
        Context of a Christian Deuteronomy," *JSNT* 35 (1989):
        19-35.

4649   Pamela Thimmes, "The Language of Community:
        Metaphors, Systems of Convictions, Ethnic, and Gender
        Issues in Luke 10:25-37 and 10:38-42," *SBLSP* 21 (1991):
        698-713.

4650   Warren Carter, "Getting Martha out of the Kitchen: Luke 10:38-42," *CBQ* 58 (1996): 264-80.

10:42

4651   M. Augsten, "Lukanische Miszelle," *NTS* 14 (1967-1968): 581-83.

4652   J. Lionel North, "Oligon de estin chreia e enos (Luke 10.42): Text, Subtext and Context," *JSNT* 66 (1997): 3-13.

11-12

4653   M. Perry, "A Judaeo-Christian Source in Luke," *JBL* 49 (1930): 181-94.

11:1-13

4654   Paul Ternant, "Le Père exauce la prière filiale (Lc 11)," *AsSeign* NS 48 (1972): 61-72.

4655   Roy A. Harrisville, "God's Mercy: Tested, Promised, Done! An Exposition of Genesis 18:20-32; Luke 11:1-13; Colossians 2:6-15," *Int* 3 (1977): 165-78.

11:1-4

4656   P. Dacquino, "La preghiera del cristano," *BibO* 5 (1963): 201-205.

4657   J. K. Elliott, "Did the Lord's Prayer Originate With John the Baptist?" *TZ* 29 (1973): 215.

11:1

4658   R. F. Collins, " 'Lord, Teach Us to Pray': A Reflection on the Prayer of Petition," *LouvS* 10 (1984-1985): 354-71.

4659   Jan Ambaum, "Gemeinsames Oder Persönliches Beten," *IKaZ* 14/4 (1985): 315-18.

11:2-13

4660   Eugene A. LaVerdiere, "God as Father," *Emmanuel* 88 (1982): 545-50.

11:2-4

4661   O. Schäfer, "Das Vaterunser, das Gebet des Christen," *TGl* 35 (1943): 1-6.

4662   W. Stiller, "Vater unser, Biblische Erwägungen," *TGl* 42 (191): 49-1.

4663   T. W. Manson, "The Lord's Prayer," *BJRL* 38 (1955-1956): 99-113, 436-48.

4664   R. Leaney, "The Lucan Text of the Lord's Prayer (Lk xi 2-4)," *NovT* 1 (1956): 103-11.

4665   W. Fresenius, "Beobachtungen und Gedanken zum Gebet des Herrn," *EvT* 20 (1960): 235-39.

4666   G. Miegge, "Le 'Notre Père' prière du temps présent," *ÉTR* 35 (1960): 237-53.

4667   E. Bammel, "A New Text of the Lord's Prayer," *ET* 73 (1961-1962): 54.

4668   Michael D. Goulder, "The Composition of the Lord's Prayer," *JTS* 14 (1963): 32-45.

4669   R. Freudenberger, "Zum Text der zweiten Vaterunserbitte," *NTS* 15 (1968-1969): 419-32.

4670   Günther Schwarz, "Matthäus vi.9-13 = Lukas xi.2-4," *NTS* 15 (1968-1969): 233-47.

4671   Georges Casalis, "Das Vater Unser und die Weltlage," *EvT* 29 (1969): 357-71.

4672   Sjef van Tilborg, "A Form-Criticism of the Lord's Prayer," *NovT* 14 (1972): 94-105.

4673   P. Edmonds, "The Lucan 'Our Father': A Summary of Luke's Teaching on Prayer?" *ET* 91 (1979-1980): 140-43.

4674   Pierre Grelot, "L'Arrière-Plan Araméen du 'Pater'," *RB* 91/4 (1984): 531-56.

4675   Robert J. Miller, "The Lord's Prayer and Other Items from the Sermon on the Mount," *Forum* 5 (1989): 177-86.

4676   W. M. Buchan, "Research on the Lord's Prayer," *ET* 100 (1989-1990): 336-39.

4677   Tjitze Baarda, "De Korte Tekst Van Het Onze Vader in Lucas 11:2-4: Een Marcionitische Coruptie?" *NedTT* 44 (1990): 273-87.

4678   Wiard Popkes, "Die letzte Bitte des Vater-Unser. Formgeschichte Beobachtungen zum Gebet Jesu," *ZNW* 81 (1990): 1-20.

4679   R. G. Kratz, "Die Gnade des täglichen Brots: Späte Psalmen auf dem Weg zum Vaterunser," *ZTK* 89 (1992): 1-40.

4680   Lewis J. Prockter, "The Blind Spot: New Testament Scholarship's Ignorance of Rabbinic Judaism," *ScrSA* 48 (1994): 1-12.

4681   Günther Schwarz, "Das Gebet der Gebete (Mt 6,9-13/Lk 11,2-4)," *BibN* 70 (1993): 21-24.

4682   Alistair I. Wilson, "The Disciples' Prayer: A Fresh Look at a Familiar Text," *RTR* 57 (1998): 136-50.

11:2

4683   Marc Philonenko, " 'Que Ton Esprit-Saint vienne sur nous et qu'il nous purifie' (Luc 11,2): l'arrière-plan qoumrânien d'une variante lucanienne du 'Notre Père'," *RHPR* 75 (1995): 61-66.

11:3

4684   Bernard Orchard, "The Meaning of τὸν ἐπιούσιον(Mt 6:11 = Lk 11:3)," *BTB* 3 (1973): 274-82.

4685   F.-M. Braun, "Le pain dont nous avons besoin. Matt. 6:11; Luke 11:3," *NRT* 100 (1978): 559-68.

4686   R. ten Kate, "Geef ons Heden ons 'Dagelijks Brood'," *NedTT* 32/2 (1978): 125-39.

4687   Pierre Grelot, "La Quatrième Demande du 'Pater' et son Arrière-Plan Sémitique," *NTS* 25 (1978-1979): 299-314.

4688   Henri Bourgoin, "Epiousios expliqué par la notion de préfixe vide," *BibL* 60 (1979): 91-96.

4689   L.-M. Dewailly, " 'Donne-nous notre pain': quel pain? Notes sur la quatrième demande du Pater," *RSPT* 64 (1980): 561-88.

4690   D. Alexandre, "En torno a la cuarta petición del padrenuestro," *EB* 45 (1987): 325-36.

4691   L. Ramaroson, " 'Notre part de nourriture'," *ScE* 43 (1991): 87-115.

4692   R. G. Kratz, "Die Gnade des täglichen Brots: Späte Psalmen auf dem Weg zum Vaterunser," *ZTK* 89 (1992): 1-40.

11:4

4693   C. B. Houk, *"Peirasmos*, The Lord's Prayer, and the Massah Tradition," *SJT* 19 (1966): 216-25.

4694   Stanley E. Porter, "Mt 6:13 and Lk 11:4: 'Lead Us Not into Temptation," *ET* 101 (1989-1990): 359-62.

4695   Kenneth Grayston, "The Decline of Temptation--and the Lord's Prayer," *SJT* 46 (1993): 279-95.

11:5-13

4696   G. Bornkamm, "Bittet, Suchet, Klopfet an," *EvT* 13 (1953): 1-5.

4697   Ernst Fuchs, "Notes bibliques de prédication: pour les temps de Pâques et de Pentecôte," *VC* 58 (1961): 214-26.

4698   R. R. Rickards, "The Translation of Luke 11,5-13," *BT* 28 (1977): 239-43.

11:5-10

4699   Curtis C. Mitchell, "Why Keep Bothering God: The Case for Persisting in Prayer," *CT* 29/18 (1985): 33-34.

11:5-9

4700   David R. Catchpole, "Q and 'The Friend at Midnight'," *JTS* 34 (1983): 407-24.

11:5-8

4701   E. W. Hubbard, "The Parable of the Friend at Midnight: God's Honor or Man's Persistence?" *RQ* 21 (1978): 154-60.

4702   A. F. Johnson, "Assurance for Man: The Fallacy of Translating *anaideia* by 'Persistence' in Luke 11:5-8," *JETS* 22 (1979): 123-31.

4703   Klaus Haacker, "Mut zum Bitten: Eine Auslegung von Lukas 11,5-8," *TBe* 17 (1986): 1-6.

4704   Christopher M. Tuckett, "Q, Prayer, and the Kingdom," *JTS* 40 (1989): 367-76.

11:6

4705   J. D. M. Derrett, "Moving Mountains and Uprooting Trees," *BibO* 30 (1988): 231-44.

11:8

4706 Klyne R. Snodgrass, "Anaideia and the Friend at Midnight (Luke 11:8)," *JBL* 116 (1997): 505-13.

11:9-13

4707 Dale Goldsmith, "Ask, and It Will Be Given . . . : Toward Writing the History of a Logion," *NTS* 35/2 (1989): 254-65.

11:11-12

4708 J. Vara, "Una sugerencia: κόρπιον lección originaria de σκορπίον en Lucas 11:11-12," *Salm* 30 (1983): 225-29.

11:13

4709 Édouard Delebecque, "Sur un hellénisme de Saint Luc," *RB* 87 (1980): 590-93.

11:14-32

4710 Kerry M. Craig and Margret A. Kristjansson, "Women Reading as Men/Women Reading as Women: A Structural Analysis for the Historical Project," *Semeia* 51 (1990): 119-36.

11:14-28

4711 E. Galbiati, "Esegesi degli Evangeli festivi," *BibO* 3 (1961): 58-64.

11:14-26

4712 Roland Meynet, "Qui Donc Esr 'Le Plus Fort'? Analyse Rhetorique de Mc 3,22-30; Mt 12,22-37; Luc 11,14-26," *RB* 90/3 (1983): 334-50.

11:14-23

4713 R. F. Collins, "Jesus' Ministry to the Deaf and Dumb," *MeliT* 35/1 (1984): 12-36.

4714 Ulrich Luz, "Q 10:2-16; 11:14-23," *SBLSP* 15 (1985): 101-102.

4715 James M. Robinson, "The Mission and Beelzebul: Pap Q 10:2-16; 11:14-23," *SBLSP* 15 (1985): 97-99.

11:14-20

4716   Ingo Hermann, " ' . . . dann ist das Gottesreich zu euch gekommen.' Eine Homilie zu Lk 11:14-20," *BibL* 1 (1960): 198-204.

4717   John S. Kloppenborg, "Q 11:14-20: Work Sheets for Reconstruction," *SBLSP* 15 (1985): 133-51.

4718   Eduard Schweizer, "The Testimony to Jesus in the Early Christian Community," *HBT* 7/1 (1985): 77-98.

11:15-23

4719   Bruce D. Chilton, "A Comparative Study of Synoptic Development: The Dispute between Cain and Abel in the Palestinian Targums and the Beelzebul Controversy in the Gospel," *JBL* 101 (1982): 553-62.

11:15

4720   W. C. B. MacLaurin, "Beelzeboul," *NovT* 20/2 (1978): 156-60.

11:16

4721   Dino Merli, "Il Segno di Giona," *BibO* 14 (1972): 61-77.

11:17-30

4722   Chrys C. Caragounis, "Kingdom of God, Son of Man and Jesus' Self-Understanding," *TynB* 40 (1989): 3-23.

11:17

4723   H. E. Bryant, "Note on Luke 11:17," *ET* 50 (1938-1939): 15-26.

4724   Frans Neirynck, "Mt 12,25a / Lc 11,17a et la rédaction des évangiles," *ETL* 62 (1986): 122-33.

11:18

4725   W. C. B. MacLaurin, "Beelzeboul," *NovT* 20/2 (1978): 156-60.

11:19

4726   Robert Shirock, "Whose Exorcists Are They? The Referents of οἱ υἱοὶ ὑμῶν at Matthew 12:27/Luke 11:19," *JSNT* 46 (1992): 41-51.

11:20

4727   Robert G. Hamerton-Kelly, "A Note on Matthew xii.28 par. Luke xi.20," *NTS* 11 (1964-1965): 167-69.

4728   Augustin George, "Par le doigt de Dieu (Lc 11:20)," *SE* 18 (1966): 461-66.

4729   Gerhard Lohfink, "Die Korrelation von Reich Gottes und Volk Gottes bei Jesus," *TQ* 165/3 (1985): 173-83.

4730   Robert W. Wall, "The Finger of God: Deuteronomy 9:10 and Luke 11:20," *NTS* 33 (1987): 144-50.

11:21-22

4731   Simon Légasse, " 'Homme Fort' de Luc XI,21-22," *NovT* 5 (1962): 5-9.

11:21

4732   L. Michael White, "Sealing the Strongman's 'Court'," *Forum* 3 (1987): 3-28.

11:24-26

4733   John J. Kilgallen, "The Return of the Unclean Spirit (Luke 11,24-26)," *Bib* 74 (1993): 45-59.

11:27-28

4734   R. C. Wahlberg, "Jesus and the Uterus Image (Lc 11,27-28)," *ITQ* 41 (1974): 235-50.

11:27

4735   Heinrich Zimmermann, " 'Selig die das Wort Gottes hören und es bewahren': Eine exegetische Studie zu Lk 11,27f.," *Cath* 29 (1975): 114-19.

11:28

4736   J. Riedl, "Selig, die das Wort Gottes hören und befolgen (Lk 11:28). Theologisch-biblische Adventsbesinnung," *BibL* 4 (1963): 21-60.

4737   H. P. Scott, "A Note on the Meaning and Translation of Luke 11:28," *ITQ* 41 (1974): 235-50.

11:29-32

4738   John Howton, "The Sign of Jonah," *SJT* 15 (1962): 288-304.

4739   Dino Merli, "Il Segno di Giona," *BibO* 14 (1972): 61-77.

4740   G. Schmitt, "Das Zeichen des Jona," *ZNW* 69 (1978): 123-29.

4741   Théo Pfrimmer, "De l'interprétation en théologie pratique," *ÉTR* 73 no 4 (1998): 543-55.

11:29-30

4742   A. K. M. Adam, "The Sign of Jonah: A Fish-Eye View," *Semeia* 51 (1990): 177-91.

11:29

4743   James Swetnam, "No Sign of Jonah," *Bib* 66/1 (1985): 126-30.

11:30

4744   Santiago G. Oporto, "The Sign of Jonah," *TD* 32/1 (1985): 49-53.

11:33-36

4745   Marc Philonenko, "La parabole sur la lampe (Luc 11:33-36) et le horoscopes qoumrâniens," *ZNW* 79/1-2 (1988): 145-51.

4746   Susan R. Garrett, "Lest the Light in You Be Darkness: Luke 11:33-36 and the Question of Commitment," *JBL* 110 (1991): 93-105.

11:33

4747   E. Alliata, "La κρύπτη di Lc 11,33 e le grotte ripostigllo delle antiche case palestinesi," *SBFLA* 34 (1984): 53-66.

11:34-36

4748   Dale C. Allison, "The Eye Is the Lamp of the Body (Matthew 6.22-23; Luke 11.34-36)," *NTS* 33 (1987): 61-83.

11:37-54

4749   Werner Bieder, "Das Volk Gottes in Erwartung von Licht und Lobpreis," *TZ* 40/2 (1984): 137-48.

4750   E. Springs Steele, "Luke 11:37-54: A Modifed Hellenistic Symposium?" *JBL* 103 (1984): 379-94.

4751   Heinz Schürmann, "Die Redekomposition wider 'dieses Geschlecht' und seine Führung in der Redequelle (vgl. Mt 23,1-39 par Lk 11,37-54)," *SNTU-A* 11 (1986): 33-81.

4752   W. Schmithals, "Zur Geschichte der Spruchquelle Q und der Tradenten der Spruchüberlieferung: Das Siebenfache Wehe Lk 11.37-54 par," *NTS* 45 (1999): 472-97.

11:39-41

4753   Leif E. Vaage, "The Woes in Q (and Matthew and Luke): Deciphering the Rhetoric of Criticism," *SBLSP* 18 (1988): 582-607.

4754   Robert J. Miller, "The Inside is (not) the Outside: Q 11:39-41 and GThom 89," *Forum* 5 (1989): 92-105.

11:39

4755   Jacob Neusner, "The Absoluteness of Christianity and the Uniqueness of Judaism: Why Salvation Is Not of the Jews," *Int* 43 (1989): 18-31.

11:40-41

4756   Günther Schwarz, " 'Gebt . . . den Inhalt als Almosen'? (Lukas 11,40.41)," *BibN* 75 (1994): 26-30.

11:41

4757   W. Auer, "Bibeltexte - falsch verstanden," *BK* 13 (1958): 85-88.

11:42

4758   Dietrich Correns, "Die Verzehntung der Raute. Luk XI,42 und M Schebi IX,I," *MeliT* 6/2 (1963): 110-12.

11:44

4759   Günther Schwarz, " 'Unkenntliche Gräber'? (Lukas XI.44)," *NTS* 23/2 (1976-1977): 345-46.

11:49-51

4760   E. Earle Ellis, "Luke 11:49-51: An Oracle of a Christian Prophet?" *ET* 74 (1962-1963): 157-58.

4761   Giuseppe Frizzi, "Carattere originale e rilevanza degli 'apostoli inviati' in Q," *RBib* 21 (1973): 401-12.

11:51

4762   J. Barton Payne, " 'Zechariah Who Perished'," *GTJ* 8/3 (1967): 33-35.

12:1-12

4763   Dennis M. Sweetland, "Discipleship and Persecution: A Study of Luke 12,1-12," *Bib* 65 (1984): 61-80.

12:1-8

4764   André Légault, "An Application of the Form-Critique Method to the Anointing in Galilee (Lc 7,36-50) and Bethany (Mt 26,6-13; Mk 14,3-9; Lk 12,1-8)," *CBQ* 16 (1954): 131-45.

12:1

4765   Athanase Negōitā and C. Daniel, "L'énigme du levain. Ad Mc. viii,15; Mt. xvi,6; et Lc. xii,1," *NovT* 9 (1967): 306-14.

12:2-7

4766   John S. Kloppenborg, "The Q Sayings on Anxiety (Q 12:2-7)," *Forum* 5 (1989): 83-98.

12:6

4767   Alfredo Scattolon, "L'agapêtos sinottico nella luce della tradizione guidaica," *RBib* 26 (1978): 2-32.

12:7

4768   Dale C. Allison, "The Hairs on Your Head Are Numbered," *ET* 102 (1990-1991): 334-36.

12:8-9

4769   G. W. H. Lampe, "St. Peter's Denial," *BJRL* 55/2 (1973): 346-68.

4770   John M. McDermott, "Luke 12:8-9: Stone of Scandal," *RB* 84 (1977): 13-37.

4771   Harry T. Fleddermann, "The Q Sayings on Confessing and Denying," *SBLSP* 17 (1987): 606-16.

12:8

4772   Barnabas Lindars, "Jesus as Advocate: A Contribution to the Christology Debate," *BJRL* 62/2 (1980): 476-97.

4773   David R. Catchpole, "The Angelic Son of Man in Luke 12:8," *NovT* 2 (1982): 255-65.

4774   D. R. Copestake, "Luke 12:8 and 'Silent Witness'," *ET* 94 (1982-1983): 335.

4775   Paul Hoffmann, "Der Menschensohn in Lukas 12:8," *NTS* 44 (1998): 357-79.

12:10

4776   I. Howard Marshall, "Hard Sayings," *Theology* 67 (1964): 65-67.

4777   J. G. Williams, "A Note on the 'Unforgivable Sin' Logion," *NTS* 12 (1965-1966): 75-77.

4778   Jan Lambrecht, "Ware Verwantschap en Eeuwige Zonde: Ontstaan en Structuur van Mc. 3:20-35," *Bij* 29/2 (1968): 114-50.

4779   Evald Lövestam, "Logiet om hädelse mot den helige Ande (Mark. 3:28f. par. Matt. 12:31f.; Luk. 12:10)," *SEÅ* 33 (1968): 101-17.

4780   M. Eugene Boring, "The Unforgivable Sin Logion Mark 3:28-29/Matt 12:31-32/Luke 12:10: Formal Analysis and History of the Tradition," *NovT* 18/4 (1976): 258-79.

4781   P. Maurice Casey, "The Son of Man Problem," *ZNW* 67/3 (1976): 147-54.

4782   Chrys C. Caragounis, "Kingdom of God, Son of Man and Jesus' Self-Understanding," *TynB* 40 (1989): 3-23.

4783   Odette Mainville, "Le péché contre l'Esprit annoncé en Lc 12.10, commis en Ac 4.16-18: Une illustration de l'unité de Luc et Actes," *NTS* 45 (1999): 38-50.

12:11-12

4784   William L. Schutter, "Luke 12:11-12/21:12-15 and the Composition of Luke-Acts," *EGLMBS* 10 (1990): 236-50.

12:11

4785   George R. Beasley-Murray, "The Parousia in Mark," *RevExp* 75/4 (1978): 565-81.

4786   Matthew Mahoney, "Luke 21:14-15: Editorial Rewriting or Authenticity?" *ITQ* 47/3 (1980): 220-38.

12:13-34

4787   Abraham J. Malherbe, "The Christianization of a Topos (Luke 12:13-34)," *NovT* 38 (1996): 123-35.

12:13-21

4788 Gilles Gaide, "Le riche insensé (Lc 12)," *AsSeign* NS 49 (1971): 82-89.

4789 H. Sawatzky, "What's Gotten Into Us?" *ET* 91 (1979-1980): 245-47.

4790 R. Wayne Stacy, "Luke 12:13-21: The Parable of the Rich Fool," *RevExp* 94 (1997): 285-92.

4791 Frank Stagg, "Luke's Theological Use of Parables," *RevExp* 94 (1997): 215-29.

12:13-14

4792 T. Gorringe, "A Zealot Option Rejected? Luke 12:13-14," *ET* 98 (1986-1987): 267-70.

12:14

4793 John Killinger, "On Not Being Everybody's Commodity," *ChrM* 16/3 (1985): 23-25.

4794 Gregory J. Riley, "Influence of Thomas Christianity on Luke 12:14 and 5:39," *HTR* 88 (1995): 229-35.

12:15-21

4795 G. W. E. Nickelsburg, "Riches, the Rich, and God's Judgment in 1 Enoch 92-105 and the Gospel according to Luke," *NTS* 25 (1978-1979): 324-44.

12:15-20

4796 Henry Chadwick, "The Shorter Text of Luke 12:15-20," *HTR* 50 (1957): 249-58.

12:15

4797 C. C. Tarelli, "A Note on Luke xii.15," *JTS* 41 (1940): 260-62.

12:16-21

4798 Erhardt Güttgemanns, "Narrative Analyse Synoptischer Texte," *LB* 25/26 (1973): 50-73.

4799 J. D. M. Derrett, "The Rich Fool: A Parable of Jesus Concerning Inheritance," *HeyJ* 18 (1977): 131-51.

4800 E. W. Seng, "Der reiche Tor: Eine Untersuchung von Lk xii,16-21 unter besonderer Berücksichtigung form—und motivgeschichtlicher Aspekte," *NovT* 20 (1978): 136-55.

12:16-20

4801   Günther Schwarz, "Ταύτη τῇ νυκτὶ τὴν ψυχήν σου ἀπαιτοῦσιν ἀπὸ σοῦ," *BibN* 25 (1984): 36-41.

12:16

4802   J. Neville Birdsall, "Luke 12:16ff. and the Gospel of Thomas," *JTS* 13 (1962): 332-36.

4803   Helen R. Graham, "Once there Was a Rich Man . . . : Five 'Rich Man' Stories in Luke," *BibTo* 26 (1988): 98-103.

12:20

4804   Günther Schwarz, "λυθῆναι απὸ τοῦ δεσμοῦ τούτου," *BibN* 15 (1981): 47.

4805   Günther Schwarz, "Ταύτη τῇ νυκτὶ τὴν ψυχήν σου ἀπαιτοῦσιν ἀπὸ σοῦ," *BibN* 25 (1984): 36-41.

12:22-31

4806   John N. Jones, " 'Think of the Lilies' and Prov 6:6-11," *HTR* 88 (1995): 175-77.

12:24

4807   J. F. Healey, "Models of Behavior: Matt 6:26," *JBL* 108 (1989): 497-98.

12:32-48

4808   Augustin George, "L'attente du maître qui vient (Lc 12)," *AsSeign* NS 50 (1974): 66-76.

12:32

4809   Wilhelm Pesch, "Zur Formgeschichte und Exegese von Lk. 12:32," *Bib* 41/1 (1960): 25-40.

12:35-59

4810   C. Küven, "Advent in der Entscheidung nach Lukas 12:35-59," *BK* 16 (1961): 109-12.

12:35-48

4811   A. G. Van Aarde, "Narrative Point of View: An Ideological Reading of Luke 12:35-48," *Neo* 22 (1988): 235-1.

4812   J. Botha, "Isers Wandering Viewpoint: A Reception-Analytical Reading of Luke 12:35-48," *Neo* 22 (1988): 253-68.

4813 H. J. B. Combrink, "Readings, Readers and Authors: An Orientation," *Neo* 22 (1988): 189-203.

4814 Bernard C. Lategan, "Reading Luke 12:35-48: An Empirical Study," *Neo* 22 (1988): 391-413.

4815 Eben H. Scheffler, "A Psychological Reading of Luke 12:35-48," *Neo* 22 (1988): 355-71.

4816 C. W. Schnell, "Historical Context in Parable Interpretation: A Criticism of Current Tradition-Historical Interpretations of Luke 12:35-48," *Neo* 22 (1988): 269-82.

4817 W. Sebothoma, "Luke 12:35-48: A Reading by a Black South African," *Neo* 22 (1988): 325-35.

4818 Dirk J. Smit, "Responsible Hermeneutics: A Systematic Theologian's Response to the Readings and Readers of Luke 12:35-48," *Neo* 22 (1988): 441-84.

4819 P. van Staden, "A Sociological Reading of Luke 12:35-48," *Neo* 22 (1988): 337-53.

4820 Sjef van Tilborg, "An Interpretation from the Ideology of the Text," *Neo* 22 (1988): 205-15.

12:35-40

4821 Richard J. Bauckham, "Synoptic Parousia Parables and the Apocalypse," *NTS* 23 (1976-1977): 162-76.

4822 P. Deterding, "Eschatological and Eucharistic Motifs in Luke 12,35-40," *CJ* 5 (1979): 85-94.

4823 Richard J. Bauckham, "Synoptic Parousia Parables Again," *NTS* 29 (1983): 129-34.

12:35-39

4824 H. Spaemann, "Advent der Christen im Gleichnis. Eine Meditation über Lk 12:35-39," *BibL* 1 (1960): 266-70.

12:39-46

4825 Harry T. Fleddermann, "The Householder and the Servant Left in Charge," *SBLSP* 16 (1986): 17-26.

12:41-48

4826 Patrick J. Hartin, "Angst in the Household: A Deconstructive Reading of the Parable of the Supervising Servant," *Neo* 22 (1988): 373-90.

12:42-46

4827 Arthur J. Dewey, "A Prophetic Pronouncement: Q 12:42-46," *Forum* 5 (1989): 99-108.

12:46

4828 Paul Ellingworth, "Luke 12:46: Is There an Anti-Climax Here?" *BT* 31 (1980): 242-43.

12:49-53

4829 Augustin George, "La venue de Jésus, cause de division entre les hommes (Lc 12)," *AsSeign* NS 51 (1972): 62-71.

4830 José Fernández-Lago, " 'Fuego he venido a traer a la tierra' (Lc 12,49-53): Estudio bíblico," *EB* 57 (1999): 239-55.

12:49

4831 P. Kutter, "Eine 'biblische' Ansprache," *BK* 5 (1950): 48-50.

12:50

4832 Gerhard Delling, "*Baptisma baptisthēnai,*" *NovT* 2 (1957-1958): 92-115.

4833 André Feuillet, "La coupe et le baptême de la Passion (Mc x,35-40; cf. Mt xx,20-23; Lc xii,50)," *RB* 74 (1967): 356-91.

4834 J. D. M. Derrett, "Christ's Second Baptism (Lk. 12:50; Mk. 10:38-40)," *ET* 100 (1988-1989): 294-95.

12:51-53

4835 T. A. Roberts, "Some Comments on Matthew x.34-36 and Luke xii.51-53," *ET* 69 (1957-1958): 304-306.

12:52-53

4836 Christoph Heil, "Die Rezeption von Micha 7:6 LXX in Q und Lukas," *ZNW* 88 (1997): 211-22.

12:54-56

4837 Jan N. Sevenster, "Geeft den Keizer, wat des Keizers is, en Gode, wat Gods is," *NedTT* 17 (1962): 21-31.

4838 Günter Klein, "Die Prüfung der Zeit (Lukas 12:54-56)," *ZTK* 61/4 (1964): 373-90.

12:57-59

4839   Georg Strecker, "Die Antithesen der Bergpredigt (Mt 5,21-48 par)," *ZNW* 69 (1978): 36-72.

13:1-35

4840   Robert Shirock, "The Growth of the Kingdom in Light of Israel's Rejection of Jesus: Structure and Theology in Luke 13:1-35," *NovT* 35 (1993): 15-29.

13:1-9

4841   Paul Ternant, "Le dernier délai de la conversion (Lc 13)," *AsSeign* NS 16 (1971): 59-72.

4842   F. W. Young, "Luke 13:1-9," *Int* 31 (1977): 59-63.

13:1-5

4843   Sherman E. Johnson, "A Note on Luke 13:1-5," *ATR* 17 (1935): 91-95.

4844   Josef Blinzler, "Die Niedermetzelung von Galiläern durch Pilatus," *NovT* 2 (1957-1958): 24-49.

4845   Günther Schwarz, "Lukas xiii.1-5—Eine Emendation," *NovT* 11 (1969): 121-26.

4846   Philip Yancey, "Riddles of Pain: Clues from the Book of Job," *CT* 29/18 (1985): 80.

13:4

4847   Michael B. Walker, "Luke xiii.4," *ET* 75 (1963-1964): 151.

13:6-9

4848   Ulrich Schoenborn, "El Jardinero Audaz: Aspectos Semánticos y Pragmáticos en Lucas 13,6-9," *RevB* 1/2 (1990): 65-84.

4849   Charles W. Hedrick, "An Unfinished Story about a Fig Tree in a Vineyard (Luke 13:6-9)," *PRS* 26 (1999): 169-92.

4850   Charles W. Hedrick, "Prolegomena to Reading Parables: Luke 13:6-9 As a Test Case," *RevExp* 94 (1997): 179-97.

13:9

4851   Günter Scholz, "Aesthetische Beobachtungen am Gleichnis vom reichen Mann und armen Lazarus und von drei anderen Gleichnissen," *LB* 43 (1978): 67-74.

13:10-17

4852   John Wilkinson, "The Case of the Bent Woman in Luke 13:10-17," *EQ* 49 (1977): 195-205.

4853   Christian Dietzfelbinger, "Vom Sinn der Sabbatheilungen Jesu," *EvT* 38 (1978): 281-97.

4854   J. D. M. Derrett, "Positive Perspectives on Two Lucan Miracles," *DR* 104 (1986): 272-87.

4855   Dennis Hamm, "The Freeing of the Bent Woman and the Restoration of Israel: Luke 13:10-17 as Narrative Theology," *JSNT* 31 (1987): 23-44.

4856   Elisabeth Schüssler Fiorenza, "Luke 13:10-17: Interpretation for Liberation and Transformation," *TD* 36 (1989): 303-19.

4857   Joel B. Green, "Jesus and a Daughter of Abraham (Luke 13:10-17): Test Case for a Lucan Perspective on Jesus' Miracles," *CBQ* 51 (1989): 643-54.

4858   Robert F. O'Toole, "Some Exegetical Reflections on Luke 13:10-17," *Bib* 73 (1992): 84-107.

4859   Judith G. Kipp, "Holy Obedience," *BLT* 38 (1993): 44-47.

4860   David M. May, "The Straightened Woman (Luke 13:10-17): Paradise Lost and Regained," *PRS* 24 (1997): 245-58.

13:10-13

4861   Gretchen E. Ziegenhals, "This Bridge Called Me Back," *CC* 106 (1989): 343-44.

13:10

4862   Christoph Burchard, "Fußnoten zum neutestamentlichen Griechisch II," *ZNW* 69 (1978): 143-57.

13:11

4863   Günther Schwarz, "καὶ ἦν συγκύπτουσα," *BibN* 20 (1983): 58.

4864   W. Radl, "Ein 'Doppeltes Leiden' in Lk. 13,11: Zu Einer Notiz von Günther Schwarz," *BibN* 31 (1986): 35-36.

13:16

4865   Günther Schwarz, "λυθῆναι απὸ τοῦ δεσμοῦ τούτου," *BibN* 15 (1981): 47.

13:18-19

4866   Otto Kuss, "Zur Senfkornparabel," *TGl* 41 (1951): 40-49.

4867   Harvey K. McArthur, "The Parable of the Mustard Seed," *CBQ* 33 (1971): 198-210.

4868   John D. Crossan, "The Seed Parables of Jesus," *JBL* 92 (1973): 244-66.

13:20-21

4869   Robert W. Funk, "Beyond Criticism in Quest of Literacy: The Parable of the Leaven," *Int* 25 (1971): 149-70.

4870   Elizabeth Waller, "The Parable of the Leaven: A Sectarian Teaching and the Inclusion of Women," *USQR* 35 (1980): 99-109.

4871   Günther Schwarz, " 'Verbarg es in drei Sea Mehl'? (Matthäus 13,33/Lukas 13,20.21)," *BibN* 86 (1997): 60-62.

13:22-30

4872   Paul Hoffmann, "Pántes ergátai adikías, Redaktion und Tradition in Lc 13,22-30," *ZNW* 58 (1967): 188-214.

4873   J. Seynaeve, "La parabole de la porte étroite: l'acceptation 'pratique' du Christ (Lc 13)," *AsSeign* NS 1 (1974): 68-77.

4874   Mitzi Minor, "Luke 13:22-30--The Wrong Question, The Right Door," *RevExp* 91 (1994): 551-57.

13:22-24

4875   Rod Parrott, "Entering the Narrow Door: Matt 7:13/Luke 13:22-24," *Forum* 5 (1989): 111-20.

13:22

4876   C. L'Eplattenier, "Lecture d'une séquence lucanienne, Luc 13:22 à 14:24," *ÉTR* 56 (1981): 282-87.

13:24

4877   J. D. M. Derrett, "The Merits of the Narrow Gate," *JSNT* 15 (1982): 20-29.

13:28-29

4878   Dale C. Allison, "Who Will Come from East and West,"
        IBS 11 (1989): 158-70.

13:28

4879   Dieter Zeller, "Das Logion Mt 8,11f./Lk 13,28f. und das
        Motiv der 'Völkerwallfahrt'," *BZ* 15 (1971): 222-37; 16
        (1972): 84-93.

4880   W. Grimm, "Zum Hintergrund von Mt 8,11f., Lk 13,28.f.,"
        BZ 16 (1972): 255-56.

13:31-33

4881   W. Grimm, "Eschatologischer Saul wider
        eschatologischen David," *NovT* 15 (1973): 114-33.

13:31

4882   B. Prete, "Il testo di Luca 13:31. Unità letteraria ed
        insegnamento cristologico," *BibO* 24 (1982): 59-79.

13:32

4883   L. H. Bunn, "Herod Antipas and 'That Fox'," *ET* 43
        (1931-1932): 380-81.

4884   J. D. M. Derrett, "The Lucan Christ and Jerusalem:
        τελειοῦμαι," *ZNW* 75 (1984): 36-43.

13:33

4885   J. Bishop, "The Power of the Single Purpose," *ET* 93
        (1982-1983): 115-16.

13:34-35

4886   F. D. Weinert, "Luke, the Temple, and Jesus' Saying about
        Jerusalem's Abandoned House (Luke 13:34-35)," *CBQ* 44
        (1982): 68-76.

13:35

4887   Dale C. Allison, "Matt. 23:39 = Luke 13:35b as a
        Conditional Prophecy," *JSNT* 18 (1983): 75-84.

14:1-11

4888   E. Galbiati, "Esegesi degli Evangeli festivi," *BibO* 1
        (1959): 20-25.

14:1-10

4889 Christian Dietzfelbinger, "Vom Sinn der Sabbatheilungen Jesu," *EvT* 38 (1978): 281-97.

14:1-6

4890 J. D. M. Derrett, "Positive Perspectives on Two Lucan Miracles," *DR* 104 (1986): 272-87.

4891 G. J. Volschenk and A. G. Van Aarde, "Sistematies verwronge kommunikasie in Lukas 14:1-6: Die dialekties-kritiese teorie van Jürgen Habermas krities bespreek," *HTS* 50 (1994): 812-40.

14:5

4892 Matthew Black, "The Aramaic Spoken by Christ and Luke 14,5," *JTS* 1 (1950): 60-62.

4893 Harald Riesenfeld, "Anteckning till Luk 14:5," *SEÅ* 49 (1984): 83-88.

14:7-11

4894 Erhardt Güttgemanns, "Narrative Analyse Synoptischer Texte," *LB* 25/26 (1973): 50-73.

4895 Timothy L. Noël, "The Parable of the Wedding Guest: A Narrative-Critical Interpretation," *PRS* 16 (1989): 17-27.

14:12-24

4896 Otto Glombitza, "Das grosse Abendmahl: Luk 14:12-24," *NovT* 5 (1962): 10-16.

4897 Daniel L. Migliore, "The Open Banquet," *PSB* 6/1 (1985): 8-13.

14:14

4898 P. Ketter, "Die Auferstehung der Gerechten und der Sünder (Luke 14:14)," *BK* 4 (1949): 10-20.

14:15-35

4899 Hans Klein, "Botschaft für viele--Nachfolge von wenigen: Überlegungen zu Lk 14,15-35," *EvT* 57 (1997): 427-37.

14:15-24

4900 J. Baker, "Christ's Challenge to Straight Thinking," *ET* 67 (1955-1956): 179-81.

4901   Eta Linnemann, "Überlegungen zur Parabel vom grossen Abendmahl, Lc 14,15-24/Mt 22,1-14," *ZNW* 51 (1960): 246-55.

4902   Dan O. Via, "The Relationship of Form to Content in the Parable: The Wedding Feast," *Int* 25 (1971): 171-84.

4903   Detlev Dormeyer, "Literarische und theologische Analyse der Parabel Lukas 14:15-24," *BibL* 15 (1974): 206-19.

4904   E. Pousset, "Les invités au banquet (Luc 14,15-24)," *Chr* 32 (1985): 81-89.

4905   Luise Schottroff, "Das Gleichnis vom grossen Gastmahl in der Logienquelle," *EvT* 47 (1987): 192-211.

4906   Victor E. Vine, "Luke 14:15-24 and Anti-Semitism," *ET* 102 (1990-1991): 262-63.

4907   Frank Stagg, "Luke's Theological Use of Parables," *RevExp* 94 (1997): 215-29.

4908   Roger W. Sullivan, "The Parable of the Great Supper (Luke 14:15-24)," *TEd* 56 (1997): 59-66.

14:16-24

4909   E. Galbiati, "Gli invitati al convito (Luke 14:16-24)," *BibO* 7 (1965): 129-35.

4910   Humphrey Palmer, "Just Married, Cannot Come," *NovT* 18/4 (1976): 241-57.

4911   R. W. Resenhöfft, "Jesu Gleichnis von den Talenten, ergänzt durch die Lukas-Fassung," *NTS* 26 (1979-1980): 318-31.

14:16-23

4912   Olivier Abel, "De l'Obligation de Croire: les Objections de Bayle au Commentaire Augustinien du 'Contrains-les d'Entrer'," *ÉTR* 61/1 (1986): 35-49.

14:23

4913   Siegfried Kreuzer, "Der Zwang des Boten: Beobachtungen zu Lk. 14:23 und 1 Kor 9:16," *ZNW* 76/1-2 (1985): 123-28.

14:24

4914   C. L'Eplattenier, "Lecture d'une séquence lucanienne, Luc 13:22 à 14:24," *ÉTR* 56 (1981): 282-87.

14:25-33

4915   P. G. Jarvis, "Expounding the Parables: Tower-Builder and King Going to War," *ET* 77 (1965-1966): 196-98.

4916   J. Seynaeve, "Exigences de la condition chrétienne (Lc 14)," *AsSeign* NS 54 (1972): 64-75.

4917   Charles E. Wolfe, "All or Nothing," *ChrM* 16/1 (1985): 32-33.

4918   Norman Mundhenk, "Problems Involving Illustrations in Luke," *BT* 44 (1993): 247-48.

4919   Christophe Singer, "La difficulté d'être disciple: Luc 14/25-35," *ÉTR* 73 (1998): 21-36.

14:26-27

4920   Leif E. Vaage, "Q and the Historical Jesus: Some Peculiar Sayings," *Forum* 5 (1989): 159-76.

14:26

4921   Roy A. Harrisville, "Jesus and the Family," *Int* 23/4 (1969): 425-38.

4922   S. A. Panimolle, "Se uno non odia la moglie e ifgli, non puo essere mio discepolo (Lc 14,26)," *ParSpirV* 12 (1984): 143-65.

4923   Ieuan Ellis, "Jesus and the Subversive Family," *SJT* 38/2 (1985): 173-88.

4924   Robert H. Stein, "Luke 14:26 and the Question of Authenticity," *Forum* 5 (1989): 187-92.

14:28-33

4925   S. Mechie, "The Parables of the Tower-Builder and the King Going to War," *ET* 48 (1936-1937): 235-36.

14:28

4926   Werner Bieder, "Das Volk Gottes in Erwartung von Licht und Lobpreis," *TZ* 40/2 (1984): 137-48.

14:31

4927   Jim Wallis, "Acting Boldly in the Spirit: A Call to Peace Pentecost 1985," *Soj* 14/4 (1985): 4-5.

14:33

4928   Thomas E. Schmidt, "Burden, Barrier, Blasphemy: Wealth in Matt. 6:33, Luke 14:33, and Luke 16:15," *TriJ* 9/2 (1988): 171-89.

14:34

4929   J. B. Bauer, "Quod si sal infatuatum fuerit," *VD* 28 (1951): 228-30.

15-16

4930   John J. Kilgallen, "Luke 15 and 16: A Connection," *Bib* 78 (1997): 369-76.

15:1-16:8

4931   Peter R. Jones, "Preaching on the Parable Genre," *RevExp* 94 (1997): 231-45.

15

4932   J. Bradley Chance, "Luke 15: Seeking the Outsiders," *RevExp* 94 (1997): 249-57.

4933   Frank Stagg, "Luke's Theological Use of Parables," *RevExp* 94 (1997): 215-29.

4934   Gerald L. Stevens, "Luke 15: Parables of God's Search for Sinners," *TEd* 56 (1997): 67-76.

4935   Ernst R. Wendland, "Finding Some Lost Aspects of Meaning in Christ's Parables of the Lost--and Found (Luke 15)," *TriJ* 17 (1996): 19-65.

15:1-32

4936   R. Waelkens, "L'analyse structurale des paraboles. Deux essais: Luke 15:1-32 et Matthieu 13:44-46," *RTL* 8 (1977): 160-78.

4937   E. P. Sanders, "Jesus and the Sinners," *JSNT* 19 (1983): 5-36.

4938   R. Krüger, " 'La sustitución del tener por el ser: Lectura semiótica de Lucas 15,1-32," *RevB* 49 (1987): 65-97.

4939   Bruce D. Chilton, "Jesus and the Repentance of E. P. Sanders," *TynB* 39 (1988): 1-18.

15:1-10

4940   F. Kamphaus, " ' . . . zu suchen, was verloren war.' Homilie zu Luke 15:1-10," *BibL* 8 (1967): 201-203.

4941   H. Sawatzky, "Problem at the Party," *ET* 91 (1979-1980): 270-72.

4942   J. Toy, "The Lost Sheep and the Lost Coin," *ET* 92 (1980-1981): 276-77.

15:1-7

4943   Wilhelm Schmidt, "Der gute Hirte: Biblische Besinnung über Luke 15:1-7," *EvT* 24/4 (1964): 173-77.

4944   P. Mourlon-Beernaert, "The Lost Sheep: Four Approaches," *TD* 29 (1981): 143-48.

15:1-2

4945   Martin Völkel, " 'Freund der Zöllner und Sünder'," *ZNW* 69 (1978): 1-10.

4946   A. Viard, "Un homme avait deux fils (Luke 15:1-2, 11-32)," *EV* 83 (1983): 53-55.

15:1

4947   Martin Völkel, "Freund der Zöllner und Sünder," *ZNW* 69 (1978): 1-10.

15:2

4948   J. J. Bartolome, "Synesthiein en la Obra Lucana: Lc 15,2; Hch 10,41; 11:3," *Sale* 46/2 (1984): 269-88.

15:3-10

4949   J. D. M. Derrett, "Fresh Light on the Lost Sheep and the Lost Coin," *NTS* 26 (1979-1980): 36-60.

15:3-7

4950   Eric F. F. Bishop, "The Parable of the Lost or Wandering Sheep," *ATR* 44 (1962): 44-57.

4951   Sasagu Arai, "Das Gleichnis vom verlorenen Schaf: Eine traditionsgeschichtliche Untersuchung," *AJBI* 2 (1976): 111-37.

15:3-6

4952   W. L. Petersen, "The Parable of the Lost Sheep in the Gospel of Thomas and the Synoptics," *NovT* 23 (1981): 128-47.

15:4-7

4953   Franz Schnider, "Das Gleichnis vom verlorenen Schaf und seine Redaktoren," *K* 19 (1977): 146-54.

4954   R. Favris, "La parabola della pecora perduta," *ParSpirV* 10 (1984): 105-19.

15:4

4955   F. Bussy, "Did a Shepherd Leave Sheep Upon the Mountains or in the Desert?" *ATR* 45 (1963): 93-94.

15:8-32

4956   Carol S. LaHurd, "Rediscovering the Lost Women in Luke 15," *BTB* 24 (1994): 66-76.

15:8-10

4957   Daniel Sheerin, "The Theotokion: Ὁ ΤΗΝ ΕΥΛΟΓΗΜΕΝΗΝ: Its Background in Patristic Exegesis of Luke 15:8-10 and Western Parallels," *VC* 43/2 (1989): 166-87.

15:10

4958   Andrew F. Walls, "In the Presence of the Angels," *NovT* 3 (1959): 314-16.

15:11-32

4959   J. E. Compton, "The Prodigal's Brother," *ET* 42 (1930-1931): 287.

4960   H. E. Sticker, "The Prodigal's Brother," *ET* 42 (1930-1931): 45-46.

4961   Charles E. Carlston, "A Positive Criterion of Authenticity?" *BR* 7 (1962): 33-44.

4962   R. Silva, "La parábola del hijo pródigo," *CuBí* 23 (1966): 259-63.

4963   J. D. M. Derrett, "Law in the New Testament: The Parable of the Prodigal Son," *NTS* 14 (1967-1968): 56-74.

4964 Jack T. Sanders, "Tradition and Redaction in Luke xv.11-32," *NTS* 15 (1968-1969): 433-38.

4965 P. Penning de Vries, "Der nie verlorene Vater," *GeistL* 44 (1971): 74-75.

4966 John J. O'Rourke, "Some Notes on Luke xv.11-32," *NTS* 18 (1971-1972): 431-33.

4967 J. Delgado Sanchez, "Consideraciones sobre la parábola del hijo pródigo," *CuBí* 29 (1972): 338-41.

4968 Gerhard Lohfink, "Das Gleichnis vom gütigen Vater. Eine Predigt zu Luke 15:11-32," *BibL* 13 (1972): 138-46.

4969 Erhardt Güttgemanns, "Narrative Analyse Synoptischer Texte," *LB* 25/26 (1973): 50-73.

4970 Ingo Broer, "Das Gleichnis vom verlorenen Sohn und die Theologie des Lukas," *NTS* 20 (1973-1974): 453-62.

4971 Gerhard Sellin, "Gleichnisstrukturen," *LB* 31 (1974): 89-115.

4972 Charles E. Carlston, "Reminiscence and Redaction in Luke 15:11-32," *JBL* 94 (1975): 368-90.

4973 Pierre Grelot, "Le père et ses deux fils: Luke 15:11-32," *RB* 84 (1977): 321-48, 538-65.

4974 James L. Price, "Luke 15:11-32," *Int* 31 (1977): 64-69.

4975 Bernard B. Scott, "The Prodigal Son: A Structuralist Interpretation," *Semeia* 9 (1977): 45-73.

4976 Mary A. Tolbert, "The Prodigal Son: An Essay in Literary Criticism from a Psychoanalytic Perspective," *Semeia* 9 (1977): 1-20.

4977 Dan O. Via, "The Prodigal Son: A Jungian Reading," *Semeia* 9 (1977): 21-43.

4978 Otfried Hofius, "Alttestamentliche Motive im Gleichnis vom verlorenen Sohn," *NTS* 24 (1977-1978): 240-48.

4979 R. G. Crawford, "A Parable of the Atonement," *EQ* 50 (1978): 2-7.

4980 Günter Scholz, "Aesthetische Beobachtungen am Gleichnis vom reichen Mann und armen Lazarus und von drei anderen Gleichnissen," *LB* 43 (1978): 67-74.

4981   R. R. Rickards, "Some Points to Consider in Translating the Parable of the Prodigal Son," *BT* 31 (1980): 243-45.

4982   M. Roy, "Jugement et sanction. Matthieu 25:31-46; Luc 15:11-32; 16:19-31," *Chr* 28 (1981): 440-49.

4983   A. Viard, "Un homme avait deux fils (Luke 15:1-2, 11-32)," *EV* 83 (1983): 53-55.

4984   H.-J. Vogel, "Der verlorene Sohn: Lukas 15,11-32," *TextK* 18 (1983): 27-34.

4985   Jacques Dupont, "Il padre del figliol prodigo (Lc 15,11-32)," *ParSpirV* 10 (1984): 120-34.

4986   G. S. Gibson, "The Sins of the Saints," *ET* 96 (1984-1985): 276-77.

4987   Roger D. Aus, "Luke 15:11-32 and R. Eliezer Ben Hyrcanus's *Rise to Fame*," *JBL* 104 (1985): 443-69.

4988   Michael R. Austin, "The Hypocritical Son," *EQ* 57 (1985): 307-15.

4989   J. G. Lees, "The Parable of the Good Father," *ET* 97/8 (1985-1986): 246-47.

4990   G. Daan Cloete and Dirk J. Smit, "Rejoicing With God," *JTSA* 66 (1989): 62-73.

4991   Nancy J. Duff, "Luke 15:11-32," *Int* 49 (1995): 66-69 .

4992   Greg Forbes, "Repentance and Conflict in the Parable of the Lost Son (Luke 15:11-32)," *JETS* 42 (1999): 211-29.

4993   Timothy J. Geddert, "The Parable of the Prodigal: Priorities," *Dir* 24 (1995): 28-36.

4994   Garrison Keillor, "Prodigal Son," *WW* 17 (1997): 289-94.

4995   Carlos Noyen, " 'Teilt meine Freude': Exegetische Randbemerkungen zu Lukas 15,11-32," *IKaZ* 22 (1993): 387-96.

4996   Robert O'Meara, " 'Luring the Crocus through the Snow': The Parable of the Man Who Had Two Sons (Luke 15:11-32)," *ABR* 46 (1998): 17-35.

4997   Eckhard Rau, "Jesu Auseinandersetzung mit Pharisäern über seine Zuwendung zu Sünderinnen und Sündern: Lk 15,11-32 und Lk 18,10-14a als Worte des historischen Jesus," *ZNW* 89 (1998): 5-29.

15:11-24

4998 R. G. Forrest, "I Believe in the Forgiveness of Sins," *ET* 92 (1980-1981): 18-19.

4999 Bill J. Leonard, "Luke 15:11-24--Being Lost, Being Found," *RevExp* 90 (1993): 117-21.

15:11-12

5000 Rudolf Hoppe, "Gleichnis und Situation," *BZ* 28/1 (1984): 1-21.

15:11

5001 Joachim Jeremias, "Zum Gleichnis vom verlorenen Sohn, Luk. 15,11," *TZ* 5 (1949): 228-31.

15:12

5002 Wolfgang Pöhlmann, "Die Abschichtung des verlorenen Sohnes (Lk 15:12f.) und die erzählte Welt der Parabel," *ZNW* 70 (1979): 194-213.

15:15

5003 J. A. Harrill, "The Indentured Labor of the Prodigal Son (Luke 15:15)," *JBL* 115 (1996): 714-17.

5004 Günther Schwarz, " 'Er hängte sich an einen Bürger' (Lukas 15,15a)," *BibN* 85 (1996): 24-25.

15:17

5005 Ian MacLeod, "Enough and to Spare," *ET* 88 (1976-1977): 114-15.

5006 J. C. Kellogg, "Enough to Spare," *ET* 94 (1982-1983): 272-73.

15:18-21

5007 Gerhard Lohfink, " 'Ich habe gesündigt gegen den Himmel und gegen dich': Eine Exegese von Lk 15,18.21," *TQ* 15 (1975): 51-1.

15:19-31

5008 C. H. Cave, "Lazarus and the Lukan Deuteronomy," *NTS* 15 (1968-1969): 319-25.

15:25-32

> 5009   Mikeal C. Parsons, "The Prodigal's Elder Brother: The History and Ethics of Reading Luke 15:25-32," *PRS* 23 (1996): 147-74.

15:30

> 5010   James Custer, "When Is Communion Communion?" *GTJ* 6/2 (1985): 403-10.

> 5011   Tom Corlett, "This Brother of Yours," *ET* 100 (1989-1990): 216.

16

> 5012   Michael Ball, "The Parables of the Unjust Steward and the Rich Man and Lazarus," *ET* 106 (1995): 329-30.

16:1-35

> 5013   Ronald G. Lunt, "Expounding the Parables: Parable of the Unjust Steward," *ET* 77 (1965-1966): 132-36.

16:1-17

> 5014   Paul S. Wilson, "The Lost Parable of the Generous Landowner and Other Texts for Imaginative Preaching," *QR* 9 (1989): 80-99.

16:1-13

> 5015   R. B. Y. Scott, "The Parable of the Unjust Steward," *ET* 49 (1937-1938): 234-35.

> 5016   W. F. Boyd, "The Parable of the Unjust Steward," *ET* 50 (1938-1939): 46.

> 5017   Lawrence M. Friedel, "The Parable of the Unjust Steward," *CBQ* 3 (1941): 337-48.

> 5018   D. R. Fletcher, "The Riddle of the Unjust Steward," *JBL* 82 (1963): 15-30.

> 5019   Joseph A. Fitzmyer, "The Story of the Dishonest Manager," *TS* 25 (1964): 23-42.

> 5020   Francis E. Williams, "Is Almsgiving the Point of the 'Unjust Steward'?" *JBL* 83 (1964): 293-97.

> 5021   L. J. Topel, "On the Injustice of the Unjust Steward: Lk 16:1-13," *CBQ* 35 (1975): 216-27.

5022   J. P. Molina, "Luc 16:1 à 13: l'injustice Mamon," *ÉTR* 53 (1978): 311-75.

5023   Dave Mathewson, "The Parable of the Unjust Steward (Luke 16:1-13): A Reexamination of the Traditional View in Light of Recent Challenges," *JETS* 38 (1995): 29-39.

5024   L. Paul Trudinger, "Ire or Irony? The Enigmatical Character of the Parable of the Dishonest Steward (Luke 16:1-13)," *DR* 116 (1998): 85-102.

16:1-9

5025   F. Hüttermann, "Stand das Gleichnis vom ungerechten Verwalter in Q?" *TGl* 27 (1935): 739-42.

5026   Charles H. Pickar, "The Unjust Steward," *CBQ* 1 (1939): 250-53.

5027   E. Galbiati, "Esegesi degli Evangeli festivi," *BibO* 3 (1961): 92-96.

5028   Heinrich Zimmermann, "Die Forderung der Gleichnisse Jesu. Das Gleichnis vom ungerechten Verwalter: Lk 16:1-9," *BibL* 2 (1961): 254-61.

5029   F. J. Moore, "The Parable of the Unjust Steward," *ATR* 47 (1965): 103-105.

5030   André Feuillet, "La parabole du mauvais riche et du pauvre Lazare (Luc 16:19-31) antithèse de la parabole de l'intendant astucieux (Luc 16:1-9)," *NRT* 101 (1979): 212-23.

5031   Jack T. Sanders, "The Criterion of Coherence and the Randomness of Charisma: Poring Through Some Aporias in the Jesus Tradition," *NTS* 44 (1998): 1-25.

16:1-8

5032   J. Maiworm, "Die Verwalter-Parabel," *TGl* 36 (1944): 149-56.

5033   J. D. M. Derrett, "Fresh Light on St. Luke 16: I. The Parable of the Unjust Steward," *NTS* 7 (1960-1961): 198-219.

5034   J. D. M. Derrett, "Fresh Light on St. Luke 16: II. Dives and Lazarus and the Preceding Sayings," *NTS* 7 (1960-1961): 364-80.

5035   Francis E. Williams, "Is Almsgiving the Point of the 'Unjust Steward'?" *JBL* 83 (1964): 293-97.

5036   Bernard B. Scott, "A Master's Praise: Luke 16:1-8," *Bib* 64 (1983): 173-88.

5037   John S. Kloppenborg, "The Dishonoured Master (Luke 16:1-8a)," *Bib* 70/4 (1989): 474-95.

5038   W. R. G. Loader, "Jesus and the Rogue in Luke 16:1-8a: The Parable of the Unjust Steward," *RB* 96 (1989): 518-32.

5039   Douglas M. Parrott, "The Dishonest Steward and Luke's Special Parable Collection," *NTS* 37 (1991): 499-515.

5040   Mary A. Beavis, "Ancient Slavery as an Interpretive Context for the New Testament Servant Parables with Special Reference to the Unjust Steward," *JBL* 111 (1992): 37-54.

5041   Thomas Hoeren, "Das Gleichnis vom ungerechten Verwalter (Lukas 16.1-8a)--zugleich ein Beitrag zur Geschichte der Restschuldbefreiung," *NTS* 41 (1995): 620-29.

5042   David T. Landry and B. May, "Honor Restored: New Light on the Parable of the Prudent Steward," *JBL* 119 (2000): 287-309.

16:1-7

5043   H. Preisker, "Lukas 16,1-7," *TLZ* 74 (1949): 85-92.

5044   H. Drexler, "Zu Lukas 16,1-7," *ZNW* 58 (1967): 286-88.

16:1-3

5045   A. King, "The Parable of the Unjust Steward," *ET* 50 (1938-1939): 474-76.

16:1

5046   Helen R. Graham, "Once there Was a Rich Man . . . : Five 'Rich Man' Stories in Luke," *BibTo* 26 (1988): 98-103.

16:3-25

5047   R. P. Casey, "An Early Armenian Fragment of Luke xvi.3-25," *JTS* 36 (1935): 70-73.

16:5-7

5048   G. Gander, "Le procédé de l'économe infidèle, décrit Luc 16:5-7, est-il répréhensible ou louable?" *VC* 27/28 (1953): 128-41.

16:6

5049   J. D. M. Derrett, "Take Thy Bond . . . and Write Fifty (Luke xvi.6): The Nature of the Bond," *JTS* 23 (1972): 438-40.

16:8-53

5050   Gregorio Ruiz, "El Clamor de las Piedras (Lk. 19:40; Hab 2:11): el Reino Choca con la Ciudad Injusta en la Fiesta de Ramos," *EE* 59/230 (1984): 297-312.

16:8-9

5051   A. Maillot, "Notules sur Luc 16:8-9," *ÉTR* 44 (1969): 127-30.

16:8

5052   I. Howard Marshall, "Luke xvi.8: Who Commended the Unjust Steward?" *JTS* 19 (1968): 617-19.

5053   Günther Schwarz, " . . . lobte den betrügerischen Verwalter? (Lukas 16,8s)," *BZ* 18 (1974): 94-95.

5054   Michael G. Steinhauser, "Noah in His Generation: An Allusion in Luke 16,8b 'εἰς τὴν γενεὰν τὴν ἑαυτῶν'," *ZNW* 79 (1988): 11-57.

5055   C. S. Mann, "Unjust Steward or Prudent Manager?" *ET* 102 (1990-1991): 234-35.

16:9-13

5056   A.-L. Descamps, "La composition littéraire de Luc xvi.9-13," *NovT* 1 (1956): 47-53.

5057   P. Rüger, "*Mamōnas*," *ZNW* 64 (1973): 127-31.

16:9-11

5058   P. Colella, "De Mamona iniquitatis," *RBib* 19 (1971): 427-28.

16:9

5059   J. C. Wansey, "The Parable of the Unjust Steward: An Interpretation," *ET* 47 (1935-1936): 39-40.

5060   O. Hof, "Luthers Auslegung von Lukas 16,9," *EvT* 8 (1948-1949): 151-66.

5061   P. Colella, "Zu Lk 16,9," *ZNW* 64 (1973): 124-26.

5062   Helen R. Graham, "Once there Was a Rich Man . . . : Five 'Rich Man' Stories in Luke," *BibTo* 26 (1988): 98-103.

16:13

5063   Hans C. Brennecke, " 'Niemand kann zwei Herren dienen': Bemerkungen zur Auslegung von Mt 6:24/Lk 16:13 in der Alten Kirche," *ZNW* 88 (1997): 157-69.

16:15

5064   Thomas E. Schmidt, "Burden, Barrier, Blasphemy: Wealth in Matt. 6:33, Luke 14:33, and Luke 16:15," *TriJ* 9/2 (1988): 171-89.

16:16-18

5065   E. Bammel, "Is Luke 16,16-18 of Baptist Provenience?" *HTR* 51 (1958): 101-106.

16:16

5066   Frederick W. Danker, "Luke 16:16: An Opposition Logion," *JBL* 77 (1958): 231-43.

5067   David R. Catchpole, "On Doing Violence to the Kingdom," *JTSA* 25 (1978): 50-61.

5068   B. E. Thiering, "Are the 'Violent Men' False Teachers?" *NovT* 21/4 (1979): 293-97.

5069   J. B. Cortés and F. M. Gatti, "On the Meaning of Luke 16:16," *JBL* 106 (1987): 247-59.

5070   Ben Witherington, "Jesus and the Baptist: Two of a Kind?" *SBLSP* 18 (1988): 225-44.

5071   Stephen Llewelyn, "The Traditionsgeschichte of Matt 11:12-13, par Luke 16:16," *NovT* 36 (1994): 330-49.

16:18

5072   Gerhard Schneider, "Jesu Wort über die Ehescheidung in der Überlieferung des Neuen Testaments," *TTZ* 80 (1971): 65-87.

5073   A.-L. Descamps, "Les textes évangéliques sur le mariage," *RTL* 9 (1978): 259-86.

5074 Augustine Stock, "Matthean Divorce Texts," *BTB* 8/1 (1978): 24-33.

5075 Charles C. Ryrie, "Biblical Teaching on Divorce and Remarriage," *GTJ* 3/2 (1982): 177-92.

5076 B. N. Wambacq, "Matthieu 5,31-32: Possibilité de Divorce ou Obligation de Rompre une Union Illiégitime," *NRT* 104/1 (1982): 34-49.

5077 Werner Stenger, "Zur Rekonstruktion eines Jesusworts anhand der synoptischen Ehescheidungslogien (Mt 5,32; 19,9; Lk 16,18; Mk 10,11f)," *K* 26 (1984): 194-205.

5078 John J. Kilgallen, "The Purpose of Luke's Divorce Text (16,18)," *Bib* 76 (1995): 229-38.

5079 Duane Warden, "The Words of Jesus on Divorce," *RQ* 39 (1997): 141-53.

16:19-31

5080 J. Maiworm, "Umgekehrte Gleichnisse," *BK* 10 (1955): 82-85.

5081 Henry J. Cadbury, "A Proper Name For Dives," *JBL* 81 (1962): 399-402.

5082 Kendrick Grobel, "Whose Name Was Neves," *NTS* 10 (1963-1964): 373-82.

5083 W. P. Huie, "The Poverty of Abundance. From Text to Sermon on Luke 16:19-31," *Int* 22 (1968): 403-20.

5084 Otto Glombitza, "Der reiche Mann und der arme Lazarus," *NovT* 12 (1970): 166-80.

5085 Augustin George, "La parabole du riche et de Lazare (Lc 16)," *AsSeign* NS 57 (1971): 80-93.

5086 Josef Zmijewski, "Die Eschatologiereden Lk 21 und Lk 17. Überlegungen zum Verständnis und zur Einordnung der lukanischen Eschatologie," *BibL* 14 (1973): 30-40.

5087 Gerhard Sellin, "Gleichnisstrukturen," *LB* 31 (1974): 89-115.

5088 E. Pax, "Der Reiche und der arme Lazarus. Eine Milieustudie," *SBFLA* 25 (1975): 254-68.

5089 Thorwald Lorenzen, "A Biblical Meditation on Luke 16,19-31," *ET* 87 (1975-1976): 39-45.

5090   E. S. Wehrli, "Luke 16:19-31," *Int* 31 (1977): 276-80.

5091   Franz Schnider and Werner Stenger, "Die offene Tür und die unüberschreitbare Kluft. Strukturanalytische Überlegungen zum Gleichnis vom reichen Mann und armen Lazarus," *NTS* 25 (1978-1979): 273-83.

5092   André Feuillet, "La parabole du mauvais riche et du pauvre Lazare (Luc 16:19-31) antithèse de la parabole de l'intendant astucieux (Luc 16:1-9)," *NRT* 101 (1979): 212-23.

5093   J. Toy, "The Rich Man and Lazarus," *ET* 91 (1979-1980): 274-75.

5094   H. J. L. Jensen, "Diesseits und jenseits des Raumes eines Textes: Textsemiotische Bemerkungen zur Erzählung 'Vom reichen Mann und armen Lazarus'," *LB* 47 (1980): 39-60.

5095   M. Roy, "Jugement et sanction. Matthieu 25:31-46; Luc 15:11-32; 16:19-31," *Chr* 28 (1981): 440-49.

5096   J. P. Sauzède, "Une série pour le Carême," *ÉTR* 58 (1983): 59-71.

5097   Vincent Tanghe, "Abraham, Son Fils et Son Envoyé (Luc 16:19-31)," *RB* 91/4 (1984): 557-77.

5098   R. F. Hock, "Lazarus and Micyllus: Greco-Roman Backgrounds to Luke 16:19-31," *JBL* 106 (1987): 447-63.

5099   J. Osei-Bonsu, "The Intermediate State in Luke-Acts," *IBS* 9 (1987): 115-30.

5100   Roger L. Omanson, "Lazarus and Simon," *BT* 40 (1989): 416-19.

5101   Eckart Reinmuth, "Ps-Philo, Liber Antiquitatum Biblicarum 33,1-5 und die Auslegung der Parabel Lk. 16:19-31," *NovT* 31 (1989): 16-38.

5102   Walter Vogels, "Having or Longing: A Semiotic Analysis of Luke 16:19-31," *ÉgT* 20/1 (1989): 27-46.

5103   Richard J. Bauckham, "The Rich Man and Lazarus: The Parable and the Parallels," *NTS* 37 (1991): 225-46.

5104   Donald L. Bretherton, "Lazarus of Bethany: Resurrection or Resuscitation?" *ET* 104 (1993): 169-73.

5105   J. G. Griffiths, "Cross-cultural Eschatology with Dives and Lazarus," *ET* 105 (1993): 7-12.

5106   George W. Knight, "Luke 16:19-31: The Rich Man and Lazarus," *RevExp* 94 (1997): 277-83.

5107   J. Mary Luti, "Send Lazarus," *CC* 115 (1998): 819.

5108   Charles A. Ray, "The Rich Man and Lazarus (Luke 16:19-31)," *TEd* 56 (1997): 77-84.

16:19-25

5109   Günter Scholz, "Aesthetische Beobachtungen am Gleichnis vom reichen Mann und armen Lazarus und von drei anderen Gleichnissen," *LB* 43 (1978): 67-74.

16:19-21

5110   Erhardt Güttgemanns, "Narrative Analyse Synoptischer Texte," *LB* 25/26 (1973): 50-73.

16:19

5111   L. T. Lefort, "Le nom du mauvais riche Lc 16,19 et la tradition copte," *ZNW* 37 (1938): 65-72.

5112   Henry J. Cadbury, "A Proper Name for Dives," *JBL* 81 (1962): 399-402.

5113   Henry J. Cadbury, "The Name for Dives," *JBL* 84 (1965): 73.

16:22-31

5114   Edward G. Kettner, "Time, Eternity, and the Intermediate State," *CJ* 12/3 (1986): 90-100.

16:22

5115   Helen R. Graham, "Once there Was a Rich Man . . . : Five 'Rich Man' Stories in Luke," *BibTo* 26 (1988): 98-103.

16:26

5116   Eric F. F. Bishop, "A Yawning Chasm," *EQ* 45 (1973): 3-5.

17:1-19

5117   Eugene C. Kreider, "The Politics of God: The Way to the Cross," *WW* 6/4 (1986): 453-62.

17:1-10

5118   R. M. Shelton, "Luke 17:1-10," *Int* 31 (1977): 280-85.

17:2

5119   Jacques Schlosser, "Lk 17,2 und die Logienquelle," *SNTU-A* 8 (1983): 70-78.

17:3-4

5120   David R. Catchpole, "Reproof and Reconciliation in the Q Community: A Study of the Tradition History of Mt 18,15-17.21-22/Lk 17,3-4," *SNTU-A* 8 (1983): 79-90.

17:3

5121   Gerhard Barth, "Auseinandersetzungen um die Kirchenzucht im Umkreis des Matthäusevangeliums," *ZNW* 69 (1978): 158-77.

5122   William R. Domeris, "Biblical Perspectives on Forgiveness," *JTSA* 54 (1986): 48-50.

17:5-10

5123   Augustin George, "La foi des apôtres (Lc 17)," *AsSeign* NS 58 (1974): 68-77.

5124   Ben Witherington, "Jesus the Savior of the Least, the Last, and the Lost," *QR* 15 (1995): 197-211.

17:6

5125   Günther Schwarz, "Πίστιν ὡς κόκκον σινάπεως," *BibN* 25 (1984): 27-35.

5126   Ferdinand Hahn, "Jesu Wort vom bergeversetzenden Glauben," *ZNW* 76 (1985): 149-69.

5127   J. D. M. Derrett, "Moving Mountains and Uprooting Trees," *BibO* 30 (1988): 231-44.

17:7-10

5128   Paul S. Minear, "A Note on Luke 17:7-10," *JBL* 93 (1974): 82-87.

17:10

5129   A. Marcus Ward, "Uncomfortable Words: IV. Unprofitable Servants," *ET* 81/7 (1969-1970): 200-203.

5130   John J. Kilgallen, "What Kind of Servants Are We?" *Bib* 63 (1982): 549-51.

5131   David P. Scaer, "Sanctification in Lutheran Theology," *CTQ* 49/2-3 (1985): 181-97.

17:11-19

5132　J. Bours, "Vom dankbaren Samariter. Eine Meditation über Lk 17:11-19," *BibL* 1 (1960): 193-98.

5133　E. Galbiati, "Esegesi degli Evangeli festivi," *BibO* 2 (1960): 171-73.

5134　Otto Glombitza, "Der dankbare Samariter," *NovT* 11 (1969): 241-46.

5135　H. D. Betz, "The Cleansing of the Ten Lepers (Luke 17:11-19)," *JBL* 90 (1971): 314-28.

5136　É. Charpentier, "L'etranger appelé au salut (Lc 17)," *AsSeign* NS 59 (1974): 68-79.

5137　J. W. Drane, "Simon the Samaritan and the Lucan Concept of Salvation History," *EQ* 47 (1975): 131-37.

5138　T. McCaughey, "Paradigms of Faith in the Gospel of St. Luke," *ITQ* 45 (1978): 177-84.

5139　M. J. Kingston, "Modern-day Leprosy," *ET* 92 (1980-1981): 371.

5140　J. D. M. Derrett, "Gratitude and the Ten Lepers," *DR* 113 (1995): 79-95.

5141　Dennis Hamm, "What the Samaritan Leper Sees: The Narrative Christology of Luke 17:11-19," *CBQ* 56 (1994): 273-87.

5142　Ben Witherington, "Jesus the Savior of the Least, the Last, and the Lost," *QR* 15 (1995): 197-211.

17:11

5143　G. Bouwman, "Samaria in Lucas-Handelingen," *Bij* 34 (1973): 40-59.

17:20-18:8

5144　André Feuillet, "La double venue du Règne de Dieu et du Fils de l'homme en Luc 17:20-18:8," *RT* 81 (1981): 5-33.

17:20-37

5145　A. Strobel, "In dieser Nacht (Luk 17:34): Zu einer älteren Form der Erwartung in Luk 17:20-37," *ZTK* 58/1 (1961): 16-29.

17:20-21

5146 Alexander Rüstow, "*Entos umōn estin*: zur Deutung von Lukas 17,20-21," *ZNW* 51 (1960): 197-224.

5147 Franz Mußner, "Wann kommt das Reich Gottes? Die Antwort Jesu Nach Lk. 17:20b-21," *BZ* 6/1 (1962): 107-11.

5148 K. S. Proctor, "Luke 17,20.21," *BT* 33 (1982): 245.

5149 Harald Riesenfeld, "Gudsriket - här eller där, mitt ibland människor eller inom dem? Till Luk 17:20-21," *SEÅ* 47 (1982): 93-101.

5150 Harald Riesenfeld, "Le règne de Dieu, parmi vous ou en vouse?" *RB* 36 (1991): 190-98.

5151 Günther Schwarz, "Οὐκ . . . μετὰ παρατηρήσεως?" *BibN* 59 (1991): 45-48.

17:20

5152 A. Strobel, "Die Passa-Erwartung als unchristliches Problem in Lukas 17,20f.," *ZNW* 49 (1958): 157-96.

5153 A. Strobel, "A Merx über Lc 17:20f," *ZNW* 51/1-2 (1960): 133-34.

5154 A. Strobel, "Zu Lk. 17:20f," *BZ* 7 (1963): 111-13.

17:21

5155 G. Smith, "The Kingdom of God is Within You," *ET* 43 (1931-1932): 378-79.

5156 P. M. S. Allen, "Luke 17:21," *ET* 49 (1937-1938): 476-77; 50 (1938-1939): 233-35.

5157 A. Sledd, "The Interpretation of Luke 17,21," *ET* 50 (1938-1939): 235-37.

5158 C. H. Roberts, "The Kingdom of Heaven (Lk. XVI1.21)," *HTR* 41 (1948): 1-8.

5159 Richard Sneed, "The Kingdom of God is Within You (Lk. 17:21)," *CBQ* 24 (1962): 363-82.

5160 D. H. C. Read, "Christ Comes Unexpectedly," *ET* 98/1 (1986-1987): 21-22.

5161 J. Ramsey Michaels, "Almsgiving and the Kingdom Within: Tertullian on Luke 17:21," *CBQ* 60 (1998): 475-83.

17:22-37

5162   W. Powell, "The Days of the Son of Man," *ET* 67
        (1955-1956): 219.

17:22

5163   E. Ashby, "The Days of the Son of Man," *ET* 67
        (1955-1956): 124-25.

5164   E. Leaney, "The Days of the Son of Man (Luke xvii. 22),"
        ET 67 (1955-1956): 28-29.

5165   Matthew Black, "The Aramaic Dimension in Q with Notes
        on Luke 17:22, Matthew 24:26," *JSNT* 40 (1990): 33-41.

17:25

5166   D. Meyer, *"Polla pathein,"* *ZNW* 55 (1964): 132.

17:26-30

5167   Jacques Schlosser, "Les jours de Noé et de Lot: À propos
        de Luc, xvii,26-30," *RB* 80 (1973): 13-36.

5168   Norman Mundhenk, "Problems Involving Illustrations in
        Luke," *BT* 44 (1993): 247-48.

17:26-29

5169   Dieter Lührmann, "Noah and Lot (Lk 17,26-29): - ein
        Nachtrag," *ZNW* 63 (1972): 130-32.

17:33

5170   X. Léon-Dufour, "Luc 17:33," *RechSR* 69 (1981): 101-12.

17:34-35

5171   Clayton N. Jefford, "The Dangers of Lying in Bed: Luke
        17:34-35 and Parallels," *Forum* 5 (1989): 106-10.

17:34

5172   A. Strobel, "In dieser Nacht (Luk 17:34): Zu einer älteren
        Form der Erwartung in Luk 17:20-37," *ZTK* 58/1 (1961):
        16-29.

5173   J. D. M. Derrett, " 'On That Night': Luke 17:34,"
        EQ 68 (1996): 35-46.

17:37

5174   John P. Brown, "The Ark of the Covenant and the Temple
        of Janus," *BZ* 30/1 (1986): 20-35.

5175   Heinz O. Guenther, "When 'Eagles' Draw Together," *Forum* 5 (1989): 140-50.

18:1-18

5176   Gerhard Delling, "Das Gleichnis vom gottlosen Richter," *ZNW* 53 (1962): 1-25.

5177   R. Deschryver, "La parabole du juge malveillant," *RHPR* 48 (1968): 355-66.

5178   J. D. M. Derrett, "Law in the New Testament: The Parable of the Unjust Judge," *NTS* 18 (1971-1972): 178-91.

5179   Mary Zimmer, "A Fierce Mother and a Widow: Models of Persistence," *RevExp* 92 (1995): 89-93.

18:1-14

5180   Frank Stagg, "Luke's Theological Use of Parables," *RevExp* 94 (1997): 215-29.

18:1-8

5181   H. G. Meecham, "The Parable of the Unjust Judge," *ET* 57 (1945-1946): 300-307.

5182   Ceslaus Spicq, "La Parabole de la Veuve Obstinée et du Juge Inerte, aux Décisions Impromptues," *RB* 68 (1961): 68-90.

5183   C. E. B. Cranfield, "The Parable of the Unjust Judge and the Eschatology of Luke-Acts," *SJT* 16 (1963): 297-301.

5184   Augustin George, "La parabole du juge qui fait attendre le jugement (Lc 18)," *AsSeign* NS 60 (1975): 68-79.

5185   Henning Paulsen, "Die Witwe und der Richter (Lk 18,1-8)," *TGl* 74 (1984): 13-39.

5186   E. D. Freed, "The Parable of the Judge and the Widow," *NTS* 33 (1987): 38-60.

5187   John M. Hicks, "The Parable of the Persistent Widow," *RQ* 33/4 (1991): 209-23.

5188   François Bovon, "Apocalyptic Traditions in the Lukan Special Material: Reading Luke 18:1-8," *HTR* 90 (1997): 383-91.

5189   Ronald Goetz, "On Petitionary Prayer: Pleading with the Unjust Judge?" *CC* 114 (1997): 96-99.

5190 Jack T. Sanders, "The Criterion of Coherence and the Randomness of Charisma: Poring Through Some Aporias in the Jesus Tradition," *NTS* 44 (1998): 1-25.

5191 Ben Witherington, "Jesus the Savior of the Least, the Last, and the Lost," *QR* 15 (1995): 197-211.

18:2-7

5192 Hermann J. Vogt, "Die Witwe als Bild der Seele in der Exegese des Origenes," *TQ* 165/2 (1985): 105-18.

18:7

5193 Herman Ljungvik, "Zur Erklärung einer Lukas-Stelle," *NTS* 10 (1963-1964): 289-94.

5194 Albert Wifstrand, "Lukas 18:7," *NTS* 11 (1964-1965): 72-74.

5195 Alessandro Sacchi, "Pazienza di Dio e Ritardo Della Parousia," *RBib* 36 (1988): 299-327.

18:8

5196 David R. Catchpole, "The Son of Man's Search for Faith (Luke 18:8)," *NovT* 19 (1977): 81-104.

5197 K. H. Tyson, "Faith on Earth," *ET* 88 (1977): 111-12.

5198 Domingo Muñoz León, "Jesus y la apocaliptica pesimista (a proposito de Lc 18:8b y Mt 24:12)," *EB* 46/4 (1988): 457-95.

18:9-23

5199 J. Kodell, "Luke and the Children: The Beginning and End of the Great Interpolation (Luke 9:46-56; 18:9-23)," *CBQ* 49 (1987): 415-30.

18:9-14

5200 F. F. Bruce, "Justification by Faith in the Non-Pauline Writing of the N.T.," *EQ* 24 (191): 66-67.

5201 J. A. Colunga, "El fariseo y el publicano," *CuBí* 13 (1956): 136-38.

5202 E. Galbiati, "Esegesi degli Evangeli festivi," *BibO* 2 (1960): 169-71.

5203 É. Charpentier, "Le chrétien: un homme 'juste' ou 'justifié'? (Lc 18)," *AsSeign* NS II/61 (1972): 66-78.

5204   E. Neuhäusler, " 'Anstösse' zur Besinnung über das Gleichnis vom Pharisäer und Zöllner," *BibL* 13 (1972): 293-96.

5205   Erhardt Güttgemanns, "Narrative Analyse Synoptischer Texte," *LB* 25/26 (1973): 50-73.

5206   Martin Hengel, "Die ganz andere Gerechtigkeit: Bibelarbeit über Lk 18,9-14," *TBe* 5 (1974): 1-13.

5207   A. Biesinger, "Vorbild und Nachahmung. Imitations-psychologische und bibeltheologische Anmerkungen zu Lk 18:9-14," *BK* 32 (1977): 42-45.

5208   Helmut Merklein, " 'Dieser ging als Gerechter nach Hause ...' Das Gottesbild Jesu und die Haltung der Menschen nach Lk 18:9-14," *BK* 32 (1977): 34-42.

5209   Martin Völkel, " 'Freund der Zöllner und Sünder'," *ZNW* 69 (1978): 1-10.

5210   André Feuillet, "Le pharisien et le publicain (Luc 18:9-14). La manifestation de la miséricorde divine en Jésus Serviteur souffrant," *EV* 91 (1981): 657-65.

5211   P. Raffin, "Le pharisien et le publicain," *EV* 82 (1982): 260-61.

5212   S. Schmitz, "Psychologische Hilfen zum Verstehen biblischer Texte?" *BK* 38 (1983): 112-18.

5213   Ralph P. Martin, "Two Worshippers, One Way to God," *ET* 96 (1984-1985): 117-18.

5214   Marion C. Barnett, "Graceless Goodness, Forgiven Folly," *ChrM* 16/1 (1985): 25-27.

5215   Thorwald Lorenzen, "The Radicality of Grace: The Pharisee and the Tax Collector as a Parable of Jesus," *FM* 3/2 (1986): 66-75.

5216   John G. Strelan, "The Pharisee Lurking: Reflections on Luke 18:9-14," *LTJ* 20/2-3 (1986): 116-20.

5217   R. Krüger, "El desenmascaramiento de un despreciador prestigioso: Lectura semiótica de la parábola del fariseo y del publicano. Lucas 18,9-14," *RevB* 49 (1987): 155-67.

5218   F. Gerald Downing, "The Ambiguity of 'The Pharisee and the Toll-Collector' (Luke 18:9-14) in the Greco-Roman World of Late Antiquity," *CBQ* 54 (1992): 80-99.

5219   Fredrick C. Holmgren, "The Pharisee and the Tax Collector: Luke 18:9-14 and Deuteronomy 26:1-15," *Int* 48 (1994): 252-61.

5220   Ben Witherington, "Jesus the Savior of the Least, the Last, and the Lost," *QR* 15 (1995): 197-211.

18:10-14

5221   Gerhard Sellin, "Gleichnisstrukturen," *LB* 31 (1974): 89-115.

5222   F. Mahr, "Der Antipharisäer. Ein Kapitel 'Bibel verfremdet' zu Lk 18:10-14," *BK* 32 (1977): 47.

5223   Franz Schnider, "Ausschließen und ausgeschlossen werden. Beobachtungen zur Struktur des Gleichnisses vom Pharisäer und Zöllner Lk 18:10-14," *BZ* 24 (1980): 42-56.

5224   J. Warren Holleran, "The Saint and the Scoundrel," *BibTo* 25 (1987): 375-79.

5225   Eckhard Rau, "Jesu Auseinandersetzung mit Pharisäern über seine Zuwendung zu Sünderinnen und Sündern: Lk 15,11-32 und Lk 18,10-14a als Worte des historischen Jesus," *ZNW* 89 (1998): 5-29.

18:12

5226   Felix Böhl, "Das Fasten an Montagen und Donnerstagen: Zur Geschichte einer Pharisäischen Praxis (Lk 18,12)," *BZ* 31 (1987): 247-50.

18:13

5227   Robert G. Hoerber, "God Be Merciful to Me a Sinner: A Note on Luke 18:13," *CTM* 33 (1962): 283-86.

18:14

5228   Patrick P. Saydon, "Some Biblico-Liturgical Passages Reconsidered," *MeliT* 18/1 (1966): 10-17.

5229   J. B. Cortés, "The Greek Text of Luke 18:14a: A Contribution to the Method of Reasoned Eclecticism," *CBQ* 46 (1984): 255-73.

18:15-19:10

5230   Stephen Fowl, "Receiving the kingdom of God as a child: Children and riches in Luke 18:15ff," *NTS* 39 (1993): 153-58.

18:15-17

5231   Daniel Patte, "Jesus' Pronouncement about Entering the Kingdom Like a Child: A Structural Exegesis," *Semeia* 29 (1983): 3-42.

18:17

5232   F. A. Schilling, "What Means the Saying about Receiving the Kingdom of God as a Little Child (τὴν βασιλείαν τοῦ θεοῦ ὡς παιδίον)? Mark 10:15; Luke 18:17," *ET* 77 (1965-1966): 56-58.

18:18-30

5233   Richard A. Ward, "Pin-Points and Panoramas: The Preacher's Use of the Aorist," *ET* 71 (1959-1960): 267-70.

5234   B. Celada, "Distribución de los bienes y seguimiento de Jesús, según Lucas 18:18-30," *CuBi* 26 (1969): 337-40.

5235   Claude Coulot, "La structuration de la péricope de l'homme riche et ses différentes lectures (Mc 10:17-31; Mt 19:16-30; Lc 18:18-30)," *RevSR* 56 (1982): 240-1.

5236   C. M. Swezey, "Luke 18:18-30," *Int* 37 (1983): 68-73.

5237   Jean P. Gérard, "Les riches dans la communauté lucanienne," *ETL* 71 (1995): 71-106.

18:18-23

5238   J. Williams, "The Rich Young Ruler and St. Paul," *ET* 41 (1929-1930): 139-40.

5239   Gregory Murray, "The Rich Young Man," *DR* 103 (1985): 144-46.

5240   Reginald H. Fuller, "The Decalogue in the NT," *Int* 43/3 (1989): 243-55.

18:18-19

5241   John W. Wenham, " 'Why Do You Ask Me about the Good?' A Study of the Relation between Text and Source Criticism," *NTS* 28 (1982): 116-25.

18:18

5242   P. Huuhtanen, "Die Perikope vom 'reichen Jüngling' unter Berücksichtigung der Akszentuierungen des Lukas," *SNTU-A* 7 (1976): 79-98.

18:25

5243   B. Celada, "Más acerca del camello y la aguja," *CuBí* 26 (1969): 157-58.

5244   Helen R. Graham, "Once there Was a Rich Man . . . : Five 'Rich Man' Stories in Luke," *BibTo* 26 (1988): 98-103.

5245   José O'Callaghan, "Examen critico de Mt 19,24," *Bib* 69 (1988): 401-405.

18:29-30

5246   J. Garcia Burillo, "El ciento por uno (Mc. 10:29-30 par)," *EB* 36 (1977): 173-203.

18:31-43

5247   E. Galbiati, "Esegesi degli Evangeli festivi," *BibO* 4 (1962): 57-63.

18:33

5248   John M. Perry, "The Three Days in the Synoptic Passion Predictions," *CBQ* 48/4 (1986): 637-54.

18:35-43

5249   T. McCaughey, "Paradigms of Faith in the Gospel of St. Luke," *ITQ* 45 (1978): 177-84.

5250   Roland Meynet, "Au coeur du texte. Analyse rhétorique de l'aveugle de Jéricho selon saint Luc," *NRT* 103 (1981): 696-710.

19:1-11

5251   W. Hülsbusch, "Begegnung vor Jerusalem," *BibL* 15 (1974): 220-25.

19:1-10

5252   W. P. Loewe, "Towards an Interpretation of Lk 19:1-10," *CBQ* 36 (1974): 321-31.

5253   F. W. Hobbie, "Luke 19:1-10," *Int* 31 (1977): 285-90.

5254   Walter Vogels, "Structural Analysis and Pastoral Work: The Story of Zacchaeus," *LV* 33 (1978): 482-92.

5255   Martin Völkel, " 'Freund der Zöllner und Sünder'," *ZNW* 69 (1978): 1-10.

5256   R. C. White, "Vindication for Zacchaeus," *ET* 91 (1979-1980): 21.

5257   J. O'Hanlon, "The Story of Zacchaeus and the Lukan Ethic," *JSNT* 12 (1981): 2-26.

5258   Eugene A. LaVerdiere, "Zacchaeus," *Emmanuel* 90 (1984): 461-65.

5259   Dennis Hamm, "Zacchaeus Revisited Once More: A Story of Vindication or Conversion?" *Bib* 2 (1991): 248-1.

5260   Robert F. O'Toole, "The Literary Form of Luke 19:1-10," *JBL* 110 (1991): 107-16.

5261   D. A. S. Ravens, "Zacchaeus: The Final Part of a Lucan Triptych," *JSNT* 41 (1991): 19-32.

5262   Jean P. Gérard, "Les riches dans la communauté lucanienne," *ETL* 71 (1995): 71-106. '

5263   Michael J. Hassold, "Eyes To See: Reflections On Luke 19:1-10," *LTJ* 29 (1995): 68-73.

5264   Robert C. Tannehill, "The Story of Zacchaeus as Rhetoric: Luke 19:1-10," *Semeia* 64 (1994): 201-21.

5265   Ben Witherington, "Jesus the Savior of the Least, the Last, and the Lost," *QR* 15 (1995): 197-211.

19:2

5266   B. Ahern, "The Zacchaeus Incident," *BibTo* 25 (1987): 348-51.

19:3

5267   Günther Schwarz, "'Οτι τῇ ἡλικίᾳ μικρὸς ἦν," *BibN* 8 (1979): 23-24.

19:8

5268   Nigel M. Watson, "Was Zacchaeus Really Reforming?" *ET* 77 (1965-1966): 282-85.

5269   A. P. Salom, "Was Zacchaeus Really Reforming?" *ET* 78 (1966-1967): 87.

5270   A. J. Kerr, "Zacchaeus's Decision to Make Fourfold Restitution," *ET* 98/3 (1986-1987): 68-71.

5271   B. W. Grindlay, "Zacchaeus and David," *ET* 99 (1987-1988): 46-47.

5272   Dennis Hamm, "Luke 19:8 Once Again: Does Zacchaeus Defend or Resolve?" *JBL* 107 (1988): 431-37.

5273   Alan C. Mitchell, "Zacchaeus Revisited: Luke 19:8 as a Defense," *Bib* 71/2 (1990): 153-76.

5274   Alan C. Mitchell, "The Use of *Sykophantein* in Luke 19:8: Further Evidence for Zacchaeus's Defense," *Bib* 72/4 (1991): 546-47.

19:10

5275   D. Howell-Jones, "Lost and Found," *ET* 92 (1980-1981): 371-72.

19:11-27

5276   R. W. Resenhöfft, "Jesu Gleichnis von den Talenten, ergänzt durch die Lukas-Fassung," *NTS* 26 (1979-1980): 318-31.

5277   Jack T. Sanders, "The Parable of the Pounds and Lucan Anti-Semitism," *TS* 42 (1981): 660-68.

5278   Luke T. Johnson, "The Lukan Kingship Parable," *NovT* 24 (1982): 139-59.

19:12-27

5279   Gerhard Sellin, "Gleichnisstrukturen," *LB* 31 (1974): 89-115.

5280   F. D. Weinert, "The Parable of the Throne Claimant Reconsidered," *CBQ* 39 (1977): 505-14.

19:11-17

5281   Andrew Goddard and Caroline Klopfenstein, "Ellul et le réalisme Politique du Christ," *FV* 93 (1994): 83-93.

19:24-40

5282   O. Samuel, "Die Regierungsgewalt des Wortes Gottes," *EvT* 3 (1936): 1-3.

19:26

5283   G. Lindeskog, "Logia-Studien," *ST* 4 (1951-191): 129-89.

19:27

5284   J. D. M. Derrett, "A Horrid Passage in Luke Explained,"
        ET 97 (1985-1986): 136-38.

19:28-21:38

5285   C. R. Hutcheon, " 'God is with Us': The Temple in Luke-
        Acts," *SVTQ* 44 (2000): 3-33.

19:28-20:19

5286   Jan W. Doeve, "Purification du Temple et Desséchement
        du Figuier," *NTS* 1 (1954-1955): 297-308.

19:28-44

5287   Brent Kinman, "Parousia, Jesus' 'A-Triumphal' Entry, and
        the Fate of Jerusalem (Luke 19:28-44)," *JBL* 118 (1999):
        279-94.

5288   Brent Kinman, "The 'A-Triumphal' Entry (Luke
        19:28-48): Historical Backgrounds, Theological Motifs
        and the Purpose of Luke," *TynB* 45 (1994): 189-93.

19:28-38

5289   T. L. Davies, "Was Jesus Compelled?" *ET* 42
        (1930-1931): 16-27.

5290   R. S. Frayn, "Was Jesus Compelled?" *ET* 43 (1931-1932):
        381-82.

5291   J. Meikle, "Was Jesus Compelled?" *ET* 43 (1931-1932):
        288.

5292   Brian A. Mastin, "The Date of the Triumphal Entry," *NTS*
        16 (1969-1970): 76-82.

5293   J. D. M. Derrett, "Law in the New Testament: The Palm
        Sunday Colt," *NovT* 13 (1971): 241-58.

19:31-34

5294   Randall Buth, "Luke 19:31-34, Mishnaic Hebrew, and
        Bible Translation: Is *Kyrioi Tou Polou* Singular?" *JBL*
        104/4 (1985): 680-85.

19:31

5295   Henry Osborn, "A Quadruple Quote in the Triumphal
        Entry Account in Warao," *BT* 18/1 (1967): 301-21.

19:35-40

5296   N. Fernández Marcos, "La unción de Salomón y la entrada
        de Jesús en Jérusalén: 1 Re 1,33-40/Lc 19,35-40," *Bib* 68
        (1987): 89-97.

19:38

5297   Heinrich Baarlink, "Friede im Himmel: die lukanische
        Redaktion von Lk 19,38 und ihre Deutung," *ZNW* 76/3
        (1985): 170-86.

19:40

5298   Gregorio Ruiz, "El Clamor de las Piedras (Lk. 19:40; Hab
        2:11): el Reino Choca con la Ciudad Injusta en la Fiesta de
        Ramos," *EE* 59/230 (1984): 297-312.

5299   Brent Kinman, " 'The stones will cry out' (Luke
        19:40)--Joy or Judgment?" *Bib* 75 (1994): 232-35.

19:41-44

5300   Brent Kinman, "Lucan Eschatology and the Missing Fig
        Tree," *JBL* 113 (1994): 669-78.

19:41

5301   Stephen Voorwinde, "Jesus' Tears--Human or Divine?"
        RTR 56 (1997): 68-81.

19:44

5302   Kairos Theologians, "The Kairos Document--Challenge to
        the Church: A Theological Comment on the Political
        Crisis in South Africa," *JTSA* 53 (1985): 61-81.

19:45-46

5303   Étienne Trocmé, "L'expulsion des marchands du Temple,"
        NTS 15 (1968-1969): 1-22.

20:1

5304   Christoph Burchard, "Fußnoten zum neutestamentlichen
        Griechisch II," *ZNW* 69 (1978): 143-57.

20:9-19

5305   H. J. Klauck, "Das Gleichnis vom Mord im Weinberg (Mk
        12,1-12; Mt 21,33-46; Lk 20,9-19)," *BibL* 11 (1970):
        118-45.

5306   J. A. T. Robinson, "The Parable of the Wicked Husbandmen: A Test of Synoptic Relationships," *NTS* 21 (1974-1975): 443-61.

5307   Klyne R. Snodgrass, "The Parable of the Wicked Husbandmen: Is the Gospel of Thomas Version the Original?" *NTS* 21 (1974-1975): 142-44.

5308   Robert W. Bertram, "The Storyteller Visits the Vineyard," *CC* 106 (1989): 255-56.

20:9-18

5309   John D. Crossan, "The Parable of the Wicked Husbandmen," *JBL* 90/4 (1971): 451-65.

5310   Donald L. Jones, "The Title υἱὸς θεοῦ in Acts," *SBLSP* 15 (1985): 451-63.

20:13

5311   Alfredo Scattolon, "L'agapêtos sinottico nella luce della tradizione giudaica," *RBib* 26 (1978): 2-32.

20:18

5312   Robert Doran, "Luke 20:18: A Warrior's Boast?" *CBQ* 45 (1983): 61-67.

20:20-26

5313   David T. Owen-Ball, "Rabbinic Rhetoric and the Tribute Passage," *NovT* 35 (1993): 1-14.

20:25

5314   Charles H. Giblin, " 'The Things of God' in the Questions Concerning Tribute to Caesar," *CBQ* 33/4 (1971): 510-27.

20:27-40

5315   Sebastián Bartina, "Jesús y los saduceos: 'El Dios de Abraham, de Isaac y de Jacob' es 'El que hace existir'," *EB* 21 (1962): 151-60.

5316   John J. Kilgallen, "The Sadducees and Resurrection From the Dead: Luke 20:27-40," *Bib* 67/4 (1986): 478-95.

20:27-38

5317   É. Charpentier, "Tous vivent pour lui," *AsSeign* NS 63 (1971): 81-94.

20:34-36

5318   C. Monanti, "Lc 20,34-36 e la filiazione divina degli uomini," *BibO* 13 (1971): 255-75.

20:37-38

5319   D. M. Cohn-Sherbok, "Jesus' Defence of the Resurrection of the Dead," *JSNT* 11 (1981): 64-73.

20:38

5320   M. Trowitzsch, "Gemeinschaft der Lebenden und der Toten. Lk. 20:38 als Text der Ekklesiologie," *ZTK* 79 (1982): 212-29.

20:41-44

5321   Fritz Neugebauer, "Die Davidsohnsfrage (Mark xii.35-7 parr) und der Menschensohn," *NTS* 21 (1974-1975): 81-108.

21-24

5322   Paul Winter, "The Treatment of his Sources by the Third Evangelist in Luke XXI-XXIV," *ST* 8 (1954-1955): 138-72.

21:1-4

5323   A. G. Wright, "The Widow's Mites: Praise or Lament? A Matter of Context," *CBQ* 44 (1982): 256-65.

5324   Gregory Murray, "Did Luke Use Mark?" *DR* 104 (1986): 268-71.

21:5-36

5325   Charles Perrot, "Essai sur le Discours eschatologique (Mc. XIII,1-37; Mt. XXIV,1-36; Lc. XXI,5-36)," *RechSR* 47 (1959): 481-514.

5326   A. del Agua Pérez, "Derás Lucano de Mc 13 a la luz de su 'teologia del Reino' Lc 21,5-36," *EB* 39 (1981): 285-313.

21:5-35

5327   Hugo Lattanzi, "Eschatologici Sermonis Domini Logica Interpretatio," *Div* 11/1 (1967): 71-92.

21:12-15

5328   William L. Schutter, "Luke 12:11-12/21:12-15 and the Composition of Luke-Acts," *EGLMBS* 10 (1990): 236-50.

21:14-15

5329   Matthew Mahoney, "Luke 21:14-15: Editorial Rewriting or Authenticity?" *ITQ* 47/3 (1980): 220-38.

21:20-24

5330   F. Flückiger, "Luk. 21,20-24 und die Zerstörung Jerusalems," *TZ* 28 (1972): 385-90.

5331   Gordon D. Fee, "A Text-Critical Look at the Synoptic Problem," *NovT* 22/1 (1980): 12-28.

21:20-22

5332   Craig R. Koester, "The Origin and Significance of the Flight to Pella Tradition," *CBQ* 51 (1989): 90-106.

21:25-36

5333   Johann H. Heinz, "The 'Summer That Will Never End': Luther's Longing For the 'Dear Last Day' in His Sermon on Luke 21 (1531)," *AUSS* 23 (1985): 181-86.

5334   Elizabeth Achtemeier, "Luke 21:25-36," *Int* 48 (1994): 401-404.

21:25-33

5335   E. Galbiati, "L'avvento liberatore (Lc. 21:25-33)," *BibO* 3 (1961): 222-24.

21:28

5336   A. Salas, " 'Vuestra liberación está cerca' (Lc 21,28): Dimension liberacionista del acto redentor," *CuBí* 31 (1974): 157-63.

21:29-34

5337   William H. Willimon, "Take Heed to Yourselves," *CC* 103/37 (1986): 1085-86.

21:29

5338   M. Pérez Fernández, " 'prope est aestas'," *VD* 46 (1968): 361-69.

21:31-34

5339   William J. Tobin, "The Petrine Primacy Evidence of the Gospels," *LV* 23/1 (1968): 27-70.

21:32

5340 Charles L. Holman, "The Idea of an Imminent Parousia in the Synoptic Gospels," *SBT* 3 (1973): 15-31.

21:34

5341 Günther Schwarz, "μήποτε βαρηθῶσιν ὑμῶν αἱ καρδίαι," *BibN* 10 (1979): 40.

21:36

5342 Martino Conti, "La via della beatitudine e della rovina secondo il Salmo I," *Ant* 61/1 (1986): 3-39.

22-23

5343 A. M. Perry, "Luke's Disputed Passion-Source," *ET* 46 (1934-1935): 256-60.

5344 M. Kiddle, "The Passion Narrative in St. Luke's Gospel," *JTS* 36 (1935): 267-80.

5345 V. Monsarrat, "Le récit de la Passion: un enseignement pour le disciple fidèle. Luc 22-23," *FV* 81 (1982): 40-47.

22:1-38

5346 X. Léon-Dufour, "Das letzte Mahl Jesu und die testamentarische Tradition nach Lk 22," *ZKT* 103 (1981): 33-55.

22:3

5347 Heinrich Baarlink, "Friede im Himmel: die lukanische Redaktion von Lk 19,38 und Ihre Deutung," *ZNW* 76/3 (1985): 170-86.

22:7-30

5348 M. Sabbe, "The Footwashing in John 13 and Its Relation to the Synoptic Gospels," *ETL* 58 (1982): 279-308.

22:7-13

5349 Joel B. Green, "Preparation for Passover: A Question of Redactional Technique," *NovT* 29 (1987): 305-19.

22:7

5350 Arthur G. Arnott, " 'The First Day of the Unleavened . . . ' Mt 26.17, Mk 14.12, Lk 22.7," *BT* 35 (1984): 235-38.

22:14-38

5351   Dennis M. Sweetland, "The Lord's Supper and the Lukan Community," *BTB* 13 (1983): 23-27.

5352   William S. Kurz, "Luke 22:14-38 and Greco-Roman and Biblical Farewell Addresses," *JBL* 104 (1985): 251-68.

5353   Robert J. Karris, "Women and Discipleship in Luke," *CBQ* 56 (1994): 1-20.

22:14-23

5354   Eugene A. LaVerdiere, "Discourse at the Last Supper," *BibTo* 71 (1974): 1540-48.

22:14-20

5355   G. J. Bahr, "The Seder of Passover and the Eucharistic Words," *NovT* 12 (1970): 181-202.

22:15-21

5356   James Custer, "When Is Communion Communion," *GTJ* 6/2 (1985): 403-10.

22:15-20

5357   Henry Chadwick, "The Shorter Text of Luke XXII.15-20," *HTR* 50 (1957): 249-58.

5358   C.-B. Amphoux, "Le dernier repas de Jésus, Lc 22/15-20 par," *ÉTR* 56 (1981): 449-54.

22:15-18

5359   N. Hook, "The Dominical Cup Saying," *Theology* 77 (1974): 625-30.

22:15

5360   C. K. Barrett, "Luke XXII,15: To Eat the Passover," *JTS* 9 (1958): 305-307.

22:17-19

5361   Brian A. Mastin, "Jesus said Grace," *SJT* 24 (1971): 449-56.

22:17

5362   Martin Rese, "Zur Problematik von Kurz- und Langtext in Luk. xxii.17ff.," *NTS* 22 (1975-1976): 15-31.

22:19-28

5363   Bart D. Ehrman, "The Cup, the Bread, and the Salvific Effect of Jesus' Death in Luke-Acts," *SBLSP* 21 (1991): 576-91.

22:19-20

5364   K. Goetz, "Das vorausweisende Demonstrativum in Lk 22,19-20 und 1 Cor 11,24," *ZNW* 38 (1939): 188-90.

5365   Pierre Benoit, "Luc XXII.19b-20," *JTS* 49 (1948): 145-47.

5366   B. H. Throckmorton, "The Longer Reading of Luke 22:19-20," *ATR* 30 (1948): 55-56.

5367   Pierson Parker, "Three Variant Readings in Luke-Acts," *JBL* 83 (1964): 165-70.

5368   J. H. Petzer, "Luke 22:19b-20 and the Structure of the Passage," *NovT* 26 (1984): 249-52.

22:19

5369   M. H. Sykes, "The Eucharist as 'Anamnesis'," *ET* 71 (1959-1960): 115-18.

5370   H. Kosmala, "Das tut zu meinem Gedächtnis," *NovT* 4 (1960): 81-94.

5371   X. Léon-Dufour, "Do This in Memory of Me," *TD* 26 (1978): 36-39.

5372   D. W. A. Gregg, "Hebraic Antecedents to the Eucharistic Anamnèsis Formula," *TynB* 30 (1979): 165-68.

5373   B. Schwank, "Das ist mein Leib, der für euch hingegeben wird (Lk 22,19)," *ErAu* 59 (1983): 279-90.

5374   B. de Margerie, " 'Hoc facite in meam commemorationem' (Lc 22,19b): Les exégeses des Pères préchaícédoniens (150-451)," *Div* 28 (1984): 43-69, 137-49.

5375   John D. Laurence, "The Eucharist as the Imitation of Christ," *TS* 47/2 (1986): 286-96.

5376   Francis G. Carpinelli, " 'Do This as My Memorial' (Luke 22:19): Lucan Soteriology of Atonement," *CBQ* 61 (1999): 74-91.

22:20

5377   J. Günther, "Das Becherwort Jesu," *TGl* 45 (1955): 47-49.

5378   Lynne C. Boughton, " 'Being Shed for You/Many': Time-Sense and Consequences in the Synoptic Cup Citations," *TynB* 48 (1997): 249-70.

22:21-39

5379   A. Vööbus, "A New Approach to the Problem of the Shorter and Longer Text in Luke," *NTS* 15 (1968-1969): 457-63.

22:21-38

5380   Philip H. Sellew, "The Last Supper Discourse in Luke 22:21-38," *Forum* 3 (1987): 70-95.

22:22

5381   Leslie C. Allen, "The Old Testament Background of (Pro)Orizein in the New Testament," *NTS* 17/1 (1970-1971): 104-108.

22:23

5382   F. G. Untergassmair, "Thesen zur Sinndeutung des Todes Jesu in der lukanischen Passionsgeschichte," *TGl* 70 (1980): 180-93.

22:24-30

5383   David J. Lull, "The Servant-Benefactor as a Model of Greatness," *NovT* 28/4 (1986): 289-305.

5384   David L. Tiede, "The King of the Gentiles and the Leader Who Serves: Luke 22:24-30," *WW* 12 (1992): 23-28.

5385   Peter K. Nelson, "The Unitary Character of Luke 22:24-30," *NTS* 40 (1994): 609-19.

5386   Ian Sloan, "The Greatest and the Youngest: Greco-Roman Reciprocity in the Farewell Address, Luke 22:24-30," *SR* 22 (1993): 63-73.

22:24-27

5387   L. Rasmussen, "Luke 22:24-27," *Int* 37 (1983): 73-76.

5388   A. W. Swamidoss, "Diakonia as Servanthood in the Synoptics," *IJT* 32 (1983): 37-51.

5389   Peter K. Nelson, "The Flow of Thought in Luke
        22:24-27," *JSNT* 43 (1991): 113-23.

22:25-27

5390   Jacques Schlosser, "La genèse de Luc XXII,25-27," *RB* 89
        (1982): 1-70.

22:25

5391   R. R. Rickards, "Lk 22:25: They Are Called 'Friends of
        the People'," *BT* 28 (1977): 445-46.

5392   Frederick W. Danker, "The Endangered Benefactor in
        Luke-Acts," *SBLSP* 11 (1981): 39-48.

22:27

5393   Jürgen Roloff, "Anfänge der soteriologischen Deutung des
        Todes Jesu (Mk. x.45 und Lk. xxii.27)," *NTS* 19
        (1972-1973): 38-64.

22:28-30

5394   Harry T. Fleddermann, "The End of Q," *SBLSP* 20 (1990):
        1-10.

22:29-30

5395   Peter K. Nelson, "Luke 22:29-30 and the Time Frame for
        Dining and Ruling," *TynB* 44 (1993): 351-61.

22:29

5396   J. Guillet, "Luc 22,29: Une jormule johannique dans
        l'évangile de Luc," *RechSR* 69 (1981): 113-22.

22:31-34

5397   James W. Thompson, "The Odyssey of a Disciple (Luke
        22,31-34)," *RQ* 23 (1980): 77-81.

22:31

5398   W. Foerster, "Lukas 22,31f.," *ZNW* 46 (1955): 129-33.

22:35-53

5399   T. M. Napier, "The Enigma of the Swords," *ET* 49
        (1937-1938): 467-70.

5400   S. K. Finlayson, "The Enigma of the Swords," *ET* 50
        (1938-1939): 563.

5401   W. Western, "The Enigma of the Swords," *ET* 50
        (1938-1939): 377.

5402   H.-W. Bartsch, "Jesu Schwertwort, Lukas xxii.35-38: Überlieferungsgeschichtliche Studien," *NTS* 20 (1973-1974): 190-203.

5403   J. Gillman, "A Temptation to Violence: The Two Swords in Luke 22:35-38," *LouvS* 9 (1982-1983): 142-53.

22:35-38

5404   Roman Heiligenthal, "Wehrlosigkeit oder Selbstschutz? Aspekte zum Verständnis des lukanischen Schwertwortes," *NTS* 41 (1995): 39-58.

22:36

5405   Paul S. Minear, "Note on Luke 22:36," *NovT* 7/2 (1964): 128-34.

22:37

5406   Richard T. France, "The Servant of the Lord in the Teaching of Jesus," *TynB* 19 (1968): 26-1.

22:38

5407   Günther Schwarz, "Κύριε, ἰδοὺ μάχαιραι ὧδε δύο," *BibN* 8 (1979): 22.

22:39-49

5408   Jerome H. Neyrey, "The Absence of Jesus' Emotions—The Lucan Redaction of Lk 22,39-49," *Bib* 61/2 (1980): 153-71.

22:39-46

5409   André Feuillet, "Le récit lucanien de l'agonie de Gethsémani (Lc 22:39-46)," *NTS* 22 (1975-1976): 397-417.

5410   Sheldon Tostengard, "Luke 22:39-46," *Int* 34 (1980): 283-88.

5411   Joel B. Green, "Jesus on the Mount of Olives (Luke 22:39-46): Tradition and Theology," *JSNT* 26 (1986): 29-48.

22:39

5412   J. Bishop, "The Place of Habit in the Spiritual Life," *ET* 91 (1980-1981): 374-75.

5413   Marion L. Soards, "On Understanding Luke 22:39," *BT* 36/3 (1985): 336-37.

22:40-46

5414   K. G. Kuhn, "Jesus in Gethsemane," *EvT* 12 (191-1953): 260-85.

5415   T. Lescow, "Jesus in Gethsemane bei Lukas und im Hebräerbrief," *ZNW* 58 (1967): 215-39.

5416   T. Lescow, "Jesus in Gethsemane," *EvT* 26 (1968): 141-59.

5417   R. S. Barbour, "Gethsemane in the Tradition of the Passion," *NTS* 16 (1969-1970): 231-51.

5418   Marlis Gielen, " 'Und führe uns nicht in Versuchung' Die 6. Vater-Unser Bitte—eine Anfechtung für das biblische Gottesbild?" *ZNW* 89 (1998): 201-16.

22:40

5419   H. N. Bate, "Luke xxii.40," *JTS* 36 (1935): 76-77.

22:42-47

5420   Tjitze Baarda, "Luke 22:42-47a: The Emperor Julian as a Witness to the Text of Luke," *NovT* 30 (1988): 289-96.

22:43-44

5421   L. Brun, "Engel und Blutschweiss Lc 22,43-44," *ZNW* 32 (1933): 265-76.

5422   Gerhard Schneider, "Engel und Blutschweiss," *BZ* 20 (1976): 112-16.

5423   W. J. Larkin, "The Old Testament Background of Luke 22:43-44," *NTS* 25 (1978-1979): 250-54.

5424   Bart D. Ehrman and Mark A. Plunkett, "The Angel and the Agony: The Textual Problem of Luke 22:43-44," *CBQ* 45 (1983): 401-16.

5425   T. van Lopik, "Once Again: Floating Words, Their Significance for Textual Criticism," *NTS* 41 (1995): 286-91.

22:48

5426   P. Maurice Casey, "The Son of Man Problem," *ZNW* 67/3 (1976): 147-54.

22:54-23:25

5427   Jean Delorme, "Le procès de Jésus ou la parole risquée (Lc 22:54-23:25)," *RechSR* 69 (1981): 123-46.

22:54-62

5428   N. J. McEleney, "Peter's Denials—How Many? To Whom?" *CBQ* 1 (1990): 467-72.

22:55-62

5429   Dietfried Gewalt, "Die Verlegnung des Petrus," *LB* 43 (1978): 113-44.

5430   Gregory Murray, "St. Peter's Denials," *DR* 103 (1985): 296-98.

22:57

5431   W. J. P. Boyd, "Peter's Denials—Mark 14:68, Luke 22:57," *ET* 67 (1955-1956): 341.

22:61

5432   Marion L. Soards, "And the Lord Turned and Looked Straight at Peter: Understanding Luke 22:61," *Bib* 67/4 (1986): 518-19.

22:62-66

5433   Michael D. Goulder, "On Putting Q to the Test," *NTS* 24 (1977-1978): 218-34.

22:63-65

5434   W. C. van Unnik, "Jesu Verhüng vor dem Synedrium," *ZNW* 29 (1930): 310-11.

22:63-64

5435   D. L. Miller, "*Empaizein:* Playing the Mock Game (Luke 22:63-64)," *JBL* 90 (1971): 309-13.

22:64

5436   Frans Neirynck, "Τίς ἐστιν ὁ παίσας σε. Mt 26,68/Lk 22,64 (diff. Mk 14,65)," *ETL* 63/1 (1987): 5-47.

22:66-71

5437   Paul Winter, "Luke XXII,66b-71," *ST* 9 (1956): 112-15.

5438   John P. Heil, "Reader-Response and the Irony of Jesus Before the Sanhedrin in Luke 22:66-71," *CBQ* 51 (1989): 271-84.

5439   Frank J. Matera, "Luke 22:66-71: Jesus Before the Presbyterion," *ETL* 65/1 (1989): 43-59.

5440   John J. Kilgallen, "Jesus' First Trial: Messiah and Son of God (Luke 22,66-71)," *Bib* 80 (1999): 401-14.

22:67-68

5441   J. D. M. Derrett, "Midrash in the New Testament: The Origin of Luke 22:67-68," *ST* 29 (1975): 147-56.

22:69

5442   Joseph Plevnik, "Son of Man Seated at the Right Hand of God: Luke 22:69 in Lucan Christology," *Bib* 72/3 (1991): 331-47.

22:70

5443   Renatus Kempthorne, "The Marcan Text of Jesus' Answer to the High Priest (Mark XIV 62)," *NovT* 19/3 (1977): 197-208.

23:1-16

5444   J. D. M. Derrett, "Daniel and Salvation History," *DR* 100 (1982): 62-68.

23:1-7

5445   J. M. Creed, "The Supposed 'Proto-Lucan' Narrative of the Trial before Pilate: A Rejoinder," *ET* 46 (1934-1935): 378-79.

23:2

5446   J. Spencer Kennard, "Syrian Coin Hoards and the Tribute Question," *ATR* 27 (1945): 248-1.

23:5

5447   David Hill, "Jesus before the Sanhedrin: On What Charge?" *IBS* 7 (1985): 174-86.

23:6-12

5448   M. Corbin, "Jésus devant Hérode," *Chr* 25 (1978): 190-97.

5449   Marion L. Soards, "Tradition, Composition, and Theology in Luke's Account of Jesus before Herod Antipas," *Bib* 66/3 (1985): 344-64.

23:8

5450   H. Hutchison, "Beware of the Sensational!" *ET* 91 (1979-1980): 117-19.

5451   Marion L. Soards, "Herod Antipas' Hearing in Luke 23:8," *BT* 37/1 (1986): 146-47.

23:9

5452   Marion L. Soards, "The Silence of Jesus before Herod: An Interpretative Suggestion," *ABR* 33 (1985): 41-45.

23:13

5453   G. Rau, "Das Volk in der lukanischen Passionsgeschichte, eine Konjektur zu Lk 23,13," *ZNW* 56 (1965): 41-51.

23:21

5454   J. M. Ford, " 'Crucify Him, Crucify Him' and the Temple Scroll," *ET* 87 (1975-1976): 275-78.

23:25-31

5455   Nicholas T. Wright, "Jesus, Israel and the Cross," *SBLSP* 15 (1985): 75-95.

23:26-32

5456   Marion L. Soards, "Tradition, Composition, and Theology in Jesus' Speech to the 'Daughters of Jerusalem' (Luke 23,26-32)," *Bib* 68/2 (1987): 221-44.

23:26

5457   Brian K. Blount, "A Socio-Rhetorical Analysis of Simon of Cyrene: Mark 15:21 and Its Parallels," *Semeia* 64 (1994): 171-98.

23:27-31

5458   Jerome H. Neyrey, "Jesus' Address to the Women of Jerusalem: A Prophetic Judgment Oracle," *NTS* 29 (1983): 74-86.

23:29

5459   Walter Käser, "Exegetische und Theologische Erwägungen zur Seligpreisung der Kinderlosen, Lk 23:29b," *ZNW* 54/3-4 (1963): 240-54.

5460   Bonaventura Rinaldi, "Beate le sterili (Lc. 23,29)," *BibO* 15 (1973): 61-64.

23:33

> 5461 Joseph A. Fitzmyer, "Crucifixion in Ancient Palestine, Qumran Literature, and the New Testament," *CBQ* 40/4 (1978): 493-513.
>
> 5462 José O'Callaghan, "Fluctuación textual en Mt 20,21.26,27," *Bib* 71/4 (1990): 553-58.

23:34-46

> 5463 John Wilkinson, "The Seven Words from the Cross," *SJT* 17 (1964): 69-82.

23:34

> 5464 J. Reid, "The Words from the Cross: I. 'Father, Forgive Them'," *ET* 41 (1929-1930): 103-107.
>
> 5465 William H. Willimon, "Following Jesus," *CC* 102 (1985): 236-37.
>
> 5466 D. A. S. Ravens, "St. Luke and Atonement," *ET* 97 (1985-1986): 291-94.
>
> 5467 J. H. Petzer, "Anti-Judaism and the Textual Problem of Luke 23:34," *FilN* 5 (1992): 199-203.

23:35-43

> 5468 W. Trilling, "Le Christ, roi crucifié (Lc 23)," *AsSeign* 65 (1973): 56-65.

23:35

> 5469 P. M. Webb, "Saved," *ET* 85 (1973-1974): 175-76.

23:39-43

> 5470 W. M. MacGregor, "The Words from the Cross: II. The Penitent Thief," *ET* 41 (1929-1930): 151-54.
>
> 5471 J. M. García Pérez, "El relato del Buen Ladron (Lc 23,39-43)," *EB* 44 (1986): 263-304.

23:43

> 5472 L. P. Hope, "The King's Garden," *ET* 48 (1936-1937): 471-73.
>
> 5473 Joseph Hong, "Understanding and Translating 'Today' in Luke 23.43," *BT* 46 (1995): 408-17.
>
> 5474 Ulrich Kellermann, "Elia als Seelenführer der Verstorbenen oder Elia-Typologie in Lk 23,43 'Heute

wirst du mit mir im Paradies sein'," *BibN* 83 (1996): 35-53.

23:44-49

5475   Joel B. Green, "The Death of Jesus and the Rending of the Temple Veil (Luke 23:44-49): A Window into Luke's Understanding of Jesus and the Temple," *SBLSP* 21 (1991): 543-57.

5476   Joel B. Green, "The Demise of the Temple as 'Culture Center' in Luke-Acts: An Exploration of the Rending of the Temple Veil (Luke 23:44-49)," *RB* 101 (1994): 495-515.

5477   C. R. Hutcheon, " 'God is with Us': The Temple in Luke-Acts," *SVTQ* 44 (2000): 3-33.

23:44-46

5478   Dennis D. Sylva, "The Temple Curtain and Jesus' Death in the Gospel of Luke," *JBL* 105/2 (1986): 239-50.

23:44-45

5479   J. F. A. Sawyer, "Why is a Solar Eclipse Mentioned in the Passion Narrative (Luke xxiii.44-45)?" *JTS* 23 (1972): 124-28.

5480   R. M. Grández, "Las tinieblas en la muerte de Jesús: Historia de la exégesis de Lc 23,44-45a," *EB* 47 (1989): 177-223.

23:46-48

5481   Hartmut Gese, "Psalm 22 und das Neue Testament," *ZTK* 65/1 (1968): 1-22.

23:46

5482   T. Yates, "The Words from the Cross - Vll," *ET* 41 (1929-1930): 427-29.

5483   Luise Abramowski and E. Goodman, "Luke xxiii.46: *paratithemai* in a Rare Syriac Rendering," *NTS* 13 (1966-1967): 290-91.

5484   Eberhard Bons, "Das Sterbewort Jesu nach Lk 23:46 und sein alttestamentlicher Hintergrund," *BZ* NS 38 (1994): 93-101.

23:47

5485   George D. Kilpatrick, "A Theme of the Lucan Passion Story and Luke XXIII.47," *JTS* 43 (1942): 34-36.

5486   Robert J. Karris, "Luke 23:47 and the Lucan View of Jesus' Death," *JBL* 105/1 (1986): 65-74.

5487   Peter Doble, "Luke 23.47: The Problem of *dikaios*," *BT* 44 (1993): 320-31.

23:49-24:43

5488   Robert J. Karris, "Women and Discipleship in Luke," *CBQ* 56 (1994): 1-20.

23:50

5489   G. Ghiberti, "Sepolcro, sepoltura e panni sepolcrali di Gesù. Riconsiderando i dati biblici relativi alla Sindone di Torino," *RBib* 27 (1979): 123-58.

23:53-54

5490   Michael D. Goulder, "On Putting Q to the Test," *NTS* 24 (1977-1978): 218-34.

23:53

5491   D. Moody Smith, "Mark 15:46: The Shroud of Turin as a Problem of History and Faith," *BA* 46/4 (1983): 251-54.

24:1-12

5492   H. Gerits, "Le message pascal au tombeau (Lc 24,1-12): La résurrection selon la présentation théologique de Lu," *EstT* 8/15 (1981): 3-63.

24:1-11

5493   Michael D. Goulder, "Mark 21:1-8 and Parallels," *NTS* 24 (1977-1978): 235-40.

5494   Luke T. Johnson, "Luke 24:1-11," *Int* 46 (1992): 57-61.

24:1

5495   Michael D. Goulder, "On Putting Q to the Test," *NTS* 24 (1977-1978): 218-34.

24:3

5496   Mikeal C. Parsons, "A Christological Tendency in P^{75}," *JBL* 105/3 (1986): 463-79.

24:4

5497   Christoph Burchard, "Fußnoten zum neutestamentlichen Griechisch II," *ZNW* 69 (1978): 143-57.

24:6

5498   Mikeal C. Parsons, "A Christological Tendency in P^{75}," *JBL* 105/3 (1986): 463-79.

5499   Domingo Muñoz León, " 'Iré delante de vosotros a Galilea' (Mt 26,32 y par). Sentido mesiánico y posible sustrato arameo del logion," *EB* 48 (1990): 215-41.

24:7-21

5500   John M. Perry, "The Three Days in the Synoptic Passion Predictions," *CBQ* 48/4 (1986): 637-54.

24:9

5501   Ralf Oppermann, "Eine Beobachtung in Bezug auf das Problem des Markus-Schlusses," *BibN* 40 (1987): 24-29.

24:12

5502   John Muddiman, "A Note on Reading Luke 24:12," *ETL* 48 (1972): 542-48.

5503   Frans Neirynck, "Παρακύψας βλέπει: Lc 24:12 et Jn 20:5," *ETL* 53 (1977): 113-1.

5504   Frans Neirynck, "'Απῆλθεν πρὸς ἑαυτόν: Lc 24:12 et Jn 20:10," *ETL* 54 (1978): 104-18.

5505   Frans Neirynck, "John and the Synoptics: The Empty Tomb Stories," *NTS* 30/2 (1984): 161-87.

5506   J. M. Ross, "The Genuineness of Luke 24:12," *ET* 98 (1986-1987): 107-108.

5507   Anton Dauer, "Zur Authentizität von Lk 24,12," *ETL* 70 (1994): 294-318.

5508   Frans Neirynck, "A Supplementary Note on Lk 24,12," *ETL* 72 (1996): 425-30.

24:13-53

5509   J. M. Nielen, "Gestalten des Neuen Testamentes," *BK* 10 (1955): 35-49.

5510   Jacob Kremer, "Die Bezeugung der Auferstehung Christi in Form von Geschichten: Zu Schwierigkeiten und

Chancen heutigen Verstehens von Lk 24,13-53," *GeistL* 61 (1988): 172-87.

24:13-35

5511 A. Ehrhardt, "Disciples of Emmaus," *NTS* 10 (1963-1964): 182-201.

5512 Joseph A. Grassi, "Emmaus Revisited (Luke 24:13-35 and Acts 8:26-40)," *CBQ* 26 (1964): 463-67.

5513 J. Wanke, " 'Wie sie ihn beim Brotbrechen erkannten': Zur Auslegung der Emmauserzählung Lk 24,13-35," *BZ* 18 (1974): 180-92.

5514 Soeur J. D'Arc, "Un grand jeu d'inclusions dans les pèlerins d'Emmaüs," *NRT* 99 (1977): 62-76.

5515 P. M. J. Stravinskas, "The Emmaus Pericope: Its Sources, Theology and Meaning for Today," *BB* 3 (1977): 97-115.

5516 André Feuillet, "L'apparition du Christ à Marie-Madeleine, Jean 20:11-18. Comparaison avec l'apparition aux disciples d'Emmaüs Luc 24:13-35," *EV* 88 (1978): 193-204, 209-23.

5517 D. Cerbelaud, "Bribes sur Emmaüs," *VS* 133 (1979): 4-7.

5518 X. Thévenot, "Emmaüs, une nouvelle Genèse? Une lecture psychanalytique de Genèse 2-3 et Luc 24:13-35," *MSR* 37 (1980): 3-18.

5519 P. J. Berry, "The Road to Emmaus," *ET* 91 (1980-1981): 204-206.

5520 Antoine Delzant, "Les Disciples d'Emmaüs (Luc 24:13-35)," *RechSR* 73/2 (1985): 177-86.

5521 Jim Forest, "In the Breaking of the Bread: Recognizing the Face of Jesus," *Soj* 14/4 (1985): 34-36.

5522 B.-J. Koet, "Some Traces of a Semantic Field of Interpretation in Luke 24:13-35," *Bij* 46 (1985): 59-73.

5523 Robert J. Karris, "Luke 24:13-35," *Int* 41 (1987): 57-61.

5524 R. F. Smith, "Did Not Our Hearts Burn Within Us?" *CThM* 15 (1988): 187-93.

5525 François Rousseau, "Un Phénomène Particulier d'Inclusions dans Luc 24:13-35," *SR* 18/1 (1989): 67-79.

5526   Mary C. Hilkert, "Retelling the Gospel Story: Preaching and Narrative," *ÉgT* 21/2 (1990): 147-67.

5527   Corina Combet-Galland and F. Smyth-Florentin, "Le pain qui fait lever les Ecritures: Emmaüs, Luc 24/13-35," *ÉTR* 68 (1993): 323-32.

5528   Christian Grappe, "Au croisement des lectures et aux origines de repas communautaire: Le récit des pèlerins d'Emmaüs: Luc 24/13-35," *ÉTR* 73 (1998): 491-501.

5529   Elisabet Hölscher and Michael Klessmann, "Die Auferstehung einer Geschichte: Eine bibliodramatische Bearbeitung von Lk 24,13-35," *EvT* 54 (1994): 391-99.

5530   Sandra H. Polaski, "Identifying the Unnamed Disciple: An Exercise in Reader-Response Criticism," *PRS* 26 (1999): 193-202.

5531   Thomas M. Rosica, "The Road to Emmaus and the Road to Gaza: Luke 24:13-35 and Acts 8:26-40," *Worship* 68 (1994): 117-31.

5532   D. Marion, "Textes évangéliques sur l'Eucharistie. V. Luc 24. 13-35: Le repas d'Emmaüs. L'Euchariste, présence du Ressuscité," *EV* 110 (2000): 1-4.

24:13-33

5533   John M. Gibbs, "Canon Cuming's 'Service-Endings in the Epistles': A Rejoinder," *NTS* 24 (1977-1978): 545-47.

5534   J.-N. Aletti, "Luc 24,13-33: Signes, accomplissement et temps," *RechSR* 75 (1987): 305-20.

24:13-32

5535   H. D. Betz, "The Origin and Nature of Christian Faith According to the Emmaus Legend (Luke 24:13-32)," *Int* 23 (1969): 32-46.

5536   Bernard P. Robinson, "The Place of the Emmaus Story in Luke-Acts," *NTS* 30/4 (1984): 481-97.

24:13-29

5537   Soeur J. D'Arc, "La catéchèse sur la route d'Emmaüs," *LV* 32 (1977): 7-20.

24:16

5538 Günther Schwarz, "Οἱ δὲ ὀφθαλμοὶ αὐτῶν ἐκρατοῦντο?" *BibN* 55 (1990): 16-17.

24:28-32

5539 Soeur J. D'Arc, "Le partage du pain à Emmaüs," *VS* 130 (1976): 896-909.

24:28-31

5540 Ronald Goetz, "Picturing a Vanishing," *CC* 107 (1990): 395.

24:30-31

5541 R. Abba, "The Unrecognized Guest," *ET* 92 (1980-1981): 210-12.

24:33-35

5542 R. Annand, " 'He Was Seen of Cephas': A Suggestion about the First Resurrection Appearance to Peter," *SJT* 11 (1958): 180-87.

24:33

5543 Joseph Plevnik, " 'The Eleven and Those with Them' According to Luke," *CBQ* 40 (1978): 205-11.

24:34-35

5544 P. Nash, "The Emmaus Road Incident," *ET* 85 (1973-1974): 178-79.

24:34

5545 J. R. Gray, "The Lord is Risen Indeed," *ET* 93 (1981-1982): 179-80.

5546 Gordon Dalbey, "Does the Resurrection Happen," *CC* 102 (1985): 319-20.

5547 Ingo Broer, " 'Der Herr ist Simon erschienen' (Lk 24,34): Zur Entstehung des Osterglaubens," *SNTU-A* 13 (1988): 81-100.

24:35

5548 J. Reid, "Old Texts in Modern Translations: Luke 24,35 (Moffatt)," *ET* 49 (1937-1938): 186-89.

24:36-53

5549 Alois Stöger, "Österliche Freude: Meditation über Lk 24,36-53," *BL* 50 (1977): 121-24.

5550 Gerard Mussies, "Variation in the Book of Acts," *FilN* 4 (1991): 165-82.

24:36-49

5551 Max A. Chevallier, " 'Pentecôtes' lucaniennes et 'Pentecôtes' johanniques," *RechSR* 69 (1981): 301-13.

5552 Thomas S. Moore, "The Lucan Great Commission and the Isaianic Servant," *BSac* 154 (1997): 47-60.

24:36-48

5553 C. Clifton Black, "Our Shepherd's Voice: Biblical Resources for the Easter Season," *QR* 14 (1994): 89-110.

24:40

5554 Mikeal C. Parsons, "A Christological Tendency in P[75]," *JBL* 105/3 (1986): 463-79.

24:42-43

5555 George D. Kilpatrick, "Luke 24:42-43," *NovT* 28/4 (1986): 306-308.

5556 Gerald O'Collins, "Did Jesus Eat the Fish (Luke 24:42-43)," *Greg* 69 (1988): 65-76.

24:44-49

5557 Jack D. Kingsbury, "Luke 24:44-49," *Int* 35 (1981): 170-74.

24:44

5558 J. A. Jáuregui, " 'Israel' y la Iglesia en la Teologia de Lucas," *EE* 61/237 (1986): 129-49.

24:46-53

5559 A. Viard, "L'ascension de Jésus et le don de l'Esprit," *EV* 87 (1977): 267-68.

24:46-48

5560 R. Trevijano Etcheverría, "La misión de la iglesia primitiva y los mandatos del Señor en los evangelios," *Salm* 25 (1978): 5-36.

24:46

5561   John M. Perry, "The Three Days in the Synoptic Passion Predictions," *CBQ* 48/4 (1986): 637-54.

24:50-53

5562   P. A. van Stempvoort, "The Interpretation of the Ascension in Luke and Acts," *NTS* 5 (1958-1959): 30-42.

5563   Eugene A. LaVerdiere, "The Ascension of the Risen Lord," *BibTo* 95 (1978): 1553-59.

5564   John F. Maile, "The Ascension in Luke-Acts," *TynB* 37 (1986): 29-59.

5565   P. Palatty, "The Ascension of Christ in Luke-Acts: An Exegetical Critical Study of Luke 24,50-53 and Acts 1,2-3.9-11," *BB* 12 (1986): 100-17, 166-81.

5566   Mikeal C. Parsons, "Narrative Closure and Openness in the Plot of the Third Gospel: The Sense of an Ending in Luke 24:50-53," *SBLSP* 16 (1986): 201-23.

5567   Carol L. Stockhausen, "Luke's Stories of the Ascension: The Background and Function of a Dual Narrative," *EGLMBS* 10 (1990): 251-63.

5568   A. W. Zwiep, "The Text of the Ascension Narratives," *NTS* 42 (1996): 219-44.

24:51-1

5569   Mikeal C. Parsons, "A Christological Tendency in P[75]," *JBL* 105/3 (1986): 463-79.

24:51

5570   G. Odasso, "L'ascensione nell'evangelo di Luca," *BibO* 13 (1971): 107-18.

John

1-3

5571   E. B. Redlich, "Saint John i-iii: A Study in Dislocations," *ET* 55 (1943-1944): 89-92.

1:1-2:11

5572   W. Van Der Spek, "Ein wunderliches Buch: Das Evangelium nach Johannes," *TextK* 21 (1984): 6-20.

1

5573   Amos B. Hulen, "The Call of the Four Disciples in John 1," *JBL* 67 (1948): 153-57.

5574   M.-É. Boismard, "La première semaine du ministère de Jésus selon Saint Jean," *VS* 94 (1956): 593-603.

5575   T. Barrosse, "The Seven Days of the New Creation in St. John's Gospel," *CBQ* 21 (1959): 507-16.

5576   Harald Sahlin, "Zwei Abschnitte aus Johannes 1 rekonstruiert," *ZNW* 51 (1960): 64-69.

5577   F.-M. Braun, "La lumière du monde (Jean 1)," *RT* 64 (1964): 341-63.

5578   Stephen S. Smalley, "Salvation Proclaimed: VIII. John 1," *ET* 93 (1981-1982): 324-29.

5579   E. A. Nida, "Rhetoric and the Translator: With Special Reference to John 1," *BT* 33 (1982): 324-28.

5580   H. Mowvley, "John 1 in the Light of Exodus 33-34," *ET* 95 (1983-1984): 135-37.

5581   I. L. Grohar, "El 'mundo' en los escritos juanicos: un ensayo de interpretación," *RevB* 47/4 (1985): 221-27.

5582   John Ashton, "The Transformation of Wisdom: A Study of the Prologue of John's Gospel," *NTS* 32/2 (1986): 161-86.

5583   Meynet Roland, "Analyse rhétorique du Prologue de Jean," *RB* 96 (1989): 481-510.

5584   M. H. Franzmann and Michael Klinger, "The Call Stories of John 1 and John 21," *SVTQ* 36/1-2 (1992): 7-15.

1:1-21

5585   L.-M. Dewailly, "La Parole parlait à Dieu?. Note d'exégèse biblique," *RTP* 1 (1967): 123-28.

1:1-18

5586   J. H. Michael, "Notes on the Johannine Prologue," *ET* 31 (1919-1920): 276-79.

5587   C. Cryer, "The Prologue of the Fourth Gospel," *ET* 32 (1920-1921): 440-43.

5588   J. Viteau, "Sur le prologue de Saint Jean," *RechSR* 2 (1922): 459-67.

5589   Millar Burrows, "The Johannine Prologue as Aramaic Verse," *JBL* 45 (1926): 57-69.

5590   B. W. Bacon, "The Anti-Marcionite Prologue to John," *JBL* 49 (1930): 43-54.

5591   U. Holzmeister, "Prologi Iohannei (1:1-18) idea principalis et divisio," *VD* 11 (1931): 65-70.

5592   Charles Masson, "Le prologue du quatrieme évangile," - *RTP* 117 (1940): 297-311.

5593   J. L. Lilly, "The Eternal Word Made Flesh," *AmER* 118 (1948): 409-21.

5594   A. R. Osborn, "The Word Became Flesh: An Exposition of John 1:1-18," *Int* 3 (1949): 42-49.

5595   V. Gregersen, "Johannes-prologens struktur," *DTT* 17 (1954): 34-36.

5596   H. C. Green, "The Composition of St. John's Prologue," *ET* 66 (1954-1955): 291-94.

5597   M.-F. Lacan, "Le Prologue de Saint Jean: Ses thèmes, sa structure, son mouvement," *LV* 33 (1957): 91-110.

5598   Rudolf Schnackenburg, "Logos Hymnus und johanneischer Prolog," *BZ* N.F. 1 (1957): 69-109.

5599   T. E. van Pollard, "Cosmology and the Prologue of the Fourth Gospel," *VC* 12 (1958): 147-53.

5600   J. A. T. Robinson, "The Relation of the Prologue to the Gospel of St. John," *NTS* 9 (1962-1963): 120-29.

5601   P. M. Galopin, "Le Verbe, témoin du Père, Jean 1:1-18,"
        BVC 53 (1963): 16-34.

5602   Ernst Haenchen, "Probleme des johanneischen 'Prologs',"
        ZTK 60 (1963): 305-34.

5603   P. Lemarche, "Le Prologue de Jean," *RechSR* 52 (1964):
        497-537.

5604   K. H. Schelkle, "Das Wort ist Fleisch geworden:
        Weihnachtspredigt zum Prolog des Johannes-
        Evangeliums," *GeistL* 37 (1964): 401-405.

5605   Raymond B. Brown, "The Prologue of the Gospel of
        John," *RevExp* 62/4 (1965): 429-39.

5606   B. Schwank, "Das Wort vom Wort," *ErAu* 42 (1966):
        183-87.

5607   R. H. Countess, "The Translation of Theos in the New
        World Translation," *JETS* 10 (1967): 153-60.

5608   Kurt Aland, "Eine Untersuchung zu Johannes 1:3-
        4: Über die Bedeutung eines Punktes," *ZNW* 59
        (1968): 174-209.

5609   P. de Surgy, "Le prologue de saint Jean," *AsSeign* 10
        (1970): 68-79.

5610   Robert Kysar, "Rudolf Bultmann's Interpretation of the
        Concept of Creation in John 1:3-4: A Study of Exegetical
        Method," *CBQ* 32 (1970): 77-85.

5611   E. L. Miller, " 'The Logos Was God'," *EQ* 53 (1981):
        65-77.

5612   E. L. Miller, "The Logic of the Logos Hymn: A New
        View," *NTS* 29 (1983): 552-61.

5613   Charles H. Giblin, "Two Complementary Literary
        Structures in John 1:1-18," *JBL* 104 (1985): 87-103.

5614   Elizabeth Johnson, "Jesus, the Wisdom of God: A Biblical
        Basis for Non-Androcentric Christology," *ETL* 61/4
        (1985): 261-94.

5615   Gérard Rochais, "La formation du prologue (Jean
        1:1-18)," *ScE* 37 (1985): 5-44, 161-87.

5616   Jeffrey L. Staley, "The Structure of John's Prologue: Its Implications for the Gospel's Narrative Structure," *CBQ* 48/2 (1986): 241-64.

5617   Peder Borgen, "Creation, Logos and the Son: Observations on John 1:1-18 and 5:17-18," *ExA* 3 (1987): 88-97.

5618   Otfried Hofius, "Struktur und Gedankengang des Logos-Hymnus in Johannes 1:1-18," *ZNW* 78/1-2 (1987): 1-25.

5619   J. van der Watt, "Die strukturele komposisie van die proloog van die Johannesevangelie heroorweeg," *SkrifK* 8/1 (1987): 68-84.

5620   F. Genuyt, "Le prologue de Jean," *SémBib* 49 (1988): 15-34.

5621   John W. Pryor, "Covenant and Community in John's Gospel," *RTR* 47 (1988): 44-51.

5622   Marc Cholin, "Le prologue de l'Evangile selon Jean: structure et formation," *ScE* 41 (1989): 343-62.

5623   J. P. Louw, "Die Johannese logos-himne," *HTS* 1 (1989): 35-43.

5624   Warren Carter, "The Prologue and John's Gospel: Function, Symbol and the Definitive Word," *JSNT* 39 (1990): 35-58.

5625   Michael Theobald, "Geist- und Inkarnationschristologie: Zur Pragmatik des Johannesprologs," *ZKT* 112/2 (1990): 129-49.

5626   Thomas H. Tobin, "The Prologue of John and Hellenistic Jewish Speculation," *CBQ* 52 (1990): 252-69.

5627   Christopher Hancock, "Saint John's Four Laws," *CT* 35 (1991): 38-42.

5628   Roland Bergmeier, "Weihnachten mit und ohne Glanz: Notizen zu Johannesprolog und Philipperhymnus," *ZNW* 85 (1994): 47-68.

5629   Walther Bindemann, "Der Johannesprolog: Ein Versuch, ihn zu verstehen," *NovT* 37 (1995): 331-54.

5630   Joseph Moingt, "Autour du Prologue de Jean: Hommage à Xavier Léon-Dufour SJ," *RechSR* 83 (1995): 171-303.

5631   J. van der Watt, "The Composition of the Prologue of John's Gospel: The Historical Jesus Introducing Divine Grace," *WTJ* 57 (1995): 311-32.

5632   Otto Schwankl, "Auf der Suche nach dem Anfang des Evangeliums: Von 1 Kor 15,3-5 zum Johannes-Prolog," *BZ* NS 40 (1996): 39-60.

5633   Simon R. Valentine, "The Johannine Prologue: A Microcosm of the Gospel," *EQ* 68 (1996): 291-304.

5634   Mary Coloe, "The Structure of the Johannine Prologue and Genesis 1," *ABR* 45 (1997): 40-55.

5635   Alison Jasper, "Communicating (1997): The Word of God," *JSNT* 67 (1997): 29-44.

1:1-17

5636   W. J. Dumbrell, "Law and Grace: The Nature of the Contrast in John 1:17," *EQ* 58/1 (1986): 25-37.

1:1-14

5637   R. Calmes, "Étude sur le prologue du quatrième évangile," *RB* 9 (1902): 5-30.

5638   R. J. Drummond, "Genesis 1 and John 1:1-14," *ET* 49 (1937-1938): 568.

5639   William Barclay, "Great Themes of the New Testament: John 1:1-14," *ET* 70 (1958): 78-82; 114-17.

5640   C. Clifton Black, "St. Thomas's Commentary on the Johannine Prologue: Some Reflections on Its Character and Implications," *CBQ* 48/4 (1986): 681-98.

5641   H. Saxby, "The Time-Scheme in the Gospel of John," *ET* 104 (1992): 9-13.

1:1-13

5642   Ronald E. Heine, "Can the Catena Fragments of Origen's Commentary on John Be Trusted?" *VC* 40/2 (1986): 118-34.

1:1-5

5643   L. H. Bunn, "Ordet, lyset, livet Joh 1:1-5," *SEÅ* 5 (1940): 95-115.

5644   F. Hickman, "That Which Was from the Beginning," *RevExp* 37 (1940): 266-81.

5645   H. van den Bussche, "De tout être la Parole était la vie," *BVC* 69 (1966): 57-65.

1:1-4

5646   Robert L. Reymond, "The Justification of Theology with a Special Application to Contemporary Christology," *Pres* 12/1 (1986): 1-16.

1:1-2

5647   Nigel Turner, "John's Eternal Word," *EQ* 22 (1950): 243-48.

5648   Charles Masson, "Pour une traduction nouvelle de Jean 1:1b et 2," *RTP* 98 (1965): 376-81.

1:1

5649   H. G. Meecham, "The Anarthrous θεός in John 1:1 and 1 Corinthians 3:16," *ET* 63 (1951-1952): 126.

5650   Bruce M. Metzger, "On the Translation of John 1:1," *ET* 63 (1951-1952): 125-26.

5651   V. Perry, "Jehovah's Witnesses and the Deity of Christ," *EQ* 35 (1963): 15-22.

5652   Philip B. Harner, "Qualitative Anarthrous Predicate Nouns: Mark 15:39 and John 1:1," *JBL* 91 (1973): 75-87.

5653   M. O'Rourke, "Sermo: Reopening the Conversation on Translating John 1:1," *VC* 31 (1977): 161-68.

5654   Günther Schwarz, "Gen 1:1; 2:2a und Joh 1:1a, 3a: Ein Vergleich," *ZNW* 73 (1982): 136-37.

5655   Darryl Wood, "John's Use of Logos," *BI* 15/1 (1988): 73-75.

5656   Norbert Brox, " 'Gott'--mit und ohne Artikel: Origenes über Joh 1,1," *BibN* 66 (1993): 32-39.

5657   A. Ototsi Mojola, "Theories of Metaphor in Translation with Some Reference to John 1:1 and 1 John 1:1," *BT* 44 (1993): 341-47.

1:2-4

5658   O. C. Quick, "Note on St. John 1:2-4," *Theology* 34 (1937): 115, 244.

1:2

5659   Charles Masson, "Pour une traduction nouvelle de Jean 1:1b et 2," *RTP* 98 (1965): 376-81.

1:3-4

5660   George D. Kilpatrick, "John 1:3-4 and Jerome," *JTS* 46 (1945): 191-92.

5661   I. de la Potterie, "De interpunctione et interpretatione versuum Jo. 1:3-4," *VD* 33 (1955): 193-208.

5662   B. Vawter, "What Came to Be in Him was Life (John 1:3b-4a)," *CBQ* 25 (1963): 401-406.

5663   Hugolinus Langkammer, "Die Zugehörigkeit des Satzteiles Ho gegonen in Johannes 1:3, 4 bei Hieronymus," *BZ* 8 (1964): 295-98.

5664   Kurt Aland, "Eine Untersuchung zu Johannes 1:3-4: Über die Bedeutung eines Punktes," *ZNW* 59 (1968): 174-209.

5665   Robert Kysar, "Rudolf Bultmann's Interpretation of the Concept of Creation in John 1:3-4: A Study of Exegetical Method," *CBQ* 32 (1970): 77-85.

5666   F. W. Schlatter, "The Problem of John 1:3b-4a," *CBQ* 34/1 (1972): 54-58.

5667   E. L. Miller, "Codex Bezae on John i.3-4: One Dot or Two?" *TZ* 32 (1976): 269-71.

5668   E. L. Miller, "P[66] and P[75] on John 1:3-4," *TZ* 41 (1985): 440-43.

5669   Peter van Minnen, "The Punctuation of John 1:3-4," *FilN* 7 (1994): 33-41.

5670   Peter Cohee, "John 1.3-4," *NTS* 41 (1995): 470-77.

1:3

5671   J. Collantes, "Un comentario gnóstico," *EE* 27 (1953): 65-83.

5672   I. de la Potterie, "De punctuatie en de exegese van Jo 1:3s in de Traditie," *Bij* 16 (1955): 117-35.

5673   T. F. Glasson, "A Trace of Xenophon in John 1:3," *NTS* 4 (1957-1958): 208-209.

5674   T. E. van Pollard, "Cosmology and the Prologue of the Fourth Gospel," *VC* 12 (1958): 147-53.

5675   Klaus Haacker, "Eine formgeschichtliche Beobachtung zu Johannes 1:3," *BZ* 12 (1968): 119-21.

5676   Günther Schwarz, "Gen 1:1; 2:2a und Joh 1:1a, 3a: Ein Vergleich," *ZNW* 73 (1982): 136-37.

5677   Georg Korting, "Johannes 1:3," *BZ* 33/1 (1989): 97-104.

1:4-10

5678   Gary K. Halbrook, " 'Light' in John's Writings," *BI* 8/2 (1982): 26-29.

1:4

5679   R. L. Twomey, "Substantial Life in John 1:4," *AmER* 134 (1956): 324-27.

5680   M.-F. Lacan, "L'œuvre du Verbe incarné: le don de la vie," *RechSR* 45 (1957): 61-78.

1:5

5681   C. K. Barrett, "Κατέλαβεν in John 1:5," *ET* 53 (1941-1942): 297.

5682   Jacob A. Dyer, "The Unappreciated Light," *JBL* 79 (1960): 170-71.

5683   J. P. Louw, "Jon 1:5-'n vertaalprobleem," *NTT* 6 (1965): 47-52.

5684   Earl Richard, "Expressions of Double Meaning and Their Function in the Gospel of John," *NTS* 31 (1985): 96-112.

5685   Tjitze Baarda, "John 1:5 in the Oration and Diatessaron of Tatian: Concerning the Reading Katalambanei," *VC* 47 (1993): 209-25.

1:6-13

5686   M. Kehl, "Der Mensch in der Geschichte Gottes: Zum Johannesprolog 6-8," *GeistL* 40 (1967): 404-409.

1:6-9

5687   Harald Sahlin, "Zwei Abschnitte aus Johannes 1 rekonstruiert," *ZNW* 51 (1960): 64-69.

1:9-28

5688   E. Galbiati, "La testimonianza di Giovanni Battista (Giov. 1:9-28)," *BibO* 4 (1962): 227-33.

1:9-11

5689   H. van den Bussche, "Il était dans le monde," *BVC* 81 (1968): 19-25.

1:9

5690   H. Schulte, "Die Übersetzung von Johannes 1:9," *BZ* 21 (1933): 182-83.

5691   C. A. Phillips, "The Use of John 1:9 in the 'Rest of the Words of Baruch'," *ET* 47 (1935-1936): 431.

5692   F. Auer, "Wie ist Johannes 1:9 zu verstehen?" *TGl* 28 (1936): 397-407.

5693   Joseph Sickenberger, "Das in die Welt kommende Licht, Johannes 1:9," *TGl* 33 (1941): 129-34.

5694   J. Mehlmann, "A Note on John 1:9," *ET* 65 (1953-1954): 93-94.

5695   T. F. Glasson, "John 1:9 and a Rabbinic Tradition," *ZNW* 49 (1958): 288-90.

5696   A. Vicent Cernuda, "Engañan la oscuridad y el mundo; la luz era y manifiesta lo verdadero," *EB* 27 (1968): 153-75, 215-32.

5697   B. Prete, "La concordanza del participio ἐρχόμενον in Giov. 1:9," *BibO* 17 (1975): 195-208.

1:10

5698   C. Schedl, "Zur Schreibung von Johannes i.10a in Papyrus Bodmer XV," *NovT* 14 (1972): 238-40.

1:11-12

5699   W. E. Reiser, "Der Eindringling: Legende zu Johannes 1:11-12," *BK* 30 (1975): 123-25.

1:11

5700   A. Médebielle, "In propria venit," *VD* 2 (1922): 38-42.

5701   A. L. Humphries, "A Note on πρὸς ἐμαυτόν and εἰς τὰ ἴδια: A Plea for a Revised Translation," *ET* 53 (1941-1942): 356.

5702 Jacob Jervell, "Han kom til sitt eget," *NTT* 54 (1953): 129-43.

5703 É. Florival, " 'Les siens ne l'ont pas recu' (Jean 1:11): Regard évangélique sur la question juive," *NRT* 89 (1967): 43-66.

5704 R. Abba, "God Comes to Man," *ET* 91 (1979): 51-52.

5705 I. Zedde, " 'E i suoi non lo accolsero'," *PV* 29 (1984): 290-300.

5706 John W. Pryor, "Jesus and Israel in the Fourth Gospel," *NovT* 32 (1990): 201-18.

1:12-13

5707 Michael Mees, "Johannes 1:12, 13 nach frühchristlicher Überlieferung," *BZ* 29/1 (1985): 107-15.

1:13-14

5708 A. Vicent Cernuda, "La doble generación de Jesucristo según Jean 1:13-14," *EB* 40 (1982): 49-117, 313-44.

1:13

5709 J. A. Oñate, " 'Qui non e sanguinibus... sed ex Deo nati sunt'," *CuBi* 2 (1945): 311-12.

5710 B. J. Le Frois, "The Spiritual Motherhood of Mary in John 1:13," *CBQ* 13 (1951): 422-31.

5711 J. Schmid, "Johannes 1:13," *BZ* N.F. 1 (1957): 118-25.

5712 E. P. Groenewald, "Uit die wil van 'n man," *NTT* 2/1 (1960): 17-22.

5713 John D. Crossan, "Mary and the Church in John 1:13," *BibTo* 20 (1965): 1318-24.

5714 B. Schwank, "Eine textkritische Fehlentscheidung (Johannes 1:13) und ihre Auswirkungen im holländischen Katechismus," *BK* 24 (1969): 16-19.

5715 W. C. Robinson, "The Virgin Birth-A Broader Base," *CT* 17/5 (1972): 238-40.

5716 Léopold Sabourin, " 'Who Was Begotten ... of God' (John 1:13)," *BTB* 6 (1976): 86-90.

5717 John W. Pryor, "Of the Virgin Birth or the Birth of Christians: The Text of John 1:13 Once More," *NovT* 27 (1985): 296-318.

1:14-18

5718   J. P. Louw, "Narrator of the Father, ΕΞΗΓΕΙΣΘΑΙ and Related Terms in Johannine Christology," *Neo* 2 (1968): 32-40.

5719   A. T. Hanson, "John i.14-18 and Exodus xxxiv," *NTS* 23 (1976-1977): 90-101.

5720   D. H. C. Read, "Inside John's Gospel: Introducing Jesus," *ET* 88 (1976-1977): 42-47.

5721   P. P. A. Kotzé, "Die betekenis en konteks van genade en waarheid in Johannes 1:14-18," *SkrifK* 8/1 (1987): 38-51.

1:14

5722   A. Médebielle, "Et Verbum caro factum est (Ioh. 1,14)," *VD* 2 (1922): 137-44.

5723   F. Hickman, "That Which Was from the Beginning," *RevExp* 37 (1940): 266-81.

5724   J. P. Arendzen, " 'Grace' (John 1:14)," *Scr* 4 (1949): 22.

5725   T. Barrosse, "The Word Became Flesh," *BibTo* 1/9 (1963): 590-95.

5726   M.-F. Lacan, "Le thème biblique: L'habitation de Dieu parmi nous," *AsSeign* 10 (1963): 58-74.

5727   J. Grangette, "Nous avons vu sa gloire," *VS* 110 (1964): 32-42.

5728   Joseph A. Grassi, " 'And the Word Became Flesh and Dwelt among Us'," *BibTo* 1/15 (1964): 975-79.

5729   Lester J. Kuyper, "Grace and Truth: An OT Description of God, and Its Use in the Johannine Gospel," *Int* 18 (1964): 3-19.

5730   H. Leroy, " 'Und das Wort ist Fleisch geworden...': Eine theologische Meditation," *BK* 20 (1965): 114-16.

5731   J. J. Navone, "We Have Seen His Glory," *BibTo* 21 (1965): 1390-96.

5732   J. Riedl, "Strukturen christologischer Glaubensentfaltung im NT," *ZKT* 87 (1965): 443-52.

5733   F. C. Grant, " 'Only-Begotten': A Footnote to the R.S.V.," *BT* 17 (1966): 11-14.

5734 Patrick P. Saydon, "Some Biblico-Liturgical Passages Reconsidered," *MeliT* 18/1 (1966): 10-17.

5735 M. Isabel, " 'Dios con nosotros': 'Y el Verbo se hizo carne y habitó entre nosotros'," *RevB* 29 (1967): 143-65.

5736 A. B. du Toit, "The Incarnate Word. A Study of John 1:14," *Neo* 2 (1968): 9-21.

5737 J. C. Meagher, "John 1:14 and the New Temple," *JBL* 88 (1969): 57-68.

5738 J. M. Rist, "St. John and Amelius," *JTS* 20 (1969): 230-31.

5739 H. Schneider, " 'The Word Was Made Flesh': An Analysis of the Theology of Revelation in the Fourth Gospel," *CBQ* 31 (1969): 344-56.

5740 Friedrich Wulf, "Gott im Menschen Jesus. Auslegung und Meditation von Johannes 1:14; Phil 2:7; Lk 2:11," *GeistL* 42 (1969): 472-73.

5741 E. Ruckstuhl, "Und das Wort wurde Fleisch," *BibL* 13 (1972): 235-38.

5742 Klaus Berger, "Zu 'Das Wort ward Fleisch' Johannes 1:14a," *NovT* 16 (1974): 161-66.

5743 R. F. Collins, " 'He Came to Dwell among Us' (John 1:14)," *MeliT* 28 (1976): 44-59.

5744 J. K. Elliott, "John 1:14 and the New Testament's Use of πλήρης," *BT* 28 (1977): 151-53.

5745 R. G. Cole, "We Beheld His Glory," *ET* 90 (1978): 50-51.

5746 Rudolf Schnackenburg, " 'Und das Wort ist Fleisch geworden'," *IKaZ* 8 (1979): 1-9.

5747 L. D. Hynson, "The Flesh Became Word: An Advent Meditation," *PSB* 3 (1980): 54-55.

5748 C. E. B. Cranfield, "John 1:14: 'Became'," *ET* 93 (1981-1982): 215.

5749 W. Robert Cook, "The 'Glory' Motif in the Johannine Corpus," *JETS* 27 (1984): 291-97.

5750 Ricardo Pietrantonio, "Un transfondo arameo para el Evangelio de Juan 1:14," *RevB* 46 (1984): 187-97.

<u>1:15</u>

5751 E. A. Cerny, "The Translation of St. John 1:15," *CBQ* 1 (1939): 363-68.

<u>1:16</u>

5752 Matthew Black, "Does an Aramaic Tradition Underlie John 1:16," *NTS* 42 (1941): 69.

5753 D. Frangipane, " 'Et gratiam pro gratia' (Jo 1:16)," *VD* 26 (1948): 3-17.

5754 Zane C. Hodges, "Problem Passages in the Gospel of John: Part 1. Grace and Grace," *BSac* 135 (1978): 34-45.

5755 Ruth B. Edwards, "χάριν ἀντὶ χάριτος (John 1:16): Grace and the Law in the Johannine Prologue," *JSNT* 32 (1988): 3-15.

<u>1:17</u>

5756 C. Van Der Waal, "The Gospel according to John and the Old Testament," *Neo* 6 (1972): 28-47.

5757 Mark W. Karlberg, "Legitimate Discontinuities between the Testaments," *JETS* 28 (1985): 9-20.

<u>1:18-34</u>

5758 J. M. Ross, "Two More Titles of Jesus," *ET* 85 (1973-1974): 281.

<u>1:18</u>

5759 Rudolf Bultmann, "Θεὸν οὐδεὶς ἑώραθκεν πώποτε," *ZNW* 29 (1930): 169-92.

5760 M.-É. Boismard, " 'Dans le sein du Père' (Jean 1:18)," *RB* 59 (1952): 23-39.

5761 Francis J. Moloney, "John 1:18: 'In the Bosom of' or 'Turned towards' the Father?" *ABR* 31 (1983): 63-71.

5762 David A. Black, "The Text of John 3:13," *GTJ* 6 (1985): 49-66.

5763 David A. Fennema, "John 1.18: 'God the Only Son'," *NTS* 31 (1985): 124-35.

5764 Robert L. Reymond, "The Justification of Theology with a Special Application to Contemporary Christology," *Pres* 12/1 (1986): 1-16.

5765 I. de la Potterie, " 'C'est lui qui a ouvert la voie': la finale du prologue johannique," *Bib* 69/3 (1988): 340-70.

5766 Otfried Hofius, "Der in des Vaters Schoss ist: Johannes 1:18," *ZNW* 80/3-4 (1989): 163-71.

5767 Joachim Kügler, "Der Sohn im Schoss des Vaters: Eine motivgeschichtliche Notiz zu Joh 1,18," *BibN* 89 (1997): 76-87.

1:19-4:54

5768 Wolfgang Roth, "Scriptural Coding in the Fourth Gospel," *BR* 32 (1987): 6-29.

1:19-2:25

5769 Mary M. Pazdan, "Nicodemus and the Samaritan Woman: Contrasting Models of Discipleship," *BTB* 17 (1987): 145-48.

1:19-2:12

5770 T. Matus, "First and Last Encounter," *BibTo* 42 (1969): 2893-97.

1:19-2:11

5771 J. Cazeaux, "C'est Moïse qui vous condamnera. . .," *LV* 29/149 (1980): 75-88.

1:19-51

5772 L. Paul Trudinger, "The Seven Days of the New Creation in St John's Gospel: Some Further Reflections," *EQ* 44 (1972): 154-58.

5773 A. Niccacci, "La fede nel Gesù storico e la fede nel Cristo risorto," *Ant* 53 (1978): 423-42.

5774 L. Schenke, "Die literarische Entstehungsgeschichte von Johannes 1:19-51," *BibN* 46 (1989): 24-57.

1:19-36

5775 B. M. F. van Iersel, "Tradition und Redaktion in Johannes 1:19-36," *NovT* 5 (1962): 245-67.

5776 M.-É. Boismard, "Les traditions johanniques concernant le Baptiste," *RB* 70 (1963): 5-42.

1:19-28

5777   André Feuillet, "The Baptism of Jesus," *TD* 14 (1966): 207-12.

5778   Francis E. Williams, "Fourth Gospel and Synoptic Tradition: Two Johannine Passages," *JBL* 86 (1967): 311-19.

5779   R. Beauvery, "Le Baptiste devant les enquêteurs (Jean 1,19-28)," *EV* 78 (1968): 707-709.

5780   A. G. Patzia, "Did John the Baptist Preach a Baptism of Fire and Holy Spirit?" *EQ* 40 (1968): 21-27.

5781   P. Proulx and Luis Alonso Schökel, "Las sandalias del Mesias Esposo," *Bib* 59 (1978): 1-37.

5782   L. S. Chafer, "For Whom Did Christ Die?" *BSac* 137 (1980): 310-26.

5783   Francis J. Moloney, "The Fourth Gospel and the Jesus of History," *NTS* 46 (2000): 42-58.

1:19-25

5784   Harald Sahlin, "Zwei Abschnitte aus Johannes 1 rekonstruiert," *ZNW* 51 (1960): 64-69.

1:19

5785   Thomas Söding, " 'Was kann aus Nazareth schon Gutes kommen?' Die Bedeutung des Judenseins Jesu im Johannesevangelium," *NTS* 46 (2000): 21-41.

1:20

5786   E. D. Freed, "Egō Eimi in John 1:20 and 4:25," *CBQ* 41 (1979): 288-91.

1:21

5787   Georg Richter, " 'Bist du Elias?' (Johannes 1:21)," *BZ* 6 (1962): 79-92, 238-56; 7 (1963): 63-80.

1:22

5788   L. W. Grensted, "John 1:22; 2 Cor. 10:9," *ET* 35 (1923-1924): 331.

1:23

5789   M. J. J. Menken, "The Quotation from Isa 40,3 in John 1,23," *Bib* 66 (1985): 190-205.

__1:26__

5790 U. Holzmeister, " 'Medius vestrum stetit quem vos nescitis'," *VD* 20 (1940): 329-32.

__1:28__

5791 D. Buzy, "Béthanie au delà du Jourdain," *RechSR* 21 (1931): 444-62.

5792 Pierson Parker, " 'Bethany beyond Jordan'," *JBL* 74 (1955): 257-61.

5793 Rainer Riesner, "Bethany beyond the Jordan (John 1:28): Topography, Theology and History in the Fourth Gospel," *TynB* 38 (1987): 29-63.

5794 Brian F. Byron, "Bethany across the Jordan: Or simply Across the Jordan," *ABR* 46 (1998): 36-54.

__1:29-42__

5795 C. B. Cousar, "John 1:29-42," *Int* 31 (1977): 401-406.

__1:29-36__

5796 C. E. Blakeway, "Behold the Lamb of God," *ET* 31 (1919-1920): 364-65.

__1:29-34__

5797 J. Giblet, "Pour rendre témoignage à la lumiere," *BVC* 16 (1956): 80-86.

5798 M. de Goedt, "Un schème de révélation dans le 4e Évangile," *NTS* 8 (1961-1962): 142-50.

5799 A. Rose, "Jésus Christ, Agneau de Dieu," *BVC* 62 (1965): 27-32.

5800 J. E. Wood, "Isaac Typology in the New Testament," *NTS* 14 (1967-1968): 583-89.

5801 P.-E. Jacquemin, "Le témoignage de Jean le Baptiste (Jean 1:29-34)," *AsSeign* 33 (1970): 22-30.

5802 Lars Hartman, "Dop, and och barnaskap. Några traditions-historiska överväganden till Mk 1:9-11 par." *SEÅ* 37-38 (1972-1973): 88-106.

5803 Simon Légasse, "Le baptême de Jésus et le baptême chrétien," *SBFLA* 27 (1977): 51-68.

5804 H. Uprichard, "The Baptism of Jesus," *IBS* 3 (1981): 187-202.

5805 S. Cipriani, "Cristo 'agnello' redentore in Giovanni," *PV* 29 (1984): 463-72.

5806 J. Daryl Charles, "Will the Court Please Call in the Prime Witness? John 1:29-34 and the 'Witness' Motif," *TriJ* 10 (1989): 71-83.

5807 Francis J. Moloney, "The Fourth Gospel and the Jesus of History," *NTS* 46 (2000): 42-58.

1:29

5808 F. Porporato, " 'Ecce Agnus Dei' (Joh. 1:29)," *VD* 10 (1930): 329-37.

5809 P. Federkiewicz, " 'Ecce Agnus Dei' (Joh. 1:29, 36)," *VD* 12 (1932): 41-47, 83-88, 117-20, 156-60, 168-71.

5810 Joachim Jeremias, "' Ἀμνὸς τοῦ θεοῦ—παῖς θεοῦ," *ZNW* 34 (1935): 115-23.

5811 P. Joüon, "L'Agneau de Dieu," *NRT* 67 (1940): 318-21.

5812 Juan Leal, "El sentido soteriológico del cordero de Dios en la exégesis catolica," *EE* 24 (1950): 134-38, 147-82.

5813 Joachim Jeremias, "Ein Anhalt für die Datierung der masoretischen Redaktion?" *ZAW* 67 (1955): 289-90.

5814 F. Gryglewicz, "Das Lamm Gottes," *NTS* 13 (1966-1967): 133-46.

5815 J. H. Roberts, "The Lamb of God" *Neo* 2 (1968): 41-56.

5816 William J. Tobin, "Reflections on the Title and Function of the 'Lamb of God'," *BibTo* 34 (1968): 2367-76.

5817 Daniel A. Negoïtsa, "L'Agneau de Dieu et le Verbe de Dieu," *NovT* 13 (1971): 24-37.

5818 E. W. Burrows, "Did John the Baptist Call Jesus 'The Lamb of God'?" *ET* 85 (1973-1974): 245-49.

5819 A. Viard, "Jésus l'agneau de Dieu," *EV* 85 (1975): 3-5.

5820 G. Ashby, "The Lamb of God," *JTSA* 21 (1977): 62-65.

5821 J. C. O'Neill, "The Lamb of God in the Testaments of the Twelve Patriarchs," *JSNT* 1 (1979): 2-30.

5822   G. L. Carey, "The Lamb of God and Atonement Theories," *TynB* 32 (1981): 97-122.

5823   D. Greeves, "The Recognized Saviour," *ET* 93 (1981-1982): 84-86.

5824   Antonio Orbe, "Cristo, sacrificio y manjar [Heracleon, frag 12]," *Greg* 66/2 (1985): 185-239.

5825   D. Brent Sandy, "John the Baptist's 'Lamb of God' Affirmation in Its Canonical and Apocalyptic Milieu," *JETS* 34 (1991): 447-59.

1:30

5826   Frédéric Manns, "Exégèse rabbinique et exégèse johannique," *RB* 92/4 (1985): 525-38.

1:31

5827   Ricardo Pietrantonio, "Los 'Ioudaioi' en el Evangelio de Juan," *RevB* 47/1-2 (1985): 27-41.

1:32-34

5828   Georg Richter, "Zu den Tauferzählungen Mk 1:9-11 und Johannes 1:32-34," *ZNW* 65 (1974): 43-56.

5829   G. Tosatto, "Il battesimo di Gesù e alcuni passi trascurati dello Pseudo-Filone," *Bib* 56 (1975): 405-409.

5830   Stephen Gero, "The Spirit as a Dove at the Baptism of Jesus," *NovT* 18 (1976): 17-35.

1:32-33

5831   K. Luke, "The Syriac Text of Matthew 11:29b and John 1:32-33," *BB* 16 (1990): 250-67.

1:32

5832   Leander E. Keck, "The Spirit and the Dove," *NTS* 17 (1970-1971): 41-67.

5833   Paul Garnet, "The Baptism of Jesus and the Son of Man Idea," *JSNT* 9 (1980): 49-65.

5834   Günther Schwarz, " 'Wie eine Taube'?" *BibN* 89 (1997): 27-29.

1:33

5835   P. Sánchez-Céspedes, "Cognovitne Iohannes Baptista mysterium Trinitatis?" *VD* 13 (1933): 75-78.

5836   B. Marconcini, "La predicazione del Battista: Interpretazione storica e applicazioni," *BibO* 15 (1973): 49-60.

5837   Ronald E. Heine, "Can the Catena Fragments of Origen's Commentary on John Be Trusted?" *VC* 40/2 (1986): 118-34.

1:34-43

5838   J. Williams, "Proposed Renderings for Some Johannine Passages," *BT* 25 (1974): 351-53.

1:34

5839   André Légault, "Le baptème de Jésus et la doctrine du Serviteur souffrant," *ScE* 13 (1961): 147-66.

1:35-51

5840   H. Spaemann, "Stunde des Lammes: Meditationen über die ersten Jüngerberufungen (Johannes 1:35-51)," *BibL* 7 (1966): 58-68.

5841   F. Agnew, "Vocatio primorum discipulorum in traditione synoptica," *VD* 46 (1968): 129-47.

5842   J. Bill, "Die Erfahrung des Anfangs: Meditationsgedanken zu Johannes 1:35-51," *GeistL* 43 (1970): 230-34.

5843   Claude Coulot, "Les figures du maître et de ses disciples dans les premières communautés chrétiennes," *RechSR* 59 (1985): 1-11.

5844   Francis J. Moloney, "The Fourth Gospel and the Jesus of History," *NTS* 46 (2000): 42-58.

1:35-42

5845   P.-E. Jacquemin, "Les premiers disciples du Messie," *AsSeign* 33 (1970): 53-61.

5846   D. H. C. Read, "From the Roots of Our Religion," *ET* 92 (1980): 21-22.

5847   R. F. Collins, "Discipleship in John's Gospel," *Emmanuel* 91 (1985): 248-55.

5848   H. J. Klauck, "Gemeinde ohne Amt: Erfahrungen mit der Kirche in den johanneischen Schriften," *BZ* 29/2 (1985): 193-220.

1:35-39

5849 M. de Goedt, "Un schème de révélation dans le 4ᵉ Évangile," *NTS* 8 (1961-1962): 142-50.

1:35

5850 John K. Thornecroft, "The Redactor and the 'Beloved' in John," *ET* 98 (1987): 135-39.

1:36

5851 P. Federkiewicz, "Ecce Agnus Dei' (Joh. 1:29, 36)," *VD* 12 (1932): 41-47, 83-88, 117-20, 156-60, 168-71.

5852 Joachim Jeremias, "'Αμνὸς τοῦ θεοῦ—παῖς θεοῦ," *ZNW* 34 (1935): 115-23.

5853 Juan Leal, "El sentido soteriológico del cordero de Dios en la exégesis catolica," *EE* 24 (1950): 134-38, 147-82.

5854 Daniel A. Negoïtsa, "L'Agneau de Dieu et le Verbe de Dieu," *NovT* 13 (1971): 24-37.

5855 D. Brent Sandy, "John the Baptist's 'Lamb of God' Affirmation in Its Canonical and Apocalyptic Milieu," *JETS* 34 (1991): 447-59.

1:38

5856 Frédéric Manns, "Exégèse rabbinique et exégèse johannique," *RB* 92/4 (1985): 525-38.

5857 Robert H. Smith, "Seeking Jesus in the Gospel of John," *CTM* 15 (1988): 48-55.

1:40-49

5858 J. Enciso Viana, "La vocación de Natanael y el Salmo 24," *EB* 19 (1960): 229-36.

5859 A. H. Maynard, "The Role of Peter in the Fourth Gospel," *NTS* 30/4 (1984): 531-48.

1:40

5860 Michael C. Perry, "Studies in Texts: The Other of the Two," *Theology* 64 (1961): 153-54.

1:41-42

5861 O. M. Rao, "The Call of Peter in the Fourth Gospel," *IJT* 10 (1961): 125-29.

1:41

5862   D. Langley, "John 1:41," *ET* 41 (1929-1930): 430.

1:43-51

5863   J. Ramsey Michaels, "Nathanael under the Fig Tree," *ET* 78 (1966-1967): 182-83.

5864   J. D. M. Derrett, "Figtrees in the New Testament," *HeyJ* 14 (1973): 249-65.

5865   L. Díez Merino, " 'Can Anything Good Come from Nazareth?' An Account of the History and Excavations Where the Word Became Incarnate," *BibTo* 69 (1973): 1385-88.

5866   E. G. Clarke, "Jacob's Dream at Bethel as Interpreted in the Targums and the New Testament," *SR* 4 (1975): 367-77.

5867   E. Leidig, "Natanael, ein Sohn des Tholomäus," *TZ* 36 (1980): 374-75.

5868   William O. Walker, "John 1:43-51 and 'The Son of Man' in the Fourth Gospel," *JSNT* 56 (1994): 31-42.

5869   Paul S. Berge, "The Beginning of the Good News: The Epiphany Gospels in Mark and John," *WW* 17 (1997): 94-101.

1:43

5870   H. Spencer, "John 1:43," *ET* 45 (1933-1934): 336.

1:45-51

5871   L. Paul Trudinger, "An Israelite in Whom There Is No Guile: An Interpretative Note on John 1:45-51," *EQ* 54 (1982): 117-20.

5872   Peter J. Gomes, "John 1:45-51," *Int* 43 (1989): 282-86.

5873   Craig R. Koester, "Messianic Exegesis and the Call of Nathanael," *JSNT* 39 (1990): 23-34.

1:45-50

5874   T. Nicklas, " 'Unter dem Feigenbaum'. Die Rolle des Lesers im Dialog zwischen Jesus und Natanael (Joh 1.45-50)," *NTS* 46 (2000): 193-203.

1:45-49

5875   D. Browne, "Who Was Nathanael?" *ET* 38 (1926-1927): 286.

5876   R. B. Y. Scott, "Who Was Nathanael?" *ET* 38 (1926-1927): 93-94.

1:45

5877   Mike Mitchell, "Philip the Apostle," *BI* 17/1 (1990): 52-54.

5878   Thomas Söding, " 'Was kann aus Nazareth schon Gutes kommen?' Die Bedeutung des Judenseins Jesu im Johannesevangelium,"*NTS* 46 (2000): 21-41.

1:47-51

5879   M. de Goedt, "Un schème de révélation dans le 4ᵉ Évangile," *NTS* 8 (1961-1962): 142-50.

1:47

5880   H. Kuhli, "Nathanael - 'wahrer Israelit' Zum angeblich attributiven Gebrauch von ἀληθῶς Ἰσραηλίτης in Johannes 1:47," *BibN* 9 (1979): 11-19.

5881   Günther Schwarz, "ἀληθῶς Ἰσραηλίτης," *BibN* 10 (1979): 41-42.

5882   Ricardo Pietrantonio, "Los 'Ioudaioi' en el Evangelio de Juan," *RevB* 47/1-2 (1985): 27-41.

5883   Tjitze Baarda, "Nathanael, 'The Scribe of Israel': John 1,47 in Ephraem's Commentary on the Diatessaron," *ETL* 71 (1995): 321-36.

1:48-50

5884   C. F. D. Moule, "A Note on 'Under the Fig Tree' in John 1:48-50," *JTS* 5 (1954): 210-11.

1:49

5885   John Ashton, "The Identity and Function of the *Ioudaioi* in the Fourth Gospel," *NovT* 27 (1985): 40-75.

5886   Ricardo Pietrantonio, "Los 'Ioudaioi' en el Evangelio de Juan," *RevB* 47/1-2 (1985): 27-41.

1:51

5887   Hans Windisch, "Angelophanien um den Menschensohn auf Erden: Zu Ioh. 1:51," *ZNW* 30 (1931): 215-33.

5888   Hans Windisch, "Johannes 1:51 und die Auferstehung Jesu," *ZNW* 31 (1932): 199-204.

5889   G. Quispel, "Nathanael und der Menschensohn (Johannes 1:51)," *ZNW* 47 (1956): 281-83.

5890   W. Michaelis, "Johannes 1:51, Gen 28:12 und das Menschensohn-Problem," *TLZ* 85 (1960): 561-78.

5891   Raymond E. Brown, "Incidents that Are Units in the Synoptic Gospels but Dispersed in St. John," *CBQ* 23 (1961): 143-60.

5892   Jerome H. Neyrey, "The Jacob Allusions in John 1:51," *CBQ* 44 (1982): 586-605.

5893   H. Maillet, " 'Au-dessus de' ou 'sur'? (Jean1/51)," *ÉTR* 59 (1984): 207-31.

5894   Christopher C. Rowland, "John 1.51, Jewish Apocalyptic and Targumic Tradition," *NTS* 30 (1984): 498-507.

5895   John W. Pryor, "The Johannine Son of Man and the Descent-Ascent Motif," *JETS* 34 (1991): 341-51.

5896   Michèle Morgen, "La promesse de Jésus à Nathanaël (Jn 1:51) éclairée par la hagaddah de Jacob-Israël," *RevSR* 67 (1993): 3-21.

2-12

5897   T. C. Smith, "The Book of Signs, John 2-12," *RevExp* 62/4 (1965): 441-57.

2-4

5898   F.-M. Braun, "Le don de Dieu et l'initiation chrétienne," *NRT* 86 (1964): 1025-48.

2:1-4:54

5899   Francis J. Moloney, "From Cana to Cana (John 2:1-4:54) and the Fourth Evangelist's Concept of Correct (and Incorrect) Faith," *Sale* 40 (1978): 817-45.

2

5900   C. Charlier, "Les noces de Cana (Jean 2)," *BVC* 1/4 (1953): 81-86.

5901 Giuseppe Segalla, "Le signe du Temple et la foi (Jean 2)," *AsSeign* 16 (1971): 50-58.

5902 A. B. Kolenkow, "The Changing Patterns: Conflicts and the Necessity of Death. John 2 and 12 and Markan Parallels," *SBLSP* 9/1 (1979): 123-25.

5903 F. Genuyt, "Les noces de Cana et la purification du temple. Analyse du chapitre 2 de l'Évangile de Jean," *SémBib* 31 (1983): 14-33.

2:1-22

5904 D. Schüler, "Jesus faz milagres? Uma análise de Jo 2:1-22," *EstT* 23/1 (1983): 73-78.

2:1-12

5905 E. Haible, "Das Gottesbild der Hochzeit von Kana: Zur biblischen Grundlegung der Eingottlehre," *MTZ* 10 (1959): 189-99.

5906 J. B. Cortés, "The Wedding Feast at Cana," *TD* 14 (1966): 14-17.

5907 M.-B. Eyquem, "La foi de Marie et les noces de Cana," *VS* 117 (1967): 169-81.

5908 Francis E. Williams, "Fourth Gospel and Synoptic Tradition: Two Johannine Passages," *JBL* 86 (1967): 311-19.

5909 P.-E. Jacquemin, "Le signe inaugural de Jésus," *AsSeign* 35 (1970): 76-88.

5910 F. S. Parnham, "The Miracle at Cana," *EQ* 42 (1970): 105-109.

5911 H. Engel, "Der Wein göttlichen Heils: Ein Versuch, heute über Johannes 2:1-12 zu predigen," *BibL* 12 (1971): 282-85.

5912 Eta Linnemann, "Die Hochzeit zu Kana und Dionysos oder das Unzureichende der Kategorien-Übertragung und Identifkation zur Erfassung der religionsgeschichtlichen Beziehungen," *NTS* 20 (1973-1974): 408-18.

5913 I. de la Potterie, "La madre di Gesù e il mistero di Cana," *CC* 96 (1979): 425-40.

5914 Ulrich Busse and A. May, "Das Weinwunder von Kana (Johannes 2:1-11). Erneute Analyse eines 'erratischen Blocks'," *BibN* 12 (1980): 35-61.

5915 R. F. Collins, "Cana (John 2:1-12) - The First of His Signs or the Key to His Signs?" *ITQ* 47 (1980): 79-95.

5916 Ingo Broer, "Noch einmal: Zur religionsgeschichtlichen 'Ableitung' von Johannes 2:1-11," *SNTU-A* 8 (1983): 103-23.

5917 F. Rauch, "Der neue Wein der Gottesliebe: Eine Hochzeitsmeditation nach Johannes 2:1-12," *GeistL* 56 (1983): 224-27.

5918 Gerhard Lohfink, "Das Weinwunder zu Kana: Eine Auslegung von Johannes 2:1-12," *GeistL* 57 (1984): 169-82.

5919 Joseph A. Grassi, "The Role of Jesus' Mother in John's Gospel: A Reappraisal," *CBQ* 48/1 (1986): 67-80.

5920 L. Paul Trudinger, "On the Third Day There Was a Wedding at Cana: Reflections on St. John 2:1-12," *DR* 104 (1986): 41-43.

5921 Allan Mayer, "Elijah and Elisha in John's Signs Source," *ET* 99 (1988): 171-73.

5922 Rainer Riesner, "Fragen um 'Kana in Galiläa'," *BK* 43 (1988): 69-71.

5923 Louis Painer, "Cana et le Temple: la pratique et la théorie," *LV* 41 (1992): 37-54.

5924 Ritva H. Williams, "The Mother of Jesus at Cana: A Social-Science Interpretation of John 2:1-12," *CBQ* 59 (1997): 679-92.

2:1-11

5925 V. Anzalone, "Jesus et Maria ad nuptias in Cana Galilaeae," *VD* 9 (1929): 364-68.

5926 Paul Gächter, "Maria in Kana," *ZKT* 55 (1931): 351-402.

5927 W. Moock, "Zu Johannes 2:1-11," *TGl* 30 (1938): 313-16.

5928 H. Grimme, "Drei Evangelienberichte in neuer Auffassung," *TGl* 34 (1942): 85-87.

5929 L. Cadoux, "Les noces de Cana," *VS* 81 (1949): 155-62.

5930   Hugh W. Montefiore, "The Position of the Cana Miracle and the Cleansing of the Temple in St. John's Gospel," *JTS* 50 (1949): 183-86.

5931   J. A. Robillard, "Le vin manqua," *VS* 90 (1953): 28-45.

5932   D. Gonzalo Maeso, "Una lección de exégesis lingüística sobre el pasaje evangélico de las bodas de Caná," *CuBí* 11 (1954): 352-64.

5933   Emmanuele Testa, "La mediazione di Maria a Cana," *SBFLA* 5 (1954-1955): 139-90.

5934   J. Michl, "Hochzeit von Kana: Kritik einer Auslegung," *TGl* 45 (1955): 334-48.

5935   Christian P. Ceroke, "Jesus and Mary at Cana: Separation or Association?" *TS* 17 (1956): 1-38.

5936   D. M. Stanley, "Cana as Epiphany," *Worship* 32 (1957-1958): 83-89.

5937   C. Armerding, "The Marriage in Cana," *BSac* 118 (1961): 320-26.

5938   Arthur M. Vincent, "Water into Wine: A Sign for the Modern Ministry," *CTM* 32 (1961): 28-38.

5939   Richard J. Dillon, "Wisdom Tradition and Sacramental Retrospect in the Cana Account," *CBQ* 24 (1962): 268-96.

5940   Jean Galot, "Réflexions doctrinales: Le mystère de Cana," *AsSeign* 16 (1962): 88-100.

5941   P.-E. Jacquemin, "Évangile du 2ᵉ Dimanche après l'Épiphanie: Le signe inaugural de Jésus," *AsSeign* 16 (1962): 32-53.

5942   S. Temple, "The Two Signs in the Fourth Gospel," *JBL* 81 (1962): 169-74.

5943   H. Leroy, "Das Weinwunder zu Kana: Eine exegetische Studie zu Johannes 2:1-11," *BibL* 4 (1963): 168-73.

5944   J. Bodson, "Cana de Galilée: L'église et l'Eucharistie," *LV* 19 (1964): 645-52.

5945   P. Hinnebusch, "Cana and the Paschal Mystery," *BibTo* 20 (1965): 1325-33.

5946   J. Ramos-Regidor, "Signo y poder: A propósito de la exégesis patrística de Jean 2:1-11," *Sale* 27 (1965): 499-562.

5947   Richard J. Dillon, "Wisdom Tradition and Sacramental Retrospect in the Cana Account," *CBQ* 24 (1966): 268-96.

5948   J. Riedl, "El 'principio' de los milagros de Jesús en Caná de Galilea," *RevB* 28 (1966): 131-47.

5949   Sebastián Bartina, " 'Cada uno a lo suyo': Una frase hecha en Os 14,19," *EB* 28 (1968): 247-49.

5950   T. Worden, "The Marriage Feast at Cana," *Scr* 20 (1968): 97-106.

5951   G. Giavini, "Il segno di Cana," *PV* 15 (1970): 349-55.

5952   Joseph A. Grassi, "The Wedding at Cana: A Pentecostal Meditation?" *NovT* 14 (1972): 131-36.

5953   J. Proust, "Lecture d'un sermon 'Les noces de Cana'," *ÉTR* 47 (1972): 121-43.

5954   P. Goodman, "The Mother of Jesus: Thoughts on Her Role," *BibTo* 87 (1976): 1006-1009.

5955   Otto Bächli, " 'Was habe ich mit dir zu schaffen?' Eine formelhafte Frage im A.T. und N.T.," *TZ* 33 (1977): 69-80.

5956   Stanley D. Toussaint, "The Significance of the First Sign in John's Gospel," *BSac* 134 (1977): 45-51.

5957   K. T. Cooper, "The Best Wine: John 2:1-11," *WTJ* 1 (1978-1979): 364-80.

5958   R. M. Mackowski, "Scholar's Qanah. A Re-Examination of the Evidence in Favor of Khirbet-Qanah," *BZ* 23 (1979): 278-84.

5959   Charles H. Giblin, "Suggestion, Negative Response, and Positive Action in St. John's Portrayal of Jesus," *NTS* 26 (1979-1980): 197-211.

5960   J.-M. Léonard, "Notule sur l'évangile de Jean: Le récit des noces de Cana et Ésaïe 25," *ÉTR* 57 (1982): 119-20.

5961   A. H. Maynard, "ΤΙ ΕΜΟΙ ΚΑΙ ΣΟΙ" *NTS* 31 (1985): 582-86.

5962   John Rena, "Women in the Gospel of John," *ÉgT* 17/2 (1986): 131-47.

5963   Timothy L. Owings, "John 2:1-11," *RevExp* 85 (1988): 533-37.

5964   Knut   Backhaus,   "Praeparatio   Evangelii: Die religionsgeschichtlichen Beziehungen zwischen Täufer- und Jesus-Bewegung im Spiegel der sog. Semeia-Quelle des vierten Evangeliums," *TGl* 81 (1991): 202-15.

5965   Wolfgang Roth, "The Six Vessels of John," *BibTo* 30/4 (1992): 241-45.

5966   J. Zumstein, "Le signe de la croix," *LV* 41 (1992): 68-82.

5967   Ulrich Busse, "The relevance of social history to the interpretation of the Gospel according to John," *SkrifK* 16 (1995): 28-38.

2:1

5968   J. B. Bauer, "Drei Tage," *Bib* 39 (1958): 354-58.

5969   Vincent Parkin, " 'On the Third Day there Was a Marriage in Cana of Galilee'," *IBS* 3 (1981): 134-44.

2:3-5

5970   Edward J. Kilmartin, "The Mother of Jesus Was There," *SE* 15/2 (1963): 213-26.

2:3-4

5971   E. Pax, "Bemerkungen zum patriarchalischen Stil," *SBFLA* 22 (1972): 315-34.

5972   Édouard Delebecque, "Les deux vins de Cana," *RT* 85 (1985): 242-52.

2:3

5973   J. R. Harris, "Western Gloss to John 2:3," *ET* 41 (1929-1930): 107-109.

5974   Martino Conti, " 'Non hanno più vino' (Gv 2,3)," *BibO* 11 (1969): 76.

5975   F. Zehrer, "Das Gespräch Jesu mit seiner Mütter auf der Hochzeit zu Kana (Johannes 2:3f) im Licht der traditions- und redaktionsgeschichtlichen Forschung," *BL* 43 (1970): 14-27.

2:4

5976   H. Smith, "John 2:4," *ET* 32 (1920-1921): 45.

5977   B. Brinkmann, "Quid mihi et tibi, mulier? Nondum venit hora mea," *VD* 14 (1934): 135-41.

5978   T. Gallus, "Quid mihi et tibi, mulier? Nondum venit hora mea," *VD* 22 (1942): 41-50.

5979   R. B. Woodworth, "The Marriage at Cana in Galilee (John 2:4," *Int* 1 (1947): 372-74.

5980   H. Preisker, "Johannes 2:4 und 19:26," *ZNW* 42 (1949): 209-14.

5981   Juan Leal, "La hora de Jesús, la hora de su madre," *EE* 26 (1952): 147-68.

5982   A. Kurfess, "Zu Johannes 2:4," *ZNW* 44 (1952-1953): 257.

5983   J. Michl, "Bemerkungen zu Johannes 2:4," *Bib* 36 (1955): 492-509.

5984   J. Michl, " 'Frau, was ist zwischen mir und dir'?" *BK* 11 (1956): 98-110.

5985   Christian P. Ceroke, "The Problem of Ambiguity in John 2:4," *CBQ* 21 (1959): 316-40.

5986   J. D. M. Derrett, "Water into Wine: The Situation at Cana," *BZ* 7 (1963): 80-97.

5987   F. Salvoni, "Nevertheless, My Hour Has Not Yet Come," *RQ* 7 (1963): 236-41.

5988   Albert Vanhoye, "Interrogation johannique et exégèse de Cana (Jean 2:4)," *Bib* 55 (1974): 157-67.

5989   A. H. Maynard, "ΤΙ ΕΜΟΙ ΚΑΙ ΣΟΙ," *NTS* 31 (1985): 582-86.

2:6

5990   J. Villescas, "John 2: The Capacity of Six Jars," *BT* 28 (1977): 447.

5991   Margaret Pamment, "Focus in the Fourth Gospel," *ET* 97/3 (1985): 71-74.

5992   John C. Thomas, "The Fourth Gospel and Rabbinic Judaism," *ZNW* 82 (1991): 159-82.

5993 Günther Schwarz, "Ana metretas dyo e treis?" *BibN* 62 (1992): 45.

2:9

5994 P. Dacquino, "Aqua vinum facta," *VD* 39 (1961): 92-96.

2:10

5995 Paul W. Meyer, "John 2:10," *JBL* 86 (1967): 191-97.

5996 Barnabas Lindars, "Two Parables in John," *NTS* 16 (1969-1970): 318-29.

5997 J. B. Bauer, " 'Literarische' Namen und 'literarische' Bräuche (zu Johannes 2:10 and 18:39)," *BZ* 26 (1982): 258-64.

2:11

5998 John Hennig, "Was ist eigentlich geschehen?" *ZRGG* 15/3 (1963): 276-86.

2:12-9:42

5999 R. Alan Culpepper, "The Gospel of John and the Jews," *RevExp* 84 (1987): 273-88.

2:12-5:18

6000 W. Van Der Spek, "Zwischen Galiläa und Judea. Auslegung von Johannes 2:12-5:18," *TextK* 26 (1985): 14-36.

2:12-25

6001 Gordon D. Fee, "The Lemma of Origen's Commentary on John, Book X—An Independent Witness to the Egyptian Textual Tradition?" *NTS* 20 (1973-1974): 78-81.

2:12-22

6002 C. Hudry-Clergeon, "Jésus et le Sanctuaire. Étude de Jean 2:12-22," *NRT* 105 (1983): 535-48.

2:13-3:21

6003 G. Ogg, "The Jerusalem Visit of John 2:13-3:21," *ET* 56 (1944-1945): 70-72.

6004 Antonio Orbe, "San Ireneo y la primera Pascua del Salvador," *EE* 44 (1969): 297-344.

2:13-25

6005 Louis Painer, "Cana et le Temple: la pratique et la théorie," *LV* 41 (1992): 37-54.

2:13-22

6006 E. C. Hoskyns, "Adversaria exegetica: The Old and New Worship of God," *Theology* 1 (1920): 143-48.

6007 F.-M. Braun, "L'expulsion des vendeurs du temple," *RB* 38 (1929): 178-200.

6008 A. Herranz Arriba, "Expulsión de los profanadores del Templo," *EB* 1 (1929-1930): 39-59, 122-42.

6009 G. P. Lewis, "Dislocations in the Fourth Gospel: The Temple Cleansing and the Visit of Nicodemus," *ET* 44 (1932-1933): 228-30.

6010 H. van den Bussche, "Le Signe du Temple," *BVC* 20 (1957): 92-100.

6011 R. A. Martin, "The Date of the Cleansing of the Temple in John 2:13-22," *IJT* 15 (1966): 52-56.

6012 C. J. Bjerkelund, "En tradisjons- og redaksjonshistorisk analyse an perikopene om tempelrendelsen," *NTT* 69 (1968): 206-18.

6013 Étienne Trocmé, "L'expulsion des marchands du Temple," *NTS* 15 (1968-1969): 1-22.

6014 Richard H. Hiers, "Purification of the Temple: Preparation for the Kingdom of God," *JBL* 90 (1971): 82-90.

6015 R. Gyllenberg, "Intåget i Jerusalem och Johannes-evangeliets uppbyggnad," *SEÅ* 41-42 (1976-1977): 81-86.

6016 Joachim Jeremias, "Zwei Miszellen. 2. Zur Geschichtlichkeit der Tempelreinigung," *NTS* 23 (1976-1977): 179-80.

6017 J. D. M. Derrett, "The Zeal of the House and the Cleansing of the Temple," *DR* 95 (1977): 79-94.

6018 Mauro Láconi, "I pellegrinaggi di Gesù al Tempio e il mistero pasquale," *PV* 29 (1984): 188-95.

6019 K. Butting, "Das Haus Gottes Israels. Kapitel 2 des Evangeliums nach Johannes," *TextK* 26 (1985): 37-47.

6020   P. Imhof, "Jesus im Tempel. Zur Gegenwart Gottes im Leib des Menschen," *GeistL* 58 (1985): 222-26.

6021   Egon Spiegel, "War Jesus gewalttätig? Bemerkungen zur Tempelreinigung," *TGl* 75 (1985): 239-47.

6022   William P. Wood, "John 2:13-22," *Int* 45 (1991): 59-63.

6023   Francis J. Moloney, "The Fourth Gospel and the Jesus of History," *NTS* 46 (2000): 42-58.

2:13-20

6024   X. Léon-Dufour, "Le signe du temple selon Jean," *RechSR* 39 (1951): 155-75.

2:13-17

6025   J. D. M. Derrett, "Fresh Light on the Lost Sheep and the Lost Coin," *NTS* 26 (1979-1980): 36-60.

2:13

6026   Margaret Pamment, "Focus in the Fourth Gospel," *ET* 97/3 (1985): 71-74.

2:14-16

6027   W. F. Howard, "The Position of the Temple-Cleansing in the Fourth Gospel," *ET* 44 (1932-1933): 284-85.

6028   E. J. Roberts, "The Position of the Temple-Cleansing in the Fourth Gospel," *ET* 44 (1932-1933): 427.

6029   R. H. Lightfoot, "The Cleansing of the Temple in St. John's Gospel," *ET* 60 (1948-1949): 64-68.

2:15

6030   H. M. Foston, "Two Johannine Parentheses," *ET* 32 (1920-1921): 520-23.

6031   H. K. Moulton, "πάντας in John 2:15," *BT* 18 (1967): 126-27.

6032   P. Colella, "Cambiamonete (Jean 2:15)," *RBib* 19 (1971): 429-30.

2:19-22

6033   H.-J. Vogel, "Die Tempelreinigung und Golgotha," *BZ* 6/1 (1962): 102-107.

2:19-20

6034   J. B. Bauer, "Drei Tage," *Bib* 39 (1958): 354-58.

2:19

6035 F. P. Cheetham, " 'Destroy this Temple, and in Three Days I Will Raise it up'," *JTS* 24 (1922-1923): 315-17.

2:20

6036 E. Power, "John 2:20 and the Date of the Crucifixion," *Bib* 9 (1928): 257-88.

6037 F. J. Badcock, "A Vote on John 2:20," *ET* 47 (1935-1936): 40-41.

6038 G. Ogg, "The Age of Jesus When He Taught," *NTS* 5 (1958-1959): 291-98.

2:21-22

6039 H. J. Flowers, "Interpolations in the Fourth Gospel," *JBL* 40 (1921): 146-58.

2:23-3:22

6040 G. Steven, "Nicodemus," *ET* 31 (1919-1920): 505-508.

2:23-3:21

6041 I. de la Potterie, "Ad dialogum Jesu cum Nicodemo (2,23-3,21). Analysis litteraria," *VD* 47 (1969): 141-50.

6042 L. J. Topel, "A Note on the Methodology of Structural Analysis in John 2:23-3:21," *CBQ* 33 (1971): 211-20.

6043 K. Tsuchido, "The Composition of the Nicodemus Episode, John ii,23-iii,21," *AJBI* 1 (1975): 91-103.

2:23-25

6044 Zane C. Hodges, "Problem Passages in the Gospel of John. Part 2: Untrustworthy Believers—John 2:23-25," *BSac* 135 (1978): 139-52.

2:23

6045 D. M. Stanley, "Israel's Wisdom Meets the Wisdom of God," *Worship* 32 (1958): 280-87.

6046 Christoph Burchard, "Fussnoten zum neutestamentlichen Griechisch (Johannes 2:23; 7:11 μὴ ἐν τῇ ἑορτῇ)," *ZNW* 61 (1970): 157-71.

6047 Georg Korting, "Binden oder lösen: Zur Verstockungs- und Befreiungstheologie in Mt 16:19; 18:18-21:35 und Joh 15:1-17; 2:23," *SNTU-A* 14 (1989): 39-91.

3-4

6048 I. de la Potterie, "Structura primae partis Evangelii Iohannis (Capita III et IV)," *VD* 47 (1969): 130-40.

3

6049 F. W. Lewis, "The Arrangement of the Texts in the Third Chapter of St. John," *ET* 37 (1925-1926): 179-81.

6050 J. H. Michael, "The Arrangement of the Text in the Third Chapter of St. John," *ET* 37 (1925-1926): 428-29.

6051 Rudolf Schnackenburg, "Die 'situationsgelösten' Redestücke in Johannes 3," *ZNW* 49 (1958): 88-99.

6052 Marinus de Jonge, "Entretien de Jésus avec Nicodème (Jean 3)," *SémBib* 10 (1978): 45-48.

6053 Jerome H. Neyrey, "John III - A Debate over Johannine Epistemology and Christianity," *NovT* 23 (1981): 115-27.

6054 William C. Grese, "Unless One Is Born Again: The Use of a Heavenly Journey in John 3," *JBL* 107 (1988): 677-93.

6055 Michel Gourgues, "Sur la structure et la christologie de Jean 3 (1993): Approche et apport d'un ouvrage récent," *ScE* 46 (1994): 221-27.

6056 Roland Bergmeier, "Gottesherrschaft, Taufe und Geist: Zur Tauftradition in Joh 3," *ZNW* 86 (1995): 53-73.

3:1-21

6057 E. C. Hoskyns, "John 3:1-21," *Theology* 1 (1920): 83-89.

6058 F. Roustang, "L'entretien avec Nicodème," *NRT* 78 (1956): 337-58.

6059 Siegfried Mendner, "Nikodemus," *JBL* 77 (1958): 293-323.

6060 M. Balagué, "Diálogo con Nicodemo," *CuBí* 16 (1959): 193-206.

6061 John Bligh, "Four Studies in St. John. 2. Nicodemus," *HeyJ* 8 (1967): 40-51.

6062 W. A. Wolfram and R. W. Fasold, "A Black English Translation of John 3:1-21 with Grammatical Annotations," *BT* 20 (1969): 48-54.

6063 G. T. Fish and W. A. Wolfram, "Correspondence," *BT* 21 (1970): 44-46.

6064   L. Stachowiak, "Spotkanie Jezusa z Nikodemen," *RoczTK* 20 (1973): 69-81.

6065   D. H. C. Read, "Nicodemus," *ET* 87 (1975-1976): 208-209.

6066   R. F. Collins, "Jesus' Conversation with Nicodemus," *BibTo* 93 (1977): 1409-19.

6067   L. Walter, "Lecture d'Évangile. Jean III,1-21: selon la foi et l'incrédulité," *EV* 87 (1977): 369-78, 385-90.

6068   Marinus de Jonge, "Entretien de Jésus avec Nicodème (Jean 3)," *SémBib* 10 (1978): 45-48.

6069   Alois Stöger, "Das österliche Sakrament der Taufe: Meditation zu Johannes 3:1-21," *BL* 52 (1979): 121-24.

6070   M. Michel, "Nicodème ou le non-lieu de la vérité," *RevSR* 55 (1981): 227-36.

6071   Francis P. Cotterell, "The Nicodemus Conversation: A Fresh Appraisal," *ET* 96 (1984-1985): 237-42.

6072   Jouette M. Bassler, "Mixed Signals: Nicodemus in the Fourth Gospel," *JBL* 108 (1989): 635-46.

6073   Michael D. Goulder, "Nicodemus," *SJT* 44 (1991): 153-68.

3:1-17

6074   Sharon H. Ringe, "On the Gospel of John: The Gospel as Healing Word," *QR* 6/4 (1986): 75-103.

6075   Glen V. Wiberg, "Listen! The Wind: A Sermon On John 3:1-17," *ExA* 12 (1996): 147-51.

6076   Margaret B. Hess, "A Curious Man," *CC* 114 (1997): 475.

3:1-15

6077   F.-M. Braun, "La vie d'en haut," *RSPT* 40 (1956): 3-24.

6078   H. A. Hoyt, "The Explanation of the New Birth," *GTJ* 8/10 (1967): 14-21.

6079   John N. Suggit, "Nicodemus, the True Jew," *Neo* 14 (1981): 90-110.

6080   Sandra M. Schneiders, "Born Anew," *TT* 44 (1987): 189-96.

6081   Gail R. O'Day, "New Birth as a New People: Spirituality and Community in the Fourth Gospel," *WW* 8 (1988): 53-61.

6082   Don Williford, "John 3:1-15--gennêthênai anôthen: A Radical Departure, A New Beginning," *RevExp* 96 (1999): 451-61.

3:1-12

6083   Rudolf Pesch, " 'Ihr müsst von oben geboren werden': Eine Auslegung von Johannes 3:1-12," *BibL* 7 (1966): 208-19.

3:1-11

6084   Mark F. Whitters, "Discipleship in John: Four Profiles," *WW* 18 (1998): 422-27.

3:1-10

6085   G. P. Lewis, "Dislocations in the Fourth Gospel: The Temple Cleansing and the Visit of Nicodemus," *ET* 44 (1932-1933): 228-30.

6086   I. de la Potterie, "Jesus et Nicodemus: de necessitate generationis ex Spiritu," *VD* 47 (1969): 193-214.

3:1-8

6087   R. G. Forrest, "The Lord God Formed Man. . .," *ET* 91 (1979-1980): 15-17.

3:1-6

6088   Daniel Patte, "Jesus' Pronouncement about Entering the Kingdom Like a Child: A Structural Exegesis," *Semeia* 29 (1983): 3-42.

3:1-3

6089   S. Agrelo, "A propósito de Jean 3:1-3," *Ant* 60 (1985): 233-39.

3:1

6090   A. J. Conyers, "Nicodemus," *BI* 16/1 (1989): 14-16.

3:2

6091   Homer A. Kent, "A Time to Teach," *GTJ* 1/1 (1980): 7-17.

6092   John W. Pryor, "Papyrus Egerton 2 and the Fourth Gospel," *ABR* 37 (1989): 1-13.

3:3-10

6093   Matthew Vellanickal, "Christian: Born of the Spirit," *BB* 2 (1976): 153-74.

3:3-5

6094   J. W. Carpenter, "Water Baptism," *RevExp* 54 (1957): 59-66.

6095   Barnabas Lindars, "John and the Synoptic Gospels: A Test Case," *NTS* 27 (1980-1981): 287-94.

6096   George R. Beasley-Murray, "John 3:3, 5: Baptism, Spirit and the Kingdom," *ET* 97 (1985-1986): 167-70.

3:3

6097   B. J. Le Frois, "The Spiritual Motherhood of Mary in John 3:3ff.," *CBQ* 14 (1952): 116-23.

6098   D. Howell-Jones, "The Second Birth," *ET* 92 (1981-1982): 85-86.

3:5-8

6099   Carroll D. Osburn, "Some Exegetical Observations on John 3:5-8," *RQ* 31/3 (1989): 129-38.

3:5

6100   H. W. Bates, "Born of Water," *BSac* 85 (1928): 230-36.

6101   J. S. Murray, "Water and Spirit," *ET* 59 (1947-1948): 138-39.

6102   H. de Julliot, "L'eau et l'esprit," *BVC* 27 (1959): 35-42.

6103   I. de la Potterie, "Naître de l'eau et naître de l'Esprit: le texte baptismal de Jean 3:5," *SE* 14/3 (1962): 417-43.

6104   M. Costa, "Simbolismo battesimale in Giovanni 7:37-39; 19:31-37; 3:5," *RBib* 13 (1965): 347-83.

6105   Donald W. B. Robinson, "Born of Water and Spirit: Does John 3:5 Refer to Baptism?" *RTR* 25 (1966): 15-23.

6106   R. Fowler, "Born of Water and the Spirit (John 3:5)," *ET* 82 (1970-1971): 159.

6107   G. Spriggs, "Meaning of 'Water' in John 3:5," *ET* 85 (1973-1974): 149-50.

6108   Georg Richter, "Zum sogenannten Tauf text Johannes 3:5," *MTZ* 26 (1975): 101-25.

6109   Zane C. Hodges, "Problem Passages in the Gospel of John. Part 3: Water and Spirit - John 3:5," *BSac* 135 (1978): 206-20.

6110   L. L. Belleville, " 'Born of Water and Spirit': John 3:5," *TriJ* 1 (1980): 125-41.

6111   Margaret Pamment, "John 3:5," *NovT* 25 (1983): 189-90.

6112   Ben Witherington, "The Waters of Birth: John 3:5 and 1 John 5:6-8," *NTS* 35/1 (1989): 155-60.

6113   John F. Brug, "A Rebirth-Washing and a Renewal-Holy Spirit," *WLQ* 92 (1995): 124-28.

3:8

6114   C. H. Smith, "Οὕτως ἐστὶν πᾶς ὁ γεγεννημένος ἐκ τοῦ πνεύματος," *ET* 81 (1969-1970): 181.

6115   Jean Doignon, "L'esprit souffle où il veut dans la plus ancienne tradition patristique latine," *RSPT* 62 (1978): 345-59.

6116   Balembo Buetubela, "Jean 3:8: l'Esprit-Saint ou le vent naturel," *RAfT* 4/8 (1980): 55-64.

6117   J. D. Thomas, "A Translation Problem - John 3:8," *RQ* 24 (1981): 219-24.

6118   Günther Schwarz, " 'Der Wind weht, wo er will'?" *BibN* 63 (1992): 47-48.

6119   Manfred Görg, "Vom Wehen des Pneuma," *BibN* 66 (1993): 5-9.

3:10

6120   Eric F. F. Bishop, " 'The Authorized Teacher of the Israel of God'," *BT* 7 (1956): 81-83.

3:13-21

6121   Marla J. Selvidge, "Nicodemus and the Woman with Five Husbands," *EGLMBS* 2 (1982): 63-75.

3:13

6122   W. H. Rigg, "St. John 3:13," *Theology* 20 (1930): 98-99.

6123   David A. Black, "The Text of John 3:13," *GTJ* 6 (1985): 49-66.

6124 John W. Pryor, "The Johannine Son of Man and the Descent-Ascent Motif," *JETS* 34 (1991): 341-51.

6125 John F. Brug, "Exegetical Brief: The Son of Man Who Is in Heaven," *WLQ* 93 (1996): 14-41.

3:14-36

6126 G. H. C. MacGregor, "A Suggested Rearrangement of the Johannine Text," *ET* 35 (1923-1924): 476-77.

3:14-21

6127 R. Beauvery, "Accueillir le dessein d'amour que Dieu révèle en Jésus," *EV* 80 (1970): 113-16.

6128 V. Mannucci, "Amour de Dieu et foi de l'homme," *AsSeign* 17 (1970): 40-50.

3:14-16

6129 André Charbonneau, "Jésus en croix (Jn 19,16b-42), Jésus élevé (3,14ss; 8,28s; 12,31ss)," *ScE* 45 (1993): 5-23.

3:14-15

6130 Michèle Morgen, "Le Fils de l'homme élevé en vue de la vie éternelle (Jn 3, 14-15 éclairé par diverses traditions juives)," *RevSR* 68 (1994): 5-17.

3:14

6131 B. Schwank, "Erhöht und verherrlicht," *ErAu* 68 (1992): 137-46.

3:15

6132 K. Stasiak, "The Man Who Came by Night," *BibTo* 20 (1982): 84-89.

3:16-21

6133 Roman Heiligenthal, "Das Heil entscheidet sich durch die Tat," *ZRGG* 36/2 (1984): 131-40.

6134 J. D. M. Derrett, "The Bronze Serpent," *EB* 49/3 (1991): 311-29.

3:16

6135 Dale Moody, "God's Only Son: The Translation of John 3:16 in the R.S.V.," *JBL* 72 (1953): 213-19.

6136 Eduard Schweizer, "Zum religionsgeschichtlichen Hintergrund der 'Sendungsformel' Gal 4:4; Röm 8:3f.; Joh 3:16f.; 1 Joh 4:9," *ZNW* 57 (1966): 199-210.

6137 H. K. Moulton, "John 3:16 - God so Loved the World" *BT* 27 (1973): 242.

6138 R. L. Roberts, "The Rendering 'Only Begotten' in John 3:16," *RQ* 16 (1973): 2-22.

6139 J. Williams, "John 3:16 [Croatian Version]," *BT* 25 (1974): 248.

6140 N. E. Block-Hoell, "Extra ecclesiam nulla salus?" *NTT* 80 (1979): 19-27.

6141 Carnegie S. Calian, "The Challenge of John 3:16 for Theological Education," *CC* 103/5 (1986): 121, 145-48.

6142 Robert H. Grundy and Russell W. Howell, "The Sense and Syntax of John 3:14-17 with Special Reference to the Use of OYTOS...OSTE in John 3:16," *NovT* 41 (1999): 24-39.

3:20-21

6143 Zane C. Hodges, "Problem Passages in the Gospel of John. Part 4: Coming to the Light - John 3:20-21," *BSac* 135 (1978): 314-22.

3:21

6144 H. J. de Jonge, "Een nieuwe tekstgetuige van het Griekse Nieuwe Testament in Nederland," *NTT* 32 (1978): 305-309.

6145 J.-F. Collange, " 'Faire la vérité' considérations éthiques sur Jean 3,21," *RHPR* 62 (1982): 415-23.

3:22-4:3

6146 G. Gardner, "Jean 3:22-4:3 parle-t-il d'un baptême administré par Jésus?" *RTP* 36 (1948): 133-37.

6147 M. Cambe, "Jésus baptise et cesse de baptiser en Judée: Jean 3:22-4:3," *ÉTR* 53 (1978): 98-102.

3:22-36

6148 Jeffrey Wilson, "The Integrity of John 3:22-36," *JSNT* 10 (1981): 34-41.

6149   Walter Klaiber, "Der irdische und der himmlische Zeuge: eine Auslegung von Johannes 3:22-36," *NTS* 36 (1990): 205-33.

3:22-30

6150   M.-É. Boismard, "Les traditions johanniques concernant le Baptiste," *RB* 70 (1963): 5-42.

6151   Francis J. Moloney, "The Fourth Gospel and the Jesus of History," *NTS* 46 (2000): 42-58.

3:22-26

6152   A. J. Walker, "Saint John's Gospel 3:22-26," *ET* 46 (1934-1935): 380-81.

6153   H. van den Bussche, "Les paroles de Dieu," *BVC* 55 (1964): 23-28.

6154   Simon Légasse, "Le baptême administré par Jésus et l'origine du baptême chrétien," *BLE* 78 (1977): 3-30.

3:23

6155   M.-É. Boismard, "Aenon, près de Salem," *RB* 80 (1973): 218-29.

3:25

6156   A. C. Bouquet, "St. John 3:25: A Suggestion," *JTS* 27 (1925-1926): 181-82.

6157   J. M. Ross, "Some Unnoticed Points in the Text of the New Testament," *NovT* 25 (1983): 59-72.

6158   John W. Pryor, "John the Baptist and Jesus: Tradition and Text in John 3.25," *JSNT* 66 (1997): 15-26.

3:29

6159   Barnabas Lindars, "The Parable of the Best Man," *NTS* 16 (1969-1970): 324-29.

6160   Mirjam Zimmermann and Ruben Zimmermann, "Der Freund des Bräutigams (Joh 3,29): Deflorations- oder Christuszeuge?" *ZNW* 90 (1999): 123-30.

3:30

6161   A. Löhr, " 'Er muss wachsen, ich aber abnehmen': Meditation zur Johanneszeit," *BibL* 8 (1967): 139-44.

3:31-36

6162 W. R. G. Loader, "The Central Structure of Johannine Christology," *NTS* 30 (1984): 188-216.

3:34

6163 J. Golub, ". . . non enim ad mensuram dat Spiritum," *VD* 43 (1965): 62-70.

6164 Gerhard L. Müller, "Der eine Gott und das Gebet zu den Heiligen," *IKaZ* 14/4 (1985): 319-33.

6165 Otfried Hofius, " 'Er gibt den Geist ohne Mass' Joh 3,34b," *ZNW* 90 (1999): 131-34.

3:35

6166 Jesse Sell, "Johannine Traditions in Logion 61 of the Gospel of Thomas," *PRS* 7/1 (1980): 24-37.

6167 John W. Pryor, "The Great Thanksgiving and the Fourth Gospel," *BZ* 35/2 (1991): 157-79.

4

6168 F. Roustang, "Les moments de l'acte de foi et ses conditions de possibilité: Essai d'interprétation du dialogue avec la Samaritaine," *RechSR* 46 (1958): 344-78.

6169 L.-H. Vincent, "Puits de Jacob ou de la Samaritaine," *RB* 65 (1958): 547-67.

6170 Gordon D. Fee, "The Text of John in Origen and Cyril of Alexandria: A Contribution to Methodology in the Recovery and Analysis of Patristic Citations," *Bib* 52 (1971): 357-94.

6171 Alois Stöger, "Erfülltes Leben: Meditation über Johannes 4," *BL* 52 (1972): 72-75.

6172 P. J. Cahill, "Narrative Art in John IV," *RSB* 2 (1982): 41-48.

6173 Gail R. O'Day, "Narrative Mode and Theological Claim: A Study in the Fourth Gospel," *JBL* 105/4 (1986): 657-68.

6174 A. Link, "Kritische Bestandsaufnahme neuer methodischer Ansätze in der Exegese des Johannesevangeliums anhand vom Johannes 4," *TGl* 81 (1991): 253-78.

6175 Elian Cuvillier, "La figure des disciples en Jean 4," *NTS* 42 (1996): 245-59.

6176 Streeter S. Stuart, "A New Testament Perspective on Worship," *EQ* 68 (1996): 209-21.

4:1-45

6177 I. Howard Marshall, "The Problem of New Testament Exegesis (John 4:1-45)," *JETS* 17 (1974): 67-73.

6178 C. Hudry-Clergeon, "De Judée en Galilée. Étude de Jean 4:1-45," *NRT* 103 (1981): 818-30.

6179 David S. Dockery, "Reading John 4:1-45: Some Diverse Hermeneutical Perspectives," *CTR* 3 (1988): 127-40.

4:1-42

6180 L. Schmid, "Die Komposition der Samaria-Szene," Johannes 4:1-42," *ZNW* 28 (1929): 148-58.

6181 U. Holzmeister, "Colloquium Domini cum muliere Samaritana," *VD* 13 (1933): 17-20, 51-55.

6182 J. Graf, "Jesus und die Samariterin," *BK* (1951): 99-114.

6183 D. Mollat, "Le puits de Jacob," *BVC* 6 (1954): 83-91.

6184 D. M. Stanley, "Samaritan Interlude," *Worship* 34 (1964): 137-44.

6185 H. Rondet, "Au puits de Jacob. Saint Augustin et la conversion d'une âme," *BLE* 70 (1969): 100-109.

6186 I. de la Potterie, "Jésus et les Samaritains," *AsSeign* 16 (1971): 34-49.

6187 Normand Bonneau, "The Woman at the Well: John 4 and Genesis 24," *BibTo* 67 (1973): 1252-59.

6188 J. S. King, "Sychar and Calvary: A Neglected Theory in the Interpretation of the Fourth Gospel," *Theology* 77 (1974): 417-22.

6189 M. P. Hogan, "The Woman at the Well," *BibTo* 82 (1976): 663-69.

6190 E. DeVries, "Johannes 4:1-42 in geest en hoofdzaak" *GTT* 78 (1978): 93-114.

6191 C. M. Carmichael, "Marriage and the Samaritan Woman," *NTS* 26 (1979-1980): 332-46.

6192 Hendrikus Boers, "Discourse Structure and Macro-Structure in the Interpretation of Texts: John 4:1-42 as an Example," *SBLSP* 10 (1980): 159-82.

6193 W. Au, "Dialogue as Catechesis," *BibTo* 22 (1984): 381-85.

6194 J. D. M. Derrett, "The Samaritan Woman's Pitcher," *DR* 102 (1984): 252-61.

6195 Marc Girard, "Jésus en Samarie: analyse des structures stylistiques et du processus de symbolisation," *ÉgT* 17/3 (1986): 275-310.

6196 J. D. M. Derrett, "The Samaritan Woman in India c. AD 200," *ZRGG* 39/4 (1987): 328-36.

6197 Niels Hyldahl, "Samtalen med den samaritanske kvinde," *DTT* 56 (1993): 153-65.

6198 Dorothy A. Lee, "The Story of the Woman at the Well: A Symbolic Reading," *ABR* 41 (1993): 35-48.

6199 Johannes Neugebauer, "Die Textbezüge von Joh 4,1-42 und die Geschichte der johanneischen Gruppe," *ZNW* 84 (1993): 135-41.

6200 Jerome H. Neyrey, "What's Wrong with This Picture? John 4, Cultural Stereotypes of Women, and Public and Private Space," *BTB* 24 (1994): 77-91.

6201 Judith M. Gundry-Volf, "Spirit, Mercy, and the Other," *TT* 51 (1995): 508-23.

6202 Musa W. Dube, "Reading for Decolonization (John 4:1-42)," *Semeia* 75 (1996): 37-59.

4:1-16

6203 G. Ferraro, "Aspetti del dialogo di Gesù con la donna di Samaria (Gv 4:1-26)," *SM* 43 (1994): 1-18.

4:1-3

6204 Simon Légasse, "Le baptême administré par Jésus et l'origine du baptême chrétien," *BLE* 78 (1977): 3-30.

4:2

6205 H. J. Flowers, "Interpolations in the Fourth Gospel," *JBL* 40 (1921): 146-58.

4:3

6206 Martin Wallraff, "Das Zeugnis des Kirchenhistorikers Sokrates zur Textkritik von 1 Joh 4,3," *ZNW* 88 (1997): 145-48.

4:4-52

6207   J. D. M. Derrett, "The Samaritan Woman's Purity," *EQ* 60 (1988): 291-98.

4:4-42

6208   Adrien Lenglet, "Jésus de passage parmi les Samaritans Jean 4:4-42," *Bib* 66/4 (1985): 493-503.

6209   Alan Neely, "Communicating the Gospel to People Who Are Different," *FM* 2/2 (1985): 13-22.

6210   Steven M. Sheeley, " 'Lift Up Your Eyes': John 4:4-42," *RevExp* 92 (1995): 81-87.

4:4-26

6211   Matthew Vellanickal, "Drink from the Source of the Living Water. A 'Dhvani' Interpretation of the Dialogue between Jesus and the Samaritan Woman," *BB* 5 (1979): 303-18.

4:5-42

6212   A. F. Wedel, "John 4:5-26 (5-42)," *Int* 31 (1977): 406-12.

6213   Fred B. Craddock, "The Witness at the Well," *CC* 107 (1990): 243.

6214   Linda M. Bridges, "John 4:5-42," *Int* 48 (1994): 173-76.

4:5-26

6215   Laurence Cantwell, "Immortal Longings in Sermone Humili: A Study of John 4:5-26," *SJT* 36 (1983): 73-86.

4:5-15

6216   Luise Schottroff, "Johannes 4:5-15 und die Konsequenzen des johanneischen Dualismus," *ZNW* 60 (1969): 199-214.

4:6-39

6217   Mark F. Whitters, "Discipleship in John: Four Profiles," *WW* 18 (1998): 422-27.

4:6

6218   Eric F. F. Bishop, "Constantly on the Road," *EQ* 41 (1969): 14-18.

4:7-9

6219   James E. Taulman, "The Samaritan Concept of the Messiah," *BI* 8/2 (1982): 62-65.

4:9

6220 George D. Kilpatrick, "John 4:9," *JBL* 87 (1968): 327-28.

6221 David R. Hall, "The Meaning of συγχράομαι in John 4:9," *ET* 83 (1972-1973): 56-57.

6222 T. E. van Pollard, "Jesus and the Samaritan Woman," *ET* 92 (1980-1981): 147-48.

6223 John C. Thomas, "The Fourth Gospel and Rabbinic Judaism," *ZNW* 82 (1991): 159-82.

6224 Thomas Söding, " 'Was kann aus Nazareth schon Gutes kommen?' Die Bedeutung des Judenseins Jesu im Johannesevangelium," *NTS* 46 (2000): 21-41.

4:10-26

6225 Jerome H. Neyrey, "Jacob Traditions and the Interpretation of John 4:10-26," *CBQ* 41 (1979): 419-37.

4:10-14

6226 Dale C. Allison, "The Living Water," *SVTQ* 30/2 (1986): 143-57.

4:11-12

6227 B. Bagatti, "Nuovi apporti archeologici sul pozzo di Giacobbe in Samaria," *SBFLA* 16 (1966): 127-64.

4:12

6228 P. W. van der Horst, "A Wordplay in John 4:12?" *ZNW* 63 (1972): 280-82.

4:13-14

6229 F. Grob, "La femme samaritaine et l'eau du puits. Jean 4/13-14," *ÉTR* 55 (1980): 86-89.

4:13

6230 J. R. Harris, "A Lost Verse of St. John's Gospel," *ET* 38 (1926-1927): 342-43.

4:16-24

6231 A. E. J. Rawlinson, "In Spirit and in Truth: An Exposition of St. John 4:16-24," *ET* 44 (1932-1933): 12-14.

4:16

6232 J. Botha, "John 4:16: A Difficult Text Speech Act Theoretically Revisited," *ScrSA* 35 (1990): 1-9.

4:17-38

6233   Marla J. Selvidge, "Nicodemus and the Woman with Five Husbands," *EGLMBS* 2 (1982): 63-75.

4:17-18

6234   Charles H. Giblin, "What Was Everything He Told Her She Did?" *NTS* 45 (1999): 148-52.

4:18

6235   L. A. Prest, "The Samaritan Woman," *BibTo* 30 (1992): 367-71.

4:19-24

6236   S. Petri, "Tillbedjan i ande och sanning: En exegeshistorisk skiss till Joh. 4:19-24," *SEÅ* 11 (1946): 47-76.

4:19

6237   Thomas Söding, " 'Was kann aus Nazareth schon Gutes kommen?' Die Bedeutung des Judenseins Jesu im Johannesevangelium," *NTS* 46 (2000): 21-41.

4:20

6238   R. J. Bull, "An Archaeological Context for Understanding John 4:20," *BA* 38 (1975): 54-59.

6239   R. J. Bull, "An Archaeological Footnote to 'Our Fathers Worshipped on This Mountain'," *NTS* 23 (1976-1977): 460-62.

6240   James E. Taulman, "The Samaritan Concept of the Messiah," *BI* 8/2 (1982): 62-65.

4:22

6241   R. Loewe, " 'Salvation' Is Not of the Jews," *JTS* 32 (1981): 341-68.

6242   I. de la Potterie, " 'Nous adorons, nous, ce que nous connaissons, car le salut vient des Juifs': Histoire de l'exégèse et interprétation de Jean 4:22," *Bib* 64 (1983): 74-115.

4:23-24

6243 Charles S. Gaede, "Evangelistic Worship: John 4:23-24 and Contemporary Christian Worship," *Para* 23 (1989): 13-19.

6244 Clifford J. Collins, "John 4:23-24, 'in Spirit and Truth': An Idiomatic Proposal," *Pres* 21 (1995): 118-21.

4:23

6245 Rudolf Schnackenburg, "Die Anbetung 'in Geist und Wahrheit' im Lichte von Qumrân-Texten," *BZ* 3 (1959): 88-94.

6246 I. de la Potterie, "Adorare il Padre nello Spirito e nella verità," *ParSpirV* 3 (1981): 140-55.

4:24

6247 J. Bennetch, "John 4:24a: A Greek Study," *BSac* 107 (1950): 71-83.

4:25-29

6248 Ferdinand Dexinger, "Der Taheb, ein 'messianischer' Heilsbringer der Samaritaner," *K* 27 (1985): 1-172.

4:25

6249 E. D. Freed, "Egō Eimi in John 1:20 and 4:25," *CBQ* 41 (1979): 288-91.

4:26

6250 Gary Hardin, "Samaritan Beliefs," *BI* 16/1 (1989): 60-64.

4:27

6251 J. Foster, "What Seekest Thou? John 4:27," *ET* 52 (1940-1941): 37-38.

6252 J. P. Louw, "A Semiotic Approach to Discourse Analysis with Reference to Translation Theory," *BT* 36/1 (1985): 101-107.

4:28

6253 Larry McGraw, "Waterpots and Other Common Vessels," *BI* 17/1 (1990): 70-73.

4:29

6254 Charles H. Giblin, "What Was Everything He Told Her She Did?" *NTS* 45 (1999): 148-52.

4:34-42

6255 L. H. Bunn, "John 4:34-42," *ET* 41 (1929-1930): 141-42.

4:35

6256 J. M. Bover, " 'Adhuc quattuor menses sunt, et messis venit'," *Bib* 3 (1922): 442-44.

6257 A. W. Argyle, "A Note on John 4:35," *ET* 82 (1970-1971): 247-48.

6258 P. W. Ensor, "The Authenticity of John 4.35," *EQ* 72 (2000): 13-21.

4:36-38

6259 A. Niccacci, "Siracide 6:19 e Giovanni 4:36-38," *BibO* 23 (1981): 149-53.

4:39-42

6260 R. Walker, "Jüngerwort und Herrenwort: Zur Auslegung von Johannes 4:39-42," *ZNW* 57 (1966): 49-54.

4:39

6261 Charles H. Giblin, "What Was Everything He Told Her She Did?" *NTS* 45 (1999): 148-52.

4:40

6262 J. L. Espinel, "Jesús y el pueblo samaritano," *CuBí* 34 (1977): 243-54.

4:41

6263 George D. Kilpatrick, "John 4:41: πλεῖον or πλείους," *NovT* 18 (1976): 131-32.

4:42

6264 E. Mathiot, "Jean 4:42," *ÉTR* 48 (1973): 265-73.

6265 Andrés Torres-Queiruga, "La teoría de la revelación en Wolfhart Pannenberg," *EE* 59/229 (1984): 139-78.

6266 Craig R. Koester, "The Savior of the World," *JBL* 109 (1990): 665-80.

6267 Thomas Söding, " 'Was kann aus Nazareth schon Gutes kommen?' Die Bedeutung des Judenseins Jesu im Johannesevangelium,"*NTS* 46 (2000): 21-41.

4:43-54

6268 Barry W. Henaut, "John 4:43-54 and the Ambivalent Narrator: A Response to Culpepper's Anatomy of the Fourth Gospel," *SR* 19/3 (1990): 287-304.

4:43-45

6269 Kikuo Matsunaga, "The Galileans in the Fourth Gospel," *AJBI* 2 (1976): 139-58.

6270 R. L. Sturch, "The πατρίς of Jesus," *JTS* 28 (1977): 94-96.

4:43-44

6271 Thomas Söding, " 'Was kann aus Nazareth schon Gutes kommen?' Die Bedeutung des Judenseins Jesu im Johannesevangelium," *NTS* 46 (2000): 21-41.

4:44

6272 L. Johnson, "John 4:44," *ET* 49 (1937-1938): 236.

6273 W. A. Wordsworth, "A Prophet in his Own Country," *ET* 49 (1937-1938): 92-93, 429-30.

6274 L. Johnson, "John 4:44," *ET* 50 (1938-1939): 93-94.

6275 G. Reim, "John IV.44 - Crux or Clue? The Rejection of Jesus at Nazareth in Johannine Composition," *NTS* 22 (1975-1976): 476-80.

6276 John W. Pryor, "John 4:44 and the Patris of Jesus," *CBQ* 49 (1987): 254-63.

6277 Gilbert Van Belle, "The Faith of the Galileans (1996): The Parenthesis in Jn 4,44," *ETL* 74 (1998): 27-44.

4:46-54

6278 Eduard Schweizer, "Die Heilung des Königlichen," *EvT* 11 (1951-1952): 64-71.

6279 André Feuillet, "La signification théologique du second miracle de Cana," *RechSR* 48 (1960): 62-75.

6280 M.-É. Boismard, "Saint Luc et la réaction du quatrième évangile (Jean 4:46-54)," *RB* 69 (1962): 185-211.

6281 S. Temple, "The Two Signs in the Fourth Gospel," *JBL* 81 (1962): 169-74.

6282 Rudolf Schnackenburg, "Zur Traditionsgeschichte von Johannes 4:46-54," *BZ* 8 (1964): 58-88.

6283   Josef Sudbrack, "Der Glaube des Hauptmanns: Die drei evangelischen Berichte von der Heilung des Hauptmanns-Knechtes," *GeistL* 39 (1966): 379-84.

6284   E. F. Siegman, "St. John's Use of the Synoptic Material," *CBQ* 30/2 (1968): 182-98.

6285   J. D. M. Derrett, "Law in the New Testament: The Syro-Phoenician Woman and the Centurion of Capernaum," *NovT* 15 (1973): 161-86.

6286   Frans Neirynck, "Foi et miracle. Le fonctionnaire royal de Capharnaüm et 4:46-54," *ETL* 53 (1977): 451-78.

6287   Charles H. Giblin, "Suggestion, Negative Response, and Positive Action in St. John's Portrayal of Jesus," *NTS* 26 (1979-1980): 197-211.

6288   Allan Mayer, "Elijah and Elisha in John's Signs Source," *ET* 99 (1988): 171-73.

6289   Frans Neirynck, "Jean 4,46-54: Une leçon de méthode," *ETL* 71 (1995): 176-84.

4:46-51

6290   Frans Neirynck, "John 4:46-51: Signs Source and/or Synoptic Gospels," *ETL* 60/4 (1984): 367-75.

4:46-54

6291   Rudolf Schnackenburg, "Zur Traditionsgeschichte von Joh 4:46-54," *BZ* 8 (1964): 58-88.

4:46-53

6292   M.-É. Boismard, "L'Évangile [du 20ᵉ Dimanche après la Pentecôte]: Guérison du fils d'un fonctionnaire royal," *AsSeign* 75 (1965): 26-37.

6293   A. Hugh Mead, "The βασιλικὸς in John 4:46-53," *JSNT* 23 (1985): 69-72.

4:46

6294   Günther Schwarz, " 'Καὶ ἦν τις βασιλοκός. . .'," *ZNW* 75 (1984): 138.

4:48

6295   Gilbert Van Belle, "Jean 4:48 et la foi du centurion," *ETL* 61 (1985): 167-69.

4:51

6296 George D. Kilpatrick, "John 4:51: παῖς or υἱός?" *JTS* 14 (1963): 393.

6297 E. D. Freed, "John 4:51: παῖς or υἱός," *JTS* 16 (1965): 448-49.

5

6298 R. Mackintosh, "Two Johannine Miracles," *ET* 37 (1925-1926): 43-44.

6299 C. H. Dodd, "Une parabole cachée dans le quatrième Évangile," *RHPR* 42 (1962): 107-15.

6300 John Bligh, "Jesus in Jerusalem," *HeyJ* 4 (1963): 115-34, 176.

6301 K. P. M. Kuzenzama, "Jean 5-6 ou Jean 6-5? Une question embarrassante de critique littéraire," *RAfT* 3 (1979): 61-69.

6302 Giovanni Bissoli, "S. Cirillo di Gerusalemme: omelia sul paralitico della piscina probatica," *SBFLA* 31 (1981): 177-90.

6303 John Painter, "Text and Context in John 5," *ABR* 35 (1987): 28-34.

6304 Jeffrey L. Staley, "Stumbling in the Dark, Reaching for the Light: Reading Character in John 5 and 9," *Semeia* 53 (1991): 55-80.

6305 Rainer Metzner, "Der Geheilte von Johannes 5—Repräsentant des Unglaubens," *ZNW* 90 (1999): 177-93.

5:1-18

6306 H. van den Bussche, "Guérison d'un paralytique à Jérusalem le jour du Sabbat," *BVC* 61 (1965): 18-28.

6307 J. Bernard, "La guérison de Bethesda: Harmonies judéo-hellénistiques d'un récit de miracle un jour de sabbat," *MSR* 33 (1976): 3-34; 34 (1977): 13-44.

6308 A. B. Kolenkow, "Healing Controversy as a Tie between Miracle and Passion Material for a Proto-Gospel," *JBL* 95 (1976): 623-38.

6309 J. Alonso Díaz, "El paralítico de Betesda," *BibFe* 8 (1982): 151-67

6310   J. Klinger, "Bethesda and the Universality of the Logos," *SVTQ* 27 (1983): 169-85.

6311   H. Van Dyke Parunak, "Transitional Techniques in the Bible," *JBL* 102 (1983): 525-48.

6312   Leonard T. Witkamp, "The Use of Traditions in John 5:1-18," *JSNT* 25 (1985): 19-47.

6313   Michael Mees, "Die Heilung des Kranken vom Bethesdateich aus Johannes 5:1-18 in frühchristlicher Sicht," *NTS* 32/4 (1986): 596-608.

6314   John C. Thomas, "The Fourth Gospel and Rabbinic Judaism," *ZNW* 82 (1991): 159-182.

6315   John C. Thomas, " 'Stop Sinning Lest Something Worse Come upon You': The Man at the Pool in John 5," *JSNT* 59 (1995): 3-20.

<u>5:1-16</u>

6316   H. Weiss, "The Sabbath in the Fourth Gospel," *JBL* 110 (1991): 311-21.

<u>5:1-15</u>

6317   Paul D. Duke, "John 5:1-5," *RevExp* 85 (1988): 539-42.

<u>5:1-10</u>

6318   Tom Thatcher, "The Sabbath Trick: Unstable Irony in the Fourth Gospel," *JSNT* 76 (1999): 53-77.

<u>5:1</u>

6319   J. M. Bover, "La fiesta de los judíos en Jean 5:1," *EE* 26 (1952): 79-82.

6320   Maria L. Rigato, "Era festa dei Giudei (Gv 5:1): quale?" *RBib* 39 (1991): 25-29.

<u>5:2-15</u>

6321   Mark F. Whitters, "Discipleship in John: Four Profiles," *WW* 18 (1998): 422-27.

<u>5:2</u>

6322   J. M. Bover, "El nombre de la piscina," *EB* 3 (1931): 192-98.

6323   D. J. Wieand, "John v.2 and the Pool of Bethesda," *NTS* 12 (1965-1966): 392-404.

6324   B. Celada, "El nombre y la realidad de Bethesdá confirmada por los manuscritos del Mar Muerto y la arqueologia," *CuBi* 25 (1968):102-103.

6325   Gary L. Donhardt, "The Pools of Bethesda," *BI* 16/1 (1989): 80-84.

6326   Manfred Görg, "Betesda: 'Beckenhausen'," *BibN* 49 (1989): 7-10.

6327   Daniel B. Wallace, "John 5:2 and the Date of the Fourth Gospel," *Bib* 71/2 (1990): 177-205.

5:3-4

6328   J. M. Bover, "Autenticidad de Juan 5:3b-4," *EB* 11 (1952): 69-72.

6329   Gordon D. Fee, "On the Inauthenticity of John 5:3b-4," *EQ* 54 (1982): 207-18.

5:4

6330   Zane C. Hodges, "Problem Passages in the Gospel of John. Part 5: The Angel at Bethesda - John 5:4," *BSac* 136 (1979): 25-39.

5:5

6331   C. H. Dodd, "Notes from Papyri: John 5:5," *JTS* 26 (1924-1925): 78.

5:6

6332   J. G. Morton, "Christ's Diagnosis of Disease at Bethesda," *ET* 33 (1921-1922): 424-25.

5:8

6333   Ivor Buse, "Joh 5:8 and the Johannine-Marcan Relationship," *NTS* 1 (1954): 134-36.

6334   D. B. Johnson, "A Neglected Variant in Gregory 33 (John 5,8)," *NTS* 18 (1971-1972): 231-32.

5:16

6335   Robert I. Vasholz, "Is the New Testament Anti-Semitic?" *Pres* 11/2 (1985): 118-23.

5:17-28

6336 H. J. de Jonge, "Een nieuwe tekstgetuige van het Griekse Nieuwe Testament in Nederland," *NTT* 32 (1978): 305-309.

5:17-18

6337 Peder Borgen, "Creation, Logos and the Son: Observations on John 1:1-18 and 5:17-18," *ExA* 3 (1987): 88-97.

5:17

6338 Henri Clavier, "Autour de Jean 5:17," *RHPR* 24 (1944): 82-90.

6339 G. Ferraro, "Il senso di 'heos arti' nel testo di Giovanni 5:17," *RBib* 20 (1972): 529-45.

6340 S. Bacchiocchi, "John 5:17: Negation or Clarification of the Sabbath?" *AUSS* 19 (1981): 3-19.

5:18-23

6341 Jesse Sell, "Johannine Traditions in Logion 61 of the Gospel of Thomas," *PRS* 7/1 (1980): 24-37.

5:18

6342 Robert I. Vasholz, "Is the New Testament Anti-Semitic?" *Pres* 11/2 (1985): 118-23.

6343 James F. McGrath, "A Rebellious Son? Hugo Odeberg and the Interpretation of John 5:18," *NTS* 44 (1998): 470-73.

6344 Craig S. Keener, "Is Subordination Within the Trinity Really Heresy? A Study of John 5:18 in Context," *TriJ* 20 (1999): 39-51.

5:19-47

6345 R. Beauvery, " 'Mon Père et votre Père' (Jean 5:19-47)," *LV* 20/104 (1971): 75-87.

5:19-30

6346 X. Léon-Dufour, "Trois chiasmes johanniques," *NTS* 7 (1960-1961): 249-55.

6347 G. Ferraro, "Il figlio ha la vita in se stesso (Gv 5,19-30)," *ParSpirV* 5 (1982): 147-58.

6348 Michael Mees, "Jesu Selbstzeugnis nach Johannes 5:19-30 in frühchristlicher Sicht," *ETL* 62/1 (1986): 102-17.

5:19-24

6349   M. Eugene Boring, "John 5:19-24," *Int* 45 (1991): 176-81.

5:24-30

6350   H. J. de Jonge, "Een recente aanwinst onder de nieuwtestamentische tekstgetuigen in Nederland," *NTT* 31 (1977): 2-7.

5:24

6351   Roland Bergmeier, "Entweltlichung. Verzicht auf religionsgeschichtliche Forschung?" *NovT* 16 (1974): 58-80.

5:25-29

6352   W. G. Essame, "Matthew xxvii.51-54 and John v.25-29," *ET* 76 (1964-1965): 103.

6353   J. van der Watt, "A New Look at John 5:25-29 in the Light of the Use of the Term 'Eternal Life' in the Gospel according to John," *Neo* 19 (1985): 71-86.

5:28-29

6354   H. J. Flowers, "Interpolations in the Fourth Gospel," *JBL* 40 (1921): 146-58.

6355   Zane C. Hodges, "Problem Passages in the Gospel of John. Part 6: Those Who Have Done Good - John 5:28-29," *BSac* 136 (1979): 158-66.

5:31-47

6356   J. Gilbet, "Le témoignage du Père," *BVC* 12 (1955): 49-59.

6357   J. Bernard, "Témoignage pour Jésus-Christ: Jean 5:31-47," *MSR* 36 (1979): 3-55.

6358   John C. Thomas, "The Fourth Gospel and Rabbinic Judaism," *ZNW* 82 (1991): 159-82.

5:31-40

6359   Urban C. Von Wahlde, "The Witnesses to Jesus in John 5:31-40 and Belief in the Fourth Gospel," *CBQ* 43 (1981): 385-404.

5:35

6360   Fritz Neugebauer, "Miszelle zu Johannes 5:35," *ZNW* 52 (1961): 130.

6361 Roland Mörchen, "Johanneisches 'Jubeln'," *BZ* 301/2 (1986): 248-50.

5:36

6362 Albert Vanhoye, "Opera Iesu donum Patris," *VD* 36 (1958): 83-92.

6363 Albert Vanhoye, "L'œuvre du Christ, don du Pere," *RechSR* 48 (1960): 377-419.

6364 Ernst Haenchen, " 'Der Vater, der mich gesandt hat'," *NTS* 9 (1962-1963): 208-16.

5:39

6365 H. I. Bell, "Search the Scriptures," *ZNW* 37 (1938): 10-13.

6366 M.-É. Boismard, "A propos de Jean 5:39: Essai de critique textuelle," *RB* 55 (1948): 5-34.

6367 Walter Magass, "II Thesen zum Bibellesen und zum 'Suchen' in den Schrift," *LB* 47 (1980): 5-20.

5:45-47

6368 S. Dillmann, "Ioh. 5:45-47 in der Pentateuchfrage," *BZ* 15 (1918-1920): 219-28.

5:45-46

6369 T. Nicklas, " 'Unter dem Feigenbaum'. Die Rolle des Lesers im Dialog zwischen Jesus und Natanael (Joh 1.45-50)," *NTS* 46 (2000): 193-203

6:1-19:42

6370 Morton Smith, "Mark 6:32-15:47 and John 6:1-19:42," *SBLSP* 8/2 (1978): 281-88.

6

6371 J. F. Springer, "The Sixth Chapter of John Not in Danger," *ATR* 6 (1923-1924): 132-40.

6372 E. Janot, "Le pain de vie: A propos des interprétations du chap. VI de l'Évangile de Saint Jean," *Greg* 11 (1930): 161-70.

6373 Paul Gächter, "Die Form der eucharistischen Rede Jesu," *ZKT* 59 (1935): 419-41.

6374 M. Balagué, "El Pedagogo Divino," *CuBí* 4 (1947): 193-200.

6375   Patrick J. Temple, "The Eucharist in St. John 6," *CBQ* 9 (1947): 442-52.

6376   D. Mollat, "Le ch. 6 de Saint Jean," *LV* 31 (1957): 107-19.

6377   D. M. Stanley, "The Bread of Life," *Worship* 32 (1957-1958): 477-88.

6378   X. Léon-Dufour, "Le mystère du Pain de Vie (Jean 6)," *RechSR* 46 (1958): 481-523.

6379   F. J. Leenhardt, "La structure du ch. 6 de l'évangile de Jean," *RHPR* 39 (1959): 1-13.

6380   Edward J. Kilmartin, "Liturgical influence on John 6," *CBQ* 22 (1960): 183-91.

6381   Cyril Vollert, "The Eucharist: Quests for Insights from Scripture," *TS* 21 (1960): 404-43.

6382   Peder Borgen, "Observations on the Midrashic Character of John 6," *ZNW* 54/3-4 (1963): 232-40.

6383   Vernon Ruland, "Sign and Sacrament: John's Bread of Life Discourse (Chapter 6)," *Int* 18 (1964): 450-62.

6384   F. J. Moore, "Eating the Flesh and Drinking the Blood. A Reconsideration," *ATR* 48 (1966): 70-75.

6385   J. Giblet, "The Eucharist in St. John's Gospel," *Conci* 40 (1968): 60-69.

6386   M.-F. Berrouard, "La multiplication des pains et le discours du pain de vie (Jean 6)," *LV* 18/94 (1969): 63-75.

6387   Michael Mees, "Sinn und Bedeutung westlicher Textvarianten in Johannes 6," *BZ* 13 (1969): 244-51.

6388   M. Herranz Marco, "El Jordán y el mar de Galilea en el marco geográfico de los Evangelios," *EB* 29 (1970): 327-52.

6389   R. Le Déaut, "Une aggadah targumique et les 'murmures' de Jean 6," *Bib* 51 (1970): 80-83.

6390   Thierry Snoy, "Le chapitre 6 de l'Évangile de Jean," *BVC* 94 (1970): 5-7.

6391   James D. G. Dunn, "John VI. A Eucharistic Discourse?" *NTS* 17 (1970-1971): 328-38.

6392   F.-M. Braun, "L'œuvre de Dieu (Jean 6)," *AsSeign* 49 (1971): 48-58.

6393   T. Preiss, "Étude sur le chapitre 6 de l'Évangile de Jean," *ÉTR* 46 (1971): 143-67.

6394   Joachim Jeremias, " 'This is My Body'. . .," *ET* 83 (1971-1972): 196-203.

6395   M. Shorter, "The Position of Chapter VI in the Fourth Gospel," *ET* 84 (1972-1973): 181-83.

6396   M. Tavernier, "Celui qui me mange vivra par moi," *AsSeign* 51 (1973): 44-51.

6397   J.-N. Aletti, "Le discours sur le pain de la vie (Jean 6). Problèmes de composition et fonction des citations de l'Ancien Testament," *RechSR* 62 (1974): 169-97.

6398   J. S. Croatto, "Riletture dell'Esodo nel cap. 6 di San Giovanni," *BibO* 17 (1975): 11-20.

6399   Francis J. Moloney, "John 6 and the Celebration of the Eucharist," *DR* 93 (1975): 243-51.

6400   M. Corbin, "Le pain de vie: La lecture de Jean VI par Saint Thomas d'Aquin," *RechSR* 65 (1977): 107-38.

6401   John D. Crossan, "It Is Witten. A Structuralist Analysis of John 6," *SBLSP* 1 (1978): 197-213.

6402   F. A. Rusch, "The Signs and the Discourse: The Rich Theology of John 6," *CThM* 5 (1978): 386-90.

6403   Matthew Vellanickal, "Jesus: The Bread of Life," *BB* 4 (1978): 30-48.

6404   John D. Crossan, "It is Written: A Structuralist Analysis of John 6," *SBLSP* 9/1 (1979): 197-214.

6405   Gary Phillips, " 'This Is a Hard Saying; Who Can Be a Listener to It?' The Creation of the Reader in John 6," *SBLSP* 9/1 (1979): 185-96.

6406   M. H. Smith, "Collected Fragments: On the Priority of John 6 to Mark 6-8," *SBLSP* 9/1 (1979): 105-108.

6407   Alois Stöger, "Christus, Brot des Lebens: Meditation über Johannes 6," *BL* 52 (1979): 192-94.

6408   J. Giblet, "La chair du fils de l'homme," *LV* 29/149 (1980): 89-103.

6409   Michel Gourgues, "Section christologique et section eucharistique en Jean VI. Une proposition," *RB* 88 (1981): 515-31.

6410   Domingo Muñoz León, "Las fuentes y estadios de composición del Cap. 6. de San Juan segúin Boismard-Lamouille," *EB* 39 (1981): 315-38.

6411   Simon Légasse, "Le pain de la vie," *BLE* 83 (1982): 243-61.

6412   Enzo Bianchi, "Un pane unico per giudei e gentili," *ParSpirV* 7 (1983): 89-98.

6413   Daniel Patte, "Narrative and Discourse in Structural Exegesis. John 6 & 1 Thessalonians," *Semeia* 26 (1983): 1-13.

6414   Gary Phillips, " 'This is a Hard Saying. Who Can Be Listener to It?' Creating a Reader in John 6," *Semeia* 26 (1983): 23-56.

6415   H. Kruse, "Jesu Seefahrten und die Stellung von Johannes 6," *NTS* 30 (1984): 508-30.

6416   Hans Weder, "Die Menschwerdung Gottes: Überlegungen zur Auslegungsproblematik des Johannesevangeliums am Beispiel von Johannes 6," *ZTK* 82/3 (1985): 325-60.

6417   Christoph Burchard, "The Importance of Joseph and Aseneth for the Study of the New Testament: A General Survey and a Fresh Look at the Lord's Supper," *NTS* 33/1 (1987): 102-34.

6418   Kenneth Durkin, "A Eucharistic Hymn in John 6?" *ET* 98 (1987): 168-70.

6419   Raymond H. Bailey, "John 6," *RevExp* 85 (1988): 95-98.

6420   G. F. Snyman, "Die wonders in Johannes 6 verklaar aan die hand van vertellersperspektiefanalise," *HTS* 44 (1988): 708-33.

6421   John Painter, "Tradition and Interpretation in John 6," *NTS* 35/3 (1989): 421-50.

6422   James W. Voelz, "The Discourse on the Bread of Life in John 6: Is It Eucharistic?" *CJ* 15 (1989): 29-37.

6423   Johannes Beutler, "Zur Struktur von Johannes 6," *SNTU-A* 16 (1991): 89-104.

6424   Thomas R. Valletta, "The 'Bread of Life' Discourse in the Context of Exodus Typology," *EGLMBS* 11 (1991): 129-43.

6425   P. Beauchamp, "Le signe des pains," *LV* 41 (1992): 55-67.

6426   Bruce W. Longenecker, "The Unbroken Messiah: A Johannine Feature and Its Social Functions," *NTS* 41 (1995): 428-41.

6:1-72

6427   Juan Fernández, "Jesus, pan de vida," *CuBí* 12 (1955): 218-24.

6:1-25

6428   L. Schenke, "Das Szenarium von Johannes 6:1-25," *TTZ* 92 (1983): 191-203.

6:1-21

6429   J. Blank, "Die johanneische Brotrede: Einführung: Brotvermehrung und Seewandel Jesu: Johannes 6:1-21," *BibL* 7 (1966): 193-207.

6430   Paul S. Berge, "John 6:1-21: The Bread which Gives Life to the World," *WW* 5 (1985): 311-20.

6431   G. F. Snyman, "Die wonders in Johannes 6 verklaar aan die hand van vertellersperspektiefanalise," *HTS* 44 (1988): 708-33.

6432   Leonard T. Witkamp, "Some Specific Johannine Features in John 6:1-21," *JSNT* 40 (1990): 43-59.

6:1-15

6433   P. E. Cousins, "The Feeding of the Five Thousand," *EQ* 39 (1967): 152-54.

6434   F. Quiévreux, "Le récit de la multiplication des pains dans le quatrième évangile," *RevSR* 41 (1967): 97-108.

6435   C. T. Ruddick, "Feeding and Sacrifice. The Old Testament Background of the Fourth Gospel," *ET* 79 (1967-1968): 340-41.

6436 M. Balagué, "Dominica 17ᵃ per annum: 1ᵃ lectura 2 R 4:42-44; 2ᵃ lectura Ef 4:1-6; 3ᵃ lectura Jean 6:1-15," *CuBí* 27 (1970): 215-22.

6437 Jean-Marie Van Cangh, "Le thème des poissons dans les récits évangéliques de la multiplication des pains," *RB* 78 (1971): 71-83.

6438 B. Maggioni, "La multiplication des pains," *AsSeign* 48 (1973): 39-49.

6439 R. Trevijano Etcheverría, "La multiplicación de los panes (Mc. 6:30-46; 8:1-10 y par.)," *Bur* 15 (1974): 435-65.

6440 Giuseppe Pace, "La prima moltiplicazione dei pani: Topografia," *BibO* 21 (1979): 85-91.

6441 B. Bagatti, "Dove avvenne la moltiplicazione dei pani?" *Salm* 28 (1981): 293-98.

6442 O. Da Spinetoli, "Il segno eucaristico nel racconto della moltiplicazione dei pani (Mt, Lc e Gv)," *ParSpirV* 7 (1983): 99-111.

6443 J. Zumstein, "Le signe de la croix," *LV* 41 (1992): 68-82.

6:1-14

6444 Allan Mayer, "Elijah and Elisha in John's Signs Source," *ET* 99 (1988): 171-73.

6:1-13

6445 J.-M. Léonard, "Multiplication des pains. 2 Rois 4/42-44 et Jean 6/1-13," *ÉTR* 55 (1980): 265-70.

6:12-13

6446 F.-M. Braun, "Quatre 'signes' johanniques de l'unité chrétienne (Jean 6:12-13, 11:47-52, 19:23-4, 21:1-11)," *NTS* 9 (1963): 147-55.

6:13

6447 Andrés Torres-Queiruga, "La plentitud de la revelacion y el problema de la historia," *Salm* 32 (1985): 153-80.

6:16-26

6448 Bruce H. Grigsby, "The Reworking of the Lake-Walking Account in the Johannine Tradition," *ET* 100 (1989-1990): 295-97.

6:16-21

6449   P. Zarrella, "Gesù cammina sulle acque: Significato teologico di Giovanni 6:16-21," *BibO* 10 (1968): 181-87.

6450   T. M. Suriano, " 'Who then Is This?' Jesus Masters the Sea," *BibTo* 79 (1975): 449-56.

6451   Diego A. Losada, "Jesús camina sobre las aguas: Un relatio apocalíptico," *RevB* 28 (1976): 311-19.

6452   J. D. M. Derrett, "Why and How Jesus Walked on the Sea," *NovT* 23 (1981): 330-48.

6453   Charles H. Giblin, "The Miraculous Crossing of the Sea," *NTS* 29 (1983): 96-103.

6:16-12

6454   Hubert Ritt, "Der 'Seewandel Jesu': Literarische und theologische Aspekte," *BZ* 23 (1979): 71-84.

6:22-59

6455   J.-N. Aletti, "Le discours sur le pain de la vie (Jean 6). Problèmes de composition et fonction des citations de l'Ancien Testament," *RechSR* 62 (1974): 169-97.

6456   J. Thomas, "Le discours dans la synagogue de Capharnaüm: Note sur Jean 6:22-59," *Chr* 29 (1982): 218-22.

6:22-50

6457   J. Blank, " 'Ich bin das Lebensbrot' Johannes 6:22-50: Die johanneische Brotrede II," *BibL* 7 (1966): 255-70.

6:22-24

6458   Frans Neirynck, "L'epanaiepsis et la critique littéraire. A propos de l'évangile de Jean," *ETL* 56 (1980): 303-38.

6:24-35

6459   M. Balagué, "Domingo 18 per annum: 1.ª lectura, Ex 16:2-4; 2.ª lectura, Ef 4:17, 20-24; 3.ª lectura, Jn 6:24-35," *CuBi* 27 (1970): 293-303.

6:25-34

6460   M. J. J. Menken, "Some Remarks on the Course of the Dialogue: John 6:25-34," *Bij* 48 (1987): 139-49.

6:26-71

    6461   David S. Yeago, "The Bread of Life: Patristic Christology and Evangelical Soteriology in Martin Luther's Sermons on John 6," *SVTQ* 39 (1995): 257-79.

6:26-58

    6462   Giuseppe Segalla, "La struttura circolare-chiasmatica di Gv 6:26-58 e il suo significato teologico," *BibO* 13 (1971): 191-98.

    6463   L. Schenke, "Die formale und gedankliche Struktur von Joh 6:26-58," *BZ* 24 (1980): 21-41.

    6464   L. Schenke, "Die literarische Vorgeschichte von Joh 6:26-58," *BZ* 29/1 (1985): 68-89.

6:26-51

    6465   G. Gamibino, "Struttura, composizione e analisi letterario-teologica di Gv. 6:26-51b," *RBib* 24 (1976): 337-58.

6:26-47

    6466   F. S. Müller, "Promissio Eucharistiae: revelaturne Eucharistia Ioh. 6:26-47 ipsis verbis an typis?" *Greg* 3 (1922): 161-77.

6:26-30

    6467   K. P. M. Kuzenzama, "Une discussion sur les 'œuvres': Approche exégétique de Jean 6:26-30," *RAfT* 7/14 (1983): 165-79.

6:26

    6468   F. Grob, " 'Vous me cherchez, non parce que vous avez vu des signes. . .' Essai d'explication cohérente de Jean 6/26," *RHPR* 60 (1980): 429-39.

6:28-29

    6469   Roland Bergmeier, "Glaube als Werk? Die 'Werke Gottes' in Damaskusschrift II,14-15 und Johannes 6:28-29," *RevQ* 6 (1967): 253-60.

    6470   Urban C. Von Wahlde, "Faith and Works in Jean 6:28-29. Exegesis or Eisegesis?" *NovT* 22 (1980): 304-15.

6:29-31

6471   R. E. Lee, "John 6:29-31," *ET* 38 (1926-1927): 188.

6:29

6472   W. G. White, "John 6:29," *ET* 30 (1918-1919): 142.

6:30

6473   J. D. M. Derrett, "*Ti ergaze* (Jn 6,30): An Unrecognized Allusion to Is 45,9," *ZNW* 84 (1993): 142-44.

6:31-59

6474   Urban C. Von Wahlde, "Literary Structure and Theological Argument in Three Discourses with the Jews in the Fourth Gospel," *JBL* 103 (1984): 575-84.

6:31-58

6475   Georg Richter, "Zur Formgeschichte und literarischen Einheit von Johannes 6:31-58," *ZNW* 60 (1969): 21-55.

6:31

6476   G. Geiger, "Aufruf an Rückkehrende. Zum Sinn des Zitats von Psalm 78:24b in Johannes 6:31," *Bib* 65 (1984): 449-64.

6477   M. J. J. Menken, "The Provenance and Meaning of the Old Testament Quotation in John 6:31," *NovT* 30 (1988): 39-56.

6478   Glenn Balfour, "The Jewishness of John's Use of the Scriptures in John 6:31 and 7:37-38," *TynB* 46 (1995): 357-80.

6:35-48

6479   K. P. M. Kuenzama, "La préhistoire de l'expression 'pain de vie': Continuité ou émergence?" *RAfT* 4 (1980): 65-83.

6:35-40

6480   X. Léon-Dufour, "Trois chiasmes johanniques," *NTS* 7 (1960-1961): 249-55.

6:35-39

6481   H. J. de Jonge, "Een recente aanwinst onder de nieuwtestamentische tekstgetuigen in Nederland," *NTT* 31 (1977): 2-7.

6:35

6482 Domingo Muñoz León, "El sustrato targúmico del Discurso del Pan de Vida. Nuevas aportaciones: La equivalencia 'venir' y 'aprender/creer' y la conexión 'vida eterna' y 'resurrección'," *EB* 36 (1977): 217-26.

6483 Dale C. Allison, "The Living Water," *SVTQ* 30/2 (1986): 143-57.

6:37

6484 A. Henderson, "Note on John 6:37," *ET* 31 (1919-1920): 37-38.

6485 Otfried Hofius, "Erwähnung und Bewahrung. Zur Auslegung von Joh 6:37," *TBe* 8 (1977): 24-29.

6486 Domingo Muñoz León, "El sustrato targúmico del Discurso del Pan de Vida. Nuevas aportaciones: La equivalencia 'venir' y 'aprender/creer' y la conexión 'vida eterna' y 'resurrección'," *EB* 36 (1977): 217-26.

6:39-40

6487 H. J. Flowers, "Interpolations in the Fourth Gospel," *JBL* 40 (1921): 146-58.

6:40

6488 Domingo Muñoz León, "El sustrato targúmico del Discurso del Pan de Vida. Nuevas aportaciones: La equivalencia 'venir' y 'aprender/creer' y la conexión 'vida eterna' y 'resurrección'," *EB* 36 (1977): 217-26.

6:41-52

6489 R. Beauvery, "Le fils de Joseph! Manne descendue du ciel? Jean 6:41-52," *AsSeign* 50 (1974): 43-49.

6:41-43

6490 R. Le Déaut, "Une aggadah targumique et les 'murmures' de Jean 6," *Bib* 51 (1970): 80-83.

6:41

6491 F. J. A. de Grijs, "Christologie und Thomasinterpretation; über von W F Schwenk," *Bij* 45 (1984): 350-73.

6:42

6492   A. Salas, "José, el padre (Mt 1:21; Jn 6:42; Lk 3:23)," *BibFe* 6 (1980): 304-32.

6493   Wendy E. Sproston, "Is Not This Jesus, the Son of Joseph (John 6:42): Johannine Christology as a Challenge to Faith," *JSNT* 24 (1985): 77-97.

6494   Thomas Söding, " 'Was kann aus Nazareth schon Gutes kommen?' Die Bedeutung des Judenseins Jesu im Johannesevangelium," *NTS* 46 (2000): 21-41.

6:44

6495   H. J. Flowers, "Interpolations in the Fourth Gospel," *JBL* 40 (1921): 146-58.

6:45

6496   Domingo Muñoz León, "El sustrato targúmico del Discurso del Pan de Vida. Nuevas aportaciones: La equivalencia 'venir' y 'aprender/creer' y la conexión 'vida eterna' y 'resurrección'," *EB* 36 (1977): 217-26.

6497   M. J. J. Menken, "The Old Testament Quotation in John 6:45: Source and Redaction," *ETL* 64/1 (1988): 164-72.

6:46

6498   Gérard Rochais, "Jésus savait-il qu'il était Dieu: réflexions critiques à propos d'un livre récent," *SR* 14/1 (1985): 85-106.

6499   S.-E. Farrell, "Seeing the Father: Part II: Perceptive Seeing and Comprehensive Seeing," *ScE* 44 (1992): 159-83.

6:48

6500   P. Schineller, "Jesus in the Gospel of John--II. 'I Am the Bread of Life'," *Emmanuel* 106 (2000): 288-89, 301.

6:51-58

6501   Joachim Jeremias, "Jo 6:51c-58 redaktionell?" *ZNW* 44 (1953): 256-57.

6502   S. A. Panimolle, "Il discorso eucaristico (Gv 6:51-58)," *ParSpirV* 7 (1983): 112-24.

6503   Joseph A. Grassi, "Eating Jesus' Flesh and Drinking His Blood: The Centrality and Meaning of John 6:51-58," *BTB* 17 (1987): 24-30.

6504   Eduard Schweizer, "Joh 6,51c-58—vom Evangelisten übernommene Tradition?" *ZNW* 82 (1991): 274.

6505   M. J. J. Menken, "John 6,51c-58: Eucharist or Christology?" *Bib* 74 (1993): 1-26.

6506   John M. Perry, "The Evolution of the Johannine Eucharist," *NTS* 39 (1993): 22-35.

6507   Eleanor B. Hanna, "Biblical Interpretation and Sacramental Practice: John Calvin's Interpretation of John 6:51-58," *Worship* 73 (1999): 211-30.

6:51-65

6508   David E. Fredrickson, "Eucharistic Symbolism in the Gospel of John," *WW* 17 (1997): 40-44.

6:51

6509   Heinz Schürmann, "Joh 6:51c—ein Schlüssel zur grossen johanneischen Brotrede," *BZ* 2 (1958): 244-62.

6:52-59

6510   M. Blanchard, "A Spiritual Interpretation of John 6:52-59," *IJT* 8 (1959): 48-50.

6511   E. Sambayya, "St. John's Discourse on the Bread of Life with Special Reference to John 6:52-59," *IJT* 8 (1959): 77-82.

6:52

6512   Rudolf Schnackenburg, "Zur Rede vom Brot aus dem Himmel: eine Beobachtung zu Joh 6,52," *BZ* 12 (1968): 248-52.

6:53-59

6513   Heinz Schürmann, "Die Eucharistie als Repräsentation und Applikation des Heilsgeschehens nach John 6:53-59," *TTZ* 68 (1959): 30-45, 108-18.

6:53-58

6514   Edward J. Kilmartin, "A First-Century Chalice Dispute," *SE* 12/3 (1960): 403-408.

6:54

6515   H. J. Flowers, "Interpolations in the Fourth Gospel," *JBL* 40 (1921): 146-58.

6516 Domingo Muñoz León, "El sustrato targúmico del Discurso del Pan de Vida. Nuevas aportaciones: La equivalencia 'venir' y 'aprender/creer' y la conexión 'vida eterna' y 'resurrección'," *EB* 36 (1977): 217-26.

6:55-58

6517 E. Galbiati, "Il pane della vita (Giov. 6:55-58)," *BibO* 5 (1963): 101-10.

6518 Alfred Vanneste, "L'évangile (de Fête-Dieu) (Jean 6:55-58): Le pain de vie descendu du ciel," *AsSeign* 54 (1966): 41-53.

6:56

6519 J. M. Ross, "Some Unnoticed Points in the Text of the New Testament," *NovT* 25 (1983): 59-72.

6:57

6520 G. Crocetti, "Le linee fondamentali del concetto di vita in Io. 6:57," *RBib* 19 (1971): 375-94.

6:58-61

6521 R. Le Déaut, "Une aggadah targumique et les 'murmures' de Jean 6," *Bib* 51 (1970): 80-83.

6:60-71

6522 G. Ferraro, "Giovanni 6,60-71. Osservazioni sulla struttura letteraria e il valore della pericope nel quarto vangelo," *RBib* 26 (1978): 33-69.

6523 L. Schenke, "Das johanneische Schisma und die 'Zwölf' (Johannes 6:60-71)," *NTS* 38 (1992): 105-21.

6:60-69

6524 R. Beauvery, " 'Voulez-vous partir, vous aussi?' Jean 6:60-69," *AsSeign* 52 (1974): 44-51.

6:60

6525 S. Ben-Chorin, "Deuteworte, Dornenkrone und Evangelienstruktur: drei exegetische Randbemerkungen," *ZRGG* 38/3 (1986): 270.

6:62

6526 J. H. Michael, "The Actual Saying Behind St. John 6:62," *ET* 43 (1931-1932): 427-28.

6527   John W. Pryor, "The Johannine Son of Man and the
        Descent-Ascent Motif," *JETS* 34 (1991): 341-51.

6:63-64

6528   D. H. C. Read, "Your Bible - Dead or Alive?" *ET* 91
        (1979-1980): 49-51.

6:63

6529   G. Boccali, "Spirito e vita," *PV* 13 (1968): 118-31.

6530   G. Boccali, "Un 'mashal' evangelico e la sua applicazione
        (Gv 6:63)," *BibO* 10 (1968): 53-58.

6531   Werner Stenger, " 'Der Geist ist es, der lebendig macht,
        das Fleisch nützt nichts'," *TTZ* 85 (1976): 116-22.

6532   G. Ghiberti, "Le mie parole sono spirito e vita (Gv 6, 63),"
        ParSpirV 5 (1982): 174-92.

6533   Gerhard A. Krodel, "John 6:63," *Int* 37 (1983): 283-88.

6:64

6534   L. Tondelli, "Caro non prodest quidquam (Ioh. 6:64)," *Bib*
        4 (1923): 320-27.

6535   Juan Leal, "Spiritus et Caro in Jo 6:64," *VD* 30 (1952):
        257-64.

6:66-71

6536   Edwin K. Broadhead, "Echoes of an Exorcism in the
        Fourth Gospel?" *ZNW* 86 (1995): 111-19.

6:67-69

6537   H. Bürkle, "Biblische Besinnung Johannes 6:67-69,"
        ZMiss 11 (1985): 66-68.

6:69

6538   H. L. N. Joubert, " 'The Holy One of God' (John 6:69),"
        Neo 2 (1968): 57-69.

6539   William R. Domeris, "The Holy One of God as a Title for
        Jesus," *Neo* 19 (1985): 9-17.

6540   William R. Domeris, "The Confession of Peter according
        to John 6:69," *TynB* 44 (1993): 155-67.

7-10

6541   L. Schenke, "Joh 7-10: Eine dramatische Szene," *ZNW*
        80/3-4 (1989): 172-92.

7:1-10:21

6542   T. Cottam, "At the Feast of Booths (John 7:1-10:21)," *ET* 48 (1936-1937): 45.

7-9

6543   C. C. Oke, "At the Feast of Booths: A Suggested Rearrangement of John 7-9," *ET* 47 (1935-1936): 425-27; 48 (1936-1937): 189.

7:1-8:59

6544   Catherine Cory, "Wisdom's Rescue: A New Reading of the Tabernacles Discourse," *JBL* 116 (1997): 95-116.

7

6545   G. H. C. MacGregor, "The Rearrangement of John 7 and 8," *ET* 33 (1921-1922): 74-78.

6546   J. Schneider, "Zur Komposition von John 7," *ZNW* 45 (1954): 108-19.

6547   C. W. F. Smith, "Tabernacles in the Fourth Gospel and Mark," *NTS* 9 (1962-1963): 130-46.

6548   D. M. Stanley, "Holy Scripture: The Feast of Tents—Jesus' Self-Revelation," *Worship* 34 (1964): 20-27.

6549   F. Mosetto, "È lui il Cristo? (Gv 7)," *PV* 29 (1984): 382-91.

6550   Diana Culbertson, "Are You Also Deceived? Reforming the Reader in John 7," *EGLMBS* 9 (1989): 148-60.

6551   Gérard Rochais, "Jean 7: une construction littéraire dramatique, à la manière d'un scénario," *NTS* 39 (1993): 355-78.

7:1-36

6552   H. W. Attridge, "Thematic Development and Source Elaboration in John 7:1-36," *CBQ* 42 (1980): 160-70.

7:1-10

6553   Alonso V. Estalayo, "Análisis literario de Jn 7:1-10," *EstT* 4/8 (1977): 3-106.

__7:2-14__

6554   Charles H. Giblin, "Suggestion, Negative Response, and
        Positive Action in St. John's Portrayal of Jesus," *NTS* 26
        (1979-1980): 197-211.

6555   K. H. Kuhn, "St. John 7:7-38," *NTS* 4 (1957-1958): 61-65.

__7:7__

6556   T. H. Olbricht, "Its Works Were Evil (John 7:7)," *RQ* 7
        (1963): 242-44.

__7:11__

6557   Christoph Burchard, "Fussnoten zum neutestamentlichen
        Griechisch (Johannes 2:23, 7:11 μὴ ἐν τῇ ἑορτῇ)," *ZNW*
        61 (1970): 157-71.

__7:12__

6558   B. Hedman, "No Middle Ground (John 7:12)," *ET* 90
        (1978-1979): 368-69.

__7:16__

6559   S. M. Ogden, "Sources of Religious Authority in Liberal
        Protestantism (John 7:16)," *JAAR* 44 (1976): 403-16.

__7:22-23__

6560   J. D. M. Derrett, "Circumcision and Perfection: A
        Johannine Equation," *EQ* 63 (1991): 211-24.

__7:35__

6561   E. Bammel, "Joh 7:35 in Manis Lebensbeschreibung,"
        NovT 15 (1973): 191-92.

__7:37-41__

6562   Harald Sahlin, "Till förståelsen av Joh. 7:37-41," *SEÅ* 11
        (1946): 77-90.

__7:37-39__

6563   J. M. Bover, "Christus fons aquae vitae (Ioh. 7:37-39),"
        VD 1 (1921): 109-14.

6564   L. Brun, " 'Floder av levende vand' (Joh. 7:37-39)," *NTT*
        29 (1928): 71-79.

6565   J. Blenkinsopp, "The Quenching of Thirst: Reflections on
        the Utterance in the Temple," *Scr* 12 (1950): 39-48.

6566   J. Blenkinsopp, "John 7:37-39: Another Note on a Notorious Crux," *NTS* 6 (1959-1960): 95-98.

6567   M. Kohler, "Des fleuves d'eau vive: Exégèse de Jean 7:37-39," *RTP* 10 (1960): 188-201.

6568   M. Costa, "Simbolismo battesimale in Giov. 7:37-39; 19:31-37; 3:5," *RBib* 13 (1965): 347-83.

6569   H. van den Bussche, "Jésus l'unique source d'eau vive," *BVC* 65 (1965): 17-23.

6570   Pierre Grelot, "La promesse de l'eau vive (Jean 7:37-39)," *AsSeign* 30 (1970): 23-28.

6571   M. Miguéns, "El Agua y el Espítitu en Jean 7:37-39," *EB* 41 (1972): 369-93.

6572   Gordon D. Fee, "Once More - John 7:37-39," *ET* 89 (1977-1978): 116-18.

6573   Zane C. Hodges, "Problem Passages in the Gospel of John: Part 7. Water - John 7:37-39," *BSac* 136 (1979): 239-48.

6574   Martin Hengel, "Jesus, Quelle des Heils: Predigt über Johannes 7,37-39," *TBe* 12 (1981): 201-205.

6575   J. Caba, "Jn 7:37-39 en la teología del IV Evangelio sobre la oración de petición," *Greg* 63 (1982): 647-75.

6576   E. Biser, "Die älteste Pfngstgeschichte: Zur Archäologie des Glaubens," *GeistL* 56 (1983): 199-213.

6577   A. Pinto da Silva, "Giovanni 7:37-39," *Sale* 45 (1983): 575-92.

6578   Dale C. Allison, "The Living Water," *SVTQ* 30/2 (1986): 143-57.

6579   Bruce H. Grigsby, "If Any Man Thirsts: Observations on the Rabbinic Background of John 7:37-39," *Bib* 67/1 (1986): 101-108.

6580   Gary Fredricks, "Rethinking the Role of the Holy Spirit in the Lives of Old Testament Believers," *TriJ* 9 (1988): 81-104.

6581   Henry M. Knapp, "The Messianic Water Which Gives Life to the World," *HBT* 19 (1997): 109-21.

7:37-38

6582   W. C. Allen, "John 7:37-38," *ET* 34 (1922-1923): 329-30.

6583 C. H. Turner, "On the Punctuation of John 7:37-38," *JTS* 24 (1922-1923): 66-70.

6584 H. Rahner, "Flumina de ventre Christi: Die patristische Auslegung von Joh 7:37-38," *Bib* 22 (1941): 269-302, 367-403.

6585 Eric F. F. Bishop, "Drinking Grapes," *ET* 57 (1945-1946): 307.

6586 F.-M. Braun, "L'eau et l'esprit," *RT* 49 (1949): 5-30.

6587 Cuthbert Lattey, "A Note on John 7:37-38," *Scr* 6 (1953-1954): 151-53.

6588 J. Cortés Quirant, " 'Torrentes de agua viva': ¿Una nueva interpretación de Jn 7:37-38?" *EB* 16 (1957): 279-306.

6589 George D. Kilpatrick, "The Punctuation of John 7:37-38," *JTS* (1960): 340-42.

6590 J. B. Cortés, "Yet Another Look at John 7:37-38," *CBQ* 29 (1967): 75-86.

6591 G. Leanza, "Testimonianze della tradizione indiretta sul alcuni Testamento (Giov. 7:7-38 e altri passi)," *RBib* 15 (1967): 407-18.

6592 Glenn Balfour, "The Jewishness of John's Use of the Scriptures in John 6:31 and 7:37-38," *TynB* 46 (1995): 357-80.

7:38

6593 F. J. Badcock, "The Feast of Tabernacles," *JTS* 24 (1922-1923): 169-74.

6594 C. F. Burney, "The Aramaic Equivalent of ἐκ τῆς κοιλίας in John 7:38," *JTS* 24 (1922-1923): 79-80.

6595 M.-É. Boismard, "De son ventre couleront des fleuves d'eau," *RB* 65 (1958): 523-46.

6596 Pierre Grelot, " 'De son ventre couleront des fleuves d'eau": La citation scriptuaire de Jean 7:38," *RB* 66 (1959): 369-74.

6597 Pierre Grelot, "A propos de Jean 7:38," *RB* 67 (1960): 224-25.

6598 Pierre Grelot, "Joh 7:38: Eau du rocher ou source du temple?" *RB* 70 (1963): 43-51.

6599 M. Balagué, "Flumina de ventre credentis (Jean 7:38)," *EB* 26 (1967): 187-201.

6600 Luis F. Ladaria, "Juan 7:38 en Hilario de Poitiers. un análisis de Tr. Ps. 64,13-16," *EE* 52 (1977): 123-28.

6601 M. J. J. Menken, "The Origin of the Old Testament Quotation in John 7:38," *NovT* 38 (1996): 160-75.

6602 Joel Marcus, "Rivers of Living Water from Jesus' Belly (John 7:38)," *JBL* 117 (1998): 328-30.

7:39

6603 H. J. Flowers, "Interpolations in the Fourth Gospel," *JBL* 40 (1921): 146-58.

6604 S. H. Hooke, "The Spirit Was Not Yet," *NTS* 9 (1963): 372-80.

6605 H. Woodhouse, "The Holy Ghost Was Not Yet Given (John 7:39)," *Theology* 67 (1964): 310-12.

7:40-52

6606 J. Mehlmann, "Propheta a Moyse promissus in Jo 7:52 citatus," *VD* 44 (1966): 79-88.

6607 S. Pancaro, "The Metamorphosis of a Legal Principle in the Fourth Gospel: A Closer Look at John 7:51," *Bib* 53 (1972): 340-61.

6608 Martin Avanzo, "Las relaciones entre los rabinos y el Pueblo," *RevB* 37 (1975): 9-15.

7:42

6609 Thomas Söding, " 'Was kann aus Nazareth schon Gutes kommen?' Die Bedeutung des Judenseins Jesu im Johannesevangelium," *NTS* 46 (2000): 21-41.

7:47

6610 J.-M. Charensol, "Épiphanies," *ÉTR* 58 (1983): 515-25.

7:48-49

6611 Martin Avanzo, "Las relaciones entre los rabinos y el Pueblo," *RevB* 37 (1975): 9-15.

7:51

6612   S. Pancaro, "The Metamorphosis of a Legal Principle in the Fourth Gospel: A Closer Look at John 7:51," *Bib* 53 (1972): 340-61.

7:52

6613   E. R. Smothers, "Two Readings in PBodmer II," *HTR* 51 (1958): 109-22.

6614   J. Mehlmann, "Propheta a Moyse promissus in Jo 7:52 citatus," *VD* 44 (1966): 79-88.

7:53-8:11

6615   Harald Riesenfeld, "Perikopen De adultera (Jo 7:53-8:11) i den fornkyrkliga traditionen," *SEÅ* 17 (1952): 106-18.

6616   R. B. Ward, "The Case for John 7:53-8:11," *RQ* 3 (1959): 130-39.

6617   F. Salvoni, "Textual Authority for John 7:53-8:11," *RQ* 4 (1960): 11-15.

6618   A. F. Johnson, "A Stylistic Trait of the Fourth Gospel in the Pericope Adulterae," *JETS* 9 (1966): 91-96.

6619   B. W. Coleman, "The Woman Taken in Adultery. Studies in Texts: John 7:53-8:11," *Theology* 73 (1970): 409-10.

6620   Domingo Muñoz León, "Jésus pardonne à la femme adultère," *AsSeign* 18 (1970): 55-65.

6621   A. A. Trites, "The Woman Taken in Adultery," *BSac* 131 (1974): 137-46.

6622   A. Viard, "La femme adultère," *EV* 84 (1974): 142-44.

6623   Simon Légasse, "Jésus et les prostituées," *RTL* 7 (1976): 137-54.

6624   H. von Campenhausen, "Zur Perikope von der Ehebrecherin," *ZNW* 68 (1977): 182-96.

6625   François Rousseau, "La femme adultère: Structure de Jean 7:53-8:11," *Bib* 59 (1978): 463-80.

6626   Zane C. Hodges, "Problem Passages in the Gospel of John. Part 8: The Woman Taken in Adultery," *BSac* 136 (1979): 318-32; 137 (1980): 41-53.

6627   S. A. James, "The Adulteress and the Death Penalty," *JETS* 22 (1979): 45-53.

6628 Barclay M. Newman, "Verses Marked with Brackets," *BT* 30 (1979): 233-36.

6629 John Ferguson, "The Woman Taken in Adultery," *ET* 93 (1981-1982): 280-81.

6630 Gary M. Burge, "A Specific Problem in the New Testament Text and Canon: The Woman Caught in Adultery," *JETS* 27 (1984): 141-48.

6631 Bart D. Ehrman, "Jesus and the Adulteress," *NTS* 34/1 (1988): 24-44.

6632 Charles P. Baylis, "The Woman Caught in Adultery: A Test of Jesus as the Greater Prophet," *BSac* 146 (1989): 171-84.

6633 Philip Comfort, "The Pericope of the Adulteress," *BT* 40 (1989): 145-47.

6634 Reginald H. Fuller, "The Decalogue in the New Testament," *Int* 43 (1989): 243-55.

6635 Andrew Nugent, "What Did Jesus Write? (John 7:53-8:11)," *DR* 108 (1990): 193-98.

6636 John P. Heil, "The Story of Jesus and the Adulteress Reconsidered," *Bib* 72/2 (1991): 182-91.

6637 J. Rius-Camps, "Origen lucano de la perícopa de la mujer adúltera (Jn 7,53-8,11)," *FilN* 6 (1993): 149-75.

6638 Daniel B. Wallace, "Reconsidering 'The Story of Jesus and the Adulteress Reconsidered'," *NTS* 39 (1993): 290-96.

6639 John P. Heil, "A Rejoinder to 'Reconsidering 'The Story of Jesus and the Adulteress Reconsidered'," *ÉgT* 25 (1994): 361-66.

6640 James I. H. McDonald, "The So-Called Pericope de adultera," *NTS* 41 (1995): 415-27.

6641 T. van Lopik, "Once Again: Floating Words, Their Significance for Textual Criticism," *NTS* 41 (1995): 286-91.

6642 Brad H. Young, " 'Save the Adulteress!' Ancient Jewish *Responsa* in the Gospels?" *NTS* 41 (1995): 59-70.

6643   Alan Watson, "Jesus and the Adulteress," *Bib* 80 (1999): 100-108.

8

6644   G. H. C. MacGregor, "The Rearrangement of John 7 and 8," *ET* 33 (1921-1922): 74-78.

6645   F. J. Leenhardt, "Abraham et la conversion de Saul de Tarse, suivi d'une note sur 'Abraham' dans Jean VIII," *RHPR* 53 (1973): 331-51.

6646   T. B. Dozeman, "Sperma Abraam in John 8 and Related Literature. Cosmology and Judgment," *CBQ* 42 (1980): 342-58.

8:1-11

6647   R. Eisler, "Jesus und die ungetreue Braut," *ZNW* 22 (1923): 305-307.

6648   Eric F. F. Bishop, "The Pericope Adulterae: A Suggestion," *JTS* 35 (1934): 40-45.

6649   Allen P. Wikgren, "The Lectionary Text of the Pericope (John 8:1-11)," *JBL* 53 (1934): 188-98.

6650   T. W. Manson, "The Pericope de Adultera," *ZNW* 44 (1952-1953): 255-57.

6651   F. A. Schilling, "The Story of Jesus and the Adulteress," *ATR* 37 (1955): 91-106.

6652   J. D. M. Derrett, "Law in the NT: The Story of the Woman Taken in Adultery," *NTS* 10 (1963-1964): 1-26.

6653   P. Gervais, "Faute et pardon. Jean 8,1-11," *Chr* 28 (1981): 431-39.

6654   Michel Gourgues, "Moi non plus je ne te condamne pas: les mots et la théologie de Luc en Jean 8:1-11 (la femme adultère)," *SR* 19/3 (1990): 305-18.

6655   Paul S. Minear, "Writing on the Ground: The Puzzle in John 8:1-11," *HBT* 13 (1991): 23-37.

8:3-11

6656   Lauree H. Meyer, "Jesus' Authority and Communal Crisis, John 8:3-11," *BLT* 30 (1985): 115-19.

6657   Dieter Lührmann, "Die Geschichte von einer Sünderin und andere apokryphe Jesusüberlieferungen bei Didymos von Alexandrien," *NovT* 32 (1990): 289-316.

8:5

6658   Josef Blinzler, "Die Strafe für Ehebruch in Bibel und Halacha: Zur Auslegung von Johannes 8:5," *NTS* 4 (1957): 32-47.

8:6-9

6659   E. Power, "Writing on the Ground," *Bib* 2 (1921): 54-57.

6660   Raimund Köbert, "Ein Satz aus Harîris 29: Makame zur Beleuchtung von Jo 8:6-9," *Bib* 29 (1948): 409-10.

8:6-8

6661   P. Humbert, "Jesus Writing on the Ground," *ET* 30 (1918-1919): 475-76.

8:6

•6662   A. F. Johnson, "A Stylistic Trait of the Fourth Gospel in the Pericope Adulterae," *JETS* 9 (1966): 91-96.

6663   Harald Schöndorf, "Jesus schreibt mit dem Finger auf die Erde: Joh 8,6b.8," *BZ* NS 40 (1996): 91-93.

8:8

6664   Harald Schöndorf, "Jesus schreibt mit dem Finger auf die Erde: Joh 8,6b.8," *BZ* NS 40 (1996): 91-93.

8:12-59

6665   Henri Troadec, "Le témoignage de la lumière, Jean 8:12-59," *BVC* 49 (1963): 16-26.

8:12-58

6666   W. Kern, "Der symmetrische Gesamtaufbau von Jo 8:12-58," *ZKT* 78 (1956): 451-54.

8:12-48

6667   Dale A. Bisnauth, "A Re-Reading of John in the Struggle for Liberation," *IRM* 79 (1990): 325-30.

8:12-30

6668   K. Tsuchido, "Tradition and Redaction in John 8:12-30," *AJBI* 6 (1980): 56-75.

8:12

6669   S. Seiser, "Das Licht-Wort Jesu (Joh 8:12) und seine Enthüllung im 'Zeichen' der Blindenheilung (Joh 9:1-38): Eine Unterrichtseinheit für das 6. Schuljahr," *BSac* 136 (1979): 53-63.

6670   P. Schineller, "Jesus in the Gospel of John—I. 'I Am the Light of the World'" *Emmanuel* 106 (2000): 224-27.

8:13-59

6671   Urban C. Von Wahlde, "Literary Structure and Theological Argument in Three Discourses with the Jews in the Fourth Gospel," *JBL* 103 (1984): 575-84.

8:13

6672   John C. Thomas, "The Fourth Gospel and Rabbinic Judaism," *ZNW* 82 (1991): 159-182.

8:17

6673   Jean-P. Charlier, "L'exégèse johannique d'un précepte légal," *RB* 67 (1960): 503-15.

6674   Jörg Augenstein, " 'Euer Gesetz'--Ein Pronomen und die johanneische Haltung zum Gesetz," *ZNW* 88 (1997): 311-13.

8:21-59

6675   Jerome H. Neyrey, "Jesus the Judge: Forensic Process in John 8:21-59," *Bib* 68/4 (1987): 509-42.

8:21-30

6676   F. J. Leenhardt, "Abraham et la conversion de Saul de Tarse, suivi d'une note sur 'Abraham' dans Jean VIII," *RHPR* 53 (1973): 331-51.

6677   R. A. Ward, "Question Marks as an Aid in Interpretation," *SouJT* 18 (1975): 69-71.

6678   T. B. Dozeman, "Sperma Abraam in John 8 and Related Literature: Cosmology and Judgment," *CBQ* 42 (1980): 342-58.

6679   E. L. Miller, "The Christology of John 8:25," *TZ* 36 (1980): 257-65.

6680   E. D. Freed, "Egō Eimi in John viii.24 in the Light of Its Context and Jewish Messianic Belief," *JTS* 33 (1982): 163-67.

8:23

6681   W. C. Robinson, "The Virgin Birth: A Broader Base," *CT* 17/5 (1972): 238-40.

8:24

6682   Heinrich Zimmermann, "Das absolute Ego eimi als die neutestamentliche Offenbarungsformel [2 pts]," *BZ* 4/1 (1960): 54-69; 4/2 (1960): 266-76.

6683   E. D. Freed, "Egō Eimi in John viii.24 in the Light of Its Context and Jewish Messianic Belief," *JTS* 33 (1982): 163-67.

8:25

6684   Robert W. Funk, "PBodmer II and John 8:25," *HTR* 51 (1958): 95-100.

6685   E. R. Smothers, "Two Readings in PBodmer II," *HTR* 51 (1958): 109-22.

6686   Patrick P. Saydon, "Some Biblico-Liturgical Passages Reconsidered," *MeliT* 18/1 (1966): 10-17.

6687   E. L. Miller, "The Christology of John 8:25," *TZ* 36 (1980): 257-65.

6688   J. D. M. Derrett, "Exercitations on John 8," *EB* 52 (1994): 433-51.

6689   Miguel A. Pertini, "La genialidad gramatical de Jn 8,25," *EB* 56 (1998): 371-404.

8:28-29

6690   André Charbonneau, "Jésus en croix (Jn 19,16b-42), Jésus élevé (3,14ss; 8,28s; 12,31ss)," *ScE* 45 (1993): 5-23.

8:28

6691   B. Schwank, "Erhöht und verherrlicht," *ErAu* 68 (1992): 137-46.

8:30-31

6692   R. A. Ward, "Question Marks as an Aid in Interpretation," *SouJT* 18/1 (1975): 69-71.

8:31-36

6693   Bernard C. Lategan, "The Truth That Sets Man Free. John 8:31-36," *Neo* 2 (1968): 70-80.

6694   J. M. Casabó Suqué, "La liberación en San Juan," *RevB* 34 (1972): 225-42.

6695   Harm W. Hollander, " 'Vrijheid' en 'slavernij' in Johannes 8:31-36," *NTT* 48 (1994): 265-74.

8:31-32

6696   Giuseppe Segalla, "Un appello alla perseveranza nella fede in Gv 8:31-32?" *Bib* 62 (1981): 387-89.

8:31

6697   James Swetnam, "The Meaning of πεπιστευκότας in John 8:31," *Bib* 61 (1980): 106-109.

8:32

6698   Johann Kinghorn, "John 8:32—The Freedom of Truth," *IRM* 79 (1990): 314-19.

8:33-47

6699   C. H. Dodd, "A l'arrière-plan d'un dialogue johannique," *RHPR* 37 (1957): 5-17.

8:33-36

6700   Ulrich Busse, "The relevance of social history to the interpretation of the Gospel according to John," *SkrifK* 16 (1995): 28-38.

8:41

6701   W. C. Robinson, "The Virgin Birth: A Broader Base," *CT* 17/5 (1972): 238-40.

6702   Joachim Kügler, "Wir stammen nicht aus einem Ehebruch (Joh 8,41). Eine Kritik an Günther Schwarz," *BibN* 16 (1981): 27-29.

6703   Günther Schwarz, "ἡμεῖς ἐκ πορνείας οὐ γεγεννήμεθα (Johannes 8:41)" *BibN* 14 (1981): 50-53.

6704   G. Vittmann, "Überlegungen zu Matthäus 1:18," *BibN* 16 (1981): 39-41.

8:44

6705   Nils A. Dahl, "Manndraperen og hans far (Joh 8:44)," *NTT* 64/3 (1963): 129-62.

6706   S. Ben-Chorin, "Antijüdische Elemente im Neuen Testament," *EvT* 40 (1980): 203-14.

6707   Domingo Muñoz León, "El principio trinitario inmanente y la interpretación del Nuevo Testamento (a propósito de la cristología epifánica restrictiva), pt 3," *EB* 41/3-4 (1983): 241-83.

6708   G. Reim, "Joh 8:44—Gotteskinder-Teufelskinder: wie antijudaistisch ist 'die wohl antijudaistischste Äusserung des NT'," *NTS* 30/4 (1984): 619-24.

6709   Timothy N. Boyd, "The New Testament Concept of Evil," *BI* 16/2 (1990): 19-23.

8:48

6710   J. Mehlmann, "John 8:48 in Some Patristic Quotations," *Bib* 44/2 (1963): 206-209.

8:53-58

6711   Edward J. Kilmartin, "A First Century Chalice Dispute," *SE* 12 (1960): 403-08.

8:56

6712   F. H. Chase, "Two Notes on St. John's Gospel," *JTS* 26 (1924-1925): 381.

6713   T. Vargha, " 'Abraham exultavit ut videret diem meum'," *VD* 10 (1930): 43-46.

6714   Pierre Grelot, "Jean 8:56 et Jubilés 16:16-29," *RevQ* 13 (1988): 621-28.

8:57

6715   G. Ogg, "The Age of Jesus When He Taught," *NTS* 5 (1958-1959): 291-98.

6716   Édouard Delebecque, "Jésus contemporain d'Abraham selon Jean 8:57," *RB* 93/1 (1986): 85-92.

6717   M. J. Edwards, " 'Not Yet Fifty Years Old': John 8:57," *NTS* 40 (1994): 449-54.

6718   Tjitze Baarda, "John 8:57B: The Contribution of the Diatessaron of Tatian," *NovT* 38 (1996): 336-43.

8:58

6719 E. D. Freed, "Who or What Was before Abraham in John 8:58?" *JSNT* 17 (1983): 52-59.

9

6720 R. Mackintosh, "Two Johannine Miracles," *ET* 37 (1925-1926): 43-44.

6721 F. Smyth-Florentin, "Guérison d'un aveugle-né," *AsSeign* 17 (1970): 17-26.

6722 R. R. Fitzgerald, "The Blind Man and the Cave," *BibTo* 93 (1977): 1420-26.

6723 G. Reim, "Joh 9 - Tradition und zeitgenössische messianische Diskussion," *BZ* 22 (1978): 245-53.

6724 John Painter, "Johannine Symbols: A Case Study in Epistemology," *JTSA* 27 (1979): 26-41.

6725 Michel Gourgues, "L'aveugle-né (Jean 9). Du miracle au signe: typologie des réactions à l'égard du Fils de l'homme," *NRT* 104 (1982): 381-95.

6726 F. Mosetto, "Esegesi agostiniana di Gv 9," *PV* 29 (1984): 473-80.

6727 P. J. Riga, "The Man Born Blind," *BibTo* 22 (1984): 168-73.

6728 Frédéric Manns, "Racines juives et nouveauté chrétienne en Jean 9," *SBFLA* 35 (1985): 69-106.

6729 J. M. Lieu, "Blindness in the Johannine Tradition," *NTS* 34/1 (1988): 83-95.

6730 Jeffrey L. Staley, "Stumbling in the Dark, Reaching for the Light: Reading Character in John 5 and 9," *Semeia* 53 (1991): 55-80.

6731 G. Cooke, "Seeing, Judging and Acting: Evangelism in Jesus' Way according to John 9," *ERT* 16/3 (1992): 251-61.

6732 J. Warren Holleran, "Seeing the Light: A Narrative Reading of John 9," *ETL* 69 (1993): 5-26; 354-82.

6733 Gilberto Marconi, "La vista del cieco: Gv 9,1-41," *Greg* 79 (1998): 625-43.

9:1-41

6734   Thomas L. Brodie, "Creative Rewriting: Key to a New Methodology (John 9:1-41)," *SBLSP* 2 (1968): 261-67.

6735   Thomas L. Brodie, "Jesus as the New Elisha: Cracking the Code (John 9:1-41)," *ET* 93 (1981-1982): 39-42.

6736   Jeffrey L. Staley, "Stumbling in the Dark, Reaching for the Light: Reading Character in John 5 and 9," *Semeia* 53 (1991): 55-80.

6737   John C. Thomas, "The Fourth Gospel and Rabbinic Judaism," *ZNW* 82 (1991): 159-182.

6738   Mark F. Whitters, "Discipleship in John: Four Profiles," *WW* 18 (1998): 422-27.

9:1-38

6739   S. Seiser, "Das Licht-Wort Jesu (Joh 8:12) und seine Enthüllung im 'Zeichen' der Blindenheilung (Joh 9:1-38): Eine Unterrichtseinheit für das 6. Schuljahr," *BSac* 136 (1979): 53-63.

9:1-14

6740   Tom Thatcher, "The Sabbath Trick: Unstable Irony in the Fourth Gospel," *JSNT* 76 (1999): 53-77.

9:1-12

6741   John Bligh, "Four Studies in St John: 1. The Man Born Blind," *HeyJ* 7 (1966): 129-44.

6742   Bruce H. Grigsby, "Washing in the Pool of Siloam: A Thematic Anticipation of the Johannine Cross," *NovT* 27 (1985): 227-35.

6743   William J. Ireland, "The Pool of Siloam," *BI* 16/2 (1990): 31-34.

9:1-3

6744   F. A. Garcia Romero, "Breve comentario a Jn 9:1-3: objeciones al supuesto cristianismo de Trifiodoro," *FilN* 2 (1989): 93-97.

9:2

6745   J. P. Comiskey, " 'Rabbi, Who Has Sinned' (John 9,2)," *BibTo* 26 (1966): 1808-14.

9:3

6746   W. Spencer, "John 9:3," *ET* 55 (1944): 110.

6747   John C. Poirier, " 'Day and Night' and the Punctuation of John 9.3," *NTS* 42 (1996): 288-94.

9:5

6748   P. Schineller, "Jesus in the Gospel of John—I. 'I Am the Light of the World'" *Emmanuel* 106 (2000): 224-27.

9:6-41

6749   David Smith, "Jesus and the Pharisees in Socio-Anthropological Perspective," *TriJ* 6/2 (1985): 151-56.

9:6

6750   J. D. M. Derrett, "John 9:6 Read With Isaiah 6:10; 20:9," *EQ* 66 (1994): 251-54.

9:7

6751   Karl Müller, "Joh 9,7 und das jüdische Verständnis des Šiloh-Spruches," *BZ* 13 (1969): 251-56.

6752   Bruce H. Grigsby, "Washing in the Pool of Siloam: A Thematic Anticipation of the Johannine Cross," *NovT* 27 (1985): 227-35.

9:25

6753   Christoph Burchard, "Ei nach einem Ausdruck des Wissens oder Nichtwissens Joh 9:25, Act 19:2, 1 Cor 1:16, 7:16," *ZNW* 52/1-2 (1961): 73-82.

9:35

6754   Mogens Müller, "Have You Faith in the Son of Man?" *NTS* 37 (1991): 291-94.

6755   John W. Pryor, "The Johannine Son of Man and the Descent-Ascent Motif," *JETS* 34 (1991): 341-51.

9:38-39

6756   Calvin L. Porter, "John IX,38.39a: A Liturgical Addition to the Text," *NTS* 13 (1966-1967): 387-94.

10

6757   J. T. Hudson, "A Disarrangement in John 10," *ET* 38 (1926-1927): 329.

6758   A. Fridrichsen, "Herdekapitlet, Joh. 10," *SEÅ* 8 (1943): 30-48.

6759   Juan Leal, "La Eucaristía y la Parábola del Buen Pastor," *EE* 27 (1953): 317-24.

6760   J. A. Emerton, "Interpretation of Psalm 82 in John 10," *JTS* 11 (1960): 329-32.

6761   J. A. Emerton, "Some New Testament Notes: I. The Interpretation of Psalm lxxxii in John 10," *JTS* NS 11 (1960): 329-32.

6762   J. E. Burns, "The Discourse on the Good Shepherd and the Rite of Ordination," *AmER* 149 (1963): 386-91.

6763   Wilfred Tooley, "The Shepherd and Sheep Image in the Teaching of Jesus," *NovT* 7/1 (1964): 15-25.

6764   M. DeCerteau, "Comme un voleur," *Chr* 12 (1965): 25-41.

6765   J. L. De Velliers, "The Shepherd and His Flock," *Neo* 2 (1968): 89-103.

6766   Mary Therest, "The Good Shepherd," *BibTo* 38 (1968): 2657-64.

6767   J. D. M. Derrett, "The Good Shepherd. St. John's Use of Jewish Halakah and Haggadah," *StTheol* 27 (1973): 25-50.

6768   J. F. O'Grady, "The Good Shepherd and the Vine and the Branches," *BTB* 8 (1978): 86-89.

6769   B. A. Ramsey, "A Note on the Disappearance of the Good Shepherd from Early Christian Art," *HTR* 76 (1983): 375-78.

6770   Ulrich Busse, "Offene Fragen zu Joh 10," *NTS* 33/4 (1987): 516-31.

<u>10</u>

6771   J. van der Watt, "Simboliek in die Evangelie van Johannes," *SkrifK* 19 (1998): 392-403.

<u>10:1-30</u>

6772   Frédéric Manns, "Traditions targumiques en Jean 10:1-30," *RevSR* 60/3-4 (1986): 135-57.

<u>10:1-21</u>

6773   J. Quasten, "The Parable of the Good Shepherd," *CBQ* 10 (1948): 1-12, 151-69.

6774   David J. Hawkin, "Orthodoxy and Heresy in John 10:1-21 and 15:1-17," *EQ* 47 (1975): 208-13.

6775   L. Stachowiak, "Dobry Pasterz: The Good Shepherd," *RoczTK* 22 (1975): 75-84.

6776   Max A. Chevallier, "L'analyse littéraire des textes du Nouveau Testament (Conseils aux étudiants)," *RHPR* 57 (1977): 367-78.

10:1-18

6777   J. M. Bover, "El símil del Buen Pastor," *EB* 14 (1955): 297-308.

6778   Paul W. Meyer, "A Note on John 10:1-18," *JBL* 75 (1956): 232-35.

6779   John J. O'Rourke, "John 10:1-18: Series Parabolarum?" *VD* 42 (1964): 22-25.

6780   O. Kiefer, "Le seul troupeau et le seul Pasteur: Jésus et les siens," *AsSeign* 25 (1969): 46-61.

6781   Miguel Rodríguez-Ruiz, "El discurso del Buen Pastor: coherencia theologico-literaria e interpretacion," *EB* 48/1 (1990): 5-45.

6782   Robert Kysar, "Johannine Metaphor—Meaning and Function: A Literary Case Study of John 10:1-18," *Semeia* 53 (1991): 81-111.

10:1-10

6783   Augustin George, "Je suis la porte des brebis," *BVC* 51 (1963): 18-25.

6784   J. P. Martin, "John 10:1-10" *Int* 32 (1978): 171-75.

10:1-5

6785   J. A. T. Robinson, "The Parable of John 10:1-5," *ZNW* 46 (1955): 233-40.

6786   Adele Reinhartz, "The Shepherd and the Sheep: John 10:1-5 Reconsidered," *EGLMBS* 9 (1989): 161-77.

10:7-9

6787   Eric F. F. Bishop, "Door of the Sheep—John 10:7-9," *ET* 71 (1960): 307-309.

10:7

6788   P. Weigandt, "Zum Text von Joh. x 7. Ein Beitrag zum
Problem der koptischen Bibelübersetzung," *NovT* 9
(1967): 43-51.

6789   J.-C. Didier, "Histoire de la présence réelle. À propos d'un
dogme récemment contesté (Jean 10:7; 15:1-5)," *EV* 87
(1977): 305-14.

10:9

6790   J. M. Ballard, "Two Translations in St. John's Gospel," *ET*
36 (1924-1925): 45.

10:11-18

6791   D. Mollat, "Le bon pasteur," *BVC* 52 (1963): 25-35.

6792   Gilles Becquet, "Jésus, Bon Pasteur, donne vie à une
nouvelle communauté (Jean 10:11-18)," *EV* 80 (1970):
242-43.

6793   C. Clifton Black, "Our Shepherd's Voice: Biblical
Resources for the Easter Season," *QR* 14 (1994): 89-110.

10:11-16

6794   Ingo Hermann, "Der gute Hirt—Bild und Wirklichkeit:
Eine Homilie zu Jo 10:11-16," *BibL* 4 (1963): 70-74.

10:11

6795   J. Gregg, " 'I Am the Good Shepherd'," *ET* 31
(1919-1920): 491-93.

6796   D. M. Stanley, "I Am the Good Shepherd," *Worship* 35
(1961): 287-93.

6797   André Feuillet, "Deux références évangéliques cachées au
Serviteur martyrisé (Is 52,13-53,12). Quelques aspects
importants du mystère rédempteur," *NRT* 106 (1984):
549-65.

10:15

6798   P. E. Kretzmann, " 'Die Schrift kann nicht gebrochen
werden'," *CTM* 6 (1936): 114-21.

6799   André Feuillet, "Deux références évangéliques cachées au
Serviteur martyrisé (Is 52,13-53,12). Quelques aspects
importants du mystère rédempteur," *NRT* 106 (1984):
549-65.

10:16

6800 A. Ross, "A Critical Note on John 10:16: Fold or Flock?" *JETS* 4/3 (1961): 99-100.

6801 Otfried Hofius, "Die Sammlung der Heiden zur Herde Israels (Joh 10,16; 11,51f.)," *ZNW* 58 (1967): 289-91.

10:17-18

6802 André Feuillet, "Deux références évangéliques cachées au Serviteur martyrisé (Is 52,13-53,12). Quelques aspects importants du mystère rédempteur," *NRT* 106 (1984): 549-65.

10:22-39

6803 J. Giblet, "Et il y eut la dédicace, Jean 10:22-39," *BVC* 66 (1965): 17-25.

6804 Urban C. Von Wahlde, "Literary Structure and Theological Argument in Three Discourses with the Jews in the Fourth Gospel," *JBL* 103 (1984): 575-84.

6805 J. C. Skedros, "The Works of Jesus: A Study of John 10:22-29," *MeliT* 10 (1991): 51-57.

6806 Jerry R. Lancaster and R. Larry Overstreet, "Jesus' Celebration of Hanukkah in John 10," *BSac* 152 (1995): 318-33.

10:22-30

6807 Robert Kysar, "John 10:22-30," *Int* 43 (1989): 66-70.

10:22-29

6808 J. M. Bover, "El viaje a Jerusalén, narrado por Lc. 9:51-11:13, fue a lafiesta de las Encenias, narrada por Ioh. 10:22-39," *EB* 3 (1931-1932): 3-10.

10:22

6809 H. Höpfl, "Das Chanukafest," *Bib* 3 (1922): 165-79.

10:24

6810 Raymond E. Brown, "Incidents that Are Units in the Synoptic Gospels but Dispersed in St. John," *CBQ* 23 (1961): 143-60.

10:28-30

6811   R. Aytoun, " 'No One Shall Match Them Out of My Hand'," *ET* 31 (1919-1920): 475-76.

10:29

6812   J. H. Michael, "The Text and Context of John 10:29," *JTS* 24 (1922-1923): 51-54.

6813   R. G. Bury, "St. John 10:29," *JTS* 41 (1940): 262-63.

6814   J. Neville Birdsall, "John 10:29," *JTS* 11 (1960): 342-44.

6815   J. Whittaker, "A Hellenistic Context for John 10:29," *VC* 24 (1970): 241-60.

6816   Jesse Sell, "Johannine Traditions in Logion 61 of the Gospel of Thomas," *PRS* 7/1 (1980): 24-37.

10:30

6817   T. E. van Pollard, "The Exegesis of John 10:30 in the Early Trinitarian Controversies," *NTS* (1956-1957): 334-49.

10:33-36

6818   A. T. Hanson, "John's Citation of Ps 82," *NTS* 11 (1964-1965): 158-62.

10:34-36

6819   Richard Jungkuntz, "Approach to the Exegesis of John 10:34-36," *CTM* 35 (1964): 556-65.

6820   J. A. Emerton, "Melchizedek and the Gods. Fresh Evidence for the Jewish Background of John X,34-36," *JTS* 17 (1966): 399-401.

10:34

6821   J. S. Ackerman, "The Rabbinic Interpretation of Psalm 82 and the Gospel of John: John 10:34 and the Prologue," *HTR* 59 (1966): 186-91.

6822   Jörg Augenstein, " 'Euer Gesetz'--Ein Pronomen und die johanneische Haltung zum Gesetz," *ZNW* 88 (1997): 311-13.

10:36

6823   J. Rovira, "Spiritus Sanctus in Christo," *VD* 6 (1926): 49-56.

6824   A. T. Hanson, "John's Citation of Psalm LXXXII Reconsidered," *NTS* 13 (1966-1967): 363-67.

10:38

6825   J. M. Ross, "Some Unnoticed Points in the Text of the New Testament," *NovT* 25 (1983): 59-72.

10:40-21:24

6826   R. Gyllenberg, "Intåget i Jerusalem och Johannesevangeliets uppbyggnad," *SEÅ* 41/42 (1976-1977): 81-86.

11-12

6827   Mario Galizzi, "Quando io sarò elevato da terra attirerò tutti a me (Gv 12:32) (Il tema della Passione in Gv cc. 11-12)," *PV* 18 (1973): 85-100.

6828   E. F. Glusman, "The Cleansing of the Temple and the Anointing at Bethany: The Order of Events in Mark 11/John 11-12," *SBLSP* 9/1 (1979): 113-17.

6829   M. DeMérode, "L'accueil triomphal de Jésus selon Jean 11-12," *RTL* I3 (1982): 49-62.

6830   L. Eslinger, "Judas Game: The Biology of Combat in the Gospel of John," *JSNT* 77 (2000): 45-73.

11:1-12:8

6831   Maria L. Rigato, "Maria di Betania nella redazione giovannea," *Ant* 66 (1991): 203-26.

11

6832   A. Henderson, "Notes on John 11," *ET* 32 (1920-1921): 123-26.

6833   T. F. Forth, "The Tomb of Lazarus and the Text of John," *Theology* 4 (1922): 232-34.

6834   Juan Leal, "De amore Iesu erga amicum Lazarum," *VD* 21 (1941): 59-64.

6835   Roderic Dunkerley, "Lazarus," *NTS* 5 (1958-1959): 321-27.

6836   Wilhelm Wilkens, "Die Erweckung des Lazarus," *TZ* 15 (1959): 22-39.

6837   Harald Sahlin, "Lasarus-gestalten i Luk 16 och Joh 11," *SEÅ* 37-38 (1972-1973): 167-74.

6838   Sandra M. Schneiders, "Death in the Community of Eternal Life: History, Theology, and Spirituality in John 11," *Int* 41 (1987): 44-56.

6839   Wilhelm H. Wuellner, "Putting Life Back into the Lazarus Story and Its Reading: The Narrative Rhetoric of John 11 as the Narration of Faith," *Semeia* 53 (1991): 113-32.

6840   Barnabas Lindars, "Rebuking the Spirit: A New Analysis of the Lazarus Story of John 11," *NTS* 38 (1992): 89-104.

6841   Delbert Burkett, "Two Accounts of Lazarus' Resurrection in John 11," *NovT* 36 (1994): 209-32.

11:1-57

6842   M. Balagué, "La resurrección de Lázaro," *CuBí* 19 (1962): 16-29.

11:1-54

6843   J. Zumstein, "Le signe de la croix," *LV* 41 (1992): 68-82.

11:1-45

6844   Werner Stenger, "Die Auferweckung des Lazarus (Joh 11: 1-45). Vorlage und johanneische Redaktion," *TTZ* 83 (1974): 17-37.

11:1-44

6845   J. P. Martin, "History and Eschatology in the Lazarus Narrative," *SJT* 17 (1964): 332-43.

6846   Dino Merli, "Lo scopo della risurrezione di Lazzaro in Giov. 11:1-44," *BibO* 12 (1970): 59-82.

6847   M. Morlet, "Le dernier signe de la glorifcation de Jésus," *AsSeign* 18 (1970): 11-25.

6848   M. Aubineau, "Un Ps. Athanase, In Lazarum (e Vat. Ottob. gr. 14) restitué à Léonce de Constantinople," *JTS* 25 (1974): 442-47.

6849   B. McNeil, "The Raising of Lazarus," *DR* 92 (1974): 269-75.

6850   C. F. D. Moule, "The Meaning of 'Life' in the Gospel and Epistles of St John: A Study of Lazarus, John 11:1-44," *Theology* 78 (1975): 114-25.

6851   L. Paul Trudinger, "The Meaning of 'Life' in St. John. Some Further Reflections," *BTB* 6 (1976): 258-63.

6852   L. Paul Trudinger, "The Raising of Lazarus—A Brief Response," *DR* 94 (1976): 287-90.

6853   J.-F. Malherbe, " 'Lectures d'un texte johannique' Questions de méthode à propos d'un séminaire interdisciplinaire," *RTL* 10 (1979): 394-99.

6854   Charles H. Giblin, "Suggestion, Negative Response, and Positive Action in St. John's Portrayal of Jesus," *NTS* 26 (1979-1980): 197-211.

6855   Ekkart Sauser, "Das Bild von der Auferweckung des Lazarus in der frühchristlichen und in der östlichen Kunst," *TTZ* 90 (1981): 276-88.

6856   A. Salas, "La resurrección de Lázaro," *BibFe* 8 (1982): 180-94.

6857   John N. Suggit, "The Raising of Lazarus," *ET* 95 (1983-1984): 106-108.

6858   Keith Pearce, "The Lucan Origins of the Raising of Lazarus," *ET* 96 (1984-1985): 359-61.

6859   Jacob Kremer, "Die Lazarusgeschichte. Ein Beispiel urkirchlicher Christusverkündigung," *GeistL* 58 (1985): 244-58.

6860   Mark W. G. Stibbe, "A Tomb with a View: John 11:1-44 in Narrative-Critical Perspective," *NTS* 40 (1994): 38-54.

11:1

6861   F. W. Lewis, "A Certain Village, Not Bethany," *ET* 32 (1920-1921): 330.

6862   Tony M. Martin, "Bethany," *BI* 1/2 (1975): 17-19.

11:5

6863   J. N. Sanders, "Those Whom Jesus Loved," *NTS* 1 (1954): 29-41.

11:9-10

6864   Iver Larsen, "Walking in the Light: A Comment on John 11:9-10," *BT* 37/4 (1986): 432-36.

11:14-15

6865   Édouard Delebecque, "Lazare est mort (note sur Jean 11:14-15)," *Bib* 67/1 (1986): 89-97.

11:17-40

6866   Francis J. Moloney, "The Faith of Martha and Mary: A Narrative Approach to John 11,17-40," *Bib* 75 (1994): 471-93.

11:17-27

6867   Guy Lafon, "Croire et vivre chez Jean XI,17-27," *RTL* 6 (1975): 130-34.

6868   H. J. de Jonge, "Een recente aanwinst onder de nieuwtestamentische tekstgetuigen in Nederland," *NTT* 31 (1977): 2-7.

11:25-27

6869   Miguel Rodríguez-Ruiz, "Significado cristológico y soteriológico de Jn 11,25-27," *EB* 55 (1997): 199-222.

11:25-26

6870   Paul S. Minear, "The promise of life in the Gospel of John," *TT* 49 (1993): 485-99.

11:25

6871   Kazimierz Romaniuk, " 'I Am the Resurrection and the Life' (John 11:25)," *Conci* 6 (1970): 10, 68-77.

11:27

6872   Raymond E. Brown, "Incidents that Are Units in the Synoptic Gospels but Dispersed in St. John," *CBQ* 23 (1961): 143-60.

11:33

6873   E. Bevan, "Note on Mark 1:41 and John 11:33, 38," *JTS* 33 (1931-1932): 186-88.

6874   Cullen I. K. Story, "The Mental Attitude of Jesus at Bethany: John 11:33, 38," *NTS* 37 (1991): 51-66.

11:35

6875   Stephen Voorwinde, "Jesus' Tears--Human or Divine?" *RTR* 56 (1997): 68-81.

11:38

6876   E. Bevan, "Note on Mark 1:41 and John 11:33, 38," *JTS* 33 (1931-1932): 186-88.

6877   Cullen I. K. Story, "The Mental Attitude of Jesus at Bethany: John 11:33, 38," *NTS* 37 (1991): 51-66.

6878   Barnabas Lindars, "Rebuking the Spirit: A New Analysis of the Lazarus Story of John 11," *NTS* 38 (1992): 89-104.

11:41-42

6879   Max Wilcox, "The 'Prayer' of Jesus in John xi.41b-42," *NTS* 24 (1977-1978): 128-32.

6880   W. Bingham Hunter, "Contextual and Genre Implications for the Historicity of John 11:41b-42," *JETS* 28 (1985): 53-70.

11:44

6881   B. Osborne, "A Folded Napkin in an Empty Tomb: John 11:44 and 20:7 Again," *HeyJ* 14 (1973): 437-40.

6882   W. E. Reiser, "The Case of the Tidy Tomb: The Place of the Napkins of John 11:44 and 20:7," *HeyJ* 14 (1973): 47-57.

11:45-12:11

6883   G. Tosatto, "La passione di Cristo in S. Giov," *PV* 15 (1970): 377-88.

11:45-54

6884   Gerhard Lohfink, "Jesus' Death and the Church Life," *TD* 32 (1985): 156-58.

11:47-53

6885   Johannes Beutler, "Two Ways of Gathering: The Plot to Kill Jesus in John 11:47-53," *NTS* 40 (1994): 399-406.

11:47-52

6886   F.-M. Braun, "Quatre 'signes' johanniques de l'unité chrétienne (Jean 6:12-13, 11:47-52, 19:23-4, 21:1-11)," *NTS* 9 (1963): 147-55.

11:49-52

6887   J. Szlaga, "Proroctwo Kajfasza," *RoczTK* 28 (1981): 55-64.

11:49-51

6888   P. Schepens, "Pontifex anni illius," *RechSR* 11 (1921): 372-74.

11:50-52

6889   S. Pancaro, " 'People of God' in St. John's Gospel?" *NTS* 16 (1969-1970): 114-29.

11:50

6890   J. Kennedy, "The Abuse of Power," *ET* 85 (1973-1974): 172-73.

11:51

6891   Otfried Hofius, "Die Sammlung der Heiden zur Herde Israels (Joh 10,16; 11,51f.)," *ZNW* 58 (1967): 289-91.

11:52

6892   Thomas Söding, " 'Was kann aus Nazareth schon Gutes kommen?' Die Bedeutung des Judenseins Jesu im Johannesevangelium," *NTS* 46 (2000): 21-41.

11:54

6893   Paul Katz, "Wieso gerade nach Efrajim? (Erwägungen zu Jh 11,54)," *ZNW* 88 (1997): 130-34.

11:55-12:11

6894   Chantal Reynier, "Le thème du parfum et l'avènement des figures en Jn 11,55-12,11," *ScE* 46 (1994): 203-20.

12

6895   L. R. Kittlaus, "Evidence from John 12 that the Author of John Knew the Gospel of Mark," *SBLSP* 9/1 (1979): 119-22.

6896   A. B. Kolenkow, "The Changing Patterns: Conflicts and the Necessity of Death. John 2 and 12 and Markan Parallels," *SBLSP* 9/1 (1979): 123-25.

6897   Bernard P. Robinson, "The Anointing by Mary of Bethany (John 12)," *DR* 115 (1997): 99-111.

12:1-43

6898   K. Tsuchido, "Tradition and Redaction in John 12:1-43," *NTS* 30/4 (1984): 609-19.

12:1-11

6899   T. W. Bevan, "The Four Anointings," *ET* 39 (1927-1928): 137-39.

6900   Frans Neirynck, "L'onction de Béthanie (12,1-11)," *ETL*
        53 (1977): 449-500.

6901   J. Ramsey Michaels, "John 12:1-11," *Int* 43 (1989):
        287-91.

12:1-8

6902   L. Von Sybel, "Die Salbungen," *ZNW* 23 (1924): 184-93.

6903   A. Lemonnyer, "L'onction de Béthanie: Notes d'exégèse
        sur Jean 12:1-8," *RechSR* 18 (1928): 105-17.

6904   Rudolf Schnackenburg, "Der johanneische Bericht von der
        Salbung in Bethanien," *MTZ* 1/1 (1950): 48-52.

6905   André Légault, "An Application of the Form-Critique
        Method to the Anointings in Galilee and Bethany," *CBQ*
        16 (1954): 131-45.

6906   J. Michl, "Der Sinn der Fusswaschung," *Bib* 40 (1959):
        697-708.

6907   A. Kassing, "Das Evangelium der Fusswaschung," *ErAu*
        36 (1960): 83-93.

6908   J. K. Elliott, "The Anointing of Jesus," *ET* 85
        (1973-1974): 105-107.

6909   Robert Holst, "The One Anointing of Jesus: Another
        Application of the Form-Critical Method," *JBL* 95 (1976):
        435-46.

6910   E. E. Platt, "The Ministry of Mary of Bethany," *TT* 34
        (1977): 29-59.

6911   Winsome Munro, "The Anointing in Mark 14:3-9 and
        John 12:1-8," *SBLSP* 9/1 (1979): 127-30.

6912   C.-P. März, "Zur Traditionsgeschichte von Mk 14,3-9 und
        Parallelen," *SNTU-A* 6/7 (1981-1982): 89-112.

6913   André Feuillet, "Le récit johannique de l'onction de
        Béthanie," *EV* 95 (1985): 193-203.

6914   James F. Coakley, "The Anointing at Bethany and the
        Priority of John," *JBL* 107 (1988): 241-56.

6915   Guy Wagner, "L'oncion de Béthanie: Essai sur la genèse
        du récit de Marc 14/3-9 et sa reprise par Matthieu, Luc et
        Jean," *ÉTR* 72 (1997): 437-46.

12:1-3

6916   H. M. Foston, "Two Johannine Parentheses," *ET* 32 (1920-1921): 520-23.

12:1

6917   J. M. Ross, "Some Unnoticed Points in the Text of the New Testament," *NovT* 25 (1983): 59-72.

12:3

6918   J. E. Bruns, "A Note on John 12,3," *CBQ* 28 (1966): 219-22.

6919   B. Prete, "Un'aporia giovannea: il testo di Giov. 12:3," *RBib* 25 (1977): 357-73.

6920   Barnabas Lindars, "Rebuking the Spirit: A New Analysis of the Lazarus Story of John 11," *NTS* 38 (1992): 89-104.

12:9

6921   G. M. Lee, "John xii 9 ὁ ὄχλος πολύς," *NovT* 22 (1980): 95.

12:12-19

6922   E. D. Freed, "The Entry into Jerusalem in the Gospel of John," *JBL* 80 (1961): 329-38.

6923   Brian A. Mastin, "The Date of the Triumphal Entry," *NTS* 16 (1969-1970): 76-82.

6924   J. D. M. Derrett, "Law in the New Testament: The Palm Sunday Colt," *NovT* 13 (1971): 241-58.

6925   H. Patsch, "Der Einzug in Jerusalem. Ein historischer Versuch," *ZTK* 68 (1971): 1-26.

6926   W. A. Visser 't Hooft, "Triumphalism in the Gospels," *SJT* 38 (1985): 491-504.

6927   Robert Lunt, "The Chronology of John 12:12-19," *BT* 38 (1987): 445-46.

12:12-15

6928   Eric Werner, " 'Hosanna' in the Gospels," *JBL* 65 (1946): 97-122.

12:12

6929   D. Moody Smith, "John 12:12ff. and the Question of John's Use of the Synoptics," *JBL* 82 (1963): 58-64.

12:13

6930   William F. Beck, "Hosanna (Matthew 21:9, 15; Mark 11:9-10; John 12:13)," *CTM* 23 (1952): 122-29.

6931   William R. Farmer, "The Palm Branches in John 12:13," *JTS* 3 (1952): 62-66.

6932   J. S. Hill, "τὰ βαῖα φοινίκων (John 12:13): Pleonasm or Prolepsis?" *JBL* 101 (1982): 133-35.

12:12-19

6933   James F. Coakley, "Jesus' Messianic Entry into Jerusalem," *JTS* NS 46 (1995): 461-82.

12:20-50

6934   Michael D. Goulder, "From Ministry to Passion in Luke and John," *NTS* 29 (1983): 561-68.

12:20-39

6935   H. van den Bussche, "Si le grain de blé ne tombe en terre," *BVC* 5 (1954): 53-67.

12:20-36

6936   R. L. Jeske, "John 12:20-36," *Int* 43 (1989): 292-95.

6937   Larry E. McKinney, "Bethsaida," *BI* 16/2 (1990): 38-41.

6938   Judith L. Kovacs, " 'Now Shall the Ruler of This World Be Driven Out': Jesus' Death as Cosmic Battle in John 12:20-36," *JBL* 114 (1995): 227-47.

12:20-33

6939   R. Beauvery, "Jésus élevé attire les hommes à lui (Jean 12:20-33)," *EV* 80 (1970): 117-19.

12:20-32

6940   A. J. Gossip, "How Christ Won Through," *ET* 37 (1925-1926): 500-505.

6941   J. E. Lone, "Thunder or Angel? (John 12:20-32)," *ET* 66 (1984-1985): 145-46.

12:20-26

6942   Augustin George, "Qui veut sauver sa vie, la perdra; qui perd sa vie, la sauvera," *BVC* 83 (1968): 11-24.

6943   R. S. Barbour, "Gethsemane in the Tradition of the Passion," *NTS* 16 (1969-1970): 231-51.

12:20

6944   Johannes Beutler, "Greeks Come to See Jesus," *Bib* 71/3 (1990): 333-47.

12:21

6945   T. Torrance, "We Would See Jesus," *EQ* 23 (1951): 171-82.

6946   W. E. Moore, " 'Sir, We Wish to See Jesus': Was This an Occasion of Temptation?" *SJT* 20 (1967): 75-93.

6947   M. D. L. Sellick, " 'To See Jesus'," *ET* 95 (1983-1984): 86-87.

12:23-32

6948   X. Léon-Dufour, "Trois chiasmes johanniques," *NTS* 7 (1960-1961): 249-55.

12:23

6949   C. C. Torrey, " 'When I am Lifted up from the Earth': John 12:23," *JBL* 51 (1932): 320-22.

12:24

6950   E. Rasco, "Christus granum frumenti," *VD* 37 (1959): 12-25, 65-77.

6951   A. W. Argyle, "Fruitfulness through Death (John 12:24)," *ET* 89 (1977-1978): 149.

12:25

6952   C. H. Dodd, "Some Johannine 'Herrnworte' with Parallels in the Synoptic Gospels," *NTS* 2 (1955): 75-86.

6953   William A. Beardslee, "Saving One's Life by Losing It (John 12:25)," *JAAR* 47 (1979): 57-72.

12:26

6954   N. Cachia, "The Servant in a Fellowship of Suffering and Life in the Lord: An Exegesis of John 12:26," *MeliT* 43 (1992): 39-60.

12:27

6955   Raymond E. Brown, "Incidents that Are Units in the Synoptic Gospels but Dispersed in St. John," *CBQ* 23 (1961): 143-60.

12:28

6956 Craig A. Evans, "The Voice from Heaven: A Note on John 12:28," *CBQ* 43 (1981): 405-408.

12:30-36

6957 G. H. C. MacGregor, "A Suggested Rearrangement of the Johannine Text," *ET* 35 (1923-1924): 476-77.

12:31-36

6958 I. de la Potterie, "L'exaltation du Fils de l'homme (Jean 12:31-36)," *Greg* 49 (1968): 460-78.

12:31-32

6959 André Charbonneau, "Jésus en croix (Jn 19,16b-42), Jésus élevé (3,14ss; 8,28s; 12,31ss)," *ScE* 45 (1993): 5-23.

12:31

6960 S. A. Fries, "Was bedeutet der Fürst der Welt in Joh 12:31; 14:30; 16:11?" *ZNW* 6 (1905): 159-79.

6961 F. B. Blomfield and H. G. Blomfield, "The Prince of this World," *Theology* 16/1 (1928): 105-107.

6962 A. Corell, "Det historiska och det homiletiska nu: Till Joh. 12:31," *SEÅ* 10 (1945): 186-91.

6963 Erich Metzing, "Textkritische Beobachtungen zu ekblethesetai exo in Joh 12,31," *ZNW* 88 (1997): 126-29.

12:32-34

6964 B. Schwank, "Erhöht und verherrlicht," *ErAu* 68 (1992): 137-46.

12:32

6965 C. C. Torrey, " 'When I Am Lifted up from the Earth', John 12:32," *JBL* 51 (1932): 320-22.

6966 Wilhelm Thüsing, " 'Wenn ich von der Erde erhöht bin. . . ': Die Erhohung Jesu nach dem Jo-Ev," *BK* 20/2 (1965): 40-42.

6967 Mario Galizzi, "Quando io sarò elevato da terra attirerò tutti a me (Gv 12:32) (Il tema della Passione in Gv cc. 11-12)," *PV* 18 (1973): 85-100.

6968 Giovanni Rinaldi, "ὑψόω (Giov. 12:32)," *BibO* 16 (1974): 138.

6969   R. L. Sturch, "The Replacement of 'Son of Man' by a Pronoun (John 12:32)," *ET* 94 (1982-1983): 333.

12:33

6970   H. J. Flowers, "Interpolations in the Fourth Gospel," *JBL* 40 (1921): 146-58.

12:34

6971   W. C. van Unnik, "The Quotation from the OT in John 12:34," *NovT* 3 (1959): 174-79.

6972   B. McNeil, "The Quotation at John xii 34," *NovT* 19 (1977): 22-23.

6973   Bruce D. Chilton, "John xii 34 and Targum Isaiah lii 13," *NovT* 22 (1980): 176-78.

6974   G. D. Bampfylde, "More Light on John XII 34," *JSNT* 17 (1983): 87-89.

12:35-43

6975   R. Kühschelm, "Verstockung als Gericht. Eine Untersuchung zu Joh 12,35-43; Lk 13,34-35; 19,41-44," *BL* 57 (1984): 234-43.

12:36

6976   Roland Mörchen, " 'Weggehen'. Beobachtungen zu Joh 12,36b," *BZ* 28 (1984): 240-42.

12:37-50

6977   F. Genuyt, "L'économie des signes," *LV* 41 (1992): 19-35.

12:40

6978   Craig A. Evans, "The Function of Isaiah 6:9-10 in Mark and John (12,40)," *NovT* 24 (1982): 124-38.

6979   B. Hollenbach, "Lest They Should Turn and Be Forgiven: Irony," *BT* 34 (1983): 312-21.

12:44-50

6980   B. Brinkmann, "De priore quodam sermone valedictorio Domini," *VD* 19 (1939): 300-307; 20 (1940): 62-63.

6981   Peder Borgen, "The Use of Tradition in John 12:44-50," *NTS* 26 (1979-1980): 18-35.

6982   Ben Engelbrecht, "He Who Believes in Me, Believes Not in Me (John 12:44)," *JTSA* 54 (1986): 39-41.

12:46

6983   Gary K. Halbrook, " 'Light' in John's Writings," *BI* 8/2 (1982): 26-29.

13-19

6984   Georg Richter, "Die Deutung des Kreuzestodes Jesu in der Leidensgeschichte des Johannesevangeliums (Joh 13-19)," *BibL* 9 (1968): 21-36.

6985   Gottfried Brakemeier, "A Santa Ceia do Novo Testamento e na prática atual," *EstT* 26/3 (1986): 247-75.

13-17

6986   Frank Stagg, "The Farewell Discourses," *RevExp* 62/4 (1965): 459-72.

6987   Heinrich Zimmermann, "Struktur und Aussageabsicht der johanneischen Abschiedsreden (Jo 13-17)," *BibL* 8 (1967): 279-90.

6988   F. J. Steinmetz, " 'Und ich gehe nimmer, wann ich gehe . . .': Zum Verständnis der johanneischen Abschiedsreden," *GeistL* 51 (1978): 85-99.

6989   Sam Fourie and Jacques Rousseau, "Eenheid in Johannes 13-17," *ScrSA* 29 (1989): 19-35.

6990   E. Bammel, "The Farewell Discourse in Patristic Exegesis," *Neo* 25/2 (1991): 193-207.

6991   J. A. du Rand, "Perspectives on Johannine Discipleship according to the Farewell Discourses," *Neo* 25/2 (1991): 311-25.

6992   Patrick J. Hartin, " 'Remain in Me': The Foundation of the Ethical and Its Consequences in the Farewell Discourses," *Neo* 25/2 (1991): 341-56.

6993   H. R. Lemmer, "A Possible Understanding by the Implied Reader, of Some of the 'Coming-Going-Being Sent' Prouncements, in the Johannine Farewell Discourses" *Neo* 25/2 (1991): 289-310

6994   Gail R. O'Day, " 'I Have Overcome the World' (John 16:33): Narrative Time in John 13-17," *Semeia* 53 (1991): 153-66.

6995   W. H. Oliver and A. G. Van Aarde, "The Community of Faith as Dwelling Place of the Father: βασιλεία τοῦ θεοῦ as 'Household of God' in the Johannine Farewell Discourses," *Neo* 25/2 (1991): 379-400.

6996   D. F. Tolmie, "The Function of Focalisation in John 13-17," *Neo* 25/2 (1991): 273-87.

6997   E. Bammel, "Die Abschiedsrede des Johannesevangeliums und ihr jüdischer Hintergrund," *Neo* 26 (1992): 1-12.

6998   Jonathan A. Draper, "The Sociological Function of the Spirit/Paraclete in the Farewell Discourses in the Fourth Gospel," *Neo* 26 (1992): 13-29.

6999   John N. Suggit, "John 13-17 Viewed through Liturgical Spectacles," *Neo* 26 (1992): 47-58.

7000   Mary M. Pazdan, "Gifts. Challenges, and Promises in John 13-17," *BibTo* 38 (2000): 75-80.

7001   John J. Pilch, "Final Words and Family Loyalty," *BibTo* 38 (2000): 81-85.

13

7002   R. A. Henderson, "The Washing of the Feet: A New Interpretation," *Theology* 10 (1925): 126-33.

7003   B. W. Bacon, "The Sacrament of Footwashing," *ET* 43 (1931-1932): 218-21.

7004   A. Fridrichsen, "Bemerkungen zur Fusswaschung Joh 13," *ZNW* 38 (1939): 94-96.

7005   J. A. du Rand, "Eksegetiese kanttekeninge by Johannes 13," *ScrSA* 1 (1980): 43-51.

7006   Frédéric Manns, "Le lavement des pieds: Essai sur la structure et la signification de Jean 13," *RechSR* 55 (1981): 149-69.

7007   F. Genuyt, "Les deux bains. Analyse sémiotique de Jean 13," *SémBib* 25 (1982): 1-21.

7008   M. Sabbe, "Footwashing in John 13 and Its Relations to the Synoptic Gospels," *ETL* 58 (1982): 279-308.

7009   Karl T. Kleinknecht, "Johannes 13, die Synoptiker und die 'Methode' der johanneischen Evangelienüberlieferung," *ZTK* 82/3 (1985): 361-88.

7010   R. Alan Culpepper, "The Johannine *Hypodeigma*: A Reading of John 13," *Semeia* 53 (1991): 133-52.

7011   David Tripp, "Meanings of Foot-Washing: John 13 and Oxyrhynchus Papyrus 840," *ET* 103 (1992): 237-39.

13:1-38

7012   Francis J. Moloney, "The Structure and Message of John 13:1-38," *ABR* 34 (1986): 1-16.

7013   J. A. du Rand, "Narratological Perspectives on John 13:1-38," *HTS* 46 (1990): 367-89.

7014   Francis J. Moloney, "A Sacramental Reading of John 13:1-38," *CBQ* 53 (1991): 237-56.

13:1-30

7015   W. L. Knox, "John 13:1-30," *HTR* 43 (1950): 161-63.

7016   G. Tosatto, "La passione di Cristo in S. Giov," *PV* 15 (1970): 377-88.

13:1-20

7017   Georg Richter, "The Washing of Feet in the Gospel of John," *TD* 14 (1966): 200-206.

7018   W. M. Eshbach, "Another Look at John 13:1-20," *BLT* 14 (1969): 117-25.

7019   James D. G. Dunn, "The Washing of the Disciples' Feet in John 13:1-20," *ZNW* 61 (1970): 247-52.

7020   H. Weiss, "Foot Washing in the Johannine Community," *NovT* 21 (1979): 298-325.

7021   G. G. Nicol, "Jesus' Washing the Feet of the Disciples: A Model for Johannine Christology?" *ET* 91 (1979-1980): 20-21.

7022   Sandra M. Schneiders, "The Foot Washing (John 13:1-20): An Experiment in Hermeneutics," *CBQ* 43 (1981): 76-92.

7023   M. Sabbe, "The Footwashing in John 13 and Its Relation to the Synoptic Gospels," *ETL* 58 (1982): 279-308.

7024   Fernando F. Segovia, "John 13,1-20. The Footwashing in the Johannine Tradition," *ZNW* 73 (1982): 31-51.

7025   John N. Suggit, "John 13:1-20: The Mystery of the Incarnation and of the Eucharist," *Neo* 19 (1985): 64-70.

7026   Michal Wojciechowski, "La source de Jean 13:1-20," *NTS* 34/1 (1988): 135-41.

7027   Ingrid R. Kitzberger, "Love and Footwashing: John 13:1-20 and Luke 7 (1992): 36-50 Read Intertextually," *BibInt* 2 (1994): 190-206.

7028   Mauro Pesce and Adriana Destro, "La lavanda dei piedi di Gv 13,1-20, il Romanzo di Esopo e i Saturnalia di Macrobio," *Bib* 80 (1999): 240-49.

13:1-17

7029   E. Lohmeyer, "Die Fusswaschung," *ZNW* 38 (1939): 74-94.

7030   Franz Mußner, "Die Fusswaschung," *GeistL* 31 (1958): 25-30.

7031   M.-É. Boismard, "Le lavement des pieds," *RB* 71 (1964): 5-24.

7032   Allen Edgington, "Footwashing as an Ordinance," *GTJ* 6/2 (1985): 425-34.

13:1-15

7033   N. Lazure, "Le lavement des pieds (Jean 13:1-15)," *AsSeign* 38 (1967): 40-50.

13:1-11

7034   Hugo Zorrilla, "A Service of Sacrifical Love: Footwashing," *Dir* 24 (1995): 74-85.

13:1-3

7035   W. K. Grossouw, "A Note on John xiii 1-3," *NovT* 8 (1966): 124-31.

13:1

7036   C. A. Phillips and J. R. Harris, "A Mediaeval Interpretation of John 13:1," *ET* 38 (1926-1927): 233.

7037   R. M. Ball, "Saint John and the Institution of the Eucharist (John 13:1)," *JSNT* 23 (1985): 59-68.

7038   Donald Farmer, "The Lord's Supper Until He Comes," *GTJ* 6/2 (1985): 391-401.

13:2-14:31

7039   Karl T. Kleinknecht, "Johannes 13, die Synoptiker und die 'Methode' der johanneischen Evangelienüberlieferung," *ZTK* 82/3 (1985): 361-88.

13:2-20

7040   Martin Connell, "Nisi Pedes, Except for the Feet: Footwashing in the Communities of John's Gospel," *Worship* 70 (1996): 517-31.

13:2-17

7041   Hans W. Huppenbauer, "Fusswaschung: ein Problem taucht auf," *ZMiss* 11/3 (1985): 183-84.

13:3-17

7042   A. Wilmart, "Un ancien texte latin de l'Év. selon saint Jean," *RB* 31 (1922): 182-202.

13:3

7043   Jesse Sell, "Johannine Traditions in Logion 61 of the Gospel of Thomas," *PRS* 7/1 (1980): 24-37.

13:4-10

7044   F.-M. Braunk, "Le lavement des pieds et la réponse de Jésus à saint Pierre," *RB* 44 (1935): 22-33.

13:7

7045   J. Huby, "Une exégèse faussement attribuée à S. Cyprien," *Bib* 14 (1933): 96.

7046   D. H. C. Read, "Happiness Is Doing What You Believe (John 13:7)," *ET* 85 (1973-1974): 240-41.

13:8-9

7047   John C. Thomas, "The Fourth Gospel and Rabbinic Judaism," *ZNW* 82 (1991): 159-82.

13:10

7048   N. M. Haring, "Historical Notes on the Interpretation of John 13:10," *CBQ* 13 (1951): 355-80.

7049   John C. Thomas, "A Note on the Text of John 13:10," *NovT* 29 (1987): 46-52.

7050   J. C. O'Neill, "John 13:10 Again," *RB* 101 (1994): 67-74.

13:11

7051   J. D. M. Derrett, "Impurity and Idolatry: John 13:11; Ezekiel 36:25," *BibO* 34 (1992): 87-92.

13:12-20

7052   Alfons Weiser, "Joh 13:12-20—Zufügung eines späteren Herausgebers?" *BZ* 12 (1968): 252-57.

13:16

7053   H. F. D. Sparks, "St. John's Knowledge of Matthew: The Evidence of John 13:16 and 15:20," *JTS* 3 (1952): 58-61.

7054   C. H. Dodd, "Some Johannine 'Herrnworte' with Parallels in the Synoptic Gospels," *NTS* 2 (1955): 75-86.

7055   Graydon F. Snyder, "John 13:16 and the Anti-Petrinism of the Johannine Tradition," *BR* 16 (1971): 5-15.

13:18-30

7056   P. Evdokimov, "Étude sur Jean 13:18-30," *EV* (1950): 201-16.

13:18

7057   Eric F. F. Bishop, " 'He That Eateth Bread with Me Hath Lifted up His Heel against Me'," *ET* 70 (1958-1959): 331-33.

13:20

7058   C. H. Dodd, "Some Johannine 'Herrnworte' with Parallels in the Synoptic Gospels," *NTS* 2 (1955): 75-86.

7059   Georg Richter, "Die Fusswaschung Joh 13:20," *MTZ* 16 (1965): 13-26.

13:21-30

7060   David L. Bartlett, "John 13:21-30," *Int* 43 (1989): 393-97.

13:21

7061   G. Ferraro, " 'Pneuma' in Giov. 13,21," *RBib* 28 (1980): 185-211.

13:27

7062   Armin J. Panning, "Exegetical Brief: 'What You Are Doing, Do (More?) Quickly' John 13:27," *WLQ* 94 (1997): 203-205.

13:29

> 7063   Donald Farmer, "The Lord's Supper Until He Comes,"
> *GTJ* 6/2 (1985): 391-401.

13:31-17:26

> 7064   H. Müller, "El Sermón de despedida y la oración
> sacerdotal," *RevB* 31 (1969): 16-25.

> 7065   Giuseppe Segalla, "Il libro dell'Adio di Gesù ai suoi," *PV*
> 15 (1970): 356-74.

> 7066   G. Leonardi, "Il significato del passaggio di Gesù al Padre
> nei Discorsi d'addio di Giovanni," *PV* 18 (1972): 101-19.

> 7067   G. Granado, "El Espíritu Santo revelado como persana en
> el sermón de la Cena," *EB* 32 (1973): 157-73.

> 7068   G. Reim, "Probleme der Abschiedsreden," *BZ* 20 (1976):
> 117-22.

> 7069   T. Onuki, "Die johanneischen Abschiedsreden und die
> synoptische Tradition. Eine traditionskritische und
> traditionsgeschichtliche Untersuchung," *AJBI* 3 (1977):
> 157-268.

> 7070   John Painter, "Glimpses of the Johannine Community in
> the Farewell Discourses," *ABR* 28 (1980): 21-38.

> 7071   E. Ruckstuhl, "Neue und alte Überlegungen zu den
> Abendmahlsworten Jesu," *SNTU-A* 5 (1980): 79-106.

> 7072   John Painter, "The Farewell Discourses and the History of
> Johannine Christianity," *NTS* 27 (1980-1981): 525-43.

> 7073   A. D. Duba, "Hints for a Morphology of Eucharistic
> Praying: A Study of John 13:31-17:26," *Worship* 57
> (1983): 365-77.

> 7074   J. P. Kaefer, "Les discours d'adieu en Jean 13:31-17:26.
> Rédaction et théologie," *NovT* 26 (1984): 253-82.

> 7075   J. Rahner, "Vergegenwärtigende Erinnerung. Die
> Ahschiedsreden, der Geist-Paraklet und die Retrospektive
> des Johannesevangeliums," *ZNW* 91 (2000): 72-90.

13:31-16:33

> 7076   J. Becker, "Die Abschiedsreden Jesu im Johannes-
> evangelium," *ZNW* 61 (1970): 215-46.

7077   M. Balagué, "Los discursos de la última cena," *CuBi* 30 (1973): 160-64.

7078   A. Lacomara, "Deuteronomy and the Farewell Discourse (John 13:31-16:33)," *CBQ* 36 (1974): 65-84.

7079   J. L. Boyle, "The Last Discourse (John 13:31-16:33) and Prayer (John 17): Some Observations on Their Unity and Development," *Bib* 56 (1975): 210-22.

13:31-14:31

7080   C. Charlier, "La présence dans l'absence," *BVC* 2 (1953): 61-75.

7081   M. Reese, "Literary Structure of John 13:31-14:31; 16:5-6; 16:16-33," *CBQ* 34 (1972): 321-31.

7082   D. B. Woll, "The Departure of 'The Way': The First Farewell Discourse in the Gospel of John (John 13:31-14:31)," *JBL* 99 (1980): 225-39.

7083   Fernando F. Segovia, "The Structure, *Tendenz*, and *Sitz im Leben* of John 13:31-14:31," *JBL* 104 (1985): 471-93.

7084   J. A. du Rand, "A Story and a Community: Reading the First Farewell Discourse from Narratological and Sociological Perspectives," *Neo* 26 (1992): 31-45.

13:31-35

7085   N. Lazure, "Louange au Fils de l'homme et commandement nouveau: Jean 13:31-35," *AsSeign* 26 (1973): 73-80.

13:31

7086   John W. Pryor, "The Johannine Son of Man and the Descent-Ascent Motif," *JETS* 34 (1991): 341-51.

13:33-17:26

7087   E. Bammel, "The Farewell Discourse of the Evangelist John and Its Jewish Heritage," *TynB* 44 (1993): 103-16.

13:33-38

7088   Lucien Cerfaux, "La charité fraternelle et le retour du Christ selon Jean 13:33-38," *ETL* 24 (1948): 321-32.

13:33-35

7089   F. C. Schäfer, "The Mark of the Christian (John 13:33-35; 17:21)," *CT* 14 (1970): 1063-66.

13:34

7090   R. P. Brown, "'Εντολὴν καινὴν," *Theology* 26 (1933): 184-93.

14-17

7091   M. Peinador, "Idea central del discurso de Jesús después de la Cena," *EB* 12 (1953): 5-28.

7092   J. Carmody, "The 'Death of God' and John 14-17," *BT* 30 (1967): 2082-90.

7093   William R. Domeris, "The Paraclete as an Ideological Construct: A Study in the Farewell Discourses," *JTSA* 67 (1989): 17-23.

7094   William R. Domeris, "The Farewell Discourse: An Anthropological Perspective," *Neo* 25/2 (1991): 233-50.

14-16

7095   S. Gallo, "Sermo Christi sacrificalis," *VD* 26 (1948): 33-43.

14

7096   Simon Légasse, "Le retour du Christ d'après l'évangile de Jean, chapitre 14 et 16: une adaptation du motif de la Parousie," *BLE* 81 (1980): 161-74.

7097   F. Porsch, "Der 'andere Paraklet': Das Wirken des Geistes nach den johanneischen Abschiedsreden," *BK* 37 (1982): 133-38.

7098   F. Mosetto, " 'Io vado, ma ritorero a voi' (Gv 14)," *PV* 14 (1984): 143-51.

7099   Heribert Wahl, "Empathie und Text: das selbst-psychologische Modell interaktiver Texthermeneutik," *TQ* 169/3 (1989): 201-22.

14:1-14

7100   G. Widengren, "En la maison de mon Père sont demeures nombreuses," *SEÅ* 37-38 (1972-1973): 9-15.

14:1-12

7101   R. Beauvery, "Évangiles et homélies. Présentation exégétique des Évangiles de Dimanche (Jean 14:1-12, 15-21)," *EV* 79 (1969): 287-91, 317-19, 633-36.

7102   G. Rossetto, "La route vers le Père: Jean 14:1-12," *AsSeign* 26 (1973): 18-30.

14:1-7

7103   O. Schäffer, "Der Sinn der Rede Jesu von den vielen Wohnungen in seines Vaters Hause und von dem Weg zu ihm," *ZNW* 32 (1933): 210-17.

14:1-4

7104   W. K. L. Clark, "John 14:1-4," *Theology* 9 (1924): 41-43.

14:1-3

7105   Alonso V. Eetelayo, "La vuelta de Cristo en el Evangelio de Juan: Análisis literario de Jn 14:1-3," *EstT* 5 (1978): 3-70.

14:2

7106   B. W. Bacon, " 'In My Father's House Are Many Mansions'," *ET* 43 (1931-1932): 477-78.

7107   Robert H. Gundry, " 'In My Father's House Are Many Monaí' (John 14:2)," *ZNW* 58 (1967): 68-72.

7108   W. H. Oliver and A. G. Van Aarde, "The Community of Faith as Dwelling Place of the Father: βασιλεία τοῦ θεοῦ as 'Household of God' in the Johannine Farewell Discourses," *Neo* 25/2 (1991): 379-400.

14:3

7109   A. L. Humphries, "A Note on πρὸς ἐμαυτόν and εἰς τὰ ἴδια: A Plea for a Revised Translation," *ET* 53 (1941-1942): 356.

14:6

7110   I. de la Potterie, " 'Je suis la Voie, la Vérité et la Vie'," *NRT* 88 (1966): 907-42.

7111   F. C. Fensham, "I Am the Way, the Truth and the Life: John 14:6," *Neo* 2 (1968): 81-88.

7112   Ted Peters, "A Christian Theology of Interreligious Dialogue," *CC* 103/30 (1986): 883-85.

7113   Gabriel Fackre, "Bible, Community, and Spirit," *HBT* 21 (1999): 66-81.

14:8-17

7114   Gordon D. Fee, "John 14:8-17," *Int* 43 (1989): 170-74.

14:9

7115   S.-E. Farrell, "Seeing the Father: Part II. Perceptive Seeing and Comprehensive Seeing," *ScE* 44 (1992): 159-83.

14:10

7116   C. H. Gordon, " 'In' of Predication or Equivalence (John 14:10)," *JBL* 100 (1981): 612-13.

14:12-24

7117   Alois Stöger, "Jesus Christus - der Lebende: Meditation zu Joh 14:12-24," *BL* 52 (1979): 257-60.

14:12-14

7118   Víctor M. Fernández, "Hacer 'obras mayores' que las de Cristo (Juan 14,21-14)," *RevB* 57 (1995): 65-91.

14:12

7119   Christian Dietzfelbinger, "Die grösseren Werke (Joh 14:12f)," *NTS* 35/1 (1989): 27-47.

14:13-14

7120   John F. Walvoord, "Prayer in the Name of the Lord Jesus Christ," *BSac* 91 (1934): 463-72.

14:15-21

7121   R. Beauvery, "Évangiles et homélies. Présentation exégétique des Évangiles de Dimanche (Jean 14:1-12, 15-21)," *EV* 79 (1969): 287-91, 317-19, 633-36.

7122   R. Massó, "La promesa del Espíritu," *CuBí* 29 (1972): 276-93.

14:16-25

7123   Christian Dietzfelbinger, "Paraklet und theologischer Anspruch im Johannesevangelium," *ZTK* 82/4 (1985): 389-408.

14:16-17

7124   J. Rieger, "Spiritus Sanctus suum praeparat adventum," *VD* 43 (1965): 19-27.

14:16

7125 E. A Ullendorff, "Mistranslation from Aramaic?" *NTS* 2 (1955): 50-52.

7126 G. M. Lee, "John xiv.16," *ET* 76 (1964-1965): 254.

7127 Margaret Pamment, "Path and Residence Metaphors in the Fourth Gospel," *Theology* 88 (1985): 118-24.

7128 T. B. Slater, "The Paraclete as Advocate in the Community of the Beloved Disciple," *AfTJ* 20/2 (1991): 101-108.

14:17

7129 W. R. Hutton, "John 14:17," *ET* 57 (1945-1946): 194.

7130 J. E. Morgan-Wynne, "A Note on John 14:17b," *BZ* 23 (1979): 93-96.

14:20

7131 Eduard Schweizer, "Joh 6,51c-58—vom Evangelisten übernommene Tradition?" *ZNW* 82 (1991): 274.

14:23-31

7132 R. Kugelmann, "The Gospel for Pentecost," *CBQ* 6 (1944): 259-75.

14:23-30

7133 Augustin George, "L'Évangile: Les venues de Dieu aux croyants," *AsSeign* 51 (1963): 63-71.

14:23-29

7134 I. John Hesselink, "John 14:23-29," *Int* 43 (1989): 174-77.

14:23

7135 W. H. Oliver and A. G. Van Aarde, "The Community of Faith as Dwelling Place of the Father: βασιλεία τοῦ θεοῦ as 'Household of God' in the Johannine Farewell Discourses," *Neo* 25/2 (1991): 379-400.

14:25-26

7136 J. Blank, "Bindung und Freiheit: Das Verhältnis der nachapostolischen Kirche zu Jesus von Nazaret," *BK* 33 (1978): 19-22.

14:26

7137 U. Holzmeister, "Paraclietus Spiritus Sanctus," *VD* 12 (1932): 135-39.

7138 Thomas D. Lea, "Comfort," *BI* 10/1 (1983): 35-36.

7139 T. B. Slater, "The Paraclete as Advocate in the Community of the Beloved Disciple," *AfTJ* 20/2 (1991): 101-108.

14:27

7140 R. L. Jeske, "John 14:27 and 16:33," *Int* 38 (1984): 403-11.

14:28

7141 Lino Cignelli, "L'esegesi di Giovanni 14,28 nella Gallia del secolo IV," *SBFLA* 24 (1974): 329-58.

7142 Lino Cignelli, "Giovanni 14,28 nell'esegesi di Origene," *SBFLA* 25 (1975): 136-63.

7143 Lino Cignelli, "Giovanni 14,28 nell'esegesi di S. Ireneo," *SBFLA* 27 (1977): 173-96.

14:30

7144 S. A. Fries, "Was bedeutet der Fürst der Welt in Joh 12:31; 14:30; 16:11?" *ZNW* 6 (1905): 159-179.

14:31

7145 I. Hammer, "Eine klare Stellung zu Joh 14:31b," *BK* 14 (1959): 33-40.

7146 Donald S. Deer, "More about the Imperatival ἵνα (John 14:31; 1 Cor 16:16; Col 2:41)," *BT* 24 (1973): 328-29.

15-16

7147 A. Niccacci, "Esame letterario di Gv 15-16," *Ant* 56 (1981): 43-71.

15:1-16:15

7148 H. Müller, "Naturaleza y consecuencia de la unión de vida de los discípulos, Juan 15:1-16:15," *RevB* 31 (1969): 86-96.

15:1-16:4

7149 Giovanni Rinaldi, "Amore e odio (Giov. 15:1-16:4a)," *BibO* 22 (1980): 97-106.

15:1-16:3

7150   Francis J. Moloney, "The Structure and Message of John 15:1-16:3," *ABR* 35 (1987): 35-49.

15

7151   Juan Leal, "La alegoría de la vid y la necesidad de la gracia," *EE* 26 (1952): 5-38.

7152   W. Grundmann, "Das Wort von Jesu Freunden und das Herrenmahl," *NovT* 3 (1959): 62-69.

7153   H. van den Bussche, "La vigne et ses fruits," *BVC* 26 (1959): 12-18.

7154   B. Sandvik, "Joh. 15 als Abendmahltext," *TZ* 23 (1967): 323-28.

15:1-17

7155   David J. Hawkin, "Orthodoxy and Heresy in John 10:1-21 and 15:1-17," *EQ* 47 (1975): 208-13.

7156   M. Provera, "La cultura della vite nelle tradizione biblica ed orientale," *BibO* 24 (1982): 97-106.

7157   Fernando F. Segovia, "The Theology and Provenance of John 15:1-17," *JBL* 101 (1982): 115-28.

7158   Georg Korting, "Binden oder lösen: Zur Verstockungs- und Befreiungstheologie in Mt 16:19; 18:18-21:35 und Joh 15:1-17; 2:23," *SNTU-A* 14 (1989): 39-91.

7159   R. Garland Young, "Ritual Cleansing," *BI* 16/2 (1990): 76-78.

15:1-11

7160   Christoph Barth, "Bible Study IV. The Disciples of the Servant. John 15:1-11," *SEAJT* 6 (1965): 14-16.

7161   Tecle Vetrali, "Gesù vite vera: Gv 15,1-11," *SEcu* 12 (1994): 267-96.

15:1-8

7162   R. Beauvery, "Les disciples, communauté à laquelle Jésus donne vie (Jean 15:1-8)," *EV* 80 (1970): 242-45.

7163   Giuseppe Segalla, "La struttura chiastica di Giov 15:1-8," *BibO* 12 (1970): 129-31.

7164   Jacobus C. de Smidt, "A Perspective on John 15:1-8," *Neo* 25/2 (1991): 251-72.

7165   Josef Ernst, "Das Johannesevangelium—ein frühes Beispiel christlicher Mystik," *TGl* 81 (1991): 323-28.

7166   Peter Bolt, "What Fruit Does the Vine Bear? Some Pastoral Implications of John 15:1-8," *RTR* 51 (1992): 11-19.

7167   C. Clifton Black, "Our Shepherd's Voice: Biblical Resources for the Easter Season," *QR* 14 (1994): 89-110.

7168   J. van der Watt, " 'Metaphorik' in Joh 15,1-8," *BZ* NS 38 (1994): 67-80.

15:1-6

7169   J. Carl Laney, "Abiding Is Believing: The Analogy of the Vine in John 15:1-6," *BSac* 146 (1989): 55-66.

7170   Joseph C. Dillow, "Abiding Is Remaining in Fellowship: Another Look at John 15:1-6," *BSac* 147 (1990): 44-53.

7171   Gary W. Derickson, "Viticulture and John 15:1-6," *BSac* 153 (1996): 34-52.

15:1-5

7172   J.-C. Didier, "Histoire de la présence réelle. A propos d'un dogme récemment contesté (Jean 10:7; 15:1-5)," *EV* 87 (1977): 305-14.

15:1

7173   F. Engel, "The Ways of Vines," *ET* 60 (1949): 111.

7174   D. M. Stanley, " 'I Am the Genuine Vine," *BibTo* 1/8 (1963): 484-91.

15:4-7

7175   Eduard Schweizer, "Joh 6,51c-58—vom Evangelisten übernommene Tradition?" *ZNW* 82 (1991): 274.

15:4

7176   F. J. Steinmetz and Friedrich Wulf, "Ausharren und bleiben! Auslegung und Meditation von Lk. 24:29, Jo. 15:4 und Phil. 1:25," *GeistL* 42 (1969): 225-30.

15:5

7177   J. Foster, "A Note on St. Polycarp (John 15:5, 8)," *ET* 77 (1966): 319.

7178   Henri J. M. Nouwen, "Bearing Fruit in the Spirit: The Gifts of God's Love (pt. 2)," *Soj* 14/7 (1985): 26-30.

15:8

7179   J. Foster, "A Note on St. Polycarp (John 15:5, 8)," *ET* 77 (1966): 319.

7180   G. M. Lee, "New Testament Gleanings: Three Notes on ἵνα," *Bib* 51 (1970): 239-40.

15:9-17

7181   R. Beauvery, "La mission des disciples: demeurer dans l'amour par l'obéissance (Jean 15:9-17)," *EV* 80 (1970): 273-75.

15:9

7182   J. Dublin, " 'Continue Ye in My Love'," *ET* 47 (1935-1936): 91-92.

15:11

7183   G. S. Gibson, "JOY (John 15:11)," *ET* 94 (1982-1983): 244-45.

15:12

7184   M. E. Iriarte, " 'Amáos unos a otros': El amor, entrega," *BibFe* 11 (1985): 273-85.

15:13

7185   G. M. Lee, "New Testament Gleanings: Three Notes on ἵνα," *Bib* 51 (1970): 239-40.

15:14

7186   G. M. Lee, "John xv 14 'Ye are My Friends'," *NovT* 15 (1973): 260.

15:18-16:4

7187   Ricardo Pietrantonio, "El sufrimiento en la persecución por causa de la palabra; Juan 15:18-16:4a," *RevB* 42 (1980): 11-19.

7188   Fernando F. Segovia, "John 15:18-16:4a: A First Addition to the Original Farewell Discourse?" *CBQ* 45 (1983): 210-30.

15:19

7189   D. Heinz, "Brief Translation Note on John 15:19," *CTM* 39 (1968): 775.

15:20

7190   H. F. D. Sparks, "St. John's Knowledge of Matthew: The Evidence of John 13:16 and 15:20," *JTS* 3 (1952): 58-61.

15:25

7191   Raymond Schwager, "Haine sans raison: La perspective de René Girard," *Chr* 31 (1984): 118-26.

7192   Jörg Augenstein, " 'Euer Gesetz'--Ein Pronomen und die johanneische Haltung zum Gesetz," *ZNW* 88 (1997): 311-13.

15:26-16:4

7193   Augustin George, "L'Évangile après l'Ascension: Les témoins de Jésus devant le monde," *AsSeign* 50 (1966): 30-40.

15:26-27

7194   Alvin Reid, "Proclamation and Witness," *BI* 16/4 (1990): 69-71.

15:26

7195   T. B. Slater, "The Paraclete as Advocate in the Community of the Beloved Disciple," *AfTJ* 20/2 (1991): 101-108.

16

7196   Simon Légasse, "Le retour du Christ d'après l'évangile de Jean, chapitre 14 et 16: une adaptation du motif de la Parousie," *BLE* 81 (1980): 161-74.

7197   F. Genuyt, "Le 'passage' de Jésus et la venue du paraclet. Analyse sémiotique du ch. 16 de l'Évangile de Jean," *SémBib* 34 (1984): 1-14.

7198   F. Genuyt, "Un temps pour se taire et un temps pour parler. La clôture interne du discours d'après le chapitre 16 de l'évangile de Jean," *LV* 34 (1985): 67-79.

16:1-15

7199   D. Moody Smith, "John 16:1-15," *Int* 33 (1979): 58-62.

16:5-15

7200   H. Liese, "Spiritus Sancti testimonium," *VD* 14 (1934): 101-107.

16:5-14

7201   Augustin George, "L'Évangile: La tâche du Paraclet," *AsSeign* 47 (1963): 28-36.

16:5-6

7202   M. Reese, "Literary Structure of John 13:31-14:31; 16:5-6; 16:16-33," *CBQ* 34 (1972): 321-31.

16:7-15

7203   L. J. Lutkemeyer, "The Role of the Paraclete," *CBQ* 8 (1946): 220-29.

16:7-11

7204   D. A. Carson, "The Function of the Paraclete in John 16:7-11," *JBL* 98 (1979): 547-66.

7205   T. B. Slater, "The Paraclete as Advocate in the Community of the Beloved Disciple," *AfTJ* 20/2 (1991): 101-108.

7206   Kelly D. Reese, "The Role of the Paraclete in John 16:7-11," *TEd* 51 (1995): 39-48.

16:8-11

7207   W. H. P. Hatch, "The Meaning of Ioh. 16:8-11," *HTR* 14 (1921): 103-105.

7208   M.-F. Berrouard, "Le Paraclet, défenseur du Christ devant la conscience du croyant," *RSPT* 33 (1949): 361-89.

7209   J. D. M. Derrett, "Advocacy at John 16:8-11," *ET* 110 (1999): 181-82.

16:8-10

7210   Werner Stenger, "Δικαιοσύνη in Jo. xvi 8:10," *NovT* 21 (1979): 2-12.

7211   Matthew Vellanickal, "The Johannine Concept of Righteousness or Dharma," *BB* 6 (1980): 382-94.

16:8

7212   A. H. Stanton, "Convince or Convict," *ET* 33 (1921-1922): 278-79.

16:10

7213   A. W. Wotherspoon, "Note on John 16:10," *ET* 33 (1921): 521-22.

16:11

7214   S. A. Fries, "Was bedeutet der Fürst der Welt in Joh 12:31; 14:30; 16:11?" *ZNW* 6 (1905): 159-179.

16:12-24

7215   J. Terry Young, "The Doctrine of the Trinity," *BI* 16/2 (1990): 82-84.

16:12-15

7216   Augustin George, "L'Esprit, guide vers la vérité plénière. Jean 16:12-15," *AsSeign* 31 (1973): 40-47.

16:13-14

7217   D. Howell-Jones, "God's Pilgrim People," *ET* 90 (1978-1979): 45-46.

16:13

7218   S. J. Stein, "Retrospection and Introspection. The Gospel according to Mary Baker Eddy," *HTR* 75 (1982): 97-116.

7219   T. B. Slater, "The Paraclete as Advocate in the Community of the Beloved Disciple," *AfTJ* 20/2 (1991): 101-108.

16:15

7220   L. Rubio Morán, "Revelación en enigmas y revelación en claridad: Análisis exégetico de Jn 16:15," *Salm* 19 (1972): 107-44.

16:16-17:26

7221   H. Müller, "El camino a la unión y su consumación por la muerte de Crist," *RevB* 31 (1969): 204-10.

16:16-33

7222   M. Reese, "Literary Structure of John 13:31-14:31; 16:5-6; 16:16-33," *CBQ* 34 (1972): 321-31.

7223   Christian Dietzfelbinger, "Die eschatologische Freude der Gemeinde in der Angst der Welt, Joh 16,16-33," *EvT* 40 (1980): 420-36.

16:16

7224   W. Moock, "Gn 5 und Jo 16:16," *TGl* 31 (1939): 435-40.

7225   G. M. Lee, "John xvi 16," *ET* 76 (1964-1965): 254.

7226   J. D. M. Derrett, "Not Seeing and Later Seeing (John 16:16)," *ET* 109 (1998): 208-209.

16:21

7227   André Feuillet, "L'heure de la femme (Jean 16:21) et l'heure de la Mère de Jésus (Jean 19:5-27)," *Bib* 47 (1966): 169-84, 361-80, 551-73.

16:23-30

7228   Augustin George, "L'Évangile: La nouveauté de Paques," *AsSeign* 48 (1965): 39-46.

16:23-24

7229   E. Macmillan, "Note on Ioh 16:23-24," *ET* 34 (1922-1923): 379.

16:26-30

7230   L. Fonck, "Duplex fructus Spiritus Sancti," *VD* (1921): 115-20.

16:32

7231   E. Fascher, "Johannes 16:32: Eine Studie zur Geschichte der Schriftauslegung und zur Traditionsgeschichte des Urchristentums," *ZNW* 39 (1940): 171-230.

7232   Frans Neirynck, "ΕΙΣ ΤΑ ΙΔΙΑ," *ETL* 55 (1979): 357-65.

16:33

7233   J. E. Bruns, "A Note on John 16:33 and I John 2:13-14," *JBL* 86 (1967): 451-53.

7234   R. L. Jeske, "John 14:27 and 16:33," *Int* 38 (1984): 403-11.

7235   Gail R. O'Day, " 'I Have Overcome the World' (John 16:33): Narrative Time in John 13-17," *Semeia* 53 (1991): 153-66.

7236   Günther Schwarz, " 'In der Welt habt ihr Angst'?" *BibN* 63 (1992): 49-51.

7237   J. D. M. Derrett, "I Have Overcome the World," *BibO* 45 (1999): 109-15.

17

7238   Augustin George, " 'L'Heure' de Jean XVII," *RB* 61 (1954): 392-97.

7239   J. Cadier, "The Unity of the Church: An Exposition of John 17," *Int* 11 (1957): 166-76.

7240   Jacques Dupont, "La preghiera di Gesù per l'unità dei cristiani," *PV* 10 (1965): 321-36.

7241   C. D. Morrison, "Mission and Ethic: An Interpretation of John 17," *Int* 19 (1965): 259-73.

7242   J. Becker, "Aufbau, Sichtung und theologiegeschichtliche Stellung des Gebetes in Johannes," *ZNW* 60 (1969): 56-83.

7243   C. Evans, "Christ at Prayer in St. John's Gospel," *LV* 24 (1969): 579-96.

7244   Béda Rigaux, "Die Jünger Jesu in Johannes 17," *TQ* 150 (1970): 202-13.

7245   Béda Rigaux, "Les destinataires du IV Évangile à la lumière de Jean 17," *RTL* 1 (1970): 289-319.

7246   E. Malatesta, "The Literary Structure of John 17," *Bib* 52 (1971): 190-214.

7247   Scott L. Tatum, "Great Prayers of the Bible," *SouJT* 14 (1972): 29-42.

7248   Paul S. Minear, "Evangelism, Ecumenism, and John Seventeen," *TT* 35 (1978): 5-13.

7249   J. Radermakers, "La prière de Jésus: Jean 17," *AsSeign* 29 (1973): 48-86.

7250   Rudolf Schnackenburg, "Strukturanalyse von Joh 17," *BZ* 17 (1973): 67-78, 196-202.

7251   P. Van Boxel, "Die präexistente Doxa Jesu im Johannes-evangelium," *Bij* 34 (1973): 268-81.

7252   Jean Delorme, "Sacerdoce du Christ et ministère. (À propos de Jean 17). Sémantique et théologie biblique," *RechSR* 62 (1974): 199-219.

7253   J. L. Boyle, "The Last Discourse (John 13:31-16:33) and Prayer (John 17): Some Observations on Their Unity and Development," *Bib* 56 (1975): 210-22.

7254   D. Marzotto, "Giovanni 17 e il Targum di Esodo 19-20," *RBib* 25 (1977): 375-88.

7255   M. L. Appold, "Christ Alive! Christ Alive! Reflections on the Prayer of Jesus in John 17," *CThM* 5 (1978): 365-73.

7256   Barclay M. Newman, "The Case of the Eclectic and the Neglected Éx of John 17," *BT* 29 (1978): 339-41.

7257   William O. Walker, "The Lord's Prayer in Matthew and in John," *NTS* 28 (1981-1982): 237-56.

7258   David A. Black, "On the Style and Significance of John 17," *CTR* 3 (1988): 141-59.

7259   Justin S. Ukpong, "Jesus' Prayer for His Followers: In Mission Perspective," *AfTJ* 18/1 (1989): 49-60.

7260   Dennis A. Laskey, "Luther's Exposition of John 17," *CThM* 18 (1991): 204-208.

7261   E. Gordon, "Our Lord's Priestly Prayer," *HTR* 92 (1992): 17-21.

7262   James R. Payton, "On Unity and Truth: Martin Bucer's Sermon on John 17," *CTJ* 27 (1992): 26-38.

7263   Ernst R. Wendland, "Rhetoric of the Word: An Interactional Discourse Analysis of the Lord's Prayer of John 17 and Its Communicative Implications," *Neo* 26 (1992): 59-88.

7264   B. W. De Wet, "Unity in John 17 and in 1QS I-IX: A comparative study," *SkrifK* 18 (1997): 34-51.

7265   John E. Staton, "A Vision of Unity--Christian Unity in the Fourth Gospel," *EQ* 69 (1997): 291-305.

7266   D. G. van der Merwe, "John 17: Jesus Assigns His Mission to His Disciples," *SkrifK* 19 (1998): 115-27.

17:1-26

7267   J. Giblet, "Sanctifie-les dans la vérité," *BVC* 19 (1957): 58-73.

7268   M. Balagué, "La oración sacerdotal (Juan 17:1-26)," *CuBi* 31 (1974): 67-90.

7269   Josef Ernst, "Das Johannesevangelium - ein frühes Beispiel christlicher Mystik," *TGl* 81 (1991): 323-28.

17:1-11

7270   Paul S. Minear, "John 17:1-11," *Int* 32 (1978): 175-79.

17:3

7271   E. Ghini, " 'Questa è la vita eterna: conoscere te!' (Gv 17,3)," *ParSpirV* 5 (1982): 193-210.

17:4

7272   Albert Vanhoye, "Opera Iesu donum Patris," *VD* 36 (1958): 83-92.

7273   Albert Vanhoye, "L'œuvre du Christ, don du Pere," *RechSR* 48 (1960): 377-419.

17:5

7274   J. M. Ballard, "Two Translations in St. John's Gospel," *ET* 36 (1924-1925): 45.

7275   J. M. Ballard, "The Translation of John 17:5," *ET* 47 (1935-1936): 284.

7276   André Laurentin, "Weattah - Kai nun: formule caractéristique des textes juridiques et liturgiques (à propos de Jean 17:5)," *Bib* 45/2 (1964): 168-97; 45/3 (1964): 413-32.

17:9-17

7277   Edward May, "Outlines on the Swedish Gospels," *CTM* 29 (1958): 277-91.

17:11-12

7278   J. Huby, "Un double Problème de Critique textuelle et d'Interprétation: Saint Jean 17:11-12," *RechSR* 27 (1937): 408-21.

7279   E. Martín Nieto, "El nombre de Dios en S. Juan 17:11-12," *EB* 11 (1952): 5-30.

17:11

7280   Gail R. O'Day, " 'I Have Overcome the World' (John 16:33): Narrative Time in John 13-17," *Semeia* 53 (1991): 153-66.

17:17

7281   P. Pous, "Sanctifica eos in veritate," *VD* (1921): 247-50.

17:18-23

7282   Edward May, "Outlines on the Swedish Gospels," *CTM* 29 (1958): 277-91.

17:18

7283   J. Riedl, "Die Funktion der Kirche nach Johannes. 'Vater, wie du mich in die Welt gesandt hast, so habe ich auch sie in die Welt gesandt' (Johannes 17:18)," *BK* 28 (1973): 12-14.

17:19

7284   J. Rovira, "Spiritus Sanctus in Christo," *VD* 6 (1926): 49-56.

17:20-26

7285   C. H. Gordon, " 'In' of Predication or Equivalence," *JBL* 100 (1981): 612-13.

7286   Herbert Giesbrecht, "The Evangelist John's Conception of the Church as Delineated in His Gospel," *EQ* 58/2 (1986): 101-19.

7287   Royce G. Gruenler, "John 17:20-26," *Int* 43 (1989): 178-83.

17:20-23

7288   J. M. Bover, "La oración de Jesús por la Iglesia," *EE* 12 (1933): 242-50.

7289   J. F. Randall, "The Theme of Unity in John 17:20-23," *ETL* 41 (1965): 373-94.

7290   Margaret Pamment, "Short Note: John xvii 20-23," *NovT* 24 (1982): 383-84.

7291   H. P. Hamann, "The New Testament Concept of the 'Church' and Its Implied Ecumenical Program, with an Appendix on John 17:20-23," *LTJ* 18 (1984): 117-28.

17:21

7292   T. E. van Pollard, " 'That They All May Be One'," *ET* 70 (1958-1959): 149-50.

7293   J. C. Earwaker, "John 17:21," *ET* 75 (1963-1964): 316-17.

7294   F. C. Schäffer, "The Mark of the Christian (John 13:33-35; 17:21)," *CT* 14 (1970): 1063-66.

7295   Martin Tetz, "Athanasius und die Einheit der Kirche: zur ökumenischen Bedeutung eines Kirchenvaters," *ZTK* 81/2 (1984): 196-219.

7296   Paolo Ricca, "Giovanni 17:21," *SEcu* 9 (1991): 49-54.

17:23-24

7297   F. C. Conybeare, "John 17:23-24," *HTR* 17 (1924): 188-89.

17:24-26

7298   Edward May, "Outlines on the Swedish Gospels," *CTM* 29 (1958): 277-91.

17:24

7299   Kosuke Koyama, "So They May See My Glory," *CC* 106 (1989): 467.

18-21

7300   Ray Summers, "The Death and Resurrection of Jesus, John 18-21," *RevExp* 62 (1955): 473-81.

18-20

7301   Tovar S. Talavero, "Problemática de la unidad en Jn. 18-20," *Salm* 19 (1972): 513-75.

18-19

7302   Albert J. de Varebeke, "La structure des scènes du récit de la Passion en Jean 18-19," *ETL* 38 (1962): 504-22.

7303   M. Weise, "Passionswoche und Epiphaniewoche im Johannes-Evangelium. Ihre Bedeutung für Komposition und Konzeption des vierten Evangelium," *KD* 12 (1966): 48-62.

7304   I. de la Potterie, "La Passion selon Saint Jean, Jean 18:1-19:42," *AsSeign* 2/21 (1969): 21-34.

7305   Raymond E. Brown, "The Passion according to John: Chapters 18-19," *Worship* 49 (1975): 126-34.

7306   David E. Garland, "John 18-19: Life Through Jesus' Death," *RevExp* 85 (1988): 485-99.

7307   Frank J. Matera, " 'On Behalf of Others,' 'Cleansing,' and 'Return': Johannine Images of Jesus' Death," *LouvS* 13 (1988): 161-78.

7308   Jeffrey L. Staley, "Reading with a Passion: John 18:1-19:42 and the Erosion of the Reader," *SBLSP* 22 (1992): 61-81.

18

7309   W. Church, "The Dislocations in the Eighteenth Chapter of John," *JBL* 49 (1930): 375-83.

7310   N. Krieger, "Der Knecht des Hohenpriesters," *NovT* 2 (1957): 73-74.

18:1-27

7311   Charles H. Giblin, "Confrontations in John 18:1-27," *Bib* 65 (1984): 210-32.

18:1-19

7312   G. Tosatto, "La passione di Cristo in S. Giov," *PV* 15 (1970): 377-88.

18:1-18

7313   Charles H. Giblin, "Two Complementary Literary Structures in John 1:1-18," *JBL* 104 (1985): 87-103.

18:1-14

7314   Edmon L. Rowell, "The Brook Kidron," *BI* 16/2 (1990): 42-52.

18:1-11

7315   Georg Richter, "Die Gefangennahme Jesu nach dem Johannesevangelium," *BibL* 10 (1969): 26-39.

7316   H. Summerall, "What Was the Cup That Jesus Had to Drink?" *CT* 14 (1970): 937-40.

7317   T. F. Glasson, "Davidic Links with the Betrayal of Jesus," *ET* 85 (1973-1974): 118-19.

7318   André Charbonneau, "L'arrestation de Jésus, une victoire d'après la facture interne de Jean 18:1-11," *SE* 34 (1982): 155-70.

7319   M. Lods, "Climat de bataille à Gethsémani," *ÉTR* 60 (1985): 425-29.

7320   Detlev Dormeyer, "Joh 18:1-14 Par Mk 14.43-53: Methodologische Überlegungen zur Rekonstruktion einer vorsynoptischen Passionsgeschichte," *NTS* 41 (1995): 218-39.

18:1-2

7321   J. D. M. Derrett, "Peter's Sword and Biblical Methodology," *BibO* 32 (1990): 180-92.

18:2

7322   Hans Reynen, "συνάγεσθαι (18:2)," *BZ* 5 (1961): 86-90.

18:4-8

7323   Sebastián Bartina, " 'Yo soy Yahweh': Nota exegética a Jo 18:4-8," *EE* 32 (1958): 403-26.

18:5-6

7324   J. H. Hingston, "John 18:5-6," *ET* 32 (1920-1921): 232.

18:6

7325   P. Mein, "A Note on John 18:6," *ET* 65 (1953-1954): 286-87.

18:8-11

7326   J. D. M. Derrett, "Peter's Sword and Biblical Methodology," *BibO* 32 (1990): 180-92.

18:9

7327   H. J. Flowers, "Interpolations in the Fourth Gospel," *JBL* 40 (1921): 146-58.

18:10-11

7328   Lamar Williamson, "Jesus of the Gospels and the Christian Vision of Shalom," *HBT* 6/2 (1984): 49-66.

7329   Arthur J. Droge, "The Status of Peter in the Fourth Gospel: A Note on John 18:10-11," *JBL* 109 (1990): 307-11.

7330   Craig S. Farmer, "Wolfgang Musculus and the Allegory of Malchus's Ear," *WTJ* 56 (1994): 285-301.

18:11

7331   Raymond E. Brown, "Incidents that Are Units in the Synoptic Gospels but Dispersed in St. John," *CBQ* 23 (1961): 143-60.

18:12-19:16

    7332   Helmut Merkel, "Peter's Curse: The Trial of Jesus," *SBT* 2/13 (1970): 66-71.

18:12-27

    7333   J. Schneider, "Zur Komposition von Johannes 18:12-27: Kaiphas und Hannas," *ZNW* 48 (1957): 111-19.

    7334   André Charbonneau, "L'interrogatoite de Jésus d'après la facture interne de Jean 18:12-27," *SE* 35 (1983): 191-210.

18:12-24

    7335   Robert T. Fortna, "Jesus and Peter at the Hight Priest's House: A Test Case for the Question of the Relation between Mark's and John's Gospels," *NTS* 24 (1977-1978): 371-83.

    7336   D. Rensberger, "The Politics of John: The Trial of Jesus in the Fourth Gospel," *JBL* 103 (1984): 395-411.

    7337   Jeffrey L. Staley, "Subversive Narrator/Victimized Reader: A Reader Response Assessment of a Text-Critical Problem, John 18.12-24," *JSNT* 51 (1993): 79-98.

18:12-14

    7338   A. Mahoney, "A New Look at an Old Problem," *CBQ* 27 (1965): 137-44.

18:14

    7339   P. Schepens, "Pontifex anni illius," *RechSR* 11 (1921): 372-74.

18:15-27

    7340   N. J. McEleney, "Peter's Denials—How Many? To Whom?" *CBQ* 52 (1990): 467-72.

    7341   Francis J. Moloney, "John 18:15-27: A Johannine View of the Church," *DR* 112 (1994): 231-48.

18:15-18

    7342   G. W. H. Lampe, "St. Peter's Denial," *BJRL* 55 (1972-1973): 346-68.

    7343   Dietfried Gewalt, "Die Verleugnung des Petrus," *LB* 43 (1978): 113-44.

7344   Kim E. Dewey, "Peter's Denial Reexamined: John's Knowledge of Mark's Gospel," *SBLSP* 9/1 (1979): 109-12.

18:15-16

7345   Frans Neirynck, "The 'Other Disciple' in John 18:15-16," *ETL* 51 (1975): 113-41.

18:19-24

7346   A. Mahoney, "A New Look at an Old Problem," *CBQ* 27 (1965): 137-44.

7347   P. Valentin, "Les comparutions de Jésus devant le Sanhédrin," *RechSR* 59 (1971): 230-36.

18:25-27

7348   G. W. H. Lampe, "St. Peter's Denial," *BJRL* 55 (1972-1973): 346-68.

7349   Dietfried Gewalt, "Die Verleugnung des Petrus," *LB* 43 (1978): 113-44.

7350   Kim E. Dewey, "Peter's Denial Reexamined: John's Knowledge of Mark's Gospel," *SBLSP* 9/1 (1979): 109-12.

7351   Craig A. Evans, " 'Peter Warming Himself': The Problem of an Editorial 'Seam'," *JBL* 101 (1982): 245-49.

18:26-30

7352   D. Mollat, "Le bon pasteur," *BVC* 52 (1963): 25-35.

18:28-19:16

7353   J. Blank, "Die Verhandlung vor Pilatus. Johannes 18:28-19:16 im Lichte johanneischer Theologie," *BZ* 3 (1959): 60-81.

7354   Ernst Haenchen, "Jesus vor Pilatus: Zur Methode der Auslegung," *TLZ* 85 (1960): 93-102.

7355   A. Jaubert, "Une discussion patristique sur la chronologie de la passion," *RechSR* 54 (1966): 407-10.

7356   Alois Bajsić, "Pilatus, Jesus und Barabbas," *Bib* 48 (1967): 7-28.

7357   Tibor Horvath, "Why Was Jesus Brought to Pilate?" *NovT* 11 (1969): 174-85.

7358   Hyam Z. Maccoby, "Jesus and Barabbas," *NTS* 16 (1969-1970): 55-60.

7359 Ernst Haenchen, "History and Interpretation in the Johannine Passion Narrative," *Int* 24 (1970): 198-219.

7360 F. Chenderlin, "Distributed Observance of the Passover: A Hypothesis," *Bib* 56 (1975): 369-93.

7361 Hans Klein, "Die lukanisch-johanneische Passionstradition," *ZNW* 67 (1976): 155-86.

7362 L. Díez Merino, "El suplicio de la cruz en la literatura judia intertestamental," *SBFLA* 26 (1976): 31-120.

7363 V. C. Pfitzner, "The Coronation of the King: The Passion of John," *CThM* 4 (1977): 10-21.

7364 Bart D. Ehrman, "Jesus' Trial before Pilate: John 18:28-19:16," *BTB* 13 (1983): 124-31.

7365 B. Marconcini, "Il significato della Passione in Giovanni," *PV* 29 (1984): 209-15.

7366 D. Rensberger, "The Politics of John: The Trial of Jesus in the Fourth Gospel," *JBL* 103 (1984): 395-411.

7367 F. Genuyt, "La comparution de Jésus devant Pilate: analyse sémiotique de Jean 18:28-19:16," *RechSR* 73 (1985): 133-46.

7368 André Charbonneau, "Qu'as-tu fait et 'd'où es-tu': le procès de Jésus chez Jean (18:28-19:16a) pt. 2," *ScE* 38/2 (1986): 317-29.

7369 Charles H. Giblin, "John's Narration of the Hearing before Pilate (John 18:28-19:16a)," *Bib* 67/2 (1986): 221-39.

7370 J. Zumstein, "Le Procès de Jésus devant Pilate (un exemple d'eschatologie johannique," *FV* 91 (1991): 89-101.

7371 Carola Diebold-Scheuermann, "Jesus vor Pilatus: Eine Gerichtsszene: Bemerkungen zur joh. Darstellungsweise," *BibN* 84 (1996): 64-74.

7372 Thomas Söding, "Die Macht der Wahrheit und das Reich der Freiheit: Zur johanneischen Deutung des Pilatus-Prozesses," *ZTK* 93 (1996): 35-58.

18:28-38

7373 D. Mollat, "Jésus devant Pilate," *BVC* 39 (1961): 23-31.

18:28

7374 Barry D. Smith, "The Chronology of the Last Supper," *WTJ* 53 (1991): 29-45.

7375 John C. Thomas, "The Fourth Gospel and Rabbinic Judaism," *ZNW* 82 (1991): 159-182.

18:29-32

7376 Manuel Benéitez, "Un Extraño interrogatorio: Jn 18,29-32," *EE* 68 (1993): 459-96.

18:31

7377 A. Vicent Cernuda, "La aporía entre Jean 18:31 y 19:6," *EB* 42/1-2 (1984): 71-88.

7378 J. Ramsey Michaels, "John 18:31 and the 'Trial' of Jesus," *NTS* 36 (1990): 474-79.

18:33-37

7379 M.-É. Boismard, "La royauté universelle du Christ (Jean 18:33-37)," *AsSeign* 88 (1966): 22-45.

18:36

7380 X. Alegre-Santamaria, "My Kingdom Is not of This World," *TD* 29 (1981): 231-35.

18:37

7381 A. M. Vitti, "Ergo Rex es tu?" *VD* 10 (1930): 289-97.

7382 J. D. M. Derrett, "Christ, King and Witness (John 18:37)," *BibO* 31 (1989): 189-98.

18:38

7383 M. Herranz Marco, "Un problema de crítica histórica en el relato de la Pasión: la liberación de Barrabás," *EB* 30 (1971): 137-60.

7384 B. Schwank, " 'Was ist Wahrheit?' (Joh 18:38)," *ErAu* 47 (1971): 487-96.

7385 Klauspeter Blaser, "Was ist Wahrheit? (Joh 18:38)," *ZMiss* 17/4 (1991): 194-96.

18:39

7386 J. B. Bauer, " 'Literarische' Namen und 'literarische' Bräuche (zu Joh 2,10 and 18,39)," *BZ* 26 (1982): 258-64.

18:40

7387   J. J. Twomey, "Barabbas Was a Robber," *Scr* 8 (1956): 115-19.

18:42

7388   G. Tosatto, "La passione di Cristo in S. Giov," *PV* 15 (1970): 377-88.

19

7389   Grant R. Osborne, "Redactional Techniques in the Crucifixion Narrative," *EQ* 51 (1979): 80-96.

19:1

7390   P. P. Flourney, "What Frightened Pilate," *BSac* 82 (1925): 314-20.

19:2-5

7391   H. S. J. Hart, "The Crown of Thorns in John 19:2-5," *JTS* 3 (1952): 66-75.

19:5-27

7392   André Feuillet, "L'heure de la femme (Jean 16:21) et l'heure de la Mère de Jésus (Jean 19:5-27)," *Bib* 47 (1966): 169-84, 361-80, 551-73.

19:5

7393   G. Siegmund, "Ecce Homo," *ErAu* 42 (1966): 91-104.

7394   J. L. Houlden, "John 19:5: 'And he said to them, Behold, the Man'," *ET* 92 (1980-1981): 148-49.

7395   John N. Suggit, "John 19:5: 'Behold the Man'," *ET* 94 (1982-1983): 333-34.

7396   Dieter Böhler, " 'Ecce Homo!' (Joh 19,5) ein Zitat aus dem Alten Testament," *BZ* NS 39 (1995): 104-108.

19:6

7397   A. Vicent Cernuda, "La aporía entre Jean 18:31 y 19:6," *EB* 42/1-2 (1984): 71-88.

19:7

7398   D. W. Head, "We Have a Law," *NovT* 11 (1969): 185-89.

19:8-11

7399   Dieter Zeller, "Jesus und die Philosophen vor dem Richter (zu Joh 19:8-11)," *BZ* NS 37 (1993): 88-92.

19:9

7400 L.-M. Dewailly, " 'D'où es-tu? (Jean 19:9)," *RB* 92 (1985): 481-96.

19:11

7401 R. Thibaut, "La réponse de Notre Seigneur à Pilate," *NRT* 54 (1927): 208-11.

7402 H. von Campenhausen, "Verständnis von Joh 19:11," *TLZ* 73 (1948): 387-92.

19:12

7403 E. Bammel, "φίλος τοῦ Καισαρος," *TLZ* 77 (1952): 205-10.

19:13

7404 J. Steele, "The Pavement," *ET* 34 (1922-1923): 562-63.

7405 L. Pujol, " 'In loco qui dicitur Lithostrotos'," *VD* 15 (1935): 180-86, 204-207, 233-37.

7406 L.-H. Vincent, "Le Lithostrotos évangélique," *RB* 59 (1952): 513-30.

7407 A. Kurfess, "ἐκάθισεν ἐπὶ βήματος," *Bib* 34 (1953): 271.

7408 I. de la Potterie, "Jesus King and Judge according to John 19:13," *Scr* 13 (1961): 97-111.

7409 John J. O'Rourke, "Two Notes on St. John's Gospel," *CBQ* 25 (1963): 124-28.

7410 M. Balagué, "Y lo sentó en el tribunal: Reparas a la nueva traducción litúrgica," *EB* 33 (1974): 63-67.

7411 A. M. Zabala, "The Enigma of John 19:13 Reconsidered," *SEAJT* 22 (1981): 16-28; 23 (1982): 87-110.

7412 Julio T. Barrera, "Posible substrato semitico del uso transitivo o intransitivo del verbo ἐκάθισεν en Jn 19:13," *FilN* 4 (1991): 51-54.

19:14

7413 J. Bonsirven, "Hora talmudica: La notion chronologique de Jean 19:14 aurait-elle un sens symbolique?" *Bib* 33 (1952): 511-15.

7414 V. Miller, "The Time of the Crucifixion," *JETS* 26 (1983): 157-66.

19:16-42

7415   S. R. Boguslawski, "Jesus' and the Bestowal of the Spirit," *IBS* 14 (1992): 106-29.

7416   André Charbonneau, "Jésus en croix (Jn 19,16b-42), Jésus élevé (3,14ss; 8,28s; 12,31ss)," *ScE* 45 (1993): 5-23.

7417   M. Sabbe, "The Johannine Account of the Death of Jesus and Its Synoptic Parallels (Jn 19:16b-42)," *ETL* 70 (1994): 34-64.

19:16-27

7418   I. de la Potterie, "La tunique sans couture, symbole du Christ grand prêtre?" *Bib* 60 (1979): 255-69.

19:17-30

7419   David A. Hubbard, "John 19:17-30," *Int* 43 (1989): 397-40.

19:17-21

7420   Joseph A. Fitzmyer, "Crucifixion in Ancient Palestine, Qumran Literature, and the New Testament," *CBQ* 40 (1978): 493-513.

19:17

7421   E. Bammel, "Johannes 9:17," *NTS* 40 (1994): 455-56.

19:18-37

7422   F. Genuyt, "L'économie des signes," *LV* 41 (1992): 19-35.

19:18

7423   Joseph A. Fitzmyer, "Crucifixion in Ancient Palestine, Qumran Literature, and the New Testament," *CBQ* 40/4 (1978): 493-513.

19:19-20

7424   Max Wilcox, "The Text of the Titulus in John 19:19-20 as Found in Some Italian Renaissance Painting," *JSNT* 27 (1986): 113-16.

19:23-24

7425   F.-M. Braun, "Quatre 'signes' johanniques de l'unité chrétienne (Jean 6:12-13, 11:47-52, 19:23-4, 21:1-11)," *NTS* 9 (1963): 147-55.

19:24-27

7426 M. de Goedt, "Un schème de révélation dans le 4ᵉ Évangile" *NTS* 8 (1961-1962): 142-50.

19:25-30

7427 Max A. Chevallier, "La fondation de 'l'Église' dans le quatrième évangile," *ÉTR* 58 (1983): 343-54.

19:25-27

7428 Dominic J. Unger, "A Note on John 19:25-27," *CBQ* 9 (1947): 111-12.

7429 André Feuillet, "Les adieux du Christ à sa mère et la maternité spirituelle de Marie," *NRT* 86 (1964): 469-89.

7430 André Feuillet, "L'heure de la femme (Jean 16:21) et l'heure de la Mère de Jésus (Jean 19:25-27)," *Bib* 47 (1966): 169-84, 361-80, 551-73.

7431 Anton Dauer, "Das Wort des Gekreuzigten an seine Mutter und den 'Jünger, den er liebte': Eine traditionsgeschichtliche und theologische Untersuchung zu Joh 19:25-27," *BZ* 11 (1967): 222-39; 12 (1968) 80-93.

7432 G. Dip, "Maria en el Nuevo Testamento," *CuBi* 24 (1967): 83-98.

7433 André Feuillet, "Christ's Farewell to His Mother," *TD* 15 (1967): 37-40.

7434 F. Longo, "Riflessioni su Giov. 19:25-27," *PV* 12 (1967): 389-94.

7435 M. Zerwick, "La hora de la Madre (J 19:25-27)," *RevB* 30 (1968): 197-205.

7436 M. Cimosa, "Maria ai piedi della Croce," *PV* 21 (1976): 377-88.

7437 S. A. Panimolle, " 'Donna-madre' del popolo di Dio (Gv 19:25-27)," *ParSpirV* 6 (1982): 136-51.

19:25-26

7438 J. G. Patrick, "Motherhood: Its Tragedy and Its Triumph," *ET* 94 (1982-1983): 145-46.

19:25

7439 Eric F. F. Bishop, "Mary Clopas," *ET* 65 (1953-1954): 382-83.

7440   Eric F. F. Bishop, "Mary (of) Clopas and Her Father," *ET* 73 (1962): 339.

19:26-27

7441   J. M. Bover, " 'Mujer, he ahí a tu Hijo': Maternidad espiritual de María para con todos los fieles, según San Juan," *EE* 1 (1922): 5-18.

7442   Josef Ernst, "Origenes und die geistige Mutterschaft Marias," *ZKT* 47 (1923): 617-21.

7443   Juan Leal, "Beata Virgo omnium spiritualis Mater ex Ioanne 19:26-27," *VD* 27 (1949): 65-73.

7444   Juan Leal, "Sentido mariológico de Jn 19:26-27," *EB* 11 (1952): 303-19.

7445   H. S. Box and M. E. Thrall, "The Blessed Virgin Mary," *Theology* 67 (1964): 360-62.

7446   Paul K. Jewett, "Can We Learn from Mariology?" *CC* 84/32 (1967): 1019-21.

7447   Hugolinus Langkammer, "Christ's 'Last Will and Testament' in the Interpretation of the Fathers of the Church and the Scholastics," *Ant* 43 (1968): 99-109.

7448   Frans Neirynck, "Short Note on John 19,26-27," *ETL* 71 (1995): 431-34.

19:26

7449   Paul Gächter, "Die geistige Mutterschaft Marias: Ein Beitrag zur Erklärung von Johannes 19:26f.," *ZKT* 47 (1923): 391-429.

7450   H. Preisker, "Johannes 2:4 und 19:26," *ZNW* 42 (1949): 209-14.

7451   I. Zudaire, "Mujer, he ahí a tu hijo," *CuBi* 11 (1954): 365-74.

19:27

7452   Frans Neirynck, "La traduction d'un verset johannique: Jean 19:27b" *ETL* 57 (1981): 83-106.

19:28-37

7453   R. Alan Culpepper, "The Death of Jesus: An Exegesis of John 19:28-37," *FM* 5 (1988): 64-70.

19:28-30

7454   R. E. O. White, "Christ's Death as John Saw It," *CT* 16 (1972): 548-51.

7455   J.-N. Aletti, "Mort de Jésus et théorie du récit," *RechSR* 73 (1985): 147-60.

7456   Leonard T. Witkamp, "Jesus' Thirst in John 19:28-30: Literal or Figurative?" *JBL* 115 (1996): 489-510.

19:28-29

7457   Robert L. Brawley, "An Absent Complement and Intertextuality in John 19:28-29," *JBL* 112 (1993): 427-43.

19:28

7458   G. D. Bampfylde, "John xix,28: A Case for a Different Translation," *NovT* 11 (1969): 247-60.

19:29

7459   Günther Schwarz, "ὑσσώπῳ περιθέντες (Johannes 19:29)," *NTS* 30/4 (1984): 625-26.

7460   F. G. Beetham and P. A. Beetham, "A Note on John 19:29," *JTS* NS 44 (1993): 163-69.

19:30

7461   Roland Bergmeier, "Tetelestai (Johannes 19:30)," *ZNW* 79/3-4 (1988): 282-90.

19:31-37

7462   M. Costa, "Simbolismo battesimale in Giov. 7:37-39; 19:31-37; 3:5," *RBib* 13 (1965): 347-83.

19:32

7463   Joseph A. Fitzmyer, "Crucifixion in Ancient Palestine, Qumran Literature, and the New Testament," *CBQ* 40/4 (1978): 493-513.

19:34-37

7464   J. Ramsey Michaels, "The Centurion's Confession and the Spear Thrust," *CBQ* 29 (1967): 102-109.

19:34

7465   R. Galdos, "Apertumne est militis lancea emortui Jesu latus?" *VD* 5 (1925): 161-68.

7466   F.-M. Braun, "L'eau et l'esprit," *RT* 49 (1949): 5-30.

7467   A. F. Sava, "The Wound in the Side of Christ," *CBQ* 19 (1957): 343-46.

7468   J. M. Ford, " 'Mingled Blood' from the Side of Christ (John xix,34)," *NTS* 15 (1968-1969): 337-38.

7469   Georg Richter, "Blut und Wasser aus der durchbohrten Seite Jesu (Joh 19:34b)," *MTZ* 21 (1970): 1-21.

7470   John Wilkinson, "The Incident of the Blood and Water in John 19:34," *SJT* 28 (1975): 149-72.

7471   L. Dunlop, "The Pierced Side: Focal Point of Johannine Theology," *BibTo* 86 (1976): 960-65.

7472   P. Bellet, "Analecta Coptica," *CBQ* 40 (1978): 37-52.

7473   Stephen Pennells, "The Spear Thrust," *JSNT* 19 (1983): 99-115.

7474   J. D. M. Derrett, " 'Dost Thou Teach Us?' (John 9:34c)," *DR* 116 (1998): 183-94.

19:35

7475   H. J. Flowers, "Interpolations in the Fourth Gospel," *JBL* 40 (1921): 146-58.

7476   F. H. Chase, "Two Notes on St. John's Gospel," *JTS* 26 (1924-1925): 381.

19:36

7477   G. A. Barton, " 'A Bone of Him Shall Not be Broken': John 19:36," *JBL* 49 (1930): 13-19.

19:37

7478   M. J. J. Menken, "The Textual Form and the Meaning of the Quotation from Zechariah 12:10 in John 19:37," *CBQ* 55 (1993): 494-511.

19:38-42

7479   E. A. Wuenschel, "The Shroud of Turin and the Burial of Christ: John's Account of the Burial," *CBQ* 8 (1946): 135-78.

7480   K. P. G. Curtis, "Three Points of Contact between Matthew and John in the Burial and Resurrection Narratives," *JTS* 23 (1972): 440-44.

19:38

7481 Linda M. Bridges, "To Be a Disciple," *BI* 16/3 (1990): 16-19.

19:39

7482 T. C. de Kruijf, " 'More than Half a Hundredweight' of Spices: Abundance and Symbolism in the Gospel of John," *Bij* 43 (1982): 234-39.

7483 Dennis D. Sylva, "Nicodemus and His Spices," *NTS* 34/1 (1988): 148-51.

19:41-20:18

7484 G. Kretschmar, "Kreuz und Auferstehung Jesu Christ. Das Zeugnis der heiligen Stätten," *ErAu* 54 (1978): 423-31; 55 (1979): 12-26.

19:40

7485 P. Savio, "Ricerche sopra la Santa Sindone," *Sale* 17 (1955): 319-90.

7486 B. Prete, "E lo legarono con bende (Giov. 19:40)," *BibO* 10 (1968): 189-96.

7487 J. Kenneth Eakins, "Burial Practices in Palestine," *BI* 1/2 (1975): 20-24.

7488 Brian Harbour, "A Proper Burial," *BI* 16/3 (1990): 31-34.

20

7489 Barnabas Lindars, "The Composition of John 20," *NTS* 7 (1960-1961): 142-47.

7490 Gert Hartmann, "Die Vorlage der Osterberichte in Joh 20," *ZNW* 55/3-4 (1964): 197-220.

7491 B. Schwank, "Die Ostererscheinungen des Johannesevangeliums und die Postmortem-Erscheinungen der Parapsychologie," *ErAu* 44 (1968): 36-53.

7492 G. Ghiberti, " 'Abbiamo veduto il Signore': Struttura e messagio dei racconti pasquali in S. Giovanni," *PV* 15 (1970): 389-414.

7493 J. Seynaeve, "De l'expérience à la foi (Jean 20)," *AsSeign* 23 (1971): 56-71.

7494 Jacques Dupont, "Recherche sur la structure de Jean 20," *Bib* 54 (1973): 482-98.

7495　G. Ghiberti, "Dall'incredulità alla fede (I racconti della Resurrezione nel Vangelo di Giovanni)," *PV* 18 (1973): 137-46.

7496　André Feuillet, "Les christophanies pascales du quatrième évangile sont-elles des signes?" *NRT* 97 (1975): 577-92.

7497　G. Ghiberti, " 'Resurrexit': Gli Atti di un simposio e la discussione successiva," *RBib* 23 (1975): 413-40.

7498　Matthew Vellanickal, "Resurrection of Jesus in St. John," *BB* 3 (1977): 131-54.

7499　D. H. C. Read, "How to Hear the Easter Story," *ET* 79 (1977-1978): 178-79.

7500　Frédéric Manns, "En marge des récits de la résurrection dans l'évangile de Jean: le verbe voir," *RevSR* 57 (1983): 10-28.

7501　I. de la Potterie, "Genèse de la foi pascale d'après Jean 20," *NTS* 30 (1984): 26-49.

7502　Brendan Byrne, "The Faith of the Beloved Disciple and the Community in John 20," *JSNT* 23 (1985): 83-97.

7503　Raymond E. Brown, "The Resurrection in John 20—A Series of Diverse Reactions," *Worship* 64 (1990): 194-206.

7504　Dorothy A. Lee, "Partnership in Easter Faith: The Role of Mary Magdalene and Thomas in John 20," *JSNT* 58 (1995): 37-49.

20:1-31

7505　C. Clifton Black, "Our Shepherd's Voice: Biblical Resources for the Easter Season," *QR* 14 (1994): 89-110.

20:1-19

7506　A. Niccacci, "La fede nel Gesù storico e la fede nel Cristo risorto (Gv 1,19-51//20,1-19)," *Ant* 53 (1978): 423-42.

20:1-18

7507　Matthew Vellanickal, "Feast of the Resurrection (John 20:1-18): Identity of the Risen Lord," *BB* 2 (1976): 91-94.

7508　Frans Neirynck, "John and the Synoptics: The Empty Tomb Stories," *NTS* 30/2 (1984): 161-87.

7509　Frans Neirynck, "Note sur Jean 20:1-18," *ETL* 62/4 (1986): 404.

7510 Frank J. Matera, "John 20:1-18," *Int* 43 (1989): 402-406.

7511 C. Bernabé, "Trasfondo derásico de Jn 20," *EB* 49 (1991): 209-28.

7512 M. Ebner, "Wer liebt mehr? Die liebende Jüngerin und der geliebte Jünger nach Joh 20,1-18," *BZ* NS 42 (1998): 39-55.

7513 B. Kowalski, "Der Gang zum leeren Grab aus pragmatischer Sicht," *GeistL* 73 (2000): 353-28.

20:1-10

7514 André Feuillet, "Le saint suaire de Turin et les évangiles. La passion et la résurrection: un unique mystère salvifique," *EV* 89 (1979): 401-16.

7515 Sandra M. Schneiders, "The Face Veil: A Johannine Sign (John 20:1-10)," *BTB* 13 (1983): 94-97.

7516 Brendan Byrne, "The Faith of the Beloved Disciple and the Community in John 20," *JSNT* 23 (1985): 83-97.

20:1-9

7517 E. Charpentier, "Jour de Pâque: le tombeau vide (Jean 20:1-9)," *EV* 79 (1969): 262-66.

7518 Jacques Winandy, "Les vestiges laissés dans le tombeau et la foi du disciple," *NRT* 110/2 (1988): 212-19.

20:1-8

7519 Frans Neirynck, "John and the Synoptics: The Empty Tomb Stories," *NTS* 30 (1984): 161-87.

20:2-10

7520 F. M. William, "Johannes am Grabe des Auferstandenen," *ZKT* 71 (1949): 204-13.

20:2

7521 Paul S. Minear, " 'We Don't Know Where . . .' John 20:2," *Int* 30 (1976): 125-39.

20:3-10

7522 Francesco Spadafora, "Sulla risurrezione di Gesu Jo 20:3-10," *RivBib* 1/2 (1953): 99-115.

7523 K. P. G. Curtis, "Luke XXIV.12 and John XX.3-10," *JTS* 22 (1971): 512-15.

7524 John Muddiman, "A Note on Reading Luke XXIV.12," *ETL* 48 (1972): 542-48.

7525 Frans Neirynck, "The Uncorrected Historic Present in Lk. XXIV.12," *ETL* 48 (1972): 548-33.

7526 André Feuillet, "La découverte du tombeau vide en Jean 20:3-10 et la foi au Christ ressuscité. Étude exégétigue et doctrinale," *EV* 87 (1977): 257-66, 273-84.

20:5-10

7527 M. Shorter, "The Sign of the Linen Cloths: The Fourth Gospel and the Holy Shroud of Turin," *JSNT* 17 (1983): 90-96.

20:5-8

7528 J. Ducatillon, "Le linceul de Jésus d'après saint Jean," *RT* 91 (1991): 421-24.

20:5-7

7529 R. Mercier, "Lo que 'el otro discipulo' vio en la tumba vacia. Juan 20:5-7," *RevB* 43 (1981): 3-32.

20:5

7530 P. Savio, "Ricerche sopra la Santa Sindone," *Sale* 17 (1955): 319-90.

7531 Frans Neirynck, "παρακύψας βλέπει Lc 24:12 et Jean 20:5," *ETL* 53 (1977): 113-52.

20:6-7

7532 M. Balagué, "La prueba de la resurrección," *EB* 25 (1966): 169-92.

20:7

7533 L. H. Duparc, "Le premier signe de la Résurrection chez saint Jean. Jean 20:7," *BVC* 86 (1969): 70-77.

7534 B. Osborne, "A Folded Napkin in an Empty Tomb: John 11:44 and 20:7 Again," *HeyJ* 14 (1973): 437-40.

7535 W. E. Reiser, "The Case of the Tidy Tomb: The Place of the Napkins of John 11:44 and 20:7," *HeyJ* 14 (1973): 47-57.

7536 F. Salvoni, "The So-Called Jesus Resurrection Proof (John 20:7)," *RQ* 22 (1979): 72-76.

<u>20:8</u>

7537   Francisco Gnidovec, "Introivit et vidit et credidit (2 pts; Jn

<u>20:10</u>

7538   Frans Neirynck, "ἀπῆλθεν πρὸς αὐτον Lc 24:12 et Jean
        20:10," *ETL* 54 (1978): 104-18.

<u>20:11-18</u>

7539   A. Webster, "My Master," *ET* 85 (1973-1974): 206-208.

7540   G. Ghiberti, "Maria Maddalena al sepolcro," *PV* 29
        (1984): 226-44.

7541   Teresa Okure, "The Significance Today of Jesus'
        Commission to Mary Magdalene," *IRM* 81 (1992): 177-88.

<u>20:16</u>

7542   Patrick P. Saydon, "Some Biblico-Liturgical Passages
        Reconsidered," *MeliT* 18/1 (1966): 10-17.

7543   J. D. M. Derrett, "Miriam and the Resurrection," *BibO* 33
        (1991): 211-19.

<u>20:17-27</u>

7544   T. Hearn, "Reach Hither, Touch Me Not," *RevExp* 59
        (1962): 200-204.

<u>20:17</u>

7545   Bruno Violet, "Ein Versuch zu Johannes 20:17," *ZNW* 24
        (1925): 78-80.

7546   W. Morris, "John 20:17," *ET* 40 (1928-1929): 527-28.

7547   W. E. P. Cotter, " 'Touch me not; for I am not yet
        ascended unto the Father'," *ET* 43 (1931-1932): 45-46.

7548   J. Maiworm, " 'Noli me tangere!': Beitrag zur Exegese
        von Johannes 20:17," *TGl* 30 (1938): 540-46.

7549   A. Vidal, " 'Noli me tangere'," *CuBi* 2 (1945): 78-81,
        221-22.

7550   Ceslaus Spicq, " 'Noli me tangere'," *RSPT* 32 (1948):
        226-27.

7551   H. Kraft, "Johannes 20:17," *TLZ* 76 (1951): 570.

7552   W. Grundmann, "Zur Rede Jesu vom Vater im
        Johannes-Evangelium: eine redaktions- und

bekenntnisgeschichtliche Untersuchung zu Joh 20:17 und seiner Vorbereitung," *ZNW* 52/3-4 (1961): 213-30.

7553 Georg Richter, "Der Vater und Gott Jesu und seiner Brüder in Joh 20:17. Ein Beitrag zur Christologie des Johannesevangeliums," *MTZ* 24 (1973): 95-114.

7554 D. C. Fowler, "The Meaning of 'Touch me not' in John 20:17," *EQ* 47 (1975): 16-25.

7555 G. Glaser, "Wie Maria Magdalena dem Auferstandenen begegnete. Meditation über Joh 20:17," *GeistL* 51 (1978): 137-40.

7556 Antonio Charbel, "Giov. 20:17a: 'Nondum enim ascendi ad Patrem'?" *BibO* 21 (1979): 79-83.

7557 Michael McGehee, "A Less Theological Reading of John 20:17," *JBL* 105/2 (1986): 299-302.

7558 Y. Ibuki, "Nondum enim ascendi (Joh 20:17)—crux interpretum," *AJBI* 3 (1987): 59-84.

7559 Mary B. D'Angelo, "A Critical Note: John 20:17 and Apocalypse of Moses 31," *JTS* 41 (1990): 529-36.

20:18

7560 Pheme Perkins, " 'I Have Seen the Lord' (John 20:18): Women Witnesses to the Resurrection," *Int* 46 (1992): 31-41.

20:19-31

7561 Gilles Becquet, "Le Christ ressuscité transfère sa mission à la communauté des croyants (Jean 20:19-31)," *EV* 80 (1970): 193-96.

20:19-29

7562 John N. Suggit, "The Eucharistic Significance of John 20:19-29," *JTSA* 16 (1976): 52-59.

20:19-23

7563 J. J. Cook, "John 20:19-23: An Exegesis," *RR* 21/2 (1967): 2-10.

7564 John R. W. Stott, "The Great Commission," *CT* 12 (1968): 723-25, 778-82, 826-29.

7565 Félix Asensio, "Los pasajes biblicos de la 'Gran Misión' y el Vaticano II," *EB* 29 (1970): 213-26.

7566 André Feuillet, "La communication de l'Esprit-Saint aux Apôtres (Jean 20:19-23) et le ministère sacerdotal de la réconciliation des hommes avec Dieu," *EV* 82 (1972): 2-7.

7567 M. G. DeDurand, "Pentecôte johannique et Pentecôte lucanienne chez certains Pères," *BLE* 79 (1978): 97-126.

7568 Reginald H. Fuller, "John 20:19-23," *Int* 32 (1978): 180-84.

7569 Eugene A. LaVerdiere, " 'Peace Be with You'," *Emmanuel* 90 (1984): 316-19.

7570 Josef Sudbrack, "Über den Frieden Jesu Christi. Anleitung zum ignatianischen Meditieren von Joh 20:19-23," *GeistL* 58 (1985): 392-95.

20:19-21

7571 Heino Falcke, "Kirchen im Friedensbund Gottes: ekklesiologische Aspekte des Friedensauftrags der Kirchen heute," *EvT* 45 (1985): 348-66.

20:19-20

7572 M.-É. Boismard, "Le réalisme des récits évangéliques," *LV* 21 (1972): 31-41.

20:21-23

7573 R. Trevijano Etcheverría, "La misión de la Iglesia primitiva y los mandatos del Señor en los evangelios," *Salm* 25 (1978): 5-36.

7574 J.-C. Basset, "Dernières paroles du ressuscité et mission de l'Église aujourd'hui. (À propos de Mt 28:18-20 et parallèles)," *RTP* 114 (1982): 349-67.

20:21

7575 Pablo A. Deiros, "Evangelism and the Third World: The Great Commission and the Great Commandment," *FM* 2/2 (1985): 42-49.

20:22-23

7576 James Swetnam, "Bestowal of the Spirit in the Fourth Gospel," *Bib* 74 (1993): 556-76.

20:22

7577   Joost van Rossum, "The 'Johannine Pentecost': John 20:22 in Modern Exegesis and in Orthodox Theology," *SVTQ* 35/2-3 (1991): 149-67.

7578   Thomas R. Hatina, "John 20,22 in Its Eschatological Context: Promise or Fulfillment?" *Bib* 74 (1993): 196-219.

20:23

7579   Henry J. Cadbury, "The Meaning of John 20:23, Matthew 16:19, and Matthew 18:18," *JBL* 58 (1939): 251-54.

7580   Julius R. Mantey, "The Mistranslation of the Perfect Tense in John 20:23, Matthew 16:19, and Matthew 18:18," *JBL* 58 (1939): 243-49.

7581   C. H. Dodd, "Some Johannine 'Herrnworte' with Parallels in the Synoptic Gospels," *NTS* 2 (1955): 75-86.

7582   J. A. Emerton, "Binding and Loosing—Forgiving and Retaining," *JTS* 13 (1962): 325-31.

7583   Julius R. Mantey, "What of Priestly Absolution," *CT* 13/9 (1969): 233-391.

7584   G. M. Lee, "Presbyters and Apostles," *ZNW* 62 (1971): 122.

7585   Julius R. Mantey, "Evidence That the Perfect Tense in John 20:23 and Matthew 16:19 Is Mistranslated," *JETS* 16/3 (1973): 129-38.

7586   Julius R. Mantey, "Distorted Translations in John 20:23; Matthew 16:18-19 and 18:18," *RevExp* 78/3 (1981): 409-16.

7587   J. D. M. Derrett, "Binding and Loosing (Matt 16:19; 18:18; John 20:23)," *JBL* 102 (1983): 112-17.

7588   B. De Margerie, "La mission sacerdotale de retenir les péchés en liant les pécheurs. Intérêt actuel et justification d'une exégèse tridentine," *RevSR* 58 (1984): 300-17.

7589   Herbert W. Basser, "Derrett's 'Binding' Reopened," *JBL* 104 (1985): 297-300.

7590   Dennis C. Duling, "Binding and Loosing: Matthew 16:19; Matthew 18:18; John 20:23," *Forum* 3 (1987): 3-31.

7591   Steven E. Hansen, "Forgiving and Retaining Sin: A Study
        of the Text and Context of John 20:23," *HBT* 19 (1997):
        24-32.

20:24-29

7592   T. M. Suriano, "Doubting Thomas: An Invitation to
        Belief," *BibTo* 53 (1971): 309-15.

7593   M.-É. Boismard, "Le réalisme des récits évangéliques," *LV*
        21 (1972): 31-41.

7594   P. Bellet, "Analecta Coptica," *CBQ* 40 (1978): 37-52.

7595   A. Hilhorst, "The Wounds of the Risen Jesus," *EB* 41/1-2
        (1983): 165-67.

20:29

7596   H. G. Wood, "The Beatitude of Faith in the Unseen," *ET*
        48 (1936-1937): 552-54.

7597   B. Prete, "Beati coloro che non vedono e credono (Giov.
        20:29)," *BibO* 9 (1967): 97-114.

7598   Ron Cameron, "Seeing Is Not Believing: The History of a
        Beatitude in the Jesus Tradition," *Forum* 4 (1988): 47-57.

20:30-21:25

7599   Fernando F. Segovia, "The Final Farewell of Jesus: A
        Reading of John 20:30-21:25," *Semeia* 53 (1991): 167-90.

20:30-31

7600   F. Segarra, "La doble conclusión del Evangelio de San
        Juan 20:30-31 y 21:24-25," *EE* 9 (1930): 32-47.

7601   Léon Vaganay, "La finale du IVᵉ Évangile," *RB* 45 (1936):
        512-28.

7602   Michael Lattke, "Joh 20:30f als Buchschluss," *ZNW*
        78/3-4 (1987): 288-92.

7603   Gilbert Van Belle, "The Meaning of Semeia in Jn
        20,30-31," *ETL* 74 (1998): 300-25.

20:31

7604   E. P. Groenewald, "The Christological Meaning of John
        20:31," *Neo* 2 (1968): 131-40.

7605   T. C. de Kruijf, " 'Hold the Faith' or 'Come to Belief'? A
        Note on John 20:31," *Bij* 36 (1975): 439-49.

7606   D. A. Carson, "The Purpose of the Fourth Gospel: John 20:31 Reconsidered," *JBL* 106 (1987): 639-51.

7607   James V. Brownson, "John 20:31 and the Purpose of the Fourth Gospel," *RR* 48 (1995): 212-16.

21

7608   Bishop Cassian, "John XXI," *NTS* (1956-1957): 132-36.

7609   S. B. Marrow, "Jo 21: Indagatio in Ecclesiologiam Joanneam," *VD* 45 (1967): 47-51.

7610   B. de Solages and J.-M. Vacherot, "Le chapitre xxi de Jean est-il de la même plume que la reste de l'Évangile?" *BLE* 80 (1970): 96-101.

7611   Stephen S. Smalley, "The Sign in John xxi," *NTS* 20 (1973-1974): 275-88.

7612   A. Shaw, "Image and Symbol in John 21," *ET* 86 (1974-1975): 311.

7613   B. de Solages and J.-M. Vacherot, "Le chapitre XXI de Jean est-il de la même plume que le reste de l'Évangile?" *BLE* 80 (1979): 96-101.

7614   J. D. M. Derrett, "Esan gar Halieis (Mark 1:16). Jesus' Fisherman and the Parable of the Net," *NovT* 22/2 (1980): 108-37.

7615   Paul S. Minear, "The Original Functions of John 21," *JBL* 102 (1983): 85-98.

7616   Lars Hartman, "An Attempt of a Text-Centered Exegesis of John 21," *StTheol* 38 (1984): 29-45.

7617   L. Paul Trudinger, "John 21 Revisited Once Again," *DR* 106 (1988): 145-48.

7618   Raymond E. Brown, "The Resurrection in John 21: Missionary and Pastoral Directives for the Church," *Worship* 64 (1990): 433-45.

7619   Frans Neirynck, "John 21," *NTS* 36 (1990): 321-36.

7620   P. Hofrichter, "Joh 21 im Makrotext des vierten Evangeliums," *TGl* 81 (1991): 302-22.

7621   John Breck, "John 21: Appendix, Epilogue or Conclusion?" *SVTQ* 36 (1992): 27-49.

7622 J. P. Duplantier, "Le pasteur et l'écrivain: Lecture de Jean 21," *LV* 41 (1992): 83-94.

7623 P. F. Ellis, "The Authenticity of John 21," *SVTQ* 36 (1992): 17-25.

7624 M. H. Franzmann and Michael Klinger, "The Call Stories of John 1 and John 21," *SVTQ* 36/1-2 (1992): 7-15.

7625 Wolfgang Schenk, "Interne Strukturierungen im Schluss-Segment Johannes 21," *NTS* 38 (1992): 507-30.

7626 Patrick E. Spencer, "Narrative Echoes in John 21: Intertextual Interpretation and Intratextual Connection," *JSNT* 75 (1999): 49-68.

21:1-25

7627 Édouard Delebecque, "La mission de Pierre et celle de Jean: note philologique sur Jean 21," *Bib* 67/3 (1986): 335-42.

7628 Gabriel M. Napole, "Pedro y el discipulo amado en Juan 21:1-25," *RevB* 52/3 (1990): 153-77.

21:1-23

7629 Timothy Wiarda, "John 21:1-23: Narrative Unity and Its Implications," *JSNT* 46 (1992): 53-71.

21:1-19

7630 B. Schwank, "Le Christ et Pierre à la fin des temps," *AsSeign* 24 (1970): 57-64.

7631 Samuel O. Abogunrin, "The Three Variant Accounts of Peter's Call: A Critical and Theological Examination of the Texts," *NTS* 31 (1985): 587-602.

21:1-14

7632 D. H. C. Read, "Ongoing Easter: The Sign of the Fish," *ET* 85 (1973-1974): 208-209.

7633 A. Shaw, "Tile Breakfast by the Shore and the Mary Magdalene Encounter as Eucharistic Narratives," *JTS* 25 (1974): 12-26.

7634 Diego A. Losada, "El relato de la pesca milagrosa," *RevB* 40 (1978): 17-26.

7635 Mathias Rissi, "Voll grosser Fische, hundertdreiundfünfzig, Joh 21:1-14," *TZ* 35 (1979): 73-89.

7636   Marion L. Soards, "Τὸν ἐπενδύτην διεζώσατο, ἦν γάρ γυμνός," *JBL* 102 (1983): 283-84.

7637   V. C. Pfitzner, "They Knew It Was the Lord: The Place and Function of John 21:1-14 in the Gospel of John," *LTJ* 20/2-3 (1986): 64-75.

7638   Sandra M. Schneiders, "John 21:1-14," *Int* 43 (1989): 70-75.

7639   S. Sabugal, "La resurreción de Jesús en el cuarto evangelio," *Sale* 53 (1991): 649-67.

7640   M. H. Franzmann and Michael Klinger, "The Call Stories of John 1 and John 21," *SVTQ* 36/1-2 (1992): 7-15.

21:1-11

7641   F.-M. Braun, "Quatre 'signes' johanniques de l'unité chrétienne (Jean 6:12-13, 11:47-52, 19:23-4, 21:1-11)," *NTS* 9 (1963): 147-55.

7642   Bernd Steinseifer, "Der Ort der Erscheinungen des Auferstandenen," *ZNW* 63/3 (1971): 232-65.

21:7

7643   D. H. Gee, "Why Did Peter Spring into the Sea? (John 21:7)," *JTS* 40 (1989): 481-89.

7644   Ulrich Busse, "The Relevance of Social History to the Interpretation of the Gospel according to John," *SkrifK* 16 (1995): 28-38.

21:9

7645   Kenneth Cardwell, "The Fish on the Fire: John 21:9," *ET* 102 (1990): 12-14.

7646   Günther Schwarz, "Blepousin anthrakian keimenen? (Johannes 21:9b)," *BibN* 55 (1990): 14-15.

21:11

7647   R. M. Grant, "One Hundred and Fifty-Three Large Fish," *HTR* 42 (1949): 273-75.

7648   J. A. Emerton, "The Hundred and Fifty-Three Fishes in John 21:11," *JTS* 9 (1958): 86-89.

7649   P. R. Ackroyd, "The 153 Fishes in John 21:11—A Further Note," *JTS* NS 10 (1959): 94.

7650 J. A. Emerton, "Some New Testament Notes: 4. Gematria in John 21:11," *JTS* 11 (1960): 335-36.

7651 N. J. McEleney, "153 Great Fishes: Gematriacal Atbash," *Bib* 58 (1977): 411-17.

7652 J. A. Romeo, "Gematria and John 21:11: The Children of God," *JBL* 97 (1978): 263-64.

7653 Bruce H. Grigsby, "Gematria and John 21:11: Another Look at Ezekiel 47:10," *ET* 95 (1983-1984): 177-78.

7654 Michal Wojciechowski, "Certains aspects algébriques de quelques nombres symboliques de la Bible," *BibN* 23 (1984): 29-31.

7655 Michael Oberweis, "Die Bedeutung der neutestamentlichen 'Rätselzahlen' 666 (Apk 13:18) und 153 (Joh 21:11)," *ZNW* 77/3-4 (1986): 226-41.

7656 O. T. Owen, "One Hundred and Fifty Three Fishes," *ET* 100 (1988): 52-54.

7657 J. M. Ross, "One Hundred and Fifty-Three Fishes," *ET* 100 (1989): 357.

7658 Kenneth Cardwell, "The Fish on the Fire: John 21:9," *ET* 102 (1990): 12-14.

7659 L. Paul Trudinger, "The 153 Fishes: A Response and a Further Suggestion," *ET* 102 (1990): 11-12.

21:14

7660 Frans Neirynck, "Note sur Jean 21:14," *ETL* 64/4 (1988): 429-32.

21:15-25

7661 B. W. Bacon, "The Motivation of John 21:15-25," *JBL* 50 (1931): 71-80.

7662 Emilio Castro, "Nachfolge Jesu: biblische Besinnung zu Johannes 21:15-25," *ZMiss* 14/3 (1988): 131-33.

21:15-19

7663 J. F. Sheehan, "Feed My Lambs," *Scr* 16 (1964): 21-27.

7664 Gilbert L. Bartholomew, "Feed My Lambs: John 21:15-19 as Oral Gospel," *Semeia* 39 (1987): 69-96.

21:15-17

7665 W. K. L. Clarke, "John 21:15-17," *Theology* 8/1 (1924): 281-82.

7666 Tomas Arvedson, "Några notiser till två ntliga perikoper," *SEÅ* 21 (1956): 27-29.

7667 Félix Gils, "Pierre et la foi au Christ ressuscité," *ETL* 38 (1962): 5-43.

7668 Otto Glombitza, "Petrus—der Freund Jesu: Überlegungen zu Johannes 21:15-17," *NovT* 6 (1963): 277-85.

7669 William J. Tobin, "The Petrine Primacy Evidence of the Gospels," *LV* 23/1 (1968): 27-70.

7670 B. A. Ramsey, "A Note on the Disappearance of the Good Shepherd from Early Christian Art," *HTR* 76 (1983): 375-78.

7671 K. L. McKay, "Style and Significance in the Language of John 21:15-17," *NovT* 27 (1985): 319-33.

21:17

7672 S. Del Páramo, "Pasce oves meas," *CuBí* 7 (1950): 334-37.

21:18-19

7673 J. D. M. Derrett, "Zonnymi, phero, allos: The Fate of Peter," *FilN* 8 (1995): 79-84.

21:20-23

7674 G. M. Lee, "John 21:20-23," *JTS* NS 1 (1950): 62-63.

21:21

7675 P. N. Bushill, "A Note on John 21:21," *ET* 47 (1935-1936): 523-24.

21:23-25

7676 L. S. Ford, "St. John 21:23-25," *Theology* 20/1 (1930): 229.

21:24-25

7677 F. Segarra, "La doble conclusión del Evangelio de San Juan 20:30-31 y 21:24-25," *EE* 9 (1930): 32-47.

7678 I. de la Potterie, "Le témoin qui demeure: le disciple que Jésus aimait," *Bib* 67/3 (1986): 343-59.

7679 Wolfgang Schenk, "Interne Strukturierungen im Schluss-Segment Johannes 21," *NTS* 38 (1992): 507-30.

7680 D. F. Tolmie, "John 21:24-25: A Case of Failed Attestation?" *SkrifK* 17 (1996): 420-26.

21:24

7681 J. Chapman, " 'We Know That His Testimony Is True'," *JTS* 31 (1929-1930): 379-87.

7682 C. H. Dodd, "Note on John 21:24," *JTS* 4 (1953): 212-13.

7683 F. W. Grosheide, "Jean 21:24 en de Canon," *GTT* 53 (1953): 117-18.

21:25

7684 C. Lo Giudice, "La fede degli Apostoli nel IV Vangelo," *Bib* 28 (1947): 59-82, 264-80.

7685 Günther Schwarz, "τὸν κόσμον χωρῆσαι (Johannes 21:25)," *BibN* 15 (1981): 46.

7686 René Kieffer, "Å gjenkjenne den ukjente," *NTT* 91/3 (1990): 129-39.

7687 J. Neville Birdsall, "The Source of Catena Comments on John 21:25," *NovT* 36 (1994): 271-79.

Acts

1-15

7688   R. A. Martin, "Syntactical Evidence of Aramaic Sources in Acts I-XV," *NTS* 11/1 (1964): 38-59.

1:1-15:35

7689   R. A. Martin, "Semitic Traditions in Some Synoptic Accounts," *SBLSP* 26 (1987): 295-335.

1-12

7690   J. Rius-Camps, "El seguimiento de Jesús, 'el Señor', y de su Espíritu en los prolegómenos de la misión," *EB* 51 (1993): 73-116.

1-6

7691   Francis Lenssen, "Biblical Communities: Christian Communities in the New Testament," *Point* 1 (1972): 24-34.

7692   J. H. Petzer, "The Textual Relationships of the Vulgate and Acts," *NTS* 39/2 (1993): 227-45.

1-5

7693   William L. Blevins, "The Early Church: Acts 1-5," *RevExp* 71/4 (1974): 463-74.

7694   Mikeal C. Parsons, "Christian Origins and Narrative Openings: The Sense of a Beginning in Acts 1-5," *RevExp* 87 (1990): 403-22.

1-2

7695   Everett Ferguson, "Apologetics in the New Testament," *RQ* 6 (1962): 180-95.

7696   P. M. J. Stravinskas, "The Role of the Spirit in Acts 1 and 2," *BibTo* 18/4 (1980): 263-68.

7697   C. W. Wibb, "The Characterization of God in the Opening Scenes of Luke and Acts," *EGLMBS* 13 (1993): 275-92.

7698 A. W. Zwiep, "The Text of the Ascension Narratives," *NTS* 42 (1996): 219-44.

1

7699 Justin Taylor, "The Making of Acts: A New Account," *RB* 97 (1990): 504-24.

7700 Gerard Mussies, "Variation in the Book of Acts," *FilN* 4 (1991): 165-82.

7701 Jürgen Wehnert, "Die Teilhabe der Christen an der Herrschaft mit Christus--eine eschatologische Erwartung des frühen Christentums," *ZNW* 88 (1997): 81-96.

1:1-26

7702 P. W. van der Horst, "Hellenistic Parallels to the Acts of the Apostles: 1:1-26," *ZNW* 74/1-2 (1983): 17-26.

7703 Mikeal C. Parsons, "Christian Origins and Narrative Openings: The Sense of a Beginning in Acts 1-5," *RevExp* 87 (1990): 403-22.

1:1-18

7704 Jerome Murphy-O'Connor, "Paul and Gallio," *JBL* 112/2 (1990): 315-17.

1:1-14

7705 Philippe Rolland, "L'organisation du Livre des Actes et de l'ensemble de l'œuvre de Luc," *Bib* 65/1 (1984): 81-86.

7706 D. W. Palmer, "The Literary Background of Acts 1:1-14," *NTS* 33/3 (1987): 427-38.

1:1-11

7707 Wayne E. Weissenbuehler, "Acts 1:1-11," *Int* 46 (1992): 61-65.

1:1-3

7708 J. Rius-Camps, "Las variantes de la recensión occidental de los Hechos de los Apóstoles," *FilN* 6 (1993): 59-68.

7709 G. Menestrina, "L'incipit dell'espitola 'Ad Diognetum,' Luca 1:1-4 et Atti 1:1-2," *BibO* 19 (1977): 215-18.

7710 André Feuillet, "Le 'Commencement' de l'Économie Chrétienne d'après He II. 3-4; Mc I.1 et Ac 1. 1-2," *NTS* 24/2 (1978): 163-74.

1:1

7711   Pierson Parker, "The 'Former Treatise' and the Date of Acts," *JBL* 84/1 (1965): 52-58.

7712   Paul S. Minear, "Dear Theo: The Kerygmatic Intention and Claim of the Book of Acts," *Int* 27/2 (1973): 131-50.

7713   Schuyler Brown, "The Prologues of Luke-Acts in Their Relation to the Purpose of the Author," *SBLSP* 5 (1975): 1-14.

7714   Vernon K. Robbins, "Prefaces in Greco-Roman Biography and Luke-Acts," *SBLSP* 8/2 (1978): 193-208.

7715   Terrance Callan, "The Preface of Luke-Acts and Historiography," *NTS* 31 (1985): 576-81.

7716   C. W. Wibb, "The Characterization of God in the Opening Scenes of Luke and Acts," *EGLMBS* 13 (1993): 275-92.

7717   L. C. A. Alexander, "What If Luke Had Never Met Theophilus?" *BibInt* 8 (2000): 161-70.

1:2-3

7718   P. Palatty, "The Ascension of Christ in Luke-Acts: An Exegetical Critical Study of Luke 24,50-53 and Acts 1,2-3.9-11," *BB* 12 (1986): 100-17, 166-81.

1:2

7719   Jacques Dupont, "Ἀνελήμφθη (Acts 1:2)," *NTS* 8 (1962): 154-57.

7720   Mikeal C. Parsons, "The Text of Acts 1:2 Reconsidered," *CBQ* 50/1 (1988): 58-71.

1:3-11

7721   Robert F. O'Toole, "Activity of the Risen Jesus in Luke-Acts," *Bib* 62/4 (1981): 471-98.

1:3-8

7722   E. J. Christiansen, "Taufe als Initiation in der Apostelgeschichte," *StTheol* 40/1 (1986): 55-79.

1:3

7723   John H. Hayes, "The Resurrection as Enthronement and the Earliest Church Christology," *Int* 22/3 (1968): 333-45.

7724   David L. Mealand, "The Phrase 'Many Proofs' in Acts 1:3 and in Hellenistic Writers," *ZNW* 80/1-2 (1989): 134-35.

1:4

7725   J. Dasiewicz, "Jeruzalem—miejscem zeslania Ducha Swietego," *RoczTK* 23 (1976): 85-96.

7726   J. Rius-Camps, "Las variantes de la recensión occidental de los Hechos de los Apóstoles," *FilN* 6 (1993): 59-68.

1:4-8

7727   John R. Donahue, "The 'Parable' of the Sheep and the Goats: A Challenge to Christian Ethics," *JTS* 47/1 (1986): 3-31.

1:4-5

7728   J. Rius-Camps, "Las variantes de la recensión occidental de los Hechos de los Apóstoles," *FilN* 6 (1993): 59-68.

1:5

7729   David L. Mealand, " 'After not Many Days' in Acts 1:5 and Its Hellenistic Context," *JSNT* 42 (1991): 69-77.

1:6-11

7730   David L. Tiede, "The Exaltation of Jesus and the Restoration of Israel in Acts 1," *SBLSP* 24 (1985): 367-75.

1:6-8

7731   David L. Tiede, "Acts 1:6-8 and the Theo-Political Claims of Christian Witness," *WW* 1/1 (1981): 41-51.

7732   Lucien Legrand, "The Spirit, the Mission and the Church: Acts 1:6-8," *BB* 8/4 (1982): 204-15.

7733   David Hill, "The Spirit and the Church's Witness: Observations on Acts 1:6-8," *IBS* 6/1 (1984): 16-26.

7734   J. A. McLean, "Did Jesus Correct the Disciples' View of the Kingdom?" *BSac* 151 (1994): 215-27.

1:6

7735   David L. Tiede, "The Exaltation of Jesus and the Restoration of Israel in Acts 1," *HTR* 79/1 (1986): 278-86.

7736   J. Rius-Camps, "Las variantes de la recensión occidental de los Hechos de los Apóstoles," *FilN* 6 (1993): 59-68.

7737   A. Buzard, "Acts 1:6 and the Eclipse of the Biblical Kingdom," *EQ* 66 (1994): 197-215.

1:7

7738   R. Y. K. Fung, "Charismatic Versus Organized Ministry? An Examination of an Alleged Antithesis," *EQ* 52/4 (1980): 195-214.

7739   Luis F. Ladaria, "Dispensatio en S. Hilario de Poitiers [De Trinitate]," *Greg* 66/3 (1985): 429-55.

1:8-11

7740   J. Rius-Camps, "Las variantes de la recensión occidental de los Hechos de los Apóstoles," *FilN* 6 (1993): 59-68.

1:8

7741   H. A. Hoyt, "The Frantic Future and the Christian Directive: Acts 1:8," *GTJ* 10/1 (1969): 36-41.

7742   A. Moretti, "Mi sarete testimoni (Atti 1,8)" *PV* 15 (1970): 421-36.

7743   T. C. G. Thornton, "To the End of the Earth: Acts 1:8," *ET* 89 (1978): 374-75.

7744   Gordon D. Fee, "Baptism in the Holy Spirit: The Issue of Separability and Subsequence," *Pneuma* 7/2 (1985): 87-99.

7745   Jaroslav J. Pelikan, "The Man Who Belongs to the World," *CC* 102 (1985): 827-31.

7746   J. A. Jáuregui, "Israel y la iglesia en la teologia de Lucas," *EE* 61 (1986): 129-49.

7747   Andreas Lindemann, "Erwägungen zum Problem einer 'Theologie der synoptischen Evangelien'," *ZNW* 77/1-2 (1986): 1-33.

7748   Warren McWilliams, "The Uttermost Part of the Earth: First-Century Views," *BI* 12/3 (1986): 66-69.

7749   Daniel R. Schwartz, "The End of the Genesis: Beginning or End of the Christian Vision?" *JBL* 105/4 (1986): 669-76.

7750   LaMoine DeVries, "Samaria," *BI* 14/2 (1989): 10-15.

1:9-11

7751 C. H. J. van Kempen, "Masters of the Text: is Every Age the Same," *RR* 40/1 (1986): 21-26.

7752 P. Palatty, "The Ascension of Christ in Luke-Acts: An Exegetical Critical Study of Luke 24,50-53 and Acts 1,2-3.9-11," *BB* 12 (1986): 100-17, 166-81.

7753 Carol L. Stockhausen, "Luke's Stories of the Ascension: The Background and Function of a Dual Narrative," *EGLMBS* 10 (1990): 251-63.

7754 G. C. Fuller, "The Life of Jesus after the Ascension," *WTJ* 56/2 (1994): 391-98.

7755 A. W. Zwiep, "The Text of the Ascension Narratives," *NTS* 42 (1996): 219-44.

1:9

7756 J. D. M. Derrett, "Akeldama (Acts 1:19)," *Bij* 56 (1995): 122-32.

1:11

7757 Gerhard Lohfink, " 'Was steht ihr da und schauet' (Apg 1.11). Die 'Himmelfahrt Jesu' im lukanischen Geschichtswerk," *BK* 20/2 (1965): 43-48.

7758 Anthony Hoekema, "Heaven: Not Just an Eternal Day Off," *CT* 29 (1985): 18-19.

1:12-14

7759 G. Betori, "La strutturazione del libro degli Atti: una proposta," *RBib* 42 (1994): 3-34.

1:13-14

7760 J. Rius-Camps, "Las variantes de la recensión occidental de los Hechos de los Apóstoles," *FilN* 6 (1993): 59-68.

1:13

7761 Bonnie B. Thurston, "τὸ ὑπερῷον in Acts 1,13," *ET* 81/1 (1968): 21-22.

7762 Roger L. Omanson, "Lazarus and Simon," *BT* 40 (1989): 416-19.

7763 Günther Schwarz, "Philippon kai Bartholomaion?" *BibN* 56 (1991): 26-30.

1:14

7764   Walter Thiele, "Eine Bemerkung zu Act 1:14," *ZNW* 53 (1962): 110-11.

7765   Curt Niccum, "A Note on Acts 1:14," *NovT* 36 (1994): 196-99.

1:15-2:47

7766   Louis Painer, "Comprenez pourquoi vous comprenez! Actes 1,15-2,47," *SémBib* 23 (1981): 20-43.

1:15-26

7767   J. M. Bover, "Un fragmento de la 'Vetus Latina' en un epistolario del siglo XIII," *EE* 6 (1927): 331-34.

7768   K. H. Rengstorf, "Die Zuwahl des Matthias," *ST* 15/1 (1961): 35-67.

7769   Otto Betz, "The Dichotomized Servant and the End of Judas Iscariot," *RevQ* 5 (1964): 43-58.

7770   R. A. Martin, "Syntactical Evidence of Aramaic Sources in Acts I-XV," *NTS* 11/1 (1964): 38-59.

7771   Everett Ferguson, "Qumran and Codex D," *RevQ* 8/29 (1972): 75-80.

7772   W. Dietrich, "Das Petrusbild des Judas—Tradition in Acta i. 15-26," *NTS* 19/4 (1973): 438-52.

7773   Max Wilcox, "The Judas-Tradition in Acts 1. 15-26," *NTS* 19/4 (1973): 438-52.

7774   E. Nellessen, "Tradition und Schrift in der Perikope von der Erwahlung des Mattias," *BZ* 19/2 (1975): 205-18.

7775   L. Desautels, "La mort de Judas," *ScE* 38 (1986): 221-39.

7776   J. Rius-Camps, "Las variantes de la recensión occidental de los Hechos de los Apóstoles," *FilN* 6 (1993): 59-68.

1:15-22

7777   Roger L. Omanson, "How Does It All Fit Together? Thoughts On Translating Acts 1:15-22 and 15:19-21," *BT* 41 (1990): 416-21.

1:16-20

7778   Jacques Dupont, "La Destinée de Judas Prophétisée par David," *CBQ* 23 (1961): 41-51.

1:18

7779   C. M. Horne, "Toward a Biblical Apologetic," *GTJ* 2 (1961): 14-18.

7780   Alasdair B. Gordon, "The Fate of Judas According to Acts 1:18," *EQ* 43/2 (1971): 97-100.

7781   J. D. M. Derrett, "Miscellanea: A Pauline Pun and Judas' Punishment," *ZNW* 72 (1981): 132-33.

7782   Thomas S. Moore, " 'To the End of the Earth': The Geographic and Ethnic Universalism of Acts 1:8 in Light of Isaianic Influence on Luke," *JETS* 40 (1997): 389-99.

1:21-22

7783   J. E. Young, "That Some Should Be Apostles," *EQ* 48 (1976): 96-104.

1:23

7784   Jenny Raed-Heimerdinger, "Barnabas in Acts (1996): A Study of His Role in the Text of Codex Bezae," *JSNT* 72 (1998): 23-66.

7785   Johan Ferreira, "The Plan of God and Preaching in Acts," *EQ* 71 (1999): 209-15.

1:24

7786   Bruno Kleinbeyer, "Apg 1:24 im Kontext der Weiheliturgie: zum Aufbau des Kapitels De ordinatione in Gegenwart und Geschichte," *ZKT* 107/1-2 (1985): 31-38.

7787   J. B. Bauer, "Kardiognostes, ein unbeachteter Aspekt," *BibN* 32/1 (1988): 114-17.

1:26

7788   John F. Brug, "Acts 1:26--Lottery of Election?" *WLQ* 95 (1998): 212-14.

2-4

7789   David L. Mealand, "Community of Goods and Utopian Allusions in Acts II-IV," *JTS* 28/1 (1977): 96-99.

2

7790   W. G. MacDonald, "Glossolalia in the New Testament," *JETS* 20 (1964): 59-68.

7791   C. F. Sleeper, "Pentecost and Resurrection," *JBL* 84 (1965): 389-99.

7792   M. F. Unger, "The Significance of Pentecost," *BSac* 122/486 (1965): 169-77.

7793   S. Svéda, "Ich gieße meinen Geist auf alles Fleisch (Joel 3,1). Alttestamentliche Geistverheißung in lukanischer Deutung," *BK* 21/2 (1966): 37-41.

7794   Joseph D. Collins, "Discovering the Meaning of Pentecost," *Scr* 20 (1968): 73-79.

7795   J. R. Fowler, "Holiness, the Spirit's Infilling, and Speaking with Tongues," *Para* 2 (1968): 7-9.

7796   Howard M. Ervin, "As the Spirit Gives Utterance," *CT* 13/14 (1969): 623-26.

7797   A. S. Wood, "Social Involvement in the Apostolic Church," *EQ* 42/4 (1970): 194-212.

7798   Anne Étienne, "Étude du récit de l'événement de Pentecôte dans Actes 2," *FV* 80/1 (1981): 47-67.

7799   Donald H. Juel, "Social Dimensions of Exegesis: The Use of Psalm 16 in Acts 2," *CBQ* 43/4 (1981): 543-56.

7800   Craig A. Evans, "The Prophetic Setting of the Pentecost Sermon," *ZNW* 74/1 (1983): 148-50.

7801   Gerald T. Sheppard, "Pentecostals and the Hermeneutics of Dispensationalism: The Anatomy of an Uneasy Relationship," *Pneuma* 6/2 (1984): 5-33.

7802   F. R. Harm, "Structural Elements Related to the Gift of the Holy Spirit in Acts," *CJ* 14/1 (1988): 28-41.

7803   J. Rius-Camps, "Pentecostes Versus Babel Estudio Crítico de Hch 2," *FilN* 1 (1988): 35-61.

7804   Murray W. Dempster, "The Church's Moral Witness: A Study of Glossolalia in Luke's Theology of Acts," *Para* 23 (1989): 1-7.

7805   H. van de Sandt, "The Fate of the Gentiles in Joel and Acts 2: An Intertextual Study," *ETL* 66/1 (1990): 56-77.

7806   Justin Taylor, "The Making of Acts: A New Account," *RB* 97 (1990): 504-24.

7807 J. A. Jáuregui, "Pentecostés, fiesta de identidad cristiana," *EE* 66 (1991): 369-96.

7808 Robert B. Sloan, "Signs and Wonders: A Rhetorical Clue to the Pentecost Discourse," *EQ* 63 (1991): 225-40.

7809 G. Daan Cloete and Dirk J. Smit, "Its Name was Called Babel. . . .," *JTSA* 86 (1994): 81-87.

7810 M. J. Cartledge, "The Nature and Function of New Testament Glossolalia," *EQ* 72 (2000): 135-50.

7811 G. Chéreau, "De Babel à la Pentecôte. Histoire d'une bénédiction," *NRT* 122 (2000): 19-36.

2:1-47

7812 David L. Tiede, "Acts 2:1-47," *Int* 33/1 (1979): 62-67.

7813 P. W. van der Horst, "Hellenistic Parallels to the Acts of the Apostles," *JSNT* 25 (1985): 49-60.

7814 Mikeal C. Parsons, "Christian Origins and Narrative Openings: The Sense of a Beginning in Acts 1-5," *RevExp* 87 (1990): 403-22.

2:1-41

7815 E. J. Christiansen, "Taufe als Initiation in der Apostelgeschichte," *StTheol* 40/1 (1986): 55-79.

7816 Gerard Mussies, "Variation in the Book of Acts," *FilN* 8 (1995): 23-61.

2:1-40

7817 G. Jankowski, "Was sollen wir tun? Erwägungen über Apostelgeschichte 2,1-40," *TextK* 8 (1980): 22-44.

2:1-21

7818 Warren E. Messmann, "Acts 2:1-21," *CTQ* 46 (1982): 52-53.

2:1-15

7819 Bill Kellermann, "In the Boldness of the Spirit: Pentecost," *Soj* 14/5 (1985): 28-31.

2:1-13

7820 Ingo Broer, "Der Geist und die Gemeinde: Zur Auslegung der lukanischen Pfingstgeschichte," *BibL* 13/4 (1972): 261-83.

7821   A. P. O'Hagan, "The First Christian Pentecost," *SBFLA* 23 (1973): 50-66.

7822   H. J. Tschiedel, "Ein Pfingstwunder im Apollonhymnos *(Hymn. Hom. Ap.* 156-64 und Apg. 2, 1-13)" *ZRGG* 27/1 (1975): 22-39.

7823   S. Sahagian, "Tonalités de la parole. 4—Temps de l'Église— Actes 2:1-13," *ÉTR* 58/3 (1983): 359-67.

7824   J. A. Jáuregui, "Pentecostes, Fiesta de Identidad Cristiana," *EE* 66 (1991): 369-96.

7825   Martin Parmentier, "Das Zungenreden bei den Kirchenvätern," *Bij* 55/4 (1994): 376-98.

7826   A. J. M. Wedderburn, "Traditions and Redaction in Acts 2:1-13," *JSNT* 55 (1994): 27-54.

7827   Bob Zerhusen, "An Overlooked Judean Diglossia in Acts 2?" *BTB* 25 (1995): 118-30.

2:1-11

7828   W. D. McHardy, "The Philoxenian Text of the Acts in the Cambridge Syriac MS Add. 2053," *JTS* 45 (1944): 175.

7829   R. K. Levang, "The Content of an Utterance in Tongues," *Para* 23 (1989): 14.

2:1-8

7830   James E. Carter, "The Tongues of Pentecost," *BI* 13/3 (1987): 29-31.

2:1-4

7831   R. A. Martin, "Syntactical Evidence of Aramaic Sources in Acts I-XV," *NTS* 11/1 (1964): 38-59.

2:1

7832   R. J. Hardy, "Three Papers on the Text of Acts: 1. The Reconstruction of the Torn Leaf of Codex Bezae; 2. And When the Day of Pentecost Was Fully Come; 3. The Greek Text of Codex Laudianus," *HTR* 16 (1923): 163-86.

7833   A. Salas, "Estaban 'todos' reunidos: Precisiones críticas sobre los 'testigos' de Pentecostés," *Salm* 28/1-2 (1981): 299-314.

7834   Timothy N. Boyd, "The Feast of Pentecost," *BI* 12/3 (1986): 70-73.

7835   Michael L. Sweeney, "The identity of 'They' in Acts 2.1,"
        BT 46 (1995): 245-48.

2:3

7836   Reinhard Neudecker, " 'Das ganze Volk sah die
        Stimmen...': Haggadische Auslegung und Pfingstbericht,"
        Bib 78 (1997): 329-49.

2:4

7837   P. C. Bori, "Chiesa primitiva, Atti 2:4," *RTP* 110 (1978):
        306.

2:5-11

7838   F. Díez Fernández, "Crónica arqueológica," *EB* 42/3-4
        (1984): 421-28.

2:6-8

7839   George L. Lasebikan, "Glossolalia: Its Relationship with
        Speech Disabilities and Personality Disorders," *AfTJ* 14/2
        (1985): 111-20.

2:7-11

7840   Werner Stenger, "Beobachtungen zur sogenannten
        Völkerliste des Pfingstwunders," *K* 21/2-3 (1979): 206-14.

2:9-11

7841   J. A. Brinkman, "The Literary Background of the
        'Catalogue of the Nations'," *CBQ* 25/3 (1963): 418-27.

7842   E. Güting, "Der Geographische Horizont der sogenannten
        Volkerliste des Lukas," *ZNW* 66/3 (1975): 149-69.

7843   Manfred Gorg, "Apg 2:9-11 in außerbiblischer Sicht,"
        BibN 1 (1976): 15-18.

2:10

7844   Colin J. Hemer, "Phrygia: A Further Note," *JTS* 28/1
        (1977): 99-101.

2:14-41

7845   Daryl D. Schmidt, "The Historiography of Acts:
        Deuteronomistic or Hellenistic," *SBLSP* 24 (1985):
        417-27.

2:14-40

7846   John J. Kilgallen, "The Unity of Peter's Pentecost Speech," *BibTo* 82 (1976): 650-56.

7847   Lawrence Wills, "The Form of the Sermon in Hellenistic Judaism and Early Christianity," *HTR* 77/3-4 (1984): 277-99.

7848   Robert B. Sloan, "Signs and Wonders: a Rhetorical Clue to the Pentecost Discourse," *EQ* 63 (1991): 225-40.

2:14-21

7849   Yoshiaki Hatori, "Evangelism: The Bible's Primary Message," *ERT* 12 (1988): 5-16.

2:14

7850   C. M. Horne, "Toward a Biblical Apologetic," *GTJ* 2 (1961): 14-18.

7851   E. Rasco, "La gloire de la résurrection et ses fruits," *AsSeign* 24 (1969): 6-14.

7852   Edwina Hunter, "Preaching from Acts: Homiletical Resources for Easter," *QR* 7 (1987): 76-102.

7853   Robert C. Tannehill, "Mission in the 1990s: Reflections on the Easter Lections from Acts," *QR* 10/1 (1990): 84-97.

2:15

7854   C. M. Horne, "Toward a Biblical Apologetic," *GTJ* 2 (1961): 14-18.

2:16-21

7855   Richard J. Dillon, "The Prophecy of Christ and His Witnesses According to the Discourses of Acts," *NTS* 32/4 (1986): 544-56.

7856   Daniel J. Treier, "The Fulfillment of Joel 2:28-32: A Multiple-Lens Approach," *JETS* 40 (1997): 13-26.

2:17

7857   Franz Mußner, "In den Letzten Tagen," *BZ* 5/2 (1961): 263-65.

7858   David W. Miller, "The Uniqueness of New Testament Church Eldership," *GTJ* 6/2 (1985): 315-27.

2:18

7859 Shirley Stephens, "Women in the New Testament Church," *BI* 9/2 (1983): 62-66.

7860 Peter R. Rodgers, "Acts 2:18: καὶ προφητεύσουσιν," *JTS* 38 (1987): 95-97.

2:21

7861 Darrell L. Bock, "Jesus as Lord in Acts and in the Gospel Message," *BSac* 143 (1986): 146-54.

2:22-36

7862 John H. Hayes, "The Resurrection as Enthronement and the Earliest Church Christology," *Int* 22/3 (1968): 333-45.

7863 Burton L. Mack, "The Innocent Transgressor: Jesus in Early Christian Myth and History," *Semeia* 33 (1985): 135-65.

2:22-32

7864 Edwina Hunter, "Preaching from Acts: Homiletical Resources for Easter," *QR* 7/1 (1987): 76-102.

2:22-28

7865 E. Rasco, "La gloire de la résurrection et ses fruits," *AsSeign* 24 (1969): 6-14.

2:22-24

7866 Eric Gans, "Christian Morality and the Pauline Revelation," *Semeia* 33 (1985): 97-108.

7867 Bill Kellermann, "In the Boldness of the Spirit: Pentecost," *Soj* 14/5 (1985): 28-31.

2:22

7868 H. K. Moulton, "Acts 2:22: Jesus—A Man Approved by God?" *BT* 30 (1979): 344-45.

7869 Eduard Schweizer, "The Testimony to Jesus in the Early Christian Community," *HBT* 7/1 (1985): 77-98.

2:23

7870 Leslie C. Allen, "The Old Testament Background of (προ)ὠρισμένη in the New Testament," *NTS* 17/1 (1970-1971): 104-108.

2:25-33

7871   W. C. Kaiser, "The Promise to David in Psalm 16 and its Application in Acts 2:25-33 and 13:32-37," *JETS* 23 (1980): 219- 29.

2:28

7872   W. E. Moore, "One Baptism," *NTS* 10/4 (1964): 504-16.

2:30

7873   Joseph A. Fitzmyer, "David, 'Being Therefore a Prophet . . . '," *CBQ* 34/3 (1972): 332-39.

7874   Robert F. O'Toole, "Acts 2:30 and the Davidic Covenant of Pentecost," *JBL* 102/2 (1983): 245-58.

2:32-39

7875   Darrell L. Bock, "Jesus as Lord in Acts and in the Gospel Message," *BSac* 143 (1986): 146-54.

2:32-36

7876   Gérard Rochais, "Jésus savait-il qu'il était Dieu: réflexions critiques à propos d'un livre récent," *SR* 14/1 (1985): 85-106.

2:32

7877   Joseph Plevnik, " 'The Eleven and Those with Them' According to Luke," *CBQ* 40/2 (1978): 205-11.

2:33-36

7878   Peter Hocken, "The Meaning and Purpose of 'Baptism in the Spirit'," *Pneuma* 7/2 (1985): 125-33.

2:33

7879   Michel Gourgues, "Exalté à la droite de Dieu," *SE* 27 (1975): 303-27.

7880   Odette Mainville, "Jésus et l'Esprit dans l'œuvre de Luc: Éclairage à Partir d'Ac 2:33," *ScE* 42 (1990): 193-208.

7881   John J. Kilgallen, "A Rhetorical and Source-traditions Study of Acts 2,33," *Bib* 77 (1996): 178-96.

2:36-47

7882   Edwina Hunter, "Preaching from Acts: Homiletical Resources for Easter," *QR* 7 (1987): 76-102.

2:36-40

7883   Otto Glombitza, "Der Schluss der Petrusrede Acta
       2:36-40. Ein Beitrag zum Problem der Predigten in Acta,"
       ZNW 52/1-2 (1961): 115-18.

2:36

7884   Gerhard Voss, " 'Zum Herrn und Messias gemacht hat
       Gott diesen Jesus' (Apg 2,36). Zur Christologie der
       lukanischen Schriften," *BK* 8/4 (1967): 236-48.

7885   Luis F. Landaria, "Eucaristía y escatología," *EE* 59/229
       (1984): 211-16.

7886   R. Fowler White, "The Last Adam and His Seed: An
       Exercise in Theological Preemption," *TriJ* 6 (1985):
       60-73.

2:38-39

7887   D. Mínguez, "Estructura dinámica de la conversión.
       Reflexión sobre Hch 2,38-39," *EE* 54/210 (1979): 383-94.

2:38

7888   R. L. Roberts, "Notes on Selected Passages," *RQ* 4 (1960):
       234-58.

7889   J. C. Davis, "Another Look at the Relationship between
       Baptism and Forgiveness of Sins in Acts 2:38," *RQ* 24/2
       (1981): 80-88.

7890   Carroll D. Osburn, "The Third Person Imperative in Acts
       2:38," *RQ* 26/2 (1983): 81-84.

7891   Gerard S. Sloyan, "Jewish Ritual of the 1st Century CE
       and Christian Sacramental Behavior," *BTB* 15 (1985):
       98-103.

7892   L. T. Tanton, "The Gospel and Water Baptism: A Study of
       Acts 2:38," *GTJ* 3/1 (1990): 27-52.

7893   Luther B. McIntyre, "Baptism and Forgiveness in Acts
       2:38," *BSac* 153 (1996): 53-62.

7894   Ashby L. Camp, "Reexamining the Rule of Concord in
       Acts 2:38," *RQ* 39 (1997): 37-42.

2:41-4:35

7895   Z. I. Herman, "Un tentativo di analisi strutturale di *Atti* 2,41-4,35 secundo il metodo di A. J. Greimas," *Ant* 56/2-3 (1981): 467-74.

2:41-47

7896   Gregory E. Sterling, " 'Athletes of Virtue': An Analysis of the Summaries in Acts," *JBL* 113/4 (1994): 679-96.

2:42-47

7897   Heinrich Zimmermann, "Die Sammelberichte der Apostel-geschichte," *BZ* 5/1 (1961): 71-82.

7898   Edgar Haulotte, "La vie en communion, phase ultime de al Pentecôte, Actes 2,42-47," *FV* 80/1 (1981): 69-75.

7899   Joseph Allen, "Renewal of the Christian Community: A Challenge for the Pastoral Ministry," *SVTQ* 29/4 (1985): 305-23.

7900   A. del Agua Pérez, "El papel de la 'escuela midrásica' en la configuración del Nuevo Testamento," *EE* 60/234 (1985): 333-49.

7901   Robrecht Michaels, "The 'Model of Church' in the First Christian Community of Jerusalem: Ideal and Reality," *LouvS* 10/4 (1985): 303-23.

7902   S. J. Joubert, "Die Gesigpunt van die Verteller en die Funksie van die Jerusalemgemeente Binne die: 'Opsommings' in Handelinge," *SkrifK* 10/1 (1989): 21-35.

7903   Gary L. Carver, "Acts 2:42-47," *RevExp* 87 (1990): 475-80.

7904   M. A. Co, "The Major Summaries in Acts: Acts 2:42-47; 4:32-35; 5:12-16: Linguistic and Literary Relationships," *ETL* 68/1 (1992): 49-85.

2:42-46

7905   Bernard P. Robinson, "The Place of the Emmaus Story in Luke-Acts," *NTS* 30/4 (1984): 481-97.

2:42

7906   R. Orlett, "The Breaking of Bread in Acts," *BibTo* 1/2 (1962): 108-13.

7907   E. Glenn Hinson, "Worship in the First Century Church," *BI* 1/2 (1975): 34-41.

7908   M. Manzanera, "Koinonia en Hch 2,42. Notas sobre su interpretación y origen historico-doctrinal," *EE* 52/202 (1977): 307-29.

7909   Léopold Sabourin, "Koinonia in the New Testament," *RSB* 1/4 (1981): 109-15.

7910   J. Timothy Coyle, "The Agape—Eucharist Relationship in 1 Corinthians 11," *GTJ* 6/2 (1985): 411-24.

7911   Donald Farmer, "The Lord's Supper Until He Comes," *GTJ* 6/2 (1985): 391-401.

7912   Paul D. Fueter, "The Therapeutic Language of the Bible," *IRM* 75 (1986): 211-21.

7913   Jean M. Prieur, "Actes 2,42 et le culte réformé," *FV* 94 (1995): 63-72.

2:44-47

7914   A. C. Michell, "The Social Function of Friendship in Acts 2:44-47 and 4:32-37," *JBL* 111 (1992): 255-72.

2:46

7915   R. Orlett, "The Breaking of Bread in Acts," *BibTo* 1/2 (1962): 108-13.

7916   John T. Pless, "Implications of Recent Exegetical Studies for the Doctrine of the Lord's Supper: A Survey of the Literature," *CTQ* 48/2-3 (1984): 203-20.

7917   J. Timothy Coyle, "The Agape—Eucharist Relationship in 1 Corinthians 11," *GTJ* 6/2 (1985): 411-24.

7918   Donald Farmer, "The Lord's Supper Until He Comes," *GTJ* 6/2 (1985): 391-401.

7919   David W. Miller, "The Uniqueness of New Testament Church Eldership," *GTJ* 6/2 (1985): 315-27.

2:47

7920   R. L. Roberts, "Notes on Selected Passages," *RQ* 4 (1960): 234-58.

7921   F. P. Cheetham, "Acts 2:47: ἔχοντες χάριν πρὸς ὅλον τὸν λαόν," *ET* 74 (1963-1964): 214-15.

7922   Édouard Delebecque, "Trois simples mots, chargés d'une lumière neuve," *RT* 80/1 (1980): 75-85.

7923   G. G. Gamba, "Significato letterale e portate dottrinale dell'inciso participiale di Atti 2,47b: ἔχοντες χάριν πρὸς ὅλον τὸν λαόν," *Salm* 43/1 (1981): 45-70.

7924   T. David Anderson, "The Meaning of ἔχοντες χάριν πρὸς in Acts 2:47," *NTS* 34/4 (1988): 604-10.

3:1-4:31

7925   Mikeal C. Parsons, "Christian Origins and Narrative Openings: The Sense of a Beginning in Acts 1-5," *RevExp* 87 (1990): 403-22.

3:1-4:22

7926   Gerard Mussies, "Variation in the Book of Acts," *FilN* 8 (1995): 23-61.

3-5

7927   Louis Painer, "Pour lire les Actes des Apôtres. 2e partie: les chapitres 3-5," *SémBib* 29 (1983): 11-18.

3-4

7928   P. W. van der Horst, "Hellenistic Parallels to Acts," *JSNT* 35 (1989): 37-46.

7929   Randall C. Webber, " 'Why Were the Heathen So Arrogant?' The Socio-Rhetorical Strategy of Acts 3-4," *BTB* 22/1 (1992): 19-25.

3

7930   F. Gryglewicz, "Die Herkunft der Hymnen des Kindheits-evangeliums des Lucas," *NTS* 21/2 (1975): 265-73.

7931   Mary C. Hilkert, "Naming Grace: A Theology of Proclamation," *Worship* 60/5 (1986): 434-49.

7932   Justin Taylor, "The Making of Acts: A New Account," *RB* 97 (1990): 504-24.

7933   Donald H. Juel, "Hearing Peter's Speech in Acts 3: Meaning and Truth in Interpretation," *WW* 12 (1992): 43-50.

3:1-11

7934   Danielle Ellul, "Actes 3:1-11," *ÉTR* 64/1 (1989): 95-99.

3:1-10

7935   R. Filippini, "Atti 3,1-10: Proposta di analisi del racconto," *RBib* 28/3 (1980): 305-17.

7936   Dennis Hamm, "Acts 3:1-10: The Healing of the Temple Beggar as Lucan Theology," *Bib* 67/3 (1986): 305-19.

7937   Paul W. Walaskay, "Acts 3:1-10," *Int* 42/2 (1988): 171-75.

3:1

7938   A. del Agua Pérez, "La sinagoga: origenes, ciclos de lectura y oración: estado de la cuestión," *EB* NS 41/3-4 (1983): 341-66.

3:2

7939   Christopher J. Cowton, "The Alms Trade: A Note on Identifying the Beautiful Gate of Acts 3.2," *NTS* 42 (1996): 475-76.

3:12-26

7940   C. H. H. Scobie, "The Use of Source Material in the Speeches of Acts III and VII," *NTS* 25/4 (1978-1979): 399-421.

7941   Dennis Hamm, "Acts 3:12-26: Peter's Speech and the Healing of the Man Born Lame," *PRS* 11/3 (1984): 199-217.

7942   Lawrence Wills, "The Form of the Sermon in Hellenistic Judaism and Early Christianity," *HTR* 77/3-4 (1984): 277-99.

3:12-23

7943   E. S. Buchanan, "Two Pages from the Fleury Palimpsest with Some Newly Discovered Readings," *JTS* 7 (1905-1906): 454-55.

3:12

7944   H. J. Klauck, "With Paul in Paphos and Lystra: Magic and Paganism in the Acts of the Apostles," *Neo* 28 (1994): 93-108.

3:13-15

7945   E. Rasco, "La gloire de la résurrection et ses fruits," *AsSeign* 24 (1969): 6-14.

7946   P. Smulders, "Some Riddles in the Apostles Creed II. Creeds and Rules of Faith," *Bij* 32/4 (1971): 350-66.

3:14

7947   George D. Kilpatrick, "Three Problems of New Testament Text," *NovT* 21/4 (1979): 289-92.

7948   Billy E. Simmons, "Christ the Holy One," *BI* 14/2 (1989): 23.

7949   Billy E. Simmons, "Christ the Just," *BI* 14/2 (1989): 39.

3:15

7950   Joseph Plevnik, " 'The Eleven and Those with Them' According to Luke," *CBQ* 40/2 (1978): 205-11.

7951   I. de la Potterie, "Gesu il capo che conduce alla vita," *ParSpirV* 5 (1982): 107-26.

7952   Billy E. Simmons, "Christ the Prince of Life," *BI* 14/2 (1989): 80.

3:17-19

7953   E. Rasco, "La gloire de la résurrection et ses fruits," *AsSeign* 24 (1969): 6-14.

3:17

7954   Eldon J. Epp, "The 'Ignorance Motif' in Acts and Anti-Judaic Tendencies in Codex Bezae," *HTR* 55 (1962): 51-62.

3:18

7955   Paul R. Berger, "Kollyrium für die blinden Augen, Apk 3:18," *NovT* 27/2 (1985): 174-95.

3:19-21

7956   Gerhard Lohfink, "Christologie und Geschichtsbild in Apg 3:19-21," *BZ* 13/2 (1969): 223-41.

7957   Klaus Haacker, "Das Bekenntnis des Paulus zur Hoffnung Israels Nach der Apostelgeschichte des Lukas," *NTS* 31 (1985): 437-51.

3:19

7958   Paul Ternant, "Repentez-vous et convertissez-vous," *AsSeign* 21 (1963): 50-79.

3:20

> 7959 Richard J. Dillon, "The Prophecy of Christ and His Witnesses according to the Discourses of Acts," *NTS* 32 (1986): 544-56.

3:21

> 7960 Mark W. Karlberg, "Legitimate Discontinuities between the Testaments," *JETS* 28 (1985): 9-20.

> 7961 Julián Carrón Pérez, "El significado de ἀποκαταστάσεως en Hch 3,21," *EB* 50 (1992): 375-94.

3:22-26

> 7962 Jacques Schlosser, "Moïse, Serviteur du Kérygme Apostolique d'après Ac 3:22-26," *RevSR* 61 (1987): 17-31.

3:22-23

> 7963 Jan de Waard, "Quotation from Deuteronomy in Acts 3:22-23 and the Palestinian Text: Additional Arguments," *Bib* 52/4 (1971): 537-40.

3:23

> 7964 C. M. Martini, "L'esclusione dalla comunità del popolo di Dio e il nuovo Israele secondo Atti 3,23," *Bib* 50/1 (1969): 1-14.

3:25

> 7965 T. E. Brawley, "For Blessing All Families of the Earth: Covenant Traditions in Luke-Acts," *CThM* 22/1 (1995): 18-26.

4-6

> 7966 W.-D. Hauschild, "Die Confessio Augustana und die altkirchliche Tradition," *KD* 26/3 (1980): 142-63.

4

> 7967 A. S. Wood, "Social Involvement in the Apostolic Church," *EQ* 42/4 (1970): 194-212.

> 7968 F. Gerald Downing, "Common Ground with Paganism in Luke and Josephus," *NTS* 28/4 (1982): 546-59.

> 7969 Kevin N. Giles, "Present-Future Eschatology in the Book of Acts (II)," *RTR* 41/1 (1982): 11-18.

4:1-31

7970   Marco Adinolfi, " 'Obbedire a Dio piuttosto che algi uomni.' La comunità cristiana e il sinedrio in Atti 4,1-31; 5,17-42," *RBib* 27/1-2 (1979): 69-93.

4:1-2

7971   Robert F. O'Toole, "Christ's Resurrection in Acts 13:13-52," *Bib* 60/3 (1979): 361-72.

4:4

7972   J. A. Jáuregui, "Israel y la iglesia en la teologia de Lucas," *EE* 61 (1986): 129-149.

4:5-20

7973   I. W. Foulkes, "Two Semantic Problems in the Translation of Acts 4:5-20," *BT* 29/1 (1978): 121-25.

4:5-12

7974   R. A. Martin, "Syntactical Evidence of Aramaic Sources in Acts I-XV," *NTS* 11/1 (1964): 38-59.

4:5

7975   Werner Bieder, "Das Volk Gottes in Erwartung von Licht und Lobpreis," *TZ* 40/2 (1984): 137-48.

4:6

7976   E. P. Sanders, "Judaism and the Grand "Christian" Abstractions: Love, Mercy, and Grace," *Int* 39 (1985): 357-372.

4:8-12

7977   Michel Coune, "Sauvés au nom de Jesus," *AsSeign* 12 (1964): 14-27.

7978   I. Fransen, "Par le nom de Jésus Christ le Nazaréen. Acts 4,8-12," *BVC* 59 (1964): 38-44.

7979   C. K. Barrett, "Salvation Proclaimed. XII. ACTS 4:8-12," *ET* 94/3 (1982): 68-71.

4:10

7980   L. Schenke, "Die Kontrast-Formel Apg 4:10b," *BZ* 26/1 (1982): 1-20.

4:11

7981   Wayne Grudem, "Does κεφαλή ('Head') Mean 'Source' or 'Authority Over' in Greek Literature: A Survey of 2,336 Examples," *TriJ* 6 (1985): 38-59.

4:12

7982   A. R. Gualtieri, "Confessional Theology in the Context of the History of Religions," *SR* 1/4 (1971): 347-60.

7983   Troy Organ, "A Cosmological Christology," *CC* 88/44 (1971): 1293-95.

7984   Magne Saebo, " 'Kein Anderer Name'," *KD* 22/3 (1976): 181-90.

7985   R. Y. K. Fung, "Charismatic Versus Organized Ministry? An Examination of an Alleged Antithesis," *EQ* 52/4 (1980): 195-214.

7986   Tokunboh Adeyemo, "The Salvation Debate and Evangelical Response: Pt. 2," *EAJT* 2/2 (1983): 4-19.

7987   Allan Boesak, "In the Name of Jesus: Acts 4:12," *JTSA* 52 (1985): 49-55.

7988   Malcolm J. McVeigh, "The Fate of Those Who've Never Heard: It Depends," *EMQ* 21/4 (1985): 370-379.

7989   Jaroslav J. Pelikan, "The Man Who Belongs to the World," *CC* 102 (1985): 827-31.

7990   Wolfgang Bienert, "Jesus Christus: das Ursakrament Gottes," *Cath* 38/4 (1984): 340-351.

7991   Hugo H. Culpepper, "Acts 4:12: Religious Pluralism, Missions Theology," *RevExp* 89 (1992): 85-87.

4:13

7992   Pieter de Villiers, "The Medium is the Message: Luke and the Language of the New Testament against a Greco-Roman Background," *Neo* 24 (1990): 247-56.

4:16-18

7993   Odette Mainville, "Le péché contre l'Esprit annoncé en Lc 12.10, commis en Ac 4.16-18: Une illustration de l'unité de Luc et Actes," *NTS* 45 (1999): 38-50.

4:17

7994   R. Y. K. Fung, "Charismatic Versus Organized Ministry? An Examination of an Alleged Antithesis," *EQ* 52/4 (1980): 195-214.

4:20

7995   E. D. Freed, "Samaritan Influence in the Gospel of John," *CBQ* 30/4 (1968): 580-87.

4:23-31

7996   R. A. Martin, "Syntactical Evidence of Aramaic Sources in Acts I-XV," *NTS* 11/1 (1964): 38-59.

7997   Raymond Schwager, "Christ's Death and the Prophetic Critique of Sacrifice," trans. P. Riordan *Semeia* 33 (1985): 109-23.

7998   Beverly R. Gaventa, "To Speak Thy Word with All Boldness Acts 4:23-31," *FM* 3/2 (1986): 76-82.

4:24-31

7999   Urban C. Von Wahlde, "The Theological Assessment of the First Christian Persecution: The Apostles' Prayer and Its Consequences in Acts 4,24-31," *Bib* 76 (1995): 523-31.

4:25-27

8000   George D. Kilpatrick, "*Laoi* at Luke ii. 31 and Acts iv. 25, 27," *JTS* 16 (1965): 127.

8001   Marion L. Soards, "Tradition, Composition, and Theology in Luke's Account of Jesus before Herod Antipas," *Bib* 66 (1985): 344-364.

4:25

8002   George D. Kilpatrick, "*Laoi* at Luke ii.31 and Acts iv.25, 27," *JTS* 16 (1965): 127.

8003   Leslie C. Allen, "The Old Testament Background of (προ)ὡρισμένῃ in the New Testament," *NTS* 17/1 (1970-1971): 104-108.

8004   L. V. Le Roux, "Style and the Text of Acts 4:25(a)," *Neo* 26 (1991): 29-32.

8005   Urban C. Von Wahlde, "The Problems of Acts 4:25a: A New Proposal," *ZNW* 86 (1995): 265-67.

4:27

8006   George D. Kilpatrick, "*Laoi* at Luke ii.31 and Acts iv.25, 27," *JTS* 16 (1965): 127.

4:30

8007   James L. Travis, "Temple Personnel," *BI* 13/3 (1987): 36-39.

4:31-5:11

8008   A. Mettayer, "Ambiguïté et terrorisms du sacré: Analyse d'un texte des Actes des Apôtres," *SR* 714 (1978): 415-24.

4:32-5:42

8009   Mikeal C. Parsons, "Christian Origins and Narrative Openings: The Sense of a Beginning in Acts 1-5," *RevExp* 87 (1990): 403-22.

4:32-5:11

8010   A.-E. Combet-Galland, "Actes 4:32-5:11," *ÉTR* 52/4 (1977): 548-53.

4:32-37

8011   John Weborg, "Giving the Soul Wings," *ChrM* 16/1 (1985): 28.

8012   A. C. Michell, "The Social Function of Friendship in Acts 2:44-47 and 4:32-37," *JBL* 111 (1992): 255-72.

4:32-35

8013   A. del Agua Pérez, "El papel de la 'escuela midrásica' en la configuración del Nuevo Testamento," *EE* 60/234 (1985): 333-49.

8014   Richard Fraser, "Office of Deacon," *Pres* 11/1 (1985): 13-19.

8015   Robrecht Michaels, "The 'Model of Church' in the First Christian Community of Jerusalem: Ideal and Reality," *LouvS* 10/4 (1985): 303-23.

8016   Dorothee Sölle, "Church: They Had Everything In Common," *TT* 42 (1985): 215-19.

8017   Mark K. Taylor, "The Community of the Resurrected Christ," *PSB* 6/3 (1985): 228-30.

8018   M. A. Co, "The Major Summaries in Acts: Acts 2:42-47; 4:32-35; 5:12-16: Linguistic and Literary Relationships," *ETL* 68/1 (1992): 49-85.

8019   Gregory E. Sterling, " 'Athletes of Virtue': An Analysis of the Summaries in Acts," *JBL* 113/4 (1994): 679-96.

4:32

8020   Josef Sudbrack, "Die Schar der Gläubigen war ein Herz und eine Seele," *GeistL* 38/3 (1965): 161-68.

8021   Birger Gerhardsson, "Einige Bemerkungen zu Apg 4,32," *StTheol* 24/2 (1970): 142-49

8022   Birger Gerhardsson, "Några anmärkningar till Apg 4:32," *SEÅ* 35 (1971): 96-103.

8023   David L. Mealand, "Community of Goods at Qumran," *TZ* 31 (1975): 129-39.

4:33

8024   Joseph Plevnik, " 'The Eleven and Those with Them' According to Luke," *CBQ* 40/2 (1978): 205-11.

4:35

8025   Simon Légasse, "L' 'Homme Fort' de Luc XI 21-22," *NovT* 5 (1962): 5-9.

4:36

8026   S. Brock, "Barnabas: υἱὸς παρακλήσεως," *JTS* 25 (1974): 93-98.

8027   Richard T. France, "Barnabas—Son of Encouragement," *ERT* 4/1 (1980): 91-101.

5

8028   J. M. Boice, "The Reliability of the Writings of Luke and Paul," *CT* 12/4 (1967): 176-78.

5:1-11

8029   Alfons Weiser, "Das Gottesurteil über Hananias und Saphira; Apg 5,1-11," *TGl* 69/2 (1979): 148-58.

8030   Brian J. Capper, " 'In der Hand des Ananias . . . ' Erwägungen zu IQS VI,20 und der urchristlichen Gütergemeinschaft," *RevQ* 12/2 (1986): 223-36.

8031   B. Prete, "Anania e Saffira (At 5:1-11): Componenti Letterarie e Dottrinali," *RBib* 36 (1989): 463-486.

8032   Daniel Marguerat, "Terreur dans l'Église: le drame d'Ananias et Saphira," *FV* 91 (1992): 77-88.

8033   Daniel Marguerat, "La mort d'Ananias et Saphire dans la stratégie narrative de Luc," *NTS* 39/2 (1993): 209-26.

8034   Daniel Marguerat, "Ananias et Saphira (Actes 5,1-11)," *LV* 42/215 (1993): 51-63.

5:1

8035   J. D. M. Derrett, "Ananias, Sapphira, and the Right of Property," *DR* 89/296 (1971): 225-32.

5:4

8036   Brian J. Capper, "The Interpretation of Acts 5:4," *JSNT* 19 (1983): 117-31.

8037   Robert F. O'Toole, " 'You Did Not Lie to Us (Human Beings) but to God' (Acts 5,4c)," *Bib* 76 (1995): 182-209.

5:12-25

8038   A. del Agua Pérez, "El papel de la 'escuela midrásica' en la configuración del Nuevo Testamento," *EE* 60/234 (1985): 333-49.

5:12-17

8039   Robrecht Michaels, "The 'Model of Church' in the First Christian Community of Jerusalem: Ideal and Reality," *LouvS* 10/4 (1985): 303-23.

5:12-16

8040   Robrecht Michaels, "The 'Model of Church' in the First Christian Community of Jerusalem: Ideal and Reality," *LouvS* 10/4 (1985): 303-23.

8041   M. A. Co, "The Major Summaries in Acts: Acts 2:42-47; 4:32-35; 5:12-16: Linguistic and Literary Relationships," *ETL* 68/1 (1992): 49-85.

8042   Gregory E. Sterling, " 'Athletes of Virtue': An Analysis of the Summaries in Acts," *JBL* 113/4 (1994): 679-96.

5:12

8043   R. Y. K. Fung, "Charismatic Versus Organized Ministry? An Examination of an Alleged Antithesis," *EQ* 52/4 (1980): 195-214.

8044   René Latourelle, "Originalité et fonctions des miracles de Jésus," *Greg* 66/4 (1985): 641-653.

5:13-14

8045   Daniel R. Schwartz, "Non-Joining Sympathizers," *Bib* 64/4 (1983): 550-55.

5:14

8046   J. A. Jáuregui, "Israel y la iglesia en la teologia de Lucas," *EE* 61 (1986): 129-49.

5:15

8047   Werner Bieder, "Der Petrusschatten, Apg 5:15," *TZ* 16 (1960): 407-409.

8048   P. W. van der Horst, "Peter's Shadow: The Religio-Historical Background of Acts V.15," *NTS* 23/2 (1977): 204-11.

5:17-42

8049   R. A. Martin, "Syntactical Evidence of Aramaic Sources in Acts I-XV," *NTS* 11/1 (1964): 38-59.

8050   Marco Adinolfi, " 'Obbedire a Dio piuttosto che algi uomni.' La comunità cristiana e il sinedrio in Atti 4,1-31; 5,17-42," *RBib* 27/1-2 (1979): 69-93.

5:17

8051   Morton Smith, "The Report about Peter in 1 Clement V. 4," *NTS* 7 (1960): 86-88.

8052   E. P. Sanders, "Judaism and the Grand "Christian" Abstractions: Love, Mercy, and Grace," *Int* 39 (1985): 357-372.

5:21-29

8053   J. A. Jáuregui, "Israel y la iglesia en la teologia de Lucas," *EE* 61 (1986): 129-149.

5:27-32

    8054   E. Rasco, "La gloire de la résurrection et ses fruits," *AsSeign* 24 (1969): 6-14.

5:30

    8055   Joseph A. Fitzmyer, "Crucifixion in Ancient Palestine, Qumran Literature, and the New Testament," *CBQ* 40/4 (1978): 493-513.

5:31

    8056   Michel Gourgues, "Exalté à la droite de Dieu," *SE* 27 (1975): 303-27.

    8057   Michael R. Austin, "Salvation and the Divinity of Jesus," *ET* 96 (1985): 271-75.

    8058   Gérard Rochais, "Jésus savait-il qu'il était Dieu: réflexions critiques à propos d'un livre récent," *SR* 14/1 (1985): 85-106.

5:32

    8059   Gerhard Lohfink, " 'Wir sind Zeugen dieser Ereignisse' (Apg 5,32). Die Einheit der neutestamentlichen Botschaft von Erhöhung und Himmelfahrt Jesu," *BK* 20/2 (1965): 49-52.

5:34

    8060   Klaus Haacker, "Verwendung und Vermeidung des Apostelbegriffs im lukanischen Werk," *NovT* 30 (1988): 9-38.

    8061   Fred A. Grissom, "Gamaliel," *BI* 14/2 (1989): 29-31.

5:35-16:5

    8062   G. Betori, "La strutturazione del libro degli Atti: una proposta," *RBib* 42 (1994): 3-34.

5:35-39

    8063   J. A. Trumbower, "The Historical Jesus and the Speech of Gamaliel," *NTS* 39/4 (1993): 500-17.

5:38-39

    8064   William J. Lyons, "The Words of Gamaliel (Acts 5:38-39) and the Irony of Indeterminacy," *JSNT* 68 (1997): 23-49.

5:40-41

    8065   E. Rasco, "La gloire de la résurrection et ses fruits," *AsSeign* 24 (1969): 6-14.

6-12

    8066   Karlmann Beyschlag, "Zur Simon-Magus-Frage," *ZTK* 78 (1971): 395-426.

    8067   John B. Polhill, "The Hellenist Breakthrough: Acts 6-12," *RevExp* 71/4 (1974): 475-86.

6:1-11:26

    8068   U. Borse, "Der Rahmentext im Umkreis der Stephanus-geschichte," *BibL* 14/3 (1973): 187-204.

6-9

    8069   Louis Painer, "Pour lire les Actes des Apôtres. 3e série: Ac. 6-9," *SémBib* 30 (1983): 34-42.

6-8

    8070   Thomas L. Brodie, "The Departure for Jerusalem as a Rhetorical Imitation of Elijah's Departure for the Jordan," *Bib* 70/1 (1989): 96-109.

    8071   G. Jankowski, "Stephanos: Eine Auslegung von Apostel-geschichte 6-8,3," *TextK* 15 (1992): 2-38.

6:1-8:3

    8072   David S. Dockery, "Acts 6-12: The Christian Mission beyond Jerusalem," *RevExp* 87 (1990): 423-37.

6-7

    8073   Edvin Larsson, "Temple-Criticism and the Jewish Heritage: Some Reflections on Acts 6-7," *NTS* 39/3 (1993): 379-95.

    8074   C. Amos, "Renewed in the Likeness of Christ: Stephen the Servant Martyr," *IBS* 16 (1994): 31-37.

6

    8075   Otto Glombitza, "Zur Charakterisiering des Stephanus in Act 6 und 7," *ZNW* 53 (1962): 238-44.

    8076   A. S. Wood, "Social Involvement in the Apostolic Church," *EQ* 42/4 (1970): 194-212.

8077   Kevin N. Giles, "Is Luke an Exponent of 'Early Protestantism'? Church Order in the Lukan Writings. Part II," *EQ* 55/1 (1983): 3-20.

8078   Armin J. Panning, "Acts 6: The 'Ministry' of the Seven," *WLQ* 93 (1996): 11-17.

6:1-15

8079   Martin Hengel, "Zwischen Jesus und Paulus. Die 'Hellenisten,' die 'Sieben' und Stephanus," *ZTK* 72/2 (1975): 151-206.

6:1-8

8080   Edvin Larsson, "Die Hellenisten und die Urgemeinde," *NTS* 33/2 (1987): 205-225.

6:1-7

8081   Barbara Hall, "La communauté chrétienne dans le livre des Actes: Actes 6:1-7 et 10:1-11:18," *FV* Suppl (1971): 146-56.

8082   B. Domagalski, "Waren die 'sieben' Diakone?" *BZ* 26/1 (1982): 21-33.

8083   Joseph B. Tyson, "Acts 6:1-7 and Dietary Regulations in Early Christianity," *PRS* 10/2 (1982): 145-61.

6:1-6

8084   J. D. McCaughey, "The Intention of the Author: Some Questions About the Exegesis of Acts 6:1-6," *ABR* 7 (1959): 27-36.

8085   J. T. Lienhard, "Acts 6:1-6: A Redactional View," *CBQ* 37/2 (1975): 228-36.

8086   Richard Fraser, "Office of Deacon," *Pres* 11/1 (1985): 13-19.

6:1-4

8087   Oscar Cullmann, "Dissensions within the Early Church," *USQR* 22/2 (1967): 83-92.

8088   LaVonne Neff, "Three Women Out of Four: How the Church Can Meet the Needs of Its Widows," *CT* 29/16 (1985): 30-33.

8089   C. J. Mork, "Women's Ordination and the Leadership of the Church," *WW* 7/4 (1987): 374-79.

6:1

8090   Everett Ferguson, "The Hellenists in the Book of Acts," *RQ* 12/4 (1969): 159-80.

8091   Rudolf Pesch, " 'Hellenisten' und 'Hebräer.' Zu Apg 9:29 und 6:1," *BZ* NS 23/1 (1979): 87-92.

8092   Craig A. Evans, "The Citation of Isaiah 60:17 in 1 Clement," *VC* 36/2 (1982): 105-107.

8093   Nikolaus Walter, "Apostelgeschichte 6.1 und die Anfänge der Urgemeinde in Jerusalem," *NTS* 29/3 (1983): 370-93.

6:2

8094   E. S. Buchanan, "Some Noteworthy Readings of the Fleury Palimpsest," *JTS* 9 (1907-1908): 98-100.

6:4

8095   André Feuillet, " 'Témoins Oculaires et Serviteurs de la Parole'," *NovT* 15/4 (1973): 241-59.

6:5

8096   Norbert Brox, "Nikolaos und Nikolaiten," *VC* 19/1 (1965): 23-30.

8097   James E. Carter, "The Chosen," *BI* 14/2 (1989): 50-52.

6:6

8098   R. Y. K. Fung, "Charismatic Versus Organized Ministry? An Examination of an Alleged Antithesis," *EQ* 52/4 (1980): 195-214.

6:7

8099   M. H. Franzmann, "The Word of the Lord Grew," *CTM* 30 (1959): 563-81.

8100   J. Kodell, " 'The Word of God Grew.' The Ecclesial Tendency of *Logos* in Acts 6:7; 12:24; 19:20," *Bib* 55/4 (1974): 505-19.

8101   M. H. Grumm, "Another Look at Acts," *ET* 96/11 (1985): 333-37.

8102   J. A. Jáuregui, "Israel y la iglesia en la teologia de Lucas," *EE* 61 (1986): 129-49.

6:8-8:2

8103   M.-É. Boismard, "Le martyre d'Étienne. Actes 6:8-8:2,"
        RechSR 69/2 (1981): 181-94.

8104   Peter Doble, "The Son of Man Saying in Stephen's
        Witnessing: Acts 6:8-8:2," *NTS* 31/1 (1985): 68-84.

6:8-15

8105   Karin Finsterbusch, "Christologie als Blasphemie: Das
        Hauptthema der Stephanusperikope in lukanischer
        Perspektive," *BibN* 92 (1998): 38-54.

6:8

8106   Charles H. Giblin, "A Prophetic Vision of History and
        Things," *BibTo* 63 (1972): 994-1001.

6:9

8107   Jeff Cranford, "The Synagogue of the Libertines," *BI* 13/3
        (1987): 40-41.

6:11-14

8108   Edvin Larsson, "Temple-Criticism and the Jewish
        Heritage: Some Reflections on Acts 6-7," *NTS* 39/3
        (1993): 379-95.

6:13-14

8109   F. D. Weinert, "Luke, Stephen, and the Temple in
        Luke-Acts," *BTB* 17 (1987): 88-90.

6:13

8110   Gerald L. Borchert, "Acts 6:13," *RevExp* 88 (1991): 73-78.

6:14

8111   E. D. Freed, "Samaritan Influence in the Gospel of John,"
        CBQ 30/4 (1968): 580-87.

8112   Sasagu Arai, "Zum 'Tempelwort' Jesu in
        Apostelgeschichte 6:14," *NTS* 34/3 (1988): 397-410.

8113   D. L. Balch, " 'You Teach All the Jews . . . to Forsake
        Moses, Telling Them not to . . . Observe the Customs',"
        SBLSP 32 (1993): 369-83.

7-8

8114   R. J. Coggins, "The Samaritans and Acts," *NTS* 28/3
        (1981-1982): 423-34.

7:2-8:3

8115   David P. Moessner, " 'The Christ Must Suffer': New Light on the Jesus-Peter, Stephen, Paul Parallels in Luke-Acts," *NovT* 28/3 (1986): 220-56.

7

8116   Otto Glombitza, "Zur Charakterisierung des Stephanus in Act 6 und 7," *ZNW* 53 (1962): 238-44.

8117   Rudolf Pesch, "Der Christ als Nachahmer Christi: Der Tod des Stephanus (Apg 7) im Vergleich mit dem Tode Christi," *BK* 24/1 (1969): 10-11.

8118   W. Harold Mare, "Acts 7: Jewish or Samaritan in Character?" *WTJ* 34/1 (1971): 1-21.

8119   Cyril J. Barber, "Moses: A Study of Hebrews 11:23-29a," *GTJ* 14/2 (1973): 14-28.

8120   G. Stemberger, "Die Stephanusrede (Apg 7) und die jüdische Tradition," *SNTU-A* 1 (1976): 154-74.

8121   Rex A. Koivisto, "Stephen's Speech: A Case Study in Rhetoric and Biblical Inerrancy," *JETS* 20/4 (1977): 353-64.

8122   Earl Richard, "Acts 7: An Investigation of the Samaritan Evidence," *CBQ* 39/2 (1977): 190-208.

8123   Robert W. Thurston, "Midrash and 'Magnet' Words in the New Testament," *EQ* 51/1 (1979): 22-39.

8124   Klaus Seybold, "Die Geschichte des 29: Psalms und ihre Theologische Bedeutung," *TZ* 36/4 (1980): 208-19.

8125   Terence L. Donaldson, "Moses Typology and the Sectarian Nature of Early Christian Anti-Judaism: A Study in Acts 7," *JSNT* 12 (1981): 27-52.

8126   Jacques Dupont, "La Structure Oratoire du Discours d'Étienne," *Bib* 66/2 (1985): 153-67.

8127   Jean Lambert, "L'Echappée Belle: Rubriques en Marge du Discours d'Étienne, Actes 7," *FV* 84/6 (1985): 25-32.

8128   D. A. DeSilva, "The Stoning of Stephen: Purging and Consolidating an Endangered Institution," *SBT* 17/2 (1989): 165-85.

7:1-53

8129 R. A. Martin, "Syntactical Evidence of Aramaic Sources in Acts I-XV," *NTS* 11/1 (1964): 38-59.

8130 Martin H. Scharlemann, "Stephen's Speech: A Lucan Creation?" *CJ* 4/2 (1978): 52-57.

8131 J. A. Jáuregui, "Israel y la iglesia en la teologia de Lucas," *EE* 61 (1986): 129-49.

7:2-53

8132 F. J. Foakes-Jackson, "Stephen's Speech in Acts," *JBL* 49 (1930): 283-86.

8133 John J. Kilgallen, "The Stephen Speech: A Literary and Redactional Study of Acts 7:2-53," *CBQ* 40 (1978): 639.

8134 Jacques Dupont, "La Structure Oratoire du Discours d'Étienne," *Bib* 66/2 (1985): 153-67.

8135 Rex A. Koivisto, "Stephen's Speech: a Theology of Errors?" *GTJ* 8 (1987): 101-14.

8136 S. Szymik, "The Literary Structure of Saint Stephen's Speech," *RoczTK* 35 (1988): 101-16.

8137 John J. Kilgallen, "The Function of Stephen's Speech," *Bib* 70/2 (1989): 173-93.

7:2-17

8138 Eckart Reinmuth, "Beobachtungen zur Rezeption der Genesis bei Pseudo-Philo (LAB 1-8) und Lukas (Apg 7:2-17)," *NTS* 43 (1997): 552-69.

7:2

8139 T. E. Brawley, "For Blessing All Families of the Earth: Covenant Traditions in Luke-Acts," *CThM* 22/1 (1995): 18-26.

7:3

8140 Wayne Litke, "Acts 7.3 and Samaritan Chronology," *NTS* 42 (1996): 156-60.

7:6

8141 Jack R. Riggs, "The Length of Israel's Sojourn in Egypt," *GTJ* 12/1 (1971): 18-35.

8142   James R. Battenfield, "A Consideration of the Identity of the Pharaoh of Genesis 47," *JETS* 15 (1972): 77-85.

7:8

8143   T. E. Brawley, "For Blessing All Families of the Earth: Covenant Traditions in Luke-Acts," *CThM* 22/1 (1995): 18-26.

7:9-16

8144   Earl Richard, "The Polemical Character of the Joseph Episode in Acts 7," *JBL* 98/2 (1979): 255-67.

7:14-18

8145   Stephen Gaselee, "Two Fayoumic Fragments of the Acts," *JTS* 11 (1909-1910): 514-17.

7:17-43

8146   J. C. Atienza, "Hechos 7,17-43 y las corrientes cristológicas dentro de la primitiva comunidad cristiana," *EB* 33/1 (1974): 31-62.

8147   M. Balagué, "Hechos 7,17-43 y las corrientes cristológicas dentro de la primitiva communidad cristiana," *EB* 33 (1974): 33-67.

7:32

8148   T. E. Brawley, "For Blessing All Families of the Earth: Covenant Traditions in Luke-Acts," *CThM* 22/1 (1995): 18-26.

7:33

8149   I. Howard Marshall, "New Wine in Old Wineskins: V. The Biblical Use of the Word 'Ekklesia'," *ET* 84/12 (1973): 359-64.

7:35-37

8150   E. J. Via, "An Interpretation of Acts 7:35-37 from the Perspective of Major Themes in Luke-Acts," *PRS* 6/3 (1979): 190-207.

7:38

8151   Albert Vanhoye, "A Mediator of Angels in Gal 3:19-20," *Bib* 59/3 (1978): 403-11.

7:42

8152 H. van de Sandt, "Why Is Amos 5,25-27 Quoted in Acts 7,42f?" *ZNW* 82 (1991): 67-87.

7:43

8153 Jerome Murphy-O'Connor, "The Damascus Document Revisited," *RB* 92 (1985): 223-46.

8154 R. Borger, "Amos 5,26, Apostelgeschichte 7,43 und urpu II, 180," *ZAW* 100/1 (1988): 70-81.

7:44-50

8155 Edvin Larsson, "Temple-Criticism and the Jewish Heritage: Some Reflections on Acts 6-7," *NTS* 39/3 (1993): 379-95.

7:46-50

8156 Dennis D. Sylva, "The Meaning and Function of Acts 7:46-50," *JBL* 106/2 (1987): 261-75.

7:48

8157 R. Le Déaut, "Actes 7,48 et Matthieu 17,4 (par.) à la lumière du targum palestinien," *RechSR* 52/1 (1964): 85-90.

8158 A. G. Van Aarde, " 'The Most High God Does Live in Houses, but not Houses Built by Men': The Relativity of the Metaphor 'Temple' in Luke-Acts," *Neo* 26 (1991): 51-64.

7:54-8:3

8159 Martin Hengel, "Zwischen Jesus und Paulus. Die 'Hellenisten,' die 'Sieben' und Stephanus," *ZTK* 72/2 (1975): 151-206.

7:54-8:1

8160 M. J. Kingston, "God Guarantees the Church," *ET* 97/10 (1986): 305-306.

7:55-60

8161 Edwina Hunter, "Preaching from Acts: Homiletical Resources for Easter," *QR* 7 (1987): 76-102.

8162 Robert C. Tannehill, "Mission in the 1990s: Reflections on the Easter Lections from Acts," *QR* 10/1 (1990): 84-97.

7:55-56

8163   J. D. M. Derrett, "The Son of Man Standing," *BibO* 30 (1988): 71-84.

8164   Simon Légasse, "Encore Hestota en Actes 7:55-56," *FilN* 3 (1990): 63-66.

7:55

8165   Rudolf Pesch, "Die Vision des Stephanus Apg 7:55f. im Rahmen der Apostelgeschichte," *BibL* 6/2 (1965): 92-107.

8166   Heinrich Baarlink, "Friede im Himmel. Die lukanische Redaktion von Lk 19,38 und Ihre Deutung," *ZNW* 76/3 (1985): 170-86.

7:56

8167   George D. Kilpatrick, "Acts 7:56: Son of Man?" *TZ* 21/3 (1965): 209.

8168   George D. Kilpatrick, "Again Acts 7:56: Son of Man?" *TZ* 34/4 (1978): 232.

7:58-8:1

8169   Peter van Minnen, "Paul the Roman Citizen," *JSNT* 56 (1994): 43-52.

7:58

8170   Thomas L. Brodie, "The Accusing and Stoning of Naboth (1 Kgs 2:18-13) as One Component of the Stephen Text," *CBQ* 45/3 (1983): 417-32.

8171   Paula Fredriksen, "Paul and Augustine: Conversion Narratives, Orthodox Traditions, and the Retrospective Self," *JTS* 37/1 (1986): 3-34.

8:1-11:18

8172   Robert F. O'Toole, "Philip and the Ethiopian Eunuch," *JSNT* 17 (1983): 25-34.

8

8173   Joseph Hanimann, " 'Nous Avons été Abreuves d'un Seul Esprit': Note sur 1 Co 12, 13b," *NRT* 94/4 (1972): 400-405.

8174   C. H. H. Scobie, "The Origins and Development of Samaritan Christianity," *NTS* 19/4 (1973): 390-414.

8175   B. E. Thiering, "Qumran Initiation and New Testament
       Baptism," *NTS* 27/5 (1981): 615-31.

8176   Roland Bergmeier, "Die Gestalt des Simon Magus in Apg
       8 und in der Simonianischen Gnosis—Aporien einer
       Gesamtdeutung," *ZNW* 77/3 (1986): 267-75.

8177   Gerd Lüdemann, "The Acts of the Apostles and the
       Beginnings of Simonian Gnosis," *NTS* 33/3 (1987):
       420-26.

8178   F. R. Harm, "Structural Elements Related to the Gift of the
       Holy Spirit in Acts," *CJ* 14/1 (1988): 28-41.

8179   Mikeal C. Parsons, " 'Making Sense of What We Read':
       The Place of Biblical Hermeneutics," *SouJT* 35/3 (1993):
       12-20.

8:1-4

8180   G. Betori, "La strutturazione del libro degli Atti: una
       proposta," *RBib* 42 (1994): 3-34.

8:1

8181   F. F. Bruce, "The Church of Jerusalem in the Acts of the
       Apostles," *BJRL* 67/2 (1985): 641-61.

8:2-25

8182   Dietrich A. Koch, "Geistbesitz, Geistverleihung und
       Wundermacht. Erwägungen zur Tradition und zur
       lukanischen Redaktion in Act 8:5-25," *ZNW* 77/1 (1986):
       64-82.

8:4-12:25

8183   John T. Squires, "The Function of Acts 8:4-12:25," *NTS*
       44 (1998): 608-17.

8:4-40

8184   David S. Dockery, "Acts 6-12: The Christian Mission
       beyond Jerusalem," *RevExp* 87 (1990): 423-37.

8:4-25

8185   O. C. Edwards, "The Exegesis of Acts 8:4-25 and Its
       Implications for Confirmation and Glossolalia: A Review
       Article of E. Haenchen's Acts Commentary," *ATR* 55
       (1973): 100-12.

8186 Kevin N. Giles, "Is Luke an Exponent of 'Early Protestantism'? Church Order in the Lukan Writings. Part I," *EQ* 54/4 (1982): 193-205.

8187 E. J. Christiansen, "Taufe als Initiation in der Apostelgeschichte," *StTheol* 40/1 (1986): 55-79.

8:4-24

8188 F. Garcá Bazán, "En torno a Hechos 8,4-24. Milagro y magia entre los gnósticos," *RevB* 40/1 (1978): 27-38.

8189 H. J. Klauck, "With Paul in Paphos and Lystra: Magic and Paganism in the Acts of the Apostles," *Neo* 28 (1994): 93-108.

8:4-13

8190 Axel von Dobbeler, "Mission und Konflikt: Beobachtungen zu prosechein in Act 8,4-13," *BibN* 84 (1996): 16-22.

8:4

8191 Paul Muench, "The New Testament Scope of Ministry," *Point* 5/1 (1976): 77-84.

8192 Eduard Schweizer, "The Testimony to Jesus in the Early Christian Community," *HBT* 7/1 (1985): 77-98.

8193 Fred A. Grissom, "The Church Scattered," *BI* 13/3 (1987): 55-58.

8:5-25

8194 Michel Gourgues, "Esprit des Commencements et Esprit des Prolongements dans les Actes: Note sur la 'Pentecôte des Samaritains'," *RB* 93/3 (1986): 376-85.

8195 Dietrich A. Koch, "Geistbesitz, Geistverleihung und Wundermacht: Erwägungen zur Tradition und zur lukanischen Redaktion in Apg 8:5-25," *ZNW* 77/1-2 (1986): 64-82.

8196 Patrick L. Dickerson, "The Sources of the Account of the Mission to Samaria in Acts 8:5-25," *NovT* 39 (1997): 210-34.

8:5-8

8197 R. Massó, "La promesa del Espíritu," *CuBí* 29 (1972): 342-48.

8:9-40

8198   Thomas L. Brodie, "Towards Unraveling the Rhetorical Imitation of Sources in Acts: 2 Kgs 5 as One Component of Acts 8:9-40," *Bib* 67/1 (1986): 41-67.

8:9-24

8199   J. D. M. Derrett, "Simon Magus," *ZNW* 73/1-2 (1982): 52-68.

8:9-11

8200   S. Haar, "Lens or Mirror: The Image of Simon and Magic in Early Christian Literature," *LTJ* 27 (1993): 113-21.

8:12

8201   E. A. Russell, "They Believed Philip Preaching," *IBS* 1 (1979): 169-76.

8:14-25

8202   David A. Handy, "Acts 8:14-25," *Int* 47 (1993): 289-94.

8:14-17

8203   R. Massó, "La promesa del Espíritu," *CuBí* 29 (1972): 342-48.

8204   Heribert Schützeichel, "Calvins Stellungnahme zu den Trienter Canones über die Sakramente im Allgemeinen," *Cath* 38/4 (1984): 317-39.

8:16

8205   W. E. Moore, "One Baptism," *NTS* 10/4 (1964): 504-16.

8:18-24

8206   Christopher R. Matthews, "The Acts Of Peter and Luke's Intertextual Heritage," *Semeia* 80 (1997): 207-22.

8:18

8207   Klaus Haacker, "Einige Fälle von 'erlebter Rede' im Neuen Testament," *NovT* 12/1 (1970): 70-77.

8:25-40

8208   D. Mínguez, "Hechos 8,25-40. Análisis estructural del relato," *Bib* 57/2 (1976): 168-91.

8209   Robert F. O'Toole, "Philip and the Ethiopian Eunuch," *JSNT* 17 (1983): 25-34.

8:26-40

8210   Joseph A. Grassi, "Emmaus Revisited," *CBQ* 26 (1964): 463-67.

8211   M. Corbin, "Connais-tu ce que tu lis? Une lecture d'Actes 8,v.26 à 40," *Chr* 24 (1977): 73-85.

8212   Paul de Meester, " 'Philippe et l'Eunuque éthiopien' ou 'le baptême d'un pèlerin de Nubie'?" *NRT* 103/3 (1981): 360-74.

8213   Bernard P. Robinson, "The Place of the Emmaus Story in Luke-Acts," *NTS* 30/4 (1984): 481-97.

8214   Clarice J. Martin, "A Chamberlain's Journey and the Challenge of Interpretation for Liberation," *Semeia* 47 (1989): 105-35.

8215   F. Scott Spencer, "The Ethiopian Eunuch and His Bible: A Social-Science Analysis," *BTB* 22 (1992): 155-65.

8216   Mikeal C. Parsons, " 'Making Sense of What We Read': The Place of Biblical Hermeneutics," *SouJT* 35 (1993): 12-20.

8217   Thomas M. Rosica, "Two Journeys of Faith," *BibTo* 31 (1993): 177-80.

8218   Thomas M. Rosica, "The Road to Emmaus and the Road to Gaza: Luke 24:13-35 and Acts 8:26-40," *Worship* 68 (1994): 117-31.

8:26-39

8219   Bo Reicke, "Der Gottesknecht im Alten und Neuen Testament," *TZ* 35/6 (1979): 342-50.

8220   John M. Gibbs, "Luke 24:13-33 and Acts 8:26-39," *NRT* 103 (1981): 360-74.

8:26-32

8221   Bruce M. Metzger, "Recently Published Greek Papyri of the New Testament," *BA* 10 (1947): 25-44.

8:26

8222   Robert Coleman, "Gaza," *BI* 16/1 (1989): 35-37.

8223   Melchor Sánchez de Toca, "Poreuou kata mesembrian (Hch 8,26)," *EB* 55 (1997): 107-15.

8:27

8224 Klaus Haacker, "Einige Fälle von 'erlebter Rede' im Neuen Testament," *NovT* 12/1 (1970): 70-77.

8225 Rice A. Pierce, "Candance, Queen of Ethiopia," *BI* 9/2 (1983): 68-73.

8226 Mike Fuhrman, "North African Jews," *BI* 13/3 (1987): 52-54.

8:29

8227 R. Wayne Jones, "Chariots," *BI* 14/2 (1989): 52-55.

8:30-38

8228 Robert F. O'Toole, "Philip and the Ethiopian Eunuch," *JSNT* 17 (1983): 25-34.

8:30

8229 Peter Trummer, "Verstehst du auch, was du liest?" *K* 22 (1980): 103-13.

8:37

8230 Antonio Orbe, "Cristo, sacrificio y manjar," *Greg* 66/2 (1985): 185-239.

8231 Jenny Heimerdinger, "La Foi de l'eunuquee Éthiopien: le Problème Textuel d'Actes 8:37," *ÉTR* 63/4 (1988): 521-28.

8232 R. J. Porter, "What Did Philip Say to the Eunuch?" *ET* 100 (1988): 54-55.

8233 Cottrel R. Carson, "Acts 8:37--A Textual Reexamination," *USQR* 51 (1997): 57-78.

8:40

8234 Sherman E. Johnson, "Caesarea Maritima," *LTJ* 20 (1985): 28-32.

8235 Eduard Schweizer, "The Testimony to Jesus in the Early Christian Community," *HBT* 7/1 (1985): 77-98.

9-15

8236 F. W. Beare, "The Sequence of Events in Acts 9-15," *JBL* 62 (1943): 295-306.

9

8237   D. M. Stanley, "Paul's Conversion in Acts: Why the Three Accounts?" *CBQ*, 15 (1953): 315-38.

8238   Gerhard Lohfink, "Eine alttestamentliche Darstellungsform für Gotteserscheinungen in den Damaskusberichten," *BZ* NS 9/2 (1965): 246-57.

8239   D. Gill, "The Structure of Acts 9," *Bib* 55/4 (1974): 546-48.

8240   O. H. Steck, "Formgeschichtliche Bemerkungen zur Darstellung des Damaskusgeschehens in der Apostelgeschichte," *ZNW* 67/1 (1976): 20-28.

8241   R. F. Collins, "Paul's Damascus Experience: Reflections on the Lukan Account," *LouvS* 11/2 (1986): 99-118.

8242   Marvin W. Meyer, "The Light and Voice on the Damascus Road," *Forum* 2 (1986): 27-35.

8243   S. R. Bechtler, "The Meaning of Paul's Call and Commissioning in Luke's Story: An Exegetical Study of Acts 9, 22, and 26," *SBT* 15 (1987): 53-77.

8244   Olubayo Obijole, "The Influence of the Conversion of St. Paul on His Theology of the Cross," *EAJT* 6/2 (1987): 27-36.

8245   Ronald D. Witherup, "Functional Redundancy in the Acts of the Apostles: A Case Study," *JSNT* 48 (1992): 67-86.

8246   Sophie Schlumberger, "Saul renversé Actes 9: Le récit d'un identité reconstruite," *FV* 94 (1995): 61-74.

9:1-31

8247   Beverly R. Gaventa, "The Overthrown Enemy: Luke's Portrait of Paul," *SBLSP* 24 (1985): 439-49.

8248   David S. Dockery, "Acts 6-12: The Christian Mission beyond Jerusalem," *RevExp* 87 (1990): 423-37.

9:1-30

8249   David P. Moessner, "The Christ Must Suffer: New Light on the Jesus—Peter, Stephen, Paul Parallels in Luke-Acts," *NovT* 28/3 (1986): 220-56.

9:1-29

8250   John T. Townsend, "Acts 9:1-29 and Early Church Tradition," *SBLSP* 27 (1988): 119-31.

9:1-20

8251   M. Trotter, "Acts in Esther," *QR* 14/4 (1994-1995): 435-47.

9:1-19

8252   Charles W. Hedrick, "Paul's Conversion-Call: A Comparative Analysis of the Three Reports in Acts," *JBL* 100/3 (1981): 415-32

8253   Dennis Hamm, "Paul's Blindness and Its Healing: Clues to Symbolic Intent," *Bib* 71/1 (1990): 63-72.

9:1-10

8254   Robert V. Thompson, "Eyesight and Insight," *ChrM* 17/1 (1986): 29-31.

9:1-9

8255   O. F. A. Meinardus, "The Site of the Apostle Paul's Conversion at Kaukab," *BA* 44/1 (1981): 57-59.

9:1-5

8256   Raymond Schwager, "Christ's Death and the Prophetic Critique of Sacrifice," trans. P. Riordan *Semeia* 33 (1985): 109-23.

9:1-2

8257   C. S. Mann, "Saul and Damascus," *ET* 99 (1988): 331-34.

9:1

8258   P. W. van der Horst, "Drohung und Hord schnaubend," *NovT* 12/3 (1970): 257-69.

9:2-3

8259   S. Sabugal, "La Mencion neotestamentaria de Damasco ¿ciudad de Siria o region de Qumran?" *ETL* 45 (1978): 403-13.

9:2

8260   Eduard Schweizer, "The Testimony to Jesus in the Early Christian Community," *HBT* 7/1 (1985): 77-98.

9:3-19

8261   Willy Rordorf and Peter W. Dunn, "Paul's Conversion in the Canonical Acts and in the Acts of Paul," *Semeia* 80 (1997): 137-44.

9:4-6

8262   Jean Doignon, "Le dialogue de Jesus et de Paul: Sa 'pointe' dans l'exégèse latine la plus ancienne," *RSPT* 64 (1980): 477-89.

9:4

8263   Elmar Salmann, "Trinität und Kirche: eine dogmatische Studie," *Cath* 38/4 (1984): 352-74.

9:7

8264   Robert G. Bratcher, "*Akouo* in Acts 9:7 and 22:9," *ET* 71 (1960): 243-45.

8265   Gert Steuernagel, "'Ακούοντες μὲν τῆς φωνῆς: Ein Genitiv in der Apostelgeschichte," *NTS* 35/4 (1988-1989): 619-24.

9:8-10

8266   S. Sabugal, "La Mencion neotestamentaria de Damasco ¿ciudad de Siria o region de Qumran?" *ETL* 45 (1978): 403-13.

9:10-20

8267   R. A. Martin, "Syntactical Evidence of Aramaic Sources in Acts I-XV," *NTS* 11/1 (1964): 38-59.

9:15

8268   Gerhard Lohfink, " 'Meinen Namen zu tragen . . . ," *BZ* 10/1 (1966): 108-15.

9:16

8269   C. Burfeind, "Paulus *muss* nach Rom. Zur politischen Dimension der Apostelgeschichte," *NTS* 46 (2000): 75-91.

9:17-19

8270   Robert V. Thompson, "Eyesight and Insight," *ChrM* 17/1 (1986): 29-31.

9:18

8271 E. S. Buchanan, "Some Noteworthy Readings of the Fleury Palimpsest," *JTS* 9 (1907-1908): 98-100.

9:19-25

8272 Charles Masson, "A Propos de Act 9:19b-25," *TZ* 18 (1962): 161-66.

9:19-22

8273 David L. Jones, "Luke's Unique Interest in Historical Chronology," *SBLSP* 28 (1989): 378-87.

9:20

8274 David L. Jones, "The Title huios theou in Acts," *SBLSP* 24 (1985): 451-63.

9:22

8275 Norbert Lohfink, "Eine alttestamentliche Darstellungsform für Gotteserscheinungen in den Damaskusberichten," *BZ* NS 9 (1965): 246-57.

8276 Robert L. Reymond, "The Justification of Theology with a Special Application to Contemporary Christology," *Pres* 12/1 (1986): 1-16.

9:23-25

8277 Mark Harding, "On the Historicity of Acts: Comparing Acts 9:23-25 with 2 Corinthians 11:32-33," *NTS* 39/4 (1993): 518-38.

9:25

8278 Jos Janssens, "Il cristiano di fronte al martirio imminente: testimonianze e dottrina nella chiesa antica," *Greg* 66/3 (1985): 405-27.

9:26-30

8279 F. F. Bruce, "Galatian Problems: 1. Autobiographical Data," *BJRL* 11/2 (1969): 292-309.

8280 J. Morgado, "Paul in Jerusalem: A Comparison of His Visits in Acts and Galatians," *JETS* 37 (1994): 55-68.

8281 R. Trevijano Etcheverría, "El contrapunto lucano (Hch 9,26-30; 11,27-30; 12,25 y 15,1-35) a Gal 1,18-20 y 2,1-10," *Salm* 44 (1997): 295-39.

9:26

8282   J. Cambier, "Le Voyage de Saint Paul à Jérusalem en Act 9:26ss et le Schéma Missionaire Théologique de Saint Luc," *NTS* 8 (1961-1962): 249-57.

8283   Norbert Lohfink, "Eine alttestamentliche Darstellungsform für Gotteserscheinungen in den Damaskusberichten," *BZ* NS 9 (1965): 246-57.

8284   John Weborg, "Giving the Soul Wings," *ChrM* 16/1 (1985): 28.

9:27

8285   Richard T. France, "Barnabas—Son of Encouragement," *ERT* 4/1 (1980): 91-101.

9:28-39

8286   Stephen Gaselee, "Two Fayoumic Fragments of the Acts," *JTS* 11 (1909-10): 514-17.

9:29

8287   Everett Ferguson, "The Hellenists in the Book of Acts," *RQ* 12/4 (1969): 159-80.

8288   Rudolf Pesch, " 'Hellenisten' und 'Hebräer.' Zu Apg 9:29 und 6:1," *BZ* NS 23/1 (1979): 87-92.

9:30

8289   Sherman E. Johnson, "Caesarea Maritima," *LTJ* 20 (1985): 28-32.

9:31-43

8290   R. A. Martin, "Syntactical Evidence of Aramaic Sources in Acts I-XV," *NTS* 11/1 (1964): 38-59.

9:31

8291   Kevin N. Giles, "Luke's Use of the Term 'Ekklesia' with Special Reference to Acts 20.28 and 9.31," *NTS* 31/1 (1985): 135-42.

8292   Eduard Schweizer, "The Testimony to Jesus in the Early Christian Community," *HBT* 7/1 (1985): 77-98.

9:32-11:18

8293   David S. Dockery, "Acts 6-12: The Christian Mission beyond Jerusalem," *RevExp* 87 (1990): 423-37.

9:34-10:1

8294   Bruce M. Metzger, "Recently Published Greek Papyri of
        the New Testament," *BA* 10 (1947): 25-44.

9:36-43

8295   M. Trotter, "Acts in Esther," *QR* 14/4 (1994-1995):
        435-47.

9:36-42

8296   Hermann-Josef Stipp, "Vier Gestalten einer Totener-
        weckungserzählung (1 Kön 17,17-24; 2Kön 4,8-37; Apg
        9,36-42; Apg 20,7-12)," *Bib* 80 (1999): 43-77.

10-11

8297   William S. Kurz, "Effects of Variant Narrators in Acts
        10-11," *NTS* 43 (1997): 570-86.

10:1-11:18

8298   François Bovon, "Tradition et rédaction en Actes
        10,1-11,18," *TZ* 26 (1970): 22-45.

8299   Edgar Haulotte, "Fondation d'une communauté de type
        universel: Actes 10,1-11,18. Étude critique sur la
        rédaction, la 'structure' et la 'tradition' du récit," *RechSR*
        58/1 (1970): 63-100.

8300   Louis Marin, "Essai d'analyse structurale d'Actes
        10,1-11,18," *RechSR* 58/1 (1970): 39-61.

8301   Barbara Hall, "La communauté chrétienne dans le livre des
        Actes: Actes 6:1-7 et 10:1-11:18," *FV* Suppl (1971):
        146-56.

8302   Mark A. Plunkett, "Ethnocentricity and Salvation History
        in the Cornelius Episode," *SBLSP* 24 (1985): 465-79.

8303   John H. Elliott, "Household and Meals vs. Temple Purity:
        Replication Patterns in Luke-Acts," *BTB* 21 (1991):
        102-108.

8304   J. Julius Scott, "The Cornelius Incident in the Light of its
        Jewish Setting," *JETS* 34 (1991): 475-84.

8305   Ronald D. Witherup, "Cornelius Over and Over and Over
        Agian: 'Functional Redundancy' in the Acts of the
        Apostles," *JSNT* 49 (1993): 45-66.

8306 Edith M. Humphrey, "Collision of Modes?--Vision and Determining Argument in Acts 10:1-11:18," *Semeia* 71 (1995): 65-84.

8307 Michael Pettem, "Luke's Great Omission and His View of the Law," *NTS* 42 (1996): 35-54.

8308 René Kieffer, "From Linguistic Methodology to the Discovery of a World of Metaphors," *Semeia* 81 (1998): 77-93.

8309 John J. Kilgallen, "Clean, Acceptable, Saved: Acts 10," *ET* 109 (1998): 301-302.

10

8310 Klaus Haacker, "Einige Fälle von 'erlebter Rede' im Neuen Testament," *NovT* 12/1 (1970): 70-77.

8311 B. E. Thiering, "Qumran Initiation and New Testament Baptism," *NTS* 27/5 (1981): 615-31.

8312 C. House, "Defilement by Association: Some Insights from the Usage of Koino/Doino in Acts 10 and 11," *AUSS* 21/2 (1983): 143-53.

8313 Jouette M. Bassler, "Luke and Paul On Impartiality," *Bib* 66/4 (1985): 546-52.

8314 Glenn N. Davis, "When Was Cornelius Saved?" *RTR* 46/2 (1987): 43-49.

8315 Robert W. Wall, "Peter, 'Son' of Jonah: the Conversion of Cornelius in the Context of Canon," *JSNT* 29 (1987): 79-90.

8316 F. R. Harm, "Structural Elements Related to the Gift of the Holy Spirit in Acts," *CJ* 14/1 (1988): 28-41.

8317 Roland Barthes, "L'Analyse Structurale du Récit. À propos d'Actes 10-11," *RechSR* 58/1 (1970): 17-37.

8318 Sherman E. Johnson, "Caesarea Maritima," *LTJ* 20 (1985): 28-32.

10:1-33

8319 J. Julius Scott, "The Cornelius Incident in the Light of Its Jewish Setting," *JETS* 34 (1991): 475-84.

10:2

> 8320 Gerhard Delling, "Zur Taufe von 'Häusern' im Urchristentum," *NovT* 7 (1965): 285-311.

10:4

> 8321 George L. Lasebikan, "Glossolalia: Its Relationship with Speech Disabilities and Personality Disorders," *AfTJ* 14/2 (1985): 111-20.

10:23-48

> 8322 José O'Callaghan, "Nuevo pergamino de la Vulgate latina," *Bib* 56/3 (1975): 410-15.

10:24-48

> 8323 Sherman E. Johnson, "Caesarea Maritima," *LTJ* 20 (1985): 28-32.

10:25-26

> 8324 H. J. Klauck, "With Paul in Paphos and Lystra: Magic and Paganism in the Acts of the Apostles," *Neo* 28 (1994): 93-108.

10:26-43

> 8325 R. A. Martin, "Syntactical Evidence of Aramaic Sources in Acts I-XV," *NTS* 11/1 (1964): 38-59.

10:26-31

> 8326 Bruce M. Metzger, "Recently Published Greek Papyri of the New Testament," *BA* 10 (1947): 25-44.

10:28-29

> 8327 Charles Perrot, "Un Fragment Christo-palestinien Découvert à Khirbet Mird: Actes des Apôtres," *RB* 70 (1963): 506-55.

10:30

> 8328 Eduard Schweizer, "The Testimony to Jesus in the Early Christian Community," *HBT* 7/1 (1985): 77-98.

10:32-41

> 8329 Charles Perrot, "Un Fragment Christo-palestinien Découvert à Khirbet Mird: Actes des Apôtres," *RB* 70 (1963): 506-55.

10:34-48

    8330   Denton Lotz, "Peter's Wider Understanding of God's Will: Acts 10:34-48," *IRM* 77 (1988): 201-207.

10:34-43

    8331   E. Plümacher, "Die Missionsreden der Apostelgeschichte und Dionys von Halikarnass," *NTS* 39/2 (1993): 161-77.

    8332   R. S. MacKenzie, "The Western Text of Acts: Some Lucanisms in Selected Sermons," *JBL* 104/4 (1985): 637-50.

    8333   Frank J. Matera, "Acts 10:34-43," *Int* 41/1 (1987): 62-66.

    8334   Robert C. Tannehill, "Mission in the 1990s: Reflections on the Easter Lections from Acts," *QR* 10/1 (1990): 84-97.

    8335   E. Plümacher, "Die Missionsreden der Apostelgeschichte und Dionys von Halikarnass," *NTS* 39 (1993): 161-77.

    8336   Ed Erwin, "Acts 10:34-43," *Int* 49 (1995): 179-82.

    8337   Robert F. O'Toole, "Eirene, an Underlying Theme in Acts 10:34-43," *Bib* 77 (1996): 461-76.

10:34-40

    8338   Pieter de Villiers, "God Raised Him on the Third Day and Made Him Manifest . . and He Commanded Us to Preach to the People," *JTSA* 70 (1990): 55-63.

10:34-35

    8339   John B. Polhill, "No Respecter of Persons: God's View of Race Relations," *BI* 12/4 (1986): 66-71.

10:34

    8340   Troy Organ, "A Cosmomogical Christology," *CC* 88/44 (1971): 1293-95.

10:36-43

    8341   Frans Neirynck, "Le Livre des Actes (6): Ac 10, 36-43 et L'Évangile," *ETL* 60/1 (1984): 109-17.

10:36

    8342   Giovanni Rinaldi, "Lógos in Atti 10:36," *BibO* 12/4-5 (1970): 223-25.

    8343   Frans Neirynck, "Acts 10:36a: τὸν λόγον ὂν," *ETL* 60/1 (1984): 118-23.

10:37-43

8344 Wilhelm Wilkens, "Die theologische Struktur der Komposition des Lukas-Evangeliums," *TZ* 34/1 (1978): 1-13.

10:37

8345 O. Knoch, "Jesus, der 'Wohltäter' und 'Befreier' des Menschen. Das Christuszeugnis der Predigt des Petrus vor Kornelius," *GeistL* 46/1 (1973): 1-7.

10:39

8346 Joseph A. Fitzmyer, "Crucifixion in Ancient Palestine, Qumran Literature, and the New Testament," *CBQ* 40/4 (1978): 493-513.

10:41

8347 J. J. Bartolome, "Synesthiein en la Obra Lucana: Lc 15,2; Hch 10,41; 11,3," *Sale* 46/2 (1984): 269-88.

10:42

8348 Leslie C. Allen, "The Old Testament Background of (προ)ώρισμένη in the New Testament," *NTS* 17/1 (1970-1971): 104-108.

8349 A. J. Mattill, "Naherwartung, Fernerwartung, and the Purpose of Luke-Acts: Weymouth Reconsidered," *CBQ* 34/3 (1972): 276-93.

10:44-48

8350 R. K. Levang, "The Content of an Utterance in Tongues," *Para* 23/1 (1989): 14-20.

10:46

8351 Robert W. Graves, "Use of γάρ in Acts 10:46," *Para* 22 (1988): 15-18.

11

8352 A. S. Wood, "Social Involvement in the Apostolic Church," *EQ* 42/4 (1970): 194-212.

8353 Francis Lenssen, "Biblical Communities: Christian Communities in the New Testament," *Point* 1 (1972): 24-34.

8354   Édouard Delebecque, "La montée de Pierre de Césarée à Jerusalem selon le Codex Bezae au chapitre 11 des Actes des Apôtres," *ETL* 58/1 (1982): 106-10.

8355   C. House, "Defilement by Association: Some Insights from the Usage of Koino/Doino in Acts 10 and 11," *AUSS* 21/2 (1983): 143-53.

11:1-18

8356   R. A. Martin, "Syntactical Evidence of Aramaic Sources in Acts I-XV," *NTS* 11/1 (1964): 38-59.

8357   David L. Tiede, "Acts 11:1-18," *Int* 42/2 (1988): 175-80.

8358   M. Trotter, "Acts in Esther," *QR* 14/4 (1994-1995): 435-47.

11:3

8359   J. J. Bartolome, "Synesthiein en la Obra Lucana: Lc 15,2; Hch 10,41; 11,3," *Sale* 46/2 (1984): 269-88.

11:5

8360   Timothy Trammell, "Joppa," *BI* 13/2 (1987): 55-59.

11:14

8361   Gerhard Delling, "Zur Taufe von 'Häusern' im Urchristentum," *NovT* 7 (1965): 285-311.

11:15

8362   John J. Kilgallen, "Did Peter Actually Fail to Get a Word in?" *Bib* 71/3 (1990): 405-10.

11:17-30

8363   R. Trevijano Etcheverría, "El contrapunto lucano (Hch 9,26-30; 11,27-30; 12,25 y 15,1-35) a Gal 1,18-20 y 2,1-10," *Salm* 44 (1997): 295-39.

11:17

8364   J. A. Jáuregui, "Israel y la iglesia en la teologia de Lucas," *EE* 61 (1986): 129-49.

11:18

8365   Troy Organ, "A Cosmomogical Christology," *CC* 88/44 (1971): 1293-95.

11:19-30

8366   David P. Moessner, "The Christ Must Suffer: New Light
        on the Jesus—Peter, Stephen, Paul Parallels in
        Luke-Acts," *NovT* 28/3 (1986): 220-56.

8367   David S. Dockery, "Acts 6-12: The Christian Mission
        beyond Jerusalem," *RevExp* 87 (1990): 423-37.

8368   D. Z. Niringiye, "Jerusalem to Antioch to the World: A
        Biblical Missions Strategy," *EMQ* 26/1 (1990): 56-61.

11:19-20

8369   Wayne Dehoney, "Cyprus," *BI* 13/3 (1987): 67-69.

11:19

8370   Fred A. Grissom, "The Church Scattered," *BI* 13/3 (1987):
        55-58.

11:20

8371   Pierson Parker, "Three Variant Readings in Luke-Acts,"
        JBL 83 (1964): 165-70.

8372   Everett Ferguson, "The Hellenists in the Book of Acts,"
        RQ 12/4 (1969): 159-80.

11:22

8373   Richard T. France, "Barnabas—Son of Encouragement,"
        ERT 4/1 (1980): 91-101.

8374   F. F. Bruce, "The Church of Jerusalem in the Acts of the
        Apostles," *BJRL* 67/2 (1985): 641-61.

11:25

8375   Richard T. France, "Barnabas—Son of Encouragement,"
        ERT 4/1 (1980): 91-101.

11:26-28

8376   Édouard Delebecque, "Saul et Luc avant le premier
        voyage missionaire: Comparaison des deux versions des
        Actes 11:26-28," *RSPT* 66/4 (1982): 551-59.

11:26

8377   Harold B. Mattingly, "The Origin of the Name
        'Christiani'," *JTS* NS 9 (1958): 26-37.

8378   Ian Macleod, "Chance Names Which Stuck," *ET* 96
        (1985): 242.

8379   Justin Taylor, "Why Were the Disciples First Called 'Christians' at Antioch?" *RB* 101 (1994): 75-94.

11:27-12:25

8380   Suzanne Poque, "Une lecture d'Actes: 11,27-12,25," *ÉTR* 55/2 (1980): 265-78.

11:27-30

8381   D. F. Robinson, "A Note on Acts 11:27-30," *JBL* 63 (1944): 169-72.

8382   Georg Strecker, "Die sogenannte zweite Jerusalemreise des Paulus," *ZNW* 53 (1962): 67-77.

8383   David R. Catchpole, "Paul, James and the Apostolic Decree," *NTS* 23/4 (1976-1977): 428-44.

8384   Ralph P. Martin, "The Setting of 2 Corinthians," *TynB* 37 (1986): 3-19.

11:27

8385   Georg Strecker, "Die sogenannte zweite Jerusalemreise des Paulus," *ZNW* 53 (1962): 67-77.

11:28

8386   H. Patsch, "Die Prophetie des Agabus," *TZ* 28 (1972): 228-32.

8387   Scott Andrew, "Claudius Caesar," *BI* 14 (1989): 62-65.

11:30

8388   F. F. Bruce, "Galatian Problems: 1. Autobiographical Data," *BJRL* 11/2 (1969): 292-309.

8389   Robert H. Stein, "The Relationship of Galatians 2:1-10 and Acts 15:1-35; Two Neglected Arguments," *JETS* 17/4 (1974): 239-42.

8390   Richard T. France, "Barnabas—Son of Encouragement," *ERT* 4/1 (1980): 91-101.

8391   J. Morgado, "Paul in Jerusalem: A Comparison of His Visits in Acts and Galatians," *JETS* 37 (1994): 55-68.

12-28

8392   T. C. Geer, "The Two Faces of Codex 33 in Acts," *NovT* 31/1 (1989): 39-47.

12-21

8393   George D. Kilpatrick, "Jesus, His Family and His Disciples," *JSNT* 15 (1982): 3-19.

12

8394   W. Radl, "Befreiung aus dem Gefängnis-die Darstellung eines Biblischen Grundthemas in Apg 12," *BZ* 27/1 (1983): 81-96.

12:1-25

8395   R. A. Martin, "Syntactical Evidence of Aramaic Sources in Acts I-XV," *NTS* 11/1 (1964): 38-59.

12:1-24

8396   David S. Dockery, "Acts 6-12: The Christian Mission beyond Jerusalem," *RevExp* 87 (1990): 123-37.

8397   Susan R. Garrett, "Exodus from Bondage: Luke 9:31 and Acts 12:1-24," *CBQ* 52 (1990): 656-80.

12:1-17

8398   Robert W. Wall, "Successors to 'The Twelve' According to Acts 12:1-17," *CBQ* 53 (1991): 628-43.

12:2

8399   Josef Blinzler, "Rechtsgeschichtliches zur Hinrichtung des Zebedäiden Jakobus," *NovT* 5 (1962): 191-206.

12:6-7

8400   Jerome D. Quinn, "Seven Times He Wore Chains," *JBL* 97 (1978): 574-76.

12:12-17

8401   F. Scott Spencer, "Out of Mind, Out of Voice: Slave-Girls and Prophetic Daughters in Luke-Acts," *BibInt* 7 (1999): 133-55.

12:12

8402   Norbert Brox, "Zur pseudepigraphischen Rahmung des Ersten Petrusbriefes," *BZ* 19/1 (1975): 78-96.

8403   C. Clifton Black, "The Presentation of John Mark in the Acts of the Apostles," *PRS* 20 (1993): 235-54.

12:13-16

8404   J. A. Harrill, "The Dramatic Function of the Running Slave Rhoda: A Piece of Greco-Roman Comedy," *NTS* 46 (2000): 150-57.

12:17

8405   Morton Smith, "The Report about Peter in 1 Clement V. 4," *NTS* 7 (1960): 86-88.

8406   Carsten P. Thiede, "Babylon, der andere Ort: Anmerkungen zu 1 Petr 5,13 und Apg 12,17," *Bib* 67/4 (1986): 532-38.

12:19

8407   Sherman E. Johnson, "Caesarea Maritima," *LTJ* 20 (1985): 28-32.

12:20-23

8408   Mark R. Strom, "An Old Testament Background to Acts 12:20-23," *NTS* 32/2 (1986): 289-92.

12:21-23

8409   H. J. Klauck, "With Paul in Paphos and Lystra: Magic and Paganism in the Acts of the Apostles," *Neo* 28 (1994): 93-108.

12:23

8410   F. C. Conybeare, "Two Notes on Acts," *ZNW* 20 (1921): 136-42.

8411   Josef Blinzler, "Rechtsgeschichtliches zur Hinrichtung des Zebedäiden Jakobus," *NovT* 5 (1962): 191-206.

12:24

8412   M. H. Franzmann, "The Word of the Lord Grew," *CTM* 30 (1959): 563-81.

8413   J. Kodell, " 'The Word of God Grew.' The Ecclesial Tendency of *Logos* in Acts 6:7; 12:24; 19:20," *Bib* 55/4 (1974): 505-19.

8414   M. H. Grumm, "Another Look at Acts," *ET* 96/11 (1985): 333-37.

12:25

8415 Jacques Dupont, "La mission de Paul à Jérusalem," *NovT* 1 (1956): 275-303.

8416 Robert H. Stein, "The Relationship of Galatians 2:1-10 and Acts 15:1-35; Two Neglected Arguments," *JETS* 17/4 (1974): 239-42.

8417 E. G. Edwards, "On Using the Textual Apparatus of the UBS Greek New Testament," *BT* 28/1 (1977): 121-42.

8418 Richard T. France, "Barnabas—Son of Encouragement," *ERT* 4/1 (1980): 91-101.

8419 J. Morgado, "Paul in Jerusalem: A Comparison of His Visits in Acts and Galatians," *JETS* 37 (1994): 55-68.

8420 R. Trevijano Etcheverría, "El contrapunto lucano (Hch 9,26-30; 11,27-30; 12,25 y 15,1-35) a Gal 1,18-20 y 2,1-10," *Salm* 44 (1997): 295-39.

13-25

8421 H. Dixon Slingerland, " 'The Jews' in the Pauline Portion of Acts," *JAAR* 54/2 (1986): 305-21.

13-19

8422 R. Alan Culpepper, "Paul's Mission to the Gentile World: Acts 13-19," *RevExp* 71/4 (1974): 487-97.

8423 James L. Blevins, "Acts 13-19: The Tale of Three Cites," *RevExp* 87 (1990): 439-50.

13-14

8424 R. L. Roberts, "Notes on Selected Passages," *RQ* 4 (1960): 234-58.

8425 David R. Catchpole, "Paul, James and the Apostolic Decree," *NTS* 23/4 (1976-1977): 428-44.

8426 Ken Kilinski, "How Churches Can Follow Antioch's Model," *EMQ* 15/1 (1979): 19-23.

8427 J. Rius-Camps, "La misión hacia el paganismo avalada por el Señor Jesús y el Espíritu Santo," *EB* 52 (1994): 341-60.

13

8428 Francis Lenssen, "Biblical Communities: Christian Communities in the New Testament," *Point* 1 (1972): 24-34.

8429   F. F. Bruce, "Was Paul a Mystic?" *RTR* 34/3 (1975): 66-75.

8430   Harold R. Cook, "Who Really Sent the First Missionaries?" *EMQ* 11/4 (1975): 233-39.

8431   Glenn N. Davis, "When Was Cornelius Saved?" *RTR* 46/2 (1987): 43-49.

13:1-4

8432   J. Fain, "Church-Mission Relationships: What We Can Learn from Acts 13:1-4," *SouJT* 2 (1994): 19-39.

13:1-3

8433   Ernest Best, "Acts 13:1-3," *JTS* 11 (1960): 344-48.

8434   S. Dockx, "L'ordination de Barnabé et de Saul d'après Actes 13:1-3," *NRT* 98/3 (1976): 238-58.

8435   D. Z. Niringiye, "Jerusalem to Antioch to the World: A Biblical Missions Strategy," *EMQ* 26/1 (1990): 56-61.

13:1-2

8436   Richard T. France, "Barnabas—Son of Encouragement," *ERT* 4/1 (1980): 91-101.

13:1

8437   Richard Glover, " 'Luke the Antiochene' and Acts," *NTS* 11/1 (1964): 97-106.

8438   A. del Agua Pérez, "El papel de la 'escuela midrásica' en la configuración del Nuevo Testamento," *EE* 60/234 (1985): 333-49.

8439   John W. Wenham, "The Identification of Luke," *EQ* 63/1 (1991): 3-44.

13:3

8440   R. L. Roberts, "Notes on Selected Passages," *RQ* 4 (1960): 234-58.

8441   Timothy N. Boyd, "The Laying on of Hands," *BI* (1989): 9-10.

13:4-12

8442   H. J. Klauck, "With Paul in Paphos and Lystra: Magic and Paganism in the Acts of the Apostles," *Neo* 28 (1994): 93-108.

8443   D. Gill, "Paul's Travels Through Cyprus (Acts 13:4-12),"
        TynB 46 (1995): 219-28.

8444   John J. Kilgallen, "Acts 13:4-12: The Role of the Magos,"
        EB 55 (1997): 223-37.

13:5

8445   C. Clifton Black, "The Presentation of John Mark in the
        Acts of the Apostles," *PRS* 20 (1993): 235-54.

13:6-12

8446   L. Yaure, "Elymas—Nehelamite—Pethor," *JBL* 79 (1960):
        297-314.

13:7-2

8447   Richard T. France, "Barnabas—Son of Encouragement,"
        ERT 4/1 (1980): 91-101.

13:9

8448   F. C. Synge, "Acts 13:9: Saul, Who is Also Paul,"
        Theology 63 (1960): 199-200.

13:13-52

8449   Robert F. O'Toole, "Christ's Resurrection in Acts
        13:13-52," *Bib* 60/3 (1979): 361-72.

8450   Joseph B. Tyson, "Jews and Judaism in Luke-Acts:
        Reading as a Godfearer," *NTS* 41 (1995): 19-38.

13:13-43

8451   Danielle Ellul, "Antoiche de Pisidie: Une predication . . .
        trois credos?" *FilN* 5 (1992): 3-14.

13:13-41

8452   C. Clifton Black, "The Rhetorical Form of the Hellenistic
        Jewish and Early Christian Sermon," *HTR* 81 (1988):
        1-18.

13:13

8453   C. Clifton Black, "The Presentation of John Mark in the
        Acts of the Apostles," *PRS* 20 (1993): 235-54.

13:14-52

8454   E. Plümacher, "Die Missionsreden der Apostelgeschichte
        und Dionys von Halikarnass," *NTS* 39 (1993): 161-77.

13:14-41

8455   Lawrence Wills, "The Form of the Sermon in Hellenistic Judaism and Early Christianity," *HTR* 77/3-4 (1984): 277-99.

13:14

8456   John W. Bowker, "Speeches in Acts: A Study in Proem and Yelammedenu Form," *NTS* 14/1 (1967-1968): 96-111.

13:15

8457   Joseph Plevnik, " 'The Eleven and Those with Them' According to Luke," *CBQ* 40/2 (1978): 205-11.

13:16-41

8458   Lars Hartman, "Davids Son. Apropa Acta 13,16-41," *SEÅ* 28-29 (1963-1964): 117-34.

8459   R. A. Martin, "Syntactical Evidence of Aramaic Sources in Acts I-XV," *NTS* 11/1 (1964): 38-59.

8460   O. J. F. Seitz, "Gospel Prologues: A Common Pattern?" *JBL* 83 (1964): 262-68.

8461   F. F. Bruce, "Is the Paul of Acts the Real Paul?" *BJRL* 58/2 (1976): 282-305.

8462   M. Dumais, "Le langage de l'Évangélisation: L'annonce missionnaire en milieu juif," *JTS* 29 (1978): 198.

8463   A. del Agua Pérez, "El papel de la 'escuela midrásica' en la configuración del Nuevo Testamento," *EE* 60/234 (1985): 333-49.

8464   R. S. MacKenzie, "The Western Text of Acts: Some Lucanisms in Selected Sermons," *JBL* 104/4 (1985): 637-50.

8465   Adriana Bottino, "Il Discorso Missionario di Paolo," *RechSR* 2 (1990): 81-97.

8466   D. A. DeSilva, "Paul's Sermon in Antioch of Pisidia," *BSac* 151 (1994): 32-49.

8467   James W. Thompson, "Paul's Preaching Ministry: Evangelistic and Pastoral Preaching in Acts," *RQ* 42 (2000): 19-26

13:18

8468   Robert P. Gordon, "Targumic Parallels to Acts XIII 18 and Didache XIV 3," *NovT* 16/4 (1974): 285-89.

13:20

8469   Eugene H. Merrill, "Paul's Use of 'About 450 Years' in Acts 13:20," *BSac* 138 (1981): 246-57.

13:26

8470   T. E. Brawley, "For Blessing All Families of the Earth: Covenant Traditions in Luke-Acts," *CThM* 22/1 (1995): 18-26.

13:29

8471   Joseph A. Fitzmyer, "Crucifixion in Ancient Palestine, Qumran Literature, and the New Testament," *CBQ* 40/4 (1978): 493-513.

13:31

8472   Edvin Larsson, "Paul: Law and Salvation," *NTS* 31 (1985): 425-36.

13:32-52

8473   H. van de Sandt, "The Quotations in Acts 13:32-52 as a Reflection of Luke's LXX: Interpretation," *Bib* 75 (1994): 26-58.

13:32-37

8474   W. C. Kaiser, "The Promise to David in Psalm 16 and its Application in Acts 2:25-33 and 13:32-37," *JETS* 23 (1980): 219- 29.

13:33-37

8475   Dale Goldsmith, "Acts 13:33-37: A *Pesher* on 2 Samuel 7," *JBL* 87/3 (1968): 321-24.

13:33-35

8476   C. Ghidelli, "Un saggio di lettura dell'AT nel libro degli Atti," *PV* 9 (1964): 83-91.

13:33

8477   George D. Kilpatrick, "Acts 13:33 and Tertullian, Adv Marc IV:xxii.8," *JTS* 11 (1960): 53.

8478   John H. Hayes, "The Resurrection as Enthronement and the Earliest Church Christology," *Int* 22/3 (1968): 333-45.

8479   Donald L. Jones, "The Title huios theou in Acts," *SBLSP* 24 (1985): 451-63.

8480   Gérard Rochais, "Jésus savait-il qu'il était Dieu: réflexions critiques à propos d'un livre récent," *SR* 14/1 (1985): 85-106.

13:38-39

8481   Edvin Larsson, "Paul: Law and Salvation," *NTS* 31 (1985): 425-36.

8482   John J. Kilgallen, "Acts 13:38-39: Culmination of Paul's Speech in Pisidia," *Bib* 69/4 (1988): 480-506.

13:38

8483   Paul Ellingworth, "Acts 13:38—A Query," *BT* 45 (1994): 242-43.

13:44

8484   Balmer H. Kelly, "Revelation 7:9-17," *Int* 40/3 (1986): 288-95.

13:45

8485   Slayden A. Yarbrough, "The Judaizers," *BI* (1989): 16-19.

13:46

8486   Richard T. France, "Barnabas—Son of Encouragement," *ERT* 4/1 (1980): 91-101.

8487   Robert C. Tannehill, "Rejection by Jews and Turning to Gentiles: the Pattern of Paul's Mission in Acts," *SBLSP* 25 (1986): 130-41.

13:47

8488   Pierre Grelot, "Note sur Actes 13:47," *RB* 88/3 (1981): 368-72.

8489   John R. Donahue, "The 'Parable' of the Sheep and the Goats: A Challenge to Christian Ethics," *JTS* 47/1 (1986): 3-31.

13:50

8490   Richard T. France, "Barnabas—Son of Encouragement," *ERT* 4/1 (1980): 91-101.

14-22

8491   Henning Paulsen, "Erwägungen zu Acta Apollonii 14-22," *ZNW* 66/1 (1975): 117-26.

14

8492   H. C. Shank, "Qoheleth's World and Life View as Seen in His Recurring Phrases," *WTJ* 37/1 (1974): 57-73.

14:2

8493   Slayden A. Yarbrough, "The Judaizers," *BI* (1989): 16-19.

14:4

8494   S. Dockx, "L'ordination de Barnabé et de Saul d'après Actes 13:1-3," *NRT* 98/3 (1976): 238-58.

14:5-14

8495   E. S. Buchanan, "Two Pages from the Fleury Palimpsest with Some Newly Discovered Readings," *JTS* 7 (1905-1906): 454-55.

14:6

8496   G. Ogg, "Derbe," *NTS* 9/4 (1963): 367-70.

14:8-18

8497   D. Wiens, "Luke on Pluralism: Flex with History," *Dir* 23 (1994): 44-53.

8498   Gerard Mussies, "Variation in the Book of Acts," *FilN* 8 (1995): 23-61.

14:8-15

8499   B. Gaertner, "Paulus und Barnabas in Lystra. Zu Apg. 14.8-15," *SEÅ* 27 (1962): 83-88.

14:11-17

8500   Cilliers Breytenbach, "Zeus und der lebendige Gott: Anmerkungen zu Apostelgeschichte 14:11-17," *NTS* 39/3 (1993): 369-413.

14:11-13

8501   F. Gerald Downing, "Common Ground with Paganism in Luke and Josephus," *NTS* 28/4 (1982): 546-59.

14:12

8502   Richard T. France, "Barnabas—Son of Encouragement," *ERT* 4/1 (1980): 91-101.

8503   L. H. Martin, "Gods or Ambassadors of God? Barnabas and Paul in Lystra," *NTS* 41/1 (1995): 152-56.

14:14

8504   E. S. Buchanan, "Some Noteworthy Readings of the Fleury Palimpṣest," *JTS* 9 (1907-1908): 98-100.

8505   W. M. Green, "Apostels—Actes 14:14," *RQ* 4 (1960): 245-47.

8506   R. L. Roberts, "Notes on Selected Passages," *RQ* 4 (1960): 234-58.

8507   S. Dockx, "L'ordination de Barnabé et de Saul d'après Actes 13:1-3," *NRT* 98/3 (1976): 238-58.

8508   Richard T. France, "Barnabas—Son of Encouragement," *ERT* 4/1 (1980): 91-101.

8509   George D. Kilpatrick, "Epithuein and Epikrinein in the Greek Bible," *ZNW* 74/1 (1983): 151-53.

14:15-23

8510   E. S. Buchanan, "More Pages from the Fleury Palimpsest," *JTS* 8 (1906-07): 96-100.

14:15-18

8511   Ernst Lerle, "Die Predigt in Lystra," *NTS* 7 (1960): 46-55.

14:15-17

8512   Colin Barnes, "Paul and Johanan ben Zakkai," *ET* 108 (1997): 366-67.

14:15

8513   C. M. Horne, "Toward a Biblical Apologetic," *GTJ* 2 (1961): 14-18.

14:16

8514   Klaus Haacker, "Gott und die Wege der Völker," *TBe* 21 (1990): 281-84.

14:17

8515   Troy Organ, "A Cosmological Christology," *CC* 88/44 (1971): 1293-95.

8516   Jacques Dupuis, "The Practice of Agape Is the Reality of Salvation," *IRM* 74 (1985): 472-77.

8517 Ernst Lerle, "Kardia als Bezeichnung für den Mageneingang," *ZNW* 76/3 (1985): 292-94.

8518 Malcolm J. McVeigh, "The Fate of Those Who've Never Heard: It Depends," *EMQ* 21/4 (1985): 370-79.

14:20

8519 G. Ogg, "Derbe," *NTS* 9/4 (1963): 367-70.

8520 Richard T. France, "Barnabas—Son of Encouragement," *ERT* 4/1 (1980): 91-101.

8521 Jimmy Albright, "Derbe," *BI* 15/1 (1988): 69-72.

14:21-23

8522 D. F. Detweiler, "Paul's Approach to the Great Commission in Acts 14:21-23," *BSac* 152/605 (1995): 33-41.

14:22

8523 A. J. Mattill, " 'The Way of Tribulation'," *JBL* 98/4 (1979): 531-46.

14:23

8524 André Feuillet, " 'Témoins Oculaires et Serviteurs de la Parole'," *NovT* 15/4 (1973): 241-59.

8525 S. Dockx, "L'ordination de Barnabé et de Saul d'après Actes 13:1-3," *NRT* 98/3 (1976): 238-58.

8526 R. Y. K. Fung, "Charismatic Versus Organized Ministry? An Examination of an Alleged Antithesis," *EQ* 52/4 (1980): 195-214.

14:27-15:35

8527 A. T. M. Cheung, "A Narrative Analysis of Acts 14:27-15:35: Literary Shaping in Luke's Account of the Jerusalem Council," *WTJ* 55/1 (1993): 137-54.

14:27-28

8528 G. Betori, "La strutturazione del libro degli Atti: una proposta," *RBib* 42 (1994): 3-34.

15

8529 E. Ravarotto, "De Hierosolymitano Concilio," *Ant* 37/2 (1962): 185-218.

8530   Stanley D. Toussaint, "The Chronological Problem of Galatians 2:1-10," *BSac* 120 (1963): 334-40.

8531   E. Schuyler English, "Was St. Peter Ever in Rome?" *BSac* 124 (1967): 314-20.

8532   Pierson Parker, "Once More, Acts and Galatians," *JBL* 86/2 (1967): 175-82.

8533   Francis Lenssen, "Biblical Communities: Christian Communities in the New Testament," *Point* 1 (1972): 24-34.

8534   Traugott Holtz, "Die Bedeutung des Apostelkonzils für Paulus," *NovT* 16 (1974): 110-33.

8535   A. Strobel, "Das Aposteldekret in Galatien: Zur Situation von Gal I und II," *NTS* 20/2 (1974): 177-90.

8536   John J. Kilgallen, "Acts: Literary and Theological Turning Points," *BTB* 7/4 (1977): 177-80.

8537   I. M. Ellis, "Codex Bezae at Acts 15," *IBS* 2 (1980): 134-40.

8538   A. Wainwright, "Where Did Silas Go? And What Was His Connection with Galatians?" *JSNT* 8 (1980): 66-70.

8539   John W. Wenham, "The Theology of Unclean Food," *EQ* 53/1 (1981): 6-15.

8540   C. K. Barrett, "Quomodo Historia Conscribenda Sit," *NTS* 28/3 (1982): 303-20.

8541   Charles Perrot, "The Decrees of the Council of Jerusalem," *TD* 30/1 (1982): 21-24.

8542   C. K. Barrett, "Apostles in Council and in Conflict," *ABR* 31 (1983): 14-32.

8543   D. H. King, "Paul and the Tannaim: A Study in Galatians," *WTJ* 45/2 (1983): 340-70.

8544   Darrell L. Whiteman, "Communicating Across Cultures," *Point* 5 (1984): 56-83.

8545   Mark A. Seifrid, "Jesus and the Law in Acts," *JSNT* 30 (1987): 39-57.

8546   Donald Hohensee, "To Eat or Not to Eat? Christians and Food Laws," *EMQ* 25/1 (1989): 74-81.

8547 Clayton N. Jefford, "Tradition and Witness in Antioch: Acts 15 and Didache 6," *PRS* 19 (1992): 409-19.

8548 J. Morgado, "Paul in Jerusalem: A Comparison of His Visits in Acts and Galatians," *JETS* 37 (1994): 55-68.

8549 J. Rius-Camps, "La misión hacia el paganismo avalada por el Señor Jesús y el Espíritu Santo," *EB* 52 (1994): 341-60.

15:1-35

8550 Veselin Kesich, "The Apostolic Council at Jerusalem," *SVTQ* 6/3 (1962): 108-17.

8551 Robert H. Stein, "The Relationship of Galatians 2:1-10 and Acts 15:1-35; Two Neglected Arguments," *JETS* 17/4 (1974): 239-42.

8552 Robert G. Hoerber, "A Review of the Apostolic Council After 1925 Years," *CJ* 214 (1976): 155-59.

8553 Alfons Weiser, "Das 'Apostel-Konzil' (Apg 15,1-35)-Ereignis, überlieferung, lukanische Deutung," *BZ* 28/2 (1984): 145-67.

8554 Royce Dickinson, "The Theology of the Jerusalem Conference: Acts 15:1-35," *RQ* 32/2 (1990): 65-83.

8555 P. Nepper-Christensen, "Apostelmødet i Jerusalem," *DTT* 56 (1993): 169-88.

8556 François Refoulé, "Le discours de Pierre à l'Assemblée de Jerusalem," *RB* 100 (1993): 239-51.

8557 A. J. M. Wedderburn, "The 'Apostolic Decree': Tradition and Redaction," *NovT* 35 (1993): 362-89.

8558 R. Trevijano Etcheverría, "El contrapunto lucano (Hch 9,26-30; 11,27-30; 12,25 y 15,1-35) a Gal 1,18-20 y 2,1-10," *Salm* 44 (1997): 295-39.

15:1-34

8559 Justin Taylor, "Ancient Texts and Modern Critics: Acts 15:1-34," *RB* 99 (1992): 373-78.

15:1-33

8560 M.-É. Boismard, "Le 'Concile' de Jérusalem (Act 15:1-33): Essai de Critique Littéraire," *ETL* 64/4 (1988): 433-40.

15:1-29

8561   Lewis Sperry, "An Introduction to the Study of Prophecy," *BSac* 100 (1943): 98-133.

8562   Brian Schwarz, "Contextualization and the Church in Melanesia," *Point* 7 (1985): 104-20.

8563   Robert P. Lightner, "Theological Perspectives on Theonomy; Pt 3: a Dispensational Response to Theonomy," *BSac* 143 (1986): 228-45.

8564   Joseph B. Tyson, "Jews and Judaism in Luke-Acts: Reading as a Godfearer," *NTS* 41 (1995): 19-38.

8565   David B. Whitlock, "An Exposition of Acts 15:1-29," *RevExp* 92 (1995): 375-78.

15:1

8566   David R. Catchpole, "Paul, James and the Apostolic Decree," *NTS* 23/4 (1976-1977): 428-44.

15:2

8567   Richard T. France, "Barnabas—Son of Encouragement," *ERT* 4/1 (1980): 91-101.

15:6-21

8568   H. van de Sandt, "An Explanation of Acts 15:6-21 in the Light of Deuteronomy 4:29-35," *JSNT* 46 (1992): 73-97.

15:6-11

8569   Barbara Hall, "La communauté chrétienne dans le livre des Actes: Actes 6:1-7 et 10:1-11:18," *FV* Suppl (1971): 146-56.

15:6

8570   J. Lionel North, "Is ἰδεῖν περί a Latinsim?" *NTS* 29/2 (1983): 265-66.

15:7-11

8571   François Refoulé, "Le discours de Pierre à l'assemblée de Jérusalem," *RB* 64 (1957): 35-47.

8572   Troy Organ, "A Cosmomogical Christology," *CC* 88/44 (1971): 1293-95.

15:8

8573   J. B. Bauer, "Kardiognostes, ein unbeachteter Aspekt," *BibN* 32/1 (1988): 114-17.

15:10-29

8574   J. A. Jáuregui, "Israel y la iglesia en la teologia de Lucas," *EE* 61 (1986): 129-49.

15:10

8575   John Nolland, "A Fresh Look at Acts 15:10," *NTS* 27/1 (1980): 105-15.

15:12

8576   Richard T. France, "Barnabas—Son of Encouragement," *ERT* 4/1 (1980): 91-101.

8577   Ronald Ross, "Brief Note on Form and Meaning," *BT* 47 (1996): 137-38.

15:13-18

8578   W. M. Aldrich, "The Interpretation of Acts 15:13-18," *BSac* 111 (1954): 317-23.

8579   W. C. Kaiser, "The Davidic Promise and the Inclusion of the Gentiles: A Test Passage for Theological Systems," *JETS* 20/2 (1977): 97-111.

15:14-17

8580   Charles Zimmerman, " 'To This Agree the Words of the Prophets'," *GTJ* 4 (1963): 28-40.

15:14

8581   Jacques Dupont, "Un Peuple d'entre les Nations," *NTS* 31/3 (1985): 321-35.

15:19-21

8582   Daniel R. Schwartz, "The Futility of Preaching Moses," *Bib* 67/2 (1986): 276-81.

8583   Roger L. Omanson, "How Does It All Fit Together? Thoughts On Translating Acts 1:15-22 and 15:19-21," *BT* 41 (1990): 416-21.

8584   Roger L. Omanson, "Acts 15:19-21: Some Further Discussion," *BT* 42 (1991): 234-41.

15:20-29

8585   Frédéric Manns, "Remarques sur Actes 15,20.29," *Ant* 53/3 (1978): 443-51.

15:20

8586   Thor Boman, "Das textkritische Problem des sogenannten Aposteldekrets," *NovT* 7/1 (1964): 26-36.

8587   A. F. J. Klijn, "The Pseudo Clementines and the Apostolic Decree," *NovT* 10/4 (1968): 305-12.

8588   H.-W. Bartsch, "Traditionsgeschichtliches zur 'Goldenen Regel' und zum Aposteldekret," *ZNW* 75/1 (1984): 128-32.

8589   Terrance Callan, "The Background of the Apostolic Decree," *CBQ* 55 (1993): 284-97.

8590   John Proctor, "Proselytes and Pressure Cookers: The Meaning and Application of Acts 15:20," *IRM* 85 (1996): 469-83.

15:21

8591   Daniel R. Schwartz, "The Futility of Preaching Moses," *Bib* 67/2 (1986): 276-81.

15:22-40

8592   B. N. Kaye, "Acts' Portrait of Silas," *NTS* 21/1 (1979): 13-26.

15:22-29

8593   Torstein Jorgensen, "Acta 15:22-29: Historiske Og Eksegetiske Problemer," *NTT* 90/1 (1989): 31-45.

15:22

8594   Richard T. France, "Barnabas—Son of Encouragement," *ERT* 4/1 (1980): 91-101.

15:23-29

8595   M. Simon, "The Apostolic Decree and Its Setting in the Ancient Church," *BJRL* 52/2 (1970): 437-60.

15:25

8596   Richard T. France, "Barnabas—Son of Encouragement," *ERT* 4/1 (1980): 91-101.

15:28-29

8597 R. L. Roberts, "Notes on Selected Passages," *RQ* 4 (1960): 234-58.

8598 H.-W. Bartsch, "Traditionsgeschichtliches zur 'Goldenen Regel' und zum Aposteldekret," *ZNW* 75/1 (1984): 128-32.

8599 Victor M. Fernández, "Santiago, la plenificación cristiana de la espiritualidad postexilica," *RevB* 53 (1991): 29-33.

8600 Harold R. Johne, "Exegetical Brief: The Prohibitions in the Jerusalem Council's Letter to Gentile Believers," *WLQ* 94 (1997): 47-48.

15:28

8601 John N. Suggit, "The Holy Spirit and We Resolved. . .," *JTSA* 79 (1992): 38-48.

15:29

8602 Thor Boman, "Das textkritische Problem des sogenannten Aposteldekrets," *NovT* 7/1 (1964): 26-36.

8603 A. F. J. Klijn, "The Pseudo Clementines and the Apostolic Decree," *NovT* 10/4 (1968): 305-12.

8604 C. K. Barrett, "The Apostolic Decree of Acts 15:29," *ABR* 35 (1987): 50-59.

8605 Terrance Callan, "The Background of the Apostolic Decree," *CBQ* 55 (1993): 284-97.

15:34

8606 Édouard Delebecque, "Silas, Paul et Barnabe a Antioche Selon le Texte 'Occidental' d'Actes, 15, 34 et 38," *RHPR* 64/1 (1984): 47-52.

15:35-37

8607 Richard T. France, "Barnabas—Son of Encouragement," *ERT* 4/1 (1980): 91-101.

15:36-16:5

8608 Jacques Dupont, "La Question du Plan des Actes des Apôtres à la lumière d'un Texte de Lucien de Samosate," *NovT* 21/3 (1979): 220-31.

15:36-40

8609   C. Clifton Black, "The Presentation of John Mark in the Acts of the Apostles," *PRS* 20 (1993): 235-54.

15:38

8610   Édouard Delebecque, "Silas, Paul et Barnabe a Antioche Selon le Texte 'Occidental' d'Actes, 15, 34 et 38," *RHPR* 64/1 (1984): 47-52.

15:39

8611   G. B. Bruzzone, "Il dissenso tra Paolo e Barnaba in Atti 15,39," *EB* 35 (1976): 121.

8612   Richard T. France, "Barnabas—Son of Encouragement," *ERT* 4/1 (1980): 91-101.

15:41

8613   Y. Tissot, "Les prescriptions des presbytres (Actes 15,41). Exégèse et origine du décret dans le texte syro-occidental des *Actes,*" *RB* 77/3 (1970): 321-46.

16:1-18:22

8614   J. Rius-Camps, "Jesús y el Espíritu Santo conducen la misión hacia Europa," *EB* 52/4 (1994): 517-34.

16

8615   Paul E. Davies, "The Macedonian Scene of Paul's Journeys," *BA* 26 (1963): 91-106.

8616   Édouard Delebecque, "De Lystres à Philippes (Ac 16) avec le Codex Bezae," *Bib* 63/3 (1982): 395-405.

8617   J. K. Howard, "New Testament Exorcism and Its Significance Today," *ET* 96/4 (1985): 105-09.

8618   I. Richter-Reimer, "Die Geschichte der Frauen rekonstruieren. Betrachtungen über die Arbeit und den Status von Lydia in Apg 16," *TextK* 14 (1991): 16-29.

8619   J. Gillman, "Hospitality in Acts 16," *LouvS* 17 (1992): 181-96.

16:1-3

8620   William O. Walker, "The Timothy-Titus Problem Reconsidered," *ET* 92/8 (1981): 231-35.

8621   S. J. D. Cohen, "Was Timothy Jewish? Patristic Exegesis, Rabbinic Law, and Matrilineal Descent," *JBL* 105/2 (1986): 251-68.

8622   Christopher Bryan, "A Further Look at Acts 16:1-3," *JBL* 107/2 (1988): 292-94.

16:1

8623   G. Ogg, "Derbe," *NTS* 9/4 (1963): 367-70.

8624   R. Y. K. Fung, "Charismatic Versus Organized Ministry? An Examination of an Alleged Antithesis," *EQ* 52/4 (1980): 195-214.

16:6-40

8625   F. Martin, "Ke geôlier et la marchande de pourpre: Actes des Apôtres 16:6-40," *SémBib* 59 (1990): 9-29.

16:6

8626   F. F. Bruce, "Galatian Problems: 2. North or South Galatians?" *BJRL* 52/2 (1970): 243-66.

8627   G. M. Lee, "The Past Participle of Subsequent Action," *NovT* 17/3 (1975): 199.

8628   Colin J. Hemer, "Phrygia: A Further Note," *JTS* 28/1 (1977): 99-101.

16:7

8629   Romano Penna, "Lo 'Spirito di Gesù' in Atti 16,7. Analisi letteraria e Teologica," *RBib* 20/3 (1972): 241-61.

16:8

8630   W. P. Bowers, "Paul's Route Through Mysia: A Note on Acts XVI.8," *JTS* 30/2 (1979): 507-11.

16:9-17:5

8631   B. Schwank, " 'Setz über nach Mazedonien und hilf uns!' Reisenotizen zu Apg 16,9-17,5," *ErAu* 39/5 (1963): 399-416.

16:9-15

8632   Otto Glombitza, "Der Schritt nach Europa: Erwägungen zu Act 16:9-15," *ZNW* 53 (1962): 77-82.

8633   M. Trotter, "Acts in Esther," *QR* 14/4 (1994-1995): 435-47.

16:10-17

8634   Susan M. Praeder, "The Problem of First Person Narration in Acts," *NovT* 29 (1987): 193-218.

16:10

8635   Richard Glover, " 'Luke the Antiochene' and Acts," *NTS* 11/1 (1964): 97-106.

16:12

8636   M. F. Unger, "Archaeology and Paul's Campaign at Philippi," *BSac* 119 (1962): 150-60.

8637   Richard S. Ascough, "Civic Pride at Philippi: The Text-Critical Problem of Acts 16:12," *NTS* 44 (1998): 93-103.

16:13-40

8638   H. Boterman, "Der Heidenapostel und sein Historiker: Zur historischen Kritik der Apostelgeschichte," *TBe* 24 (1993): 62-84.

16:14

8639   R. Stephen Cherry, "Acts 16:14f.," *ET* 75 (1964-1965): 114.

8640   A. J. Conyers, "Lydia of Thyatira," *BI* 13/3 (1987): 81-83.

16:15

8641   Gerhard Delling, "Zur Taufe von 'Häusern' im Urchristentum," *NovT* 7 (1965): 285-311.

16:16-34

8642   M. Trotter, "Acts in Esther," *QR* 14/4 (1994-1995): 435-47.

16:16-24

8643   Monique Veillé, "Écriture et prédication: Actes 16,16-24," *ÉTR* 54/2 (1979): 271-78.

16:16-18

8644   Paul R. Trebilco, "Paul and Silas—'Servants of the Most High God'," *JSNT* 36 (1989): 51-73.

8645   H. J. Klauck, "With Paul in Paphos and Lystra: Magic and Paganism in the Acts of the Apostles," *Neo* 28 (1994): 93-108.

8646   F. Scott Spencer, "Out of Mind, Out of Voice: Slave-Girls and Prophetic Daughters in Luke-Acts," *BibInt* 7 (1999): 133-55.

16:16

8647   Colin J. Hemer, "The Adjective 'Phrygia'," *JTS* 27/1 (1976): 122-26.

16:19-21

8648   Craig S. de Vos, "Finding a Charge that Fits: The Accusation against Paul and Silas at Philippi (Acts 16.19-21)," *JSNT* 74 (1999): 51-63.

16:19

8649   B. N. Kaye, "Acts' Portrait of Silas," *NTS* 21/1 (1979): 13-26.

16:20-21

8650   Daniel R. Schwartz, "The Accusation and the Accusers at Philippi," *Bib* 65/3 (1984): 357-63.

16:22

8651   F. F. Bruce, "St. Paul in Macedonia," *BJRL* 61/2 (1979): 337-54.

16:25-34

8652   Eugene A. LaVerdiere, "The Eucharist in the New Testament and the Early Church—VI: The Breaking of the Bread. The Eucharist in the Acts of the Apostles," *Emmanuel* 100 (1994): 324-35.

16:25

8653   B. N. Kaye, "Acts' Portrait of Silas," *NTS* 21/1 (1979): 13-26.

16:27-36

8654   Craig S. de Vos, "The Significance of the Change from οἶκος to οἰκία in Luke's Account of the Philippian Gaoler," *NTS* 41/2 (1995): 292-96.

16:29

8655   B. N. Kaye, "Acts' Portrait of Silas," *NTS* 21/1 (1979): 13-26.

16:30-34

8656   J. Ramsey Michaels, "Apostolic Hardships and Righteous Gentiles," *JBL* 84 (1965): 27-37.

16:31

8657   Gerhard Delling, "Zur Taufe von 'Häusern' im Urchristentum," *NovT* 7 (1965): 285-311.

16:35-39

8658   Peter van Minnen, "Paul the Roman Citizen," *JSNT* 56 (1994): 43-52.

16:37-38

8659   Mark Black, "Paul and Roman Law in Acts," *RQ* 24/4 (1981): 209-18.

8660   Wolfgang Stegemann, "War der Apostel Paulus ein Römischer Bürger?" *ZNW* 78/3-4 (1987): 200-29.

17

8661   Everett Ferguson, "Apologetics in the New Testament," *RQ* 6 (1962): 180-95.

8662   Paul E. Davies, "The Macedonian Scene of Paul's Journeys," *BA* 26 (1963): 91-106.

8663   Lucien Legrand, "The Unknown God of Athens: Acts 17 and the Religion of the Gentiles," *IJT* 30/3 (1981): 158-67.

8664   Dean W. Zweck, "The Areopagus Speech of Acts 17," *LTJ* 21 (1987): 111-22.

17:1-10

8665   Néstor O. Míguez, "Lectura Socio-Politica de Hechos 17:1-10," *RevB* 50/2-3 (1988): 183-206.

17:1-9

8666   H. Boterman, "Der Heidenapostel und sein Historiker: Zur historischen Kritik der Apostelgeschichte," *TBe* 24 (1993): 62-84.

17:2-3

8667   Robert L. Reymond, "The Justification of Theology with a Special Application to Contemporary Christology," *Pres* 12/1 (1986): 1-16.

17:4-15

8668   Édouard Delebecque, "Paul à Thessalonique et à Bérée selon le texte occidental des Actes," *RT* 82/4 (1982): 605-15.

17:4

8669   B. N. Kaye, "Acts' Portrait of Silas," *NTS* 21/1 (1979): 13-26.

17:5-7

8670   Edwin A. Judge, "The Decrees of Caesar at Thessalonica," *RTR* 39/1 (1971): 1-7.

17:10-13

8671   Jacob Kremer, "Einführung in die Problematik heutiger Acta-Forschung anhand von Apg 17,10-13," *ETL* 48 (1978): 11-20.

17:10

8672   B. N. Kaye, "Acts' Portrait of Silas," *NTS* 21/1 (1979): 13-26.

17:11

8673   E. Nestle, "Act 17:11," *ZNW* 15 (1914): 91-92.

8674   Frederick W. Danker, "Menander and the New Testament," *NTS* 10 (1963-1964): 365-68.

17:14-15

8675   B. N. Kaye, "Acts' Portrait of Silas," *NTS* 21/1 (1979): 13-26.

17:14

8676   Wayne A. Meeks, "Who Went Where and How? A Consideration of Acts 17:14," *BT* 44/2 (1993): 201-206.

17:15-16

8677   R. E. Wycherley, "St. Paul at Athens," *JTS* 9/2 (1968): 619-21.

8678   Colin J. Hemer, "Paul at Athens: A Topographical Note," *NTS* 20/3 (1974): 341-50.

8679   Gil Lain, "Ancient Athens," *BI* (1989): 24-29.

17:16-34

8680   Jean Calloud, "Paul devant l'Aréopage d'Athènes: Actes 17:16-34," *RechSR* 69/2 (1981): 209-48.

8681   C. Manus, "The Areopagus Speech (Acts 17:16-34): a Study of Luke's Approach to Evangelism and its Significance in the African Context," *AfTJ* 14/1 (1985): 3-18.

8682   Joel Marcus, "Paul at the Areopagus: Window on the Hellenistic World," *BTB* 18 (1988): 143-48.

8683   Raymond H. Bailey, "Acts 17:16-34," *RevExp* 87 (1990): 481-85.

8684   P. Sciberras, "The Figure of Paul in the Acts of the Apostles: The Areopagus Speech," *MeliT* 43 (1992): 1-15.

8685   K. O. Sandnes, "Paul and Socrates: The Aim of Paul's Areopagus Speech," *JSNT* 50 (1993): 13-26.

8686   H. J. Klauck, "With Paul in Paphos and Lystra: Magic and Paganism in the Acts of the Apostles," *Neo* 28 (1994): 93-108.

8687   D. Wiens, "Luke on Pluralism: Flex with History," *Dir* 23 (1994): 44-53.

8688   P. Bossuyt and J. Radermakers, "Rencontre de l'incroyant et inculturation. Paul à Athènes," *NRT* 117/1 (1995): 19-43.

8689   J. Daryl Charles, "Engaging the (Neo) Pagan Mind: Paul's Encounter with Athenian Culture as a Model for Cultural Apologetics (Acts 17:16-34)," *TriJ* 16 (1995): 47-62.

17:16-32

8690   Robert G. Hoerber, "Paul at Athens," *CJ* 21 (1995): 202-205.

17:16-31

8691   Mark R. Shaw, "Is There Salvation Outside the Christian Faith," *EAJT* 2/2 (1983): 42-62.

17:16-21

8692   N. Clayton Croy, "Hellenistic Philosophies and the Preaching of the Resurrection (Acts 17:18, 32)," *NovT* 39 (1997): 21-39.

17:18-20

8693 Bruce W. Winter, "On Introducing Gods to Athens: An Alternative Reading of Acts 17:18-20," *TynB* 47 (1996): 71-90.

17:18

8694 George D. Kilpatrick, "The Acts of the Apostles, 17:18," *TZ* 42/5 (1986): 431-32.

8695 K. L. McKay, "Foreign Gods Identified in Acts 17:18?" *TynB* 45 (1994): 411-12.

17:22-34

8696 F. F. Bruce, "Paul and the Athenians," *ET* 88/11 (1976): 8-12.

17:22-33

8697 Heinz Külling, "Zur Bedeutung des Agnostos Thoes," *TZ* 36/2 (1980): 22-23.

17:22-32

8698 J.-C. Lebram, "Der Aufbau der Areopagrede," *ZNW* 55/3-4 (1964): 221-43.

17:22-31

8699 Wolfgang Nauck, "Die Tradition und Komposition der Aeropagrede," *ZTK* 53 (1956): 11-52.

8700 Kenneth O. Gangel, "Paul's Areopagus Speech," *BSac* 127 (1970): 308-12.

8701 A.-M. Dubarle, "Le discours à l'Aréopage (Actes 17:22-31) et son arrièreplan biblique," *RSPT* 57/4 (1973): 576-610.

8702 Jacques Dupont, "Le discours à l'Aréopage: Lieu de Rencoutre entre Christianisme et Hellénisme," *Bib* 60/4 (1979): 530-46.

8703 F. Gerald Downing, "Common Ground with Paganism in Luke and Josephus," *NTS* 28/4 (1982): 546-59.

8704 R. S. MacKenzie, "The Western Text of Acts: Some Lucanisms in Selected Sermons," *JBL* 104/4 (1985): 637-50.

8705 Stephen R. Spencer, "Is Natural Theology Biblical?" *GTJ* 9 (1988): 59-72.

8706   Robert C. Tannehill, "Mission in the 1990s: Reflections on the Easter Lections from Acts," *QR* 10/1 (1990): 84-97.

8707   James W. Thompson, "Paul's Preaching Ministry: Evangelistic and Pastoral Preaching in Acts," *RQ* 42 (2000): 19-26.

17:22-23

8708   Dean W. Zweck, "The Exordium of the Areopagus Speech, Acts 17:22,23," *NTS* 35/1 (1989): 94-103.

17:22

8709   C. M. Horne, "Toward a Biblical Apologetic," *GTJ* 2 (1961): 14-18.

8710   H. Armin Moellering, "Deisidaimonia: A Footnote to Acts 17:22," *CTM* 34 (1963): 466-71.

8711   R. E. Wycherley, "St. Paul at Athens," *JTS* 9/2 (1968): 619-21.

8712   Colin J. Hemer, "Paul at Athens: A Topographical Note," *NTS* 20/3 (1974): 341-50.

8713   Gil Lain, "Ancient Athens," *BI* (1989): 24-29.

17:23-31

8714   Pierre Auffret, "Essai sur la Structure Littéraire du Discours d'Athenes," *NovT* 20/3 (1978): 185-202.

17:24-30

8715   B. E. Shields, "The Areopagus Sermon and Romans 1:18ff.: A Study in Creation Theology," *RQ* 20/1 (1977): 23-40.

17:24-27

8716   Lawrence Wills, "The Form of the Sermon in Hellenistic Judaism and Early Christianity," *HTR* 77/3-4 (1984): 277-99.

17:24

8717   É. des Places, "Des temples faits de main d'homme" *Bib* 42/2 (1961): 217-23.

17:25

8718   É. des Places, "Actes 17:25," *Bib* 46 (1965): 219-22.

17:26

8719 Roger Lapointe, "Que Sont les Kaiaoi d'Act 17,26? Étude Semantique et Stylistique," *ÉgT* 3/3 (1972): 323-38.

17:27-29

8720 H. U. von Balthasar, "Toward a Theology of Christian Prayer," *CICR* 12 (1985): 245-57.

17:27

8721 É. des Places, "Actes 17:27," *Bib* 48/1 (1967): 1-6.

17:28

8722 É. des Places, "Ipsius enim et genus sumus," *Bib* 43/3 (1962): 388-95.

8723 Peter Colaclides, "Acts 17:28a and Bacchae 506," *VC* 27/3 (1973): 161-64.

8724 Walter Magass, "Theologie und Wetterregel: Semiotische Variationen über Arats 'Phainomena'," *LB* 49 (1981): 7-26.

8725 Gary M. Poulton, "The Poets of Ancient Greece," *BI* 13/4 (1987): 13-16.

8726 M. J. Edwards, "Quoting Aratus: Acts 17,28," *ZNW* 83 (1992): 26-29.

17:29

8727 Michael R. Austin, "Salvation and the Divinity of Jesus," *ET* 96 (1985): 271-75.

17:30-31

8728 É. des Places, "Actes 17:30-31," *Bib* 52/4 (1971): 526-34.

8729 Robert F. O'Toole, "Christ's Resurrection in Acts 13:13-52," *Bib* 60/3 (1979): 361-72.

17:31

8730 Gerhard Schneider, "Urchristliche Gottesverkündigung in Hellenistischer Umwelt," *BZ* 13/1 (1969): 59-75.

8731 Leslie C. Allen, "The Old Testament Background of (προ)ὡρισμένη in the New Testament," *NTS* 17/1 (1970-1971): 104-108.

17:32-34

8732   N. Clayton Croy, "Hellenistic Philosophies and the Preaching of the Resurrection (Acts 17:18, 32)," *NovT* 39 (1997): 21-39.

17:34

8733   J. G. Griffiths, "Was Damaris an Egyptian?" *BZ* 8/2 (1964): 293-95.

8734   D. Gill, "Dionysios and Damaris: A Note on Acts 17:34," *CBQ* 61 (1999): 483-90.

18

8735   Leander E. Keck, "Listening to and Listening for: From Text to Sermon," *Int* 27/2 (1973): 184-202.

8736   F. R. Harm, "Structural Elements Related to the Gift of the Holy Spirit in Acts," *CJ* 14/1 (1988): 28-41.

18:1-18

8737   H. Dixon Slingerland, "Acts 18:1-18: The Gallio Inscription, and Absolute Pauline Chronology," *JBL* 110 (1991): 439-49.

18:1-17

8738   H. Dixon Slingerland, "Acts 18:1-17 and Lüdemann's Pauline Chronology," *JBL* 109 (1990): 686-90.

8739   H. Boterman, "Der Heidenapostel und sein Historiker: Zur historischen Kritik der Apostelgeschichte," *TBe* 24 (1993): 62-84.

18:1

8740   R. E. Wycherley, "St. Paul at Athens," *JTS* 9/2 (1968): 619-21.

8741   Colin J. Hemer, "Paul at Athens: A Topographical Note," *NTS* 20/3 (1974): 341-50.

8742   Gil Lain, "Ancient Athens," *BI* (1989): 24-29.

18:2

8743   Robert G. Hoerber, "The Decree of Claudius in Acts 18:2," *CTM* 31 (1960): 690-94.

8744   F. F. Bruce, "Christianity Under Claudius," *BJRL* 44 (1962): 309-26.

18:3

8745   H. Szesnat, "What Did the σκηνοποιός Paul Produce?"
        Neo 27 (1993): 391-402.

18:5

8746   B. N. Kaye, "Acts' Portrait of Silas," *NTS* 21/1 (1979):
        13-26.

18:8

8747   Gerhard Delling, "Zur Taufe von 'Häusern' im
        Urchristentum," *NovT* 7 (1965): 285-311.

18:11-17

8748   Klaus Haacker, "Die Gallio-Episode und die paulinische
        Chronologie," *BZ* 16/2 (1972): 252-55.

18:15

8749   J. Lionel North, "Is ἰδεῖν περί a Latinsim?" *NTS* 29/2
        (1983): 265-66.

18:18-22

8750   Friedrich W. Horn, "Paulus, das Nasiräat und die
        Nasiräer," *NovT* 39 (1997): 117-37.

8751   G. G. Gamba, "Il voto di Paolo a Cencre e l' 'armatore'
        Teofilo. Ipotesi interpretativa a proposito di Atti 18,18,"
        Sale 61 (1999): 443-61.

18:21-23

8752   Sherman E. Johnson, "Caesarea Maritima," *LTJ* 20 (1985):
        28-32.

18:21

8753   J. M. Ross, "The Extra Words in Acts 18:21," *NovT* 34
        (1992): 247-49.

18:22

8754   J. Morgado, "Paul in Jerusalem: A Comparison of His
        Visits in Acts and Galatians," *JETS* 37 (1994): 55-68.

18:23

8755   F. F. Bruce, "Galatian Problems: 2. North or South
        Galatians?" *BJRL* 52/2 (1970): 243-66.

8756   Colin J. Hemer, "Phrygia: A Further Note," *JTS* 28/1
        (1977): 99-101.

18:24-19:10

8757   Kevin N. Giles, "Is Luke an Exponent of 'Early Protestantism'? Church Order in the Lukan Writings. Part I," *EQ* 54/4 (1982): 193-205.

18:24-19:7

8758   Michael Wolter, "Apollos und die Ephesinischen Johannesjünger," *ZNW* 78/1-2 (1987): 49-73.

18:24

8759   George D. Kilpatrick, "Apollos—Apelles," *JBL* 89/1 (1970): 77.

8760   Mikeal C. Parsons, "Ancient Alexandria," *BI* (1989): 30-34.

18:25

8761   James D. G. Dunn, "The Birth of a Metaphor: Baptized in the Spirit (I)," *ET* 89/5 (1978-1979): 134-38.

18:26

8762   G. G. Blum, "Das Amt der Frau im Neuen Testament," *NovT* 7 (1964): 142-61.

18:27-19:6

8763   L. G. Fonseca, "Novum Fragmentum papyraceum Actuum Apostolorum," *VD* 7 (1927): 157-59.

8764   M.-J. Lagrange, "Un nouveau papyrus contenant un fragment des Actes," *RB* 36 (1927): 549-60.

8765   H. A. Sanders, "A Papyrus Fragment of Acts in the Michigan Collection," *HTR* 20 (1927): 1-20.

8766   A. C. Clark, "The Michigan Fragment of the Acts," *JTS* 29 (1927-1928): 18-28.

18:27

8767   Werner Bieder, "Das Volk Gottes in Erwartung von Licht und Lobpreis," *TZ* 40/2 (1984): 137-48.

18:28

8768   Robert L. Reymond, "The Justification of Theology with a Special Application to Contemporary Christology," *Pres* 12/1 (1986): 1-16.

19-20

8769   T. Y. Mullins, "A Comparison between 2 Timothy and the Book of Acts," *AUSS* 31 (1993): 199-203.

19

8770   Donald K. Campbell, "Paul's Ministry at Ephesus," *BSac* 118 (1961): 304-10.

8771   Joseph Hanimann, " 'Nous Avons été Abreuves d'un Seul Esprit': Note sur 1 Co 12, 13b," *NRT* 94/4 (1972): 400-405.

8772   B. E. Thiering, "Qumran Initiation and New Testament Baptism," *NTS* 27/5 (1981): 615-31.

8773   Richard B. Cunningham, "Wide Open Doors and Many Adversaries," *RevExp* 89 (1992): 89-98.

8774   Peter Lampe, "Acta 19 im Spiegel der ephesischen Inschriften," *BZ* 36/1 (1992): 59-76.

19:1-7

8775   J. K. Parratt, "The Rebaptism of the Ephesian Disciples," *ET* 79/6 (1968): 182-83.

8776   C. B. Kaiser, "The 'Rebaptism' of the Ephesian Twelve: Exegetical Study on Acts 19:1-7," *RR* 31/1 (1977): 57-61.

8777   F. W. Norris, " 'Christians Only, But Not the Only Christians'," *RQ* 28/2 (1985): 97-105.

8778   Hermann Lichtenberger, "Täufergemeinden und frühchristliche Täuferpolemik im letzten Drittel," *ZTK* 84/1 (1987): 36-57.

19:1-6

8779   R. K. Levang, "The Content of an Utterance in Tongues," *Para* 23/1 (1989): 14-20.

19:1

8780   Klaus Haacker, "Einige Fälle von 'erlebter Rede' im Neuen Testament," *NovT* 12/1 (1970): 70-77.

8781   George D. Kilpatrick, "Apollos—Apelles," *JBL* 89/1 (1970): 77.

8782   W. A. Strange, "The Text of Acts 19:1," *NTS* 38 (1992): 145-48.

19:2

8783   Christoph Burchard, "Ei nach einem Ausdruck des Wissens oder Nichtwissens Joh 9:25, Act 19:2, 1 Cor 1:16, 7:16," *ZNW* 52/1-2 (1961): 73-82.

19:4

8784   John J. Kilgallen, "Paul's Speech to the Ephesian Elders: Its Structure," *ETL* 70 (1994): 112-21.

19:5

8785   W. E. Moore, "One Baptism," *NTS* 10/4 (1964): 504-16.

8786   Gerard S. Sloyan, "Jewish Ritual of the 1st Century CE and Christian Sacramental Behavior," *BTB* 15 (1985): 98-103.

19:6

8787   Timothy N. Boyd, "The Laying on of Hands," *BI* (1989): 9-10.

19:11-20

8788   H. J. Klauck, "With Paul in Paphos and Lystra: Magic and Paganism in the Acts of the Apostles," *Neo* 28 (1994): 93-108.

19:12-16

8789   L. G. Fonseca, "Novum Fragmentum papyraceum Actuum Apostolorum," *VD* 7 (1927): 157-59.

8790   M.-J. Lagrange, "Un nouveau papyrus contenant un fragment des Actes," *RB* 36 (1927): 549-60.

8791   H. A. Sanders, "A Papyrus Fragment of Acts in the Michigan Collection," *HTR* 20 (1927): 1-20.

8792   A. C. Clark, "The Michigan Fragment of the Acts," *JTS* 29 (1927-1928): 18-28.

19:12

8793   T. J. Leary, "The 'Aprons' of St. Paul—Acts 19:12," *JTS* 41 (1990): 527-29.

19:13-20

8794   Édouard Delebecque, "La mésaventure des fils de Scévas selon ses deux versions," *RSPT* 66/2 (1982): 225-32.

19:14

8795   Brian A. Mastin, "A Note on Acts 19:14," *Bib* 59/1 (1978): 97-99.

8796   W. A. Strange, "The Sons of Sceva and the Text of Acts 19:14," *JTS* 38 (1987): 97-106.

19:15-17

8797   Chrys C. Caragounis, "Divine Revelation," *ERT* 12 (1988): 226-39.

19:18

8798   Robert L. Reymond, "The Justification of Theology with a Special Application to Contemporary Christology," *Pres* 12/1 (1986): 1-16.

19:20-22

8799   G. Betori, "La strutturazione del libro degli Atti: una proposta," *RBib* 42 (1994): 3-34.

19:20

8800   M. H. Franzmann, "The Word of the Lord Grew," *CTM* 30 (1959): 563-81.

8801   A. W. Argyle, "Acts 19:20," *ET* 75 (1964): 151.

8802   J. Kodell, " 'The Word of God Grew.' The Ecclesial Tendency of *Logos* in Acts 6:7; 12:24; 19:20," *Bib* 55/4 (1974): 505-19.

8803   M. H. Grumm, "Another Look at Acts," *ET* 96/11 (1985): 333-37.

19:21

8804   C. Burfeind, "Paulus *muss* nach Rom. Zur politischen Dimension der Apostelgeschichte," *NTS* 46 (2000): 75-91.

19:22-27

8805   S. Sabugal, "La Mencion neotestamentaria de Damasco ¿ciudad de Siria o region de Qumran?" *ETL* 45 (1978): 403-13.

19:23-41

8806   R. E. Oster, "Acts 19:23-41 and an Ephesian Inscription," *HTR* 77/2 (1984): 233-37.

8807   Larry J. Kreitzer, "A Numismatic Clue to Acts 19.23-41: The Ephesian Cistophori of Claudius and Agrippina," *JSNT* 30 (1987): 59-70.

8808   Robert F. Stoops, "Riot and Assembly: the Social Context of Acts 19:23-41," *JBL* 108 (1989): 73-91.

19:24-40

8809   Édouard Delebecque, "La révolte des orfèvres à Éphèse et deux versions," *RT* 83/3 (1983): 419-29.

8810   Reinhard Selinger, "Die Demetriosunruhen (Apg 19:23-40): Eine Fallstudie aus rechthistorischer Perspektive," *ZNW* 88 (1997): 242-59.

19:24

8811   F. Sokolowski, "A New Testimony on the Cult of Artemis of Ephesus," *HTR* 58/4 (1965): 427-31.

19:27

8812   Steven M. Baugh, "Phraseology and the Reliability of Acts," *NTS* 36/2 (1990): 290-94.

19:35-40

8813   Lawrence Wills, "The Form of the Sermon in Hellenistic Judaism and Early Christianity," *HTR* 77/3-4 (1984): 277-99.

19:37

8814   T. C. G. Thornton, "The Destruction of Idols: Sinful or Meritorius?" *JTS* 37/1 (1986): 121-29.

8815   Steven M. Baugh, "Phraseology and the Reliability of Acts," *NTS* 36/2 (1990): 290-94.

20-28

8816   Harold S. Songer, "Paul's Mission to Jerusalem: Acts 20-28," *RevExp* 71/4 (1974): 499-510.

8817   Harold S. Songer, "Acts 20-28: From Ephesus to Rome," *RevExp* 87 (1990): 451-63.

20

8818   Paul E. Davies, "The Macedonian Scene of Paul's Journeys," *BA* 26 (1963): 91-106.

8819 Thomas L. Budesheim, "Paul's *Abschiedsrede* in the Acts of the Apostles," *HTR* 69/1 (1976): 9-30.

8820 W.-D. Hauschild, "Die Confessio Augustana und die altkirchliche Tradition," *KD* 26/3 (1980): 142-63.

20:1-21:14

8821 A. Moda, "Paolo prigioniero e martire. Gli avvenimenti gerosolimitiani," *BibO* 34 (1992): 193-252.

20:3-6

8822 Édouard Delebecque, "Les deux Versions du Voyage de Saint Paul de Corinthe à Troas," *Bib* 64/4 (1983): 556-64.

20:4

8823 G. Ogg, "Derbe," *NTS* 9/4 (1963): 367-70.

20:7-12

8824 Bernard Morel, "Eutychus et les Fondements Bibliques du Culte," *ÉTR* 37/1 (1962): 41-47.

8825 Bernard Trémel, "A propos d'Actes 20,7-12: puissance du thaumaturge ou du témoin?" *RTP* 30/4 (1980): 359-69.

8826 D. H. C. Read, "Eutychus—Or the Perils of Preaching," *PSB* 6/3 (1985): 168-78.

8827 A. D. Bulley, "Hanging in the Balance: A Semiotic Study of Acts 20:7-12," *ÉgT* 25 (1994): 171-88.

8828 Eugene A. LaVerdiere, "The Eucharist in the New Testament and the Early Church—VI: The Breaking of the Bread. The Eucharist in the Acts of the Apostles," *Emmanuel* 100 (1994): 324-35.

8829 Hermann-Josef Stipp, "Vier Gestalten einer Totenerweckungserzählung (1 Kön 17,17-24; 2Kön 4,8-37; Apg 9,36-42; Apg 20,7-12)," *Bib* 80 (1999): 43-77.

20:7

8830 C. H. Dodd, "New Testament Translation Problems I," *BT* 27/3 (1976): 301-11.

8831 Bernard P. Robinson, "The Place of the Emmaus Story in Luke-Acts," *NTS* 30/4 (1984): 481-97.

8832 J. Timothy Coyle, "The Agape—Eucharist Relationship in 1 Corinthians 11," *GTJ* 6/2 (1985): 411-24.

20:9

8833 Donald S. Deer, "Getting the 'Story' Straight in Acts 20:9," *BT* 39 (1988): 246-47.

8834 T. Naden, "Another Stor(e)y," *BT* 41/2 (1990): 243.

20:11

8835 Bernard P. Robinson, "The Place of the Emmaus Story in Luke-Acts," *NTS* 30/4 (1984): 481-97.

8836 J. Timothy Coyle, "The Agape—Eucharist Relationship in 1 Corinthians 11," *GTJ* 6/2 (1985): 411-24.

20:13-37

8837 D. Wiens, "Luke on Pluralism: Flex with History," *Dir* 23 (1994): 44-53.

20:14

8838 Werner Bieder, "Das Volk Gottes in Erwartung von Licht und Lobpreis," *TZ* 40/2 (1984): 137-48.

20:17-38

8839 Alberto Casalegno, "Il discorso di Miletoi," *RBib* 25/1 (1977): 29-58.

8840 J. S. Petofi, "La struttura della comunicazione in Atti 20:17-38," *RBib* 29/3-4 (1981): 359-78.

8841 Lewis R. Donelson, "Cult Histories and the Sources of Acts," *Bib* 68/1 (1987): 1-21.

8842 Colin J. Hemer, "The Speeches of Acts: 1. The Ephesian Elders at Miletus," *TynB* 40 (1989): 77-85.

8843 Colin J. Hemer, "The Speeches of Acts. 2. The Areopagus Address," *TynB* 40/2 (1989): 239-59.

20:17-35

8844 Lawrence Wills, "The Form of the Sermon in Hellenistic Judaism and Early Christianity," *HTR* 77/3-4 (1984): 277-99.

8845 Robert L. Reymond, "The Justification of Theology with a Special Application to Contemporary Christology," *Pres* 12/1 (1986): 1-16.

20:17-30

8846   Phillip Sigal, "Aspects of Dual Covenant Theology: Salvation," *HBT* 5/2 (1983): 1-48.

20:18-35

8847   J. Cheryl Exum and Charles H. Talbert, "The Structure of Paul's Speech to the Ephesian Elders," *CBQ* 29/2 (1967): 233-36.

8848   F. F. Bruce, "Is the Paul of Acts the Real Paul?" *BJRL* 58/2 (1976): 282-305.

8849   F. Zeilinger, "Lukas, Anwalt des Paulus. Überlegungen zur Abschiedsrede von Milet Apg 20,18-35," *BL* 54/3 (1981): 167-72.

8850   Evald Lövestam, "En gammaltestamentlig nyckel till Paulus-talet I Miletos," *SEÅ* 51 (1986): 137-47.

8851   Evald Lövestam, "Paul's Address at Miletus," *ST* 41/1 (1987): 1-10.

8852   John J. Kilgallen, "Paul's Speech to the Ephesian Elders: Its Structure," *ETL* 70 (1994): 112-21.

8853   Steve Walton, "Leadership and Lifestyle (1997): Luke's Paul, Luke's Jesus and the Paul of 1 Thessalonians," *TynB* 48 (1997): 377-80.

20:28

8854   I. Howard Marshall, "New Wine in Old Wineskins: V. The Biblical Use of the Word 'Ekklesia'," *ET* 84/12 (1973): 359-64.

8855   Kevin N. Giles, "Luke's Use of the Term ecclesia (ἐκκλήσια) with Special Reference to Acts 20:28 and 9:31," *NTS* 31 (1985): 135-42.

8856   K. G. E. Dolfe, "The Greek Word of 'Blood' and the Interpretation of Acts 20:28," *SEÅ* 55 (1990): 64-70.

20:29

8857   K. A. D. Smelik, "John Chrysostom's Homilies Against the Jews: Some Comments," *NTT* 39 (1985): 194-200.

20:32

8858   André Feuillet, " 'Témoins Oculaires et Serviteurs de la Parole'," *NovT* 15/4 (1973): 241-59.

20:35

8859   Eduard Schweizer, "The Testimony to Jesus in the Early Christian Community," *HBT* 7/1 (1985): 77-98.

8860   John J. Kilgallen, "Acts 20:35 and Thucydides," *JBL* 112 (1993): 312-14.

8861   Robert F. O'Toole, "What Role Does Jesus' Saying in Acts 20:35 Play in Paul's Address to the Ephesian Elders?" *Bib* 75 (1994): 329-49.

21

8862   R. J. Hardy, "Three Papers on the Text of Acts: 1. The Reconstruction of the Torn Leaf of Codex Bezae; 2. And When the Day of Pentecost Was Fully Come; 3. The Greek Text of Codex Laudianus," *HTR* 16 (1923): 163-86.

21:8

8863   Richard Glover, " 'Luke the Antiochene' and Acts," *NTS* 11/1 (1964): 97-106.

8864   Timothy Trammell, "Caesarea Maritima," *BI* (1989): 38-48.

21:10

8865   H. Patsch, "Die Prophetie des Agabus," *TZ* 28 (1972): 228-32.

21:14-26

8866   Matthew Black, "A Palestinian Syriac Palimpsest Leaf of Acts 21:14-26," *BJRL* 23 (1939): 201-14.

21:15-27

8867   Friedrich W. Horn, "Paulus, das Nasiräat und die Nasiräer," *NovT* 39 (1997): 117-37.

21:15-26

8868   A. Moda, "Paolo prigioniero e martire. Gli avvenimenti gerosolimitiani," *BibO* 34 (1992): 193-252.

21:16-17

8869   Édouard Delebecque, "La dernière étape du troisième voyage missionnaire de saint Paul selon les deux versions des Actes des Apôtres," *RTL* 14/4 (1983): 446-55.

21:17-26

8870   Giovanni Rinaldi, "Giacomo, Paolo e i Giudei," *RBib* 14/4 (1966): 407-23.

21:17

8871   J. Morgado, "Paul in Jerusalem: A Comparison of His Visits in Acts and Galatians," *JETS* 37 (1994): 55-68.

21:21

8872   D. L. Balch, " 'You Teach All the Jews . . . to Forsake Moses, Telling Them not to . . . Observe the Customs'," *SBLSP* 32 (1993): 369-83.

21:23-30

8873   John Fischer, "Paul in His Jewish Context," *EQ* 57 (1985): 211-36.

21:25

8874   Thor Boman, "Das textkritische Problem des sogenannten Aposteldekrets," *NovT* 7/1 (1964): 26-36.

8875   A. F. J. Klijn, "The Pseudo Clementines and the Apostolic Decree," *NovT* 10/4 (1968): 305-12.

8876   Terrance Callan, "The Background of the Apostolic Decree," *CBQ* 55 (1993): 284-97.

21:26-22:22

8877   Ronald D. Petry, "A Summary of Two Bible Studies by Graydon Snyder," *BLT* 43 (1998): 55-58.

21:26

8878   E. P. Sanders, "Judaism and the Grand "Christian" Abstractions: Love, Mercy, and Grace," *Int* 39 (1985): 357-72.

21:27-23:22

8879   A. Moda, "Paolo prigioniero e martire. Gli avvenimenti gerosolimitiani," *BibO* 34 (1992): 193-252.

21:27-26:32

8880   Simon Légasse, "L'apologétique à l'égard de Rome dans le procès de Paul," *RechSR* 69/2 (1981): 249-55.

21:37

8881   Larry V. Crutchfield, "The Fortress Antonia," *BI* (1989): 2-3, 7-8.

22-28

8882   Jacob Jervell, "Paulus—der Lehrer Israels," *NovT* 10/2 (1968): 164-90.

22

8883   D. M. Stanley, "Paul's Conversion in Acts: Why the Three Accounts?" *CBQ*, 15 (1953): 315-38.

8884   Gerhard Lohfink, "Eine alttestamentliche Darstellungsform für Gotteserscheinungen in den Damaskusberichten," *BZ* NS 9/2 (1965): 246-57.

8885   Boyd Reese, "The Apostle Paul's Exercise of His Rights as a Roman Citizen as Recorded in the Book of Acts," *EQ* 47/3 (1975): 138-45.

8886   Thomas L. Budesheim, "Paul's *Abschiedsrede* in the Acts of the Apostles," *HTR* 69/1 (1976): 9-30.

8887   O. H. Steck, "Formgeschichtliche Bemerkungen zur Darstellung des Damaskusgeschehens in der Apostelgeschichte," *ZNW* 67/1 (1976): 20-28.

8888   S. R. Bechtler, "The Meaning of Paul's Call and Commissioning in Luke's Story: An Exegetical Study of Acts 9, 22, and 26," *SBT* 15 (1987): 53-77.

8889   Gert Steuernagel, "'Ακούοντες μὲν τῆς φωνῆς: Ein Genitiv in der Apostelgeschichte," *NTS* 35/4 (1988-1989): 619-24.

8890   Ronald D. Witherup, "Functional Redundancy in the Acts of the Apostles: A Case Study," *JSNT* 48 (1992): 67-86.

22:3

8891   A. I. Baumgarten, "The Name of the Pharisees," *JBL* 102/3 (1983): 411-28.

8892   E. P. Sanders, "Judaism and the Grand "Christian" Abstractions: Love, Mercy, and Grace," *Int* 39 (1985): 357-72.

8893   Mark R. Fairchild, "Paul's Pre-Christian Zealot Associations: A Re-Examination of Galatians 1.14 and Acts 22.3," *NTS* 45 (1999): 514-32.

22:4-16

8894   Charles W. Hedrick, "Paul's Conversion-Call: A Comparative Analysis of the Three Reports in Acts," *JBL* 100/3 (1981): 415-32.

22:6-21

8895   Roy A. Harrisville, "Acts 22:6-21," *Int* 42 (1988): 181-85.

22:6-16

8896   Dennis Hamm, "Paul's Blindness and Its Healing: Clues to Symbolic Intent," *Bib* 71/1 (1990): 63-72.

8897   Willy Rordorf and Peter W. Dunn, "Paul's Conversion in the Canonical Acts and in the Acts of Paul," *Semeia* 80 (1997): 137-44.

22:8

8898   Colin J. Hemer, "The Name of Paul," *TynB* 36 (1985): 179-83.

22:9

8899   Robert G. Bratcher, "*Akouo* in Acts 9:7 and 22:9," *ET* 71 (1960): 243-45.

22:14-21

8900   David P. Moessner, "The Christ Must Suffer: New Light on the Jesus—Peter, Stephen, Paul Parallels in Luke-Acts," *NovT* 28/3 (1986): 220-56.

22:17-22

8901   C. R. A. Morray-Jones, "Paradise Revisited: The Jewish Mystical Background of Paul's Apostolate," *HTR* 86 (1993): 265-92.

22:22-29

8902   Peter van Minnen, "Paul the Roman Citizen," *JSNT* 56 (1994): 43-52.

22:25-29

8903   Mark Black, "Paul and Roman Law in Acts," *RQ* 24/4 (1981): 209-18.

22:30-23:11

8904   D. Cox, "Paul Before the Sanhedrin: Acts 22:30-23:11," *SBFLA* 21 (1971): 54-75.

23:3-6

8905   E. P. Sanders, "Judaism and the Grand "Christian" Abstractions: Love, Mercy, and Grace," *Int* 39 (1985): 357-72.

23:8-9

8906   Benedict T. Viviano, "Sadducees, Angels, and Resurrection," *JBL* 111 (1992): 496-98.

23:10

8907   Larry V. Crutchfield, "The Fortress Antonia," *BI* (1989): 2-3, 7-8.

23:11

8908   C. Burfeind, "Paulus *muss* nach Rom. Zur politischen Dimension der Apostelgeschichte," *NTS* 46 (2000): 75-91.

23:12-16

8909   W. H. P. Hatch, "Six Coptic Fragments of the New Testament from Nitria," *HTR* 26 (1933): 99-108.

23:23-26:32

8910   A. Moda, "Paolo prigioniero e martire. Gli avvenimenti di Cesarea," *BibO* 35 (1993): 21-59.

23:23

8911   George D. Kilpatrick, "Acts 23:23 Dexiolbous," *JTS* 14 (1963): 393-94.

8912   Sherman E. Johnson, "Caesarea Maritima," *LTJ* 20 (1985): 28-32.

23:24-26

8913   F. F. Bruce, "The Full Name of the Procurator Felix," *JSNT* 1 (1978): 33-36.

24

8914   Boyd Reese, "The Apostle Paul's Exercise of His Rights as a Roman Citizen as Recorded in the Book of Acts," *EQ* 47/3 (1975): 138-45.

8915   Giovanni Rinaldi, "Procurator Felix: note prosopografiche in margine ad una rilettura di At 24," *RBib* 39 (1991): 423-66.

24:1-21

8916   Bruce W. Winter, "The Importance of the Captatio Benevolentiae in the Speeches of Tertullus and Paul in Acts 24:1-21," *JTS* 42 (1991): 505-31.

24:6-8

8917   Édouard Delebecque, "Saint Paul avec ou sans le tribun Lysias en 58 à Cesarée. Texte court ou texte long?" *RT* 81/3 (1981): 426-34.

24:25-27

8918   F. F. Bruce, "The Full Name of the Procurator Felix," *JSNT* 1 (1978): 33-36.

24:27

8919   Sherman E. Johnson, "Caesarea Maritima," *LTJ* 20 (1985): 28-32.

25:1-26:32

8920   Robert F. O'Toole, "Luke's Notion of 'Be Imitators of Me as I Am of Christ' in Acts 25-26," *BTB* 8/4 (1978): 155-61.

25:6-12

8921   Peter van Minnen, "Paul the Roman Citizen," *JSNT* 56 (1994): 43-52.

25:8

8922   A. Moda, "Paolo prigioniero e martire. Gli avvenimenti di Cesarea," *BibO* 35 (1993): 21-59.

25:10

8923   C. Burfeind, "Paulus *muss* nach Rom. Zur politischen Dimension der Apostelgeschichte," *NTS* 46 (2000): 75-91.

25:11

8924   H. W. Tajra, "L'appel à César: séparation d'avec le Christianisme?" *ÉTR* 56/4 (1981): 593-98.

25:21

8925   Giuseppe Scarpat, "Ancora Sulla Data di Composizione Della Sapientia Salomonis. Il Termine Diagnosis," *RBib* 36 (1988): 363-75.

26

8926   D. M. Stanley, "Paul's Conversion in Acts: Why the Three Accounts?" *CBQ*, 15 (1953): 315-38.

8927   Gerhard Lohfink, "Eine alttestamentliche Darstellungsform für Gotteserscheinungen in den Damaskusberichten," *BZ* NS 9/2 (1965): 246-57.

8928   Boyd Reese, "The Apostle Paul's Exercise of His Rights as a Roman Citizen as Recorded in the Book of Acts," *EQ* 47/3 (1975): 138-45.

8929   O. H. Steck, "Formgeschichtliche Bemerkungen zur Darstellung des Damaskusgeschehens in der Apostelgeschichte," *ZNW* 67/1 (1976): 20-28.

8930   Robert F. O'Toole, "Acts 26: The Christological Climax of Paul's Defense," *TLZ* 104 (1979): 825.

8931   W. G. Marx, "A New Theophilus," *EQ* 52/1 (1980): 17-26.

8932   S. R. Bechtler, "The Meaning of Paul's Call and Commissioning in Luke's Story: An Exegetical Study of Acts 9, 22, and 26," *SBT* 15 (1987): 53-77.

8933   Ronald D. Witherup, "Functional Redundancy in the Acts of the Apostles: A Case Study," *JSNT* 48 (1992): 67-86.

26:2-23

8934   John J. Kilgallen, "Paul before Agrippa: Some Considerations," *Bib* 69/2 (1988): 170-95.

26:2-22

8935   Robert J. Kepple, "The Hope of Israel: The Resurrection of the Dead, and Jesus: A Study of Their Relationship in Acts with Particular Regard to the Understanding of Paul's Trial Defense," *JETS* 20/3 (1977): 231-41.

26:2

8936   A. O. Collins, "Herod Agrippa II," *BI* (1989): 68-71.

26:5

8937   Dick Avi, "Church: Mission and Development," *Point* 8/1 (1979): 29-38.

8938   A. I. Baumgarten, "The Name of the Pharisees," *JBL* 102/3 (1983): 411-28.

26:6-8

8939   Robert F. O'Toole, "Christ's Resurrection in Acts 13:13-52," *Bib* 60/3 (1979): 361-72.

26:7

8940   I. Peri, "Gelangen zur Vollkommenheit: Zur lateinischen Interpretation von Katantao in Eph 4:13," *BZ* 23/2 (1979): 269-78.

26:12-23

8941   Dennis Hamm, "Paul's Blindness and Its Healing: Clues to Symbolic Intent," *Bib* 71/1 (1990): 63-72.

26:12-18

8942   Charles W. Hedrick, "Paul's Conversion-Call: A Comparative Analysis of the Three Reports in Acts," *JBL* 100/3 (1981): 415-32.

8943   Willy Rordorf and Peter W. Dunn, "Paul's Conversion in the Canonical Acts and in the Acts of Paul," *Semeia* 80 (1997): 137-44.

26:12

8944   Bobby D. Box, "Damascus," *BI* 13/4 (1987): 23-27.

26:16-23

8945   David P. Moessner, "The Christ Must Suffer: New Light on the Jesus—Peter, Stephen, Paul Parallels in Luke-Acts," *NovT* 28/3 (1986): 220-56.

26:16-18

8946   Edward Fudge, "Paul's Apostolic Self-Consciousness at Athens," *JETS* 14/3 (1971): 193-98.

26:22-23

8947   Robert F. O'Toole, "Christ's Resurrection in Acts 13:13-52," *Bib* 60/3 (1979): 361-72.

26:28-29

8948   Paul Harlé, "Un 'Private-Joke' de Paul dans le livre des Actes," *NTS* 24/4 (1978): 527-33.

26:33

8949   Bent Noack, "Si passibilis Christus," *SEÅ* 37/38 (1972-1973): 211-21.

27-28

8950   A. Acworth, "Where Was St. Paul Shipwrecked? A Re-examination of the Evidence," *JTS* 24/1 (1973): 190-93.

8951   G. B. Miles and G. W. Trompf, "Luke and Antiphon: The Theology of Acts 27-28 in the Light of Pagan Beliefs about Divine Retribution, Pollution, and Shipwreck," *HTR* 69/3 (1976): 259-67.

8952   D. Ladouceur, "Hellenistic Preconceptions of Shipwreck and Pollution, as a Context for Acts 27-28," *HTR* 73 (1980): 435-49.

8953   Colin J. Hemer, "First Person Narrative in Acts 27-28," *TynB* 36 (1985): 79-109.

8954   Jürgen Wehnert, "Gestrandet: Zu einer neuen These über den Schiffbruch des Apostels Paulus auf dem Wege nach Rom," *ZTK* 87 (1990): 67-99.

8955   Jürgen Wehnert, " . . . und da erfuhren wir, daß die Insel Kephallenia heißt. Zur neuesten Auslegung von Apg 27-28 und ihrer Methode," *ZTK* 88 (1991): 169-80.

8956   Daniel Marguerat, " 'Et quand nous sommes entrés dans Rome': L'énigme de la fin du livre des Actes," *RHPR* 73/1 (1993): 1-21.

8957   A. Moda, "Paolo prigioniero e martire. Gli avvenimenti di Cesarea," *BibO* 35 (1993): 21-59.

8958   Dennis R. MacDonald, "The Shipwrecks of Odysseus and Paul," *NTS* 45 (1999): 88-107.

27:1-28:16

8959   Susan M. Praeder, "Acts 27:1-28:16: Sea Voyages in Ancient Literature and the Theology of Luke-Acts," *CBQ* 46/4 (1984): 683-706.

8960   Alfred Suhl, "Gestrandet! Bemerkungen zum Streit über die Romfahrt des Paulus," *ZTK* 88/1 (1991): 1-28.

8961   J. M. Gilchrist, "The Historicity of Paul's Shipwreck," *JSNT* 61 (1996): 29-51.

27

8962   R. W. Orr, "Paul's Voyage and Shipwreck," *EQ* 35/2 (1963): 103-104.

8963   P. Pokorný, "Die Romfahrt des Paulus und der antike Roman," *ZNW* 64/3-4 (1973): 233-44.

8964   Michael Oberweis, "Ps. 33 als Interpretationsmodell für Act 27," *NovT* 30/2 (1988): 169-83.

8965   C. Sant and J. Sammut, "Paulus war doch auf Malta!" *TGl* 80 (1990): 327-32.

27:1-13

8966   E. S. Buchanan, "More Pages from the Fleury Palimpsest," *JTS* 8 (1906-1907): 96-100.

8967   M.-É. Boismard and A. Lamouille, "Le Texte Occidental des Actes des Apôtres: à propos de Actes 27:1-13," *ETL* 63/1 (1987): 48-58.

27:1-10

8968   J. Rouge, "Actes 27:1-10," *VC* 14/4 (1960): 193-203.

27:1-5

8969   A. Moda, "Paolo prigioniero e martire. Gli avvenimenti romani," *BibO* 35 (1993): 89-118.

27:4-13

8970   James M. Robinson and Robert A. Kraft, "A Sahidic Parchment Fragment of Acts 27:4-13 at the University Museum, Philadelphia (E 16690 Coptic 1)," *JBL* 94/2 (1975): 256-65.

27:6-13

8971   A. Moda, "Paolo prigioniero e martire: Gli avvenimenti romani," *BibO* 35 (1993): 89-118.

27:7-12

8972   B. Schwank, " 'Wir umsegelten Kreta bei Salmone.' Reisebericht zu Apg 27,7-12," *ErAu* 48/1 (1972): 16-25.

27:10

8973   A. Moda, "Paolo prigioniero e martire: Gli avvenimenti romani," *BibO* 35 (1993): 89-118.

27:13

8974   R. Alan Culpepper, "Crete," *BI* (1989): 72-75.

27:14-26

8975   A. Moda, "Paolo prigioniero e martire: Gli avvenimenti romani," *BibO* 35 (1993): 89-118.

27:18-19

8976   David J. Clark, "What Went Overboard First?" *BT* 26/1 (1975): 144-46.

27:24

8977   C. Burfeind, "Paulus *muss* nach Rom. Zur politischen Dimension der Apostelgeschichte," *NTS* 46 (2000): 75-91.

27:27

8978   B. Schwank, " 'Als wir schon die vierzehnte Nacht auf der Adria trieben'," *ErAu* 66 (1990): 44-49.

27:33-38

8979   A. Moda, "Paolo prigioniero e martire: Gli avvenimenti romani," *BibO* 35 (1993): 89-118.

8980   Eugene A. LaVerdiere, "The Eucharist in the New Testament and the Early Church—VI: The Breaking of the Bread. The Eucharist in the Acts of the Apostles," *Emmanuel* 100 (1994): 324-35.

28

8981   N. Heutger, " 'Paulus auf Malta' im Lichte der maltesischen Topographie," *BZ* 28/1 (1984): 86-88.

28:1-10

8982   B. Schwank, "Also doch Malta? Spurensuche auf Kefalonia," *BK* 45 (1990): 43-46.

28:1-6

8983   H. J. Klauck, "With Paul in Paphos and Lystra: Magic and Paganism in the Acts of the Apostles," *Neo* 28 (1994): 93-108.

28:1

8984   W. Jürgen, "Und da erfuhren wir, dass die Insel Kephallenia heisst: Zur neuesten Auslegung von Apg 27-28 und ihrer Methode," *ZTK* 88/2 (1991): 169-80.

28:4

8985   Giovanni Rinaldi, "Nota: Dike in Atti 28:4," *BibO* 24/133 (1982): 186.

28:7

8986   Alfred Suhl, "Zum Titel πρώτῳ τῆς νήσου," *BZ* 36 (1992): 220-26.

28:13-14

8987   Marco Adinolfi, "San Paolo á Pozzuoli," *RBib* 8/3 (1960): 206-24.

28:14-16

8988   G. Betori, "La strutturazione del libro degli Atti: una proposta," *RBib* 42 (1994): 3-34.

28:14

8989   B. Schwank, " 'Und so kamen wir nach Rom (Apg 28,14).' Reisenotizen zu den letzten beiden Kapiteln der Apostelgeschichte," *ErAu* 36/3 (1960): 169-93.

28:16-31

8990   B. Prete, "L'arrivo di Paolo a Roma e il suo significato secondo Atti 28:16-31," *RBib* 31/2 (1983): 147-87.

8991   B.-J. Koet, "Paul in Rome (Acts 28:16-31): A Farewell to Judaism?" *Bij* 48 (1987): 397-415.

8992   Daniel Marguerat, " 'Et quand nous sommes entrés dans Rome': L'énigme de la fin du livre des Actes," *RHPR* 73 (1993): 1-21.

28:17-28

8993   Joseph B. Tyson, "Jews and Judaism in Luke-Acts (1992): Reading as a Godfearer," *NTS* 41 (1995): 19-38.

28:17-31

8994   Robert H. Smith, "The Theology of Acts," *CTM* 42/8 (1971): 527-35.

28:17-28

8995   A. Moda, "Paolo prigioniero e martire. Gli avvenimenti di Cesarea," *BibO* 35 (1993): 21-59.

8996   Joseph B. Tyson, "Jews and Judaism in Luke-Acts: Reading as a Godfearer," *NTS* 41 (1995): 19-38.

28:25-28

8997   H. van de Sandt, "Acts 28,28: No Salvation for the People of Israel? An Answer in the Perspective of the LXX," *ETL* 70/4 (1994): 341-58.

28:25

8998   François Bovon, " 'Schön hat der Heilige Geist durch den Propheten Jesaja zu euren Vätern gesprochen'," *ZNW* 75/3 (1984): 226-32.

28:26

8999   Heinrich Baarlink, "Friede im Himmel. Die lukanische Redaktion von Lk 19,38 und Ihre Deutung," *ZNW* 76/3 (1985): 170-86.

28:28

9000   J. Riedl, "Sabed que Dios envía su salud a los gentiles," *RevB* 27 (1965): 153-55, 162.

9001   Robert C. Tannehill, "Israel in Luke-Acts: A Tragic Story," *JBL* 104/1 (1985): 69-85.

28:30-31

9002   David E. Garland, "Rome," *BI* 13/4 (1987): 41-49.

9003   David L. Mealand, "The Close of Acts and Its Hellenistic Greek Vocabulary," *NTS* 36 (1990): 583-97.

9004   A. Moda, "Paolo prigioniero e martire. Gli avvenimenti di Cesarea," *BibO* 35 (1993): 21-59.

28:30

9005   E. Hansack, "Er lebte . . . von seinem eigenen Einkommen," *BZ* 19/2 (1975): 249-53.

9006   Franz Saum, " 'Er Lebte . . . von seinem eigenen Einkommen'," *BZ* 20/2 (1976): 226-29.

9007 E. Hansack, "Nochmals zu Apostelgeschichte 28,30. Erwiderung auf F. Saums kritische Anmerkungen," *BZ* 21/1 (1977): 118-21.

28:31

9008 Gerhard Delling, "Das Letzte Wort der Apostelgeschichte," *NovT* 15/3 (1973): 193-204.

9009 Frank Stagg, "The Unhindered Gospel," *RevExp* 71/4 (1974): 451-62.

Romans

1-11

9010   K. Prümm, "Röm. 1-11 und 2 Kor. 3, *Bib* 31 (1950): 164-203.

9011   L. Ramaroson, "Un 'nouveau plan' de Rm 1,16-11,36," *NRT* 94 (1972): 943-58.

1-8

9012   E. Ortigues, "La composition de l'épître aux Romains (i-viii)," *VC* 29-30 (1954): 52-81.

9013   Ulrich Luz, "Zum Aufbau von Röm. 1-8," *TZ* 25 (1960): 161-81.

9014   André Feuillet, "La vie nouvelle du chrétien d'après Romains i-viii," *RT* 83 (1983): 5-39.

1-6

9015   Carl A. Raschke, "On Rereading Romans 1-6 or Overcoming the Hermeneutics of Suspicion," *ExA* 1 (1985): 146-55.

1-5:11

9016   André Feuillet, "La citation d'Habacuc II.4 et les huit premièrs chapitres de l'épître aux Romains," *NTS* 6 (1959): 52-80.

1-3

9017   G. Bornkamm, "Die Offenbarung des Zornes Gottes," *ZNW* 34 (1935): 239-62.

9018   S. Lewis Johnson, "Studies in Romans. Part IX," *BSac* 131 (1974): 163-72.

9019   F. F. Bruce, "Paul and the Athenians," *ET* 88 (1976): 8-12.

9020   Walter B. Russell, "An Alternative Suggestion for the Purpose of Romans," *BSac* 145 (1988): 174-84.

1-2

9021   Everett Ferguson, "Apologetics in the New Testament," *RQ* 6 (1962): 180-95.

9022   William C. Martin, "The Bible and Natural Law," *RQ* 17/4 (1974): 193-221.

9023   W. C. Bouzard, "The Theology of Wisdom in Romans 1 & 2: A Proposal," *WW* 7/3 (1987): 281-91.

1

9024   J. L. Lilly, "Exposition of the Missal Epistles from Romans," *CBQ* 3 (1941): 159-66.

9025   H. P. Owen, "The Scope of Natural Revelation in Romans i and Acts xvii," *NTS* 5 (1958-1959) 133-43.

9026   Morna D. Hooker, "Adam in Romans i," *NTS* 6 (1959-1960): 297-306.

9027   Morna D. Hooker, "A Further Note on Romans i," *NTS* 13 (1966-1967): 131-83.

1:1-17

9028   A. B. du Toit, "Persuasion in Romans 1:1-17," *BZ* 33/2 (1989): 192-209.

9029   Robert Jewett, "Ecumenical Theology for the Sake of Mission: Romans 1:1-17," *SBLSP* 15 (1992): 598-612.

1:1-7

9030   Peter Stuhlmacher, "Theologische Probleme des Römerbriefpräskripts," *EvT* 27 (1967): 374-89.

9031   J. Duplacy, "Le fils de Dieu né de la race de David," *AsSeign* 8 (1972): 12-16.

9032   A. Viard, "L'évangile et l'accomplissement des promesses de Dieu (Romains 1,1-7)," *EV* 87 (1977): 618-19.

9033   Beverly R. Gaventa, "Homiletical Resources: Advent as Apocalypse," *QR* 6/3 (1986): 54-83.

9034   Simon Légasse, "Paul et César: Romains 13,1-7: Essai de synthèse," *RB* 101 (1994): 516-32.

9035   Samuel Byrskog, "Epistolography, Rhetoric and Letter Prescript: Romans 1.1-7 as a Test Case," *JSNT* 65 (1997): 27-46.

1:1-6

9036   J. Duplacy, "Paul apôtre du Fils de Dieu auprès des nations," *AsSeign* 8 (1962): 20-36.

1:1-5

9037   Chip Anderson, "Romans 1:1-5 and the Occasion of the Letter: The Solution to the Two-Congregation Problem in Rome," *TriJ* 14 (1993): 25-40.

1:1-2

9038   Charles H. Giblin, " 'As It Is Written.' A Basic Problem in Noematics," *CBQ* 20 (1958): 477-98.

1:1

9039   A. O. Collins, "First-Century Slavery," *BI* 14/3 (1988): 36-39.

9040   Alton H. McEachern, "Paul: A Brief Biography," *BI* 14/3 (1988): 14-18.

1:3-4

9041   Eduard Schweizer, "Rom. 1,3f. und Gegensatz von Fleisch und Geist vor und bei Paulus," *EvT* 15 (1955): 563-71.

9042   J. Riedl, "Strukturen christologischer Glaubensentfaltung im Neuen Testament," *ZKT* 87 (1965): 443-52.

9043   H.-W. Bartsch, "Zur vorpaulinischen Bekenntnisformel im Eingang des Römerbriefs," *TZ* 23 (1967): 329-39.

9044   Leslie C. Allen, "The Old Testament Background of (προ)ορίζειν in the New Testament," *NTS* 17/1 (1970-1971): 104-108.

9045   Eta Linnemann, "Tradition und Interpretation in Rom. 1,3f.," *EvT* 31 (1971): 264-75.

9046   James D. G. Dunn, "Jesus—Flesh and Spirit: An Exposition of Romans 1.3-4," *JTS* 24 (1973): 40-68.

9047   J. Pikaza, "Constituido Hijo de Dios en la resurrección (Rm 1,3-4)," *CuBí* 32 (1975): 197-206.

9048   Vern S. Poythress, "Is Romans 1,3-4 a Pauline Confession After All?" *ET* 87 (1976) 180-83.

9049   P.-É. Langevin, "Quel est le 'Fils de Dieu' de Romains
       1,3-4?" *SE* 29 (1977) 145-77.

9050   Michael Theobald, " 'Sohn Gottes' als christologische
       Grundmetapher bei Paulus," *TQ* 174 (1994): 185-207.

9051   L. Schenke, "Gibt es im Markusevangelium eine
       Präexistenzchristologie?" *ZNW* 91 (2000): 45-71.

1:3

9052   Klaus Haacker, "Exegetische Probleme des Römerbriefs,"
       NovT 20/1 (1978): 1-21.

9053   Paul Beasley-Murray, "Romans 1:3f: an Early Confession
       of Faith in the Lordship of Jesus," *TynB* 31 (1980):
       147-54.

9054   Guy Wagner, "La filiation davidique de Jésus chez Paul,
       Marc, et Matthieu," *ÉTR* 66 (1991): 419-22.

1:4

9055   J. Trinidad, "Praedestinatus Filius Dei... ex resurrectione
       mortuorum (Rom. 1,4)," *VD* 20 (1940): 145-50.

9056   M.-É. Boismard, "Constitué fils de Dieu," *RB* 60 (1953)
       5-17.

9057   T. Fahy, "Romans 1:4," *ITQ* 23 (1956): 412.

9058   S. H. Hooke, "The Translation of Romans i.4," *NTS* 9
       (1962-1963): 370-71.

9059   B. Schneider, "κατὰ πνεῦμα ἁγιωσύνης (Romans 1,4),"
       Bib 48 (1967): 359-88.

1:5

9060   Junji Kinoshita, "Romans—Two Writings Combined,"
       NovT 7 (1965): 258-77.

9061   Gerhard Friedrich, "Muss upakoē pisteōs Rom 1,5 mit
       'Glaubens-gehorsam' übersetzt werden?" *ZNW* 72 (1981):
       118-23.

9062   Giuseppe Segalla, "L'obbedienza Di Fede (Rm 1:5; 16:26)
       Tema Della Lettera Ai Romani," *RivBib* 36 (1988):
       329-42.

9063   Don B. Garlington, "The Obedience of Faith in the Letter
       to the Romans," *WTJ* 52 (1990): 201-24.

9064 R. B. Hays, "Pistis and Pauline Christology: What Is at Stake?" *SBLSP* 30 (1991): 714-29.

1:8-17

9065 William Baird, "Romans 1:8-17," *Int* 33 (1979): 398-403.

1:8-15

9066 G. Eichholz, "Der ökumenische und missionarische Horizont der Kirche. Eine exegetische Studie zu Röm. 1,8-15," *EvT* 21 (1961): 15-27.

1:8

9067 B. E. Shields, "The Areopagus Sermon and Romans 1:18ff.: A Study in Creation Theology," *RQ* 20/1 (1977): 23-40.

9068 Steve Kraftchick, "Paul's Use of Creation Themes: A Test of Romans 1-8," *ExA* 3 (1987): 72-87.

1:9

9069 S. Lyonnet, "Deus cui servio in spiritu meo (Rom 1,9)," *VD* 41 (1963): 52-59.

1:11

9070 J. K. Parratt, "Laying on of Hands in Paul," *ET* 79 (1967-1968): 151-52.

9071 John J. Kilgallen, "Reflections on Charisma(ta) in the New Testament," *SM* 41 (1992): 289-323.

1:13

9072 Junji Kinoshita, "Romans—Two Writings Combined," *NovT* 7 (1965): 258-77.

9073 M. A. Krüger, "Tina Karpon, 'Some Fruit' in Romans 1:13," *WTJ* 49 (1987): 167-73.

1:14-17

9074 Otto Glombitza, "Von der Scham des Gläubigen," *NovT* 4 (1960-1961): 74-80.

1:14

9075 D. Jones-Howell, "Our Universal Debts," *ET* 89 (1977-1978): 372-73.

1:15

9076   N. Hutchison, "Have You Heard the Good News," *ET* 89 (1977-1978) 274-75.

1:16-3:26

9077   Normand Bonneau, "Stages of Salvation History In Romans 1:16-3:26," *ÉgT* 23/2 (1992): 177-94.

1:16-32

9078   Gerhard O. Forde, "The Normative Character of Scripture for Matters of Faith and Life: Human Sexuality in Light of Romans 1:16-32," *WW* 14 (1994): 305-14.

1:16-18

9079   Bill J. Leonard, "A Place to Believe: Romans 1:16-18," *RevExp* 86 (1989): 93-78.

1:16-17

9080   J. Cambier, "Justice de Dieu, salut de tous les hommes et foi," *RB* 71 (1964): 537-83.

9081   M. D. Tolbert, "Life Situation and Purpose of Romans," *RevExp* 73/4 (1976): 391-99.

9082   David S. Dockery, "Romans 1:16-17," *RevExp* 86 (1989): 87-91.

1:16

9083   B. Prete, "La formula *dunamis Theou* in Rom. 1,16," *RivBib* 23 (1975): 299-328.

9084   André Feuillet, "La situation privilegiée des Juifs d'après Rm. 3,9," *NRT* 105 (1983): 33-46.

9085   Harold S. Songer, "The Greeks: What Was Hellenism?" *BI* 9/2 (1983): 3, 9-11.

9086   Stanley N. Olson, "Epistolary Uses of Expressions of Self-Confidence," *JBL* 103 (1984): 585-597.

1:17

9087   S. Lyonnet, "De justitia Dei in epistola ad Romanos 1,17 et 3,21-22," *VD* 25 (1947): 23-34.

9088   Hans C. Cavallin, " 'The Righteous Shall Live by Faith': A Decisive Argument for the Traditional Interpretations," *ST* 32 (1978): 33-43.

9089   R. M. Moody, "The Habakkuk Quotation in Romans 1:17," *ET* 92 (1981) 205-208.

9090   R. B. Hays, "Pistis and Pauline Christology: What Is at Stake?" *SBLSP* 30 (1991): 714-29.

9091   Douglas A. , Campbell, "Romans 1:17—A Crux Interpretum for Pistis Christou Debate," *JBL* 113 (1994): 265-85.

1:18-5:11

9092   X. Jacques, "Colère de Dieu (Romains 1,18-5,11)," *Chr* 25 (1978) 100-10.

1:18-4:25

9093   Hendrikus Boers, "We Who Are by Inheritance Jews: Not from the Gentiles, Sinners," *JBL* 111/1 (1992): 273-81.

1:18-3:20

9094   J.-N. Aletti, "Rm 1:18-3:20—Incohérence ou Cohérence de l'argumentation Paulinienne?" *Bib* 69/1 (1988): 47-62.

9095   Thomas H. Tobin, "Controversy and Continuity in Romans 1:18-3:20," *CBQ* 55 (1993): 298-318.

1:18-2:29

9096   René Lafontaine, "Pour une nouvelle évangélisation. L'emprise universelle de la justice de Dieu selon l'épître aux Romains 1,18-2,29," *NRT* 108 (1986): 641-65.

9097   William O. Walker, "Romans 1.18-2.29: A Non-Pauline Interpolation?" *NTS* 45 (1999): 533-52.

1:18-2:3

9098   F. Flückiger, "Zur Unterscheidung von Heiden und Juden in Röm. 1,18-2,3," *TZ* 10 (1954): 154-58.

1:18-32

9099   S. Schulz, "Die Anklage in Röm. 1,18-32," *TZ* 14 (1958): 161-73.

9100   D. M. Coffey, "Natural Knowledge of God: Reflections on Romans 1:18-32," *TS* 31 (1970): 674-91.

9101   J. Pikaza, "Constituido Hijo de Dios en la resurrección (Rm 1,3-4)," *CuBí* 32 (1975): 197-206.

9102   Wiard Popkes, "Zum Aufbau und Charakter von Römer 1.18-32," *NTS* 28 (1982): 490-501.

9103   R. B. Hays, "Awaiting the Redemption of Our Bodies: Drawing on Scripture and Tradition in the Church Debate on Homosexuality," *Soj* 20 (1991): 17-21.

9104   Calvin L. Porter, "Romans 1:18-32: The Role in the Developing Argument," *NTS* 40 (1994): 210-28.

9105   Kathy L. Gaca, "Paul's Uncommon Declaration in Romans 1:18-32 and Its Problematic Legacy for Pagan and Christian Relations," *HTR* 92 (1999): 165-98.

9106   Nélio Schneider, " 'Homossexualidade' no Novo Testamento: Observaçoes exegéticas e hermenêuticas," *EstT* 39 (1999): 27-35.

1:18-23

9107   André Feuillet, "La connaissance naturelle de Dieu par les hommes, d'après Romains 1,18-23," *LV* 14 (1954): 63-80.

9108   Leander E. Keck, "Romans 1:18-23," *Int* 40/4 (1986): 402-406.

1:18-22

9109   H. Schlier, "Von den Heiden. Römer 1,18-22," *EvT* 5 (1938): 113-24.

1:18-20

9110   W. Vandermarck, "Natural Knowledge of God in Romans: Patristic and Medieval Interpretations," *TS* 34 (1973): 36-52.

9111   James Barr, "La Foi Biblique et la Théologie Naturelle," *ÉTR* 64/3 (1989): 355-68.

1:18

9112   J. Y. Campbell, "Great Texts Reconsidered: Romans 1,18," *ET* 50 (1938-1939): 229-33.

9113   F. E. Gäbelein, "The Christian Dynamic. A Sermon on Romans 1:18," *Int* 6 (1952): 178-83.

9114   H.-M. Schenke, "Aporien im Römerbrief," *TLZ* 92 (1967): 881-88.

9115 H. J. Eckstein, "Denn Gottes Zorn wird von Himmel Her offenbar werden: Exegetische Erwägungen zu Röm 1:18," *ZNW* 78/1-2 (1987): 74-89.

1:19-21

9116 H. Ott, "Röm 1,19 ff. als dogmatisches Problems," *TZ* 15 (1959): 40-50.

9117 J. L. McKenzie, "Natural Law in the New Testament," *BR* 9 (1964): 3-13.

1:19-20

9118 H. Schlier, "Über die Erkenntnis Gottes bei den Heiden (Nach dem Neuen Testament)," *EvT* 2 (1935): 9-26.

1:19

9119 H. Rosin, "Τὸ γνωστὸν τοῦ θεοῦ," *TZ* 17 (1961): 161-65.

1:20

9120 K. Adam, "Die natürliche Gotterkenntnis," *TQ* 126 (1946): 1-18.

9121 L. Peretto, "Il pensiero di S. Ireneo su Rom. 1,20," *RivBib* 8 (1960): 304-23.

9122 John J. O'Rourke, "Romans 1,20 and Natural Revelation," *CBQ* 23 (1961): 301-306.

9123 F. J. A. de Grijs, "Theologische aantekeningen over enige wijzen, waarop Romeinen 1,20 is verstaan in de traditie van de rooms-katholieke kerk," *Bij* 30 (1969): 66-83.

1:21-32

9124 G. Bouwman, "Noch einmal Römer 1,21-32," *Bib* 54 (1973): 411-14.

1:21

9125 Edward Adams, "Abraham's Faith and Gentile Disobedience: Textual Links between Romans 1 and 4," *JSNT* 65 (1997): 47-66.

1:22-31

9126 E. Klostermann, "Die adäquate Vergeltung in Rm 1,22-31," *ZNW* 32 (1933): 1-6.

1:23-27

9127 K. Halter, "A Note on the Old Testament Background of Rom 1,23-27," *BibN* 69 (1993): 21-23.

1:23

9128 Niels Hyldahl, "A Reminiscence of the Old Testament at Romans i. 23," *NTS* 2 (1955-1956): 285-88.

9129 Ugo Vanni, "'Omoiōma in Paolo: Un'interpretazione esegetico- teologica alla luce del'uso dei LXX," *Greg* 58 (1977): 321-45, 431-70.

9130 Klaus Haacker, "Exegetische probleme des Römerbriefs," *NovT* 20/1 (1978): 1-21.

9131 F. M. Gillman, "Another Look at Romans 8:3: 'In the Likeness of Sinful Flesh'," *CBQ* 49 (1987): 597-604.

9132 Terrance Callan, "Paul and the Golden Calf," *EGLMBS* 10 (1990): 1-17.

1:24-27

9133 Leland J. White, "Does the Bible Speak about Gays or Same-Sex Orientation? A Test Case in Biblical Ethics," *BTB* 25 (1995): 14-23.

1:26-27

9134 James B. DeYoung, "The Meaning of 'Nature' in Romans 1 and Its Implications for Biblical Proscriptions of Homosexual Behavior," *JETS* 31 (1988): 429-41.

9135 Abraham Smith, "The New Testament and Homosexuality," *QR* 11 (1991): 18-32.

9136 David E. Malick, "The Condemnation of Homosexuality in Romans 1:26-27," *BSac* 150 (1993): 327-40.

9137 Halvor Moxnes, "Hedningenes synder? Polemikken mot 'homoseksualitet' i Det nye testamente," *NTT* 94/1 (1993): 1-34.

9138 Arland J. Arland, "Being Faithful to the Scriptures: Romans 1:26-27 as a Case in Point," *WW* 14 (1994): 315-25.

9139 John W. Martens, "Romans 2:14-16: A Stoic Reading," *NTS* 40 (1994): 55-67.

9140 Margaret Davies, "New Testament Ethics and Ours: Homosexuality and Sexuality in Romans 1:26-27," *BibInt* 3/3 (1995): 315-55.

9141 Mark D. Smith, "Ancient Bisexuality and the Interpretation of Romans 1:26-27," *JAAR* 64 (1996): 223-56.

9142 Daniel A. Helminiak, "Ethics, Biblical and Denominational: A Response to Mark Smith," *JAAR* 65 (1997): 855-59.

9143 James E. Miller, "Pederasty and Romans 1:27: A Response To Mark Smith," *JAAR* 65 (1997): 861-65.

9144 John Nolland, "Romans 1:26-27 and the Homosexuality Debate," *HBT* 22 (2000): 32-57.

1:26

9145 James E. Miller, "The Practices of Romans 1:26: Homosexual or Heterosexual?" *NovT* 37 (1995): 1-11.

1:28

9146 David E. Garland, "Rome's Reprobate Mind," *BI* 10/1 (1983): 18-26.

2-3

9147 E. F. Synge, "St. Paul's Boyhood and Conversion and His Attitude to Race," *ET* 94/9 (1983): 260-63.

2:1-3:20

9148 J. Cambier, "Le jugment des tous les hommes par Dieu seul, selon la vérité dans Rom 2:1-3:20," *ZNW* 67 (1976): 187-213. ET *TD* 26 (1978): 107-13.

2

9149 Klyne R. Snodgrass, "Justification by Grace—To the Doers: An Analysis of the Place of Romans 2 in the Theology of Paul," *NTS* 32/1 (1986): 72-93.

9150 J.-N. Aletti, "Romains 2: Sa cohérence et sa fonction," *Bib* 77 (1996): 153-77.

2:1-29

9151 G. P. Carras, "Romans 2:1-29: A Dialogue on Jewish Ideals," *Bib* 73/2 (1992): 183-207.

2:1

9152   F. J. Steinmetz and Friedrich Wulf, " 'Richtet nicht!' Auslegung und Meditation von Röm 2,1, Mt 7,1f. und Rom 8,1," *GeistL* 42 (1969): 71-74.

2:1-5

9153   Junji Kinoshita, "Romans—Two Writings Combined," *NovT* 7 (1965): 258-77.

2:6

9154   Russell Pregeant, "Grace and Recompense: Reflections on a Pauline Paradox," *JAAR* 47/1 (1979): 73-96.

2:10

9155   Charles H. Cosgrove, "Justification in Paul: A Linguistic and Theological Reflection," *JBL* 106/4 (1987): 653-70.

2:11-29

9156   Jouette M. Bassler, "Divine Impartiality in Paul's Letter to the Romans," *NovT* 26/1 (1984): 43-58.

2:12-16

9157   Jeffrey S. Lamp, "Paul, the Law, Jews, and Gentiles: A Contextual and Exegetical Reading of Romans 2:12-16," *JETS* 42 (1999): 37-51.

2:13

9158   Russell Pregeant, "Grace and Recompense: Reflections on a Pauline Paradox," *JAAR* 47/1 (1979): 73-96.

9159   Andreas Lindemann, "Die Gerechtigkeit aus dem Gesetz. Erwägungen zur Auslegung und zur Textgeschichte von Römer 10,5," *ZNW* 73 (1982): 231-50.

9160   Vítor Westhelle, "Labor: A Suggestion For Rethinking the Way of the Christian," *WW* 6/2 (1986): 194-206.

9161   Charles H. Cosgrove, "Justification in Paul: A Linguistic and Theological Reflection," *JBL* 106/4 (1987): 653-70.

9162   Don B. Garlington, "The Obedience of Faith in the Letter to the Romans. Part 2: The Obedience of Faith and Judgment by Works," *WTJ* 53 (1991): 47-72.

9163   Hendrikus Boers, "We Who Are by Inheritance Jews: Not from the Gentiles, Sinners," *JBL* 111/1 (1992): 273-81.

2:14-29

9164 X. Jacques, "La conscience Romains 2,14-29," *Chr* 28 (1981): 414-21.

2:14-16

9165 F. Fluckiger, "Die Werke des Gesetzes bei den Heiden (nach Rom. 2,14ff)," *TZ* 8 (1951): 17-42.

9166 Otto Kuss, "Die Heiden und die Werke des Gesetzes," *MTZ* 5 (1954): 77-98.

9167 John W. Martens, "Romans 2:14-16: A Stoic Reading," *NTS* 40 (1994): 55-67.

2:14-15

9168 F. Kuhr, "Rm 2,14f. und die Verheissung bei Jeremi. 31,31ff," *ZNW* 55 (1964): 243-61.

9169 Mark D. Mathewson, "Moral Intuitionism and the Law Inscribed on Our Hearts," *JETS* 42 (1999): 629-43.

2:14

9170 Paul J. Achtemeier, " 'Some Things in Them Hard to Understand': Reflection on an Approach to Paul," *Int* 38/3 (1984): 254-67.

2:15-16

9171 Hendrikus Boers, "We Who Are by Inheritance Jews: Not from the Gentiles, Sinners," *JBL* 111/1 (1992): 273-81.

2:15

9172 Bo Reicke, "Syneidesis in Röm. 2,15," *TZ* 12 (1956): 157-61.

9173 Lloyd Gaston, "Works of Law as a Subjective Genitive," *SR* 13/1 (1984): 39-46.

9174 Ramez Atallah, "The Objective Witness to Conscience: An Egyptian Parallel to Romans 2:15," *ERT* 18 (1994): 4-13.

2:16

9175 E. Driessen, "Secundum Evangelium meum (Rom 2,16; 16,25; 2 Tim 2,8)," *VD* 24 (1944): 25-32.

9176 Rudolf Bultmann, "Glossen im Römerbrief," *TLZ* 72 (1947): 197-202.

9177 Helmut Saake, "Echtheitskritische Überlegungen zur Interpolations-Hypothese von Römer ii. 16," *NTS* 19 (1972-1973): 486-89.

9178 Klaus Haacker, "Exegetische Probleme des Römerbriefs," *NovT* 20/1 (1978): 1-21.

2:17-24

9179 O. Olivieri, "Sintassi, senso e reporto col contesto di Rom. 2,17-24," *Bib* 11 (1930): 188-215.

2:17

9180 Junji Kinoshita, "Romans—Two Writings Combined," *NovT* 7 (1965): 258-77.

2:22

9181 Don B. Garlington, "Hierosylein and the Idolatry of Israel," *NTS* 36 (1990): 142-51.

2:25-29

9182 John M. G. Barclay, "Paul and Philo on Circumcision: Romans 2:25-9 in Social and Cultural Context," *NTS* 44 (1998): 536-56.

2:27-29

9183 Stephen Westerholm, "Letter and Spirit: The Foundation of Pauline Ethics," *NTS* 30/2 (1984): 229-48.

2:29

9184 B. Schneider, "The Meaning of St. Paul's Antithesis: 'The Letter and the Spirit'," *CBQ* 15 (1953): 163-207.

9185 M. Morreale de Castro, "La antitesis paulina entre la letra y el espíritu en la traducción y commentario de Juan Valdés," *EB* 13 (1954): 167-83.

3:1-11:36

9186 Charles D. Myers, "Chiastic Inversion in the Argument of Romans 3-8," *NovT* 35/1 (1993): 30-47.

3-8

9187 Walter Diezinger, "Unter Toten freigeworden. Eine Untersuchung zu Röm. iii-viii," *NovT* 5 (1962): 268-98.

9188 Charles D. Myers, "Chiastic Inversion in the Argument of Romans 3-8," *NovT* 35/1 (1993): 30-47.

<u>3</u>

9189   Marco Nobile, "Teologie e Teologia nella Bibbia: pluralismo di penssiero e sistema teologico," *Ant* 66/4 (1991): 469-81.

<u>3:1-9</u>

9190   Stanley Stowers, "Paul's Dialogue with a Fellow Jew in Romans 3:1-9," *CBQ* 46/4 (1984): 707-22.

<u>3:1-8</u>

9191   O. Olivieri, "Quid ergo amplius Judaeo est," *Bib* 10 (1939): 31-52.

9192   John S. Piper, "The Righteousness of God in Romans 3,1-8," *TZ* 36/1 (1980): 3-16.

9193   W. S. Campbell, "Romans III as a Key to the Structure and Thought of the Letter," *NovT* 23/1 (1981): 21-40.

9194   David R. Hall, "Romans 3.1-8 Reconsidered," *NTS* 29/2 (1983): 183-97.

9195   Paul J. Achtemeier, " 'Some Things in Them Hard to Understand': Reflection on an Approach to Paul," *Int* 38/3 (1984): 254-67.

9196   Heikki Räisänen, "Zum Verständnis von Röm 3:1-8," *SNTU-A* 10 (1985): 93-108.

9197   Charles H. Cosgrove, "What If Some Have Not Believed: The Occasion and Thrust of Romans 3:1-8," *ZNW* 78/1-2 (1987): 90-105.

9198   Paul J. Achtemeier, "Romans 3:1-8: Structure and Argument," *ATR* 11 (1990): 77-87.

9199   Charles D. Myers, "Chiastic Inversion in the Argument of Romans 3-8," *NovT* 35/1 (1993): 30-47.

<u>3:1-4</u>

9200   S. Lewis Johnson, "Studies in Romans. Part VIII: Divine Faithfulness, Divine Judgment, and the Problem of Antinomianism," *BSac* 130 (1973): 329-37.

<u>3:1-2</u>

9201   André Feuillet, "La situation privilegiée des Juifs d'après Rm. 3,9," *NRT* 105 (1983): 33-46.

<u>3:1</u>

9202   S. Lewis Johnson, "Studies in Romans. Part VII: The Jews
        and the Oracles of God," *BSac* 130 (1973): 235-49.

<u>3:4</u>

9203   Bengt Lofstedt, "Notes on St. Paul's Letter to the
        Romans," *FilN* 1/2 (1988): 209-10.

<u>3:5</u>

9204   S. Lyonnet, "De Justitia Dei in Epistola ad Romanos 10,3
        et 3,5," *VD* 25 (1947): 118-21.

9205   C. J. Bjerkelund, " 'Nach menschlicher Weise rede ich'.
        Funktion und Sinn des paulinischen Ausdrucks," *ST* 26
        (1972): 63-100.

<u>3:7-8</u>

9206   Herman Ljungvik, "Zum Römerbrief 3, 7-8," *ZNW* 32
        (1933): 207-10.

9207   A. Fridrichsen, "Nochmals Römer 3,7-8," *ZNW* 34 (1935):
        306-308.

<u>3:8</u>

9208   I. J. Canales, "Paul's Accusers in Romans 3:8 and 6:1,"
        EQ 57 (1985): 237-45.

<u>3:9-6:23</u>

9209   Ricardo Pietrantonio, "Esta la Justicia Enraizada en el
        NT," *RBib* 48/2 (1986): 89-119.

<u>3:9</u>

9210   F. C. Synge, "The Meaning of proekhometha in Romans
        3:9," *ET* 81 (1969-1970): 351.

9211   André Feuillet, "La situation privilegiée des Juifs d'après
        Rm. 3,9," *NRT* 105 (1983): 33-46.

9212   T. C. de Kruijf, "Is Anybody Any Better off?" *Bij* 46
        (1985): 234-44.

<u>3:10-18</u>

9213   H.-M. Schenke, "Aporien im Römerbrief," *TLZ* 92 (1967):
        881-88.

3:17-21

9214   Charles H. Giblin, "Three Monotheistic Texts in Paul," *CBQ* 37/4 (1975): 527-47.

3:18

9215   Romano Penna, "La Funzione Strutturale di 3:1-8 Nella Lettera ai Romani," *Bib* 69/4 (1988): 507-42.

3:19

9216   E. Pax, "Ein Beitrag zur biblischen Toposforschung," *SBFLA* 15 (1964-1965): 302-17.

3:20-21

9217   R. B. Hays, "Psalm 143 and the Logic of Romans 3," *JBL* 99 (1980): 107-15.

3:20

9218   Junji Kinoshita, "Romans—Two Writings Combined," *NovT* 7 (1965): 258-77.

9219   Charles H. Cosgrove, "Justification in Paul: A Linguistic and Theological Reflection," *JBL* 106/4 (1987): 653-70.

9220   C. E. B. Cranfield, "The Works of the Law in the Epistle to the Romans," *JSNT* 43 (1991): 89-101.

9221   Nikolaus Walter, "Gottes Erbarmen mit 'allem Fleisch' (Röm 3:20/Gal 2:16)—Ein 'Femininer' Zug im paulinischen Gottesbild?" *BZ* 35/1 (1991): 99-102.

9222   Hendrikus Boers, "We Who Are by Inheritance Jews: Not from the Gentiles, Sinners," *JBL* 111/1 (1992): 273-81.

9223   James D. G. Dunn, "Yet Once More—'The Works of the Law': A Response," *JSNT* 46 (1992): 99-117.

3:21-5:21

9224   Harold S. Songer, "New Standing before God: Romans 3:21-5:21," *RevExp* 73/4 (1976): 415-24.

3:21-4:25

9225   U. Wilckens, "Zu Römer 3,21-4,25. Antwort an G. Klein," *EvT* 11 (1964): 586-610.

9226   Don B. Garlington, "The Obedience of Faith in the Letter to the Romans. Part 3: The Obedience of Christ and the Obedience of the Christian," *WTJ* 55/1 (1993): 87-112.

3:21-4:24

9227   Günter Klein, "Exegetische Probleme in Römer 3,21-4,25," *EvT* 24 (1964): 676-83.

3:21-31

9228   John H. Reumann, "The Gospel of the Righteousness of God," *Int* 20/4 (1966): 432-52.

9229   George Howard, "Romans 3:21-31 and the Inclusion of the Gentiles," *HTR* 63 (1970): 223-33.

9230   James L. Price, "God's Righteousness Shall Prevail," *Int* 28/3 (1974): 259-80.

9231   W. J. Dumbrell, "Justification in Paul: A Covenantal Perspective," *RTR* 51/3 (1992): 91-101.

3:21-28

9232   Rudolf Schnackenburg, "Notre justification par la foi en Jésus Christ sans les oeuvres de la loi (Rm 3)," *AsSeign* 40 (1973): 10-15.

9233   Karl P. Donfried, "Romans 3:21-28," *Int* 34/1 (1980): 59-64.

3:21-26

9234   J. M. Bover, "El pensamiento generador de la teologia de S. Pablo," *Bib* 20 (1939): 142-72.

9235   W. S. Campbell, "Romans III as a Key to the Structure and Thought of the Letter," *NovT* 23/1 (1981): 21-40.

9236   Luke T. Johnson, "Rom 3:21-26 and the Faith of Jesus," *CBQ* 44/1 (1982): 77-90.

9237   J. A. Ziesler, "Salvation Proclaimed IX. Romans 3.21-26," *ET* 93 (1982): 356-59.

9238   Z. I. Herman, "Giustificazione e perdono in Romani 3,21-26," *Ant* 60 (1985): 240-78.

9239   A. Maillot, "Les Théologies de la Mort du Christ Chez Paul," *FV* 85/6 (1986): 33-45.

9240   R. B. Hays, "Pistis and Pauline Christology: What Is at Stake?" *SBLSP* 30 (1991): 714-29.

3:21-23

9241   P.-G. Klumbies, "Der eine Gott des Paulus: Röm 3,21-31 als Brennpunkt paulinischer Theologie," *ZNW* 85/3-4 (1994): 192-206.

3:21-22

9242   S. Lyonnet, "De justitia Dei in epistola ad Romanos 1,17 et 3,21-22," *VD* 25 (1947): 23-34.

3:21

9243   Jouette M. Bassler, "Divine Impartiality in Paul's Letter to the Romans," *NovT* 26/1 (1984): 43-58.

9244   J. Claude Piguet, "La Foi et les Oeuvres: Un Dialogue Inter-disciplinaire," *RTP* 118/3 (1986): 291-96.

9245   Steve Lemke, "The Law and the Prophets," *BI* 14/3 (1988): 23-25.

3:22-26

9246   S. R. Boguslawski, "Implicit Faith in Karl Rahner: A Pauline View," *ITQ* 51/4 (1985): 300-308.

3:22

9247   James D. G. Dunn, "Once More, Pistis Christou," *SBLSP* 30 (1991): 730-44.

3:23

9248   R. H. Allaway, "Fall or Fall-Short?" *ET* 97/4 (1986): 108-10.

3:24-26

9249   E. Driessen, "Promissio Redemptoris apud S. Paulum," *VD* 21 (1941) 233-38; 264-71; 298-305.

9250   Ernst Käsemann, "Zum Verständnis von Röm. 3,24-26," *ZNW* 43 (1950-1951): 150-54.

9251   John H. Reumann, "The Gospel of the Righteousness of God," *Int* 20/4 (1966): 432-52.

9252   Charles H. Talbert, "A Non-Pauline Fragment at Romans 3:24-26?" *JBL* 85/3 (1966): 287-96.

9253   Randal A. Argall, "Critical Investigation of Stuhlmacher's Exegesis of Rom 3:24-26 in the Light of NT Hermeneutics," *CTJ* 19 (1984): 280-281.

3:24

9254 Henri Clavier, "Notes sur un Motclef du Johannisme et de la Sotériologie Biblique: Hilasmos," *NovT* 10/4 (1968): 287-304.

9255 R. G. Crawford, "Is the Penal Theory of the Atonement Scriptural?" *SJT* 23/3 (1970): 257-72.

9256 Norman H. Young, "Did St. Paul Compose Romans iii,24f?" *ABR* 22 (1974): 23-32.

3:25-26

9257 H. G. Meecham, "Ro 3,25f. 4,25—The Meaning of διά with the Accusative," *ET* 50 (1938-1939): 564.

9258 V. Taylor, "Great Texts Reconsidered: Romans 3,25ff.," *ET* 50 (1938-1939): 295-300.

9259 John S. Piper, "The Demonstration of the Righteousness of God in Romans 3:25-26," *JSNT* 7 (1980): 2-32.

9260 Ben F. Meyer, "The Pre-Pauline Formula in Rom. 3.25-26a," *NTS* 29/2 (1983): 198-208.

3:25

9261 I. Logan, "The Strange Word 'Propitiation'," *ET* 46 (1934-1935) 522-27.

9262 J. M. Bover, "Quem proposuit Deus propositionem (Rom. 3,25)," *VD* 18 (1938): 137-42.

9263 J. M. Creed, "*Paresis* in Dionysius of Halicarnassus and in St. Paul," *JTS* 41 (1940): 28-30.

9264 T. W. Manson, "ἱλαστήριον," *JTS* 46 (1945): 1-10.

9265 S. Lyonnet, "Propter remissionem praecedentium delictorum (Rom 3,25)," *VD* 28 (1950): 282-87.

9266 L. Morris, "The Meaning of ilasterion in Romans iii. 25," *NTS* 2 (1955-1956): 33-43.

9267 T. Fahy, "Exegesis of Romans 3:25f.," *ITQ* 23 (1956): 69-73.

9268 S. Lyonnet, "Notes sur l'exégèse de l'épître aux Romains," *Bib* 38 (1957): 35-61.

9269 E. C. Blackman, "Romans 3,26b: A Question of Translation," *JBL* 87 (1968): 203-204.

9270   T. C. G. Thornton, "Propitiation or Expiation?" *ET* 80 (1968-1969): 53-55.

9271   David Greenwood, "Jesus as Hilasterion in Romans 3:25," *BTB* 3 (1973): 316-22.

9272   C. M. Robeck, "What is the Meaning of Hilasterion in Romans 3:25?" *SBT* 4/1 (1974): 21-36.

9273   Hans Hübner, "Sühne und Versöhnung," *KD* 29/4 (1983): 284-305.

9274   Olubayo Obijole, "St. Paul's Understanding of the Death of Christ in Romans 3:25: the Yoruba Hermeneutical Perspective," *AfTJ* 15/3 (1986): 196-201.

9275   Nico S. L. Fryer, "The Meaning and Translation of Hilasterion in Romans 3:25," *EQ* 59 (1987): 99-116.

9276   Hans Hübner, "Rechtfertigung und Sühne bei Paulus: Eine hermeneutische und theologische Besinnung," *NTS* 39/1 (1993): 80-93.

9277   Bruce W. Longenecker, "Pistis in Romans 3.25: Neglected Evidence for the 'Faithfulness of Christ'?" *NTS* (1993): 478-80.

3:26

9278   James D. G. Dunn, "Once More, Pistis Christou," *SBLSP* 30 (1991): 730-44.

3:27-4:25

9279   Junji Kinoshita, "Romans—Two Writings Combined," *NovT* 7 (1965): 258-77.

9280   Harold S. Songer, "New Standing before God: Romans 3:21-5:21," *RevExp* 73/4 (1976): 415-24.

3:27-4:8

9281   Klaus Haacker, "Justification, salut et foi (1997): Etude sur les rapports entre Paul, Jacques et Pierre," *ÉTR* 73 (1998): 177-88.

3:27-31

9282   Klyne R. Snodgrass, "Spheres of Influence: A Possible Solution to the Problem of Paul and the Law," *JSNT* 32 (1988): 93-113.

3:27-30

9283 R. W. Thompson, "The Inclusion of the Gentiles in Rom 3:27-30," *Bib* 69/4 (1988): 543-46.

3:27

9284 Gerhard Friedrich, "Das Gesetz des Glaubens Römer 3,27," *TZ* 10 (1954): 401-16.

9285 Heikki Räisänen, "Das 'Gesetz des Glaubens' (Rom. 3.27) und das 'Gesetz des Geistes' (Rom. 8.2)," *NTS* 26/1 (1979): 101-17.

9286 Jan Lambrecht, "Why is Boasting Excluded: A Note on Rom 3:27 and 4:2," *ETL* 61/4 (1985): 365-369.

9287 R. W. Thompson, "Paul's Double Critique of Jewish Boasting: A Study of Rom 3:27 in Its Context," *Bib* 67/4 (1986): 520-531.

3:28

9288 Ulrich Luck, "Der Jakobusbrief und die Theologie des Paulus," *TGl* 61 (1971): 161-79.

9289 John D. Hannah, "The Meaning of Saving Faith: Luther's Interpretation of Romans 3:28," *BSac* 140 (1983): 322-34.

9290 Phillip Sigal, "A Prolegomenon to Paul's Judaic Thought: The Death of Jesus and the Akedah," *EGLMBS* 4 (1984): 222-36.

9291 C. E. B. Cranfield, "The Works of the Law in the Epistle to the Romans," *JSNT* 43 (1991): 89-101.

3:29-30

9292 Charles H. Giblin, "Three Monotheistic Texts in Paul," *CBQ* 37/4 (1975): 527-47.

9293 Jan Lambrecht, "Paul's Logic in Romans 3:29-30," *JBL* 119 (2000): 526-28.

3:30

9294 Luke T. Johnson, "Rom 3:21-26 and the Faith of Jesus," *CBQ* 44/1 (1982): 77-9O.

9295 Stanley Stowers, "Ek Pisteos and Dia Tes Pisteos," *JBL* 108 (1989): 665-74.

<u>3:31</u>

9296 R. W. Thompson, "The Alleged Rabbinic Background of Rom 3:31," *ETL* 63/1 (1987): 136-48.

<u>4</u>

9297 T. Fahy, "Faith and the Law: Epistle to the Romans Ch. 4," *ITQ* 28 (1961): 207-14.

9298 Günter Klein, "Römer 4 und die Idee der Heilsgeschichte" *EvT* 23 (1963): 424-47.

9299 L. Goppelt, "Paulus und die Heilsgeschichte: Schlussfolgerungen aus Röm. iv und I. Kor. 1-13," *NTS* 13 (1966-1967): 31-42.

9300 Günter Klein, "Heil und Geschichte nach Römer iv," *NTS* 13 (1966-1967): 43-47.

9301 F. Muliyil, "The 'Children of Abraham' in St. Paul's Letters," *IJT* 20/1-2 (1971): 92-97.

9302 Lloyd Gaston, "Abraham and the Righteousness of God," *HBT* 2 (1980): 39-68.

9303 William Baird, "Abraham in the New Testament: Tradition and the New Identity," *Int* 42 (1988): 367-79.

9304 Anthony J. Guerra, "Romans 4 as Apologetic Theology," *HTR* 81 (1988): 251-70.

9305 J.-N. Aletti, "L'acte de croire pour l'apôtre Paul," *RechSR* 77/2 (1989): 233-50.

9306 J. Smit Sibinga, "Serta Paulina: On Composition Technique in Paul," *FilN* 10 (1997): 35-54.

<u>4:1-25</u>

9307 D. Yubero, "Presencia secular de Abraham," *CuBi* 12 (1955): 8-15.

9308 R. B. Hays, "Pistis and Pauline Christology: What Is at Stake?" *SBLSP* 30 (1991): 714-29.

<u>4:1-15</u>

9309 Michael Cranford, "Abraham in Romans 4: The Father of All Who Believe," *NTS* 41 (1995): 71-88.

4:1-8

9310   W. J. Dumbrell, "Justification in Paul: A Covenantal Perspective," *RTR* 51/3 (1992): 91-101.

4:1

9311   R. B. Hays, " 'Have We Found Abraham To Be Our Forefather According to the Flesh?': A Reconsideration of Rom 4:1," *NovT* 27 (1985): 76-98.

4:2

9312   Jan Lambrecht, "Why Is Boasting Excluded? A Note on Rom 3:27 and 4:2," *ETL* 61 (1985): 365-69.

4:3-5

9313   Wayne G. Strickland, "Preunderstanding and Daniel Fuller's Law-Gospel Continuum," *BSac* 144 (1987): 181-93.

4:3

9314   Richard Holst, "The Meaning of 'Abraham Believed God' in Romans 4:3," *WTJ* 59 (1997): 319-26.

4:5

9315   A. B. Kolenkow, "The Ascription of Romans 4:5," *HTR* 60 (1967): 228-30.

9316   Richard K. Moore, "Romans 4:5 In TEV: A Plea For Consistency," *BT* 39 (1988): 126-29.

4:11-12

9317   F. Porporato, "De Paulina pericopa Rom. 4,11-12," *VD* 17 (1937): 173-79.

4:12-21

9318   R. B. Hays, "Pistis and Pauline Christology: What Is at Stake?" *SBLSP* 30 (1991): 714-29.

4:12

9319   James Swetnam, "The Curious Crux at Romans 4,12," *Bib* 61/1 (1980): 110-15.

4:13-25

9320   A. B. du Toit, "Gesetzesgerechtigkeit und Glaubensgerechtigkeit in Rom 4:13-25: In Gespräch mit E. P. Sanders," *HTS* 44/1 (1988): 71-80.

4:13-16

> 9321   Guy Lafon, "La pensée du social et la théologie: Loi et grâce en Romains 4,13-1," *RechSR* 75 (1987): 9-38.

4:14

> 9322   John J. O'Rourke, "Pistis in Romans," *CBQ* 35/2 (1973): 188-94.

4:15

> 9323   Bengt Lofstedt, "Notes on St. Paul's Letter to the Romans," *FilN* 1/2 (1988): 209-10.

4:16

> 9324   John J. O'Rourke, "Pistis in Romans," *CBQ* 35/2 (1973): 188-94.

4:17

> 9325   Otfried Hofius, "Eine altjüdische Parallele zu Röm. IV. 17b," *NTS* 18/1 (1971): 93-94.

4:18-25

> 9326   R. Baulès, "La foi justifiante," *AsSeign* 41 (1971): 9-14.

4:18-22

> 9327   Hendrikus Boers, "Polarities at the Roots of New Testament Thought: Methodological Considerations," *PRS* 11 (1984): 55-75.

4:20

> 9328   Edward Adams, "Abraham's Faith and Gentile Disobedience: Textual Links between Romans 1 and 4," *JSNT* 65 (1997): 47-66.

4:21

> 9329   William Neil, "Paul's Certainties: God's Promises are Sure—Romans iv 21," *ET* 69 (1957-1958): 146-48.

4:22

> 9330   Bengt Lofstedt, "Notes on St. Paul's Letter to the Romans," *FilN* 1/2 (1988): 209-10.

4:23-25

> 9331   R. B. Hays, "Have We Found Abraham To Be Our Forefather According to the Flesh: A Reconsideration of Rom 4:1," *NovT* 27 (1985): 76-98.

4:25

9332 H. G. Meecham, "Ro 3,25f. 4,25—The Meaning of διά with the Accusative," *ET* 50 (1938-1939): 564.

9333 D. M. Stanley, "Ad historiam Exegeseos Rom 4,25," *VD* 29 (1951): 257-74.

9334 S. Lyonnet, "La valeur sotériologique de la résurrection du Christ selon saint Paul," *Greg* 39 (1958): 296-309.

9335 J. M. González-Ruiz, "Muerto por nuestros pecados y resucitado por nuestra justificaión?" *Bib* 40 (1959): 837-58.

9336 M. Peinador, "Un texto de San Pablo a la luz del paralelismo," *CuBí* 16 (1959): 339-49.

9337 H. Patsch, "Zum alttestamentlichen Hintergrund von Römer 4,25 und I Petrus 2,24," *ZNW* 60 (1969): 273-79.

9338 Antonio Charbel, "Nota a Rom 4'25: construzione semiticia?" *BibO* 17 (1975): 194.

9339 Antonio Charbel, "Ancora su Rom. 4,25: construzione semiticia?" *BibO* 18 (1976): 28.

5

9340 Rudolf Bultmann, "Adam und Christus nach Rm 5," *ZNW* 50 (1959): 145-65.

9341 X. Léon-Dufour, "Situation littéraire de Rom V," *RechSR* 51 (1963): 83-95.

9342 H. Müller, "Der rabbinische Qal-Wachomer-Schluss in paulinischer Typologie (zur Adam-Christus-Typologie in Rm 5)," *ZNW* 58 (1967): 73-92.

9343 G. R. Castellino, "Il peccato di Adamo," *BibO* 16 (1974): 145-62.

9344 J.-N. Aletti, "La Présence d'un Modèle Rhétorique en Romains: Son Rôle et Son Importance," *Bib* 71/1 (1990): 1-24.

9345 Stanley E. Porter, "The Argument of Romans 5: Can A Rhetorical Question Make A Difference?" *JBL* 110 (1991): 655-77.

5-8

9346   P. Rossano, "Il concetto di 'Hamartia' in Rom. 5-8," *RivBib* 4 (1956): 289-313.

9347   Bryant M. Kirkland, "God's Gifts," *PSB* 7/3 (1986): 268-275.

9348   Stanley N. Olson, "Romans 5-8 as Pastoral Theology," *WW* 4 (1986): 390-397.

9349   P. Roland, "L'antithèse de Rm 5-8," *Bib* 69/3 (1988): 396-400.

5:1

9350   Günter Klein, "Der Friede Gottes und der Friede der Welt: Eine exegetische Vergewisserung am Neuen Testament," *ZTK* 83/3 (1986): 325-55.

9351   Robert Jewett, "The God of Peace in Romans: Reflections on Crucial Lutheran Texts," *CThM* 25 (1998): 186-94.

5:1-21

9352   Harold S. Songer, "New Standing before God: Romans 3:21-5:21," *RevExp* 73/4 (1976): 415-24.

9353   M. L. Reid, "A Rhetorical Analysis of Romans 1:1-5:21 with Attention to the Rhetorical Function of 5:1-21," *PRS* 19/3 (1992): 255-72.

5:1-11

9354   Nils A. Dahl, "Two notes on Romans 5," *ST* 5 (1952): 37-48.

9355   Robert P. Meye, "Theological Education as Character Formation," *TEd* 24/1 (1988): 96-126.

9356   Patricia M. McDonald, "Romans 5:1-11 as a Rhetorical Bridge," *JSNT* 40 (1990): 81-96.

9357   Theodore Pulcini, "In Right Relationship With God: Present Experience and Future Fulfillment: An Exegesis of Romans 5:1-11," *SVTQ* 1-2 (1992): 61-85.

5:1-8

9358   Don B. Garlington, "The Obedience of Faith in the Letter to the Romans. Part 3: The Obedience of Christ and the Obedience of the Christian," *WTJ* 55/1 (1993): 87-112.

<u>5:1-5</u>

9359   J. L. Lilly, "Exposition of the Missal Epistles from Romans," *CBQ* 3 (1941): 159-66.

9360   R. Jacob, "Dieu, notre Joie," *AsSeign* 31 (1973): 36-39.

9361   Roy A. Harrisville, "Romans 5:1-5," *Int* 45 (1991): 181-85.

<u>5:2</u>

9362   J. M. Bover, "Gloriamur in spe (Rom. 5,2)," *Bib* 22 (1941): 41-45.

<u>5:3-5</u>

9363   Ulrich Luck, "Weisheit und Leiden," *TLZ* 92 (1967): 253-58.

<u>5:5</u>

9364   Mikeal C. Parsons, "The Holy Spirit: A History of Interpretation," *BI* 14/3 (1988): 33-35.

<u>5:6-11</u>

9365   John F. Walvoord, "Reconciliation," *BSac* 120 (1963): 3-12.

9366   D. G. Lafont, "La fierté des sauvés (Rm 5,6-11)," *AsSeign* 42 (1970): 12-17.

9367   J. P. Sampley, "Overcoming Traditional Methods by Synthesizing the Theology of Individual Letters," *SBLSP* 25 (1986): 603-13.

9368   James L. Jarrard, "Romans 5:6-11—While We Were Yet Sinners," *RevExp* 90 (1993): 123-28.

<u>5:7</u>

9369   F. Wisse, "The Righteous Man and the Good Man in Romans v.7," *NTS* 19 (1972-1973): 91-93.

9370   George R. Beasley-Murray, "Righteous and Good: There Was a Difference!" *BI* 3/1 (1976): 25.

9371   C. P. Bammel, "Patristic Exegesis of Romans 5:7," *JTS* NS 47 (1996): 532-42.

<u>5:8</u>

9372   Charles A. Wanamaker, "Christ as Divine Agent in Paul," *SJT* 39/4 (1986): 517-28.

5:10

9373   W. Thomas Sawyer, "Reconciled," *BI* 10/1 (1983): 33-34.

5:11

9374   George R. Beasley-Murray, "Atonement," *BI* 3/1 (1976): 27.

5:12-8:39

9375   Étienne Trocmé, "From 'I' to 'We': Christian Life According to Romans, Chapters 7 and 8," trans. M. Benedict, *ABR* 35 (1987): 73-76.

5:12-7:25

9376   Junji Kinoshita, "Romans—Two Writings Combined," *NovT* 7 (1965): 258-77.

5:12-19

9377   Leslie Houlden, "Fall and Salvation: A Case of Difficulty," *ET* 109 (1998): 234-37.

5:12-24

9378   Ugo Vanni, "L'analisi letteraria del contesto di Rom. v, 12-24," *RivBib* 11 (1963): 115-44.

5:12-21

9379   A.-M. Dubarle, "Le péché original dans Saint Paul," *RSPT* 40 (1956): 213-54.

9380   B. Mariani, "La persana di Adamo e il peccato originale secondo S. Paolo: Rom. 5,12-21," *Div* 2 (1958): 486-519.

9381   R. Raponi, "Rom. 5,12-21 e il peccato originale," *Div* 2 (1958): 520-59.

9382   William Barclay, "Romans v. 12-21," *ET* 70 (1959-1960): 132-35, 172-75.

9383   Harold O. Forshey, "The Doctrine of the Fall and Original Sin in the Second Century," *RQ* 3/3 (1960): 119-29.

9384   W. B. Neenan, "Doctrine of Original Sin in Scripture," *ITQ* 28 (1961): 54-64.

9385   Bernard Ramm, "The Fall and Natural Evil," *SouJT* 5 (1963): 21-32.

9386   E. McIver, "The Cosmic Dimensions of Salvation in the Thought of St. Paul," *Worship* 40 (1966): 156-64.

9387   Bruce J. Malina, "Some Observations on the Origin of Sin in Judaism and St. Paul," *CBQ* 31 (1969): 18-34.

9388   André Feuillet, "Le règne de la mort et le règne de la vie (Rom. v,12-21)," *RB* 77 (1970): 481-521.

9389   Chrys C. Caragounis, "Romans 5:15-16 in the Context of 5:12-21: Contrast or Comparison?" *NTS* 31 (1985): 142-148.

9390   Brendan Byrne, "The Type of the One to Come (Rom 5:14): Fate and Responsibility in Romans 5:12-21," *ABR* 36 (1988): 19-30.

9391   Karl Kertelge, "The Sin of Adam in the Light of Christ's Redemptive Act According to Romans 5:12-21," *CICR* 18 (1991): 502-13.

9392   Don B. Garlington, "The Obedience of Faith in the Letter to the Romans. Part 3: The Obedience of Christ and the Obedience of the Christian," *WTJ* 55 (1993): 281-97.

9393   Alfred Vanneste, "Le péché originel: un débat sans issue?" *ETL* 70/4 (1994): 359-83.

9394   J.-N. Aletti, "Romains 5,12-21: Logique, sens et fonction," *Bib* 78 (1997): 3-32.

5:12-19

9395   R. Jacob, "La nouvelle solidarité humaine," *AsSeign* 14 (1973): 322-38.

5:12-16

9396   André Feuillet, "La citation d'Habacuc II.4 et les huit premièrs chapitres de l'épître aux Romains," *NTS* 6 (1959): 52-80.

5:12-14

9397   S. Lyonnet, "Original Sin snd Romans 5:12-14," *TD* 5 (1957): 54-58.

9398   Ugo Vanni, "Rom. 5,12-14 alla luce del contesto," *RivBib* 11 (1963): 337-66.

9399   K. Condon, "The Biblical Doctrine of Original Sin," *ITQ* 34 (1967): 20-36.

9400   Denis Biju-Duval, "La Traduzione Di Rm 5:12-14," *RevB* 38 (1990): 353-73.

<u>5:12</u>

9401   S. Lyonnet, "Le sens de ἐφ' ᾧ en Rom. 5,12 et l'exégèse des Pères grecs," *Bib* 36 (1955): 436-56.

9402   J. M. González-Ruiz, "El pecado original segun San Pablo," *EB* 17 (1958): 147-88.

9403   S. Lyonnet, "Le sens de πειράζειν en Sg 2,24 et la doctrine du péché original," *Bib* 39 (1958): 27-36.

9404   Adrin Hastings, "The Salvation of Unbaptized Infants," *DR* 249 (1959): 172-78.

9405   L. Ligier, "In quo omnes peccaverunt," *NRT* 82 (1960): 337-48.

9406   S. Lyonnet, "À propos de Romains 5,12 dans l'oeuvre de saint Augustin," *Bib* 45 (1964): 541-42.

9407   J. Cambier, "Péchés des Hommes et Péché d'Adam en Rom. v. 12," *NTS* 11 (1964-1965): 217-55.

9408   S. Lyonnet, "Augustin et Rm 5,12 avant la controverse pélagienne," *NRT* 99 (1967): 842-49.

9409   Frederick W. Danker, "Romans v. 12: Sin under Law," *NTS* 14 (1967-1968): 424-39.

9410   D. G. Lafont, "Il n'y a pas de commune mesure! (Rm 5,12.15)," *AsSeign* 43 (1969): 13-18.

9411   Kazimierz Romaniuk, "Nota su Rom. 5,12," *RivBib* 19 (1971): 327-34.

9412   A. J. M. Wedderburn, "The Theological Structure of Romans v. 12," *NTS* 19 (1972-1973): 339-54.

9413   M. Miguéns, "A Particular Notion of Sin," *AmER* 167 (1973): 30-40.

9414   David Weaver, "The Exegesis of Romans 5:12 among the Greek Fathers and Its Implications for the Doctrine of Original Sin: The 5th-12th Centuries," *SVTQ* 29 (1985): 133-59, 231-57.

9415   R. H. Allaway, "Fall or Fall-Short?" *ET* 97/4 (1986): 108-10.

9416   John T. Kirby, "The Syntax of Romans 5:12: A Rhetorical Approach," *NTS* 33/2 (1987): 283-86.

9417 Joseph A. Fitzmyer, "The Consecutive Meaning of ἐφ᾽ ᾧ in Romans 5:12," *NTS* 39 (1993): 321-39.

5:13-14

9418 Meredith Kline, "Gospel Until the Law: Rom 5:13-14 and the Old Covenant," *JETS* 34 (1991): 433-46.

9419 John C. Poirier, "Romans 5:13-14 and the Universality of Law," *NovT* 38 (1996): 344-58.

5:13

9420 A. Marmorstein, "Paulus uad die Rabbinen," *ZNW* 30 (1931): 271-85.

9421 Gerhard Friedrich, "ἁμαρτία οὐκ ἐλλογεῖται. Rom. 5,13," *TLZ* 77 (1952): 523-28.

5:14

9422 L. Campeau, "Regnavit mors ab Adam usque ad Moysen," *SE* 5 (1953): 57-66.

9423 Klaus Haacker, "Exegetische Probleme des Römerbriefs," *NovT* 20/1 (1978): 1-21.

9424 R. R. Lara, "Por qué murieron los que no pecaron. Una luxury antigua de Rom 5,14," *CuBí* 36 (1979): 173-195.

5:15-21

9425 D. G. Lafont, "Sur l'interprétation de Romains v, 15-21," *RechSR* 45 (1957): 481-513.

5:15-17

9426 Brendan Byrne, "Christ's Pre-Existence in Pauline Soteriology," *TS* 58 (1997): 308-30.

5:15-16

9427 Chrys C. Caragounis, "Romans 5:15-16 in the Context of 5:12-21: Contrast or Comparison?" *NTS* 31 (1985): 142-48.

9428 John J. Kilgallen, "Reflections on Charisma(ta) in the New Testament," *SM* 41 (1992): 289-323.

5:15

9429 J. M. Bover, "In Rom. 5,15: exegesis logica," *Bib* 4 (1923): 94-96.

5:20-7:6

9430   Z. I. Herman, "La novita cristiana secondo Romani 5,20-7,6. Alcune osservazioni esegetiche," *Ant* 61 (1986): 225-73.

5:20

9431   Otto Eissfeldt, "Das Gesetz ist zwischeneingekommen," *TLZ* 91 (1966): 1-6.

6:1-8:13

9432   Brendan Byrne, "Living Out the Righteousness of God: The Contribution of Rom 6:1-8:13 to an Understanding of Paul's Ethical Presuppositions," *CBQ* 43 (1981): 557-81.

6-7

9433   Walter Diezinger, "Unter Toten Freigeworden. Eine Untersuchung zu Rom. iii-viii," *NovT* 5 (1962): 268-98.

6

9434   Kenneth S. Wuest, "Victory Over Indwelling Sin in Romans Six," *BSac* 116 (1959): 43-50.

9435   A. B. du Toit, "Dikaiosyne in Rom 6. Beobachtungen zur ethischen Dimension der paulinischen Gerechtigkeits-auffassung," *ZTK* 76 (1979): 261-91.

9436   M. H. Grumm, "The Gospel Call: Imperatives in Romans," *ET* 93 (1982): 239-42.

9437   A. J. M. Wedderburn, "Hellenistic Christian Traditions in Romans 6," *NTS* 29 (1983): 337-55.

9438   Georg Strecker, "Indicative and Imperative According to Paul," *BR* 35 (1987): 60-72.

9439   A. J. M. Wedderburn, "The Soteriology of the Mysteries and Pauline Baptismal Theology," *NovT* 29 (1987): 53-72.

9440   James W. Aageson, " 'Control' in Pauline Language and Culture: A Study of Romans 6," *NTS* 42 (1996): 75-89.

6:1-14

9441   James L. Price, "Romans 6:1-14," *Int* 4 (1980): 65-69.

9442   Gerhard Sellin, " 'Die Auferstehung ist schon geschehen'. Zur Spiritualisierung apokalyptischer Terminologie im Neuen Testaments," *NovT* 25 (1983): 220-37.

9443 Simon Légasse, "Etre baptisé dans la mort du Christ: étude de Romains 6:1-14," *RB* 98 (1991): 544-59.

9444 C. E. B. Cranfield, "Romans 6:1-14 Revisited," *ET* 106 (1994): 40-43.

6:1-11

9445 Otto Kuss, "Zur paulinischen und nachpaulinischen Tauflehre," *TGl* 42 (1932): 401-25.

9446 Rudolf Schnackenburg, "Todes- und Lebensgemeinschaft mit Christus. Neue Studien zu Röm 6,1-11," *MTZ* 6 (1955): 32-53.

9447 James D. G. Dunn, "Salvation Proclaimed. VI. Romans 6:1-11: Dead and Alive," *ET* 93 (1982): 259-64.

9448 Bo Frid, "Römer 6,4-5. εἰς τὸν θάνατον und τῷ ὁμοιώματι τοῦ θανάτου αὐτοῦ als Schlüssel zu Duktus und Gedankengang in Rom 6,11," *BZ* 30 (1986): 188-203.

9449 Robert Schlarb, "Röm 6:1-11 in der Auslegung der frühen Kirchenväter," *BZ* 33/1 (1989): 104-13.

6:1-5

9450 P.-É. Langevin, "Le baptême dans la mort-résurrection. Exégèse de Rm 6,1-5," *SE* 17 (1965): 29-65.

6:1

9451 I. J. Canales, "Paul's Accusers in Romans 3:8 and 6:1," *EQ* 57 (1985): 237-45.

6:2-10

9452 Vincent Tanghe, "Die Vorlage in Römer 6," *ETL* 73 (1997): 411-14.

6:3-14

9453 William J. Fogleman, "Romans 6:3-14," *Int* 47 (1993): 294-98.

6:3-11

9454 W. Dress, "Taufpredigt über Rom 6,3," *EvT* 2 (1935): 421-23.

9455 F. Ogara, "Complantati. . . similitudini mortis eius, simul et resurrectionis erimus," *VD* 15 (1935): 194-203.

9456   J. L. Lilly, "Exposition of the Missal Epistles from Romans," *CBQ* 3 (1941): 353-63.

9457   E. Druwé, " 'Medebegraven en verrezen met Christus': Röm vi,3-11 und O. Casel," *Bij* 10 (1949): 201-24.

9458   G. Ferloni, "Le Epistole della Liturgia," *BibO* 3 (1961): 97-100.

9459   J. Cambier, "La liberté des baptisés," *AsSeign* 60 (1963): 15-27.

9460   L. Fazekaš, "Taufe als Tod in Röm. 6,3ff," *TZ* 22 (1966): 305-18.

9461   Adalberto Sisti, "Simbolismo e realtà nel battesimo," *BibO* 11 (1969): 77-86.

9462   A. Viard, "Mort et résurrection," *EV* 83 (1983) 87-88.

6:3-4

9463   Franz G. Cremer, "Der 'Heilstod' Jesu im paulinischen Verständnis von Taufe und Eucharistie," *BZ* 14 (1970): 227-39.

6:3

9464   William B. Badke, "Baptised into Moses—Baptised into Christ: A Study in Doctrinal Development," *EQ* 60 (1988): 23-29.

6:4-11

9465   B. Rey, "L'homme nouveau d'après S. Paul," *RSPT* 48 (1964): 603-29; 49 (1965): 161-95.

6:4-6

9466   P. Rossano, "Consepolti... concrocefissi," *RivBib* 48 (1954): 51-55.

6:4-5

9467   Bo Frid, "Römer 6,4-5. εἰς τὸν θάνατον und τῷ ὁμοιώματι τοῦ θανάτου αὐτοῦ als Schlüssel zu Duktus und Gedankengang in Rom 6,11," *BZ* 30 (1986): 188-203.

6:5

9468   Paul Gächter, "Zur Exegese von Röm 6,5," *ZKT* 54 (1930): 88-92.

9469   Otto Kuss, "Zu Röm 6,5a," *TGl* (1951): 430-37.

9470 Ugo Vanni, "'Omoiōma in Paolo: Un'interpretazione esegetico- teologica alla luce del'uso dei LXX," *Greg* 58 (1977): 321-45, 431-70.

9471 Klaus Haacker, "Exegetische Probleme des Römerbriefs," *NovT* 20/1 (1978): 1-21.

9472 F. A. Morgan, "Romans 6,5a: United to a Death Like Christ's," *ETL* 59 (1983): 267-302.

<u>6:7</u>

9473 K. G. Kuhn, "Röm 6,7," *ZNW* 30 (1931): 305-10.

9474 Robin Scroggs, "Romans vi.7: ʽὸ γὰρ ἀποθανων δεδικαίωται ἀπὸ τῆς ἁμαρτίας'," *NTS* 10 (1963): 104-108.

9475 S. Lyonnet, "Qui enim mortuus est, iustificatus est a peccato," *VD* 42 (1964): 17-21.

9476 E. Klaar, "Röm 6,7: ὸ γὰρ ἀποθανων δεδικαίωται ἀπὸ τῆς ἁμαρτίας," *ZNW* 59 (1968): 131-34.

<u>6:12-14</u>

9477 Joel Marcus, "Let God Arise and End the Reign of Sin: A Contribution to the Study of Pauline Parenesis," *Bib* 69/3 (1988): 386-95.

<u>6:13</u>

9478 J. H. Michael, "The Text of Romans 6:13 in the Chester Beatty Papyrus," *ET* 49 (1937-1938): 235.

9479 W. H. Hagen, "Two Deutero-Pauline Glosses in Romans 6," *ET* 92 (1981): 364-67.

<u>6:17-18</u>

9480 Rudolf Bultmann, "Glossen im Römerbrief," *TLZ* 72 (1947): 197-202.

<u>6:17</u>

9481 F. Ogara, "Complantati. . . similitudini mortis eius, simul et resurrectionis erimus," *VD* 15 (1935): 194-203.

9482 J. Kurzinger, "Τύπος διδαχῆς und der Sinn von Röm 6,17f," *Bib* 39 (1958): 156-76.

9483 F. W. Beare, "On the Interpretation of Romans vi.17," *NTS* 5 (1958-1959): 206-10.

9484 U. Borse, "Abbild der Lehre," *BZ* 12 (1968): 95-103.

9485 Klaus Haacker, "Exegetische Probleme des Römerbriefs," *NovT* 20/1 (1978): 1-21.

6:19-23

9486 Adalberto Sisti, "Servizio del peccato e di Dio," *BibO* 6 (1964): 119-28.

6:19

9487 C. J. Bjerkelund, " 'Nach menschlicher Weise rede ich'. Funktion und Sinn des paulinischen Ausdrucks," *ST* 26 (1972): 63-100.

9488 W. H. Hagen, "Two Deutero-Pauline Glosses in Romans 6," *ET* 92 (1981): 364-67.

6:23

9489 Stephen Bigham, "Death and Orthodox Iconography," *SVTQ* 29/4 (1985): 325-41.

9490 John J. Kilgallen, "Reflections on Charisma(ta) in the New Testament," *SM* 41 (1992): 289-323.

6:26-27

9491 E. Vallauri, "I gemiti ddlo Spirito Santo," *RivBib* 27 (1979): 95-113.

7-8

9492 Pierre Grelot, "La vie dans l'Esprit," *Chr* 29 (1982): 83-98.

7:1-8:8

9493 Bruce Morrison and John Woodhouse, "The Coherence of Romans 7:1-8:8," *RTR* 47 (1988): 8-16.

7

9494 D. M. Davies, "Free From the Law. An Exposition of the Seventh Chapter of Romans," *Int* 7 (1953): 156-62.

9495 E. Ellwein, "Das Rätsel von Römer 7," *KD* 1 (1955): 247-68.

9496 S. Lyonnet, "L'histoire du salut selon le ch. 7 de l'épître aux Romains," *Bib* 43 (1962): 117-51.

9497 J. Kurzinger, "Der Schlüssel zum Verständnis von Röm 7," *BZ* 7 (1963): 270-74.

9498 Karl Kertelge, "Exegetische Überlegungen zum Verständnis der paulinischen Anthropologie nach Römer 7," *ZNW* 62 (1971): 105-14.

9499 S. Yagi, "Weder persönlich noch generell—zum neutestamentlichen Denken anhand Röm vii," *AJBI* 2 (1976): 159-73.

9500 André Feuillet, "Loi de Dieu, loi du Christ et loi de l'Esprit d'après les épîtres pauliniennes," *NovT* 22 (1980): 29-65.

9501 G. Bader, "Römer 7 als Skopus einer theologischen Handlungstheorie," *ZTK* 78 (1981): 31-56.

9502 C. P. Bammel, "Philocalia IX, Jerome, Epistle 121, and Origen's Exposition of Romans vii," *JTS* 32 (1981): 50-81.

9503 Paul J. Achtemeier, " 'Some Things in Them Hard to Understand': Reflection on an Approach to Paul," *Int* 38/3 (1984): 254-67.

9504 T. C. de Kruijf, "Is Anybody Any Better off?" *Bij* 46 (1985): 234-44.

9505 John M. Espy, "Paul's 'Robust Conscience' Re-examined," *NTS* 31 (1985): 161-188.

9506 Mark W. Karlberg, "Israel's History Personified: Romans 7:7-13 in Relation to Paul's Teaching on the 'Old Man'," *TriJ* 7/1 (1986): 65-74.

9507 Alan F. Segal, "Romans 7 and Jewish Dietary Law," *SR* 15/3 (1986): 361-374.

9508 J. A. Ziesler, "The Role of the Tenth Commandment in Romans 7," *JSNT* 33 (1988): 41-56.

9509 J.-D. Causse, "Le renversement diabolique du symbolique: Réflexions à partie de Romains 7,' *ÉTR* 75 (2000): 363-72.

7:1-6

9510 A. Gieniusz, "Rom 7,1-6: Lack of Imagination? Function of the Passage in the Argumentation of Rom 6,1-7,6," *Bib* 74 (1993): 389-400.

9511 David Hellholm, "Die argumentative Funktion von Römer 7:1-6," *NTS* 43 (1997): 385-411.

7:1-4

9512   John D. Earnshaw, "Reconsidering Paul's Marriage Analogy in Romans 7:1-4," *NTS* 40 (1994): 68-88.

7:2-3

9513   Robert Macina, "Pour Éclairer le Terme: Digamoi," *RevSR* 61 (1987): 54-73.

7:3

9514   Walter Diezinger, "Unter Toten Freigeworden. Eine Untersuchung zu Rom. iii-viii," *NovT* 5 (1962): 268-98.

7:6

9515   M. Morreale de Castro, "La antitesis paulina entre la letra y el espíritu en la traducción y commentario de Juan Valdés," *EB* 13 (1954): 167-83.

9516   Stephen Westerholm, "Letter and Spirit: The Foundation of Pauline Ethics," *NTS* 30/2 (1984): 229-48.

7:7-8:4

9517   E. de los Rios, "Peccatum et lex. Animadversions in Rom. 7,7-25," *VD* 11 (1931): 23-28.

9518   Pierre Benoit, "La loi et la Croix d'après saint Paul," *RB* 47 (1948): 481-509.

7:7-25

9519   Robert Jewett, "The Basic Human Dilemma: Weakness or Zealous Violence? Romans 7:7-25 and 10:1-18," *ExA* 13 (1997): 96-109.

7:7-13

9520   S. Lyonnet, "Quaestiones ad Rom-7,7-13," *VD* 40 (1962): 163-83.

9521   Katrine Krarup, "Det apologetiske sigte i Paulus' apologi for loven," *DTT* 57/3 (1995): 199-216.

7:7-12

9522   Ernst Fuchs, "Existentiale Interpretation von Röm 7,7-12 und 21-23," *ZTK* 59 (1962): 285-314.

9523   Douglas J. Moo, "Israel and Paul in Romans 7:7-12," *NTS* 32/1 (1986): 122-135.

9524   Daniel Roquefort, "Romains 7:7s Selon Jacques Lacan,"
        ÉTR 61/3 (1986): 343-352.

9525   Herbert Braun, "Römer 7,7-25 und das Selbstverständnis
        des Qumran- Frommen," *ZTK* 56 (1959): 1-18.

9526   Ole Modalsli, "Gal. 2,19-21; 5,16-18 und Rom 7,7-25," *TZ*
        21 (1965): 22-37.

9527   J. Blank, "Der gespaltene Mensch. Zur Exegese von Röm
        7,7-25," *BibL* 9 (1968): 10-20.

9528   K. F. Nickle, "Romans 7:7-25," *Int* 33 (1979): 181-87.

9529   Pheme Perkins, "Pauline Anthropology in Light of Nag
        Hammadi," *CBQ* 48/3 (1986): 512-522.

9530   Stanley E. Porter, "The Pauline Concept of Original Sin,
        in Light of Rabbinic Background," *TynB* 41 (1990): 3-30.

7:7-8

9531   André Feuillet, "La citation d'Habacuc ii.4 et les huit
        premièrs chapitres de l'épître aux Romains," *NTS* 6
        (1959): 52-80.

7:9

9532   W. Keuck, "Dienst des Geistes und des Fleisches," *TQ* 141
        (1961): 257-80.

9533   Antonio Orbe, "S. Metodio y la exegesis de Rom. 7,9a:
        'Ego autem vivebam sine lege aliqusndo'," *Greg* 50
        (1969): 93-137.

7:14-8:17

9534   George R. Beasley-Murray, "Flesh and Spirit," *BI* 3/1
        (1976): 38.

7:14-25

9535   P. Althaus, "Zur Auslegung von Röm. 7,14 ff.," *TLZ* 77
        (1952): 475-80.

9536   James D. G. Dunn, "Rom. 7,14-25 in the Theology of
        Paul," *TZ* 31 (1975): 257-73.

9537   B. L. Martin, "Some Reflections on the Identity of Ego in
        Romans 7:14-25," *SJT* 34 (1981): 39-47.

9538   A van den Beld, "Romeinen 7:14-25 en het probleem van
        de akrasía," *Bij* 46 (1985): 39-58.

9539   Don B. Garlington, "Romans 7:14-25 and the Creation Theology of Paul," *TriJ* 11 (1990): 197-235.

9540   Mark A. Seifrid, "The Subject of Rom 7:14-25," *NovT* 34 (1992): 313-33.

7:15-21

9541   Guy Lafon, "Un moi sans oeuvre," *RechSR* 78 (1990): 165-74.

7:15

9542   Ronald V. Huggins, "Alleged Classical Parallels to Paul's 'What I Want To Do I Do Not Do, But What I Hate, That I Do'," *WTJ* 54 (1992): 153-61.

7:17

9543   C. Mack Roark, "Sin and Evil in Paul's Theology," *BI* 14/3 (1988): 70-72.

7:21-23

9544   Ernst Fuchs, "Existentiale Interpretation von Röm 7,7-12 und 21-23," *ZTK* 59 (1962): 285-314.

7:22-8:3

9545   F. Müller, "Zwei Marginalien im Brief des Paulus an die Römer," *ZNW* 40 (1941): 249-54.

7:22-25

9546   Timothy F. Merrill, "Achard of Saint Victor and the Medieval Exegetical Tradition: Rom 7:22-25 in a Sermon on the Feast of the Resurrection," *WTJ* 48/1 (1986): 47-62.

7:23

9547   Jean Doignon, "Touches d'inspiration Origéniennes dans l'enseignement traditionnel d'Hilaire de Poitiers sur Romains 7,23," *RevSR* 67 (1993): 53-59.

7:24-25

9548   E. W. Smith, "The Form and Religious Background of Romans vii 24-25a," *NovT* 13 (1971): 127-35.

7:25

9549   James D. G. Dunn, "Rom 7,25 in the Theology of Paul," *TD* 24 (1976): 230-36.

9550 Hermann Lichtenberger, "Der Beginn der Auslegungs-geschichte von Römer 7: Röm 7:25b," *ZNW* 88 (1997): 284-95.

8

9551 Rudolf Schnackenburg, "Leben auf Hoffnung hin. Christliche Existenz nach Röm 8," *BL* 39 (1966): 316-19.

9552 Ernst Fuchs, "Der Anteil des Geistes am Glauben des Paulus. Ein Beitrag zum Verständnis von Römer 8," *ZTK* 72 (1975): 293-302.

9553 Hans Hübner, "Der Heilige Geist in der Heiligen Schrift," *KD* 36 (1990): 181-208.

9554 Philip Yancey, "Distress Signals: God Hears Our Groans," *CT* 34 (1990): 33-35.

9555 E. J. Vledder, "A Holistic View of the Holy Spirit as Agent of Ethical Responsibility," *HTS* 47 (1991): 503-25.

9556 A. G. Van Aarde, "Aanneming tot kind van God (yiothesia) by Paulus in Romeine 8 teen die agtergrond van die Jerusalemse tempelkultus--Deel II," *SkrifK* 19 (1998): 96-114.

9557 Richard J. Dillon, "The Spirit as Taskmaster and Troublemaker in Romans 8," *CBQ* 60 (1998): 682-702.

8:1-39

9558 Nils A. Dahl, "Two Notes on Romans 5," *ST* 5 (1952): 37-48.

9559 Giuseppe De Virgilio, "Spirito e libertà nel cristiano secondo Paolo," *BibO* 36 (1994): 87-100.

8:1-17

9560 Friedrich W. Horn, "Wandel im Geist: Zur pneumatologischen Begründung der Ethik bei Paulus," *KD* 38 (1992): 149-70.

8:1-11

9561 F. Lang, "Römer 8,1-11 in der Revision des Luthertextes von 1975," *ZTK* 5 (1981): 20-31.

8:1-2

9562 Chuck Lowe, " 'There Is No Condemnation' (Romans 8:1): But Why Not?" *JETS* 42 (1999): 231-50.

8:1

9563   E. Thurneysen, "Predigt über Röm. 8,1," *EvT* 2 (1935): 1-8.

9564   G. Crespy, "Rom. 8:1," *ÉTR* 30/4 (1955): 20-22.

9565   F. J. Steinmetz and Friedrich Wulf, " 'Richtet nicht': Auslegung und Meditation von Röm. 2,1, Mt 7,1f. and Röm 8,1," *GeistL* 42/1 (1969): 71-75.

8:2-4

9566   S. Lyonnet, "Le Nouveau Testament à la lumière de l'Ancien, à propos de Rom 8,2-4," *NRT* 87 (1965): 561-87.

8:2

9567   Heikki Räisänen, "Das 'Gesetz des Glaubens' (Rom. 3.27) und das 'Gesetz des Geistes' (Rom. 8.2)," *NTS* 26/1 (1979): 101-17.

9568   Romano Penna, "Il motivo della 'Aqedah sullo sfondo di Röm. 8:2," *RivBib* 33 (1985): 425-60.

9569   E. A. Obeng, "The Origins of the Spirit Intercession Motif in Romans 8.26," *NTS* 32 (1986): 621-32.

8:3-4

9570   Eduard Schweizer, "Zum religionsgeschichtlichen Hintergrund der "Sendungsformel" Gal 4,4f; Röm 8,3f; Joh 3,16f; 1 Joh 4,9," *ZNW* 57 (1966): 199-210.

8:3

9571   G. Giavini, " 'Damnavit peccatum in carne': Rom. 8,3 nel suo contesto," *RivBib* 17 (1969): 233-48.

9572   T. C. G. Thornton, "The meaning of kai penamartiss in Romans viii. 3," *JTS* 22 (1971): 515-17.

9573   Ugo Vanni, "'Omoiōma in Paolo: Un'interpretazione esegetico- teologica alla luce del'uso dei LXX," *Greg* 58 (1977): 321-45, 431-70.

9574   A. Vicent Cernuda, "La génesis humana de Jesucristo según S. Pablo," *EB* 37 (1978): 57-77.

9575   Marco Adinolfi, "L'invio del Figlio in Rom 8:3," *RBib* 33 (1985): 291-317.

9576 V. P. Branick, "The Sinful Flesh of the Son of God Rom 8:3): A Key of Image of Pauline Theology," *CBQ* 47 (1985): 246-62.

9577 Everett Ferguson, "Alexander Campbell's 'Sermon on the Law': A Historical and Theological Examination," *RQ* 29/2 (1987): 71-85.

9578 Cilliers Breytenbach, "Oor Die Vertaling Van Peri Hamartias in Romeine 8:3," *HTS* 45 (1989): 30-33.

9579 M. Dwaine Greene, "A Note On Romans 8:3," *BZ* 35/1 (1991): 103-106.

9580 Michael Theobald, " 'Sohn Gottes' als christologische Grundmetapher bei Paulus," *TQ* 174 (1994): 185-207.

9581 J. F. Bayes, "The Translation of Romans 8:3," *ET* 111 (1999): 14-16.

8:4

9582 H. van de Sandt, "Research into Rom. 8,4a: The Legal Claim of the Law," *Bij* 37 (1976): 252-69.

9583 H. van de Sandt, "An Explanation of Rom. 8:4a," *Bij* 37/4 (1976): 361-78.

9584 R. W. Thompson, "How Is the Law Fulfilled in Us? An Interpretation of Rom 8:4," *LouvS* 11 (1986): 31-40.

9585 J. A. Ziesler, "The Just Requirement of the Law (Romans 8:4)," *ABR* 35 (1987): 77-82.

8:7-9

9586 William L. Hendricks, "Paul's Use of 'Flesh'," *BI* 9/2 (1983): 50-52.

8:9-13

9587 R. Baulès, "Vivre selon l'esprit (Rm 8)," *AsSeign* 45 (1974): 10-15.

8:9-11

9588 K. Gatzweiler, "Le chrétien, un homme renouvelé par l'Esprit," *AsSeign* 18 (1970): 6-10.

8:9

9589 K. H. Schelkle, " 'Ihr seid Geistliche'. Eine Predigt," *GeistL* 35 (1962): 241-44.

8:10

9590   Robert T. Fortna, "Romans 8:10 and Paul's Doctrine of the Spirit," *ATR* 41 (1959): 77-84.

9591   C. Mack Roark, "Sin and Evil in Paul's Theology," *BI* 14/3 (1988): 70-72.

8:11-23

9592   Luis F. Ladaria, "Presente y Futuro en la Escatología Cristiana," *EE* 60/234 (1985): 351-59.

8:11

9593   Michael Theobald, " 'Sohn Gottes' als christologische Grundmetapher bei Paulus," *TQ* 174 (1994): 185-207.

8:12-30

9594   Oscar Cullmann, "Le prière selon les Épitres pauliniennes," *TZ* 35 (1979): 90-101.

8:12-17

9595   F. Ogara, "Ipse Spiritus testimonium reddit spiritui nostro, quod sumus filii Dei," *VD* 16 (1936): 200-208.

9596   Adalberto Sisti, "La vita nello spirito," *BibO* 10 (1968): 197-206.

9597   A. T. Hanson, "The Domestication of Paul: A Study in the Development of Early Christian Theology," *BJRL* 63/2 (1981): 402-18.

8:14-30

9598   S. C. Keesmaat, "Exodus and the Intertextual Transformation of Tradition in Romans 8:14-30," *JSNT* 54 (1994): 29-56.

8:14-27

9599   Piero Stefani, "I gemiti dello Spirito: Ro 8,14-27: note esegetiche e messaggio," *SEcu* 15 (1997): 291-300.

8:14-17

9600   R. Baulès, "Fils et héritiers de Dieu dans l'Esprit," *AsSeign* 31 (1973): 22-27.

8:14

9601   J. K. Sanders, "Led by the Spirit," *ET* 90 (1979): 307-308.

9602 Watson E. Mills, "Sons of God: The Roman View," *BI* 10/1 (1983): 37-39.

9603 W. Nicol, "Hoe Direk Lei Die Gees? 'N Dogmatiese en Eksegetiese Ondersoek Rondom Romeine 8:14," *SKrifK* 7/2 (1986): 173-97.

8:15

9604 S. V. McCasland, "Abba, Father," *JBL* 72 (1953): 79-91.

9605 Joachim Jeremias, "Abba," *TLZ* 79 (1954): 213-14.

9606 Kazimierz Romaniuk, "Spiritus clamans," *VD* 40 (1962): 190-98.

9607 J. Becker, "Quid locutio πάλιν εἰς φόβον in Rom 8,15 proprie valeat," *VD* 45 (1967): 162-67.

8:16-25

9608 T. Fahy, "St. Paul: Romans 8:16-25," *ITQ* 23 (1956): 178-81.

8:16

9609 A. Roosen, "Testimonium Spiritus," *VD* 28 (1950): 214-26.

9610 Tim Rayborn, "A Child's Place in the First Century," *BI* 14/3 (1988): 55-59.

8:17-30

9611 J. C. Beker, "Suffering and Triumph in Paul's Letter to the Romans," *HBT* 7/2 (1985): 105-119.

9612 J. C. Beker, "Vision of Hope for a Suffering World: Romans 8:17-30," *PSB* suppl 3 (1994): 26-32.

8:17-25

9613 J. L. Wu, "The Spirit's Intercession in Romans 8:26-27: An Exegetical Note," *ET* (1993): 13.

8:18-39

9614 E. Lewis, "A Christian Theodicy. An Expositian of Romans 8:18-39," *Int* 11 (1957): 495-20.

9615 John Ferguson, "The Christian Hope," *ET* 97/7 (1986): 204-205.

9616 Sheldon Tostengard, "Light in August: Romans 8:18-39," *WW* 7 (1987): 316-22.

8:18-30

9617   G. W. H. Lampe, "The New Testament Doctrine of *Ktisis*," *SouJT* 17 (1964): 449-62.

8:18-27

9618   John Bolt, "The Relation Between Creation and Redemption in Romans 8:18-27," *CTJ* 30 (1995): 34-51.

8:18-26

9619   Bernard Ramm, "The Fall and Natural Evil," *SouJT* 5 (1963): 21-32.

8:18-25

9620   P. S. Watson, "The Travail of Creation," *ET* 91 (1980): 208-209.

9621   Wayne G. Rollins, "Greco-Roman Slave Terminology and Pauline Metaphors for Salvation," *SBLSP* 26 (1987): 100-10.

9622   J. Mark Lawson, "Romans 8:18-25—The Hope of Creation," *RevExp* 91 (1994): 559-65.

8:18-23

9623   F. Ogara, "Exspectatio creaturae revelationem filiorum Dei exspectat," *VD* 18 (1938): 193-201.

9624   J. L. Lilly, "Exposition of the Missal Epistles from Romans," *CBQ* 4 (1942): 341-48.

9625   A.-M. Dubarle, "Lois de l'univers et vie chrétienne," *AsSeign* 58 (1964): 14-26.

9626   Adalberto Sisti, "La speranza della gloria," *BibO* 10 (1968): 123-34.

9627   Michael A. Bullmore, "The Four Most Important Biblical Passages for a Christian Environmentalism," *TriJ* 19 (1998): 139-62.

8:18-22

9628   U. Gerber, "Röm. viii 18 ff. als exegetisches Problem der Dogmatik," *NovT* 8 (1966): 58-81.

8:19-30

9629   Friedrich Wulf, "Von der Sehnsucht des Christen," *GeistL* 44 (1971): 391-94.

<u>8:19-23</u>

9630   S. Lyonnet, "Redemptio a 'cosmic' secundum Rom 8,19-23," *VD* 44 (1966): 225-42.

<u>8:19-22</u>

9631   A. Viard, "Exspectatio creaturae," *RB* 59 (1952): 337-54.

9632   A.-M. Dubarle, "Le gémissement des créatures dans l'ordre divin du cosmos," *RSPT* 38 (1954): 445-65.

<u>8:19</u>

9633   G. Bertram, "ἀποκαραδοκία," *ZNW* 49 (1958): 264-70.

9634   G. Kehnscherper, "Theologischc und homiletische Aspekte von Rom 8,19," *TLZ* 104 (1979): 411-24.

9635   D. R. Denton, "ἀποκαραδοκία" *ZNW* 73 (1982): 138-40.

<u>8:20-21</u>

9636   E. Hill, "The Construction of Three Passages from St. Paul," *CBQ* 23 (1961): 296-301.

9637   R. H. Allaway, "Fall or Fall-Short?" *ET* 97/4 (1986): 108-10.

<u>8:22-23</u>

9638   W. D. Stacey, "Paul's Certainties: God's Purpose in Creation—Romans viii. 22-23," *ET* 69 (1957-1958): 178-81.

9639   Gail R. O'Day, "Hope Beyond Brokenness: A Markan Reflection On the Gift of Life," *CThM* 15 (1988): 244-51.

<u>8:22</u>

9640   Lucien Richard, "Toward a Renewed Theology of Creation: Implications for the Question of Human Rights," *ÉgT* 17/2 (1986): 149-70.

9641   D. T. Tsumura, "An OT Background to Rom 8:22," *NTS* 40 (1994): 620-21.

<u>8:23</u>

9642   C. C. Oke, "The Interpreter's Forum: A Suggestion with Regard to Romans 8:23," *Int* 11 (1957): 455-60.

9643   James Swetnam, "On Romans 8,23 and the 'Expectation of Sonship'," *Bib* 48 (1967): 102-108.

9644 F. de la Calle, "La 'huiothesian' de Rom. 8,23," *EB* 30 (1971): 77-98.

8:24

9645 J. Bishop, "The Neglected Virtues," *ET* 89 (1977): 49-50.

8:26-28

9646 Klaus Haacker, "Ratlos, aber getrost," *TBe* 22 (1991): 289-92.

8:26-27

9647 K. Niederwimmer, "Das Gebet des Geistes," *TZ* 20 (1964): 252-65.

9648 J. Cambier, "La prière de l'Esprit, fondement de l'esperance," *AsSeign* 47 (1970): 11-17.

9649 M. de Goedt, "L'intercession de l'Esprit dans la prière chrétienne," *Conci* 79 (1972): 25-35.

9650 G. W. MacRae, "A Note on Romans 8:26-27," *HTR* 73 (1980): 227-30.

9651 G. W. MacRae, "Romans 8:26-27," *Int* 34 (1980): 288-92.

9652 Peter T. O'Brien, "Romans 8:26, 27: A Revolutionary Approach To Prayer?" *RTR* 46 (1987): 65-73.

9653 J. L. Wu, "The Spirit's Intercession in Romans 8:26-27: An Exegetical Note," *ET* (1993): 13.

8:26

9654 A. J. M. Wedderburn, "Romans 8.26—Towards a Theology of Glossolalia?" *SJT* 28 (1975): 369-77.

9655 George R. Beasley-Murray, "Intercession," *BI* 3/1 (1976): 43.

9656 O. Bayer, "Glückliche Skepsis (Röm 8:26f)," *TBe* 16 (1985): 99-102.

9657 E. A. Obeng, "The Origins of the Spirit Intercession Motif in Romans 8:26," *NTS* 32/4 (1986): 621-632.

9658 E. A. Obeng, "The Reconciliation of Rom 8:26f to New Testament Writings and Themes," *SJT* 39/2 (1986): 165-174.

9659 Geoffrey V. Smith, "The Function of 'Likewise' (Osautos) in Romans 8:26," *TynB* 49 (1998): 29-38.

8:28-30

9660   J. Cambier, "Dieu veut sauver les élus," *AsSeign* 48 (1972): 10-15.

8:28-29

9661   D. Edmond Hiebert, "Romans 8:28-29 and the Assurance of the Believer," *BSac* 148 (1991): 170-83.

9662   Robert A. Peterson, "Though all hell should endeavor to shake: God's Preservation of His Saints," *Pres* 17 (1991): 40-57.

8:28

9663   J. G. Griffiths, "Romans 8,28," *ET* 49 (1937-1938): 474-76.

9664   E. C. Blackman, "A Further Note on Romans 8,28," *ET* 50 (1938-1939): 378-79.

9665   J. G. Griffiths, "Romans 8:28," *ET* 61 (1949-1950): 286.

9666   H. G. Wood, "Paul's Certainties: God's Providential Care and Continual Help—Romans viii. 28, *ET* 69 (1957-1958): 292-95.

9667   J. B. Bauer, "Τοῖς ἀγαπῶσιν τὸν θεόν, Rm 8,28," *ZNW* 50 (1959): 106-12.

9668   C. E. B. Cranfield, "Romans 8,28," *SJT* 19 (1966): 204-15.

9669   J. M. Ross, "Panta synergei, Rom. viii.28," *TZ* 34 (1978): 82-85.

9670   Oda Wischmeyer, "Theon Agapan bei Paulus: Eine Traditionsgeschichtliche Miszelle," *ZNW* 78/1-2 (1987): 141-44.

9671   Hildebrecht Hommel, "Denen, die Gott Lieben: Erwägungen zu Römer 8:28," *ZNW* 80/1-2 (1989): 126-29.

8:29

9672   T. Fahy, "Romans 8:29," *ITQ* 23 (1956): 401-12.

9673   J. Kurzinger, "Συμμόρφους τῆς εἰκίνος τοῦ υἱοῦ αὐτοῦ," *BZ* 2 (1958): 294-99.

9674   Leslie C. Allen, "The Old Testament Background of (Pro)Orizein in the New Testament," *NTS* 17/1 (1970): 104-08.

9675   Friedrich Wulf, "Der Erstgeborene unter vielen Brüdern," *GeistL* 43 (1970): 466-69.

9676   Ulrich Schoenborn, "Solidariedade dos Crucificados: Eclesiogênese e Credibilidade Contextual," *EstT* 25/3 (1985): 225-47.

8:31-39

9677   G. Schille, "Die Liebe Gottes in Christus, Beobachtungen zu Rm 8,31-39," *ZNW* 59 (1968): 230-44.

9678   P. Fielder, "Röm 8,31-39 als Brennpunkt paulinischer Frohbotschaft," *ZAW* 68 (1977): 23-34.

9679   Gerhard Delling, "Die Entfaltung des 'Deus pro nobis' in Röm 8,31-39," *SNTU-A* 4 (1979): 76-96.

9680   Andreas H. Snyman, "Style and the Rhetorical Situation of Romans 8:31-39," *NTS* 34/2 (1988): 218-31.

9681   L. T. Tisdale, "Romans 8:31-39," *Int* 42 (1988): 68-72.

9682   Isabelle Parlier, "La folle justice de Dieu: Romains 8:31-39," *FV* 91 (1992): 103-10.

9683   Francis C. Rossow, "The Hound of Heaven, A Twitch upon the Thread, and Romans 8:31-39," *CJ* 23 (1997): 91-98.

8:31-34

9684   R. Baulès, "L'amour soverain de Dieu," *AsSeign* 15 (1973): 31-36.

8:32

9685   A. W. Argyle, "Romans 8,32," *JTS* 4 (1953): 214-15.

9686   Friedrich Wulf, "Er hat seinen eigenen Sohn nicht geschont. Zeitgemässe Gedanken zum Weihnachtsgeheimnis," *GeistL* 34 (1961): 407-409.

9687   E. Meile, "Isaaks Opferung. Eine Note an Nils Alstrup Dahl," *ST* 34 (1980): 111-28.

9688   Daniel R. Schwartz, "Two Pauline Allusions to the Redemptive Mechanism of the Crucifixion," *JBL* 102 (1983): 259-68.

9689   Robert D. Preus, "Clergy Mental Health and the Doctrine of Justification," *CTQ* 48/2-3 (1984): 113-23.

8:33

9690   Charles H. Cosgrove, "Justification in Paul: A Linguistic and Theological Reflection," *JBL* 106/4 (1987): 653-70.

8:34

9691   T. Fahy, "Romans 8:34," *ITQ* 25 (1958): 387.

9692   T. Worden, "Christ Jesus who Died or rather who has been raised up," *Scr* 10 (1958): 33-43; 11 (1959): 51-58.

8:35-39

9693   J. L. Lilly, "Exposition of the Missal Epistles from Romans," *CBQ* 4 (1942): 73-79.

9694   S. Lyonnet, "L'amour efficace du Christ," *AsSeign* 49 (1971): 12-16.

8:35-36

9695   Gerhard Münderlein, "Interpretation einer Tradition," *KD* 11 (1965): 136-42.

8:38-39

9696   G. J. Jeffrey, "Paul's Certainties: The Love of God in Christ—Romans viii. 38, 39," *ET* 69 (1957-1958): 359-61.

9697   James L. Jaquette, "Life and Death, Adiaphora, and Paul's Rhetorical Strategies," *NovT* 38 (1996): 30-54.

9-11

9698   H. Bleienstein, "Israel in der Heilsgeschichte," *GeistL* 6 (1931): 165-70.

9699   E. S. Berry, "The Conversion of the Jews," *AmER* 89 (1933): 414-17.

9700   P. Raith, "The Conversion of the Jews. Restoration of Israel and Juda," *AmER* 89 (1933): 234-45.

9701   R. M. Hawkins, "The Rejection of Israel: An Analysis of Romans IX-XI," *ATR* 23 (1941): 329-35.

9702   Pierre Benoit, "La question juive selon Rom. ix-xi d'après K. L. Schmidt," *RB* 55 (1948): 310-12.

9703   J. M. Bover, "La reprobation de Israel en Rom 9-11," *EE* 25 (1951): 63-82.

9704   George B. Caird, "Expository Problems: Predestination—Romans ix.-xi," *ET* 68 (1956-1957): 324-27.

9705   B. Martin Sanchez, "El destino de Israel," *CuBí* 18 (1961): 79-96.

9706   C. Journet, "L'économie de la loi mosaïque," *RT* 63 (1963): 5-36, 193-224, 515-47.

9707   J. Prado, "La Iglesia del futuro, según San Pablo," *EB* 22 (1963): 255-302.

9708   Bent Noack, "Current and Backwater in the Epistle to the Romans," *ST* 19 (1965): 155-66.

9709   Bruno Corsani, "I capitoli 9-11 della lettera ai Romani," *BibO* 14 (1972): 31-47.

9710   Dieter Zeller, "Israel unter dem Ruf Gottes (Röm 9-11)," *IKaZ* 2 (1973) 289-301.

9711   H. U. von Balthasar, "Aktualität des Themas Kirche aus Juden und Heiden," *IKaZ* 5 (1976): 239-45.

9712   G. S. Worgul, "Romans 9-11 and Ecclesiology," *BTB* 7 (1977): 99-109.

9713   J. A. Fischer, "Dissent within a Religious Community: Romans 9-11," *BTB* 10 (1980): 105-10.

9714   W. S. Campbell, "The Freedom and Faithfulness of God in Relation to Israel," *JSNT* 13 (1981): 27-45.

9715   A. T. Hanson, "Vessels of Wrath or Instruments of Wrath? Romans ix.22-33," *JTS* 32 (1981): 433-43.

9716   A. Maillot, "Essai sur les citations vétérotestamentaires contenues dans Romains 9 à 11. Ou comment se servir de la Torah pour montrer que le 'Christ est la fin de la Torah'," *ÉTR* 57 (1981): 55-73.

9717   André Feuillet, "Les privilèges et l'incrédulité d'Israël d'après les chapitres 9-11 de l'épître aux Romains. Quelques suggestions pour un dialogue fructueux entre Juifs et Chrétiens," *EV* 92 (1982): 497-506.

9718   Phillip Sigal, "Aspects of Dual Covenant Theology: Salvation," *HBT* 5/2 (1983): 1-48.

9719   James W. Aageson, "Scripture and Structure in the Development of the Argument in Romans 9-11," *CBQ* 48/2 (1986): 265-289.

9720   Otfried Hofius, "Das Evangelium und Israel. Erwägungen zu Römer 9-11," *ZTK* 83 (1986): 297-324.

9721   Donald Sneen, "The Root, the Remnant, and the Branches," *WW* 6/4 (1986): 398-409.

9722   J. Winkel, "Argumentationsanalyse von Röm 9-11," *LB* 58 (1986): 65-79.

9723   James W. Aageson, "Typology, Correspondence, and the Application of Scripture in Romans 9-11," *JSNT* 31 (1987): 51-72.

9724   Mary A. Getty, "Paul on the Covenants and the Future of Israel," *BTB* 17 (1987): 92-99.

9725   Paul W. Gooch, "Sovereignty and Freedom: Some Pauline Compatibilisms," *SJT* 40/4 (1987): 531-42.

9726   Barnabas Lindars, "The Old Testament and Universalism in Paul," *BJRL* 69 (1987): 511-27.

9727   François Refoulé, "Unité de l'épître aux Romains et Histoire du Salut," *RSPT* 71 (1987): 219-42.

9728   Mary A. Getty, "Paul and the Salvation of Israel: A Perspective on Romans 9-11," *CBQ* 50 (1988): 456-69.

9729   Robert A. Guelich, "The Church and Israel: Romans 9-11," *ExA* 4 (1988): 1-123.

9730   Elizabeth Johnson, "Jews and Christians in the New Testament: John, Matthew, and Paul," *RR* 42 (1988): 113-28.

9731   Daniel L. Migliore, "The Church and Israel: Romans 9-11: The 1989 Frederick Neumann Symposium on the Theological Interpretation of Scripture," *PSB* 1 (1990): 1-139.

9732   Étienne Trocmé, "Comment le Dieu d'Abraham, d'Isaac et de Jacob Peut-il Être a la Fois Fidèle et Libre? (épître aux Romains, chap 9 à 11)," *FV* 89 (1990): 7-10.

9733   François Refoulé, "Cohérence ou incohérence de Paul en Romains 9-11," *RB* 36 (1991): 51-79.

9734   Larry J. Kreitzer, "Romans 9-11: Albert Schweitzer's 1929 New Testament, and the Call to Christian Mission," *TEd* 50 (1994): 5-14.

9735   Ronald W. Pierce, "Covenant Conditionally and a Future for Israel," *JETS* 37 (1994): 27-38.

9736   F. Thielman, "Unexpected Mercy: Echoes of a Biblical Motif in Romans 9-11," *SJT* 47 (1994): 169-81.

9737   Klaus Haacker, "Die Geschichtstheologie von Röm 9-11 im Lichte philonischer Schriftauslegung," *NTS* 43 (1997): 209-22.

9-11

9738   M. E. Lodahl, "Arguing 'According to the Scriptures': A Path toward Christian Affirmation of God's People Israel," *QR* 20 (2000): 265-80.

9739   Franz Mußner, "Die 'Verstockung' Israels nach Röm 9-11," *TTZ* 109 (2000): 191-98.

9:1-11:36

9740   I. Fransen, "Le Dieu de toute consolation," *BVC* 49 (1963): 27-32.

9741   Junji Kinoshita, "Romans—Two Writings Combined," *NovT* 7 (1965): 258-77.

9

9742   Egon Brandenburger, "Paulinische Schriftauslegung in der Kontroverse um das Verheissungswort Gottes (Röm 9)," *ZTK* 82 (1985): 1-47.

9743   J.-N. Aletti, "L'argumentation Paulinienne en Rm 9," *Bib* 68/1 (1987): 41-56.

9744   Martin Rese, "Israel und Kirche in Römer 9," *NTS* 34/2 (1988): 208-17.

9745   Martin Parmentier, "Greek Church Fathers on Romans 9," *Bij* 50 (1989): 139-54; 51 (1990): 2-20.

9746   Thomas R. Schreiner, "Does Romans 9 Teach Individual Election unto Salvation? Some Exegetical and Theological Reflections," *JETS* 36 (1993): 25-40.

9:1-18

9747   T. Fahy, "A Note on Romans 9:1-18," *ITQ* 32 (1965): 261-62.

9:1-13

9748 Michael Cranford, "Election and Ethnicity: Paul's View of Israel in Romans 9.1-13," *JSNT* 50 (1993): 27-41.

9:1-5

9749 J. Bernard, "Le mystère de la foi," *AsSeign* 50 (1974): 16-21.

9750 Eldon J. Epp, "Jewish-Gentile Continuity in Paul: Torah and/or Faith (Romans 9:1-5)," *HTR* 79/1-3 (1986): 80-90.

9:3

9751 P. Bratsiotis, "Eine exegetische Notiz zu Röm. ix 3 und x 1," *NovT* 5 (1961-1962): 299-300.

9:3-5

9752 W. L. Lorimer, "Romans ix. 3-5, Hebrews vii. 23 f.," *NTS* 13 (1966-1967): 385-87.

9:4-5

9753 Martin Rese, "Die Vorzüge Israels in Röm. 9,4f. und Eph. 2, 12. Exegetische Anmerkungen zum Thema Kirche und Israel," *TZ* 31 (1975): 211-22.

9:4

9754 C. J. Roetzel, "Διαθῆκαι in Romans 9,4," *Bib* 51 (1970): 377-90.

9:5

9755 H.-W. Bartsch, "Rom. 9, 5 und 1. Clem. 32, 4. Eine notwendige Konjektur im Römerbrief," *TZ* 21 (1965): 401-409.

9:6-29

9756 Lloyd Gaston, "Israel's Enemies in Pauline Theology," *NTS* 28 (1982): 400-23.

9:6-13

9757 F. Thielman, "Unexpected Mercy: Echoes of a Biblical Motif in Romans 9-11," *SJT* 47/2 (1994): 169-81.

9:11

9758 J. Louis Martyn, "Paul and His Jewish-Christian Interpreters," *USQR* 42/1-2 (1988): 1-15.

9:16

9759   B. Moack, "Celui qui court," *ST* 24 (1970): 113-16.

9:17

9760   Bengt Lofstedt, "Notes on St. Paul's Letter to the Romans," *FilN* 1/2 (1988): 209-10.

9:19-23

9761   J. M. González-Ruiz, "Justicia y Misericordia divina en la election y reprobación de los hombres," *EB* 8 (1949): 365-77.

9762   A. T. Hanson, "The Domestication of Paul: A Study in the Development of Early Christian Theology," *BJRL* 63/2 (1981): 402-18.

9:22-24

9763   Paul Ellingworth, "Translation and Exegesis: A Case Study," *Bib* 59 (1978) 396-402.

9:22-23

9764   A. T. Hanson, "Vessels of Wrath or Instruments of Wrath? Romans ix.22-33," *JTS* 32 (1981): 433-43.

9:25-26

9765   W. E. Glenny, "The 'People of God' in Romans 9:25-26," *BSac* 152 (1995): 42-59.

9:25

9766   Christoph Burchard, "Rom 9:25 ἐν τῷ Ὡσηέ," *ZNW* 76 (1985): 131.

9:27-29

9767   Paul E. Dinter, "Paul and the Prophet Isaiah," *BTB* 13/2 (1983): 48-52.

9:29

9768   Michael Winger, "Unreal Conditions in the Letters of Paul," *JBL* 105/1 (1986): 110-12.

9:30-10:30

9769   R. Bring, "Paul and the Old Testament," *ST* 25 (1971): 21-60.

9:30-10:13

9770   Werner Führer, "Herr ist Jesus: die Rezeption der urchristlichen Kyrios-Akklamation durch Paulus—Römer 10:9," *KD* 33 (1987): 137-49.

9771   David B. Capes, "YHWH and His Messiah: Pauline Exegesis and the Divine Christ," *HBT* 16 (1994): 121-43.

9:30-10:4

9772   C. E. B. Cranfield, "Romans 9:30-10:4," *Int* 34 (1980): 70-74.

9:30-10:3

9773   Thomas R. Schreiner, "Israel's Failure to Attain Righteousness in Romans 9:30-10:3," *TriJ* 12 (1991): 209-20.

9:30-33

9774   François Refoulé, "Notes sur Romains IX,30-33," *RB* 92 (1985): 161-86.

9775   S. R. Bechtler, "Christ, the τέλος of the Law: The Goal of Romans 10:4," *CBQ* 56 (1994): 288-308.

9776   Wolfgang Reinbold, "Paulus und das Gesetz: Zur Exegese von Röm 9,30-33," *BZ* NS38/2 (1994): 253-64.

9777   Jan Lambrecht, "The Caesura between Romans 9.30-3 and 10.1-4," *NTS* 45 (1999): 141-47.

9:32

9778   T. David Gordon, "Why Israel Did Not Obtain Torah-Righteousness: A Translation Note On Rom 9:32," *WTJ* 54 (1992): 163-66.

9:33-10:11

9779   Paul E. Dinter, "Paul and the Prophet Isaiah," *BTB* 13/2 (1983): 48-52.

9:33

9780   Douglas A. Oss, "The Interpretation of the 'Stone' Passages by Peter and Paul: A Comparative Study," *JETS* 32 (1989): 181-200.

10:1-18

9781   Robert Jewett, "The Basic Human Dilemma: Weakness or Zealous Violence? Romans 7:7-25 and 10:1-18," *ExA* 13 (1997): 96-109.

10:1-15

9782   Arthur J. Dewey, "A Re-hearing of Romans 10:1-15," *SBLSP* 29 (1990): 273-82.

10:1-13

9783   P.-É. Langevin, "The Christology of Romans 10:1-13," *TD* 28 (1980): 45-48.

10:1-4

9784   S. R. Bechtler, "Christ, the τέλος of the Law: The Goal of Romans 10:4," *CBQ* 56 (1994): 288-308.

9785   Jan Lambrecht, "The Caesura between Romans 9.30-3 and 10.1-4," *NTS* 45 (1999): 141-47.

10:1

9786   P. Bratsiotis, "Eine exegetische Notiz zu Röm. ix 3 und x 1," *NovT* 5 (1961-1962): 299-300.

10:3

9787   S. Lyonnet, "De Justitia Dei in Epistola ad Romanos 10,3 et 3,5," *VD* 25 (1947): 118-21.

10:4

9788   H. Hellbradt, "Christus das *Telos* des Gesetzes," *EvT* 3 (1936): 331-46.

9789   F. Flückiger, "Christus, des Gesetzes *telos*," *TZ* 11 (1955): 153-57.

9790   E. E. Schneider, "Finis legis Christus, Röm. 10,4," *TZ* 20 (1964): 410-22.

9791   R. Bring, "Das Gesetz und die Gerechtigkeit Gottes. Eine Studie zur Frage nach der Bedeutung des Ausdruckes *telos nomou* in Röm. 10:4," *ST* 20 (1966): 1-36.

9792   J. W. Deenick, "The Fourth Commandment and Its Fulfillment," *RTR* 28/2 (1969): 54-61.

9793   François Refoulé, "Romains, 10:4: Encore une Fois," *RB* 91/3 (1984): 321-350.

9794 C. Thomas Rhyne, "Nomos Dikaiosynēs and the Meaning of Romans 10:4," *CBQ* 47 (1985): 486-99.

9795 W. C. Linss, "Exegesis of Telos in Romans 10:4," *BR* 33 (1988): 5-12.

9796 Julian V. Hills, " 'Christ was the Goal of the Law . . .' (Romans 10: 4)," *JTS* 44 (1993): 585-92.

9797 S. R. Bechtler, "Christ, the Telos of the Law: The Goal of Romans 10:4," *CBQ* 56 (1994): 288-308.

9798 Alain Gignac, "Le Christ, τέλος de la loi (Rm 10,4), une lecture en termes de continuité et de discontinuité, dans le adre du paradigme paulinien de l'élection," *ScE* 46 (1994): 55-81.

10:13-18

9799 F. Müller, "Zwei Marginalien im Brief des Paulus an die Römer," *ZNW* 40 (1941): 249-54.

10:14-17

9800 Dietfried Gewalt, "Die 'fides ex auditu' und die Taubstummen. Zur Auslegungsgeschichte von Gal. 3,2 und Rom. 10,14-17," *LB* 58 (1986): 45-64.

10:14

9801 A. Rakotoharintsifa, "Paul aux prises avec le Judaïsme: la question de la Loi et l'exemple de Romains 10,1-4," *FV* 92 (1993): 89-100.

10:17

9802 Bernhard Hanssler, "Autorität in der Kirche," *IKaZ* 14/6 (1985): 493-504.

9803 Peter Stuhlmacher, "Ex Auditu and the Theological Interpretation of Holy Scripture," *ExA* 2 (1986): 1-6.

10:20

9804 William L. Schutter, "Philo's Psychology of Prophetic Inspiration and Romans 10:20," *SBLSP* 28 (1989): 624-33.

10:4-9

9805 Mary A. Getty, "Romans 10:4 in an Apocalyptic Perspective," *EGLMBS* 3 (1983): 85-107.

10:4-6

9806　George Howard, "Christ the End of the Law: the Meaning of Romans 10:4 ff," *JBL* 88 (1969): 331-37.

10:4-5

9807　Thomas R. Schreiner, "Paul's View of the Law in Romans 10:4-5," *WTJ* 55 (1993): 113-35.

10:5-10

9808　Johan S. Vos, "Die hermeneutische Antinomie bei Paulus," *NTS* 38 (1992): 254-70.

10:5

9809　Andreas Lindemann, "Die Gerechtigkeit aus dem Gesetz. Erwägungen zur Auslegung und zur Textgeschichte von Römer 10,5," *ZNW* 73 (1982): 231-50.

9810　Alain Gignac, "Citation de Lévitique 18,5 en Romains 10,5 et Galates 3,12: Deux lectures différentes des rapports Christ-Torah?" *ÉgT* 25/3 (1994): 367-403.

10:6-17

9811　Gerhard Delling, " 'Nahe ist dir das Wort'. Wort—Geist— Glaube bei Paulus," *TLZ* 99 (1974): 401-12.

10:6-8

9812　A. M. Goldberg, "Torah aus der Unterwelt?" *BZ* 14 (1970): 127-31.

9813　Mark A. Seifrid, "Paul's Approach to the Old Testament in Romans 10:6-8," *TriJ* 6 (1985): 3-37.

10:6-7

9814　J. Heller, "Himmel- und Höllenfahrt nach Römer 10,6-7," *EvT* 32 (1972): 478-86.

9815　George R. Beasley-Murray, "Heaven and the Deep," *BI* 3/1 (1976): 53.

10:8-13

9816　P.-É. Langevin, "Le salut par la foi," *AsSeign* 14 (1913): 47-53.

9817　A. Viard, "Le salut et la foi en Jésus-Christ," *EV* 83 (1983): 38-39.

10:8

9818   H. J. Eckstein, "Nahe ist dir das Wort: Exegetische Erwägungen zu Röm 10:8," *ZNW* 79/3-4 (1988): 204-20.

10:9

9819   Livingston Blauvelt, "Does the Bible Teach Lordship Salvation?" *BSac* 143 (1986): 37-45.

11

9820   Gordon Zerbe, "Jews and Gentiles as People of the Covenant: The Background and Message of Romans 11," *Dir* 12/3 (1983): 20-28.

11:1

9821   Mark D. Given, "Restoring the Inheritance in Romans 11:1," *JBL* 118 (1999): 89-96.

11:3-4

9822   Christopher D. Stanley, "The Significance of Romans 11:3-4 for the Text History of the LXX Book of Kingdoms," *JBL* 112 (1993): 43-54.

11:4

9823   A. T. Hanson, "The Oracle in Romans xi 4," *NTS* 19 (1972-1973): 300-302.

11:11-36

9824   Mark Harding, "The Salvation of Israel and the Logic of Romans 11:11-36," *ABR* 46 (1998): 55-69.

11:11-15

9825   Dale C. Allison, "The Background of Romans 11:11-15 in Apocalyptic and Rabbinic Literatures," *SBT* 10 (1980): 229-34.

9826   V. Jegher-Bucher, "Erwählung und Verwerfung im Römerbrief? Eine Untersuchung von Röm 11,11-15," *TZ* 47/4 (1991): 326-36.

11:12

9827   Franz Mußner, "Fehl- und Falschübersetzungen von Röm 11 in der 'Einheitsübersetzung'," *TQ* 170/2 (1990): 137-39.

9828   Terence L. Donaldson, " 'Riches for the Gentiles' (Rom 11:12): Israel's Rejection and Paul's Gentile Mission," *JBL* 112 (1993): 81-98.

11:13-32

9829   Francisco Montagnini, "Nul ne peut faire échec au plan du salut," *AsSeign* 51 (1972): 9-14.

11:16-24

9830   Pieter J. Maartens, "A Critical Dialogue of Structure and Reader in Romans 11:16-24," *HTS* 53 (1997): 1030-51.

9831   Pieter J. Maartens, "Inference and Relevance in Paul's Allegory of the Wild Olive Tree," *HTS* 53 (1997): 1000-29.

11:17-24

9832   A. C. Baxter and J. A. Ziesler, "Paul and Arboriculture: Romans 11:17-24," *JSNT* 24 (1985): 25-32.

11:17-21

9833   Walter Riggans, "Romans 11:17-21," *ET* 98 (1987): 205-206.

11:20

9834   Franz Mußner, "Fehl- und Falschübersetzungen von Röm 11 in der 'Einheitsübersetzung'," *TQ* 170/2 (1990): 137-39.

11:25-32

9835   Otto Glombitza, "Apostolische Sorge," *NovT* 7 (1964-1965): 312-18.

9836   Richard A. Batey, " 'So All Israel Will Be Saved'. An Interpretation of Romans 11:15-32," *Int* 20 (1966): 218-28.

9837   H. Celada, "Llamada permanente a la conciencia cristiana respecto a Israel, en la carta de San Pablo a la Romanos: Un trabajo de Eliseo Rodriguez," *CuBi* 34 (1977): 279-93

9838   Jennifer A. Glancy, "Israel vs Israel in Romans 11:25-32," *USQR* 45/3-4 (1991): 191-203.

11:25-31

9839   F. Thielman, "Unexpected Mercy: Echoes of a Biblical Motif in Romans 9-11," *SJT* 47/2 (1994): 169-81.

11:25-28

9840   Franz Mußner, "Fehl- und Falschübersetzungen von Röm 11 in der 'Einheitsübersetzung'," *TQ* 170/2 (1990): 137-39.

11:25-27

9841   D. Sänger, "Rettung der Heiden und Erwählung Israels: Einige vorläufige Erwägungen zu Römer 11,25-27," *KD* 32/2 (1986): 99-119.

9842   Reidar Hvalvik, "A 'Sonderweg' for Israel: A Critical Examination of a Current Interpretation of Romans 11:25-27," *JSNT* 38 (1990): 87-107.

11:25-26

9843   Seyoon Kim, "The 'Mystery' of Rom 11 (1996): 25-6 Once More," *NTS* 43 (1997): 412-29.

11:25

9844   Roger D. Aus, "Paul's Travel Plans to Spain and the 'Full Number of the Gentiles' of Rom. xi 25," *NovT* 21 (1979): 232-62.

11:26

9845   F. J. Caubet Iturbe, "Et sic omnis Israel salvus fieret, Rom. 11,26," *EB* 21 (1962): 127-50.

9846   Franz Mußner, "All Israel Will Be Saved (Rom 11:26)," *TD* 26 (1978): 113-16.

9847   H. Ponsot, "Et ainsi tout Israël sera sauvé: Rom. xi,26a," *RB* 89 (1982): 406-17.

9848   P. W. van der Horst, " 'Only Then Will All Israel Be Saved': A Short Note on the Meaning of καὶ οὕτως in Romans 11:26," *JBL* 119 (2000): 521-25.

11:29

9849   Ceslaus Spicq, "'Αμεταμέλητος dans Rom. xi,29," *RB* 67 (1960): 210-19.

9850   John J. Kilgallen, "Reflections on Charisma(ta) in the New Testament," *SM* 41 (1992): 289-323.

11:31

9851   L. Villuendas, "El actual pueblo judio y su conversión," *CuBi* 17 (1960): 269-77.

9852   D. Judant, "À propos de la destinée d'Israël. Remarques concernant un verest de l'épître aux Romains," *Div* 23 (1979): 108-25.

11:33-36

9853   F. Ogara, "Ex ipso et per opossum et in ipso sunt omnia," *VD* 15 (1935): 164-71.

9854   Adalberto Sisti, "Il mistero di Dio," *BibO* S (1963): 95-100.

9855   P.-É. Bonnard, "Les trésors de la miséricorde," *AsSeign* 53 (1964): 13-19.

9856   Markus Barth, "Theologie—ein Gebet (Rom 11:33-36). Abschieds-Vorlesung an der Universität Basel, gehalten am 21. Februar 1985," *TZ* 41 (1985): 330-48.

11:33

9857   J. Mehlmann, "'Ανεξιχνίαστος = investigabilis," *Bib* 40 (1959): 902-14.

9858   H.-M. Dion, "La notion paulinienne de 'richesse de Dieu' et ses sources," *SE* 18 (1966): 139-48.

12-15

9859   R. Alan Culpepper, "God's Righteousness in the Life of His People: Romans 12-15," *RevExp* 73/4 (1976): 451-63.

9860   L. Pohle, "Der Staat—Regnum Christi oder Instrumentum Diaboli: Zu K. Barths und O. Cullmanns Theologie des Staates," *IKaZ* 15/2 (1986): 145-52.

9861   C. J. Roetzel, "Sacrifice in Romans 12-15," *WW* 6/4 (1986): 410-419.

9862   François Vouga, "L'épître aux Romains comme document ecclésiologique," *ÉTR* 61 (1986): 485-95.

9863   James L. Bailey and Stanley P. Saunders, "God's Merciful Community," *CThM* 14 (1987): 325-33.

9864   Jeremy Moiser, "Rethinking Romans 12-15," *NTS* 36 (1990): 571-82.

12-14

9865   Peter L. Samuelson, "A New Vision of Righteousness: Paul's Exhortations in Romans 12-15," *WW* 10 (1990): 295-297, 300, 302-303.

12

9866   K. Flender, "Weisung statt Ermahnung—Einführung in die Bibelarbeit über Röm 12," *BK* 28 (1973): 81-84.

9867   K. H. Schelkle, "Der Christ in der Gemeinde. Eine Auslegung von Rom 12," *BK* 28 (1973): 74-80.

9868   David G. Peterson, "Worship and Ethics in Romans 12," *TynB* 44 (1993)

12:1-5

9869   J. L. Lilly, "Exposition of the Missal Epistles from Romans," *CBQ* 4 (1942): 338-44.

9870   Adalberto Sisti, "Epistole," *BibO* 4 (1962): 30-33.

12:1-2

9871   H. Asmussen, "Das Opfer der Gemeinde," *EvT* 1 (1934-1935): 49-55.

9872   H. E. Stoessel, "Notes on Romans 12:1-2. The Renewal of the Mind and Internalizing the Truth," *Int* 17 (1963): 161-75.

9873   O. Knoch, "Wandelt euch durch ein neues Denken: Meditation über Röm 12,1ff," *BK* 19 (1964): 89-93.

9874   H. Schlier, "Der Christ und die Welt," *GeistL* 38 (1965): 416-25.

9875   S. Lyonnet, "Le culte spirituel," *AsSeign* 53 (1970): 11-14.

9876   H. D. Betz, "Das Problem der Grundlagen der paulinischen Ethik (Rom 12:1-2)," *ZTK* 85/2 (1988): 199-218.

9877   Mikeal C. Parsons, "Being Precedes Act: Indicative and Imperative in Paul's Writing," *EQ* 60 (1988): 99-127.

9878 Christine Ledger, "Be Transformed by the Renewing of Your Mind: Reflections on Romans 12:1-2," *IRM* 80 (1991): 71-88.

9879 George Smiga, "Romans 12:1-2 and 15:30-32 and the Occasion of the Letter to the Romans," *CBQ* 53 (1991): 257-73.

9880 D. Edmond Hiebert, "Presentation and Transformation: An Exposition of Romans 12:1-2," *BSac* 151 (1994): 309-24.

<u>12:1</u>

9881 George W. Harrison, "Old Testament Sacrifices and Offerings," *BI* 1/2 (1975): 54-59.

9882 Nikolaus Walter, "Christusglaube und heidnische Religiosität in paulinischen Gemeinden," *NTS* 25 (1979): 422-42.

9883 Paul Müller, "Der Begriff 'Das Erbauliche' bei Sören Kierkegaard," *KD* 31 (1985): 116-34.

<u>12:3</u>

9884 C. E. B. Cranfield, "Metron pisteôs in Romans xii. 3," *NTS* 8 (1961-1962): 345-51.

9885 J. Neville Birdsall, "Emetrēsen in Rom. xii. 3," *JTS* 14 (1963):

<u>12:6-8</u>

9886 Albert L. Garcia, "Spiritual Gifts and the Work of the Kingdom," *CTQ* 49/2-3 (1985): 149-60.

<u>12:6</u>

9887 George R. Beasley-Murray, "He That Ruleth," *BI* 3/1 (1976): 61.

9888 Elsie A. McKee, "Calvin's Exegesis of Romans 12:8—Social, Accidental or Theological?" *CTJ* 23 (1988): 6-18.

<u>12:9-21</u>

9889 Charles H. Talbert, "Tradition and Redaction in Romans 12:9-21," *NTS* 16 (1969-1970): 83-93.

9890 P. Kanjuparambil, "Imperatival Participles in Romans 12:9-21," *JBL* 102 (1983): 285-88.

9891   David A. Black, "The Pauline Love Command: Structure, Style, and Ethics in Romans 12:9-21," *FilN* 2 (1989): 3-22.

9892   Timothy R. Sensing, "From Exegesis to Sermon in Romans 12:9-21," *RQ* 40 (1998): 171-87.

12:9-15

9893   F. A. J. MacDonald, "Pity or Compassion?" *ET* 92 (1981): 344-46.

12:11

9894   Wayne Hollaway, "First-Century Businesses," *BI* 14/3 (1988): 66-69.

12:14-21

9895   Marcus J. Borg, "A New Context for Romans xiii," *NTS* 19/2 (1972-1973): 205-18.

9896   Kent L Yinger, "Romans 12:14-21 and Nonretaliation in Second Temple Judaism: Addressing Persecution within the Community," *CBQ* 60 (1998): 74-96.

12:15

9897   D. H. C. Read, "A Church that Can Laugh—and Weep," *ET* 88 (1976): 23-25.

12:16-13:8

9898   T. C. de Kruijf, "The Literary Unity of Rom 12:16-13:8a: A Network of Inclusions," *Bij* 48 (1987): 319-26.

12:16

9899   R. G. Bury, "Romans 12,16; 1 Corinthians 13,7," *ET* 49 (1937-1938): 430.

12:19-21

9900   K. Stendahl, "Hate, Non-Retaliation, and Love: 1 QS x, 17-20 and Rom. 12:19-21," *HTR* 55 (1962): 343-55.

12:20

9901   William Klassen, "Coals of Fire: Sign of Repentance or Revenge?" *NTS* 9 (1962-1963): 337-50.

9902   S. Bartine, "Carbones encendidos, sobre la cabeza o sobre el veneno?" *EB* 31 (1972): 201-203.

9903   L. Gaugusch, "Die Staatslehre des Apostels Paulus nach Rom. 13," *TGl* 26 (1934): 529-50.

9904 J. Koch-Mehrin, "Die Stellung des Christen zum Staat nach Röm. 13 und Apok. 13," *EvT* 7 (1947-1948): 378-401.

9905 A. Strobel, "Zum Verständnis von Rm 13," *ZNW* 47 (1956): 67-93.

9906 A. Molnar, "Romains 13 dans l'interprétation de la première Réforme," *ÉTR* 46 (1971): 231-40.

9907 Marcus J. Borg, "A New Context for Romans xiii," *NTS* 19 (1972-1973): 205-18.

9908 Horst Goldstein, "Die politischen Paränesen in 1 Pdr 2 und Röm 13," *BibL* 14 (1973): 88-104.

13:1-7

9909 H. M. Gale, "Paul's View of the State. A Discussion of the Problem in Romans 13:1-7," *Int* 6 (1952): 409-14.

9910 K. H. Schelkle, "Staat und Kirche in der patristischen Auslegung von Rm 13,1-7," *ZNW* 44 (1952-1953): 223-36.

9911 Otto Kuss, "Paulus über die staatliche Gewalt," *TGl* 45 (1955): 321-34.

9912 R. Morgenthaler, "Roma—Sedes Satanae. Röm, 13,1 ff. im Lichte von Luk. 4,5-8," *TZ* 12 (1956): 289-304.

9913 Ernst Käsemann, "Römer 13, 1-7 in unserer Generation," *ZTK* 56 (1959): 316-76.

9914 C. E. B. Cranfield, "Some Observations on Romans xiii. 1-7," *NTS* 6 (1959-1960): 241-49.

9915 F. Neygebauer, "Zur Auslegung von Röm. 13,1-7," *KD* 8 (1962): 151-72.

9916 K. Neufeld, "Das Jason. Ein Deutungsversuch im Anschluss an Röm 13,1-7," *BibL* 12 (1971): 32-45.

9917 Marcus J. Borg, "A New Context for Romans xiii," *NTS* 19/2 (1972-1973): 205-18.

9918 R. Bring, "Der paulinische Hintergrund der lutherischen Lehre von den zu Reichen oder Regimenten," *ST* 27 (1973): 107-26.

9919 T. J. Reese, "Pauline Politics: Rom 13:1-7," *BTB* 3 (1973): 323-31.

9920 J. Friedrich, "Zur historischen Situation und Intention von Röm 13,1-7," *ZTK* 73 (1976): 131-66.

9921 A. Molnar, "Peter Chelčickys Deutung von Röm 13,1-7," *TLZ* 101 (1976): 481-89.

9922 Franz Laub, "Der Christ und die staatliche Gewalt—Zum Verständnis der 'politischen' Paränese Röm 13,1-7 in der gegenwärtigen Diskussion," *MTZ* 30 (1979): 257-65.

9923 Kazimierz Romaniuk, "Il Cristiano e l'autorità civile in Romani 13,1-7," *RivBib* 27 (1979): 261-69.

9924 Roman Heiligenthal, "Strategien konformer Ethik im Neuen Testament am Beispiel von Röm. 13.1-7," *NTS* 29 (1983): 55-61.

9925 Harold J. Dyck, "The Christian and the Authorities in Romans 13:1-7," *Dir* 14/1 (1985): 44-50.

9926 R. G. Crawford, "Theological Bombshell in South Africa," *ET* 98/1 (1986): 9-13.

9927 James D. G. Dunn, "Romans 13:1-7: A Charter for Political Quietism?" *ExA* 2 (1986): 55-68.

9928 Richard T. France, "Liberation in the New Testament," *EQ* 58/1 (1986): 3-23.

9929 Jeffrey E. Shearier, "The Ethics of Obedience: A Lutheran Development," *CJ* 12/2 (1986): 55-63.

9930 David C. Steinmetz, "Calvin and Melanchthon on Romans 13:1-7," *ExA* 2 (1986): 74-81.

9931 Susan Boyer, "Exegesis of Romans 13:1-7," *BLT* 32 (1987): 208-16.

9932 Jonathan A. Draper, "Humble Submission to Almighty God and Its Biblical Foundation: Contextual Exegesis of Romans 13:1-7," *JTSA* 63 (1988): 30-38.

9933 James I. H. McDonald, "Romans 13:1-7: A Test Case for New Testament Interpretation," *NTS* 35/4 (1989): 540-49.

9934 Dag Thorkildsen, "Fra Martin Luther til Eivind Berggrav: Fortolkning og bruk av Rom 13.1-7," *NTT* 90/2 (1989): 105-23.

9935 Winsome Munro, "Romans 13:1-7: Apartheid's Last Biblical Refuge," *BTB* 20 (1990): 161-68.

9936   Stanley E. Porter, "Romans 13:1-7 as Pauline Political Rhetoric," *FilN* 3 (1990): 115-37.

9937   J. Botha, "Creation of New Meaning: Rhetorical Situations and the Reception of Romans 13:1-7," *JTSA* 79 (1992): 24-37.

9938   P. Arzt, "Über die Macht des Staates nach Röm 13, 1-7," *SNTU-A* 18 (1993): 163-81.

9939   Jean F. Racine, "Romains 13,1-7: simple préservation de l'ordre social?" *EB* 51/2 (1993): 187-205.

9940   N. A. Røsaeg, "Rom 13, 1-7 i sosialpolitisk kontekst," *NTT* 94 (1993): 35-54.

9941   J. Botha, "Social Values in the Rhetoric of Pauline Paraenetic Literature," *Neo* 28 (1994): 109-26.

9942   William R. Herzog, "Dissembling, a Weapon of the Weak: The Case of Christ and Caesar in Mark 12:13-17 and Romans 13:1-7," *PRS* 21 (1994): 339-60.

9943   Simon Légasse, "Paul et César. Romains 13,1-7. Essai de synthèse," *RB* 101 (1994): 516-32.

9944   Matthew G. Neufeld, "Submission to Governing Authorities: A Study of Romans 13:1-7," *Dir* 23 (1994): 90-97.

9945   William R. Herzog, "Dissembling, a Weapon of the Weak: The Case of Christ and Caesar in Mark 12:13-17 and Romans 13:1-7," *PRS* 21 (1994): 339-60.

9946   P. J. Strauss, "God's Servant Working for Your Own Good: Notes from Modern South Africa on Calvin's Commentary on Romans 13:1-7 and the State," *HTS* 54 (1998): 24-35.

13:1

9947   Oscar Cullmann, "Zur neuesten Diskussion über die *eksouslai* in Röm. 13,1," *TZ* 10 (1954): 321-36.

9948   Jacques Ellul, "Petite Note Complémentaire Sur Romains 13:1," *FV* 89 (1990): 81-83.

13:3-4

9949   J. Héring, "*Serviteurs de Dieu*. Contribution à l'exégèse de Romains 13:34," *RHPR* 30 (1950): 31-40.

9950 Bruce W. Winter, "The Public Honouring of Christian Benefactors: Romans 13:3-4 and 1 Peter 2:14-15," *JSNT* 34 (1988): 87-103.

13:3

9951 W. L. Lorimer, "Romans xiii. 3, Hebrews iii. 13," *NTS* 12 (1965-1966): 389-91.

9952 C. Mack Roark, "Sin and Evil in Paul's Theology," *BI* 14/3 (1988): 70-72.

13:4

9953 H. Armin Moellering, "The Sword Is Not a Feather Duster," *CJ* 24 (1998): 5-6.

13:5

9954 M. E. Thrall, "The Pauline Use of *Suneidēsis*," *NTS* 14 (1967-1968): 118-25.

9955 Page Lee, "Conscience in Romans 13:5," *FM* 8 (1990): 85-93.

13:7

9956 A. Strobel, "Furcht, wem Furcht gebührt, zum profangriechischen Hintergrund vom Rm 13,7," *ZNW* 55 (1964): 58-62.

13:8-10

9957 R. Swaeles, "La charité fraternelle accomplissement de la Loi," *AsSeign* 54 (1972): 10-15.

9958 A. Bencze, "An Analysis of Romans xiii. 8-10," *NTS* 20 (1973-1974): 90-92.

13:8

9959 Willi Marxsen, "Der *eteros nomos* Röm. 13, 8," *TZ* 11 (1955): 230-37.

13:17

9960 J. Kallas, "Romans xiii. 17: An Interpolation," *NTS* 11 (1964-1965): 365-74.

9961 R. J. Karros, "Rom 14:1-15:13 and the Occasion of Romans," *CBQ* 35 (1973): 155-78.

9962   Robert H. Stein, "The Argument of Romans 13:1-7," *NovT* 31 (1989): 325-43.

14-23

9963   Martin Dreher, "Vida Religiosa Consagrada no Protestantismo Brasileiro," *EstT* 25/2 (1985): 185-97.

14:1-15:13

9964   Junji Kinoshita, "Romans—Two Writings Combined," *NovT* 7 (1965): 258-77.

14:1-15:7

9965   Susan Miller, "Romans 14:1-15:7--Unity in the Essentials, Opinions in the Non-Essentials, Charity in Everything," *RevExp* 95 (1998): 103-108.

14:2

9966   William Ratliff, "Foods of the Ancient World," *BI* 14/3 (1988): 73-75.

14:7-9

9967   E. Wolf, "Trauansprache über Römer 14,7-9," *EvT* 31 (1971): 507-10.

9968   R. Baulès, "Le chrétien appartient au Seigneur," *AsSeign* 55 (1974): 10-15.

9969   James L. Jaquette, "Life and Death, Adiaphora, and Paul's Rhetorical Strategies," *NovT* 38 (1996): 30-54.

14:12

9970   Jacob A. Loewen, "A New Look at Section Headings in West African Translations," *BT* 36/2 (1985): 237-241.

14:13

9971   George R. Beasley-Murray, "Stumbling-blocks and Scandals:" *BI* 3/1 (1976): 64-65.

14:14

9972   G. W. S. Friedrichsen, "The Gothic Text of Romans xiv 14 in Cod. Guelferbytanus," *JTS* 38 (1937): 245-47.

9973   Owen E. Evans, "Paul's Certainties: What God Requires of Man—Romans iv. 14," *ET* 69 (1957-1958): 199-202.

14:17

9974   Jack P. Lewis, " 'The Kingdom of God . . . Is Righteousness, Peace, and Joy in the Holy Spirit' (Rom 14:17): A Survey of Interpretation," *RQ* 40 (1998): 53-68.

9975   Gary S. Shogren, "Is the Kingdom of God about Eating and Drinking or Isn't It?" *NovT* 42 (2000): 238-56.

15

9976   Robert Jewett, "Form and Function of the Homiletic Benediction," *ATR* 51 (1969): 18-34.

15:1-7

9977   Ernst Käsemann, "Römer 15, 1-7 in unserer Generation," *ZTK* 56 (1959): 316-76.

15:4-6

9978   A. T. Hanson, "The Domestication of Paul: A Study in the Development of Early Christian Theology," *BJRL* 63/2 (1981): 402-18.

15:8-9

9979   J. Ross Wagner, "The Christ, Servant of Jew and Gentile: A Fresh Approach to Romans 15:8-9," *JBL* 116 (1997): 473-85.

9980   Jan Lambrecht, "Syntactical and Logical Remarks on Romans 15:8-9a," *NovT* 42 (2000): 257-61.

15:14-16:24

9981   Robert Jewett, "Ecumenical Theology for the Sake of Mission: Romans 1:1-17," *SBLSP* 15 (1992): 598-612.

15:14-33

9982   John Knox, "Romans 15,14-33 and Paul's Conception of His Apostolic Mission," *JBL* 83 (1964): 1-11.

9983   François Vouga, "L'épître aux Romains comme Document Ecclésiologique (Rm 12-15)," *ÉTR* 61/4 (1986): 485-495.

9984   Benjamin Fiore, "Friendship in the Exhortation of Romans (15:14-33)," *EGLMBS* 7 (1987): 95-103.

9985   Peter Müller, "Grundlinien paulinischer Theologie (Röm 15:14-33)," *KD* 35 (1989): 212-35.

15:14-16

9986   N. Krieger, "Zum Römerbrief," *NovT* 3 (1959-1960): 146-48.

15:14

9987   Klaus Haacker, "Exegetische Probleme des Römerbriefs," *NovT* 20/1 (1978): 1-21.

15:17-21

9988   Paul Bowers, "Fulfilling the Gospel: The Scope of the Pauline Mission," *JETS* 30 (1987): 185-98.

15:19

9989   A. S. Greyser, "Un essai d'explication de Rom. xv. 19," *NTS* 6 (1959-1960): 156-59.

9990   Lynn Jones, "Illyricum," *BI* 15/1 (1988): 58-61.

15:20

9991   J. D. M. Derrett, "Paul as Master-Builder," *EQ* 69 (1997): 129-37.

15:23-24

9992   Arthur J. Dewey, "Social-Historical Observations on Romans (15:23-24)," *EGLMBS* 7 (1987): 49-57.

15:24

9993   Walter L. Liefeld, "Can Deputation Be Defended Biblically?" *EMQ* 22/4 (1986): 360-365.

9994   Timothy Trammell, "Spain in the Day of Paul," *BI* 14/3 (1988): 79-83.

15:25-31

9995   Víctor M. Fernández, " 'La gran colecta para Jerusalen' o 'La gracia y el dinero' (Rom 15,25-31; 2 Cor 8-9)," *RevB* 58 (1996): 183-89.

15:26

9996   G. W. Peterman, "Romans 15:26: Make a Contribution or Establish Fellowship?" *NTS* 40 (1994): 457-63.

15:28

9997   L. Radermacher, *"Sphragizesthai*: Rm 15, 28," *ZNW* 32 (1933): 87-89.

9998   H.-W. Bartsch, ". . .wenn ich ihnen diese Frucht versiegelt habe. Röm 15,28," *ZNW* 63 (1972): 95-107.

15:30

9999   Klaus Haacker, "Exegetische Probleme des Römerbriefs," *NovT* 20/1 (1978): 1-21.

15:33

10000   Robert Jewett, "The God of Peace in Romans: Reflections on Crucial Lutheran Texts," *CThM* 25 (1998): 186-94.

16

10001   F. M. Young, "Romans 16: A Suggestion," *ET* 47 (1935-1936): 44.

10002   H.-M. Schenke, "Aporien im Römerbrief," *TLZ* 92 (1967): 881-88.

10003   James I. H. McDonald, "Was Romans xvi a Separate Letter?" *NTS* 16 (1969-1970): 369-72.

10004   Karl P. Donfried, "A Short Note on Romans 16," *JBL* 89 (1970): 441-49.

10005   Elisabeth Schüssler Fiorenza, "Missionaries, Apostles, Coworkers: Romans 16 and the Reconstruction of Women's Early Christian History," *WW* 6/4 (1986): 420-33.

10006   A. B. du Toit, "The ecclesiastical situation of the first generation Roman Christians," *HTS* 53 (1997): 498-512.

16:1-4

10007   Wendy J. Cotter, "Women's Authority Roles in Paul's Churches: Countercultural or Conventional?" *NovT* 36 (1994): 350-72.

16:1-2

10008   Daniel C. Arichea, "Who Was Phoebe? Translating Diakonos in Romans 16:1," *BT* 39 (1988): 401-409.

10009   C. F. Whelan, "Amica Pauli: The Role of Phoebe in the Early Church," *JSNT* 49 (1993): 67-85.

16:1

10010   G. G. Blum, "Das Amt der Frau im Neuen Testament," *NovT* 7 (1964): 142-61.

16:2

10011   Marco Zappella, "A Proposito di Febe Prostatis (Rm 16:2)," *RivBib* 37 (1989): 167-71.

10012   Ray R. Schulz, "A Case for 'President' Phoebe in Romans 16:2," *LTJ* 24 (1990): 124-27.

16:3-16

10013   François Refoulé, "A contre-courant: Romains 16,3-16," *RHPR* 70 (1990): 409-20.

16:3-5

10014   Marlis Gielen, "Zur Interpretation der paulinischen Formel He kat' Oikon Ekklesia," *ZNW* 77/1-2 (1986): 109-25.

16:4

10015   R. E. Oster, " 'Congregations of the Gentiles' (Rom 16:4): A Culture-Based Ecclesiology in the Letters of Paul," *RQ* 40 (1998): 39-52.

16:5

10016   Glenn McCoy, "The Churches of Achaia," *BI* 9/2 (1983): 79-83.

16:7

10017   B. W. Bacon, "Andronicus," *ET* 42 (1930-1931): 300-304.

10018   Peter Lampe, "Iunia/Iunias: Sklavenherkunft im Kreise der vor-paulinischen Apostel (Röm 16:7)," *ZNW* 76 (1985): 132-34.

10019   Ray R. Schulz, "Romans 16:7: Junia or Junias?" *ET* 98 (1987): 108-10.

10020   R. S. Cervin, "A Note Regarding the Name 'Junia(s)' in Romans 16:7," *NTS* 40 (1993): 464-70.

10021   John Thorley, "Junia, a Woman Apostle," *NovT* 38 (1996): 18-29.

16:17-20

10022   W. Schmithals, "Die Irrlehrer von Rm 16, 17-20," *ST* 13 (1959): 51-69.

16:18

10023   Juan Mateos, "Analisis de un Campo Lexematico: Eulogia en el Nuevo Testamento," *FilN* 1 (1988): 5-25.

10024 J. Lionel North, " 'Good Wordes and Faire Speeches':
       More Materials and a Pauline Pun," *NTS* 42 (1996):
       600-14.

<u>16:20</u>

10025 U. Borse, "Das Schlusswort des Römerbriefes:
       Segensgruss (16,24) statt Doxologie," *SNTU-A* 19 (1994):
       173-92.

10026 Robert Jewett, "The God of Peace in Romans: Reflections
       on Crucial Lutheran Texts," *CThM* 25 (1998): 186-94.

<u>16:23</u>

10027 David W. J. Gill, "Erastus the Aedile," *TynB* 40 (1989):
       293-301.

10028 U. Borse, "Das Schlusswort des Römerbriefes:
       Segensgruss (16,24) statt Doxologie," *SNTU-A* 19 (1994):
       173-92.

10029 Justin J. Meggitt, "The Social Status of Erastus (Rom
       16:23)," *NovT* 38 (1996): 218-23.

<u>16:25-27</u>

10030 K. Gatzweiler, "Gloire au-Dieu Sauveur," *AsSeign* 8
       (1972): 34-38.

10031 U. Borse, "Das Schlusswort des Römerbriefes:
       Segensgruss (16,24) statt Doxologie," *SNTU-A* 19 (1994):
       173-92.

<u>16:25</u>

10032 L.-M. Dewailly, "Mystère et silence dans Rom. xvi. 25,"
       NTS 14 (1967-1968): 111-18.

<u>16:26</u>

10033 Don B. Garlington, "The Obedience of Faith in the Letter
       to the Romans: The Meaning of Hypakoe Pisteos," *WTJ* 52
       (1990): 201-24.

1 Corinthians

1:1-6:20

> 10034 I. Fransen, "Le champ du Seigneur," *BVC* 44 (1962): 31-38.

1-4

> 10035 Glen O. Peterman, "Equipping God's People for Ministry in 1 Corinthians 1-4," *RR* 21 (1967): 56-64.
>
> 10036 Gerhard Sellin, "Das 'Geheimins' der Weisheit und das Rätsel der 'Christtuspartei'," *ZNW* 73/1-2 (1982): 69-96.
>
> 10037 John B. Polhill, "The Wisdom of God and Factionalism: 1 Corinthians 1-4," *RevExp* 80/3 (1983): 325-39.
>
> 10038 L. L. Welborn, "On the Discord in Corinth: 1 Corinthians 1-4 and Ancient Politics," *JBL* 106/1 (1987): 85-111.
>
> 10039 Peter Lampe, "Theological Wisdom and the 'Word about the Cross': The Rhetorical Scheme in 1 Corinthians 1-4," *Int* 44 (1990): 117-31.
>
> 10040 E. Borghi, "Il tema σοφία in 1 Cor 1-4," *RivBib* 40/4 (1992): 421-58.
>
> 10041 Thomas Söding, "Kreuzestheologie und Rechtfertigungslehre. Zur Verbindung von Christologie und Soteriologie im Ersten Korintherbrief und im Galaterbrief," *Cath* 46/1 (1992): 31-60.

1-3

> 10042 Wilhelm H. Wuellner, "Haggadic Homily Genre in 1 Corinthians 1-3," *JBL* 89/2 (1970): 199-204.
>
> 10043 V. P. Branick, "Source and Redaction Analysis of 1 Corinthians 1-3," *JBL* 101/2 (1982): 251-69.
>
> 10044 Michael D. Goulder, "Σοφία in 1 Corinthians," *NTS* 37/4 (1991): 516-34.

1-2

10045 Niels Hyldahl, "The Corinthian 'Parties' and the Corinthian Crisis," *StTheol* 45/1 (1991): 19-32.

1

10046 Markus Barth, "A Chapter on the Church—The Body of Christ," *Int* 12 (1958): 131-56.

10047 Paul Ellingworth, "Translating 1 Corinthians," *BT* 31/2 (1980): 234-38.

10048 Halvor Moxnes, "Paulus og den norske vaerematen: 'skam' og 'aere' i Romerbrevet," *NTT* 86/3 (1985): 129-40.

1:1-9

10049 É. Beaucamp, "Grâce et fidélité," *BVC* 15 (1956): 58-65.

10050 É. Samain, "L'église communion de foi au Christ," *AsSeign* NS33 (1970): 15-21.

10051 Max A. Chevallier, "L'unité plurielle de l'église d'après le Nouveau Testament," *RHPR* 66 (1986): 3-20.

10052 Ronald Byars, "Sectarian Division and the Wisdom of the Cross: Preaching from First Corinthians," *QR* 9/4 (1989): 65-97.

1:2

10053 Cullen I. K. Story, "The Nature of Paul's Stewardship with Special Reference to 1 and 2 Corinthians," *EQ* 48/4 (1976): 212-29.

10054 P.-É. Langevin, "Ceux qui invoquent le nom du Seigneur," *SE* 19 (1967): 393-407; 21 (1969): 71-122.

1:4-9

10055 F. S. Malan, "Die Funksie en boodskap van die 'voorword' in 1 Korintiërs," *HTS* 49 (1993): 561-75.

1:4-8

10056 F. Ogara, "In omnibus divites facti estis in illo, in omni verbo et in omni scientia," *VD* 16 (1936): 225-32.

10057 J. L. Lilly, "Missal Epistles from 1 Corinthians," *CBQ* 13 (1951): 79-85.

1:4-7

10058 Hermann von Lips, "Der Apostolat des Paulus - ein Charisma: semantische Aspekte zu charis-charisma und anderen Wortpaaren im Sprachgebrauch des Paulus," *Bib* 66/3 (1985): 305-43.

1:5-10

10059 M. L. Barré, "To Marry or to Burn: Purousthai in 1 Cor. 7:9," *CBQ* 36/2 (1974): 193-202.

1:7-9

10060 P. von der Osten-Sacken, "Gottes Treue bis zur Parusie: Formgeschichtliche Beobachtungen zu 1 Kor. 1:7b-9," *ZNW* 68/3-4 (1977): 176-99.

1:7

10061 John J. Kilgallen, "Reflections on Charisma(ta) in the New Testament," *SM* 41 (1992): 289-323.

1:3-9

10062 R. Feuillet, "Action de grâces pour les dons de Dieu," *AsSeign* NS5 (1969): 37-43.

1:10-4:21

10063 Victor P. Furnish, "Belonging to Christ: A Paradigm for Ethics in First Corinthians," *Int* 44/2 (1990): 145-57.

1:10-2:5

10064 D. L. Gragg, "Discourse Ananlysis of 1 Corinthians 1:10-2:5," *LB* 65 (1991): 37-57.

1:10-17

10065 William B. Badke, "Baptised into Moses-Baptised into Christ: A Study in Doctrinal Development," *EQ* 60/1 (1988): 23-29.

1:10

10066 F. Ogara, "Ut id ipsum dicatis omnes et non sint in vobis schismata," *VD* 16 (1936): 257-66, 289-94, 321-29.

10067 Thomas Wieser, "Community-Its Unity, Diversity, And Universality," *Semeia* 33 (1985): 83-95.

1:12-7:16

10068 Craig Blumberg, "The Structure of 2 Corinthians 1-7," *CTR* 4 (1989): 3-20.

1:12

10069 W. O. Fitch, "Paul, Apollos, Cephas, Christ," *Theology* 74/607 (1971): 18-24.

10070 Phillip Vielhauer, "Paulus und die Kephaspartei in Korinth," *NTS* 21/3 (1974): 341-52.

1:12-27

10071 Dennis Ormseth, "Showing the Body: Reflections on 1 Corinthians 12-13 for Epiphany," *WW* 6 (1986): 97-103.

1:16

10072 Christoph Burchard, "Ei nach einem Ausdruck des Wissens oder Nichtwissens Joh 9:25, Act 19:2, 1 Cor 1:16, 7:16," *ZNW* 52/1-2 (1961): 73-82.

10073 Gerhard Delling, "Zur Taufe von 'Häusern' im Urchristentum," *NovT* 7 (1965): 285-311.

1:17-3:4

10074 Terrance Callan, "Competition and Boasting: Toward a Psychological Portrait of Paul," *StTheol* 40 (1986): 137-56.

1:17-2:16

10075 Maurice Sachot, "Comment le christianisme est-il devenu religion," *RevSR* 59 (1985): 95-118.

1:17

10076 Kenneth E. Bailey, "Recovering the Poetic Structure of 1 Corinthians 1:17," *NovT* 17/4 (1975): 265-96.

10077 Marie Hendrickx, "Sagesse de la parole (1 Cor 1, 17) selon saint Thomas d'Aquinas," *NRT* 110/3 (1988): 336-50.

10078 Nigel M. Watson, " 'The Philosopher Should Bathe and Brush His Teeth'—Congruence between Word and Deed in Graeco-Roman Philosophy and Paul's Letters to the Corinthians," *ABR* 42 (1994): 1-16.

1:17-25

10079 J. L. Lilly, "Missal Epistles from 1 Corinthians," *CBQ* 13 (1951): 199-207.

10080 E. L Bode, "La follia della Croce," *BibO* 12 (1970): 257-63.

1:18-3:4

10081 Victor P. Furnish, "Theology in 1 Corinthians: Initial Soundings," *SBLSP* 28 (1989): 246-64.

1:18-2:5

10082 Benjamin Fiore, " 'Covert Allusion' in 1 Corinthians 1-4," *CBQ* 47/1 (1985): 85-102.

1:18

10083 Luis F. Ladaria, "Presente y futuro en la escatología cristiana," *EE* 60 (1985): 351-59.

10084 J. Louis Martyn, "Paul and His Jewish-Christian Interpreters," *USQR* 42/1-2 (1988): 1-15.

1:18-31

10085 Gail P. Corrington, "Paul and the two wisdoms: 1 Corinthians 1:18-31 and the hellenistic mission," *EGLMBS* 6 (1986): 72-84.

10086 Alan Padgett, "Feminism in First Corinthians: A Dialogue with Elisabeth Schüssler Fiorenza," *EQ* 58/2 (1986): 121-32.

10087 Molly T. Marshall, "1 Corinthians 1:18-31," *RevExp* 85/4 (1988): 683-86.

10088 Ronald Byars, "Sectarian Division and the Wisdom of the Cross: Preaching from First Corinthians," *QR* 9/4 (1989): 65-97.

10089 Molly T. Marshall, "Forsaking a Theology of Glory: 1 Corinthians 1:18-31," *ExA* 7 (1991): 101-104.

10090 John B. Trotti, "1 Corinthians 1:18-31," *Int* 45 (1991): 63-66.

10091 Francis Watson, "Christ, Community, and the Critique of Ideology: A Theological Reading of 1 Cor 1:18-31," *NTT* 46/2 (1992): 132-49.

1:18-25

10092 Karl Müller, "1 Kor 1,18-25: Die eschatologisch- kritische Funktion der Verkündigung des Kreuzes," *BZ* 10/2 (1966): 246-72.

10093 Angelo Penna, "La δύναμις θεοῦ: reflessioni in margine a 1 Cor. 1:18-25," *RBib* 15 (1967): 281-94.

10094 Gordon H. Clark, "Wisdom in First Corinthians," *JETS* 15/4 (1972): 197-205.

1:20

10095 Lars Hartman, "Universal Reconciliation (Col 1.20)," - *SNTU-A* 10 (1985): 109-21.

10096 Daniel Hoffman, "The Authority of Scripture and Apostolic Doctrine in Ignatius of Antioch," *JETS* 28 (1985): 71-79.

10097 · Markus Lautenschlager, "Abschied vom Disputierer. Zur Bedeutung von συζητητὴς in 1 Kor 1,20," *ZNW* 83/3-4 (1992): 276-85.

1:22-24

10098 S. Cipriani, "Sapientia crucis e sapienza 'umana' in Paolo," *RBib* 36 (1988): 343-61.

1:22-23

10099 Gregory M. Corigan, "Paul's Shame for the Gospel," *BTB* 16/1 (1986): 23-27.

1:22

10100 Jos Janssens, "Il cristiano di fronte al martirio imminente: testimonianze e dottrina nella chiesa antica," *Greg* 66/3 (1985): 405-27.

10101 R. Garland Young, "Greek Wisdom," *BI* 14/2 (1989): 20-22.

1:23

10102 Kazimierz Romaniuk, "Nos autem praedicamus Christum et hunc crucifixum," *VD* 47 (1969): 232-36.

1:25

10103 L. D. Hurst, "Re-enter the Pre-existent Christ in Philippians 2:5-11," *NTS* 32 (1986): 449-57.

1:26-31

10104 Gail R. O'Day, "Jeremiah 9:22-23 and 1 Corinthians 1:26-31: A Study in Intertextuality," *JBL* 109/2 (1990): 259-67.

1:26

10105 D. Sänger, "Die δυνατοί in 1 Kor 1:26," *ZNW* 76 (1985): 285-91.

10106 Francisco Montagnini, " 'Videte vocationem vestram' (1 Cor 1,26)," *RBib* 39/2 (1991): 217-21.

1:27

10107 Robert T. Osborn, "The Christian Blasphemy," *JAAR* 53 (1985): 339-63.

1:29-31

10108 Sigfred Pedersen, "Theologische Überlegungen zur Isagogik des Römerbriefs," *ZNW* 76/1-2 (1985): 47-67.

1:30

10109 Wilhelm Bender, "Bemerkungen zur Übersetzung von 1 Korinther 1:30," *ZNW* 71/3-4 (1980): 263-68.

2

10110 D. W. Martin, "Spirit in 1 Cor. 2," *CBQ* 5 (1943): 381-95.

10111 Norman M. Pritchard, "Profession of Faith and Admission to Communion in the Light of 1 Corinthians 2 and Other Passages," *SJT* 33/1 (1980): 55-70.

2:1-13

10112 C. B. Cousar, "1 Corinthians 2:1-13," *Int* 44 (1990): 169-73.

2:1-11

10113 Ronald Byars, "Sectarian Division and the Wisdom of the Cross: Preaching from First Corinthians," *QR* 9/4 (1989): 65-97.

2:1-5

10114 Timothy H. Lim, "Not in Persuasive Words of Wisdom but in the Demonstration of the Spirit and Power," *NovT* 29/2 (1987): 137-49.

2:1

10115 James L. Blevins, " 'Wisdom' in Paul's Writings," *BI* 8/2 (1982): 15-17.

2:2-16

10116 A. Rose, "L'épouse dans l'assemblée liturgique," *BVC* 34 (1960): 13-19.

2:4-7

10117 James L. Blevins, " 'Wisdom' in Paul's Writings," *BI* 8/2 (1982): 15-17.

2:6-3:4

10118 Benjamin Fiore, " 'Covert Allusion' in 1 Corinthians 1-4," *CBQ* 47/1 (1985): 85-102.

2:6-16

10119 Martin Widmann, "1 Kor 2:6-16: Ein Einspruch gegen Paulus," *ZNW* 70/1-2 (1979): 44-53.

10120 W. C. Kaiser, "A Neglected Text in Bibliography Discussions: 1 Corinthians 2:6-16," *WTJ* 43/2 (1981): 301-319.

10121 Jerome Murphy-O'Connor, "Interpolations in 1 Corinthians," *CBQ* 48 (1986): 81-94.

10122 William O. Walker, "1 Corinthians 2:6-16: A Non-Pauline Interpolation?" *JSNT* 47 (1992): 75-94.

10123 R. B. Gaffin, "Some Epistemological Reflections on 1 Corinthians 2:6-16," *WTJ* 57 (1995): 103-24.

2:6-15

10124 Paul W. Gooch, "Margaret, Bottom, Paul, and the Inexpressible," *WW* 6/3 (1986): 313-25.

2:6-8

10125 E. Driessen, "Promissio Redemptoris apud S. Paulum," *VD* 21 (1941): 233-38, 264-71, 280-305.

10126 P. Bormann, "Bemerkungen zu zwei lesenswerten Aufsätzen," *TGl* 50 (1960): 112-14.

2:6

10127 William Baird, "Among the Mature: The Idea of Wisdom in 1 Corinthians 2:6," *Int* 13 (1959): 425-32.

10128 V. P. Branick, "Apocalyptic Paul?" *CBQ* 47 (1985): 664-75.

2:7

10129 Leslie C. Allen, "The Old Testament Background of (Pro)Orizein in the New Testament," *NTS* 17/1 (1970): 104-08.

10130 Galen W. Wiley, "A Study of 'Mystery' in the New Testament," *GTJ* 6/2 (1985): 349-60.

10131 J. K. Grider, "Predestination as Temporal Only," *WTJ* 22 (1987): 56-64.

2:9

10132 André Feuillet, "The Enigma of 1 Cor 2:9," *TD* 14 (1966): 143-48.

10133 Eckhard Nordheim, "Das Zitat des Paulus in 1 Kor 2:9 und seine Beziehung zum koptischen Testament Jakobs," *ZNW* 65/1-2 (1974): 112-120.

10134 H. Ponsot, "D'Isaie 64:3 à 1 Corinthiens 2:9," *RB* 90/2 (1983): 229-42.

10135 Bo Frid, "The Enigmatic ἀλλά in 1 Corinthians 2:9," *NTS* 31 (1985): 603-11.

10136 Luis F. Ladaria, "Presente y futuro en la escatología cristiana," *EE* 60 (1985): 351-59.

10137 Oda Wischmeyer, "Theon agapan bei Paulus: eine traditionsgeschichtliche Miszelle," *ZNW* 78/1-2 (1987): 141-44.

2:10-12

10138 Michael A. G. Haykin, "The Spirit of God: The Exegesis of 1 Cor 2:10-12 by Origen and Athanasius," *SJT* 35/6 (1982): 513-28.

2:12-15

10139 David R. Nichols, "The Problem of Two-Level Christianity at Corinth," *Pneuma* 11 (1989): 99-112.

2:13

10140 James L. Blevins, " 'Wisdom' in Paul's Writings," *BI* 8/2 (1982): 15-17.

2:14-3:4

10141   Stanley D. Toussaint, "The Spiritual Man," *BSac* 125/498
        (1968): 139-146.

2:15-16

10142   John D. Lawrence, "The Eucharist as the Imitation of
        Christ," *TS* 47 (1986): 286-96.

10143   Roger L. Omanson, "Acknowledging Paul's Quotations,"
        BT 43/2 (1992): 201-13.

2:16

10144   W. L. Willis, "The 'Mind of Christ' in 1 Corinthians
        2:16," *Bib* 70/1 (1989): 110-122.

3-6

10145   Michael D. Goulder, "Did Luke Know Any of the Pauline
        Letters," *PRS* 13 (1986): 97-112.

3

10146   Brendan Byrne, "Ministry and Maturity in 1 Corinthians
        3," *ABR* 35 (1987): 83-87.

10147   John Proctor, "Fire in God's House: Influence of Malachi
        3 in the NT," *JETS* 36 (1993): 9-14.

3:1-9

10148   C. Thomas Rhyne, "1 Corinthians 3:1-9," *Int* 44 (1990):
        174-79.

3:1-3

10149   J. Francis, " 'As Babes in Christ': Some Proposals
        regarding 1 Corinthians 3:1-3," *JSNT* 7 (1980): 41-60.

10150   David R. Nichols, "The Problem of Two-Level
        Christianity at Corinth," *Pneuma* 11 (1989): 99-112.

3:1-2

10151   Wilhelm Thüsing, " 'Milch' und 'feste Speise'," *TTZ* 76
        (1967): 233-46, 261-80.

10152   Beverly R. Gaventa, "Our Mother St Paul (1995): Toward
        the Recovery of a Neglected Theme," *PSB* NS 17 (1996):
        29-44.

3:5-4:5

10153 Benjamin Fiore, " 'Covert Allusion' in 1 Corinthians 1-4," *CBQ* 47/1 (1985): 85-102.

10154 David W. Kuck, "Paul and Pastoral Ambition: A Reflection on 1 Corinthians 3-4," *CThM* 19/3 (1992): 174-83.

3:5-17

10155 Max A. Chevallier, "L'unité plurielle de l'église d'après le Nouveau Testament," *RHPR* 66 (1986): 3-20.

3:5-11

10156 Sigfred Pedersen, "Theologische Überlegungen zur Isagogik des Römerbriefs," *ZNW* 76/1-2 (1985): 47-67.

3:5

10157 Gerhard L. Miller, "Purgatory," *TD* 33/4 (1986): 31-36.

3:6-9

10158 Richard J. Bauckham, "The Parable of the Vine: Rediscovering a Lost Parable of Jesus," *NTS* 33/1 (1987): 84-101.

3:9-17

10159 Jay Shanor, "Paul as Master Builder: Construction Terms in First Corinthians," *NTS* 34/3 (1988): 461-71.

3:9

10160 E. Peterson, "Ἔργον in der Bedeutung 'Bau' bei Paulus," *Bib* 22 (1941): 439-41.

10161 Victor P. Furnish, " 'Fellow Workers in God's Service'," *JBL* 80 (1961): 364-70.

3:10-3:23

10162 A. Miranda, "L' 'uomo spirituale' nella Prima ai Corinzi," *RBib* 43 (1995): 485-519.

3:10-15

10163 S. Cipriani, "Insegna 1 Cor. 3,10-15 la dottrina del Purgatorio?" *RBib* 7 (1959): 25-43.

10164 Charles W. Fishburne, "1 Cor. 3:10-15 and the Testament of Abraham," *NTS* 17/1 (1970): 109-15.

10165 Craig A. Evans, "How Are the Apostles Judged? A Note On 1 Corinthians 3:10-15," *JETS* 27/2 (1984): 149-50.

10166 Gerhard L. Müller, "Fegfeuer: zur Hermeneutik eines umstrittenen Lehrstücks in der Eschatologie," *TQ* 166 (1986): 25-39.

10167 Harm W. Hollander, "The Testing by Fire of the Builder's Works: 1 Corinthians 3.10-15," *NTS* 40 (1994): 89-104.

3:10-13

10168 J. D. M. Derrett, "Paul as Master-Builder," *EQ* 69 (1997): 129-37.

3:10

10169 Hermann von Lips, "Der Apostolat des Paulus - ein Charisma: semantische Aspekte zu charis-charisma und anderen Wortpaaren im Sprachgebrauch des Paulus," *Bib* 66/3 (1985): 305-43.

3:13

10170 Harm W. Hollander, "Revelation by Fire: 1 Corinthians 3:13," *BT* 44 (1993): 242-44.

3:15

10171 J. R. Busto Saiz, "Se salvará como atravesando fuego? 1 Cor 3:15b reconsiderado," *EE* 68 (1993): 333-38.

3:16-23

10172 M. Trimaille, "La communauté, sanctuaire de Dieu, et son unité dans le Christ," *AsSeign* NS38 (1970): 34-41.

3:16-17

10173 A.-M. Denis, "La fonction apostolique et la liturgie nouvelle en esprit: l'Apôtre, constructeur du temple spirituel," *RSPT* 42 (1958): 408-26.

10174 Jonathan A. Draper, "The Tip of an Ice-berg: The Temple of the Holy Spirit," *JTSA* 59 (1987): 57-65.

10175 Brian S. Rosner, "Temple and Holiness in 1 Corinthians 5," *TynB* 42/1 (1991): 137-45.

3:16

10176　Friedrich W. Horn, "Wandel im Geist: zur pneumatologischen Begründung der Ethik bei Paulus," *KD* 38 (1992): 149-70.

3:18

10177　Dennis Ormseth, "Showing the Body: Reflections on 1 Corinthians 12-13 for Epiphany," *WW* 6 (1986): 97-103.

3:20

10178　Roy A. Harrisville, "Paul and the Psalms: A Formal Study," *WW* 5 (1985): 168-79.

3:21

10179　Sigfred Pedersen, "Theologische Überlegungen zur Isagogik des Römerbriefs," *ZNW* 76/1-2 (1985): 47-67.

4:1-5

10180　J. L. Lilly, "Missal Epistles from 1 Corinthians," *CBQ* 13 (1951): 308-13, 432-38.

10181　Michel Coune, "L'apôtre sera jugé," *AsSeign* 7 (1967): 16-31.

10182　Jouette M. Bassler, "1 Corinthians 4:1-5," *Int* 44 (1990): 179-83.

4:2

10183　W. Hulitt Gloer, "Stewards in the First Century," *BI* 11/1 (1985): 31-33.

4:4

10184　Charles H. Cosgrove, "Justification in Paul: A Linguistic and Theological Reflection," *JBL* 106/4 (1987): 653-70.

4:6-13

10185　Benjamin Fiore, " 'Covert Allusion' in 1 Corinthians 1-4," *CBQ* 47/1 (1985): 85-102.

4:6

10186　Morna D. Hooker, "Beyond the Things Which Are Written: An Examination of 1 Corinthians 4:6," *NTS* 10 (1963): 127-32.

10187 John Strugnell, "A Plea Conjectural Emendation in the New Testament with a Coda on 1 Cor. 4:6," *CBQ* 36/4 (1974): 543-58.

10188 Jerome Murphy-O'Connor, "Interpolations in 1 Corinthians," *CBQ* 48 (1986): 81-94.

10189 L. L. Wellborn, "A Conciliatory Principle in 1 Cor. 4:6," *NovT* 29/4 (1987): 300-46.

10190 Roger L. Omanson, "Acknowledging Paul's Quotations," *BT* 43/2 (1992): 201-13.

10191 David R. Hall, "A Disguise for the Wise: μετεσχηματισμός in 1 Corinthians 4.6," *NTS* 40 (1994): 143-49.

10192 B. J. Dodd, "Pauls's Paradigmatic 'I' and 1 Corinthians 6:12," *JSNT* 59 (1995): 39-58.

10193 James C. Hanges, "1 Corinthians 4:6 and the Possibility of Written Bylaws in the Corinthian Church," *JBL* 117 (1998): 275-98.

10194 Ronald L. Tyler, "First Corinthians 4:6 and Hellenistic Pedagogy," *CBQ* 60 (1998): 97-103.

10195 J. Ross Wagner, " 'Not Beyond the Things Which Are Written': A Call to Boast Only in the Lord," *NTS* 44 (1998): 279-87.

4:7

10196 Sigfred Pedersen, "Theologische Überlegungen zur Isagogik des Römerbriefs," *ZNW* 76/1-2 (1985): 47-67.

4:8-9

10197 William Klassen, "The King as 'Living Law' with Particular Reference to Musonius Rufus," *SR* 14/1 (1985): 63-71.

4:8

10198 David R. Nichols, "The Problem of Two-Level Christianity at Corinth," *Pneuma* 11 (1989): 99-112.

10199 Mark A. Plunkett, "Eschatology at Corinth," in *EGLMBS* 9 (1989): 195-211.

4:9-20

10200 W. D. Spencer, "The Power in Paul's Teaching (1 Cor 4:9-20)," *JETS* 32/1 (1989): 51-61.

4:12

10201 Jürgen Sauer, "Traditionsgeschichtliche Erwägungen zu den synoptischen und paulinischen Aussagen über Feindesliebe und Wiedervergeltungsverzicht," *ZNW* 76/1-2 (1985): 1-28.

4:14-21

10202 Benjamin Fiore, " 'Covert Allusion' in 1 Corinthians 1-4," *CBQ* 47/1 (1985): 85-102.

10203 E. M. Lassen, "The Use of the Father Image in Imperial Propaganda and 1 Corinthians 4:14-21," *TynB* 42/1 (1991): 127-36.

4:14-15

10204 Dennis Ormseth, "Showing the Body: Reflections on 1 Corinthians 12-13 for Epiphany," *WW* 6 (1986): 97-103.

4:15

10205 M. Saillard, "C'est moi qui, par l'Évangile, vous ai enfantés dans le Christ," *RechSR* 56 (1968): 5-42.

10206 Norman H. Young, "Paidagogos: The Social Setting of a Pauline Metaphor," *NovT* 29 (1987): 150-76.

4:17

10207 Kenneth E. Bailey, "The Structure of 1 Corinthians and Paul's Theological Method with Special Reference to 4:17," *NovT* 25/2 (1983): 152-81.

10208 M. C. Griffths, "Today's Missionary, Yesterday's Apostle," *EMQ* 21/2 (1985): 154-65.

4:18

10209 Luis F. Ladaria, "Presente y futuro en la escatología cristiana," *EE* 60 (1985): 351-59.

4:20

10210 Günter Haufe, "Reich Gottes bei Paulus und in der Jesustradition," *NTS* 31 (1985): 467-72.

5-6

10211 Paul S. Pinear, "Christ and the Congregation: 1 Corinthians 5-6," *RevExp* 80/3 (1983): 341-50.

10212 Arthur J. Dewey, "Paulos pornographos: the mapping of sacred space," *EGLMBS* 6 (1986): 104-13.

10213 Gerhard Sellin, "1 Korinther 5-6 und der 'Vorbrief' nach Korinth. Indizien für eine Mehrschichtigkeit von Kommunikationsakten im ersten Korintherbrief," *NTS* 37/4 (1991): 535-58.

10214 R. Trevijano Etcheverría, "A propósito del incestuoso (1 Cor 5-6)," *Salm* 38/2 (1991): 129-53.

10215 Will Deming, "The Unity of 1 Corinthians 5-6," *JBL* 115 (1996): 289-312.

5

10216 B. N. Wambacq, "Matthieu 5, 31-32: Possibilité de Divorce ou Obligation de Rompre une Union Illiégitime," *NRT* 104/1 (1982): 34-49.

10217 Colin G. Kruse, "The Offender and the Offence in 2 Corinthians 2:5 and 7:12," *EQ* 60 (1988): 129-39.

10218 Peter Zaas, "Catalogues and Context: 1 Corinthians 5 and 6," *NTS* 34/4 (1988): 622-629.

10219 J. J. Engelbrecht, "Kerklike Tug Volgens 1 Korintiers 5 en 6 (Ecclesiastical Discipline According to 1 Cor 5 & 6)," *HTS* 45/2 (1989): 387-400.

10220 G. Harris, "The Beginnings of Church Discipline: 1 Corinthians 5," *NTS* 37/1 (1991): 1-21.

10221 Brian S. Rosner, "Temple and Holiness in 1 Corinthians 5," *TynB* 42/1 (1991): 137-45.

5:1

10222 G. Al Wright, "First-Century AD Greek Morals," *BI* 14/2 (1989): 35-38.

5:1-13

10223 David W. Miller, "The Uniqueness of New Testament Church Eldership," *GTJ* 6/2 (1985): 315-27.

5:1-8

10224 James Benedict, "The Corinthian Problem of 1 Corinthians 5:1-8," *BLT* 32 (1987): 70-73.

10225 James T. South, "A Critique of the 'Curse/Death' Interpretation of 1 Corinthians 5:1-8," *NTS* 39 (1993): 539-61.

5:1-5

10226 V. C. Pfitzner, "Purified Community-Purified Sinner: Expulsion from the Communion According to Matthew 18:15-18 and 1 Corinthians 5:1-5," *ABR* 30 (1982): 34-55.

10227 A. C. Perriman, "Paul and the Parousia: 1 Corinthians 15:50-57 and 2 Corinthians 5:1-5," *NTS* 35/4 (1989): 512-21.

5:2

10228 Brian S. Rosner, "᾿Ουσχὶ μᾶλλον ἐπενθήσατε': Corporate Responsibility in 1 Corinthians 5," *NTS* 38/3 (1992): 470-73.

5:3-5

10229 Jerome Murphy-O'Connor, "1 Corinthians 5:3-5," *RB* 84/2 (1977): 239-45.

5:4

10230 G. A. Cole, "1 Cor 5:4: 'With my Spirit'," *ET* 8 (1987): 205.

5:5

10231 J. Cambier, "La Chair et l'Esprit en 1 Cor. 5:5," *NTS* 15/2 (1969): 221-32.

10232 N. George Joy, "Is the Body Really to be Destroyed?" *BT* 39/4 (1988): 429-36.

10233 Barth Campbell, "Flesh and Spirit in 1 Cor 5:5: An Exercise in Rhetorical Criticism of the New Testament," *JETS* 36 (1993): 331-42.

10234 V. George Shillington, "Atonement Texture in 1 Corinthians 5.5," *JSNT* 71 (1998): 29-50.

10235 Brian S. Rosner, " 'Drive out the wicked person' A Biblical Theology of Exclusion," *EQ* 71 (1999): 25-36.

5:6

10236 A. Schon, "Eine weitere metrische Stelle bei St. Paulus," *Bib* 30 (1949): 510-13.

10237 Luis F. Ladaria, "Presente y futuro en la escatología cristiana," *EE* 60 (1985): 351-59.

5:6-8

10238 J. K. Howard, " 'Christ Our Passover': A Study of the Passover- Exodus Theme in 1 Corinthians," *EQ* 41/2 (1969): 97-108.

5:7-8

10239 F. Ogara, "Dominica Resurrectionis," *VD* 13 (1933): 97-103.

10240 L. D. Hurst, "Apollos, Hebrews, and Corinth: Bishop Montefiore's Theory Examined," *SJT* 38/4 (1985): 505-13.

5:7

10241 Christian Grappe, "Essai sur l'arrière-plan Pascal des récits de la dernière nuit de Jésus," *RHPR* 65/2 (1985): 105-25.

10242 Antonio Orbe, "Cristo, sacrificio y manjar," *Greg* 66/2 (1985): 185-239.

10243 P. Colella, "Cristo nostra pasqua? 1 Cor 5:7," *BibO* 28 (1986): 197-217.

5:12

10244 B. J. Dodd, "Pauls's Paradigmatic 'I' and 1 Corinthians 6:12," *JSNT* 59 (1995): 39-58.

5:16-21

10245 Paul D. Hanson, "The Identity and Purpose of the Church," *TT* 42 (1985): 342-52.

6-7

10246 David R. Catchpole, "The Synoptic Divorce Material as a Traditio-Historical Problem," *BJRL* 57/1 (1974): 92-127.

10247 Jens Christensen, "Paulus livsfornaegteren? For og imod Vilhelm Gronbechs Paulustolkning," *DTT* 53/1 (1990): 1-18.

6

10248 William Klassen, "The King as 'Living Law' with Particular Reference to Musonius Rufus," *SR* 14/1 (1985): 63-71.

10249 Peter Zaas, "Catalogues and Context: 1 Corinthians 5 and 6," *NTS* 34/4 (1988): 622-629.

10250 J. J. Engelbrecht, "Kerklike Tug Volgens 1 Korintiers 5 en 6 (Ecclesiastical Discipline According to 1 Cor 5 & 6)," *HTS* 45/2 (1989): 387-400.

6:1-11

10251 Erich Dinkler, "Zum Problem der Ethik bei Paulus: Rechtsnahme und Rechtsverzicht," *ZTK* 49 (1952): 167-200.

10252 Peter Richardson, "Judgment in Sexual Matters in 1 Corinthians 6:1-11," *NovT* 25/1 (1983): 37-58.

10253 Reginald H. Fuller, "An exegetical paper: 1 Corinthians 6:1-11," *ExA* 2 (1986): 96-104.

10254 V. George Shillington, "People of God in the Courts of the World: A Study of 1 Corinthians 6:1-11," *Dir* 15 (1986): 40-50.

10255 Robert D. Taylor, "Toward a Biblical Theology of Litigation: A Law Professor Looks at 1 Cor 6:1-11," *ExA* 2 (1986): 105-16.

10256 Lloyd A. Lewis, "The Law Courts in Corinth: An Experiment in the Power of Baptism," *ATR* suppl. 11 (1990): 88-98.

10257 J. D. M. Derrett, "Judgement and 1 Corinthians 6," *NTS* 37/1 (1991): 22-36.

10258 Alan C. Mitchell, "Rich and Poor in the Courts of Corinth: Litigiousness and Status in 1 Corinthians 6:1-11," *NTS* 39 (1993): 562-86.

10259   Nélio Schneider, " 'Homossexualidade' no Novo Testamento: Observaçoes exegéticas e hermenêuticas," *EstT* 39 (1999): 27-35.

6:1-8

10260   Bruce W. Winter, "Civil Litigation in Secular Corinth and the Church. The Forensic Background to 1 Corinthians 6.1-8," *NTS* 37/4 (1991): 559-72.

6:1-6

10261   Brian S. Rosner, "Moses Appointing Judges. An Antecedent to 1 Cor 6,1-6?" *ZNW* 82 (1991): 275-78.

6:4

10262   Brent Kinman, " 'Appoint the Despised as Judges!'," *TynB* 48 (1997): 345-54.

6:9-11

10263   Brian S. Rosner, "The Origin and Meaning of 1 Corinthians 6,9-11 in Context," *BZ* NS 40 (1996): 250-53.

6:9-10

10264   Randolph A. Nelson, "Homosexuality and Social Ethics," *WW* 5 (1985): 380-94.

10265   John R. W. Stott, "Homosexual Marriage: Why Same Sex Partnerships Are Not a Christian Option," *CT* 29/17 (1985): 21-28.

10266   David L. Tiede, "Will Idolaters, Sodomizers, or the Greedy Inherit the Kingdom of God? A Pastoral Exposition of 1 Cor 6:9-10," *WW* 10 (1990): 147-55.

10267   Abraham Smith, "The New Testament and Homosexuality," *QR* 11 (1991): 18-32.

6:9

10268   W. L. Petersen, "Can ἀρσενοκοῖται Be Translated by 'Homosexuals'?" *VC* 40 (1986): 187-91.

10269   David F. Wright, "Translating arsenokoitai," *VC* 41/4 (1987): 396-98.

10270   David E. Malick, "The Condemnation of Homosexuality in 1 Corinthians 6:9," *BSac* 150 (1993): 479-92.

6:11

10271 Günter Haufe, "Reich Gottes bei Paulus und in der Jesustradition," *NTS* 31 (1985): 467-72.

6:12-7:40

10272 G. Claudel, "1 Kor 6:12-7:40 neu gelesen," *TTZ* 94 (1985): 20-36.

10273 G. Claudel, "Une lecture de 1 Co 6,12-7,40," *SémBib* 41 (1986): 3-19.

6:12-7:16

10274 Walter J. Bartling, "Sexuality, Marriage, and Divorce in 1 Corinthians 6:12-7:16," *CTM* 39/6 (1968): 355-66.

6:12-30

10275 Janice R. Huie, "A Call to Christian Integrity: preaching from 1 Corinthians," *QR* 7 (1987): 83-104.

10276 Robert Jewett, "Paul's Dialogue with the Corinthians . . . and Us," *QR* 13 (1993): 89-112.

6:12-20

10277 Jerome Murphy-O'Connor, "Corinthian Slogans in 1 Cor. 6:12-20," *CBQ* 40/3 (1978): 391-96.

10278 Brendan Byrne, "Eschatologies of Resurrection and Destruction: The Ethical Significance of Paul's Dispute with the Corinthians," *DR* 104/357 (1986): 280-98.

10279 Terrance Callan, "Toward a Psychological Interpretation of Paul's Sexual Ethic," *EGLMBS* 6 (1986): 57-71.

10280 Roy B. Ward, "Porneia and Paul," *EGLMBS* 6 (1986): 219-28.

10281 Brian S. Rosser, "Temple Prostitution in 1 Corinthians 6:12-20," *NovT* 40 (1998): 336-51.

6:12

10282 Roger L. Omanson, "Acknowledging Paul's Quotations," *BT* 43/2 (1992): 201-13.

10283 B. J. Dodd, "Paul's Paradigmatic 'I' and 1 Corinthians 6:12," *JSNT* 59 (1995): 39-58.

6:13-20

10284 W. J. McGarry, "St. Paul's Magnificent Appeal for Purity," *AmER* 92 (1935): 47-56.

10285 Michel Coune, "La dignité chrétienne du corps," *AsSeign* NS33 (1970): 46-52.

6:14

10286 Udo Schnelle, "1 Kor. 6:14: Eine nachpaulinische Glosse," *NovT* 25/3 (1983): 217-19.

10287 Jerome Murphy-O'Connor, "Interpolations in 1 Corinthians," *CBQ* 48 (1986): 81-94.

6:16-17

10288 Stanley E. Porter, "How Should ὁ κολλώμενος in 1 Cor 6,16.17 Be Translated?" *ETL* 67/1 (1991): 105-106.

6:17-20

10289 L. D. Hurst, "Apollos, Hebrews, and Corinth: Bishop Montefiore's Theory Examined," *SJT* 38/4 (1985): 505-13.

6:17

10290 O. Wieslaw J. Roslon, " 'A Ten, Kto Przylgnie do Pana, Stanowi z nim Jednego Ducha' (1 Kor 6, 17)," *RoczTK* 12 (1965): 58-73.

6:18

10291 Brendan Byrne, "Sinning Against One's Own Body: Paul's Understanding of the Sexual Relationship in 1 Corinthians 6:18," *CBQ* 45/4 (1983): 608-16.

10292 Brian S. Rosner, "A Possible Quotation of Test. Reuben 5:5 in 1 Corinthians 6:18a," *JTS* 43/1 (1992): 123-27.

10293 Bruce Fisk, "Porneuein as Body Violation: The Unique Nature of Sexual Sin in 1 Corinthians 6:18," *NTS* 42 (1996): 540-58.

10294 J. D. M. Derrett, "Right and Wrong Sticking (1 Cor 6,18)?" *EB* 55 (1997): 89-106.

6:19-20

10295 Jonathan A. Draper, "The Tip of an Ice-berg: The Temple of the Holy Spirit," *JTSA* 59 (1987): 57-65.

10296 George L. Klein, "Hosea 3:1-3—Background to 1 Cor 6:19b-20?" *CTR* 3 (1989): 373-75.

6:19

10297 Harold S. Songer, "The Temple in Roman Thought," *BI* 11/1 (1985): 14-18.

10298 Friedrich W. Horn, "Wandel im Geist: zur pneumatologischen Begründung der Ethik bei Paulus," *KD* 38 (1992): 149-70.

7

10299 P. Schoonenberg, "Le sens de la virginité," *Chr* 5 (1958): 32-44.

10300 E. Neuhäusler, "Ruf Gottes und Stand des Christen: Bemerkungen zu 1 Kor 7," *BZ* 3 (1959): 43-60.

10301 Terri Williams, "The Forgotten Alternative in First Corinthians 7," *CT* 17/17 (1973): 870-72.

10302 Elaine H. Pagels, "Paul and Women: A Response to Recent Discussion," *JAAR* 42/3 (1974): 538-49.

10303 Darrell J. Doughty, "The Presence and Future of Salvation in Corinth," *ZNW* 66/1-2 (1975): 61-90.

10304 Marco Adinolfi, "Il Matrimonio Nella Liberta Dell' Etica Escatologica di 1 Cor. 7,"*Ant* 51/2-3 (1976): 133-69.

10305 J. Cambier, "Doctrine Paulinienne du Mariage chrétien. Etude critique de 1 Co 7 et d'Ep 5, 21-33 et Essai de leur Traduction actuelle," *ÉgT* 10/1 (1979): 13-59.

10306 J. Carl Laney, "Paul and the Permanence of Marriage in 1 Corinthians 7," *JETS* 25/3 (1982): 283-94.

10307 David E. Garland, "The Christian's Posture Toward Marriage and Celibacy: 1 Corinthians 7," *RevExp* 80/3 (1983): 351-62.

10308 Jeremy Moiser, "A Reassessment of Paul's View of Marriage With Reference to 1 Cor. 7," *JSNT* 18 (1983): 103-22.

10309 Terrance Callan, "Toward a Psychological Interpretation of Paul's Sexual Ethic," *EGLMBS* 6 (1986): 57-71.

10310   Margaret Y. MacDonald, "Women Holy in Body and Spirit: The Social Setting of 1 Corinthians 7," *NTS* 36/2 (1990): 161-81.

7:1-40

10311   G. J. Laughery, "Paul: Anti-marriage? Anti-sex? Ascetic? A Dialogue with 1 Corinthians 7:1-40," *EQ* 69 (1997): 109-28.

7:1-11

10312   H. J. Richards, "Christ on Divorce," *Scr* 11 (1959): 22-32.

7:1-9

10313   William A. Heth, "Unmarried 'for the Sake of the Kingdom' in the Early Church," *GTJ* 8 (1987): 55-88.

7:1-7

10314   Wolfgang Schrage, "Zur Frontstellung der paulinischen Ehebewertung in 1 Kor 7:1-7," *ZNW* 67/3-4 (1976): 214-34.

10315   R. F. Collins, "The Unity of Paul's Paraenesis in 1 Thess. 4:3-8. 1 Cor. 7:1-7, A Significant Parallel," *NTS* 29/3 (1983): 420-29.

7:1-5

10316   Alan Padgett, "Feminism in First Corinthians: A Dialogue with Elisabeth Schüssler Fiorenza," *EQ* 58/2 (1986): 121-32.

10317   R. E. Oster, "Use, Misuse and Neglect of Archaeological Evidence in Some Modern Works on 1 Corinthians)," *ZNW* 83/1-2 (1992): 52-73.

7:1

10318   Gordon D. Fee, "1 Corinthians 7:1 in The NIV," *JETS* 23/4 (1980): 307-14.

10319   William E. Phipps, "Is Paul's Attitude Towards Sexual Relations Contained in 1 Cor. 7.1?" *NTS* 28/1 (1982): 125-31.

10320   William J. Ireland, "Letter-Writing in the First Century AD," *BI* 14/2 (1989): 56-58.

10321   Roger L. Omanson, "Acknowledging Paul's Quotations," *BT* 43/2 (1992): 201-13.

7:2

10322   Roy B. Ward, "Porneia and Paul," *EGLMBS* 6 (1986): 219-28.

7:6-24

10323   Bruce W. Winter, "1 Corinthians 7:6-7: A Caveat and a Framework for 'the Sayings' in 7:8-24," *TynB* 48 (1997): 57-65.

7:7-8

10324   Christian Wolff, "Niedrigkeit und Verzicht in Wort und Weg Jesu und in der apostolischen Existenz des Paulus," *NTS* 34/2 (1988): 183-96.

7:7

10325   Hermann von Lips, "Der Apostolat des Paulus - ein Charisma: semantische Aspekte zu charis-charisma und anderen Wortpaaren im Sprachgebrauch des Paulus," *Bib* 66/3 (1985): 305-43.

10326   John J. Kilgallen, "Reflections on Charisma(ta) in the New Testament," *SM* 41 (1992): 289-323.

10327   B. J. Dodd, "Pauls's Paradigmatic 'I' and 1 Corinthians 6:12," *JSNT* 59 (1995): 39-58.

7:8-9

10328   Robert Macina, "Pour éclairer le terme: digamoi," *RevSR* 61 (1987): 54-73.

7:9

10329   M. L. Barré, "To Marry or to Burn: Purousthai in 1 Cor. 7:9," *CBQ* 36/2 (1974): 193-202.

7:10-16

10330   H. G. Coiner, "Those 'Divorce and Remarriage' Passages," *CTM* 39/6 (1968): 367-84.

10331   Richard N. Soulen, "Marriage and Divorce: A Problem in New Testament Interpretation," *Int* 23/4 (1969): 439-50.

7:10-15

10332   Brian F. Byron, "1 Cor. 7:10-15: A Basis for Future Catholic Discipline on Marriage and Divorce?" *TS* 34/3 (1973): 429-45.

7:10-11

10333   E. Vogt, "Zu 1 Kor 7,10-11," *TGl* 31 (1939): 68-76.

10334   M. Zerwick, "De matrimonio et divortio in Evangelio," *VD* 38 (1960): 193-212.

10335   Wilfrid J. Harrington, "Jesus' Attitude towards Divorce," *ITQ* 37 (1970): 199-209.

10336   Augustine Stock, "Matthean Divorce Texts," *BTB* 8/1 (1978): 24-33.

10337   Jerome Murphy-O'Connor, "The Divorced Woman in 1 Cor 7:10-11," *JBL* 100/4 (1981): 601-606.

7:10

10338   Roger L. Omanson, "Some Comments about Style and Meaning: 1 Corinthians 9:15 and 7:10," *BT* 34/1 (1983): 135-39.

10339   Nikolaus Walter, "Paulus und die urchristliche Jesustradition," *NTS* 31 (1985): 498-522.

7:12-15

10340   J. B. Bauer, "Das sogenannte Privilegium Paulinum," *BL* 20 (1952-1953): 82-83.

7:12

10341   John J. O'Rourke, "A Note on an Exception: Mt 5:32 (19:9) and 1 Cor 7:12 Compared," *HeyJ* 5 (1964): 299-302.

7:14

10342   Lester J. Kuyper, "Exegetical Study on 1 Corinthians 7:14," *RR* 31/1 (1977): 62-64.

10343   Jerome Murphy-O'Connor, "Works Without Faith in 1 Cor. 7:14," *RB* 84/3 (1977): 349-61.

7:15

10344   H. U. Willi, "Das Privilegium Paulinum (1 Kor 7,15f) Pauli eigene Lebenserinnerung?" *BZ* 22/1 (1978): 100-108.

10345   William A. Heth, "Divorce and Remarriage: The Search for an Evangelical Hermeneutic," *TriJ* 16 (1995): 63-100.

10346   Robert G. Olender, "The Pauline Privilege: Inference or Exegesis?" *FM* 16 (1998): 94-117.

10347   Gerald L. Borchert, "1 Corinthians 7:15 and the Church's Historic Misunderstanding of Divorce and Remarriage," *RevExp* 96 (1999): 125-29.

7:16

10348   Christoph Burchard, "Ei nach einem Ausdruck des Wissens oder Nichtwissens Joh 9:25, Act 19:2, 1 Cor 1:16, 7:16," *ZNW* 52/1-2 (1961): 73-82.

10349   Sakae Kubo, "1 Corinthians 7:16: Optimistic or Pessimistic?" *NTS* 24/4 (1978): 539-544.

7:17-24

10350   Gregory W. Dawes, "But If You Can Gain Your Freedom (1 Corinthians 7:17-24)," *CBQ* 52 (1990): 681-97.

7:17

10351   Sigfred Pedersen, "Theologische Überlegungen zur Isagogik des Römerbriefs," *ZNW* 76/1-2 (1985): 47-67.

7:19

10352   F. Thielman, "The Coherence of Paul's View of the Law: The Evidence of First Corinthians," *NTS* 38/2 (1992): 235-53.

7:20-24

10353   Daniel Marguerat, "Paul: un génie théologique et ses limites," *FV* 84/5 (1985): 65-76.

7:21-22

10354   Will Deming, "A Diatribe Pattern in 1 Corinthians 7:21-22: A New Perspective on Paul's Directions to Slaves," *NovT* 37 (1995): 130-37.

7:21

10355   J. A. Harrill, "Paul and Slavery: The Problem of 1 Cor 7:21," *BR* 39 (1994): 5-28.

7:22

10356   Lucien Cerfaux, "Service du Christ et liberté," *BVC* 8 (1954-1955): 7-15.

7:25-40

10357 Diane Payette-Bucci, "Voluntary Childlessness," *Dir* 17 (1988): 26-41.

10358 P. Genton, "1 Corinthiens 7,25-40. Notes exégétiques," *ÉTR* 67/2 (1992): 249-53.

7:25-38

10359 M. Navarro Puerto, "La παρθένος: Un futuro significativo en el aquí y ahora de la comunidad (1 Cor 7,25-38)," *EB* 49/3 (1991): 353-87.

7:25-35

10360 X. Leon-Dufour, "L'appel au célibat consacré," *AsSeign* 95 (1966): 17-32.

7:25-28

10361 William A. Heth, "Unmarried 'for the Sake of the Kingdom' in the Early Church," *GTJ* 8 (1987): 55-88.

7:25

10362 K. G. E. Dolfe, "1 Cor 7,25 Reconsidered (Paul a Supposed Adviser)," *ZNW* 83/1-2 (1992): 115-18.

7:26

10363 B. B. Blue, "The House Church at Corinth and the Lord's Supper: Famine, Food Supply, and the *Present Distress*," *CTR* 5/2 (1991): 221-39.

10364 Roger L. Omanson, "Acknowledging Paul's Quotations," *BT* 43/2 (1992): 201-13.

7:27

10365 Bruce W. Winter, "Secular and Christian Responses to Corinthian Famines," *TynB* 40 (1989): 86-106.

7:29-35

10366 F. Puzo, "Maria y Maria (Nota exegetica a Lc. 10,38-42 y 1 Cor 7,29-35)," *EE* 34 (1960): 851-57.

10367 Janice R. Huie, "A Call to Christian Integrity: Preaching from 1 Corinthians," *QR* 7 (1987): 83-104.

7:29-31

10368 Y. Congar, "In the World and not of the World," *Scr* 9 (1957): 53-64.

10369   Romano Penna, "San Paolo (1 Cor 7, 29b-31a) e Diogene il Cinico," *Bib* 58/2 (1977): 237-45.

10370   H. Russell Botman, "Exegesis and Proclamation—1 Corinthians 7:29-31: 'To Live . . . as if It Were not'," *JTSA* 65 (1988): 73-79.

10371   Robert Jewett, "Paul's Dialogue with the Corinthians . . . and Us," *QR* 13 (1993): 89-112.

7:29

10372   V. P. Branick, "Apocalyptic Paul?" *CBQ* 47 (1985): 664-75.

7:30

10373   F. J. Steinmetz, " 'Weinen mit den Weinenden': Auslegung und Meditation von Lk 6,25; 1 Kor 7,30; Rom 12,15," *GeistL* 42 (1969): 391-94.

7:31

10374   A. Vicent Cernuda, "Engañan la oscuridad y el mundo; la luz era y manifiesta lo verdadero," *EB* 27 (1968): 153-75, 215-32.

10375   I. L. Grohar, "El 'mundo' en los escritos juanicos: un ensayo de interpretación," *RevB* 47 (1985): 221-27.

10376   Luis F. Ladaria, "Presente y futuro en la escatología cristiana," *EE* 60 (1985): 351-59.

7:32-35

10377   D. L. Balch, "1 Cor 7:32-35 and Stoic Debates About Marriage, Anxiety and Distraction," *JBL* 102/3 (1983): 429-39.

7:34-40

10378   William A. Heth, "Unmarried 'for the Sake of the Kingdom' in the Early Church," *GTJ* 8 (1987): 55-88.

7:34

10379   Roger L. Omanson, "Acknowledging Paul's Quotations," *BT* 43/2 (1992): 201-13.

<u>7:35</u>

10380 David E. Fredrickson, "No Noose is Good News: Leadership as a Theological Problem in the Corinthian Correspondence," *WW* 16 (1996): 420-26.

<u>7:36-38</u>

10381 R. Kugelmann, "1 Cor. 7,36-38," *CBQ* 10 (1948): 63-71, 458-59.

10382 John J. O'Rourke, "Hypotheses regarding 1 Corinthians 7,36-38," *CBQ* 20 (1958): 292-98.

10383 Roger L. Omanson, "Translations: Text and Interpretation," *EQ* 57 (1985): 195-210.

<u>7:36</u>

10384 Bruce W. Winter, "Puberty or Passion? The Referent of hyperakmos in 1 Corinthians 7:36," *TynB* 49 (1998): 71-89.

<u>7:37</u>

10385 Juan Leal, "Super virgine sua (1 Cor. 7,37)," *VD* 35 (1957): 97-102.

<u>7:39-40</u>

10386 Robert Macina, "Pour éclairer le terme: digamoi," *RevSR* 61 (1987): 54-73.

<u>7:39</u>

10387 Richard H. Hiers, "Binding and 'Loosing': The Matthean Authorizations," *JBL* 104 (1985): 233-50.

10388 J. B. Bauer, "Was las Tertullian 1 Kor 7,39?" *ZNW* 77 (1986): 284-87.

<u>8-11</u>

10389 Michael D. Goulder, "Did Luke Know Any of the Pauline Letters," *PRS* 13 (1986): 97-112.

10390 E. de la Serna, "¿'Ver-juzgar-actuar' in San Pablo?" *RevB* 52/2 (1990): 85-98.

<u>8:1-11:1</u>

10391 Harold S. Songer, "Problems Arising from Worship of Idols: 1 Corinthians 8:1-11:1," *RevExp* 80/3 (1983): 363-75.

10392   John C. Brunt, "Rejected, Ignored, or Misunderstood? The Fate of Paul's Approach to the Problem of Food Offered to Idols in Early Christianity," *NTS* 31 (1985): 113-24.

10393   Jan Lambrecht, "Universalism in 1 Cor 8:1-11:1?" *Greg* 77 2 (1996): 333-39.

10394   B. J. Oropeza, "Laying to Rest the Midrash: Paul's Message on Meat Sacrificed to Idols in Light of the Deuteronomic Tradition," *Bib* 79 (1998): 57-68.

8-10

10395   Michel Coune, "Le problème des idolothytes et l'éducation de la syneidêsis," *RechSR* 51 (1963): 497-534.

10396   Eugene J. Cooper, "Man's Basic Freedom and Freedom of Conscience in the Bible: Reflections on 1 Corinthians 8-10," *ITQ* 42/4 (1975): 272-83.

10397   Richard A. Horsley, "Consciousness and Freedom Among the Corinthians: 1 Corinthians 8-10," *CBQ* 40/4 (1978): 574-89.

10398   Gordon D. Fee, "Eidolothuta Once Again: An Interpretation of 1 Corinthians 8-10," *Bib* 61/2 (1980): 172-97.

10399   Bruce Fisk, "Eating Meat Offered to Idols: Corinthian Behavior and Pauline Response in 1 Corinthians 8-10," *TriJ* 10/1 (1989): 49-70.

10400   Lamar Cope, "First Corinthians 8-10: Continuity or Contradiction?" *ATR* suppl. 11 (1990): 114-23.

10401   Thomas Söding, "Starke und Schwache: Der Götzenopferstreit in 1 Kor 8-10 als Paradigma paulinischer Ethik," *ZNW* 85 (1994): 69-92.

8

10402   J. M. Ford, "Levirate Marriage in St. Paul," *NTS* 10 (1964): 361-65.

10403   J. M. Ford, "St. Paul, the Philogamist: 1 Cor. 8 in Early Patristic Exegesis," *NTS* 11/4 (1965): 326-48.

10404   Paul W. Gooch, "Conscience in 1 Corinthians 8 and 10," *NTS* 33/2 (1987): 244-54.

10405 K.-K. Yeo, "The Rhetorical Hermeneutic of 1 Corinthians 8 and Chinese Ancester Worship," *BibInt* 3 (1994): 294-311.

8:1-13

10406 L. D. Hurst, "Apollos, Hebrews, and Corinth: Bishop Montefiore's Theory Examined," *SJT* 38/4 (1985): 505-13.

10407 Janice R. Huie, "A Call to Christian Integrity: Preaching from 1 Corinthians," *QR* 7 (1987): 83-104.

10408 Robert Jewett, "Paul's Dialogue with the Corinthians . . . and Us," *QR* 13 (1993): 89-112.

8:1-11

10409 Michael D. Goulder, "Did Luke Know any of the Pauline Letters?" *PRS* 13/2 (1986): 97-112.

8:1-10

10410 E. de la Serna, "Ver-juzgar-actuar en San Pablo?" *RevB* 52/2 (1990): 85-98.

8:1-6

10411 Richard A. Horsley, "Gnosis in Corinth: 1 Corinthians 8: 1-6," *NTS* 27/1 (1980): 32-51.

8:1

10412 James E. Taulman, "The Greek Gods," *BI* 14/2 (1989): 66-69.

8:3

10413 Oda Wischmeyer, "Theon agapan bei Paulus: eine traditionsgeschichtliche Miszelle," *ZNW* 78/1-2 (1987): 141-44.

8:6

10414 M. M. Sagnard, "À propos de 1 Cor. 8,6," *ETL* 26 (1950): 54-58.

10415 Hugolinus Langkammer, "Jednostki Literackie i Teologiczne w i Kor 8, 6," *RoczTK* 15/1 (1968): 97-109.

10416 E. Earle Ellis, "Traditions in 1 Corinthians," *NTS* 32/4 (1986): 481-502.

8:7-9:27

> 10417 J. F. M. Smit, "The Rhetorical Disposition of First Corinthians 8:7-9:27," *CBQ* 59 (1997): 476-91.

8:7-13

> 10418 Gregory W. Dawes, "The Danger of Idolatry: First Corinthians 8:7-13," *CBQ* 58 (1996): 82-98.

8:8-11

> 10419 W. J. McGarry, "St. Paul and the Weaker Brother," *AmER* 94 (1936): 609-17.

8:8

> 10420 Jerome Murphy-O'Connor, "Food and Spiritual Gifts in 1 Cor. 8:8," *CBQ* 41/2 (1979): 292-98.

8:10

> 10421 B. N. Wambacq, "Quid S. Paulus de usu carnium docuerit," *VD* 19 (1939): 18-21, 60-69.

> 10422 James Custer, "When is Communion Communion," *GTJ* 6 (1985): 403-10.

> 10423 R. E. Oster, "Use, Misuse and Neglect of Archaeological Evidence in Some Modern Works on 1 Corinthians)," *ZNW* 83/1-2 (1992): 52-73.

8:13-9:27

> 10424 B. J. Dodd, "Pauls's Paradigmatic 'I' and 1 Corinthians 6:12," *JSNT* 59 (1995): 39-58.

9

> 10425 Gerhard Dautzenberg, "Der Verzicht auf das apostolische Unterhaltsrecht. Eine exegetische Untersuchung zu 1 Kor 9," *Bib* 50 (1969): 212-32.

> 10426 W. L. Willis, "An Apostolic Apologia? The Form and Function of 1 Corinthians 9," *JSNT* 24 (1985): 33-48.

> 10427 Wilhelm H. Wuellner, "Where Is Rhetorical Criticism Taking Us?" *CBQ* 49 (1987): 448-63.

> 10428 Harry P. Nasuti, "The Woes of the Prophets and the Rights of the Apostle: The Internal Dynamics of 1 Corinthians 9," *CBQ* 50/2 (1988): 246-64.

10429 J. Smit Sibinga, "Serta Paulina: On Composition Technique in Paul," *FilN* 10 (1997): 35-54.

10430 J. Smit Sibinga, "The Composition of 1 Cor 9 and Its Context," *NovT* 40 (1998): 136-63.

9:1-2

10431 Joseph Plevnik, " 'The Eleven and Those with Them' According to Luke," *CBQ* 40/2 (1978): 205-11.

9:1

10432 Ulrich Luck, "Die Bekehrung des Paulus und das paulinische Evangelium: zur Frage der Evidenz in Botschaft und Theologie des Apostels," *ZNW* 76/3-4 (1985): 187-208.

9:4-10:5

10433 Adalberto Sisti, "Guardare fissi alla meta," *BibO* 5 (1963): 14-21.

9:5

10434 J. B. Bauer, "Uxores circumducere (1 Kor 9,5)," *BZ* 3 (1959): 94-102.

9:6-13

10435 H. Rosman, "Tolle' lege," *VD* 20 (1940): 120-21.

9:8-12

10436 J. F. M. Smit, " 'You Shall Not Muzzle a Threshing Ox': Paul's Use of the Law of Moses in 1 Cornithians 9:8-12," *EB* 58 (2000): 239-63.

9:8-10

10437 W. C. Kaiser, "The Current Crisis in Exegesis and the Apostolic Use of Deuteronomy 25:4 in 1 Corinthians 9:8-10," *JETS* 21/1 (1978): 3-18.

9:8-9

10438 F. Thielman, "The Coherence of Paul's View of the Law: The Evidence of First Corinthians," *NTS* 38/2 (1992): 235-53.

10439 Harm W. Hollander, "The Meaning of the Term 'Law' (NOMOS) in 1 Corinthians," *NovT* 40 (1998): 117-35.

9:9-18

10440 A. Miranda, "L' 'uomo spirituale' nella Prima ai Corinzi," *RBib* 43 (1995): 485-519.

9:9-11

10441 David I. Brewer, "1 Corinthians 9:9-11: A Literal Interpretation of 'Do not Muzzle the Ox'," *NTS* 38 (1992): 554-65.

9:9

10442 Eduard Lohse, " 'Kümmert sich Gott etwa um die Ochsen?': Zu 1 Kor 9:9," *ZNW* 88 (1997): 314-15.

9:13-23

10443 Richard A. Krause, " 'All Things to All Men': Where is the Limit? An Exegetical Study of 1 Corinthians 9:19-23," *WLQ* 93 (1996): 83-105.

9:13-14

10444 Armando J. Levoratti, "Tú no has querido sacrificio ni oblación: Salmo 40:7; Hebreos 10:5; pt 1," *RevB* 48 (1986): 1-30.

9:14-27

10445 G. Didier, "Le salaire du désintéressement (1 Cor. 9,14-27)," *RechSR* 43 (1955): 228-52.

9:14-18

10446 Ernst Käsemann, "Eine paulinische Variation des 'Amor Fati'," *ZTK* 56 (1959): 138-154.

9:14-15

10447 David Horrell, " 'The Lord Commanded...But I Have Not Used...': Exegetical and Hermeneutical Reflections on 1 Corinthians 9:14-15," *NTS* 43 (1997): 587-603.

9:14

10448 Nikolaus Walter, "Paulus und die urchristliche Jesustradition," *NTS* 31 (1985): 498-522.

9:15-16

10449 Sigfred Pedersen, "Theologische Überlegungen zur Isagogik des Römerbriefs," *ZNW* 76/1-2 (1985): 47-67.

9:15

> 10450 Roger L. Omanson, "Some Comments about Style and Meaning: 1 Corinthians 9:15 and 7:10," *BT* 34/1 (1983): 135-39.

9:16-23

> 10451 Janice R. Huie, "A Call to Christian Integrity: Preaching from 1 Corinthians," *QR* 7 (1987): 83-104.

> 10452 Robert Jewett, "Paul's Dialogue with the Corinthians . . . and Us," *QR* 13 (1993): 89-112.

9:16

> 10453 Siegfried Kreuzer, "Der Zwang des Boten: Beobachtungen zu Lk 14,23 und 1 Kor 9,16," *ZNW* 76(1/2) (1985); 123-28.

9:19-23

> 10454 Peter Richardson, "Pauline Inconsistency," *NTS* 26/3 (1980): 347-62.

> 10455 Heikki Räisänen, "Galatians 2:16 and Paul's Break with Judaism," *NTS* 31 (1985): 543-53.

> 10456 Kenneth V. Neller, "1 Corinthians 9:19-23," *RQ* 29/3 (1987): 129-42.

> 10457 F. Thielman, "The Coherence of Paul's View of the Law: The Evidence of First Corinthians," *NTS* 38/2 (1992): 235-53.

9:19

> 10458 R. F. Hock, "Paul's Tentmaking and the Problem of His Social Class," *JBL* 97/4 (1978): 555-64.

9:20-22

> 10459 Harm W. Hollander, "The Meaning of the Term 'Law' (NOMOS) in 1 Corinthians," *NovT* 40 (1998): 117-35.

9:20

> 10460 E. G. Edwards, "On Using the Textual Apparatus of the UBS Greek New Testament," *BT* 28/1 (1977): 121-42.

9:22

> 10461 David A. Black, "A Note on 'The Weak' in 1 Corinthians 9:22," *Bib* 64/2 (1983): 240-42.

10462   David Stanley, "The Apostle Paul as Saint," *SM* 35 (1986): 71-97.

9:24-10:5

10463   G. Martelet, "But et sens d'une double comparison," *AsSeign* 22 (1965): 19-27.

10464   F. Ogara, "Bibebant... de spiritali consequente eos petra, petra autem erat Christus," *VD* 16 (1936): 33-40.

9:24-27

10465   Robert Jewett, "Paul's Dialogue with the Corinthians . . . and Us," *QR* 13 (1993): 89-112.

10466   Otto Schwankl, " 'Lauft so, dass ihr gewinnt' (1996): Zur Wettkampfmetaphorik in 1 Kor 9," *BZ* NS 41 (1997): 174-91.

10467   Amphilochios Papathomas, "Das agonistische Motiv 1 Kor 9:24ff im Spiegel zeitgenössischer dokumentarischer Quellen," *NTS* 43 (1997): 223-41.

9:24-26

10468   Roman Garrison, "Paul's Use of the Athlete Metaphor in 1 Corinthians 9," *SR* 22/2 (1993): 209-17.

9:24

10469   François Refoulé, "Note sur Romains 9:30-33," *RB* 92 (1985): 161-86.

10470   Timothy N. Boyd, "Paul's Use of Analogy," *BI* 14/2 (1989): 24-28.

9:27

10471   Daniel Hoffman, "The Authority of Scripture and Apostolic Doctrine in Ignatius of Antioch," *JETS* 28 (1985): 71-79.

10-13

10472   Colin G. Kruse, "The Relationship Between the Opposition to Paul Reflected in 2 Corinthians 1-7 and 10-13," *EQ* 61/3 (1989): 195-202.

10-11

10473   Paul S. Minear, "Paul's Teaching on the Eucharist in First Corinthians," *Worship* 44 (1970): 83-92.

10474 Christoph Burchard, "The Importance of Joseph and Aseneth for the Study of the New Testament: A General Survey and a Fresh Look at the Lord's Supper," *NTS* 33/1 (1987): 102-34.

10

10475 Paul W. Gooch, "Conscience in 1 Corinthians 8 and 10," *NTS* 33/2 (1987): 244-54.

10:1-22

10476 Wayne A. Meeks, "And Rose Up To Play: Midrash and Paraenesis in 1 Corinthians 10:1-22," *JSNT* 16 (1982): 64-78.

10477 Terrance Callan, "Paul and the Golden Calf," *EGLMBS* 10 (1990): 1-17.

10478 J. F. M. Smit, " 'Do Not Be Idolaters': Paul's Rhetoric in First Corinthians 10:1-22," *NovT* 39 (1997): 40-53.

10:1-13

10479 Tjitze Baarda, "1 Corinthe 10:1-13: Een Schets (1 Corinthians 10:1-13: A Sketch)," *GTT* 76/1 (1976): 1-14.

10480 E. Earle Ellis, "Traditions in 1 Corinthians," *NTS* 32/4 (1986): 481-502.

10481 William Baird, "1 Corinthians 10:1-13," *Int* 44 (1990): 286-90.

10482 G. D. Collier, " 'That We Might Not Crave Evil': The Structure and Argument of 1 Corinthians 10:1-13," *JSNT* 55 (1994): 55-75.

10483 Ellen B. Aitken, "ta dromena kai ta legomena: The Eucharistic Memory of Jesus' Words in First Corinthians," *HTR* 90 (1997): 359-70.

10:1-12

10484 B. J. Oropeza, "Apostasy in the Wilderness: Paul's Message to the Corinthians in a State of Eschatological Liminality," *JSNT* 75 (1999): 69-86.

10:1-11

10485 A. Rose, "L'Église au desert," *BVC* 13 (1956): 49-59.

10486 Andrew J. Bandstra, "Interpretation in 1 Corinthians 10:1-11," *GTJ* 6/1 (1971): 5-21.

10:1-6

    10487 A. Miranda, "L' 'uomo spirituale' nella Prima ai Corinzi," *RBib* 43 (1995): 485-519.

10:1-2

    10488 J. Bonduelle, "Les trois temps de notre exode: Tous, en Moïse, furent baptisés dans la nuée et dans la mer (1 Cor. 10,2)," *VS* 84 (1951): 276-302.

10:2

    10489 Michael A. G. Haykin, " 'In the Cloud and in the Sea': Basil of Caesarea and the Exegesis of 1 Cor 10:2," *VC* 40 (1986): 135-44.

    10490 William B. Badke, "Baptised into Moses-Baptised into Christ: A Study in Doctrinal Development," *EQ* 60/1 (1988): 23-29.

10:3-7

    10491 James Custer, "When is Communion Communion," *GTJ* 6 (1985): 403-10.

10:6-16

    10492 Charles Perrot, "Les Exemples du Desert," *NTS* 29/4 (1983): 437-52.

10:6-13

    10493 F. Ogara, "Haec... in figura contingebant illis," *VD* 15 (1935): 227-32.

10:6

    10494 Norbert Baumert, "Eis to mit Infinitiv," *FilN* 11 (1998): 7-23.

10:11

    10495 I. Peri, "Gelangen zur Vollkommenheit: Zur lateinischen Interpretation von Katantao in Eph 4:13," *BZ* 23/2 (1979): 269-78.

10:13

    10496 R. J. Foster, "The Meaning of 1 Cor X,13," *Scr* 2 (1947): 45.

10497 D. M. Ciocchi, "Understanding Our Ability to Endure Temptation: A Theological Watershed," *JETS* 35/4 (1992): 463-79.

10498 Marlis Gielen, " 'Und führe uns nicht in Versuchung' Die 6. Vater-Unser Bitte—eine Anfechtung für das biblische Gottesbild?" *ZNW* 89 (1998): 201-16.

10:14-22

10499 Donald Farner, "The Lord's Supper until He Comes," *GTJ* 6/2 (1985): 391-401.

10500 David T. Adamo, "The Lord's Supper in 1 Cor. 10:14-22; 11:17-34," *AfTJ* 18/1 (1989): 36-48.

10:14-21

10501 M.-É. Boismard, "L'Eucharistie selon saint Paul," *LV* 31 (1957): 93-106.

10:15-16

10502 Sigfred Pedersen, "Theologische Überlegungen zur Isagogik des Römerbriefs," *ZNW* 76/1-2 (1985): 47-67.

10:15

10503 James Custer, "When is Communion Communion," *GTJ* 6 (1985): 403-10.

10:16-17

10504 Peter E. Fink, "The Challenge of God's Koinonia," *Worship* 59 (1985): 386-403.

10:16

10505 Phillip Sigal, "Another Note to 1 Corinthians 10:16," *NTS* 29/1 (1983): 134-39.

10506 Guillermo J. Garlatti, "La eucaristia como memoria y proclamacion de la muerte del Señor: aspectos de la cena del Señor según San Pablo [2 pts]," *RevB* 46/4 (1984): 321-41; (1984) 47/1-2 (1985): 1-25.

10507 Walter Kasper, "The Unity and Multiplicity of Aspects in the Eucharist," *CICR* 12 (1985): 115-38.

10508 Andrew B. McGowan, " 'First Regarding the Cup . . .': Papias and the Diversity of Early Eucharistic Practice," *JTS* 46 (1995): 551-55.

10:18-22

10509 James Custer, "When is Communion Communion," *GTJ* 6 (1985): 403-10.

10:20-21

10510 Roy B. Ward, "Porneia and Paul," *EGLMBS* 6 (1986): 219-28.

10:22

10511 Brian S. Rosner, " 'Stronger Than He?' The Strength of 1 Corinthians 10:22b," *TynB* 43/1 (1992): 171-79.

10:23-11:1

10512 Duane F. Watson, "1 Corinthians 10:23-11:1 in the Light of Greco-Roman Rhetoric," *JBL* 108/2 (1989): 301-18.

10:23-30

10513 J. F. M. Smit, "The Function of First Corinthians 10,23-30: A Rhetorical Anticipation," *Bib* 78 (1997): 377-88.

10:23-24

10514 Morna D. Hooker, "Interchange in Christ and Ethics," *JSNT* 25 (1985): 3-17.

10:23

10515 Dennis Ormseth, "Showing the Body: Reflections on 1 Corinthians 12-13 for Epiphany," *WW* 6 (1986): 97-103.

10516 B. J. Dodd, "Pauls's Paradigmatic 'I' and 1 Corinthians 6:12," *JSNT* 59 (1995): 39-58.

10:25

10517 David W. J. Gill, "The Meat-Market at Corinth," *TynB* 43/2 (1992): 389-93.

10518 Dietrich A. Koch, " 'Alles, was en makello verkauft wird, esst...': Die macella von Pompeji, Gerasa und Korinth und ihre Bedeutung für die Auslegung von 1 Kor 10,25," *ZNW* 90 (1999): 194-219.

10:26

10519 Roy A. Harrisville, "Paul and the Psalms: A Formal Study," *WW* 5 (1985): 168-79.

11-14

10520   R. Fowler White, "Richard Gaffin and Wayne Grudem on 1 Cor 13:10: A Comparison of Cessationist and Noncessationist Argumentation," *JETS* 35/2 (1992): 173-81.

11

10521   G. G. Blum, "Das Amt der Frau im Neuen Testament," *NovT* 7 (1964): 142-61.

10522   Elaine H. Pagels, "Paul and Women: A Response to Recent Discussion," *JAAR* 42/3 (1974): 538-49.

10523   Bruce W. Winter, "The Lord's Supper at Corinth: An Alternative Reconstruction," *RTR* 37/3 (1978): 73-82.

11:1-16

10524   E. Haulotte, "Le 'voile' des femmes dans l'assemblée liturgique (1 Co 11,1-16)," *VD* 22 (1942): 237-71.

10525   Cindy Weber-Han, "Sexual Equality according to Paul: An Exegetical Study of 1 Corinthians 11:1-16 and Ephesians 5:21-33," *BLT* 22/3 (1977): 167-70.

10526   Leonidas Kalugila, "Women in the Ministry of Priesthood in the Early Church: An Inquiry," *AfTJ* 14/1 (1985): 35-45.

11:2-34

10527   David K. Lowery, "The Head Covering and the Lord's Supper in 1 Corinthians 11:2-34," *BSac* 143 (1986): 155-63.

11:2-16

10528   J. W. Roberts, "The Veils in 1 Corinthians 11:2-16," *RQ* 3 (1959): 183-98.

10529   Graydon F. Snyder, "Jesus Power: A Confrontation with Women's Lib at Corinth," *BLT* 16/3 (1971): 161-67.

10530   James B. Hurley, "Did Paul Require Veils or the Silence of Women? A Consideration of 1 Corinthians 11:2-16 and 1 Corinthians 14:33b-36," *WTJ* 35/2 (1973): 190-202.

10531   William O. Walker, "1 Corinthians 11:2-16 and Paul's Views Regarding Women," *JBL* 94/1 (1975): 94-110.

10532   Jerome Murphy-O'Connor, "The Non-Pauline Character of 1 Corinthians 11:2-16," *JBL* 95/4 (1976): 615-21.

10533   Bruce K. Waltke, "1 Corinthians 11:2-16: An Interpretation," *BSac* 135 (1978): 46-57.

10534   Jerome Murphy-O'Connor, "Sex and Logic in 1 Corinthians 11:2-16," *CBQ* 42/4 (1980): 482-500.

10535   Alan Padgett, "Paul on Women in the Church: The Contradictions of Coiffure in 1 Corinthians 11:2-16," *JSNT* 20 (1984): 69-86.

10536   Lyle D. Vander Broek, "Women and the Church: Approaching Difficult Passages," *RR* 38 (1985): 225-31.

10537   Terrance Callan, "Toward a Psychological Interpretation of Paul's Sexual Ethic," *EGLMBS* 6 (1986): 57-71.

10538   Alan Padgett, "Feminism in First Corinthians: A Dialogue with Elisabeth Schüssler Fiorenza," *EQ* 58/2 (1986): 121-32.

10539   David M. Scholer, "Feminist Hermeneutics and Evangelical Biblical Interpretation," *JETS* 30 (1987): 407-20.

10540   Thomas P. Shoemaker, "Unveiling of Equality: 1 Corinthians 11:2-16," *BTB* 17/2 (1987): 60-63.

10541   Jerome Murphy-O'Connor, "1 Corinthians 11:2-16 Once Again," *CBQ* 50/2 (1988): 265-74.

10542   Cynthia L. Thompson, "Hairstyles, Head-Coverings, and St. Paul. Portraits from Roman Corinth," *BA* 51/2 (1988): 99-115.

10543   H. van de Sandt, "1 Kor. 11:2-16 als een retorische eenheid," *Bij* 49/4 (1988): 410-25.

10544   Danielle Ellul, "Sois belle et tais -toi!" Est-ce vraiment ce que Paul a dit? A propos de 1 Co 11:2-16," *FV* 88/5 (1989): 49-58.

10545   David W. J. Gill, "The Importance of Roman Portraiture for Head-Coverings in 1 Corinthians 11:2-16," *TynB* 41 (1990): 245-60.

10546   Gail P. Corrington, "The 'Headless Woman': Paul and the Language of the Body in 1 Cor 11:2-16," *PRS* 18/3 (1991): 223-31.

10547 K. T. Wilson, "Should Women Wear Headcoverings?" *BSac* 148/592 (1991): 442-62.

10548 R. E. Oster, "Use, Misuse and Neglect of Archaeological Evidence in Some Modern Works on 1 Corinthians)," *ZNW* 83/1-2 (1992): 52-73.

10549 L. Ann Jervis, " 'But I Want You to Know . . . .': Paul's Midrashic Intertextual Response to the Corinthian Worshipers," *JBL* 112 (1993): 231-46.

10550 I. R. Reimer, "Da Memória à Novidade de Vida," *EstT* 33/3 (1993): 201-12.

10551 Harold R. Holmyard, "Does 1 Corinthians 11:2-16 Refer to Women Praying and Prophesying in Church?" *BSac* 154 (1997): 461-72.

10552 K.-K. Yeo, "Differentiation and Mutuality of Male-Female Relations in 1 Corinthians 11:2-16," *BR* 43 (1998): 7-21.

10553 Jason D. BeDuhn, " 'Because of the Angels': Unveiling Paul's Anthropology in 1 Corinthians 11," *JBL* 118 (1999): 295-320.

10554 Marlis Gielen, "Beten und Prophezeien mit unverhülltem Kopf? Die Kontroverse zwischen Paulus und der korinthischen Gemeinde um die Wahrung der Geschlechtsrollensymbolik in 1 Kor 11,2-16," *ZNW* 90 (1999): 220-49.

11:3-17

10555 J. K. Howard, "Neither Male nor Female: An Examination of the Status of Women in the New Testament," *EQ* 55/1 (1983): 31-42.

11:3-16

10556 G. W. Trompf, "On Attitudes Toward Women in Paul and Paulinist Literature: 1 Corinthians 11:3-16 and Its Context," *CBQ* 42/2 (1980): 196-215.

10557 Jerome Murphy-O'Connor, "Interpolations in 1 Corinthians," *CBQ* 48 (1986): 81-94.

10558 William O. Walker, "The Vocabulary of 1 Corinthians 11:3-16: Pauline or Non-Pauline?" *JSNT* 35 (1989): 75-88.

11:3

10559   Joseph A. Fitzmyer, "Another Look at Kephalē in 1 Corinthians 11:3," *NTS* 35/4 (1989): 503-11.

10560   Wayne Grudem, "The Meaning of Kephale ('head'): A Response to Recent Studies," *TriJ* 11 (1990): 3-72.

10561   A. C. Perriman, "The Head of a Woman: The Meaning of κεφαλὴ in 1 Cor. 11:3," *JTS* 45 (1994): 602-22.

11:4-21

10562   F. Thielman, "The Coherence of Paul's View of the Law: The Evidence of First Corinthians," *NTS* 38/2 (1992): 235-53.

11:4

10563   R. E. Oster, "When Men Wore Veils to Worship: The Historical Context of 1 Corinthians 11:4," *NTS* 34/4 (1988): 481-505.

11:6-8

10564   Wesley Carr, "The Rulers of this Age—1 Corinthians 11:6-8," *NTS* 23/1 (1976): 20-35.

11:6

10565   Halvor Moxnes, "Paulus og den norske vaerematen: 'skam' og 'aere' i Romerbrevet," *NTT* 86/3 (1985): 129-40.

11:7-12

10566   Gregory E. Sterling, " 'Wisdom among the Perfect': Creation Traditions in Alexandrian Judaism and Corinthian Christianity," *NovT* 37/4 (1995): 355-84.

11:9

10567   T. Gallus, "Non est creatus vir propter mulierem, sed mulier propter virum (1 Cor 11,9)," *VD* 22 (1942): 141-51.

11:10

10568   I. Mezzacasa, "Propter angels," *VD* 11 (1931): 39-42.

10569   C. Rösch, "Um tar Engel willen (1 Kor. 11,10)," *TGl* 24 (1932): 363-65.

10570 Morna D. Hooker, "Authority on Her Head: An Examination of 1 Corinthians 11:10," *NTS* 10 (1964): 410-17.

10571 André Feuillet, "Le Signe de Puissance sur la Tête de la Femme: 1 Co 11, 10," *NRT* 95/9 (1973): 945-54.

10572 Günther Schwarz, "Exousian echein epi tes kephales? (1. Korinther 11:10)," *ZNW* 70/3-4 (1979): 249.

10573 Robert C. Newman, "The Ancient Exegesis of Genesis 6:2,4," *GTJ* 5/1 (1984): 13-36.

10574 David R. Hall, "A Problem of Authority," *ET* 102 (1990): 39-42.

10575 Jacques Winandy, "Un curieux *casus pendens:* 1 Corinthiens 11.10 et son interprétation," *NTS* 38/4 (1992): 621-29.

11:11-13

10576 Nikolaus Walter, "Paulus und die urchristliche Jesustradition," *NTS* 31 (1985): 498-522.

11:11-12

10577 Madeleine Boucher, "Some Unexplored Parallels to 1 Corinthians 11,11-12 and Gal 3,28: The NT on the Role of Women," *CBQ* 31 (1969): 50-58.

11:11

10578 K. Wennemer, "Jedoch ist weder die Frau ohne den Mann, noch der Mann ohne die Frau im Herrn (1 Kor 11,11)," *GeistL* 26 (1953): 288-97.

11:12

10579 K. H. Schelkle, "1 Cor 11:12: 'Woman from Man, Man from Woman'," *TD* 32/2 (1985): 145-47.

11:13

10580 Joseph A. Fitzmyer, "Kephalē in 1 Corinthians 11:3," *Int* 47/1 (1993): 52-59.

11:14-15

10581 Halvor Moxnes, "Paulus og den norske vaerematen: 'skam' og 'aere' i Romerbrevet," *NTT* 86/3 (1985): 129-40.

11:15

10582 Alan Padgett, "The Significance of ἀντί in 1 Corinthians 11:15," *TynB* 45 (1994): 181-87.

11:16

10583 T. Engberg-Pedersen, "1 Corinthians 11:16 and the Character of Pauline Exhortation," *JBL* 110/4 (1991): 679-89.

11:17-34

10584 L. Dequeker and W. Zuidema, "L'Eucharistie selon saint Paul," *Conci* 40 (1968): 45-53.

10585 John C. Middlekauff, "The Lord's Supper: 1 Corinthians 11:17-34," *BLT* 24 (1979): 225-29.

10586 J. Timothy Coyle, "The Agape/Eucharist Relationship in 1 Corinthians 11," *GTJ* 6/2 (1985): 411-24.

10587 Donald Farner, "The Lord's Supper until He Comes," *GTJ* 6/2 (1985): 391-401.

10588 Daniel Marguerat, "Paul: un génie théologique et ses limites," *FV* 84/5 (1985): 65-76.

10589 Stephen C. Barton, "Paul's Sense of Place: An Anthropological Approach to Community Formation in Corinth," *NTS* 32/2 (1986): 225-46.

10590 Peter Stuhlmacher, "Das neutestamentliche Zeugnis vom Herrenmahl," *ZTK* 84/1 (1987): 1-35.

10591 Otfried Hofius, "Herrenmahl und Herrenmahlsparadosis," *ZTK* 85/4 (1988): 371-408.

10592 David T. Adamo, "The Lord's Supper in 1 Cor. 10:14-22; 11:17-34," *AfTJ* 18/1 (1989): 36-48.

10593 E. de la Serna, "Ver-juzgar-actuar en San Pablo?" *RevB* 52/2 (1990): 85-98.

10594 Victor P. Furnish, "Belonging to Christ: A Paradigm for Ethics in First Corinthians," *Int* 44/2 (1990): 145-57.

10595 B. B. Blue, "The House Church at Corinth and the Lord's Supper: Famine, Food Supply, and the *Present Distress*," *CTR* 5/2 (1991): 221-39.

10596 T. Engberg-Pedersen, "Proclaiming the Lord's Death: 1 Corinthians 11:7-34 and the Forms of Paul's Theological Argument," *SBLSP* (1991): 592-617.

10597 Peter Lampe, "Das korinthische Herrenmahl im Schnittpunkt hellenistisch-römischer Mahlpraxis und paulinischer Theologia Crucis (1Kor 11,17-34)," *ZNW* 82/3-4 (1991): 183-213.

10598 Craig R. Koester, "Promise and Warning: The Lord's Supper in 1 Corinthians," *WW* 17 (1997): 45-53.

10599 A. A. Das, "1 Corinthians 11:17-34 Revisited," *CTQ* 62 (1998): 187-208.

11:17-22

10600 Willem S. Vorster, "On Early Christian Communities and Theological Perspectives," *JTSA* 59 (1987): 26-34.

11:19

10601 R. A. Campbell, "Does Paul Acquiesce in Divisions at the Lord's Supper?" *NovT* 33/1 (1991): 61-70.

11:20-25

10602 John D. Lawrence, "The Eucharist as the Imitation of Christ," *TS* 47 (1986): 286-96.

11:20

10603 Gerard S. Sloyan, "Jewish Ritual of the 1st Century CE and Christian Sacramental Behavior," *BTB* 15 (1985): 98-103.

10604 Joe O. Lewis, "Paul and the Lord's Supper," *BI* 14/2 (1989): 73-75.

11:21-34

10605 James Custer, "When is Communion Communion," *GTJ* 6 (1985): 403-10.

11:21-23

10606 Paul D. Fueter, "The Therapeutic Language of the Bible," *IRM* 75 (1986): 211-21.

11:21

10607 J. D. M. Derrett, "Intoxication, Joy, and Wrath: 1 Cor 11:21 and Jn 2:10," *FilN* 2/1 (1989): 41-56.

11:23-32

10608 M.-É. Boismard, "L'Eucharistie selon saint Paul," *LV* 31 (1957): 93-106.

11:23-30

10609 Hyam Z. Maccoby, "Paul and the Eucharist," *NTS* 37/2 (1991): 247-67.

11:23-29

10610 Edward J. Kilmartin, "The Eucharistic Cup in the Primitive Liturgy," *CBQ* 24 (1962): 32-43.

10611 Ceslaus Spicq, "L'authentique participation au repas du Seigneur (1 Co 11,23-29)," *AsSeign* 54 (1966): 27-40.

11:23-26

10612 William L. Craig, "The Historicity of the Empty Tomb of Jesus," *NTS* 31 (1985): 39-67.

10613 William R. Farmer, "Peter and Paul, and the Tradition concerning 'the Lord's Supper' in 1 Corinthians 11:23-26," *CTR* 2 (1987): 119-40.

10614 Ellen B. Aitken, "ta dromena kai ta legomena: The Eucharistic Memory of Jesus' Words in First Corinthians," *HTR* 90 (1997): 359-70.

10615 Andrew B. McGowan, " 'Is There a Liturgical Text in This Gospel?': The Institution Narratives and Their Early Interpretative Communities," *JBL* 118 (1999): 73-87.

11:23-25

10616 A. Grail, "Sacrement de la Croix," *LV* 7 (1952): 11-27.

10617 Pierre Benoit, "Les récits de l'institution et leur portée," *LV* 31 (1957): 49-76.

10618 J. Betz, "Die Eucharistie als sakramentale Gegenwart des Heilsereignisses 'Jesus,' nach dem ältesten Abendmahls-bericht," *GeistL* 33 (1960): 166-75.

10619 Walter Kasper, "The Unity and Multiplicity of Aspects in the Eucharist," *CICR* 12 (1985): 115-38.

10620 Charles H. Talbert, "Paul on the Covenant," *RevExp* 84 (1987): 299-313.

10621 Bonnie B. Thurston, "Do This: A Study on the Institution of the Lord's Supper," *RQ* 30/4 (1988): 207-17.

10622 Martin Karrer, "Der Kelch des neuen Bundes: Erwägungen zum Verständnis des Herrenmahls nach 1 Kor 11:23b-25," *BZ* 34/2 (1990): 198-221.

10623 Peter Lampe, "The Eucharist: Identifying with Christ on the Cross," *Int* 48 (1994): 36-49.

10624 Nikolaus Walter, "Paulus und die urchristliche Jesustradition," *NTS* 31 (1985): 498-522.

10625 Guillermo J. Garlatti, "La eucaristia como memoria y proclamacion de la muerte del Señor: aspectos de la cena del Señor según San Pablo [2 pts]," *RevB* 46/4 (1984): 321-41; (1984) 47/1-2 (1985): 1-25.

11:23-24

10626 Peder Borgen, "Nattverdtradisjonen i 1.Kor. 10 og 11 som evangelietradisjon," *SEÅ* 51-52 (1985-1986): 32-39.

11:23

10627 Christian Grappe, "Essai sur l'arrière-plan Pascal des récits de la dernière nuit de Jésus," *RHPR* 65/2 (1985): 105-25.

11:24-25

10628 F. Porporato, "Hoc facite in meam commemorationem," *VD* 13 (1933): 264-70.

10629 Peter Henrici, "Do This in Remembrance of Me: The Sacrifice of Christ and the Sacrifice of the Faithful," *CICR* 12 (1985): 146-57.

10630 R. A. D. Clancy, "The Old Testament Roots of Remembrance in the Lord's Supper," *CJ* 19/1 (1993): 35-50.

11:24

10631 Jakob J. Petuchowski, "Do This In Remembrance of Me (1 Cor. 11:24)," *JBL* 76 (1957): 293-98.

10632 Otfried Hofius, "Τὸ σῶμα τὸ ὑπὲρ ὑμῶν 1 Cor 11:24," *ZNW* 80/1-2 (1989): 80-88.

11:25

10633   R. Kugelmann, "This Is My Blood of the New Covenant," *Worship* 35 (1961): 421-24.

10634   Homer A. Kent, "The New Covenant and the Church," *GTJ* 6/2 (1985): 289-98.

10635   Niels Hyldahl, "Μετὰ τὸ δειπνῆσαι, 1 Kor 11,25 (og Luk 22, 20)," *SEÅ* 51/52 (1986-1987): 100-107.

11:26

10636   Otfried Hofius, " 'Bis dass kommt': 1 Kor. xi. 26," *NTS* 14/3 (1968): 439-41.

10637   Franz G. Cremer, "Der 'Heilstod,' Jesu im paulinischen Verständnis von Taufe und Eucharistie," *BZ* 14 (1970): 227-39.

10638   Beverly R. Gaventa, " 'You Proclaim the Lord's Death': 1 Corinthians 11:26 and Paul's Understanding of Worship," *RevExp* 80/3 (1983): 377-87.

10639   Ray C. Jones, "The Lord's Supper and the Concept of Anamnesis," *WW* 6 (1986): 434-45.

11:27-34

10640   H. U. von Balthasar, "The Holy Church and the Eucharistic Sacrifice," *CICR* 12 (1985): 139-45.

11:27-33

10641   Peter E. Fink, "The Challenge of God's Koinonia," *Worship* 59 (1985): 386-403.

11:27-32

10642   M. P. Surburg, "Structural and Lexical Features in 1 Corinthians 11:27-32," *CJ* 26 (2000): 200-17.

11:27-29

10643   J. M. R. Tillard, "L'Eucharistie, Purification de l'Église Peregrinante," *NRT* 84 (1962): 449-74; 579-97.

11:27

10644   George A. F. Knight, "The Cup of Wrath," *Int* 12 (1958): 412-17.

11:28

10645 J. E. Sanchez Caro, " 'Probet autem seipsum homo' (1 Cor 11:28). Influjo de la praxis penitential Eclesiástica en la interpretacion de un texto biblico," *Salm* 32 (1985): 293-334.

10646 Edward A. Engelbrecht, " 'Let a man Examine Himself': Context and Communion Preparation," *CJ* 23 (1997): 118-21.

11:29-30

10647 Mauro Pesce, "Manigiare e bere il proprio giudizio. Una concezione culturale comune a 1 Cor e a Sota?" *RBib* 38/4 (1990): 495-513.

11:30

10648 Nélio Schneider, " 'Por Isso Há Vocês Muitos Fracos e Doentes, e Vários já Dormiram' (1 Co 11.30)--Pecado e Sacrificio na Ceia do Senhor," *EstT* 36 (1996): 119-28.

10649 Sebastian Schneider, "Glaubensmängel in Korinth: Eine neue Deutung der 'Schwachen, Kranken, Schlafenden' in Kor 11,30," *FilN* 9 (1996): 3-19.

12-16

10650 Stephen S. Smalley, "Spiritual Gifts and 1 Corinthians 12-16," *JBL* 87/4 (1968): 417-33.

12-14

10651 Daniel Fraikin, "Charismes et Ministères" à la Lumière de 1 Cor 12-14," *ÉgT* 9/3 (1978): 455-63.

10652 David L. Baker, "The Interpretation of 1 Corinthians 12-14," *EQ* 46/4 (1974): 224-34.

10653 Bert Dominy, "Paul and Spiritual Gifts: Reflections on 1 Corinthians 12-14," *SouJT* 26/1 (1983): 49-68.

10654 Charles H. Talbert, "Paul's Understanding of the Holy Spirit: The Evidence of 1 Corinthians 12-14," *PRS* 11/4 (1984): 95-108.

10655 D. B. Martin, "Tongues of Angels and Other Status Indicators," *JAAR* 59/3 (1991): 547-89.

10656 U. Heckel, "Paulus und die Charismatiker. Zur theologischen Einordnung der Geistesgaben in 1 Kor 12-14," *TBe* 23/3 (1992): 117-38.

12-13

10657 Gail P. Corrington, "The Beloved Community: A Roycean Interpretation of Paul," *EGLMBS* 7 (1987): 27-38.

12

10658 A. Alvarez de Linera, "El glosolalo y su intérpret," *EB* 9 (1950): 193-208.

10659 J. M. Bover, "Los carismas espirituales en San Pablo," *EB* 9 (1950): 295-328.

10660 Walter J. Bartling, "The Congregation of Christ: A Charismatic Body: An Exegetical Study of 1 Corinthians 12," *CTM* 40/2 (1969): 68-80.

10661 Robert L. Thomas, " 'Tongues. . . Will Cease'," *JETS* 17/2 (1974): 81-89.

10662 Terrance Callan, "Prophecy and Ecstasy in Greco-Roman Religion and in 1 Corinthians," *NovT* 27/2 (1985): 125-40.

10663 Dennis Ormseth, "Showing the Body: Reflections on 1 Corinthians 12-13 for Epiphany," *WW* 6 (1986): 97-103.

10664 Thomas A. Jackson, "Concerning Spiritual Gifts: A Study of 1 Corinthians 12," *FM* 7/1 (1989): 61-69.

10665 E. J. Vledder and A. G. Van Aarde, "A Holistic View of the Holy Spirit as Agent of Ethical Responsibility," *HTS* 47 (1991): 503-25.

10666 Enrique Nardoni, "Charism in the Early Church since Rudolph Sohm: An Ecumenical Challenge," *TS* 53 (1992): 646-62.

10667 Ola Tjorhom, "Enhet og mangfold innenfor Kristi legeme i 1 Kor 12—og i dag," *NTT* 94/4 (1993): 247-63.

12:1-31

10668 B. Hennen, "Ordines sacri. Ein Deutungsversuch zu 1 Cor 12,1-31 und Rom 12,3-8," *TQ* 119 (1938): 427-69.

12:1-13

10669 Gary W. Charles, "1 Corinthians 12:1-13," *Int* 44/1 (1990): 65-68.

12:1-11

10670   Adalberto Sisti, "Unita nella varieta," *BibO* 7 (1965): 187-95.

10671   A. Miranda, "L' 'uomo spirituale' nella Prima ai Corinzi," *RBib* 43 (1995): 485-519.

12:1-3

10672   K. Maly, "1 Kor 12:1-3: Eine Regel zur Unterscheidung der Geister? *BZ* 10 (1967): 57-95.

10673   Traugott Holtz, "Das Kennzeichen des Geistes," *NTS* 18/3 (1972): 365-76.

10674   Michel Bouttier, "Complexio Oppositorum: Sur les Formules de 1 Cor. 12:13; GAL. 3:26-28; Col. 3:10-11," *NTS* 23/1 (1976): 1-19.

10675   Andre Mehat, "L'Enseignement sur 'Les Choses de ˙L'Esprit'," *RHPR* 63/4 (1983): 395-415.

10676   Johan S. Vos, "Das Rätsel von 1 Kor 12:1-3," *NovT* 35 (1993): 251-69.

12:1

10677   David R. Nichols, "The Problem of Two-Level Christianity at Corinth," *Pneuma* 11 (1989): 99-112.

12:2

10678   T. Paige, "1 Corinthians 12.2: A Pagan *Pompe?*" *JSNT* 44 (1991): 57-65.

12:3-13

10679   Heinz Schürmann, "Unité dans l'Esprit et diversité spirituelle (1 Co 12,3b-7.12-13)," *AsSeign* NS30 (1970): 35-41.

12:3

10680   Norbert Brox, "Ἀνάθεμα Ἰησοῦς," *BZ* 12 (1968): 103-11.

10681   W. F. Albright, "Two Texts in 1 Corinthians," *NTS* 16/3 (1970): 271-76.

10682   J. D. M. Derrett, "Cursing Jesus (1 Cor. 12:3): The Jews as Religious 'Persecutors'," *NTS* 21/4 (1975): 544-54.

12:10

10683   Gerhard   Dautzenberg,   "Zum   religionsgeschichten
        Hintergrund der Diakrisis (1 Kor 12:10)," *BZ* 15/1 (1971):
        93-104.

10684   Wayne Grudem, "A Response to Gerhard Dautzenberg on
        1 Cor. 12:10," *BZ* 22/2 (1978): 253-70.

10685   George L. Lasebikan, "Glossolalia: Its Relationship with
        Speech Disabilities and Personality Disorders," *AfTJ* 14/2
        (1985): 111-20.

12:12-13

10686   Luther L. Grubb, "The Church Reaching Tomorrow's
        World," *GTJ* 12/3 (1971): 13-22.

12:12

10687   J. Havet, " 'Christ collectif,' ou 'Christ individual,' en 1
        Cor. 12,12," *ETL* 23 (1947): 499-520.

12:13

10688   Joseph Hanimann, "Nous Avons été Abreuves d'un seul
        Esprit: Note Sur 1 Co 12, 13b," *NRT* 94/4 (1972):
        400-405.

10689   Daniel Marguerat, "Paul: un génie théologique et ses
        limites," *FV* 84/5 (1985): 65-76.

10690   Warren McWilliams, "Paul's View of Freedom," *BI* 12/3
        (1986): 50-53.

10691   B. Macías, "1 Cor 12.13: Una conjetura renacentista: . .
        .καὶ πάντες ἕν πνεῦμα ἐποτίσθημεν," *FilN* (1994): 209-13.

12:14-26

10692   R. E. Oster, "Use, Misuse and Neglect of Archaeological
        Evidence in Some Modern Works on 1 Corinthians),"
        ZNW 83/1-2 (1992): 52-73.

12:14

10693   Timothy N. Boyd, "Paul's Use of Analogy," *BI* 14/2
        (1989): 24-28.

12:20

10694 George L. Lasebikan, "Glossolalia: Its Relationship with Speech Disabilities and Personality Disorders," *AfTJ* 14/2 (1985): 111-20.

12:22-27

10695 L. D. Hurst, "Apollos, Hebrews, and Corinth: Bishop Montefiore's Theory Examined," *SJT* 38/4 (1985): 505-13.

12:26

10696 Thomas Söding, " 'Ihr aber seid der Leib Christi' (1 Kor 12,26). Exegetische Beobachtungen an einem zentralen Motiv paulinischer Ekklesiologie," *Cath* 45/2 (1991): 135-62.

12:28-31

10697 Hermann von Lips, "Der Apostolat des Paulus - ein Charisma: semantische Aspekte zu charis-charisma und anderen Wortpaaren im Sprachgebrauch des Paulus," *Bib* 66/3 (1985): 305-43.

10698 John J. Kilgallen, "Reflections on Charisma(ta) in the New Testament," *SM* 41 (1992): 289-323.

12:28

10699 A. del Agua Pérez, "El papel de la 'escuela midrásica' en la configuración del Nuevo Testamento," *EB* 60 (1985): 333-49.

10700 M. C. Griffths, "Today's Missionary, Yesterday's Apostle," *EMQ* 21/2 (1985): 154-65.

10701 George W. Knight, "Two Offices and Two Orders of Elders: A New Testament Study," *Pres* 11/1 (1985): 1-12.

10702 Jerry R. Young, "Shepherds, Lead," *GTJ* 6/2 (1985): 329-35.

10703 James E. Carter, "Paul's View of Church Administration," *BI* 12/3 (1986): 77-79.

10704 P. Roberts, "Seers or Overseers?" *ET* 108 (1997): 301-305.

12:31

10705 Gerhard Iber, "Zum Verständnis von 1 Cor. 12:31," *ZNW* 54 (1963): 43-52.

10706   J. P. Louw, "The Function of Discourse in a Sociosemiotic Theory of Translation: Illustrated by the Translation of *Zeloute* in 1 Corinthians 12:31," *BT* 39/3 (1988): 329-35.

10707   J. F. M. Smit, "Two Puzzles: 1 Corinthians 12:31 and 13:3: A Rhetorical Solution," *NTS* 39 (1993): 246-64.

10708   W. C. van Unnik, "The Meaning of 1 Corinthians 12:31," *NovT* 35 (1993): 142-59.

12:4-9

10709   Hermann von Lips, "Der Apostolat des Paulus - ein Charisma: semantische Aspekte zu charis-charisma und anderen Wortpaaren im Sprachgebrauch des Paulus," *Bib* 66/3 (1985): 305-43.

12:4-6

10710   Fred B. Craddock, "From Exegesis To Sermon: 1 Corinthians 12:4-6," *RevExp* 80/3 (1983): 417-25.

12:4-5

10711   James E. Carter, "Paul's View of Church Administration," *BI* 12/3 (1986): 77-79.

12:4

10712   Watson E. Mills, "Charismatic Gifts in the New Testament Church," *BI* 1/2 (1975): 28-33.

10713   Luis F. Ladaria, "Presente y futuro en la escatología cristiana," *EE* 60 (1985): 351-59.

10714   John J. Kilgallen, "Reflections on Charisma(ta) in the New Testament," *SM* 41 (1992): 289-323.

12:7-11

10715   John F. Walvoord, "The Holy Spirit and Spiritual Gifts," *BSac* 143 (1986): 109-22.

12:8-11

10716   Donald Gee, "The Gifts and Fruit of the Spirit," *Para* 21 (1987): 21-26.

12:8-10

10717   Andrew G. Hadden, "Gifts of the Spirit in Assemblies of God Writings," *Para* 24 (1990): 20-32.

10718 David S. Lim, "Many Gifts, One Spirit," *Para* 26 (1992): 3-7.

12:9-10

10719 John J. Kilgallen, "Reflections on Charisma(ta) in the New Testament," *SM* 41 (1992): 289-323.

13

10720 H.-C. Desroches, "Le 'portrait,' de la charité," *VS* 74 (1946): 518-36.

10721 J. Brennan, "The Exegesis of 1 Cor. 13," *ITQ* 21 (1954): 270-78.

10722 Ceslaus Spicq, "L'Agapè de 1 Cor. 13. Un example de contribution de la sémantique à l'exégèse neo-testamentaire," *ETL* 31 (1955): 357-70.

10723 John W. Bowman, "The Three Imperishables," *Int* 13 (1959): 433-43.

10724 Stanley D. Toussaint, "First Corinthians Thirteen and the Tongues Question," *BSac* 120 (1963): 311-16.

10725 Nils Johansson, "1 Cor. 13 and 1 Cor. 14," *NTS* 10 (1964): 383-92.

10726 Jack T. Sanders, "First Corinthians 13," *Int* 20/2 (1966): 159-87.

10727 Arthus G. Vella, " 'Agape' in 1 Corinthians 13," (part 1) *MeliT* 18/1 (1966): 22-31; 18/2 (1966): 56-66; 19/1-2 (1967): 44-54.

10728 Adalberto Sisti, "L'inno della carità," *BibO* 10 (1968): 39-51.

10729 Terrance Callan, "Prophecy and Ecstasy in Greco-Roman Religion and in 1 Corinthians," *NovT* 27/2 (1985): 125-40.

10730 Dennis Ormseth, "Showing the Body: Reflections on 1 Corinthians 12-13 for Epiphany," *WW* 6 (1986): 97-103.

10731 J. F. M. Smit, "The Genre of 1 Corinthians 13 in the Light of Classical Rhetoric," *NovT* 33/3 (1991): 193-216.

10732 E. Stuart, "Love is . . . Paul," *ET* 102/9 (1991): 264-66.

10733 C. J. Waters, " 'Love is . . . Paul'—A Response," *ET* 103/3 (1991): 75.

10734 Steven L. Cox, "1 Corinthians 13--An Antidote to Violence: Love," *RevExp* 93 (1996): 529-36.

13:1

10735 Ivor H. Jones, "Musical Instruments in the Bible," *BT* 37 (1986): 101-16.

10736 William W. Klein, "Noisy Gong or Acoustic Vase? A Note 1 Corinthians 13:1," *NTS* 32/2 (1986): 286-89.

10737 Todd K. Sanders, "A New Approach to 1 Corinthians 13:1," *NTS* 36 (1990): 614-18.

13:3

10738 J. H. Petzer, "Contextual Evidence in Favor of Kauchesomai in 1 Corinthians 13:3," *NTS* 35/2 (1989): 229-53.

10739 J. F. M. Smit, "Two Puzzles: 1 Corinthians 12:31 and 13:3: A Rhetorical Solution," *NTS* 39 (1993): 246-64.

13:4-7

10740 J. J. McGovern, "The Gamut of Charity," *Worship* 35 (1961): 155-59.

13:7

10741 Emily Wong, "1 Corinthians 13:7 and Christian Hope," *LouvS* 17/2-3 (1992): 232-42.

13:8-13

10742 M. Miguéns, "1 Cor 13:8-13 Reconsidered," *CBQ* 37/1 (1975): 76-97.

10743 Myron J. Houghton, "A Reexamination of 1 Corinthians 13:8-13," *BSac* 153 (1996): 344-56.

13:8-12

10744 Walter Kasper, "Die Hoffnung auf die endgültige Ankunft Jesu Christi in Herrlichkeit," *IKaZ* 14/1 (1985): 1-14.

13:10

10745 R. L. Roberts, " 'That which Is Perfect': 1 Cor. 13:10," *RQ* 3 (1959): 199-204.

10746 John R. McRay, "Τὸ τέλειον in 1 Corinthians 13:10," *RQ* 14 (1971): 168-83.

10747 Randy Tate, "Christian Childishness and 'That Which is Perfect'," *Para* 24/1 (1990): 11-15.

10748 R. Fowler White, "Richard Gaffin and Wayne Grudem on 1 Cor 13:10: A Comparison of Cessationist and Noncessationist Argumentation," *JETS* 35/2 (1992): 173-81.

13:12

10749 J. Beumer, "Tunc... cognoscam, sicut et cognitus sum (1 Cor 13,12)," *VD* 22 (1942): 166-73.

10750 D. H. Gill, "Through a Glass Darkly: A Note on 1 Corinthians 13,12," *CBQ* 25 (1963): 427-29.

10751 Raoul Mortley, "The Mirror and 1 Cor. 13:12 in the Epistemology of Clement of Alexandria,"*VC* 30/2 (1976): 109-20.

10752 Richard Seaford, "1 Corinthians 13:12," *JTS* 35/1 (1984): 117-20.

10753 Luis F. Ladaria, "Presente y futuro en la escatología cristiana," *EE* 60 (1985): 351-59.

10754 Michael Johnson, "Face to Face," *EGLMBS* 11 (1991): 222-37.

13:13

10755 M.-F. Lacan, "Les trois qui demeurent. 1 Cor 13,13," *RechSR* 46 (1958): 321-43.

10756 Frans Neirynck, "De grote drie bij een nieuwe vertaling van 1 Cor. xiii, 13," *ETL* 39 (1963): 595-615.

10757 Wolfgang Weiss, "Glaube—Liebe—Hoffnung: Zu der Trias bei Paulus," *ZNW* 84/3-4 (1993): 196-217.

14

10758 Eduard Schweizer, "The Service of Worship," *Int* 13 (1959): 400-407.

10759 G. G. Blum, "Das Amt der Frau im Neuen Testament," *NovT* 7 (1964): 142-61.

10760 Nils Johansson, "1 Cor. 13 and 1 Cor. 14," *NTS* 10 (1964): 383-92.

10761 Robert L. Thomas, " 'Tongues... Will Cease'," *JETS* 17/2 (1974): 81-89.

10762 Watson E. Mills, "Glossolalia in Asia Minor," *BI* 8/2 (1982): 81-85.

10763 Terrance Callan, "Prophecy and Ecstasy in Greco-Roman Religion and in 1 Corinthians," *NovT* 27/2 (1985): 125-40.

10764 Pui Lan Kwok, "The Feminist Hermeneutics of Elisabeth Schüssler Fiorenza: An Asian Feminist Response," *EAJT* 3/2 (1985): 147-53.

10765 Alan Padgett, "Feminism in First Corinthians: A Dialogue with Elisabeth Schüssler Fiorenza," *EQ* 58/2 (1986): 121-32.

10766 R. K. Levang, "The Content of an Utterance in Tongues," *Para* 23/1 (1989): 14-20.

10767 Edward A. Engelbrecht, " 'To Speak in a Tongue': The Old Testament and Early Rabbinic Background of a Pauline Expression," *CJ* 22 (1996): 295-302.

10768 Bob Zerhusen, "The Problem Tongues in 1 Cor 14: A Reexamination," *BTB* 27 (1997): 139-52.

14:1-12

10769 A. Miranda, "L' 'uomo spirituale' nella Prima ai Corinzi," *RBib* 43 (1995): 485-519.

14:1-9

10770 Jean Cantinat, "Charismes et bien commun de L'Église," *BVC* 63 (1956): 16-25.

14:2

10771 George L. Lasebikan, "Glossolalia: Its Relationship with Speech Disabilities and Personality Disorders," *AfTJ* 14/2 (1985): 111-20.

14:13-27

10772 George L. Lasebikan, "Glossolalia: Its Relationship with Speech Disabilities and Personality Disorders," *AfTJ* 14/2 (1985): 111-20.

14:20-25

10773 Wayne Grudem, "1 Corinthians 14:20-25: Prophecy and Tongues as Signs of God's Attitude," *WTJ* 41/2 (1979): 381-96.

10774   Bruce C. Johanson, "Tongues: A Sign for Unbelievers?"
        NTS 25/2 (1979): 180-203.

10775   Karl O. Sanders, "Prophecy--A Sign for Believers (1 Cor
        14,20-25)," *Bib* 77 (1996): 1-15.

14:20-22

10776   D. E. Lanier, "With Stammering Lips and Another
        Tongue: 1 Cor 14:20-22 and Isa 28:11-12," *CTR* 5/2
        (1991): 259-85.

14:20

10777   H. U. von Balthasar, "Jesus als Kind und sein Lob des
        Kindes," *IKaZ* 14/2 (1985): 101-108.

14:21

10778   Harm W. Hollander, "The Meaning of the Term 'Law'
        (NOMOS) in 1 Corinthians," *NovT* 40 (1998): 117-35.

14:22-25

10779   Walter Rebell, "Gemeinde als Missionsfaktor im
        Urchristentum: 1 Kor 14:24f, als Schlüsselsituation," *TZ*
        44/2 (1988): 117-34.

14:22

10780   J. F. M. Smit, "Tongues and Prophecy: Deciphering 1 Cor
        14,22," *Bib* 75 (1994): 175-90.

14:23-26

10781   Marlis Gielen, "Zur Interpretation der paulinischen Formel
        He kat' oikon ekklesia," *ZNW* 77 (1986): 109-25.

14:26-33

10782   W. E. Richardson, "Liturgical Order and Glossolalia in
        1 Corinthians 14.26c-33a," *NTS* 32 (1986): 144-53. See
        AUSS 24 (1986): 47-48.

14:33-40

10783   J. Smit Sibinga, "Serta Paulina: On Composition
        Technique in Paul," *FilN* 10 (1997): 35-54.

14:33-38

10784   W. A. Maier, "An Exegetical Study of 1 Corinthians
        14:33b-38," *CTQ* 55/2-3 (1991): 81-104.

14:33-36

10785 James B. Hurley, "Did Paul Require Veils or the Silence of Women? A Consideration of 1 Corinthians 11:2-16 and 1 Corinthians 14:33b-36," *WTJ* 35/2 (1973): 190-202.

10786 Stephen C. Barton, "Paul's Sense of Place: An Anthropological Approach to Community Formation in Corinth," *NTS* 32/2 (1986): 225-46.

10787 D. W. Odell-Scott, "In Defense of an Egalitarian Interpretation of 1 Cor 14:34-36: A Reply to Murphy-O'Connor's Critique," *BTB* 17/3 (1987): 100-103.

10788 Robert W. Allison, "Let Women be Silent in the Churches: What Did Paul Really Say, and What Did It Mean?" *JSNT* 32 (1988): 27-60.

10789 I. R. Reimer, "Da Memória à Novidade de Vida," *EstT* 33/3 (1993): 201-12.

14:33-35

10790 D. J. Nadeau, "Le problème des femmes en 1 Cor 14:33-35," *ÉTR* 69 (1994): 63-65.

10791 Harold R. Holmyard, "Does 1 Corinthians 11:2-16 Refer to Women Praying and Prophesying in Church?" *BSac* 154 (1997): 461-72.

14:34-36

10792 D. W. Odell-Scott, "In Defense of an Egalitarian Interpretation of 1 Cor 14:34-36," *BTB* 17 (1987): 100-103.

14:34-35

10793 J. K. Howard, "Neither Male nor Female: An Examination of the Status of Women in the New Testament," *EQ* 55/1 (1983): 31-42.

10794 Jerome Murphy-O'Connor, "Interpolations in 1 Corinthians," *CBQ* 48 (1986): 81-94.

10795 J. H. Petzer, "Reconsidering the Silent Women of Corinth—A Note on 1 Corinthians 14:34-35," *ThEv* 26 (1993): 132-38.

10796 Peter F. Lockwood, "Does 1 Corinthians 14:34-35 Exclude Women from the Pastoral Office?" *LTJ* 30 (1996): 30-38.

10797   David W. Bryce, " 'As in All the Churches of the Saints':
         A Text-Critical Study of 1 Corinthians 14:34,35," *LTJ* 31
         (1997): 31-39.

10798   Curt Niccum, "The Voice of the Manuscripts on the
         Silence of Women: The External Evidence for 1
         Corinthians 14:34-35," *NTS* 43 (1997): 242-55.

10799   Philip B. Payne, "Ms 88 as Evidence for a Text without 1
         Cor 14:34-35," *NTS* 44 (1998): 152-58.

10800   D. W. Odell-Scott, "Editorial Dilemma: The Interpretation
         of 1 Corinthians 14:34-35 in the Western Manuscripts of
         D, G and 88," *BTB* 30 (2000): 68-74.

14:34

10801   B. M. F. van Iersel, "Keep Quiet about Women in the
         Church (with Apologies to 1 Corinthians 14.34)," *Conci* 5
         (1994): 137-39.

10802   Anders Eriksson, " 'Women Tongue Speakers, Be Silent'
         (1997): A Reconstruction through Paul's Rhetoric," *BibInt*
         6 (1998): 80-104.

10803   Harm W. Hollander, "The Meaning of the Term 'Law'
         (NOMOS) in 1 Corinthians," *NovT* 40 (1998): 117-35.

14:35

10804   Winsome Munro, "Women, Text and the Canon: The
         Strange Case of 1 Corinthians 14:35," *BTB* 18/1 (1988):
         26-31.

14:36

10805   I. Peri, "Gelangen zur Vollkommenheit: Zur lateinischen
         Interpretation von Katantao in Eph 4:13," *BZ* 23/2 (1979):
         269-78.

14:37-40

10806   A. Miranda, "L' 'uomo spirituale' nella Prima ai Corinzi,"
         RBib 43 (1995): 485-519.

15

10807   Ernest Lussier, "The Biblical Theology on Purgatory,"
         AmER 142 (1960): 225-33.

10808   S. Lyonnet, "Redemption through Death and
         Resurrection," *Worship* 35 (1961): 281-87.

10809　Y.-B. Trémel, "À l'image du dernier Adam. Lecture de 1 Cor. 15," *VS* 108 (1963): 395-406.

10810　Franz Mußner, " 'Schichten' in der paulinischen Theologie dargetan an 1 Kor 15," *BZ* 9 (1965): 59-70.

10811　C. F. Sleeper, "Pentecost and Resurrection," *JBL* 84 (1965): 389-99.

10812　John H. Schütz, "Apostolic Authority and the Control of Tradition: 1 Cor. 15," *NTS* 15/4 (1969): 439-57.

10813　Jacob Kremer, "La résurrection de Jésus, principe et modèle de notre résurrection, d'après saint Paul," *Conci* 60 (1970): 71-80.

10814　Elaine H. Pagels, " 'The Mystery of the Resurrection': A Gnostic Reading of 1 Corinthians 15," *JBL* 93/2 (1974): 276-88.

10815　Gerald L. Borchert, "The Resurrection: 1 Corinthians 15," *RevExp* 80/3 (1983): 401-15.

10816　Robert B. Sloan, "Resurrection in 1 Corinthians," *SouJT* 26/1 (1983): 69-91.

10817　Günter Haufe, "Individuelle Eschatologie des Neuen Testaments," *ZTK* 83/4 (1986): 436-63.

10818　Ben F. Meyer, "Did Paul's View of the Resurrection of the Dead Undergo Development?" *TS* 47 (1986): 363-87.

10819　G. W. E. Nickelsburg, "An ἐκτρώμη, Though Appointed from the Womb: Paul's Apostolic Self-Description in 1 Corinthians 15 and Galatians 1," *HTR* 79/1-3 (1986): 198-205.

10820　A. G. Pérez Gordo, "¿Es 1 Co 15 una homilia?" *Bur* 27 (1986): 9-98.

10821　J. N. Vorster, "Resurrection Faith in 1 Corinthians 15," *Neo* 23/2 (1989): 287-307.

10822　Edgar M. Krentz, "Images of the Resurrection in the New Testament," *CTM* 18 (1991): 98-108.

10823　Andreas Lindemann, "Paulus und die korinthische Eschatologie. zur These von einer 'Entwicklung' im paulinischen Denken," *NTS* 37/3 (1991): 373-99.

10824 Gerhard Barth, "Zur Frage nach der in 1 Korinther 15 bekämpften Auferstehungsleugnung," *ZNW* 83/3-4 (1992): 187-201.

10825 Jeremy Moiser, "1 Corinthians 15," *IBS* 14/1 (1992): 10-30.

10826 Johan S. Vos, "Argumentation und Situation in 1 Kor 15," *NovT* 41 (1999): 313-33.

15:1-20

10827 Ted Peters, "What Is the Gospel?" *PRS* 13 (1986): 21-43.

15:1-19

10828 Ronald J. Sider, "St. Paul's Understanding of the Nature and Significance of the Resurrection in 1 Corinthians 15:1-19," *NovT* 19/2 (1977): 124-41.

15:1-11

10829 Karl Kertelge, "Das Apostelamt des Paulus, sein Ursprung und seine Bedeutung," *BZ* 14 (1970): 161-81.

10830 P. von der Osten-Sacken, "Die Apologie des Paulinischen Apostolats in 1 Kor 15:1-11," *ZNW* 64/3-4 (1973): 245-62.

10831 J. Smit Sibinga, "1 Cor 15:8/9 and Other Divisions in 1 Cor 15:1-11," *NovT* 39 (1997): 54-59.

15:1-10

10832 J. Cambier, "L'affirmation de la résurrection du Christ (1 Co 15,1-10)," *AsSeign* 65 (1963): 12-30.

15:1-3

10833 Knox Chamblin, "Revelation and Tradition in the Pauline Euangelion," *WTJ* 48 (1986): 1-16.

15:1

10834 Dieter Lührmann, "Confesser sa foi à l'époque apostolique," *RTP* 117 (1985): 93-110.

10835 J. Terry Young, "The Gospel of Jesus Christ," *BI* 15/1 (1988): 16-17.

15:2

10836 W. M. Aldrich, "Perseverence," *BSac* 115 (1958): 9-19.

15:3-12

10837   William L. Craig, "The Historicity of the Empty Tomb of Jesus," *NTS* 31 (1985): 39-67.

15:3-8

10838   William Baird, "What Is the Kerygma? A Study of 1 Cor 15:3-8 and Gal 1:11-17," *JBL* 76 (1957): 181-91.

10839   P. Seidemsticker, "Das antiochenische Glaubens-bekenntnis 1 Kor 15,3-7 im Lichte seiner Traditionsgeschichte," *TGl* 57 (1967): 286-323.

10840   P. Seidemsticker, "The Resurrection Seen from Antioch," *TD* 17 (1969): 104-109.

10841   Byung-Mu Ahn, "The Body of Jesus-Event Tradition," *EAJT* 3/2 (1985): 293-309.

10842   R. Y. K. Fung, "Revelation and Tradition: The Origins of Paul's Gospel," *EQ* 57 (1985): 23-41.

10843   Christian Grappe, "Essai sur l'arrière-plan Pascal des récits de la dernière nuit de Jésus," *RHPR* 65/2 (1985): 105-25.

15:3-7

10844   Barnabas Lindars, "Jesus Risen: Bodily Resurrection but no Empty Tomb," *Theology* 89 (1986): 90-96.

15:3-5

10845   Hans Conzelmann, "On the Analysis of the Confessional Formula in 1 Corinthians 15:3-5," *Int* 20/1 (1966): 13-25.

10846   John S. Kloppenborg, "An Analysis of the Pre-Pauline Formula 1 Cor. 15:3b-5 in Light of Some Recent Literature," *CBQ* 40:3 (1978): 351-67.

10847   Randall C. Webber, "A Note on 1 Corinthians 15:3-5," *JETS* 26/3 (1983): 265-69.

10848   Rinaldo Fabris, "San Pietro apostolo nella prima chiesa," *SM* 35 (1986): 41-70.

10849   Otto Schwankl, "Auf der Suche nach dem Anfang des Evangeliums: Von 1 Kor 15,3-5 zum Johannes-Prolog," *BZ* NS 40 (1996): 39-60.

15:3-4

10850   Jacques Dupont, "Ressuscité le troisième jour," *Bib* 40 (1959): 742-61.

10851   Kenneth O. Gangel, "According to the Scriptures," *BSac* 128 (1968): 123-28.

15:3

10852   C. de Beus, "Paulus en de traditie over de opstanding in 1 Cor. 15:3," *NTT* 22/3 (1968): 185-99.

10853   Erhardt Güttgemanns, "Christos in 1 Kor. 15.3b: Titel oder Eigenname?" *EvT* 28/10 (1968): 533-54.

10854   Jean-Marie van Cangh, "Mort pour nos péchés selon les Écritures," *RTL* 1 (1970): 191-99.

10855   Christophe Senft, "Paul et Jésus," *FV* 84/5 (1985): 49-56.

10856   F. Pastor-Ramos, " 'Murió por nuestros pecados' (1 Cor 15,3; Gal 1,4). Observaciones sobre el origen de esta fórmula en Is 53," *EE* 61 (1986): 385-93.

10857   Akira Satake, "1 Ko 15,3 und das Verhalten von Paulus den Jerusalemern gegenüber," *AJBI* 16 (1990): 100-11.

15:4

10858   Harvey K. McArthur, " 'On the Third Day'," *NTS* 18/1 (1971): 81-86.

15:5-7

10859   Félix Gils, "Pierre et la foi au Christ ressuscité," *ETL* 38 (1962): 5-43.

15:5

10860   William O. Walker, "Acts and the Pauline Corpus Reconsidered," *JSNT* 24 (1985): 3-23.

15:6

10861   Eric F. F. Bishop, "The Risen Christ and the Five Hundred Brethren," *CBQ* 18 (1956): 341-44.

10862   Victor Hasler, "Credo und Auferstehung in Korinth," *TZ* 40/1 (1984): 12-33.

10863   H. U. von Balthasar, "Gottes Reich und die Kirche," *IKaZ* 15 (1986): 124-30.

15:8-10

10864   Harm W. Hollander and G. E. van de Hout, "The Apostle Paul Calling Himself an Abortion: 1 Corinthians 15:8

within the Context of 1 Corinthians 15:8-10," *NovT* 38 (1996): 224-36.

15:8

10865 Peter R. Jones, "1 Corinthians 15:8: Paul the Last Apostle," *TynB* 36 (1985): 3-34.

10866 Ulrich Luck, "Die Bekehrung des Paulus und das paulinische Evangelium: zur Frage der Evidenz in Botschaft und Theologie des Apostels," *ZNW* 76/3-4 (1985): 187-208.

10867 David Stanley, "The Apostle Paul as Saint," *SM* 35 (1986): 71-97.

10868 M. Schäfer, "Paulus, 'Fehlgeburt' oder 'unvernünftiges Kind'? Ein Interpretationsvorschlag zu 1 Kor 15,8," *ZNW* 85 (1994): 207-17.

10869 Harm W. Hollander and G. E. van de Hout, "Calling Himself an Abortion: 1 Corinthians 15:8 within the Context of 1 Corinthians 15:8-10," *NovT* 38 (1996): 224-36.

15:10

10870 Hermann von Lips, "Der Apostolat des Paulus - ein Charisma: semantische Aspekte zu charis-charisma und anderen Wortpaaren im Sprachgebrauch des Paulus," *Bib* 66/3 (1985): 305-43.

15:12-58

10871 Mark A. Plunkett, "Eschatology at Corinth," in *EGLMBS* 9 (1989): 195-211.

15:12-22

10872 C. Ghidelli, "Notre résurrection dans le Christ," *AsSeign* 96 (1967): 18-30.

15:12-20

10873 Theodor G. Bucher, "Nochmals zur Beweisführung in 1. Korinther 15,12-20," *TZ* 36/3 (1980): 129-52.

10874 C. Zimmer, "Das argumentum resurrectionis 1 Kor 15,12-20," *LB* 65 (1991): 25-36.

10875 Johan S. Vos, "Die Logik des Paulus in 1 Kor 15,12-20," *ZNW* 90 (1999): 78-97.

<u>15:12-19</u>

10876 Ulrich Luck, "Die Bekehrung des Paulus und das paulinische Evangelium: zur Frage der Evidenz in Botschaft und Theologie des Apostels," *ZNW* 76/3-4 (1985): 187-208.

<u>15:12</u>

10877 Michael Bachmann, "Zur Gedankenführung in 1. Kor. 15:12 ff.," *TZ* 34/5 (1978): 265-76.

10878 Karl A. Plank, "Resurrection Theology: The Corinthian Controversy Re-Examined," *PRS* 8/1 (1981): 41-54.

10879 Michael Bachmann, "Rezeption von 1 Kor. 15 (v. 12ff) unter logischem und unter philologischem Aspekt," *LB* 51 (1982): 79-103.

10880 R. Trevijano Etcheverría, "Los que dicen que no hay resurrección (1 Cor 15,12)," *Salm* 33 (1986): 275-302.

10881 H. Binder, "Zum geschichtlichen Hintergrund von 1 Kor 15,12," *TZ* 46/3 (1990): 193-201.

10882 Michael Bachmann, "Zum 'argumentum resurrectionis' von 1 Kor 15,12ff nach Christoph Zimmer, Augustin und Paulus," *LB* 67 (1992): 29-39.

<u>15:14</u>

10883 Gordon Dalbey, "Does the Resurrection Happen?" *CC* 102 (1985): 319-20.

<u>15:17-19</u>

10884 V. P. Branick, "Apocalyptic Paul?" *CBQ* 47 (1985): 664-75.

<u>15:17</u>

10885 Sigfred Pedersen, "Theologische Überlegungen zur Isagogik des Römerbriefs," *ZNW* 76/1-2 (1985): 47-67.

<u>15:20-28</u>

10886 William Dykstra, "1 Corinthians 15:20-28: An Essential Part of Paul's Argument against Those Who Deny the Resurrection," *CTJ* 4/2 (1969): 195-211.

10887 Gerhard Barth, "Erwägungen zu 1. Korinther 15:20-28," *EvT* 30/10 (1970): 515-27.

10888 Wilber B. Wallis, "The Problem of an Intermediate Kingdom in 1 Corinthians 15:20-28," *JETS* 18/4 (1975): 229-42.

10889 D. A. Templeton, "Paul the Parasite. Notes on the Imagery of Corinthians 15:20-28," *HeyJ* 26 (1985): 1-4.

10890 W. Schmithals, "The Pre-Pauline Tradition in 1 Corinthians 15:20-28," trans. Clayton N. Jefford, *PRS* 20 (1993): 357-80.

10891 C. E. Hill, "Paul's Understanding of Christ's Kingdom in 1 Corinthians 15:20-28," *NovT* 30/4 (1988): 297-320.

15:20-26

10892 E.-B. Allo, "Saint Paul et la 'double résurrection,' corporelle," *RB* 41 (1932): 188-209.

15:20-24

10893 Robert D. Culver, "A Neglected Millennial Passage from Saint Paul," *BSac* 113 (1956): 141-52.

15:20-22

10894 Stanley E. Porter, "The Pauline Concept of Original Sin in Light of Rabbinic Background," *TynB* 41 (1990): 3-30.

15:20

10895 F. J. Steinmetz and Friedrich Wulf, "Mit Christus auferstanden. Auslegung und Meditation von 1 Kor 15, 20; Eph 2,6 und 2 Tim 2,18," *GeistL* 42 (1969): 146-50.

10896 Timothy N. Boyd, "Paul's Use of Analogy," *BI* 14/2 (1989): 24-28.

15:21-28

10897 David L. Turner, "The Continuity of Scripture and Eschatology: Key Hermeneutical Issues," *GTJ* 6/2 (1985): 275-87.

15:21-22

10898 R. H. Allaway, "Fall or Fall-short," *ET* 97 (1986): 108-10.

15:22

10899 Mark W. Karlberg, "Legitimate Discontinuities between the Testaments," *JETS* 28 (1985): 9-20.

15:23-28

10900 Uta Heil, "Theologische Interpretation von 1 Kor 15,23-28," *ZNW* 84/1-2 (1993): 27-35.

15:23-24

10901 Frank Pack, "Does 1 Corinthians 15:23-24 Teach a Premillennial Reign of Christ on Earth?" *RQ* 3 (1959): 205-13.

15:23

10902 Luis F. Ladaria, "Presente y futuro en la escatología cristiana," *EE* 60 (1985): 351-59.

15:24-28

10903 J. Prado, "La Iglesia del futuro, según San Pablo," *EB* 22 (1963): 255-302.

10904 H. U. von Balthasar, "Gottes Reich und die Kirche," *IKaZ* 15 (1986): 124-30.

10905 John F. Jansen, "1 Corinthians 15:24-28 and the Future of Jesus Christ," *SJT* 40/4 (1987): 543-70.

15:24

10906 Juan Leal, "Deinde finis (1 Cor. 15,24a)," *VD* 37 (1959): 225-31.

15:25-27

10907 Wilber B. Wallis, "The Use of Psalm 8 and 110 in 1 Corinthians 15:25-27 and in Hebrews 1 and 2," *JETS* 15/1 (1972): 25-29.

15:25

10908 Roy A. Harrisville, "Paul and the Psalms: A Formal Study," *WW* 5 (1985): 168-79.

15:26

10909 V. P. Branick, "Apocalyptic Paul?" *CBQ* 47 (1985): 664-75.

15:27-28

10910 G. Pelland, "Un passage difficile de Novatien sur 1 Cor 15:27-28," *Greg* 66 (1985): 25-52.

15:27

10911 Roy A. Harrisville, "Paul and the Psalms: A Formal Study," *WW* 5 (1985): 168-79.

15:28

10912 David E. Fredrickson, "God, Christ, and All Things in 1 Corinthians 15:28," *WW* 18 (1998): 254-63.

15:29

10913 B. M. Foschini, "Those Who Are Baptized for the Dead," *CBQ* 12 (1950): 260-76, 379-88; 13 (1951): 46-78, 172-98, 276-83.

10914 Ole Wierod, "Daben i 1 Kor 15:29," *DTT* 50/1 (1987): 54-58.

10915 Joel R. White, " 'Baptized on Account of the Dead': The Meaning of 1 Corinthians 15:29 in Its Context," *JBL* 116 (1997): 487-99.

15:31

10916 Donald S. Deer, "Whose Pride/Rejoicing/Glory(ing) in 1 Corinthians 15:31?" *BT* 38/1 (1987): 126-28.

15:31-32

10917 Jerome Murphy-O'Connor, "Interpolations in 1 Corinthians," *CBQ* 48 (1986): 81-94.

15:32-34

10918 Brendan Byrne, "Eschatologies of Resurrection and Destruction: The Ethical Significance of Paul's Dispute with the Corinthians," *DR* 104/357 (1986): 280-98.

15:32

10919 Robert E. Osborne, "Paul and the Wild Beasts," *JBL* 85/2 (1966): 225-30.

15:34

10920 Homer A. Kent, "A Fresh Look at 1 Corinthians 15:34: An Appeal for Evangelism or a Call to Purity?" *GTJ* 4/1 (1983): 3-14.

15:35-56

10921 William L. Craig, "The Historicity of the Empty Tomb of Jesus," *NTS* 31 (1985): 39-67.

15:35-54

> 10922 Ronald J. Sider, "The Pauline Conception of the Resurrection Body in 1 Corinthians 15:35-54," *NTS* 21/3 (1974): 428-39.

15:35-44

> 10923 Normand Bonneau, "The Logic of Paul's Argument on the Resurrection Body in 1 Cor 15:35-44a," *SE* 45 (1993): 79-92.

15:36

> 10924 Gerhard Ebeling, "Des Todes Tod: Luthers Theologie der Konfrontation mit dem Tode," *ZTK* 84/2 (1987): 62-94.

15:39-49

> 10925 A. Miranda, "L' 'uomo spirituale' nella Prima ai Corinzi," *RBib* 43 (1995): 485-519.

15:42-51

> 10926 Alan F. Segal, "Paul and Ecstasy," *SBLSP* 25 (1986): 555-80.

15:42-44

> 10927 V. P. Branick, "Apocalyptic Paul?" *CBQ* 47 (1985): 664-75.

15:42

> 10928 Vincenz Buchheit, "Resurrectio carnis bei Prudentius," *VC* 40 (1986): 261-85.

15:44-49

> 10929 Gregory E. Sterling, " 'Wisdom among the Perfect': Creation Traditions in Alexandrian Judaism and Corinthian Christianity," *NovT* 37/4 (1995): 355-84.

15:44-48

> 10930 Jerome Murphy-O'Connor, "Interpolations in 1 Corinthians," *CBQ* 48 (1986): 81-94.

15:44

> 10931 Leonard Audet, "Avec quel corps les justes ressuscitent-ils? analyse de 1 Corinthiens 15:44," *SR* 1/3 (1971): 165-77.

15:45-49

10932   M. Trimaille, "Notre résurrection à l'image de Jésus, nouvel Adam," *AsSeign* NS38 (1970): 51-58.

10933   Mark W. Karlberg, "Legitimate Discontinuities between the Testaments," *JETS* 28 (1985): 9-20.

10934   S. P. Botha, "1 Corinthians 15:49b: A Hortative or Future Reading," *HTS* 49 (1993): 760-74.

15:45-47

10935   Louis Painchaud, "Le sommaire anthropogonique de (NH II, 117:38-118:2) à la lumière de 1 Co 15:45-47," *VC* 44 (1990): 382-93.

15:45

10936   John F. Walvoord, "The Present Work of Christ in Heaven," *BSac* 121 (1964): 195-208, 291-302.

10937   B. Schneider, "The Corporate Meaning and Background of 1 Cor 15,45b," *CBQ* 29 (1967): 450-67.

10938   J. J. Buckley, "An Interpretation of Logion 114 in the Gospel of Thomas," *NovT* 27 (1985): 245-72.

15:50

10939   Antonio Orbe, "Cristo, sacrificio y manjar," *Greg* 66/2 (1985): 185-239.

15:51

10940   P. Oppenheim, "1 Kor. 15,51. Eine kritische Untersuchung zu Text und Auffassung bei den Vätern," *TQ* 112 (1931): 92-135.

10941   Alberto Vaccari, "Il testo 1 Cor. 15,51," *Bib* 13 (1932): 73-76.

10942   A. Romeo, " 'Omnes quid em resurgemus' seu 'Omnes quidem nequaquam dormiemus'," *VD* 14 (1934): 142-48, 250-55, 267-75, 313-20, 328-36, 375-78.

10943   P. Brandhuber, "Die sekundären Lesarten bei 1 Kor. 15,51. Ihre Verbreitung und Entstehung," *Bib* 18 (1937): 303-33, 418-38.

15:54

10944   A. Dirksen, "Death Is Swallowed in Victory (1 Cor. 15: 54)," *AmER* 96 (1937): 347-56.

15:56

10945   Christophe Senft, "Paul et Jésus," *FV* 84/5 (1985): 49-56.

10946   Friedrich W. Horn, "1 Korinther 15,56—ein exegetischer Stachel," *ZNW* 82 (1991): 88-105

10947   Thomas Söding, " 'Die Kraft der Sünde ist das Gesetz' (1 Kor 15:56): Anmerkungen zum Hintergrund und zur Pointe einer gesetzeskritischen Sentenz des Apostels Paulus," *ZNW* 83/1-2 (1992): 74-84.

10948   Harm W. Hollander, "The Meaning of the Term 'Law' (NOMOS) in 1 Corinthians," *NovT* 40 (1998): 117-35.

15:57

10949   W. J. McGarry, "Victory through Our Lord (1 Cor. 15:57)," *AmER* 96 (1937): 337-47.

16:1-4

10950   W. C. Linss, "The First World Hunger Appeal," *CThM* 12 (1985): 211-19.

16:1

10951   Bruce W. Winter, "Secular and Christian Responses to Corinthian Famines," *TynB* 40 (1989): 86-106.

16:9

10952   Richard B. Cunningham, "Wide Open Doors and Many Adversaries (1 Corinthians 16:9; Acts 19)," *RevExp* 89 (1992): 89-98.

16:10-11

10953   Christopher R. Hutson, "Was Timothy Timid? On the Rhetoric of Fearlessness (1 Corinthians 16:10-11) and Cowardice (2 Timothy 1:7)," *BR* 42 (1997): 58-73.

16:12

10954   M. C. Griffths, "Today's Missionary, Yesterday's Apostle," *EMQ* 21/2 (1985): 154-65.

16:15

10955 L. Hertling, "1 Kor, 16,15 und 1 Clem. 42," *Bib* 20 (1939): 276-83.

16:18

10956 Juan Mateos, "Analisis de un campo lexematico: eulogia en el Nuevo Testamento," *FilN* 1 (1988): 5-25.

16:19

10957 Marlis Gielen, "Zur Interpretation der paulinischen Formel He kat' oikon ekklesia," *ZNW* 77 (1986): 109-25.

16:22

10958 John J. O'Rourke, "Question and Answer: Maranatha," *Scr* 13 (1961): 24-32.

10959 W. F. Albright, "Two Texts in 1 Corinthians," *NTS* 16/3 (1970): 271-76.

10960 W. Dunphy, "Maranatha: Development in Early Christianity," *ITQ* 37 (1970): 294-309.

16:23

10961 H. Duesberg, "La proximité de Dieu dans la liturgie de l'Avent," *BVC* 8 (1954-1955): 16-30.

2 Corinthians

<u>1-9</u>

10962 U. Borse, "Die Geschichte und theologische Einordnung des Römerbriefes," *BZ* 16 (1972): 70-83.

10963 F. F. Bruce, "Galatian Problems: 4. The Date of the Epistle," *BJRL* 54/2 (1972): 250-67.

10964 J. M. Gilchrist, "Paul and the Corinthians—The Sequence of Letters and Visits," *JSNT* 34 (1988): 47-69.

10965 D. A. DeSilva, "Measuring Penultimate against Ultimate Reality: An Investigation of the Integrity and Argumentation of 2 Corinthians," *JSNT* 52 (1993): 41-70.

10966 A. A. Myrick, " 'Father' Imagery in 2 Corinthians 1-9 and Jewish Paternal Tradition," *TynB* 47 (1996): 163-71.

<u>1-7</u>

10967 Colin G. Kruse, "The Relationship between the Opposition to Paul Reflected in 2 Corinthians 1-7 and 10-13," *EQ* 61 (1989): 195-202.

10968 Paul B. Duff, "2 Corinthians 1-7: Sidestepping the Division Hypothesis Dilemma," *BTB* 24 (1994): 16-26.

<u>1-3</u>

10969 Scott Hafemann, "The Comfort and Power of the Gospel: The Argument of 2 Corinthians 1-3," *RevExp* 86 (1989): 325-44.

<u>1-2</u>

10970 C. Roiné, "Notes de lecture sur 2 Corinthiens 1-2," *SémBib* 73 (1994): 45-55.

<u>1:1-2:13</u>

10971 Robert G. Hamerton-Kelly, "A Girardian Interpretation of Paul: Rivalry, Mimesis and Victimage in the Corinthian Correspondence," *Semeia* 33 (1985): 65-81.

10972 N. H. Taylor, "The Composition and Chronology of Second Corinthians," *JSNT* 44 (1991): 67-87.

10973 L. L. Welborn, "Like Broken Pieces of a Ring: 2 Corinthians 1.1-2.13; 7.5-16 and Ancient Theories of Literary Unity," *NTS* 42 (1996): 559-83.

1:3-7

10974 David E. Fredrickson, "Christ's Many Friends: The Presence of Jesus in 2 Corinthians 1-7," *WW* Suppl 3 (1997): 163-74.

1:7

10975 John J. Kilgallen, "Reflections on Charisma(ta) in the New Testament," *SM* 41 (1992): 289-323.

1:8

10976 F. J. Steinmetz, "so dass wir keinen: Ausweg mehr sahen (2 Kor 1,8). Apostolische Mühsal bei Paulus - und heute," *GeistL* 41 (1968): 321-26.

1:9

10977 Colin J. Hemer, "A Note on 2 Corinthians 1:9," *TynB* 23 (1972): 103-107.

1:11

10978 Hermann von Lips, "Der Apostolat des Paulus - ein Charisma: semantische Aspekte zu charis-charisma und anderen Wortpaaren im Sprachgebrauch des Paulus," *Bib* 66/3 (1985): 305-343.

1:12-14

10979 Stanley N. Olson, "Epistolary Uses of Expressions of Self-Confidence," *JBL* 103 (1984): 585-97.

1:12

10980 J. W. Roberts, "Exegetical Helps: The Genitive With Nouns of Action," *RQ* 1 (1957): 35-40.

1:13

10981 Mark A. Seifrid, "Paul's Approach to the Old Testament in Rom 10:6-8," *TriJ* 6 (1985): 3-37.

1:14

10982 Sigfred Pedersen, "Theologische Überlegungen zur Isagogik des Römerbriefs," *ZNW* 76/1-2 (1985): 47-67.

1:15-22

10983 David E. Fredrickson, "Christ's Many Friends: The Presence of Jesus in 2 Corinthians 1-7," *WW* Suppl 3 (1997): 163-74.

1:15

10984 Gordon D. Fee, "CARIS in 2 Corinthians i.15: Apostolic Parousia and Paul-Corinth Chronology," *NTS* 24 (1978): 533-38.

1:17

10985 J. M. Bover, "El 'sí' y el 'no': Un caso interesante de crítica textual," *EB* 5 (1946): 95-99.

10986 F. Young, "Note on 2 Corinthians 1.17b," *JTS* 37 (1986): 404-15.

10987 L. L. Welborn, "The Dangerous Double Affirmation: Character and Truth in 2 Corinthians 1:17," *ZNW* 86 (1995): 34-52.

1:17-23

10988 R. Alan Culpepper, "The Judaizers," *BI* 8 (1982): 61-63.

1:17-18

10989 David Wenham, "2 Corinthians 1.17,18: Echo of a Dominical Logion," *NovT* 28 (1986): 271-79.

1:18-22

10990 M. Trimaille and Michel Coune, "Les Apôtre, envoyés authentiques du Dieu fidèle (2 Co 1,18-22)," *AsSeign* 38 (1970): 42-50.

1:18

10991 E. Peterson, "1 Cor. 1,18f und die Thematik des jüdischen Busstages," *Bib* 32 (1951): 97-103.

10992 David Stanley, "The Apostle Paul as Saint," *SM* 35 (1986): 71-97.

1:19-20

> 10993 J. D. M. Derrett, "Nαί (2 Corinthians 1:19-20)," *FilN* 4 (1991): 205-209.

1:20

> 10994 Edmund Hill, "Construction of Three Passages from St Paul," *CBQ* 23 (1961): 296-301.

> 10995 Walter Kasper, "Hope in the Final Coming of Jesus Christ in Glory," *CICR* 12 (1985): 368-84.

1:21-22

> 10996 L. L. Belleville, "Paul's Polemic and Theology of the Spirit in Second Corinthians," *CBQ* 58 (1996): 281-304.

1:22

> 10997 J. Rieger, "Siegel und Angeld," *BibL* 7 (1966): 158-61.

> 10998 Luis F. Ladaria, "Presente y futuro en la escatología cristiana," *EE* 60 (1985): 351-59.

> 10999 A. J. Kerr, "Arrabon," *JTS* 39 (1988): 92-97.

> 11000 Eldon Woodcock, "The Seal of the Holy Spirit," *BSac* 155 (1998): 139-63.

1:24

> 11001 Bernhard Hanssler, "Autorität in der Kirche," *IKaZ* 14/6 (1985): 493-504.

2:1-5

> 11002 Walter Magass, "Theophrast und Paulus: exemplarisch für Umstände und Ethos in Korinth und Saloniki," *K* 26/3-4 (1984): 154-65.

2:1

> 11003 J. M. Gilchrist, "Paul and the Corinthians—The Sequence of Letters and Visits," *JSNT* 34 (1988): 47-69.

2:2

> 11004 K. Scholtissek, "Ihr seid ein Brief Christi: Zu einer ekklesiologischen Metapher bei Paukus," *BZ* 44 (2000): 183-205

2:4

11005   Francis Watson, "2 Corinthians X-XIII and Paul's Painful Letter to the Corinthians," *JTS* 35 (1984): 324-46.

11006   A. A. Myrick, " 'Father' Imagery in 2 Corinthians 1-9 and Jewish Paternal Tradition," *TynB* 47 (1996): 163-71.

2:5-4:6

11007   David E. Fredrickson, "Christ's Many Friends: The Presence of Jesus in 2 Corinthians 1-7," *WW* Suppl 3 (1997): 163-74.

2:5

11008   Colin G. Kruse, "The Offender and the Offence in 2 Corinthians 2:5 and 7:12," *EQ* 60 (1988): 129-39.

2:7

11009   Colin G. Kruse, "The Offender and the Offence in 2 Corinthians 2:5 and 7:12," *EQ* 60 (1988): 129-39.

2:13-14

11010   Jerome Murphy-O'Connor, "Paul and Macedonia: The Connection between 2 Corinthians 2:13 and 2:14," *JSNT* 25 (1985): 99-103.

11011   A. C. Perriman, "Between Troas and Macedonia: 2 Corinthians 2:13-14," *ET* 101 (1989): 39-41.

2:14-3:18

11012   Guy Wagner, "Alliance de la lettre, alliance de l'esprit: essai d'analyse de 2 Corinthiens 2:14 a 3:18," *ÉTR* 60/1 (1985): 55-65.

11013   Robert W. Scholla, "Into the Image of God: Pauline Eschatology and the Transformation of Believers," *Greg* (1997): 33-54.

2:14-17

11014   A.-M. Denis, "La fonction apostolique et la liturgie nouvelle en esprit," *RSPT* 42 (1958): 426-36.

11015   M. E. Thrall, "A Second Thanksgiving Period in 2 Corinthians," *JSNT* 16 (1982): 101-24.

11016   James I. H. McDonald, "Paul and the Preaching Ministry," *JSNT* 17 (1983): 35-50.

2:14-16

11017 Heinz Schürmann, "Verkündigung - ein existentieles Geschehen. 2 Kor 2,14-16 als Meditation," *BibL* 4 (1963): 130-37.

11018 Bonnie B. Thurston, "2 Corinthians 2:14-16a: Christ's Incense," *RQ* 29/2 (1987): 65-69.

11019 Jan Lambrecht, "The Defeated Paul, Aroma of Christ: An Exegetical Study of 2 Corinthians 2:14-16b," *LouvS* 20 (1995): 170-86.

2:14

11020 Lamar Williamson, "Led in Triumph: Paul's Use of θριαμβεύειν," *Int* 22 (1968): 317-32.

11021 R. B. Egan, "Lexical Evidence on Two Pauline Passages," *NovT* 19 (1977): 34-62.

11022 P. Marshall, "A Metaphor of Social Shame: θριαμβεύειν," in 2 Corinthians 2:14," *NovT* 25 (1983): 302-17.

11023 Guy Wagner, "Alliance de la lettre, alliance de l'Esprit. Essai d'analyse de 2 Corinthiens 2:14 à 3:18," *ÉTR* 60 (1985): 55-65.

11024 Paul B. Duff, "Metaphor, Motif, and Meaning: The Rhetorical Strategy behind the Image 'Led in Triumph' in 2 Corinthians 2:14," *CBQ* 53 (1991): 79-92.

2:15-3:18

11025 T. E. Provence, " 'Who is Sufficient for These Things?' An Exegesis of 2 Corinthians ii 15-iii 18," *NovT* 24 (1982): 54-81.

2:16

11026 F. T. Fallon, "Self's Sufficiency or God's Sufficiency: 2 Corinthians 2:16," *HTR* 76 (1983): 369-74.

2:17

11027 C. Daniel, "Une mention paulinienne des Esséniens de Qumrân," *RevQ* 5 (1966): 553-67.

11028 Mikeal C. Parsons, "Peddlers of God's Word," *BI* 11/3 (1985): 79-83.

2:20

11029   Jeffrey A. Gibbs, "The Grace of God as the Foundation for
          Ethics," *CTQ* 48/2-3 (1984): 185-201.

3:1-4:6

11030   K. Prümm, "Der Abschnitt über die Doxa des Apostolats
          2 Kor 3,1-4,6 in der Deutung des hl. Johannes
          Chrysostomus," *Bib* 30 (1949): 161-96.

11031   Earl Richard, "Polemics, Old Testament, and Theology. A
          Study of 2 Corinthians III,I-IV,6," *RB* 88 (1981): 340-67.

3

11032   D. L. Balch, "Backgrounds of 1 Corinthians 7: Sayings of
          the Lord in Q; Moses as as Ascetic *theios anēr* in 2
          Corinthians 3," *NTS* 18 (1972): 351-64.

11033   Paul R. Thorsell, "The Spirit in the Present Age:
          Preliminary Fulfillment of the Predicted New Covenant
          According to Paul," *JETS* 41 (1998): 397-413.

3:1-18

11034   Maurice Carrez, "La méthode de G. von Rad appliquée à
          quelques textes pauliniens: petit essai de vérification,"
          RSPT 55 (1971): 81-95.

3:1-16

11035   Herbert Ulonska, "Die Doxa des Mose: Zum Problem des
          Alten Testaments in 2 Kor 3:1-16," *EvT* 26/7 (1966):
          378-88.

3:1-11

11036   Randall C. Gleason, "Paul's Covenantal Contrasts in 2
          Corinthians 3:1-11," *BSac* 154 (1997): 61-79.

3:1-6

11037   P. De Surgy, "Le ministère apostolique de la nouvelle
          alliance (2 Co 3)," *AsSeign* 39 (1972): 36-43.

3:1-3

11038   William Baird, "Letters of Recommendation: A Study of
          2 Corinthians 3:1-3," *JBL* 80 (1961): 166-72.

11039   L. L. Belleville, "Paul's Polemic and Theology of the
          Spirit in Second Corinthians," *CBQ* 58 (1996): 281-304.

3:1

11040   Hans Hübner, "Der Heilige Geist in der Heiligen Schrift,"
        KD 36 (1990): 181-208.

3:3

11041   Kendell H. Easley, "The Pauline Usage of Pneumati as a
        Reference to the Spirit of God," *JETS* 27 (1984): 299-313.

3:4-9

11042   H. Liese, "De Spiritu et littera," *VD* 11 (1931): 225-29.

11043   F. Ogara, "Fiduciam... talem habemus per Christum ad
        Deum," *VD* 18 (1938): 227-34.

11044   P. De Surgy, "Ministres de l'alliance nouvelle," *AsSeign*
        66 (1966): 19-31.

3:6-14

11045   J. Carmignac, "2 Corinthiens iii.6,14 et le Début de la
        Formation du Nouveau Testament," *NTS* 24 (1978):
        384-86.

3:6

11046   B. Schneider, "The Meaning of St. Paul's Antithesis 'the
        Letter and the Spirit'," *CBQ* 15 (1953): 163-207.

11047   Homer A. Kent, "The New Covenant and the Church,"
        GTJ 6/2 (1985): 289-98.

11048   Thomas R. Schreiner, "Paul and Perfect Obedience to the
        Law: An Evaluation of the View of E. P. Sanders," *WTJ*
        47/2 (1985): 245-78.

11049   A. Stimpfle, " 'Buchstabe und Geist.' Zur Geschichte
        eines Missverständnisses von 2 Kor 3,6," *BZ* 39 (1995):
        181–202.

3:7-4:6

11050   Joseph A. Fitzmyer, "Glory Reflected on the Face of
        Christ and a Palestinian Jewish Motif," *TS* 42 (1981):
        630-44.

3:7-18

11051   S. Schulz, "Die Decke des Moses," *ZNW* 49 (1958): 1-30.

3:7-18

> 11052 A. T. Hanson, "The Midrash in 2 Corinthians 3: A Reconsideration," *JSNT* 9 (1980): 2-28.

3:7-18

> 11053 A. del Agua Pérez, "El papel de la 'escuela midrásica' en la configuración del Nuevo Testamento," *EE* 60/234 (1985): 333-49.

3:7-18

> 11054 Terrance Callan, "Paul and the Golden Calf," *EGLMBS* 10 (1990): 1-17.

3:7-18

> 11055 David E. Fredrickson, "Free Speech in Pauline Political Theology," *WW* 12 (1992): 345-51.

3:7-14

> 11056 Scott Hafemann, "The Glory and Veil of Moses in 2 Corinthians 3:7-14: An Example of Paul's Contextual Exegesis of the OT—A Proposal," *HBT* 14 (1992): 31-49.

3:10

> 11057 Edmund Hill, "Construction of Three Passages from St Paul," *CBQ* 23 (1961): 296-301.

3:12-18

> 11058 W. C. van Unnik, "With Unveiled Face: An Exegesis of 2 Corinthians 3:12-18," *NovT* 6 (1963): 153-69.

> 11059 J. M. Turner, "The Glory in the Face," *ET* 96 (1985): 144-45.

3:13-16

> 11060 M. A. Molina Palma, "La remoción del velo o del acceso a la libertad. Ensago hermenéutico," *EB* 41 (1983): 285-324.

3:13

> 11061 Mark A. Seifrid, "Paul's Approach to the Old Testament in Romans 10:6-8," *TriJ* 6 (1985): 3-37.

3:14

11062   L. Dequeker, "Het Nieuwe Verbond bij Ieremia, bij Paulus en in de brief aan de Hebreën. La nouvelle Alliance chez Jérémie, chez Paul et dans l'épître aux Hébreux," *Bij* 33 (1972): 234-61.

11063   William J. Dalton, "Is the Old Covenant Abrogated (2 Corinthians 3:14)?" *ABR* 35 (1987): 88-94.

11064   Pierre Grelot, "Note sur 2 Corinthiens 3:14," *NTS* 33/1 (1987): 135-44.

11065   Philip B. Harner, "Notes on the Accusative Absolute," *EGLMBS* 6 (1987): 120-27.

3:16

11066   R. Le Déaut, "Traditions targumiques dans le Corpus Paulien?" *Bib* 42/1 (1961): 28-48.

11067   Kurt Schubert, " 'Einmal aber wird der Schleier weggenommen': Die messianischen Erwärtungen im Judentum," *BK* 17 (1962): 50-53.

3:17-18

11068   W. Schmithals, "Zwei gnostische Glossen im Zweiten Korintherbrief," *EvT* 18 (1958): 552-73.

3:17

11069   H. M. Hughes, "2 Corinthians 3,17," *ET* 45 (1933-1934): 235-36.

11070   Cuthbert Lattey, "Dominus autem Spiritus est," *VD* 20 (1940): 187-89.

11071   K. Prümm, "Israels Kehr zum Geist," *ZKT* 72 (1950): 385-442.

11072   K. Prümm, "Die katholische Auslegung von 2 Kor 3,17a in den letzten vier Jahrzehnten nach ibren Hauptrichtungen," *Bib* 31 (1950): 316-45, 459-82; 32 (1951) 1-24.

11073   S. Lyonnet, "S. Cyrille d'Alexandrie et 2 Cor. 3,17," *Bib* 32 (1951): 25-31.

11074   James D. G. Dunn, "2 Corinthians 3:17: The Lord is the Spirit," *JTS* 21 (1970): 309-20.

11075 A. Giglioli, "Il Signore è lo Spirito," *RivBib* 20 (1972): 263-76.

11076 David Greenwood, "The Lord Is the Spirit: Some Considerations of 2 Corinthians 3:17," *CBQ* 34 (1972): 467-72.

11077 Emily Wong, "The Lord is the Spirit (2 Corinthians 3:17a)," *ETL* 61/1 (1985): 48-72.

11078 J. G. Ziegler, "Wo der Geist des Herrn wirkt, da ist Freiheit," *TTZ* 105 (1996): 139-50.

3:18-4:6

11079 Alan F. Segal, "Paul and Ecstasy," *SBLSP* 25 (1986): 555-80.

11080 Wiard Popkes, "New Testament Principles of Wholeness," *EQ* 64 (1992): 319-32.

3:18

11081 Jean Doignon, "Le Libellé singulier de II Corinthiens 3.18 chez Hilaire de Poitiers: Essai d'explication," *NTS* 26 (1979): 118-26.

11082 Jacob Kremer, "Christliche Schriftauslegung," *BL* 52 (1979): 18-21.

11083 Jan Lambrecht, "Transformation in 2 Corinthians 3,18," *Bib* 64 (1983): 243-54.

11084 Jeffrey A. Gibbs, "The Grace of God as the Foundation for Ethics," *CTQ* 48/2-3 (1984): 185-201.

11085 J. LeBourlier, "L'Ancien Testament, miroir de la gloire du Seigneur Jesus. Une lecture du chapitre 3 de la deuxième épître aux Corinthiens," *BLE* 97 (1996): 321-29.

4-7

11086 John B. Polhill, "Reconciliation at Corinth: 2 Corinthians 4-7," *RevExp* 86 (1989): 345-57.

4:4

11087 Norbert Brox, "Non huius aevi deus: zu Tertullian, Adv Marc V 11, 10," *ZNW* 59/3-4 (1968): 259-61.

11088 Jeffrey A. Gibbs, "The Grace of God as the Foundation for Ethics," *CTQ* 48/2-3 (1984): 185-201.

4:5-7

11089 C. E. B. Cranfield, "Minister and Congregation in the Light of 2 Corinthians 4:5-7: An Exposition," *Int* 19 (1965): 163-67.

4:5

11090 David E. Fredrickson, "No Noose is Good News: Leadership as a Theological Problem in the Corinthian Correspondence," *WW* 16 (1996): 420-26.

4:6-11

11091 Michel Bouttier, "Le tesson (2 Co 4)," *AsSeign* 40 (1973): 37-42.

4:6-9

11092 Alan C. Thompson, "2 Corinthians 4:6-9," *RevExp* 94 (1997): 455-60.

4:6

11093 H. T. Barrow, "A Leper's Portrait of Jesus Christ," *ET* 90 (1979): 111-12.

11094 D. H. C. Read, "Light for Another Year," *ET* 93 (1981): 82-83.

4:7-6:2

11095 David E. Fredrickson, "Christ's Many Friends: The Presence of Jesus in 2 Corinthians 1-7," *WW* Suppl 3 (1997): 163-74.

4:7-5:10

11096 Walter Kasper, "Hope in the Final Coming of Jesus Christ in Glory," *CICR* 12 (1985): 368-84.

11097 Roy Metts, "Death, Discipleship, and Discourse Strategies: 2 Corinthians 5:1-10—Once Again," *CTR* 4 (1989): 57-76.

4:7-15

11098 Ernest Best, "2 Corinthians 4:7-15. Life through Death," *IBS* 8 (1986): 2-7.

11099　Linda M. Bridges, "2 Corinthians 4:7-15," *RevExp* 86 (1989): 391-96.

11100　M. J. Cartledge, "A Model of Hermeneutical Method—An Exegetical Missiological Reflection upon Suffering in 2 Corinthians 4:7-15," *ERT* 17 (1993): 472-83.

4:7-12

11101　H. K. Neely, "Views of Martyrdom in the Early Church," *BI* 8 (1982): 79-83.

4:7-10

11102　Paul B. Duff, "Apostolic Suffering and the Language of Processions in 2 Corinthians 4:7-10," *BTB* 21 (1991): 158-65.

4:7

11103　W. Auer, "Bibeltexte - falsch verstanden," *BK* 13 (1958): 85-88.

11104　Herbert G. Grether, "Treasure in Earthen Vessels," *SEAJT* 5 (1963): 6-8.

11105　John D. Laurence, "The Eucharist as the Imitation of Christ," *TS* 47/2 (1986): 286-96.

4:10-11

11106　Maurice Carrez, "Que représente la vie de Jésus pour l'apôtre Paul?" *RHPR* 68/2 (1988): 155-61.

11107　Christian Wolff, "Niedrigkeit und Verzicht in Wort und Weg Jesu und in der apostolischen Existenz des Paulus," *NTS* 34/2 (1988): 183-96.

4:13-5:10

11108　Jerry W. McCant, "Competing Pauline Eschatologies: An Exegetical Comparison of 1 Corinthians 15 and 2 Corinthians 5," *WTJ* 29 (1994): 23-49.

4:13-18

11109　J. Cadier, "2 Corinthians 4:13-18," *ÉTR* 30, (1955): 69-72.

4:13-14

11110　Jerome Murphy-O'Connor, "Faith and Resurrection in 2 Corinthians 4:13-14," *RB* 95 (1988): 543-50.

11111   Kazimierz Romaniuk, "Résurrection existentielle ou eschatologique en 2 Co 4:13-14?" *BZ* 34/2 (1990): 248-52.

4:13

11112   Roy A. Harrisville, "Paul and the Psalms: A Formal Study," *WW* 5 (1985): 168-79.

4:15

11113   Bent Noack, "Note on 2 Corinthians 4:15," *StTheol* 17/2 (1963): 129-32.

11114   Hermann von Lips, "Der Apostolat des Paulus - ein Charisma: semantische Aspekte zu charis-charisma und anderen Wortpaaren im Sprachgebrauch des Paulus," *Bib* 66/3 (1985): 305-343.

4:16

11115   V. P. Branick, "Apocalyptic Paul?" *CBQ* 47 (1985): 664-75.

4:18

11116   Luis F. Ladaria, "Presente y futuro en la escatología cristiana," *EE* 60 (1985): 351-59.

5-7

11117   Gregory K. Beale, "The Old Testament Background of Reconciliation in 2 Corinthians 5-7 and Its Bearing on the Literary Problem of 2 Corinthians 6:14-7:1," *NTS* 35 (1989): 550-81.

5:1-10

11118   L. Brun, "Zur Auslegung von 2 Kor. 5:1-10," *ZNW* 28 (1929): 207-29.

11119   R. F. Hettlinger, "2 Corinthians 5:1-10," *SJT* 10 (1957): 74-94.

11120   E. Earle Ellis, "2 Corinthians 5:1-10 in Pauline Eschatology," *NTS* 6 (1959-1960): 211-24.

11121   Ronald Berry, "Death and Life in Christ: The Meaning of 2 Corinthians 5:1-10," *SJT* 14 (1961): 60-76.

11122   Guy Wagner, "Le tabernacle et la vie 'en Christ': exégèse de 2 Corinthiens 5:1 à 10," *RHPR* 41 (1961): 379-93.

11123   K. Hanhart, "Paul's Hope in the Face of Death," *JBL* 88 (1969): 445-57.

11124   Frederick W. Danker, "Consolation in 2 Corinthians 5:1-10," *CTM* 39 (1968): 552-56.

11125   C. Demke, "Zur Auslegung von 2. Korinther 5,1-10," *EvT* 29 (1969): 589-602.

11126   Ronald Cassidy, "Paul's Attitude to Death in 2 Corinthians 5:1-10," *EQ* 43 (1971): 210-17.

11127   Murray J. Harris, "2 Corinthians 5:1-10: watershed in Paul's eschatology?" *TynB* 22 (1971): 32-57.

11128   U. Borse, "Zur Todes - und Jenseitserwartung Pauli nach 2 Kor 5,1-10," *BibL* 13 (1972): 29-38.

11129   William Lillie, "An Approach to 2 Corinthians 5,1-10," *SJT* 30 (1977): 59-70.

11130   K. H. Schelkle, "Entmythologisierung in existentialer Interpretation," *TQ* 165/4 (1985): 257-66.

11131   J. Osei-Bonsu, "Does 2 Corinthians 5:1-10 Teach the Reception of the Resurrection Body at the Moment of Death?" *JSNT* 28 (1986): 81-101.

11132   William L. Craig, "Paul's Dilemma in 2 Corinthians 5:1-10: A 'Catch-22'?" *NTS* 34/1 (1988): 145-47.

11133   R. O. Zorn, "2 Corinthians 5:1-10: Individual Eschatology or Corporate Solidarity, Which?" *RTR* 48 (1989): 93-104.

11134   T. F. Glasson, "2 Corinthians 5:1-10 Versus Platonism," *SJT* 43/2 (1990): 145-55.

11135   Peter W. Macky, "St Paul's Collage of Metaphors in 2 Corinthians 5:1-10: Ornamental or Exploratory," *EGLMBS* 11 (1991): 162-73.

11136   Nikolaus Walter, "Hellenistische Eschatologie bei Paulus?" *TQ* 176 (1996): 53-64.

5:1-5

11137   C. L. Mitton, "Paul's Certainties: The Gift of the Spirit and Life beyond Death - 2 Corinthians v. 1-5," *ET* (1957-1958): 260-63.

11138   John Gillman, "A Thematic Comparison: 1 Corinthians
15:50-57 and 2 Corinthians 5:1-5," *JBL* 107 (1988):
439-54.

11139   A. C. Perriman, "Paul and the Parousia: 1 Corinthians
15:50-57 and 2 Corinthians 5:1-5," *NTS* 35 (1989):
512-21.

5:2

11140   R. Wonneberger, "Der Beitrag der generativen Syntax zur
Exegese. Ein Beispiel und neue Thesen," *Bij* 36 (1975):
312-17.

5:3

11141   David Wenham, "Being 'Found' on the Last Day: New
Light on 2 Peter 3:10 and 2 Corinthians 5:3," *NTS* 33/3
(1987): 477-79.

5:5

11142   A. J. Kerr, "Arrabon," *JTS* 39 (1988): 92-97.

11143   Kurt Erlemann, "Der Geist als arrabon (2Kor 5,5) im
Kontext der paulinischen Eschatologie," *ZNW* 83/3-4
(1992): 202-23.

11144   L. L. Belleville, "Paul's Polemic and Theology of the
Spirit in Second Corinthians," *CBQ* 58 (1996): 281-304.

11145   Eldon Woodcock, "The Seal of the Holy Spirit," *BSac* 155
(1998): 139-63.

5:6

11146   Jerome Murphy-O'Connor, "'Being at Home in the Body':
We Are in Exile from the Lord," *RB* 93 (1986): 214-21.

11147   Helge K. Nielsen, "Og det selv om vi ved. Om
oversaettelsen af 2 Kor 5,6," *DTT* 49 (1986): 62-69.

5:11-6:2

11148   David L. Turner, "Paul and the Ministry of Reconciliation
in 2 Corinthians 5:11-6:2," *CTR* 4 (1989): 77-95.

5:11-21

11149   W. Fürst, "2 Korinther 5, 11-21, Auslegung und
Meditation," *EvT* 28 (1968): 221-38.

11150 Anne Étienne, "Réconciliation: un aspect de la théologie paulinienne," *FV* 84 (1985): 49-57.

11151 Marion L. Soards, "The Righteousness of God in the Writings of the Apostle Paul," *BTB* 15 (1985): 104-109.

5:11

11152 Stanley N. Olson, "Epistolary Uses of Expressions of Self-Confidence," *JBL* 103 (1984): 585-97.

5:12-20

11153 J. C. O'Neill, "The Absence of the 'in Christ' Theology in 2 Corinthians 5," *ABR* 35 (1987): 99-106.

5:13

11154 Moyer Hubbard, "Was Paul Out of His Mind? Re-reading 2 Corinthians 5.13," *JSNT* 70 (1998): 39-64.

5:14

11155 Ceslaus Spicq, "L'étreinte de la Charité (2 Cor. V, 14)," *ST* 8 (1955): 123-32.

11156 José A. Fidalgo Herranz, "La SS Trinidad en la Suma contra los Gentiles: fuentes biblicas," *EB* 42 (1984): 363-89.

11157 Raymond Schwager, "Christ's Death and the Prophetic Critique of Sacrifice," *Semeia* 33 (1985): 109-23.

5:14-6:2

11158 Ferdinand Hahn, " 'Siehe, jetzt ist der Tag des Heils': Neuschöpfung und Versöhnung nach 2 Korinther 5,14-6,2," *EvT* 33 (1973): 244-53.

5:14-21

11159 J. Cadier, "2 Corinthians 5:14-21," *ÉTR* 30 (1955): 58-63.

11160 D. Von Allmen, "Réconciliation du monde et christologie cosmique," *RHPR* 48 (1968): 32-45.

11161 P.-É. Bonnard, "Conversation biblique avec Jean Delumeau," *FV* 84 (1985): 77-81.

11162 J. P. Sampley, "Overcoming Traditional Methods by Synthesizing the Theology of Individual Letters," *SBLSP* 25 (1986): 603-13.

11163   W. Hulitt Gloer, "2 Corinthians 5:14-21," *RevExp* 86 (1989): 397-405.

5:14-17

11164   Thor Hall, "Let Religion Be Religion: From Text to Sermon on 2 Corinthians 5:14-17," *Int* 23 (1969): 158-89.

11165   John D. Laurence, "The Eucharist as the Imitation of Christ," *TS* 47/2 (1986): 286-96.

5:14-15

11166   H. U. von Balthasar, "Jesus and Forgiveness," *CICR* 11 (1984): 322-34.

5:15

11167   Helmut Gollwitzer, "Hinfort nicht mehr," *EvT* 14 (1954): 1-6.

5:16

11168   W. Schmithals, "Zwei gnostische Glossen im Zweiten Korintherbrief," *EvT* 18 (1958): 552-73.

11169   J. B. Soucek, "Wir kennen Christus nicht mehr nach dem Fleisch," *EvT* 19 (1959): 300-14.

11170   J. W. Fraser, "Paul's Knowledge of Jesus: 2 Corinthians v. 16 once more," *NTS* 17 (1970-1971): 293-313.

11171   A. J. M. Wedderburn, "Paul and Jesus: The Problem of Continuity," *SJT* 38 (1985): 189-203.

5:17-21

11172   C. B. Cousar, "2 Corinthians 5:17-21," *Int* 35 (1981): 180-83.

11173   A. Viard, "Réconciliés avec Dieu par le Christ," *EV* 83 (1983): 77-78.

5:17

11174   V. P. Branick, "Apocalyptic Paul?" *CBQ* 47 (1985): 664-75.

11175   Anthony Hoekema, "How We See Ourselves," *CT* 29 (1985): 36-38.

11176   Ulrich Luck, "Die Bekehrung des Paulus und das paulinische Evangelium: zur Frage der Evidenz in

Botschaft und Theologie des Apostels," *ZNW* 76/3-4 (1985): 187-208.

11177 Gerhard Sauter, "Leiden und 'Handeln' [theologische Hermeneutik des Politischen]," *EvT* 45 (1985): 435-58.

11178 Gail P. Corrington, "The Beloved Community: A Roycean Interpretation of Paul," *EGLMBS* 7 (1987): 27-38.

11179 Mikeal C. Parsons, "The New Creation," *ET* 99 (1987): 3-4.

5:18-21

11180 Nikolaus Walter, "Christusglaube und heidnische Religiosität in paulinischen Gemeinden," *NTS* 25 (1979): 422-42.

11181 Charles A. Wanamaker, "Christ as Divine Agent in Paul," *SJT* 39/4 (1986): 517-28.

5:18-20

11182 Theodore Mueller, "Justification: Basic Linguistic Aspects and the Art of Communicating It," *CTQ* 46 (1982): 21-38.

11183 Traian Valdman, "Uno sguardo ortodosso sulla giustificazione in Lutero," *SEcu* 1 (1983): 277-88.

11184 David Stanley, "The Apostle Paul as Saint," *SM* 35 (1986): 71-97.

5:18

11185 H. U. von Balthasar, "Jesus and Forgiveness," *CICR* 11 (1984): 322-34.

5:19-20

11186 R. Weth, "Heil im gekreuzigten Gott," *EvT* 31 (1971): 227-44.

5:19

11187 Otfried Hofius, "Gott hat unter uns aufgerichtet das Wort von der Versöhnung," *ZNW* 71 (1980): 3-20.

11188 R. Bieringer, "2 Kor 5:19a und die Versöhnung der Welt," *ETL* 63/4 (1987): 295-326.

11189 Otfried Hofius, "2 Kor 5:19a und das Imperfekt," *TLZ* 118 (1993) 790-95.

5:20

11190 Bernhard Hanssler, "Autorität in der Kirche," *IKaZ* 14/6 (1985): 493-504.

11191 W. Hulitt Gloer, "Ambassadors for Christ," *BI* 15/1 (1988): 30-32.

5:20-21

11192 J. R. Gray, "Christ Made Sin for Us," *ET* 87 (1976): 173-75.

5:21

11193 Morna D. Hooker, "Interchange in Christ," *JTS* 22 (1971): 349-61.

11194 H. U. von Balthasar, "Jesus and Forgiveness," *CICR* 11 (1984): 322-34.

11195 V. P. Branick, "Apocalyptic Paul?" *CBQ* 47 (1985): 664-75.

11196 Paul Ellingworth, "For Our Sake God Made Him Share Our Sin (2 Corinthians 5:21, Good News Bible)," *BT* 38 (1987): 237-41.

11197 Bradley H. McLean, "Christ as a Pharmakos in Pauline Soteriology," *SBLSP* 30 (1991): 187-206.

6:1-10

11198 G. Ferloni, "Le epistole della liturgia," *BibO* 3 (1961): 32-37.

11199 David L. Mealand, " 'As having nothing, and yet possessing everything'," *ZNW* 67 (1976): 277-79.

6:1

11200 Hermann von Lips, "Der Apostolat des Paulus - ein Charisma: semantische Aspekte zu charis-charisma und anderen Wortpaaren im Sprachgebrauch des Paulus," *Bib* 66/3 (1985): 305-343.

6:4-7:1

11201 Joseph A. Fitzmyer, "Qumran and the Interpolated Paragraph in 2 Corinthians 6:14-7:1," *CBQ* 23 (1961): 271-80.

6:5

11202 Eric F. F. Bishop, "Why of Sleepless Nights," *EQ* 37 (1965): 29-31.

11203 J. Müller-Bardorff, "Nächtlicher Gottesdienst im apostolischen Zeitalter," *TLZ* 81 (1956): 347-52.

6:6

11204 Kendell H. Easley, "The Pauline Usage of Pneumati as a Reference to the Spirit of God," *JETS* 27 (1984): 299-313.

11205 L. L. Belleville, "Paul's Polemic and Theology of the Spirit in Second Corinthians," *CBQ* 58 (1996): 281-304.

6:8-10

11206 Ulrich Luck, "Die Bekehrung des Paulus und das paulinische Evangelium: zur Frage der Evidenz in Botschaft und Theologie des Apostels," *ZNW* 76/3-4 (1985): 187-208.

6:9-10

11207 Walter Magass, "Theophrast und Paulus: exemplarisch für Umstände und Ethos in Korinth und Saloniki," *K* 26/3-4 (1984): 154-65.

6:11-13

11208 M. C. Griffths, "Today's Missionary, Yesterday's Apostle," *EMQ* 21/2 (1985): 154-65.

6:11

11209 Roy A. Harrisville, "Paul and the Psalms: A Formal Study," *WW* 5 (1985): 168-79.

6:14-7:1

11210 Gerhard Sass, "Noch einmal; 2Kor 6,14-7,1: Literarkritische Waffen gegen einen 'unpaulinischen' Paulus?" *ZNW* 84 (1993): 36-64.

11211 H. D. Betz, "2 Corinthians 6:14-7:1: An Anti-Pauline Fragment?" *JBL* 92 (1973): 88-108.

11212 Gordon D. Fee, "2 Corinthians vi.14-vii.1 and Fond offered to Idols," *NTS* 23 (1977): 140-61.

11213 M. E. Thrall, "The Problem of 2 Corinthians vi.14-vii.1 in Some Recent Discussion," *NTS* 24 (1977-1978): 132-48.

11214 J. D. M. Derrett, "2 Corinthians 6,14ff. A Midrash on Deuternomony 22,10," *Bib* 50 (1978): 231-50.

11215 D. Rensberger, "2 Corinthians 6:14-7:1 - A Fresh Examination," *SBT* 8 (1978): 25-49.

11216 Lawrence Wills, "The Form of the Sermon in Hellenistic Judaism and Early Christianity," *HTR* 77 (1984): 277-99.

11217 Jerome Murphy-O'Connor, "Relating 2 Corinthians 6:14-7:1 to Its Context," *NTS* 33 (1987): 272-75.

11218 Jerome Murphy-O'Connor, "Philo and 2 Corinthians 6:14-7:1," *RB* 95 (1988): 55-69.

11219 Gregory K. Beale, "The Old Testament Background of Reconciliation in 2 Corinthians 5-7 and Its Bearing on the Literary Problem of 2 Corinthians 6:14-7:1," *NTS* 35 (1989): 550-81.

11220 Elizabeth Waller, "The Rhetorical Structure of 2 Corinthians 6:14-7:1: Is the So-Called 'Non-Pauline Interpolation' a Clue to the Redactor of 2 Corinthians?" *EGLMBS* 10 (1990): 151-65.

11221 N. H. Taylor, "The Composition and Chronology of Second Corinthians," *JSNT* 44 (1991): 67-87.

11222 D. A. DeSilva, "Recasting the Moment of Decision: 2 Corinthians 6:14-7:1 in Its Literary Context," *AUSS* 31 (1993): 3-16.

11223 Paul B. Duff, "The Mind of the Redactor: 2 Corinthians 6:14-7:1 in Its Secondary Context," *NovT* 35 (1993): 160-80.

11224 Franz Zeilinger, "Die Echtheit von 2 Cor 6:14-7:1," *JBL* 112 (1993): 71-80.

11225 Michael D. Goulder, "2 Corinthians 6:14-7:1 as an Integral Part of 2 Corinthians," *NovT* 36 (1994): 47-57.

11226 J. M. Scott, "The Use of Scripture in 2 Corinthians 6.16c-18 and Paul's Restoration Theology," *JSNT* 56 (1994): 73-99.

11227 D. A. DeSilva, "Meeting the Exigency of a Complex Rhetorical Situation: Paul's Strategy in 2 Corinthian1 through 7," *AUSS* 34 (1996): 5-22.

6:14

11228 Traian Valdman, "Uno sguardo ortodosso sulla giustificazione in Lutero," *SEcu* 1 (1983): 277-88.

11229 William J. Webb, "Unequally Yoked together with Unbelievers," *BSac* 149 (1992): 27-44; 162-79.

6:16-18

11230 J. M. Scott, "The Use of Scripture in 2 Corinthians 6.16c-18 and Paul's Restoration Theology," *JSNT* 56 (1994): 73-99.

6:16

11231 Elmar Salmann, "Trinität und Kirche: eine dogmatische Studie," *Cath* 38 (1984): 352-74.

6:18

11232 Willem A. VanGemeren, " 'Abba' in the Old Testament?" *JETS* 31 (1988): 385-98.

11233 John W. Olley, "A Precursor of the NRSV? 'Sons and Daughters' in 2 Corinthians 6.18," *NTS* 44 (1998): 204-11.

7:1

11234 R. E. Ker, "Fear or Love? A Textual Note," *ET* 72 (1961): 195-96.

7:2-4

11235 Robert G. Hamerton-Kelly, "A Girardian Interpretation of Paul: Rivalry, Mimesis and Victimage in the Corinthian Correspondence," *Semeia* 33 (1985): 65-81.

7:2-4

11236 N. H. Taylor, "The Composition and Chronology of Second Corinthians," *JSNT* 44 (1991): 67-87.

7:3

11237 Jan Lambrecht, "Om samen te sterven en samen te leven. Uitleg van 2 Kor 7,3," *Bij* 37 (1976): 234-51.

7:5-8:24

11238 N. H. Taylor, "The Composition and Chronology of Second Corinthians," *JSNT* 44 (1991): 67-87.

7:5-16

11239　Margaret M. Mitchell, "New Testament Envoys in the Context of Greco-Roman Diplomatic and Epistolary Conventions," *JBL* 111 (1992): 641-62.

11240　D. A. DeSilva, "Meeting the Exigency of a Complex Rhetorical Situation: Paul's Strategy in 2 Corinthians 1 through 7," *AUSS* 34 (1996): 5-22.

11241　L. L. Welborn, "Like Broken Pieces of a Ring: 2 Corinthians 1.1-2.13; 7.5-16 and Ancient Theories of Literary Unity," *NTS* 42 (1996): 559-83.

7:7

11242　John J. Kilgallen, "Reflections on Charisma(ta) in the New Testament," *SM* 41 (1992): 289-323.

7:8

11243　Francis Watson, "2 Corinthians X-XIII and Paul's Painful Letter to the Corinthians," *JTS* 35 (1984): 324-46.

7:9

11244　M. L. Barré, "Paul as 'Eschatologic Person': A New Look at 2 Corinthians 11:29," *CBQ* 37 (1975): 500-26.

7:10

11245　Anthony Hoekema, "How We See Ourselves," *CT* 29 (1985): 36-38.

8-9

11246　C. H. Buck, "The Collection for the Saints," *HTR* 43 (1950): 1-29.

11247　Klaus Berger, "Almosen für Israel: Zum historischen Kontext der paulinischen Kollekte," *NTS* 23 (1977): 180-204.

11248　Ulrich Schoenborn, "La inversion de la gracia: apuntes sobre 2 Corintios 8:9," *RevB* 50 (1988): 207-18.

11249　Richard R. Melick, "The Collection for the Saints: 2 Corinthians 8-9," *CTR* 4 (1989): 97-117.

11250　Charles H. Talbert, "Money Management in Early Mediterranean Christianity: 2 Corinthians 8-9," *RevExp* 70 (1989): 359-70.

11251 Stanley Stowers, "Peri men gar and the Integrity of 2 Corinthians 8 and 9," *NovT* 32 (1990): 340-48.

11252 D. A. DeSilva, "Meeting the Exigency of a Complex Rhetorical Situation: Paul's Strategy in 2 Corinthians 1 through 7," *AUSS* 34 (1996): 5-22.

8:1-15

11253 Richard S. Ascough, "The Completion of a Religious Duty: The Background of 2 Corinthians 8.1-15," *NTS* 42 (1996): 584-99.

8:1-10

11254 W. C. Linss, "The First World Hunger Appeal," *CThM* 12 (1985): 211-19.

8:1-9

11255 Gerhard Aho, "2 Corinthians 8:1-9,13-14," *CTQ* 46 (1982): 58-60.

8:1

11256 Del Olsen, "Macedonia," *BI* 1/2 (1975): 50-53,65.

11257 Helmut Koester, "The Churches of Macedonia," *BI* 11/3 (1985): 40-49.

11258 Hermann von Lips, "Der Apostolat des Paulus - ein Charisma: semantische Aspekte zu charis-charisma und anderen Wortpaaren im Sprachgebrauch des Paulus," *Bib* 66/3 (1985): 305-343.

8:2

11259 V. P. Branick, "Apocalyptic Paul?" *CBQ* 47 (1985): 664-75.

8:4

11260 Léopold Sabourin, "Koinonia in the New Testament," *RSB* 1/4 (1981): 109-15.

8:6

11261 Robert N. Stapp, "Titus," *BI* 1/2 (1975): 42,48-49.

8:7

11262 Hermann von Lips, "Der Apostolat des Paulus - ein Charisma: semantische Aspekte zu charis-charisma und anderen Wortpaaren im Sprachgebrauch des Paulus," *Bib* 66/3 (1985): 305-343.

8:8-15

11263 C. Thomas Rhyne, "2 Corinthians 8:8-15," *Int* 41 (1987): 408-13.

8:9

11264 George W. Buchanan, "Jesus and the Upper Class," (Matt 13:55; 2 Corinthians 8:9) *NovT* 7/3 (1965): 195-206.

11265 Fred B. Craddock, "The Poverty of Christ. An Investigation of 2 Corinthians 8:9," *Int* 22 (1968): 158-70.

11266 R. Brindle, "Geld und Gnade (zu 2 Kor 8:9)," *TZ* 41 (1985): 264-71.

11267 Hermann von Lips, "Der Apostolat des Paulus - ein Charisma: semantische Aspekte zu charis-charisma und anderen Wortpaaren im Sprachgebrauch des Paulus," *Bib* 66/3 (1985): 305-343.

11268 Brendan Byrne, "Christ's Pre-Existence in Pauline Soteriology," *TS* 58 (1997): 308-30.

8:13-14

11269 Gerhard Aho, "2 Corinthians 8:1-9,13-14," *CTQ* 46 (1982): 58-60.

11270 Renato Iori, "Uso e significato di isotns 2 Cor 8:13-14," *RivBib* 36 (1989): 425-38.

8:17-23

11271 M. C. Griffths, "Today's Missionary, Yesterday's Apostle," *EMQ* 21/2 (1985): 154-65.

8:17-22

11272 K. L. McKay, "Observations on the Epistolary Aorist in 2 Corinthians," *NovT* 37 (1995): 154-58.

8:18-19

11273 J. E. Morgan-Wynne, "2 Corinthians 8:18f. and the Question of a Traditionsgrundlage for Acts," *JTS* 30 (1979): 172-73.

8:23

11274 H. Evans, "An Apostolic Partner," *ET* 90 (1979): 207-209.

8:24-9:5

11275 Jan Lambrecht, "Paul's Boasting about the Corinthians: A Study of 2 Corinthians 8:24-9:5," *NovT* 40 (1998): 352-68.

9:3-12

11276 W. C. Linss, "The First World Hunger Appeal," *CThM* 12 (1985): 211-19.

9:5

11277 Vernon Kleinig, "Providence and Worship: The Aaronic Blessing," *LTJ* 19 (1985): 120-24.

9:5-6

11278 Juan Mateos, "Analisis de un campo lexematico: eulogia en el Nuevo Testamento," *FilN* 1 (1988): 5-25.

9:8

11279 Hermann von Lips, "Der Apostolat des Paulus - ein Charisma: semantische Aspekte zu charis-charisma und anderen Wortpaaren im Sprachgebrauch des Paulus," *Bib* 66/3 (1985): 305-343.

9:9

11280 Roy A. Harrisville, "Paul and the Psalms: A Formal Study," *WW* 5 (1985): 168-79.

9:13

11281 Jonathan F. Grothe, "Confessing Christ in a Pluralistic Age," *CJ* 16 (1990): 217-30.

9:14

11282 Hermann von Lips, "Der Apostolat des Paulus - ein Charisma: semantische Aspekte zu charis-charisma und anderen Wortpaaren im Sprachgebrauch des Paulus," *Bib* 66/3 (1985): 305-343.

10-13

11283 F. F. Bruce, "St. Paul in Rome 5. Concluding Observations," *BJRL* 50 (1968): 262-79.

11284 U. Borse, "Die Geschichte und theologische Einordnung des Römerbriefes," *BZ* 16 (1972): 70-83.

11285 F. F. Bruce, "Galatian Problems. 4. The Date of the Epistle," *BJRL* 54 (1972): 250-67.

11286 M. L. Barré, "Qumran and the 'Weakness' of Paul," *CBQ* 42 (1980): 216-27.

11287 Ernst Fuchs, "La falblase, gloire de l'apostolat selon Paul," *ÉTR* 55 (1980): 231-53.

11288 Doyle Kee, "Who Were the 'Super-Apostles' of 2 Corinthians 10-13?" *RQ* 23 (1980): 65-76.

11289 M. V. Abraham, "Diakonia in the Early Letters of Paul," *IJT* 32 (1983): 61-67.

11290 Francis Watson, "2 Corinthians X-XIII and Paul's Painful Letter to the Corinthians," *JTS* 35 (1984): 324-46.

11291 Robert G. Hamerton-Kelly, "A Girardian Interpretation of Paul: Rivalry, Mimesis and Victimage in the Corinthian Correspondence," *Semeia* 33 (1985): 65-81.

11292 J. M. Gilchrist, "Paul and the Corinthians—The Sequence of Letters and Visits," *JSNT* 34 (1988): 47-69.

11293 David E. Garland, "Paul's Apostolic Authority: The Power of Christ Sustaining Weakness," *RevExp* 86 (1989): 371-89.

11294 Colin G. Kruse, "The Relationship between the Opposition to Paul Reflected in 2 Corinthians 1-7 and 10-13," *EQ* 61 (1989): 195-202.

11295 J. A. Loubser, "Exegesis and Proclamation: Winning the Struggle, How to Treat Heretics. 2 Corinthians 12:1-10," *JTSA* 75 (1991): 75-83.

11296 N. H. Taylor, "The Composition and Chronology of Second Corinthians," *JSNT* 44 (1991): 67-87.

11297 L. L. Welborn, "The Identification of 2 Corinthians 10-13 with the 'Letter of Tears'," *NovT* 37 (1995): 138-53.

10-12

11298 Christopher Forbes, "Comparison, Self-Praise and Irony: Paul's Boasting and the Conventions of Hellenistic Rhetoric," *NTS* 32/1 (1986): 1-30.

10:1-18

11299 Terrance Callan, "Competition and Boasting: Toward a Psychological Portrait of Paul," *StTheol* 40/2 (1986): 137-56.

10:1

> 11300   Ragnar Leivestad, "Meekness and Gentleness of Christ, 2 Corinthians 10:1," *NTS* 12 (1966): 156-64.

10:5

> 11301   D. B. Lockerbie, "Thinking Like a Christian. Part 1: The Starting Point," *BSac* 143 (1986): 3-13.

10:7-12

> 11302   Richard F. Ward, "2 Corinthians 10:7-12," *RevExp* 87 (1990): 605-609.

10:8

> 11303   M. C. Griffths, "Today's Missionary, Yesterday's Apostle," *EMQ* 21/2 (1985): 154-65.

10:10

> 11304   Richard F. Ward, "Pauline Voice and Presence as Strategic Communication," *SBLSP* 29 (1990): 283-92.

10:12-18

> 11305   Kasper Wong, " 'Lord' in 2 Corinthians 10:17,' *LouvS* 17 (1992): 243-53.

10:13-16

> 11306   James F. Strange, "2 Corinthians 10:13-16 Illuminated by a Recently Published Inscription," *BA* 46 (1983): 167-68.

> 11307   James F. Strange, "Enigmatic Bible Passage. 2 Corinthians 10:13-16 Illuminated by a Recently Published Inscription," *BA* 46 (1983): 167-68.

> 11308   J. D. M. Derrett, "Paul as Master-Builder," *EQ* 69 (1997): 129-37.

10:13

> 11309   L. D. Hurst, "Apollos, Hebrews, and Corinth: Bishop Montefiore's Theory Examined," *SJT* 38/4 (1985): 505-13.

10:14-16

> 11310   M. C. Griffths, "Today's Missionary, Yesterday's Apostle," *EMQ* 21/2 (1985): 154-65.

10:17

> 11311   Kasper Wong, " 'Lord' in 2 Corinthians 10:17,' *LouvS* 17 (1992): 243-53.

11:1-21

11312 H. S. Shoemaker, "2 Corinthians 11:1-21," *RevExp* 86 (1989): 407-14.

11:1-15

11313 John T. Anderson, "The Body of Satan according to Paul," *EGLMBS* 13 (1993): 103-12.

11:1

11314 Christfried Böttrich, "2Kor 11,1 als Programmwort der 'Narrenrede'," *ZNW* 88 (1997): 135-39.

11:2-4:30

11315 Sigfred Pedersen, "Theologische Überlegungen zur Isagogik des Römerbriefs," *ZNW* 76/1-2 (1985): 47-67.

11:2-16

11316 Cynthia L. Thompson, "Hairstyles, Head-Coverings, and St. Paul. Portraits from Roman Corinth," *BA* 51 (1988): 99-115.

11:2-4

11317 J. A. Mazzeo, "Dante and the Pauline Modes of Vision," *HTR* 50 (1957): 275-306.

11:2-3

11318 Richard A. Batey, "Paul's Bride Image: A Symbol of Realistic Eschatology," *Int* 17 (1963): 176-82.

11:2

11319 R. Infante, "Imagine nuziale e tensione escatologica nel Nuovo Testamento. Note a 2 Cor. 11:2 e Eph 5:25-27," *RivBib* 33 (1985): 45-61.

11320 R. Bieringer, "Paul's Divine Jealousy: The Apostle and His Communities in Relationship," *LouvS* 17 (1992): 197-231.

11:3

11321 Abraham J. Malherbe, "Through the Eye of the Needle: Simplicity or Singleness?" *RQ* 5 (1961): 119-29.

11322 Jack Levison, "Is Eve to Blame: A Contextual Analysis of Sirach 25:24," *CBQ* 47 (1985): 617-23.

11:4

11323 J. P. Jossua, "Christ autre ou autre Christ?" *LV* 112 (1973): 55-70.

11324 Jerome Murphy-O'Connor, "Another Jesus," *RB* 97 (1990): 238-51.

11325 L. L. Belleville, "Paul's Polemic and Theology of the Spirit in Second Corinthians," *CBQ* 58 (1996): 281-304.

11:5-23

11326 M. E. Thrall, "Super-Apostles, Servants of Christ, and Servants of Satan," *JSNT* 6 (1980): 42-57.

11327 S. E. McClelland, " 'Super-Apostles, Servants of Christ, Servants of Satan': A Response," *JSNT* 14 (1982): 82-87.

11:5

11328 Stanley N. Olson, "Epistolary Uses of Expressions of Self-Confidence," *JBL* 103 (1984): 585-97.

11:6

11329 Watson E. Mills, "Paul's Training and Knowledge," *BI* 11/3 (1985): 50-53.

11330 Richard F. Ward, "Pauline Voice and Presence as Strategic Communication," *SBLSP* 29 (1990): 283-92.

11:7

11331 R. F. Hock, "Paul's Tentmaking and the Problem of His Social Class," *JBL* 97 (1978): 555-64.

11:8

11332 Chrys C. Caragounis, "Opsonion: A Reconsideration of Its Meaning," *NovT* 16 (1974): 35-57.

11:9-12

11333 W. Pratscher, "Der Verzicht des Paulus auf finanziellen Unterhalt durch seine Gemeinden: ein Aspekt seiner Missionsweise," *NTS* 25 (1979): 284-98.

11:9

11334 R. Trevijano Etcheverría, "La mision en Tesalonica (1 Tes 1:1-2,16)," *Salm* 32 (1985): 263-91.

11:13

11335   Takaaki Haraguchi, "Das Unterhaltsrecht des frühchristlichen Verkündigers: Eine Untersuchung zur Bezeichnung ergátes im Neuen Testament," *ZNW* 84 (1993): 178-95.

11:15

11336   Mark A. Seifrid, "Paul's Approach to the Old Testament in Rom 10:6-8," *TriJ* 6 (1985): 3-37.

11:16-12:13

11337   Aida B. Spencer, "The Wise Fool (and the Foolish Wise)," *NovT* 23 (1981): 349-6O.

11:16-29

11338   Paul Ellingworth, "Grammar, Meaning, and Verse Divisions in 2 Corinthians 11:16-29," *BT* 43 (1993): 245-46.

11:22-28

11339   Walter Magass, "Theophrast und Paulus: exemplarisch für Umstände und Ethos in Korinth und Saloniki," *K* 26/3-4 (1984): 154-65.

11:22

11340   L. D. Hurst, "Apollos, Hebrews, and Corinth: Bishop Montefiore's Theory Examined," *SJT* 38/4 (1985): 505-13.

11:23-33

11341   S. B. Andrews, "Too Weak Not to Lead: The Form and Function of 2 Corinthians 11:23b-33," *NTS* 41 (1995): 263-76.

11342   Jan Lambrecht, "Strength in Weakness," *NTS* 43 (1997): 285-90.

11:23-30

11343   H. Binder, "Die angebliche Krankheit des Paulus," *TZ* 32 (1976): 1-13.

11:23-29

11344   Robert Hodgson, "Paul the Apostle and First Century Tribulation Lists," *ZNW* 74 (1983): 59-80.

11:23

11345 John N. Collins, "Georgi's 'Envoys' in 2 Corinthians 11:23," *JBL* 93 (1974): 88-96.

11:24

11346 Sven Gallas, " 'Fünfmal vierzig weniger einen . . .': Die an Paulus vollzogenen Synagogalstrafen nach 2 Kor 11,24," *ZNW* 81/3-4 (1990): 178-91.

11347 Simon Légasse, "Paul fut-il un juif apostat?" *BLE* 95 (1994): 183-96.

11:27

11348 Eric F. F. Bishop, "Why of Sleepless Nights," *EQ* 37 (1965): 29-31.

11349 Eric F. F. Bishop, "In Famine and Drought," *EQ* 38 (1966): 169-71.

11:29

11350 John H. Dobson, "Emphatic Personal Pronouns in the New Testament," *BT* 22 (1971): 58-61.

11351 M. L. Barre, "Paul as 'Eschatologic Person': A New Look at 2 Corinthians 11:29," *CBQ* 37 (1975): 500-26.

11:30

11352 Kasper Wong, " 'Lord' in 2 Corinthians 10:17,' *LouvS* 17 (1992): 243-53.

11:32-33

11353 William O. Walker, "Acts and the Pauline Corpus Reconsidered," *JSNT* 24 (1985): 3-23.

11354 Étienne Trocmé, "Le rempart de Damas: un faux pas de Paul?" *RHPR* 69 (1989): 475-79.

11355 Justin Taylor, "The Ethnarch of King Aretas at Damascus: A Note on 2 Corinthians 11:32-33," *RB* 99 (1992): 719-28.

11356 Mark Harding, "On the Historicity of Acts: Comparing Acts 9:23-25 with 2 Corinthians 11:32-33," *NTS* 39/4 (1993): 518-38.

11:32

11357 E. A. Knauf, "Zum Ethnarchen des Aretas 2 Kor 11:32," *ZAW* 74 (1983): 145-47.

12:1-12

11358 C. R. A. Morray-Jones, "Paradise Revisited: The Jewish Mystical Background of Paul's Apostolate. Part 1: The Jewish Sources," *HTR* 86 (1993): 177-217.

11359 C. R. A. Morray-Jones, "Paradise Revisited: The Jewish Mystical Background of Paul's Apostolate. Part 2: Paul's Heavenly Ascent and Its Significance," *HTR* 86 (1993): 265-92.

12:1-10

11360 Helmut Saake, "Paulus als Ekstatiker: pneumatologische Beobachtungen zu 2 Kor 12:1-10," *NovT* 15/2 (1973): 153-60.

11361 Andrew T. Lincoln, " 'Paul the Visionary': The Setting and Significance of the Rapture to Paradise in 2 Corinthians 12:1-10," *NTS* 25 (1979): 204-20.

11362 R. M. Price, "Punished in Paradise (An Exegetical Theory on 2 Corinthians 12:1-10)," *JSNT* 7 (1980): 33-40.

11363 Brad H. Young, "The Ascension Motif of 2 Corinthians 12 in Jewish, Christian and Gnostic Texts," *GTJ* 9 (1988): 73-103.

11364 Daniel L. Akin, "Triumphalism, Suffering, and Spiritual Maturity: An Exposition of 2 Corinthians 12:1-10 in Its Literary, Theological, and Historical Context," *CTR* 4 (1989): 119-44.

11365 P. de Salis, "L'écharde dans la chair: Une signe visible de la présence de Dieu? La dimension dramatique de la vie: perspectives à partir de 2 Corinthiens 12:1-10," *RTP* 127 (1995): 27-41.

12:1-6

11366 Robert E. Osborne, "St. Paul's Silent Years," *JBL* 84 (1965): 59-65.

12:1-5

11367 William Baird, "Visions, Revelation, and Ministry: Reflections on 2 Corinthians 12:1-5 and Gal 1:11-17," *JBL* 104/4 (1985): 651-62.

11368 Michael D. Goulder, "Vision and Knowledge," *JSNT* 56 (1994): 53-71.

11369 B. Otzen, "Himmelrejser og himmelvisioner i jødisk Apokalyptik," *DTT* 58 (1995): 16-26.

12:2-4

11370 John T. Anderson, "The Cosmological Roots of Pauline Metaphors," *EGLMBS* 11 (1991): 153-61.

12:4

11371 W. Thomas Sawyer, "Paradise," *BI* 8 (1982): 77-78.

12:5

11372 Kasper Wong, " 'Lord' in 2 Corinthians 10:17,' *LouvS* 17 (1992): 243-53.

12:6

11373 J. Cambier, "Le critère paulinien de l'apostolat en 2 Cor 12:6s," *Bib* 43/4 (1962): 481-518.

12:7

11374 T. Y. Mullins, "Paul's Thorn in the Flesh," *JBL* 76 (1957): 299-303.

11375 P. Nisbet, "The Thorn in the Flesh," *ET* 80 (1968-1969): 126.

11376 Josef Zmijewski, "Kontextbezug und Deutung von 2 Kor 12,7a," *BZ* 21 (1977): 265-72.

11377 M. L. Barré, "Qumran and the 'Weakness' of Paul," *CBQ* 42 (1980): 216-27.

11378 David M. Park, "Paul's σκόλοψ τῇ σαρκί: Thorn or Stake?" *NovT* 22 (1980): 179-83.

11379 Laurie Woods, "Opposition to a Man and His Message: Paul's 'Thorn in the Flesh'," *ABR* 39 (1991): 44-53.

11380 T. J. Leary, "A Thorn in the Flesh--2 Corinthians 12:7," *JTS* 43 (1992): 520-22.

11381 U. Heckel, "Der Dorn im Fleisch: Die Krankheit des Paulus in 2 Kor 12,7 und Gal 4,13f," *ZNW* 84/1-2 (1993): 65-92.

12:7-12

11382 David Stanley, "The Apostle Paul as Saint," *SM* 35 (1986): 71-97.

12:7-10

11383 H. D. Betz, "Eine Christus-Aretalogie bei Paulus (2 Kor 12:7-10)," *ZTK* 66/3 (1969): 288-305.

11384 J. Bernard, "Lorsque je suis faible, c'est alors que je suis fort," *AsSeign* 45 (1974): 34-39.

11385 Jerry W. McCant, "Paul's Thorn of Rejected Apostleship," *NTS* 34/4 (1988): 550-72.

12:7-9

11386 N. G. Smith, "The Thorn that Stayed: An Exposition of 2 Corinthians 12:7-9," *Int* 13 (1959): 409-16.

11387 J. J. Thierry, "Der Dorn im Fleische (2 Kor 12:7-9)," *NovT* 5 (1962): 301-10.

11388 Paul A. Mickey, "Strength in Weakness: From Text to Sermon on 2 Corinthians 12:7-9," *Int* 22 (1968): 288-300.

11389 Peter Jensen, "Faith and Healing in Christian Theology," *Point* No 2 (1982): 153-59.

12:8

11390 D. G. M. MacKay, "Suffering," *ET* 91 (1980): 147-48.

11391 Christian Grappe, "Essai sur l'arrière-plan Pascal des récits de la dernière nuit de Jésus," *RHPR* 65/2 (1985): 105-25.

12:9-10

11392 Gerald O'Collins, "Power Made Perfect in Weakness: 2 Corinthians 12:9-10," *CBQ* 33 (1971): 528-37.

12:9

11393 John N. Suggit, "Man: The Creature of God, His Glory and His Humiliation," *ScrSA* 14 (1985): 1-15.

11394 W. Auer, "Bibeltexte - falsch verstanden," *BK* 13 (1958): 85-88.

11395 Hermann von Lips, "Der Apostolat des Paulus - ein Charisma: semantische Aspekte zu charis-charisma und anderenWortpaaren im Sprachgebrauch des Paulus," *Bib* 66/3 (1985): 305-343.

12:10

11396 Helmut Saake, "Paulus als Ekstatiker: pneumatologische Beobachtungen zu 2 Kor 12:1-10," *Bib* 53/3 (1972): 404-10.

12:12

11397 Gail P. Corrington, "Paul and the Two Wisdoms: 1 Corinthians 1:18-31 and the Hellenistic Mission," - *EGLMBS* 6 (1985): 72-84.

11398 A. O. Igenoza, "African Weltanschauung and Exorcism: The Quest for the Contextualization of the Kerygma," *AfTJ* 14/3 (1985): 179-93.

11399 R. Trevijano Etcheverría, "La mision en Tesalonica (1 Tes 1:1-2,16)," *Salm* 32 (1985): 263-91.

12:24

11400 H. J. Klauck, "Die Himmelfahrt des Paulus (2 Kor 12:24) in der koptischen Paulusapokalypse aus Nag Hammadi," *SNTU-A* 10 (1985): 151-90.

13:1-2

11401 Lawrence H. Schiffman, "The Qumran Law of Testimony," *RevQ* 8 (1975): 603-12.

13:4

11402 Jan Lambrecht, "Philological and Exegetical Notes on 2 Corinthians 13:4," *Bij* 46 (1985): 261-69.

13:5

11403 Perry C. Brown, "What Is the Meaning of 'Examine Yourselves' in 2 Corinthians 13:5?" *BSac* 154 (1997): 175-88.

13:6

11404 Stanley N. Olson, "Epistolary Uses of Expressions of Self-Confidence," *JBL* 103 (1984): 585-97.

13:8

11405 Walter Kasper, "Hope in the Final Coming of Jesus Christ in Glory," *CICR* 12 (1985): 368-84.

13:11-13

11406   J. Depasse-Livet, "L'existence chrétienne: participation à la vie trinitaire," *AsSeign* 31 (1973): 10-13.

13:13

11407   J. W. Roberts, "Exegetical Helps: The Genitive With Nouns of Action," *RQ* 1 (1957): 35-40.

11408   Léopold Sabourin, "Koinonia in the New Testament," *RSB* 1/4 (1981): 109-15.

11409   Laurent Gagnebin, "De Trinitate: questions de méthode," *ÉTR* 61/1 (1986): 63-73.

11410   A. S. Di Marco, "Koinonia pneumatos--pneuma koinonias: circolaità e ambivalenza linguistica e filologica," *FilN* 1 (1988): 63-76.

11411   L. L. Belleville, "Paul's Polemic and Theology of the Spirit in Second Corinthians," *CBQ* 58 (1996): 281-304.

13:14

11412   James C. McKinnell, "The Lord's Supper: Its Relevance for Faith and Worship," *BLT* 7/2 (1962): 44-59.

Galatians

1-2

11413 Georg Strecker, "Die sogenannte zweite Jerusalemreise des Paulus," *ZNW* 53 (1962): 67-77.

11414 Jack T. Sanders, "Paul's Autobiographical Statements in Galatians 1-2," *JBL* 85 (1966): 335-43.

11415 A. Strobel, "Das Aposteldekret in Galatien: Zur Situation von Gal I und II," *NTS* 20 (1974): 177-90.

11416 J. F. M. Smit, "Paulus, de Galaten en het Judaïsme. Een narratieve analyse van Galaten 1-2," *TT* 25 (1985): 337-62.

11417 H. A. Brehm, "Paul's Relationship with the Jerusalem Apostles in Galatians 1 and 2," *SouJT* 37 (1994): 11-16.

11418 A. A. Das, "Oneness in Christ: The Nexus Indivulsus Between Justification and Sanctification in Paul's Letter to the Galatians," *CJ* 21 (1995): 173-86.

1:1-2:21

11419 L. L. Cranford, "A Rhetorical Reading of Galatians," *SouJT* 37 (1994): 410.

1:1-2:14

11420 David S. Dockery, "Introduction to the Epistle and Paul's Defense of his Apostleship," *RevExp* 91 (1994): 153-64.

1:1-17

11421 Jean Calloud, " 'Humanité. . . Vous avez dit: Humanité'!. . ." *SémBib* 98 (2000): 31-49.

1:1-12

11422 Benoît Standaert, "La rhétorique antique et l'épître aux galates," *FV* 84 (1985): 33-40.

1:1-10

11423 Silverio Zedda, "Le courage de la fidélité au Christ," *AsSeign* Ns 40 (1973): 62-65.

1:1-5

11424 David Cook, "The Prescript as Programme in Galatians," *JTS* NS 43 (1992): 511-19.

11425 L. L. Cranford, "A Rhetorical Reading of Galatians," *SouJT* 37 (1994): 410.

11426 Johan S. Vos, "Paul's Argumentation in Galatians 1-2," *HTR* 87 (1994): 1-16.

1:1-2

11427 M. V. Abraham, "Diakonia in the Early Letters of Paul," *IJT* 32 (1983): 61-67.

1:1

11428 Bernhard Hanssler, "Autorität in der Kirche," *IKaZ* 14/6 (1985): 493-504.

11429 Tjitze Baarda, "Marcion's Text of Galatians 1:1 concerning the Reconstruction of the First Verse of the Marcionite Corpus Paulinum," *VC* 42 (1988): 236-56.

11430 L. L. Cranford, "A Rhetorical Reading of Galatians," *SouJT* 37 (1994): 410.

1:2

11431 Louis Panier, "Pour une approche sémiotique de l'épître aux galates," *FV* 84 (1985): 19-32.

1:4

11432 V. P. Branick, "Apocalyptic Paul?" *CBQ* 47 (1985): 664-75.

11433 Christophe Senft, "Paul et Jésus," *FV* 84 (1985): 49-56.

11434 Federico Ramos, "Murió por nuestros pecados: observaciones sobre el origen de esta formula en Is 53," *EE* 61 (1986): 385-93.

11435 Michael Bachmann, "4QMMT und Galaterbrief התורה מעשי und ΕΡΓΑ ΝΟΜΟΥ," *ZNW* 89 (1998): 91-113.

1:5

11436 John Knox, "On the Meaning of Galatians 1:15," *JBL* 106 (1987): 301-304.

1:6-23

11437 Christiane Dieterlé, "Être juste ou vivre," *FV* 84/5 (1985): 5-18.

1:6-10

11438 Erich Grässer, "Das eine Evangelium: Hermeneutische Erwägungen zu Gal 1:6-10," *ZTK* 66 (1969): 306-44.

1:6-9

11439 Johan S. Vos, "Paul's Argumentation in Galatians 1-2," *HTR* 87 (1994): 1-16.

11440 Troy Martin, "Apostasy to Paganism: The Rhetorical Stasis of the Galatian Controversy," *JBL* 114 (1995): 437-61.

1:6

11441 F. F. Bruce, "Galatian Problems. 3. The 'Other' Gospel," *BJRL* 53 (1970-1971): 253-71.

11442 F. F. Bruce, "Galatian Problems: 4. The Date of the, Epistle," *BJRL* 54/2 (1972): 250-67.

1:7

11443 Heikki Räisänen, "Galatians 2:16 and Paul's Break with Judaism," *NTS* 31 (1985): 543-53.

1:8

11444 Jerome H. Neyrey, "Bewitched in Galatia: Paul and Cultural Anthropology," *CBQ* 50 (1988): 72-100.

1:10-12

11445 Johan S. Vos, "Paul's Argumentation in Galatians 1-2," *HTR* 87 (1994): 1-16.

1:10

11446 André Feuillet, "Chercher à persuader Dieu (Ga 1:10a): le début de l'épître aux Galates et la scène matthéenne de Césarée de Philippe," *NovT* 12 (1970): 350-60.

11447 L. D. Hurst, "Re-enter the Pre-existent Christ in Philippians 2:5-11," *NTS* 32 (1986): 449-57.

11448 Michael Winger, "Unreal Conditions in the Letters of Paul," *JBL* 105 (1986): 110-12.

11449   B. J. Dodd, "Christ's Slave, People Pleasers and Galatians 1.10," *NTS* 42 (1996): 90-104.

1:11-2:21

11450   Christiane Dieterlé, "Être juste ou vivre," *FV* 84/5 (1985): 5-18.

11451   Donald J. Verseput, "Paul's Gentile Mission and the Jewish Christian Community: A Study of the Narrative in Galatians 1 and 2," *NTS* 39 (1993): 36-58.

1:11-2:14

11452   N. H. Taylor, "Paul's Apostolic Legitimacy: Autobiographical Reconstruction in Galatians 1:11-2:14," *JTSA* 83 (1993): 65-77.

11453   H. A. Brehm, "Paul's Relationship with the Jerusalem Apostles in Galatians 1 and 2," *SouJT* 37 (1994): 11-16.

1:11-20

11454   John T. Townsend, "Acts 9:1-29 and Early Church Tradition," *SBLSP* 27 (1988): 119-31.

1:11-17

11455   William Baird, "What Is the Kerygma? A Study of 1 Corinthians 15,3-8 and Galatians 1,11-17," *JBL* 76 (1957): 181-91.

11456   James L. Blevins, "Paul's Conflict with the Jerusalem Church," *BI* 10/4 (1984): 32-35.

11457   William Baird, "Visions, Revelation, and Ministry: Reflections on 2 Corinthians 12:1-5 and Galatians 1:11-17," *JBL* 104 (1985): 651-62.

11458   R. Y. K. Fung, "Revelation and Tradition: The Origins of Paul's Gospel," *EQ* 57 (1985): 23-41.

11459   Heikki Räisänen, "Paul's Conversion and the Development of His View of the Law," *NTS* 33 (1987): 404-19.

11460   Pieter F. Craffert, "Paul's Damascus Experience as Reflected in Galatians 1: Call or Conversion?" *ScrSA* (1989): 36-47.

11461   R. G. Hoerser, "Paul's Conversion/Call," *CJ* 22 (1996): 186-88.

1:11-12

11462 Knox Chamblin, "Revelation and Tradition in the Pauline Euangelion," *WTJ* 48 (1986): 1-16.

11463 Bernard C. Lategan, "Is Paul Defending his Apostleship in Galatians? The Function of Galatians 1:11-12 and 2:19-20 in the Development of Paul's Argument," *NTS* 34 (1988): 411-30.

1:12-2:14

11464 F. F. Bruce, "Galatian Problems: 1. Autobiographical Data," *BJRL* 11/2 (1969): 292-309.

1:12

11465 Marion L. Soards, "The Righteousness of God in the Writings of the Apostle Paul," *BTB* 15 (1985): 104-109.

1:13-2:14

11466 Benoît Standaert, "La rhétorique antique et l'épître aux galates," *FV* 84 (1985): 33-40.

11467 Paul E. Koptak, "Rhetorical Identification in Paul's Autobiographical Narrative: Galatians 1:13-2:14," *JSNT* 40 (1990): 97-113.

11468 Johan S. Vos, "Paul's Argumentation in Galatians 1-2," *HTR* 87 (1994): 1-16.

11469 Niels Hyldahl, "Gerechtigkeit durch Glauben. Historische und theologische Beobachtungen zum Galaterbrief," *NTS* 46 (2000): 425-44.

1:13-15

. 11470 Jan W. Doeve, "Paulus der Pharisäer und Galater 1:13-15," *NovT* 6 (1963): 170-81.

1:13-14

11471 F. F. Bruce, "Galatian Problems: 1. Autobiographical Data," *BJRL* 11/2 (1969): 292-309.

11472 William O. Walker, "Acts and the Pauline Corpus Reconsidered," *JSNT* 24 (1985): 3-23.

1:13

11473 F. F. Bruce, "The Church of Jerusalem in the Acts of the Apostles," *BJRL* 67 (1985): 641-61.

11474   Paula Fredriksen, "Paul and Augustine: Conversion Narratives, Orthodox Traditions, and the Retrospective Self," *JTS* NS 37 (1986): 3-34.

11475   Niels Hyldahl, "Gerechtigkeit durch Glauben. Historische und theologische Beobachtungen zum Galaterbrief," *NTS* 46 (2000): 425-44.

1:14

11476   P.-É. Bonnard, "Conversation biblique avec Jean Delumeau," *FV* 84 (1985): 77-81.

11477   Nicholas T. Wright, "Paul, Arabia, and Elijah," *JBL* 115 (1996): 683-92.

11478   Mark R. Fairchild, "Paul's Pre-Christian Zealot Associations: A Re-Examination of Galatians 1.14 and Acts 22.3," *NTS* 45 (1999): 514-32.

1:15-16

11479   François Refoulé, "Le parallèle Matthieu 16/16-17--Galates 1/15-16 réexaminé," *ÉTR* 67/2 (1992): 161-75.

1:15

11480   Ulrich Luck, "Die Bekehrung des Paulus und das paulinische Evangelium: zur Frage der Evidenz in Botschaft und Theologie des Apostels," *ZNW* 76 (1985): 187-208.

1:16

11481   Peter Hocken, "The Meaning and Purpose of 'Baptism in the Spirit'," *Pneuma* 7 (1985): 125-33.

11482   Marion L. Soards, "The Righteousness of God in the Writings of the Apostle Paul," *BTB* 15 (1985): 104-109.

11483   A. M. Artola, " 'Revelar en mi a su Hijo para que le anunciara': La dimensión inspiracional de la visión de Damasco," *EB* 50 (1992): 359-73.

11484   Michael Bachmann, "4QMMT und Galaterbrief התורה מעשי und ΕΡΓΑ ΝΟΜΟΥ," *ZNW* 89 (1998): 91-113.

1:17-18

11485   Jerome Murphy-O'Connor, "Ierosolgma/Ierogsalem in Galatians," *ZNW* 90 (1999): 280-81.

1:17

11486 William O. Walker, "Acts and the Pauline Corpus Reconsidered," *JSNT* 24 (1985): 3-23.

11487 Jerome Murphy-O'Connor, "Paul in Arabia," *CBQ* 55 (1993): 732-37.

11488 Johan S. Vos, "Paul's Argumentation in Galatians 1-2," *HTR* 87 (1994): 1-16.

11489 Nicholas T. Wright, "Paul, Arabia, and Elijah," *JBL* 115 (1996): 683-92.

1:18-20

11490 O. Bauernfeind, "Die Begegnung zwischen Paulus und Kephas Gal 1,18- 20," *ZNW* 47 (1956): 268-76.

11491 R. Trevijano Etcheverría, "Los primeros viajes de San Pablo a Jerusalén," *Salm* 42 (1995): 173-209.

11492 R. Trevijano Etcheverría, "El contrapunto lucano (Hch 9,26-30; 11,27-30; 12,25 y 15,1-35) a Gal 1,18-20 y 2,1-10," *Salm* 44 (1997): 295-39.

1:18-19

11493 A. Pénicaud, "Paul et l'autobiographie dans l'Épître aux Galates," *SémBib* 95 (1999): 3-20.

1:18

11494 O. Bauernfeind, "Die erste Begegnung zwischen Paulus und Kephas Gal. 1, 18," *TLZ* 81 (1956): 343-44.

11495 James D. G. Dunn, "Once More Gal 1:18," *ZNW* 76 (1985): 138-39.

11496 Nikolaus Walter, "Paulus und die urchristliche Jesustradition," *NTS* 31 (1985): 498-522.

11497 Paul J. Achtemeier, "An Elusive Unity: Paul, Acts, and the Early Church," *CBQ* 48 (1986): 1-26.

11498 E. J. Vardaman, "The Roman Census," *BI* 16/1 (1989): 70-73.

11499 Günther Schwarz, "Zum Wechsel von Kephas zu Petros in Gal 1 und 2," *BibN* 62 (1992): 46-50.

1:19

11500 H. Koch, "Zur Jakobusfrage Gal 1,19," *ZNW* 33 (1934): 204-209.

11501 L. Paul Trudinger, "A Note on Galatians i 19," *NovT* 17 (1975) 200-202.

11502 F. F. Bruce, "The Church of Jerusalem in the Acts of the Apostles," *BJRL* 67 (1985): 641-61.

1:21-24

11503 F. F. Bruce, "Galatian Problems: 1. Autobiographical Data," *BJRL* 11/2 (1969): 292-309.

1:21

11504 E. M. B. Green, "Syria and Cilicia," *ET* 71 (1959-1960): 52-53.

1:22

11505 F. F. Bruce, "The Church of Jerusalem in the Acts of the Apostles," *BJRL* 67 (1985): 641-61.

1:23

11506 E. Bammel, "Galater 1:23," *ZNW* 59 (1968): 108-12.

2

11507 Olof Linton, "The Third Aspect," *ST* 3 (1950-1951): 79-95.

11508 Pierson Parker, "Once More, Acts and Galatians," *JBL* 86/2 (1967): 175-82.

11509 C. K. Barrett, "Apostles in Council and in Conflict," *ABR* 31 (1983): 14-32.

11510 Geert Hallbäck, "Jerusalem og Antiokia i Gal 2: En historisk hypotese," *DTT* 53 (1990): 300-16.

2:1-14

11511 Traugott Holtz, "Die Bedeutung des Apolstelkonzils für Paulus," *NovT* (1974): 110-48.

11512 James D. Hester, "The Use and Influence of Rhetoric in Galatians 2:1-14," *TZ* 42 (1986): 386-408.

11513 Ralph P. Martin, "The Setting of 2 Corinthians," *TynB* 37 (1986): 3-19.

11514 Philip F. Esler, "Making and Breaking an Agreement Mediterranean Style: A New Reading of Galatians 2:1-14," *BibInt* 3 (1995): 285-314.

2:1-10

11515 Robert G. Hoerber, "Galatians 2:1-10 and the Acts of the Apostles," *CTM* 31 (1960): 482-91.

11516 Stanley D. Toussaint, "Chronological Problem of Galatians 2:1-10," *BSac* 120 (1963): 334-40.

11517 Robert H. Stein, "Relationship of Galatians 2:1-10 and Acts 15:1-35: Two Neglected Arguments," *JETS* 17 (1974): 239-42.

11518 David R. Catchpole, "Paul, James and the Apostolic Decree," *NTS* 23/4 (1976-1977): 428-44.

11519 Paul J. Achtemeier, "An Elusive Unity: Paul, Acts, and the Early Church," *CBQ* 48 (1986): 1-26.

11520 J. Morgado, "Paul in Jerusalem: A Comparison of His Visits in Acts and Galatians," *JETS* 37 (1994): 55-68.

11521 R. Trevijano Etcheverría, "Los primeros viajes de San Pablo a Jerusalén," *Salm* 42 (1995): 173-209.

11522 P. Rolin, "Pierre, Paul, Jacques à Jérusalem,"*FV* 96 (1997): 99-114.

11523 W. Schmithals, "Probleme des 'Apostelkonzils'," *HTS* 53 (1997): 6-35.

11524 R. Trevijano Etcheverría, "El contrapunto lucano (Hch 9,26-30; 11,27-30; 12,25 y 15,1-35) a Gal 1,18-20 y 2,1-10," *Salm* 44 (1997): 295-39.

11525 A. Pénicaud, "Paul et l'autobiographie dans l'Épître aux Galates," *SémBib* 95 (1999): 3-20.

2:1-5

11526 William O. Walker, "Why Paul Went to Jerusalem: The Interpretation of Galatians 2:1-5," *CBQ* 54 (1992): 503-10.

2:1

11527 Gert Haendler, "Cyprians Auslegung zu Galater 2:11ff," *TLZ* 97 (1972): 561-68.

11528 E. J. Vardaman, "The Roman Census," *BI* 16/1 (1989): 70-73.

11529 Jerome Murphy-O'Connor, "Ierosolgma/Ierogsalem in Galatians," *ZNW* 90 (1999): 280-81.

2:2-9

11530 W. Foerster, "Die dokountes in Gal 2," *ZNW* 36 (1937): 286-92.

11531 E. Heitsch, "Glossen zum Galaterbrief," *ZNW* 86 (1995): 173-88.

2:2

11532 J. D. M. Derrett, "Running in Paul: The Midrashic Potential of Hab 2:2," *Bib* 66 (1985): 560-67.

11533 E. Heitsch, "Glossen zum Galaterbrief," *ZNW* 86 (1995): 173-88.

2:3-5

11534 Bernard Orchard, "A Note on the Meaning of Galatians ii. 3-5," *JTS* 43 (1942): 173-77.

11535 Donald W. B. Robinson, "The Circumcision of Titus, and Paul's 'Liberty'," *ABR* 12 (1964): 24-42.

2:3-4

11536 Bernard Orchard, "Ellipsis between Galatians 2:3 and 2:4," *Bib* 54 (1973): 469-81.

11537 A. C. M. Blommerde, "Is There an Ellipsis between Galatians 2,3 and 2,4?" *Bib* 56 (1975): 100-102.

2:4

11538 C. H. Roberts, "A Note on Galatians ii 4," *JTS* 40 (1939): 55-56.

11539 John N. Suggit, "The Right Hand of Fellowship," *JTSA* 49 (1984): 51-54.

2:6

11540 K. Heussi, "Galater 2 und der Lebensausgang der jerusalemischen Urapostel," *TLZ* 77 (1952): 67-72.

11541 Kurt Aland, "Wann starb Petrus?" *NTS* 2 (1955-1956): 267-75.

11542 David M. Hay, "Paul's Indifference to Authority," *JBL* 88 (1969): 36-44.

2:6-10

11543 Victor M. Fernández, "Santiago, la plenificación cristiana de la espiritualidad postexilica," *RevB* 53 (1991): 29-33.

2:6-9

11544 Günter Klein, "Galater 2:6-9 und die Geschichte der Jerusalemer Urgemeinde," *ZTK* 57 (1960): 275-95.

2:6

11545 James L. Jaquette, "Paul, Epictetus, and Others on Indifference to Status," *CBQ* 56 (1994): 68-80.

2:7-14

11546 Rinaldo Fabris, "San Pietro apostolo nella prima chiesa," *SM* 35 (1986): 41-70.

2:7-9

11547 . Bradley H. McLean, "Galatians 2:7-9 and the Recognition of Paul's Apostolic Status at the Jerusalem Conference," *NTS* 37 (1991): 67-76.

11548 Paul S. Berge, "Peter and Cephas and Paul: God's Apostolate and Mission in Galatians 2:7-9," *WW* Suppl 1 (1992): 127-37.

11549 Michael Bachmann, "4QMMT und Galaterbrief התורה מעשי und ΕΡΓΑ ΝΟΜΟΥ," *ZNW* 89 (1998): 91-113.

2:7-8

11550 Andreas Schmidt, "Das Missionsdekret in Galater 2:7-8 als Vereinbarung vom ersten Besuch Pauli in Jerusalem," *NTS* 38 (1992): 149-52.

2:9

11551 R. Annand, "Note on the Three 'Pillars' (Galatians ii. 9)," *ET* 67 (1955-1956): 178.

11552 John N. Suggit, "The Right Hand of Fellowship," *JTSA* 49 (1984): 51-54.

11553 A. J. Conyers, "James: A Pillar of the Church," *BI* 15/1 (1988): 22-25.

11554 Günther Schwarz, "Zum Wechsel von Kephas zu Petros in Gal 1 und 2," *BibN* 62 (1992): 46-50.

11555   David Wenham and A. D. A. Moses, " 'There Are Some Standing Here . . .': Did They Become the 'Reputed Pillars' of the Jerusalem Church? Some Reflections on Mark 9:1, Galatians 2:9 and the Transfiguration," *NovT* 36 (1994): 146-63.

2:10

11556   Leander E. Keck, "The Poor among the Saints in the New Testament," *ZNW* 56 (1965): 100-29.

11557   Dietfried Gewalt, "Neutestamentliche Exegese und Soziologie," *EvT* 31 (1971): 87-99

11558   David R. Hall, "St Paul and Famine Relief: A Study in Galatians 2:10," *ET* 82 (1971): 309-11.

11559   Niels Hyldahl, "Gerechtigkeit durch Glauben. Historische und theologische Beobachtungen zum Galaterbrief," *NTS* 46 (2000): 425-44.

2:11-21

11560   Markus Barth, "Jew and Gentile; White Man and Negro: An Exegesis of Galatians 2:11-21," *Kata* 1 (1965): 27-31.

11561   Markus Barth, "Justification," *Int* 22 (1968): 147-57.

11562   J. F. M. Smit, "Hoe kun je de heidenen verplichten als Joden te leven: Paulus en de torah in Galaten 2:11-21," *Bij* 46 (1985): 118-40.

11563   Bengt Holmberg, "Sociologiska perspektiv pa Gal 2:11-14," *SEÅ* 55 (1990): 71-92.

11564   Paul C. Böttger, "Paulus und Petrus in Antiochien: zum Verständnis von Galater 2:11-21," *NTS* 37 (1991): 77-100.

11565   Eduard Lohse, "St. Peter's Apostleship in the Judgment of St. Paul, the Apostle to the Gentiles: An Exegetical Contribution to an Ecumenical Debate," *Greg* 72 (1991): 419-35.

11566   A. Pénicaud, "Paul et l'autobiographie dans l'Épître aux Galates," *SémBib* 95 (1999): 3-20.

2:11-17

11567   James D. G. Dunn, "Echoes of Intra-Jewish Polemic in Paul's Letter to the Galatians," *JBL* 112 (1993): 459-77.

2:11-16

11568 V. Jegher-Bucher, "Formgeschichtliche Betrachtung zu Galater 2,11-16," *TZ* 46 (1990): 305-21.

2:11-14

11569 Inge Lönning, "Paulus und Petrus," *ST* 24 (1970): 1-69.

11570 Gerhard Schneider, "Contestation dans le Nouveau Testament," *Conci* 68 (1971): 83-89.

11571 Traugott Holtz, "Der antiochenische Zwischenfall," *NTS* 32 (1986): 344-61.

11572 Peter S. Cameron, "An Exercise in Translation: Galatians 2:11-14," *BT* 40 (1989): 135-45.

2:11

11573 M. V. Abraham, "Diakonia in the Early Letters of Paul," *IJT* 32 (1983): 61-67.

11574 E. J. Vardaman, "Antioch of Syria," *BI* 14/1 (1987): 22-26.

11575 Günther Schwarz, "Zum Wechsel von Kephas zu Petros in Gal 1 und 2," *BibN* 62 (1992): 46-50.

2:12

11576 James D. G. Dunn, "4QMMT and Galatians: Galatians 2:12, 2:16, 3:6, 4:10, 6:16," *NTS* 43 (1997): 147-53.

11577 Norman H. Young, "Who's Cursed and Why?" *JBL* 117 (1998): 79-92.

2:13

11578 E. P. Sanders, "Judaism and the Grand 'Christian' Abstractions: Love, Mercy, and Grace," *Int* 39 (1985): 357-72.

11579 D. Sänger, "'Verflucht ist jeder, der am Holze hängt' (Gal 3,13b). Zur Rezeption einer früben antichristlichen Polemik," *ZNW* 85 (1994): 279-85.

2:14-21

11580 Louis Panier, "Pour une approche sémiotique de l'épître aux Galates," *FV* 84 (1985): 19-32.

2:14

11581   Franz Mußner, "Gesetz - Abraham - Israel," *K* 25 (1983): 200-22.

11582   Günther Schwarz, "Zum Wechsel von Kephas zu Petros in Gal 1 und 2," *BibN* 62 (1992): 46-50.

2:15-3:22

11583   David E. Garland, "Paul's Defense of the Truth of the Gospel Regarding Gentiles," *RevExp* 91 (1994): 165-81.

11584   F. Martin, "La Loi dans l'Épître aux Galates: Essai l'interprétation," *SémBib* 95 (1999): 21-29.

2:15-21

11585   Günter Klein, "Individualgeschichte und Weltgeschichte bei Paulus: Eine Interpretation ihres Verhältnisses im Galaterbrief," *EvT* 24 (1964): 126-65.

11586   Victor Hasler, "Glaube und Existenz: hermeneutische Erwägungen zu Gal 2:15-21," *TZ* 25 (1969): 241-51.

11587   H. Feld, " 'Christus Diener der Sünde:' Zum Ausgang des Streites zwischen Petrus und Paulus," *TQ* 153 (1973): 119-31.

11588   Christiane Dieterlé, "Être juste ou vivre," *FV* 84/5 (1985): 5-18.

11589   Benoît Standaert, "La rhétorique antique et l'épître aux galates," *FV* 84 (1985): 33-40.

11590   Pheme Perkins, "Not through the Law," *CC* 106 (1989): 587.

11591   Samuel Vollenweider, "Grosser Tod und grosses Leben: ein Beitrag zum buddhistisch-christlichen Gespräch im Blick auf die Mystik des Paulus," *EvT* 51 (1991): 365-82.

11592   J. Fairweather, "The Epistle to the Galatians and Classical Rhetoric: Parts 1 & 2," *TynB* 45 (1994): 1-38.

11593   Jack Albright, "Stand Firm in Freedom: Summer Lections from Galatians," *QR* 15 (1995): 89-106.

2:15-17

11594   E. Heitsch, "Glossen zum Galaterbrief," *ZNW* 86 (1995): 173-88.

2:16-21

11595 H.-J. Iwand, "Predigt über Galater 2,16-21," *EvT* 14 (1954): 289-97.

2:16

11596 Heikki Räisänen, "Galatians 2:16 and Paul's Break with Judaism," *NTS* 31 (1985): 543-53.

11597 R. Trevijano Etcheverría, "La mision en Tesalonica (1 Tes 1:1-2,16)," *Salm* 32 (1985): 263-91.

11598 Charles H. Cosgrove, "Justification in Paul: A Linguistic and Theological Reflection," *JBL* 106 (1987): 653-70.

11599 James D. G. Dunn, "Once More, πίστις χριστοῦ," *SBLSP* 30 (1991): 730-44.

11600 Nikolaus Walter, "Gottes Erbarmen mit 'allem Fleisch' (Röm 3:20/Gal 2:16): ein 'femininer' Zug im paulinischen Gottesbild?" *BZ* NS 35 (1991): 99-102.

11601 James D. G. Dunn, "4QMMT and Galatians: Galatians 2:12, 2:16, 3:6, 4:10, 6:16," *NTS* 43 (1997): 147-53.

11602 William O. Walker, "Translation and Interpretation of ἐὰν μὴ in Galatians 2:16," *JBL* 116 (1997): 515-20.

11603 Michael Bachmann, "4QMMT und Galaterbrief התורה מעשי und ΕΡΓΑ ΝΟΜΟΥ," *ZNW* 89 (1998): 91-113.

11604 A. A. Das, "Another Look at GREEKp.73 in Galatians 2:16," *JBL* 119 (2000): 529-39.

2:17-18

11605 Jan Lambrecht, "Once again Galatians 2:17-18 and 3:21," *ETL* 63 (1987): 148-53.

11606 Don B. Garlington, "Role Reversal and Paul's Use of Scripture in Galatians 3:10-13," *JSNT* 65 (1997): 85-121.

2:17

11607 Guy Wagner, "Le Repas du Seigneur et la justification par la foi: exégèse de Galates 2:17," *ÉTR* 36 (1981): 245-54.

11608 Robert G. Hamerton-Kelly, "Sacred Violence and 'Works of Law': 'Is Christ then an Agent of Sin'?" *CBQ* 52 (1990): 55-75.

2:18-21

11609   Jan Lambrecht, "Transgressor by Nullifying God's Grace: A Study of Galatians 2:18-21," *Bib* 72 (1991): 217-36.

2:18

11610   Norman H. Young, "Who's Cursed and Why?" *JBL* 117 (1998): 79-92.

2:19-31

11611   Ole Modalsli, "Gal 2:19-21; 5:16-18 und Rom 7:7-25," *TZ* 21 (1965): 22-37.

2:19-20

11612   Bernard C. Lategan, "Is Paul Defending His Apostleship in Galatians? The Function of Galatians 1:11-12 and 2:19-20 in the Development of Paul's Argument," *NTS* 34 (1988): 411-30.

2:19

11613   Jos Janssens, "Il cristiano di fronte al martirio imminente: testimonianze e dottrina nella chiesa antica," *Greg* 66 (1985): 405-27.

11614   Silverio Zedda, "Morto alla legge mediante la legge: testo autobiografico sulla conversione di San Paolo?" *RivBib* 37 (1989): 81-95.

11615   E. Heitsch, "Glossen zum Galaterbrief," *ZNW* 86 (1995): 173-88.

2:20

11616   Traian Valdman, "Uno sguardo ortodosso sulla giustificazione in Lutero," *SEcu* 1 (1983): 277-88.

11617   Georges Chantraine, "Prayer within the Church," *CICR* 12 (1985): 258-75.

11618   Frank Chikane, "The Incarnation in the Life of the People in Southern Africa," *JTSA* 51 (1985): 37-50.

11619   John D. Laurence, "The Eucharist as the Imitation of Christ," *TS* 47/2 (1986): 286-96.

11620   James D. G. Dunn, "Once More, πίστις χριστοῦ," *SBLSP* 30 (1991): 730-44.

11621 R. B. Hays, "Pistis and Pauline Christology: What Is at Stake?" *SBLSP* 30 (1991): 714-29.

11622 J. G. Janzen, "Coleridge and πίστις χριστοῦ," *ET* 107 (1996): 265-68.

2:21

11623 Eckart Reinmuth, "Nicht vergeblich bei Paulus und Pseudo-Philo, Liber antiquitatum biblicarum," *NovT* 33 (1991): 97-123.

3:1-5:12

11624 Otto Merk, "Der Beginn der Paränese im Galaterbrief," *ZNW* 60 (1969): 83-104.

3-4

11625 Günther Baumbach, "Antijudaismus im Neuen Testament: Fragestellung und Lösungsmöglichkeit," *K* 25 (1983): 68-85.

11626 François Vouga, "La construction de l'histoire en Galates 3-4," *ZNW* 75 (1984): 259-69.

11627 Bruce Corley, "Reasoning 'By Faith': Whys and Wherefores of the Law in Galatians," *SouJT* 37 (1994): 17-22.

3:1-4:31

11628 Günter Klein, "Individualgeschichte und Weltgeschichte bei Paulus: Eine Interpretation ihres Verhältnisses im Galaterbrief," *EvT* 24 (1964): 126-65.

11629 L. L. Cranford, "A Rhetorical Reading of Galatians," *SouJT* 37 (1994): 410.

3:1-4:7

11630 Michael Bachmann, "4QMMT und Galaterbrief התורה מעשי und ΕΡΓΑ ΝΟΜΟΥ," *ZNW* 89 (1998): 91-113.

3

11631 J. Dwight Pentecost, "Purpose of the Law," *BSac* 128 (1971): 227-33.

11632 B. Geoncet, "Galates III," *SémBib* 76 (1994): 49-59.

11633 R. A. Pyne, "The 'Seed,' the Spirit, and the Blessing of Abraham," *BSac* 152 (1995): 211-22.

3:1-29

11634   Charles H. Talbert, "Paul on the Covenant," *RevExp* 84 (1987): 299-313.

3:1-18

11635   Tom Thatcher, "The Plot of Galatians 3:1-18," *JETS* 40 (1997): 401-10.

3:1-15

11636   Ernst Baasland, "Persecution: A Neglected Feature in the Letter to the Galatians," *StTheol* 38 (1984): 135-50.

3:1-14

11637   In-Gyu Hong, "The Perspective of Paul in Galatians," *Scr* 36 (1991): 1-16.

11638   In-Gyu Hong, "Does Paul Misrepresent the Jewish Law? Law and Covenant in Galatians 3:1-14," *NovT* 36 (1994): 164-82.

3:1-5

11639   Christiane Dieterlé, "Être juste ou vivre," *FV* 84/5 (1985): 5-18.

11640   John F. Johnson, "Paul's Argument from Experience: A Closer Look at Galatians 3:1-5," *CJ* 19 (1993): 234-37.

11641   Niels Hyldahl, "Gerechtigkeit durch Glauben. Historische und theologische Beobachtungen zum Galaterbrief," *NTS* 46 (2000): 425-44.

3:1

11642   P. G. Bretscher, "Light from Galatians 3:1 on Pauline Theology," *CTM* 34 (1963): 77-97.

11643   James D. G. Dunn, "Works of the Law and the Curse of the Law," *NTS* 31 (1985): 523-42.

11644   John D. Laurence, "The Eucharist as the Imitation of Christ," *TS* 47/2 (1986): 286-96.

11645   Jerome H. Neyrey, "Bewitched in Galatia: Paul and Cultural Anthropology," *CBQ* 50 (1988): 72-100.

11646   Basil S. Davis, "The Meaning of Proegraphe in the Context of Galatians 3.1," *NTS* 45 (1999): 194-212.

3:2

11647 Sam K. Williams, "The Hearing of Faith: ἀκοῆς πίστεως in Galatians 3," *NTS* 35 (1989): 82-93.

11648 Michael Bachmann, "4QMMT und Galaterbrief התורה מעשי und ΕΡΓΑ ΝΟΜΟΥ," *ZNW* 89 (1998): 91-113.

3:5

11649 J. K. Parratt, "Laying on of Hands in Paul," *ET* 79 (1967-1968): 151-52.

11650 J. K. Parratt, "Romans 1:11 and Galatians 3:5: Pauline Evidence for the Laying on of Hands?" *ET* 79 (1968): 151-52.

11651 A. O. Igenoza, "African Weltanschauung and Exorcism: The Quest for the Contextualization of the Kerygma," *AfTJ* 14/3 (1985): 179-93.

11652 Sam K. Williams, "The Hearing of Faith: ἀκοῆς πίστεως in Galatians 3," *NTS* 35 (1989): 82-93.

11653 Michael Bachmann, "4QMMT und Galaterbrief התורה מעשי und ΕΡΓΑ ΝΟΜΟΥ," *ZNW* 89 (1998): 91-113.

3:6-29

11654 F. Martin, "La Loi dans l'Épître aux Galates: Essai l'interprétation," *SémBib* 95 (1999): 21-29.

3:6-14

11655 Benoît Standaert, "La rhétorique antique et l'épître aux galates," *FV* 84 (1985): 33-40.

3:6-9

11656 H. Wayne Johnson, "The Paradigm of Abraham in Galatians 3:6-9," *TriJ* 8 (1987): 179-99.

11657 E. Heitsch, "Glossen zum Galaterbrief," *ZNW* 86 (1995): 173-88.

3:6

11658 Franz Mußner, "Gesetz - Abraham - Israel," *K* 25 (1983): 200-22.

11659 James D. G. Dunn, "4QMMT and Galatians: Galatians 2:12, 2:16, 3:6, 4:10, 6:16," *NTS* 43 (1997): 147-53.

3:7

> 11660   Norman H. Young, "Who's Cursed and Why?" *JBL* 117 (1998): 79-92.

3:8-14

> 11661   Thomas R. Schreiner, "Paul and Perfect Obedience to the Law: An Evaluation of the View of E. P. Sanders," *WTJ* 47/2 (1985): 245-78.

3:8

> 11662   A. J. M. Wedderburn, "Some Observations on Paul's Use of the Phrases 'in Christ' and 'with Christ'," *JSNT* 25 (1985): 83-97.

> 11663   Michael Bachmann, "4QMMT und Galaterbrief התורה מעשי und ΕΡΓΑ ΝΟΜΟΥ," *ZNW* 89 (1998): 91-113.

3:10-4:7

> 11664   Daniel Boyarin, "Was Paul an 'Anti-Semite'? A Reading of Galatians 3-4," *USQR* 47 (1993): 47-80.

3:10-22

> 11665   F. Martin, "La Loi dans l'Épître aux Galates: Essai l'interprétation," *SémBib* 95 (1999): 21-29.

3:10-14

> 11666   James D. G. Dunn, "Works of the Law and the Curse of the Law," *NTS* 31 (1985): 523-42.

> 11667   Christopher D. Stanley, "Under a Curse: A Fresh Reading of Galatians 3:10-14," *NTS* 36 (1990): 481-511.

> 11668   Normand Bonneau, "The Logic of Paul's Argument on the Curse of the Law in Galatians 3:10-14," *NovT* 39 (1997): 60-80.

> 11669   Norman H. Young, "Who's Cursed and Why?" *JBL* 117 (1998): 79-92.

3:10-13

> 11670   Christophe Senft, "Paul et Jésus," *FV* 84 (1985): 49-56.

> 11671   Joseph P. Braswell, "The Blessing of Abraham Versus 'the Curse of the Law': Another Look at Galatians 3:10-13," *WTJ* 53 (1991): 73-91.

11672 Don B. Garlington, "Role Reversal and Paul's Use of Scripture in Galatians 3:10-13," *JSNT* 65 (1997): 85-121.

3:10-12

11673 R. Bring, "Die Erfüllung des Gesetzes durch Christus," *KD* 5 (1959): 1-22.

11674 Wayne G. Strickland, "Preunderstanding and Daniel Fuller's Law-Gospel Continuum," *BSac* 144 (1987): 181-93.

11675 E. Heitsch, "Glossen zum Galaterbrief," *ZNW* 86 (1995): 173-88.

3:10

11676 Hans Hübner, "Galatians 3:10 und die Herkunft des Paulus," *KD* 19 (1973): 215-31.

11677 Thomas R. Schreiner, "Is Perfect Obedience to the Law Possible: A Re-examination of Galatians 3:10," *JETS* 27 (1984): 151-60.

11678 Mark W. Karlberg, "Legitimate Discontinuities between the Testaments," *JETS* 28 (1985): 9-20.

11679 Thomas R. Schreiner, "Paul and Perfect Obedience to the Law: An Evaluation of the View of E. P. Sanders," *WTJ* 47/2 (1985): 245-78.

11680 Michael Cranford, "The Possibility of Perfect Obedience: Paul and an Implied Premise in Galatians 3:10 and 5:3," *NovT* 36 (1994): 242-58.

11681 Michael Bachmann, "4QMMT und Galaterbrief התורה מעשי und ΕΡΓΑ ΝΟΜΟΥ," *ZNW* 89 (1998): 91-113.

11682 Norman H. Young, "Who's Cursed and Why?" *JBL* 117 (1998): 79-92.

3:11-12

11683 François Refoulé, "Romains, 10:4: encore une fois," *RB* 91 (1984): 321-50.

11684 Johan S. Vos, "Die hermeneutische Antinomie bei Paulus," *NTS* 38 (1992): 254-70.

3:11

11685 H. Manse, "Dēlon: Zu Gal 3:11," *ZNW* 34 (1935): 299-303.

11686   Dietrich A. Koch, "Der Text von Hab 2:4b in der Septuaginta und im Neuen Testament," *ZNW* 76 (1985): 68-85.

3:12

11687   Alain Gignac, "Citation de Lévitique 18,5 en Romains 10,5 et Galates 3,12: Deux lectures différentes des rapports Christ-Torah?" *ÉgT* 25 (1994): 367-403.

3:13-14

11688   Terence L. Donaldson, "The 'Curse of the Law' and the Inclusion of the Gentiles. Galatians 3:13-14," *NTS* 32 (1986): 94-112.

3:13

11689   Morna D. Hooker, "Interchange in Christ," *JTS* NS 22 (1971): 349-61.

11690   Traian Valdman, "Uno sguardo ortodosso sulla giustificazione in Lutero," *SEcu* 1 (1983): 277-88.

11691   V. P. Branick, "Apocalyptic Paul?" *CBQ* 47 (1985): 664-75.

11692   Ardel Caneday, "Redeemed from the Curse of the Law: The Use of Deuteronomy 21:22-23 in Galatians 3:13," *TriJ* 10 (1989): 185-209.

11693   Robert G. Hamerton-Kelly, "Sacred Violence and the Curse of the Law: The Death of Christ as a Sacrificial Travesty," *NTS* 36 (1990): 98-118.

11694   Bradley H. McLean, "Christ as a Pharmakos in Pauline Soteriology," *SBLSP* 30 (1991): 187-206.3:22

3:15-29

11695   Charles H. Giblin, "Three Monotheistic Texts in Paul," *CBQ* 37 (1975): 527-47.

3:15-22

11696   F. Martin, "La Loi dans l'Épître aux Galates: Essai l'interprétation," *SémBib* 95 (1999): 21-29.

3:15-18

11697   Charles H. Cosgrove, "Arguing Like a Mere Human Being: Galatians 3:15-18 in Rhetorical Perspective," *NTS* 34 (1988): 536-49.

3:15-17

11698 E. Bammel, "Gottes διαθήκη und das jüdische Rechts-
denken," *NTS* 6 (1959-1960) 313-19.

3:15

11699 Joachim Jeremias, "OMOS," *ZNW* (1961): 127-28.

3:17-25

11700 Robert P. Lightner, "Theological Perspectives on
Theonomy; pt 3: A Dispensational Response to
Theonomy," *BSac* 143 (1986): 228-45.

3:17

11701 Jack R. Riggs, "The Length of Israel's Sojourn in Egypt,"
GTJ 12/1 (1971): 18-35.

11702 James R. Battenfield, "A Consideration of the Identity of
the Pharaoh of Genesis 47," *JETS* 15 (1972): 77-85.

3:19-25

11703 David J. Lull, "The Law Was Our Pedagogue: A Study in
Galatians 3:19-25," *JBL* 105 (1986): 481-98.

3:19-20

11704 Daniel B. Wallace, "Galatians 3:19-20: A Crux
Interpretum for Paul's View of the Law," *WTJ* 52 (1990):
225-45.

3:19

11705 Andrew J. Bandstra, "The Law and Angels: Antiquities
15.136 and Galatians 3:19," *CTJ* 24 (1989): 223-40.

3:20

11706 R. Bring, "Der Mittler und das Gesetz," *KD* 12 (1966):
292-309.

11707 Ulrich W. Mauser, "Galater 3:20: die Universalität des
Heils," *NTS* 13 (1967): 258-70.

11708 M. Pérez Fernández, "El numeral ehis en Pablo como
título cristológico," *EB* NS 41 (1983): 325-40.

11709 Michael Bachmann, "4QMMT und Galaterbrief התורה
מעשי und ΕΡΓΑ ΝΟΜΟΥ," *ZNW* 89 (1998): 91-113.

3:21-4:11

11710 L. L. Belleville, " 'Under Law'. Structural Analysis and the Pauline Concept of Law in Galatians 3:21-4:11," *JSNT* 26 (1986): 53-78.

3:21

11711 Michael Winger, "Unreal Conditions in the Letters of Paul," *JBL* 105 (1986): 110-12.

11712 Jan Lambrecht, "Once again Galatians 2:17-18 and 3:21," *ETL* 63 (1987): 148-53.

11713 François Refoulé, "Romains, 10:4: encore une fois," *RB* 91 (1984): 321-50.

3:22-25

11714 Jean Calloud, " 'Humanité. . . Vous avez dit: Humanité'!. . ." *SémBib* 98 (2000): 31-49.

3:22

11715 James D. G. Dunn, "Once More, πίστις χριστοῦ," *SBLSP* 30 (1991): 730-44.

11716 R. B. Hays, "πίστις and Pauline Christology: What Is at Stake?" *SBLSP* 30 (1991): 714-29.

3:23-4:5

11717 Joseph Moingt, "Prêtre 'selon le Nouveau Testament': à propos d'un livre récent *RechSR* 69 (1981): 573-98.

3:23-29

11718 H. Hesse, "Predigt über Galater 3,23-29," *EvT* 3 (1936): 289-96.

11719 V. P. Branick, "Apocalyptic Paul?" *CBQ* 47 (1985): 664-75.

11720 Gerald L. Borchert, "A Key to Pauline Thinking: Galatians 3:23-29: Faith and the New Humanity," *RevExp* 91 (1994): 145-51.

11721 Jack Albright, "Stand Firm in Freedom: Summer Lections from Galatians," *QR* 15 (1995): 89-106.

3:23-25

11722 J. Louis Martyn, "The Apocalyptic Gospel in Galatians," *Int* 54 (2000): 246-66.

3:23

11723 Dieter Lührmann, "Confesser sa foi à l'époque apostolique," *RTP* 117 (1985): 93-110.

3:24-25

11724 John Fischer, "Paul in His Jewish Context," *EQ* 57 (1985): 211-36.

11725 T. David Gordon, "A Note on παιδαγωγός in Galatians 3:24-25," *NTS* 35 (1989): 150-54.

3:24

11726 Erdmann Schott, "Lex paedagogus noster fuit in Christo Jesu (Vulgata): zu Luthers Auslegung von Gal 3:24," *TLZ* 95 (1970): 561-70.

11727 Norman H. Young, "Paidagogos: The Social Setting of a Pauline Metaphor," *NovT* 29 (1987): 150-76.

11728 A. T. Hanson, "The Origin of Paul's Use of παιδαγωγός for the Law," *JSNT* 34 (1988): 71-76.

3:26-4:7

11729 Jean Calloud, " 'Humanité. . . Vous avez dit: Humanité'!. . ." *SémBib* 98 (2000): 31-49.

3:26-29

11730 Joseph M. Pathrapankal, "Faith and Conversion: A Study in the Context of the Covenantal Significance of Baptism," *IJT* 16 (1967): 166-79.

11731 Roman Heiligenthal, "Soziologische Implikationen der paulinischen Rechtfertigungslehre im Galaterbrief am Beispiel der 'Werke des Gesetzes'," *K* 26 (1984): 38-53.

11732 Sheila E. McGinn, "Galatians 3:26-29 and the Politics of the Spirit," *EGLMBS* 13 (1993): 89-101.

11733 Ben Wiebe, "Two Texts on Women: A Test of Interpretation," *HBT* 16 (1994): 54-85.

11734 Michael Bachmann, "4QMMT und Galaterbrief התורה מעשי und ΕΡΓΑ ΝΟΜΟΥ," *ZNW* 89 (1998): 91-113.

3:26-27

11735 Simon Légasse, "Foi et baptême chez saint Paul's Etude de Galates 3,26-27," *BLE* 74 (1973): 81-102.

3:27-28

11736 Walter H. Principe, "The Dignity and Rights of the Human Person as Saved, as Being Saved, as to Be Saved by Christ," *Greg* 65 (1984): 389-430.

11737 J. Louis Martyn, "Apocalyptic Antinomies in Paul's Letter to the Galatians," *NTS* 31 (1985): 410-24.

11738 Wanda Deifelt, "Os tortuosos caminhos de Deus: Igreja e homossexualidade," *EstT* 39 (1999): 36-48.

3:27

11739 Norman H. Young, "Who's Cursed and Why?" *JBL* 117 (1998): 79-92.

3:28-29

11740 Stanley E. Porter, "Wittgenstein's Classes of Utterances and Pauline Ethical Texts," *JETS* 32 (1989): 85-97.

3:28

11741 J. J. Buckley, "An Interpretation of Logion 114 in the Gospel of Thomas," *NovT* 27 (1985): 245-72.

11742 LeRoy S. Capper, "The Imago Dei and Its Implications for Order in the Church," *Pres* 11 (1985): 21-33.

11743 Leonidas Kalugila, "Women in the Ministry of Priesthood in the Early Church: An Inquiry," *AfTJ* 14 (1985): 35-45.

11744 Daniel Marguerat, "Paul: un génie théologique et ses limites," *FV* 84 (1985): 65-76.

11745 Richard I. Pervo, "Wisdom and Power: Petronius' Satyricon and the Social World of Early Christianity," *ATR* 67 (1985): 307-25.

11746 Jean Y. Thériault, "La femme chrétienne dans les textes pauliniens," *ScE* 37 (1985): 297-317.

11747 Joyce Hollyday, "Voices out of the Silence: Recovering the Biblical Witness of Women," *Soj* 15 (1986): 20-23.

11748 H. Wayne House, "A Biblical View of Women in the Ministry," *BSac* 145 (1988): 47-56; 141-61; 301-18; 387-99.

11749 Lone Fatum, "Women, Symbolic Universe and Structures of Silence: Challenges and Possibilities in Androcentric Texts," *StTheol* 43 (1989): 61-80.

11750	Thomas Hopko, "Galatians 3:28: An Orthodox Interpretation," *SVTQ* 35 (1991): 169-86.

11751	Stephen D. Lowe, "Rethinking the Female Status/Function Question: The Jew/Gentile Relationship as Paradigm," *JETS* 34 (1991): 59-75.

11752	Wolfgang Stegemann, "Zu ihrem Gedächtnis . . . eine feministisch-theologische Rekonstruktion der christlichen Ursprünge," *EvT* 51 (1991): 383-95.

11753	Wayne Litke, "Beyond Creation: Galatians 3:28, Genesis and the Hermaphrodite Myth," *SR* 24 (1995): 173-78.

11754	F. Gerald Downing, "A Cynic Preparation for Paul's Gospel for Jew and Greek, Slave and Free, Male and Female," *NTS* 42 (1996): 454-62.

11755	Christopher D. Stanley, " 'Neither Jew nor Greek': Ethnic Conflict in Graeco-Roman Society," *JSNT* 64 (1996): 101-24.

11756	G. Rohser, "Mann und Frau in Christus. Eine Verhältnisbestimmung von Gal 3,28 und 1 Kor 11,2-16," *SNTU-A* 22 (1997): 57-78.

3:38

11757	Madeleine Boucher, "Some Unexplored Parallels to 1 Corinthains 11:11-12 and Galatians 3:28: The News Testament on the Role of Women," *CBQ* 31 (1969): 50-58.

4-6

11758	Morna D. Hooker, "Interchange in Christ and Ethics," *JSNT* 25 (1985): 3-17.

4:1-11

11759	Bo Reicke, "The Law and This World According to Paul," *JBL* 70 (1951): 259-76.

4:1-9

11760	Derek R. Moore-Crispin, "Galatians 4:1-9: The Use and Abuse of Parallels," *EQ* 61 (1989): 203-23.

4:1-7

11761	W. M. Calder, "Adoption and Inheritance in Galatia," *JTS* 31 (1930): 372-73.

11762   H. Diem, "Weihnachtspredigt über Gal. 4,1-7," *EvT* 1 (1934-1935): 327-33.

11763   A. Marcello Buscemi, "Gal 4:12-20: un argomento di amicizia," *SBFLA* 34 (1984): 67-108.

11764   V. P. Branick, "Apocalyptic Paul?" *CBQ* 47 (1985): 664-75.

4:1

11765   C. Kenny Cooper, "Ancient Inheritance Practices," *BI* 14/1 (1987): 80-83.

4:2

11766   Traian Valdman, "Uno sguardo ortodosso sulla giustificazione in Lutero," *SEcu* 1 (1983): 277-88.

11767   Georges Chantraine, "Prayer within the Church," *CICR* 12 (1985): 258-75.

4:3-11

11768   T. C. G. Thornton, "Jewish New Moon Festivals, Galatians 4:3-11 and Colossians 2:16," *JTS* NS 40 (1989): 97-100.

4:3

11769   Eduard Schweizer, "Slaves of the Elements and Worshipers of Angels: Galatians 4:3, 9 and Colossians 2:8, 18, 20," *JBL* 107 (1988): 455-68.

11770   David R. Bundrick, "τὰ στοιχεῖα τοῦ κόσμου (Gal 4:3)," *JETS* 34 (1991): 353-64.

11771   Dietrich Rusam, "Neue Belege zu den στοιχεῖα τοῦ κόσμου (Gal 4,3.9; Kol 2,8.20)," *ZNW* 83 (1992): 119-25

11772   Wayne E. Oates, "A Biblical Perspective on Addiction," *RevExp* 91 (1994): 71-75.

11773   Clinton E. Arnold, "Returning to the Domain of the Powers: στοιχεῖα as Evil Spirits in Galatians 4:3,9," *NovT* 38 (1996): 55-76.

4:4-7

11774   Augustin George, "La venue du Fils nous fait fibres, et fils," *AsSeign* 11 (1971): 60-65.

11775 G. Daan Cloete, "Christmas: Heirs of God, the Father, through Jesus, the Son, Incarnated," *JTSA* 85 (1993): 53-60.

<u>4:4-6</u>

11776 P. K. Walker, "A Meditation on Galatians 4:4-6," *Theology* 63 (1960): 150-52.

11777 J. Louis Martyn, "The Apocalyptic Gospel in Galatians," *Int* 54 (2000): 246-66.

<u>4:4-5</u>

11778 Christophe Senft, "Paul et Jésus," *FV* 84 (1985): 49-56.

<u>4:4</u>

11779 Eduard Schweizer, "Zum religionsgeschichtlichen Hintergrund der Sendungsformel," *ZNW* 57 (1966): 199-210.

11780 William E. Hull, "The Fullness of Time," *BI* 1/1 (1974): 54-58.

11781 Richard Gist, "The Fullness of Time," *BI* 14/1 (1987): 30-33.

11782 Michael Bachmann, "4QMMT und Galaterbrief התורה מעשי und ΕΡΓΑ ΝΟΜΟΥ," *ZNW* 89 (1998): 91-113.

<u>4:5</u>

11783 James D. G. Dunn, "Works of the Law and the Curse of the Law," *NTS* 31 (1985): 523-42.

11784 John Ellington, "Adoption in Modern Translations," *BT* 36 (1985): 437-40.

11785 Norman H. Young, "Who's Cursed and Why?" *JBL* 117 (1998): 79-92.

<u>4:6</u>

11786 S. V. McCasland, "Abba, Father," *JBL* 72 (1953): 79-91.

11787 Joachim Jeremias, "Abba," *TLZ* 79 (1954): 213-14.

11788 Pheme Perkins, "God in the New Testament: Preliminary Soundings," *TT* 42 (1985): 332-41.

11789 E. A. Obeng, "Abba, Father: The Prayer of the Sons of God," *ET* 99 (1988): 363-66.

11790 S. C. Keesmaat, "Paul and His Story: Exodus and Tradition in Galatians," *HBT* 18 (1996): 133-68.

4:7

11791 Traian Valdman, "Uno sguardo ortodosso sulla giustificazione in Lutero," *SEcu* 1 (1983): 277-88.

4:8-11

11792 Troy Martin, "Apostasy to Paganism: The Rhetorical Stasis of the Galatian Controversy," *JBL* 114 (1995): 437-61.

4:9

11793 Eduard Schweizer, "Slaves of the Elements and Worshipers of Angels: Galatians 4:3, 9 and Colossians 2:8, 18, 20," *JBL* 107 (1988): 455-68.

11794 Dietrich Rusam, "Neue Belege zu den στοιχεῖα τοῦ κόσμου (Gal 4,3.9; Kol 2,8.20)," *ZNW* 83 (1992): 119-25

11795 Clinton E. Arnold, "Returning to the Domain of the Powers: στοιχεῖα as Evil Spirits in Galatians 4:3,9," *NovT* 38 (1996): 55-76.

4:10

11796 James D. G. Dunn, "Echoes of Intra-Jewish Polemic in Paul's Letter to the Galatians," *JBL* 112 (1993): 459-77.

11797 Troy Martin, "Pagan and Judeo-Christian Time-Keeping Schemes in Galatian 4:10 and Colossians 2:16," *NTS* 42 (1996): 105-19.

11798 James D. G. Dunn, "4QMMT and Galatians: Galatians 2:12, 2:16, 3:6, 4:10, 6:16," *NTS* 43 (1997): 147-53.

4:11

11799 Tom Thatcher, "The Plot of Galatians 3:1-18," *JETS* 40 (1997): 401-10.

4:12-6:18

11800 J. F. M. Smit, "Redactie in de brief aan de Galaten. Retorische analyse van Gal. 4:12-6:18," *TT* 26 (1986): 113-44.

4:12-20

11801 A. Marcello Buscemi, "Gal 4:12-20: un argomento di amicizia," *SBFLA* 34 (1984): 67-108.

11802 A. J. Goddard and S. A. Cummins, "Ill or Ill-Treated? Conflict and Persecution as the Context of Paul's Original Ministry in Galatia," *JSNT* 52 (1993): 93-126.

11803 Niels Hyldahl, "Gerechtigkeit durch Glauben. Historische und theologische Beobachtungen zum Galaterbrief," *NTS* 46 (2000): 425-44.

4:13-15

11804 Louis Panier, "Pour une approche sémiotique de l'épître aux Galates," *FV* 84 (1985): 19-32.

4:13-14

11805 U. Heckel, "Der Dorn im Fleisch: Die Krankheit des Paulus in 2 Kor 12,7 und 4,13f," *ZNW* 84/1-2 (1993): 65-92.

11806 Jerome Murphy-O'Connor, "Galatians 4:13-14 and the Recipients of Galatians,"*RB* 105 (1998): 202-207.

11807 Troy Martin, "Whose Flesh? What Temptation? (Galatians 4.13-14)," *JSNT* 74 (1999): 65-91.

4:13

11808 F. F. Bruce, "Galatian Problems: 4. The Date of the Epistle," *BJRL* 54/2 (1972): 250-67.

4:14

11809 Peter Jensen, "Faith and Healing in Christian Theology," *Point* 2 (1982): 153-59.

4:17

11810 F. R. M. Hitchcock, "The Meaning of ἐκκλεῖσια in Galatians. iv 17," *JTS* 40 (1939): 149-51.

11811 James D. G. Dunn, "Echoes of Intra-Jewish Polemic in Paul's Letter to the Galatians," *JBL* 112 (1993): 459-77.

11812 Christopher C. Smith, " ἐκκλεῖσια in Galatians 4:17: The Motif of the Excluded Lover as a Metaphor of Manipulation," *CBQ* 58 (1996): 480-99.

4:19

11813   R. Hermann, "Uber den Sinn des μορφῦσθαι χριστον ἐν
        ὑμῖν in Gal. 4, 19," *TLZ* 80 (1955): 713-26.

11814   Beverly R. Gaventa, "Our Mother St. Paul: Toward the
        Recovery of a Neglected Theme," *PSB* NS 17 (1996):
        29-44.

4:20

11815   Gerhard Wilhelmi, "ἀλλάξαι τὴν φωνήν μου? Galater
        4:20," *ZNW* 65 (1974): 151-54.

4:21-5:1

11816   Donald W. B. Robinson, "The Distinction between Jewish
        and Gentile Believers in Galatians," *ABR* 13 (1965):
        29-48.

11817   J. Louis Martyn, "Apocalyptic Antinomies in Paul's Letter
        to the Galatians," *NTS* 31 (1985): 410-24.

11818   A. C. Perriman, "The Rhetorical Strategy of Galatians
        4:21-5:1," *EQ* 65 (1993): 27-42.

11819   Susan M. Elliott, "Choose Your Mother, Choose Your
        Master: Galatians 4:21-5:1 in the Shadow of the Anatolian
        Mother of the Gods," *JBL* 118 (1999): 661-83.

4:21-31

11820   Benoît Standaert, "La rhétorique antique et l'épître aux
        galates," *FV* 84 (1985): 33-40.

11821   Kenneth J. Thomas, "Covenant in Relation to Hagar and
        Ishmael in Galatians," *BT* 37 (1986): 445-46.

11822   G. Bouwman, "De twee testamenten: een exegese van Gal
        4:21-31," *Bij* 48 (1987): 259-76.

11823   Paul K. Jewett, "Children of Grace," *TT* 44 (1987):
        170-78.

11824   Charles H. Talbert, "Paul on the Covenant," *RevExp* 84
        (1987): 299-313.

11825   John Fischer, "Covenant, Fulfillment and Judaism in
        Hebrews," *ERT* 13 (1989): 175-87.

11826   Karen H. Jobes, "Jerusalem, Our Mother: Metalepsis and
        Intertextuality in Galatians 4:21-31," *WTJ* 55 (1993):
        299-320.

11827 Patrick G. Barker, "Allegory and Typology in Galatians 4:21-31," *SVTQ* 38 (1994): 193-209.

11828 Stephen Fowl, "Who Can Read Abraham's Story? Allegory and Interpretative Power in Galatians," *JSNT* 55 (1994): 77-95.

11829 Richard N. Longenecker, "Graphic Illustrations of a Believer's New Life in Christ: Galatians 4:21-31," *RevExp* 91 (1994): 183-99.

11830 J. A. Loubser, "The Contrast Slavery/Freedom as Persuasive Device in Galatians," *Neo* 28 (1994): 163-76.

4:21-30

11831 Charles H. Cosgrove, "The Law Has Given Sarah No Children," *NovT* 29 (1987): 219-35.

4:21

11832 Thomas R. Schreiner, "Paul and Perfect Obedience to the Law: An Evaluation of the View of E. P. Sanders," *WTJ* 47/2 (1985): 245-78.

4:22

11833 Franz Mußner, "Gesetz - Abraham - Israel," *K* 25 (1983): 200-22.

4:23-24

11834 J. G. Janzen, "Hagar in Paul's Eyes and in the Eyes of Yahweh (Genesis 16): A Study in Horizons," *HBT* 13 (1991): 1-22.

4:24

11835 Ronald E. Heine, "Gregory of Nyssa's Apology for Allegory," *VC* 38 (1984): 360-70.

4:25-26

11836 Jerome Murphy-O'Connor, "Ierosolgma/Ierogsalem in Galatians," *ZNW* 90 (1999): 280-81.

4:25

11837 Michel Bouttier, "Petite suite paulinienne," *ÉTR* 60 (1985): 265-72.

11838 Michael G. Steinhauser, "Galatians 4:25a: Evidence of Targumic Tradition in Galatians 4:21-31?" *Bib* 70 (1989): 234-40.

11839 Nicholas T. Wright, "Paul, Arabia, and Elijah," *JBL* 115 (1996): 683-92.

4:29-30

11840 R. Le Déaut, "Traditions targumiques dans le Corpus Paulien?" *Bib* 42 (1961): 28-48.

4:29

11841 Ernst Baasland, "Persecution: A Neglected Feature in the Letter to the Galatians," *StTheol* 38 (1984): 135-50.

5-6

11842 J. Scott Duvall, "Pauline Lexical Choice Revisited: A Paradigmatic Analysis of Selected Terms of Exhortation in Galatians 5 and 6," *FilN* 7 (1994): 17-31.

11843 A. A. Das, "Oneness in Christ: The Nexus Indivulsus Between Justification and Sanctification in Paul's Letter to the Galatians," *CJ* 21 (1995): 173-86.

5:1-6:18

11844 J. Scott Duvall, " 'Identity-Performance-Result': Tracing Paul's Argument in Galatians 5 and 6," *SouJT* 37 (1994): 30-38.

11845 Gordon D. Fee, "Freedom and the Life of Obedience," *RevExp* 91 (1994): 201-17.

5:1-6:17

11846 Frank J. Matera, "The Culmination of Paul's Argument to the Galatians: Galatians 5:1-6:17," *JSNT* 32 (1988): 79-91.

5:1-6:10

11847 L. L. Cranford, "A Rhetorical Reading of Galatians," *SouJT* 37 (1994): 410.

5

11848 Stanley D. Toussaint, "Contrast between the Spiritual Conflict in Romans 7 and Galatians 5," *BSac* 123 (1966): 310-14.

11849 K. A. D. Smelik, "John Chrysostom's Homilies against the Jews: Some Comments," *NTT* 39 (1985): 194-200.

11850 Paul D. Duke, "The Imperative of Freedom: Galatians 5," *FM* 8 (1990): 94-100.

5:1-12

11851 Benoît Standaert, "La rhétorique antique et l'épître aux galates," *FV* 84 (1985): 33-40.

5:1-2

11852 Jean Calloud, " 'Humanité. . . Vous avez dit: Humanité'!. . ." *SémBib* 98 (2000): 31-49.

5:1

11853 Günter Haufe, "Reich Gottes bei Paulus und in der Jesustradition," *NTS* 31 (1985): 467-72.

11854 Gerhard Sauter, "Leiden und 'Handeln'," *EvT* 45 (1985): 435-58.

11855 Ulrich Schoenborn, "Solidariedade dos crucificados: eclesiogênese e credibilidade contextual," *EstT* 25 (1985): 225-47.

11856 Frances T. Gench, "Galatians 5:1,13-25," *Int* 46 (1992): 290-95.

11857 Molly T. Marshall, "Galatians 5:1,13-14: Free Yet Enslaved," *RevExp* 91 (1994): 233-37.

11858 Jack Albright, "Stand Firm in Freedom: Summer Lections from Galatians," *QR* 15 (1995): 89-106.

11859 Jan Lambrecht, "Is Gal. 5:1 1b a Parenthesis? A Response to Tjitze Baarda," *NovT* 38 (1996): 237-41.

5:2-3

11860 Mark W. Karlberg, "Legitimate Discontinuities between the Testaments," *JETS* 28 (1985): 9-20.

5:3

11861 Thomas R. Schreiner, "Paul and Perfect Obedience to the Law: An Evaluation of the View of E. P. Sanders," *WTJ* 47/2 (1985): 245-78.

11862 Norman H. Young, "Who's Cursed and Why?" *JBL* 117 (1998): 79-92.

5:4

11863   Michael Martin, "Fallen from Grace," *BI* 14/1 (1987): 37-39.

5:5

11864   R. Trevijano Etcheverría, "La mision en Tesalonica (1 Tes 1:1-2,16)," *Salm* 32 (1985): 263-91.

11865   Michael Bachmann, "4QMMT und Galaterbrief התורה מעשי und EPΓA NOMOY," *ZNW* 89 (1998): 91-113.

5:6

11866   Arthur L. Mulka, "Fides quae per caritatem operatur," *CBQ* 28 (1966): 174-88.

11867   Daniel C. Stevens, "Christian Educational Foundations and the Pauline Triad: A Call to Faith, Hope, and Love," *CEJ* 5 (1984): 5-16.

11868   J. Louis Martyn, "Apocalyptic Antinomies in Paul's Letter to the Galatians," *NTS* 31 (1985): 410-24.

11869   Jean Y. Thériault, "La femme chrétienne dans les textes pauliniens," *ScE* 37 (1985): 297-317.

5:7

11870   J. D. M. Derrett, "Running in Paul: The Midrashic Potential of Hab 2:2," *Bib* 66 (1985): 560-67.

5:9

11871   C. L. Mitton, "New Wine in Old Wineskins," *ET* 84 (1973): 339-43.

5:11

11872   Tjitze Baarda, "τί ἔτι διώκομαι in Galatians 5:11: apodosis or parenthesis?" *NovT* 34 (1992): 250-56.

11873   Jan Lambrecht, "Is Galatians 5:11b a Parenthesis? A Response to Tjitze Baarda," *NovT* 38 (1996): 237-41.

5:13-6:10

11874   Friedrich W. Horn, "Wandel im Geist: zur pneumatologischen Begründung der Ethik bei Paulus," *KD* 38 (1992): 149-70.

11875   J. C. O'Neill, "The Holy Spirit and the Human Spirit in Galatians," *ETL* 71 (1995): 107-20.

5:13-26

11876 W. B. Russell, "Does the Christian Have 'Flesh' in Galatians 5:13-26?" *JETS* 36 (1993): 179-87.

11877 W. B. Russell, "The Apostle Paul's Redemptive-Historical Argumentation in Galatians 5:13-26," *WTJ* 57 (1995): 333-57.

5:13-25

11878 P.-É. Bonnard, "Conversation biblique avec Jean Delumeau," *FV* 84 (1985): 77-81.

11879 Frances T. Gench, "Galatians 5:1,13-25," *Int* 46 (1992): 290-95.

11880 Jack Albright, "Stand Firm in Freedom: Summer Lections from Galatians," *QR* 15 (1995): 89-106.

5:13-18

11881 J. Scott Duvall, " 'Identity-Performance-Result': Tracing Paul's Argument in Galatians 5 and 6," *SouJT* 37 (1994): 30-38.

5:13-15

11882 John C. Brunt, "More on the Topos as a New Testament Form," *JBL* 104 (1985): 495-500.

5:13-14

11883 Molly T. Marshall, "Galatians 5:1,13-14: Free Yet Enslaved," *RevExp* 91 (1994): 233-37.

11884 Jean Calloud, " 'Humanité. . . Vous avez dit: Humanité'!. . ." *SémBib* 98 (2000): 31-49.

5:13

11885 Elmer L. Gray, "Liberty," *BI* 12/3 (1986): 28.

11886 J. Louis Martyn, "The Apocalyptic Gospel in Galatians," *Int* 54 (2000): 246-66.

5:14

11887 Oda Wischmeyer, "Das Gebot der Nächstenliebe bei Paulus: eine traditionsgeschichtliche Untersuchung," *BZ* NS 30 (1986): 161-87.

11888 Stephen Westerholm, "On Fulfilling the Whole Law," *SEÅ* 55 (1990): 229-37.

11889 Norman H. Young, "Who's Cursed and Why?" *JBL* 117 (1998): 79-92.

5:16-26

11890 Moisés Martínez-Peque, "Unidad de forma y contenido en Gál 5:16-26," *EB* 45 (1987): 105-24.

5:16-24

11891 Anthony Hoekema, "The Struggle between Old and New Natures in the Converted Man," *JETS* 5 (1962): 42-50.

5:16-18

11892 Ole Modalsli, "Gal 2:19-21; 5:16-18 und Rom 7:7-25," *TZ* 21 (1965): 22-37.

5:16-17

11893 J. Louis Martyn, "Apocalyptic Antinomies in Paul's Letter to the Galatians," *NTS* 31 (1985): 410-24.

5:17

11894 David J. Lull, "The Law Was Our Pedagogue: A Study in Galatians 3:19-25," *JBL* 105 (1986): 481-98.

11895 J. C. O'Neill, "The Holy Spirit and the Human Spirit in Galatians," *ETL* 71 (1995): 107-20.

11896 John J. Kilgallen, "The Strivings of the Flesh...(Galatians 5,17)," *Bib* 80 (1999): 113-14.

5:18-20

11897 Traian Valdman, "Uno sguardo ortodosso sulla giustificazione in Lutero," *SEcu* 1 (1983): 277-88.

5:18

11898 Robert P. Lightner, "Theological Perspectives on Theonomy; pt 3: A Dispensational Response to Theonomy," *BSac* 143 (1986): 228-45.

5:19-21

11899 V. P. Branick, "Apocalyptic Paul?" *CBQ* 47 (1985): 664-75.

11900 Louis Panier, "Pour une approche sémiotique de l'épître aux Galates," *FV* 84 (1985): 19-32.

5:19

11901 Vítor Westhelle, "Labor: A Suggestion for Rethinking the Way of the Christian," *WW* 6 (1986): 194-206.

5:22-23

11902 Donald Gee, "The Gifts and Fruit of the Spirit," *Para* 21 (1987): 21-26.

11903 John Painter, "The Fruit of the Spirit is Love: Galatians 5:22-23, An Exegetical Note," *JTSA* 5 (1973): 57-59.

11904 John R. W. Stott, "The Unforbidden Fruit: Why Power, Knowledge, Orthodoxy, Faith, and Service Are Not the Mark of a True Christian," *CT* 36 (1992): 34-36.

11905 Charles S. Hawkins, "Galatians 5:22-23 and 2 Samuel 13—Remembering Tamar," *RevExp* 93 (1996): 537-42.

5:23

11906 R. A. Campbell, " 'Against Such Things there Is No Law'? Galatians 5:23b again," *ET* 107 (1996): 271-72.

5:25-6:10

11907 Thomas A. Rand, "A Call to Koinonia: A Rhetorical Analysis of Galatians 5:25-6:10," *EGLMBS* 15 (1995): 79-92.

5:25

11908 Mikeal C. Parsons, "Being Precedes Act: Indicative and Imperative in Paul's Writing," *EQ* 60 (1988): 99-127.

6:1-16

11909 Jack Albright, "Stand Firm in Freedom: Summer Lections from Galatians," *QR* 15 (1995): 89-106.

11910 Jan Lambrecht, "Paul's Coherent Admonition in Galatians 6,1-6: Mutual Help and Individual Attentiveness," *Bib* 78 (1997): 33-56.

6:1-5

11911 Don B. Garlington, "Burden Bearing and the Recovery of Offending Christians," *TriJ* 12 (1991): 151-83.

6:1-2

11912 David W. Miller, "The Uniqueness of New Testament Church Eldership," *GTJ* 6 (1985): 315-27.

<u>6:1</u>

11913 Louis Panier, "Pour une approche sémiotique de l'épître aux Galates," *FV* 84 (1985): 19-32.

<u>6:4</u>

11914 R. Trevijano Etcheverría, "La mision en Tesalonica (1 Tes 1:1-2,16)," *Salm* 32 (1985): 263-91.

<u>6:5</u>

11915 David W. Kuck, " 'Each Will Bear His Own Burden': Paul's Creative Use of an Apocalyptic Motif," *NTS* 40 (1994): 289-97.

<u>6:6</u>

11916 Nikolaus Walter, "Paulus und die urchristliche Jesustradition," *NTS* 31 (1985): 498-522.

<u>6:7-10</u>

11917 Frank Stagg, "Galatians 6:7-10," *RevExp* 88 (1991): 247-51.

<u>6:7</u>

11918 J. Lionel North, "Sowing and Reaping: More Examples of a Classical Maxim," *JTS* NS 43 (1992): 523-27.

<u>6:8</u>

11919 Richard Vinson, "Life Everlasting," *BI* 16/1 (1989): 74-76.

<u>6:9-10</u>

11920 Wolfgang Schenk, "Die Paränese Hebr 13:16 im Kontext des Hebräerbriefs: einer Fallstudie semiotisch-orientierter Textinterpretation und Sachkritik," *StTheol* 39 (1985): 73-106.

<u>6:10</u>

11921 Jeffrey A. Gibbs, "The Grace of God as the Foundation for Ethics," *CTQ* 48/2-3 (1984): 185-201.

<u>6:11-18</u>

11922 U. Borse, "Die Wundmale und der Todesbescheid," *BZ* NS 14 (1970): 88-111.

11923 Wolfgang Harnisch, "Einübung des neuen Seins: paulinische Paränese am Beispiel des Galaterbriefs," *ZTK* 84 (1987): 279-96.

11924   Jeffrey A. D. Weima, "Gal 6:11-18: A Hermeneutical Key to the Galatian Letter," *CTJ* 28 (1993): 90-107.

6:11-15

11925   Benoît Standaert, "La rhétorique antique et l'épître aux galates," *FV* 84 (1985): 33-40.

6:13

11926   J. Louis Martyn, "Apocalyptic Antinomies in Paul's Letter to the Galatians," *NTS* 31 (1985): 410-24.

11927   A. B. du Toit, "Galatians 6:13: A Possible Solution to an Old Exegetical Problem," *Neo* 28 (1994): 157-61.

6:14-16

11928   Michael Bachmann, "4QMMT und Galaterbrief התורה מעשי und ΕΡΓΑ ΝΟΜΟΥ," *ZNW* 89 (1998): 91-113.

6:14

11929   Traian Valdman, "Uno sguardo ortodosso sulla giustificazione in Lutero," *SEcu* 1 (1983): 277-88.

6:15

11930   Mikeal C. Parsons, "The New Creation," *ET* 99 (1987): 3-4.

11931   Michael Bachmann, "4QMMT und Galaterbrief התורה מעשי und ΕΡΓΑ ΝΟΜΟΥ," *ZNW* 89 (1998): 91-113.

11932   J. Louis Martyn, "The Apocalyptic Gospel in Galatians," *Int* 54 (2000): 246-66.

6:16

11933   Franz Mußner, "Gesetz - Abraham - Israel," *K* 25 (1983): 200-22.

11934   James D. G. Dunn, "4QMMT and Galatians: Galatians 2:12, 2:16, 3:6, 4:10, 6:16," *NTS* 43 (1997): 147-53.

11935   Norman H. Young, "Who's Cursed and Why?" *JBL* 117 (1998): 79-92.

11936   Gregory K. Beale, "Peace and Mercy Upon the Israel of God: The Old Testament Background of Galatians 6,16b," *Bib* 80 (1999): 204-23.

6:17

11937   William Klassen, "Galatians 6:17," *ET* 81 (1970): 378.

Ephesians

<u>1</u>

11938 Peter T. O'Brien, "Ephesians 1: An Unusual Introduction to a New Testament Letter," *NTS* 25 (1978-1979): 504-16.

<u>1-3</u>

11939 Jack T. Sanders, "Hymnic Elements in Ephesians 1-3," - ZNW 56 (1965): 214-32.

11940 Carey C. Newman, "Election and Predestination in Ephesians 1:4-6a: An Exegetical-Theological Study of the Historical, Christological Realization of God's Purpose," *RevExp* 93 (1996): 237-47.

<u>1:1-23</u>

11941 Billy E. Simmons, "Perspectives on Salvation," *TEd* 54 (1996): 41-51.

<u>1:1-14</u>

11942 Victor A. Bartling, "Church in God's Eternal Plan: A Study in Ephesians 1:1-14," *CTM* 36 (1965): 198-204.

11943 P. Kessler, "Unsere Berufung zum göttlichen Leben Betrachtung über den Prolog des Epheserbriefes," *BL* 40 (1967): 119-22.

<u>1:1</u>

11944 S. Garofalo, "Rettifica su Eph. 1:1," *Bib* 16 (1935): 342-43.

11945 Mark Santer, "Text of Ephesians 1:1," *NTS* 15 (1969): 247-48.

11946 Ian A. Moir, "A Mini-Guide to New Testament Textual Criticism," *BT* 36 (1985): 122-29.

<u>1:3-14</u>

11947 E. Driessen, "Aeternum Dei propositum de salute hominis et de redintegratione omnium rerum per Christuni," *VD* 24 (1944): 120-24, 151-57, 184-91.

11948 J. Trinidad, "The Mystery Hidden in God: A Study of Ephesians 1:3-14," *Bib* 31 (1950): 1-26.

11949 R. Pottier, "The Expectation of the Creature," *Scr* 4 (1951): 256-62.

11950 C. Maurer, "Der Hymnus von Epheser I als Schlüssel zum ganzen Briefe," *EvT* 11 (1951-1952): 151-72.

11951 G. Perez, "El plan divino de la salvación," *CuBi* 11 (1954): 149-60.

11952 John Coutts, "Ephesians 1:3-14 and 1 Peter 13-12," *NTS* 3 (1956-1957): 115-27.

11953 Hugo Lattanzi, "Cristo nella gerarchia degli esseri secondo le Lettere della cattività e quella ai Romani," *Div* 2 (1958): 472-85.

11954 J. Cambier, "La bénédiction d'Eph 1:3-14," *ZNW* 54 (1963): 58-104.

11955 H.-M. Dion, "La prédestination chez saint Paul," *RechSR* 53 (1965): 5-43.

11956 Franz Mußner, "Le peuple de Dieu selon Ephésiens 1,3-14," *Conci* 10 (1965): 87-96.

11957 Michel Coune, "Dieu veuille illuminer les yeux de notre coeur," *AsSeign* NS 11 (1971): 75-79.

11958 Michel Coune, "À la louange de sa gloire," *AsSeign* NS 46 (1974): 37-42.

11959 Donald Jayne, "We and 'You' in Ephesians 1:3-14," *ET* 85 (1974): 151-52.

11960 L. Ramaroson, "La grande bénédiction," *SE* 33 (1981): 93-103.

11961 Mark W. Karlberg, "Legitimate Discontinuities between the Testaments," *JETS* 28 (1985): 9-20.

11962 Charles J. Robbins, "The Composition of Ephesians 1:3-14," *JBL* 105 (1986): 677-87.

11963 Beatriz M. Couch, "Blessed Be He Who Has Blessed: Ephesians 1:3-14," *IRM* 77 (1988): 213-20.

11964 J. H. Barkhuizen, "The Strophic Structure of the Eulogy of Ephesians 1:3-14," *HTR* 46 (1990): 390-413.

11965   Ronald Olson, " 'Thinking and Practicing Reconciliation':
The Ephesian Texts for Pentecost 8-14," *WW* 17 (1997):
322-28.

11966   Eldon Woodcock, "The Seal of the Holy Spirit," *BSac* 155
(1998): 139-63.

1:3-10

11967   P. Kessler, "Eph 1,3-10," *BL* 40 (1967): 119-22.

1:3-6

11968   L. Rimbault, "Éph 1:3-6," *ÉTR* 30 (1955): 16-17.

1:3-5

11969   Peter Hocken, "The Meaning and Purpose of 'Baptism in
the Spirit'," *Pneuma* 7 (1985): 125-33.

1:3

11970   Andrew T. Lincoln, "A Re-examination of 'The
Heavenlies' in Ephesians," *NTS* 19 (1973): 468-83.

11971   T. B. Cargal, "Seated in the Heavenlies: Cosmic Mediators
in the Mysteries of Mithras and the Letter to the
Ephesians," *SBLSP* 33 (1994): 804-21.

11972   Carey C. Newman, "Ephesians 1:3: A Primer to Paul's
Grammar of God," *RevExp* 95 (1998): 89-101.

1:4

11973   Otfried Hofius, "Erwählt vor Grundlegung der Welt (Eph
1:4)," *ZNW* 62 (1971): 123-28.

11974   Robert R. Hann, "Election, the Humanity of Jesus, and
Possible Worlds," *JETS* 29 (1986): 295-305.

1:5

11975   P. A. Drago, "La nostra adozione a figli di Dio in Ef. 1,5,"
RBib 19 (1971): 203-19.

11976   John Ellington, "Adoption in Modern Translations," *BT* 36
(1985): 437-40.

1:5-7

11977   Allen Mawhinney, "Baptism, Servanthood, and Sonship,"
WTJ 49 (1987):

1:9-10

11978 Galen W. Wiley, "A Study of 'Mystery' in the New Testament," *GTJ* 6 (1985): 349-60.

1:10

11979 J. A. Allan, "The 'In Christ' Formula in Ephesians," *NTS* 5 (1958-1959): 54-62.

11980 Jean M. Dufort, "La récapitulation paulinienne dans l'exégèse des Pères," *SE* 12 (1960): 21-38.

11981 Gerhard L. Müller, "Der eine Gott und das Gebet zu den Heiligen," *IKaZ* 14 (1985): 319-33.

11982 T. Otero Lazaro, "Reflexiones sobre el significado de πλήρωμα en las cartas a los Colosenses y Efesios," *Bur* 39 (1998): 9-30.

1:11-23

11983 Romano Penna, "La proiezione dell'esperienza comunitaria sul piano storico (Ef 2,11-22) e cosmico (Ef 1,20-23)," *RBib* 26 (1978): 163-86.

1:13-14

11984 Richard D. Patterson, "Though All Hell Should Endeavor to Shake: God's Preservation of His Saints," *Pres* 17 (1991): 40-57.

1:13

11985 Kendell H. Easley, "The Pauline Usage of pneumati as a Reference to the Spirit of God," *JETS* 27 (1984): 299-313.

1:14

11986 B. Ahern, "The Indwelling Spirit, Pledge of our Inheritance," *CBQ* 9 (1947): 179-89.

11987 D. A. Conchas, "Redemptio acquisitionis (Eph. 1,14)," *VD* 30 (1952): 14-29, 81-91, 154-69.

11988 J. Rieger, "Siegel und Angeld," *BibL* 7 (1966): 158-61.

11989 Alastair J. Alastair, "Arrabon," *JTS* 39 (1988): 92-97.

1:15-2:10

11990 L. Ramaroson, "Une lecture de Éphésiens 1,15-2,10," *Bib* 58 (1977): 388-410.

1:15-23

11991 L. Rimbault, "Éph. 1:15-23," *ÉTR* 30 (1955): 68-69.

11992 A. Viard, "Ascension (Ep 1,17-23)," *EV* 83 (1983): 120-21.

1:15-18

11993 Michel Coune, "Dieu veuille illuminer les yeux de notre coeur (Ep 1)," *AsSeign* NS 11 (1971): 75-79.

1:15

11994 Ian A. Moir, "A Mini-Guide to New Testament Textual Criticism," *BT* 36 (1985): 122-29.

1:16-23

11995 Henry J. Eggold, "The Ascension of our Lord," *CTQ* 46 (1982): 50-51.

1:17

11996 William R. Schoedel, "Blameless Mind 'Not on Loan' but 'by Nature'," *JTS* NS 15 (1964): 308-16.

11997 Peter Hocken, "The Meaning and Purpose of 'Baptism in the Spirit'," *Pneuma* 7 (1985): 125-33.

1:18

11998 A. C. Robertson, "Hope in Ephesians 1:18: A Contextual Approach," *JTSA* 55 (1986): 62-63.

1:19-23

11999 Erwin Penner, "The Enthronement of Christ in Ephesians," *Dir* 12 (1983): 12-19.

1:20-23

12000 Félix Asensio, "El protagonismo del 'Hombre-Hijo del Hombre' del Salmo 8," *EB* NS 41 (1983): 17-51.

1:20

12001 Andrew T. Lincoln, "A Re-examination of 'The Heavenlies' in Ephesians," *NTS* 19 (1973): 468-83.

12002 Thomas G. Allen, "Exaltation and Solidarity with Christ: Ephesians 1:20 and 2:6," *JSNT* 28 (1986): 103-20.

12003 T. B. Cargal, "Seated in the Heavenlies: Cosmic Mediators in the Mysteries of Mithras and the Letter to the Ephesians," *SBLSP* 33 (1994): 804-21.

1:21

12004 Pierre Benoit, "Pauline Angelology and Demonology: Reflexions on Designations of Heavenly Powers and on Origin of Angelic Evil according to Paul," *RSB* 3 (1983): 1-18.

12005 Walter Kasper, "Die Hoffnung auf die endgültige Ankunft Jesu Christi in Herrlichkeit," *IKaZ* 14 (1985): 1-14.

12006 Thomas G. Allen, "God the Namer: A Note on Ephesians 1:21b," *NTS* 32 (1986): 470-75.

1:22-23

12007 C. F. D. Moule, "A Note on Ephesians 1:22-23," *ET* 60 (1949): 53.

1:22-23

12008 George Howard, "The Head-Body Metaphors of Ephesians," *NTS* 20 (1974): 350-56.

12009 I. de la Potterie, "Le Christ, Plérôme de l'Église (Ep 1,22-23)," *Bib* 58 (1977): 500-24.

12010 D. H. C. Read, "The Gospel in the Galaxies: What Message for Mars?" *ET* 89 (1978): 212-13.

1:22

12011 Max A. Chevallier, "L'unité plurielle de l'église d'après le Nouveau Testament," *RHPR* 66 (1986): 3-20.

1:23

12012 A. E. N. Hitchcock, "Ephesians 1:23," *ET* 22 (1910-1911): 91.

12013 Johannes L. Johannes, "Die Katholizität der Kirche: eine neue Interpretation nach alter Tradition," *Greg* 42 (1961): 193-241.

12014 R. Fowler, "Ephesians i. 23," *ET* 76 (1964-1965): 294.

12015 Alastair R. McGlashan, "Ephesians 1:23," *ET* 76 (1965): 132-33.

12016 R. Hermans and L. Geysels, "Efeziërs 1,23: Het pleroma van Gods heilswerk. Eph. 1,23: Le plérôme de l'oeuvre salvifique de Dieu," *Bij* 28 (1967): 279-93.

12017   Roy Yates, "Re-examination of Ephesians 1:23," *ET* 83 (1972): 146-51.

12018   G. S. Gibson, "The Church - Pattern for Her Life," *ET* 91 (1980): 306-307.

12019   R. R. Jeal, "A Strange Style of Expression, Ephesians 1:23," *FilN* 10 (1997): 129-38.

12020   T. Otero Lazaro, "Reflexiones sobre el significado de πλήρωμα en las cartas a los Colosenses y Efesios," *Bur* 39 (1998): 9-30.

2

12021   Jean P. Lichtenberg, "Situation et destinée d'Israel à la lumière de Romains 9-11 et d'Ephésiens 2," *FV* 64 (1965): 488-518.

2:1-3:13

12022   Harald Riesenfeld, "Var de kristna i Efesos fortfarande hedningar? till Ef 2:1-3:13," *SEÅ* 60 (1995): 129-40

2:1-22

12023   Andrew T. Lincoln, "The Church and Israel in Ephesians 2," *CBQ* 49 (1987): 605-24.

12024   Charles A. Ray, "Removing the Wall," *TEd* 54 (1996): 53-59.

2:1-10

12025   Martinus C. de Boer, "On Confronting the Past," *PSB* NS 6 (1985): 138-41.

2:1-3

12026   Mark R. Shaw, "Is There Salvation outside the Christian Faith?" *EAJT* 2 (1983): 42-62.

12027   Peter T. O'Brien, "Divine Analysis and Comprehensive Solution: Some Priorities from Ephesians 2," *RTR* 53 (1994): 130-42.

2:1

12028   Ernest Best, "Dead in Trespasses and Sins (Eph. 2. 1)," - *JSNT* 13 (1981): 9-25.

2:2

12029 Jean Doignon, "Variations inspirées d'Origène sur le 'prince de l'air' (Eph 2,2) chez Hilaire de Poitiers," *ZNW* 81 (1990): 143-48.

2:3-4

12030 Cándido Pozo, "El hombre pecador," *Greg* 65 (1984): 365-87.

2:4-10

12031 A. Viard, "La vie nouvelle accordée par Dieu aux croyants dans le Christ," *EV* 79 (1979): 86-88.

2:4

12032 Palémon Glorieux, "La révélation du Pére," *MSR* 42 (1985): 21-41.

2:6

12033 Andrew T. Lincoln, "A Re-examination of 'The Heavenlies' in Ephesians," *NTS* 19 (1973): 468-83.

12034 Thomas G. Allen, "Exaltation and Solidarity with Christ: Ephesians 1:20 and 2:6," *JSNT* 28 (1986): 103-20.

12035 T. B. Cargal, "Seated in the Heavenlies: Cosmic Mediators in the Mysteries of Mithras and the Letter to the Ephesians," *SBLSP* 33 (1994): 804-21.

2:8-10

12036 R. H. Countess, "Thank God for the Genitive!" *JETS* 12 (1969): 117-22.

12037 Andrew T. Lincoln, "Ephesians 2:8-10: A Summary of Paul's Gospel?" *CBQ* 45 (1983): 617-30.

2:8-9

12038 D. H. C. Read, "What Makes an Evangelical?" *ET* 89 (1978): 309-11.

2:8

12039 Roy L. Aldrich, "Gift of God," *BSac* 122 (1965): 248-53.

12040 Theodore Mueller, "Justification: Basic Linguistic Aspects and the Art of Communicating It," *CTQ* 46 (1982): 21-38.

12041 Palémon Glorieux, "La révélation du Père," *MSR* 42 (1985): 21-41.

2:10

12042   D. Edmond Hiebert, "God's Creative Masterpiece," *Dir* 23 (1994): 116-24.

12043   David P. Kuske, "Does Ephesians 2:10 Teach Sanctification or Not?" *WLQ* 92 (1995): 51-52.

2:11-3:21

12044   Cullen I. K. Story, "Peace: A Bible Study on Ephesians 2:11-3:21," *ERT* 9 (1985): 8-17.

2:11-22

12045   J. T. Cleland, "Someone There Is Who Doesn't Love a Wall: From Text to Sermon on Ephesians 2:11-22," *Int* 21 (1967): 147-57.

12046   G. Giavini, "La structure littéraire d'Eph 2:11-22," *NTS* 16 (1970): 209-11.

12047   N. J. McEleney, "Conversion, Circumcision and the Law," *NTS* 20 (1974): 319-41.

12048   P. S. Watson, "The Blessed Trinity," *ET* 90 (1979): 242-43.

12049   Mark W. Karlberg, "Legitimate Discontinuities between the Testaments," *JETS* 28 (1985): 9-20.

12050   William R. Long, "Ephesians 2:11-22," *Int* 45 (1991): 281-83.

12051   Bruce W. Fong, "Addressing the Issue of Racial Reconciliation According to the Principles of Eph 2:11-22," *JETS* 38 (1995): 565-80.

12052   Craig McMahan, "The Wall Is Gone!" *RevExp* 93 (1996): 261-66.

12053   Ronald Olson, " 'Thinking and Practicing Reconciliation': The Ephesian Texts for Pentecost 8-14," *WW* 17 (1997): 322-28.

2:11-21

12054   Klauspeter Blaser, "Christus: unser Friede? Biblische Besinnung zu Eph 2,11-21," *ZMiss* 19 (1993): 66-71.

2:11-19

12055   Günter Klein, "Der Friede Gottes und der Friede der Welt: eine exegetische Vergewisserung am Neuen Testament," *ZTK* 83 (1986): 325-55.

2:11-12

12056   R. J. McKelvey, "Christ the Cornerstone," *NTS* 8 (1962): 352-59.

2:12

12057   Martin Rese, "Die Vorzüge Israels in Rbm. 9, 4f. und Eph. 2,12. Exegetische Anmerkungen zum Thema Kirche und Israel," *TZ* 31 (1975): 211-22.

2:14-18

12058   Helmut Merklein, "Zur Tradition und Komposition von Eph 2:14-18," *BZ* NS 17 (1973): 79-102.

12059   Walter Kirchschlager, "Christus, unser Friede - Gedanken zu Eph 2,14-18," *BL* 48 (1975): 173-79.

12060   L. Ramaroson, "Le Christ, notre paix (Ep 2,14-18)," *SE* 31 (1979): 373-82.

12061   Gerhard Wilhelmi, "Der Versöhner-Hymnus in Eph 2:14ff," *ZNW* 78 (1987): 145-52.

12062   Rowan Williams, "Resurrection and Peace," *Theology* 92 (1989): 481-90.

2:14-16

12063   Emmanuele Testa, "Gesù pacificatore universale," *SBFLA* 19 (1969): 5-64.

12064   Michael S. Moore, "Ephesians 2:14-16: A History of Recent Interpretation," *EQ* 54 (1982): 163-69.

12065   Anne Étienne, "Réconciliation: un aspect de la théologie paulinienne," *FV* 84 (1985): 49-57.

2:14

12066   Josef Sudbrack, ". . .er ist unser Friede und unsere Versöhnung (Eph. 2,14)," *GeistL* 56 (1983): 143-44.

2:15

12067   C. J. Roetzel, "Jewish Christian - Gentile Christian Relations: A Discussion of Ephesians 2 15a," *ZAW* 74 (1983): 81-89.

2:18

12068   F. Greeves, "One God," *ET* 87 (1976): 268-69.

12069   Elmar Salmann, "Trinität und Kirche: eine dogmatische Studie," *Cath* 38 (1984): 352-74.

12070   D. M. Coffey, "A Proper Mission of the Holy Spirit," *TS* 47 (1986): 227-50.

2:19-22

12071   Wolfgang Nauck, "Eph. 2, 19-22, ein Tauflied?" *EvT* 13 (1953): 362-71.

12072   F. F. Bruce, "New Wine in Old Wineskins," *ET* 84 (1973): 231-35.

12073   Joseph Moingt, "Prêtre 'selon le Nouveau Testament': à propos d'un livre récent," *RechSR* 69 (1981): 573-98.

12074   Ricardo Pietrantonio, "Un estudio bíblico sobre la Iglesia: explicación de la metodología de los Estudios Bíblicos," *RevB* 46 (1984): 275-86.

12075   Derwood C. Smith, "Cultic language in Ephesians 2:19-22: A Test Case," *RQ* 31 (1989): 207-17.

2:19

12076   S. Clive Thexton, "The Communion of Saints," *ET* 88 (1976): 25-26.

12077   H. O. Morton, "No Walls in Heaven," *ET* 89 (1977-1978): 109-11.

12078   Joseph Allen, "Renewal of the Christian Community: A Challenge for the Pastoral Ministry," *SVTQ* 29 (1985): 305-23.

2:20-22

12079   Horace D. Hummel, "Are Law and Gospel a Valid Hermeneutical Principle?" *CTQ* 46 (1982): 181-207.

12080   Léopold Sabourin, "Paul and His Thought in Recent Research," *RSB* 2 (1982): 62-73; 3 (1983): 117-31.

2:20

12081   Francis Lenssen, "Biblical Communities: Christian Communities in the New Testament," *Point* 1 (1972): 24-34.

12082   R. Fowler White, "Gaffin and Grudem on Eph 2:20: In Defense of Gaffin's Cessationist Exegesis," *WTJ* 54 (1992): 303-20.

3

12083   Charles C. Ryrie, "Mystery in Ephesians 3," *BSac* 123 (1966): 24-31.

3:1-21

12084   Gerald L. Stevens, "Building on Paul's Foundation," *TEd* 54 (1996): 61-66.

3:2-6

12085   A. Viard, "La révélation du mystère du Christ," *EV* 82 (1982): 359-61.

3:3-6

12086   W. Harold Mare, "Paul's Mystery in Ephesians 3," *JETS* 8 (1965): 77-84.

3:3

12087   Peter Hocken, "The Meaning and Purpose of 'Baptism in the Spirit'," *Pneuma* 7 (1985): 125-33.

3:5

12088   Kendell H. Easley, "The Pauline Usage of pneumati as a Reference to the Spirit of God," *JETS* 27 (1984): 299-313.

3:7

12089   Jean Y. Thériault, "La femme chrétienne dans les textes pauliniens," *ScE* 37 (1985): 297-317.

3:10

12090   Pierre Benoit, "Pauline Angelology and Demonology: Reflexions on Designations of Heavenly Powers and on Origin of Angelic Evil according to Paul," *RSB* 3 (1983): 1-18.

3:12

12091 Palémon Glorieux, "La révélation du Pére," *MSR* 42 (1985): 21-41.

3:13-21

12092 Adalberto Sisti, "Il progresso nella vita interiore," *BibO* 9 (1967): 197-208.

12093 P. Dacquino, "Preghiera di San Paolo per la perseveranza dei suoi cristiani," *BibO* 5 (1963): 41-46.

12094 F. Ogara, "Scire... supereminentem scientiae caritatem Christi," *VD* 15 (1935): 260-70.

12095 H. Liese, "De interiore homine," *VD* 12 (1932): 257-63.

3:13

12096 George Thompson, "Ephesians 3:13 and 2 Timothy 2:10 in the Light of Colossians 1:24," *ET* 71 (1960): 187-89.

3:14-21

12097 Cynthia A. Jarvis, "Ephesians 3:14-21," *Int* 45 (1991): 283-88.

12098 Ronald Olson, " 'Thinking and Practicing Reconciliation': The Ephesian Texts for Pentecost 8-14," *WW* 17 (1997): 322-28.

3:14-19

12099 Lucien Cerfaux, "À genoux en présence de Dieu," *BVC* 10 (1955): 87-90.

3:15

12100 Palémon Glorieux, "La révélation du Pére," *MSR* 42 (1985): 21-41.

3:17

12101 Adalberto Sisti, "Enraizados y fundados en la caridad," *CuBi* 29 (1972): 153-57.

3:18-19

12102 J.-A. Ubieta, "Mystère du Christ et maturité chrétienne," *AsSeign* NS 32 (1971): 87-96.

12103 P. Géoltrain, "Notes sur la connaissance de Dieu chez l'apôtre Paul," *FV* 64 (1965): 465-81.

3:19

12104 T. Otero Lazaro, "Reflexiones sobre el significado de πλήρωμα en las cartas a los Colosenses y Efesios," *Bur* 39 (1998): 9-30.

3:21

12105 E. E. Rees, "The Cosmic Christ," *ET* 41 (1929-1930): 335-36.

4:1-25

12106 Claudio Basevi, "La missione di Cristo e dei cristiani nella Lettera agli Efesini: una lettura di Ef 4:1-25," *RBib* 38 (1990): 27-55.

4:1-24

12107 H. Liese, "In vinculo pacis," *VD* 13 (1933): 289-94.

12108 Pierre Benoit, "Exhortation à l'unité (Ep 4,1-24)," *AsSeign* 71 (1963): 14-26.

12109 J. Prado, "La Iglesia del futuro según San Pablo," *EB* 22 (1963); 255-302.

4:1-16

12110 B. C. Wintle, "Patterns of Ministry in the Later Pauline Letters," *IJT* 32 (1983): 68-76.

12111 L. Michael White, "Social Authority in the House Church Setting and Ephesians 4:1-16," *RQ* 29 (1987): 209-28.

12112 David P. Kuske, "Ministry According to Ephesians 4:1-16," *WLQ* 91 (1994): 205-16.

12113 L. Thomas Strong, "An Essential Unity," *TEd* 54 (1996): 67-74.

12114 Ronald Olson, " 'Thinking and Practicing Reconciliation': The Ephesian Texts for Pentecost 8-14," *WW* 17 (1997): 322-28.

4:1-7

12115 E. John Hamlin, "People of the Servant," *SEAJT* 6-7 (1965): 16-22.

4:1-6

12116 M. Balague, "Dominica 17. per annum: lectura Ef 4:1-6," *CuBi* 27 (1970): 215-22.

12117   R. Baulès, "Vivre l'unité," *AsSeign* NS 48 (1972): 33-38.

12118   David S. Dockery, "Ephesians 4:1-6," *RevExp* 88 (1991): 79-82.

4:1-3

12119   Judith G. Kipp, "Of Sunbeams and Spiders," *BLT* 38 (1993): 40-43.

4:3

12120   L. Davies, "I wrote afore in few words (Eph 3,3)," *ET* 46 (1934-1935): 568.

12121   F. J. Steinmetz, "Bewahrt die Einheit des Geistes'(Eph 4,3): Eine paulinische Gewissenserforschung zum Thema 'Kritik and der Kirche'," *GeistL* 54 (1981): 201-12.

4:4-6

12122   R. R. W. Bishop, "Logic versus Experience in the Order of Credal Formulae," *NTS* 1 (1954-1955): 42-44.

4:4-5

12123   J. A. T. Robinson, "The One Baptism as a Category of New Testament Soteriology," *SJT* 6 (1953): 257-74.

4:5

12124   W. E. Moore, "One Baptism," *NTS* 10 (1964): 504-16.

12125   E. R. Rogers, "Yet Once More—'One Baptism'?" *RTR* 50 (1991): 41-49.

4:7-11

12126   Erwin Penner, "The Enthronement of Christ in Ephesians," *Dir* 12 (1983): 12-19.

4:7-10

12127   J. Cambier, "La signification christologique d'Eph 4:7-10," *NTS* 9 (1963): 262-75.

12128   J. Clifford Hindley, "The Christ of Creation in New Testament Theology," *IJT* 15 (1966): 89-105.

4:8-10

12129   Max A. Chevallier, "L'unité plurielle de l'église d'après le Nouveau Testament," *RHPR* 66 (1986): 3-20.

4:8

12130 Geoffrey V. Smith, "Paul's Use of Psalms 68:18 in Ephesians 4:8," *JETS* 18 (1975): 181-89.

12131 Richard A. Taylor, "The Use of Psalm 68:18 in Ephesians 4:8 in Light of the Ancient Versions," *BSac* 148 (1991): 319-36.

12132 Richard Dormandy, "The Ascended Christ and His Gifts," *ET* 109 (1998): 206-207.

4:9-10

12133 W. Hall Harris, "The Ascent and Descent of Christ in Ephesians 4:9-10," *BSac* 151 (1994): 198-214.

4:9

12134 Ian A. Moir, "A Mini-Guide to New Testament Textual Criticism," *BT* 36 (1985): 122-29.

12135 Larry J. Kreitzer, "The Plutonium of Hierapolis and the Descent of Christ into the 'Lowermost Parts of the Earth'," *Bib* 79 (1998): 381-93.

4:11

12136 Dikran Y. Haddidian, "Tous de euangelistas in Ephesians 4:11," *CBQ* 28 (1966): 317-21.

12137 Hywel R. Jones, "Are There Apostles Today," *ERT* 9 (1985): 107-16.

12138 George W. Knight, "Two Offices (Elders or Bishops and Deacons) and Two Orders of Elders: A New Testament Study," *Pres* 11 (1985): 1-12.

4:11-16

12139 P. Menoud, "Éphésiens 4:11-16," *ÉTR* 30 (1955): 75-76.

12140 F. Ross Kinsler, "The Church and Health Care: Theological Bases for Church Involvement," *Point* 10 (1981): 161-69.

12141 Joseph Moingt, "Prêtre 'selon le Nouveau Testament': à propos d'un livre récent," *RechSR* 69 (1981): 573-98.

4:11-13

12142 E. John Hamlin, "People of the Servant," *SEAJT* 6-7 (1965): 16-22.

12143   Jerry R. Young, "Shepherds, Lead," *GTJ* 6 (1985): 329-35.

12144   John Vooys, "No clergy or Laity: All Christians Are Ministers in the Body of Christ, Ephesians 4:11-13," *Dir* 20 (1991): 87-95.

4:11-12

12145   Paul Muench, "The New Testament Scope of Ministry," *Point* 5 (1976): 77-84.

12146   Bert E. Downs, "The Spiritual Gift of Teaching," *CEJ* 6 (1985): 62-67.

12147   John J. Kilgallen, "Reflections on Charisma(ta) in the New Testament," *SM* 41 (1992): 289-323.

12148   T. David Gordon, " 'Equipping' Ministry in Ephesians 4?" *JETS* 37 (1994): 69-78.

4:12

12149   J. M. Bover, "In aedificationem corporis Christi," *EB* 3 (1944): 313-42.

12150   H. P. Hamann, "The Translation of Ephesians 4:12: A Necessary Revision," *CJ* 14 (1988): 42-49.

4:13-24

12151   Léopold Sabourin, "Paul and His Thought in Recent Research," *RSB* 2 (1982): 62-73; 3 (1983): 117-31.

4:13-15

12152   Guy Bedouelle, "Reflection on the Place of the Child in the Church: 'Suffer the Little Children to Come unto Me'," *CICR* 12 (1985): 349-67.

4:13

12153   I. Peri, "Gelangen zur Vollkommenheit: Zur lateinischen Interpretation von *katantaō* in Eph 4,13," *BZ* 23 (1979): 269-78.

12154   Richard L. Strauss, "Like Christ: An Exposition of Ephesians 4:13," *BSac* 143 (1986): 260-65.

12155   T. Otero Lazaro, "Reflexiones sobre el significado de πλήρωμα en las cartas a los Colosenses y Efesios," *Bur* 39 (1998): 9-30.

4:15-16

12156   George Howard, "The Head-Body Metaphors of Ephesians," *NTS* 20 (1974): 350-56.

4:15

12157   Jean D. Dubois, "Ephesians 4:15—On the Use of Coptic Versions for New Testament Textual Criticism," *NovT* 16 (1974): 30-34.

12158   Wayne Grudem, "Does Kephale ('Head') Mean 'Source' or 'Authority over' in Greek Literature: A Survey of 2,336 Examples," *TriJ* NS 6 (1985): 38-59.

4:16

12159   G. H. Whitaker, "sunarmologou/menon καὶ sumbibazo/menon. Eph. iv 16," *JTS* 31 (1930): 48-49.

12160   S. Tromp, "Caput influit sensum et motum," *Greg* 39 (1958): 353-66.

4:17-6:17

12161   Roman Heiligenthal, "Das Heil entscheidet sich durch die Tat," *ZRGG* 36 (1984): 131-40.

4:17-5:21

12162   Don H. Stewart, "The New Community in the Purpose of God," *TEd* 54 (1996): 75-81.

4:17-32

12163   Eugene F. Klug, "Will of God in the Life of a Christian," *CTM* 33 (1962): 453-68.

4:17-24

12164   M. Balague, "Domingo 18 per annum: lectura Ef 4,17.20-24," *CuBi* 27 (1970): 293-303.

12165   James A. Hyde, "Ephesians 4:17-24," *RevExp* 89 (1992): 403-407.

4:17-22

12166   Michel Coune, "L'homme nouveau," *AsSeign* NS 49 (1971): 41-47.

4:18

12167   R. Rubinkiewicz, "Psalm 68:19 (=Eph. 4:18): Another Textual Tradition or Targum," *NovT* 17 (1975): 219-24.

4:22-24

12168 B. Rey, "L'homme nouveau d'après S. Paul," *RSPT* 48 (1964): 603-24; 49 (1965): 161-95.

12169 LeRoy S. Capper, "The Imago Dei and Its Implications for Order in the Church," *Pres* 11 (1985): 21-33.

4:23-28

12170 F. Ogara, "Scire... supereminentem scientiae caritatem Christi," *VD* 15 (1935): 260-70.

12171 Michel Coune, "Revêtir l'homme nouveau (Ep 4,23-28)," *AsSeign* 74 (1963): 16-32.

4:25-5:2

12172 Ronald Olson, " 'Thinking and Practicing Reconciliation': The Ephesian Texts for Pentecost 8-14," *WW* 17 (1997): 322-28.

4:25

12173 J. P. Sampley, "Scripture and Tradition in the Community as Seen in Ephesians 4:25ff," *StTheol* 26 (1972): 101-109.

4:26

12174 Daniel B. Wallace, "Orgizesthe in Ephesians 4:26: Command or Condition?" *CTR* 3 (1989): 353-72.

4:28

12175 W. Morris, "Ephesians 4,28," *ET* 41 (1929-1930): 237.

4:29

12176 J. A. Finclay, "Ephesians 4,29," *ET* 46 (1934-1935): 429.

4:30-32

12177 P. van der Berghe, "Oui, cherchez à imiter Dieu," *AsSeign* NS 50 (1974): 37-41.

4:30

12178 Eldon Woodcock, "The Seal of the Holy Spirit," *BSac* 155 (1998): 139-63.

5:22-6:9

12179 Ernest Best, "The Haustafel in Ephesians," IBS 16 (1994): 146-60.

<u>5</u>

12180   Martin Neuhauser, "The Theology of Christian Marriage,"
        Point 5 (1976): 44-60.

<u>5:1-9</u>

12181   H. Liese, "Filii lucis, non iam tenebrarum," *VD* 12 (1932):
        33-38.

12182   F. Ogara, "Imitatores Dei... lux in Domino (Eph. 5,1-9),"
        VD 17 (1936): 33-38, 70-73.

<u>5:1</u>

12183   Palémon Glorieux, "La révélation du Pére," *MSR* 42
        (1985): 21-41.

12184   Carlos I. González, "Fausto Socino: la salvación del
        hombre en las fuentes del racionalismo," *Greg* 66 (1985):
        457-90.

<u>5:12-13</u>

12185   T. Engberg-Pedersen, "Ephesians 5:12-13: Elenchein and
        Conversion in the New Testament," *ZNW* 80 (1989):
        89-110.

<u>5:12</u>

12186   Larry J. Kreitzer, " 'Crude Language' and 'Shameful
        Things Done in Secret'," *JSNT* 71 (1998): 51-77 S

<u>5:14</u>

12187   Bent Noack, "Das Zitat in Ephes. 5:14," *ST* 5 (1951):
        52-64.

12188   Friedrich Wulf, "Wach auf, der du schläfst (Eph 5,14):
        Weckruf zum Advent," *GeistL* 51 (1978): 401-406.

12189   Tracy L. Howard, "The Meaning of 'Sleep' in 1
        Thessalonians 5:10: A Reappraisal," *GTJ* 6 (1985):
        337-48.

<u>5:15-20</u>

12190   C. Bigaré, "Sagesse chrétienne pour le temps présent,"
        AsSeign NS 51 (1972): 38-43.

12191   Austin C. Lovelace, "Make a Joyful Noise to the Lord:
        Biblical Foundations of Church Music," *Point* 2 (1973):
        15-27.

12192   Ronald Olson, " 'Thinking and Practicing Reconciliation':
        The Ephesian Texts for Pentecost 8-14," *WW* 17 (1997):
        322-28.

5:18-20

12193   Peter W. Gosnell, "Ephesians 5:18-20 and Mealtime
        Propriety," *TynB* 44 (1993): 363-71.

5:18

12194   Kendell H. Easley, "The Pauline Usage of pneumati as a
        Reference to the Spirit of God," *JETS* 27 (1984): 299-313.

12195   Carolyn D. Baker, "The Full Significance of Plerousthe in
        Ephesians 5:18," *Para* 22 (1988): 19-21.

12196   Dennis Leggett, "Be Filled with the Spirit: Ephesians
        5:18," *Para* 23 (1989): 9-12.

5:21-6:24

12197   Frank Stagg, "The Domestic Code and Final Appeal,
        Ephesians 5:21-6:24," *RevExp* 76 (1979): 541-52.

5:21-6:9

12198   John W. Bowman, "The Gospel and the Christian Family.
        An Exposition of Ephesians 5:22 to 6:9," *Int* 1 (1947):
        436-49.

12199   Winsome Munro, "Colossians 3:18-4:1 and Ephesians
        5:21-6:9: Evidences of a Late Literary Stratum?" *NTS* 18
        (1972): 434-47.

12200   A. S. Di Marco, "Ef. 5,21-6,9: teologia della famiglia,"
        RBib 31 (1983): 189-207.

12201   Frank Stagg, "The Gospel, Haustafel, and Women," *FM* 2
        (1985): 59-63.

12202   Margaret Gary, "Beating the Wedding-Sermon Blues: A
        New Look at Intimacy," *CThM* 13 (1986): 106-107.

12203   Lee McGlone, "Genesis 2:18-24; Ephesians 5:21-6:9,"
        RevExp 86 (1989): 243-47.

12204   Joe E. Trull, "Is the Head of the House at Home? (Eph
        5:21-6:9)," *TEd* 54 (1996): 83-94.

5:21-33

12205 Richard A. Batey, "Jewish Gnosticism and the 'Hieros Gamos' of Ephesians 5:21-33," *NTS* 10 (1964): 121-27.

12206 J. Pierron, "Comme le Christ a aimé l'Église," *AsSeign* 97 (1967): 16-30.

12207 David A. Fennema, "Unity in Marriage: Ephesians 5:21-33," *RR* 25 (1971): 62-71.

12208 R. Baulès, "L'époux et l'épouse dans le Christ," *AsSeign* NS 52 (1974): 37-42.

12209 J. Cambier, "Doctrine paulinienne du mariage chrétien: Étude critique de 1 Co 7 et d'Ep 5,21-33 et essai de leur traduction actuelle," *ÉgT* 10 (1979): 13-59.

12210 Julian C. Bridges, "Major Life Shapers: Marriage and the Family," *PRS* 12 (1985): 49-66.

12211 David M. Park, "The Structure of Authority in Marriage: An Examination of hupotasso and kephale in Ephesians 5:21-33," *EQ* 59 (1987): 117-24.

12212 Orsay Groupe, "Une lecture féministe des 'codes domestiques'," *FV* 88 (1989): 59-69.

12213 François Wessels, "Exegesis and Proclamation: Ephesians 5:21-33," *JTSA* 67 (1989): 67-75.

12214 Carol J. Westphal, "Coming Home," *RR* 42 (1989): 177-88.

12215 John E. Toews, "Paul's Radical Vision for the Family," *Dir* 19 (1990): 29-38.

12216 H. U. von Balthasar, "A Word on Humanae Vitae," *CICR* 20 (1993): 437-50.

12217 Jostein Ådna, "Die eheliche Liebesbeziehung als Analogie zu Christi Beziehung zur Kirche: Eine traditions-geschichtliche Studie zu Epheser 5,21-33," *ZTK* 92 (1995): 434-65.

5:21

12218 Richard D. Balge, "Ephesians 5:21--A Transitional Verse," *WLQ* 95 (1998): 41-43.

5:22-33

12219 J. A. Robillard, "Le symbolisme du mariage selon S. Paul," *RSPT* 21 (1932): 242-48.

12220 Robert Macina, "Pour éclairer le terme: digamoi," *RevSR* 61 (1987): 54-73.

5:22-29

12221 E. Neuhäusler, "Das Geheimnis ist gross: Einführung in die Grundbegriffe der Eheperikope, Eph 5,22-29," *BibL* 4 (1963): 155-67.

5:22-25

12222 Bernhard Hanssler, "Autorität in der Kirche," *IKaZ* 14 (1985): 493-504.

5:22-23

12223 J. Cambier, "Le grand mystère concernant le Christ et son Église Ephésiens 5:22-33," *Bib* 47 (1966): 43-90; 223-42.

12224 B. Celada, "Esposa y novia seductora a la vez: Profundidades de un texto de san Pablo en su carta a los fieles de Efeso (Ef 5:22-33)," *CuBi* 32 (1975): 27-30.

12225 Andreas J. Kostenberger, "The Mystery of Christ and the Church: Head and Body, 'One Flesh'," *TriJ* 12 (1991): 79-94.

5:22

12226 Elmar Salmann, "Trinität und Kirche: eine dogmatische Studie," *Cath* 38 (1984): 352-74.

12227 Ian A. Moir, "A Mini-Guide to New Testament Textual Criticism," *BT* 36 (1985): 122-29.

5:23-32

12228 Max A. Chevallier, "L'unité plurielle de l'église d'après le Nouveau Testament," *RHPR* 66 (1986): 3-20.

5:23

12229 Wayne Grudem, "Does Kephale ('Head') Mean 'Source' or 'Authority over' in Greek Literature: A Survey of 2,336 Examples," *TriJ* NS 6 (1985): 38-59.

12230 Wayne Grudem, "The Meaning of Kephale: A Response to Recent Studies," *TriJ* 11 (1990): 3-72.

5:28-33

12231   Richard A. Batey, "The *mia sarks* Union of Christ and the Church," *NTS* 13 (1966-1967): 270-81.

5:30

12232   Peter R. Rodgers, "The Allusion to Genesis 2:23 at Ephesians 5:30," *JTS* NS 41 (1990): 92-94.

5:31-32

12233   James Knight, "Pastoral Theology for Marriage in Melanesia," *Point* 5 (1976): 72-130.

5:31

12234   T. A. Burkill, "Two into One: The Notion of Carnal Union in Mark 10,8, 1 Kor 6,16, Eph 5,31," *ZNW* 62 (1971): 115-20.

5:32

12235   Gerard S. Sloyan, "Jewish Ritual of the 1st Century CE and Christian Sacramental Behavior," *BTB* 15 (1985): 98-103.

12236   Marion L. Soards, "The Righteousness of God in the Writings of the Apostle Paul," *BTB* 15 (1985): 104-109.

5:5

12237   Stanley E. Porter, "iste ginoskontes in Ephesians 5,5: Does Chiasm Solve a Problem?" *ZNW* 81 (1990): 270-76.

5:6-14

12238   Roman Heiligenthal, "Das Heil entscheidet sich durch die Tat," *ZRGG* 36 (1984): 131-40.

5:8-14

12239   James A. Harnish, "Listening in Time," *QR* 15 (1995): 427-40.

5:9-10

12240   James Knight, "Pastoral Theology for Marriage in Melanesia," *Point* 5 (1976): 72-130.

5:9

12241   Ian A. Moir, "A Mini-Guide to New Testament Textual Criticism," *BT* 36 (1985): 122-29.

6:6

12242 Jean Doignon, "Servi facientes voluntatem Dei ex animo: un éclatement de la notion de servitude chez Ambroise, Jérôme, Augustin?" *RSPT* 68 (1984): 201-11.

6:10-20

12243 J. L. Espinel, "Los eriostianos en guerra contra el mal en el mundo según Ef 6,10-20," *CuBí* 34 (1977): 31-45.

12244 Paul T. Eckel, "Ephesians 6:10-20," *Int* 45 (1991): 288-93.

12245 Robert A. Guelich, "Spiritual Warfare: Jesus, Paul and Peretti," *Pneuma* 13 (1991): 33-64.

12246 Andrew T. Lincoln, " 'Stand, therefore...' Ephesians 6:10-20 as Peroratio," *BibInt* 3 (1995): 99-114.

12247 William F. Warren, "Engaging the Forces of Evil (Eph 6:10-20)," *TEd* 54 (1996): 95-103.

12248 Ronald Olson, " 'Thinking and Practicing Reconciliation': The Ephesian Texts for Pentecost 8-14," *WW* 17 (1997): 322-28.

6:10-18

12249 Arthur E. Travis, "Christian's Warfare: An Exegetical Study of Ephesians Six," *SouJT* 6 (1963): 71-80.

6:10-17

12250 Donald P. Senior, "The New Testament and Peacemaking: Some Problem Passages," *FM* 4 (1986): 71-77.

6:10-12

12251 Galen W. Wiley, "A Study of 'Mystery' in the New Testament," *GTJ* 6 (1985): 349-60.

6:12

12252 D. E. H. Whiteley, "Ephesians vi. 12 Evil Powers," *ET* 68 (1956-1957): 100-103.

12253 Andrew T. Lincoln, "A Re-examination of 'The Heavenlies' in Ephesians," *NTS* 19 (1973): 468-83.

12254 Pierre Benoit, "Pauline Angelology and Demonology: Reflexions on Designations of Heavenly Powers and on Origin of Angelic Evil according to Paul," *RSB* 3 (1983): 1-18.

12255   Clinton E. Arnold, "The 'Exorcism' of Ephesians 6:12 in Recent Research: A Critique of Wesley Carr's View of the Role of Evil Powers in First Century AD Belief," *JSNT* 30 (1987): 71-87.

12256   T. B. Cargal, "Seated in the Heavenlies: Cosmic Mediators in the Mysteries of Mithras and the Letter to the Ephesians," *SBLSP* 33 (1994): 804-21.

12257   Ronald Olson, "Thinking and Practicing Reconciliation," *WW* 17 (1997): 322-28.

12258   M. E. Gudorf, "The Use of πάλη in Ephesians 6:12," *JBL* 117 (1998): 331-35.

6:13

12259   Nlenanya Onwu, "The Hermeneutical Model: The Dilemma of the African Theologian," *AfTJ* 14 (1985): 145-60.

6:14-18

12260   Raymond L. Cox, "The Unrecognized Armament," *Para* 21 (1987): 14-17.

6:18

12261   Kendell H. Easley, "The Pauline Usage of pneumati as a Reference to the Spirit of God," *JETS* 27 (1984): 299-313.

6:19-20

12262   Gene R. Smillie, "Ephesians 6:19-20: A Mystery for the Sake of Which the Apostle is an Ambassador in Chains," *TriJ* 18 (1997): 199-222.

6:21-24

12263   Billy E. Simmons, "Perspectives on Salvation," *TEd* 54 (1996): 41-51.

Philippians

1:1-11

12264 Wendell R. Debner, "Christ and the Church: The Ministry of the Baptized," *WW* 7 (1987): 417-23.

1:1

12265 George W. Knight, "Two Offices and Two Orders of Elders: A New Testament Study," *Pres* 11 (1985): 1-12.

12266 David W. Miller, "The Uniqueness of New Testament Church Eldership," *GTJ* 6 (1985): 315-27.

12267 T. C. Skeat, "Did Paul Write to 'Bishops and Deacons' at Philippi? A Note on Philippians 1:1," *NovT* 37 (1995): 12-15.

1:3

12268 Léopold Sabourin, "Koinonia in the New Testament," *RSB* 1 (1981): 109-15.

12269 R. Trevijano Etcheverría, "La mision en Tesalonica," *Salm* 32 (1985): 263-91.

1:4-11

12270 Gilles Gaide, "L'amour de Dieu en nous," *AsSeign* NS 6 (1969): 62-69.

1:4-6

12271 J. Mas, "Filipenses 1:4-6,8-11," *CuBi* 27 (1970): 343-46.

1:5

12272 L.-M. Dewailly, " La part prise à l'Évangile (Phil. 1, 5)," *RB* 80 (1973): 247-60.

12273 Léopold Sabourin, "Koinonia in the New Testament," *RSB* 1 (1981): 109-15.

1:6-11

12274 F. Ogara, "Socios gaudii mei omnes vos esse," *VD* 15 (1935): 324-30.

12275 Adalberto Sisti, "Nell'attesa del giorno di Cristo," *BibO* 7 (1965): 265-78.

1:6

12276 J. G. Janzen, "Creation and New Creation in Philippians 1:6," *HBT* 18 (1996): 27-54.

1:7

12277 Jacques Schlosser, "La communauté en charge de l'Evangile: A propos de Ph 1,7," *RHPR* 75 (1995): 67-76.

1:8-11

12278 J. Mas, "Filipenses 1:4-6,8-11," *CuBi* 27 (1970): 343-46.

1:8

12279 U. Holzmeister, "Viscera Christi," *VD* 16 (1936): 161-65.

1:12-13

12280 C. Ray Burchette, "Paul's Persecutions," *BI* 10/1 (1983): 66-71.

1:15-17

12281 H. W. Bateman, "Were the Opponents at Philippi Necessarily Jewish," *BSac* 155 (1998): 39-61.

1:19-27

12282 Wendell R. Debner, "Christ and the Church: The Ministry of the Baptized," *WW* 7 (1987): 417-23.

1:19-26

12283 Thomas F. Dailey, "To Live or Die: Paul's Eschatological Dilemma in Philippians 1:19-26," *Int* 44 (1990): 18-28.

1:20-27

12284 C. Bigaré, "Soit que je vive, soit que je meure (Ph 1)," *AsSeign* NS 56 (1974): 9-14.

1:20-24

12285 G. Gappert, " 'Aufbrechen' und 'Bleiben'. Eine österliche Besinnung zu Phil 1,20-24," *BL* 8 (1967): 63-67.

1:20

12286 G. Bertram, "ἀποκαραδοκία," *ZNW* 49 (1958): 264-70.

12287 D. R. Denton, "ἀποκαραδοκία," *ZNW* 73 (1982): 138-40.

12288   Arthur J. Droge, "Mori lucrum: Paul and Ancient Theories of Suicide," *NovT* 30 (1988): 263-86.

12289   Samuel Vollenweider, "Die Waagschalen von Leben und Tod: Zum antiken Hintergrund von Phil 1,21-26," *ZNW* 85 (1994): 93-115.

12290   James L. Jaquette, "Life and Death, Adiaphora, and Paul's Rhetorical Strategies," *NovT* 38 (1996): 30-54.

1:21-24

12291   André Feuillet, "Mort du Christ et mort du chrétien d'après les épitres pauliniennes," *RB* 66 (1959): 481-513.

1:21

12292   P. Joüon, "Notes philologiques sur quelques versets de l'épître aux Philippiens," *RechSR* 28 (1948): 88-93, 299-310.

12293   Friedrich Wulf, "Denn Leben ist für mich Christus und Sterben ist Gewinn," *GeistL* 30 (1957): 241-45.

12294   A. Giglioli, "Mihi enim vivere Christus est," *RivBib* 16 (1968): 305-16.

12295   D. W. Palmer, "To Die Is Gain (Philippians 1:21)," NovT 17 (1975): 203-18.

12296   Will K. Morris, "Rejoice Always," *ChrM* 16 (1985): 24.

1:22-23

12297   G. M. Lee, "Philippians 1:22-3," *NovT* 12 (1970): 361.

1:22

12298   Rodney R. Reeves, "To Be or Not to Be? That Is not the Question: Paul's Choice in Philippians 1:22," *PRS* 19 (1992): 273-89.

1:23-24

12299   C.-J. De Vogel, "Reflexions on Philippians 1:23-24," *NovT* 19 (1977): 262-74.

1:23

12300   Anne Hetzel, "L'accompagnement des mourants," *FV* 84 (1985): 29-45.

12301   Anthony Hoekema, "Heaven: Not Just an Eternal Day off," *CT* 29 (1985): 18-19.

12302 Günter Klein, "Aspekte ewigen Lebens im Neuen Testament: ein theologischer Annähungsversuch," *ZTK* 82 (1985): 48-70.

12303 Will K. Morris, "Rejoice Always," *ChrM* 16 (1985): 24.

12304 Enrique Treiyer, "S'en aller et etre avec Christ: Philippiens 1:23," *AUSS* 34 (1996): 47-64.

1:25

12305 F. J. Steinmetz and Friedrich Wulf, "Ausharren und bleiben! Auslegung und Meditation von Lk 24,29; Jo 15,4 und Phil 1,25," *GeistL* 24 (1969): 225-29.

1:27-4:3

12306 David E. Garland, "The Composition and Unity of Philippians: Some Neglected Literary Factors," *NovT* 27 (1985): 141-73.

1:27-2:18

12307 James P. Berkeley, "Self-Emptying of the Church," *Found* 9 (1966): 70-74.

1:27-30

12308 Nikolaus Walter, "Christusglaube und heidnische Religiosität in paulinischen Gemeinden," *NTS* 25 (1979): 422-42.

1:27-28

12309 H. W. Bateman, "Were the Opponents at Philippi Necessarily Jewish," *BSac* 155 (1998): 39-61.

12310 George W. Murray, "Paul's Corporate Witness in Philippians," *BSac* 155 (1998): 316-26.

1:27

12311 R. Roberts, "Old Texts in Modern Translations: Philippians 1:27," *ET* 49 (1937-1938): 325-28.

12312 Raymond R. Brewer, "The Meaning of *politeuesthe* in Philippians 1:27," *JBL* 73 (1954): 76-83.

12313 David R. Hall, "Fellow-Workers with the Gospel," *ET* 85 (1973-1974): 119-20.

12314 E. C. Miller, "*Politeuesthe* in Philippians 1:27: Some Philological and Thematic Observations," *JSNT* 15 (1982): 86-96.

1:28

12315 Gerald F. Hawthorne, "The Interpretation and Translation of Philippians 1:28b," *ET* 95 (1983): 80-81.

2:1-11

12316 William Barclay, "Philippians 2:1-11," *ET* 70 (1959-1960): 4-7, 40-44.

12317 James A. Sanders, "Dissenting Deities and Philippians 2:1-11," *JBL* 88 (1969): 279-90.

12318 Joachim Gnilka, "La carrière du Christ, appel à l'union et à la charité (Ph 2)," *AsSeign* NS 57 (1971): 12-19.

2:1-6

12319 Wendell R. Debner, "Christ and the Church: The Ministry of the Baptized," *WW* 7 (1987): 417-23.

2:1-5

12320 A. Moreno García , "Aproximación al sentido de Filipenses 2,1-5," *EB* 47 (1989): 529-58.

2:1-4

12321 David A. Black, "Paul and Christian Unity: A Formal Analysis of Philippians 2:1-4," *JETS* 28 (1985): 299-308.

2:1

12322 Léopold Sabourin, "Koinonia in the New Testament," *RSB* 1 (1981): 109-15.

12323 A. S. Di Marco, "Koinonia pneumatos (2 Cor 13:13; Flp 2:1)--pneuma koinonias: circolaità e ambivalenza linguistica e filologica," *FilN* 1 (1988): 63-76.

2:2

12324 J. Randall O'Brien, "Like-Mindedness," *BI* 14/1 (1987): 27.

2:3

12325 Anthony Hoekema, "How We See Ourselves," *CT* 29 (1985): 36-38.

2:5-11

12326 Ernst Käsemann, "Kritische Analyse von Phil. 2, 5-11," *ZTK* 47 (1950): 313-60.

12327 C. M. Horne, "Let This Mind Be in You," *JETS* 3 (1960): 37-44.

12328 Christoph Barth, "True Servant: Philippians 2:5-11," *SEAJT* 6 (1965): 12-14.

12329 Adalberto Sisti, "Sull'esempio di Cristo," *BibO* 7 (1965): 61-68.

12330 I. Howard Marshall, "The Christ-Hymn in Philippians," *TynB* 19 (1968): 104-27.

12331 John G. Gibbs, "Relation between Creation and Redemption according to Philippians 2:5-11," *NovT* 12 (1970): 270-83.

12332 K.-A. Bauer, "Der Weg der Diakonie. Predigt über Phil 2,5-1 1," *EvT* 36 (1976): 280-84.

12333 John G. Strelan, "Who Heals the Healers," *Point* 10 (1981): 170-79.

12334 David A. Black, "Paul and Christian Unity: A Formal Analysis of Philippians 2:1-4," *JETS* 28 (1985): 299-308.

12335 Albert Verwilghen, "Ph 2:5-11 dans l'oeuvre de Cyprien et dans les écrits d'auteurs anonymes africains du IIIIeme siécle," *Sale* 47 (1985): 707-34.

12336 L. D. Hurst, "Re-Enter the Pre-Existent Christ in Philippians 2:5-11," *NTS* 32 (1986): 449-57.

12337 A. Maillot, "Les théologies de la mort du Christ chez Paul," *FV* 85 (1986): 33-45.

12338 John B. Webster, "Christology, Imitability and Ethics," *SJT* 39 (1986): 309-26.

12339 John B. Webster, "The Imitation of Christ," *TynB* 37 (1986): 95-120.

12340 Nicholas T. Wright, "ἁρπαγμός and the Meaning of Philippians 2:5-11," *JTS* 37 (1986): 321-52.

12341 John Breck, "Biblical chiasmus: Exploring Structure for Meaning," *BTB* 17 (1987): 70-74.

12342   François Rousseau, "Une disposition des versets de Philippiens 2:5-11," *SR* 17 (1988): 191-98.

12343   Olaf H. Schumann, "Mission in der Weise Jesu Christi: Reflexionen im Anschluss an Phil 2:5-11," *ZMiss* 14 (1988): 168-71.

12344   Alan Neely, "Mission as kenosis: Implications for Our Times," *PSB* NS 10 (1989): 202-23.

12345   James W. McClendon, "Philippians 2:5-11," *RevExp* 88 (1991): 439-44.

12346   Robert A. Wortham, "Christology as Community: Identity in the Philippians Hymn—The Philippians Hymn as Social Drama," *PRS* 23 (1996): 269-87.

12347   Markus Bockmuehl, " 'The Form of God': Variations on a Theme of Jewish Mysticism," *JTS* NS 48 (1997): 1-23.

2:5-8

12348   J. Guillet, "Forme du Christ et formation du chrétien, Philippiens," *Chr* 30 (1983): 82-87.

12349   Paul D. Hanson, "The Identity and Purpose of the Church," *TT* 42 (1985): 342-52.

2:5

12350   U. Holzmeister, "Hoc sentite in vobis, quod et in Christo Jesu," *VD* 22 (1942): 225-28.

12351   P. Joüon, "Notes philologiques sur quelques versets de l'épître aux Philippiens," *RechSR* 28 (1948): 88-93, 299-310.

12352   P. A. van Stempvoort, "De betekenis van Filippenzen 2:5 t/m 11," NTT 19 (1964): 97-111.

12353   Andrew J. Bandstra, "Adam and the Servant in Philippians 2:5ff," *CTJ* 1 (1966): 213-16.

12354   A. Losie, "A Note on the Interpretation of Philippians 2:5," *ET* 90 (1978): 52-53.

2:6-11

12355   F. Ogara, "Hoc sentite in vobis, quod et in Christo Iesu," *VD* 15 (1935): 99-109.

12356   A. A. Stephenson, "Christ's Self-abasement," *CBQ* 1 (1939): 296-313.

12357 André Feuillet, "L'Homme-Dieu considéré dans sa condition terrestre," *RB* 51 (1942): 58-79.

12358 A. Ehrhardt, "Jesus Christ and Alexander the Great," *JTS* 46 (1945): 45-51.

12359 V. Larrañaga, "El nombre sobre todo nombre dado a Jesús desde su Resurrección gloriosa," *EB* 6 (1947): 287-305.

12360 A. Ehrhardt, "Ein antikes Herrscherideal," *EvT* 8 (1948-1949): 101-10.

12361 Jacques Dupont, "Jésus-Christ dans son abaissement et son exaltation, d'après Phil. 2,6-11," *RechSR* 37 (1950): 500-14.

12362 L. Bouyer, " Arpagmos," *RechSR* 39 (1951): 281-88.

12363 Max Meinertz, "Zum Verständnis des Christushymnus Phil. 2,5-11," *TTZ* 61 (1952): 186-92.

12364 G. Perez, "Humillación y exaltación de Cristo," *CuBí* 13 (1956): 4-10, 84-88.

12365 J. M. Furness, "Arpagmos eauton ekenōse," *ET* 69 (1957-1958): 93-94.

12366 Hugo Lattanzi, "Cristo nella gerarchia degli esseri secondo le Lettere della cattività e quelle ai Romani," *Div* 2 (1958): 472-85.

12367 P. Dacquino, "Il testo cristologico di Fil. 2,6-11," *RivBib* 7 (1959): 221-29.

12368 L. Krinetzki, "Der Einfluss von Is 52,13-53,12 Par auf Phil 2,6-11," *TQ* 139 (1959): 157-93, 291-336.

12369 J. M. Furness, "The Authorship of Philippians ii. 6-11," *ET* 70 (1959-1960): 240-43.

12370 Paul Neuenzeit, "Der Hymnus auf die Entäusserung Christi," *BK* 16 (1961): 9-13.

12371 Georg Strecker, "Redaktion und Tradition im Christushymnus Phil 2:6-11," *ZNW* 55 (1964): 63-78.

12372 André Feuillet, "L'hymne christologique de l'épître aux Philippiens 2:6-11," *RB* 72 (1965): 352-80, 481-507.

12373 John Harvey, "New Look at the Christ Hymn in Philippians 2:6-11," *ET* 76 (1965): 337-39.

12374   L. Krinetzki, "Le serviteur de Dieu," *AsSeign* 37 (1965): 37-45.

12375   D. F. Hudson, "A Further Note on Philippians ii. 6-11," *ET* 77 (1965-1966): 29.

12376   Joseph Coppens, "Les affinités littéraires de l'hymne christologique Phil 2, 6-11," *ETL* 42 (1966): 238-41.

12377   M. Dhainaut, "Les abaissements volontaires du Christ: Philippiens 2,6-11," *BVC* 71 (1966): 44-57.

12378   E. B. F. Kinniburgh, "The Humility of God: A Discussion of Philippians 2: 6-11," *BT* 16 (1966): 16-19.

12379   Joseph Coppens, "Une nouvelle structuration de l'hymne christologique de l'Epître aux Philippiens," *ETL* 43 (1967): 197-202.

12380   Charles H. Talbert, "Problem of Pre-existence in Philippians 2:6-11," *JBL* 86 (1967): 141-53.

12381   J. M. Furness, "Behind the Philippian Hymn," *ET* 79 (1967-1968): 178-82.

12382   L. Paul Trudinger, "Arpagmos and the Christological Significance of the Ascension," *ET* 79 (1967-1968): 279.

12383   Norman K. Bakken, "New Humanity: Christ and the Modern Age," *Int* 22 (1968): 71-82.

12384   Donald W. B. Robinson, "Arnagmos: The Deliverance Jesus Refused?" *ET* 80 (1968-1969): 253-54.

12385   K. Gamber, "Der Christus-Hymnus im Philipperbrief in liturgiegeschichtlicher Sicht," *Bib* 51 (1970): 369-76.

12386   Pierre Grelot, "Heurs et malheurs de la traduction liturgique," *ÉgT* 3 (1971): 449-59.

12387   Pierre Grelot, "Deux notes critiques sur Philippiens 2,6-11," *Bib* 54 (1973): 169-96.

12388   T. F. Glasson, "Two Notes on the Philippians Hymn 2:6-11," *NTS* 21 (1974): 133-39.

12389   P. Dacquino, "L'umiltà e l'esaltazione dell'Adamo escatologico," *BibO* 17 (1975): 241-51.

12390   J. Thomas, "L'Hymne de l'Épître aux Philippiens," *Chr* 22 (1975): 334-45.

12391 Jerome Murphy-O'Connor, "Christological Anthropology in Philippians 11:6-11," *RB* 83 (1976): 25-50.

12392 George Howard, "Philippians 2:6-11 and the Human Christ," *CBQ* 40 (1978): 368-87.

12393 A. Viard, "Abaissement et élévation du Christ Jésus," *EV* 78 (1978): 57-59.

12394 E. Lupoeri, "La morte di Croce: Contributi per un'analisi di Fil. 2,6-11," *RBib* 27 (1979): 271-311.

12395 B. Eckman, "A Quantitative Metrical Analysis of the Philippians Hymn," *NTS* 26 (1980): 258-66.

12396 Charles J. Robbins, "Rhetorical Structure of Philippians 2:6-11," *CBQ* 42 (1980): 73-82.

12397 A. Spreafico, "*Theos/anthrōpos:* Fil. 2,6-11," *RBib* 28 (1980): 407-15.

12398 J.-C. Basset, "Théologie de la croix et culture indienne. L'interprétation de V. Chakkarai à la lumière de Philippiens 2:6-11," *RHPR* 63 (1983): 417-34.

12399 T. Nagata, "A Neglected Literary Feature of the Christ-Hymn in Philippians 2:6-11," *AJBI* 9 (1983): 184-229.

12400 A. Viard, "Jésus crucifié, Seigneur du monde (Ph 2,6-11)," *EV* 83 (1983): 79-80.

12401 Norman K. Bakken, "Uma nova criaçao: o Cristo para o nosso tempo," *EstT* 24 (1984): 118-28.

12402 Byung-Mu Ahn, "The Body of Jesus-Event Tradition," *EAJT* 3 (1985): 293-309.

12403 A. M. Artola, "La mística cristopática de San Pablo de la Cruz," *EE* 60 (1985): 135-56.

12404 Christophe Senft, "Paul et Jésus," *FV* 84 (1985): 49-56.

12405 Guy Wagner, "Le scandale de la croix expliqué par le Chant du Serviteur d'Esaïe 53. Réflexion sur Philippiens 2:6-11," *ÉTR* 61 (1986): 177-87.

12406 Teresia Yai-Chow Wong, "The Problem of Pre-existence in Philippians 2:6-11," *ETL* 62 (1986): 267-82.

12407 Pheme Perkins, "Christology, Friendship and Status: The Rhetoric of Philippians," *SBLSP* 26 (1987): 509-20.

12408   Charles A. Wanamaker, "Philippians 2:6-11: Son of God or Adamic Christology?" *NTS* 33 (1987): 179-93.

12409   David A. Black, "The Authorship of Philippians 2:6-11: Some Literary-Critical Observations," *CTR* 2 (1988): 269-89.

12410   Joseph A. Fitzmyer, "The Aramaic Background of Philippians 2:6-11," *CBQ* 50 (1988): 470-83.

12411   Ulrich B. Müller, "Der Christushymnus Phil 2:6-11," *ZNW* 79 (1988): 17-44.

12412   J. Botha, "Die Kolossense-himne (Kol 1:15-20)," *HTS* suppl 1 (1989): 54-82.

12413   Sheila Briggs, "Can an Enslaved God Liberate? Hermeneutical Reflections on Philippians 2:6-11," *Semeia* 47 (1989): 137-53.

12414   Michel Gourgues, "La foi chrétienne primitive face à la croix: le témoignage des formulaires pré-pauliniens," *ScE* 41 (1989): 49-69.

12415   Andreas H. Snyman, "Die Filippense-himne (Fil 2:6-11)," HTS suppl 1 (1989): 44-53.

12416   Roselyne Dupont-Roc, "De l'hymne christologique à une vie de koinonia: Etude sur la lettre aux Philippiens," *EB* 49 (1991): 451-72.

12417   Steve Kraftchick, "A Necessary Detour: Paul's Metaphorical Understanding of the Philippian Hymn," *HBT* 15 (1993): 1-37.

12418   Roland Bergmeier, "Weihnachten mit und ohne Glanz: Notizen zu Johannesprolog und Philipperhymnus," *ZNW* 85 (1994): 47-68.

12419   Roland Bergmeier, "Weihnachten mit und ohne Glanz: Notizen zu Johannesprolog und Philipperhymnus," *ZNW* 85 (1994): 47-68.

12420   L. Schenke, "Gibt es im Markusevangelium eine Präexistenzchristologie?" *ZNW* 91 (2000): 45-71.

2:6-9

12421   Paul Gilbert, "La christologie sotériologique de Kant," *Greg* 66 (1985): 491-515.

2:6-8

12422   Albert Verwilghen, "Ph 2:6-8 dans l'oeuvre de Tertullien," *Sale* 47 (1985): 433-65.

12423   Brendan Byrne, "Christ's Pre-Existence in Pauline Soteriology," *TS* 58 (1997): 308-30.

2:6-7

12424   D. R. Griffiths, "Arpagmos and *eauton ekenōsen* in Philippians 2:6-7," *ET* 69 (1957-1958): 237-39.

12425   W. Powell, *"Arpagmos eauton ekenōsen,"* *ET* 71 (1959-1960): 88.

12426   Pierre Grelot, "La traduction et l'interprétation de Ph 2, 6-7. Quelques éléments d'enquête patristique," *NRT* 93 (1971): 897-922; 1009-26.

12427   Pierre Grelot, "Deux expressions difficiles de Philippiens 2:6-7," *Bib* 53 (1972): 495-507.

12428   Joe Gaquare, "Indigenisation as incarnation: the concept of a Melanesian Christ," *Point* 6 (1977): 146-53.

12429   H. Binder, "Erwägungen zu Phil 2:6-7b," *ZNW* 78/3 (1987): 230-43.

12430   F. M. Gillman, "Another Look at Romans 8:3: 'In the Likeness of Sinful Flesh'," *CBQ* 49 (1987): 597-604.

2:6

12431   W. Foerster, *"Ouk arpagmon êgêsato* bei den griechischen Kirchenvätern," *ZNW* 29 (1930): 115-28.

12432   A. Ehrhardt, "Nochmals: Ein antikes Herrscherideal," EvT 8 (1948-1949): 569-72.

12433   H. Kruse, "ἁρπαγμός," *VD* 27 (1949): 355-60.

12434   H. Kruse, "Iterum 'ἁρπαγμός'," *VD* 29 (1951): 206-14.

12435   Tomas Arvedson, "Phil. 2,6 und Mt. 10,39," *StTheol* 5 (1952): 49-51.

12436   Mauro Láconi, "Non rapinam arbitratus est. . .," *RivBib* 5 (1957): 126-40.

12437   Ralph P. Martin, *"Morphē* in Philippians 2:6," *ET* 70 (1959-1960): 183-84.

12438   David H. Wallace, "Note on *Morphe*," *TZ* 22 (1966): 19-25.

12439   Roy W. Hoover, "ἁρπαγμός Enigma: A Philological Solution," *HTR* 64 (1971): 95-119.

12440   J. Carmignac, "L'Importance de la place d'une négation," *NTS* 18 (1971-1972): 131-66.

12441   Ceslaus Spicq, "Note sur morphe dans les papyrus et quelques inscriptions," *RB* 80 (1973): 37-45.

12442   Michael R. Austin, "Salvation and the Divinity of Jesus," *ET* 96 (1985): 271-75.

12443   Rolf Gögler, "Inkarnationsglaube und Bibeltheologie bei Origenes," *TQ* 165 (1985): 82-94.

12444   J. C. O'Neill, "Hoover on ἁρπαγμός Reviewed, with a Modest Proposal concerning Philippians 2:6," *HTR* 81 (1988): 445-49.

12445   Markus Bockmuehl, " 'The Form of God': Variations on a Theme of Jewish Mysticism," *JTS* NS 48 (1997): 1-23.

12446   J. C. O'Neill, "Goethe and Philippians 2:6," *ET* 11 (1999): 359.

12447   Samuel Vollenweider, "Der 'Raub' der Gottgleichheit: Ein religionsgeschichtlicher Vorschlag zu Phil 2.6(-11)," *NTS* 45 (1999): 413-33.

2:7-8

12448   Frank Chikane, "The Incarnation in the Life of the People in Southern Africa," *JTSA* 51 (1985): 37-50.

2:7

12449   Joachim Jeremias, "Zu Phil 2:7: *Heauton ekenosen*," *NovT* 6 (1963): 182-88.

12450   Joseph Coppens, "Phil 2:7 et Is 53:12, le problème de la 'kénose'," *ETL* 41 (1965): 147-50.

12451   P. Schoonenberg, "Il s'anéantit Lui-même," *Conci* 11 (1966): 45-60.

12452   Friedrich Wulf, "Gott im Menschen Jesus. Auslegung und Meditation von Jo 1,14; Phil 2,7; Lk 2,11," *GeistL* 42 (1969): 472-73.

12453 Ugo Vanni, " '*Homoiōma*' in Paolo: Un'interpretazione esegetico-teologica alla luce dell'uso dei LXX," *Greg* 58 (1977): 321-45; 431-70.

12454 F. M. Gillman, "Another Look at Romans 8:3: 'In the Likeness of Sinful Flesh'," *CBQ* 49 (1987): 597-604.

2:8

12455 G. Lefebvre, "La croix, mystère d'obéissance," *VS* 96 (1957): 339-48.

12456 Marcel Doucet, "La volonté humaine du Christ, spécialement en son agonie: Maxime le Confesseur, interprète de l'Ecriture," *ScE* 37 (1985): 123-59.

2:9-11

12457 Siefried Wagner, "Das Reich des Messias: zur Theologie der alttestamentlichen Königspsalmen," *TLZ* 109 (1984): 865-74.

12458 Larry J. Kreitzer and D. W. Rrook, " 'Singing in a New Key.' Philippians 2:9-11 and the 'Andante' of Beethoven's Kreutzer Sonata," *ET* 109 (1998): 231-33.

2:9

12459 Ian G. Scott, "Jesus is Lord," *ET* 96 (1985): 305-307.

2:10-11

12460 Frank Stagg, "The Name 'Jesus'," *BI* 14/1 (1987): 73.

2:10

12461 Geevarghese Osthathios, "Conviction of Truth and Tolerance of Love," *IRM* 74 (1985): 490-96.

2:11-13

12462 J. C. Campbell, "The Christian and His Life-Style," *ET* 92 (1981): 314-15.

2:11

12463 K. Gamber, "In gloria est Dei Patris. Zu einer Textänderung in der Neo-Vulgata," *BZ* 24 (1980): 262-66.

2:12-19

12464 Joseph R. Jeter, "Sermons on the Fruit of the Spirit," - Impact 15 (1985): 1-64.

2:12-18

12465 Ernst Fuchs, "Andacht über Philipper 2:12-18," *EvT* 7 (1947-1948): 97-98.

2:12-13

12466 P. Joüon, "Notes philologiques sur quelques versets de l'épître aux Philippiens," *RechSR* 28 (1948): 88-93, 299-310.

12467 R. C. Sproul, "Heresies of Holiness," *CT* 30 (1965): 30-31.

12468 Sigfred Pedersen, "Mit Furcht und Zittern (Phil. 2,12-13)," *StTheol* 32 (1978): 1-31.

12469 Norbert Baumert, "Wirket euer Heil mit Furcht und Zittern (Phil 2,12f)," *GeistL* 52 (1979): 1-9.

12470 Beat Weber, "Philipper 2,12-13: Text - Kontext - Intertext," *BibN* 85 (1996): 31-37.

2:12

12471 Otto Glombitza, "Mit Furcht und Zittern - zum Verständnis von Philip. 2:12," *NovT* 3 (1959-1960): 100-106.

12472 Mikeal C. Parsons, "Being Precedes Act: Indicative and Imperative in Paul's Writing," *EQ* 60 (1988): 99-127.

2:13

12473 W. H. Robinson, "Your Life has a Plan," *ET* 88 (1976): 79-80.

2:14-16

12474 George W. Murray, "Paul's Corporate Witness in Philippians," *BSac* 155 (1998): 316-26.

2:15

12475 S. K. Finlayson, "Lights, Stars or Beacons," *ET* 77 (1966): 181.

2:16

12476 J. D. M. Derrett, "Running in Paul: The Midrashic Potential of Hab 2:2," *Bib* 66 (1985): 560-67.

2:17

12477 U. Holzmeister, " 'Gaudete in Domino semper' et 'beati qui lugent'," *VD* 22 (1942): 257-62.

12478 A.-M. Denis, "Versé en libation. Versé en son sang?" *RechSR* 45 (1957): 567-70.

12479 A.-M. Denis, "La fonction apostolique et la liturgie nouvelle en esprit," *RSPT* 42 (1958): 617-50.

12480 David G. Peterson, "Further Reflections on Worship in the New Testament," *RTR* 44 (1985): 34-41.

2:20

12481 P. Joüon, "Notes philologiques sur quelques versets de l'épître aux Philippiens," *RechSR* 28 (1948): 88-93, 299-310.

12482 Panayotis Christou, "ἰσόψυχος, Phil. 2:20," *JBL* 70 (1951): 293-96.

2:22

12483 George W. Murray, "Paul's Corporate Witness in Philippians," *BSac* 155 (1998): 316-26.

2:25-30

12484 Bernhard Mayer, "Paulus als Vermittler zwischen Epaphroditus und der Gemeinde von Philippi: Bemerkungen zu Phil 2:25-30," *BZ* NS 31 (1987): 176-88.

12485 George W. Murray, "Paul's Corporate Witness in Philippians," *BSac* 155 (1998): 316-26.

2:26-27

12486 Peter Jensen, "Faith and Healing in Christian Theology," *Point* 11 (1982): 153-59.

2:27

12487 Will K. Morris, "Rejoice Always," *ChrM* 16 (1985): 24.

2:30

12488 H. J. de Jonge, "Eine Konjektur Joseph Scaligers zu Philipper ii 30," *NovT* 17 (1975): 297-302.

12489 David G. Peterson, "Further Reflections on Worship in the New Testament," *RTR* 44 (1985): 34-41.

3:1

12490 P. Joüon, "Notes philologiques sur quelques versets de l'épître aux Philippiens," *RechSR* 28 (1948): 88-93, 299-310.

12491   M. Zerwick, "Gaudium et pax custodia cordium," *VD* 31 (1953): 101-104.

3:2-4:3

12492   Detlev Dormeyer, "The Implicit and Explicit Readers and the Genre of Philippians 3:2-4:3, 8-9: Response to the Commentary of Wolfgang Schenk," *Semeia* 48 (1989): 147-59.

3:2-21

12493   D. A. DeSilva, "No Confidence in the Flesh: The Meaning and Function of Philippians 3:2-21," *TriJ* 15 (1994): 27-54.

12494   Darrell J. Doughty, "Citizens of Heaven: Philippians 3:2-21," *NTS* 41 (1995): 102-22.

3:2-17

12495   Stephen Fowl, "Who's Characterizing Whom and the Difference This Makes: Locating and Centering Paul," *SBLSP* 32 (1993): 537-53.

3:2-14

12496   Ulrich Schoenborn, "El yo y los demas en el discurso paulino," *RevB* 51 (1989): 163-80.

3:2-11

12497   Robert H. Gundry, "Grace, Works, and Staying Saved in Paul," *Bib* 66 (1985): 1-38.

12498   Marion L. Soards, "The Righteousness of God in the Writings of the Apostle Paul," *BTB* 15 (1985): 104-109.

12499   Heikki Räisänen, "Paul's Conversion and the Development of His View of the Law," *NTS* 33 (1987): 404-19.

3:2-7

12500   Benjamin Fiore, "Invective in Romans and Philippians," *EGLMBS* 10 (1990): 181-89.

3:2-6

12501   P.-É. Bonnard, "Conversation biblique avec Jean Delumeau," *FV* 84 (1985): 77-81.

3:2

12502   Kenneth Grayston, "The Opponents in Philippians 3," *ET* 97 (1986): 170-72.

3:3-11

12503   Ulrich Luck, "Die Bekehrung des Paulus und das paulinische Evangelium: zur Frage der Evidenz in Botschaft und Theologie des Apostels," *ZNW* 76 (1985): 187-208.

3:3

12504   A. Boyd Luter, "Worship as Service: The New Testament Usage of latreuo," *CTR* 2 (1988): 335-44.

3:4-11

12505   J. Guillet, "Forme du Christ et formation du chrétien, Philippiens," *Chr* 30 (1983): 82-87.

3:4

12506   Günther Baumbach, "Antijudaismus im Neuen Testament: Fragestellung und Lösungsmöglichkeit," *K* 25 (1983): 68-85.

3:5-6

12507   William O. Walker, "Acts and the Pauline Corpus Reconsidered," *JSNT* 24 (1985): 3-23.

3:5

12508   P. Joüon, "Notes philologiques sur quelques versets de l'épître aux Philippiens," *RechSR* 28 (1948): 88-93, 299-310.

3:6

12509   M. Goguel, "*Kata dikaiosunēn tēn en nomō(i) genomenos amemptos* (Phil. 3:6)," *JBL* 53 (1934): 257-67.

12510   Thomas R. Schreiner, "Paul and Perfect Obedience to the Law: An Evaluation of the View of E. P. Sanders," *WTJ* 47 (1985): 245-78.

3:7-16

12511   J. T. Forestell, "Christian Perfection and Gnosis in Philippians 3,7-16," *CBQ* 15 (1953): 163-207.

3:7-15

12512   Ellen L. Babinsky, "Philippians 3:7-15," *Int* 49 (1995): 70-72.

3:7-9

12513   P.-É. Bonnard, "Conversation biblique avec Jean Delumeau," *FV* 84 (1985): 77-81.

3:8-14

12514   Gilles Gaide, "C'est dans le Christ que nous nous glorifions," *AsSeign* NS 18 (1970): 48-54.

12515   A. Viard, "Le salut et la connaissance du Christ Jésus," *EV* 83 (1983): 78-79.

3:8-12

12516   David Stanley, "The Apostle Paul as Saint," *SM* 35 (1986): 71-97.

3:8-9

12517   Mark R. Shaw, "Is There Salvation outside the Christian Faith," *EAJT* 2 (1983): 42-62.

3:8

12518   D. H. C. Read, "And the Winner is... the Star of the Saint," *ET* 90 (1978): 46-47.

3:9

12519   Mark A. Seifrid, "Paul's Approach to the Old Testament in Romans 10:6-8," *TriJ* NS 6 (1985): 3-37.

12520   James D. G. Dunn, "Once More, *Pistis Christou*," *SBLSP* 30 (1991): 730-44.

3:10-11

12521   P. Joüon, "Notes philologiques sur quelques versets de l'épître aux Philippiens," *RechSR* 28 (1948): 88-93, 299-310.

12522   A. C. Perriman, "The Pattern of Christ's Sufferings: Colossians 1:24 and Philippians 3:10-11," *TynB* 42 (1991): 62-79.

3:10

12523   B. Ahern, "The Fellowship of His Sufferings," *CBQ* 22 (1960): 1-32.

12524 Léopold Sabourin, "Koinonia in the New Testament," *RSB* 1 (1981): 109-15.

12525 Christian Wolff, "Niedrigkeit und Verzicht in Wort und Weg Jesu und in der apostolischen Existenz des Paulus," *NTS* 34 (1988): 183-96.

12526 Michael Wolter, "Der Apostel und seine Gemeinden als Teilhaber am Leidensgeschick Jesu Christi: Beobachtungen zur paulinischen Leidenstheologie," *NTS* 36 (1990): 535-57.

3:11

12527 Donald L. Norbie, "If by Any Means," *EQ* 32 (1960): 224-26.

12528 I. Peri, "Gelangen zur Vollkommenheit: Zur lateinischen Interpretation von Katantao in Eph 4:13," *BZ* 23/2 (1979): 269-78.

12529 J. Terry Young, "Resurrection Theology," *BI* 14/1 (1987): 65-67.

12530 Randall E. Otto, " 'If Possible I May Attain the Resurrection from the Dead'," *CBQ* 57 (1995): 324-40.

3:12-21

12531 Wendell R. Debner, "Christ and the Church: The Ministry of the Baptized," *WW* 7 (1987): 417-23.

3:12-15

12532 R.-H. Esnault, "Philippians 3:12-15," *ÉTR* 30 (1955): 22-26.

3:12-14

12533 G. S. Gibson, "A Divine Discontent," *ET* 94 (1983): 372-73.

12534 François Refoulé, "Note sur Romains 9:30-33," *RB* 92 (1985): 161-86.

3:12

12535 E. Lopez, "En torno a Fil 3,12," *EB* 34 (1975) 121-23.

3:15

12536 P. Joüon, "Notes philologiques sur quelques versets de
l'épître aux Philippiens," *RechSR* 28 (1948): 88-93,
299-310.

3:17-4:3

12537 F. Ogara, "Nostra conversatio in caelis est," *VD* 18 (1948):
321-28.

3:17-4:1

12538 Bernard Trémel, "La voie de la perfection chrétienne,"
AsSeign NS 15 (1973): 37-42.

12539 A. Viard, "Tenez bon dans le Seigneur," *EV* 83 (1983):
55-56.

3:17

12540 P. Joüon, "Notes philologiques sur quelques versets de
l'épître aux Philippiens," *RechSR* 28 (1948): 88-93,
299-310.

12541 Friedrich Wulf, "Seid meine Nachahmer, Brüder!" *GeistL*
34 (1961): 241-47.

3:18

12542 Daniel B. Wallace, "The Semantics and Exegetical
Significance of the Object-Complement Construction in
the New Testament," *GTJ* 6 (1985): 91-112.

3:19

12543 P. Joüon, "Notes philologiques sur quelques versets de
l'épître aux Philippiens," *RechSR* 28 (1948): 88-93,
299-310.

12544 Mark A. Seifrid, "Paul's Approach to the Old Testament
in Romans 10:6-8," *TriJ* NS 6 (1985): 3-37.

12545 Jeremy Moiser, "The Meaning of *koilia* in Philippians
3:19," *ET* 108 (1998): 365-66.

3:20-21

12546 N. Flanagan, "A Note on Philippians 3,20-21," *CBQ* 18
(1956): 8-9.

12547 J. Becker, "Erwägungen zu Phil 3:20-21," *TZ* 27 (1971):
16-29.

12548 John H. Reumann, "Philippians 3:20-21: A Hymnic Fragment?" *NTS* 30 (1984): 593-609.

12549 Per Bilde, "Eskatologi, soteriologi og kosmologi hos Paulus på grundlag af Fil.3,20-21 og beslægtede tekster: Et bidrag til debatten om Gronbechs Paulus-bog," *DTT* 54 (1991): 209-27.

3:20

12550 Paul C. Böttger, "Die eschatologische Existenz der Christen: Erwägungen zu Philipper 3:20," *ZNW* 60 (1969): 244-63.

12551 Michael R. Austin, "Salvation and the Divinity of Jesus," *ET* 96 (1985): 271-75.

12552 Gary Hardin, "A Theology of Heaven," *BI* 14/1 (1987): 18-21.

3:21

12553 Gedaliahu A. G. Stroumsa, "Form(s) of God: Some Notes on Metatron and Christ," *HTR* 76 (1983): 269-88.

12554 Eugene F. Klug, "The Doctrine of Man: Christian Anthropology," *CTQ* 48 (1984): 141-52.

12555 Luis F. Landaria, "Eucaristía y escatología," *EE* 59 (1984): 211-16.

12556 Jean Doignon, "Comment Hilaire de Poitiers a-t-il lu et compris le verset de Paul, Philippiens 3:21?" *VC* 43 (1989): 127-37.

4:1

12557 Ceslaus Spicq, "ἐπιποθεῖν désirer ou chérir?" *RB* 64 (1957): 184-95.

4:2-3

12558 Marco Adinolfi, "Le collaboratrici ministeriali di Paolo nelle lettere ai Romani e ai Filippesi," *BibO* 17 (1975): 21-32.

12559 Francis X. Malinowski, "The Brave Women of Philippi," *BTB* 15 (1985): 60-64.

4:2

12560 Wendy J. Cotter, "Women's Authority Roles in Paul's Churches: Countercultural or Conventional?" *NovT* 36 (1994): 350-72.

4:3

12561 Charles R. Smith, "The Book of Life," *GTJ* 6 (1985): 219-30.

12562 George W. Murray, "Paul's Corporate Witness in Philippians," *BSac* 155 (1998): 316-26.

4:4-20

12563 Carl Loeliger, "Biblical Concepts of Salvation," *Point* 6 (1977): 134-45.

4:4-13

12564 Charles B. Bugg, "Philippians 4:4-13," *RevExp* 88 (1991): 253-57.

4:4-9

12565 P. Dacquino, "La gioia cristiana," *BibO* 3 (1961): 182-83.

4:4-7

12566 Gilles Gaide, "La joie et la paix dans le Seigneur," *AsSeign* 5 (1966): 32-40.

12567 Adalberto Sisti, "Gioia e pace," *BibO* 8 (1966): 263-72.

12568 Gilles Gaide, "Joie et paix dans le Seigneur," *AsSeign* NS 7 (1969): 59-64.

12569 Josef Sudbrack, "Mut zur Freude! Paulus an die Gemeinde von Philippi," *GeistL* 43 (1970): 81-86.

4:4

12570 T. Camelot, "Réjouissez-vous dans le Seigneur toujours," *VS* 89 (1953): 474-81.

12571 Will K. Morris, "Rejoice Always," *ChrM* 16 (1985): 24.

4:6-9

12572 C. Bigaré, "La paix de Dieu dans le Christ Jésus," *AsSeign* NS 58 (1974): 11-15.

12573 Paul A. Holloway, "Notes and Observations Bona Cognitare: An Epicurean Consolation in Philippians 4:8-9," *HTR* 91 (1998): 89-96.

4:6-7

12574 J. S. Stewart, "Old Texts in Modern Translation: Philippians 4:6-7," *ET* 49 (1937-1938): 269-71.

12575 Kenneth S. Kantzer, "Disturbing the Peace: Born This Day in the City of David a Tough-Minded Peacemaker," *CT* 29 (1985): 18.

4:7

12576 M. Zerwick, "Gaudium et pax custodia cordium," *VD* 31 (1953): 101-104.

4:8-9

12577 Paul A. Holloway, "*Bona Cognitare*: An Epicurean Consolation in Philippians 4:8-9," *HTR* 91 (1998): 89-96.

4:10-20

12578 Otto Glombitza, "Der Dank des Apostels: zum Verständnis von Philipper 4:10-20," *NovT* 7 (1964): 135-41.

12579 Pheme Perkins, "Christology, Friendship and Status: The Rhetoric of Philippians," *SBLSP* 26 (1987): 509-20.

12580 G. W. Peterman, "Thankless Thanks: The Epistolary Social Convention in Philippians 4:10-20," *TynB* 42 (1991): 261-70.

4:10

12581 Norbert Baumert, "Ist Philipper 4:10 richtig übersetzt?" *BZ* NS 13 (1969): 256-62.

4:11

12582 G. Priero, "Didici sufficiens esse," *RivBib* 10 (1962): 59-63.

4:12-20

12583 B. Rolland, "Saint Paul et la pauvreté," *AsSeign* NS 59 (1974): 10-15.

4:16

12584 L. Morris, "*Kai apaks kai dis*," *NovT* 1 (1956): 205-208.

12585 Roger L. Omanson, "Translations: Text and Interpretation," *EQ* 57 (1985): 195-210.

12586 Gerald L. Borchert, "Thessalonica," *BI* 14/1 (1987): 62-64.

4:18-19

12587   P. Joüon, "Notes philologiques sur quelques versets de l'épître aux Philippiens," *RechSR* 28 (1948): 88-93, 299-310.

4:18

12588   David G. Peterson, "Further Reflections on Worship in the New Testament," *RTR* 44 (1985): 34-41.

4:19

12589   H.-M. Dion, "La notion paulinienne de 'richesse de Dieu' et ses sources," *SE* 18 (1966): 139-48.

4:21

12590   George W. Murray, "Paul's Corporate Witness in Philippians," *BSac* 155 (1998): 316-26.

4:22

12591   Peter Lampe, "Iunia-Iunias: Sklavenherkunft im Kreise der vorpaulischen Apostel," *ZNW* 76 (1985): 132-34.

Colossians

1

12592 Franz Zeilinger, "Versöhnung - Gedanken zum Kolosser-brief," *BibL* 49 (1976): 434-37.

12593 Michel Bouttier, "Petite suite paulinienne," *ÉTR* 60 (1985): 265-72.

1:1-28

12594 Robert P. Roth, "Christ and the Powers of Darkness: Lessons from Colossians," *WW* 6 (1986): 336-44.

1:1-14

12595 T. R. Gildmeister, "Christology and the Focus of Faith: Readings from Paul's Letter to the Colossians in Year C," *QR* 18 (1998): 89-110.

1:3-3:4

12596 L. Ramaroson, "Structure de Colossiens 1:3-3:4," *SE* 29 (1977): 313-19.

1:3-11

12597 Z. Kiernikowski, "Identitià e dinamisnlo della vita cristiana secondo Col. 1:3-11," *RivBib* 33 (1985): 63-79; 191-228.

1:3-12

12598 J. van der Watt, "Colossians 1:3-12 Considered as an Exordium," *JTSA* 57 (1986): 32-42.

1:4-6

12599 Daniel C. Stevens, "Christian Educational Foundations and the Pauline Triad: A Call to Faith, Hope, and Love," *CEJ* 5 (1984): 5-16.

1:9-2:3

12600 J. C. O'Neill, "The Source of Christology in Colossians," *NTS* 26 (1979-1980): 87-100.

1:9-19

12601 Otto A. Piper, "The Savior's Eternal Work. An Exegesis of Colossians 1:9-29," *Int* 3 (1949): 286-98.

1:9

12602 Léopold Sabourin, "Paul and His Thought in Recent Research," *RSB* 2 (1982): 62-73; 3 (1983): 117-31.

12603 Henri Crouzel, "Die Spiritualität des Origenes: Ihre Bedeutung für die Gegenwart," *TQ* 165 (1985): 132-42.

1:12-20

12604 P. Menoud, "Col. 1: 12-20," *ÉTR* 30 (1955): 5-8.

12605 Paul Lamarche, "La primauté du Christ," *AsSeign* NS 46 (1974): 59-64.

12606 W. R. G. Loader, "The Apocalyptic Model of Sonship: Its Origin and Development in New Testament Tradition," *JBL* 97 (1978): 525-54.

12607 T. E. van Pollard, "Colossians 1:12-20: A Reconsideration," *NTS* 27 (1980-1981): 572-75.

1:12-14

12608 Gary S. Shogren, "Presently Entering the Kingdom of Christ: The Background and Purpose of Colossians 1:12-14," *JETS* 31 (1988): 173-80.

1:13-29

12609 P. Kessler, "Er hat uns errettet," *BibL* 41 (1968): 33-36.

1:13-20

12610 J. M. Bissen, "De primatu Christi absoluto apud Coloss. 1,13-20," *Ant* 11 (1936): 3-26.

12611 F.-X. Durrwell, "Le Christ, premier et dernier," *BVC* 54 (1963): 16-28

12612 John Behr, "Colossians 1:13-20: A Chiastic Reading," *SVTQ* 40 (1996): 247-64.

12613 J. H. Roberts, "Die belydenisuitspraak Kolossense 1:13-20," *HTS* 53 (1997): 476-97.

1:13

12614 F. Ogara, "Qui nos transtulit in regnum Filii dilectionis suae," *VD* 17 (1937): 296-302.

12615 T. Torrance, "The Pre-eminence of Jesus Christ," *ET* 89 (1977): 54-55.

1:14-20

12616 C. C. Marcheselli, "La comunità cristiana di Colossi esprime la sua fede in Gesù Cristo," *RivBib* 31 (1983): 273-91.

1:15-28

12617 T. R. Gildmeister, "Christology and the Focus of Faith: Readings from Paul's Letter to the Colossians in Year C," *QR* 18 (1998): 89-110.

1:15-23

12618 D. Von Allmen, "Réconciliation du monde et christologie cosmique de 2 Cor 5:14-21 à Col 1:15-23," *RHPR* 48 (1968): 32-45.

1:15-20

12619 James M. Robinson, "A Formal Analysis of Colossians 1:15-20," *JBL* 76 (1957): 270-87.

12620 Werner Förster, "Die Grundzüge der Ptolemäischen Gnosis," *NTS* 6 (1959-1960): 16-31.

12621 E. Bammel, "Versuch zu Col 1,15-20," *ZNW* 52 (1961): 88-95.

12622 Paul Ellingworth, "Colossians i. 15-20 and Its Context," *ET* 73 (1961-1962): 252-53.

12623 G. W. H. Lampe, "New Testament Doctrine of *Ktisis*," *SJT* 17 (1964): 449-62.

12624 Ralph P. Martin, "An Early Christian Hymn," *EQ* 36 (1964): 195-205.

12625 H. Bürke, "Die Frage nach dem kosmischen Christus als Beispiel einer ökumenisch orientierten Theologie," *KD* 11 (1965): 103-15.

12626 Kurt Scharf, "Scope of the Redemptive Task, Colossians 1:15-20," *CTM* 36 (1965): 291-300.

12627 Fred B. Craddock, " 'All Things in Him': A Critical Note on Colossians 1:15-20," *NTS* 12 (1965-1966): 78-80.

12628 A. F. Thompson, "The Colossian Vision in Theology and Philosophy," *IJT* 15 (1966): 121-29.

12629 Emmanuele Testa, "Gesù pacificatore universale," *SBFLA* 19 (1969): 5-64.

12630 B. Vawter, "The Colossians Hymn and the Principle of Redaction," *CBQ* 33 (1971): 62-81.

12631 Eduard Schweizer, "Lord of the Nations," *SEAJT* 13 (1972): 13-21.

12632 Wolfgang Pöhlmann, "Die hymnischen All-Prädikationen in Kol 1:15-20," *ZNW* 64 (1973): 53-74.

12633 J.-N. Aletti, "Créés dans le Christ," *Chr*1 23 (1976): 343-56.

12634 Frédéric Manns, "Col. 1,15-20 midrash chrétien de Gen. 1,1," *RevSR* 53 (1979): 100-10.

12635 Wayne McCown, "The Hymnic Structure of Colossians 1:15-20," *EQ* 51 (1979): 156-62.

12636 Roland Bergmeier, "Königlosigkeit als nachvalentinianisches Heilsprädikat," *NovT* 24 (1982): 316-39.

12637 Larry R. Helyer, "Colossians 1:15-20: Pre-Pauline or Pauline?" *JETS* 26 (1983): 167-79.

12638 G. E. Long, "The Economy of Grace," *ET* 95 (1983): 17-18.

12639 Wolfgang Schenk, "Christus, das Geheimnis der Welt, als dogmatisches und ethisches Grundprinzip des Kolosserbriefes," *EvT* 43 (1983): 138-55.

12640 Gedaliahu A. G. Stroumsa, "Form(s) of God: Some Notes on Metatron and Christ," *HTR* 76 (1983): 269-88.

12641 F. F. Bruce, "Colossian Problems: The 'Christ Hymn' of Colossians 1:15-20," *BSac* 141 (1984): 99-111.

12642 Steven M. Baugh, "The Poetic Form of Colossians 1:15-20," *WTJ* 47 No 2 (1985): 227-44.

12643 Anne Étienne, "Réconciliation: un aspect de la théologie paulinienne," *FV* 84 (1985):49-57.

12644 Eduard Schweizer, "Unterwegs mit meinen Lehrern," *EvT* 45 (1985): 322-37.

12645 Antonio Orbe, "Deus facit, homo fit: un axioma de san Ireneo," *Greg* 69 (1988): 629-61.

12646 J. Botha, "Die Kolossense-himne (Kol 1:15-20)," *HTS* suppl 1 (1989): 54-82.

12647 Jarl Fossum, "Colossians 1:15-18a in the Light of Jewish Mysticism and Gnosticism," *NTS* 35 (1989): 183-201.

12648 Michel Gourgues, "La foi chrétienne primitive face à la croix: le témoignage des formulaires pré-pauliniens," *ScE* 41 (1989): 49-69.

12649 Joseph Sittler, "Called to Unity," *CThM* 16 (1989): 5-13.

12650 Eduard Schweizer, "Colossians 1:15-20," *RevExp* 87 (1990): 97-104.

12651 Nicholas T. Wright, "Poetry and Theology in Colossians 1:15-20," *NTS* 36 (1990): 444-68.

12652 Larry R. Helyer, "Recent Research on Colossians 1:15-20," *GTJ* 12 (1991): 51-67.

12653 Larry R. Helyer, "Cosmic Christology and Colossians 1:15-20," *JETS* 37 (1994): 235-46.

12654 Harold Van Broeckhoven, "The Social Profiles in the Colossian Debate," *JSNT* 66 (1997): 73-90.

12655 Jeffrey S. Lamp, "Wisdom in Col 1:15-20: Contribution and Significance," *JETS* 41 (1998): 45-53.

1:15-18

12656 B. R. Brinkman, " 'Creation' and 'Creature'. 1. Some Texts and Tendencies," *Bij* 18 (1957): 129-39.

12657 T. F. Glasson, "Colossians 1,15-18 and Sirach 24," *JBL* 86 (1967): 214-16.

1:15-16

12658 David Schneider, "Colossians 1:15-16 and the Philippine Spirit World," *SEAJT* 15 (1974): 91-101.

1:15

12659 G. W. H. Lampe, "New Testament Doctrine of *Ktisis*," *SJT* 17 (1964): 449-62.

12660 Jeffrey A. Gibbs, "The Grace of God as the Foundation for Ethics," *CTQ* 48 (1984): 185-201.

12661 Henri Crouzel, "Die Spiritualität des Origenes: Ihre Bedeutung für die Gegenwart," *TQ* 165 (1985): 132-42.

12662 Rolf Gögler, "Inkarnationsglaube und Bibeltheologie bei Origenes," *TQ* 165 (1985): 82-94.

12663 Terence E. Fretheim, "The Color of God: Israel's God-Talk and Life Experience," *WW* 6 (1986): 256-65.

12664 Larry R. Helyer, "Arius Revisited: The Firstborn over All Creation," *JETS* 31 (1988): 59-67.

1:16-20

12665 John D. Laurence, "The Eucharist as the Imitation of Christ," *TS* 47 (1986): 286-96.

1:16

12666 André Feuillet, "La Création de l'Univers 'dans le Christ' d'après l'Épître aux Colossiens (i. 16a)," *NTS* 12 (1965-1966): 1-9.

12667 Pierre Benoit, "Pauline Angelology and Demonology: Reflexions on Designations of Heavenly Powers and on Origin of Angelic Evil according to Paul," *RSB* 3 (1983): 1-18.

12668 Walter Kasper, "Hope in the Final Coming of Jesus Christ in Glory," *CICR* 12 (1985): 368-84.

1:17-19

12669 David E. Garland, "First-Century Philosophers and Monotheism," *BI* 12/3 (1986): 16-19.

1:18

12670 Wayne Grudem, "Does *Kephale* ('Head') Mean 'Source' or 'Authority over' in Greek Literature: A Survey of 2,336 Examples," *TriJ* NS 6 (1985): 38-59.

12671 Bernhard Hanssler, "Autorität in der Kirche," *IKaZ* 14 (1985): 493-504.

1:19-33

12672 Traian Valdman, "Uno sguardo ortodosso sulla giustificazione in Lutero," *SEcu* 1 (1983): 277-88.

1:19

12673 Johannes L. Witte, "Die Katholizität der Kirche: eine neue Interpretation nach alter Tradition," *Greg* 42 (1961): 193-241.

12674 Gerhard Münderlein, "Die Erwählung durch das Pleroma--Kol 1:19," *NTS* 8 (1961-1962): 264-76.

12675 Hugolinus Langkammer, "Die Einwohnung der 'absoluten Seinsfülle' in Christus. Bemerkungen zu Kol 1,19," *BZ* NS 12 (1968): 258-63.

1:20

12676 Peter T. O'Brien, "Colossians 1:20 and the Reconciliation of All Things," *RTR* 33 (1974): 45-53.

12677 Carmelo Granado Bellido, "Simbolismo del vestido: interpretación patrística de Gen 49:11," *EE* 59 (1984): 313-57.

1:21-23

12678 Robert A. Peterson, "The Perseverance of the Saints: A Theological Exegesis of Four Key New Testament Passages," *Pres* 17 (1991): 95-112.

1:21

12679 Henry J. Stob, "Natural Law Ethics: An Appraisal," *CTJ* 20 (1985): 58-68.

1:23

12680 Léopold Sabourin, "Paul and His Thought in Recent Research," *RSB* 2 (1982): 62-73; 3 (1983): 117-31.

12681 Eugene W. Bunkowske, "Was Luther a Missionary?" *CTQ* 49 (1985): 161-79.

12682 Jean Y. Thériault, "La femme chrétienne dans les textes pauliniens," *ScE* 37 (1985): 297-317.

1:24-29

12683 M. J. Kingston, "Suffering," *ET* 94 (1983): 144-45.

1:24-25

12684 Michael Cahill, "The Neglected Parallelism in Colossians 1:24-25," *ETL* 68 (1992): 142-47.

1:24

12685 P. Dacquino, "Al valore della sofferenza cristiana," *BibO* 8 (1906): 241-44.

12686 W. R. G. Moir, "Colossians 1,24," *ET* 42 (1930-1931): 479-80.

12687 George Thompson, "Ephesians 3:13 and 2 Timothy 2:10 in the Light of Colossians 1:24," *ET* 71 (1960): 187-89.

12688 H. Gustafson, "The Afflictions of Christ: What is Lacking?" *BR* 8 (1963): 28-42.

12689 C. Lavergne, "La joie de saint Paul d'après Colossiens 1:24," *RT* 68 (1968): 419-34.

12690 Roy Yates, "Note on Colossians 1:24," *EQ* 42 (1970): 88-92.

12691 L. Paul Trudinger, "Further Brief Note on Colossians 1:24," *EQ* 45 (1973): 36-38.

12692 Richard J. Bauckham, "Colossians 1:24 Again: The Apocalyptic Motif," *EQ* 47 (1975): 168-70.

12693 Gerhard Sauter, "Leiden und 'Handeln'," *EvT* 45 (1985): 435-58.

12694 A. C. Perriman, "The Pattern of Christ's Sufferings: Colossians 1:24 and Philippians 3:10-11," *TynB* 42 (1991): 62-79.

1:26-2:3

12695 Galen W. Wiley, "A Study of 'Mystery' in the New Testament," *GTJ* 6 (1985): 349-60.

1:28

12696 Juan Leal, "Ut exhibeamus omnem hominem perfectum in Christo," *VD* 18 (1938): 178-86.

1:29

12697 Jean Y. Thériault, "La femme chrétienne dans les textes pauliniens," *ScE* 37 (1985): 297-317.

2:1

12698 Ernest Best, "Dead in Trespasses and Sins," *JSNT* 13 (1981): 9-25.

2:6-19

12699 Holly D. Hayes, "Colossians 2:6-19," *Int* 49 (1995): 285-88.

<u>2:6-15</u>

12700 Roy A. Harrisville, "God's Mercy - Tested, Promised, Done! An Exposition of Genesis 18:20-32; Luke 11:1-13; Colossians 2:6-15," *Int* 31 (1977): 165-78.

12701 J. C. O'Neill, "The Source of Christology in Colossians," *NTS* 26 (1979-1980): 87-100.

12702 Robert P. Roth, "Christ and the Powers of Darkness: Lessons from Colossians," *WW* 6 (1986): 336-44.

<u>2:8-20</u>

12703 J. Huby, "*Stoikeia* dans Bardesane et saint Paul," *Bib* 15 (1934): 365-68.

<u>2:8-15</u>

12704 Cyril S. Rodd, "Salvation Proclaimed. XI. Colossians 28-15," *ET* 94 (1982): 36-41.

<u>2:8-10</u>

12705 G. Bornkamm, "Die Häresie des Kolosserbriefes," *TLZ* 73 (1948): 11-20.

<u>2:8</u>

12706 Eduard Schweizer, "Slaves of the Elements and Worshipers of Angels," *JBL* 107 (1988): 455-68.

12707 Dietrich Rusam, "Neue Belege zu den stoicheia tou kosmou," *ZNW* 83 (1992): 119-25.

<u>2:9</u>

12708 Anton Anwander, "Zu Kol 2:9," *BZ* NS 9 (1965): 278-80.

<u>2:10</u>

12709 Pierre Benoit, "Pauline Angelology and Demonology: Reflexions on Designations of Heavenly Powers and on Origin of Angelic Evil according to Paul," *RSB* 3 (1983): 1-18.

12710 Wayne Grudem, "Does *Kephale* ('Head') Mean 'Source' or 'Authority over' in Greek Literature: A Survey of 2,336 Examples," *TriJ* NS 6 (1985): 38-59.

<u>2:11-15</u>

12711 Otto Kuss, "Zur paulinischen und nachpaulinischen Tauflehre," *TGl* 42 (1952): 401-25.

2:11-13

12712 Gerhard Sellin, " 'Die Auferstehung ist schon geschehen'. Zur Spiritualisierung apokalyptischer Terminologie im Neuen Testament," *NovT* 25 (1983): 220-37.

12713 Kenneth Grayston, "The Opponents in Philippians 3," *ET* 97 6 (1986): 170-72.

2:11-12

12714 Robert A. Coughenour, "Fullness of Life in Christ: Exegetical Study on Colossians 2:11-12," *RR* 31 (1977): 52-56.

12715 Paul D. Gardner, "Circumcised in Baptism - Raised through Faith: A Note on Colossians 2:11-12," *WTJ* 45 (1983): 172-77.

2:11

12716 Lynn Jones, "Circumcision Among Jews of the Dispersion," *BI* 12/3 (1986): 24-27.

12717 Everett Ferguson, "Spiritual Circumcision in Early Christinaity," *SJT* 41 (1988): 485-97.

2:12-14

12718 C. Bigaré, "La croix, source de vie (Col 2)," *AsSeign* NS 48 (1972): 55-60.

2:12

12719 Harold H. Buls, "Luther's Translation of Colossians 2:12," *CTQ* 45 (1981): 13-16.

12720 Gerard S. Sloyan, "Jewish Ritual of the 1st century CE and Christian Sacramental Behavior," *BTB* 15 (1985): 98-103.

2:13

12721 William L. Craig, "The Historicity of the Empty Tomb of Jesus," *NTS* 31 (1985): 39-67.

2:14

12722 A. Vallisoleto, "Delens chirographum," *VD* 12 (1932): 181-85.

12723 O. A. Blanchette, "Does the χειρόγραφον of Colossians 2:14 Represent Christ Himself," *CBQ* 23 (1961): 306-12.

12724 Wesley Carr, "Two Notes on Colossians," *JTS* 24 (1973): 492-500.

12725 Nikolaus Walter, "Die 'Handschrift in Satzungen' Kol 2,14," *ZNW* 70 (1979): 115-18.

12726 Roy Yates, "Colossians and Gnosis," *JSNT* 27 (1986): 49-68.

12727 Roy Yates, "Colossians 2,14: Metaphor of Forgiveness," *Bib* 71/2 (1990): 248-59.

2:15

12728 A. Vallisoleto, "Et spolian principatus et potestates," *VD* 13 (1933): 187-92.

12729 Lamar Williamson, "Led in Triumph: Paul's Use of *Thriambeuo*," *Int* 22 (1968): 317-32.

12730 R. B. Egan, "Lexical Evidence on Two Pauline Passages," *NovT* 19 (1977): 34-62.

12731 Pierre Benoit, "Pauline Angelology and Demonology: Reflexions on Designations of Heavenly Powers and on Origin of Angelic Evil according to Paul," *RSB* 3 (1983): 1-18.

12732 Colin Gunton, "Christus Victor Revisited: A Study in Metaphor and the Transformation of Meaning," *JTS* NS 36 (1985): 129-45.

12733 Roy Yates, "Colossians 2:15: Christ Triumphant," *NTS* 37 (1991): 573-91.

2:16-3:17

12734 Gregory T. Christopher, "A Discourse Analysis of Colossians 2:16-3:17," *GTJ* 11 (1990): 205-20.

2:16

12735 Paul Giem, "σαββάτων in Colossians 2:16," *AUSS* 19 (1981): 195-210.

12736 T. C. G. Thornton, "Jewish New Moon Festivals, Galatians 4:3-11 and Colossians 2:16," *JTS* NS 40 (1989): 97-100.

12737   Troy Martin, "Pagan and Judeo-Christian Time-Keeping Schemes in Galatians 4:10 and Colossians 2:16," *NTS* 42 (1996): 105-19.

2:17

12738   Troy Martin, "But Let Everyone Discern the Body of Christ," *JBL* 114 (1995): 249-55.

2:17-18

12739   Ian A. Moir, "Some Thoughts on Col. 2,17-18," *TZ* 35 (1979): 363-65.

2:18

12740   Fred O. Francis, "Humility and Angelic Worship in Colossians 2:18," *StTheol* 16 (1962): 109-34.

12741   S. Lyonnet, "L'Épître aux Colossiens (Col 2:18) et les mystères d'Apollon Clarien," *Bib* 43 (1962): 417-35.

12742   Wesley Carr, "Two Notes on Colossians," *JTS* 24 (1973): 492-500.

12743   Roy Yates, "The Worship of Angels," *ET* 97 (1985): 12

12744   Eduard Schweizer, "Slaves of the Elements and Worshipers of Angels," *JBL* 107 (1988): 455-68.

12745   Michael D. Goulder, "Vision and Knowledge," *JSNT* 56 (1994): 53-71.

2:19

12746   S. Tromp, "aput influit sensum et mortum," *Greg* 39 (1958): 353-66.

12747   Wayne Grudem, "Does *Kephale* ('Head') Mean 'Source' or 'Authority over' in Greek Literature: A Survey of 2,336 Examples," *TriJ* NS 6 (1985): 38-59.

2:20

12748   Eduard Schweizer, "Slaves of the Elements and Worshipers of Angels," *JBL* 107 (1988): 455-68.

12749   Dietrich Rusam, "Neue Belege zu den stoicheia tou kosmou," *ZNW* 83 (1992): 119-25.

2:23

12750   Bo Reicke, "Zum sprachlichen Verständnis von Kol. 2,23," *StTheol* 6 (1953): 39-53.

12751 B. Hollenbach, "Col. 2.23: Which Things Lead to the Fulfilment of the Flesh," *NTS* 25 (1978-1979): 254-61.

3:1-4:6

12752 Roy Yates, "The Christian Way of Life: The Paraenetic Material in Colossians 3:1-4:6," *EQ* 63 (1991): 241-51.

3:1-17

12753 C. F. D. Moule, "New Life in Colossians 3:1-17," *RevExp* 70 (1973): 481-93.

3:1-11

12754 M. Trimaille, "Mort et résurrection dans la vie des baptisés (Col 3)," *AsSeign* NS 49 (1971): 72-81.

3:1-8

12755 G. Crespy, "Col. 3:1-8," *ÉTR* 30 (1955): 76-79.

3:1-6

12756 John R. Levison, "2 Apoc Bar 48:42-52:7 and the Apocalyptic Dimension of Colossians 3:1-6," *JBL* 108 (1989): 93-108.

3:1-4

12757 T. Camelot, "Ressuscités avec le Christ," *VS* 84 (1951): 354-63.

12758 Erich Grässer, "Kol 3, 1-4 als Beispiel einer Interpretation secundum homines recipientes," *ZTK* 64 (1967): 139-68.

12759 Gilles Gaide, "Le Christ, votre vie," *AsSeign* 21 (1969): 84-89.

12760 A. Viard, "Une vie nouvelle avec le Christ (Col.3,1-4)," *EV* 78 (1978): 59-60.

12761 Edouard Delebecque, "Sur un problème de temps chez Saint Paul," *Bib* 70 (1989): 389-95.

3:1

12762 Friedrich Wulf, "Suchet, was droben ist, wo Christus ist, sitzend sur Rechten Gottes," *GeistL* 41 (1968): 161-64.

12763 Traian Valdman, "Uno sguardo ortodosso sulla giustificazione in Lutero," *SEcu* 1 (1983): 277-88.

12764 D. H. C. Read, "Gentle Jesus or Cosmic Christ," *ET* 96 (1985): 213-14.

3:3

12765 Léopold Sabourin, "Paul and His Thought in Recent Research," *RSB* 2 (1982): 62-73; 3 (1983): 117-31.

12766 Luis F. Ladaria, "Presente y futuro en la escatología cristiana," *EE* 60 (1985): 351-59.

3:5-15

12767 B. Rey, "L'homme nouveau d'après S. Paul," *RSPT* 48 (1964): 603-629; 49 (1965): 161-95.

12768 B. Rey, "L'existence pascale di baptisé: Lecture de Colossiens 3:5-15," *VS* 113 (1967): 696-718.

3:5-11

12769 P. Joüon, "Note sur Col 3,5-11," *RechSR* 26 (1936): 185-89.

3:9-11

12770 Kenneth Grayston, "The Opponents in Philippians 3," *ET* 97 6 (1986): 170-72.

3:9

12771 Stanley E. Porter, "P Oxy 744.4 and Colossians 3:9," *Bib* 73 (1992): 565-67.

3:10-11

12772 Michel Bouttier, "Complexio Oppositorum: sur les Formules de 1 Cor. xii. 13; Gal. iii.26-8; Col. iii. 10, 11," *NTS* 23 (1976-1977): 1-19.

3:10

12773 Jeffrey A. Gibbs, "The Grace of God as the Foundation for Ethics," *CTQ* 48 (1984): 185-201.

12774 LeRoy S. Capper, "The Imago Dei and Its Implications for Order in the Church," *Pres* 11 (1985): 21-33.

12775 Mikeal C. Parsons, "The New Creation," *ET* 99 (1987): 3-4.

3:11

12776 Walter H. Principe, "The Dignity and Rights of the Human Person as Saved, as Being Saved, as to Be Saved by Christ," *Greg* 65 (1984): 389-430.

12777 Troy Martin, "The Scythian Perspective in Colossians 3:11," *NovT* 37 (1995): 249-61.

12778 Douglas A. Campbell, "Unravelling Colossians 3:11b," *NTS* 42 (1996): 120-32.

12779 Douglas A. Campbell, "The Scythian Perspective in Colossians 3:11: A Response to Troy Martin," *NovT* 39 (1997): 81-84.

3:12-21

12780 C. Bigaré, "Amour et union dans le Seigneur (Col 3)," *AsSeign* NS 11 (1971): 13-18.

12781 A. Viard, "Famille et vie chrétienne (Col. 3,12-2 1)," *EV* 78 (1978): 329-30; 82 (1982) 358-59.

3:12-17

12782 F. Ogara, "Caritatem habete, quod est vinculum perfectionis," *VD* 17 (1937): 335-43.

12783 T. Maertens, "Aimez-vous dans le Seigneur," *AsSeign* 14 (1961): 13-24.

12784 H. J. Spital, "Christliches Leben ist Leben aus der Freude. Eine Homilie über Kol 3,12-17," *BibL* 2 (1961): 53-59.

3:12-14

12785 Joseph Allen, "Renewal of the Christian Community: A Challenge for the Pastoral Ministry," *SVTQ* 29 (1985): 305-23.

3:16-4:1

12786 William Lillie, "Pauline House-Tables," *ET* 86 (1975): 179-83.

3:16-17

12787 Austin C. Lovelace, "Make a Joyful Noise to the Lord: Biblical Foundations of Church Music," *Point* 2 (1973): 15-27.

3:17

12788 Traian Valdman, "Uno sguardo ortodosso sulla giustificazione in Lutero," *SEcu* 1 (1983): 277-88.

3:18-4:1

12789 Winsome Munro, "Colossians 3:18-4:1 and Ephesians 5:21-6:9: Evidences of a Late Literary Stratum?" *NTS* 18 (1971-1972): 434-47.

12790 E. Glenn Hinson, "Christian Household in Colossians 3:18-4:1," *RevExp* 70 (1973): 495-506.

12791 Frank Stagg, "The Gospel, Haustafel, and Women: Mark 1:1; Colossians 3:18-4:1," *FM* 2 (1985): 59-63.

12792 Robert L. Richardson, "From 'Subjection to Authority' to 'Mutual Submission': The Ethic of Subordination in 1 Peter," *FM* 4 (1987): 70-80.

3:18-19

12793 Orsay Groupe, "Une lecture féministe des 'codes domestiques'," *FV* 88 (1989): 59-69.

4:3-4

12794 Gene R. Smillie, "Ephesians 6:19-20: A Mystery for the Sake of Which the Apostle is an Ambassador in Chains," *TriJ* 18 (1997): 199-222.

4:3

12795 Markus Bockmuehl, "A Note on the Text of Colossians 4:3," *JTS* NS 39 (1988): 489-94.

4:5

12796 W. D. Thomas, "Luke, the Beloved Physician (Col 4,5)," *ET* 95 (1983-1984): 279-81.

4:6

12797 Urban C. Von Wahlde, "Mark 9:33-50: Discipleship: The Authority that Serves," *BZ* NS 29 (1985): 49-67.

4:7-17

12798 Lamar Cope, "On Rethinking the Philemon-Colossians Connection," *BR* 30 (1985): 45-50.

12799 Bonnie B. Thurston, "Paul's Associates in Colossians 4:7-17," *RQ* 41 (1999): 45-55.

12800 George E. Ladd, "Paul's Friends in Colossians 4:7-16," *RevExp* 70 (1973): 507-14.

994:10

12801 James A. Brooks, "Barnabas: All We Know," *BI* 12/3
(1986): 58-61.

12802 Rice A. Pierce, "Mark: All We Know," *BI* 12/3 (1986):
54-57.

4:12-13

12803 D. Edmond Hiebert, "Epaphras, Man of Prayer," *BSac* 136
(1979): 54-64.

4:14

12804 H. Evans, "Luke - the Good Companion," *ET* 91 (1980):
372-74.

4:15

12805 Marlis Gielen, "Zur Interpretation der paulinischen Formel
τὴν κατ᾽ οἶκον αὐτῆς ἐκκλησίαν," *ZNW* 77 (1986):
109-25.

4:16

12806 C. P. Anderson, "Who Wrote 'The Epistle from
Laodicea'?" *JBL* 85 (1966): 436-40.

1 Thessalonians

<u>1:1-13</u>

12807 R. Trevijano Etcheverría, "La mision en Tesalonica," *Salm* 32 (1985): 263-91.

<u>1:1-10</u>

12808 H. Schlier, "Auslegung des 1. Thessalonicherbriefes (1,1-10)," *BibL* 3 (1962): 16-25.

<u>1:1</u>

12809 Hendrikus Boers, "Form-Critical Study of Paul's Letters: 1 Thessalonians as a Case Study," *NTS* 22 (1976): 140-58.

12810 Gordon D. Fee, "On Text and Commentary on 1 and 2 Thessalonians," *SBLSP* 31 (1992): 165-83.

<u>1:2-10</u>

12811 Hendrikus Boers, "Form-Critical Study of Paul's Letters: 1 Thessalonians as a Case Study," *NTS* 22 (1976): 140-58.

<u>1:3</u>

12812 Daniel C. Stevens, "Christian Educational Foundations and the Pauline Triad: A Call to Faith, Hope, and Love," *CEJ* 5 (1984): 5-16.

12813 Wolfgang Weiss, "Glaube—Liebe—Hoffnung: Zu der Trias bei Paulus," *ZNW* 84 (1993): 196-217.

<u>1:4</u>

12814 S. Lewis Johnson, "Divine Love in Recent Theology," *TriJ* NS 5 (1984): 175-87.

<u>1:5-10</u>

12815 É. Charpentier, "La foi vécue est contagieuse," *AsSeign* NS 61 (1972): 10-17.

<u>1:5-8</u>

12816 James Ware, "The Thessalonians as a Missionary Congregation: 1 Thessalonians 1,5-8," *ZNW* 83 (1992): 126-31.

<u>1:5</u>

12817 Kendell H. Easley, "The Pauline Usage of *pneumati* as a Reference to the Spirit of God," *JETS* 27 (1984): 299-313.

12818 A. Hutter, "Note sur la traduction de 1 Thessaloniciens 1:5 dans la TOB," *ÉTR* 60 (1985): 259-60.

<u>1:6</u>

12819 James L. Boyce, "Graceful imitation: 'Imitators of Us and the Lord'," *WW* Suppl 1 (1992): 139-46.

12820 G. P. Benson, "Note on 1 Thessalonians 1:6," *ET* 107 (1996): 143-44.

<u>1:7</u>

12821 Gordon D. Fee, "On Text and Commentary on 1 and 2 Thessalonians," *SBLSP* 31 (1992): 165-83.

<u>1:9-10</u>

12822 Johannes Munck, "1 Thessalonians 1:9-10 and the Missionary Preaching of Paul: Textual Exegesis and Hermeneutic Reflexions," *NTS* 9 (1963): 95-110.

12823 P.-É. Langevin, "Le Seigneur Jésus selon un texte prépaulinien, 1 Th 1:9-10," *SE* 17 (1965): 263-82; 473-512.

12824 Jerome H. Neyrey, "Eschatology in 1 Thessalonians: The Theological Factor in 1:9-10; 2:4-5; 3:11-13; 4:6 and 4:13-18," *SBLSP* 19 (1980): 219-31.

12825 Barnabas Lindars, "The Sound of the Trumpet: Paul and Eschatology," *BJRL* 67 (1985): 766-82.

12826 Richard N. Longenecker, "The Nature of Paul's Early Eschatology," *NTS* 31 (1985): 85-95.

<u>1:10</u>

12827 Ivan Havener, "The Pre-Pauline Christological Credal Formulae of 1 Thessalonians," *SBLSP* 20 (1981): 105-28.

12828 Frank England, "Afterthought: An Excuse or an Opportunity?" *JTSA* 92 (1995): 56-59.

2

12829 Abraham J. Malherbe, "Gentle as a Nurse: The Cynic Background to 1 Thessalonians 2," *NovT* 12 (1970): 203-17.

2:1-18

12830 R. Trevijano Etcheverría, "La mision en Tesalonica," *Salm* 32 (1985): 263-91.

2:1-16

12831 H. Schlier, "Auslegung des 1. Thessalonicherbriefes (1,1-10)," *BibL* 3 (1962): 89-97.

2:1-12

12832 Hendrikus Boers, "Form-Critical Study of Paul's Letters: 1 Thessalonians as a Case Study," *NTS* 22 (1976): 140-58.

12833 Karl P. Donfried, "The Cults of Thessalonica and the Thessalonian Correspondence," *NTS* 31 (1985): 336-56.

12834 Bruce W. Winter, "The Entries and Ethics of Orators and Paul (1 Thessalonians 2:1-12)," *TynB* 44 (1993): 55-74.

12835 Jeffrey A. D. Weima, "An Apology for the Apologetic Function of I Thessalonians 2:1-12," *JSNT* 68 (1997): 73-99.

2:1-6

12836 A.-M. Denis, "L'Apôtre Paul, prophète 'messianique' des Gentils: étude thématique de I Thess 2:1-6," *ETL* 33 (1957): 245-318.

2:2-3

12837 William Horbury, "1 Thessalonians 2:3 as Rebutting the Charge of False Prophecy," *JTS* 33 (1982): 492-508.

2:3-12

12838 John T. Townsend, "2 Thessalonians 2:3-12," *SBLSP* 19 (1980): 233-46.

2:4-5

12839 Jerome H. Neyrey, "Eschatology in 1 Thessalonians: The Theological Factor in 1:9-10; 2:4-5; 3:11-13; 4:6 and 4:13-18," *SBLSP* 19 (1980): 219-31.

2:7-13

12840 J. Vanderhägen, "Quand l'amour de Dieu vous atteignait," *AsSeign* NS 62 (1970): 13-20.

2:7-11

12841 Gerald G. Small, "The Use of Spiritual Gifts in the Ministry of Oversight," *CEJ* 1 (1980): 21-34.

2:7

12842 Charles Crawford, "The 'Tiny' Problem of 1 Thessalonians 2:7: The Case of the Curious Vocative," *Bib* 54 (1973): 69-72.

12843 Stephen Fowl, "A Metaphor in Distress: A Reading of *nepioi* in 1 Thessalonians 2:7," *NTS* 36 (1990): 469-73.

12844 Gordon D. Fee, "On Text and Commentary on 1 and 2 Thessalonians," *SBLSP* 31 (1992): 165-83.

12845 Beverly R. Gaventa, "Our Mother St. Paul: Toward the Recovery of a Neglected Theme," *PSB* NS 17 (1996): 29-44.

2:8

12846 L. Morris, "Kai apaks kai dis," *NovT* 1 (1956): 205-208.

12847 Norbert Baumert, "*Omeiromenoi* in 1 Thessalonians 2:8," *Bib* 68 (1987): 552-63.

2:9

12848 Néstor O. Míguez , "La composicion social de la iglesia en Tesalonica," *RevB* 51 (1989): 65-89.

2:11-12

12849 P. Vang, "Sanctification in Thessalonians," *SouJT* 42 (1999): 50-65.

2:12

12850 Günter Haufe, "Reich Gottes bei Paulus und in der Jesustradition," *NTS* 31 (1985): 467-72.

12851 Gordon D. Fee, "On Text and Commentary on 1 and 2 Thessalonians," *SBLSP* 31 (1992): 165-83.

2:13-16

12852 R. Schippers, "Pre-Synoptic Tradition in 1 Thessalonians 2:13-16," *NovT* 8 (1966): 223-34.

12853   Birger A. Pearson, "1 Thessalonians 2:13-16: A Deutero-Pauline Interpolation," *HTR* 64 (1971): 79-94.

12854   Joseph Coppens, "Diatribe antijuive dans 1 Thess 2:13-16," *ETL* 51 (1975): 90-95.

12855   Hendrikus Boers, "Form-Critical Study of Paul's Letters: 1 Thessalonians as a Case Study," *NTS* 22 (1976): 140-58.

12856   George E. Okeke, "1 Thessalonians 2:13-16: The Fate of the Unbelieving Jews," *NTS* 27 (1980): 127-36.

12857   Daryl D. Schmidt, "1 Thessalonians 2:13-16: Linguistic Evidence for an Interpolation," *JBL* 102 (1983): 269-79.

12858   Karl P. Donfried, "The Cults of Thessalonica and the Thessalonian Correspondence," *NTS* 31 (1985): 336-56.

12859   Jon A. Weatherly, "The Authenticity of 1 Thessalonians 2:13-16: Additional Evidence," *JSNT* 42 (1991): 79-98.

12860   Peter Wick, "Ist I Thess 2,13-16 antijüdisch?: Der rhetorische Gesamtzusammenhang des Briefes als Interpretationshilfe für eine einzelne Perikope," *TZ* 50 (1994): 9-23.

2:13

12861   P. Vang, "Sanctification in Thessalonians," *SouJT* 42 (1999): 50-65.

2:14-16

12862   Ingo Broer, "Antisemitismus und Judenpolemik im Neuen Testament: ein Beitrag zum besseren Verständnis von 1 Thess 2:14-16," *BibN* 20 (1983): 59-91.

12863   N. Samuel Murrell, "The Human Paul of the New Testament: Anti-Judaism in 1 Thessalonians 2:14-16," *EGLMBS* 14 (1994): 169-86.

2:14-15

12864   Frank D. Gilliard, "The Problem of the Antisemitic Comma between 1 Thessalonians 2:14 and 15," *NTS* 35 (1989): 481-502.

2:15-16

12865   J. W. Simpson, "The Problems Posed by 1 Thessalonians 2:15-16 and a Solution," *HBT* 12 (1990): 42-72.

2:15

12866   E. Bammel, "Judenverfolgung und Naherwartung: zur Eschatologie des Ersten Thessalonicherbriefs," *ZTK* 56 (1959): 294-315.

12867   Günther Baumbach, "Antijudaismus im Neuen Testament: Fragestellung und Lösungsmöglichkeit," *K* 25 (1983): 68-85.

12868   Gordon D. Fee, "On Text and Commentary on 1 and 2 Thessalonians," *SBLSP* 31 (1992): 165-83.

12869   Frank D. Gilliard, "Paul and the Killing of the Prophets in 1 Thessalonians 2:15," *NovT* 36 (1994): 259-70.

12870   Eduard Verhoef, "Die Bedeutung des Artikels ton in 1 Thess 2,15," *BibN* 80 (1995): 41-46.

2:16

12871   Mark A. Seifrid, "Paul's Approach to the Old Testament in Romans 10:6-8," *TriJ* NS 6 (1985): 3-37.

2:17-3:13

12872   H. Schlier, "Auslegung des 1. Thessalonicherbriefes (1,1-10)," *BibL* 3 (1962): 174-84.

3

12873   Robert Jewett, "Form and Function of the Homiletic Benediction," *ATR* 51 (1969): 18-34.

3:1-2

12874   A. Wainwright, "Where Did Silas Go? And What Was His Connection with Galatians?" *JSNT* 8 (1980): 66-70.

3:2-3

12875   Norbert Baumert, "Wir lassen uns nicht beirren: semantische Fragen in 1 Thess 3:2f," *FilN* 5 (1992): 45-60.

3:2

12876   Gordon D. Fee, "On Text and Commentary on 1 and 2 Thessalonians," *SBLSP* 31 (1992): 165-83.

3:3-4

12877   G. Daan Cloete, "In the Meantime, Trouble for the Peacemakers: Matthew 5:10-12," *JTSA* 52 (1985): 42-48.

3:3

12878   Henry Chadwick, "1 Thessalonians 3:3," *JTS* 1 (1950): 156-58.

3:6-10

12879   Margaret M. Mitchell, "New Testament Envoys in the Context of Greco-Roman Diplomatic and Epistolary Conventions: The Example of Timothy and Titus," *JBL* 111 (1992): 641-62.

3:6-9

12880   R. Trevijano Etcheverría, "La mision en Tesalonica," *Salm* 32 (1985): 263-91.

3:6

12881   Ceslaus Spicq, "ἐπιποθεῖν: Désirer ou chérir?" *RB* 64 (1957): 184-95.

3:11-13

12882   Jerome H. Neyrey, "Eschatology in 1 Thessalonians: The Theological Factor in 1:9-10; 2:4-5; 3:11-13; 4:6 and 4:13-18," *SBLSP* 19 (1980): 219-31.

3:11

12883   James A. Hewett, "1 Thessalonians 3,11," *ET* 87 (1975-1976): 54-55.

3:12-4:2

12884   J. Vanderhägen, "Le désir de l'Apôtre," *AsSeign* NS 5 (1969): 62-70.

3:13

12885   Lucien Cerfaux, "Les 'Saints' de Jérusalem," *ETL* 2 (1925): 510-29.

12886   Gordon D. Fee, "On Text and Commentary on 1 and 2 Thessalonians," *SBLSP* 31 (1992): 165-83.

12887   E. Bammel, "Judenverfolgung und Naherwartung: zur Eschatologie des Ersten Thessalonicherbriefs," *ZTK* 56 (1959): 294-315.

12888   P. Vang, "Sanctification in Thessalonians," *SouJT* 42 (1999): 50-65.

3:17

12889   Andreas Lindemann, "Zum Abfassungszweck des zweiten Thessalonicherbriefes," *ZNW* 68 (1977): 35-47.

4-5

12890   M. A. Molina Palma, "La provisionalidad responsable: el tiempo Cristiano en perspectiva escatologica," *EB* 45 (1987): 337-46.

12891   Michael D. Goulder, "Did Luke Know Any of the Pauline Letters," *PRS* 13 (1986): 97-112.

4:1-5:22

12892   Hendrikus Boers, "Form-Critical Study of Paul's Letters: 1 Thessalonians as a Case Study," *NTS* 22 (1976): 140-58.

4

12893   B. Martin Sanchez, "Cap 4. de la I. Ep. a los Tesalonicenses," *CuBi* 17 (1960): 351-54.

12894   Günter Haufe, "Individuelle Eschatologie des Neuen Testaments," *ZTK* 83 (1986): 436-63.

12895   Ben F. Meyer, "Did Paul's View of the Resurrection of the Dead undergo Development?" *TS* 47 (1986): 363-87.

12896   T. F. Glasson, "Theophany and Parousia," *NTS* 34 (1988): 259-70.

4:1-12

12897   H. Schlier, "Auslegung des 1. Thessalonicherbriefes (1,1-10)," *BibL* 3 (1962): 240-49.

12898   Robert Hodgson, "The Testimony Hypothesis," *JBL* 98 (1979): 361-78.

12899   Robert Hodgson, "1 Thessalonians 4:1-12 and the Holiness Tradition (HT)," *SBLSP* 21 (1982): 199-215.

12900   R. F. Collins, "The Function of Paraenesis in 1 Thessalonians 4:1-12; 5:12-22," *ETL* 74 (1998): 398-414.

4:1-8

12901   Marco Adinolfi, "La santità del matrimonio in 1 Tess. 4.1-8," *RBib* 24 (1976): 165-84.

12902   Marco Adinolfi, "Etica 'commerciale' e motivi parenetici in 1 Tess. 4,1-8," *BibO* 19 (1977): 9-20.

12903   William Klassen, "Foundations for Pauline Sexual Ethics as Seen in 1 Thessalonians 4:1-8," *SBLSP* 14 (1978): 159-81.

4:1-7

12904   F. Ogara, "Haec est. . . voluntas Dei, sanctificatio vestra," *VD* 18 (1938): 65-72.

12905   Adalberto Sisti, "Le Epistole della liturgia," *BibO* 4 (1962): 64-68.

12906   G. Brillet, "Dieu veut nous sanctifier dans le Christ," *AsSeign* 28 (1963): 16-26.

4:1-3

12907   Karl P. Donfried, "The Cults of Thessalonica and the Thessalonian Correspondence," *NTS* 31 (1985): 336-56.

4:1

12908   Gordon D. Fee, "On Text and Commentary on 1 and 2 Thessalonians," *SBLSP* 31 (1992): 165-83.

4:3-18

12909   John C. Brunt, "More on the *topos* as a New Testament Form," *JBL* 104 (1985): 495-500.

4:3-17

12910   E. Bammel, "Judenverfolgung und Naherwartung: zur Eschatologie des Ersten Thessalonicherbriefs," *ZTK* 56 (1959): 294-315.

4:3-8

12911   Heinrich Baltensweiler, "Erwägungen zu I Thess 4:3-8," *TZ* 19 (1963): 1-13.

12912   R. F. Collins, "The Unity of Paul's Paraenesis in 1 Thessalonians 4:3-8: 1 Corinthians 7:1-7: A Significant Parallel," *NTS* 29 (1983): 420-29.

12913   P. Vang, "Sanctification in Thessalonians," *SouJT* 42 (1999): 50-65.

4:4

12914   J. Whitton, "A Neglected Meaning for *skeuos* in 1 Thessalonians 4:4," *NTS* 28 (1982): 142-43.

12915 Karl P. Donfried, "The Cults of Thessalonica and the Thessalonian Correspondence," *NTS* 31 (1985): 336-56.

12916 Roger L. Omanson, "Translations:Text and Interpretation," *EQ* 57 (1985): 195-210.

12917 Michael McGehee, "A Rejoinder to Two Recent Studies Dealing with 1 Thessalonians 4:4," *CBQ* 51 (1989): 82-89.

12918 Simon Légasse, "Vas suum possidere," *FilN* 10 (1997): 105-15.

12919 Torleif Elgvin, " 'To Master His Own Vessel': 1 Thess 4:4 in Light of New Qumran Evidence," *NTS* 43 (1997): 604-19.

4:5-9

12920 Karl P. Donfried, "The Cults of Thessalonica and the Thessalonian Correspondence," *NTS* 31 (1985): 336-56.

4:6

12921 R. Beauvery, "*pleonektein* in 1 Thessalonians 4:6a," *VD* 33 (1955): 78-85.

12922 Severin M. Grill, "In das Gewerbe seines Nächsten eingreifen 1 Thess 4:6," *BZ* NS 11 (1967): 118.

12923 Marco Adinolfi, "Le frodi di I Tess. 4,6a e l'epicterato," *BibO* 18 (1976): 29-38.

12924 Jerome H. Neyrey, "Eschatology in 1 Thessalonians: The Theological Factor in 1:9-10; 2:4-5; 3:11-13; 4:6 and 4:13-18," *SBLSP* 19 (1980): 219-31.

4:7-12

12925 Néstor O. Míguez , "La composicion social de la iglesia en Tesalonica," *RevB* 51 (1989): 65-89.

4:8

12926 Friedrich W. Horn, "Wandel im Geist: zur pneumatologischen Begründung der Ethik bei Paulus," *KD* 38 (1992): 149-70.

4:9-12

12927 John S. Kloppenborg, "Philadelphia, Theodidaktos and the Dioscuri: Rhetorical Engagement in 1 Thessalonians 4:9-12," *NTS* 39 (1993): 265-89.

4:9

12928 T. I. Tambyah, "Theodidaktoi," *ET* 44 (1932-1933): 527-28.

12929 Gordon D. Fee, "On Text and Commentary on 1 and 2 Thessalonians," *SBLSP* 31 (1992): 165-83.

4:11-12

12930 Ronald Russell, "The Idle in 2 Thessalonians 3:6-12: An Eschatological or a Social Problem?" *NTS* 34 (1988): 105-19.

4:13-5:11

12931 H. Schlier, "Auslegung des 1. Thessalonicherbriefes (1,1-10)," *BibL* 4 (1962): 19-30.

12932 Z. I. Herman, "Il significato della morte e della risurrezione di Gesù nel contesto escatologico di 1 Ts. 4,13-5,11," *Ant* 55 (1980): 327-51.

12933 James M. Reese, "A Linguistic Approach to Paul's Exhortation in 1 Thessalonians 4:13-5:11," *SBLSP* 19 (1980): 209-18.

12934 Günter Klein, "Aspekte ewigen Lebens im Neuen Testament: ein theologischer Annäherungsversuch," *ZTK* 82 (1985): 48-70.

12935 Barnabas Lindars, "The Sound of the Trumpet: Paul and Eschatology," *BJRL* 67 (1985): 766-82.

12936 Tracy L. Howard, "The Literary Unity of 1 Thessalonians 4:13-5:11," *GTJ* 9 (1988): 163-90.

4:13-18

12937 E.-B. Allo, "S. Paul et la 'double résurrection' corporelle," *RB* 41 (1932): 188-209.

12938 P. Rossano, "A che punto siamo con 1 Thess 1. 4,13-17?" *RBib* 4 (1956): 72-80.

12939 P. Nepper-Christensen, "Das verborgene Herrnwort: eine Untersuchung über 1 Thess 4:13-18," *StTheol* 19 (1965): 136-54.

12940 Willi Marxsen, "Auslegung von 1 Thess 4:13-18," *ZTK* 66 (1969): 22-37.

12941 P.-É. Langevin, "Nous serons pour toujours avec le Seigneur," *AsSeign* NS 63 (1971): 13-19.

12942 J. Julius Scott, "Paul and Late-Jewish Eschatology: a Case Study: 1 Thessalonians 4:13-18 and 2 Thessalonians 2:1-12," *JETS* 15 (1972): 133-43.

12943 Jerome H. Neyrey, "Eschatology in 1 Thessalonians: The Theological Factor in 1:9-10; 2:4-5; 3:11-13; 4:6 and 4:13-18," *SBLSP* 19 (1980): 219-31.

12944 Luis F. Landaria, "Eucaristía y escatología," *EE* 59 (1984): 211-16.

12945 Joseph Plevnik, "The Taking up of the Faithful and the Resurrection of the Dead in 1 Thessalonians 4:13-18," *CBQ* 46 (1984): 274-83.

12946 John Gillman, "Signals of Transformation in 1 Thessalonians 4:13-18," *CBQ* 47 (1985): 263-81.

12947 Richard N. Longenecker, "The Nature of Paul's Early Eschatology," *NTS* 31 (1985): 85-95.

12948 Helmut Merklein, "Der Theologe als Prophet: zur Funktion prophetischen Redens im theologischen Diskurs des Paulus," *NTS* 38 (1992): 402-29.

12949 J. Smit Sibinga, "Serta Paulina: On Composition Technique in Paul," *FilN* 10 (1997): 35-54.

4:13-17

12950 Anselm Wimmer, "Trostworte des Apostels Paulus an Hinterbliebene in Thessalonich," *Bib* 36 (1955): 273-86.

4:13-14

12951 Tracy L. Howard, "The Meaning of 'Sleep' in 1 Thessalonians 5:10: A Reappraisal," *GTJ* 6 (1985): 337-48.

12952 Edward G. Kettner, "Time, Eternity, and the Intermediate State," *CJ* 12 (1986): 90-100.

4:13

12953 Karl P. Donfried, "The Cults of Thessalonica and the Thessalonian Correspondence," *NTS* 31 (1985): 336-56.

12954 Gordon D. Fee, "On Text and Commentary on 1 and 2 Thessalonians," *SBLSP* 31 (1992): 165-83.

4:14-17

12955 Gebhard Löhr, "1 Thess 4:15-17: das 'Herrenwort'," *ZNW* 71 (1980): 269-73.

12956 K. H. Schelkle, "Entmythologisierung in existentialer Interpretation," *TQ* 165 (1985): 257-66.

4:14

12957 Paul Ellingworth, "Which Way Are We Going? A Verb of Movement, Especially in 1 Thessalonians 4:14b," *BT* 25 (1974): 426-31.

4:15-17

12958 Andreas Lindemann, "Zum Abfassungszweck des zweiten Thessalonicherbriefes," *ZNW* 68 (1977): 35-47.

4:15

12959 E. M. B. Green, "A Note on 1 Thessalonians 4:15,17," *ET* 69 (1958): 285-86.

12960 Nikolaus Walter, "Paulus und die urchristliche Jesustradition," *NTS* 31 (1985): 498-522.

4:17

12961 E. M. B. Green, "A Note on 1 Thessalonians 4:15,17," *ET* 69 (1958): 285-86.

12962 Randall E. Otto, "The Meeting in the Air," *HBT* 19 (1997): 192-212.

4:18

12963 Tracy L. Howard, "The Meaning of 'Sleep' in 1 Thessalonians 5:10: A Reappraisal," *GTJ* 6 (1985): 337-48.

5

12964 Robert Jewett, "Form and Function of the Homiletic Benediction," *ATR* 51 (1969): 18-34.

12965 R. F. Collins, "1 Thessalonians and the Liturgy of the Early Church," *BTB* 10 (1980): 51-64.

12966 V. P. Branick, "Apocalyptic Paul?" *CBQ* 47 (1985): 664-75.

5:1-11

12967 Gerhard Friedrich, "1 Thessalonicher 5:1-11, der apologetische Einschub eines Späteren," *ZTK* 70 (1973): 288-315.

12968 Joseph Plevnik, "1 Thessalonians 5:1-11: Its Authenticity, Intention and Message," *Bib* 60 (1979): 71-90.

12969 John C. Brunt, "More on the *topos* as a New Testament Form," *JBL* 104 (1985): 495-500.

12970 Richard N. Longenecker, "The Nature of Paul's Early Eschatology," *NTS* 31 (1985): 85-95.

5:1-10

12971 Béda Rigaux, "Tradition et rédaction dans I Th v 1-10," *NTS* 21 (1975): 318-40.

5:1-6

12972 J. Vanderhägen, "Espérer le jour du Seigneur," *AsSeign* NS 64 (1969): 10-17.

5:1

12973 E. Lucchesi, "Précédents non bibliques à l'expression néo-testamentaire: 'Les temps et les moments'," *JTS* 28 (1977): 537-40.

5:3

12974 Nikolaus Walter, "Paulus und die urchristliche Jesustradition," *NTS* 31 (1985): 498-522.

5:4

12975 Gordon D. Fee, "On Text and Commentary on 1 and 2 Thessalonians," *SBLSP* 31 (1992): 165-83.

5:8

12976 Wolfgang Weiss, "Glaube—Liebe—Hoffnung: Zu der Trias bei Paulus," *ZNW* 84 (1993): 196-217.

5:9-11

12977 Tracy L. Howard, "The Meaning of 'Sleep' in 1 Thessalonians 5:10: A Reappraisal," *GTJ* 6 (1985): 337-48.

5:9-10

12978 James L. Jaquette, "Life and Death, Adiaphora, and Paul's Rhetorical Strategies," *NovT* 38 (1996): 30-54.

5:10

12979 Thomas R. Edgar, "The Meaning of 'Sleep' in 1 Thessalonians 5:10," *JETS* 22 (1979): 345-49.

12980 Markus Lautenschlager, "εἴτε γρηγορῶμεν εἴτε καθεύδωμεν: Zum Verhältnis von Heiligung und Heil in 1 Thess 5,10," *ZNW* 81 (1990): 38-59.

5:11

12981 O. Semmelroth, "Erbauet einer den anderen," *GeistL* 30 (1957): 262-71.

5:12-28

12982 C. J. Roetzel, "1 Thessalonians 5:12-28," *SBLSP* 11 (1972): 367-83.

5:12-22

12983 R. F. Collins, "The Function of Paraenesis in 1 Thessalonians 4:1-12; 5:12-22," *ETL* 74 (1998): 398-414.

5:12-18

12984 H. Schlier, "Auslegung des 1. Thessalonicherbriefes (1,1-10)," *BibL* 4 (1962): 96-103.

5:12-13

12985 M. C. Griffths, "Today's Missionary, Yesterday's Apostle," *EMQ* 21 (1985): 154-65.

12986 George W. Knight, "Two Offices and Two Orders of Elders: A New Testament Study," *Pres* 11 (1985): 1-12.

5:14-15

12987 Abraham J. Malherbe, "Pastoral Care in the Thessalonian Church," *NTS* 36 (1990): 375-91.

5:14

12988 Ceslaus Spicq, "Les Thessaloniciens 'inquiets' étaient-ils des paresseux," *StTheol* 10 (1956): 1-13.

12989 Ronald Russell, "The Idle in 2 Thessalonians 3:6-12: An Eschatological or a Social Problem?" *NTS* 34 (1988): 105-19.

5:15

12990 Jürgen Sauer, "Traditionsgeschichtliche Erwägungen zu den synoptischen und paulinischen Aussagen über Feindesliebe und Wiedervergeltungsverzicht," *ZNW* 76 (1985): 1-28.

5:16-24

12991 P.-É. Langevin, "Conseils et prière," *AsSeign* NS 7 (1969): 34-39.

5:17

12992 Clay Smith, "Adialeiptos Proseuchesthe: Is Paul Serious?" *Pres* 22 (1996): 113-20.

5:19

12993 W. C. van Unnik, "Den Geist löschet nicht aus," *NovT* 10 (1968): 255-69.

12994 F. P. Green, "Quench not the Spirit," *ET* 88 (1977): 240-41.

12995 P. Vang, "Sanctification in Thessalonians," *SouJT* 42 (1999): 50-65.

5:21

12996 Gordon D. Fee, "On Text and Commentary on 1 and 2 Thessalonians," *SBLSP* 31 (1992): 165-83.

5:23-28

12997 Hendrikus Boers, "Form-Critical Study of Paul's Letters: 1 Thessalonians as a Case Study," *NTS* 22 (1976): 140-58.

12998 R. F. Collins, "1 Thessalonians and the Liturgy of the Early Church," *BTB* 10 (1980): 51-64.

5:23-24

12999 P.-É. Langevin, "L'intervention de Dieu, selon I Thes 5:23-24: déjà le salut par grâce," *ScE* 41 (1989): 71-92.

5:23

13000 Werner Förster, "Die Grundzüge der ptolemäischen Gnosis," *NTS* 6 (1959): 16-31.

13001 P. A. van Stempvoort, "Eine stilistische Lösung einer alten Schwierigkeit in 1 Thessalonicher 5:23," *NTS* 7 (1961): 262-65.

13002 Roland   Bergmeier,   "Königlosigkeit   als nachvalentinianisches Heilsprädikat," *NovT* 24 (1982): 316-39.

13003 Antonio Orbe, "Deus facit, homo fit: un axioma de san Ireneo," *Greg* 69 (1988): 629-61.

5:25

13004 Gordon D. Fee, "On Text and Commentary on 1 and 2 Thessalonians," *SBLSP* 31 (1992): 165-83.

2 Thessalonians

1:1-12

13005 A. Schulz, "Gemeinde auf dem Weg. Auslegung des 2. Thessalonicherbriefe," *BibL* 8 (1967): 33-41.

1:3-10

13006 Duane A. Dunham, "2 Thessalonians 1:3-10: A Study in Sentence Structure," *JETS* 24 (1981): 39-46.

1:3

13007 Roger D. Aus, "Liturgical Background of the Necessity and Propriety of Giving Thanks according to 2 Thessalonians 1:3," *JBL* 92 (1973): 432-38.

1:5-12

13008 Karl P. Donfried, "The Cults of Thessalonica and the Thessalonian Correspondence," *NTS* 31 (1985): 336-56.

1:5

13009 Jouette M. Bassler, "The Enigmatic Sign: 2 Thessalonians 1:5," *CBQ* 46 (1984): 496-510.

1:6-10

13010 Vern S. Poythress, "2 Thessalonians 1 Supports Amillennialism," *JETS* 37 (1994): 529-38.

1:7-8

13011 T. F. Glasson, "Theophany and Parousia," *NTS* 34 (1988): 259-70.

1:7

13012 Pierre Benoit, "Pauline Angelology and Demonology: Reflexions on Designations of Heavenly Powers and on Origin of Angelic Evil according to Paul," *RSB* 3 (1983): 1-18.

1:8

13013 Peter Katz, "ἐν πυρὶ φλογός," *ZNW* 46 (1955): 133-38.

1:9

13014 Edward Fudge, "The Final End of the Wicked," *JETS* 27 (1984): 325-34.

13015 Charles L. Quarles, "The *'APO* of 2 Thessalonians 1:9 and the Nature of Eternal Punishment," *WTJ* 59 (1997): 201-11.

1:11-2:12

13016 A. Schulz, "Ausschauen in Nüchternheit. Auslegung des 2. Thessalonicherbriefes," *BibL* 8 (1967): 110-19.

1:11-2:2

13017 A. M. Artola, "Le Christ se manifeste dans la communauté chrétienne," *AsSeign* NS 62 (1970): 75-80.

2:1-17

13018 Klauspeter Blaser, "Biblische Besinnung: 2. Thessalonicherbrief 2,1-17," *ZMiss* 22 (1996): 206-209.

2:1-12

13019 H. P. Hamann, "A Brief Exegesis of 2 Thessalonians 2:1-12 with Guideline for the Application of the Prophecy Contained Therein," *CTM* 24 (1953): 418-33.

13020 M. Brunec, "De 'Homine peccati' in 2 Thess. 2,1-12," *VD* 35 (1957): 3-33.

13021 Béda Rigaux, "L'Antichrist," *AsSeign* 6 (1965): 28-39.

13022 J. Julius Scott, "Paul and Late-Jewish Eschatology: a Case Study: 1 Thessalonians 4:13-18 and 2 Thessalonians 2:1-12," *JETS* 15 (1972): 133-43.

13023 Andreas Lindemann, "Zum Abfassungszweck des zweiten Thessalonicherbriefes," *ZNW* 68 (1977): 35-47.

13024 Glenn Holland, "Let No One Deceive You in Any Way: 2 Thessalonians as a Reformulation of the Apocalyptic Tradition," *SBLSP* 24 (1985): 327-41.

13025 Richard N. Longenecker, "The Nature of Paul's Early Eschatology," *NTS* 31 (1985): 85-95.

2:2

13026 John Knox, "A Note on 2 Thessalonians 2:2," *ATR* 18 (1936): 72-73.

2:3-12

13027   J. W. Moran, "Is Antichrist a Man?" *AmER* 92 (1935): 578-85.

13028   M. Miguéns, "L'apocalisse 'secondo Paolo'," *BibO* 2 (1960): 142-48.

13029   F. Marin, "Pequeña apocalipsis de 2 Tes 2,3-12," *EE* 51 (1976): 29-56.

13030   F. Marin, "2 Tes 2,3-12. Intentos de comprensión y nuevo planteamiento," *EE* 54 (1979): 527-37.

13031   John T. Townsend, "1 Thessalonians 2:3-12," *SBLSP* 19 (1980): 233-50.

13032   Karl P. Donfried, "The Cults of Thessalonica and the Thessalonian Correspondence," *NTS* 31 (1985): 336-56.

2:6-7

13033   Oscar Cullmann, "Le caractère eschatologique du devoir messianique et de la conscience apostolique de S. Paul," *RHPR* 16 (1936): 210-45.

13034   J. M. González-Ruiz, "La incredulidad de Israel y los impedimentos del Anticristo, segun 2 Tes. 2,6-7," *EB* 10 (1951): 189-203.

13035   P. Andriessen, "Celui qui retient la venue du Seigneur," *Bij* 21 (1960): 20-30.

13036   Joseph Coppens, "Les deux obstacles au retour glorieux du Saveur," *ETL* 46 (1970): 383-89.

13037   Roger D. Aus, "God's Plan and God's Power: Isaiah 66 and the Restraining Factors of 2 Thessalonians 2:6-7," *JBL* 96 (1977): 537-53.

13038   M. Barnouin, "Problèmes de traduction concernant 2 Thess 2:6-7," *NTS* 23 (1977): 482-98.

13039   Gerhard A. Krodel, "The 'Religious Power of Lawlessness' (*katechon*) as Precursor of the 'Lawless One' (*anomos*) 2 Thessalonians 2:6-7," *CThM* 17 (1990): 440-46.

13040   L. J. Lietaert Peerbolte, "The *katechon/katechon* of 2 Thessalonians 2:6-7," *NovT* 39 (1997): 138-50.

2:6

13041 Paul S. Dixon, "The Evil Restraint in 2 Thessalonians 2:6," *JETS* 33 (1990): 445-49.

2:7

13042 P. H. Furfey, "The Mystery of Lawlessness," *CBQ* 8 (1946): 179-91.

13043 M. Barnouin, "Un 'lieu intermédiaire' mythique en 2 Thess 2:7," *NTS* 40 (1994): 471.

2:8

13044 Ermanno Genre, "Huldrych Zwingli: la militance du pasteur réformé," *ÉTR* 60 (1985): 513-26.

13045 Walter Kasper, "Die Hoffnung auf die endgültige Ankunft Jesu Christi in Herrlichkeit," *IKaZ* 14 (1985): 1-14.

2:13-3:5

13046 Joseph D. Stinson, "Expository Notes on Selected Lections," *QR* 6 (1986): 84-91.

2:13-3:3

13047 A. Schulz, "Die Kunst zu trösten," *BibL* 8 (1967): 179-85.

2:13-16

13048 Karl P. Donfried, "Paul and Judaism: 1 Thessalonians 2:13-16 as a Test Case," *Int* 38 (1984): 242-53.

2:13

13049 S. Lewis Johnson, "Divine Love in Recent Theology," *TriJ* NS 5 (1984): 175-87.

2:15

13050 M. C. Griffths, "Today's Missionary, Yesterday's Apostle," *EMQ* 21 (1985): 154-65.

2:16-3:5

13051 A. M. Artola, "Prière et apostolat," *AsSeign* NS 63 (1971): 76-81.

3

13052 Robert Jewett, "Form and Function of the Homiletic Benediction," *ATR* 51 (1969): 18-34.

3:1-3

13053 J. D. M. Derrett, "Running in Paul: The Midrashic Potential of Hab 2:2," *Bib* 66 (1985): 560-67.

3:1

13054 L.-M. Dewailly, "Course et gloire de la Parole (2 Thess 3:1)," *RB* 71 (1964): 25-41.

3:4-14

13055 M. C. Griffths, "Today's Missionary, Yesterday's Apostle," *EMQ* 21 (1985): 154-65.

3:4-18

13056 A. Schulz, "Die Pflicht des Christen, zu arbeiten," *BibL* 8 (1967): 256-64.

3:6-16

13057 Bruce W. Winter, "If a Man Does not Wish to Work... A Cultural and Historical Setting for 2 Thessalonians 3:6-16," *TynB* 40 (1989): 303-15.

3:6-13

13058 Ronald Russell, "The Idle in 2 Thessalonians 3:6-12: An Eschatological or a Social Problem?" *NTS* 34 (1988): 105-19.

3:6

13059 John F. Brug, "2 Thessalonians 3:6,14,15--Admonish Him as a Brother," *WLQ* 96 (1999): 208-17.

3:7-12

13060 A. M. Artola, "L'apôtre-ouvrier se donne en modèle," *AsSeign* NS 64 (1969): 71-76.

3:10

13061 Robert Jewett, "Tenement Churches and Communal Meals in the Early Church: The Implications of a Form-Critical Analysis of 2 Thessalonians 3:10," *BR* 38 (1993): 23-43.

3:14-15

13062 John F. Brug, "2 Thessalonians 3:6,14,15--Admonish Him as a Brother," *WLQ* 96 (1999): 208-17.

1 Timothy

<u>1:1</u>

13063   Michael R. Austin, "Salvation and the Divinity of Jesus," *ET* 96 (1985): 271-75.

<u>1:3-11</u>

13064   Stephen Westerholm, "The Law and the 'Just Man' (1 Timothy 1:3-11)," *StTheol* 36 (1982): 79-95.

<u>1:3</u>

13065   Gordon D. Fee, "Reflections on Church Order in the Pastoral Epistles, with Further Reflection on the Hermeneutics of *ad hoc* Documents," *JETS* 28 (1985): 141-51.

13066   M. C. Griffths, "Today's Missionary, Yesterday's Apostle," *EMQ* 21 (1985): 154-65.

<u>1:4</u>

13067   Benedict T. Viviano, "The Genres of Matthew 1-2: Light from 1 Timothy 1:4," *RB* 97 (1990): 31-53.

<u>1:5</u>

13068   Mark A. Seifrid, "Paul's Approach to the Old Testament in Romans 10:6-8," *TriJ* NS 6 (1985): 3-37.

<u>1:8-11</u>

13069   John R. W. Stott, "Homosexual Marriage: Why Same Sex Partnerships Are Not a Christian Option," *CT* 29 (1985): 21-28.

<u>1:8-10</u>

13070   Randolph A. Nelson, "Homosexuality and Social Ethics," *WW* 5 (1985): 380-94.

<u>1:9-10</u>

13071   Abraham Smith, "The New Testament and Homosexuality," *QR* 11 (1991): 18-32.

1:10

13072 David F. Wright, "Translating *arsenokoitai* (1 Corinthians 6:9; 1 Timothy 1:10)," *VC* 41 (1987): 396-98.

13073 J. A. Harrill, "The Vice of Slave Dealers in Greco-Roman Society: The Use of a *Topos* in 1 Timothy 1:10," *JBL* 118 (1999): 97-122.

1:12-17

13074 Benoît Standaert, "Paul, exemple vivant de l'Évangile de grâce," *AsSeign* NS 55 (1974): 62-69.

13075 Gerhard Lohfink, "Die Vermittlung des Paulinismus zu den Pastoralbriefen," *BZ* NS 32 (1988): 169-88.

1:13

13076 Michael Wolter, "Paulus, der bekehrte Gottesfeind: zum Verständnis von 1 Tim 1:13," *NovT* 31 (1989): 48-66.

1:17

13077 C. C. Oke, "A Doxology not to God but Christ," *ET* 67 (1955-1956): 367-68.

1:18

13078 Michael A. G. Haykin, "The Fading Vision: The Spirit and Freedom in the Pastoral Epistles," *EQ* 57 (1985): 291-305.

13079 Jerry R. Young, "Shepherds, Lead," *GTJ* 6 (1985): 329-35.

2

13080 Vernon C. Grounds, "The Battle for Shalom," *CT* 30 (1986): 18-20.

2:1-8

13081 André Lemaire, "Conseils pour une liturgie authentique," *AsSeign* NS 56 (1974): 62-66.

13082 Geoffrey Wainwright, "Praying for Kings: The Place of Human Rulers in the Divine Plan of Salvation," *ExA* 2 (1986): 117-27.

2:1-7

13083 Gilles Gaide, "La prière missionnaire," *AsSeign* 98 (1967): 15-24.

2:1

13084 Frank Stagg, "The Gospel, Haustafel, and Women: Mark 1:1; Colossians 3:18-4:1," *FM* 2 (1985): 59-63.

2:2

13085 Jarl H. Ulrichsen, "Die sieben Häupter und die zehn Hörner zur Datierung der Offenbarung des Johannes," *StTheol* 39 (1985): 1-20.

2:3-4

13086 Robert R. Hann, "Election, the Humanity of Jesus, and Possible Worlds," *JETS* 29 (1986): 295-305.

2:3

13087 Palémon Glorieux, "La révélation du Pére," *MSR* 42 (1985): 21-41.

2:4

13088 J. Alonso Díaz, "La salvación universal a partir de la exegesis de 1 Tim 2,4," *CuBí* 28 (1971): 350-61.

2:4

13089 Rolf Gögler, "Inkarnationsglaube und Bibeltheologie bei Origenes," *TQ* 165 (1985): 82-94.

2:5-6

13090 Robert Javelet, "Marie, la femme médiatrice," *RevSR* 58 (1984): 162-71.

13091 Jürgen Denker, "Identidad y mundo vivencial (Lebenswelt): en torno a Marcos 10:35-45 y Timoteo 2:5s," *RevB* 46 (1984): 159-69.

13092 Michael R. Austin, "Salvation and the Divinity of Jesus," *ET* 96 (1985): 271-75.

13093 Malcolm J. McVeigh, "The Fate of Those Who've Never Heard: It Depends," *EMQ* 21 (1985): 370-79.

2:6

13094 C. Samuel Storms, "Defining the Elect: A Review Article," *JETS* 27 (1984): 205-18.

2:7

13095 Neal F. McBride and W. Creighton Marlowe, "Biblical Distinctives between the Content and Character of Teaching and Preaching," *CEJ* 1 (1981): 68-74.

2:8-15

13096 Lyle D. Vander Broek, "Women and the Church: Approaching Difficult Passages," *RR* 38 (1985): 225-31.

13097 Alan Padgett, "Wealthy Women at Ephesus: 1 Timothy 2:8-15 in Social Context," *Int* 41 (1987): 19-31.

13098 Carol J. Westphal, "Coming Home," *RR* 42 (1989): 177-88.

13099 Gloria N. Redekop, "Let the Women Learn: 1 Timothy 2:8-15 Reconsidered," *SR* 19 (1990): 235-45.

13100 Gordon P. Hugenberger, "Women in Church Office: Hermeneutics or Exegesis? A Survey of Approaches to 1 Timothy 2:8-15," *JETS* 35 (1992): 341-60.

13101 Ronald W. Pierce, "Evangelicals and Gender Roles in the 1990s: 1 Timothy 2:8-15: A Test Case," *JETS* 36 (1993): 343-55.

13102 Royce G. Gruenler, "The Mission-Lifestyle Setting of 1 Timothy 2:8-15," *JETS* 41 (1998): 215-38.

2:8

13103 Everett Ferguson, "*Topos* in 1 Timothy 2:8," *RQ* 33 (1991): 64-73.

2:9-15

13104 Gordon D. Fee, "Reflections on Church Order in the Pastoral Epistles, with Further Reflection on the Hermeneutics of *ad hoc* Documents," *JETS* 28 (1985): 141-51.

13105 Andreas J. Köstenberger, "The Crux of the Matter: Paul's Pastoral Pronouncements Regarding Women's Roles in 1 Timothy 2:9-15," *FM* 14 (1996): 24-48.

2:11-15

13106 Aida B. Spencer, "Eve at Ephesus," *JETS* 17 (1974): 215-22.

13107 Krijn A. van der Jagt, "Women Are Saved through Bearing Children," *BT* 39 (1988): 201-208.

13108 P. W. Barnett, "Wives and Women's Ministry (1 Timothy 2:11-15)," *EQ* 61 (1989): 225-38.

13109 Ann L. Bowman, "Women in Ministry: An Exegetical Study of 1 Timothy 2:11-15," *BSac* 149 (1992): 193-213.

13110 Steven M. Baugh, "The Apostle among the Amazons," *WTJ* 56 (1994): 153-71.

13111 Ben Wiebe, "Two Texts on Women: A Test of Interpretation," *HBT* 16 (1994): 54-85.

2:11-12

13112 Lewis R. Donelson, "The Structure of Ethical Argument in the Pastorals," *BTB* 18 (1988): 108-13.

2:12

13113 George W. Knight, "αὐθεντέω in Reference to Women in 1 Timothy 2:12," *NTS* 30 (1984): 143-57.

13114 Robert W. Allison, "Let Women Be Silent in the Churches (1 Corinthians 14:33b-36): What Did Paul Really Say, and What Did It Mean?" *JSNT* 32 (1988): 27-60.

13115 Leland E. Wilshire, "The *TLG* Computer and Further Reference to αὐθεντέω in 1 Timothy 2:12," *NTS* 34 (1988): 120-34.

13116 A. C. Perriman, "What Eve Did, What Women Shouldn't Do: The Meaning of *authenteo* in 1 Timothy 2:12," *TynB* 44 (1993): 129-42.

13117 Leland E. Wilshire, "1 Timothy 2:12 Revisited," *EQ* 65 (1993): 43-55.

13118 Robert L. Saucy, "Women's Prohibition to Teach Men: An Investigation into Its Meaning and Contemporary Application," *JETS* 37 (1994): 79-97.

2:13-15

13119 Jack Levison, "Is Eve to Blame: A Contextual Analysis of Sirach 25:24," *CBQ* 47 (1985): 617-23.

2:14-15

13120 R. Falconer, "1 Timothy 2:14,15," *JBL* 60 (1941): 375-79.

13121 J. B. Bauer, "Die Arbeit als Heilsdimension," *BL* 24 (1956-1957): 198-201.

2:14

13122 Gerald L. Bray, "The Fall Is a Human Reality," *ERT* 9 (1985): 334-38.

2:15

13123 S. Jebb, "Suggested Interpretation of 1 Timothy 2:15," *ET* 81 (1969-1970): 221-22.

13124 Jarl H. Ulrichsen, "Noen bemerkninger til 1 Tim 2:15," *NTT* 84 (1983): 19-25.

13125 Curtis C. Mitchell, "Why Keep Bothering God: The Case for Persisting in Prayer," *CT* 29 (1985): 33-34.

13126 David R. Kimberley, "1 Timothy 2:15: A Possible Understanding of a Difficult Text," *JETS* 35 (1992): 481-86.

13127 Stanley E. Porter, "What Does it Mean to be 'Saved by Childbirth'?" *JSNT* 49 (1993): 87-102.

13128 Jarl H. Ulrichsen, "Heil durch Kindergebären: zu 1 Tim 2:15 und seiner syrischen Version," *SEÅ* 58 (1993): 99-104.

3:1-17

13129 Gerald G. Small, "The Use of Spiritual Gifts in the Ministry of Oversight," *CEJ* 1 (1980): 21-34.

3:1-7

13130 Max A. Chevallier, "L'unité plurielle de l'église d'après le Nouveau Testament," *RHPR* 66 (1986): 3-20.

13131 Ed Glasscock, "The Biblical Concept of Elder," *BSac* 144 (1987): 66-78.

3:1

13132 U. Holzmeister, "Si quis episcopatum desiderat, bonum opus desiderat," *Bib* 12 (1931): 41-69.

13133 Peter Trummer, "Einehe nach den Pastoralbriefen. Zum Verständnis der Termini μιᾶς γυναικὸς ἀνήρ und ἑνὸς ἀνδρὸς γυνή," *Bib* 51 (1970): 471-84.

13134 José O'Callaghan, "1 Tim 3:16: 4:1.3 en 7Q4?" *Bib* 53 (1972): 362-67.

13135 Frank Stagg, "The Gospel, Haustafel, and Women: Mark 1:1; Colossians 3:18-4:1," *FM* 2 (1985): 59-63.

13136 J. Lionel North, " 'Human Speech' in Paul and the Paulines: The Investigation and Meaning of *anthropinos o logos*," *NovT* 37 (1995): 50-67.

3:11

13137 Jennifer H. Stoefel, "Women Deacons in 1 Timothy: A Linguistic and Literary Look at 'Women Likewise . . . '," *NTS* 41 (1995): 442-57.

3:12

13138 S. Lyonnet, "Unius uxoris vir," *VD* 45 (1967): 3-10.

13139 Peter Trummer, "Einehe nach den Pastoralbriefen. Zum Verständnis der Termini μιᾶς γυναικὸς ἀνήρ und ἑνὸς ἀνδρὸς γυνή," *Bib* 51 (1970): 471-84.

3:15

13140 Gordon D. Fee, "Reflections on Church Order in the Pastoral Epistles, with Further Reflection on the Hermeneutics of *ad hoc* Documents," *JETS* 28 (1985): 141-51.

13141 E. Butzer, "Die Witwen der Pastoralbriefe," *TextK* 20 (1998): 35-52.

3:16

13142 Werner Stenger, "Der Christushymnus in 1 Tim 3,16: Aufbau, Christologie, Sitz im Leben," *TTZ* 78 (1969): 33-48.

13143 Eduard Schweizer, "Lord of the Nations," *SEAJT* 13 (1972): 13-21.

13144 Werner Stenger, "Textkritik als Schicksal," *BZ* 19 (1973): 240-47.

13145 Frédéric Manns, "Judeo-Christian Context of 1 Timothy 3:16," *TD* 29 (1981): 119-22.

13146 Kendell H. Easley, "The Pauline Usage of *pneumati* as a Reference to the Spirit of God," *JETS* 27 (1984): 299-313.

13147 Jerome Murphy-O'Connor, "Redactional Angels in 1 Timothy 3:16," *RB* 91 (1984): 178-87.

13148 Luis F. Ladaria, "Dispensatio en S Hilario de Poitiers," *Greg* 66 (1985): 429-55.

13149 Fika J. J. Van Rensburg, "Die Timoteus-himne (1 Tim 3:16)," *HTS* suppl 1 (1989): 83-97.

3:2-7

13150 F. Ross Kinsler, "Theology by the People," *West African Religion* 20 (1983): 17-36.

3:2

13151 S. Lyonnet, "Unius uxoris vir," *VD* 45 (1967): 3-10.

13152 David J. Valleskey, "The Pastor Must Be 'Above Reproach': An Examination of *anepilemeptos* (1 Timothy 3:2) and *aneekletos* (Titus 1:6) with Applications to the Public Ministry of the Gospel," *WLQ* 96 (1999): 194-207.

3:8-13

13153 B. C. Wintle, "Patterns of Ministry in the Later Pauline Letters," *IJT* 32 (1983): 68-76.

4:1-14

13154 Barth Campbell, "Rhetorical Design in 1 Timothy 4," *BSac* 154 (1997): 189-204.

4:1-5

13155 Gerald T. Sheppard, "The Use of Scripture within the Christian Ethical Debate concerning Same-Sex Oriented Persons," *USQR* 40 (1985): 13-35.

4:1-3

13156 William L. Lane, "1 Timothy 4:1-3: An Early Instance of Over-Realized Eschatology?" *NTS* 11 (1965): 164-67.

13157 Michael A. G. Haykin, "The Fading Vision: The Spirit and Freedom in the Pastoral Epistles," *EQ* 57 (1985): 291-305.

4:1

13158 José O'Callaghan, "1 Tim 3:16; 4:1.3 en 7Q4?" *Bib* 53 (1972): 362-67.

4:2

13159 Abraham J. Malherbe, "In Season and Out of Season: 2 Timothy 4:2," *JBL* 103 (1984): 235-43.

4:3

13160 C. Daniel, "Une mention paulinienne des Esséniens de Qumrân," *RevQ* 5 (1966): 553-67.

13161 José O'Callaghan, "1 Tim 3:16: 4:1.3 en 7Q4?" *Bib* 53 (1972): 362-67.

4:6-16

13162 M. L. Reid, "An Exegesis of 1 Timothy 4:6-16," *FM* 9 (1991): 51-63.

4:7-8

13163 Ceslaus Spicq, "Gymnastique et morale," *RB* 54 (1947): 229-42.

4:10

13164 C. Samuel Storms, "Defining the Elect: A Review Article," *JETS* 27 (1984): 205-18.

13165 Steven M. Baugh, "Savior of All People: 1 Timothy 4:10 in Context," *WTJ* 54 (1992): 331-40.

13166 Mark J. Goodwin, "The Pauline Background of the Living God as Interpretative Context for 1 Timothy 4:10," *JSNT* 61 (1996): 65-85.

4:13-14

13167 Michael A. G. Haykin, "The Fading Vision: The Spirit and Freedom in the Pastoral Epistles," *EQ* 57 (1985): 291-305.

4:13

13168 G. M. Lee, "The Books and the Parchments: 1 Timothy 4:13," *Theology* 74 (1971): 168-69.

4:14

13169 Otfried Hofius, "Zur Auslegungsgeschichte von presbyterion 1 Tim 4:14," *ZNW* 62 (1971): 128-29.

13170 Jerry R. Young, "Shepherds, Lead," *GTJ* 6 (1985): 329-35.

13171 John J. Kilgallen, "Reflections on *charisma(ta)* in the New Testament," *SM* 41 (1992): 289-323.

5:3-16

13172   F. C. Synge, "Studies in texts: 1 Timothy 5:3-161,"
        Theology 68 (1965): 200-201.

13173   Josef Ernst, "Die Witwenregel des ersten
        Timotheusbriefes, ein Brief auf die biblischen Ursprünge
        des weiblichen Ordenswesens?" *TGl* 59 (1969): 434-45.

13174   Jouette M. Bassler, "The Widow's Tale: A Fresh Look at
        1 Timothy 5:3-16," *JBL* 103 (1984): 23-41.

13175   Gail P. Corrington, "Salvation, Celibacy, and Power:
        'Divine Women' in Late Antiquity," *SBLSP* 24 (1985):
        321-25.

13176   Bonnie B. Thurston, "The Widows as the 'Altar of God',"
        SBLSP 24 (1985): 279-89.

13177   Robert Macina, "Pour éclairer le terme: digamoi," *RevSR*
        61 (1987): 54-73.

13178   David M. Scholer, "Feminist Hermeneutics and
        Evangelical Biblical Interpretation," *JETS* 30 (1987):
        407-20.

13179   Bruce W. Winter, "Providentia for the Widows of 1
        Timothy 5:3-16," *TynB* 39 (1988): 83-99.

13180   E. Butzer, "Die Witwen der Pastoralbriefe," *TextK* 20
        (1998): 35-52.

5:8

13181   R. A. Campbell, "*Kai malista oikeion*—A New Look at 1
        Timothy 5:8," *NTS* 41 (1995): 157-60.

5:9

13182   Peter Trummer, "Einehe nach den Pastoralbriefen. Zum
        Verständnis der Termini μιᾶς γυναικὸς ἀνήρ und ἑνὸς
        ἀνδρὸς γυνή," *Bib* 51 (1970): 471-84.

5:10

13183   Allen Edgington, "Footwashing as an Ordinance," *GTJ* 6
        (1985): 425-34.

5:11-15

13184   Gordon D. Fee, "Reflections on Church Order in the
        Pastoral Epistles, with Further Reflection on the

Hermeneutics of *ad hoc* Documents," *JETS* 28 (1985): 141-51.

5:14

13185   William A. Heth, "Unmarried 'for the Sake of the Kingdom' (Matthew 19:12) in the Early Church," *GTJ* 8 (1987): 55-88.

5:17

13186   Gerald G. Small, "The Use of Spiritual Gifts in the Ministry of Oversight," *CEJ* 1 (1980): 21-34.

13187   Gordon D. Fee, "Reflections on Church Order in the Pastoral Epistles, with Further Reflection on the Hermeneutics of *ad hoc* Documents," *JETS* 28 (1985): 141-51.

13188   Frank Stagg, "The Gospel, Haustafel, and Women: Mark 1:1; Colossians 3:18-4:1," *FM* 2 (1985): 59-63.

13189   Elsie A. McKee, "Les anciens et l'interprétation de 1 Tim 5:17 chez Calvin: une curiosité dans l'histoire de l'exégèse," *RTP* 120 (1988): 411-17.

13190   Georg Schöllgen, "Die 'diple time' von 1 Timothy 5:17," *ZNW* 80 (1989): 232-39.

13191   B. R. Keller, "Timothy 5:17—Did All πρεσβύτεροι Proclaim God's Word?" *WLQ* 96 (1999): 43-49

5:18

13192   A. E. Harvey, " 'The Workman is Worthy of His Hire': Fortunes of a Proverb in the Early Church," *NovT* 2 (1982): 209-21.

5:19-23

13193   J. W. Fuller, "Of Elders and Triads in 1 Timothy 5:19-23," *NTS* 29 (1983): 258-63.

5:19-20

13194   D. A. Mappes, "The Discipline of a Sinning Elder," *BSac* 154 (1997): 333-43.

5:20

13195   A. Burge Troxel, "Accountability without Bondage: Shepherd Leadership in the Biblical Church," *CEJ* 2 (1982): 39-46.

5:22

13196 George D. Kilpatrick, "1 Timothy 5:22 and Tertullian *De Baptismo* 18:1," *JTS* NS 16 (1965): 127-28.

5:23

13197 Peter Jensen, "Faith and Healing in Christian Theology," *Point* 11 (1982): 153-59.

6:1

13198 Frank Stagg, "The Gospel, Haustafel, and Women: Mark 1:1; Colossians 3:18-4:1," *FM* 2 (1985): 59-63.

6:3-21

13199 Jukka Thurén, "Die Struktur der Schlussparänese 1 Tim 6:3-21," *TZ* 26 (1970): 241-53.

13200 Peter Dschulnigg, "Warnung vor Reichtum und Ermahnung der Reichen: 1 Tim 6:6-10,17-19 im Rahmen des Schlussteils 6:3-21," *BZ* NS 37 (1993): 60-77.

6:5-10

13201 Frederick E. Brenk, "Old Wineskins Recycled: *autarkeia* in 1 Timothy 6:5-10," *FilN* 3 (1990): 39-52.

6:7

13202 M. J. J. Menken, "*Oti* en 1 Tim 6:7," *Bib* 58 (1977): 532-41.

6:9-10

13203 Titus M. Kivunzi, "Biblical Basis for Financial Stewardship," *EAJT* 3 (1985): 24-34.

6:11-17

13204 Richard C. Brand, "The Evolution of a Slogan," *ET* 89 (1978): 247-48.

6:11-16

13205 H. Obendiek, "Das gute Bekenntnis nach 1. Tim 6,11-16," *EvT* 6 (1946-1947): 234-57.

13206 L. Deiss, "Jusqu'à l'épiphanie de notre Seigneur Jésus Christ," *AsSeign* NS 57 (1971): 74-79.

6:11-14

> 13207 Christian Grappe, "Essai sur l'arrière-plan Pascal des récits de la dernière nuit de Jésus," *RHPR* 65 (1985): 105-25.

6:12-16

> 13208 R.-H. Esnault, "1 Timothy 6:12-16," *ÉTR* 30 (1955): 40-45.

6:17-19

> 13209 Werner Bieder, "Reiche als Mitarbeiter der Befreiung?" *ZMiss* 17 (1991): 66-69.

6:20

> 13210 Egbert Schlarb, "Miszelle zu 1 Tim 6:20," *ZNW* 77 (1986): 276-81.

2 Timothy

1:3-12

13211 Gerhard Lohfink, "Die Vermittlung des Paulinismus zu den Pastoralbriefen," *BZ* NS 32 (1988): 169-88.

1:5

13212 Ceslaus Spicq, "Loïs, ta grand'maman," *RB* 84 (1977): 362-64.

1:6-14

13213 André Lemaire, "Conseils pour le ministère," *AsSeign* NS 58 (1974): 61-66.

1:6-8

13214 Michael A. G. Haykin, "The Fading Vision: The Spirit and Freedom in the Pastoral Epistles," *EQ* 57 (1985): 291-305.

1:6

13215 F. A. J. MacDonald, "The Three R's," *ET* 89 (1978): 343-44.

13216 H. Booth, "Stir It up," *ET* 91 (1980): 369-70.

13217 John J. Kilgallen, "Reflections on *charisma(ta)* in the New Testament," *SM* 41 (1992): 289-323.

1:7

13218 Robert A. White, "Christian Faith, the Soviet Threat, and a Theology of the Enemy," *RR* 39 (1985): 16-23.

13219 Christopher R. Hutson, "Was Timothy Timid? On the Rhetoric of Fearlessness (1 Corinthians 16:10-11) and Cowardice (2 Timothy 1:7)," *BR* 42 (1997): 58-73.

1:8-10

13220 M. Saillard, "Annoncer l'Évangile, c'est révéler le dessein de Dieu," *AsSeign* NS 15 (1973): 24-30.

13221 A. Viard, "L'Évangile du Christ, principe de vie et d'immortalité," *EV* 78 (1978): 25-26.

1:8

13222   David R. Hall, "Fellow-Workers with the Gospel," *ET* 85 (1973-1974): 119-20.

1:11

13223   J. M. Bover, "Illuminavit vitam," *Bib* 28 (1947): 136-46.

13224   Neal F. McBride and W. Creighton Marlowe, "Biblical Distinctives between the Content and Character of Teaching and Preaching," *CEJ* 1 (1981): 68-74.

1:12

13225   William Barclay, "Paul's Certainties: Our Security in God—2 Timothy 1:12," *ET* 69 (1957-1958): 324-27.

13226   A. M. Besnard, "'Je sais en qui j'ai mis ma foi," *VS* 98 (1958): 5-22.

13227   A. Sohier, "Je sais à qui j'ai donné ma foi," *BVC* 37 (1961): 75-78.

1:13-14

13228   Michael A. G. Haykin, "The Fading Vision: The Spirit and Freedom in the Pastoral Epistles," *EQ* 57 (1985): 291-305.

1:16-17

13229   W. D. Thomas, "New Testament Characters, 12: Onesiphorus," *ET* 96 (1985): 116-17.

2:2

13230   Alvin Thompson, "Design for Growth," *CEJ* 2 (1982): 57-63.

2:8

13231   F. A. J. MacDonald, "From Interest to Faith," *ET* 93 (1981): 83-84.

2:8-12

13232   L. Deiss, "Souviens-toi de Jésus Christ," *AsSeign* NS 59 (1974): 61-66.

2:10

13233   George Thompson, "Ephesians 3:13 and 2 Timothy 2:10 in the Light of Colossians 1:24," *ET* 71 (1960): 187-89.

2:11-13

13234 Gerhard Lohfink, "Die Vermittlung des Paulinismus zu den Pastoralbriefen," *BZ* NS 32 (1988): 169-88.

2:11

13235 U. Holzmeister, "Assurmptionis Deiparae mysterium verbis S. Pauli 2 Tim. 2,1 Is explicatur," *VD* 18 (1938): 225-26.

2:12

13236 William Klassen, "The Ling as 'Living Law' with Particular Reference to Musonius Rufus," *SR* 14 (1985): 63-71.

2:17

13237 Neal F. McBride and W. Creighton Marlowe, "Biblical Distinctives between the Content and Character of Teaching and Preaching," *CEJ* 1 (1981): 68-74.

2:18

13238 F. J. Steinmetz and Friedrich Wulf, "Mit Christus auferstanden. Auslegung und Meditation von 1 Kor 15,20; Eph 2,6 und 2 Tim 2,18," *GeistL* 42 (1969): 146-50.

13239 Gerhard Sellin, " 'Die Auferstehung ist schon geschehen': Zur Spiritualisierung apokalyptischer Terminologie im Neuen Testament," *NovT* 25 (1983): 220-37.

2:22

13240 W. Metzger, "Die νεωτερικαῖ ἐπιθυμία in 2 Timothy 2:22," *TZ* 33 (1977): 129-36.

2:23-26

13241 L. H. Bunn, "2 Timothy 2:23-26," *ET* 41 (1929-1930): 235-37.

2:26

13242 J. P. Wilson, "The Translation of 2 Timothy 2:26," *ET* 49 (1937-1938): 45-46.

3:5

13243 Charles Nichols, "God's Blueprint for the Church," *CEJ* 1 (1981): 29-31.

3:6-7

13244   Gordon D. Fee, "Reflections on Church Order in the Pastoral Epistles, with Further Reflection on the Hermeneutics of *ad hoc* Documents," *JETS* 28 (1985): 141-51.

3:8

13245   H. F. D. Sparks, "On the Form *Mambres* in the Latin Versions of 2 Timothy 3:8," *JTS* 40 (1939): 257-58.

13246   K. Koch, "Das Lamm, das Ägypten vernichtet, ein Fragment aus Jammes und Jambres und sein geschichtlicher Hintergrund," *ZNW* 57 (1966): 79-93.

3:14-4:5

13247   Martin Camroux, "Opening up the Word of God," *ET* 97 (1985): 51-52.

3:14-4:2

13248   Monika K. Hellwig, "Making Homilies for Our Times," *TT* 43 (1987): 561-68.

3:14-17

13249   Donald E. Cook, "Scripture and Inspiration 2 Timothy 3:14-17," *FM* 1 (1984): 56-61.

13250   Giuseppe de Virgilio, "Ispirazione ed efficacia della Scrittura in 2 Tm 3:14-17," *RivBib* 38 (1990): 485-94.

3:15-17

13251   H. Rosman, "Tolle, lege," *VD* 20 (1940): 118-20.

3:16-17

13252   T. P. McGonigal, " 'Every Scripture Is Inspired': An Exegesis of 2 Timothy 3:16-17," *SBT* 8 (1978): 53-64.

13253   George W. Knight, "From Hermeneutics to Practice: Scriptural Normativity and Culture, Revisited," *Pres* 12 (1986): 93-104.

3:16

13254   Harry Buis, "The Significance of 2 Timothy 3:16 and 2 Peter 1:21," *RR* 14 (1961): 43-49.

13255   R. J. A. Sheriffs, "Note on a Verse in the New English Bible," *EQ* 34 (1962): 91-95.

13256 J. W. Roberts, "Note on the Adjective after *pas* in 2 Timothy 3:16," *ET* 76 (1965): 359.

13257 Martin Tetz, "Athanasius und die Einheit der Kirche: zur ökumenischen Bedeutung eines Kirchenvaters," *ZTK* 81 (1984): 196-219.

13258 Antonio Piñero, "Sobre el sentido de qeo/pneustoj: 2 Tim 3:16," *FilN* 1 (1988): 143-53.

13259 Douglas A. Oss, "The Influence of Hermeneutical Frameworks in the Theonomy Debate," *WTJ* 51 (1989): 227-58.

13260 A. M. Artola, "El momento de la inspiración en la constitución de la escritura según 2 Tim 3,16," *EE* 57 (1999): 61-82.

4:2

13261 Neal F. McBride and W. Creighton Marlowe, "Biblical Distinctives between the Content and Character of Teaching and Preaching," *CEJ* 1 (1981): 68-74.

13262 Nickolas Kurtaneck, "Are Seminaries Preparing Prospective Pastors to Preach the Word of God?" *GTJ* 6 (1985): 361-71.

4:6-22

13263 M. C. Bligh, "Seventeen Verses Written for Timothy," *ET* 109 (1998): 364-69.

4:6-18

13264 Pierre Dornier, "Paul au soir de sa vie," *AsSeign* NS 61 (1972): 60-65.

4:6-8

13265 David Cook, "2 Timothy 4:6-8 and the Epistle to the Philippians," *JTS* NS 33 (1982): 168-71.

13266 M. Peaston, "Disengagement," *ET* 93 (1982): 180-82.

4:7

13267 J. J. Twomey, "I have Fought the Good Fight," *Scr* 10 (1958): 110-15.

13268 J. M. T. Barton, "Bonum certamen certavi... fidem servavi," *Bib* 40 (1959): 878-84.

4:8

13269 A. Sohier, "Je sais à qui j'ai donné ma foi," *BVC* 37 (1961): 75-78.

4:9-21

13270 T. Y. Mullins, "A Comparison between 2 Timothy and the Book of Acts," *AUSS* 31 (1993): 199-203.

4:9-18

13271 K. H. Schelkle, "Jesus und Paulus lesen die Bibel," *BK* 36 (1981): 277-79.

4:11

13272 M. C. Griffths, "Today's Missionary, Yesterday's Apostle," *EMQ* 21 (1985): 154-65.

4:13

13273 Peter Trummer, "Mantel und Schriften, 2 Tim 4:13: zur Interpretation einer persönlichen Notiz in den Pastoralbriefen," *BZ* NS 18 (1974): 193-207.

13274 T. C. Skeat, " 'Especially the Parchments': A Note on 2 Timothy 4:13," *JTS* 30 (1979): 173-77.

Titus

Commentaries in the Light of Philosophical and Logical Analysis," *BibInt* 2 (1994): 207-23.

1:12

13286 G. M. Lee, "Ephimenides in the Epistle to Titus," *NovT* 22 (1980): 96.

1:15

13287 Gerhard Lohfink, "Die Vermittlung des Paulinismus zu den Pastoralbriefen," *BZ* NS 32 (1988): 169-88.

2:1-10

13288 Frank Stagg, "The Gospel, Haustafel, and Women: Mark 1:1; Colossians 3:18-4:1," *FM* 2 (1985): 59-63.

13289 Alan Padgett, "The Pauline Rationale for Submission: Biblical Feminism and the *Hina* Clauses of Titus 2:1-10," *EQ* 59 (1987): 39-52.

2:7-8

13290 Jerry R. Young, "Shepherds, Lead," *GTJ* 6 (1985): 329-35.

2:10-14

13291 S. C. Mott, "Greek Ethics and Christian Conversion: The Philonic Background of Titus 2:10-14 and 3:3-7," *NovT* 20 (1978): 22-48.

2:11-15

13292 L. Deiss, "'La grâce de Dieu s'est manifestée," *AsSeign* NS 10 (1970): 26-31.

13293 U. Holzmeister, "Apparuit gratia Dei Salvatoris nostri," *VD* 11 (1931): 353-56.

13294 F. Ogara, "Apparuit gratia Dei Salvatoris nostri," *VD* 15 (1935): 363-72.

13295 Adalberto Sisti, "La Pedagogia di Dio," *BibO* 9 (1967): 253-62.

13296 F. Buchholz, "Predigt über Titus 2:11-15," *EvT* 7 (1947-1948): 257-63.

2:11-14

13297 A. Viard, "La grâce de Dieu et le salut des hommes," *EV* 82 (1982): 340-41.

2:11

13298 T. Vargha, "Apparuit gratia Dei," *VD* 14 (1934): 3-6.

13299 Friedrich Wulf, "Erschienen ist die Gnade Gottes," *GeistL* 40 (1967): 401-403.

2:13

13300 Michael R. Austin, "Salvation and the Divinity of Jesus," *ET* 96 (1985): 271-75.

3:1-2

13301 Geoffrey Wainwright, "Praying for Kings: The Place of Human Rulers in the Divine Plan of Salvation," *ExA* 2 (1986): 117-27.

3:3-7

13302 S. C. Mott, "Greek Ethics and Christian Conversion: The Philonic Background of Titus 2:10-14 and 3:3-7," *NovT* 20 (1978): 22-48.

13303 Gerhard Lohfink, "Die Vermittlung des Paulinismus zu den Pastoralbriefen," *BZ* NS 32 (1988): 169-88.

3:4-8

13304 Michael A. G. Haykin, "The Fading Vision: The Spirit and Freedom in the Pastoral Epistles," *EQ* 57 (1985): 291-305.

3:4-7

13305 L. Deiss, "La bonté et la 'philanthropie' de Dieu notre Sauveur," *AsSeign* NS 10 (1970): 32-37.

13306 Thomas Söding, "Gottes Menschenfreundlichkeit: Eine exegetische Meditation von Titus 3," *GeistL* 71 (1998): 410-422.

3:4-5

13307 W. Keuck, "Sein Erbarmen: Zum Titusbrief," *BL* 3 (1962): 279-84.

3:5

13308 John F. Brug, "A Rebirth-Washing and a Renewal-Holy Spirit," *WLQ* 92 (1995): 124-28.

3:13

13309 Walter L. Liefeld, "Can Deputation Be Defended Biblically?" *EMQ* 22 (1986): 360-65.

Philemon

<u>1-3</u>

13310   Josef Zmijewski, "Beobachtungen zur Struktur des Philemonbriefes, *BibL* 15 (1974): 273-96.

13311   J. H. Roberts, "Filemon in Diskussie: Enkele Hoogtepunte in die Stand van Sake," *ScrSA* 21 (1987): 24-50.

<u>1</u>

13312   Mary A. Getty, "The Letter to Philemon," *BibTo* 22 (1984): 137-44.

13313   Marion L. Soards, "Some Neglected Theological Dimensions of Paul's Letter to Philemon," *PRS* 17 (1990): 209-19.

<u>2-4</u>

13314   Brian M. Rapske, "The Prisoner Paul in the Eyes of Onesimus," *NTS* 37 (1991): 187-203.

<u>2</u>

13315   Lamar Cope, "On Rethinking the Philemon-Colossians Connection," *BR* 30 (1985): 45-50.

13316   John M. G. Barclay, "Paul, Philemon and the Dilemma of Christian Slave-Ownership," *NTS* 37 (1991): 161-86.

<u>3</u>

13317   Sara C. Winter, "Methodological Observations on a New Testament Interpretation of Paul's Letter to Philemon," *USQR* 39 (1984): 203-12.

13318   Peter Lampe, "Keine 'Sklavenflucht' des Onesimus," *ZNW* 76 (1985): 135-37.

<u>4-7</u>

13319   J. Dwight Pentecost, "Grace for the Sinner: An Exposition of Philemon 4-7," *BSac* 129 (1972): 218-25.

13320   Josef Zmijewski, "Beobachtungen zur Struktur des Philemonbriefes, *BibL* 15 (1974): 273-96.

13321   F. Forrester Church, "Rhetorical Structure and Design in Paul's Letter to Philemon," *HTR* 71 (1978): 17-33.

13322   Mary A. Getty, "The Letter to Philemon," *BibTo* 22 (1984): 137-44.

13323   Sara C. Winter, "Methodological Observations on a New Testament Interpretation of Paul's Letter to Philemon," *USQR* 39 (1984): 203-12.

13324   J. H. Roberts, "Filemon in Diskussie: Enkele Hoogtepunte in die Stand van Sake," *ScrSA* 21 (1987): 24-50.

13325   Sara C. Winter, "Paul's Letter to Philemon," *NTS* 33 (1987): 1-15.

13326   Brian M. Rapske, "The Prisoner Paul in the Eyes of Onesimus," *NTS* 37 (1991): 187-203.

4-5

13327   Marion L. Soards, "Some Neglected Theological Dimensions of Paul's Letter to Philemon," *PRS* 17 (1990): 209-19.

4

13328   Lamar Cope, "On Rethinking the Philemon-Colossians Connection," *BR* 30 (1985): 45-50.

13329   W. Thomas Sawyer, "Philemon: His Life and Times," *BI* 14/2 (1989): 81-83.

5-7

13330   P. N. Harrison, "Onesimus and Philemon," *ATR* 32 (1950): 268-94.

5

13331   John G. Nordling, "Onesmius Fugitivus: A Defense of the Runaway Slave Hypothesis in Philemon," *JSNT* 41 (1991): 97-119.

<u>6-7</u>

13332 Marion L. Soards, "Some Neglected Theological Dimensions of Paul's Letter to Philemon," *PRS* 17 (1990): 209-19.

<u>6</u>

13333 ALfred Suhl, "Der Philemonbrief als Beispiel paulinischer Paränese," *K*NS 15 (1973): 267-79.

13334 M. M. de Gaulmyn, "L'Épître de Paul à Philémon," *SémBib* 11 (1978): 7-23.

<u>7</u>

13335 Alfred Suhl, "Der Philemonbrief als Beispiel paulinischer Paränese," *K*NS 15 (1973): 267-79.

13336 M. M. de Gaulmyn, "L'Épître de Paul à Philémon," *SémBib* 11 (1978): 7-23.

13337 Mary A. Getty, "The Letter to Philemon," *BibTo* 22 (1984): 137-44.

<u>8-22</u>

13338 J. H. Roberts, "Filemon in Diskussie: Enkele Hoogtepunte in die Stand van Sake," *ScrSA* 21 (1987): 24-50.

<u>8-21</u>

13339 M. M. de Gaulmyn, "L'Épître de Paul à Philémon," *SémBib* 11 (1978): 7-23.

<u>8-20</u>

13340 Alfred Suhl, "Der Philemonbrief als Beispiel paulinischer Paränese," *K*NS 15 (1973): 267-79.

13341 Josef Zmijewski, "Beobachtungen zur Struktur des Philemonbriefes, *BibL* 15 (1974): 273-96.

<u>8-16</u>

13342 F. Forrester Church, "Rhetorical Structure and Design in Paul's Letter to Philemon," *HTR* 71 (1978): 17-33.

<u>8-12</u>

13343 Josef Zmijewski, "Beobachtungen zur Struktur des Philemonbriefes, *BibL* 15 (1974): 273-96.

<u>8-11</u>

13344 J. Dwight Pentecost, "For Love's Sake: An Exposition of Philemon 8-11," *BSac* 129 (1972): 344-51.

<u>8</u>

13345 Mary A. Getty, "The Letter to Philemon," *BibTo* 22 (1984): 137-44.

<u>9</u>

13346 Josef Zmijewski, "Beobachtungen zur Struktur des Philemonbriefes, *BibL* 15 (1974): 273-96.

13347 F. Forrester Church, "Rhetorical Structure and Design in Paul's Letter to Philemon," *HTR* 71 (1978): 17-33.

13348 John H. Elliott, "Philemon and House Churches," *BibTo* 22 (1984): 145-50.

13349 Marion L. Soards, "Some Neglected Theological Dimensions of Paul's Letter to Philemon," *PRS* 17 (1990): 209-19.

13350 J. Neville Birdsall, "πρεσβύτης in Philemon 9: A Study in Conjectural Emendation," *NTS* 39 (1993): 625-30.

<u>10-17</u>

13351 J. H. Roberts, "Filemon in Diskussie: Enkele Hoogtepunte in die Stand van Sake," *ScrSA* 21 (1987): 24-50.

<u>10-13</u>

13352 John M. G. Barclay, "Paul, Philemon and the Dilemma of Christian Slave-Ownership," *NTS* 37 (1991): 161-86.

<u>10-11</u>

13353 M. M. de Gaulmyn, "L'Épître de Paul à Philémon," *SémBib* 11 (1978): 7-23.

<u>10</u>

13354 Alfred Suhl, "Der Philemonbrief als Beispiel paulinischer Paränese," *K* NS 15 (1973): 267-79.

13355 John G. Nordling, "Onesmius Fugitivus: A Defense of the Runaway Slave Hypothesis in Philemon," *JSNT* 41 (1991): 97-119.

13356   Perry V. Kea, "Paul's Letter to Philemon: A Short Analysis of Its Values," *PRS* 23 (1996): 223-32.

11

13357   P. N. Harrison, "Onesimus and Philemon," *ATR* 32 (1950): 268-94.

13358   Brian M. Rapske, "The Prisoner Paul in the Eyes of Onesimus," *NTS* 37 (1991): 187-203.

12-14

13359   John H. Elliott, "Philemon and House Churches," *BibTo* 22 (1984): 145-50.

12

13360   Josef Zmijewski, "Beobachtungen zur Struktur des Philemonbriefes, *BibL* 15 (1974): 273-96.

13361   M. M. de Gaulmyn, "L'Épître de Paul à Philémon," *SémBib* 11 (1978): 7-23.

13362   John G. Nordling, "Onesmius Fugitivus: A Defense of the Runaway Slave Hypothesis in Philemon," *JSNT* 41 (1991): 97-119.

13363   Brian M. Rapske, "The Prisoner Paul in the Eyes of Onesimus," *NTS* 37 (1991): 187-203.

13-14

13364   Josef Zmijewski, "Beobachtungen zur Struktur des Philemonbriefes, *BibL* 15 (1974): 273-96.

13365   John M. G. Barclay, "Paul, Philemon and the Dilemma of Christian Slave-Ownership," *NTS* 37 (1991): 161-86.

13

13366   Josef Zmijewski, "Beobachtungen zur Struktur des Philemonbriefes, *BibL* 15 (1974): 273-96.

13367   John H. Elliott, "Philemon and House Churches," *BibTo* 22 (1984): 145-50.

13368   Brian M. Rapske, "The Prisoner Paul in the Eyes of Onesimus," *NTS* 37 (1991): 187-203.

15

13369 John M. G. Barclay, "Paul, Philemon and the Dilemma of Christian Slave-Ownership," *NTS* 37 (1991): 161-86.

13370 John G. Nordling, "Onesmius Fugitivus: A Defense of the Runaway Slave Hypothesis in Philemon," *JSNT* 41 (1991): 97-119.

16

13371 P. N. Harrison, "Onesimus and Philemon," *ATR* 32 (1950): 268-94.

13372 Josef Zmijewski, "Beobachtungen zur Struktur des Philemonbriefes, *BibL* 15 (1974): 273-96.

13373 M. M. de Gaulmyn, "L'Épître de Paul à Philémon," *SémBib* 11 (1978): 7-23.

13374 Carolyn Osiek, "Slavery in the New Testament World," *BibTo* 22 (1984): 151-55.

13375 Perry V. Kea, "Paul's Letter to Philemon: A Short Analysis of Its Values," *PRS* 23 (1996): 223-32.

17-22

13376 F. Forrester Church, "Rhetorical Structure and Design in Paul's Letter to Philemon," *HTR* 71 (1978): 17-33.

13377 J. H. Roberts, "Filemon in Diskussie: Enkele Hoogtepunte in die Stand van Sake," *ScrSA* 21 (1987): 24-50.

17-20

13378 John H. Elliott, "Philemon and House Churches," *BibTo* 22 (1984): 145-50.

17

13379 M. M. de Gaulmyn, "L'Épître de Paul à Philémon," *SémBib* 11 (1978): 7-23.

13380 John M. G. Barclay, "Paul, Philemon and the Dilemma of Christian Slave-Ownership," *NTS* 37 (1991): 161-86.

18

13381 John H. Elliott, "Philemon and House Churches," *BibTo* 22 (1984): 145-50.

13382 John M. G. Barclay, "Paul, Philemon and the Dilemma of Christian Slave-Ownership," *NTS* 37 (1991): 161-86.

18-19

13383 Peter Lampe, "Keine 'Sklavenflucht' des Onesimus," *ZNW* 76 (1985): 135-37.

18

13384 John G. Nordling, "Onesmius Fugitivus: A Defense of the Runaway Slave Hypothesis in Philemon," *JSNT* 41 (1991): 97-119.

19-22

13385 J. H. Roberts, "Filemon in Diskussie: Enkele Hoogtepunte in die Stand van Sake," *ScrSA* 21 (1987): 24-50.

19

13386 M. M. de Gaulmyn, "L'Épître de Paul à Philémon," *SémBib* 11 (1978): 7-23.

13387 John M. G. Barclay, "Paul, Philemon and the Dilemma of Christian Slave-Ownership," *NTS* 37 (1991): 161-86.

20

13388 Josef Zmijewski, "Beobachtungen zur Struktur des Philemonbriefes, *BibL* 15 (1974): 273-96.

13389 M. M. de Gaulmyn, "L'Épître de Paul à Philémon," *SémBib* 11 (1978): 7-23.

13390 John M. G. Barclay, "Paul, Philemon and the Dilemma of Christian Slave-Ownership," *NTS* 37 (1991): 161-86.

21-22

13391 J. H. Roberts, "Filemon in Diskussie: Enkele Hoogtepunte in die Stand van Sake," *ScrSA* 21 (1987): 24-50.

21

13392 Marion L. Soards, "Some Neglected Theological Dimensions of Paul's Letter to Philemon," *PRS* 17 (1990): 209-19.

13393 John M. G. Barclay, "Paul, Philemon and the Dilemma of Christian Slave-Ownership," *NTS* 37 (1991): 161-86.

22

13394 M. M. de Gaulmyn, "L'Épître de Paul à Philémon," *SémBib* 11 (1978): 7-23.

13395 John H. Elliott, "Philemon and House Churches," *BibTo* 22 (1984): 145-50.

13396 Marion L. Soards, "Some Neglected Theological Dimensions of Paul's Letter to Philemon," *PRS* 17 (1990): 209-19.

13397 Michael A. G. Haykin, "Praying Together: A Note on Philemon 22," *EQ* 66 (1994): 331-35.

23-25

13398 J. H. Roberts, "Filemon in Diskussie: Enkele Hoogtepunte in die Stand van Sake," *ScrSA* 21 (1987): 24-50.

23

13399 P. N. Harrison, "Onesimus and Philemon," *ATR* 32 (1950): 268-94.

13400 John H. Elliott, "Philemon and House Churches," *BibTo* 22 (1984): 145-50.

Hebrews

1:1-14

13401 John P. Meier, "Structure and Theology in Heb 1:1-14,"
        Bib 66 (1985): 168-89.

1:1-12

13402 C. Bourgin, "Qui est Jésus-Christ?" *AsSeign* NS 10 (1970):
        25-44.

1:1-6

13403 C. Bourgin, "Qui est Jésus-Christ?" *AsSeign* NS 10 (1970):
        38-47.

1:1-4

13404 Rudolf Schnackenburg, "Zum Offenbarungsgedanken in
        der Bibel," *BZ* 7 (1963): 2-13.

13405 T. Starmare, "La pienezza della Rivelazione," *BibO* 9
        (1967): 145-64.

13406 Murray J. Harris, "The Translation and Significance of *Ho
        theos* in Hebrews 1:8-9," *TynB* 36 (1985): 129-62.

13407 Thomas G. Smothers, "A Superior Model: Hebrews
        1:1-4:13," *RevExp* 82 (1985): 333-43.

13408 David A. Black, "Hebrews 1:1-4: A Study in Discourse
        Analysis," *WTJ* 49 (1987): 175-94.

13409 M. J. Paul, "The Order of Melchizedek (Ps 110:4 and Heb
        7:3)," *WTJ* 49 (1987): 195-211.

13410 Daniel J. Ebert, "The Chiastic Structure of the Prologue to
        Hebrews," *TriJ* 13 (1992): 163-79.

1:1-3

13411 D. C. Welander, "Hebrews 1:1-3," *ET* 65 (1954): 315.

13412 Ronald H. Nash, "Notion of Mediator in Alexandrian
        Judaism and the Epistle to the Hebrews," *WTJ* 40 (1977):
        89-115.

1:1-2

13413 Albert Vanhoye, "Thema sacerdotii praeparatur in Heb. 1, 1-2,18," *VD* 47 (1969): 284-97.

13414 Mark R. Shaw, "Is There Salvation outside the Christian Faith," *EAJT* 2 (1983): 42-62.

13415 Jeffrey A. Gibbs, "The Grace of God as the Foundation for Ethics," *CTQ* 48 (1984): 185-201.

13416 Palémon Glorieux, "La révélation du Pére," *MSR* 42 (1985): 21-41.

1:2-4

13417 Albert Vanhoye, "Christologia a qua initium sumit epistola ad Hebraeos," *VD* 43 (1965): 3-14, 49-61, 113-23.

1:2

13418 A. M. Vitti, "Quem constituit heredem universorum, per quem fecit et saecula," *VD* 21 (1941): 40-48, 82-87.

13419 Hugolinus Langkammer, "Den er zum Erben von allem eingesetzt hat," *BZ* NS 10 (1966): 273-80.

1:3

13420 Albert Vanhoye, "De sessione caelesti in epistola ad Hebraeos," *VD* 44 (1966): 131-34.

13421 Janusz Frankowski, "Early Christian Hymns Recorded in the New Testament: A Reconsideration of the Question in the Light of Hebrews 1:3," *BZ* NS 27 (1983): 183-94.

13422 Rolf Gögler, "Inkarnationsglaube und Bibeltheologie bei Origenes," *TQ* 165 (1985): 82-94.

13423 Bernhard Heininger, "Sündenreinigung (Hebr 1,3): Christologie Anmerkungen zum Exordium des Hebräerbriefs," *BZ* NS 41 (1997): 54-68.

1:5-10:18

13424 David A. Black, "The Problem of the Literary Structure of Hebrews: An Evaluation and a Proposal," *GTJ* 7 (1986): 163-77.

1:5-14

13425 John P. Meier, "Symmetry and Theology in the Old Testament Citations of Hebrews 1:5-14," *Bib* 66 (1985): 504-33.

13426 Thomas G. Smothers, "A Superior Model: Hebrews 1:1-4:13," *RevExp* 82 (1985): 333-43.

1:5-13

13427 H. W. Bateman, "Two First-Century Messianic Uses of the OT: Hebrews 1:5-13 and 4QFlor 1.1-19," *JETS* 38 (1995): 11-27.

1:5-6

13428 Murray J. Harris, "The Translation and Significance of *Ho theos* in Hebrews 1:8-9," *TynB* 36 (1985): 129-62.

1:5

13429 A. del Agua Pérez, "Procedimientos derásicos del Sal 2:7b en el Nuevo Testamento: Tu eres mi hijo, yo te he engendrado hoy," *EB* NS 42 (1984): 391-414.

1:6-13

13430 T. F. Glasson, "Plurality of Divine Persons and the Quotations in Hebrews 1:6ff," *NTS* 12 (1966): 270-72.

1:6

13431 A. M. Vitti, "Et cum iterum introducit Primogenitum in orbem terrae," *VD* 14 (1934): 306-12, 368-74.

13432 T. F. Glasson, "Plurality of Divine Persons and the Quotations in Hebrews 1:6ff," *NTS* 12 (1966): 270-72.

13433 A. Vicent Cernuda, "La introducción del Primogénito, según Hebr 1:6," *EB* NS39 (1981): 107-53.

1:8

13434 Murray J. Harris, "The Translation and Significance of *Ho theos* in Hebrews 1:8-9," *TynB* 36 (1985): 129-62.

1:9

13435 I. de la Potterie, "L'onction du Christ," *NRT* 80 (1958): 225-52.

1:13-14

13436 Murray J. Harris, "The Translation and Significance of *Ho theos* in Hebrews 1:8-9," *TynB* 36 (1985): 129-62.

1:14

13437 Eugene F. Klug, "The Doctrine of Man: Christian Anthropology," *CTQ* 48 (1984): 141-52.

2:1-4

13438 Thomas G. Smothers, "A Superior Model: Hebrews 1:1-4:13," *RevExp* 82 (1985): 333-43.

13439 Alan Mugridge, "Warnings in the Epistle to the Hebrews: An Exegetical and Theological Study," *RTR* 46 (1987): 74-82.

13440 Scot McKnight, "The Warning Passages of Hebrews: A Formal Analysis and Theological Conclusions," *TriJ* 13 (1992): 21-59.

2:1

13441 P. Teodorico, "Metafore nautiche in Ebr. 2,1 et 6,19," *RivBib* 6 (1958): 34-49.

2:2

13442 Ronald Williamson, "The Incarnation of the Logos in Hebrews," *ET* 95 (1983): 4-8.

2:3

13443 Gerald L. Borchert, "A Superior Book: Hebrews," *RevExp* 82 (1985): 319-22.

2:5-9

13444 Thomas G. Smothers, "A Superior Model: Hebrews 1:1-4:13," *RevExp* 82 (1985): 333-43.

2:5

13445 Albert Vanhoye, "L'οἰκουμέν dans l'Épître aux Hébreux," *Bib* 45 (1964): 248-53.

2:6-8

13446 P. Giles, "Son of Man in the Epistle to the Hebrews," *ET* 86 (1975): 328-32.

2:9-11

13447 Albert Vanhoye, "Destinée des hommes et chemin du Christ," *AsSeign* NS 58 (1974): 34-40.

2:9

13448 J. C. Neill, "Hebrews 2:9," *JTS* NS17 (1966): 79-82.

13449 J. K. Elliott, "Jesus Apart from God," *ET* 83 (1971-1972): 339-44.

13450 J. K. Elliott, "When Jesus Was Apart from God: An Examination of Hebrews 2:9," *ET* 83 (1972): 339-41.

13451 C. Samuel Storms, "Defining the Elect," *JETS* 27 (1984): 205-18.

13452 S. Brock, "Hebrews 2:9 in Syriac Tradition," *NovT* 27 (1985): 236-44.

2:10-18

13453 Colin J. A. Hickling, "John and Hebrews: The Background of Hebrews 2:10-18," *NTS* 29 (1983): 112-16.

2:10

13454 Palémon Glorieux, "La révélation du Père," *MSR* 42 (1985): 21-41.

13455 J. Julius Scott, "Archegos: The Salvation History of the Epistle to the Hebrews," *JETS* 29 (1986): 47-54.

13456 Alan C. Mitchell, "The Use of *prepein* and Rhetorical Propriety in Hebrews 2:10," *CBQ* 54 (1992): 681-701.

2:11

13457 J.-C. Dhotel, "La 'sanctification' du Christ d'après Hébreux 2:11," *RechSR* 47 (1959): 514-43; 48 (1960): 420-52.

2:14-15

13458 Eugene F. Klug, "The Doctrine of Man: Christian Anthropology," *CTQ* 48 (1984): 141-52.

2:14

13459 Thomas E. Schmidt, "The Letter *Tau* as the Cross: Ornament and Content in Hebrews 2,14," *Bib* 76 1 (1995): 75-84.

2:15-18

13460 Donald G. Miller, "Why God Became Man: From Text to Sermon on Hebrews 2:5-18," *Int* 23 (1969): 408-24.

2:16

13461 K. G. E. Dolfe, "Hebrews 2,16 under the Magnifying Glass," *ZNW* 84 (1993): 289-94.

2:17-18

13462 Albert Vanhoye, "Le Christ, grand-prêtre selon Héb. 2,17-18," *NRT* 91 (1969): 449-74.

3:1-4:13

13463 Peter E. Enns, "Creation and Re-Creation: Psalm 95 and Its Interpretation in Hebrews 3:1-4:13," *WTJ* 55 (1993): 255-80.

3:1-6

13464 Thomas G. Smothers, "A Superior Model: Hebrews 1:1-4:13," *RevExp* 82 (1985): 333-43.

13465 Brett R. Scott, "Jesus' Superiority over Moses in Hebrews 3:1-6," *BSac* 155 (1998): 201-10.

3:2-5

13466 E. A. C. Pretorius, "Christusbeeld en Kerkmodel in die Hebreërbrief," *ThEv* 15 (1982): 3-6.

13467 Erich Grässer, "Mose und Jesus: zur Auslegung von Hebr 3:1-6," *ZNW* 75 (1984): 2-23.

3:6

13468 Gerald L. Borchert, "A Superior Book: Hebrews," *RevExp* 82 (1985): 319-22.

13469 Scott C. Layton, "Christ over His House (Hebrew 3:6) and Hebrew *'shr l-hbyt*," *NTS* 37 (1991): 473-77.

3:7-4:13

13470 Thomas G. Smothers, "A Superior Model: Hebrews 1:1-4:13," *RevExp* 82 (1985): 333-43.

13471 Erich Grässer, "Das wandernde Gottesvolk: zum Basismotiv des Hebräerbriefes," *ZNW* 77 (1986): 160-79.

13472   Scot McKnight, "The Warning Passages of Hebrews: A Formal Analysis and Theological Conclusions," *TriJ* 13 (1992): 21-59.

3:7-4:11

13473   Albert Vanhoye, "Longue marche ou accès tout proche? Le contexte biblique de Hébreux 3:7-4:11," *Bib* 49 (1968): 9-26.

3:7-4

13474   Albert Vanhoye, "Longue marche ou accès tout proche? Le contexte biblique de Hébreux 3,7-4,11," *Bib* 49 (1968): 9-26.

3:8

13475   Gerald L. Borchert, "A Superior Book: Hebrews," *RevExp* 82 (1985): 319-22.

3:11

13476   Albert Vanhoye, "Longue marche ou accès tout proche? Le contexte biblique de Hébreux 3,7-4,11," *Bib* 49 (1968): 9-26.

3:12-4:2

13477   Alan Mugridge, "Warnings in the Epistle to the Hebrews: An Exegetical and Theological Study," *RTR* 46 (1987): 74-82.

3:12-14

13478   Robert A. Peterson, "The Perseverance of the Saints: A Theological Exegesis of Four Key New Testament Passages," *Pres* 17 (1991): 95-112.

3:12

13479   Gerald L. Borchert, "A Superior Book: Hebrews," *RevExp* 82 (1985): 319-22.

3:13

13480   W. L. Lorimer, "Romans xiii. 3, Hebrews, iii. 13," *NTS* 12 (1965-1966): 389-91.

3:14

13481   Enrique Nardoni, "Partakers in Christ (Hebrews 3:14),"
        NTS 37 (1991): 456-72.

3:16

13482   E. A. C. Pretorius, "Christusbeeld en Kerkmodel in die
        Hebreërbrief," *ThEv* 15 (1982): 3-6.

13483   Erich Grässer, "Mose und Jesus: zur Auslegung von Hebr
        3:1-6," *ZNW* 75 (1984): 2-23.

4:1-13

13484   Ann Hoch Cowdery, "Hebrews 4:1-13," *Int* 48 (1994):
        282-86.

4:12-13

13485   G. W. Trompf, "The Conception of God in Hebrews
        4:12-13," *StTheol* 25 (1971): 123-32.

13486   P. Proulx and Luis Alonso Schökel, "Heb 4:12-13:
        componentes y estructura," *Bib* 54 (1973): 331-39.

13487   Albert Vanhoye, "La parole qui juge," *AsSeign* NS 59
        (1974): 36-42.

13488   Charles M. Wood, "On Being Known," *TT* 44 (1987):
        197-206.

4:12

13489   Palémon Glorieux, "La révélation du Père," *MSR* 42
        (1985): 21-41.

4:13

13490   Ronald Williamson, "The Incarnation of the Logos in
        Hebrews," *ET* 95 (1983): 4-8.

4:14-5:10

13491   Gerhard Friedrich, "Das Lied vom Hohenpriester im
        Zusammenhang von Hebr. 4,14-5,10," *TZ* 18 (1962):
        95-115.

4:14-16

13492   C. Bourgin, "La Passion du Christ et la nôtre," *AsSeign* NS
        21 (1969): 15-20.

13493   Harold S. Songer, "A Superior Priesthood: Hebrews 4:14-7:27," *RevExp* 82 (1985): 345-59.

4:14

13494   K. Galling, "Durch die Himmel hindurchgeschritten," *ZNW* 43 (1950-1951): 263-64.

13495   Gerald L. Borchert, "A Superior Book: Hebrews," *RevExp* 82 (1985): 319-22.

4:15

13496   Ronald Williamson, "Hebrews 4:15 and the Sinlessness of Jesus," *ET* 86 (1974): 4-8.

4:16

13497   William Klassen, "The King as 'Living Law' with Particular Reference to Musonius Rufus," *SR* 14 (1985): 63-71.

13498   David G. Peterson, "Further Reflections on Worship in the New Testament," *RTR* 44 (1985): 34-41.

5:1-10

13499   Harold S. Songer, "A Superior Priesthood: Hebrews 4:14-7:27," *RevExp* 82 (1985): 345-59.

13500   Michael Bachmann, "Hohepriesterliches Leiden: Beobachtungen zu Heb 5:1-10," *ZNW* 78 (1987): 244-66.

5:1-6

13501   A. M. Javierre, "Réalité et transcendance du sacerdoce du Christ," *AsSeign* NS 61 (1972): 36-43.

5:4

13502   William Horbury, "The Aaronic Priesthood in the Epistle to the Hebrews," *JSNT* 19 (1983): 43-71.

13503   Harold S. Songer, "A Superior Priesthood: Hebrews 4:14-7:27," *RevExp* 82 (1985): 345-59.

5:5-10

13504   Lucien Cerfaux, "Le sacre du grand prêtre, d'après Hébreux 5,5-10," *BVC* 21 (1958): 54-58.

13505   Lucien Cerfaux, "Die Weihe des Hohenpriesters," *BL* 26 (1958-1959): 17-21.

5:5

13506 A. del Agua Pérez, "Procedimientos derásicos del Sal 2:7b en el Nuevo Testamento: Tu eres mi hijo, yo te he engendrado hoy," *EB* NS42 (1984): 391-414.

5:6-10

13507 Joseph A. Fitzmyer, "Now this Melchizedek," *CBQ* 25 (1963): 305-21.

13508 R. A. Stewart, "The Sinless High-Priest," *NTS* 14 (1967-1968): 126-35.

13509 Paul Ellingworth, "Like the Son of God: Form and Content in Hebrews 7:1-10," *Bib* 64 (1983): 255-262.

13510 H. J. de Jonge, "Traditie en exegese: de hogepriester-christologie en Melchizedek in Hebreeën," *NTT* 37 (1983): 1-19.

13511 Harold S. Songer, "A Superior Priesthood: Hebrews 4:14-7:27," *RevExp* 82 (1985): 345-59.

13512 Mark Kiley, "Melchisedek's Promotion to Archiereus and the Translation of *ta stoicheia tes arches*," *SBLSP* 25 (1986): 236-45.

13513 M. J. Paul, "The Order of Melchizedek (Ps 110:4 and Heb 7:3)," *WTJ* 49 (1987): 195-211.

13514 Jerome H. Neyrey, "Without Beginning of Days or End of Life (Hebrews 7:3): Topos for a True Deity," *CBQ* 53 (1991): 439-55.

13515 T. C. de Kruijf, "The Priest-King Melchizedek: The Reception of Gen 14,18-20 in Hebrews Mediated by Psalm 110," *Bij* 54 (1993): 393-406.

5:7-10

13516 Joachim Jeremias, "Hbr 5:7-10," *ZNW* 44 (1952): 107-11.

13517 Rueben E. Omark, "Saving of the Savior: Exegesis and Christology in Hebrews 5:7-10," *Int* 12 (1958): 39-51.

13518 Georg Braumann, "Hebrews 5:7-10," *ZNW* 51 (1960): 278-80.

13519 Egon Brandenburger, "Text und Vorlagen von Hebr 5:7-10: ein Beitrag zur Christologie des Hebräerbriefs," *NovT* 11 (1969): 190-224.

13520 Jukka Thurén, "Gebet und Gehorsam des Erniedrigten," *NovT* 13 (1971): 136-46.

5:7-9

13521 C. Bourgin, "La Passion du Christ et la nôtre," *AsSeign* NS 21 (1969): 15-20.

5:7-8

13522 Mathias Rissi, "Die Menschlichkeit Jesu nach Hebr 5:7-8," *TZ* 11 (1955): 28-45.

5:7

13523 A. M. Vitti, "Exauditus est pro sua reverentia," *VD* 14 (1934): 86-92, 108-14.

13524 A. Strobel, "Die Psalmengrundlage der Gethsemane-Parallele, Hebr 5:7ff," *ZNW* 45 (1954): 252-66.

13525 E. Rasco, "La oración sacerdotal de Cristo en la tierra segun He 5,7," *Greg* 43 (1962): 723-55.

13526 Thor Boman, "Der Gebetskampf Jesu," *NTS* 10 (1963-1964): 261-73.

13527 T. Lescow, "Jesus in Gethsemane bei Lukas und im Hebräerbrief," *ZNW* 58 (1967): 215-39.

13528 P. Andriessen, "Angoisse de la mort dans l'épître aux Hébreux," *NRT* 96 (1974): 282-92.

5:9

13529 Edward Fudge, "The Final End of the Wicked," *JETS* 27 (1984): 325-34.

5:11-6:12

13530 Kenneth S. Wuest, "Hebrews Six in the Greek New Testament," *BSac* 119 (1962): 45-53.

13531 Scot McKnight, "The Warning Passages of Hebrews: A Formal Analysis and Theological Conclusions," *TriJ* 13 (1992): 21-59.

5:11-6:3

> 13532 H. P. Owen, "The 'Stages of Ascent' in Hebrews 5:11-6:3," *NTS* 3 (1956): 243-53.

5:11

> 13533 Gerald L. Borchert, "A Superior Book: Hebrews," *RevExp* 82 (1985): 319-22.

5:14

> 13534 J. A. L. Lee, "Hebrews 5:14 and Exis: A History of Misunderstanding," *NovT* 39 (1997): 151-76.

6:1-8

> 13535 Harold S. Songer, "A Superior Priesthood: Hebrews 4:14-7:27," *RevExp* 82 (1985): 345-59.

> 13536 Wayne R. Kempson, "Hebrews 6:1-8," *RevExp* 91 (1994): 567-73.

6:1-6

> 13537 Gerald L. Borchert, "A Superior Book: Hebrews," *RevExp* 82 (1985): 319-22.

6:1

> 13538 P. R. P. Barker, "Studies in Texts: Hebrews 6:1f," *Theology* 65 (1962): 282-84.

> 13539 J. Clifford Adams, "Exegesis of Hebrews 6:1f," *NTS* 13 (1967): 378-85.

6:2

> 13540 Edward Fudge, "The Final End of the Wicked," *JETS* 27 (1984): 325-34.

6:4-8

> 13541 Herbert H. Hohenstein, "Study of Hebrews 6:4-8: The Passage in the General Setting of the Whole Epistle," *CTM* 27 (1956): 433-44.

> 13542 Alan Mugridge, "Warnings in the Epistle to the Hebrews: An Exegetical and Theological Study," *RTR* 46 (1987): 74-82.

> 13543 Randall C. Gleason, "The Old Testament Background of the Warning in Hebrews 6:4-8," *BSac* 155 (1998): 62-91.

6:4-6

13544   Charles E. Carlston, "Eschatology and Repentance in the Epistle to the Hebrews," *JBL* 78 (1959): 296-302.

13545   Philip E. Hughes, "Hebrews 6:4-6 and the Peril of Apostasy," *WTJ* 35 (1973): 137-55.

6:4

13546   Peter Jensen, "Faith and Healing in Christian Theology," *Point* 11 (1982): 153-59.

13547   Dave Mathewson, "Reading Heb 6:4-6 in Light of the Old Testament," *WTJ* 61 (1999): 209-25.

6:7

13548   Gerald L. Borchert, "A Superior Book: Hebrews," *RevExp* 82 (1985): 319-22.

6:9-20

13549   Harold S. Songer, "A Superior Priesthood: Hebrews 4:14-7:27," *RevExp* 82 (1985): 345-59.

6:9-11

13550   Gerald L. Borchert, "A Superior Book: Hebrews," *RevExp* 82 (1985): 319-22.

6:12-20

13551   David R. Worley, "Fleeing to Two Immutable Things, God's Oath-Taking and Oath-Witnessing: The Use of Litigant Oath in Hebrews 6:12-20," *RQ* 36 (1994): 223-36.

6:13-20

13552   Gerald L. Borchert, "A Superior Book: Hebrews," *RevExp* 82 (1985): 319-22.

6:18-20

13553   Marinus de Jonge, "De berichten over het scheuren van het voorhangsel bij Jezus' dood in de synoptische evangeliën," *NTT* 21 (1966): 90-114.

6:20-7:3

13554   T. C. de Kruijf, "The Priest-King Melchizedek: The Reception of Gen 14,18-20 in Hebrews Mediated by Psalm 110," *Bij* 54 (1993): 393-406.

6:20

13555 Joseph A. Fitzmyer, "Now this Melchizedek," *CBQ* 25 (1963): 305-21.

13556 R. A. Stewart, "The Sinless High-Priest," *NTS* 14 (1967-1968): 126-35.

13557 Paul Ellingworth, "Like the Son of God: Form and Content in Hebrews 7:1-10," *Bib* 64 (1983): 255-262.

13558 H. J. de Jonge, "Traditie en exegese: de hogepriester-christologie en Melchizedek in Hebreeën," *NTT* 37 (1983): 1-19.

13559 Harold S. Songer, "A Superior Priesthood: Hebrews 4:14-7:27," *RevExp* 82 (1985): 345-59.

13560 M. J. Paul, "The Order of Melchizedek (Ps 110:4 and Heb 7:3)," *WTJ* 49 (1987): 195-211.

13561 Jerome H. Neyrey, "Without Beginning of Days or End of Life (Hebrews 7:3): Topos for a True Deity," *CBQ* 53 (1991): 439-55.

13562 T. C. de Kruijf, "The Priest-King Melchizedek: The Reception of Gen 14,18-20 in Hebrews Mediated by Psalm 110," *Bij* 54 (1993): 393-406.

7-13

13563 James Swetnam, "Form and Content in Hebrews 7-13," *Bib* 55 (1974): 333-48.

7-9

13564 Gerald L. Borchert, "A Superior Book: Hebrews," *RevExp* 82 (1985): 319-22.

7:1-17

13565 Joseph A. Fitzmyer, "Now this Melchizedek," *CBQ* 25 (1963): 305-21.

13566 R. A. Stewart, "The Sinless High-Priest," *NTS* 14 (1967-1968): 126-35.

13567 Paul Ellingworth, "Like the Son of God: Form and Content in Hebrews 7:1-10," *Bib* 64 (1983): 255-262.

13568 H. J. de Jonge, "Traditie en exegese: de hogepriester-christologie en Melchizedek in Hebreeën," *NTT* 37 (1983): 1-19.

13569 Harold S. Songer, "A Superior Priesthood: Hebrews 4:14-7:27," *RevExp* 82 (1985): 345-59.

13570 M. J. Paul, "The Order of Melchizedek (Ps 110:4 and Heb 7:3)," *WTJ* 49 (1987): 195-211.

13571 Jerome H. Neyrey, "Without Beginning of Days or End of Life (Hebrews 7:3): Topos for a True Deity," *CBQ* 53 (1991): 439-55.

13572 T. C. de Kruijf, "The Priest-King Melchizedek: The Reception of Gen 14,18-20 in Hebrews Mediated by Psalm 110," *Bij* 54 (1993): 393-406.

7:1-10

13573 Paul Ellingworth, "Like the Son of God: Form and Content in Hebrews 7:1-10," *Bib* 64 (1983): 255-262.

13574 Harold S. Songer, "A Superior Priesthood: Hebrews 4:14-7:27," *RevExp* 82 (1985): 345-59.

7:1

13575 Joseph A. Fitzmyer, "Now this Melchizedek," *CBQ* 25 (1963): 305-21.

7:3

13576 Jerome H. Neyrey, "Without Beginning of Days or End of Life (Hebrews 7:3): Topos for a True Deity," *CBQ* 53 (1991): 439-55.

13577 Mark A. Seifrid, "Paul's Approach to the Old Testament in Romans 10:6-8," *TriJ* NS6 (1985): 3-37.

7:11-19

13578 Harold S. Songer, "A Superior Priesthood: Hebrews 4:14-7:27," *RevExp* 82 (1985): 345-59.

7:11

13579 William Horbury, "The Aaronic Priesthood in the Epistle to the Hebrews," *JSNT* 19 (1983): 43-71.

13580 Harold S. Songer, "A Superior Priesthood: Hebrews 4:14-7:27," *RevExp* 82 (1985): 345-59.

7:14

13581 E. A. C. Pretorius, "Christusbeeld en Kerkmodel in die Hebreërbrief," *ThEv* 15 (1982): 3-6.

13582 Erich Grässer, "Mose und Jesus: zur Auslegung von Hebr 3:1-6," *ZNW* 75 (1984): 2-23.

7:20-28

13583 Harold S. Songer, "A Superior Priesthood: Hebrews 4:14-7:27," *RevExp* 82 (1985): 345-59.

7:23-24

13584 W. L. Lorimer, "Hebrews 7:23f," *NTS* 13 (1967): 386-87.

7:24

13585 Paul Ellingworth, "The Unshakable Priesthood: Hebrews 7:24," *JSNT* 23 (1985): 125-26.

7:25

13586 David G. Peterson, "Further Reflections on Worship in the New Testament," *RTR* 44 (1985): 34-41.

7:28

13587 T. J. Finney, "A Proposed Reconstruction of Hebrews 7:28a in p46," *NTS* 40 (1994): 472-473.

8-9

13588 David J. MacLeod, "The Cleansing of the True Tabernacle," *BSac* 152 (1995): 60-71.

8:1-9:10

13589 Roger L. Omanson, "A Superior Covenant: Hebrews 8:1-10:18," *RevExp* 82 (1985): 361-73.

8:1-6

13590 David G. Peterson, "Further Reflections on Worship in the New Testament," *RTR* 44 (1985): 34-41.

8:5

13591 E. A. C. Pretorius, "Christusbeeld en Kerkmodel in die Hebreërbrief," *ThEv* 15 (1982): 3-6.

13592 L. D. Hurst, "How 'Platonic' Are Hebrews 8:5 and Hebrews 9:23f?" *JTS* NS34 (1983): 156-68.

13593 Erich Grässer, "Mose und Jesus: zur Auslegung von Hebr 3:1-6," *ZNW* 75 (1984): 2-23.

13594 Hermut Löhr, " 'Umriss' und 'Schatten': Bemerkungen zur Zitierung von Ex 25,40 in Hebr 8," *ZNW* 84 (1993): 218-32.

8:8

13595 Johannes L. P. Wolmarans, "The Text and Translation of Hebrews 8:8," *ZNW* 75 (1984): 139-44.

9-10

13596 Gary S. Selby, "The Meaning and Function of *syneidesis* in Hebrews 9 and 10," *RQ* 28 (1986): 145-54.

9:1-17

13597 Wilhelm Thüsing, "Lasst uns hinzutreten (Hebr 10:22): zur Frage nach dem Sinn der Kulttheologie im Hebräerbrief," *BZ* NS9 (1965): 1-17.

9:1-14

13598 Paul Ellingworth, "Jesus and the Universe in Hebrews," *EQ* 58 (1986): 337-350.

9:1-10

13599 Otfried Hofius, "Das 'erste' und das 'zweite' Zelt, ein Beitrag zur Auslegung von Hbr 9,1-10," *ZNW* 61 (1970): 271-77.

9:2

13600 Léopold Sabourin, "Liturge du Sanctuaire et de la Tente Véritable," *NTS* 18 (1971-1972): 87-90.

9:3-4

13601 Harold S. Camacho, "The Altar of Incense in Hebrews 9:3-4," *AUSS* 24 (1986): 5-12.

9:4-5

13602 Olaf Moe, "Das irdische und das himmlische Heiligtum: Zur Auslegung von Hebr 9:4f," *TZ* 9 (1953): 23-29.

9:4

13603 William Horbury, "The Aaronic Priesthood in the Epistle to the Hebrews," *JSNT* 19 (1983): 43-71.

13604 Harold S. Songer, "A Superior Priesthood: Hebrews 4:14-7:27," *RevExp* 82 (1985): 345-59.

9:6-10

13605 Steve Stanley, "Hebrews 9:6-10: The 'Parable' of the Tabernacle," *NovT* 37 (1995): 385-99.

9:9-10

13606 James Swetnam, "On the Imagery and Significance of Hebrews 9:9-10," *CBQ* 28 (1966): 155-73.

13607 Nello Casalini, "I sacrifici dell'antica alleanza nel piano salvifico di Dio secondo la lettera agli Ebrei," *RivBib* 35 (1987): 443-64.

9:9

13608 Gerald L. Borchert, "A Superior Book: Hebrews," *RevExp* 82 (1985): 319-22.

9:10-23

13609 John Murray, "Christian Baptism," *WTJ* 13 (1951): 105-50.

9:11-28

13610 Roger L. Omanson, "A Superior Covenant: Hebrews 8:1-10:18," *RevExp* 82 (1985): 361-73.

9:11-15

13611 C. Bourgin, " La notivelle alliance dans le sang du Christ," *AsSeign* NS 32 (1971): 40-45.

9:11

13612 J. M. Bover, "Las variante mellonton y genomenon en Hebrews 9:11," *Bib* 32 (1951): 232-36.

13613 Albert Vanhoye, "Par la tente plus grande et plus parfaite (He 9:11)," *Bib* 46 (1965): 1-28.

13614 James Swetnam, "Greater and More Perfect Tent: A Contribution to the Discussion of Hebrews 9:11," *Bib* 47 (1966): 91-106.

13615 P. Andriessen, "Das grössere und vollkornmenere Zelt," *BZ* 15 (1971): 76-92.

9:12

13616 Edward Fudge, "The Final End of the Wicked," *JETS* 27 (1984): 325-34.

13617 Franz Laub, "Ein für allemal hineingegangen in das Allerheiligste (Hebr 9:12)--zum Verständnis des Kreuzestodes im Hebräerbrief," *BZ* NS35 (1991): 65-85.

9:14

13618 Albert Vanhoye, "Esprit éternel et feu du sacrifice en He 9:14," *Bib* 64 (1983): 263-274.

9:15-18

13619 James Swetnam, "Suggested Interpretation of Hebrews 9:15-18," *CBQ* 27 (1965): 373-90.

9:16-17

13620 K. M. Campbell, "Covenant or Testament? Hebrews 9:16,17 Reconsidered," *EQ* 44 (1972): 107-111.

9:19

13621 E. A. C. Pretorius, "Christusbeeld en Kerkmodel in die Hebreërbrief," *ThEv* 15 (1982): 3-6.

13622 Erich Grässer, "Mose und Jesus: zur Auslegung von Hebr 3:1-6," *ZNW* 75 (1984): 2-23.

9:22

13623 T. C. G. Thornton, "Meaning of *ahimatekchysia* in Hebrews 9:22," *JTS* NS15 (1964): 63-65.

9:23

13624 L. D. Hurst, "How 'Platonic' Are Hebrews 8:5 and Hebrews 9:23f?" *JTS* NS34 (1983): 156-68.

9:24-28

13625 Albert Vanhoye, "L'intervention décisive du Christ," *AsSeign* NS 63 (1971): 47-52.

10:1-18

13626 Roger L. Omanson, "A Superior Covenant: Hebrews 8:1-10:18," *RevExp* 82 (1985): 361-73.

10:1-4

13627 Nello Casalini, "I sacrifici dell'antica alleanza nel piano salvifico di Dio secondo la lettera agli Ebrei," *RivBib* 35 (1987): 443-64.

10:1

13628 David G. Peterson, "Further Reflections on Worship in the New Testament," *RTR* 44 (1985): 34-41.

10:5-10

13629 P. Andriessen, "Le seul sacrifice qui plaît à Dieu," *AsSeign* NS 8 (1972): 58-63.

13630 Armando J. Levoratti, "Tú no has querido sacrificio ni oblación: Salmo 40:7; Hebreos 10:5; pt 2," *RevB* 48 (1986): 193-237.

10:5-7

13631 Karen H. Jobes, "The Function of *paronomasia* in Hebrews 10:5-7," *TriJ* 13 (1992): 181-91.

10:19-13:17

13632 David A. Black, "The Problem of the Literary Structure of Hebrews: An Evaluation and a Proposal," *GTJ* 7 (1986): 163-77.

10:19-39

13633 R. Alan Culpepper, "A Superior Faith: Hebrews 10:19-12:2," *RevExp* 82 (1985): 375-90.

13634 Scot McKnight, "The Warning Passages of Hebrews: A Formal Analysis and Theological Conclusions," *TriJ* 13 (1992): 21-59.

10:19-25

13635 Nils A. Dahl, "A New and Living Way: The Approach to God according to Hebrews 10:19-25," *Int* 5 (1951): 401-12.

13636   Otto Glombitza, "Erwägungen zum kunstvollen Ansatz der Paraenese im Brief an die Hebräer 10:19-25," *NovT* 9 (1967): 132-50.

10:20

13637   Joachim Jeremias, "Hebrér 10:20: tout' estin tes sarkos autou," *ZNW* 62 (1971): 131.

13638   Norman H. Young, *"Tout' estin tes sarkos autou*: Apposition, Dependent or Explicative?" *NTS* 20 (1973): 100-104.

10:22

13639   David G. Peterson, "Further Reflections on Worship in the New Testament," *RTR* 44 (1985): 34-41.

10:26-31

13640   Alan Mugridge, "Warnings in the Epistle to the Hebrews: An Exegetical and Theological Study," *RTR* 46 (1987): 74-82.

10:26-29

13641   Charles E. Carlston, "Eschatology and Repentance in the Epistle to the Hebrews," *JBL* 78 (1959): 296-302.

10:28

13642   E. A. C. Pretorius, "Christusbeeld en Kerkmodel in die Hebreërbrief," *ThEv* 15 (1982): 3-6.

13643   Erich Grässer, "Mose und Jesus: zur Auslegung von Hebr 3:1-6," *ZNW* 75 (1984): 2-23.

10:30-31

13644   James Swetnam, "Hebrews 10,30-31: A Suggestion," *Bib* 75 (1994): 388-94.

10:32-13:17

13645   D. Kim, "Perseverance in Hebrews," *SkrifK* 18 (1997): 280-90.

10:33

13646   Henry J. Cadbury, *"Theatrizō*No Longer a New Testament *hapax legomenon*," *ZNW* 29 (1930): 60-63.

10:37-38

13647 J. D. M. Derrett, "Running in Paul: The Midrashic Potential of Habakkuk 2:2," *Bib* 66 (1985): 560-67.

11-13

13648 Harold S. Songer, "A Superior Priesthood: Hebrews 4:14-7:27," *RevExp* 82 (1985): 345-59.

13649 Alan Mugridge, "Warnings in the Epistle to the Hebrews: An Exegetical and Theological Study," *RTR* 46 (1987): 74-82.

11:1-12:2

13650 Merland Ray Miller, "What is the Literary Form of Hebrews 11," *JETS* 29 (1986): 419-27.

11

13651 G. Schille, "Katechese und Taufliturgie: Erwägungen zu Hbr 11," *ZNW* 51 (1960): 112-31.

13652 François Bovon, "Le Christ, la foi et la sagesse dans l'épître aux Hébreux," *RTP* 18 (1968): 129-44.

13653 Gerald L. Borchert, "A Superior Book: Hebrews," *RevExp* 82 (1985): 319-22.

13654 Kimberly F. Baker, "Hebrews 11--The Promise of Faith," *RevExp* 94 (1997): 439-45.

13655 V. Rhee, "Chiasm and the Concept of Faith in Hebrews 11," *BSac* 155 (1998): 327-45.

11:1-3

13656 R. Alan Culpepper, "A Superior Faith: Hebrews 10:19-12:2," *RevExp* 82 (1985): 375-90.

13657 Richard A. Spencer, "Hebrews 11:1-3, 8-16," *Int* 49 (1995): 288-92.

11:1

13658 Heinrich Dörrie, "Zu Hbr 11:1," *ZNW* 46 (1955): 196-202.

13659 Klaus Haacker, "Der Glaube im Hebräerbrief und die hermeneutische Bedeutung des Holocaust," *TZ* 39 (1983): 152-65.

13660 Luis F. Ladaria, "Presente y futuro en la escatología cristiana," *EE* 60 (1985): 351-59.

13661 Robert G. Hoerber, "On the Translation of Hebrews 11:1," *CJ* 21 (1995): 77-79.

13662 E. Mengelle, "La estructura de Hebreos 11, 1," *Bib* 78 (1997): 534-42.

11:3

13663 Klaus Haacker, "Creatio ex auditu: zum Verständnis von Hbr 11:3," *ZNW* 60 (1969): 279-81.

11:4-7

13664 R. Alan Culpepper, "A Superior Faith: Hebrews 10:19-12:2," *RevExp* 82 (1985): 375-90.

11:6

13665 David G. Peterson, "Further Reflections on Worship in the New Testament," *RTR* 44 (1985): 34-41.

11:7

13666 Bernhard Heininger, "Hebr 11.7 und das Henochorakel am Ende der Welt," *NTS* 44 (1998): 115-32.

11:8-16

13667 Richard A. Spencer, "Hebrews 11:1-3, 8-16," *Int* 49 (1995): 288-92.

11:8-12

13668 R. Alan Culpepper, "A Superior Faith: Hebrews 10:19-12:2," *RevExp* 82 (1985): 375-90.

11:13-16

13669 R. Alan Culpepper, "A Superior Faith: Hebrews 10:19-12:2," *RevExp* 82 (1985): 375-90.

11:17-22

13670 R. Alan Culpepper, "A Superior Faith: Hebrews 10:19-12:2," *RevExp* 82 (1985): 375-90.

11:17-19

    13671 Jody L. Vaccaro, "Digging for Buried Treasure (1998): Origen's Spiritual Interpretation of Scripture," *CICR* 25 (1998): 757-75.

11:23-28

    13672 R. Alan Culpepper, "A Superior Faith: Hebrews 10:19-12:2," *RevExp* 82 (1985): 375-90.

11:23-24

    13673 E. A. C. Pretorius, "Christusbeeld en Kerkmodel in die Hebreërbrief," *ThEv* 15 (1982): 3-6.

    13674 Erich Grässer, "Mose und Jesus: zur Auslegung von Hebr 3:1-6," *ZNW* 75 (1984): 2-23.

11:29-31

    13675 R. Alan Culpepper, "A Superior Faith: Hebrews 10:19-12:2," *RevExp* 82 (1985): 375-90.

11:31

    13676 William H. Willimon, "Best Little Harlot's House in Jericho," *CC* 100 (1983): 956-58.

11:32-12:2

    13677 Murphy Davis, "Turning Dreams into Deeds: Faith in the Unseen Realities," *Soj* 14 (1985): 21-22.

11:32-38

    13678 R. Alan Culpepper, "A Superior Faith: Hebrews 10:19-12:2," *RevExp* 82 (1985): 375-90.

11:33-38

    13679 Michel van Esbroeck, "Hébreux 11:33-38 dans l'ancienne version géorgienne," *Bib* 53 (1972): 43-64.

11:39-40

    13680 R. Alan Culpepper, "A Superior Faith: Hebrews 10:19-12:2," *RevExp* 82 (1985): 375-90.

12:1-29

13681   Scot McKnight, "The Warning Passages of Hebrews: A Formal Analysis and Theological Conclusions," *TriJ* 13 (1992): 21-59.

12:1-3

13682   Gerald L. Borchert, "A Superior Book: Hebrews," *RevExp* 82 (1985): 319-22.

12:1-2

13683   Klaus Haacker, "Der Glaube im Hebräerbrief und die hermeneutische Bedeutung des Holocaust," *TZ* 39 (1983): 152-65.

13684   R. Alan Culpepper, "A Superior Faith: Hebrews 10:19-12:2," *RevExp* 82 (1985): 375-90.

13685   David A. Black, "A Note on the Structure of Hebrews 12:1-2," *Bib* 68 (1987): 543-51.

12:1

13686   Alberto Vaccari, "Hebr 12,1: lectio emendatior," *Bib* 39 (1958): 471-77.

13687   J. D. Robb, "Hebrews 12:1," *ET* 79 (1968): 254.

12:2

13688   J. Julius Scott, "Archegos: The Salvation History of the Epistle to the Hebrews," *JETS* 29 (1986): 47-54.

13689   N. Clayton Croy, "A Note on Hebrews 12:2," *JBL* 114 (1995): 117-119.

13690   Boyce J. Littleton, "Exposition of Hebrews 12:2," *FM* 16 (1999): 22-29.

13691   Andrew Neamtu, "An Exegesis on the Greek Text of Hebrews 12:2," *FM* 16 (1999): 30-38.

12:3-11

13692   Peter R. Jones, "A Superior Life: Hebrews 12:3-13:25," *RevExp* 82 (1985): 391-405.

12:4-17

13693 Bill Kellermann, "The Curse and Blessing of the Wilderness: The Risky Inheritance of Hebrews," *Soj* 14 (1985): 24-27.

12:12-17

13694 Gerald L. Borchert, "A Superior Book: Hebrews," *RevExp* 82 (1985): 319-22.

13695 Peter R. Jones, "A Superior Life: Hebrews 12:3-13:25," *RevExp* 82 (1985): 391-405.

13696 Alan Mugridge, "Warnings in the Epistle to the Hebrews: An Exegetical and Theological Study," *RTR* 46 (1987): 74-82.

12:14-17

13697 Robert A. Peterson, "The Perseverance of the Saints: A Theological Exegesis of Four Key New Testament Passages," *Pres* 17 (1991): 95-112.

12:17

13698 Charles E. Carlston, "Eschatology and Repentance in the Epistle to the Hebrews," *JBL* 78 (1959): 296-302.

13699 R. Talbot Watkins, "New English Bible and the Translation of Hebrews 12:17," *ET* 73 (1961): 29-30.

12:18-24

13700 Peter R. Jones, "A Superior Life: Hebrews 12:3-13:25," *RevExp* 82 (1985): 391-405.

12:18

13701 David G. Peterson, "Further Reflections on Worship in the New Testament," *RTR* 44 (1985): 34-41.

12:21

13702 E. A. C. Pretorius, "Christusbeeld en Kerkmodel in die Hebreërbrief," *ThEv* 15 (1982): 3-6.

13703 Erich Grässer, "Mose und Jesus: zur Auslegung von Hebr 3:1-6," *ZNW* 75 (1984): 2-23.

12:22

13704   Ceslaus Spicq, "La Panégyrie de Hebr 12:22," *StTheol* 6 (1952): 30-38.

13705   David G. Peterson, "Further Reflections on Worship in the New Testament," *RTR* 44 (1985): 34-41.

12:23

13706   Charles R. Smith, "The Book of Life," *GTJ* 6 (1985): 219-30.

12:25-29

13707   Peter R. Jones, "A Superior Life: Hebrews 12:3-13:25," *RevExp* 82 (1985): 391-405.

13708   Alan Mugridge, "Warnings in the Epistle to the Hebrews: An Exegetical and Theological Study," *RTR* 46 (1987): 74-82.

12:25-28

13709   Erich Grässer, "Das wandernde Gottesvolk: zum Basismotiv des Hebräerbriefes," *ZNW* 77 (1986): 160-79.

13

13710   Robert Jewett, "Form and Function of the Homiletic Benediction," *ATR* 51 (1969): 18-34.

13:1-16

13711   Wolfgang Schenk, "Die Paränese Hebr 13:16 im Kontext des Hebräerbriefs: einer Fallstudie semiotisch-orientierter Textinterpretation und Sachkritik," *StTheol* 39 (1985): 73-106.

13:1-6

13712   Peter R. Jones, "A Superior Life: Hebrews 12:3-13:25," *RevExp* 82 (1985): 391-405.

13:4

13713   L. D. Hurst, "Apollos, Hebrews, and Corinth: Bishop Montefiore's Theory Examined," *SJT* 38 (1985): 505-13.

13:5

13714   Peter Katz, "Hebrews 13:5: The Biblical Source of the Quotation," *Bib* 33 (1952): 523-25.

13:7-17

13715 Peter R. Jones, "A Superior Life: Hebrews 12:3-13:25," *RevExp* 82 (1985): 391-405.

13:7-16

13716 Gerald L. Borchert, "A Superior Book: Hebrews," *RevExp* 82 (1985): 319-22.

13:9-16

13717 Olaf Moe, "Das Abendmahl im Hebräerbrief: Zur Auslegung von Hebr 13:9-16," *StTheol* 4 (1950): 102-108.

13:9-14

13718 Helmut Koester, "Outside the Camp: Hebrews 13:9-14," *HTR* 55 (1962): 299-315.

13719 Peter Walker, "Jerusalem in Hebrews 13:9-14 and the Dating of the Epistle," *TynB* 45 (1994): 39-71.

13:10

13720 Antony Snell, "We Have an Altar," *RTR* 23 (1964): 16-23.

13:15-16

13721 A. Boyd Luter, "Worship as Service: The New Testament Usage of *latreuo*," *CTR* 2 (1988): 335-44.

13:17-19

13722 L. D. Hurst, "Apollos, Hebrews, and Corinth: Bishop Montefiore's Theory Examined," *SJT* 38 (1985): 505-13.

13:17

13723 A. Burge Troxel, "Accountability without Bondage: Shepherd Leadership in the Biblical Church," *CEJ* 2 (1982): 39-46.

13724 Timothy M. Willis, " 'Obey Your Leaders': Hebrews 13 and Leadership in the Church," *RQ* 36 (1994): 316-26.

13:18-21

13725 Peter R. Jones, "A Superior Life: Hebrews 12:3-13:25," *RevExp* 82 (1985): 391-405.

13:20-21

13726   C. E. B. Cranfield, "Hebrews 13:20-21," *SJT* 20 (1967): 437-41.

13:22

13727   L. Paul Trudinger, "*Kai gar dia bracheon epesteila Hymin*: A Note on Hebrews 13:22," *JTS* NS 23 (1972): 128-30.

James

1:1-27

13728 H. Rusche, "Standhaben in Gott: Einführung in die Grundgedanken des Jakobusbriefes," *BibL* 5 (1964): 153-63.

1:1

13729 S. R. Llewelyn, "The Prescript of James," *NovT* 39 (1997): 385-93.

1:2-19

13730 M. E. Isaacs, "Suffering in the Lives of Christians," *RevExp* 97 (2000): 183-93.

1:2-18

13731 Johannes Thomas, "Anfechtung und Vorfreude," *KD* 14 (1968): 183-206.

13732 D. Edmond Hiebert, "Unifying Theme of the Epistle of James," *BSac* 135 (1978): 221-31.

1:2-8

13733 Patrick J. Hartin, "Call to Be Perfect through Suffering (James 1,2-4): The Concept of Perfection in the Epistle of James and the Sermon on the Mount," *Bib* 77 (1996): 477-92.

1:2-4

13734 Ulrich Luck, "Weisheit und Leiden: zum Problem Paulus und Jakobus," *TLZ* 92 (1967): 253-58.

13735 Patrick J. Hartin, "Call to Be Perfect through Suffering," *Bib* 77 (1996): 477-92.

1:5-8

13736 David W. Perkins, "The Wisdom We Need: James 1:5-8, 3:13-18," *TEd* 34 (1986): 12-25.

1:6

13737 Hendrik F. Stander, "'n Interpretasie van die beeld van die brander in Jakobus 1:6," *SkrifK* 15 (1994): 383-90.

1:8

13738 O. J. F. Seitz, "Antecedents and Signification of the Term *dipsukhos*," *JBL* 66 (1947): 211-19.

13739 Stanley E. Porter, "Is *dipsuchos* (James 1:8; 4:8) a 'Christian' Word?" *Bib* 71 (1990): 469-98.

1:9-18

13740 Donald J. Verseput, "Wisdom, 4Q185, and the Epistle of James," *JBL* 117 (1998): 691-707.

1:10

13741 George M. Stulac, "Who Are 'the Rich' in James," *Pres* 16 (1990): 89-102.

1:12-18

13742 D. Bertrand, "Jacques 1,12-18," *Chr* 30 (1983) 212-18.

1:12-15

13743 William Stringfellow, "Temptation: Pursuit by the Power of Death," *Soj* 15 (1986): 34-38.

1:12

13744 A. C. Deane, "The Beatitude of Endurance," *ET* 48 (1936-1937): 342-43.

1:13

13745 Peter H. Davids, "Meaning of *apeirastos* in James 1:13," *NTS* 24 (1978): 386-92.

1:17-27

13746 R. Gantoy, "Accueil et mise en pratique de la Parole," *AsSeign* 53 (1970): 39-49.

1:17-21

13747 R. Gantoy, "Une catéchèse apostolique pour notre temps," *AsSeign* 47 (1963): 15-27.

13748 Adalberto Sisti, "Doni e doveri," *BibO* 6 (1964): 17-27.

1:17

13749   Heinrich Greeven, "Jede Gabe ist gut: Jak 1-17," *TZ* 14 (1958): 1-13.

13750   C.-B. Amphoux, "À propos de Jacques 1,17," *RHPR* 50 (1970): 127-36.

13751   Donald J. Verseput, "James 1:17 and the Jewish Morning Prayers," *NovT* 39 (1997): 177-91.

1:18

13752   F. Ogara, "Voluntarie genuit nos verbo veritatis ut simus initium aliquod creaturae eius," *VD* 15 (1935): 130-38.

13753   C.-M. Edsmann, "Schöpferwille und Geburt Jac 1.18: Eine Studie zur altchristlichen Kosmologie," *ZNW* 38 (1939): 11-44.

13754   Leonard E. Elliott-Binns, "James 1:18: Creation or Redemption?" *NTS* 3 (1956): 148-61.

1:19-2:26

13755   Ricardo Pietrantonio, "Esta la justicia enraizada en el NT," *RevB* 48 (1986): 89-119.

1:19-27

13756   A. Calmet, "Vraie et fausse sagesse," *BVC* 58 (1964): 19-28.

13757   C. E. B. Cranfield, "Message of James," *SJT* 18 (1965): 182-93.

1:21

13758   Leonard E. Elliott-Binns, "James 1:21 and Ezekiel 16:36: An Odd Coincidence," *ET* 66 (1955): 273.

13759   Frédéric Manns, "Une tradition liturgique juive sous-jacente à Jacques 1:21b," *RevSR* 62 (1988): 85-89.

1:22-27

13760   Adalberto Sisti, "La parola e le opere," *BibO* 6 (1964): 78-85.

13761   Ceslaus Spicq, "La vraie vie chrétienne," *AsSeign* 48 (1965): 21-38.

1:22-25

13762   R. E. Glaze, "The Relationship of Faith to Works in James 1:22-25 and 2:14-26," *TEd* 34 (1986): 35-42.

13763   Luke T. Johnson, "The Mirror of Remembrance," *CBQ* 50 (1988): 632-45.

1:22-24

13764   John J. Pilch, "Mirrors and Glass," *BibTo* 36 (1998): 382-86.

1:23-24

13765   José O'Callaghan, "New Testament Papyri in Qumran Cave 7?" *JBL* 91 (1972): 1-14.

1:23

13766   Gilberto Marconi, "Una nota sullo specchio di Gc 1:23," *Bib* 70 (1989): 396-402.

1:25

13767   Friedrich Nötscher, "Gesetz der Freiheit im NT und in der Mönchsgemeinde am Toten Meer," *Bib* 34 (1953): 193-94.

13768   Corrado Marucci, "Das Gesetz der Freiheit im Jakobusbrief," *ZKT* 117 (1995): 317-31.

1:26-27

13769   Luis Alonso Schökel, "Culto y justicia en Sant 1,26-27," *Bib* 56 (1975): 537-44.

13770   Donald J. Verseput, "Reworking the Puzzle of Faith and Deeds in James 2:14-26," *NTS* 43 (1997): 97-115.

1:26

13771   Floyd Lewis, "The Conversation of a Christian," *TEd* 34 (1986): 43-47.

1:27

13772   D. J. Roberts, "Short Comments: 'Pure Religion'," *ET* 83 (1971-1972): 215-16.

13773   Bruce C. Johanson, "Short Comment: 'Pure Religion' in James 1,27," *ET* 84 (1972-1973): 118-19.

13774   David E. Garland, "Severe Trials, Good Gifts, and Pure Religion: James 1," *RevExp* 83 (1986): 383-94.

2:1-13

13775   H. Rusche, "Der Erbarmer hält Gericht: Einführung in die Grundgedanken des Jakobusbriefes," *BibL* 5 (1964): 236-47.

13776   Dirk J. Smit, "Exegesis and Proclamation: 'Show No Partiality. . .' (James 2:1-13)," *JTSA* 71 (1990): 59-68.

13777   Nancy J. Vyhmeister, "The Rich Man in James 2: Does Ancient Patronage Illumine the Text?" *AUSS* 33 (1995): 265-83.

2:1-5

13778   O. Knoch, "Riches et pauvres dans l'Église," *AsSeign* NS 54 (1972): 28-32.

13779   Kenneth G. Phifer, "James 2:1-5," *Int* 36 (1982): 278-82.

2:1

13780   Johannes Brinktrine, "Zu Jak 2:1," *Bib* 35 (1954): 40-42.

2:2-4

13781   Roy B. Ward, "Partiality in the Assembly: James 2:2-4," *HTR* 62 (1969): 87-97.

2:8-11

13782   Oda Wischmeyer, "Das Gebot der Nächstenliebe bei Paulus: eine traditionsgeschichtliche Untersuchung," *BZ* NS 30 (1986): 161-87.

2:11

13783   Johannes Brinktrine, "Zn Jak 2,11," *Bib* 35 (1954): 40-41.

13784   George D. Kilpatrick, "Übertreter des Gesetzes, Jak. 2,2," *TZ* 23 (1967): 433.

2:12

13785   Corrado Marucci, "Das Gesetz der Freiheit im Jakobusbrief," *ZKT* 117 (1995): 317-31.

<u>2:14-26</u>

13786 A. Fernandez, "Fides et opera apud S. Paulum et S. Iacobum," *VD* 12 (1932): 177-80.

13787 Joachim Jeremias, "Paul and James," *ET* 66 (1955): 368-71.

13788 C. E. B. Cranfield, "Message of James," *SJT* 18 (1965): 182-93.

13789 Roy B. Ward, "The Works of Abrahamm," *HTR* 61 (1968): 283-90.

13790 Gary M. Burge, " 'And Threw Them Thus on Paper': Rediscovering the Poetic Form of James 2:14-26," *SBT* 7 (1977): 31-45.

13791 Thorwald Lorenzen, "Faith without Works Does Not Count before God: James 2:14-26," *ET* 89 (1978): 231-35.

13792 Christoph Burchard, "Zu Jakobus 2:14-26," *ZNW* 71 (1980): 27-45.

13793 Hans Heinz, "Jakobus 2:14-26 in der Sicht Martin Luthers," *AUSS* 19 (1981): 141-46.

13794 R. E. Glaze, "The Relationship of Faith to Works in James 1:22-25 and 2:14-26," *TEd* 34 (1986): 35-42.

13795 Mark Proctor, "Faith, Works, and the Christian Religion in James 2:14-26," *EQ* 69 (1997): 307-32.

13796 Donald J. Verseput, "Reworking the Puzzle of Faith and Deeds in James 2:14-26," *NTS* 43 (1997): 97-115.

13797 Klaus Haacker, "Justification, salut et foi: Étude sur les rapports entre Paul, Jacques et Pierre," *ÉTR* 73 (1998): 177-88.

13798 S. Dowd, "Faith That Works: James 2:14-26," *RevExp* 97 (2000): 195-205.

<u>2:14-22</u>

13799 H. Rusche, "Vom lebendigen Glauben und vom rechten Beten. Einführung in die Grundgesdanken des Jakobusbriefes," *BibL* 6 (1965): 26-37.

2:14

13800 J. Claude Piguet, "La foi et les oeuvres: un dialogue interdisciplinaire," *RTP* 118 (1986): 291-96.

13801 G. Z. Heide, "The Soteriology of James 2:14," *GTJ* 12 (1991): 69-97.

2:18-19

13802 Christiaan E. Donker, "Der Verfasser des Jak und sein Gegner: zum Problem des Einwandes in Jak 2:18-19," *ZNW* 72 (1981): 227-40.

2:18

13803 Heinz Neitzel, "Eine alte crux interpretum im Jakobusbrief 2:18," *ZNW* 73 (1982): 286-93.

13804 Scot McKnight, "James 2:18a: The Unidentifiable Interlocutor," *WTJ* 52 (1990): 355-64.

2:19

13805 J. Beumer, "Et daemones credunt (jac. 2,19). Ein Beitrag zur positiven Bewertung der *fides informis*," *Greg* 22 (1949): 231-51.

13806 T. W. Lund, "Belief and Worship," *ET* 90 (1979): 366-67.

2:21-26

13807 Irving Jacobs, "Midrashic Background for James 2:21-26," *NTS* 22 (1976): 457-64.

2:21-23

13808 C. J. Bekker and S. J. Nortjé, "Die gebruik van die offer' van Isak as 'n motief vir die verkondiging van Jesus as die lydende Christus," *HTS* 51 (1995): 454-64.

2:22

13809 John G. Lodge, "James and Paul at Cross-Purposes: James 2:22," *Bib* 62 (1981): 195-213.

2:24

13810 Ulrich Luck, "Der Jakobusbrief und die Theologie des Paulus," *TGl* 61 (1971): 161-79.

2:25

13811 A. T. Hanson, "Rahab the Harlot in Early Christian Theology," *JSNT* 1 (1978): 53-60.

3:1-12

13812 Floyd Lewis, "The Conversation of a Christian," *TEd* 34 (1986): 43-47.

13813 Duane F. Watson, "The Rhetoric of James 3:1-12 and a Classical Pattern of Argumentation," *NovT* 35 (1993): 48-64.

3:5

13814 Leonard E. Elliott-Binns, "Meaning of Hyle in James 3:5," *NTS* 2 (1955): 48-50.

3:6

13815 Hans Scharen, "Gehenna in the Synoptics," *BSac* 149 (1992): 324-37.

3:9

13816 Jeffrey A. Gibbs, "The Grace of God as the Foundation for Ethics," *CTQ* 48 (1984): 185-201.

3:13-4:10

13817 Luke T. Johnson, "James 3:13-4:10 and the *topos peri phthonou*," *NovT* 25 (1983): 327-47.

3:13-18

13818 A. Calmet, "Vraie et fausse sagesse," *BVC* 58 (1964): 19-28.

13819 David W. Perkins, "The Wisdom We Need: James 1:5-8, 3:13-18," *TEd* 34 (1986): 12-25.

3:13

13820 Patrick J. Hartin, " 'Who Is Wise and Understanding among You?' (James 3:13): An Analysis of Wisdom, Eschatology and Apocalypticism in the Epistle of James," in *SBLSP* 35 (1996): 483-503.

3:16-4:3

13821 Jean Cantinat, "Sagesse, justice, plaisirs," *AsSeign* NS 56 (1974): 36-40.

13822 Pheme Perkins, "James 3:16-4:3," *Int* 36 (1982): 283-87.

4:1-5:6

13823 F. Genuyt, "Parcours: ' 'Épître de Jacques 4:1-5:6," *SémBib* 23 (1981): 44-56.

4

13824 William L. Blevins, "A Call to Repent, Love Others, and Remember God: James 4," *RevExp* 83 (1986): 419-26.

4:1-10

13825 H. Rusche, "Vom lebendigen Glauben und vome rechten Beten. Einführung in die Grundgesdanken des Jakobusbriefes," *BibL* 6 (1965): 26-37.

4:1-4

13826 Michael J. Townsend, "James 4:1-4: A Warning against Zealotry?" *ET* 87 (1976): 211-13.

4:11-12

13827 A.-M. Cocagnac, "Simples méditations sur quelques textes de la Bible," *VS* 96 (1957): 5-31.

4:13-5:6

13828 Bent Noack, "Jacobus wider die Reichen," *ST* 18 (1964): 10-25.

4:13-17

13829 Harold T. Bryson, "What Is Your Life? James 4:13-17," *TEd* 34 (1986): 60-62.

4:4-6

13830 Lewis J. Prockter, "James 4:4-6: Midrash on Noah," *NTS* 35 (1989): 625-27.

4:5-6

13831 Wiard Popkes, "James and Scripture: An Exercise in Intertextuality" *NTS* 454 (1999): 213-29.

4:5

13832 Joachim Jeremias, "Jac 4,5: *Epipothei*," *ZNW* 50 (1959): 137-38.

13833 S. S. Laws, "Does Scripture Speak in Vain? A Reconsideration of James 4:5," *NTS* 20 (1974): 210-15.

13834 E. A. C. Pretorius, "Drie nuwe verklaringsopsies in die Jakobusbrief," *HTS* 44 (1988): 650-64.

4:6

13835 Luis Alonso Schökel, "James 5,2 and 4,6," *Bib* 54 (1973): 73-76.

4:8

13836 O. J. F. Seitz, "Antecedents and Signification of the Term *dipsukhos*," *JBL* 66 (1947): 211-19.

13837 Stanley E. Porter, "Is *dipsuchos* (James 1:8; 4:8) a 'Christian' Word?" *Bib* 71 (1990): 469-98.

5

13838 Roger L. Omanson, "The Certainty of Judgment and the Power of Prayer: James 5," *RevExp* 83 (1986): 427-38.

13839 Wiard Popkes, "James and Scripture: An Exercise in Intertextuality" *NTS* 454 (1999): 213-29.

5:1-6

13840 George Peck, "James 5:1-6," *Int* 42 (1988): 291-96.

13841 Patrick J. Hartin, " 'Come Now, You Rich, Weep and Wail . . .'," *JTSA* 84 (1993): 57-63.

5:2-3

13842 Moisés Mayordomo-Marín, "Jak 5,2.3a: Zukünftiges Gericht oder gegenwärtiger Zustand?" *ZNW* 83 (1992): 132-37.

5:2

13843 Luis Alonso Schökel, "James 5,2 and 4,6," *Bib* 54 (1973): 73-76.

5:5

13844 Ernst Lerle, "Kardia als Bezeichnung für den Mageneingang," *ZNW* 76 (1985): 292-94.

5:6-20

13845   F. Genuyt, "Épître de Saint-Jacques 5:6-20," *SémBib* 24 (1981): 28-36.

5:6

13846   E. A. C. Pretorius, "Drie nuwe verklaringsopsies in die Jakobusbrief," *HTS* 44 (1988): 650-64.

5:7-12

13847   Gilberto Marconi, "La debolezza in forma di attesa: appunti per un'esegesi di Gc 5:7-12," *RivBib* 37 (1989): 173-83.

5:7-11

13848   Ceslaus Spicq, "Exhortation à la patience," *AsSeign* NS 7 (1969): 12-15.

13849   Patrick J. Hartin, "Call to Be Perfect through Suffering (James 1,2-4): The Concept of Perfection in the Epistle of James and the Sermon on the Mount," *Bib* 77 (1996): 477-92.

5:7-10

13850   A. Viard, "Invitation à la patience," *EV* 87 (1977): 617-18.

5:11

13851   Robert P. Gordon, "*Kai to telos kyriou eidete* (James 5:11)," *JTS* 26 (1975): 91-95.

5:12

13852   Gerhard Dautzenberg, "Ist das Schwurverbot Mt 5,33-37; Jak 5,12 ein Beispiel für die Torakritik Jesu?" *BZ* NS 25 (1981): 47-66.

13853   David Wenham, "2 Corinthians 1:17,18: Echo of a Dominical Logion," *NovT* 28 (1986): 271-79.

13854   Julián Carrón Pérez, "The Second Commandment in the New Testament: Your Yes Is Yes, Your No Is No," *CICR* 20 (1993): 5-25.

13855   William R. Baker, " 'Above All Else': Contexts of the Call for Verbal Integrity in James 5:12," *JSNT* 54 (1994): 57-71.

13856   Bernd Kollmann, "Das Schwurverbot Mt 5,33-37/Jak 5,12 im Spiegel antiker Eidkritik," *BZ* NS 40 (1996): 179-93.

5:13-20

13857   Gilberto Marconi, "La malattia come 'punto di vista': esegesi di Gc 5:13-20," *RivBib* 38 (1990): 57-72.

13858   Robert J. Karris, "Some New Angles on James 5:13-20," *RevExp* 97 (2000): 207-19.

5:13-18

13859   John Wilkinson, "Healing in the Epistle of James," *SJT* 24 (1971): 326-45.

13860   Francois Vouga, "Jacques 5:13-18," *ÉTR* 53 (1978): 103-109.

13861   Keith Warrington, "The Significance of Elijah in James 5:13-18," *EQ* 66 (1994): 217-27.

5:13-15

13862   Joseph Coppens, "Jacq. V,13-15 et l'onction des malades," *ETL* 53 (1977): 201-207.

5:14-16

13863   Douglas J. Moo, "Divine Healing in the Health and Wealth Gospel," *TriJ* 9 (1988): 191-209.

13864   Gary S. Shogren, "Will God Heal Us? A Re-examination of James 5:14-16a," *EQ* 61 (1989): 99-108.

5:14-15

13865   K. Condon, "The Sacrament of Healing," *Scr* 11 (1959): 331-41.

5:14

13866   Charles H. Pickar, "Is Anyone Sick Among You?" *CBQ* 7 (1945): 165-74.

5:16

13867   G. C. Bottini, "Confessione e intercessione in Giacomo 5:16," *SBFLA* 33 (1983): 193-226.

<u>5:17</u>

13868   B. E. Thiering, "The Three and a Half Years of Elijah,"
        NovT 23 (1981): 41-55.

1 Peter

1:1-2:10

13869   Eugene A. LaVerdiere, "Covenant Theology in 1 Peter 1:1-2:10," *BibTo* 42 (1969): 2909-16.

13870   Max A. Chevallier, "1 Pierre 1:1 à 2:10: structure littéraire et conséquences exégétiques," *RHPR* 51 (1971): 129-42.

13871   John H. Elliott, "Salutation and Exhortation to Christian Behavior on the Basis of God's Blessings," *RevExp* 79 (1982): 415-25.

13872   R. I. Hamlin, "Expositor's Corner: First Peter," *TEd* 12 (1982): 83-88.

1:1-12

13873   F. W. Grosheide, "1 Petrus 1:1-12," *GTT* 60 (1960): 6-7.

1:1-6

13874   J. Ramsey Michaels, "Jewish and Christian Apocalyptic Letters: 1 Peter, Revelation, and 2 Baruch 78-87," *SBLSP* 26 (1987): 268-75.

1:1-3

13875   Philip L. Tite, "The Compositional Function of the Petrine Prescript: A Look at 1 Peter 1:1-3," *JETS* 39 (1996): 47-56.

1:1-2

13876   Martin H. Scharlemann, "An Apostolic Salutation: An Exegetical Study of 1 Peter 1:1-2," *CJ* 1 (1975): 108-18.

13877   Colin J. Hemer, "The Address of 1 Peter," *ET* 89 (1978): 239-43.

13878   D. Edmond Hiebert, "Designation of the Readers in 1 Peter 1:1-2," *BSac* 137 (1980): 64-75.

1:1

13879 Max A. Chevallier, "L'unité plurielle de l'église d'après le Nouveau Testament," *RHPR* 66 (1986): 3-20.

1:2

13880 F. Agnew, "1 Peter 1:2 - An Alternative Translation," *CBQ* 45 (1983): 68-73.

1:3-12

13881 John Coutts, "Ephesians i. 3-14 and 1 Peter i. 3-12," *NTS* 3 (1956-1957): 115-27.

13882 Martin H. Scharlemann, "An Apostolic Descant: An Exegetical Study of 1 Peter 1:3-12," *CJ* 2 (1976): 9-17.

13883 D. Edmond Hiebert, "Peter's Thanksgiving for Our Salvation," *SM* 137 (1980): 85-103.

13884 R. Kühschelm, " 'Lebendige Hoffnung'- zu 1 Petr 1,3-12," *BL* 56 (1983): 202-206.

1:3-9

13885 L. Cothenet, "Béni soit Dieu," *AsSeign* NS 23 (1971): 26-32.

13886 David W. Kendall, "1 Peter 1:3-9," *Int* 41 (1987): 66-71.

1:3-7

13887 Daniel C. Stevens, "Christian Educational Foundations and the Pauline Triad: A Call to Faith, Hope, and Love," *CEJ* 5 (1984): 5-16.

1:3-6

13888 Werner C. Graendorf, "Biblical Principles for Ministering to Older Adults," *CEJ* 4 (1983): 38-45.

1:3-5

13889 F. W. Grosheide, "Kol 3,1-4, 1 Petr 1,3-5; 1 Jo 3,1-2," *GTT* 54 (1954): 139-47.

13890 Joel C. Gregory, "Interpretation in Preaching," *SouJT* 27 (1985): 8-18.

1:3

13891 Donald G. Miller, "The Resurrection as the Source of Living Hope: An Exposition of 1 Peter 1:3," *HBT* 17 (1995): 132-41.

1:5-7

13892 Johannes Thomas, "Anfechtung und Vorfreude," *KD* 14 (1968): 183-206.

1:5

13893 David Horrell, "Whose Faith(fulness) Is It in 1 Peter 1:5?" *JTS* NS 48 (1997): 110-15.

1:6-7

13894 John Proctor, "Fire in God's House: Influence of Malachi 3 in the New Testament," *JETS* 36 (1993): 9-14.

1:8

13895 Troy Martin, "The Present Indicative in the Eschatological Statements of 1 Peter 1:6, 8," *JBL* 111 (1992): 307-12.

1:9

13896 Gerhard Dautzenberg, "Soteria psychon (1 Petr 1:9)," *BZ* NS 8 (1964): 262-76.

13897 J. A. Davidson, "The Congregation: Priest and Servant," *ET* 85 (1974): 336-37.

1:10-12

13898 Raju D. Kunjummen, "The Single Intent of Scripture: Critical Examination of a Theological Construct," *GTJ* 7 (1986): 81-110.

13899 Duane Warden, "The Prophets of 1 Peter 1:10-12," *RQ* 31 (1989): 1-12.

13900 Maria L. Rigato, "Quali i profeti di cui nella 1 Pt 1:10?" *RivBib* 38 (1990): 73-90.

1:11

13901 George D. Kilpatrick, "1 Peter 1:11 τίνα ἢ ποῖον καίρον," *NovT* 38 (1986): 91-92.

1:12

13902   K. Shimada, "A Critical Note on 1 Peter 1,12," *AJBI* 7 (1981): 146-53.

1:13-2:12

13903   Robert Hodgson, "The Testimony Hypothesis," *JBL* 98 (1979): 361-78.

1:13-2:10

13904   M.-É. Boismard, "La typologie baptismale dans la première épître de saint Pierre," *VS* 94 (1956): 339-52.

1:13-25

13905   W. P. Esterhuyse, "Kerk en politiek," *ScrSA* 24 (1988): 38-48.

1:13

13906   J. R. Harris, "An Emendation to 1 Peter 1,13," *ET* 41 (1929-1930): 43.

13907   E. Vallauri, " 'Succincti lumbos mentis vestrae' (1 Piet. 1, 13). Nota per una traduzione," *BibO* 24 (1982): 19-22.

1:14

13908   Douglas W. Kennard, "Petrine Redemption: Its Meaning and Extent," *JETS* 30 (1987): 399-405.

1:17-21

13909   K. Gatzweiler, "Prix et exigencies de la condition chrétienne," *AsSeign* 24 (1970): 16-20.

1:18

13910   Roland Bergmeier, "Die Buchrolle und das Lamm (Apk 5 und 10)," *ZNW* 76 (1985): 225-42.

13911   Douglas W. Kennard, "Petrine Redemption: Its Meaning and Extent," *JETS* 30 (1987): 399-405.

1:20

13912   R. Le Déaut, "Le Targum de Gen 22, 8 et 1 Pt 1,20," *RechSR* 49 (1961): 103-106.

13913   G. Martelet, "Das Lamm, erwählt vor der Grundlegung der Welt," *IKaZ* 9 (1980): 36-44.

1:22-23

13914   Martin Evang, "*Ek kardias allelous agapesate ektenos*: zum Verständnis der Aufforderung und ihrer Begründungen in 1 Petr 1:22f," *ZNW* 80 (1989): 111-23.

1:23

13915   Eugene A. LaVerdiere, "A Grammatical Ambiguity in 1 Peter 1:23," *CBQ* 36 (1974): 89-94.

13916   Traian Valdman, "Uno sguardo ortodosso sulla giustificazione in Lutero," *SEcu* 1 (1983): 277-88.

1:24

13917   Frederick W. Danker, "1 Peter 1:24, 2:17: A Consolatory Pericope," *ZNW* 58 (1967): 93-102.

1:25

13918   Martin H. Scharlemann, "Why the *Kuriou* in 1 Peter 1:25?" *CTM* 30 (1959): 352-56.

2:1-10

13919   P. Ketter, "Das allgemeine Priestertum der Gläubigen nach dem ersten Petrusbrief," *TTZ* 56 (1947): 43-51.

13920   Albert Vanhoye, "La maison spirituelle," *AsSeign* NS 43 (1964): 16-29.

13921   Klyne R. Snodgrass, "1 Peter 2:1-10: Its Formation and Literary Affinities," *NTS* 24 (1977-1978): 97-106.

13922   J. M. Turner, "The People of God," *ET* 91 (1980): 244-45.

2:2-10

13923   Peter H. Hobbie, "1 Peter 2:2-10," *Int* 47 (1993): 170-73.

2:2-4

13924   N. Hillyer, " 'Spiritual Mile....Spiritual House," *TynB* 20 (1969): 126.

2:2

13925   Dan G. McCartney, "*Logikos* in 1 Peter 2,2," *ZNW* 82 (1991): 128-32.

2:3-8

13926 W. B. Stanford, "St. Peter's Silence on the Petrine Claims," *Theology* 48 (1945): 15.

2:3-5

13927 Joseph Moingt, "Prêtre 'selon le Nouveau Testament': a propos d'un livre récent," *RechSR* 69 (1981): 573-98.

2:3

13928 Jerome D. Quinn, "Notes on the Text of the P72 1 Peter 2:3; 5:14; and 5:9," *CBQ* 27 (1965): 241-49.

2:4-10

13929 Ernest Best, "1 Peter 2:4-10: A Reconsideration," *NovT* 11 (1969): 270-93.

13930 Albert Vanhoye, "La foi qui construit l'Église," *AsSeign* NS 26 (1973): 12-17.

13931 L. F. Colecchia, "Rilievi su 1 Piet. 2,4-10," *RivBib* 25 (1977): 179-94.

13932 A. T. M. Cheung, "The Priest as the Redeemed Man: A Biblical- Theological Study of the Priesthood," *JETS* 29 (1986): 265-75.

13933 Rinaldo Fabris, "San Pietro apostolo nella prima chiesa," *SM* 35 (1986): 41-70.

13934 Thomas D. Lea, "The Priesthood of All Christians according to the New Testament," *SouJT* 30 (1988): 15-21.

13935 Douglas A. Oss, "The Interpretation of the 'Stone' Passages by Peter and Paul: A Comparative Study," *JETS* 32 (1989): 181-200.

13936 Pierre Prigent, "1 Pierre 2:4-10," *RHPR* 72 (1992): 53-60.

2:4-8

13937 Thomas D. Lea, "How Peter Learned the Old Testament," *SouJT* 22 (1980): 96-102.

2:5

13938 J. S. Marshall, "A Spiritual House an Holy Priesthood," *ATR* 28 (1946): 227-28.

13939 André Feuillet, "Les 'sacrifices spirituels' du sacerdoce royal des baptisés et leur préparation dans l'Ancien Testament," *NRT* 96 (1974): 704-28.

13940 D. Hill, "To Offer Spiritual Sacrifices: Liturgical Formulations and Christian Paraenesis in 1 Peter," *JSNT* 16 (1982): 45-63.

13941 David G. Peterson, "Further Reflections on Worship in the New Testament," *RTR* 44 (1985): 34-41.

2:9-12

13942 Werner Bieder, "Das Volk Gottes in Erwartung von Licht und Lobpreis," *TZ* 40 (1984): 137-48.

2:9-10

13943 William Klassen, "The King as 'Living Law' with Particular Reference to Musonius Rufus," *SR* 14 (1985): 63-71.

2:9-10

13944 Valdir R. Steuernagel, "An Exiled Community as a Missionary Community: A Study Based on 1 Peter 2:9, 10," *ERT* 10 (1986): 8-18.

2:9

13945 M. García Cordero, "El Sacerdocio real en 1 P 2,9," *CuBí* 16 (1959): 321-23.

13946 Phillip Sigal, "Reflections on Targumic and New Testament studies," *EGLMBS* 1 (1981): 1-25.

13947 S. Halas, "Sens dynamique de l'expression λαός en 1 P 2.9," *Bib* 65 (1984): 254-58.

13948 Elmar Salmann, "Trinität und Kirche: eine dogmatische Studie," *Cath* 38 (1984): 352-74.

13949 David G. Peterson, "Further Reflections on Worship in the New Testament," *RTR* 44 (1985): 34-41.

13950 Ugo Vanni, "La promozione del regno come responsabilità sacerdotale dei Cristiani secondo l'Apocalisse e la Prima Lettera di Pietro," *Greg* 68 (1987): 9-56.

2:11-3:12

> 13951   Donald P. Senior, "The Conduct of Christians in the World," *RevExp* 79 (1982): 427-38.

> 13952   D. L. Balch, "Early Christian Criticism of Patriarchal Authority: 1 Peter 2:11-3:12," *USQR* 39 (1984): 161-73.

2:11-19

> 13953   G. Perez and J. F. Hernandez, "Epistolas Dominicales," *CuBi* 13 (1956): 92-98.

> 13954   Adalberto Sisti, "Il cristiano nel mondo," *BibO* 8 (1966): 70-79.

2:11-17

> 13955   Geoffrey Wainwright, "Praying for Kings: The Place of Human Rulers in the Divine Plan of Salvation," *ExA* 2 (1986): 117-27.

2:11-12

> 13956   Max A. Chevallier, "L'unité plurielle de l'église d'après le Nouveau Testament," *RHPR* 66 (1986): 3-20.

2:11

> 13957   Marinus de Jonge, "Vreemdelingen en bijwoners: Enige opmerkingen naar aanleiding van 1 Petr 2.11 en verwante teksten," *NTT* 11 (1956-1957): 18-36.

2:12

> 13958   H. G. Meecham, "A Note on 1 Peter 2:12," *ET* 65 (1953-1954): 93.

> 13959   David G. Peterson, "Further Reflections on Worship in the New Testament," *RTR* 44 (1985): 34-41.

2:13-3:8

> 13960   Robert L. Richardson, "From 'Subjection to Authority' to 'Mutual Submission': The Ethic of Subordination in 1 Peter," *FM* 4 (1987): 70-80.

2:13-3:7

> 13961   Frank Stagg, "The Gospel, Haustafel, and Women: Mark 1:1; Colossians 3:18-4:1," *FM* 2 (1985): 59-63.

2:13-17

13962 Simon Légasse, "La soumission aux autorités d'après 1 Pierre 2:13-17: version spécifique d'une parénèse traditionelle," *NTS* 34 (1988): 378-96.

2:13-15

13963 David R. Plaster, "The Christian and War: A Matter of Personal Conscience," *GTJ* 6 (1985): 435-55.

2:13-14

13964 Manfred Spieker, "Nuclear Weapons and the Sermon on the Mount," *CICR* 11 (1984): 382-403.

13965 S. A. James, "Divine Justice and the Retributive Duty of Civil Government," *TriJ* NS 6 (1985): 199-210.

2:13

13966 H. Teichert, "1 Petr 2,13—eine crux interpretum?" *TLZ* 74 (1949): 303-304.

13967 Roger L. Omanson, "Translations: Text and Interpretation," *EQ* 57 (1985): 195-210.

13968 Jarl H. Ulrichsen, "Die sieben Häupter und die zehn Hörner. Zur Datierung der Offenbarung des Johannes," *StTheol* 39 (1985): 1-20.

2:14-15

13969 Bruce W. Winter, "The Public Honouring of Christian Benefactors: Romans 13:3-4 and 1 Peter 2:14-15," *JSNT* 34 (1988): 87-103.

2:14

13970 W. C. van Unnik, "A Classical Parallel to 1 Peter ii,14 and 20," *NTS* 2 (1955-1956): 198-202.

2:17

13971 E. Bammel, "The Commands in 1 Peter 2:17," *NTS* 11 (1965): 279-80.

13972 Frederick W. Danker, "1 Peter 1:24, 2:17: A Consolatory Pericope," *ZNW* 58 (1967): 93-102.

13973 James I. Packer, "How to Recognize a Christian Citizen," *CT* 29 (1985): 4-8.

13974   Jarl H. Ulrichsen, "Die sieben Häupter und die zehn
        Hörner. Zur Datierung der Offenbarung des Johannes,"
        StTheol 39 (1985): 1-20.

13975   Ernest Best, "A First Century Sect," *IBS* 8 (1986): 115-21.

13976   Scot Snyder, "1 Peter 2:17: A Reconsideration," *FilN* 4
        (1991): 211-15.

2:18-25

13977   James W. Thompson, " 'Be Submissive to Your Masters':
        A Study of 1 Peter 2:18-25," *RQ* 9 (1966): 66-78.

13978   Marie L. Lamau, "Exhortation aux esclaves et hymne au
        Christ souffrant dans la Première Epître de Pierre," *MSR* 43
        (1986): 121-43.

2:20

13979   W. C. van Unnik, "A Classical Parallel to 1 Peter 2:14 and
        20," *NTS* 2 (1956): 198-202.

2:21-25

13980   Horst Goldstein, "Die Kirche als Schar derer, die ihrem
        leidenden Herrn mit dem Ziel der Gottesgemeinschaft
        nachfolgen. Zum Gemeindeverständnis von 1 Peter 2,21-25
        und 3,18-22," *BibL* 15 (1974): 38-54.

13981   D. Edmond Hiebert, "Selected Studies from 1 Peter. Part 1:
        Following Christ's Example," *BSac* 139 (1982): 32-45.

13982   T. P. Osborne, "Guide Lines for Christian Suffering: A
        Source Critical and Theological Study of 1 Peter 2,21-25,"
        Bib 64 (1983): 381-408.

2:21

13983   James H. Burtness, "Sharing the Suffering of God in the
        Life of the World," *Int* 23 (1969): 277-88.

2:22-25

13984   Michel Gourgues, "La foi chrétienne primitive face à la
        croix: le témoignage des formulaires pré-pauliniens," *ScE*
        41 (1989): 49-69.

2:22-24

13985　Raymond Schwager, "Christ's Death and the Prophetic Critique of Sacrifice," *Semeia* 33 (1985): 109-23.

2:24

13986　H. Patsch, "Zum alttestamentlichen Hintergrund von Römer 4:25 und 1 Petrus 2:24," *ZNW* 60 (1969): 273-79.

2:25

13987　Sebastián Bartina, "Pedro manifiesta su poder primacial," *CuBí* 21 (1964): 333-36.

13988　R. Trevijano Etcheverría, "La mision en Tesalonica (1 Tes 1:1-2,16)," *Salm* 32 (1985): 263-91.

3-4

13989　D. Völter, "Bemerkungen zu 1. Pe 3 und 4," *ZNW* 9 (1908): 74-77.

3:1-20

13990　R. Fowler White, "The Last Adam and His Seed: An Exercise in Theological Preemption," *TriJ* NS 6 (1985): 60-73.

3:1-7

13991　Lyle D. Vander Broek, "Women and the Church: Approaching Difficult Passages," *RR* 38 (1985): 225-31.

13992　Orsay Groupe, "Une lecture féministe des 'codes domestiques'," *FV* 88 (1989): 59-69.

13993　T. K. Seim, "Hustavlen 1 Pet 3.1-7 og dens tradisjonshistoriske sammenheng," *NTT* 91 (1990): 101-14.

3:1-6

13994　James R. Slaughter, "Sarah as a Model for Christian Wives (Part 3)," *BSac* 153 (1996): 357-65.

13995　James R. Slaughter, "Winning Unbelieving Husbands to Christ (Part 2)," *BSac* 153 (1996): 199-211.

13996　James R. Slaughter, "Instructions to Christian Wives in 1 Peter 3:1-6: Submission of Wives (1 Pet 3:1a) in the Context of 1 Peter," *BSac* 153 (1996): 63-74.

3:2

13997   Dennis D. Sylva, "Translating and Interpreting 1 Peter 3:2," *BT* 34 (1983): 144-47.

3:5-6

13998   Jacques Schlosser, "1 Pierre 3,5b-6," *Bib* 64 (1983): 409-10.

3:5

13999   G. Ghiberti, "Le 'sante donne' di una volta," *RivBib* 36 (1988): 287-97.

3:6

14000   Mark Kiley, "Like Sara: The Tale of Terror behind 1 Peter 3:6," *JBL* 106 (1987): 689-92.

14001   Dorothy I. Sly, "1 Peter 3:6b in the Light of Philo and Josephus," *JBL* 110 (1991): 126-29.

14002   Troy Martin, "The TestAbr and the Background of 1Pet 3,6," *ZNW* 90 (1999): 139-46.

3:7

14003   A. Fridrichsen, "Scholia in Novum Testamentum: '3. Till 1 Petr 3,7'," *SEÅ* 12 (1947): 127-31.

14004   Carl D. Gross, "Are the Wives of 1 Peter 3:7 Christians?" *JSNT* 35 (1989): 89-96.

3:8-15

14005   Juan Fernández, "Epístola del domingo quinto después de Pentecostés," *CuBí* 10 (1962): 290-304.

14006   Adalberto Sisti, "Testimonianza di virtù cristiane," *BibO* 8 (1966): 117-26.

14007   D. K. Patterson, "Roles in Marriage: A Study in Submission," *TEd* 13 (1983): 70-79.

3:9-12

14008   John S. Piper, "Hope as the Motivation of Love: 1 Peter 3:9-12," *NTS* 26 (1980): 212-31.

3:9

14009 Juan Mateos, "Analisis de un campo lexematico: eulogia en el Nuevo Testamento," *FilN* 1 (1988): 5-25.

3:10

14010 P. Lecomte, "Aimer la vie. 1 Pierre 3/10 (Psaume 34/13)," *ÉTR* 56 (1981): 288-93.

3:13-4:11

14011 Roger L. Omanson, "Suffering for Righteousness' Sake," *RevExp* 79 (1982): 439-50.

3:13-17

14012 Max A. Chevallier, "L'unité plurielle de l'église d'après le Nouveau Testament," *RHPR* 66 (1986): 3-20.

3:14-15

14013 George Howard, "The Tetragram and the New Testament," *JBL* 96 (1977): 63-83

3:15

14014 John Knox, "Pliny and 1 Peter: A Note on 1 Peter 4:14-16 and 3:15," *JBL* 72 (1953): 187-89.

14015 D. A. Pailin, "1 Believe (2): The Ground of Faith," *ET* 88 (1977): 269-71.

3:17-4:6

14016 A. Steuer, "1 Petr 3,17-4,6 ," *TGl* 30 (1938): 675-78.

3:17

14017 J. Ramsey Michaels, "Eschatology in 1 Peter 3:17," *NTS* 13 (1967): 394-401.

3:18-22

14018 Sherman E. Johnson, "Preaching to the Dead," *JBL* 79 (1960): 48-51.

14019 B. Schwank, "Des éléments mythologiques dans une profession de foi," *AsSeign* NS 14 (1973): 41-44.

14020 Horst Goldstein, "Die Kirche als Schar derer, die ihrem leidenden Herrn mit dem Ziel der Gottesgemeinschaft nachfolgen. Zum Gemeindeverständnis von 1 Peter 2,21-25 und 3,18-22," *BibL* 15 (1974): 38-54.

14021   K. Shimada, "The Christological Credal Formula in 1 Peter 3:18-22," *AJBI* 5 (1979): 154-76.

14022   Barnabas Lindars, "Enoch and Christology," *ET* 92 (1981): 295-99.

14023   A. T. Hanson, "Salvation Proclaimed. I. 1 Peter 3:18-22," *ET* 93 (1982): 100-108.

14024   D. Edmond Hiebert, "Selected Studies from 1 Peter. Part 2: The Suffering and Triumphant Christ," *BSac* 139 (1982): 146-58.

14025   Ted Peters, "What Is the Gospel?" *PRS* 13 (1986): 21-43.

14026   John H. Skilton, "A Glance at Some Old Problems in First Peter," *WTJ* 58 (1996): 1-9.

3:18-21

14027   F. C. Synge, "1 Peter 3:18-21," *ET* 82 (1971): 311.

3:18-20

14028   John S. Feinberg, "1 Peter 3:18-20, Ancient Mythology, and the Intermediate State," *WTJ* 48 (1986): 303-36.

14029   Martin H. Scharlemann, "He Descended into Hell: An Interpretation of 1 Peter 3:18-20," *CJ* 15 (1989): 311-22.

3:18-19

14030   T. H. Bindley, "1 Peter 3,18f. ," *ET* 41 (1929-1930): 44.

3:18-19

14031   Edward G. Kettner, "Time, Eternity, and the Intermediate State," *CJ* 12 (1986): 90-100.

3:18

14032   T. H. Bindley, "1 Peter 3:18f," *ET* 41 (1929-1930): 44.

3:19-20

14033   A. M. Vitti, "Descensus Christi ad inferos ex 1 Petri 3, 19-20," *VD* 7 (1927): 111-18.

14034 Joachim Jeremias, "Zwischen Karfreitag und Ostern: Descensus und Ascensus in der Karfreitagstheologie des Neuen Testamentes," *ZNW* 42 (1949): 194-201.

14035 Wayne Grudem, "Christ Preaching through Noah: 1 Peter 3:19-20 in the Light of Dominant Themes in Jewish Literature," *TriJ* NS 7 (1986): 3-31.

3:19

14036 S. Odeland, "Kristi praediken for 'aanderne i forvaring'," *NTT* 2 (1901): 116-44, 185-229.

14037 J. Frings, "Zu 1 Petr 3, 19 und 4, 6," *BZ* 17 (1925-1926): 75-88.

14038 Edgar J. Goodspeed, "Some Greek Notes: IV Enoch in 1 Peter 3:19," *JBL* 73 (1954): 91-92.

14039 C. E. B. Cranfield, "The Interpretation of 1. Peter iii. 19 and iv. 6," *ET* 69 (1957-1958): 369-72.

14040 William J. Dalton, "Interpretation and Tradition: An Example from 1 Peter," *Greg* 49 (1968): 11-37.

14041 William J. Dalton, "The Interpretation of 1 Peter 3,19 and 4,6: Light from 2 Peter," *Bib* 60 (1979): 547-55.

14042 Geevarghese Osthathios, "Conviction of Truth and Tolerance of Love," *IRM* 74 (1985): 490-96.

3:20-21

14043 G. de Ru, "De heilige doop: gebed of gave? (1 Petrus 3:20b, 21)," *NTT* 20 (1966): 255-68.

3:20

14044 Eric F. F. Bishop, "*Oligoi* in 1 Peter 3:20," *CBQ* 13 (1951): 44-45.

3:21

14045 M. L. Smith, "1 Peter 3:21: e)perw⁻thma," *ET* 24 (1912-1913): 46-47.

14046 G. C. Richards, "1 Peter iii 21 ," *JTS* 32 (1931): 77.

14047 Tomas Arvedson, "συνειδήσεως ἀγαθῆς ἐπενρώτημα: En studie til 1 Petr. 3,21," *SEÅ* 15 (1950): 55-61.

14048 Oscar S. Brooks, "1 Peter 3:21: The Clue to the Literary Structure of the Epistle," *NovT* 16 (1974): 290-305.

14049 David Tripp, "Eperōtēma (1 Peter 3:21): A Liturgist's Note," *ET* 92 (1981): 267-70.

14050 Douglas W. Kennard, "Petrine Redemption: Its Meaning and Extent," *JETS* 30 (1987): 399-405.

3:22

14051 Pierre Benoit, "Pauline Angelology and Demonology: Reflexions on Designations of Heavenly Powers and on Origin of Angelic Evil according to Paul," *RSB* 3 (1983): 1-18.

4:1

14052 A. Strobel, "Macht Leiden von Sünde frei? Zur Problematik von 1 Petr 4:1f," *TZ* 19 (1963): 412-25.

14053 I. T. Blazen, "Suffering amd Cessation from Sin according to 1 Peter 4:1," *AUSS* 21 (1983): 27-50.

4:5

14054 J. Ramsey Michaels, "Jewish and Christian Apocalyptic Letters: 1 Peter, Revelation, and 2 Baruch 78-87," *SBLSP* 26 (1987): 268-75.

4:6

14055 J. Frings, "Zu 1 Petr 3, 19 und 4, 6," *BZ* 17 (1925-1926): 75-88.

14056 Eduard Schweizer, "1. Petrus 4,6," *TZ* 8 (1952): 152-54.

14057 C. E. B. Cranfield, "The Interpretation of 1. Peter iii. 19 and iv. 6," *ET* 69 (1957-1958): 369-72.

14058 William J. Dalton, "The Interpretation of 1 Peter 3,19 and 4,6: Light from 2 Peter," *Bib* 60 (1979): 547-55.

14059 Geevarghese Osthathios, "Conviction of Truth and Tolerance of Love," *IRM* 74 (1985): 490-96.

4:7-11

14060 Adalberto Sisti, "La vita cristiana nell'attesa della parusia," *BibO* 7 (1965): 123-28.

14061   Günter Klein, "Aspekte ewigen Lebens im Neuen Testament: ein theologischer Annäherungsversuch," *ZTK* 82 (1985): 48-70.

4:7

14062   J. Ramsey Michaels, "Jewish and Christian Apocalyptic Letters: 1 Peter, Revelation, and 2 Baruch 78-87," *SBLSP* 26 (1987): 268-75.

4:10

14063   John J. Kilgallen, "Reflections on Charisma(ta) in the New Testament," *SM* 41 (1992): 289-323.

4:12-19

14064   Max A. Chevallier, "L'unité plurielle de l'église d'après le Nouveau Testament," *RHPR* 66 (1986): 3-20.

14065   Dennis E. Johnson, "Fire in God's House: Imagery from Malachi 3 in Peter's Theology of Suffering," *JETS* 29 (1986): 285-94.

4:13-16

14066   B. Schwank, "Le 'chrétien normal' selon le Nouveau Testament," *AsSeign* NS 29 (1970): 26-30.

4:14-16

14067   John Knox, "Pliny and 1 Peter: A Note on 1 Peter 4:14-16 and 3:15 ," *JBL* 72 (1953): 187-89.

4:14

14068   A. Garcia del Moral, "Critica textual de 1 Ptr. 4, 14," *EB* 20 (1961): 45-77.

14069   A. Garcia del Moral, "Sentido trinitario de la expresión 'Espiritu de Yavé' de Is. XI, 2 en 1 Pdr. IV, 14," *EB* 20 (1961): 169-206.

14070   P. R. Rogers, "The Longer Reading of 1 Peter 4:14," *CBQ* 43 (1981): 93-95.

14071   Douglas W. Kennard, "Petrine Redemption: Its Meaning and Extent," *JETS* 30 (1987): 399-405.

4:15

14072   A. Bischoff, "*allotriepiskopos* ," *ZNW* 7 (1906): 271-74.

14073   J. B. Bauer, "Aut maleficus aut alieni speculator (1 Petr 4,15," *BZ* 22 (1978): 109-15.

4:17

14074   William L. Schutter, "Ezekiel 9:6, 1 Peter 4:17, and Apocalyptic Hermeneutics," *SBLSP* 26 (1987): 276-84.

5:1-5

14075   John H. Elliott, "Ministry and Church Order in the New Testament: A Traditio-Historical Analysis," *CBQ* 32 (1970): 367-91.

5:2-3

14076   Wolfgang Nauck, "Probleme des frühchristlichen Amtsverständnisses," *ZNW* 48 (1957): 200-20.

5:2

14077   J. A. Davidson, "The Congregation: Priest and Servant," *ET* 85 (1974): 336-37.

14078   Bernhard Hanssler, "Autorität in der Kirche," *IKaZ* 14 (1985): 493-504.

14079   George W. Knight, "Two Offices and Two Orders of Elders: A New Testament Study," *Pres* 11 (1985): 1-12.

5:4

14080   J. Ramsey Michaels, "Jewish and Christian Apocalyptic Letters: 1 Peter, Revelation, and 2 Baruch 78-87," *SBLSP* 26 (1987): 268-75.

5:5

14081   Anthony Hoekema, "How We See Ourselves," *CT* 29 (1985): 36-38.

5:6-11

14082   G. Perez and J. F. Hernandez, "Epistolas Dominicales," *CuBí* 13 (1956): 144-48.

5:7

14083   E. Smarte, "What's Your Number?" *ET* 88 (1977): 269.

5:9

14084   Jerome D. Quinn, "Notes on the Text of the P72 1 Peter 2:3; 5:14; and 5:9," *CBQ* 27 (1965): 241-49.

14085   J. Ramsey Michaels, "Jewish and Christian Apocalyptic Letters: 1 Peter, Revelation, and 2 Baruch 78-87," *SBLSP* 26 (1987): 268-75.

5:12

14086   J. Ramsey Michaels, "Jewish and Christian Apocalyptic Letters: 1 Peter, Revelation, and 2 Baruch 78-87," *SBLSP* 26 (1987): 268-75.

5:13

14087   G. G. Gamba, "L'Evangelista Marco Segretario-'Interprete' della prima lettera di Pietro?" *Sale* 44 (1982): 61-70.

14088   Carsten P. Thiede, "Babylon, der andere Ort: Anmerkungen zu 1 Petr 5:13 und Apg 12:17," *Bib* 67 (1986): 532-38.

14089   Judith K. Applegate, "The Co-Elect Woman of 1 Peter," *NTS* 38 (1992): 587-604.

5:14

14090   Jerome D. Quinn, "Notes on the Text of the P72 1 Peter 2:3; 5:14; and 5:9," *CBQ* 27 (1965): 241-49.

5:18-21

14091   Otto Kuss, "Zur paulinischen und nachpaulinischen Tauflehre," *TGl* 42 (1952): 401-25.

2 Peter

1-3

14092 M. A. Molina Palma, "La provisionalidad responsable: el tiempo Cristiano en perspectiva escatologica," *EB* 45 (1987): 337-46.

1:1

14093 Michael R. Austin, "Salvation and the Divinity of Jesus," *ET* 96 (1985): 271-75.

1:1-9

14094 Douglas W. Kennard, "Petrine Redemption: Its Meaning and Extent," *JETS* 30 (1987): 399-405.

1:4

14095 Michael R. Austin, "Salvation and the Divinity of Jesus," *ET* 96 (1985): 271-75.

14096 Frank Chikane, "The Incarnation in the Life of the People in Southern Africa," *JTSA* 51 (1985): 37-50.

14097 Albert M. Wolters, "Partners of the Deity: A Covenantal Reading of 2 Peter 1:4," *CTJ* 25 (1990): 28-44.

1:5-11

14098 D. Edmond Hiebert, "The Necessary Growth in the Christian Life: An Exposition of 2 Peter 1:5-11," *BSac* 141 (1984): 43-54.

1:16-2:3

14099 Ben Witherington, "A Petrine Source in 2 Peter," *SBLSP* 24 (1985): 187-92.

1:16-21

14100 Jerome H. Neyrey, "The Apologetic Use of the Transfiguration in 2 Peter 1:16-21," *CBQ* 42 (1980): 504-19.

14101 T. Sorg, "Die Bibel--Grund des Glaubens. Predigt über 2. Petrus 1,16-21," *TBe* 14 (1983): 162-66.

1:16-18

14102   Robert J. Miller, "Is There Independent Attestation for the Transfiguration in 2 Peter?" *NTS* 42 (1996): 620-25.

1:18-22

14103   Douglas W. Kennard, "Petrine Redemption: Its Meaning and Extent," *JETS* 30 (1987): 399-405.

1:19-21

14104   Inge Lönning, "Tradisjon og skrift: eksegese av 2 Petr 1:19-21," *NTT* 72 (1971): 129-54.

14105   D. Edmond Hiebert, "The Prophetic Foundation of the Christian Life: An Exposition of 2 Peter 1:19-21," *BSac* 141 (1984): 158-68.

1:19

14106   J. Smit Sibinga, "Une citation du Cantique dans la Secunda Petri," *RB* 73 (1966): 107-18.

1:20

14107   J. P. Louw, "Wat wordt in 2 Petrus 1:20 gesteld?" *NTT* 19 (1965): 202-12.

1:21

14108   Harry Buis, "The significance of 2 Timothy 3:16 and 2 Peter 1:21," *RR* 14 (1961): 43-49.

14109   A. M. Artola, "El momento de la inspiración en la constitución de la Escritura según 2 Tim 3,16," *EB* 57 (1999): 61-82.

2:1-3

14110   D. Edmond Hiebert, "A Portrayal of False Teachers: An Exposition of 2 Peter 2:1-3," *BSac* 141 (1984): 255-65.

2:1

14111   Andrew D. Chang, "Second Peter 2:1 and the Extent of the Atonement," *BSac* 142 (1985): 52-63.

14112   Douglas W. Kennard, "Petrine Redemption: Its Meaning and Extent," *JETS* 30 (1987): 399-405.

2:4-9

14113   Jerome H. Neyrey, "The Form and Background of the Polemic in 2 Peter," *JBL* 99 (1980): 407-31.

2:5

14114   Ronald A. Veenker, "Noah, Herald of Righteousness," *EGLMBS* 6 (1986): 204-18.

2:6

14115   T. Desmond Alexander, "Lot's Hospitality: A Clue to His Righteousness," *JBL* 104 (1985): 289-291.

14116   John Makujina, "The 'Trouble' with Lot in 2 Peter: Locating Peter's Source for Lot's Torment," *WTJ* 60 (1998): 255-69.

2:13

14117   Patrick W. Skehan, "Note on 2 Peter 2:13," *Bib* 41 (1960): 69-71.

14118   J. Timothy Coyle, "The Agape - Eucharist Relationship in 1 Corinthians 11," *GTJ* 6 (1985): 411-24.

14119   Donald Farner, "The Lord's Supper until He Comes," *GTJ* 6 (1985): 391-401.

2:18-22

14120   Duane A. Dunham, "An Exegetical Study of 2 Peter 2:18-22," *BSac* 140 (1983): 40-54.

14121   Douglas W. Kennard, "Petrine Redemption: Its Meaning and Extent," *JETS* 30 (1987): 399-405.

2:20-22

14122   Robert A. Peterson, "Apostasy," *Pres* 19 (1993): 17-31.

3

14123   Henry M. Morris, "Biblical Creationism and Modern Science," *BSac* 125 (1968): 20-28.

14124   Roselyne Dupont-Roc, "Le motif de la création selon 2 Pierre 3," *RB* 101 (1994): 95-114.

14125   G. Z. Heide, "What Is New about the New Heaven and the New Earth? A Theology of Creation from Revelation 21 and 2 Peter 3," *JETS* 40 (1997): 37-56.

14126 Gert Malan, "Die metafoor: 'Dag van die Here' in 2 Petrus en die dood as marginale ervaring," *HTS* 55 (1999): 656-70.

3:1-13

14127 D. Von Allmen, "L'apocalyptique juive et le retard de la parousie en 2 Pierre 3:1-13," *RTP* 16 (1966): 255-74.

3:3-7

14128 Sam Meier, "2 Peter 3:3-7—An Early Jewish and Christian Response to Eschatological Skepticism," *BZ* NS 32 (1988): 255-57.

3:5-9

14129 Jerome H. Neyrey, "The Form and Background of the Polemic in 2 Peter," *JBL* 99 (1980): 407-31.

3:6-7

14130 Carsten P. Thiede, "A Pagan Reader of 2 Peter: Cosmic Conflagration in 2 Peter 3 and the Octavius of Minucius Felix," *JSNT* 26 (1986): 79-96.

3:9

14131 Thomas H. Duke, "An Exegetical Analysis of 2 Peter 3:9," *FM* 16 (1999): 6-13.

3:10-13

14132 R. Larry Overstreet, "A Study of 2 Peter 3:10-13," *BSac* 137 (1980): 354-71.

14133 Carsten P. Thiede, "A Pagan Reader of 2 Peter: Cosmic Conflagration in 2 Peter 3 and the Octavius of Minucius Felix," *JSNT* 26 (1986): 79-96.

3:10

14134 Hellmut Lenhard, "Ein Beitrag zur Übersetzung von 2 Ptr 3:10d," *ZNW* 52 (1961): 128-29.

14135 Frederick W. Danker, "2 Peter 3:10 and Psalm of Solomon 17:10," *ZNW* 53 (1962): 82-86.

14136 David Wenham, "Being 'Found' on the Last Day: New Light on 2 Peter 3:10 and 2 Corinthians 5:3," *NTS* 33 (1987): 477-79.

14137   Albert M. Wolters, "Worldview and Textual Criticism in 2 Peter 3:10," *WTJ* 49 (1987): 405-13.

14138   G. van den Heever, "In Purifying Fire: World View and 2 Peter 3:10," *Neo* 27 (1993): 107-18.

3:13

14139   Anthony Hoekema, "Heaven: Not Just an Eternal Day off," *CT* 29 (1985): 18-19.

3:14-18

14140   D. Edmond Hiebert, "Directives for Living in Dangerous Days: An Exposition of 2 Peter 3:14-18," *BSac* 141 (1984): 330-40.

1 John

<u>1-4</u>

14141   Marinus de Jonge, "An Analysis of 1 John 1:1-4," *BT* (1978): 322-30.

<u>1-2</u>

14142   J. A. du Rand, "A Discourse Anaylsis of 1 John," *Neo* 13 (1981): 1-42.

<u>1:1-2:27</u>

14143   Duane F. Watson, "An Epideictic Strategy for Increasing Adherence to Community Values: 1 John 1:1-2:27," *EGLMBS* 11 (1991): 144-52.

<u>1:1-2:2</u>

14144   Robert Brusic, "A River Ride with 1 John," *WW* 17 (1997): 212-20.

<u>1:1-13</u>

14145   Charles P. Baylis, "The Meaning of Walking 'in the Darkness'," *BSac* 149 (1992): 214-22.

<u>1:1-5</u>

14146   H. H. Wendt, "Zum zweiten und dritten Johannesbrief," *ZAW* 23 (1924): 27-31.

<u>1:1-4</u>

14147   R. C. Briggs, "Contemporary Study of the Johannine Epistles," *RevExp* 67 (1970): 415-22.

14148   Donald E. Cook, "Interpretation of 1 John 1-5," *RevExp* 67 (1970): 445-59.

14149   Peter R. Jones, "A Structural Anaylsis of 1 John," *RevExp* 67 (1970): 433-44.

14150   J. A. du Rand, "A Discourse Analysis of 1 John," *Neo* 13 (1981): 1-42.

14151   J. Blank, "Die Irrlehrer des ersten Johannesbriefes," *K* 26
        (1984): 166-93.

14152   Kenneth Tollefson, "Certainty within the Fellowship:
        Dialectical Discourse in 1 John," *BTB* 29 (1999): 79-89.

1:1-3

14153   J. M. Lieu, " 'Authority to Become Children of God': A
        Study of 1 John," *NovT* 23 (1981): 210-28.

1:1-2

14154   Jerry Horner, "Introduction to the Johannine Letters,"
        SouJT 21 (1970): 41-51.

14155   André Feuillet, "Témoins oculaires et serviteurs de la
        parole," *NovT* 15 (1973): 241-59.

14156   H. J. Klauck, "Gemeinde ohne Amt: Erfahrungen mit der
        Kirche in den johanneischen Schriften," *BZ* NS 29 (1985):
        193-220.

1:1

14157   H. H. Wendt, "Zum zweiten und dritten Johannesbrief,"
        ZAW 23 (1924): 27-31.

14158   L. M. Rogers, "1 John 1,9," *ET* 45 (1933-1934): 527.

14159   Ben Witherington, "The Waters of Birth: John 3:5 and 1
        John 5:6-8," *NTS* 35 (1989): 155-60.

14160   A. Ototsi Mojola, "Theories of Metaphor in Translation
        with Some Reference to John 1:1 and 1 John 1:1," *BT* 44
        (1993): 341-47.

14161   Kenneth Tollefson, "Certainty within the Fellowship:
        Dialectical Discourse in 1 John," *BTB* 29 (1999): 79-89.

1:2

14162   Charles P. Baylis, "The Meaning of Walking 'in the
        Darkness'," *BSac* 149 (1992): 214-22.

1:10-2:1

14163   Kenneth Tollefson, "Certainty within the Fellowship:
        Dialectical Discourse in 1 John," *BTB* 29 (1999): 79-89.

1:10

14164   Jerry Horner, "Introduction to the Johannine Letters," *SouJT* 21 (1970): 41-51.

14165   W. Pratscher, "Gott ist grösser als unser Herz: Zur Interpretation von 1 Joh 3, 19f," *TZ* 32 (1976): 272-81.

14166   F.-M. Braun, "La Réduction du Pluriel au Singulier dans l'Evangile et la Première Lettre de Jean," *NTS* 24 (1977-1978): 55.

14167   P. P. A. Kotzé, "The Meaning of 1 John 3:9 with Reference to 1 John 1:8 and 10," *Neo* 13 (1981): 68-83.

14168   Charles P. Baylis, "The Meaning of Walking 'in the Darkness'," *BSac* 149 (1992): 214-22.

14169   Wendy E. Sproston, "Witnesses to What Was ἀπ᾽ ἀρχῆς: 1 John's Contribution to Our Knowledge of Tradition in the Fourth Gospel," *JSNT* 48 (1992): 43-65.

1:12-13

14170   J. M. Lieu, " 'Authority to Become Children of God': A Study of 1 John," *NovT* 23 (1981): 210-28.

1:14

14171   J. C. Coetzeé, "The Holy Spirit in 1 John," *Neo* 13 (1981): 43-67.

1:16

14172   A. P. Salom, "Some Aspects of the Grammatical Style of 1 John," *JBL* 74 (1955): 99.

1:22-24

14173   Thomas B. Hoffman, "1 John and the Qumran Scrolls," *BTB* 8 (1978): 117-25.

1:28

14174   Dale Moody, "The Theology of the Johannine Letters," *SouJT* 21 (1970): 7-22.

1:3-17

14175   Pheme Perkins, "*Koinonia* in 1 John 1:3-17: The Social Context of Division in the Johannine Letters," *CBQ* 45 (1983): 631-41.

1:3-7

14176   Terry Griffith, "A Non-Polemical Reading of 1 John," *TynB* 49 (1998): 253-76.

1:3-6

14177   R. E. Glaze, "Fellowship," *BI* 8 (1982): 25-26.

1:3

14178   Léopold Sabourin, "*Koinonia* in the New Testament," *RSB* 1 (1981): 109-15.

14179   Pheme Perkins, "*Koinonia* in 1 John 1:3-17: The Social Context of Division in the Johannine Letters," *CBQ* 45 (1983): 631-41.

14180   Christian D. Kettler, "The Vicarious Repentance of Christ in the Theology of John McLeod Campbell and R. C. Moberly," *SJT* 38 (1985): 529-43.

14181   Charles P. Baylis, "The Meaning of Walking 'in the Darkness'," *BSac* 149 (1992): 214-22.

1:4-5

14182   I. L. Grohar, "El 'mundo' en los escritos juanicos: un ensayo de interpretación," *RevB* 47 (1985): 221-27.

1:4

14183   Huber Drumwright, "Problem Passages in the Johannine Epistles," *SouJT* 21 (1970): 53-64.

14184   Jerry Horner, "Introduction to the Johannine Letters," *SouJT* 21 (1970): 41-51.

14185   John H. Dobson, "Emphatic Personal Pronouns in the New Testament," *BT* 22 (1971): 58-60.

14186   J. M. Lieu, " 'Authority to Become Children of God': A Study of 1 John," *NovT* 23 (1981): 210-28.

1:5-2:28

14187   Peter R. Jones, "A Structural Anaylsis of 1 John," *RevExp* 67 (1970): 433-44.

1:5-2:27

14188   Donald E. Cook, "Interpretation of 1 John 1-5," *RevExp* 67 (1970): 445-59.

14189   J. C. Coetzee, "The Holy Spirit in 1 John," *Neo* 13 (1981): 43-67.

14190   Kenneth Tollefson, "Certainty within the Fellowship: Dialectical Discourse in 1 John," *BTB* 29 (1999): 79-89.

1:5-2:17

14191   J. A. du Rand, "A Discourse Analysis of 1 John," *Neo* 13 (1981): 1-42.

1:5-2:11

14192   Thomas B. Hoffman, "1 John and the Qumran Scrolls," *BTB* 8 (1978): 117-25.

14193   Fernando F. Segovia, "The Structure, Tendenz, and Sitz im Leben of John 13:31-14:31," *JBL* 104 (1985): 471-93.

1:5-2:2

14194   Huber Drumwright, "Problem Passages in the Johannine Epistles," *SouJT* 21 (1970): 53-64.

14195   Kenneth Tollefson, "Certainty within the Fellowship: Dialectical Discourse in 1 John," *BTB* 29 (1999): 79-89.

1:5-10

14196   Zane C. Hodges, "Fellowship and Confession in 1 John 1:5-10," *BSac* 129 (1972): 48-60.

1:6-10

14197   Ronald A. Ward, "The Theological Patterns of the Johannine Letters," *SouJT* 21 (1970): 23-39.

1:6-2:11

14198   Terry Griffith, "A Non-Polemical Reading of 1 John," *TynB* 49 (1998): 253-76.

1:6-2:6

14199   Peter R. Jones, "A Structural Analysis of 1 John," *RevExp* 67 (1970): 433-44.

1:6-2:2

14200   Dale Moody, "The Theology of the Johannine Letters," *SouJT* 21 (1970): 7-22.

1:6-2:1

14201 Charles P. Baylis, "The Meaning of Walking 'in the Darkness'," *BSac* 149 (1992): 214-22.

1:6-7

14202 John Breck, "Biblical Chiasmus: Exploring Structure for Meaning," *BTB* 17 (1987): 70-74.

14203 Kenneth Tollefson, "Certainty within the Fellowship: Dialectical Discourse in 1 John," *BTB* 29 (1999): 79-89.

1:6

14204 Frank Stagg, "Orthodoxy and Orthopraxy in the Johannine Epistles," *RevExp* 67 (1970): 423-32.

14205 P. P. A. Kotzé, "The Meaning of 1 John 3:9 with Reference to 1 John 1:8 and 10," *Neo* 13 (1981): 68-83.

14206 Pheme Perkins, "*Koinonia* in 1 John 1:3-17: The Social Context of Division in the Johannine Letters," *CBQ* 45 (1983): 631-41.

14207 Charles P. Baylis, "The Meaning of Walking 'in the Darkness'," *BSac* 149 (1992): 214-22.

1:7-8

14208 Dale Moody, "The Theology of the Johannine Letters," *SouJT* 21 (1970): 7-22.

1:7

14209 Frank Stagg, "Orthodoxy and Orthopraxy in the Johannine Epistles," *RevExp* 67 (1970): 423-32.

14210 J. M. Lieu, " 'Authority to Become Children of God': A Study of 1 John," *NovT* 23 (1981): 210-28.

14211 Charles P. Baylis, "The Meaning of Walking 'in the Darkness'," *BSac* 149 (1992): 214-22.

1:8-10

14212 Huber Drumwright, "Problem Passages in the Johannine Epistles," *SouJT* 21 (1970): 53-64.

14213 Frank Stagg, "Orthodoxy and Orthopraxy in the Johannine Epistles," *RevExp* 67 (1970): 423-32.

14214 W. Pratscher, "Gott ist grösser als unser Herz: Zur Interpretation von 1 Joh 3, 19f," *TZ* 32 (1976): 272-81.

14215 P. P. A. Kotzé, "The Meaning of 1 John 3:9 with Reference to 1 John 1:8 and 10," *Neo* 13 (1981): 68-83.

14216 Cándido Pozo, "El hombre pecador," *Greg* 65 (1984): 365-87.

1:9-10

14217 Dale Moody, "The Theology of the Johannine Letters," *SouJT* 21 (1970): 7-22.

1:9

14218 J. P. Thornton-Duesberg, "1 John 1,9," *ET* 45 (1933-1934): 183-84.

14219 L. M. Rogers, "1 John 1.9," *ET* 45 (1933-1934): 527.

14220 A. P. Salom, "Some Aspects of the Grammatical Style of 1 John," *JBL* 74 (1955): 101-102.

14221 Ronald A. Ward, "The Theological Patterns of the Johannine Letters," *SouJT* 21 (1970): 23-39.

2:1-5

14222 N. Lazure, "Les voies de la connaissance de Dieu," *AsSeign* NS 24 (1970): 21-28.

2:1-2

14223 Jerry Horner, "Introduction to the Johannine Letters," *SouJT* 21 (1970): 41-51.

2:1

14224 R. C. Briggs, "Contemporary Study of the Johannine Epistles," *RevExp* 67 (1970): 415-22.

14225 Huber Drumwright, "Problem Passages in the Johannine Epistles," *SouJT* 21 (1970): 53-64.

14226 J. M. Lieu, " 'Authority to Become Children of God': A Study of 1 John," *NovT* 23 (1981): 210-28.

14227 Charles P. Baylis, "The Meaning of Walking 'in the Darkness'," *BSac* 149 (1992): 214-22.

2:2-17

14228 J. A. du Rand, "A Discourse Anaylsis of 1 John," *Neo* 13 (1981): 1-42.

2:2

14229 Henri Clavier, "Notes sur un mot-clef du Johannisme et de la sotériologie biblique: *hilasmos*," *NovT* 10 (1968): 287-304.

14230 T. C. G. Thornton, "Propitiation or Expiation?" *ET* 80 (1968-1969): 53-55.

14231 Huber Drumwright, "Problem Passages in the Johannine Epistles," *SouJT* 21 (1970): 53-64.

14232 Dale Moody, "Propitiation=Expiation," *BI* 8 (1982): 15-16.

14233 C. Samuel Storms, "Defining the Elect," *JETS* 27 (1984): 205-18.

14234 Giuseppe Segalla, "*Holos ho kosmos* como figura de la humanidad salvada por Jesus en 1 Jn 2,2b," *RevB* 55 (1993): 129-40.

14235 Kenneth Tollefson, "Certainty within the Fellowship: Dialectical Discourse in 1 John," *BTB* 29 (1999): 79-89.

2:3-11

14236 J. A. du Rand, "A Discourse Anaylsis of 1 John," *Neo* 13 (1981): 1-42.

14237 Kenneth Tollefson, "Certainty within the Fellowship: Dialectical Discourse in 1 John," *BTB* 29 (1999): 79-89.

2:3-7

14238 James D. G. Dunn, "Prophetic 'I'-Sayings and the Jesus Tradition: The importance of Testing Prophetic Utterances within Early Christianity," *NTS* 24 (1977-1978): 190.

2:3-6

14239 A. S. Suitbertus, "Die Vollkommenheitslehre des ersten Johannesbriefes," *Bib* 39 (1958): 452-62.

14240 H.-M. Schenke, "Determination und Ethik im ersten Johannesbrief," *ZTK* 60 (1963): 206-15.

14241 Harold S. Songer, "The Life Situation of the Johannine Epistles," *RevExp* 67 (1970): 399-409.

14242 J. A. du Rand, "A Discourse Analysis of 1 John," *Neo* 13 (1981): 1-42.

2:3-5

14243 Kenneth Tollefson, "Certainty within the Fellowship: Dialectical Discourse in 1 John," *BTB* 29 (1999): 79-89.

2:3

14244 K. Weiss, "Orthodoxie und Heterodoxie im 1. Johannesbrief," *ZNW* 58 (1967-1968): 251-53.

14245 Frank Stagg, "Orthodoxy and Orthopraxy in the Johannine Epistles," *RevExp* 67 (1970): 423-32.

14246 A. B. du Toit, "The Role and Meaning of Statements of 'Certainty' in the Structural Composition of 1 John," *Neo* 13 (1981): 84-100.

2:4-4:6

14247 Donald E. Cook, "Interpretation of 1 John 1-5," *RevExp* 67 (1970): 445-59.

2:4-6

14248 Jerry Horner, "Introduction to the Johannine Letters," *SouJT* 21 (1970): 41-51.

2:4

14249 Frank Stagg, "Orthodoxy and Orthopraxy in the Johannine Epistles," *RevExp* 67 (1970): 423-32.

14250 G. Sánchez Mielgo, "Perspectivas eclesiologicas en la primfera carta de Juan," *EV* 4 (1974): 9-64.

14251 A. B. du Toit, "The Role and Meaning of Statements of 'Certainty' in the Structural Composition of 1 John," *Neo* 13 (1981): 84-100.

2:5

14252 A. S. Suitbertus, "Die Vollkommenheitslehre des ersten Johannesbriefes," *Bib* 39 (1958): 452-62.

14253 K. Weiss, "Orthodoxie und Heterodoxie im 1. Johannesbrief," *ZNW* 58 (1967-1968): 251-53.

14254 Joseph Coppens, "Miscellanées bibliques. 52. *Agape* et *Agapan* dans les Lettres johanniques," *ETL* 45 (1969): 125-27.

14255 J. M. Lieu, " 'Authority to Become Children of God': A Study of 1 John," *NovT* 23 (1981): 210-28.

14256 Wendy E. Sproston, "Witnesses to What Was ἀπ᾽ ἀρχῆς: 1 John's Contribution to Our Knowledge of Tradition in the Fourth Gospel," *JSNT* 48 (1992): 43-65.

2:6

14257 A. P. Salom, "Some Aspects of the Grammatical Style of 1 John," *JBL* 74 (1955): 101-102.

14258 Frank Stagg, "Orthodoxy and Orthopraxy in the Johannine Epistles," *RevExp* 67 (1970): 423-32.

14259 Ronald A. Ward, "The Theological Patterns of the Johannine Letters," *SouJT* 21 (1970): 23-39.

14260 Terry Griffith, "A Non-Polemical Reading of 1 John," *TynB* 49 (1998): 253-76.

2:7-24

14261 A. P. Salom, "Some Aspects of the Grammatical Style of 1 John," *JBL* 74 (1955): 101-102.

2:7-17

14262 Peter R. Jones, "A Structural Analysis of 1 John," *RevExp* 67 (1970): 433-44.

14263 G. Giurisato, "Struttura della Prima lettera di Giovanni," *RBib* 21 (1973): 361-81.

2:7-8

14264 J. A. du Rand, "A Discourse Analysis of 1 John," *Neo* 13 (1981): 1-42.

2:7

14265 J. A. T. Robinson, "The Destination and Purpose of the Johannine Epistles," *NTS* 7 (1960): 57.

14266 R. C. Briggs, "Contemporary Study of the Johannine Epistles," *RevExp* 67 (1970): 415-22.

14267 G. Sánchez Mielgo, "Perspectivas eclesiologicas en la primfera carta de Juan," *EV* 4 (1974): 9-64.

14268 Wendy E. Sproston, "Witnesses to What Was ἀπ᾿ ἀρχῆς: 1 John's Contribution to Our Knowledge of Tradition in the Fourth Gospel," *JSNT* 48 (1992): 43-65.

2:8

14269 Raymond E. Brown, "The Qumran Scrolls and the Johannine Gospel and Epistles," *CBQ* 17 (1955): 403-19, 559-74.

14270 George D. Kilpatrick, "Two Johannine Idioms in the Johannine Epistles," *JTS* 12 (1961): 272-80.

14271 A. Vicent Cernuda, "Eengañan la oscuridady el mundo: la luz era y manifiesta lo verdadero," *EB* 27 (1968): 153-75, 215-32.

2:8-9

14272 Charles P. Baylis, "The Meaning of Walking 'in the Darkness'," *BSac* 149 (1992): 214-22.

2:8

14273 Jerry Horner, "Introduction to the Johannine Letters," *SouJT* 21 (1970): 41-51.

14274 Thomas B. Hoffman, "1 John and the Qumran Scrolls," *BTB* 8 (1978): 117-25.

2:9-11

14275 H.-M. Schenke, "Determination und Ethik im ersten Johannesbrief," *ZTK* 60 (1963): 206-15.

14276 Frank Stagg, "Orthodoxy and Orthopraxy in the Johannine Epistles," *RevExp* 67 (1970): 423-32.

14277 Ronald A. Ward, "The Theological Patterns of the Johannine Letters," *SouJT* 21 (1970): 23-39.

14278 G. Sánchez Mielgo, "Perspectivas eclesiologicas en la primfera carta de Juan," *EV* 4 (1974): 9-64.

14279 Thomas B. Hoffman, "1 John and the Qumran Scrolls," *BTB* 8 (1978): 117-25.

14280 J. A. du Rand, "A Discourse Analysis of 1 John," *Neo* 13 (1981): 1-42.

14281 Wendy E. Sproston, "Witnesses to What Was ἀπ᾽ ἀρχῆς: 1 John's Contribution to Our Knowledge of Tradition in the Fourth Gospel," *JSNT* 48 (1992): 43-65.

2:9

14282 Raymond E. Brown, "The Qumran Scrolls and the Johannine Gospel and Epistles," *CBQ* 17 (1955): 403-19, 559-74.

14283 John Breck, "Biblical Chiasmus: Exploring Structure for Meaning," *BTB* 17 (1987): 70-74.

14284 Terry Griffith, "A Non-Polemical Reading of 1 John," *TynB* 49 (1998): 253-76.

2:10

14285 G. Lefebvre, "Le précepte du Seigneur," *VS* 96 (1957): 40-55.

14286 J. W. Carlton, "Preaching from the Johannine Epistles," *RevExp* 67 (1970): 444-47.

14287 Harold S. Songer, "The Life Situation of the Johannine Epistles," *RevExp* 67 (1970): 399-409.

2:11

14288 Jerry Horner, "Introduction to the Johannine Letters," *SouJT* 21 (1970): 41-51.

14289 J. M. Lieu, "Blindness in the Johannine Tradition," *NTS* 34 (1988): 83-95.

2:12-27

14290 H. H. Wendt, "Zum zweiten und dritten Johannesbrief," *ZAW* 23 (1924): 27-31.

2:12-17

14291 Dale Moody, "The Theology of the Johannine Letters," *SouJT* 21 (1970): 7-22.

2:12-14

14292 Marinus de Jonge, "A Translator's Handbook on the Letters of John," *BT* 22 (1971): 11-18.

14293 H. H. Wendt, "Zum zweiten und dritten Johannesbrief," *ZAW* 23 (1924): 27-31.

14294 A. S. Suitbertus, "Die Vollkommenheitslehre des ersten Johannesbriefes," *Bib* 39 (1958): 453-54.

14295 Bent Noack, "On 1 John 2:12-14," *NTS* 6 (1959-1960): 236-41.

14296 G. Sánchez Mielgo, "Perspectivas eclesiologicas en la primfera carta de Juan," *EV* 4 (1974): 9-64.

14297 J. A. du Rand, "A Discourse Analysis of 1 John," *Neo* 13 (1981): 1-42.

14298 Duane F. Watson, "1 John 2:12-14 as Distributio, Conduplicatio, and Expolitio: A Rhetorical Understanding," *JSNT* 35 (1989): 97-110.

2:12

14299 J. M. Lieu, " 'Authority to Become Children of God': A Study of 1 John," *NovT* 23 (1981): 210-28.

2:13-14

14300 J. E. Bruns, "Note on John 16:33 and 1 John 2:13-14," *JBL* 86 (1967): 451-53.

2:13

14301 A. B. du Toit, "The Role and Meaning of Statements of 'Certainty' in the Structural Composition of 1 John," *Neo* 13 (1981): 84-100.

2:14

14302 S. de Giacino, ". . . a voi, giovani, che siete forti," *BibO* 2 (1960): 81-85.

14303 A. B. du Toit, "The Role and Meaning of Statements of 'Certainty' in the Structural Composition of 1 John," *Neo* 13 (1981): 84-100.

2:15-17

14304 Ronald A. Ward, "The Theological Patterns of the Johannine Letters," *SouJT* 21 (1970): 23-39.

14305 J. A. du Rand, "A Discourse Analysis of 1 John," *Neo* 13 (1981): 1-42.

14306   Wendy E. Sproston, "Witnesses to What Was ἀπ᾿ ἀρχῆς:
        1 John's Contribution to Our Knowledge of Tradition in the
        Fourth Gospel," *JSNT* 48 (1992): 43-65.

2:16

14307   P. Jouon, "1 Jo. 2,16 la présomption des richesses," *RechSR*
        28 (1938): 479-81.

14308   N. Lazure, "La convoitise de la chair en 1 Jean 2:16," *RB*
        76 (1969): 161-205.

2:17

14309   A. Vicent Cernuda, "Enganan la oscuridad y ci mundo; la
        luz era y manifiesta lo verdadero," *EB* 27 (1968): 153-75,
        215-32.

14310   I. L. Grohar, "El 'mundo' en los escritos juanicos: un
        ensayo de interpretación," *RevB* 47 (1985): 221-27.

14311   Luis F. Ladaria, "Presente y futuro en la escatología
        cristiana," *EE* 60 (1985): 351-59.

2:18-3:24

14312   D. Edmond Hiebert, "An Expositional Study of 1 John,"
        BSac 146 (1989): 76-93, 198-216, 301-19, 420-36.

2:18-3:2

14313   Kenneth Durkin, "A Eucharistic Hymn in John 6?" *ET* 98
        (1987): 168-70.

2:18-28

14314   Peter R. Jones, "A Structural Analysis of 1 John," *RevExp*
        67 (1970): 433-44.

2:18-27

14315   Dale Moody, "The Theology of the Johannine Letters,"
        SouJT 21 (1970): 7-22.

14316   J. A. du Rand, "A Discourse Analysis of 1 John," *Neo* 13
        (1981): 1-42.

14317   J. Blank, "Die Irrlehrer des ersten Johannesbriefes," *K* 26
        (1984): 166-93.

2:18-22

14318   Huber Drumwright, "Problem Passages in the Johannine Epistles," *SouJT* 21 (1970): 53-64.

2:18-21

14319   J. A. du Rand, "A Discourse Analysis of 1 John," *Neo* 13 (1981): 1-42.

2:18-19

14320   R. C. Briggs, "Contemporary Study of the Johannine Epistles," *RevExp* 67 (1970): 415-22.

14321   John Painter, "The 'Opponents' in 1 John," *NTS* 32 (1986): 48-71.

14322   Duane F. Watson, "A Rhetorical Analysis of 2 John according to Greco-Roman Convention," *NTS* 35 (1989): 104-30.

14323   David M. Scholer, "1 John 4:7-21," *RevExp* 87 (1990): 309-14.

2:18

14324   R. C. Briggs, "Contemporary Study of the Johannine Epistles," *RevExp* 67 (1970): 415-22.

14325   J. M. Lieu, " 'Authority to Become Children of God': A Study of 1 John," *NovT* 23 (1981): 210-28.

14326   Warren McWilliams, "Interpretations of the Antichrist," *BI* 16/3 (1990): 50-53.

2:19-27

14327   H. J. Klauck, "Gemeinde ohne Amt: Erfahrungen mit der Kirche in den johanneischen Schriften," *BZ* NS 29 (1985): 193-220.

2:19

14328   Frank Stagg, "Orthodoxy and Orthopraxy in the Johannine Epistles," *RevExp* 67 (1970): 423-32.

14329   Pheme Perkins, "*Koinonia* in 1 John 1:3-17: The Social Context of Division in the Johannine Letters," *CBQ* 45 (1983): 631-41.

14330 John W. Pryor, "Covenant and Community in John's Gospel," *RTR* 47 (1988): 44-51.

14331 Wendy E. Sproston, "Witnesses to What Was ἀπ᾽ ἀρχῆς: 1 John's Contribution to Our Knowledge of Tradition in the Fourth Gospel," *JSNT* 48 (1992): 43-65.

14332 Robert A. Peterson, "Apostasy," *Pres* 19 (1993): 17-31.

14333 Terry Griffith, "A Non-Polemical Reading of 1 John," *TynB* 49 (1998): 253-76.

2:20

14334 Frank Stagg, "Orthodoxy and Orthopraxy in the Johannine Epistles," *RevExp* 67 (1970): 423-32.

14335 J. C. Coetzee, "The Holy Spirit in 1 John," *Neo* 13 (1981): 43-67.

14336 Pheme Perkins, "*Koinonia* in 1 John 1:3-17: The Social Context of Division in the Johannine Letters," *CBQ* 45 (1983): 631-41.

14337 John Breck, "The Function of *pas* in 1 John 2:20," *SVTQ* 35 (1991): 187-206.

14338 David A. Black, "An Overlooked Stylistic Argument in Favor of *panta* in 1 John 2:20," *FilN* 5 (1992): 205-208.

2:21

14339 Frank Stagg, "Orthodoxy and Orthopraxy in the Johannine Epistles," *RevExp* 67 (1970): 423-32.

2:22

14340 Terry Griffith, "A Non-Polemical Reading of 1 John," *TynB* 49 (1998): 253-76.

2:23

14341 R. C. Briggs, "Contemporary Study of the Johannine Epistles," *RevExp* 67 (1970): 415-22.

14342 Jerry Horner, "Introduction to the Johannine Letters," *SouJT* 21 (1970): 41-51.

14343 Ronald A. Ward, "The Theological Patterns of the Johannine Letters," *SouJT* 21 (1970): 23-39.

2:24-25

14344   Harold S. Songer, "The Life Situation of the Johannine Epistles," *RevExp* 67 (1970): 399-409.

2:24

14345   Ronald A. Ward, "The Theological Patterns of the Johannine Letters," *SouJT* 21 (1970): 23-39.

2:25

14346   John B. Polhill, "An Analysis of 2 and 3 John," *RevExp* 67 (1970): 461-71.

14347   Charles P. Baylis, "The Meaning of Walking 'in the Darkness'," *BSac* 149 (1992): 214-22.

2:26

14348   J. M. Lieu, " 'Authority to Become Children of God': A Study of 1 John," *NovT* 23 (1981): 210-28.

2:27

14349   Jerry Horner, "Introduction to the Johannine Letters," *SouJT* 21 (1970): 41-51.

14350   Frank Stagg, "Orthodoxy and Orthopraxy in the Johannine Epistles," *RevExp* 67 (1970): 423-32.

14351   J. C. Coetzee, "The Holy Spirit in 1 John," *Neo* 13 (1981): 43-67.

14352   P. P. A. Kotzé, "The Meaning of 1 John 3:9 with Reference to 1 John 1:8 and 10," *Neo* 13 (1981): 68-83.

14353   J. M. Lieu, " 'Authority to Become Children of God': A Study of 1 John," *NovT* 23 (1981): 210-28.

14354   Pheme Perkins, "*Koinonia* in 1 John 1:3-17: The Social Context of Division in the Johannine Letters," *CBQ* 45 (1983): 631-41.

2:28-4:6

14355   J. C. Coetzee, "The Holy Spirit in 1 John," *Neo* 13 (1981): 43-67.

14356   Kenneth Tollefson, "Certainty within the Fellowship: Dialectical Discourse in 1 John," *BTB* 29 (1999): 79-89.

2:28-3:24

14357 P. P. A. Kotzé, "The Meaning of 1 John 3:9 with Reference to 1 John 1:8 and 10," *Neo* 13 (1981): 68-83.

2:28-3:10

14358 Dale Moody, "The Theology of the Johannine Letters," *SouJT* 21 (1970): 7-22.

2:28-3:3

14359 J. A. du Rand, "A Discourse Analysis of 1 John," *Neo* 13 (1981): 1-42.

14360 Kenneth Tollefson, "Certainty within the Fellowship: Dialectical Discourse in 1 John," *BTB* 29 (1999): 79-89.

2:28

14361 Ronald A. Ward, "The Theological Patterns of the Johannine Letters," *SouJT* 21 (1970): 23-39.

14362 W. Pratscher, "Gott ist grösser als unser Herz: Zur Interpretation von 1 Joh 3, 19f," *TZ* 32 (1976): 272-81.

2:29-4:6

14363 Peter R. Jones, "A Structural Analysis of 1 John," *RevExp* 67 (1970): 433-44.

2:29

14364 Frank Stagg, "Orthodoxy and Orthopraxy in the Johannine Epistles," *RevExp* 67 (1970): 423-32.

14365 W. Pratscher, "Gott ist grösser als unser Herz: Zur Interpretation von 1 Joh 3, 19f," *TZ* 32 (1976): 272-81.

14366 Wendy E. Sproston, "Witnesses to What Was ἀπ᾿ ἀρχῆς: 1 John's Contribution to Our Knowledge of Tradition in the Fourth Gospel," *JSNT* 48 (1992): 43-65.

14367 Kenneth Tollefson, "Certainty within the Fellowship: Dialectical Discourse in 1 John," *BTB* 29 (1999): 79-89.

3

14368 J. A. du Rand, "A Discourse Analysis of 1 John," *Neo* 13 (1981): 1-42.

3:1-11

14369 Palémon Glorieux, "La révélation du Pére," *MSR* 42 (1985): 21-41.

3:1-10

14370 Bill J. Leonard, "Cerinthus," *BI* 8 (1982): 53-54.

3:1-7

14371 Robert Brusic, "A River Ride with 1 John," *WW* 17 (1997): 212-20.

3:1-2

14372 F. Smyth-Florentin, "Voyez quel grand amour le Père nous a donné," *AsSeign* NS 25 (1969): 32-38.

3:1

14373 Jerry Horner, "Introduction to the Johannine Letters," *SouJT* 21 (1970): 41-51.

14374 A. B. du Toit, "The Role and Meaning of Statements of 'Certainty' in the Structural Composition of 1 John," *Neo* 13 (1981): 84-100.

14375 Eugene F. Klug, "The Doctrine of Man: Christian Anthropology," *CTQ* 48 (1984): 141-52.

3:2

14376 F. C. Synge, "1 John 3,2," *JTS* 3 (1952): 79.

14377 R. C. Briggs, "Contemporary Study of the Johannine Epistles," *RevExp* 67 (1970): 415-22.

14378 Ronald A. Ward, "The Theological Patterns of the Johannine Letters," *SouJT* 21 (1970): 23-39.

14379 W. Pratscher, "Gott ist grösser als unser Herz: Zur Interpretation von 1 Joh 3, 19f," *TZ* 32 (1976): 272-81.

14380 P. P. A. Kotzé, "The Meaning of 1 John 3:9 with Reference to 1 John 1:8 and 10," *Neo* 13 (1981): 68-83.

14381 Luis F. Ladaria, "Presente y futuro en la escatología cristiana," *EE* 60 (1985): 351-59.

3:3-5

14382   Ronald A. Ward, "The Theological Patterns of the Johannine Letters," *SouJT* 21 (1970): 23-39.

3:3

14383   Frank Stagg, "Orthodoxy and Orthopraxy in the Johannine Epistles," *RevExp* 67 (1970): 423-32.

3:4-17

14384   Terry Griffith, "A Non-Polemical Reading of 1 John," *TynB* 49 (1998): 253-76.

3:4-10

14385   Huber Drumwright, "Problem Passages in the Johannine Epistles," *SouJT* 21 (1970): 53-64.

14386   J. A. du Rand, "A Discourse Analysis of 1 John," *Neo* 13 (1981): 1-42.

3:4-8

14387   Huber Drumwright, "Problem Passages in the Johannine Epistles," *SouJT* 21 (1970): 53-64.

3:4

14388   J. A. Clapperton, " *Tēn Amartian*," *ET* 47 (1935-1936): 92-93.

14389   I. de la Potterie, "Le péché, c'est l'iniquité," *NRT* 78 (1956): 785-97.

14390   Raymond E. Gingrich, "Adumbrations of Our Lord's Return: Global Iniquity," *GTJ* 8 (1967): 17-32.

14391   Ronald A. Ward, "The Theological Patterns of the Johannine Letters," *SouJT* 21 (1970): 23-39.

3:5

14392   Ben Witherington, "The Waters of Birth: John 3:5 and 1 John 5:6-8," *NTS* 35 (1989): 155-60.

3:6-15

14393   Frank Stagg, "Orthodoxy and Orthopraxy in the Johannine Epistles," *RevExp* 67 (1970): 423-32.

3:6

14394 P. Galtier, "Le chrétien impeccable," *MSR* 4 (1947): 137-54.

14395 Huber Drumwright, "Problem Passages in the Johannine Epistles," *SouJT* 21 (1970): 53-64.

14396 A. B. du Toit, "The Role and Meaning of Statements of 'Certainty' in the Structural Composition of 1 John," *Neo* 13 (1981): 84-100.

3:7-10

14397 Harold S. Songer, "The Life Situation of the Johannine Epistles," *RevExp* 67 (1970): 399-409.

3:7

14398 R. C. Briggs, "Contemporary Study of the Johannine Epistles," *RevExp* 67 (1970): 415-22.

14399 Frank Stagg, "Orthodoxy and Orthopraxy in the Johannine Epistles," *RevExp* 67 (1970): 423-32.

14400 John Breck, "Biblical Chiasmus: Exploring Structure for Meaning," *BTB* 17 (1987): 70-74.

3:8

14401 Jerry Horner, "Introduction to the Johannine Letters," *SouJT* 21 (1970): 41-51.

14402 Ronald A. Ward, "The Theological Patterns of the Johannine Letters," *SouJT* 21 (1970): 23-39.

14403 Thomas B. Hoffman, "1 John and the Qumran Scrolls," *BTB* 8 (1978): 117-25.

3:9

14404 P. Galtier, "Le chrétien impeccable," *MSR* 4 (1947): 137-54.

14405 Sakae Kubo, "1 John 3:9: Absolute or Habitual?" *AUSS* 7 (1969): 47-56.

14406 Huber Drumwright, "Problem Passages in the Johannine Epistles," *SouJT* 21 (1970): 53-64.

14407 W. Pratscher, "Gott ist grösser als unser Herz: Zur Interpretation von 1 Joh 3, 19f," *TZ* 32 (1976): 272-81.

14408   P. P. A. Kotzé, "The Meaning of 1 John 3:9 with Reference to 1 John 1:8 and 10," *Neo* 13 (1981): 68-83.

14409   J. de Waal Dryden, "The Sense of *sperma* in 1 John 3:9," *FilN* 21-22 (1998): 85-100.

3:10-24

14410   Peter R. Jones, "A Structural Analysis of 1 John," *RevExp* 67 (1970): 433-44.

3:10-12

14411   Thomas B. Hoffman, "1 John and the Qumran Scrolls," *BTB* 8 (1978): 117-25.

3:10

14412   Jerry Horner, "Introduction to the Johannine Letters," *SouJT* 21 (1970): 41-51.

14413   J. Du Preez, "Social Justice: Motive for the Mission of the Church," *JTSA* 53 (1985): 36-46.

3:11-18

14414   Frank Stagg, "Orthodoxy and Orthopraxy in the Johannine Epistles," *RevExp* 67 (1970): 423-32.

14415   J. A. du Rand, "A Discourse Analysis of 1 John," *Neo* 13 (1981): 1-42.

14416   Sue Richard, "To Whom Am I a Neighbor: Luke 10:25-37 and 1 John 3:11-18," *BLT* 32 (1987): 180-84.

14417   Wendy E. Sproston, "Witnesses to What Was ἀπ᾿ ἀρχῆς: 1 John's Contribution to Our Knowledge of Tradition in the Fourth Gospel," *JSNT* 48 (1992): 43-65.

3:11-15

14418   Wilhelm Vischer, "Predigt über 1. Joh. 3, 11-15," *EvT* 17 (1957): 49-52.

3:11

14419   David M. Scholer, "1 John 4:7-21," *RevExp* 87 (1990): 309-14.

3:12

14420   J. B. Bauer, "Il misfatto di Caino nel giudizio di S. Giovanni," *RivBib* 2 (1954): 325-28.

14421 Kenneth Tollefson, "Certainty within the Fellowship: Dialectical Discourse in 1 John," *BTB* 29 (1999): 79-89.

3:13-18

14422 F. Ogara, "Scimus quoniam translati sumus de morte ad vitam," *VD* 18 (1938): 161-67.

14423 Jacques Dupont, "Comment aimer ses frères," *AsSeign* 55 (1962): 24-31.

3:13-15

14424 Jerry Horner, "Introduction to the Johannine Letters," *SouJT* 21 (1970): 41-51.

3:13

14425 Dale Moody, "The Theology of the Johannine Letters," *SouJT* 21 (1970): 7-22.

14426 Thomas B. Hoffman, "1 John and the Qumran Scrolls," *BTB* 8 (1978): 117-25.

3:14-16

14427 E. Bethge, "Predigt über 1. Joh. 3,14-16," *EvT* 22 (1962): 617-21.

3:14-15

14428 A. B. du Toit, "The Role and Meaning of Statements of 'Certainty' in the Structural Composition of 1 John," *Neo* 13 (1981): 84-100.

3:14

14429 Harold S. Songer, "The Life Situation of the Johannine Epistles," *RevExp* 67 (1970): 399-409.

14430 W. Pratscher, "Gott ist grösser als unser Herz: Zur Interpretation von 1 Joh 3, 19f," *TZ* 32 (1976): 272-81.

14431 Wendy E. Sproston, "Witnesses to What Was ἀπ΄ ἀρχῆς: 1 John's Contribution to Our Knowledge of Tradition in the Fourth Gospel," *JSNT* 48 (1992): 43-65.

3:15

14432 Ronald A. Ward, "The Theological Patterns of the Johannine Letters," *SouJT* 21 (1970): 23-39.

14433   Raymond Schwager, "La mort de Jésus: René Girard et la théologie; tr by M Guervel," *RechSR* 73 (1985): 481-502.

3:16-24

14434   Robert Brusic, "A River Ride with 1 John," *WW* 17 (1997): 212-20.

3:16

14435   Eduard Schweizer, "Zum religionsgeschichtlichen Hintergrund der Sendungsformel," *ZAW* 57 (196): 199-210.

14436   John D. Laurence, "The Eucharist as the Imitation of Christ," *TS* 47 (1986): 286-96.

14437   Rick Davis, "The Love of God," *BI* 16/4 (1990): 51-53.

3:17

14438   J. M. Lieu, " 'Authority to Become Children of God': A Study of 1 John," *NovT* 23 (1981): 210-28.

3:18-24

14439   I. de la Potterie, "Aimer ses frères et croire en Jesus Christ," *AsSeign* NS 26 (1973): 39-45.

3:18-19

14440   Thomas B. Hoffman, "1 John and the Qumran Scrolls," *BTB* 8 (1978): 117-25.

3:18

14441   Joseph Allen, "Renewal of the Christian Community: A Challenge for the Pastoral Ministry," *SVTQ* 29 (1985): 305-23.

14442   Wendy E. Sproston, "Witnesses to What Was ἀπ᾽ ἀρχῆς: 1 John's Contribution to Our Knowledge of Tradition in the Fourth Gospel," *JSNT* 48 (1992): 43-65.

3:19-24

14443   Dale Moody, "The Theology of the Johannine Letters," *SouJT* 21 (1970): 7-22.

14444   Harold S. Songer, "The Life Situation of the Johannine Epistles," *RevExp* 67 (1970): 399-409.

14445   J. A. du Rand, "A Discourse Analysis of 1 John," *Neo* 13 (1981): 1-42.

14446　Kenneth Tollefson, "Certainty within the Fellowship: Dialectical Discourse in 1 John," *BTB* 29 (1999): 79-89.

3:19-21

14447　Ceslaus Spicq, "La justification du charitable," *Bib* 40 (1959): 915-27.

14448　Joachim Kügler, " 'Wenn das Herz uns auch verurteilt . . .': Ägyptische Anthropologie in 1 Joh 3,19-21?'' *BibN* 66 (1993): 10-14.

3:19-20

14449　W. Pratscher, "Gott ist grösser als unser Herz: Zur Interpretation von 1 Joh 3, 19f," *TZ* 32 (1976): 272-81.

3:20

14450　A. Škrinjar, "Major est Deus corde nostro," *VD* 20 (1940): 340-50.

14451　James L. Boyer, "Relative Clauses in the Greek New Testament: A Statistical Study," *GTJ* 9 (1988): 233-56.

3:21-22

14452　John D. Crossan, "Aphorism in Discourse and Narrative," *Semeia* 43 (1988): 121-40.

3:21

14453　Ronald A. Ward, "The Theological Patterns of the Johannine Letters," *SouJT* 21 (1970): 23-39.

14454　Thomas B. Hoffman, "1 John and the Qumran Scrolls," *BTB* 8 (1978): 117-25.

14455　P. P. A. Kotzé, "The Meaning of 1 John 3:9 with Reference to 1 John 1:8 and 10," *Neo* 13 (1981): 68-83.

3:22

14456　Jerry Horner, "Introduction to the Johannine Letters," *SouJT* 21 (1970): 41-51.

3:23-24

14457　Kenneth Tollefson, "Certainty within the Fellowship: Dialectical Discourse in 1 John," *BTB* 29 (1999): 79-89.

3:23

14458   Franz Mußner, "Eine neutestamentliche Kurzformel für das
        Christentum," *TTZ* 79 (1970): 49-52.

14459   Duane F. Watson, "A Rhetorical Analysis of 2 John
        according to Greco-Roman Convention," *NTS* 35 (1989):
        104-30.

14460   David M. Scholer, "1 John 4:7-21," *RevExp* 87 (1990):
        309-14.

14461   Terry Griffith, "A Non-Polemical Reading of 1 John," *TynB*
        49 (1998): 253-76.

3:24-4:6

14462   Peter R. Jones, "A Structural Analysis of 1 John," *RevExp*
        67 (1970): 433-44.

3:24-25

14463   Thomas B. Hoffman, "1 John and the Qumran Scrolls,"
        BTB 8 (1978): 117-25.

3:24

14464   Frank Stagg, "Orthodoxy and Orthopraxy in the Johannine
        Epistles," *RevExp* 67 (1970): 423-32.

3:25

14465   Thomas B. Hoffman, "1 John and the Qumran Scrolls,"
        BTB 8 (1978): 117-25.

4-6

14466   Urban C. Von Wahlde, "The Theological Foundation of the
        Presbyter's Argument in 2 John," *ZAW* 76 (1985): 209-24.

4:1-6

14467   Dale Moody, "The Theology of the Johannine Letters,"
        SouJT 21 (1970): 7-22.

4:1-6

14468   J. A. du Rand, "A Discourse Analysis of 1 John," *Neo* 13
        (1981): 1-42.

14469   James D. Hernando, "Discerning of Spirits: 1 John 4:1-6,"
        Para 26 (1992): 6-9.

4:1-3

14470 R. C. Briggs, "Contemporary Study of the Johannine Epistles," *RevExp* 67 (1970): 415-22.

14471 Frank Stagg, "Orthodoxy and Orthopraxy in the Johannine Epistles," *RevExp* 67 (1970): 423-32.

14472 James A. Brooks, "Gnosticism," *BI* 8 (1982): 49-52.

14473 Duane F. Watson, "A Rhetorical Analysis of 2 John according to Greco-Roman Convention," *NTS* 35 (1989): 104-30.

4:1-2

14474 J. C. Coetzee, "The Holy Spirit in 1 John," *Neo* 13 (1981): 43-67.

4:1

14475 J. M. Lieu, " 'Authority to Become Children of God': A Study of 1 John," *NovT* 23 (1981): 210-28.

4:2-3:15

14476 Terry Griffith, "A Non-Polemical Reading of 1 John," *TynB* 49 (1998): 253-76.

4:2-3

14477 Wendy E. Sproston, "Witnesses to What Was ἀπ᾽ ἀρχῆς: 1 John's Contribution to Our Knowledge of Tradition in the Fourth Gospel," *JSNT* 48 (1992): 43-65.

4:2

14478 Harold S. Songer, "The Life Situation of the Johannine Epistles," *RevExp* 67 (1970): 399-409.

14479 Frank Stagg, "Orthodoxy and Orthopraxy in the Johannine Epistles," *RevExp* 67 (1970): 423-32.

14480 A. B. du Toit, "The Role and Meaning of Statements of 'Certainty' in the Structural Composition of 1 John," *Neo* 13 (1981): 84-100.

14481 Frank Chikane, "The Incarnation in the Life of the People in Southern Africa," *JTSA* 51 (1985): 37-50.

14482 H. J. Klauck, "Gemeinde ohne Amt: Erfahrungen mit der Kirche in den johanneischen Schriften," *BZ* NS 29 (1985): 193-220.

14483 Ben Witherington, "The Waters of Birth: John 3:5 and 1 John 5:6-8," *NTS* 35 (1989): 155-60.

14484 David M. Scholer, "1 John 4:7-21," *RevExp* 87 (1990): 309-14.

14485 Martinus C. de Boer, "The Death of Jesus Christ and His Coming in the Flesh," *NovT* 33 (1991): 326-46.

4:3

14486 Huber Drumwright, "Problem Passages in the Johannine Epistles," *SouJT* 21 (1970): 53-64.

14487 Bart D. Ehrman, "1 John 4:3 and the Orthodox Corruption of Scripture," *ZNW* 79 (1988): 221-43.

14488 Martin Wallraff, "Das Zeugnis des Kirchenhistorikers Sokrates zur Textkritik von 1 Joh 4,3," *ZAW* 88 (1997): 145-48.

4:4-6

14489 Thomas B. Hoffman, "1 John and the Qumran Scrolls," *BTB* 8 (1978): 117-25.

14490 Pheme Perkins, "*Koinonia* in 1 John 1:3-17: The Social Context of Division in the Johannine Letters," *CBQ* 45 (1983): 631-41.

4:4

14491 R. C. Briggs, "Contemporary Study of the Johannine Epistles," *RevExp* 67 (1970): 415-22.

14492 J. M. Lieu, " 'Authority to Become Children of God': A Study of 1 John," *NovT* 23 (1981): 210-28.

4:5-6

14493 Jerry Horner, "Introduction to the Johannine Letters," *SouJT* 21 (1970): 41-51.

4:5

14494 Pheme Perkins, "*Koinonia* in 1 John 1:3-17: The Social Context of Division in the Johannine Letters," *CBQ* 45 (1983): 631-41.

14495 H. J. Klauck, "Gemeinde ohne Amt: Erfahrungen mit der Kirche in den johanneischen Schriften," *BZ* NS 29 (1985): 193-220.

4:6

14496 Harold S. Songer, "The Life Situation of the Johannine Epistles," *RevExp* 67 (1970): 399-409.

14497 J. M. Lieu, " 'Authority to Become Children of God': A Study of 1 John," *NovT* 23 (1981): 210-28.

14498 A. B. du Toit, "The Role and Meaning of Statements of 'Certainty' in the Structural Composition of 1 John," *Neo* 13 (1981): 84-100.

4:7-5:21

14499 Peter R. Jones, "A Structural Analysis of 1 John," *RevExp* 67 (1970): 433-44.

4:7-5:13

14500 Donald E. Cook, "Interpretation of 1 John 1-5," *RevExp* 67 (1970): 445-59.

4:7-5:5

14501 J. C. Coetzee, "The Holy Spirit in 1 John," *Neo* 13 (1981): 43-67.

14502 J. A. du Rand, "A Discourse Analysis of 1 John," *Neo* 13 (1981): 1-42.

4:7-5:3

14503 Peter R. Jones, "A Structural Analysis of 1 John," *RevExp* 67 (1970): 433-44.

4:7-21

14504 David M. Scholer, "1 John 4:7-21," *RevExp* 87 (1990): 309-14.

4:7-20

14505 Frank Stagg, "Orthodoxy and Orthopraxy in the Johannine Epistles," *RevExp* 67 (1970): 423-32.

4:7-12

14506 Peter R. Jones, "A Structural Analysis of 1 John," *RevExp* 67 (1970): 433-44.

14507 Kenneth Tollefson, "Certainty within the Fellowship: Dialectical Discourse in 1 John," *BTB* 29 (1999): 79-89.

4:7-11

14508 Ronald A. Ward, "The Theological Patterns of the Johannine Letters," *SouJT* 21 (1970): 23-39.

4:7-10

14509 C. Bourgin, "L'Église fraternité dans l'amour divin," *AsSeign* NS 27 (1970): 24-29.

4:7-8

14510 J.-M. Perrin, "Voir vos frères, c'est voir Dieu," *VS* 72 (1945): 372-89.

14511 Kenneth Tollefson, "Certainty within the Fellowship: Dialectical Discourse in 1 John," *BTB* 29 (1999): 79-89.

4:7

14512 A. Boutry, "Quiconque aime, est né de Dieu," *BVC* 82 (1968): 66-70.

14513 Marinus de Jonge, "Geliefden, laten wij elkander liefhebben, want de liefde is uit God, 1 Joh 4:7," *NTT* 22 (1968): 352-67.

14514 J. M. Lieu, " 'Authority to Become Children of God': A Study of 1 John," *NovT* 23 (1981): 210-28.

14515 John Breck, "Biblical Chiasmus: Exploring Structure for Meaning," *BTB* 17 (1987): 70-74.

4:8-10

14516 Peggy Starkey, "Agape: A Christian Criterion for Truth in the Other World Religions," *IRM* 74 (1985): 425-63.

4:8

14517 André Feuillet, "Dieu est amour," *EV* 81 (1971): 537-48.

14518 R. Prenter, "Der Gott, der Liebe ist," *TLZ* 96 (1971): 401-13.

14519 Dany Dideberg, "Esprit Saint et charité. L'exégèse augustinienne de 1 Jn 4, 8 et 16," *NRT* 97 (1975): 97-109, 229-50.

14520 Wendy E. Sproston, "Witnesses to What Was ἀπ᾽ ἀρχῆς: 1 John's Contribution to Our Knowledge of Tradition in the Fourth Gospel," *JSNT* 48 (1992): 43-65.

4:9

14521 Eduard Schweizer, "Zum religionsgeschichtlichen Hintergrund der 'Sendungsformel' Gal 4,4f Röm 8,3f; Joh 3,16f 1 Joh 4,9," *ZNW* 57 (1966): 199-210.

4:10

14522 Henri Clavier, "Notes sur un mot-clef du Johannisme et de la sotériologie biblique: *hilasmos*," *NovT* 10 (1968): 287-304.

14523 T. C. G. Thornton, "Propitiation or Expiation?" *ET* 80 (1968-1969): 53-55.

14524 Ronald A. Ward, "The Theological Patterns of the Johannine Letters," *SouJT* 21 (1970): 23-39.

4:11-16

14525 C. Bourgin, "L'amour fraternel chrétien, expérience de Dieu," *AsSeign* NS 29 (1970): 31-37.

4:11

14526 Frank Stagg, "Orthodoxy and Orthopraxy in the Johannine Epistles," *RevExp* 67 (1970): 423-32.

14527 Thomas B. Hoffman, "1 John and the Qumran Scrolls," *BTB* 8 (1978): 117-25.

4:12

14528 Dale Moody, "The Theology of the Johannine Letters," *SouJT* 21 (1970): 7-22.

14529 Ronald A. Ward, "The Theological Patterns of the Johannine Letters," *SouJT* 21 (1970): 23-39.

14530 P. W. van der Horst, "Wordplay in 1 John 4:12?" *ZNW* 63 (1972): 280-82.

14531 J. A. du Rand, "The Structure of 3 John," *Neo* 13 (1981): 121-31.

14532 Wendy E. Sproston, "Witnesses to What Was ἀπ᾽ ἀρχῆς: 1 John's Contribution to Our Knowledge of Tradition in the Fourth Gospel," *JSNT* 48 (1992): 43-65.

4:13-18

14533 Harold S. Songer, "The Life Situation of the Johannine Epistles," *RevExp* 67 (1970): 399-409.

14534 Peter R. Jones, "A Structural Analysis of 1 John," *RevExp* 67 (1970): 433-44.

4:13

14535 Frank Stagg, "Orthodoxy and Orthopraxy in the Johannine Epistles," *RevExp* 67 (1970): 423-32.

14536 J. C. Coetzee, "The Holy Spirit in 1 John," *Neo* 13 (1981): 43-67.

4:14

14537 I. L. Grohar, "El 'mundo' en los escritos juanicos: un ensayo de interpretación," *RevB* 47 (1985): 221-27.

14538 Marinus de Jonge, "The Testaments of the Twelve Patriarchs: Christian and Jewish," *NTT* 39 (1985): 265-75.

4:15

14539 Dale Moody, "The Theology of the Johannine Letters," *SouJT* 21 (1970): 7-22.

4:16

14540 G.-M. Behler, "Nous avons cru en l'amour," *VS* 119 (1968): 296-318.

14541 Ronald A. Ward, "The Theological Patterns of the Johannine Letters," *SouJT* 21 (1970): 23-39.

14542 R. Prenter, "Der Gott, der Liebe ist," *TLZ* 96 (1971): 401-13.

14543   Dany Dideberg, "Esprit Saint et charité. L'exégèse augustinienne de 1 Jn 4, 8 et 16," *NRT* 97 (1975): 97-109, 229-50.

14544   A. B. du Toit, "The Role and Meaning of Statements of 'Certainty' in the Structural Composition of 1 John," *Neo* 13 (1981): 84-100.

4:17-5:3

14545   Peter R. Jones, "A Structural Analysis of 1 John," *RevExp* 67 (1970): 433-44.

4:17-21

14546   Robert Brusic, "A River Ride with 1 John," *WW* 17 (1997): 212-20.

4:17-18

14547   Kenneth Tollefson, "Certainty within the Fellowship: Dialectical Discourse in 1 John," *BTB* 29 (1999): 79-89.

4:17

14548   Ronald A. Ward, "The Theological Patterns of the Johannine Letters," *SouJT* 21 (1970): 23-39.

14549   R. E. Glaze, "Boldness," *BI* 12/2 (1986): 61.

4:18-23

14550   Thomas B. Hoffman, "1 John and the Qumran Scrolls," *BTB* 8 (1978): 117-25.

4:19-24

14551   Dale Moody, "The Theology of the Johannine Letters," *SouJT* 21 (1970): 7-22.

4:19

14552   Ronald A. Ward, "The Theological Patterns of the Johannine Letters," *SouJT* 21 (1970): 23-39.

4:20

14553   Norman K. Bakken, "The New Humanity: Christ and the Modern Age: A Study in the Christ-Hymn: Philippians 2:6-11," *Int* 22 (1968): 71-82.

14554   Frank Stagg, "Orthodoxy and Orthopraxy in the Johannine Epistles," *RevExp* 67 (1970): 423-32.

14555 Ronald A. Ward, "The Theological Patterns of the Johannine Letters," *SouJT* 21 (1970): 23-39.

14556 Palémon Glorieux, "La révélation du Pére," *MSR* 42 (1985): 21-41.

14557 Wendy E. Sproston, "Witnesses to What Was ἀπ᾽ ἀρχῆς: 1 John's Contribution to Our Knowledge of Tradition in the Fourth Gospel," *JSNT* 48 (1992): 43-65.

14558 Terry Griffith, "A Non-Polemical Reading of 1 John," *TynB* 49 (1998): 253-76.

4:24

14559 Dale Moody, "The Theology of the Johannine Letters," *SouJT* 21 (1970): 7-22.

14560 Ronald A. Ward, "The Theological Patterns of the Johannine Letters," *SouJT* 21 (1970): 23-39.

5:1-13

14561 Dale Moody, "The Theology of the Johannine Letters," *SouJT* 21 (1970): 7-22.

5:1-12

14562 D. Edmond Hiebert, "An Expositional Study of 1 John," *BSac* 147 (1990): 216-30.

5:1-6

14563 I. de la Potterie, "Le croyant qui a vaincu le monde," *AsSeign* NS 23 (1970): 34-43.

14564 Gerhard Aho, "1 John 5:1-6," *CTQ* 46 (1982): 43-44.

14565 Robert Brusic, "A River Ride with 1 John," *WW* 17 (1997): 212-20.

5:1-5

14566 Abidan P. Shah, "A Greek Exposition of 1 John 5:1-5," *FM* 16 (1999): 39-47.

14567 Alan H. West, "Faith in Jesus Christ Overcomes the World: An Exegesis on 1 John 5:1-5," *FM* 16 (1999): 48-59.

5:1

14568   David M. Scholer, "1 John 4:7-21," *RevExp* 87 (1990): 309-14.

14569   Charles P. Baylis, "The Meaning of Walking 'in the Darkness'," *BSac* 149 (1992): 214-22.

14570   Terry Griffith, "A Non-Polemical Reading of 1 John," *TynB* 49 (1998): 253-76.

5:2-3

14571   Kenneth Tollefson, "Certainty within the Fellowship: Dialectical Discourse in 1 John," *BTB* 29 (1999): 79-89.

5:2

14572   Harold S. Songer, "The Life Situation of the Johannine Epistles," *RevExp* 67 (1970): 399-409.

14573   A. B. du Toit, "The Role and Meaning of Statements of 'Certainty' in the Structural Composition of 1 John," *Neo* 13 (1981): 84-100.

5:3-12

14574   Peter R. Jones, "A Structural Analysis of 1 John," *RevExp* 67 (1970): 433-44.

5:3-4

14575   Jerry Horner, "Introduction to the Johannine Letters," *SouJT* 21 (1970): 41-51.

5:3

14576   Ronald A. Ward, "The Theological Patterns of the Johannine Letters," *SouJT* 21 (1970): 23-39.

14577   David M. Scholer, "1 John 4:7-21," *RevExp* 87 (1990): 309-14.

5:4-10

14578   F. Ogara, "Quis est, qui vincit mundum, nisi qui credit quoniam Jesus est Filius Dei?" *VD* 18 (1938): 97-103.

5:4-8

14579   M. Miguéns, "Tres testigos: Espiritu, agua, sangre," *SBFLA* 22 (1972): 74-94.

5:4

14580   Colin Gunton, "Christus Victor Revisited: A Study in Metaphor and the Transformation of Meaning," *JTS* NS 36 (1985): 129-45.

5:5-8

14581   Martinus C. de Boer, "Jesus the Baptizer: 1 John 5:5-8 and the Gospel of John," *JBL* 107 (1988): 87-106.

5:5

14582   Terry Griffith, "A Non-Polemical Reading of 1 John," *TynB* 49 (1998): 253-76.

5:6-21

14583   J. C. Coetzee, "The Holy Spirit in 1 John," *Neo* 13 (1981): 43-67.

5:6-13

14584   J. A. du Rand, "A Discourse Analysis of 1 John," *Neo* 13 (1981): 1-42.

5:6-12

14585   Huber Drumwright, "Problem Passages in the Johannine Epistles," *SouJT* 21 (1970): 53-64.

5:6-8

14586   F.-M. Braun, "L'eau et l'Esprit," *RT* 49 (1949): 5-30.

14587   Eduard Schweizer, "Das johanneische Zeugnis vom Herrenmahl," *EvT* 12 (1952-1953): 341-63.

14588   A. Calmet, "Le témoignage de l'eau, du sang, de l'Esprit," *BVC* 53 (1963): 35-36.

14589   Frank Stagg, "Orthodoxy and Orthopraxy in the Johannine Epistles," *RevExp* 67 (1970): 423-32.

14590   Ben Witherington, "The Waters of Birth: John 3:5 and 1 John 5:6-8," *NTS* 35 (1989): 155-60.

5:6

14591   Frank Stagg, "Orthodoxy and Orthopraxy in the Johannine Epistles," *RevExp* 67 (1970): 423-32.

14592   Terry Griffith, "A Non-Polemical Reading of 1 John," *TynB* 49 (1998): 253-76.

5:7-8

14593   A. Greiff, "Die drei Zeugen in 1 Joh 5,7f," *TQ* 114 (1933): 465-80.

14594   M. del Alamo, "El 'Comma Joaneo'," *EB* 2 (1943): 75-105.

14595   T. Ayuso-Marazuela, "Nuevo estudio sobre el 'Comma Johanneum'," *Bib* 28 (1947): 83-112, 216-35; 29 (1948) 52-76.

14596   Walter Thiele, "Beobachtungen zum Comma Johanneum," *ZNW* 50 (1959): 61-73.

14597   M. Miguéns, "Tres testigos: Espiritu, agua, sangre," *SBFLA* 22 (1972): 74-94.

5:7

14598   Walter Thiele, "Beobachtungen zum Comma Johanneum," *ZNW* 50 (1959): 61-73.

14599   Franz Posset, "John Bugenhagen and the Comma Johanneum," *CTQ* 49 (1985): 245-51.

14600   Charles P. Baylis, "The Meaning of Walking 'in the Darkness'," *BSac* 149 (1992): 214-22.

5:8

14601   J. C. Coetzee, "The Holy Spirit in 1 John," *Neo* 13 (1981): 43-67.

5:9

14602   Jerry Horner, "Introduction to the Johannine Letters," *SouJT* 21 (1970): 41-51.

5:10

14603   David M. Scholer, "1 John 4:7-21," *RevExp* 87 (1990): 309-14.

5:11-12

14604   Charles P. Baylis, "The Meaning of Walking 'in the Darkness'," *BSac* 149 (1992): 214-22.

14605   Kenneth Tollefson, "Certainty within the Fellowship: Dialectical Discourse in 1 John," *BTB* 29 (1999): 79-89.

5:12-14

> 14606 Jerry Horner, "Introduction to the Johannine Letters," *SouJT* 21 (1970): 41-51.

5:12-13

> 14607 Harold S. Songer, "The Life Situation of the Johannine Epistles," *RevExp* 67 (1970): 399-409.

5:12

> 14608 R. C. Briggs, "Contemporary Study of the Johannine Epistles," *RevExp* 67 (1970): 415-22.

5:13-21

> 14609 Peter R. Jones, "A Structural Analysis of 1 John," *RevExp* 67 (1970): 433-44.

5:13-15

> 14610 Kenneth Tollefson, "Certainty within the Fellowship: Dialectical Discourse in 1 John," *BTB* 29 (1999): 79-89.

5:13

> 14611 J. M. Lieu, " 'Authority to Become Children of God': A Study of 1 John," *NovT* 23 (1981): 210-28.

> 14612 A. B. du Toit, "The Role and Meaning of Statements of 'Certainty' in the Structural Composition of 1 John," *Neo* 13 (1981): 84-100.

> 14613 David M. Scholer, "1 John 4:7-21," *RevExp* 87 (1990): 309-14.

5:14-21

> 14614 Donald E. Cook, "Interpretation of 1 John 1-5," *RevExp* 67 (1970): 445-59.

> 14615 J. A. du Rand, "A Discourse Analysis of 1 John," *Neo* 13 (1981): 1-42.

> 14616 Kenneth Tollefson, "Certainty within the Fellowship: Dialectical Discourse in 1 John," *BTB* 29 (1999): 79-89.

5:14-17

> 14617 Dale Moody, "The Theology of the Johannine Letters," *SouJT* 21 (1970): 7-22.

14618 J. A. du Rand, "A Discourse Analysis of 1 John," *Neo* 13 (1981): 1-42.

5:14-15

14619 John D. Crossan, "Aphorism in Discourse and Narrative," *Semeia* 43 (1988): 121-40.

5:16-18

14620 A. H. Dammers, "Hard Sayings," *Theology* 66 (1963): 370-72.

14621 Huber Drumwright, "Problem Passages in the Johannine Epistles," *SouJT* 21 (1970): 53-64.

14622 Terry Griffith, "A Non-Polemical Reading of 1 John," *TynB* 49 (1998): 253-76.

5:16-17

14623 L. Paul Trudinger, "Concerning Sins, Mortal and Otherwise. A Note on 1 John 5,16-17," *Bib* 52 (1971): 541-42.

14624 Kenneth Tollefson, "Certainty within the Fellowship: Dialectical Discourse in 1 John," *BTB* 29 (1999): 79-89.

5:16

14625 Pheme Perkins, "*Koinonia* in 1 John 1:3-17: The Social Context of Division in the Johannine Letters," *CBQ* 45 (1983): 631-41.

14626 David M. Scholer, "1 John 4:7-21," *RevExp* 87 (1990): 309-14.

5:17

14627 Ronald A. Ward, "The Theological Patterns of the Johannine Letters," *SouJT* 21 (1970): 23-39.

5:18-21

14628 Dale Moody, "The Theology of the Johannine Letters," *SouJT* 21 (1970): 7-22.

5:18-20

14629 Albert Segond, "1re Epître de Jean, chap 5:18-20," *RHPR* 45 (1965): 349-51.

14630 Harold S. Songer, "The Life Situation of the Johannine Epistles," *RevExp* 67 (1970): 399-409.

5:19

14631 Thomas B. Hoffman, "1 John and the Qumran Scrolls," *BTB* 8 (1978): 117-25.

14632 Charles P. Baylis, "The Meaning of Walking 'in the Darkness'," *BSac* 149 (1992): 214-22.

5:20

14633 George D. Kilpatrick, "Two Johannine Idioms in the Johannine Epistles," *JTS* 12 (1961): 272-73.

14634 Ronald A. Ward, "The Theological Patterns of the Johannine Letters," *SouJT* 21 (1970): 23-39.

14635 J. M. Lieu, " 'Authority to Become Children of God': A Study of 1 John," *NovT* 23 (1981): 210-28.

14636 A. B. du Toit, "The Role and Meaning of Statements of 'Certainty' in the Structural Composition of 1 John," *Neo* 13 (1981): 84-100.

14637 Charles P. Baylis, "The Meaning of Walking 'in the Darkness'," *BSac* 149 (1992): 214-22.

5:21

14638 Dale Moody, "The Theology of the Johannine Letters," *SouJT* 21 (1970): 7-22.

14639 M. J. Edwards, "Martyrdom and the First Epistle of John," *NovT* 31 (1989): 164-71.

14640 Julian V. Hills, "Little Children, Keep Yourselves from Idols: 1 John 5:21 Reconsidered," *CBQ* 51 (1989): 285-310.

14641 Terry Griffith, " 'Little Children, Keep Yourselves from Idols' (1 John 5:21)," *TynB* 48 (1997): 187-90.

5:24

14642 Wendy E. Sproston, "Witnesses to What Was ἀπ᾽ ἀρχῆς: 1 John's Contribution to Our Knowledge of Tradition in the Fourth Gospel," *JSNT* 48 (1992): 43-65.

2 John

1-3

14643 John B. Polhill, "An Analysis of 2 and 3 John," *RevExp* 67 (1970): 461-71.

14644 J. A. du Rand, "The Structure and Message of 2 John," *Neo* 13 (1981): 101-20.

1

14645 H. J. Klauck, " *Kyria ekklesia* in Bauers Wörterbuch und die Exegese des zweiten Johannesbriefes," *ZNW* 81 (1990): 135-38.

14646 Huber Drumwright, "Problem Passages in the Johannine Epistles," *SouJT* 21 (1970): 53-64.

2

14647 Dale Moody, "The Theology of the Johannine Letters," *SouJT* 21 (1970): 7-22.

14648 Duane F. Watson, "A Rhetorical Analysis of 2 John according to Greco-Roman Convention," *NTS* 35 (1989): 104-30.

3

14649 Klauspeter Blaser, "Zum 2. Johannesbrief: 'Das Gebot, das ihr von Anfang an gehört habt, lautet: Ihr sollt in der Liebe leben'," *ZMiss* 22 (1996): 2-6.

14650 Dale Moody, "The Theology of the Johannine Letters," *SouJT* 21 (1970): 7-22.

4-6

14651 Urban C. Von Wahlde, "The Theological Foundation of the Presbyter's Argument in 2 John," *ZNW* 76 (1985): 209-24.

14652 John B. Polhill, "An Analysis of 2 and 3 John," *RevExp* 67 (1970): 461-71.

14653 Duane F. Watson, "A Rhetorical Analysis of 2 John according to Greco-Roman Convention," *NTS* 35 (1989): 104-30.

4

14654 Huber Drumwright, "Problem Passages in the Johannine Epistles," *SouJT* 21 (1970): 53-64.

14655 Jerry Horner, "Introduction to the Johannine Letters," - *SouJT* 21 (1970): 41-51.

14656 Dale Moody, "The Theology of the Johannine Letters," *SouJT* 21 (1970): 7-22.

14657 Ronald A. Ward, "The Theological Patterns of the Johannine Letters," *SouJT* 21 (1970): 23-39.

14658 J. A. du Rand, "The Structure and Message of 2 John," *Neo* 13 (1981): 101-20.

5-6

14659 Klauspeter Blaser, "Zum 2. Johannesbrief: 'Das Gebot, das ihr von Anfang an gehört habt, lautet: Ihr sollt in der Liebe leben'," *ZMiss* 22 (1996): 2-6.

14660 J. A. du Rand, "The Structure and Message of 2 John," *Neo* 13 (1981): 101-20.

6

14661 Dale Moody, "The Theology of the Johannine Letters," *SouJT* 21 (1970): 7-22.

7-11

. 14662 J. A. du Rand, "The Structure and Message of 2 John," *Neo* 13 (1981): 101-20.

7-8

14663 Francisco Gnidovec, "Introivit et vidit et credidit," *EB* NS 41 (1983): 137-55, 415-20.

14664 Huber Drumwright, "Problem Passages in the Johannine Epistles," *SouJT* 21 (1970): 53-64.

14665 Jerry Horner, "Introduction to the Johannine Letters," - *SouJT* 21 (1970): 41-51.

<u>7</u>

14666   R. C. Briggs, "Contemporary Study of the Johannine Epistles," *RevExp* 67 (1970): 415-22.

14667   Dale Moody, "The Theology of the Johannine Letters," *SouJT* 21 (1970): 7-22.

<u>9-11</u>

14668   Duane F. Watson, "A Rhetorical Analysis of 2 John according to Greco-Roman Convention," *NTS* 35 (1989): 104-30.

<u>9</u>

14669   Dale Moody, "The Theology of the Johannine Letters," *SouJT* 21 (1970): 7-22.

<u>10-11</u>

14670   John B. Polhill, "An Analysis of 2 and 3 John," *RevExp* 67 (1970): 461-71.

14671   Duane F. Watson, "A Rhetorical Analysis of 2 John according to Greco-Roman Convention," *NTS* 35 (1989): 104-30.

<u>10</u>

14672   H. H. Wendt, "Zum zweiten und dritten Johannesbrief," *ZAW* 23 (1924): 27-31.

14673   R. C. Briggs, "Contemporary Study of the Johannine Epistles," *RevExp* 67 (1970): 415-22.

14674   Jerry Horner, "Introduction to the Johannine Letters," - *SouJT* 21 (1970): 41-51.

<u>11</u>

14675   H. H. Wendt, "Zum zweiten und dritten Johannesbrief," *ZAW* 23 (1924): 27-31.

14676   Pheme Perkins, "*Koinonia* in 1 John 1:3-17: The Social Context of Division in the Johannine Letters," *CBQ* 45 (1983): 631-41.

<u>12-13</u>

14677   John B. Polhill, "An Analysis of 2 and 3 John," *RevExp* 67 (1970): 461-71.

14678 J. A. du Rand, "The Structure and Message of 2 John," *Neo* 13 (1981): 101-20.

13

14679 H. H. Wendt, "Zum zweiten und dritten Johannesbrief," *ZAW* 23 (1924): 27-31.

14680 Huber Drumwright, "Problem Passages in the Johannine Epistles," *SouJT* 21 (1970): 53-64.

14681 Jerry Horner, "Introduction to the Johannine Letters," - *SouJT* 21 (1970): 41-51.

14682 Ronald A. Ward, "The Theological Patterns of the Johannine Letters," *SouJT* 21 (1970): 23-39.

3 John

1-15

14683 Jens W. Taeger, "Der konservative Rebell: zum Widerstand des Diotrephes gegen den Presbyter," *ZNW* 78 (1987): 267-87.

1-4

14684 D. Edmond Hiebert, "Studies in 3 John. Part 1: An Exposition of 3 John 1-4," *BSac* 44 (1987): 53-65.

14685 John B. Polhill, "An Analysis of 2 and 3 John," *RevExp* 67 (1970): 461-71.

1-2

14686 J. A. du Rand, "The Structure of 3 John," *Neo* 13 (1981): 121-31.

2

14687 Dale Moody, "The Theology of the Johannine Letters," *SouJT* 21 (1970): 7-22.

3-4

14688 J. A. du Rand, "The Structure of 3 John," *Neo* 13 (1981): 121-31.

4

14689 Huber Drumwright, "Problem Passages in the Johannine Epistles," *SouJT* 21 (1970): 53-64.

14690 Dale Moody, "The Theology of the Johannine Letters," *SouJT* 21 (1970): 7-22.

5-11

14691 J. A. du Rand, "The Structure of 3 John," *Neo* 13 (1981): 121-31.

5-10

14692   D. Edmond Hiebert, "Studies in 3 John. Part 2: An
        Exposition of 3 John 5-10," *BSac* 44 (1987): 194-207.

5-8

14693   John B. Polhill, "An Analysis of 2 and 3 John," *RevExp* 67
        (1970): 461-71.

6

14694   Walter L. Liefeld, "Can Deputation Be Defended
        Biblically?" *EMQ* 22 (1986): 360-65.

7

14695   Jerry Horner, "Introduction to the Johannine Letters," -
        SouJT 21 (1970): 41-51.

8

14696   H. J. Klauck, "Gemeinde ohne Amt: Erfahrungen mit der
        Kirche in den johanneischen Schriften," *BZ* NS 29 (1985):
        193-220.

9-10

14697   John B. Polhill, "An Analysis of 2 and 3 John," *RevExp* 67
        (1970): 461-71.

14698   Pheme Perkins, "*Koinonia* in 1 John 1:3-17: The Social
        Context of Division in the Johannine Letters," *CBQ* 45
        (1983): 631-41.

14699   Margaret M. Mitchell, " 'Diotrephes Does Not Receive
        Us': The Lexicographical and Social Content of 3 John
        9-10," *JBL* 117 (1998): 299-320.

9

14700   R. W. Orr, "Diotrephes: The First Gnostic Bishop?" *EQ* 33
        (1961): 172-73.

14701   Melvin R. Storm, "Diotrephes: A Study of Rivalry in the
        Apostolic Church," *RQ* 35 (1993): 193-202.

11-14

14702   D. Edmond Hiebert, "Studies in 3 John. Part 3: An
        Exposition of 3 John 11-14," *BSac* 44 (1987): 293-304.

11-12

14703 John B. Polhill, "An Analysis of 2 and 3 John," *RevExp* 67 (1970): 461-71.

11

14704 Dale Moody, "The Theology of the Johannine Letters," *SouJT* 21 (1970): 7-22.

14705 Tibor Horvath, "3 John 11: An Early Ecumenical Creed?" *ET* 85 (1974): 339-40.

12

14706 J. A. du Rand, "The Structure of 3 John," *Neo* 13 (1981): 121-31.

13-15

14707 John B. Polhill, "An Analysis of 2 and 3 John," *RevExp* 67 (1970): 461-71.

14708 J. A. du Rand, "The Structure of 3 John," *Neo* 13 (1981): 121-31.

15

14709 H. J. Klauck, "Gemeinde ohne Amt: Erfahrungen mit der Kirche in den johanneischen Schriften," *BZ* NS 29 (1985): 193-220.

Jude

<u>2</u>

14710 John J. Gunther, "The Alexandrian Epistle of Jude," *NTS* 30 (1984): 549-62.

<u>3-4</u>

14711 John J. Gunther, "The Alexandrian Epistle of Jude," *NTS* 30 (1984): 549-62.

14712 D. Edmond Hiebert, "An Exposition of Jude 3-4," *BSac* 142 (1985): 142-51.

<u>3</u>

14713 Andrew J. Bandstra, "Onward Christian Soldiers--Praying in Love, with Mercy: Preaching on the Epistle of Jude," *CTJ* 32 (1997): 136-39.

<u>4</u>

14714 C. H. Landon, "The Text of Jude 4," *HTS* 49 (1993): 823-43.

<u>5-16</u>

14715 Andrew J. Bandstra, "Onward Christian Soldiers--Praying in Love, with Mercy: Preaching on the Epistle of Jude," *CTJ* 32 (1997): 136-39.

<u>5-7</u>

14716 Jarl Fossum, "Kyrios Jesus as the Angel of the Lord in Jude 5-7," *NTS* 33 (1987): 226-43.

<u>5</u>

14717 George D. Kilpatrick, "Land of Egypt in the New Testament," *JTS* NS 17 (1966): 70.

14718 Carroll D. Osburn, "The Text of Jude 5," *Bib* 62 (1981): 107-15.

6-9

14719   John J. Gunther, "The Alexandrian Epistle of Jude," *NTS* 30 (1984): 549-62.

6

14720   J. Daryl Charles, "Jude's Use of Pseudepigraphical Source-Material as Part of a Literary Strategy," *NTS* 37 (1991): 130-45.

7

14721   M. A. Kruger, "Τούτοις in Jude 7," *Neo* 27 (1993): 119-32.

8-10

14722   John J. Gunther, "The Alexandrian Epistle of Jude," *NTS* 30 (1984): 549-62.

9

14723   J. Daryl Charles, "Jude's Use of Pseudepigraphical Source-Material as Part of a Literary Strategy," *NTS* 37 (1991): 130-45.

11-16

14724   John J. Gunther, "The Alexandrian Epistle of Jude," *NTS* 30 (1984): 549-62.

12-16

14725   D. Edmond Hiebert, "An Exposition of Jude 12-16," *BSac* 142 (1985): 238-49.

12-13

14726   Carroll D. Osburn, "1 Enoch 80:2-8 (67:5-7) and Jude 12-13," *CBQ* 47 (1985): 296-303.

12

14727   William Whallon, "Should We Keep, Omit, or Alter the *hoi* in Jude 12?" *NTS* 34 (1988): 156-59.

13

14728   John P. Oleson, "An Echo of Hesiod's Theogony vv 190-2 in Jude 13," *NTS* 25 (1979): 492-503.

<u>14-15</u>

14729   J. Daryl Charles, "Jude's Use of Pseudepigraphical Source-Material as Part of a Literary Strategy," *NTS* 37 (1991): 130-45.

<u>14</u>

14730   Carroll D. Osburn, "Christological Use of 1 Enoch 1:9 in Jude 14,15," *NTS* 23 (1977): 334-41.

<u>15</u>

14731   Carroll D. Osburn, "Christological Use of 1 Enoch 1:9 in Jude 14,15," *NTS* 23 (1977): 334-41.

<u>16-18</u>

14732   John J. Gunther, "The Alexandrian Epistle of Jude," *NTS* 30 (1984): 549-62.

<u>17-23</u>

14733   D. Edmond Hiebert, "An Exposition of Jude 17-23," *BSac* 142 (1985): 355-66.

14734   Andrew J. Bandstra, "Onward Christian Soldiers--Praying in Love, with Mercy: Preaching on the Epistle of Jude," *CTJ* 32 (1997): 136-39.

<u>20-21</u>

14735   Andrew J. Bandstra, "Onward Christian Soldiers--Praying in Love, with Mercy: Preaching on the Epistle of Jude," *CTJ* 32 (1997): 136-39.

<u>20</u>

14736   William J. Hassold, "Keep Yourselves in the Love of God: An Interpretation of Jude 20, 21," *CTM* 23 (1952): 884-94.

<u>21</u>

14737   William J. Hassold, "Keep Yourselves in the Love of God: An Interpretation of Jude 20, 21," *CTM* 23 (1952): 884-94.

<u>22-23</u>

14738   Carroll D. Osburn, "Text of Jude 22-23," *ZNW* 63 (1972): 139-44.

14739   J. M. Ross, "Church Discipline in Jude 22-23," *ET* 100 (1989): 297-98.

14740   Sara C. Winter, "Jude 22-23: A Note on the Text and Translation," *HTR* 87 (1994): 215-22.

14741   J. S. Allen, "A New Possibility for the Three-Clause Format of Jude 22-3," *NTS* 44 (1998): 133-43.

<u>22</u>

14742   Werner Bieder, "Judas 22f: *hous de eleate en phobo*," *TZ* 6 (1950): 75-77.

Revelation

<u>1-11</u>

14743 Martin Hopkins, "The Historical Perspective of Apocalypse 1-11," *CBQ* 27 (1965): 42-47.

<u>1-3</u>

14744 A. Škrinjar, "Antiquitas christiana: de angelis septem ecclesiarum," *VD* 22 (1942): 18-24, 51-56.

14745 Augustin George, "Un appel à la fidelité, les lettres aux sept églises d'Asie," *BVC* 15 (1956): 80-86.

14746 Peter Wood, "Local Knowledge in the Letters of the Apocalypse," *ET* 73 (1962): 263-264.

14747 E. Pax, "Jüdische und christliche Funde im Bereiche der 'sieben Kirchen' der Apokalypse," *BibL* 8 (1967): 264-78.

14748 O. F. A. Meinardus, "The Christian Remains of the Seven Churches of the Apocalypse," *BA* 37 (1974): 69-82.

14749 B. Graham, "Seven Churches of Asia," *CT* 23 (1978): 20-23.

14750 Francisco Contreras-Molina, "Las cartas a las siete iglesias," *EB* 46 (1988): 141-72.

14751 John T. Kirby, "The Rhetorical Situations of Revelation 1-3," *NTS* 34 (1988): 197-207.

14752 James L. Blevins, "Revelation 1-3," *RevExp* 87 (1990): 615-21.

<u>1-2</u>

14753 Stefania Cantore, "I sette spiriti." *ParSpirV* 4 (1981): 202-14.

1

14754   André Feuillet, "Jalons pour une meilleure intelligence de l'Apocalypse. Le prologue et la vision inaugurale," *EV* 85 (1975): 65-72.

14755   Erhardt Güttgemanns, "Die Semiotik des Traums in apokalyptischen Texten am Beispiel von Apokalypse Johannis 1" *LB* 59 (1987): 7-54.

1:1-20

14756   Gregory L. Linton, "Reading the Apocalypse as an Apocalpse," *SBLSP* 30 (1991): 161-86.

1:1-3

14757   Rudolf Pesch, "Offenbarung Jesu Christi. Eine Auslegung von Apk. l,1-3," *BibL* 11 (1970): 15-29.

1:1

14758   J. Szlaga, "Apokaliptyczne 'co ma nastapić niebawem' a oczekiwanie paruzji," *RuchB* 28 (1975): 230-34.

14759   Gregory K. Beale, "The Influence of Daniel upon the Structure and Theology of John's Apocalypse," *JETS* 27 (1984): 413-24.

1:4-18

14760   Gerhard Aho, "The Second Sunday of Easter," *CTQ* 49 (1985): 295-96.

14761   Wendell W. Frerichs, "God's Song of Revelation: from Easter to Pentecost in the Apocalypse," *WW* 6 (1986): 216-28.

1:4-8

14762   J. M. Ford, " 'He That Cometh' and the Divine Name (Apoc. 1:4-8; 4:8)," *JSNT* 1 (1970): 144-47.

14763   Ugo Vanni, "Un esempio di dialogo liturgico in Ap. 1,4-8," *Bib* 57 (1976): 453-67.

14764   Richard G. Kapfer, "Last Sunday after Trinity: Revelation 1:4b-8," *CTQ* 46 (1982): 82-83.

14765   Ugo Vanni, "Liturgical Dialogue as a Literary Form in the Book of Revelation," *NTS* 37 (1991): 348-72.

1:4-5

14766   J. A. Walther, "The Address in Revelation 1:4,5a," *HBT* 17 (1995): 165-80.

1:4

14767   P. Jouon, "Apocalypse 1,4," *RechSR* 21 (1931): 486-87.

14768   A. Škrinjar, "Les sept esprits (Apoc. 1,4; 3,1; 4.5; 5,6)," *Bib* 16 (1935): 1-24, 113-40.

14769   J. D. Robb, "Ho Erchomenos ('Who is to Come'—NEB)," *ET* 73 (1962): 338-39.

1:5-8

14770   Michel Coune, "Un royaume de prêtres. Ap. 1,5-8," *AsSeign* 20 (1973): 9-16.

1:5-6

14771   F. E. Gäbelein, "Great Doxology: Revelation 1:5, 6," *BSac* 98 (1941): 194-202.

14772   P. von der Osten-Sacken, "Chistologie, Taufe, Homologie: Ein Beitrag zur Apc. Joh. 1,5-6," *ZNW* 58 (1967): 255-66.

14773   Elisabeth Schüssler Fiorenza, "Redemption as Liberation: Apoc. 1:5f and 5:9f," *CBQ* 36 (1974): 220-32.

14774   André Feuillet, "Les chrétiens prêtres et rois d'après l'Apocalypse. Contribution à l'étude de la conception chrétienne du sacerdoce," *RT* 75 (1975): 40-66.

14775   Christian Wolff, "Die Gemeinde des Christus in der Apokalypse des Johannes," *NTS* 27 (1981): 186-97.

14776   Andrew J. Bandstra, " 'A Kingship and Priests:' Inaugurated Eschatology in the Apocalypse," *CTJ* 27 (1992): 10-25.

1:5

14777   Stefania Cantore, "Colui che ci ama (Ap. 1,5)," *ParSpirV* 10 (1984): 205-14.

14778   Ugo Vanni, "La promozione del regno come responsabilità sacerdotale dei cristiani secondo l'Apocalisse e la Prima Lettera di Pietro," *Greg* 68 (1987): 9-56.

1:6

14779 R. Clark, "Imperial Priesthood of the Believer," *BSac* 92 (1935): 442-49.

14780 A. Gelston, "Royal Priesthood," *EQ* 31 (1959): 152-63.

14781 A. R. Sikora, "Miejsce realizacji kapłaństwa chrześcijan wedlug Apokalipsy św. Jana," *RoczTK* 43 (1996): 161-84.

14782 R. B. Y. Scott, "Behold, He Cometh with Clouds," *NTS* 5 (1958-1959): 127-32.

1:7

14783 Armando J. Levoratti, "El maná escondido (Apoc. 2:1 7)," *RevB* 46 (1984): 257-73.

14784 H. U. von Balthasar, "Die göttlichen Gerichte in der Apokalypse," *IKaZ* 14 (1985): 28-34.

1:8

14785 J. D. Robb, "Ho Erchomenos ('Who is to Come'—NEB)," *ET* 73 (1962): 338-39.

14786 B. Schwank, "Das A und Ω einer 'biblischen Theologie'," *SNTU-A* 21 (1996): 132-45.

1:9-20

14787 L. Ramlot, "Apparition du ressuscité au déporté de Patmos (Apoc. 1, 9-20)," *BVC* 36 (1960): 16-25.

14788 Jon Paulien, "The Role of the Hebrew Cultus, Sanctuary, and Temple in the Plot and Structure of the Book of Revelation," *AUSS* 33 (1995): 245-64.

1:9-17

14789 Vern S. Poythress, "Johannine Authorship and the Use of Intersentence Conjunctions in the Book of Revelation," *WTJ* 47 (1985): 329-36.

1:9-11

14790 B. W. Bacon, "Adhuc in corpore constituto," *HTR* 23 (1930): 305-307.

14791 B. Duda, "J'ai été mort et me voici vivant (Ap. 1,9-1 la. 12-13.17-19)," *AsSeign* 23 (1971): 44-54.

1:9-10

14792 J. E. Brown, "Living in Two Worlds," *ET* 93 (1981): 22-24.

1:9

14793 J. Frings, "Das Patmosexil des Johannes nach Apoc. 1.9," *TQ* 104 (1923): 20-31.

14794 Robert H. Smith, "Why John Wrote the Apocalypse," *CThM* 22 (1995): 356-61.

1:10-16

14795 James H. Charlesworth, "The Jewish Roots of Christology: the Discovery of the Hypostatic Voice," *SJT* 39 (1986): 19-41.

1:10

14796 J. M. Fenasse, "Le Jour du Seigneur (Apoc. 1,10)," *BVC* 61 (1965): 29-43.

14797 Wilfrid Stott, "Note on the Word KYPIAKH [Kyriakos] in Revelation 1:10," *NTS* 12 (1965): 70-75.

14798 Kenneth A. Strand, "Another Look at Lord's Day in the Early Church and in Revelation 1:10," *NTS* 13 (1967): 174-81.

14799 Ugo Vanni, "Il 'Giorno del Signore' in Apoc. 1,10: giorno di purificazione e di discernimento," *RivBib* 26 (1978): 187-99.

14800 Ugo Vanni, "L'eucaristia nel 'giorno del Signore' dell'Apocalisse," *ParSpirV* 7 (1983): 174-85.

14801 Barbara W. Snyder, "Triple-Form and Space/Time Transitions: Literary Structuring Devices in the Apocalypse," *SBLSP* 30 (1991): 440-50.

1:11-13

14802 Armando J. Levoratti, "El maná escondido (Apoc. 2:17)," *RevB* 46 (1984): 257-73.

1:12-19

14803 Giovanni Rinaldi, "Astéras heptá," *BibO* 20 (1978): 303.

1:12-13

14804 B. Duda, "J'ai été mort et me voici vivant (Ap. 1,9-11a. 12-13.17-19)," *AsSeign* 23 (1971): 44-54.

1:13-20

14805 Christopher C. Rowland, "The Vision of the Risen Christ in Revelation. 1:13ff: The Debt of an Early Christology to an Aspect of Jewish Angelology," *JTS* 31 (1980): 1-11.

14806 Harald Sahlin, "Wie wurde ursprünglich die Benennung 'Der Menschensohn' verstanden?" *StTheol* 37 (1983): 147-79.

1:13-18

14807 Franciszek Sieg, "ὅμοιον υἱὸν ἀνθρώπου (Offb. 1,13): Schlußfolgerungen aus der Untersuchung," *FilN* 7 (1994): 3-16.

1:13-16

14808 Eugenio Romero Posé, "Ecclesia in filio hominis (exégesis ticoniana al Apoc. 1,13-16)," *Bur* 25 (1984): 43-82.

1:13-14

14809 J. H. Michael, "A Slight Misplacement in Revelation 1,13-14," *ET* 42 (1930-1931): 380-81.

14810 C. C. Oke, "The Misplacement in Revelation 1,13-14," *ET* 43 (1931-1932): 237.

1:13

14811 P. Joüon, "Apocalypse, 1,13," *RechSR* 24 (1934): 365-66.

14812 T. B. Salter, "*Homoion huion anthrōpou* in Revelation 1.13 and 14.14." *BT* 44 (1993): 349-50.

14813 Franciszek Sieg, "ὅμοιον υἱὸν ἀνθρώπου (Offb. 1,13): Schlußfolgerungen aus der Untersuchung," *FilN* 7 (1994): 3-16.

14814 T. B. Slater, "More on Revelation 1:13 and 14:14," *BT* 47 (1996): 146-49.

1:15-26

> 14815 Paul Gächter, "Die Wahl des Matthias (Apk. 1,15-26)," *ZKT* 71 (1949): 318-46.

1:16

> 14816 Sebastián Bartina, "En su mano derecha siete asteres (Apoc. 1,16)," *EE* 26 (1952): 71-87.
>
> 14817 Sebastián Bartina, "Una espada salia de la boca de su vestido," *EB* 20 (1961): 207-17.
>
> 14818 H. U. von Balthasar, "Die göttlichen Gerichte in der Apokalypse," *IKaZ* 14 (1985): 28-34.
>
> 14819 Michal Wojciechowski, "Seven Churches and Seven Celestial Bodies," *BibN* 45 (1988): 48-50.

1:17-19

> 14820 B. Duda, "J'ai été mort et me voici vivant (Ap. 1,9-11a. 12-13.17-19)," *AsSeign* 23 (1971): 44-54.

1:17-18

> 14821 David E. Aune, "The Apocalypse of John and Graeco-Roman Revelatory Magic," *NTS* 33 (1987): 481-501.

1:18

> 14822 A. Škrinjar, "Fui mortuus, et ecce sum vivens in saecula saeculorum (Apo. 1,18 et 2,8)," *VD* 17 (1937): 97-106.

1:19

> 14823 W. C. van Unnik, "A Formula Describing Prophecy," *NTS* 9 (1963): 86-94.
>
> 14824 Robert L. Thomas, "John's Apocalyptic Outline," *BSac* 123 (1966): 334-41.
>
> 14825 Armando J. Levoratti, "El maná escondido (Apoc. 2:17)," *RevB* 46 (1984): 257-73.
>
> 14826 Christopher R. Smith, "Revelation 1:19: An Eschatologically Escalated Prophetic Connection," *JETS* 33 (1990): 461-66.
>
> 14827 J. Ramsey Michaels, "Revelation 1:19 and the Narrative Voices of the Apocalypse," *NTS* 37 (1991): 604-20.

14828 Gregory K. Beale, "The Interpretative Problem of Revelation," *NovT* 34 (1992): 360-87.

1:29

14829 Armando J. Levoratti, "El maná escondido (Apoc. 2:17)," *RevB* 46 (1984): 257-73.

14830 Petros Vasiliadis, "The Translation of *martyria Iesou* in Revelation," *BT* 36 (1985): 129-34.

2-3

14831 P. A. Bielmeier, "Der ἄγγελος der sieben Gemeinden in Apc. 2 und 3," *TGl* 25 (1933): 207-208.

14832 A. Škrinjar, "Praemia in Apoc. 2 et 3 victoriae proposita," *VD* 13 (1933): 182-86, 232-39, 277-280, 295-301, 333-40.

14833 J. Merle Rife, "The Literary Background of Revelation 2-3," *JBL* (1941): 179-82.

14834 M. Hubert, "L'architecture des lettres aux sept églises," *RB* 67 (1960): 349-53.

14835 Birger Gerhardsson, "De Kristologiska Utsagorna i sänderbreven I Uppenbarelseboken (kap. 2-3)," *SEÅ* 30 (1965): 70-90.

14836 Robert L. Thomas, "Chronological Interpretation of Revelation 2-3," *BSac* 124 (1967): 321-31.

14837 Menno J. Brunk, "Seven Churches of Revelation Two and Three," *BSac* 126 (1969): 240-46.

14838 André Feuillet, "Jalons pour une meilleure intelligence de l'Apocalypse. Les lettres aux églises (chpt. 2 et 3)," *EV* 85 (1975): 209-23.

14839 Jean D. Dubois, "L'hérésie dans les lettres aux églises (Apoc. 2-3)," *FV* 75 (1976): 3-11.

14840 R. Trevijano Etcheverría, "La mision en las iglesias de Asia (Apoc. 2-3)," *Salm* 27 (1979): 205-30.

14841 Daniel Bach, "La structure au service de la prédication. Les sept lettres d'Apocalypse 2-3--fournissent-elles un canevas de lecture théologique?" *ÉTR* 56 (1981): 294-305.

14842 James E. Rosscup, "The 'Overcomer' of the Apocalypse," *GTJ* 3 (1982): 261-86.

14843 Wiard Popkes, "Die Funktion der Sendschreiben in der Apokalypse: Zugleich ein Beitrag zur Spätgeschichte der neutestamentlichen Gleichnisse," *ZNW* 74 (1983): 90-107.

14844 William H. Shea, "The Covenantal Form of the Letters to the Seven Churches," *AUSS* 21 (1983): 71-84.

14845 James L. Boyer, "Are the Seven Letters of Revelation 2-3 Prophetic?" *GTJ* 6 (1985): 267-73.

14846 Jeremy H. Knowles, "Gloryland from Revelation. Letters to the Seven Churches," *BibTo* 23 (1985): 173-81.

14847 Robert L. Muse, "Revelation 2-3: A Critical Analysis of Seven Prophetic Messages," *JETS* 29 (1986): 147-61.

14848 Michal Wojciechowski, "Seven Churches and Seven Celestial Bodies," *BibN* 45 (1988): 48-50.

14849 David E. Aune, "The Form and Function of the Proclamations to the Seven Churches," *NTS* 36 (1990): 182-204.

14850 Anne-Marit Enroth, "The Hearing Formula in the Book of Revelation," *NTS* 36 (1990): 598-608.

14851 John J. Pilch, "Lying and Deceit in the Letters to the Seven Churches: Perspectives from Cultural Antbropology," *BTB* 22 (1992): 126-35.

14852 C. H. H. Scobie, "Local References in the Letters to the Seven Churches," *NTS* 39 (1993): 606-24.

14853 Stephen L. Homcy, " 'To Him Who Overcomes:' A Fresh Look at What 'Victory' Means for the Believer according to the Book of Revelation," *JETS* 38 (1995): 193-201.

14854 R. Rubinkiewicz, "Nawrócenie i pokuta w Księdze Apokahipsy św. Jana," *RoczTK* 43 (1996): 149-60.

2

14855 W. M. Mackay, "Another Look at the Nicolaitans," *EQ* 45 (1973): 111-15.

2:1-7

14856 Wilhelm Thüsing, "Die Bekehrung zur Liebe. Meditation über Apk. 2,1-7," *BibL* 5 (1964): 194-97.

14857 F. Meyer, "Rückkehr zur 'ersten Liebe.' Meditation über den Brief an die Gemeinde von Ephesus (Apk. 2,1-7)," *BibL* 9 (1968): 303-306.

14858 D. A. Carson, "A Church that Does All the Right Things, But. . . ," *CT* 23 (1979): 994-97.

14859 Jean Calloud, "Note sur la lettre à l'église d'Ephèse, Apocalypse 2,1-7," *SémBib* 44 (1986): 38-51.

2:1

14860 Franciszek Sieg, "ὅμοιον υἱὸν ἀνθρώπου (Offb. 1,13): Schlußfolgerungen aus der Untersuchung," *FilN* 7 (1994): 3-16.

2:6

14861 Norbert Brox, "Nikolaos und Nikolaiten," *VC* 19 (1965): 23-30.

14862 Armando J. Levoratti, "El maná escondido (Apoc. 2:17)," *RevB* 46 (1984): 257-73.

14863 Roman Heiligenthal, "Wer waren die 'Nikolaiten'? Ein Beitrag zur Theologiegeschichte des frühen Christentumes," *ZNW* 82 (1991): 133-37.

14864 K. A. Fox, "The Nicolaitans, Nicolaus and the Early Church," *SR* 23 (1994): 485-96.

2:7

14865 Attilio Gangemi, "L'arbero della vita (Ap. 2,7)," *RivBib* 23 (1975): 383-97.

14866 Francesco Saracino, "Quello che ho Spirito dice (Apoc. 2,7 eec.)," *RivBib* 29 (1981): 3-31.

2:8-11

14867 P. Hoyos, "La fidelidad en el combate y el premio (Ape. 2, 8-1 1)," *RivBib* 20 (1958): 73-77, 127-33, 190-93.

14868 Colin J. Hemer, "The Sardis Letter and the Croesus Tradition," *NTS* 19 (1972): 94-97.

14869 Emanuel Messias de Oliveira, "Na perseverança da luta, a certeza da vitória: Um exemplo das primieras communidades (Ap. 2,8-11)," *EB* 15 (1987): 69-76.

14870 Wolfgang Schrage, "Meditation zu Offenbarung 2.8-11," *EvT* 48 (1988): 388-403.

2:8

14871 A. Škrinjar, "Fui mortuus, et ecce sum vivens in saecula saeculoruni (Apo. 1,18 et 2,8)," *VD* 17 (1937): 97-106.

14872 Franciszek Sieg, "ὅμοιον υἱὸν ἀνθρώπου (Offb. 1,13): Schlußfolgerungen mis der Untersuchung," *FilN* 7 (1994): 3-16.

2:11

14873 Attilio Gangemi, "La morte seconda (Ap. 2,11)," *RivBib* 24 (1976): 3-11.

2:12-17

14874 F. Meyer, "Der weiße Stein mit dem neuen Namen. Meditation über das Sendschreiben an Pergamon (Apk. 2,12-1 7)," *BibL* 10 (1969): 291-94.

2:12

14875 R. North, "Thronus Satanae Pergamenus (Apoc. 2,12.13.17)," *VD* 28 (1950): 65-76.

14876 Franciszek Sieg, "ὅμοιον υἱὸν ἀνθρώπου (Offb. 1,13): Schlußfolgerungen aus der Untersuchung," *FilN* 7 (1994): 3-16.

2:13

14877 R. North, "Thronus Satanae Pergamenus (Apoc. 2,12.13.17)," *VD* 28 (1950): 65-76.

14878 Gerard Mussies, "Antipas," *NovT* 7 (1964): 242-44.

14879 Donald S. Deer, "Whose Faith/Loyalty in Revelation 2.13 and 14.12?" *BT* 38 (1987): 328-30.

2:15

14880 Norbert Brox, "Nikolaos und Nikolaiten," *VC* 19 (1965): 23-30.

14881 Roman Heiligenthal, "Wer waren die 'Nikolaiten'? Ein Beitrag zur Theologiegeschichte des frühen Christentumes," *ZNW* 82 (1991): 133-37.

14882 K. A. Fox, "The Nicolaitans. Nicolaus and the Early Church," *SR* 23 (1994): 485-96.

2:16

14883 Sebastián Bartina, " 'Una espada salia de la boca de su vestido'," *EB* 20 (1961): 207-17.

14884 David E. Aune, "The Apocalypse of John and Graeco-Roman Revelatory Magic," *NTS* 33 (1987): 481-501.

2:17

14885 R. North, "Thronus Satanae Pergamenus (Apoc. 2,12.13.17)," *VD* 28 (1950): 65-76.

14886 Attilio Gangemi, "La manna nascosta e il nome nuovo," *RivBib* 25 (1977): 337-56.

14887 Armando J. Levoratti, "El maná escondido (Apoc. 2:17)," *RevB* 46 (1984): 257-73.

2:18-3:6

14888 H. U. von Balthasar, "Die göttlichen Gerichte in der Apokalypse," *IKaZ* 14 (1985): 28-34.

2:18-29

14889 Adela Y. Collins, "Women's History and the Book of Revelation," *SBLSP* 26 (1997): 80-91.

2:18

14890 Franciszek Sieg, "ὅμοιον υἱὸν ἀνθρώπου (Offb. 1,13): Schlußfolgerungen aus der," *FilN* 7 (1994): 3-16:

2:20-23

14891 Ugo Vanni, "La figura della donna nell'Apocalisse," *SM* 40 (1991): 57-94.

2:20

14892 Tina Pippin, "Jezebel Re-Vamped," *Semeia* 69-70 (1995): 221-23.

2:26-28

14893 Attilio Gangemi, "La stella del mattino (Apoc. 2,26-28)," *RivBib* 26 (1978): 241-74.

3:1

14894 A. Škrinjar, "Les sept esprits," *Bib* 16 (1935): 1-24, 113-40.

14895 H. U. von Balthasar, "Die göttlichen Gerichte in der Apokalypse," *IKaZ* 14 (1985): 28-34.

14896 Franciszek Sieg, "ὅμοιον υἱὸν ἀνθρώπου (Offb. 1,13): Schlußfolgerungen aus der Untersuchung," *FilN* 7 (1994): 3-16.

3:2-3

14897 Colin J. Hemer, "The Sardis Letter and the Croesus Tradition," *NTS* 19 (1972): 94-97.

3:3

14898 Richard J. Bauckham, "Synoptic Parousia Parables and the Apocalypse," *NTS* 23 (1977): 162-76.

14899 Richard J. Bauckham, "Synoptic Parousia Parables Again," *NTS* 29 (1983): 129-34.

3:5

14900 J. W. Fuller, " 'I Will Not Erase His Name from the Book of Life'," *JETS* 26 (1983): 297-306.

3:7-13

14901 W. M. Calder, "The Montanists (Apoc. 3, 7-13)," *BJRL* 7 (1923): 309-54.

3:7

14902 Franciszek Sieg, "ὅμοιον υἱὸν ἀνθρώπου (Offb. 1,13): Schlußfolgerungen aus der Untersuchung," *FilN* 7 (1994): 3-16.

3:8-11

14903   P. Morgan, "Receiving Gifts," *ET* 90 (1979): 110-11.

3:8

14904   Evald Lövestam, "Apokalypsen 3:8b," *SEÅ* 30 (1965): 91-101.

3:10

14905   Schuyler Brown, "The Hour of the Trial," *JBL* 85 (1966): 308-14.

14906   Jeffrey L. Townsend, "The Rapture in Revelation 3:10," *BSac* 137 (1980): 252-66.

14907   Thomas R. Edgar, "Robert H. Gundry and Revelation 3:10," *GTJ* 3 (1982): 19-49.

14908   Theodore Mueller, " 'The Word of My Patience' in Revelation 3:10," *CTQ* 46 (1982): 231-34.

14909   David G. Winfrey, "The Great Tribulation: Kept 'Out of' or 'Through'?" *GTJ* 3 (1982): 3-18.

3:11

14910   David E. Aune, "The Apocalypse of John and Graeco-Roman Revelatory Magic," *NTS* 33 (1987): 481-501.

3:12

14911   Dale C. Allison, "4 Q 403 Fragment I, Col I, 38-46 and the Revelation to John," *RevQ* 12 (1986): 409-14.

14912   Richard H. Wilkinson, "The *stylos* of Revelation 3:12 and Ancient Coronation Rites," *JBL* 107 (1988): 498-501.

3:14

14913   Lou H. Silberman, "Farewell to *Ho Amen*," *JBL* 82 (1963): 213-15.

14914   L. Paul Trudinger, "*Amen*, and the Case for a Semitic Original of the Apocalypse," *NovT* 14 (1972): 277-79.

14915   Franciszek Sieg, "ὅμοιον υἱὸν ἀνθρώπου (Offb. 1,13): Schlußfolgerungen aus der Untersuchung," *FilN* 7 (1994): 3-16.

14916 Gregory K. Beale, "The Old Testament Background of Revelation 3,14," *NTS* 42 (1996): 133-52.

3:15-18

14917 Stanley E. Porter, "Why the Laodiceans Received Lukewarm Water," *TynB* 38 (1987): 143-49.

3:15-16

14918 A. Eberhardt, "Das Sendschreiben nach Laodizea," *EvT* 17 (1957): 431-45.

3:15

14919 J. B. Bauer, "Salvator 'nihil medium' amat," *VD* 34 (1956): 352-55.

3:18

14920 M. J. S. Rudwick and E. M. B. Green, "The Laodicean Lukewarmness," *ET* 69 (1957-1958): 176-78.

14921 Paul R. Berger, "Kollyrium für die blinden Augen, Apk. 3:18," *NovT* 27 (1985): 174-95.

3:19

14922 H. U. von Balthasar, "Die göttlichen Gerichte in der Apokalypse," *IKaZ* 14 (1985): 28-34.

3:20

14923 André Feuillet, "Le Cantique des Cantiques et l'Apocalypse. Étude de deux reminiscences du Cantique dans l'Apocalypse johannique," *RechSR* 49 (1961): 321-53.

14924 J. Bours, " 'Siehe, ich stehe vor der Tür.' Eine Meditation zu Apk. 3,20," *BibL* 4 (1963): 271-77.

14925 Timothy Wiarda, "Revelation 3:20: Imagery and Literary Context," *JETS* 38 (1995): 203-12.

3:21

14926 Jarl H. Ulrichsen, "Die sieben Häupter und die zehn Hörner: Zur Datierung der Offenbarung des Johannes," *StTheol* 39 (1985): 1-20.

4:1-22:5

14927 Francisco Montagnini, "Apocalisse 4:1-22:5: L'ordine nel caos," *RivBib* 5 (1957): 180-87.

4-11

14928 Martin Hopkins, "History in the Apocalypse," *BT* 20 (1965): 1340-44.

4-6

14929 François Martin, "Préparation de la rencontre des groupes sémiotique et Bible: Brest 27-31 aout," *SémBib* 57 (1990): 40-56.

4-5

14930 H. J. Flowers, "The Vision of Revelation IV-V," *ATR* 12 (1930): 525-30.

14931 Lucetta Mowry, "Revelation 4-5 and Early Christian Liturgical Usage," *JBL* (1952): 75-84.

14932 André Feuillet, "Jalons pour une meilleure intelligence de l'Apocalypse. Introduction à la partie prophétique," *EV* 85 (1975): 433-43.

14933 Frédéric Matins, "Traces d'une Haggadah pascale chrétienne dans l'Apocalypse de Jean?" *Ant* 56 (1981): 265-95.

14934 Larry W. Hurtado, "Revelation 4-5 in the Light of Jewish Apocalyptic Analogies," *JSNT* 25 (1985): 105-24.

14935 R. Dean Davis, "The Heavenly Court Scene of Revelation 4-5," *AUSS* 25 (1987): 301-302.

14936 Stephen L. Homcy, " 'To Him Who Overcomes:' A Fresh Look at What 'Victory' Means for the Believer According to the Book of Revelation," *JETS* 38 (1995): 193-201.

4:1-5:15

14937 J. A. du Rand, "Die narratiewe Funksie van die Liedere in Openbaring 4:1-5:15," *SkrifK* 12 (1991): 26-35.

4

14938 F. W. Grosheide, "Visioen of werkelijkheid? Apoc. 4 en verwante plaatsen," *GTT* 53 (1953): 1-7.

14939 A. Rüd, "Gottesbild md Gottesverehrung in Apocalypse 4 und 5,6 14," *BL* 24 (1956): 326-32.

14940 André Feuillet, "Quelques énigmes des chapitres 4 à 7 de l'Apocalypse. Suggestions pour l'interprétation du langage image de la Révélation johannique," *EV* 86 (1976): 455-59.

4:1-10

14941 André Feuillet, "Les vingt-quatre vieillards de l'Apocalypse," *RB* 65 (1958): 5-32.

4:1-5

14942 Jon Paulien, "The Role of the Hebrew Cultus, Sanctuary, and Temple in the Plot and Structure of the Book of Revelation," *AUSS* 33 (1995): 245-64.

4:1

14943 Paul Neuenzeit, " 'Ich will dir zeigen, was geschehen muß.' (Apk. 4,1). Zum Problem der Tragik im neutestamentlichen Existenzverständnis," *BibL* 1 (1960): 223-36.

14944 Giovanni Rinaldi, "La porta aperta nel cielo (Ap. 4,1)," *CBQ* 25 (1963): 336-47.

14945 Gregory K. Beale, "The Influence of Daniel upon the Structure and Theology of John's Apocalypse," *JETS* 27 (1984): 413-24.

4:2

14946 Barbara W. Snyder, "Triple-Form and Space/Time Transitions: Literary Structuring Devices in the Apocalypse" *SBLSP* 30 (1991): 440-50.

4:4

14947 A. Škrinjar, "Vingtiquattuor senoires (Apoc. 4, 4. 10; 5, 5-14, etc.)," *VD* 16 (1936): 333-38, 361-68.

14948 Gregory M. Stevenson, "Conceptual Background to Golden Crown Imagery in the Apocalypse of John," *JBL* 114 (1995): 257-72.

4:5

14949 A. Škrinjar, "Les sept esprits (Apoc. 1,4; 3,1; 4,5; 5,6),"*Bib* 16 (1935): 1-24, 113-40.

4:6-11

14950 W. Moock, "Zum Geheimnis Offb. 4, 6-11," *TGl* 28 (1936): 609-12.

4:6-8

14951 Sebastián Bartina, "El toro apocaliptico lleno de 'ojos,' (Ap. 4,6-8; Ct 4, 9)," *EB* 21 (1962): 329-36.

14952 J. Lévêque, "Les quatre vivants de l'Apocalypse," *Chr* 26 (1979): 333-39.

4:6

14953 Raymond R. Brewer, "Revelation 4:6 and Translations Thereof," *JBL* 71 (1952): 227-31.

14954 Robert G. Hall, "Living Creatures in the Midst of the Throne: Another Look at Revelation 4:6," *NTS* 36 (1990): 609-13.

14955 Christfried Böttrich, "Das 'gläserne Meer' in Apk. 4,6/15,2," *BibN* 80 (1995): 5-15.

4:8

14956 N. Walker, "The Origin of the 'Thrice-Holy' (Apoc. 4:8)," *NTS* 5 (1959): 132-33.

14957 J. D. Robb, "Ho Erchomenos ('Who is to Come'—NEB)," *ET* 73 (1962): 338-39.

4:10

14958 A. Škrinjar, "Vingtiquattuor seniores (Apoc. 4, 4. 10; 5, 5-14 etc)," *VD* 16 (1936): 333-38, 361-68.

14959 Gregory M. Stevenson, "Conceptual Background to Golden Crown Imagery in the Apocalypse of John," *JBL* 114 (1995): 257-72.

5-8

14960 W. S. Taylor, "The Seven Seals in the Revelation of John," *JTS* (1930): 266-71.

5

14961 E. A. Russell, "A Roman Law Parallel to Revelation Five," *BSac* 115 (1958): 258-64.

14962 William H. Shea, "Revelation 5 and 19 as Literary Reciprocals," *AUSS* 22 (1984): 249-57.

14963 J. Daryl Charles, "Imperial Pretensions and the Throne-Vision of the Lamb: Observations on the Function of Revelation 5," *CTR* 7 (1993): 85-97.

14964 Peder Borgen, "Moses, Jesus, and the Roman Emperor. Observations in Philo's Writings and the Revelation of John," *NovT* 38 (1996): 145-59.

5:1-14

14965 N. Mulde, "Christus, der Vollender der Geschichte. Meditationsgedanken zu Apk. 5,1-14," *GeistL* 38 (1965): 387-92.

14966 H. U. von Balthasar, "Die göttlichen Gerichte in der Apokalypse," *IKaZ* 14 (1985): 28-34.

14967 Roland Bergmeier, "Die Buchrolle und das Lamm (Apk. 5 und 10)," *ZNW* 76 (1985): 225-42.

14968 Paul J. Achtemeier, "Revelation 5:1-14," *Int* 40 (1986): 283-88.

14969 J. Daryl Charles, "An Apocalyptic Tribute to the Lamb," *JETS* 34 (1991): 461-73.

5:1-5

14970 H. Müller, "Die himmlische Ratsversammlung. Motivgeschichtliches zu Apc. 5:1-5," *ZNW* 54 (1963): 254-67.

5:1-3

14971 O. Roller, "Das Buch mit sieben Siegeln," *ZNW* 36 (1937): 98-113.

5:1

14972 K. Staritz, "Zu Offenbarung Johannis 5,1," *ZNW* 30 (1931): 157-70.

5:5

14973 Henry S. Coffin, "To Him That Overcometh: A Meditation," *Int* 5 (1951): 40-45.

14974 M. Hasitschka, " 'Überwunden hat der Löwe aus dem Stamm Juda' (Offb. 5,5). Funktion und Herkunft des Bildes vom Lamm in der Offenbarung des Johannes," *ZKT* 116 (1994): 487-93.

5:6-14

14975   A. Rüd, "Gottesbild und Gottesverehrung in Apocalypse 4 und 5,6-14," *BL* 24 (1956): 326-32.

5:6-13

14976   Jarl H. Ulrichsen, "Die sieben Häupter und die zehn Hörner: Zur Datierung der Offenbarung des Johannes," *StTheol* 39 (1985): 1-20.

5:6

14977   A. Škrinjar, "Les sept esprits (Apoc. 1,4; 3,1; 4,5; 5,6)," *Bib* 16 (1935): 1-24, 113-40.

14978   Sebastián Bartina, "Los siete ojos del cordero (Ap. 5, 6)," *EB* 21 (1962): 325-28.

14979   Jacobus C. de Smidt, "Die Oë van die Gees in die Boek Openbaring—'n Teologiese Perspektief," *ScrSA* 54 (1995): 159-76.

5:8-14

14980   H. Asmussen, "Predigt über Offenbarung 5,8-14," *EvT* 1 (1934-1935): 455-61.

5:9-10

14981   Elisabeth Schüssler Fiorenza, "Redemption as Liberation: Apoc. 1:5f and 5:9f," *CBQ* 36 (1974): 220-32.

14982   Andrew J. Bandstra, " 'A Kingship and Priests:' Inaugurated Eschatology in the Apocalypse," *CTJ* 27 (1992): 10-25.

5:10

14983   A. Gelston, "Royal Priesthood," *EQ* 31 (1959): 152-63.

        W. J. Rewak, "The 'Reign of the Saints'," *BibTo* 12 (1965): 1345-50.

14985   Ugo Varmi, "La promozione del regno come responsabilità sacerdotale del cristiani secondo l'Apocalisse e la Prima Lettera di Pietro," *Greg* 68 (1987): 9-56.

14986 A. R. Sikora, "Miejsce realizacji kaplánstwa chrześcijan wedlug Apokalipsy św. Jana," *RoczTK* 43 (1996): 161-84.

5:11-14

14987 C. Augrain, "La grande doxologie (Ap. 5,11-14)," *AsSeign* 24 (1970): 29-35.

14988 Wendell W. Frerichs, "God's Song of Revelation: from Easter to Pentecost in the Apocalypse," *WW* 6 (1986): 216-28.

5:11

14989 J. H. Michael, "Ten Thousand Times Ten Thousand," *ET* 46 (1934-1935): 567.

5:18-20

14990 Albert Segond, "Lire l'Épître de Jean, chap. 5:18-20," *RHPR* 45 (1965): 349-51.

6:1-16:21

14991 R. Schinzer, "Die sieben Siegel, Posaunen und Schalen und die Absicht der Offenbarung Johannis," *TBe* 11 (1980): 52-66.

6

14992 Daniel K. K. Wong, "The First Horseman of Revelation 6," *BSac* 153 (1996): 212-26.

6:1-18

14993 G. Baldensperger, "Les cavaliers de l'Apocalypse (6, 1-18)," *RHPR* 4 (1924): 1-31.

6:1-8

14994 F. Dornseiff, "Die Apokalypsen Reiter (Apc. 6, 1ff)," *ZNW* 38 (1939): 196-97.

14995 J. S. Considine, "The Rider on the White Horse: Apocalypse 6:1-8," *CBQ* 6 (1944): 406-22.

14996 Mathias Rissi, "The Rider on the White Horse: A Study of Revelation 6:1-8," *Int* 18 (1964): 407-18.

14997 André Feuillet, "Le premier cavalier de l'Apocalypse," *ZNW* 57 (1966): 229-59.

14998 F. Meyer, "Die furchtbaren Reiter. Meditation zu Apk. 6,1-8," *BibL* 12 (1971): 45-48.

14999 Michael Bachmann, "Der erste apokalyptische Reiter und die Anlage des letzten Buches der Bibel," *Bib* 67 (1986): 240-75.

15000 Michael Bachmann, "Die apokalyptischen Reiter: Dürers Holzschnitt und die Auslegungsgeschichte von Apk. 6:1-8," *ZTK* 86 (1989): 33-58.

6:2

15001 K. Pieper, "Der Charakter des ersten apokalyptischen Reiters (Apk. 6,2)," *TGl* 37 (1947): 54-57.

15002 Zane C. Hodges, "The First Horseman of the Apocalypse," *BSac* 119 (1962): 324-34.

15003 Allen Kerkeslager, "Apollo, Greco-Roman Prophecy, and the Rider on the White Horse in Revelation 6:2," *JBL* 112 (1993): 116-21.

15004 Daniel K. K. Wong, "The First Horseman of Revelation 6," *BSac* 153 (1996): 212-26.

6:5-6

15005 Ugo Vanni, "Il terzo 'sigillo' dell'Apocalisse (Ap. 6,5-6): Simbolo dell'ingiustizia sociale?" *Greg* 59 (1978): 691-719.

6:8

15006 J. H. Michael, "The Position of the Wild Beasts in Revelation 6:8b," *ET* (1947): 166.

6:9-17

15007 F. Meyer, "Das fünfte und sechste Siegel. Anregungen zu einer Meditation über Offenbarung 6,9-17," *BibL* 13 (1972): 284-89.

6:9-11

15008 P. van den Eynde, "Le Dieu du désordre. Commentaire synthétique d'Apocalypse 6, 9-11," *BVC* 74 (1967): 39-51.

15009 André Feuillet, "Revelation 6:9-11—A New Interpretation: Abstract of 'Les martyrs de l'humanité et l'agneau égorgé.

Une interpretation nouvelle de la prière des égorgés en Ap. 6, 9-11," *TD* 26 (1978): 258-61.

15010   John P. Heil, "The Fifth Seal as a Key to the Book of Revelation," *Bib* 74 (1993): 220-43.

6:9

15011   Michel Gourgues, "The Thousand-Year Reign: Terrestrial or Celestial?" *CBQ* 47 (1985): 676-81.

6:10

15012   J. M. Ford, "Shalom in the Johannine Corpus," *HBT* 6 (1984): 67-89.

6:12-7:17

15013   Andrew E. Steinmann, "The Tripartite Structure of the Sixth Seal, the Sixth Trumpet, and the Sixth Bowl of John's Apocalypse," *JETS* 35 (1992): 69-79.

15014   J. van Ruiten, "Der alttestamentliche Hintergrund von Apokalypse 6:12-17," *EB* 53 (1995): 239-60.

6:12-7:3

15015   D. Holwerda, "Ein neuer Schlüßel zum 17. Kapitel der johanneischen Offenbarung," *EB* 53 (1995): 387-96.

6:12-16

15016   Peter Maser, "Sonne und Mond: exegetische Erwägungen zum Fortleben der spätantik-jüdischens in der früh-christlichen Kunst," *K* 25 (1983): 41-67.

6:13-22

15017   Armando J. Levoratti, "El maná escondido (Apoc. 2:17)," *RevB* 46 (1984): 257-73.

6:16

15018   H. U. von Balthasar, "Die göttlichen Gerichte in der Apokalypse," *IKaZ* 14 (1985): 28-34.

7

15019   André Feuillet, "Les 144.000 Israélites marqués d'un sceau," *NovT* 9 (1967): 191-224.

15020   Terence J. Keegan, "Revelation: A Source of Encouragement," *BibTo* 19 (1981): 373-77.

15021 Albert Geyser, "The Twelve Tribes in Revelation: Judean and Judeo-Christian Apocalypticism," *NTS* 28 (1982): 388-99.

15022 Ross E. Winkle, "Another Look at the List of Tribes in Revelation 7," *AUSS* 27 (1989): 53-67.

15023 Christopher R. Smith, "The Tribes in Revelation 7 and the Literary Competence of John the Seer," *JETS* 38 (1995): 213-18.

7:1-17

15024 Jonathan A. Draper, "The Heavenly Feast of Tabernacles: Revelation 7:1-17," *JSNT* 19 (1983): 133-47.

7:1-12

15025 A. M. Vitti, "Servi Dei nostri (Apoc. 7,1-12)," *VD* 10 (1930): 321-29.

7:2-12

15026 R. E. Murphy, "The Epistle for All Saints (Ap. 7:2-12)," *AmER* 121 (1949): 203-209.

15027 Joseph Comblin, "Le rassemblement de l'Israël de Dieu (Ap. 7,2-12)," *AsSeign* 89 (1963): 15-33.

15028 E. Nellessen, "Aufbruch und Vollendung der Königsherrschaft. Eine Meditation zu den Perikopen des Allerheiligenfestes," *BibL* 9 (1968): 222-29.

7:2-4

15029 A. R. Carmona, "Presente y futuro de la Iglesia," *CuBi* 30 (1973): 19-25.

15030 Joseph Comblin, "Le rassemblement du peuple de Dieu. Ap. 7,2-4. 9-14," *AsSeign* 66 (1973): 42-49.

7:4

15031 J. M. Bover, "144,000 signati," *EE* 11 (1932): 535-47.

7:5-8

15032 Christopher R. Smith, "The Portrayal of the Church as the New Israel in the Names and Order of the Tribes in Revelation 7.5-8," *JSNT* 39 (1990): 111-18.

15033 Richard J. Bauckham, "The List of the Tribes in Revelation 7 Again," *JSNT* 42 (1991): 99-115.

7:9-17

15034 A. Viard, "Une foule immense devant le trône de Dieu," *EV* 83 (1983): 91-92.

15035 Wendell W. Frerichs, "God's Song of Revelation: From Easter to Pentecost in the Apocalypse," *WW* 6 (1986): 216-28.

15036 Balmer H. Kelly, "Revelation 7:9-17," *Int* 40 (1986): 288-95.

7:9-14

15037 A. R. Carmona, "Presente y futuro de la iglesia," *CuBí* 30 (1973): 19-25.

15038 Joseph Comblin, "Le rassemblement du peuple de Dieu: Ap. 7, 2-4. 9-14," *AsSeign* 66 (1973): 42-49.

7:9

15039 C. Augrain, "La vision de la foule innombrable (Ap. 7,9.14b-17)," *AsSeign* 25 (1969): 39-44.

15040 J. M. James, "All Saints Entering the Marketplace with Open Hands," *ET* 90 (1978): 18-19.

7:10

15041 Paul Ellingworth, "Salvation to our God," *BT* 34 (1983): 444-45.

7:12

15042 J. E. Burkhart, "Reshaping Table Blessings. 'Blessing. . . and Thanksgiving to Our God'," *Int* 48 (1994): 50-60.

7:14-17

15043 C. Augrain, "La vision de la foule innombrable (Ap. 7,9.1 4b-17)," *AsSeign* 25 (1969): 39-44.

15044 Kirsten Nielsen, "Shepherd, Lamb, and Blood: Imagery in the Old Testament, Use and Reuse," *StTheol* 46 (1992): 121-32.

7:14

15045 A. Škrinjar, "Hi sunt qui venerunt de tribulatione magna (Apc. 7,14)," *VD* 23 (1943): 115-21, 138-46.

7:37-39

15046 Jean Daniélou, "Le symbolisme de l'eau vive," *RevSR* 32 (1958): 335-46.

8-9

15047 Elian Cuvillier, "Jugement et destruction du monde dans l'Apocalypse de Jean: Notes exégétiques sur Apoc. 8-9 et Apoc. 15-16," *FV* 91 (1992): 53-67.

8:1

15048 W. Ernest Beet, "Silence in Heaven," *ET* 44 (1932): 74-76.

Manuel Beneitez, "Algunas reflexiones en torno al 'séptimo sello' del Apocalipsis (Ape. 8,1)," *EE* 63 (1988): 29-62.

8:2-6

15050 Jon Paulien, "The Role of the Hebrew Cultus, Sanctuary, and Temple in the Plot and Structure of the Book of Revelation," *AUSS* 33 (1995): 245-64.

8:9

15051 C. C. Oke, "Revelation 8:9," *ET* 43 (1931-1932): 428-29.

9:1-4

15052 Giovanni Rinaldi, "Il raduno nel cielo (Apoc. 9,1-4)," *BibO* 4 (1962): 161-63.

9:8

15053 J. Michl, "Sie hatten Haare wie Weiberhaare (Apok. 9,8)," *BZ* 23 (1935): 266-88.

15054 J. Michl, "Zu Apk. 9,8," *Bib* 23 (1942): 192-93.

15055 Ugo Vanni, "La figura della donna nell'Apocalisse," *SM* 40 (1991): 57-94.

15056 Robert P. Gordon, "Loricate Locusts in the Targum to Nahum iii 17 and Revelation ix 9," *VT* 33 (1983): 338-39.

9:10-26

15057 A. Wikenhauser, "Doppelträume," *Bib* 29 (1948): 100-11.

9:12

15058   Gerard Mussies, "*Dyo* in Apocalypse 9:12 and 16," *NovT* 9 (1967): 51-54.

9:13-11:14

15059   Andrew E. Steinmann, "The Tripartite Structure of the Sixth Seal, the Sixth Trumpet, and the Sixth Bowl of John's Apocalypse," *JETS* 35 (1992): 69-79.

9:13-14

15060   Dale C. Allison, "4 Q 403 Fragment 1, Col 1, 38-46 and the Revelation to John," *RevQ* 12 (1986): 409-14.

9:16

15061   Gerard Mussies, "*Dyo* in Apocalypse 9:12 and 16," *NovT* 9 (1967): 51-54.

10

15062   Roland Bergmeier, "Die Buchrolle und das Lamm (Apk. 5 und 10)," *ZNW* 76 (1985): 225-42.

15063   Friedrich W. Horn, "Die sieben Donner: Erwägungen zu Offenbarung 10," *SNTU-A* 17 (1992): 215-29.

10:3

15064   J. H. Michael, "The Unrecorded Thunder-Voices (Apoc. 10, 3)," *ET* 36 (1924-1925): 424-27.

10:4

15065   Jean-Pierre Ruiz, "Hearing and Seeing but Not Saying: A Look at Revelation 10:4 and 2 Corinthians 12:4," *SBLSP* 33 (1994): 182-202.

11-12

15066   E.-B. Allo, "À propos d'Apocalypse 11 et 12," *RB* 31 (1922): 572-83.

15067   L. Gry, "Les chapitres XI et XII de l'Apocalypse," *RB* 31 (1922): 203-14.

11

15068   André Feuillet, "Essai d'interprétation du Chapitre XI de l'Apocalypse," *NTS* 4 (1957-1958): 183-200.

11:1-14

15069 Allan McNicol, "Revelation 11:1-14 and the Structure of the Apocalypse," *RQ* 22 (1979): 193-202.

11:1-13

15070 Charles H. Giblin, "Revelation 11:1-13: Its Form, Function, and Contextual Integration," *NTS* 30 (1984): 433-59.

11:1

15071 Kenneth A. Strand, "An Overlooked Old Testament Background to Revelation 11:1," *AUSS* 22 (1984): 317-25.

15072 Michael Bachmann, "Himmlisch: der 'Tempel Gottes' von Apk. 11.1," *NTS* 40 (1994): 474-80.

11:3-13

15073 Laurentius van den Eerenbeemt, "Elias propheta in novissimis diebus (Apoc. 11, 3-13)," *VD* 4 (1924): 259-63.

15074 J. S. Considine, "The Two Witnesses: Apoc. 11:3-13," *CBQ* 8 (1946): 377-92.

15075 Richard J. Bauckham, "The Martyrdom of Enoch and Elijah: Jewish or Christian?" *JBL* 95 (1976): 447-58.

15076 Johannes M. Nützel, "Zum Schicksal der eschatologischen Propheten," *BZ* 20 (1976): 59-94.

15077 A. Greve, " 'Mine to vidner.' Et forsog pa at identificere de to Jerusalemitiske vidner (Apok. 11,3-13)," *DTT* 40 (1977): 128-38.

15078 Jean-P. Charlier, "Mort et résurrection du témoin de Dieu selon le cinquième évangile," *VS* 133 (1979): 324-36.

11:3-12

15079 Kenneth A. Strand, "The Two Witnesses of Revelation 11:3-12," *AUSS* 19 (1981): 127-35.

11:3-7

15080 F. Diekamp, "Nikomedes ein unbekannter Erklärer der Apokalypse," *Bib* 14 (1933): 448-51.

11:4

15081 Kenneth A. Strand, "The Two Olive Trees of Zechariah 4 and Revelation 11," *AUSS* 20 (1982): 257-61.

11:8-17

15082 Jarl H. Ulrichsen, "Die sieben Häupter und die zehn Hörner: Zur Datiering der Offenbarung des Johannes," *StTheol* 39 (1985): 1-20.

11:11-12

15083 Édouard Delebecque, " 'Je vis' dans l'Apocalypse," *RT* 88 (1988): 460-66.

11:12

15084 James R. Royse, " 'Their Fifteen Enemies:' The Text of Revelation 11:12 in P47 and 1611," *JTS* 31 (1980): 78-80.

11:19-12:18

15085 J. A. Colunga, "La mujer del Apocalipsis (Apoc. 11,19-12,18)," *Salm* 1 (1954): 675-87.

11:19

15086 Francisco Montagnini, "L'église à la recherche du Christ. Ap. 1 1,19a; 12, 1-6.10ab," *AsSeign* 66 (1973): 22-27.

15087 Jon Paulien, "The Role of the Hebrew Cultus, Sanctuary, and Temple in the Plot and Structure of the Book of Revelation," *AUSS* 33 (1995): 245-64.

12-14

15088 J. M. Ford, "Shalom in the Johannine Corpus," *HBT* 6 (1984): 67-89.

12-13

15089 Jean Calloud, "Apocalypse 12-13: Essai d'analyse sémiotique," *FV* 75 (1976): 26-78.

15090 Elian Cuvillier, "Apocalypse 20: Prédiction ou Prédication?" *ÉTR* 59 (1984): 345-54.

15091 Jan W. van Henten, "Dragon Myth and Imperial Ideology in Revelation 12-13," *SBLSP* 33 (1994): 496-515.

12

15092 J. M. Bover, "El cap. 12 del Apoc. y el Gen. 3," *EE* 1 (1922): 319-36.

15093 F. X. Steinmetzer, "Der apokalyptische Drache," *TGl* 28 (1936): 281-90.

15094   J. Lortzing, "Die inneren Beziehungen zwischen Jo. 2,1-11 und Offenbarung 12," *TGl* 29 (1937): 498-529.

15095   Sherman E. Johnson, "Notes and Comments: Apocalypse 12," *ATR* 21 (1939): 314.

15096   Joseph Sickenberger, "Die Messiasmutter im 12. Kapitel der Apokalypse," *TQ* 126 (1946): 357-427.

15097   R. E. Murphy, "Allusion to Mary in the Apocalypse: Newman's Interpretation of the Twelfth Chapter," *TS* 10 (1949): 565-73.

15098   Dominic J. Unger, "Cardinal Newman and Apocalypse XII," *TS* 11 (1950): 356-67.

15099   B. J. Le Frois, "The Woman Clothed with the Sun," *AmER* 126 (1952): 161-8O.

15100   F.-M. Braun, "La femme et le dragon," *BVC* 7 (1954): 63-72.

15101   F.-M. Braun, "La femme vêtue de soleil (Apoc. XII)," *RT* 55 (1955): 639-69.

15102   Lucien Cerfaux, "La vision de la femme et du dragon de l'Apocalypse en relation avec le Protévangile," *ETL* 31 (1955): 21-33.

15103   A. Romeo, "La donna ravvolta dal sole (Apoc. 12)," *RivBib* 4 (1956): 218-32, 314-29.

15104   André Feuillet, "Le messie et sa mère d'après le chapitre XII de l'Apocalypse," *RB* 66 (1959): 55-86.

15105   J. Michl, "Die Deutung der apokalyptischen Frau in der Gegenwart," *BZ* 3 (1959): 301-10.

15106   P. P. James, "Mary and the Great Sign," *AmER* 147 (1960): 321-29.

15107   S. Gahan, " 'The Woman Clothed with the Sun' according to St. Lawrence of Brindisi," *AmER* 147 (1962): 395-402.

15108   J. E. Bruns, "The Contrasted Women of Apocalypse 12 and 17," *CBQ* 26 (1964): 459-63.

15109   A. Molnar, "Apocalypse 12 dans l'interprétation Hussite," *RHPR* 45 (1965): 212-31.

15110 Simone Petrement, "Une suggestion de Simone Weil à propos d'Apocalypse 12," *NTS* 11 (1965): 291-96.

15111 Francisco Montagnini, "Le signe d'Apocalypse 12 à la lumière de la christologie du Nouveau Testament," *NRT* 89 (1967): 401-16.

15112 Josef Ernst, "Die 'himmlische Frau' im 12. Kapitel der Apokalvpse," *TGl* 58 (1968): 39-59.

15113 Francisco Montagnini, "La chiesa alla ricérca di Cristo (Apoc. 12)," *BibO* 15 (1973): 27-32.

15114 Henri D. Saffrey, "Relire l'Apocalypse à Patmos," *RB* 82 (1975): 385-417.

15115 Akira Satake, "Sieg Christi-Heil der Christen. Eine Betrachtung von Apc. XII," *AJBI* 1 (1975): 105-25.

15116 Roger D. Aus, "The Relevance of Isaiah 66:7 to Revelation 12 and 2 Thessalonians 1," *ZNW* 67 (1976): 252-68.

15117 J. Pikaza, "Apocalipsis XII. El nacimiento pascual del salvador," *Salm* 23 (1976): 217-56.

15118 André Feuillet, "Le chapitre XII de l'Apocalypse. Son caractère synthétique et sa richesse doctrinale," *EV* 88 (1978): 674-83.

15119 André Feuillet, "Der Sieg der Frau nach dem Protoevangelium," *IKaZ* 7 (1978): 26-35.

15120 Michèle Morgen, "Apocalypse 12, un targum de l'Ancien Testament," *FV* 80 (1981) 63-74.

15121 Tecle Vetrali, "La donna dell'Apocalisse," *ParSpirV* 6 (1982): 152-70.

15122 W. Radl, "Befreiung aus dem Gefängnis," *BZ* 27 (1983): 81-96.

15123 Hildegard Gollinger, "Das 'grosse Zeicht en.' Offb. 12--das zentrale Kapitel der Offenharung des Johannes," *BK* 39 (1984): 66-75.

15124 William H. Shea, "The Parallel Literary Structure of Revelation 12 and 20," *AUSS* 23 (1985): 37-54.

15125 Ivan M. Benson, "Revelation 12 and the Dragon of Antiquity," *RQ* 29 (1987): 97-102.

15126 Enzo Bianchi, "In adorazione: all'agnello o alla bestia?" *ParSpirV* 15 (1987): 229-46.

15127 Allan Boesak, "The Woman and the Dragon: Struggle and Victory in Revelation 12," *Soj* 16 (1987): 27-31.

15128 Catherine Keller, "Die Frau in der Wüste: ein feministisch-theologischer Midrasch zu Offenbarung 12," *EvT* 50 (1990): 414-32.

15129 Stephen L. Homcy, " 'To Him Who Overcomes:' A Fresh Look at What 'Victory' Means for the Believer According to the Book of Revelation," *JETS* 38 (1995): 193-201.

15130 Joy A. Schroeder, "Revelation 12: Female Figures and Figures of Evil," *WW* 15 (1995): 175-81.

15131 D.-E. Guery, "Les signes de la femme et du dragon: Apocalypse 12," *LV* 45 (1996): 23-33.

12:1-17

15132 A. Kassing, "Das Weib und der Drache," *BK* 15 (1960): 114-16.

15133 Charles Hauret, "Eve transfigurée: de la Genèse à l'Apocalypse," *RHPR* 59 (1979): 327-39.

15134 Emmanuele Testa, "La struttura di Ap. 12,1-17," *SBFLA* 34 (1984): 225-38.

12:1-9

15135 Bill Kellermann, "O Holy Nightmare: Incarnation and Apocalypse," *Soj* 14 (1985): 34-36.

12:1-6

15136 Francisco Montagnini, "L'église à la recherche du Christ: Ap. 11,1 9a; 12, 1-6.10ab," *AsSeign* 66 (1973): 22-27.

12:1-5

15137 Gregory H. Dix, "The Heavenly Wisdom and the Divine Logos in Jewish Apocalyptic: A Study of the Vision of the Woman and the Man-Child (Apoc. 12, 1-5, 13-17)," *JTS* 26 (1924-1925): 1-12.

15138 Ugo Vanni, "La figuta della donna nell'Apocalisse," *SM* 40 (1991) 57-94.

12:1

15139 L. Fonck, "Apocalypse 12,1," *VD* 2 (1922): 353-57.

15140 A. Rivera, "Inimicitias ponam . . . signum magnum apparuit. (Gen. 3,15; Apoc. 12,1)," *VD* 21 (1941): 113-22, 183-89.

15141 Dominic J. Unger, "Did Saint John See the Virgin Mary in Glory?" *CBQ* 11 (1949): 249-62, 392-405; 12 (1950) 75-83, 155-61. 292-300, 405-15.

15142 J. Gallus, "Scholion ad 'Mulierem' Apocalypseos (12,1)," *VD* 30 (1952): 334-40.

12:2

15143 Josef Blinzler, "Rechtsgeschichtliches zur Hinrichtung des Zebedaiden Jakobus (Apk. xii 2)," *NovT* 5 (1961-1962): 191-206.

12:3

15144 Michel Gourgues, "The Thousand-Year Reign: Terrestrial or Celestial?" *CBQ* 47 (1985): 676-81.

12:4-5

15145 Hans K. La Rondelle, "The Biblical Concept of Armageddon," *JETS* 28 (1985): 21-31.

12:6-17

15146 Ugo Vanni, "La figura della donna nell'Apocalisse," *SM* 40 (1991): 57-94.

12:7-12

15147 H. U. von Balthasar, "Die göttlichen Gerichte in der Apokalypse," *IKaZ* 14 (1985): 28-34.

12:8-18

15148 Jarl H. Ulrichsen, "Die sieben Häupter und die zehn Hörner: zur Datierung der Offenbarung des Johannes," *StTheol* 39 (1985): 1-20.

12:9

15149   P. Joüon, "Le grand dragon et l'ancien serpent (Apoc. 12:9 et Gen. 3:14)," *RechSR* 17 (1927): 444-46.

15150   J. P. Jossua, "Die alte Schlange wurde 'gestürzt' (Offb. 12.9)," *Conci* 11 (1975): 207-14.

15151   Petros Vasiliadis, "The Translation of *martyria Iesou* in Revelation," *BT* 36 (1985): 129-34.

12:10

15152   Francisco Montagnini, "L'église à la recherche du Christ: Ap. 11,1 9a; 12, 1-6.1Oab," *AsSeign* 66 (1973): 22-27.

12:13-17

15153   Gregory H. Dix, "The Heavenly Wisdom and the Divine Logos in Jewish Apocalyptic: A Study of the Vision of the Woman and the Man-Child (Apoc. 12, 1-5, 13-17)," *JTS* 26 (1924-1925): 1-12.

15154   Bill Kellermann, "O Holy Nightmare: Incarnation and Apocalypse," *Soj* 14 (1985): 34-36.

12:13

15155   C. Rösch, "Mulier, draco et bestiae in Apoc. 12:13," *VD* 8 (1928): 271-75.

12:15-16

15156   Paul S. Minear, "Far as the Curse Is Found: The Point of Revelation 12:15-16," *NovT* 33 (1991): 71-77.

12:17

15157   Michel Gourgues, "The Thousand-Year Reign: Terrestrial or Celestial?" *CBQ* 47 (1985): 676-81.

15158   Hans K. La Rondelle, "The Biblical Concept of Armageddon," *JETS* 28 (1985): 21-31.

15159   Petros Vasiliadis, "The Translation of *martyria Iesou* in Revelation," *BT* 36 (1985): 129-34.

15160   Michael Topham, "A Human Being's Measurement, Which Is an Angel's," *ET* 100 (1989): 217-18.

13

15161   J. Koch-Mehrin, "Die Stellung des Christen zum Staat nach Röm. 13 und Apok. 13," *EvT* 7 (1947-1948): 378-401.

15162   William Barclay, "Revelation 13," *ET* 70 (1958-1959): 260-64, 292-96.

15163   John F. Walvoord, "Prophecy of the Ten-Nation Confederacy," *BSac* 124 (1967): 99-105.

15164   Jarl H. Ulrichsen, "Dyret i Åpenbaringen: en skisse til tidshistorisk forståelse av kapitlene 13 og 17," *NTT* 87 (1986): 167-77.

15165   D. A. DeSilva, "The 'Image of the Beast' and the Christians in Asia Minor: Escalation of Sectarian Tension in Revelation 13," *TriJ* 12 (1991): 185-208.

13:1-18

15166   Albert H. Baldinger, "A Beastly Coalition. An Expository Sermon on the Revelation 13:1-18," *Int* 2 (1948): 444-50.

13:1-14

15167   Jarl H. Ulrichsen, "Die sieben Häupter und die zehn Hörner: Zur Datierung der Offenbarung des Johannes," *StTheol* 39 (1985): 1-20.

13:1-10

15168   George W. Buchanan, "The Word of God and the Apocalyptic Vision," *SBLSP* 17 (1978): 183-92.

13:1

15169   Michel Gourgues, "The Thousand-Year Reign: Terrestrial or Celestial?" *CBQ* 47 (1985): 676-81.

13:2

15170   K. Hanhart, "The Four Beasts of Daniel's Vision in the Night in the Light of Revelation 13:2," *NTS* 27 (1981): 576-83.

13:3

15171   Larry J. Kreitzer, "Hadrian and the Nero Redivivus Myth," *ZNW* 79 (1988): 92-115.

13:5

15172 Gregory K. Beale, "A Reconsideration of the Text of Daniel in the Apocalypse," *Bib* 67 (1986): 539-43.

13:6

15173 J. Neville Birdsall, "Revelation 13:6," *JTS* 14 (1963): 399-400.

13:7

15174 H. U. von Balthasar, "Die göttlichen Gerichte in der Apokalypse," *IKaZ* 14 (1985): 28-34.

13:10

15175 J. Schmid, "Zur Textkritik der Apokalypse (13:10; 18:2)," *ZNW* 43 (1950-1951): 112-28.

13:11

15176 Michel Gourgues, "The Thousand-Year Reign: Terrestrial or Celestial?" *CBQ* 47 (1985): 676-81.

13:13-15

15177 Steven J. Scherrer, "Signs and Wonders in the Imperial Cult: A New Look at a Roman Religious Institution in the Light of Revelation 13:13-15," *JBL* 103 (1984): 599-610.

13:15-17

15178 Hans K. La Rondelle, "The Biblical Concept of Armageddon," *JETS* 28 (1985): 21-31.

13:16

15179 Edwin A. Judge, "The Mark of the Beast, Revelation 13:16," *TynB* 42 (1991): 158-60.

13:17-18

15180 Evert M. Bruins, "The Number of the Beast," *NTT* 23 (1969): 401-407.

13:18

15181 C. Bruston, "La tête égorgée et le chiffre 666," *ZNW* 5 (1904): 258-61.

15182 B. Sanders, "The Number of the Beast in Revelation 13, 18," *JBL* 37 (1918): 95-99.

15183   W. Hadorn, "Die Zahl 666, ein Hinweis auf Trajan," *ZNW* 19 (1919-1920): 11-28.

15184   G. Menken, "Het getal 666," *GTT* 36 (1935): 136-52.

15185   E. Vogt, "El número 666 del Apocalipsis," *RevB* 6 (1944): 192-94.

15186   F. Cramer, "Die symbolische Zah 666 in der Apocalypse 13,18," *TGl* 44 (1954): 63-64.

15187   Thomas Brady, "The Number of the Beast in Seventeenth- and Eighteenth-Century England," *EQ* 45 (1973): 219-40.

15188   W. Baines, "The Number of the Beast in Revelation 13:18," *HeyJ* 16 (1975): 195-96.

15189   David Brady, "1666: The Year of the Beast," *BJRL* 61 (1978-1979): 314-36.

15190   Gregory K. Beale, "The Danielic Background for Revelation 13:18 and 17:9," *TynB* 31 (1980): 163-70.

15191   Michael Oberweis, "Die Bedeutung der neutestamentlichen 'Rätselzahlen' 666 (Apk. 13:18) und 153 (Joh. 21:11)," *ZNW* 77 (1986): 226-41.

14-15

15192   Kirsten Nielsen, " 'Gud Herren kaldte på ilden til dom.' Dommedagsmotivet og dets forskydninger," *DTT* 58 (1995): 3-15.

14

15193   Sebastián Bartina, "Un nuevo semitisrno en Apocalipsis 14: Tierra o ciudad," *EB* 27 (1968): 347-49.

14:1-5

15194   R. McCormack, "A Note on Apocalypse 14,1-5," *ET* 32 (1920-1921): 473.

15195   J. M. Ford, "Shalom in the Johannine Corpus," *HBT* 6 (1984): 67-89.

15196   H. U. von Balthasar, "Die göttlichen Gerichte in der Apokalypse," *IKaZ* 14 (1985): 28-34.

15197 Elisabeth Schüssler Fiorenza, "The Followers of the Lamb: Visionary Rhetoric and Social-Political Situation," *Semeia* 36 (1986): 123-46.

15198 Adela Y. Collins, "Women's History and the Book of Revelation," *SBLSP* 26 (1987): 80-91.

14:4-5

15199 E. Power, "A Pretended Interpolation in the Apocalypse (Apoc. 14:4e, 5ab)," *Bib* 4 (1923): 108-12.

14:4

15200 T. I. Tambyah, "Virgins in Revelation 14.4," *ET* 32 (1920): 139.

15201 A. Škrinjar, "Virgines enim sunt (Apoc. 14, 4)," *VD* 15 (1935): 331-39.

15202 Ugo Vanni, "Questi seguono l'agnello dovunque vada (Ap. 14,4)," *ParSpirV* 2 (1980): 171-92.

14:6-13

15203 Heinz Giesen, "Evangelium and Paränese: zum Verständnis der Gerichtsaussagen in Offenbarung 14,6-13," *SNTU-A* 21 (1996): 92-131.

14:6-7

15204 Willem Altink, "1 Chronicles 16:8-36 as Literary Source for Revelation 14:6-7," *AUSS* 22 (1984): 187-96.

15205 Willem Altink, "Theological Motives for the Use of 1 Chronicles 16:8-36 as Background for Revelation 14:6-7:" *AUSS* 24 (1986): 211-21.

15206 Gregory K. Beale, "A Reconsideration of the Text of Daniel in the Apocalypse," *Bib* 67 (1986): 539-43.

14:6

15207 Lucien Cerfaux, "L'évangile éternel (Apoc. 14:6)," *ETL* 39 (1963): 672-81.

14:8

15208 Hans K. La Rondelle, "The Biblical Concept of Armageddon," *JETS* 28 (1985): 21-31.

14:12

15209 Donald S. Deer, "Whose Faith/Loyalty in Revelation 2.13 and 14.12?" *BT* 38 (1987): 328-30.

14:13

15210 A. Grillmeier, "Ihre Werke folgen Ihnen nach (Offb 14,13)," *GeistL* 37 (1964): 321-24.

14:14-20

15211 André Feuillet, "La moisson et la vendange de l'Apocalypse (14,14-20): la signification chrétienne de la Révélation johannique," *NRT* 94 (1972): 113-32; (1972): 225-50.

15212 J. Pintard, "La moisson et la vendange dans l'Apocalypse (14,14-20): Pour encourager les confesseurs de la foi," *EV* 82 (1972): 374-77.

14:14

15213 M. Goguel, "Note sur l'Apocalypse 14,14," *RHPR* 5 (1925): 66-69.

15214 Harald Sahlin, "Wie wurde ursprünglich die Benennung 'Der Menschensoln' verstanden?" *StTheol* 37 (1983): 147-79.

15215 Ugo Vanni, "La figura della donna nell'Apocalisse," *SM* 40 (1991): 57-94.

15216 T. B. Salter, "*Homoioon huion anthrōpou* in Revelation 1.13 and 14.14," *BT* 44 (1993): 349-50.

15217 Gregory M. Stevenson, "Conceptual Background to Golden Crown Imagery in the Apocalypse of John," *JBL* 114 (1995): 257-72.

15218 J. A. du Rand, "Die eskatologiese betekenis van Sion as agtergrond tot die teologie van die boek Openbaring," *SkrifK* 7 (1996): 48-61.

15219 T. B. Slater, "More on Revelation 1:13 and 14:14," *BT* 47 (1996): 146-49.

15-16

15220 J. M. Ford, "Shalom in the Johanmine Corpus," *HBT* 6 (1984): 67-89.

15221 Elian Cuvillier, "Jugement et destruction du monde dans l'Apocalypse de Jean: Notes exégétiques sur Apoc. 8-9 et Apoc. 15-16," *FV* 91 (1992): 53-67.

15

15222 Roland Meynet, "Le cantique de Moïse et le cantique de l'agneau (Ap. 15 et Ex. 15)," *Greg* 73 (1992): 19-55.

15:1

15223 H. U. von Balthasar, "Die göttlichen Gerichte in der Apokalypse," *IKaZ* 14 (1985): 28-34.

15:2

15224 David E. Aune, "A Latinism in Revelation 15:2," *JBL* 110 (1991): 691-92.

15225 Christfried Böttrich, "Das 'gläserne Meer' in Apk. 4,6/15,2," *BibN* 80 (1995): 5-15.

15:3-4

15226 J. A. du Rand, "The Song of the Lamb Because of the Victory of the Lamb," *Neo* 29 (1995): 203-10.

15:5-8

15227 Jon Paulien, "The Role of the Hebrew Cultus, Sanctuary, and Temple in the Plot and Structure of the Book of Revelation," *AUSS* 33 (1995): 245-64.

16-22

15228 Charles H. Giblin, "Structural and Thematic Correlations in the Theology of Revelation 16-22," *Bib* 55 (1974): 487-504.

16

15229 Gerard Mussies, "*Dyo* in Apocalypse 9:12 and 16," *NovT* 9 (1967): 51-154.

15230 J. M. Ford, "The Structure and Meaning of Revelation 16," *ET* 98 (1987): 327-31.

15231 Roland E. Loasby, " 'Har-Magedon' according to the Hebrew in the Setting of the Seven Last Plagues of Revelation 16," *AUSS* 27 (1989): 129-32.

16:4-7

15232 Adela Y. Collins, "The History-of-Religions Approach to Apocalypticism and the 'Angel of the Waters'," *CBQ* 39 (1977): 367-81.

16:4-6

15233 Peter Staples, "Revelation 16:4-6 and Its Vindication Formula," *NovT* 14 (1972): 280-93.

16:9

15234 A. Wikenhauser, "Religionsgeschichtliche Parallelen in Apk. 16,9," *BZ* 23 (1935): 180-86.

16:12-16

15235 J. H. Michael, " 'Har-Magedon'," *JTS* 38 (1937): 168-172.

15236 Andrew E. Steinmann, "The Tripartite Structure of the Sixth Seal, the Sixth Trumpet, and the Sixth Bowl of John's Apocalypse," *JETS* 35 (1992): 69-79.

16:13-16

15237 Hans K. La Rondelle, "The Biblical Concept of Armageddon," *JETS* 28 (1985): 21-31.

16:14-15

15238 Joseph Jenson, "What Are They Saying about Armageddon?" *CThM* 13 (1986): 292-301.

16:16

15239 Joachim Jeremias, "Har Magedon (Apc. 16,16)," *ZNW* 31 (1932): 73-77.

15240 C. C. Torrey, "Armageddon," *HTR* 31 (1938): 237-48.

15241 I. H. Eybers, "Shephelah and Armageddon: What Do They Signify?" *ThEv* 10 (1977): 7-13.

15242 William H. Shea, "The Location and Significance of Armageddon in Revelation 16:16," *AUSS* 18 (1980): 157-62.

15243 Hans K. La Rondelle, "The Etymology of *Har-Magedon*," *AUSS* 27 (1989): 69-73.

15244 Michael Oberweis, "Erwägungen zur apokalyptischen Ortsbezeichnung 'Harmagedon'," *Bib* 76 (1995): 305-24.

15245 Meredith Kline, "Har-Magedon: The End of the Millennium," *JETS* 39 (1996): 207-22.

16:17-21

15246 Richard J. Bauckham, "The Eschatological Earthquake in the Apocalypse of John," *NovT* 19 (1977): 224-33.

16:17

15247 H. U. von Balthasar, "Die göttlichen Gerichte in der Apokalypse," *IKaZ* 14 (1985): 28-34.

17-22

15248 Barbara W. Snyder, "Triple-Form and Space/Time Transitions: Literary Structuring Devices in the Apocalypse," *SBLSP* 30 (1991): 440-450.

17-18

15249 Thomas R. Edgar, "Babylon: Ecclesiastical, Political, or What?" *JETS* 25 (1982): 333-41.

15250 Charles H. Dyer, "The Identity of Babylon in Revelation 17-18," *BSac* 144 (1987): 305-16, 433-49.

17

15251 J. E. Bruns, "The Contrasted Women of Apocalypse 12 and 17," *CBQ* 26 (1964): 459-63.

15252 John F. Walvoord, "Prophecy of the Ten-Nation Confederacy," *BSac* 124 (1967): 99-105.

15253 R. Beauvery, "L'Apocalypse au risque de la numismatique. Babylone, la grande prostituée et le sixième roi Vespasien et la Déesse Rome," *RB* 90 (1983): 243-60.

15254 Jarl H. Ulrichsen, "Dyret i Åpenbaringen: en skisse til tidshistorisk forståelse av kapitlene 13 og 17," *NTT* 87 (1986): 167-77.

17:1-11

15255 Sjef van Tilborg, "Metaphorical versus Visionary Language," *Neo* 28 (1994): 77-91.

17:1-8

15256 Jarl H. Ulrichsen, "Die sieben Häupter und die zehn Hörner: Zur Datierung der Offenbarung des Johannes," *StTheol* 39 (1985): 1-20.

17:1-6

15257 Ugo Vanni, "La figura della donna nell'Apocalisse," *SM* 40 (1991): 57-94.

17:3-6

15258 Tina Pippin, "Eros and the End: Reading for Gender in the Apocalypse of John," *Semeia* 59 (1992): 193-210.

17:4

15259 Gregory K. Beale, "The Origin of the Title 'King of Kings and Lord of Lords' in Revelation 17:4," *NTS* 31 (1985): 618-20.

17:5-8

15260 H. U. von Balthasar, "Die göttlichen Gerichte in der Apokalypse," *IKaZ* 14 (1985): 28-34.

17:5

15261 Hans K. La Rondelle, "The Biblical Concept of Armageddon," *JETS* 28 (1985): 21-31.

17:8-13

15262 D. Holwerda, "Ein neuer Schlüßel zum 17. Kapitel der johanneischen Offenbarung," *EB* 53 (1995): 387-96.

17:8-11

15263 Larry J. Kreitzer, "Hadrian and the Nero Redivivus Myth," *ZNW* 79 (1988): 92-115.

17:9-14

15264 M. Miguéns, "Los 'reyes' de Apoc. 17,9-14," *EB* 32 (1973): 5-24.

17:9-12

15265 A.   Strobel, "Abfassung und Geschichtstheologie der Apokalypse nach Kap. 17:9-12," *NTS* 10 (1964): 433-45.

17:9

15266 Gregory K. Beale, "The Danielic Background for Revelation 13:18 and 17:9," *TynB* 31 (1980): 163-70.

17:12-14

15267 Hans K. La Rondelle, "The Biblical Concept of Armageddon," *JETS* 28 (1985): 21-31.

17:12

15268 F. Diekamp, "Nikomedes, ein unbekannter Erklärer der Apokalypse," *Bib* 14 (1933): 448-51.

15269 Gregory K. Beale, "A Reconsideration of the Text of Daniel in the Apocalypse," *Bib* 67 (1986): 539-43.

18-22

15270 V. Monsarrat, "Apoc. 18-22: Quelques pistes de travail," *FV* 75 (1976): 79-82.

18

15271 William H. Shea, "Chiasm in Theme and by Form in Revelation 18," *AUSS* 20 (1982): 249-56.

15272 Kenneth A. Strand, "Two Aspects of Babylon's Judgment Portrayed in Revelation 18," *AUSS* 20 (1982): 53-60.

15273 Dieter Georgi, "Who Is the True Prophet (Horace or St. John)?" *HTR* 79 (1986): 100-26.

18:2

15274 J. Schmid, "Zur Textkritik der Apokalypse (13:10; 18:2)," *ZNW* 43 (1950-1951): 112-28.

15275 Hans K. La Rondelle, "The Biblical Concept of Armageddon," *JETS* 28 (1985): 21-31.

18:6-7

15276 Susan M. Elliott, "Who Is Addressed in Revelation 18:6-7?" *BR* 40 (1995): 98-113.

18:6

15277 Kenneth A. Strand, "Some Modalities of Symbolic Usage in Revelation 18," *AUSS* 24 (1986): 37-46.

18:10-19

15278 Gregory K. Beale, "A Reconsideration of the Text of Daniel in the Apocalypse," *Bib* 67 (1986): 539-43.

18:17

15279 R. Harris, "A New Reading in the Text of the Apocalypse," *ET* 48 (1936-1937): 429.

15280 Hans Conzelmann, "Miszelle zu Apk. 18:17," *ZNW* 66 (1975): 288-90.

18:21

15281 H. U. von Balthasar, "Die göttlichen Gerichte in der Apokalypse," *IKaZ* 14 (1985): 28-34.

18:23

15282 Ugo Vanni, "La figura della donna nell'Apocalisse," *SM* 40 (1991): 57-94.

19-21

15283 Jan Fekkes, " 'His Bride Has Prepared Herself': Revelation 19-21 and Isaian Nuptial Imagery," *JBL* 109 (1990): 269-87.

15284 M. Eugene Boring, "Revelation 19-21: End Without Closure," *PSB* Supplement 3 (1994): 57-84.

19

15285 Gregory K. Beale, "The Influence of Daniel upon the Structure and Theology of John's Apocalypse," *JETS* 27 (1984): 413-24.

15286 Elian Cuvillier, "Apocalypse 20: prédiction ou prédication?" *ÉTR* 59 (1984): 345-54.

15287 William H. Shea, "Revelation 5 and 19 as Literary Reciprocals," *AUSS* 22 (1984): 249-57.

19:1-10

    15288   Jon Paulien, "The Role of the Hebrew Cultus, Sanctuary, and Temple in the Plot and Structure of the Book of Revelation," *AUSS* 33 (1995): 245-64.

19:1-8

    15289   Ugo Vanni, "La figura della donna nell'Apocalisse," *SM* 40 (1991): 57-94.

19:1-7

    15290   J. Schreiner, "Sonntag nach Christi Himmelfahrt. Homilie zu Apk. 19.1-7," *BibL* 8 (1967): 68-70.

19:6

    15291   M. Eugene Boring, "The Theology of Revelation: 'The Lord Our God the Almighty Reigns'," *Int* 40 (1986): 257-69.

19:9

    15292   Ugo Vanni, " 'Beati gli invitati alla cena delle nozze dell'agnello' (Ap. 19,9): la speranza nell'Apocalisse," *ParSpirV* 9 (1984): 227-42.

19:10

    15293   J. M. Ford, "'For the Testimony of Jesus is the Spirit of Prophecy," *ITQ* 42 (1975): 284-91.

    15294   Fred D. Mazzaferri, "*Martyria Iēsoû* Revisited," *BT* 39 (1988): 114-22.

19:11-20:6

    15295   Gerard Rochais, "Le règne des mille ans et la seconde mort: origines et sens. Ap. 19,11-20,6," *NRT* 103 (1981): 831-56.

19:11-20:3

    15296   Richard A. Ostella, "Significance of Deception in Revelation 20:3," *WTJ* 37 (1975): 236-38.

19:11-21

    15297   Hans K. La Rondelle, "The Biblical Concept of Armageddon," *JETS* 28 (1985): 21-31.

15298 R. Fowler White, "Reexamining the Evidence for Recapitulation in Revelation 20:1-10," *WTJ* 51 (1989): 319-44.

19:11-16

15299 Mathias Rissi, "Die Erscheinung Christi nach Offenbarung 19:11-16," *TZ* 21 (1965): 81-95.

15300 J. M. Ford, "Shalom in the Johannine Corpus," *HBT* 6 (1984): 67-89.

19:13

15301 Carroll D. Osburn, "Alexander Campbell and the Text of Revelation 19:13," *RQ* 25 (1982): 129-38.

19:15

15302 Sebastián Bartina, " 'Una espada salia de la boca de su vestido'," *EB* 20 (1961): 207-17.

19:16-17

15303 Jarl H. Ulrichsen, "Die sieben Häupter und die zehn Hörner: Zur Datierung der Offenbarung des Johannes," *StTheol* 39 (1985): 1-20.

19:16

15304 Patrick W. Skehan, "King of Kings, Lord of Lords (Apoc. 19:16)," *CBQ* 10 (1948): 398.

15305 J. M. Ford, "Shalom in the Johannine Corpus," *HBT* 6 (1984): 67-89.

19:20

15306 Michel Gourgues, "The Thousand-Year Reign: Terrestrial or Celestial?" *CBQ* 47 (1985): 76-681.

19:21

15307 Sebastián Bartina, " 'Una espada salia de la boca de su vestido'," *EB* 20 (1961): 207-17.

20-22

15308 Paul Gächter, "The Original Sequence of Apocalypse 20-22," *TS* 10 (1949): 485-521.

15309 J. Séguy, "Millénium, troisième âge, et Jérusalem céleste," *LV* 45 (1996): 55-68.

20-21

15310   C. Bouma, "Jeruzalem de [groote] stad," *GTT* 36 (1935): 91-98.

20

15311   George E. Ladd, "Revelation 20 and the Millennium," *RevExp* 57 (1960): 167-75.

15312   Ray Summers, "Revelation 20: An Interpretation," *RevExp* 57 (1960): 176-83.

15313   Norman Shepherd, "The Resurrections of Revelation 20," *WTJ* 37 (1974): 34-43.

15314   Sydney H. T. Page, "Revelation 20 and Pauline Eschatology," *JETS* 23 (1980): 31-43.

15315   T. F. Glasson, "The Last Judgment in Revelation 20 and Related Writings," *NTS* 28 (1982): 528-39.

15316   Douglas M. L. Judisch, "Postmillennialism and the Augustana," *CTQ* 47 (1983): 158-62.

15317   William H. Shea, "The Parallel Literary Structure of Revelation 12 and 20," *AUSS* 23 (1985): 37-54.

15318   Gregory K. Beale, "Review Article: J. Webb Mealy, *After the Thousand Years*," *EQ* 66 (1994): 229-49.

15319   Jacobus C. de Smidt, "Revelation 20: Prelude to the Omega Point in The New Heaven and Earth," *ScrSA* 49 (1994): 75-87.

20:1-10

15320   D. Danner, "A History of Interpretation of Revelation 20:1-10 in the Restoration Movement," *RQ* 7 (1963): 217-35.

15321   Derwood C. Smith, "The Millennial Reign of Jesus Christ. Some Observations on Revelation 20:1-10," *RQ* 16 (1973): 219-30.

15322   Jeffrey L. Townsend, "Is the Present Age the Millennium?" *BSac* 140 (1983): 206-24.

15323   Elian Cuvillier, "Apocalypse 20: Prédiction ou Prédication?" *ÉTR* 59 (1984): 345-54.

15324 H. Zegwaart, "Apocalyptic Eschatology and Pentecostalism: The Relevance of John's Millennium for Today," *Pneuma* 10 (1988): 3-25.

15325 R. Fowler White, "Reexamining the Evidence for Recapitulation in Revelation 20:1-10," *WTJ* 51 (1989): 319-44.

15326 Ugo Vanni, "Il regno millenario di Cristo e del Suoi (Apc. 20, 1-10)," *SM* 42 (1993): 67-95.

15327 R. Fowler White, "Making Sense of Revelation 20:1-10? Harold Höhner versus Recapitulation," *JETS* 37 (1994): 539-51.

20:1-8

15328 Merrill C. Tenney, "The Importance and Exegesis of Revelation 20, 1-8," *BSac* 111 (1954): 137-48.

20:1-6

15329 H. Höpfl, "De regno mille annorum in Apocalypsi (Apoc. 20:1.6)," *VD* 3 (1923): 206-10; 237-41.

15330 J. A. Colunga, "El Milenio (Apoc. XX. 1-6)," *Salm* 3 (1956): 220-27.

15331 Michel Gourgues, "The Thousand-Year Reign: Terrestrial or Celestial?" *CBQ* 47 (1985): 676-81.

15332 Adela Y. Collins, "Reading the Book of Revelation in the 20th Century," *Int* 40 (1986): 229-42.

15333 Vern S. Poythress, "Genre and Hermeneutics in Revelation 20:1-6," *JETS* 36 (1993): 41-54.

20:4-6

15334 Elisabeth Schüssler Fiorenza, "Die tausendjährige Herrschaft der Auferstandenen (Apk. 20,4-6)," *BibL* 13 (1972): 107-24.

15335 James A. Hughes, "Revelation 20:4-6 and the Question of the Millennium," *WTJ* 35 (1973): 281-302.

15336 Jack S. Deere, "Premillennialism in Revelation 20:4-6," *BSac* 135 (1978): 58-73.

15337 Michel Gourgues, "The Thousand-Year Reign: Terrestrial or Celestial?" *CBQ* 47 (1985): 676-81.

20:4

15338 Petros Vasiliadis, "The Translation of *martyria Iesou* in Revelation," *BT* 36 (1935): 129-34.

20:5-15

15339 C. L. Feltoe, "The 'First Resurrection' and the 'Second Death' (Apoc. 20,5f)," *Theology* 4 (1922): 291-93.

20:5-6

15340 Meredith Kline, "The First Resurrection," *WTJ* 37 (1975): 366-75.

15341 J. Ramsey Michaels, "The First Resurrection: A Response," *WTJ* 39 (1976): 100-109.

15342 Philip E. Hughes, "The First Resurrection: Another Interpretation," *WTJ* 39 (1977): 315-18.

20:5

15343 J. Hofbauer, ". . . et regnabunt cum Christo mille annis (Apoc. 20,5)," *VD* 45 (1967): 331-36.

15344 Roy L. Aldrich, "Divisions of the First Resurrection," *BSac* 128 (1971): 117-19.

20:6

15345 A. Gelston, "Royal Priesthood," *EQ* 31 (1959): 152-63.

15346 Ugo Vanni, "La promozione del regno come responsahilitá sacerdotale dei cristiani secondo l'Apocalisse e la Prima Lettera di Pietro," *Greg* 68 (1987): 9-56.

15347 A. R. Sikora, "Miejsce realizacji kaptaństwa chrześcijan wedlug Apokalipsy św. Jana," *RoczTK* 43 (1996): 161-84.

20:8-9

15348 A. Vivian, "Gog e Magog nella tradizione biblica, Ebraica e Cristiana," *RivBib* 25 (1977): 389-421.

20:9

15349 Joseph Comblin, "La ville bien-aimée. Apocalypse 20. 9." *VS* 112 (1965): 631-48.

20:10

15350 Michel Gourgues, "The Thousand-Year Reign: Terrestrial or Celestial?" *CBQ* 47 (1985): 676-81.

15351 Kirsten Nielsen, "'Gud Herren kaldte på ilden til dom. Dommedagsmotivet og dets forskydninger," *DTT* 58 (1995): 3-15.

20:11-15

15352 J. H. Michael, "A Vision of the Final Judgement," *ET* 63 (1952) 199-201.

15353 H. U. von Balthasar, "Die göttlichen Gerichte in der Apokalypse," *IKaZ* 14 (1985): 28-34.

20:14

15354 Jean-Hervé Nicolas, "La seconde mort du pécheur et la fidélité de Dieu," *RT* 79 (1979): 25-49.

21:1-22:5

15355 Joseph Comblin, "La liturgie de la nouvelle Jérusalem," *ETL* 29 (1953): 5-40.

15356 Wilhelm Thüsing, "Die Vision des 'neuen Jerusalem' (Apk. 2 1,1-22.5) als Verheissung und Gottesverkündigung," *TTZ* 77 (1968): 17-34.

15357 H. U. von Balthasar, "Die göttlichen Gerichte in der Apokalypse," *IKaZ* 14 (1985): 28-34.

15358 C. Deutsch, "Transformation of Symbols: The New Jerusalem in Revelation 21:1-22:5," *ZNW* 78 (1987): 106-26.

15359 Robert H. Gundry, "The New Jerusalem: People as Place, Not Place for People," *NovT* 29 (1987): 254-64.

21

15360 H. Wulf, "Das himmlische Jerusalem," *GeistL* 34 (1961): 321-25.

15361 Michel Coune, "L univers nouveau," *AsSeign* 26 (1973): 67-72.

15362 Joseph M. Baumgarten, "Duodecimal Courts of Qumran, Revelation, and the Sanhedrin," *JBL* 95 (1976): 59-78.

15363 William Tabbernee, "Revelation 21 and the Montanist 'New Jerusalem'," *ABR* 37 (1989): 52-60.

15364 Claudio Doglio, "Compimento della storia e liturgia in Ap. 21," *ParSpirV* 25 (1992): 139-54.

15365 G. Schille, "Der Apokalyptiker Johannes und die Edelsteine (Apk. 21)," *SNTU-A* 17 (1992): 231-44.

15366 J. H. de Wit, "Dc afdaling van het nieuwe Jeruzalem. Bevrijding en Hermeneutiek," *GTT* 95 (1995): 181-94.

21:1-23

15367 Wendell W. Frerichs, "God's Song of Revelation: From Easter to Pentecost in the Apocalypse," *WW* 6 (1986): 216-28.

21:1-8

15368 Rudolph W. Raber, "Revelation 21:1-8," *Int* 40 (1986): 296-301.

15369 Ugo Vanni, "La figura della donna nell'Apocalisse," *SM* 40 (1991): 57-94.

15370 G. Daan Cloete and Dirk J. Smit, " 'And I Saw a New Heaven and a New Earth, for the First. . . Were Passed Away' (Revelation 21:1-8)," *JTSA* 81 (1992): 55-65.

15371 Jon Paulien, "The Role of the Hebrew Cultus, Sanctuary, and Temple in the Plot and Structure of the Book of Revelation," *AUSS* 33 (1995): 245-64.

21:1-5

15372 J. Michl, "Selige Menschen in einer neuen Schöpfung nach Apokalypse 21, 1-5," *BK* 16 (1961): 113-15.

15373 J. van Ruiten, "The Intertextual Relationship Between Isaiah 65:17-20 and Revelation 21:1-5," *EB* 51 (1993): 473-510.

21:2-3

15374 Michel Coune, "La Jérusalem céleste (Ap. 21.2-5)," *AsSeign* 91 (1964): 23-28.

21:3

15375   Christopher C. Rowland, "John 1:51. Jewish Apocalyptic and Targumic Tradition," *NTS* 30 (1984): 498-507.

21:4

15376   J. R. Gray, "The End of Tears," *ET* 93 (1982): 279-80.

21:5-8

15377   Friedrich Wulf, " 'Siehe, ich mache alles neu!' Meditation zu Apk. 21,5-8," *GeistL* 41 (1968): 391-93.

21:5

15378   Josef Sudbrack, "'Siehe, ich mache alles neu' (Offb. 21,5): Besinnung von einem spielenden Kind," *GeistL* 53 (1980): 228-30.

21:6

15379   B. Schwank, "Das A und Ω: einer 'biblischen Theologie'," *SNTU-A* 21 (1996): 132-45.

21:9-22:5

15380   J. A. du Rand, "The Imagery of the Heavenly Jerusalem," *Neo* 22 (1988): 65-86.

21:9-22

15381   Ugo Vanni, "La figura della donna nell'Apocalisse," *SM* 40 (1991): 57-94.

21:10-23

15382   A. Viard, "La nouvelle Jérusalem et la venue du Christ (Ap. 21,10-23; 22,12-20)," *EV* 83 (1983): 101-102.

21:10-14

15383   C. Brutsch, "La nouvelle Jérusalem (Ap. 21.10-14.22-23)," *AsSeign* 27 (1970): 30-36.

21:12-17

15384   Michael Topham, "The Dimensions of the New Jerusalem," *ET* 100 (1989): 417-19.

21:13

15385   J. H. Michael, "East, North, South. West," *ET* 49 (1937-1938): 141-42.

21:18-21

15386 U. Jart, "The Precious Stones in the Revelation of St. John xxi.18-21," *StTheol* 24 (1970): 150-81.

21:19-20

15387 T. F. Glasson, "Order of Jewels in Revelation 21:19-20: A Theory Eliminated," *JTS* 26 (1975): 95-100.

15388 William W. Reader, "The Twelve Jewels of Revelation 21:19-20: Tradition History and Modern Interpretations," *JBL* 100 (1981): 433-57.

15389 Roland Bergmeier, " 'Jerusalem, du hochgebaute Stadt'," *ZNW* 75 (1984): 86-106.

15390 Jacob A. Loewen, "A Suggestion for Translating the Names of Precious Stones," *BT* 35 (1984): 229-34.

15391 Michal Wojciechowski, "Apocalypse 21:19-20: des titres christologiques cachés dans la liste des pierres préieuses," *NTS* 33 (1987): 153-54.

21:21

15392 Eric Burrows, "The Pearl in the Apocalypse," *JTS* 43 (1942): 177-79.

21:22-26

15393 Jacques Ellul, "Pour qui, pour quoi travaillons-nous?" *FV* 79 (1980): 74-82.

15394 Robert M. Johnston, "The Eschatological Sabbath in John's Apocalypse: A Reconsideration," *AUSS* 25 (1987): 39-50.

21:22-23

15395 C. Brutsch, "La nouvelle Jérusalem (Ap. 21,10-14.22-23)," *AsSeign* 27 (1970): 30-36.

21:22

15396 Michael J. Marx, "The City of God in Revelation 21:22," *Worship* 27 (1953): 136-37.

15397 Lucius Nereparampil, "New Worship and New Temple," *BB* 16 (1990): 216-33.

21:25

15398 E. H. Robertson, "The City of God," *ET* 92 (1981): 115-16.

22

15399 Joseph Comblin, "L homme rétrouvé: la rencontre de l'époux et de l'épouse (Ap. 22)," *AsSeign* 29 (1979): 38-46.

15400 Donald S. Deer, "Notes on the Translation of Revelation, Chapter 22, into Kituba," *BT* 24 (1973): 207-15.

22:1-2

15401 G. G. Nicol, "The Threat and the Promise," *ET* 94 (1983): 136-39.

22:1

15402 Sang H. Lee, "The Water of Life: A Sermon Bible Study," *PSB* 4 (1983): 173-77.

22:2

15403 R. Schran, "Zu Apc. 22,2: Die Frage nach dem Standort des Lebensbaumes," *BZ* 24 (1938): 191-98.

15404 Édouard Delebecque, "Où situer l'arbre de vie dans la Jérusalem céleste? Note sur Apocalypse XXII, 2," *RT* 88 (1988): 124-30.

22:6-21

15405 Bethel Müller, "Die Epiloog van die Openbaring aan Johannes (22:6-21)," *ScrSA* 6 (1982): 57-64.

15406 Ugo Vanni, "Liturgical Dialogue as a Literary Form in the Book of Revelation," *NTS* 37 (1991): 348-72.

22:6

15407 Gregory K. Beale, "The Influence of Daniel upon the Structure and Theology of John's Apocalypse," *JETS* 27 (1984): 413-24.

22:7

15408 R. Trevijano Etcheverría, "El discurso profetico de este libro (Apoc. 22:7,10,18-19)," *Salm* 29 (1982): 283-308.

15409 David E. Aune, "The Apocalypse of John and Graeco-Roman Revelatory Magic," *NTS* 33 (1987): 481-501.

22:10

15410 R. Trevijano Etcheverría, "El discurso profético de este libro," *Salm* 29 (1982): 283-308.

22:12-20

15411 A. Viärd, "La nouvelle Jérusalem et la venue du Christ," *EV* 83 (1983): 101-102.

22:12

15412 David E. Aune, "The Apocalypse of John and Graeco-Roman Revelatory Magic," *NTS* 33 (1987): 481-501.

22:13

15413 A. Škrinjar, "Ego sum A et Ω (Apo. 22,13)," *VD* 17 (1937): 10-20.

15414 J. M. Fenasse, "Terme et début: voilà ce que je suis," *BVC* 54 (1963): 43-50.

15415 B. Schwank, "Das A und Ω: einer 'biblischen Theologie'," *SNTU-A* 21 (1996): 132-45.

22:14

15416 Michael J. Marx, "The City of God," *Worship* 27 (1952-1953): 136-37.

22:16

15417 Michael S. Moore, "Jesus Christ: 'Superstar' (Revelation xxii 16b)," *NovT* 24 (1982): 82-91.

15418 David E. Aune, "The Prophetic Circle of John of Patmos and the Exegesis of Revelation 22:16," *JSNT* 37 (1989): 103-16.

22:17

15419 Stefania Cantore, "Chi Ascolta Dica: 'Vieni'!" *ParSpirV* 1 (1980): 158-74.

15420 Ugo Vanni, "The Ecclesial Assembly, 'Interpreting Subject' of the Apocalypse," *RSB* 4 (1984): 79-85.

15421 Ugo Vanni, "Lo Spirito e la sposa (Ap. 22.17)," *ParSpirV* 13 (1986): 191-206.

22:18-19

15422   B. Olsson, "Der Epilog der Offenbarung Johannis," *ZNW* 31 (1932): 84-86.

15423   R. Trevijano Etcheverría, "El discurso profetico de este libro (Apoc. 22:7,10,18-19)," *Salm* 29 (1982): 283-308.

22:18

15424   Robert L. Thomas, "The Spiritual Gift of Prophecy in Revelation 22:18," *JETS* 32 (1989): 201-16.

22:20

15425   C. F. D. Moule, "A Re-consideration of the Content of *Maranatha*," *NTS* 6 (1959-1960): 307-10.

15426   S. Schulz, "*Maranatha* und *Kyrios* Jesus," *ZNW* 53 (1962): 125-44.

15427   Ugo Vanni, " 'Vieni, Signore Gesù!' (Ap. 22,20)," *ParSpirV* 8 (1983): 227-42.

15428   David E. Aune, "The Apocalypse of John and Graeco-Roman Revelatory Magic," *NTS* 33 (1987): 481-501.

15429   J.-C. Sagne, " 'Oui, je viens bientôt': le désir et l'espérance," *LV* 45 (1996): 43-54.

Index

Baird, William 9065, 9303,
10127, 10481, 10838,
11038, 11367, 11455,
11457

Bajsić, Alois 3539, 7356

Baker, Carolyn D. 12195

Baker, David L. 10652

Baker, J. 4900

Baker, Kimberly F. 13654

Baker, William R. 13855

Bakken, Norman K. 1364,
1634, 1675, 1719, 12383,
12401, 14553

Balagué, M. 6060, 6374, 6436,
6459, 6599, 6842, 7077,
7268, 7410, 7532, 8147,
12116, 12164

Balch, D. L. 8113, 8872,
10377, 11032, 13952

Baldensperger, G. 14993

Baldi, Donato 2517

Baldinger, Albert H. 15166

Balducelli, Roger 1137

Balembo, Buetubela 535

Balfour, Glenn 6478, 6592

Balge, Richard D. 12218

Ball, Michael 5012

Ball, R. M. 7037

Ballard, J. M. 6790, 7274, 7275

Ballard, Paul H. 1230

Baltensweiler, Heinrich 415,
1117, 2827, 4509, 12911

Balthasar, H. U. von 8720,
9711, 10640, 10777,
10863, 10904, 11166,
11185, 11194, 12216,
14784, 14818, 14888,
14895, 14922, 14966,
15018, 15147, 15174,
15196, 15223, 15247,
15260, 15281, 15353,
15357

Baly, D. 2732

Bamberg, C. 4440

Bammel, C. P. 9371, 9502

Bammel, E. 716, 1416, 2890,
4268, 4667, 5065, 6561,
6990, 6997,
7087, 7403, 7421, 11506, 11698,
12621, 12866, 12887,
12910, 13971

Bampfylde, G. D. 6974, 7458

Bandstra, Andrew J. 10486,
11705, 12353, 14712,
14734, 14735, 14776,
14982

Banks, Robert 364, 1922

Barbaglio, Giuseppe 2534,
3370

Barber, Cyril J. 8119

Barbour, R. S. 1261, 3417,
5417, 6943

Barclay, John M. G. 9182,
13316, 13352, 13365,
13369, 13380, 13382,
13387, 13390, 13393

Buzard, A. 7737

Buzy, D. 5791

Buzzetti, C. 1006, 1614, 1664, 1737, 1779, 1844, 1914, 2178, 3450, 3828

Byargeon, Rick W. 495

Byars, Ronald 10052, 10088, 10113

Byrne, Brendan 7502, 7516, 9390, 9426, 9432, 10146, 10278, 10291, 10918, 11268, 12423

Byron, Brian F. 5794, 10332

Byrskog, Samuel 9035

Byskov, M. 4107

Caba, J. 1090, 6575

Cabaniss, Allen 1835

Cachia, N. 6954

Cadbury, Henry J. 1014, 1080, 5081, 5112, 5113, 7579, 13646

Cadier, J. 7239, 11109, 11159

Cadoux, A. T. 1359

Cadoux, L. 5929

Cahill, Michael 12684

Cahill, P. J. 6172

Caird, George B. 403, 2345, 2715, 9704

Calder, W. M. 11761, 14901

Calian, Carnegie S. 6141

Callan, Terrance 3771, 7715, 8589, 8605, 8876, 9132, 10074, 10279, 10309,

10477, 10537, 10662, 10729, 10763, 11054, 11299

Calle, F. de la 9644

Calloud, Jean 1832, 1916, 8680, 11421, 11714, 11729, 11852, 11884, 14859, 15089

Calmes, R. 5637

Calmet, A. 2817, 13756, 13818, 14588

Camacho, Harold S. 13691

Cambe, M. 6147

Cambier, J. 8282, 9080, 9148, 9407, 9459, 9648, 9660, 10231, 10305, 10832, 11373, 11954, 12127, 12209, 12223

Camelot, T. 12570, 12757

Cameron, Peter S. 11572

Cameron, Ron 7598

Camp, Ashby L. 7894

Campbell, Barth 10233, 13154

Campbell, Cynthia M. 1537, 8770

Campbell, Douglas A. 9091, 12778, 12779

Campbell, J. C. 12462

Campbell, J. Y. 9112

Campbell, K. M. 355, 13620

Campbell, R. A. 10601, 11906, 13181

Campbell, W. S. 9193, 9235, 9714

NEW TESTAMENT
TOOLS AND STUDIES

edited by

Bruce M. Metzger, PPPPh.D., D.D., L.H.D., D. Theol., D. Litt.

and

Bart D. Ehrman, Ph.D.